# *Adoption Searches Made Easier*

By Joseph J. Culligan
*Licensed Private Investigator*

National Association of Investigative Specialists
Hall of Fame Member

FJA, Inc.

Other books by Joseph J. Culligan:

*You, Too, Can Find Anybody (also on video)*
*When In Doubt, Check Him Out (also on video)*
*Requirements To Become A P.I. In The 50 States And Elsewhere*

*Adoption Searches Made Easier*

Library of Congress Catalog Number: 95-61932
ISBN: 1-57296-100-7
Printed in the United States of America

Culligan, Joseph J.
  Adoption Searches Made Easier / by Joseph J. Culligan
  p. cm.

1. Public records--United States--Handbooks, manuals, etc.  2. Investigations--United States--Handbooks, manuals, etc.  I. Title.

JK2445.P82C85 1996        353.0071'4
                          QBI95-20808

...s the most significant chapter in the entire book because it will help
decid... ...to conduct your search depending on the information
...able ...you in the right direction and make certain
...t you ...It will save you an enormous ...is the facts you have
...nount ...alent to a
...nd ma
...road ...red
desir ...the
ado ...the
add ...use
pr ...ty l
...p ...d in
...ati

---

---

determin...
transferred to micro...
county or state archive.
If these books are found they should yield the...

**This book has been written so families will not have to endure the suffering that this poor woman has!**

# Table of Contents

# Introduction

As the title clearly states, it is the express purpose of this book to make adoption searches easier. I have purposely used the word easier because, as a general rule, attempting to find birthparents, adoptees, or an adoptee's siblings is never easy. In fact, these types of investigations are normally the most challenging cases a private investigator faces.

What makes these cases so interesting is that there are two distinct but related ingredients to each situation. First the searching individual has to uncover the identity of the party he or she is searching for. This is not made easier by the searcher's normal lack of information, the passage of a great deal of time since the adoption was completed, and the fact that most government and private institution's records dealing with an adoption are, by law, sealed and made unavailable to the searcher.

The second problem arises after the searcher has successfully uncovered the identity of the object of his or her search. Let's assume that an adoptee is successful in uncovering the name of the birthmother. The adoptee, in this example, is a 23 years old female. She was adopted out at birth. Her birthmother at that time was a 17 year old unwed mother. Twenty-three years have passed! What has happened to the birthmother during all those years? Did she marry? Did she divorce? How many times has her last name changed? Did she move to a different state or perhaps a different country? Did she die? The point is that it may be difficult to track down her present whereabouts given the length of time that has passed and various events that may have taken place in the birthmother's life.

The format of this book follows the natural progression of the adoption search itself. In *ADOPTION SEARCHES MADE EASIER*, I have described in detail the many different approaches a searcher can use to uncover an identity specifically related to an adoption search. This book is unique in revealing a number of sources of information that previously were known and used only by private investigators.

In *YOU, TOO, CAN FIND ANYBODY* I have gone into a detailed explanation of the techniques I employ in locating the present whereabouts of someone such as a missing relative, childhood sweetheart, military buddy, or even someone who owes you money. The information presented is

also useful to anyone who wishes to do a background check on a specific individual. These techniques are equally suitable to adoption and non-adoption searchers.

In response to my three books *YOU, TOO, CAN FIND ANYBODY, WHEN IN DOUBT CHECK HIM OUT, and REQUIREMENTS TO BECOME A P.I. IN THE 50 STATES AND ELSEWHERE*, I have received thousands of letters from people asking me how to conduct an adoption search. This book, *ADOPTION SEARCHES MADE EASIER*, is my response to all those searching individuals who are desperately either trying to find their true identity and/ or trying to reunite their biological families. I am sure you will find *ADOPTION SEARCHES MADE EASIER* complete and easy to use. I have openly discussed techniques and sources that I personally use when doing the same type of investigations. The pages which follow will guide and illuminate your search and I hope you will be successful in your endeavor.

As I have said before in my other books, if you find the person you are looking for using this book and you think that your case would translate into good television, then write to me immediately. I do not want to delay your reunion and I can't promise you that your story will fit into a talk show's schedule at that moment but, as I am sure you are aware, I do many shows each month on national television where I reunite families who did the "finding" themselves. I have appeared on Maury Povich, Ricki Lake, Montel Williams, Hard Copy, Leeza, and Donahue among other television programs. I may be contacted by writing to: 4995 Northwest 79th Avenue, Suite 115, Miami, Florida 33166.

# *1*

# *How much do you know?*

The first step in any successful adoption search is determining and organizing the information that is available. Generally speaking most people who begin a search don't have very much information. Consequently it is of uppermost importance to gather, list and evaluate the information you do have.

You will have different information depending on whether you are a *birthparent, adoptee, adoptive parent, or a sibling of an adoptee.* The reason this is true is because of the different age and vantage point you held during the time of the adoption. For example, if you are a birthmother you will know where you gave birth, when you gave birth, and the details pertaining to the adoption.

As the adoptee you may have been an infant at the time of the adoption and therefore you will have no first-hand recollection as to the date or place of birth, or the details surrounding your adoption. Your information must come from other sources such as your adoptive parents, your official adoption records, a birth index, a docket calendar, etc.

If you are a sibling of an adoptee you may have been old enough to remember some of the circumstances surrounding the birth and the adoption. You may also have heard the facts from an involved third party such as a relative or close family friend. You may have been adopted out together but being older you may remember more of the details such as place, date, and final destination.

In order to help you collect and organize the information presently available to you I have designed the following specific worksheets for adoptees, birthparent, and sibling. Please fill them out in as much detail as possible before you proceed to chapter 2.

## ADOPTEE'S WORKSHEET

ADOPTEE'S NAME _____

DATE OF BIRTH (DOB) _____

ACTUAL DATE OF BIRTH (DOB) _____

BIRTH PLACE _____

ACTUAL BIRTH PLACE _____

BIRTHMOTHER'S NAME _____

DATE OF BIRTH (DOB) _____

SOCIAL SECURITY NUMBER _____

MAIDEN NAME _____

LAST KNOWN ADDRESS _____

_____

NAMES OF ANY RELATIVES _____

_____

NAMES OF ANY FRIENDS _____

_____

OCCUPATION _____

EDUCATION _____

UNUSUAL TRAITS _____

BIRTHFATHER'S NAME _____

DATE OF BIRTH (DOB) _____

SOCIAL SECURITY NUMBER _____

LAST KNOWN ADDRESS _____
_____

NAME OF ANY RELATIVES _____
_____

NAME OF ANY FRIENDS _____
_____

OCCUPATION _____

EDUCATION _____

UNUSUAL TRAITS _____
_____

TYPE OF ADOPTION AGENCY:
☐ PUBLIC AGENCY  ☐ PRIVATE AGENCY

NAME AND ADDRESS OF ADOPTION AGENCY:
_____
_____
_____

ATTORNEY'S NAME AND ADDRESS:

_____

_____

DOCTOR'S NAME AND ADDRESS:

_____

_____

SOCIAL WORKER'S NAME AND ADDRESS:

_____

_____

_____

WHEN WAS CONSENT DECREE SIGNED?

_____

WHERE WAS CONSENT DECREE SIGNED?

_____

WHEN WAS THE ADOPTION PETITION SIGNED?

_____

WHERE WAS THE ADOPTION PETITION FILED?

_____

WHO FILED THE PETITION?

_____

HOW OLD WHERE YOU AT THE TIME OF THE ADOPTION?

_____

WHERE YOU BAPTIZED? ☐ YES ☐ NO
NAME & ADDRESS OF THE CHURCH

_____

_____

_____

DID YOU EVER MEET EITHER OF YOUR BIRTHPARENTS?
☐ YES ☐ NO

# ANY OTHER INFORMATION THAT MIGHT BE IMPORTANT

_____

_____

_____

_____

_____

# BIRTHMOTHER'S WORKSHEET

CHILD'S NAME _____

DATE OF BIRTH (DOB) _____ SEX ☐ M ☐ F

BIRTH PLACE _____

BIRTHFATHER'S NAME _____

DATE OF BIRTH (DOB) _____

SOCIAL SECURITY NUMBER _____

LAST KNOWN ADDRESS _____

_____

NAMES OF ANY OF HIS RELATIVES _____

_____

NAMES OF ANY OF HIS FRIENDS _____

_____

OCCUPATION_____

EDUCATION _____

UNUSUAL TRAITS _____

_____

TYPE OF ADOPTION AGENCY:

☐ PUBLIC AGENCY ☐ PRIVATE AGENCY

NAME AND ADDRESS OF ADOPTION AGENCY

_____

_____

_____

ATTORNEY'S NAME AND ADDRESS

_____

_____

_____

DOCTOR'S NAME AND ADDRESS

_____

_____

_____

SOCIAL WORKER'S NAME AND ADDRESS

_____

_____

_____

WHERE WAS CONSENT DECREE SIGNED?

_____

WHEN WAS CONSENT DECREE SIGNED?

_____

WHEN WAS THE ADOPTION PETITION SIGNED?

_____

WHERE WAS THE ADOPTION PETITION FILED?

_____

WHO FILED THE PETITION?

_____

HOW OLD WHERE YOU AT THE TIME OF THE ADOPTION?

_____

DID YOU EVER MEET YOUR BIRTHCHILD? ☐ YES ☐ NO

ANY OTHER INFORMATION THAT MIGHT BE IMPORTANT

_____

_____

_____

_____

_____

_____

# BIRTHFATHER'S WORKSHEET

CHILD'S NAME _____

DATE OF BIRTH (DOB) _____ SEX ☐ M ☐ F

BIRTH PLACE _____

BIRTHMOTHER'S NAME _____

BIRTHMOTHER'S MAIDEN NAME

_____

DATE OF BIRTH (DOB) _____

SOCIAL SECURITY NUMBER _____

LAST KNOWN ADDRESS _____

_____

NAMES OF ANY OF HER RELATIVES _____

_____

NAMES OF ANY OF HER FRIENDS _____

_____

OCCUPATION_____

EDUCATION _____

UNUSUAL TRAITS _____

_____

TYPE OF ADOPTION AGENCY:
☐ PUBLIC AGENCY ☐ PRIVATE AGENCY
NAME AND ADDRESS OF ADOPTION AGENCY

_____

_____

_____

ATTORNEY'S NAME AND ADDRESS

_____

_____

_____

DOCTOR'S NAME AND ADDRESS

_____

_____

_____

SOCIAL WORKER'S NAME AND ADDRESS

_____

_____

WHEN WAS CONSENT DECREE SIGNED?
_____

WHERE WAS CONSENT DECREE SIGNED?
_____

WHEN WAS THE ADOPTION PETITION SIGNED?
_____

WHERE WAS THE ADOPTION PETITION FILED?
_____

WHO FILED THE PETITION?
_____

HOW OLD WHERE YOU AT THE TIME OF THE ADOPTION?
_____

DID YOU EVER MEET YOUR BIRTHCHILD? ☐ YES ☐ NO

ANY OTHER INFORMATION THAT MIGHT BE IMPORTANT?

_____

_____

_____

_____

_____

# SIBLING'S WORKSHEET

CHILD'S NAME _____

DATE OF BIRTH (DOB) _____ SEX ☐ M ☐ F

BIRTH PLACE _____

BIRTHMOTHER'S NAME _____

BIRTHMOTHER'S MAIDEN NAME

_____

DATE OF BIRTH (DOB) _____

SOCIAL SECURITY NUMBER _____

LAST KNOWN ADDRESS _____

_____

NAMES OF ANY OF HER RELATIVES _____

_____

NAMES OF ANY OF HER FRIENDS _____

_____

OCCUPATION_____

EDUCATION _____

UNUSUAL TRAITS _____

_____

BIRTHFATHER'S NAME _____

DATE OF BIRTH (DOB) _____

SOCIAL SECURITY NUMBER _____

LAST KNOWN ADDRESS _____

_____

NAME OF ANY OF HIS RELATIVES _____

_____

NAME OF ANY OF HIS FRIENDS _____

_____

OCCUPATION_____

EDUCATION _____

UNUSUAL TRAITS _____

_____

TYPE OF ADOPTION AGENCY:
☐ PUBLIC AGENCY ☐ PRIVATE AGENCY

NAME AND ADDRESS OF ADOPTION AGENCY

_____

_____

_____

ATTORNEY'S NAME AND ADDRESS

_____

_____

_____

DOCTOR'S NAME AND ADDRESS

_____

_____

_____

SOCIAL WORKER'S NAME AND ADDRESS

_____

_____

_____

WHEN WAS CONSENT DECREE SIGNED?

_____

WHERE WAS CONSENT DECREE SIGNED?

_____

WHEN WAS THE ADOPTION PETITION SIGNED?

_____

WHERE WAS THE ADOPTION PETITION FILED?

_____

WHO FILED THE PETITION?

_____

HOW OLD WHERE YOU AT THE TIME OF THE ADOPTION?

_____

DID YOU EVER MEET YOUR SIBLING? ☐YES ☐NO

_____

ANY OTHER INFORMATION THAT MIGHT BE IMPORTANT?

_____

_____

_____

_____

# _Notes_

**Adoption Searches Made Easier**

# *Rules of the Game* 2

In order to play any game successfully one needs to know the rules of the game. When it comes to adoption searches knowing the rules and understanding how to use them is vital to a successful search.

If the searcher knows the state in which the adoption took place, it is essential to read the statutes of that state that pertain to adoption. It is necessary to read the present statutes as well as the statutes that were in effect in the year that the adoption took place. It is important to remember that each state's adoption laws are different and unique to that state.

These laws will provide you with the following important information:

### 1. Are the adoption records open or sealed?

In most states the adoption records are sealed. This means that a searcher is not legally allowed to view or obtain the original records of the adoption. If the records are open then the information the searcher is looking for is available. The only task left is to find the object of the search (see my other book YOU, TOO, CAN FIND ANYBODY).

### 2. Under what circumstances can sealed adoption records be opened?

Depending on the state, the statute will provide for some valid reasons for allowing the sealed adoption records to be opened and made available to the petitioner. Some but not all of those valid reasons could be:

A) a valid need for a medical history of a birthparent or the child at the time of birth;

B) a question dealing with an birthright;

C) a humanitarian need to know;

D) evidence required in a criminal proceedings;

F) strong evidence suggests the adoption was illegal, or proper procedures as specified by state statute were not followed;

E) discretion of the court of jurisdiction.

## 3. By law what procedural steps have to be followed for the adoption to be considered legal?

In most cases the statutes will define what necessary procedures have to be followed for the adoption to be legal. In many cases these procedures will help a searcher find and follow the documents generated by this adoption (the paper trail). For example, a state may require that an adoption may only be finalized by decree through a county court after the adoptee has resided with the prospective adoptive parents for one year. In this state the searcher under normal circumstances should begin to search the appropriate county court records one year after the birth of the adoptee. Knowing and understanding the procedural steps of a specific state will help determine the proper course of action for your search.

## 4. What information is a searcher legally entitled to? Is the information identifying or non-identifying? Which agency is responsible for dispersing the information?

State statutes may require that a state agency such as the Office of Vital Statistics or the state public adoption agency disburse information to a searcher upon request. The type of information available such as identifying or non-identifying may also be specified by state statute.

## 5. How can a party to an adoption waive their right of confidentiality? How can a party to an adoption contact another party to the same adoption?

Some state statutes provide for the parties to an adoption to waive their right of confidentiality. For example if a birthmother is searching for her birthchild she may be entitled to waive her right of confidentiality by writing a letter to the appropriate agency. This letter will be placed in the adoption record. If, at any time after the filing of this letter, the birthchild writes the agency for identifying information the information will be released.

Some states provide for direct contact by allowing a party to an adoption to place a letter in the adoption record addressed to another party of the same adoption. For example a birthfather might write a letter to his birthchild in which he identifies himself. If the birthchild requests information regarding the birthparents the state will forward the waiting letter.

This is only a partial list of the important information that is contained in the state's statutes pertaining to adoption. Copies of the state's statutes may be available in your local library or a law library located in the county courthouse, or law school.

The following is an example of a letter written for the purpose of waiving a birthparent's right of confidentiality:

Mrs. Fran J. Lenox
150 Brown Street
Flint, MI 48502
Telephone: (313) 555-0896

October 25, 1995

State Adoption Office
Department of Social Services
Adoption Services Division
235 S. Grand Ave., 4th Floor
Lansing, Michigan 48909

Dear Official:

On June 23, 1964 I gave birth to a baby girl that your agency, with my consent, put out for adoption. At that time my name was Fran J. Hicks and I was 15 years of age. The birth occurred at Saint Michaels Hospital in Battle Creek, Michigan and the doctor's name was Fredrick T. Sonit.

In the eventuality that my birthdaughter contacts your agency searching for identifying information on her birthmother, I hereby waive my rights of confidentiality and would appreciate it if you send her all of the information that she requests including my present name and address.

Thank you in advance for your time and effort in my behalf.

Sincerely,

*Fran Lenox*

Mrs. Fran J. Lenox

The following is an example of a cover letter that would be sent along with a sealed, personal letter from an adoptee to a birthparent:

**Jane L. Keefe**
1123 Oberlin Road
Dubuque, Iowa 52001

June 11, 1995

State Adoption Office
Department of Social Services
Adoption Service Division
235 S. Grand Ave., 4th Floor
Lansing, Michigan 48909

Dear Official:

I was born on June 23, 1964, in Saint Michaels Hospital in Battle Creek, Michigan.

In the eventuality that my birthparent(s) contacts your agency searching for identifying information on their daughter, I hereby waive my rights of confidentiality and I would appreciate it if you would send the sealed letter I have enclosed.

Thank you in advance for your time and effort on my behalf.

Sincerely,

*Jane L. Keefe*

Jane L. Keefe

To be assured that your sealed letter has been received by the agency contacted, you may ask the agency to fill out and return a performance receipt which may also be named a Disclosure Agreement. The following is an example of such an agreement:

---

## DISCLOSURE AGREEMENT

Current Full Name
Present Address
City, State, Zip

Present Date

I placed the following information into the file as requested by you.

Affidavit, Waiver of Confidentiality, update of information, personal letter, tape, and/or picture. (State the above that you have submitted.)

Placed into the file of: _____

_____

This ___ day of ___19 ___

Signatures: _____

Agency or Court: _____

Address: _____

City: _____ State: _____ Zip: _____

NOTE TO AGENCY, COURT, ETC, Please fill out the information on this Disclosure Agreement and return to me. A self-addressed, stamped envelope is enclosed for your convenience.

---

# *3*

# *Birth Indexes*

A wise, old adage states that "A journey of a thousand miles must begin with a single step." This is, of course, true for an adoptee searching for the identity of birthparents. The question is how to begin this journey on the right path and in the right direction. The answer to the puzzle is to start from the very beginning.

If the adoptee was adopted out by an adoption agency, either public or private, the adoptee is normally entitled to some background information. There are two distinct types of information that may be dispersed:

**IDENTIFYING INFORMATION** is provided by some agencies depending on what the state statutes will permit, what the policy of the agency is, and whether or not the birthparent(s) have waived their right to confidentiality. This information will reveal the last known name(s), address(es), and other relevant information pertaining to the adoptee's birthparent(s). The following are examples of identifying information written to a birthparent and another written to an adoptee:

**THE HARDING McGUIRE SERVICE**
SERVICE AND CARING SINCE 1927

December 4, 1995

Mrs. Roger Moorehead
1247 Willowband Road
Holloway, CT 23893

Dear Mrs. Moorehead,

I would like to introduce myself to you as your social worker. I was
assigned to assist you in obtaining the identifying information you
requested on your birth child.

Your birth child was born Mary Anne Litglow on 10/28/78 in Dallas
Parkland Hospital in Dallas, Texas. Shortly after her birth you signed a
consent decree and the child was taken from you and given to Tom
Jason Willowman and his wife Betty Sue Willowman. They lived at 2370
North Jessup Drive, Corpus Christie, Texas. They legally adopted the
child on 1/11/80 and changed the child's name to Lucy May Willowman.
The adoption decree was finalized in the Nueces County District Court in
Corpus Christi, Texas (case # FAM 78/56734/001).

I hope this information assists you in your search for your birth child.
Best of luck and feel free to contact me at 214 - 654-8923.

Sincerely,

*Roberta St James*

Roberta St James, C.S.W.
Adoption Department

Registrant's # 123-56-429367
William K. Tasken

Date of Adoption: 4/23/43

## *IDENTIFYING INFORMATION:*

Concerning the biological parents at the time of birth of said child.

### MOTHER

Name: Nancy Jane Hopkins

Address: 2376 Wayne Road
   Akron, Ohio 34657

Social Security #: no information available

Date of Birth: 8/11/28

Heritage:
 Nationality: American

Ethnic Background: German/Swedish

Race: Caucasian

### FATHER

Name: Ronald William Polotsky

Address: 535 Thames Avenue
   Youngstown, Ohio 56732

Social Security #: 145-55-6666

Date of Birth: 1/25/23

Heritage:
 Nationality: American

Ethnic Background: Russian/Polish

Race: Caucasian

This report was completed by Jane R. Dolye, CSW   on June 7, 1988.

**NON-IDENTIFYING INFORMATION** is what is normally provided by most agencies due to state's statutes which prohibits the release of identifying data and/or birthparent(s) not waiving their rights of confidentiality. This information generally lists the birthparents age at the time of birth, as well as a sketchy account of their economic, educational and social circumstances. In many instances the adoptees actual date and place of birth is also included.

The good news is that **NON-IDENTIFYING INFORMATION** may contain valuable information that could lead to uncovering of the birthparents' identity. Each report is different but there are almost always clues, that properly interpreted and researched, may open additional doors that may inevitably allow the adoptee to reach his or her desired final destination. If unknown, the adoptee is looking for his or her correct date and place of birth. Once this information is known, the adoptee may be able to utilize one of the most revealing yet least known of records kept by local or state government, **the birth indexes**.

Normally when a child is born in a private or public hospital, that birth must by law be recorded. It is first recorded by the hospital and kept on file in the hospital records department. In addition, as required by statute, forms describing the birth are sent to the appropriate county or city government. The government enters and saves these records in various department(s) and keeps them indefinitely. One of the places that government possibly maintains birth records is a journal called the **birth index**. Here all births for a certain town, city, or county are recorded on an annual basis.

The actual format of the records vary but generally they all contain the name of the child (if a name was given), the name and address of the birthmother, the time, date, and place of birth, the attending physician, and the name of the hospital. Depending on the particular locale this annual birth index may be stored at the county courthouse, the city or county library, a government office, and if it is old enough, a copy or the original may be stored at the state archives. The important point is that the birth index for the appropriate year may contain a great deal of the information

that the adoptee is searching for. Therefore the searcher must try to find where the appropriate birth index, if it exists, is being stored.

A great deal of the state's historical material and records are stored in the state archives for safekeeping. If the adoption is more than a few years old a good place to begin your search is the state archive (see chapter 10). A clear, concise letter addressed to the state archivist will normally save a great deal of time and provide the searcher with a significant amount of information regarding the availability of the birth index required. The sample letter written by Norma Davis (on page 3-6) covers all of the important questions the searcher is interested in. One important point is never use the word *adoption* when dealing with a government employee unless it is absolutely necessary. Substitute the word *adoption* with *genealogical research* or *tracing the family tree*.

**Mrs. Norma Davis**
1123 Bird Road South
Bridgeport, N.Y. 13030

October 31, 1995

State Archivist
California State Archives
Office of the Secretary of State
1020 O Street
Sacramento, CA 95814

Dear Archivist;

I am involved with a genealogical research project and would like to know if you house the birth index for Santa Barbara County for 1941. If you do store this index, do you provide research and, if so, what is the hourly fee? If you do not provide research would it be possible for you to recommend a good local researcher?

If you do not store this index at the archive, would you know where it is stored?

Please send a reply to the above address at your earliest possible convenience. Thanking you in advance for your time and effort in my behalf.

Sincerely,

*Norma Davis*

Norma Davis

The following is an example of the birth index from the Texas Department of Health Resources for the year 1975:

| TEXAS DEPARTMENT OF HEALTH RESOURCES<br>RECORDS AND STATISTICS<br>BIRTHS FOR THE YEAR 1975 | | | |
|---|---|---|---|
| NAME | COUNTY | DATE | FILE # |
| HIGHFILL HOLLY M | DALLAS | DEC 8 | 194572 |
| HIGHFILL MARTHA J | NUECES | JAN 28 | 39182 |
| HIGHLEY NATASHA L | HARRIS | AUG 11 | 143755 |
| HIGHNOTE DAVID D | TAYLOR | MAR 29 | 41286 |
| HIGHSAW CHALANDA D | COLLIN | OCT 17 | 157296 |
| HIGHSMITH CHRISTINA L | CASS | AUG 31 | 137325 |
| HIGHSMITH ROBERT W | HARRIS | JAN 6 | 4175 |
| HIGHSMITH SHELLEY D | DALLAS | AUG 31 | 47060 |
| HIGHSMITH WILLIAM D | TOM GREEN | JUL 7 | 111668 |
| HIGHT AMY D | ECTOR | APR 28 | 66977 |
| HIGHT ANGELA K | MENARD | JUN 19 | 91182 |
| HIGHT BRANDI M | JEFFERSON | FEB 20 | 20130 |
| HIGHT CHARLES C | JOHNSON | MAY 8 | 72758 |
| HIGHT COBY C | JEFFERSON | OCT 21 | 166123 |
| HIGHT GENEVA F | NUECES | JUL 3 | 109114 |
| HIGHT JERE H | DALLAS | APR 17 | 47095 |
| HIGHT KAREN L | HARRIS | JAN 13 | 17766 |
| HIGHT PAULA G | EASTLAND | AUG 23 | 140293 |
| HIGHT SPENCER C | TARRANT | NOV 10 | 188774 |
| HIGHT TERRY B | HARRIS | FEB 6 | 34482 |
| HIGHTOWER ALLEN T | WALKER | NOV 22 | 189365 |
| HIGHTOWER ANTHONY R | NACOGDOCHES | DEC 13 | 221418 |
| HIGHTOWER APRIL D | DALLAS | APR 9 | 47038 |
| HIGHTOWER BRANDY M | WASHINGTON | MAY 21 | 94995 |
| HIGHTOWER CARLTON D | WALKER | AUG 2 | 132900 |
| HIGHTOWER CHRISTOPHER T | HARRIS | FEB 24 | 18623 |
| HIGHTOWER CLIFFORD C JR | BELL | MAR 1 | 25610 |
| HIGHTOWER COREY A | TAYLOR | JUL 3 | 111394 |
| HIGHTOWER CRAWYTON L | DALLAS | SEP 28 | 158952 |
| HIGHTOWER DERRICK D | HARRIS | NOV 15 | 200775 |

The following letter is a good example of non-identifying information that is more revealing than the agency probably intended. The significant information in the letter describes a large family (4 sisters and 4 brothers) where the father was a park superintendent in Connecticut. Furthermore, the birthmother had taken college courses while in the 9th grade of high school which would lead one to believe that there was a college not to far from the park. Therefore, one could look at a map of Connecticut, see how many state parks there were which were close to a college and easily narrow down the possibilities.

---

CHAPLIN SPENCER
SERVICE AND CARING SINCE 1918

February 12, 1995

Mr. Thomas Blanker
5555 Fifth Street
Long River, NJ 08757

Dear Mr. Blanker;

    I would like to introduce myself to you as your social worker. I was assigned to assist you in obtaining the information you requested on your birth parents. I apologize for the delay.

    You were born on 11/17/59 in New York at 9:15 a.m. after a normal and spontaneous 8 hour labor. You were 6 lbs. 7 oz. and were 20 inches long. You had honey-blonde hair, blue eyes a loggish shaped head and a fair complexion. You were jaundiced at birth. You gained 5 lbs. in 2 months and developed into a large, well developed, good-looking baby who enjoyed food and being held. You were in a loving foster home until placement with your adoptive parents on 3/18/58. Your birth mother had prenatal care throughout her pregnancy and was in good physical health. She lived at home the first 8 months of pregnancy and lived in a maturity shelter in New York for the last month due to confidential reasons. Her friends thought she went to help her sister who lived out of town as she was due to have a child.

Your birth mother was a 14 year old, White, Protestant girl of Irish and English descent. **She was in the 9th grade and was taking some college courses**. She had blonde hair, brown eyes, a round face and a fair complexion. She was a student and was in the 9th grade. She had taken some college courses as well. **She lived with her family in a State Park in Connecticut as her father was Park Superintendent**.

Your maternal grandmother was a 49 year old woman who completed high school. She was a heavy woman in need of a hernia operation. She raised eight children the youngest was two years younger than your birthmother.

*Over*

Your maternal grandfather was a 51 year old man who had some high school. He was reported to be in good physical health.

**Your birth mother had 3 sisters and 4 brothers.** Her oldest sister was 28 years old, was a college graduate and worked in the social service field. Her other sister was 23, attended a teacher's college, was married and was expecting a child and her youngest sister was in the 7th grade. Her oldest brother was 21 and had 2 years of high school and was a park laborer. Her 20 year old brother had 2 years of college and was a laboratory technician.

Her 18 year old brother had 1 year of high school and was a clerk, and her youngest brother, 17, had 2 years of high school and was a trained mechanic.

Your birth father was a 17 year old, single, Caucasian, protestant, young man who was part Swedish. He was in high school and left when he found out that your birth mother was pregnant. He wanted to contribute financially towards her care in the maternity residence etc. and got a job as a clerk. Your birth father was of medium height and was described as being very nice. He was originally a friend of your birth mother's brother. They dated for a period of time before they discovered she was pregnant. Originally they had decided to marry, but were advised by an attorney that your birth mother would have to go before the Children's Court as she was only 14 years old to get permission to marry. There were complications surrounding this plan and decided not to marry at this time. They spoke of marriage perhaps in the future.

Your paternal grandmother was in her late 30's and was healthy. She was a housewife. Your paternal grandfather was in his late 30's or early 40's, was healthy and was a construction worker. Your birth father had 4 siblings. He had a sister, 13, who was in the 8th grade, a twin brother and sister who was 1-1/2 years old and a 3 year old brother.

Both of your birth parents were very involved in planning for you. Your birth mother was seen regularly for counseling during this period of time. They struggled with their decision but decided that it would be in your best interest if you were placed in a stable two parent family. They felt that they were too young to raise you in the way that you deserved.

I hope that this information helps to answer some of your questions about your origins. Please let me know your thoughts about this information and feel free to contact me at 212-555-6821. Please leave a message for me and I will contact you as soon as possible.

Sincerely,

*Pam Slinger*

Pam Slinger, C.S.W.
Adoption Department

# _Notes_

**Adoption Searches Made Easier**

# *The Courthouse*

Most adoptions in the United States are processed through and sanctioned by the court of jurisdiction. This means that whether the adoption was done through an agency, public or private, or through a third party such as an attorney or physician, the various required papers and necessary appearances leading to a lawful adoption were properly executed in a court of law. For those who are searching, this legal paper trail is perhaps the most revealing source of information available. To properly take advantage of this resource however, it is essential that you understand how the system works and what motions and petitions are required to be filed. This information is normally described in detail as part of the specific state's statutes that pertains to adoption.

The following is a generic description of the adoption process:

1. The birthmother, and after 1972 (*Stanley vs. Illinois*) the birthfather, are required to sign a <u>Consent To Adopt Decree</u> before or after the birth of the child(ren). The definition of consent decree is "*a solemn contract or agreement of the parties, made under sanction of the court...*" What this means is that a contract is established between the adoption agency, third party, or perhaps even the adoptive parents and the birthparent(s). The birthparent(s) gives up all parental rights and responsibilities to the child(ren) and permits the child(ren) to be adopted out. Normally this agreement can be revoked for a period of time (normally one year) but that is not always the case. The important factor here is that this agreement is sanctioned by the court and must be duly recorded. In some states this agreement to sever all paternal rights and responsibilities for a specific child is also called a <u>Relinquishment</u> or a <u>Surrender</u>.

2. Depending on state statute sometime either before or after the child is

adopted out to adoptive parents a <u>Petition to Adopt</u> must be filed with the appropriate court. A Petition to Adopt is *"an application made to a court ex parte, or where there are no parties in opposition, praying for the exercise of judicial powers of the court in relation to some matter which is not the subject for a suit or action, or for authority to do some act which requires the sanction of the court; as for the appointment of a guardian, for a child without parents."* This adoption petition is an intermediate step (interlocutory) that normally allows for a one year trial period before a final adoption decree is granted. In some states the birthparent(s) may reclaim the child during this probationary period. The important point is that there must have been an appearance in the jurisdictional court by the adoptive parents or their lawyer or both and a representative from the adoption agency or agent. This appearance and the results of the appearance is what is important to the searcher.

3. Depending upon state statute and especially since 1972 (*Stanley vs. Illinois*) most states require that when a Petition to Adopt is filed in the jurisdictional court, proper notice of the filing must be given to the birthparents or legal guardians of the child. If the court or its agents are not able to contact the birthparents or legal guardians directly a notice of the intent to adopt must be published in a newspaper in the same county as the birthparents or legal guardians last known residence.

A searcher should research the newspaper used to place legal notices for the county that the birth occurred as well as the county where the petition was filed if they are different. The notice can appear any time after the Petition to Adopt was filed up to the month prior to the hearing for the Final Adoption Decree.

For the birthparent who is searching this notice is very important because it will normally reveal the name of the couple looking to adopt the child(ren). Once the birthparent knows the name of the adoptive parent(s) the search for the child(ren) becomes much easier.

For the adoptee the legal notice normally lists the adoptee's original name as well as the name of the caseworker assigned by the court to do the home study required for adoption. This name may be of great help in gathering more facts about the adoption.

4. After some legally defined period of time depending on state statute the adoptive parents may be granted a <u>Final Adoption Decree</u>. A final decree is *"one which fully and finally disposes of the whole litigation, determining all questions raised by the case, and leaving nothing that requires further judicial action."* In a final adoption decree the adoptive parents permanently and legally become the adoptive child(ren)'s parents and the birth certificate may be amended depending on state law to show the child(ren)'s new name and the adoptive parents as the child(ren)'s parents. The interested parties once again are required to appear in the appropriate court and the result of the court's determination must also be duly recorded.

State law might require that the actual Consent to Adopt Decree, Adoption Petition, and Final Adoption Decree be included with the sealed records and not available to the searcher. However the court normally maintains a daily record of who appeared before the court and why. This journal is sometimes called the <u>Docket Appearance Book</u> and it may be stored at the appropriate county courthouse, county library, or state archive. The court also maintains another log sometimes called the <u>Minute Book</u> where the results of each appearance before the court is recorded. This minute book also may be stored in the county courthouse, county library, or state archives. The searcher must do some detective work to determine the present location of these important court diaries because they may contain identifying information that may be vital to the search.

For a birthparent looking for a birthchild the information contained in either the docket appearance book, or the minute book normally will yield the name and address (at that time) of the adoptive parents. With this information it should be relatively simple to locate the child(ren) regardless of how much time has passed.

For the adoptee the docket book and the minute book might yield a number of new and interesting facts. It may reveal the original name of the adoptee, the name of the attorney that represented his/her adopted parents, the name of the agency (public or private) that did the adoption or the name of the third party that was involved with the adoption.

The records might also include the name of the caseworker that did the family study and reports for the adoption agency or the court. This wealth of new information will be valuable in gathering additional facts. Each new piece to the puzzle draws the searcher closer to his/her successful conclusion to the investigation.

The following four documents are examples of the paper trail generated by an adoption. This adoption procedure in the court of jurisdiction starts with a Petition to Adopt (Figure 1).

## <u>Figure 1</u>

STATE OF SOUTH CAROLINA   )
)
COUNTY OF CHARLESTON    )

IN THE COURT OF COMMON PLEAS

IN THE MATTER OF THE PETITION OF )
      JAMES L. CURTIS AND      )
      CHRISTINE CURTIS       )     No. 83-16504-FC02
)
     to adopt            )
)
MARY BETH ST. JAMES       )

### PETITION TO ADOPT

TO THE HONORABLE DAVID K. JUSTICE,
                      JUDGE OF SAID COURT.

    YOUR PETITIONERS,
JAMES L. CURTIS and his wife, CHRISTINE:

1:     That they reside at 1000 Any Street, in the city of Charleston, South Carolina.

2:     That they desire to adopt MARY BETH ST. JAMES a female minor child who is about 3 weeks of age and was born on the 15th day of March, 1974 at Charleston General Hospital, South Carolina; that the said child is in the custody of and resides with the petitioners herein.

3:      That BETTY ST. JAMES is the mother; that she is not of legal age and resides in the City of Miami, County of Dade and State of Florida.

4:      That BETTY ST. JAMES, the mother of the said child is unable to support and maintain the said child and has surrendered the said child to the Department of Social Services.

5:      That the petitioners are reputable persons of good moral character with sufficient ability and financial means to rear, nurture and educate the said child in a suitable and proper manner.

YOUR PETITIONERS make MARY BETH ST. JAMES, a minor and BETTY ST. JAMES, mother of said minor, parties defendant to this cause, and

ASK THE COURT:
(a) To appoint a Guardian ad Litem to represent the interests of the minor defendant in this proceeding.
(b) For leave to adopt as their own child, the said MARY BETH ST. JAMES.
(c) For leave to change the name of the said child to MARJORIE CURTIS.

_____

_____

STATE OF SOUTH CAROLINA    )
                           ) as
COUNTY OF CHARLESTON       )

JAMES L. CURTIS AND CHRISTINE CURTIS,

his wife, being first duly sworn on oath, depose and say that they subscribed to the above and foregoing petition, know the contents thereof, and that the matters and things alleged therein are true.

_____

_____

SUBSCRIBED and SWORN to before me
this 3rd day of April 1974 .

_____
Notary Public

Figure 2 represents a docket appearance book and minute book combined. This document reveals the names of the adoptive parents, the birthmother, the birthchild, the name of the adoptive parents' attorney, as well as the presiding judge's identification number. The document also details each procedural step along the adoption process as well as the date that it occurred.

STATE OF SOUTH CAROLINA
COUNTY OF CHARLESTON

IN THE COURT OF COMMON PLEAS

Case No. 83-16504 FC02
PETITIONERS

BOOK 036   PAGE 105

JAMES L. CURTIS AND
CHRISTINE CURTIS
                vs

JUDGE ___ 25

ACTION 51
  ADOPTION

RESPONDENTS

BETTY ST. JAMES AND
MARY BETH ST. JAMES, an infant
under the age of fourteen years

Attorneys
Richard Bells, Esq.
5000 Any Street
Charleston, SC 29405
(803) 555-2815

| 1974 | | PROGRESS OF CASE | Debit | Credit |
|---|---|---|---|---|
| 04 | 03 | Petition for adoption | | |
| | 03 | Summons Issued-Return 4/18/74(Joe Smith,Father) | | |
| | 09 | Certificate of Mailing | | |
| | 23 | Answer from Dept. of Social Services | | |
| 05 | 10 | Motion for Default (against Joe Smith, Father) | | |
| | 25 | Notice of hearing 06-24-74 | | |
| | 25 | Notice of appearance ORB 27164-2844 (4-27-74) | | |
| 06 | 03 | Consent of adoption | | |
| 07 | 02 | Final Judgement ORB 27164-2971-1610 (7-13-74) | | |
| | 10 | One Certified Copy of Final Decree to Bureau of Vital Statistics n/c | | |
| | 15 | One Certified Copy of Final Decree to Dept. of Social Services | | |
| | 15 | File sealed | | |

**Figure 2**

Figure 3 is an example of the legal notice placed in the newspaper(s) prior to the hearing for the Final Adoption Decree. This notice discloses the name of the birthmother, birthchild, birthfather, adoptive parents, and the adoptive parents' attorney and the date of the hearing.

## Figure 3

### The Charleston Evening Gazette          April 27, 1974

NOTICE OF ADOPTION
IN THE FAMILY COURT FOUR-
TEENTH JUDICIAL CIRCUIT
CASE NO: 83-16504-FC02
STATE OF SOUTH CAROLINA
COUNTY OF COLLETON
JAMES L CURTIS AND
CHRISTINE CURTIS
Plaintiff,
-versus-
BETTY ST. JAMES AND MARY
BETH ST. JAMES, an infant under
the age of fourteen years
Respondents,
TO: Joe Smith
Respondent Above-Named, the
father of MARY BETH ST. JAMES
YOU ARE HEREBY NOTIFIED
pursuant to the provisions of S.C.
Code Ann, Section 20-7-1734 (Cum,
Supp. 1973) that the Respondent,
above-named, Mary Beth St. James,
has been placed with the Petitioners
above-named, for the purposes of
adoption.
YOU ARE FURTHER NOTIFIED
that an adoption action has been filed
on April 17, 1974 at 2:16 PM in the
Court of Common Pleas, 2144
Melbourne Street, PO Box 70219,
Charleston, SC 29402 in Case
Number 83-16504-FC02.

YOU ARE FURTHER NOTIFIED
that within thirty (30) days of

receiving this Notice, you shall
respond in writing by filing with the
Court of Common Pleas for
Charleston County, South Carolina,
notice and reasons to contest,
intervene or otherwise respond in the
pending adoption action:
   YOU ARE FURTHER NOTIFIED
the Court must be informed
of your current address and
of any changes in address
during the adoption proceeding;
and
   YOU ARE FURTHER NOTIFIED
that failure to file a response within
thirty (30) days of receiving Notice
constitutes consent to adoption of the
child and forfeiture of all rights and
obligations with respect to the child
BE SO NOTIFIED BY:
RICHARD BELLS, ESQUIRE
5000 Any Street
Suite 100
Charleston, SC 29402
(803) 555-2815
Dated: April 27, 1974

Figure 4 is an example of the Final Adoption Decree. It discloses the name of the birthmother, birthchild, the adoptive parents, the adoptive parents' attorney, the new name of the birthchild, and the name of the presiding judge.

## Figure 4

| | |
|---|---|
| STATE OF SOUTH CAROLINA, ) | IN THE COURT OF COMMON PLEAS |
| COUNTY OF CHARLESTON. ) | |

| | |
|---|---|
| JAMES L. CURTIS and ) | Case No. 83-16504-FC02 |
| CHRISTINE CURTIS, ) | |
| ) | |
| Petitioners, ) | |
| ) | FINAL ADOPTION DECREE |
| - versus - ) | |
| ) | |
| BETTY ST JAMES and ) | |
| MARY BETH ST JAMES, ) | |
| an infant under the age of ) | |
| fourteen years, ) | |
| ) | |
| Respondents. ) | |

THIS MATTER comes before me on the Report of T. L. Nelson, Master in Equity for Charleston County, filed herein on 17th day of April, 1974. Upon reading the said Report and on consideration of the same, and it appearing that the petitioners have had custody of the infant Respondent since her birth, that the Petitioners have caused the said infant Respondent to be medically examined and thoroughly checked and that they have been advised and are satisfied that the said Respondent is normal in all respects and is in good physical health and has no mental defects, and that the natural mother has appeared in this action and consents to the adoption and change of name, and that the punitive father is unknown, but that he is not a party to this proceeding.

IT IS ORDERED, ADJUDGED AND DECREED That the said Master's Report be, and the same is hereby, ratified, approved, confirmed, and made the judgment of this Court.

IT IS FURTHER ORDERED, ADJUDGED AND DECREED That the prayer of the Petitioners, James L. Curtis and Christine Curtis, for the adoption of the infant Respondent, Mary Beth St James, be granted and that the name of said infant shall henceforth be Lily Anne Curtis and that as the legally adopted child of the said James L. Curtis and Christine Curtis said Lily Anne Curtis be entitled to inherit from them as their lawful child.

AND, IT IS FURTHER ORDERED That the Clerk of this Court do prepare, within thirty days after this Decree becomes final, a certificate of this Decree on forms furnished by the State Registrar of Vital Statistics, as in and by Section 10-2586.1, Code of Laws of South Carolina for 1952, required: and that the State Registrar do, upon receipt of such certified certificate of adoption, prepare a supplementary certificate of birth in the new name of the adopted child, via., Lily Anne Curtis, free of any reference to or indication of the fact that said Lily Anne Curtis is adopted and showing James L. Curtis to be the real father of the said infant, Lily Anne Curtis, and showing Christine Curtis to be the real mother of the said infant, Lily Anne Curtis, and that said State Registrar do transmit a certified certificate of adoption for said Lily Anne Curtis to the State of Florida wherein said infant was born, as in and by Section 32-1119, Code of Laws of South Carolina for 1952, required.

AND, IT IS FURTHER ORDERED That this Decree be entered up forthwith.

AND, IT IS FURTHER ORDERED That the file in the Office of the Clerk of Court containing these proceedings be sealed.

AND, IT IS SO ORDERED!

Charleston, S.C.

April 17, 1974

_____
Judge, Ninth Judicial Circuit

The County Courthouse Directory (pages 4-10 through 4-267), is a listing of the names and mailing addresses of the courts of jurisdiction that hear adoption cases in the counties of the United States. This easy-to-use reference, divided by state, is provided to assist in locating and contacting the appropriate court.

# County Courthouse Directory
## ALASKA

Superior Court Clerk
Sitka Superior Court
304 Lake Street, Room 203
Sitka, AK 99835-7599

Superior Court Clerk
Wrangell Superior Court
Box 869
Wrangell, AK 99929-0869

Superior Court Clerk
Barrow Superior Court
Box 2700
Barrow, AK 99723-2700

Superior Court Clerk
Kotzebue Superior Court
Box 317
Kotzebue, AK 99752-0317

Superior Court Clerk
Nome Superior Court
Box 1110
Nome, AK 99762-1110

Clerk of Courts
Anchorage Superior Courts
303 K Street
Anchorage, AK 99501-2083

District Court Clerk
Homer District Court
3670 Lake Street, #400
Homer, AK 99607-9647

Superior Court Clerk
Kenai Superior Court
125 Trading Bay Dr,#100
Kenai, AK 99611-7717

Superior Court Clerk
Kodiak Superior Court
202 Marine Way
Kodiak, AK 99614-9987

Clerk of Courts
Palmer Superior Courts
435 S. Denali
Palmer, AK 99645-6437

Superior Court Clerk
Valdez Superior Court
Box 127
Valdez, AK 99686-0127

Superior Court Clerk
Bethel Superior Court
Box 130
Bethel, AK 99559

Clerk of Courts
Fairbanks Superior Courts
604 Barnette Street,#342
Fairbanks, AK 99701-4572

**Adoption Searches Made Easier**

# ALABAMA

**AUTAUGA COUNTY**
Circuit Court Clerk
Autauga County Circuit Court
4th and Court
Prattville, AL 36067

**BALDWIN COUNTY**
Circuit Court Clerk
Baldwin County Circuit Court
PO Box 1149
Bayminette, AL 36507

**BARBOUR COUNTY**
Circuit Court Clerk
Barbour County Circuit Court
PO Box 237
Clayton, AL 36016

**BIBB COUNTY**
Circuit Court Clerk
Bibb County Circuit Court
Bibb County Courthouse
Centerville, AL 35042

**BLOUNT COUNTY**
Circuit Court Clerk
Blount County Circuit Court
2nd Avenue E
Oneonta, AL 35121

**BULLOCK COUNTY**
Circuit Court Clerk
Bullock County Circuit Court
217 North Prairie
Union Springs, AL 36089

**BUTLER COUNTY**
Circuit Court Clerk
Butler County Circuit Court
PO Box 134
Greenville, AL 36037

**CALHOUN COUNTY**
Circuit Court Clerk
Calhoun County Courthouse
25 West 11th Street
Anniston, AL 36201

**CHAMBERS COUNTY**
Circuit Court Clerk
Chambers County Courthouse
Courthouse Square
La Fayette, AL 36862

**CHEROKEE COUNTY**
Circuit Court Clerk
Cherokee County Courthouse
Courthouse Square
Centre, AL 35960

**CHILTON COUNTY**
Circuit Court Clerk
Chilton County Circuit Court
PO Box 1946
Clanton, AL 35045

**CHOCTAW COUNTY**
Circuit Court Clerk
Choctaw County Courthouse
Courthouse Square
Butler, AL 36904

## CLARKE COUNTY
Circuit Court Clerk
Clarke County Circuit Court
117 Court Street.
Grove Hill, AL 36451

## CLAY COUNTY
Circuit Court Clerk
Clay County Courthouse
PO Box 816
Ashland, AL 36251

## CLEBURNE COUNTY
Circuit Court Clerk
Cleburne Cty Circuit Court
406 Vickery Street
Heflin, AL 36264

## COFFEE COUNTY
Circuit Court Clerk
Coffee Cty Circuit Court
230-M Court Ave
Elba, AL 36323

## COLBERT COUNTY
Circuit Court Clerk
Colbert County Courthouse
Courthouse Square
Tuscumbia, AL 35674

## CONECUH COUNTY
Circuit Court Clerk
Conecuh County Courthouse
PO Box 107
Evergreen, AL 36401

## COOSA COUNTY
Circuit Court Clerk
Coosa County Circuit Court
PO Box 98
Rockford, AL 35136

## COVINGTON COUNTY
Circuit Court Clerk
Covington Cty Courthouse
Courthouse Square
Andalusia, AL 36420

## CRENSHAW COUNTY
Circuit Court Clerk
Crenshaw Cty Circuit Court
PO Box 167
Luverne, AL 36049

## CULLMAN COUNTY
Circuit Court Clerk
Cullman County Courthouse
Rm 303
Cullman, AL 35055

## DALE COUNTY
Circuit Court Clerk
Dale County Circuit Court
PO Box 1350
Ozark, AL 36361

## DALLAS COUNTY
Circuit Court Clerk
Dallas County Circuit Court
PO Box 1158
Selma, AL 36701

## DE KALB COUNTY
Circuit Court Clerk
De Kalb Cty Circuit Court
PO Box 1149
Fort Payne, AL 35967

## ELMORE COUNTY
Circuit Court Clerk
Elmore Cty Circuit Court
200 Commerce
Wetumpka, AL 36092

## ESCAMBIA COUNTY
Circuit Court Clerk
Escambia Cty Circuit Court
PO Box 856
Brewton, AL 36427

## ETOWAH COUNTY
Circuit Court Clerk
Etowah Cty Circuit Court
800 Forrest Ave
Gadsden, AL 35999-0798

## FAYETTE COUNTY
Circuit Court Clerk
Fayette Cty Circuit Court
PO Box 206
Fayette, AL 35555

## FRANKLIN COUNTY
Circuit Court Clerk
Franklin Cty Circuit Court
PO Box 143
Russellville, AL 35653

## GENEVA COUNTY
Circuit Court Clerk
Geneva County Circuit Court
PO Box 86
Geneva, AL 36340

## GREENE COUNTY
Circuit Court Clerk
Green County Circuit Court
PO Box 307
Eutaw, AL 35462

## HALE COUNTY
Circuit Court Clerk
Hale County Courthouse
Courthouse Square
Greensboro, AL 36744

## HENRY COUNTY
Circuit Court Clerk
Henry County Circuit Court
PO Box 337
Abbeville, AL 36310

## HOUSTON COUNTY
Circuit Court Clerk
Houston Cty Circuit Court
PO Drawer 6406
Dothan, AL 36302

## JACKSON COUNTY
Circuit Court Clerk
Jackson Cty Circuit Court
PO Box 397
Scottsboro, AL 35768

## JEFFERSON COUNTY
Circuit Court Clerk
Jefferson Cty Circuit Court
801 North 21st, Rm 207
Birmingham, AL 35263

## LAMAR COUNTY
Circuit Court Clerk
Lamar County Circuit Court
North Pond Street
Vernon, AL 35592

## LAUDERDALE COUNTY
Circuit Court Clerk
Lauderdale Cty Circuit Court
200 S. Court, Room 502
Florence, AL 35631

## LAWRENCE COUNTY
Circuit Court Clerk
Lawrence Cty Circuit Court
14330 Court Street
Moulton, AL 35650

## LEE COUNTY
Circuit Court Clerk
Lee County Circuit Court
2311 Hamilton Road
Opelika, AL 36803

## LIMESTONE COUNTY
Circuit Court Clerk
Limestone Cty Circuit Court
PO Box 964
Athens, AL 35611

## LOWNDES COUNTY
Circuit Court Clerk
Lowndes County Circuit Court
PO Box 876
Hayneville, AL 36040

## MACON COUNTY
Circuit Court Clerk
Macon County Circuit Court
PO Box 723
Tuskegee, AL 36083

## MADISON COUNTY
Circuit Court Clerk
Madison County Courthouse,
100 Courthouse Square, #217
Huntsville, AL 35801

## MARENGO COUNTY
Circuit Court Clerk
Marengo County Circuit Court
101 Coats Ave
Linden, AL 36748

## MARION COUNTY
Circuit Court Clerk
Marion County Circuit Court
PO Box 1595
Hamilton, AL 35570

## MARSHALL COUNTY
Circuit Court Clerk
Marshall County Circuit Court
PO Box 248
Guntersville, AL 35976

## MOBILE COUNTY
Circuit Court Clerk
Mobile County Circuit Court
PO Box 298
Mobile, AL 36601

## MONROE COUNTY
Circuit Court Clerk
Monroe County Courthouse
Courthouse Square
Monroeville, AL 36460

## MONTGOMERY COUNTY
Circuit Court Clerk
Montgomery Cty Circuit Court
PO Box 1667
Montgomery, AL 36102-1667

## MORGAN COUNTY
Circuit Court Clerk
Morgan County Circuit Court
302 Lee Street
Decatur, AL 35602

## PERRY COUNTY
Circuit Court Clerk
Perry County Circuit Court
PO Box 505
Marion, AL 36756

## PICKENS COUNTY
Circuit Court Clerk
Pickens County Circuit Court
PO Box 418
Carrollton, AL 35447

## PIKE COUNTY
Circuit Court Clerk
Pike County Courthouse
PO Box 948
Troy, AL 36081

## RANDOLPH COUNTY
Circuit Court Clerk
Randolph County Courthouse
PO Box 328
Wedowee, AL 36278

## RUSSELL COUNTY
Circuit Court Clerk
Russell County Courthouse
PO Box 518
Phenix City, AL 36867

## SHELBY COUNTY
Circuit Court Clerk
Shelby County Circuit Court
PO Box 1810
Columbiana, AL 35051

## ST. CLAIR COUNTY
Circuit Court Clerk
St. Clair County Courthouse
PO Box 476
Ashville, AL 35953

## SUMTER COUNTY
Circuit Court Clerk
Sumter County Courthouse
PO Box 936
Livingston, AL 35470

**TALLADEGA COUNTY**
Circuit Court Clerk
Talladega County Circuit Court
148 N. East Street
Talladega, AL 35160-0755

**TALLAPOOSA COUNTY**
Circuit Court Clerk
Tallapoosa County Courthouse
101 North Broadnax, Rm 132
Dadeville, AL 36853

**TALLAPOOSA COUNTY - WESTERN DIVISION**
Circuit Court Clerk
PO Box 189
Alex City, AL 35010

**TUSCALOOSA COUNTY**
Circuit Court Clerk
Tuscaloosa County Courthouse,
714 Greensboro Ave
Tuscaloosa, AL 35401

**WALKER COUNTY**
Circuit Court Clerk
1802 2nd Avenue
Courthouse Square
Jasper, AL 35501

**WASHINGTON COUNTY**
Circuit Court Clerk
Washington County Courthouse
PO Box 548
Chatom, AL 36518

**WILCOX COUNTY**
Circuit Court Clerk
County Courthouse
Water Street
Camden, AL 36726

**WINSTON COUNTY**
Circuit Court Clerk
Winston County Circuit Court
PO Box 309
Double Springs, AL 35553

# ARKANSAS

**ARKANSAS COUNTY**
Circuit Court Clerk
Arkansas County Circuit Court
PO Box 719
Stuttgart, AR 72160

**ASHLEY COUNTY**
Circuit Court Clerk
Ashley County Circuit Court
Courthouse
Hamburg, AR 71646

**BAXTER COUNTY**
Circuit Court Clerk
Baxter County Courthouse
Courthouse Square
Mountain Home, AR 72653

**BENTON COUNTY**
Circuit Court Clerk
Benton County Courthouse
102 N.E. A Street
Bentonville, AR 72712

## BOONE COUNTY
Circuit Court Clerk
Boone County Circuit Court
PO Box 957
Harrison, AR 72601

## BRADLEY COUNTY
Circuit Court Clerk
Bradley County Circuit Court
101 East Cedar
Warren, AR 71671

## CALHOUN COUNTY
Circuit Court Clerk
Calhoun County Circuit Court
PO Box 626
Hampton, AR 71744

## CARROLL COUNTY
Circuit Court Clerk
Carroll County Circuit Court
44 South Main
Eureka Springs, AR 72632

## CHICOT COUNTY
Circuit Court Clerk
Chicot County Courthouse
Courthouse Square
Lake Village, AR 71653

## CLARK COUNTY
Circuit Court Clerk
Clark County Circuit Court
PO Box 576
Arkadelphia, AR 71923

## CLAY COUNTY
Circuit Court Clerk
Clay County Circuit Court
PO Box 29
Piggott, AR 72454

## CLEBURNE COUNTY
Circuit Court Clerk
Cleburne County Circuit Court
301 West Main
Heber Springs, AR 72543

## CLEVELAND COUNTY
Circuit Court Clerk
Cleveland County Circuit Court
Main and Magnolia
Rison, AR 71665

## COLUMBIA COUNTY
Circuit Court Clerk
Columbia County Courthouse
PO Box 327
Magnolia, AR 71753

## CONWAY COUNTY
Circuit Court Clerk
Conway County Circuit Court
115 Moose Street, Rm 206
Morrilton, AR 72110

## CRAIGHEAD COUNTY
Circuit Court Clerk
Craighead County Circuit Court
511 South Main
Jonesboro, AR 72403

## CRAWFORD COUNTY
Circuit Court Clerk
Crawford County Circuit Court
Courthouse
Van Buren, AR 72956

## CRITTENDEN COUNTY
Circuit Court Clerk
Crittenden County Circuit Court
PO Box 70
Marion, AR 72364

## CROSS COUNTY
Circuit Court Clerk
Cross County Courthouse
705 East Union, Room 9
Wynne, AR 72396

## DALLAS COUNTY
Circuit Court Clerk
Dallas County Courthouse
202 3rd Street W
Fordyce, AR 71742-3299

## DESHA COUNTY
Circuit Court Clerk
Desha County Circuit Court
PO Box 309
Arkansas City, AR 71630

## DREW COUNTY
Circuit Court Clerk
Drew County Circuit Court
210 South Main
Monticello, AR 71655

## FAULKNER COUNTY
Circuit Court Clerk
Faulkner County Courthouse,
801 Locust, Room 15
Conway, AR 72032

## FRANKLIN COUNTY
Circuit Court Clerk
Franklin County Courthouse
Courthouse Square
Ozark, AR 72949

## FULTON COUNTY
Circuit Court Clerk
Fulton County Circuit Court
PO Box 485
Salem, AR 72576

## GARLAND COUNTY
Circuit Court Clerk
Garland County Circuit Court
Courthouse
Hot Springs, AR 71901

## GRANT COUNTY
Circuit Court Clerk
Grant County Courthouse
101 West Center, Room 106
Sheridan, AR 72150

## GREENE COUNTY
Circuit Court Clerk
Greene County Circuit Court
3rd and Court
Paragould, AR 72450

## HEMPSTEAD COUNTY
Circuit Court Clerk
Hempstead County Circuit Court
PO Box 1420
Hope, AR 71801

## HOT SPRING COUNTY
Circuit Court Clerk
Hot Spring County Circuit Court
200 Locust Street
Malvern, AR 72104

## HOWARD COUNTY
Circuit Court Clerk
Howard County Courthouse,
421 North Main, Room 7
Nashville, AR 71852

## INDEPENDENCE COUNTY
Circuit Court Clerk
Independence Cty Courthouse
Main and Broad Street
Batesville, AR 72501

## IZARD COUNTY
Circuit Court Clerk
Izard County Circuit Court
PO Box 95
Melbourne, AR 72556

## JACKSON COUNTY
Circuit Court Clerk
Jackson County Circuit Court
Courthouse
Newport, AR 72112

## JEFFERSON COUNTY
Circuit Court Clerk
Jefferson County Circuit Court
Main and Barraque Street
Pine Bluff, AR 71611

## JOHNSON COUNTY
Circuit Court Clerk
Johnson County Circuit Court
PO Box 217
Clarksville, AR 72830

## LAFAYETTE COUNTY
Circuit Court Clerk
Lafayette County Courthouse
PO Box 986
Lewisville, AR 71845

## LAWRENCE COUNTY
Circuit Court Clerk
Lawrence County Circuit Court
PO Box 581
Walnut Ridge, AR 72476

## LEE COUNTY
Circuit Court Clerk
Lee County Circuit Court
15 East Chestnut
Marianna, AR 72360

## LINCOLN COUNTY
Circuit Court Clerk
Lincoln County Circuit Court
300 South Drew
Star City, AR 71667

## LITTLE RIVER COUNTY
Circuit Court Clerk
Little River Cty Circuit Court
PO Box 575
Ashdown, AR 71822

## LOGAN COUNTY
Circuit Court Clerk
Logan County Circuit Court
Courthouse
Booneville, AR 72927

## LONOKE COUNTY
Circuit Court Clerk
Lonoke County Circuit Court
PO Box 231
Lonoke, AR 72086

## MADISON COUNTY
Circuit Court Clerk
Madison County Circuit Court
PO Box 416
Huntsville, AR 72740

## MARION COUNTY
Circuit Court Clerk
Marion County Circuit Court
PO Box 385
Yellville, AR 72687

## MILLER COUNTY
Circuit Court Clerk
Courthouse, Room 109
412 Laurel
Texarkana, AR 75502

## MISSISSIPPI COUNTY
Circuit Court Clerk
Mississippi Circuit Court
2nd and Walnut
Blytheville, AR 72316

## MONROE COUNTY
Circuit Court Clerk
Monroe County Circuit Court
123 Madison Street
Clarendon, AR 72029

## MONTGOMERY COUNTY
Circuit Court Clerk
Montgomery Cty Circuit Court
PO Box 377
Mount Ida, AR 71957

## NEVADA COUNTY
Circuit Court Clerk
Nevada County Circuit Court
PO Box 204
Prescott, AR 71857

## NEWTON COUNTY
Circuit Court Clerk
Newton County Circuit Court
PO Box 410
Jasper, AR 72641

## OUACHITA COUNTY
Circuit Court Clerk
Ouachita County Circuit Court
145 Jefferson Street
Camden, AR 71701

**PERRY COUNTY**
Circuit Court Clerk
Perry County Circuit Court
PO Box 358
Perryville, AR 72126

**PHILLIPS COUNTY**
Circuit Court Clerk
Phillips Cty Circuit Court
Courthouse
Helena, AR 72342

**PIKE COUNTY**
Circuit Court Clerk
Pike County Circuit Court
PO Box 219
Murfreesboro, AR 71958

**POINSETT COUNTY**
Circuit Court Clerk
Poinsett County Circuit Court
PO Box 46
Harrisburg, AR 72432

**POLK COUNTY**
Circuit Court Clerk
Polk County Circuit Court
507 Church Street
Mena, AR 71953

**POPE COUNTY**
Circuit Court Clerk
Pope County Circuit Court
100 West Main Street
Russellville, AR 72801

**PRAIRIE COUNTY - ND**
Circuit Court Clerk
Prairie County Circuit Court
PO Box 1011
Des Arc, AR 72040

**PRAIRIE COUNTY - SD**
Circuit Court Clerk
DeValls Bluff Courthouse
PO Box 283
DeValls Bluff, AR 72401

**PULASKI COUNTY**
Circuit Court Clerk
Courthhouse Ste 380
201 West 3rd
Little Rock, AR 72201

**RANDOLPH COUNTY**
Circuit Court Clerk
Randolph County Courthouse
201 South Marr
Pocahontas, AR 72455

**SALINE COUNTY**
Circuit Court Clerk
Saline County Circuit Court
PO Box 1560
Benton, AR 72015

**SCOTT COUNTY**
Circuit Court Clerk
Scott County Circuit Court
PO Box 464
Waldron, AR 72958

## SEARCY COUNTY
Circuit Court Clerk
Searcy County Circuit Court
PO Box 813
Marshall, AR 72650

## SEBASTIAN COUNTY
Circuit Court Clerk
Sebastian Cty Circuit Court
PO Box 1179
Fort Smith, AR 72902


Circuit Court Clerk
Greenwood District
PO Box 310
Greenwood, AR 72936

## SEVIER COUNTY
Circuit Court Clerk
Sevier County Courthouse
115 North 3rd
DeQueen, AR 71832

## SHARP COUNTY
Circuit Court Clerk
Sharp County Circuit Court
PO Box 307
Ashflat, AR 72513

## STONE COUNTY
Circuit Court Clerk
Stone County Circuit Court
PO Drawer 120
Mountain View, AR 72560

## ST. FRANCIS COUNTY
Circuit Court Clerk
St. Francis Cty Circuit Court
PO Box 1775
Forrest City, AR 72335

## UNION COUNTY
Circuit Court Clerk
Union County Circuit Court
Courthouse
El Dorado, AR 71730

## VAN BUREN COUNTY
Circuit Court Clerk
Van Buren County Circuit Court
PO Box 180
Clinton, AR 72031

## WASHINGTON COUNTY
Circuit Court Clerk
Washington County Circuit Court
280 North College, Ste 302
Fayetteville, AR 72701

## WHITE COUNTY
Circuit Court Clerk
White County Circuit Court
301 West Arch
Searcy, AR 72143

## WOODRUFF COUNTY
Circuit Court Clerk
Woodruff County Circuit Court
PO Box 492
Augusta, AR 72006

## YELL COUNTY
Circuit Court Clerk
Yell County Circuit Court
PO Box 219
Danville, AR 72833

# ARIZONA

## APACHE COUNTY
Superior Court Clerk
Apache Cty Superior Court
PO Box 365
St. Johns, AZ 85936

## COCHISE COUNTY
Superior Court Clerk
Cochise Cty Superior Court
Quality Hill
Bisbee, AZ 85603

## COCONINO COUNTY
Superior Court Clerk
Coconino County Courthouse
100 East Birch
Flagstaff, AZ 86001

## GILA COUNTY
Superior Court Clerk
Gila Cty Superior Court
1400 East Ash Street
Globe, AZ 85501

## GRAHAM COUNTY
Superior Court Clerk
Graham Cty Superior Court
800 Main Street
Safford, AZ 85546

## GREENLEE COUNTY
Superior Court Clerk
Greenlee Cty Superior Court
PO Box 1027
Clifton, AZ 85533

## LA PAZ COUNTY
Superior Court Clerk
La Paz Cty Superior Court
PO Box 730
Parker, AZ 85344

## MARICOPA COUNTY
Superior Court Clerk
Maricopa Cty Superior Court
201 West Jefferson
Phoenix, AZ 85003

## MOHAVE COUNTY
Superior Court Clerk
Mohave Cty Superior Court
PO Box 7000
Kingman, AZ 86402-7000

## NAVAJO COUNTY
Superior Court Clerk
Navajo Cty Superior Court
PO Box 668
Holbrook, AZ 86025

## PIMA COUNTY
Superior Court Clerk
Pima County Superior Court
110 West Congress
Tucson, AZ 85701

## PINAL COUNTY
Superior Court Clerk
Pinal Cty Superior Court
PO Box 889
Florence, AZ 85232

## SANTA CRUZ COUNTY
Superior Court Clerk
Santa Cruz Cty Superior Court
PO Box 1265
Nogales, AZ 85628

## YAVAPAI COUNTY
Superior Court Clerk
Yavapai Cty Superior Court
Yavapai County Courthouse
Prescott, AZ 86301

## YUMA COUNTY
Superior Court Clerk
Yuma County Superior Court
168 2nd Ave
Yuma, AZ 85364

# CALIFORNIA

## ALAMEDA COUNTY
Superior Court Clerk
Alameda Cty Superior Court
1225 Fallon Street, Rm 107
Oakland, CA 94612

Superior Court Clerk
Eastern Alameda Court
5672 Stoneridge Dr
Pleasanton, CA 94566

## ALPINE COUNTY
Superior Court Clerk
Alpine County Superior Court
PO Box 515
Markleeville, CA 96120

## AMADOR COUNTY
Superior Court Clerk
Amador Cty Superior Court
108 Court Street
Jackson, CA 95642

## BUTTE COUNTY
Superior Court Clerk
Butte County Superior Court
25 County Center Dr
Oroville, CA 95965

## CALAVERAS COUNTY
Superior Court Clerk
Calaveras Cty Superior Court
891 Mountain Ranch Rd
San Andreas, CA 95249

## COLUSA COUNTY
Superior Court Clerk
Colusa County Superior Court
546 Jay Street
Colusa, CA 95932

## CONTRA COSTA COUNTY
Superior Court Clerk
Contra Costa Cty Court
725 Court Street
Martinez, CA 94553

## DEL NORTE COUNTY
Superior Court Clerk
Del Norte Cty Superior Court
450 H. Street
Cresent City, CA 95531

## EL DORADO COUNTY
Superior Court Clerk
El Dorado Cty Superior Court
495 Main Street
Placerville, CA 95667

## FRESNO COUNTY
Superior Court Clerk
Fresno Cty Superior Court
1100 Van Ness Ave
Fresno, CA 93717

## GLENN COUNTY
Superior Court Clerk
Glenn County Superior Court
526 W. Sycamore
Willows, CA 95988

## HUMBOLDT COUNTY
Clerk of Court
Humboldt Cty Superior Court
825 5th Street
Eureka, CA 95501

## IMPERIAL COUNTY
Clerk of Court
Imperial Superior Court
939 Main Street
El Centro, CA 92243

## INYO COUNTY
Clerk of Court
Inyo Superior Court
PO Drawer F
Independence, CA 93526

## KERN COUNTY
Superior Court Clerk
Kern County Superior Court
1415 Truxtun Ave
Bakersfield, CA 93301

## KINGS COUNTY
Clerk of Court
Kings Cty Superior Court
1400 West Lacey Boulevard
Hanford, CA 93230

## LAKE COUNTY
Clerk of Court
Lake Superior Court
255 North Forbes
Lakeport, CA 95453

## LASSEN COUNTY
Clerk of Courts
Lassen Superior Court
220 South Lassen Street
Susanville, CA 96130

## LOS ANGELES COUNTY
Superior Court Clerk
Los Angeles Cty Court
111 North Hill Street
Los Angeles, CA 90012

## MADERA COUNTY
Superior Court Clerk
Madera Cty Superior Court
209 W. Yosemite
Madera, CA 93637

## MARIN COUNTY
Superior Court Clerk
Marin County Superior Court
PO Box E
San Rafael, CA 94913-3904

## MARIPOSA COUNTY
Superior Court Clerk
Mariposa Cty Superior Court
5088 Bullion Street
Mariposa, CA 95338

## MENDOCINO COUNTY
Superior Court Clerk
Mendocino Cty Superior Court
PO Box 996
Ukiah, CA 95482

## MERCED COUNTY
Superior Court Clerk
Merced Cty Superior Court
2222 M Street
Merced, CA 95340

## MODOC COUNTY
Superior Court Clerk
Modoc County Superior Court
200 Court Street
Alturas, CA 96101

## MONO COUNTY
Superior Court Clerk
Mono County Superior Court
PO Box 537
Bridgeport, CA 93517

## MONTEREY COUNTY
Superior Court Clerk
Monterey Cty Superior Court
240 Church Street
Salinas, CA 93902

## NAPA COUNTY
Clerk of Court
Napa County Superior Court
PO Box 880
Napa, CA 94559-0880

## NEVADA COUNTY
Superior Court Clerk
Nevada County Superior Court
201 Church Street
Nevada City, CA 95959-6126

## ORANGE COUNTY
Superior Court Clerk
Orange Cty Superior Court
700 Civic Center Dr W
Santa Ana, CA 92702-0838

## PLACER COUNTY
Superior Court Clerk
Placer Cty Superior Court
101 Maple Street
Auburn, CA 95603

**PLUMAS COUNTY**
Clerk of Courts
Plumas Cty Superior Court
PO Box 10207
Quincy, CA 95971

**RIVERSIDE COUNTY**
Consolidated Court Clerk
Riverside Cty Courts
4100 Main Street
Riverside, CA 92501

**SACRAMENTO COUNTY**
Clerk of Courts
Sacramento Superior Court
720 9th Street
Sacramento, CA 95814

**SAN BENITO COUNTY**
Clerk of Courts
San Benito Superior Court
440 5th Street
Hollister, CA 95023

**SAN BERNARDINO**
Superior Court Clerk
San Bernardino Superior Court
351 N. Arrowhead
San Bernardino, CA 92415

**SAN DIEGO COUNTY**
Superior Court Clerk
San Diego Cty Superior Court
220 West Broadway, Rm 3005
San Diego, CA 92112

**SAN FRANCISCO COUNTY**
Clerk of Court
San Francisco Superior Court
850 Bryant Street, Rm 306
San Francisco, CA 94103

**SAN JOAQUIN COUNTY**
Superior Court Clerk
San Joaquin Superior Court
222 East Weber Street, Rm 303
Stockton, CA 95202

**SAN LUIS OBISPO COUNTY**
Superior Court Clerk
San Luis Obispo Superior Court
1050 Monterey, Rm 102
San Luis Obispo, CA 93408

**SAN MATEO COUNTY**
Clerk of Court
San Mateo Superior Courts
401 Marshall Street
Redwood City, CA 94063

**SANTA BARBARA COUNTY**
Superior Court Clerk
Santa Barbara Superior Court
PO Box 159
Santa Barbara, CA 93102-0159

**SANTA CLARA COUNTY**
Superior Court Clerk
Santa Clara Superior Court
191 North First Street
San Jose, CA 95113

## SANTA CRUZ COUNTY
Clerk of Court
Santa Cruz Superior Court
701 Ocean Street
Santa Cruz, CA 95060

## STANISLAUS COUNTY
Superior Court Clerk
Stanislaus Superior Court
PO Box 1098
Modesto, CA 95353

## SHASTA COUNTY
Clerk of Court
Shasta Superior Court
1500 Court Street
Redding, CA 96001

## SUTTER COUNTY
Clerk of Court
Sutter Cty Consolidated Court
446 2nd Street
Yuba City, CA 95991

## SIERRA COUNTY
Superior Court Clerk
Sierra Superior Court
Courthouse Square
Downieville, CA 95936

## TEHAMA COUNTY
Superior Court Clerk
Tehama Cty Superior Court
633 Washington
Red Bluff, CA 96080

## SISKIYOU COUNTY
Clerk of Court
Siskiyou Superior Court
311 4th Street
Yreka, CA 96097

## TRINITY COUNTY
Superior Court Clerk
Trinity Cty Superior Court
PO Box 1258
Weaverville, CA 96093

## SOLANO COUNTY
Superior Court Clerk
Solano County Superior Court
600 Union Ave
Fairfield, CA 94533

## TULARE COUNTY
Clerk of Court
Tulare Superior Court
County Civil Center
Visalia, CA 93291

## SONOMA COUNTY
Clerk of Court
Sonoma Superior Court
600 Administration Dr.
Santa Rosa, CA 95406

## TUOLUMNE COUNTY
Superior Court Clerk
Tuolumne Superior Court
2 South Green Street
Sonora, CA 95370

**VENTURA COUNTY**
Clerk of Court
Ventura Superior Court
800 South Victoria Ave
Ventura, CA 93009

**YOLO COUNTY**
Superior Court Clerk
Yolo Superior Court
PO Box 1820
Woodland, CA 95695

**YUBA COUNTY**
Clerk of Court
Yuba Superior Courts
215 5th Street
Marysville, CA 95901

# COLORADO

**ADAMS COUNTY**
District Court Clerk
Adams County District Court
1931 East Bridge Street
Brighton, CO 80601

**ALAMOSA COUNTY**
District Court Clerk
Alamosa County Courthouse
702 4th Street
Alamosa, CO 81101

**ARAPAHOE COUNTY**
County Court Clerk
Arapahoe County Court
5606 South Court Pl
Littleton, CO 80120

**ARCHULETA COUNTY**
Clerk of Combined Courts
Archuleta County Courts
PO Box 148
Pagosa Springs, CO 81147

**BACA COUNTY**
Clerk of the Courts
Baca County Courts
741 Main Street
Springfield, CO 81073

**BENT COUNTY**
Clerk of the Courts
Bent County Courts
Bent County Courthouse
Las Animas, CO 81054

**BOULDER COUNTY**
Clerk of the Courts
Boulder County Courts
PO Box 4249
Boulder, CO 80306

**CHAFFEE COUNTY**
Clerk of the Courts
Chaffee County Courts
PO Box 279
Salida, CO 81201

**CHEYENNE COUNTY**
Clerk of the Courts
Cheyenne County Courts
PO Box 696
Cheyenne Wells, CO 80810

## CLEAR CREEK COUNTY

Clerk of the Courts
Clear Creek County Courts
PO Box 367
Georgetown, CO 80444

## CONEJOS COUNTY

Clerk of the Courts
Conejos County Courts
PO Box 128
Conejos, CO 81129

## COSTILLA COUNTY

Clerk of the Courts
Costilla County Courts
401 Church Place
San Luis, CO 81152

## CROWLEY COUNTY

Clerk of the Courts
Crowley County Courts
6th and Main
Ordway, CO 81063

## CUSTER COUNTY

Clerk of the Courts
Custer County Courts
PO Box 60
Westcliffe, CO 81252

## DELTA COUNTY

Clerk of the Courts
Delta County Courts
501 Palmer, Rm 338
Delta, CO 81416

## DENVER COUNTY

District Court Clerk
Denver Cty District Court
1437 Bannock, Rm 256
Denver, CO 80202

## DOLORES COUNTY

Clerk of the Courts
Delores County Courts
PO Box 511
Dove Creek, CO 81324

## DOUGLAS COUNTY

District Court Clerk
Douglas Cty District Court
355 South Wilcox
Castle Rock, CO 80104-1918

## EAGLE COUNTY

Clerk of the Courts
Eagle County Courts
PO Box 597
Eagle, CO 81631

## EL PASO COUNTY

District Court Clerk
El Paso Cty District Court
20 East Vermijo
Colorado Springs, CO 80903

## ELBERT COUNTY

Clerk of the Courts
Elbert County Courts
PO Box 232
Kiowa, CO 80117

## FREMONT COUNTY
Clerk of the Courts
Fremont County Courts
615 Macon, Rm 204
Canon City, CO 81212

## GARFIELD COUNTY
Clerk of the Court
Garfield County Court
109 8th Street, Suite 104
Glenwood Springs, CO 81601

## GILPIN COUNTY
Clerk of the Courts
Gilpin County Courts
142 Lawrence Street
Central City, CO 80427

## GRAND COUNTY
Clerk of the Courts
Grand County Courts
PO Box 192
Hot Sulphur Springs, CO 80451

## GUNNISON COUNTY
Clerk of the Courts
Gunnison County Courts
200 East Virginia Ave
Gunnison, CO 81230

## HINSDALE COUNTY
Clerk of the Courts
Hinsdale County Courts
300 Henson Street
Lake City, CO 81235

## HUERFANO COUNTY
Clerk of the Courts
Huerfano County Courts
401 Main Street
Walsenburg, CO 81089

## JACKSON COUNTY
Clerk of the Courts
Jackson County Courts
PO Box 308
Walden, CO 80480

## JEFFERSON COUNTY
Clerk of the Courts
Jefferson County Court
100 Jefferson County Pkwy
Golden, CO 80401-6002

## KIOWA COUNTY
Clerk of the Courts
Kiowa County Courts
PO Box 353
Eads, CO 81036

## KIT CARSON COUNTY
Clerk of the Court
Kit Carson County Court
PO Box 547
Burlington, CO 80807

## LA PLATA COUNTY
County Court Clerk
La Plata County Court
PO Box 498
Durango, CO 81302

**LAKE COUNTY**
Clerk of the Courts
Lake County Courts
PO Box 55
Leadville, CO 80461

**MINERAL COUNTY**
Clerk of the Courts
Mineral County Courts
PO Box 337
Creede, CO 81130

**LARIMER COUNTY**
Clerk of the Courts
Larimer County Courts
PO Box 2066
Ft. Collins, CO 80522

**MOFFAT COUNTY**
Clerk of the Courts
Moffat County Courts
221 West Victory Way
Craig, CO 81625

**LAS ANIMAS COUNTY**
Clerk of the Courts
Las Animas County Courts
200 East 1st Street, Room 301
Trinidad, CO 81082

**MONTEZUMA COUNTY**
County Court Clerk
Montezuma County Court
601 North Mildred Rd.
Cortez, CO 81321

**LINCOLN COUNTY**
Clerk of the Courts
Lincoln County Courts
PO Box 128
Hugo, CO 80821

**MONTROSE COUNTY**
District Court Clerk
Montrose District Court
PO Box 368
Montrose, CO 81402

**LOGAN COUNTY**
District Court Clerk
District County Court
PO Box 71
Sterling, CO 80751

**MORGAN COUNTY**
County Court Clerk
Morgan County Court
PO Box 695
Ft. Morgan, CO 80701

**MESA COUNTY**
District Court Clerk
Mesa County Court Clerk
PO Box 20000-5030
Grand Junction, CO 81502

**OTERO COUNTY**
Clerk of the Courts
Otero County Courts
Otero County Courthouse, Rm 201
La Junta, CO 81050

## OURAY COUNTY
Clerk of the Courts
Ouray County Courts
PO Box 643
Ouray, CO 81427

## PARK COUNTY
Clerk of the Courts
Park County Courts
PO Box 190
Fairplay, CO 80440

## PHILLIPS COUNTY
Clerk of the Courts
Phillips County Courts
Phillips County Courthouse
Holyoke, CO 80734

## PITKIN COUNTY
Clerk of the Courts
Pitkin County Courts
506 East Main Street
Aspen, CO 81611

## PROWERS COUNTY
Clerk of the Courts
Prowers County Courts
PO Box 1178
Lamar, CO 81052

## PUEBLO COUNTY
Clerk of the Courts
Pueblo County Courts
320 West 10th
Pueblo, CO 81003

## RIO BLANCO COUNTY
Clerk of the Courts
Rio Blanco County Courts
PO Box 1150
Meeker, CO 81641

## RIO GRANDE COUNTY
Clerk of the Courts
Rio Grande County Courts
PO Box W
Del Norte, CO 81132

## ROUTT COUNTY
Clerk of the Courts
Routt County Courts
PO Box 773117
Steamboat Springs, CO 80477

## SAGUACHE COUNTY
Clerk of the Courts
Saguache County Courts
PO Box 164
Saguache, CO 81149

## SAN JUAN COUNTY
Clerk of the Courts
San Juan County Courts
PO Box 441
Silverton, CO 81433

## SAN MIGUEL COUNTY
Clerk of the Courts
San Miguel County Courts
PO Box 919
Telluride, CO 81435

## SEDGWICK COUNTY
Clerk of the Courts
Sedgwick County Courts
3rd and Pine
Julesburg, CO 80737

## SUMMIT COUNTY
County Court Clerk
Summit County Court
501 North Park Ave
Breckenridge, CO 80424

## TELLER COUNTY
Clerk of the Courts
Teller County Courts
PO Box 997
Cripple Creek, CO 80813

## WASHINGTON COUNTY
Clerk of the Courts
Washington County Courts
PO Box 455
Akron, CO 80720

## WELD COUNTY
District Court Clerk
Weld County District Court
9th Avenue and 9th Street
Greeley, CO 80632

## YUMA COUNTY
Clerk of the Courts
Yuma County Courts
PO Box 347
Wray, CO 80758

# CONNECTICUT

## FAIRFIELD COUNTY
Clerk of Superior Court
Judicial District Court
146 White Street
Danbury, CT 06810

Clerk of Superior Court
Judicial District Court
1061 Main Street
Bridgeport, CT 06604

Clerk of Superior Court
Judicial District Court
123 Hoyt Street
Stamford, CT 06905

Clerk of Superior Court
Judicial District Court
17 Belden Ave
Norwalk, CT 06850

## HARTFORD COUNTY
Clerk of Superior Court
Judicial District Court
95 Washington Street
Hartford, CT 06106

Clerk of Superior Court
Judicial District Court
177 Columbus Blvd
New Britain, CT 06051

## LITCHFIELD COUNTY
Clerk of Superior Court
Judicial District Court
15 West Street
Litchfield, CT 06759

## MIDDLESEX COUNTY
Clerk of Superior Court
Judicial District Court
1 Court Street
Middletown, CT 06457

## NEW HAVEN COUNTY
Clerk of Superior Court
Judicial District Court
14 West River Street
Milford, CT 06460

Clerk of Superior Court
Judicial District Court
106 Elizabeth Street
Derby, CT 06418

Clerk of Superior Court
Judicial District Court
235 Church Street
New Haven, CT 06510

Clerk of Superior Court
Judicial District Court
54 W. Main Street
Meriden, CT 06450

## NEW LONDON COUNTY
Clerk of Superior Court
Judicial District Court
70 Huntington Street
New London, CT 06320

Clerk of Superior Court
Judicial District Court
Courthouse Square
Norwich, CT 06360

## TOLLAND COUNTY
Clerk of Superior Court
Judicial District Court
69 Brooklyn Street
Rockville, CT 06066

## WINDHAM COUNTY
Clerk of Superior Court
Judicial District Court
155 Church Street
Putnam, CT 06260

Clerk of Superior Court
Judicial District Court
108 Valley Street
Willamantic, CT 06226

# DISTRICT OF COLUMBIA

## D.C. SUPERIOR COURT
Superior Court Clerk
Superior Court of DC
500 Indiana Avenue N.W.
Washington, DC 20001

# DELAWARE

## KENT COUNTY
Office of Prothonotary
38 The Green
Dover, DE 19901

## NEW CASTLE COUNTY
Office of the Prothonotary
1020 North King Street
Wilmington, DE 19801

Court of Common Pleas
1000 North King Street
Wilmington, DE 19801

## SUSSEX COUNTY
Office of the Prothonotary
Sussex County Courthouse
The Circle
Georgetown, DE 19947

Court of Common Pleas
Sussex County Courthouse
The Circle
Georgetown, DE 19947

# FLORIDA

## ALACHUA COUNTY
Clerk of Court
Circuit and County Court
PO Box 600
Gainesville, FL 32602

## BAKER COUNTY
Clerk of Court
Circuit and County Court
339 East MacClenny Ave
MacClenny, FL 32063

## BAY COUNTY
Clerk of Court
Circuit and County Court
PO Box 2269
Panama City, FL 32402

## BRADFORD COUNTY
Clerk of Court
Circuit and County Court
PO Drawer B
Starke, FL 32091

## BREVARD COUNTY
Clerk of Court
Circuit and County Courts
700 South Park
Titusville, FL 32781

## BROWARD COUNTY
Clerk of Court
Circuit and County Court
201 SE 6th Street
Ft. Lauderdale, FL 33301

## CALHOUN COUNTY
Clerk of Court
Circuit and County Court
425 East Central Ave
Blountstown, FL 32424

## CHARLOTTE COUNTY
Clerk of Court
Circuit and County Court
116 West Olympia
Punta Gorda, FL 33951

## CITRUS COUNTY
Clerk of Court
Circuit and County Court
110 North Apopka
Inverness, FL 32650

## CLAY COUNTY
Clerk of Circuit Court
Clay County Courthouse
PO Box 698
Green Cove Springs,FL 32043

## COLLIER COUNTY
Clerk of Court
Collier County
PO Box 413044
Naples, FL 33941-3044

## COLUMBIA COUNTY
Clerk of Court
County and Circuit Court
PO Drawer 2069
Lake City, FL 32056-2069

## DADE COUNTY
Clerk of Court
Circuit and County Court
73 West Flagler Street
Miami, FL 33130

## DE SOTO COUNTY
Clerk of Court
Circuit and County Court
PO Box 591
Arcadia, FL 33821

## DIXIE COUNTY
Clerk of Court
Circuit and County Court
PO Box 1206
Cross City, FL 32628

## DUVAL COUNTY
Clerk of Court
Circuit and County Court
330 East BAY ST
Jacksonville, FL 32202

## ESCAMBIA COUNTY
Clerk of Court
County Civil Division
190 Governmental Center
Pensacola, FL 32501

## FLAGLER COUNTY
Clerk of Court
Circuit and County Court
200 East Moody
Bunnell, FL 32110

## FRANKLIN COUNTY
Clerk of Court
Circuit and Civil Court
PO Box 340
Apalachicola, FL 32329

## GADSDEN COUNTY

Clerk of Court
Gadsden County Courthouse
PO Box 1649
Quincy, FL 32353-1649

## GILCHRIST COUNTY

Clerk of Court
Gilchrist Cty Courthouse
PO Box 37
Trenton, FL 32693

## GLADES COUNTY

Clerk of Court
Circuit and County Court
PO Box 10
Moore Haven, FL 33471

## GULF COUNTY

Clerk of Court
Gulf County
1000 5th Street
Port Street Joe, FL 32456

## HAMILTON COUNTY

Clerk of Court
Circuit and County Court
207 NE First Street
Jasper, FL 32052

## HARDEE COUNTY

Clerk of Court
Circuit and County Court
PO Drawer 1749
Wauchula, FL 33873

## HENDRY COUNTY

Clerk of Circuit Court
Hendry County Courthouse
PO Box 1760
LaBelle, FL 33935

## HERNANDO COUNTY

Clerk of Court
Circuit and County Court
20 North Main Street
Brooksville, FL 34601

## HIGHLANDS COUNTY

Clerk of Court
Highlands Cty Courthouse
430 South Commerce Ave
Sebring, FL 33871

## HILLSBOROUGH COUNTY

Clerk of Court
Circuit and County Court
PO Box 1110
Tampa, FL 33601

## HOLMES COUNTY

Clerk of Court
Circuit and County Court
PO Box 397
Bonifay, FL 32425

## INDIAN RIVER COUNTY

Clerk of Court
Circuit and County Court
PO Box 1028
Vero Beach, FL 32960

**JACKSON COUNTY**
Clerk of Court
Circuit and County Court
PO Drawer 510
Marianna, FL 32447

**JEFFERSON COUNTY**
Clerk of Court
Circuit and County Court
Courthouse Square
Monticello, FL 32344

**LAFAYETTE COUNTY**
Clerk of Court
Lafayette Cty Courthouse
PO Box 88
Mayo, FL 32066

**LAKE COUNTY**
Clerk of Court
Lake County Courthouse
PO Box 7800
Tavares, FL 32778

**LEE COUNTY**
Clerk of Circuit Court
Circuit and County Court
PO Box 310
Ft. Myers, FL 33902

**LEON COUNTY**
Clerk of Circuit Court
Circuit and County Court
301 S. Monroe
Tallahassee, FL 32302

**LEON COUNTY**
County Court Clerk
Leon County Court
1920 Thomasville Rd
Tallahassee, FL 32303

**LEVY COUNTY**
Clerk of Court
Levy County Courthouse
PO Box 610
Bronson, FL 32621

**LIBERTY COUNTY**
Clerk of Court
Liberty Cty Courthouse
PO Box 399
Bristol, FL 32321

**MADISON COUNTY**
Clerk of Court
Madison County Courthouse
PO Box 237
Madison, FL 32341

**MANATEE COUNTY**
Clerk of Court
Manatee County Courthouse
PO Box 1000
Bradenton, FL 34206

**MARION COUNTY**
Clerk of Circuit Court
Marion Cty Circuit Court
PO Box 1030
Ocala, FL 34478-1030

## MARTIN COUNTY
Clerk of Court
Martin County Courthouse
PO Box 9016
Stuart, FL 34995

## MONROE COUNTY
Circuit Court Clerk
Monroe Cty Circuit Court
500 Whitehead Street
Key West, FL 33040

## NASSAU COUNTY
Circuit Court Clerk
Nassau County Circuit Court
416 Centre
Fernandina Beach, FL 32034

## OKALOOSA COUNTY
Circuit Court Clerk
Okaloosa Cty Circuit Court
Box 1265
Crestview, FL 32536-1265

## OKEECHOBEE COUNTY
Clerk of Court
County Circuit Court
304 NW 2nd Street
Okeechobee, FL 34972

## ORANGE COUNTY
Clerk of Courts
Records Management Division
150 North Orange Avenue
Orlando, FL 32801

## OSCEOLA COUNTY
Clerk of Court
Osceola County Courthouse
12 South Vernon Ave
Kissimmee, FL 32741-5491

## PALM BEACH COUNTY
County Court Clerk
Palm Beach County Court
100 North Dixie, Rm 137
West Palm Beach, FL 33402

## PASCO COUNTY
Clerk of Court
Pasco Circuit and Cty Court
38053 Live Oak Ave
Dade City, FL 33525

## PINELLAS COUNTY
Clerk of Court
Pinellas County Courts
545 1st Ave
Clearwater, FL 34619

## POLK COUNTY
County Court Clerk
Polk County Court
PO Box 9000
Bartow, FL 33830-9000

## PUTNAM COUNTY
Circuit Court Clerk
Putnam Cty Circuit Court
410 Street John's
Palatka, FL 32078

## SANTA ROSA COUNTY
Court Clerk
Santa Rosa Courts
801 Caroline
Milton, FL 32572

## SARASOTA COUNTY
Clerk of Court
Sarasota Courts
2000 Main, First Floor
Sarasota, FL 34230-3079

## SEMINOLE COUNTY
Circuit Court Clerk
Seminole County Circuit Court
301 North Park Ave
Sanford, FL 32771

## ST. JOHN COUNTY
Circuit Court Clerk
St. John County Circuit Court
PO Drawer 300
St. Augustine, FL 32085

## ST. LUCIE COUNTY
Circuit Court Clerk
St. Lucie Cty Circuit Court
PO Drawer 700
Ft. Pierce, FL 34954

## SUMTER COUNTY
Circuit Court Clerk
Sumter County Circuit Court
209 North Florida Street
Bushnell, FL 33513

## SUWANNEE COUNTY
Circuit Court Clerk
Suwannee County Circuit Court
Suwannee County Courthouse
Live Oak, FL 32060

## TAYLOR COUNTY
Circuit Court Clerk
Taylor County Circuit Court
PO Box 620
Perry, FL 32347

## UNION COUNTY
Circuit Court Clerk
Union County Circuit Court
Courthouse Square
Lake Butler, FL 32054

## VOLUSIA COUNTY
Circuit Court Clerk
Volusia County Circuit Court
PO Box 43
DeLand, FL 32721

## WAKULLA COUNTY
Circuit Court Clerk
Wakulla County Circuit Court
PO Box 337
Crawfordville, FL 32326

## WALTON COUNTY
Circuit Court Clerk
Walton County Circuit Court
PO Box 1260
De Funiak Springs, FL 32433

**WASHINGTON COUNTY**
Circuit Court Clerk
Washington Cty Circuit Court
PO Box 647
Chipley, FL 32428

# GEORGIA

**APPLING COUNTY**
Superior Court Clerk
Appling County Superior Court
Appling County Courthouse
Baxley, GA 31513

**ATKINSON COUNTY**
Superior Court Clerk
Atkinson County Superior Court
PO Box 6
Pearson, GA 31642

**BACON COUNTY**
Superior Court Clerk
Bacon County Superior Court
PO Box 376
Alma, GA 31510

**BAKER COUNTY**
Superior Court Clerk
Baker County Superior Court
PO Box 10
Newton, GA 31770

**BALDWIN COUNTY**
Superior Court Clerk
Baldwin County Superior Court
PO Drawer 987
Milledgeville, GA 31061

**BANKS COUNTY**
Superior Court Clerk
Banks County Superior Court
PO Drawer C
Homer, GA 30547

**BARROW COUNTY**
Superior Court Clerk
Barrow County Superior Court
30 North Broad Street
Winder, GA 30680

**BARTOW COUNTY**
Superior Court Clerk
Bartow County Superior Court
135 West Cherokee Ave
Cartersville, GA 30120

**BEN HILL COUNTY**
Superior Court Clerk
Ben Hill County Superior Court
401 East Central Ave
Fitzgerald, GA 31750

**BERRIEN COUNTY**
Superior Court Clerk
Berrien County Superior Court
101 East Marion Ave
Nashville, GA 31639

**BIBB COUNTY**
Superior Court Clerk
Bibb County Superior Court
601 Mulberry Street
Macon, GA 31202-1015

## BLECKLEY COUNTY
Superior Court Clerk
Bleckley County Superior Court
306 S.E. 2nd
Cochran, GA 31014

## BRANTLEY COUNTY
Superior Court Clerk
Brantley County Superior Court
PO Box 1067
Nahunta, GA 31553

## BROOKS COUNTY
Superior Court Clerk
Brooks County Superior Court
PO Box 630
Quitman, GA 31643

## BRYAN COUNTY
Superior Court Clerk
Bryan County Superior Court
401 College Street
Pembroke, GA 31321

## BULLOCH COUNTY
Superior Court Clerk
Bulloch County Superior Court
North Main Street
Statesboro, GA 30458

## BURKE COUNTY
Superior Court Clerk
Burke County Superior Court
PO Box 803
Waynesboro, GA 30830

## BUTTS COUNTY
Superior Court Clerk
Butts County Superior Court
26 and 3rd Street
Jackson, GA 30233

## CALHOUN COUNTY
Superior Court Clerk
Calhoun County Superior Court
PO Box 68
Morgan, GA 31766

## CAMDEN COUNTY
Superior Court Clerk
Camden County Superior Court
PO Box 578
Woodbine, GA 31569

## CANDLER COUNTY
Superior Court Clerk
Candler County Superior Court
PO Box 830
Metter, GA 30439

## CARROLL COUNTY
Superior Court Clerk
Carroll County Superior Court
311 Noonan Street
Carrollton, GA 30117

## CATOOSA COUNTY
Superior Court Clerk
Catoosa County Superior Court
Courthouse
Ringgold, GA 30736

## CHARLTON COUNTY
Superior Court Clerk
Charlton County Superior Court
Charlton County Courthouse
Folkston, GA 31537

## CHATHAM COUNTY
State Court Clerk
Superior and State Court
Chatham County Courthouse
Savannah, GA 31401

## CHATTAHOOCHEE COUNTY
Superior Court Clerk
County Superior Court
PO Box 120
Cusseta, GA 31805

## CHATTOOGA COUNTY
Superior Court Clerk
Chattooga Cty Superior Court
PO Box 159
Summerville, GA 30747

## CHEROKEE COUNTY
Superior Court Clerk
Cherokee Cty Superior Court
100 North Street, Rm 3
Canton, GA 30114

## CLARKE COUNTY
Superior Court Clerk
Clarke County Superior Court
PO Box 1805
Athens, GA 30603

## CLAY COUNTY
Superior Court Clerk
Clay County Superior Court
PO Box 550
Ft. Gaines, GA 31751

## CLAYTON COUNTY
Superior Court Clerk
Clayton County Superior Court
Clayton County Courthouse
Jonesboro, GA 30236

## CLINCH COUNTY
Superior Court Clerk
Clinch County Superior Court
PO Box 433
Homerville, GA 31634

## COBB COUNTY
Superior Court Clerk
Cobb County Superior Court
32 Waddell Street
Marietta, GA 30090-9640

## COFFEE COUNTY
Superior Court Clerk
Coffee County Superior Court
Coffee County Courthouse
Douglas, GA 31533

## COLQUITT COUNTY
Superior Court Clerk
Colquitt Cty Superior Court
PO Box 886
Moultrie, GA 31776

## COLUMBIA COUNTY
Superior Court Clerk
Columbia Cty Superior Court
PO Box 100
Appling, GA 30802

## COOK COUNTY
Superior Court Clerk
Cook County Superior Court
212 North Hutchinson Ave
Adel, GA 31620

## COWETA COUNTY
Superior Court Clerk
Coweta County Superior Court
PO Box 943
Newman, GA 30264

## CRAWFORD COUNTY
Superior Court Clerk
Crawford Cty Superior Court
PO Box 419
Knoxville, GA 31050

## CRISP COUNTY
Superior Court Clerk
Crisp County Superior Court
PO Box 747
Cordele, GA 31015

## DADE COUNTY
Superior Court Clerk
Dade County Superior Court
PO Box 417
Trenton, GA 30752

## DAWSON COUNTY
Superior Court Clerk
Dawson County Superior Court
W 3rd Street and Tucker Ave
Dawsonville, GA 30534

## DE KALB COUNTY
Superior Court Clerk
De Kalb Cty Superior Court
556 North McDonoegh Street
Decatur, GA 30030

## DECATUR COUNTY
Superior Court Clerk
Decatur County Superior Court
PO Box 336
Bainbridge, GA 31717

## DODGE COUNTY
Superior Court Clerk
Dodge Cty Superior Court
PO Box 4276
Eastman, GA 31023

## DOOLY COUNTY
Superior Court Clerk
Dooly County Superior Court
PO Box 326
Vienna, GA 31092-0326

## DOUGHERTY COUNTY
Superior Court Clerk
Dougherty Cty Superior Court
PO Box 1827
Albany, GA 31703

## DOUGLAS COUNTY
Superior Court Clerk
Douglas Cty Superior Court
6754 Broad Street
Douglasville, GA 30134

## EARLY COUNTY
Superior Court Clerk
Early County Superior Court
39 Court Square
Blakely, GA 31723

## ECHOLS COUNTY
Superior Court Clerk
Echols County Superior Court
PO Box 213
Statenville, GA 31648

## EFFINGHAM COUNTY
Superior Court Clerk
Effingham Cty Superior Court
PO Box 387
Springfield, GA 31329

## ELBERT COUNTY
Superior Court Clerk
Elbert County Superior Court
12 South Oliver Street
Elberton, GA 30635

## EMANUEL COUNTY
Superior Court Clerk
Emanuel County Superior Court
PO Box 627
Swainsboro, GA 30401

## EVANS COUNTY
Superior Court Clerk
Evans Cty Superior Court
PO Box 845
Claxton, GA 30417

## FANNIN COUNTY
Superior Court Clerk
Fannin Cty Superior Court
PO Box 1300
Blue Ridge, GA 30513

## FAYETTE COUNTY
Superior Court Clerk
Fayette County Superior Court
PO Box 130
Fayetteville, GA 30214

## FLOYD COUNTY
Superior Court Clerk
Floyd County Superior Court
4th Ave
Rome, GA 30161

## FORSYTH COUNTY
Superior Court Clerk
Forsyth Cty Superior Court
100 Courthouse Square,Rm110
Cumming, GA 30130

## FRANKLIN COUNTY
Superior Court Clerk
Franklin Cty Superior Court
PO Box 70
Carnesville, GA 30521

**FULTON COUNTY**
Superior Counrt Clerk
Fulton County Superior Court
136 Pryor Street, Room 606
Atlanta, GA 30303

**GILMER COUNTY**
Superior Court Clerk
Gilmer County Superior Court
No. 1 West Side Square
Ellijay, GA 30540

**GLASCOCK COUNTY**
Superior Court Clerk
Glascock Cty Superior Court
PO Box 231
Gibson, GA 30810

**GLYNN COUNTY**
Superior Court Clerk
Glynn County Superior Court
PO Box 1355
Brunswick, GA 31521

**GORDON COUNTY**
Superior Court Clerk
Gordon County Superior Court
PO Box 367
Calhoun, GA 30703

**GRADY COUNTY**
Superior Court Clerk
Grady County Superior Court
250 North Broad Street
Cairo, GA 31728

**GREENE COUNTY**
Superior Court Clerk
Greene County Superior Court
113 East North Main Street
Greensboro, GA 30642

**GWINNETT COUNTY**
Superior Court Clerk
Gwinnett County Superior Court
PO Box 880
Lawrenceville, GA 30246

**HABERSHAM COUNTY**
Superior Court Clerk
Habersham Cty Superior Court
PO Box 108
Clarkesville, GA 30523

**HALL COUNTY**
Superior Court Clerk
Hall County Superior Court
PO Box 1275
Gainesville, GA 30503

**HANCOCK COUNTY**
Superior Court Clerk
Hancock County Superior Court
PO Box 451
Sparta, GA 31087

**HARALSON COUNTY**
Superior Court Clerk
Haralson Cty Superior Court
PO Box 373
Buchanan, GA 30113

## HARRIS COUNTY
Superior Court Clerk
Harris Cty Superior Court
PO Box 528
Hamilton, GA 31811

## HART COUNTY
Superior Court Clerk
Hart County Superior Court
PO Box 386
Hartwell, GA 30643

## HEARD COUNTY
Superior Court Clerk
Heard County Superior Court
PO Box 249
Franklin, GA 30217

## HENRY COUNTY
Superior Court Clerk
Henry County Superior Court
Henry County Courthouse
McDonough, GA 30253

## HOUSTON COUNTY
Superior Court Clerk
Houston Cty Superior Court
800 Carroll Street
Perry, GA 31069

## IRWIN COUNTY
Superior Court Clerk
Irwin Cty Superior Court
PO Box 186
Ocilla, GA 31774

## JACKSON COUNTY
Superior Court Clerk
Jackson County Superior Court
PO Box 7
Jefferson, GA 30549

## JASPER COUNTY
Superior Court Clerk
Jasper County Superior Court
Jasper County Courthouse
Monticello, GA 31064

## JEFF DAVIS COUNTY
Superior Court Clerk
Jeff Davis Cty Superior Court
PO Box 248
Hazelhurst, GA 31539

## JEFFERSON COUNTY
Superior Court Clerk
Jefferson Cty Superior Court
PO Box 151
Louisville, GA 30434

## JENKINS COUNTY
Superior Court Clerk
Jenkins Cty Superior Court
PO Box 659
Millen, GA 30442

## JOHNSON COUNTY
Superior Court Clerk
Johnson Cty Superior Court
PO Box 321
Wrightsville, GA 31096

## JONES COUNTY
Superior Court Clerk
Jones County Superior Court
PO Box 159
Gray, GA 31032

## LAMAR COUNTY
Superior Court Clerk
Lamar County Superior Court
326 Thomaston Street
Barnesville, GA 30204

## LANIER COUNTY
Superior Court Clerk
Lanier County Superior Court
Lanier County Courthouse
Lakeland, GA 31635

## LAURENS COUNTY
Superior Court Clerk
Laurens County Superior Court
10177 Jefferson Street
Dublin, GA 31040

## LEE COUNTY
Superior Court Clerk
Lee County Superior Court
PO Box 597
Leesburg, GA 31763

## LIBERTY COUNTY
Superior Court Clerk
Liberty Cty Superior Court
PO Box 50
Hinesville, GA 31313

## LINCOLN COUNTY
Superior Court Clerk
Lincoln Cty Superior Court
PO Box 340
Lincolnton, GA 30817

## LONG COUNTY
Superior Court Clerk
Long County Superior Court
PO Box 458
Ludowici, GA 31316

## LOWNDES COUNTY
Superior Court Clerk
Lowndes County Superior Court
PO Box 1349
Valdosta, GA 31601

## LUMPKIN COUNTY
Superior Court Clerk
Lumpkin County Superior Court
279 Courthouse Hill
Dahlonega, GA 30533

## MACON COUNTY
Superior Court Clerk
Macon County Superior Court
PO Box 337
Oglethorpe, GA 31068

## MADISON COUNTY
Superior Court Clerk
Madison County Superior Court
PO Box 247
Danielsville, GA 30633

## MARION COUNTY
Superior Court Clerk
Marion County Superior Court
PO Box 41
Buena Vista, GA 31803

## MCDUFFIE COUNTY
Superior Court Clerk
McDuffie County Superior Court
PO Box 158
Thomson, GA 30824

## MCINTOSH COUNTY
Superior Court Clerk
McIntosh County Superior Court
PO Box 1661
Darien, GA 31305

## MERIWETHER COUNTY
Superior Court Clerk
Meriwether County Superior Court
PO Box 160
Greenville, GA 30222

## MILLER COUNTY
Superior Court Clerk
Miller County Superior Court
PO Box 66
Colquitt, GA 31737

## MITCHELL COUNTY
Superior Court Clerk
Mitchell County Superior Court
11 Broad Street
Camilla, GA 31730

## MONROE COUNTY
Superior Court Clerk
Monroe County Superior Court
PO Box 450
Forsyth, GA 31029

## MONTGOMERY COUNTY
Superior Court Clerk
Montgomery Cty Superior Court
PO Box 311
Mount Vernon, GA 30445

## MORGAN COUNTY
Superior Court Clerk
Morgan County Superior Court
149 East Jefferson
Madison, GA 30650

## MURRAY COUNTY
Superior Court Clerk
Murray County Superior Court
PO Box 1000
Chatsworth, GA 30705

## MUSCOGEE COUNTY
Superior Court Clerk
Muscogee County Superior Court
PO Box 2145
Columbus, GA 31994

## NEWTON COUNTY
Superior Court Clerk
Newton County Superior Court
1124 Clark Street
Covington, GA 30209

**Adoption Searches Made Easier**

## OCONEE COUNTY
Superior Court Clerk
Oconee County Superior Court
23 North Main Street
Watkinsville, GA 30677

## OGLETHORPE COUNTY
Superior Court Clerk
Oglethorpe County Superior Court
PO Box 68
Lexington, GA 30648

## PAULDING COUNTY
Superior Court Clerk
Paulding County Superior Court
Courthouse Square
Dallas, GA 30132

## PEACH COUNTY
Superior Court Clerk
Peach County Superior Court
PO Box 389
Ft. Valley, GA 31030

## PICKENS COUNTY
Superior Court Clerk
Pickens County Superior Court
PO Box 130
Jasper, GA 30143

## PIERCE COUNTY
Superior Court Clerk
Pierce County Superior Court
84 and Main Street
Blackshear, GA 31516

## PIKE COUNTY
Superior Court Clerk
Pike County Superior Court
PO Box 10
Zebulon, GA 30295

## POLK COUNTY
Superior Court Clerk
Polk County Superior Court
PO Box 948
Cedartown, GA 30125

## PULASKI COUNTY
Superior Court Clerk
Pulaski County Superior Court
PO Box 88
Haskinsville, GA 31036

## PUTNAM COUNTY
Superior Court Clerk
Putnam County Superior Court
Putnam County Courthouse
Eatonton, GA 31024

## QUITMAN COUNTY
Superior Court Clerk
Quitman County Superior Court
PO Box 307
Georgetown, GA 31754

## RABUN COUNTY
Superior Court Clerk
Rabun County Superior Court
PO Box 893
Clayton, GA 30525

## RANDOLPH COUNTY
Superior Court Clerk
Randolph County Superior Court
PO Box 98
Cuthbert, GA 31740

## RICHMOND COUNTY
Superior Court Clerk
Richmond County Superior Court
401 Walton Way
Augusta, GA 30911

## ROCKDALE COUNTY
Superior Court Clerk
Rockdale County Superior Court
922 Court Street
Conyers, GA 30207

## SCHLEY COUNTY
Superior Court Clerk
Schley County Superior Court
PO Box 7
Ellaville, GA 31806

## SCREVEN COUNTY
Superior Court Clerk
Screven County Superior Court
216 Mims Rd
Sylvania, GA 30467

## SEMINOLE COUNTY
Superior Court Clerk
Seminole County Superior Court
PO Box 672
Donalsonville, GA 31745

## SPALDING COUNTY
Superior Court Clerk
Spalding County Superior Court
PO Box 163
Griffin, GA 30224

## STEPHENS COUNTY
Superior Court Clerk
Stephens County Superior Court
150 West Doyle Street
Toccoa, GA 30577

## STEWART COUNTY
Superior Court Clerk
Stewart County Superior Court
PO Box 910
Lumpkin, GA 31815

## SUMTER COUNTY
Superior Court Clerk
Sumter County Superior Court
PO Box 333
Americus, GA 31709

## TALBOT COUNTY
Superior Court Clerk
Talbot County Superior Court
PO Box 325
Talbotton, GA 31827

## TALIAFERRO COUNTY
Superior Court Clerk
Taliaferro Cty Superior Court
PO Box 182
Crawfordville, GA 30631

## TATTNALL COUNTY
Superior Court Clerk
Tattnall County Superior Court
PO Box 56
Reidsville, GA 30453

## TAYLOR COUNTY
Superior Court Clerk
Taylor County Superior Court
PO Box 248
Butler, GA 31006

## TELFAIR COUNTY
Superior Court Clerk
Telfair County Superior Court
Telfair County Courthouse
McRae, GA 31055

## TERRELL COUNTY
Superior Court Clerk
Terrell County Superior Court
PO Box 189
Dawson, GA 31742

## THOMAS COUNTY
Superior Court Clerk
Thomas County Superior Court
225 North Broad Street
Thomasville, GA 31799

## TIFT COUNTY
Superior Court Clerk
Tift County Superior Court
PO Box 354
Tifton, GA 31793

## TOOMBS COUNTY
Superior Court Clerk
Toombs County Superior Court
100 Courthouse Square
Lyons, GA 30436

## TOWNS COUNTY
Superior Court Clerk
Towns County Superior Court
48 River Street, Ste E
Hiawassee, GA 30546

## TREUTLEN COUNTY
Superior Court Clerk
Treutlen Cty Superior Court
PO Box 356
Soperton, GA 30457

## TROUP COUNTY
Superior Court Clerk
Troup County Superior Court
118 Ridley Ave
La Grange, GA 30241

## TURNER COUNTY
Superior Court Clerk
Turner County Superior Court
219 East College Street
Ashburn, GA 31714

## TWIGGS COUNTY
Superior Court Clerk
Twiggs County Superior Court
PO Box 228
Jeffersonville, GA 31044

## UNION COUNTY
Superior Court Clerk
Union County Superior Court
114 Courthouse Street
Blairsville, GA 30512

## UPSON COUNTY
Superior Court Clerk
Upson County Superior Court
PO Box 469
Thomaston, GA 30286-0469

## WALKER COUNTY
Superior Court Clerk
Walker County Superior Court
PO Box 448
Lafayette, GA 30728

## WALTON COUNTY
Superior Court Clerk
Walton County Superior Court
116 South Broad Street
Monroe, GA 30655

## WARE COUNTY
Superior Court Clerk
Ware County Superior Court
PO Box 776
Waycross, GA 31502

## WARREN COUNTY
Superior Court Clerk
Warren County Superior Court
PO Box 346
Warrenton, GA 30828

## WASHINGTON COUNTY
Superior Court Clerk
Washington County Superior Court
PO Box 231
Sandersville, GA 31082

## WAYNE COUNTY
Superior Court Clerk
Wayne County Superior Court
PO Box 918
Jesup, GA 31545

## WEBSTER COUNTY
Superior Court Clerk
Webster County Superior Court
PO Box 117
Preston, GA 31824

## WHEELER COUNTY
Superior Court Clerk
Wheeler County Superior Court
PO Box 38
Alamo, GA 30411

## WHITE COUNTY
Superior Court Clerk
White County Superior Court
1650 South Main Street
Cleveland, GA 30528

## WHITFIELD COUNTY
Superior Court Clerk
Whitfield County Superior Court
300 West Crawford Street
Dalton, GA 30722

## WILCOX COUNTY
Superior Court Clerk
Wilcox County Superior Court
103 Broad Street
Abbeville, GA 31001

## WILKES COUNTY
Superior Court Clerk
Wilkes County Superior Court
23 East Court Street
Washington, GA 30673

## WILKINSON COUNTY
Superior Court Clerk
Wilkinson County Superior Court
PO Box 250
Irwinton, GA 31042

## WORTH COUNTY
Superior Court Clerk
Worth County Superior Court
201 North Main
Sylvester, GA 31791

# HAWAII

## HAWAII COUNTY
Circuit Court Clerk
Third Circuit Court
PO Box 1007
Hilo, HI 96721

## HONOLULU COUNTY
Circuit Court Clerk
First Circuit Court
777 Punchbowl Street
Honolulu, HI 96809

## KAUAI COUNTY
Circuit Court Clerk
Fifth Circuit Court
3059 Umi Street
Lihue, HI 96766

## MAUI COUNTY
Circuit Court Clerk
Second Circuit Court
2145 Main Street
Wailuku, HI 96793

# IOWA

## ADAIR COUNTY
District Court Clerk
Adair County Courthouse
Courthouse
Greenfield, IA 50849

## ADAMS COUNTY
District Court Clerk
Adams County District Court
Courthouse
Corning, IA 50841

## ALLAMAKEE COUNTY
District Court Clerk
Allamakee Cty District Court
PO Box 248
Waukon, IA 52172

## APPANOOSE COUNTY
District Court Clerk
Appanoose County Courthouse
Courthouse Square
Centerville, IA 52544

## AUDUBON COUNTY
District Court Clerk
Audubon County Courthouse
Courthouse
Audubon, IA 50025

## BENTON COUNTY
District Court Clerk
Benton County District Court
PO Box 719
Vinton, IA 52349

## BLACK HAWK COUNTY
District Court Clerk
Black Hawk County Courthouse
Courthouse Square
Waterloo, IA 50703

## BOONE COUNTY
District Court Clerk
Boone County Courthouse
Courthouse Square
Boone, IA 50036

## BREMER COUNTY
District Court Clerk
Bremer County District Court
415 East Bremer
Waverly, IA 50677

## BUCHANAN COUNTY
District Court Clerk
Buchanan Cty District Court
PO Box 259
Independence, IA 50644

## BUENA VISTA COUNTY
District Court Clerk
Buena Vista Cty District Court
PO Box 1186
Storin Lake, IA 50588

## BUTLER COUNTY
District Court Clerk
Butler County District Court
PO Box 307
Allison, IA 50602

## CALHOUN COUNTY
District Court Clerk
Calhoun County District Court
416 4th Street
Rockwell City, IA 50579

## CARROLL COUNTY
District Court Clerk
Carroll County Courthouse
Courthouse
Carroll, IA 51401

## CASS COUNTY
District Court Clerk
Cass County Courthouse
Courthouse Square
Atlantic, IA 50022

## CEDAR COUNTY
District Court Clerk
Cedar County District Court
PO Box 111
Tipton, IA 52772

## CERRO GORDO COUNTY
District Court Clerk
Cerro Gordo Cty Courthouse
220 North Washington
Mason City, IA 50401

## CHEROKEE COUNTY
District Court Clerk
Cherokee County Courthouse
Drawer F
Cherokee, IA 51012

## CHICKASAW COUNTY
District Court Clerk
Chickasaw County Courthouse
Courthouse Square
New Hampton, IA 50659

## CLARKE COUNTY
District Court Clerk
Clarke County Courthouse
Courthouse Square
Osceola, IA 50213

## CLAY COUNTY
District Court Clerk
Clay County District Court
PO Box 4104
Spencer, IA 51301

## CLAYTON COUNTY
District Court Clerk
Clayton County Courthouse
111 High Street
Elkader, IA 52043

## CLINTON COUNTY
District Court Clerk
Clinton County Courthouse
612 North Second Street
Clinton, IA 52732

## CRAWFORD COUNTY
District Court Clerk
Crawford County District Court
PO Box 546
Denison, IA 51442

## DALLAS COUNTY
District Court Clerk
Dallas County District Court
801 Court Street
Adel, IA 50003

## DAVIS COUNTY
District Court Clerk
Davis County Courthouse
Courthouse Square
Bloomfield, IA 52537

## DECATUR COUNTY
District Court Clerk
Decatur County Courthouse
207 North Main Street
Leon, IA 50144

## DELAWARE COUNTY
District Court Clerk
Delaware County Courthouse
Courthouse Square
Manchester, IA 52057

## DES MOINES COUNTY
District Court Clerk
Des Moines Cty Courthouse
PO Box 158
Burlington, IA 52601

## DICKINSON COUNTY
District Court Clerk
Dickinson County Courthouse
PO Drawer O N
Spirit Lake, IA 51360

## DUBUQUE COUNTY
District Court Clerk
Dubuque Cty District Court
720 Central
Dubuque, IA 52001

## EMMET COUNTY
District Court Clerk
Emmet County Courthouse
Courthouse Square
Estherville, IA 51334

## FAYETTE COUNTY
District Court Clerk
Fayette Cty District Court
PO Box 458
West Union, IA 52175

## FLOYD COUNTY
District Court Clerk
Floyd County Courthouse
Courthouse Square
Charles City, IA 50616

## FRANKLIN COUNTY
District Court Clerk
Franklin County District Court
PO Box 28
Hampton, IA 50441

## FREMONT COUNTY
District Court Clerk
Fremont County District Court
PO Box 549
Sidney, IA 51652

## GREENE COUNTY
District Court Clerk
Greene County Courthouse
114 North Chestnut
Jefferson, IA 50129-2144

## GRUNDY COUNTY
District Court Clerk
Grundy County Courthouse
Courthouse Square
Grundy Center, IA 50638

## GUTHRIE COUNTY
District Court Clerk
Guthrie County Courthouse
Courthouse Square
Guthrie Center, IA 50115

## HAMILTON COUNTY
District Court Clerk
Hamilton County District Court
2500 Superior Street
Webster City, IA 50595

## HANCOCK COUNTY
District Court Clerk
Hancock County District Court
855 State Street
Garner, IA 50438

## HARDIN COUNTY
District Court Clerk
Hardin County Courthouse
Box 495
Eldora, IA 50627

## HARRISON COUNTY
District Court Clerk
Harrison County Courthouse
Courthouse Square
Logan,IA 51546

## HENRY COUNTY
District Court Clerk
Henry County District Court
PO Box 176
Mount Pleasant, IA 52641

## HOWARD COUNTY
District Court Clerk
Howard County Courthouse
Courthouse Square
Cresco, IA 52136

## HUMBOLDT COUNTY
District Court Clerk
Humboldt County Courthouse
Courthouse Square
Dakota City, IA 50529

## IDA COUNT
District Court Clerk
Ida County Courthouse
Courthouse Square
Ida Grove, IA 51445

## IOWA COUNTY
District Court Clerk
Iowa County District Court
PO Box 266
Marengo, IA 52301

## JACKSON COUNTY
District Court Clerk
Jackson County District Court
201 West Platt
Maquoketa, IA 52060

## JASPER COUNTY
District Court Clerk
Jasper County District Court
PO Box 666
Newton, IA 50208

## JEFFERSON COUNTY
District Court Clerk
Jefferson County District Court
Box 984
Fairfield, IA 52556

## JOHNSON COUNTY
District Court Clerk
Johnson County Courthouse
PO Box 2510
Iowa City, IA 52244

## JONES COUNTY
District Court Clerk
Jones County Courthouse
Courthouse Square
Anamosa, IA 52205

## KEOKUK COUNTY
District Court Clerk
Keokuk County Courthouse
Courthouse Square
Sigourney, IA 52591

## KOSSUTH COUNTY
District Court Clerk
Kossuth County Courthouse
114 West State Street
Algona, IA 50511

## LEE COUNTY
District Court Clerk
Lee County District Court
PO Box 1443
Ft. Madison, IA 52627

## LINN COUNTY
District Court Clerk
Linn County District Court
PO Box 1090
Cedar Rapids, IA 52406

## LOUISA COUNTY
District Court Clerk
Louisa County District Court
PO Box 268
Wapello, IA 52653

## LUCAS COUNTY
District Court Clerk
Lucas County Courthouse
Courthouse Square
Chariton, IA 50049

## LYON COUNTY
District Court Clerk
Lyon County Courthouse
Courthouse Square
Rock Rapids, IA 51246

## MADISON COUNTY
District Court Clerk
Madison County District Court
PO Box 152
Winterset, IA 50273

## MAHASKA COUNTY
District Court Clerk
Mahaska County Courthouse
Courthouse Square
Oskaloosa, IA 52577

## MARION COUNTY
District Court Clerk
Marion County District Court
PO Box 497
Knoxville, IA 50138

## MARSHALL COUNTY
District Court Clerk
Marshall County Courthouse
Courthouse Square
Marshalltown, IA 50158

## MILLS COUNTY
District Court Clerk
Mills County Courthouse
Courthouse Square
Glenwood, IA 51534

## MITCHELL COUNTY
District Court Clerk
Mitchell County Courthouse
508 State Street
Osage, IA 50461

## MONONA COUNTY
District Court Clerk
Monona County District Court
610 Iowa Ave
Onawa, IA 51040

## MONROE COUNTY
District Court Clerk
Monroe County Courthouse
Courthouse Square
Albia, IA 52531

## MONTGOMERY COUNTY
District Court Clerk
Montgomery County Courthouse
Courthouse Square
Red Oak, IA 51566

## MUSCATINE COUNTY
District Court Clerk
Muscatine County Courthouse
Courthouse Square
Muscatine, IA 52761

## OSCEOLA COUNTY
District Court Clerk
Osceola County Courthouse
PO Box 156
Sibley, IA 51249

## O'BRIEN COUNTY
District Court Clerk
O'Brien County Courthouse
Courthouse Square
Primghar, IA 51245

## PAGE COUNTY
District Court Clerk
Page County Courthouse
112 East Main
Clarinda, IA 51632

## PALO ALTO COUNTY
District Court Clerk
Palo Alto County Courthouse
PO Box 387
Emmetsburg, IA 50536

## PLYMOUTH COUNTY
District Court Clerk
Plymouth County District Court
215 4th Avenue S.E.
Le Mars, IA 51031

## POCAHONTAS COUNTY
District Court Clerk
Pocahontas County Courthouse
Courthouse Square
Pocahontas, IA 50574

## POLK COUNTY
District Court Clerk
Polk County Courthouse
5th and Mulberry Rm 201
Des Moines, IA 50309

## POTTAWATTAMIE COUNTY
District Court Clerk
Pottawattamie Cty Court
227 South 6th Street
Council Bluffs, IA 51501

## POWESHIEK COUNTY
District Court Clerk
Poweshiek County District Court
PO Box 218
Montezuma, IA 50171

## RINGGOLD COUNTY
District Court Clerk
Ringgold County Courthouse
Courthouse Square
Mount Ayr, IA 50854

## SAC COUNTY
District Court Clerk
Sac County Courthouse
PO Box 368
Sac City, IA 50583

## SCOTT COUNTY
District Court Clerk
Scott County District Court
416 West 4th Street
Davenport, IA 52801

## SHELBY COUNTY
District Court Clerk
Shelby County District Court
PO Box 431
Harlan, IA 51537

## SIOUX COUNTY
District Court Clerk
Sioux County Courthouse
PO Box 40
Orange City, IA 51041

## STORY COUNTY
District Court Clerk
Story County District Court
PO Box 408
Nevada, IA 50201

## TAMA COUNTY
District Court Clerk
Tama County District Court
PO Box 306
Toledo, IA 52342

## TAYLOR COUNTY
District Court Clerk
Taylor County Courthouse
Courthouse Square
Bedford, IA 50833

## UNION COUNTY
District Court Clerk
Union County Courthouse
Courthouse Square
Creston, IA 50801

## VAN BUREN COUNTY
District Court Clerk
Van Buren County Courthouse
Courthouse Square
Keosauqua, IA 52565

## WAPELLO COUNTY
District Court Clerk
Wapello County Courthouse
101 West 4th
Ottumwa, IA 52501

## WARREN COUNTY
District Court Clerk
Warren County District Court
PO Box 379
Indianola, IA 50125

## WASHINGTON COUNTY
District Court Clerk
Washington Cty District Court
PO Box 391
Washington, IA 52353

## WAYNE COUNTY
District Court Clerk
Wayne County District Court
PO Box 424
Corydon, IA 50060

## WEBSTER COUNTY
District Court Clerk
Webster County Courthouse
Courthouse Square
Ft. Dodge, IA 50501

## WINNEBAGO COUNTY
District Court Clerk
Winnebago Cty District Court
126 South Clark
Forest City, IA 50436

## WINNESHIEK COUNTY
District Court Clerk
Winneshiek Cty District Court
201 West Main
Decorah, IA 52101

## WOODBURY COUNTY
District Court Clerk
Woodbury County Courthouse
7th and Douglas
Sioux City, IA 51101

## WORTH COUNTY
District Court Clerk
Worth County Courthouse
Courthouse Square
Northwood, IA 50459

## WRIGHT COUNTY
District Court Clerk
Wright County District Court
PO Box 306
Clarion, IA 50525

# IDAHO

## ADA COUNTY
District Court Clerk
Ada County District Clerk
514 West Jeffereson
Boise, ID 83702-5931

## ADAMS COUNTY
District Court Clerk
Adams County District Court
PO Box 48
Council, ID 83612

## BANNOCK COUNTY
District Court Clerk
Bannock County District Court
PO Box 4847
Pocatello, ID 83205

## BEAR LAKE COUNTY
District Court Clerk
Bear Lake Cty District Court
PO Box 190
Paris, ID 83261

## BENEWAH COUNTY
District Court Clerk
Benewah County Courthouse
701 College
St. Marie's, ID 83861

## BINGHAM COUNTY
District Court Clerk
Bingham County District Court
501 North Maple
Blackfoot, ID 83221

## BLAINE COUNTY
District Court Clerk
Blaine County District Court
PO Box 1006
Hailey, ID 83333

## BOISE COUNTY
District Court Clerk
Boise County District Court
PO Box 126
Idaho City, ID 83631

## BONNER COUNTY
District Court Clerk
Bonner County District Court
215 South First
Sandpoint, ID 83864

## BONNEVILLE COUNTY
District Court Clerk
Bonneville Cty District Court
605 North Capitol
Idaho Falls, ID 83402

## BOUNDARY COUNTY
District Court Clerk
Boundary County District Court
315 Kootneai
Bonners Ferry, ID 83805-0419

## BUTTE COUNTY
District Court Clerk
Butte County District Court
PO Box 171
Arco, ID 83213

## CAMAS COUNTY
District Court Clerk
Camas County District Court
PO Box 430
Fairfield, ID 83327

## CANYON COUNTY
District Court Clerk
Canyon County District Court
1115 Albany
Caldwell, ID 83605

## CARIBOU COUNTY
District Court Clerk
Caribou County District Court
159 South Main
Soda Springs, ID 83276

## CASSIA COUNTY
District Court Clerk
Cassia County District Court
1451 Overland
Burley, ID 83318

## CLARK COUNTY
District Court Clerk
Clark County District Court
PO Box 205
Dubois, ID 83423

## CLEARWATER COUNTY
District Court Clerk
Clearwater County District Court
150 Michigan
Orofino, ID 83544

## CUSTER COUNTY
District Court Clerk
Custer County District Court
PO Box 385
Challis, ID 83226

## ELMORE COUNTY
District Court Clerk
Elmore County District Court
150 South 4th E., Ste 5
Mountain Home, ID 83647

## FRANKLIN COUNTY
District Court Clerk
Franklin County District Court
39 West Oneida
Preston, ID 83263

## FREMONT COUNTY
District Court Clerk
Fremont County District Court
PO Box 42
St. Anthony, ID 83445

## GEM COUNTY
District Court Clerk
Gem County District Court
415 East Main, Rm 300
Emmett, ID 83617

## GOODING COUNTY
District Court Clerk
Gooding County District Court
PO Box 477
Gooding, ID 83330

## IDAHO COUNTY
District Court Clerk
Idaho County District Court
320 West Main
Grangeville, ID 83530

## JEFFERSON COUNTY
District Court Clerk
Jefferson County District Court
PO Box 71
Rigby, ID 83442

## JEROME COUNTY
District Court Clerk
Jerome County District Court
PO Box 407
Jerome, ID 83338

## KOOTENAI COUNTY
District Court Clerk
Kootenai County District Court
324 West Garden
Coeur D'Alene, ID 83814

## LATAH COUNTY
District Court Clerk
Latah County District Court
PO Box 8068
Moscow, ID 83843

## LEMHI COUNTY
District Court Clerk
Lemhi County District Court
206 Courthouse Dr
Salmon, ID 83467

## LEWIS COUNTY
District Court Clerk
Lewis County District Court
PO Box 39
Nezperce, ID 83543

## LINCOLN COUNTY
District Court Clerk
Lincoln County District Court
Drawer A
Shoshone, ID 83352

## MADISON COUNTY
District Court Clerk
Madison County District Court
PO Box 389
Rexburg, ID 83340

## MINIDOKA COUNTY
District Court Clerk
Minidoka County District Court
PO Box 474
Rupert, ID 83350

## NEZ PERCE COUNTY
District Court Clerk
Nez Perce Cty District Court
PO Box 896
Lewiston, ID 83501

## ONEIDA COUNTY
District Court Clerk
Oneida County District Court
10 Court Street
Malad City, ID 83252

## OWYHEE COUNTY
District Court Clerk
Owyhee County Courthouse
Courthouse Square
Murphy, ID 83650

## PAYETTE COUNTY
District Court Clerk
Payette County District Court
1130 3rd Ave
N. Payette, ID 83661

## POWER COUNTY
District Court Clerk
Power County District Court
543 Bannock Ave
American Falls, ID 83211

## SHOSHONE COUNTY
District Court Clerk
Shoshone County District Court
700 Bank Street
Wallace, ID 83873

## TETON COUNTY
District Court Clerk
Teton County District Court
PO Box 770
Driggs, ID 83422

## TWIN FALLS COUNTY
District Court Clerk
Twin Falls Cty District Court
PO Box 126
Twin Falls, ID 83301

## VALLEY COUNTY
District Court Clerk
Valley County District Court
PO Box 650
Cascade, ID 83611

## WASHINGTON COUNTY
District Court Clerk
Washington Cty District Court
PO Box 670
Weiser, ID 83672

# ILLINOIS

## ADAMS COUNTY
Circuit Court Clerk
Courthouse
521 Vermont Street
Quincy, IL 62301

## ALEXANDER COUNTY
Circuit Court Clerk
Alexander Cty Circuit Court
2000 Washington Ave.
Cairo, IL 62914

## BOND COUNTY
Circuit Court Clerk
Bond County Circuit Court
200 West College
Greenville, IL 62246

## BOONE COUNTY
Circuit Court Clerk
Boone County Circuit Court
601 North Main
Belvidere, Il 61008

## BROWN COUNTY
Circuit Court Clerk
Brown County Circuit Court
Courthouse
Mount Sterling, IL 62353

## BUREAU COUNTY
Circuit Court Clerk
Bureau County Circuit Court
700 South Main Street
Princeton, IL 61356

## CALHOUN COUNTY
Circuit Court Clerk
Calhoun County Circuit Court
PO Box 486
Hardin, IL 62047

## CARROLL COUNTY
Circuit Court Clerk
Carroll County Circuit Court
PO Box 32
Mount Carroll, IL 61053

## CASS COUNTY
Circuit Court Clerk
Cass County Circuit Court
PO Box 203
Virginia, IL 62691

## CHAMPAIGN COUNTY
Circuit Court Clerk
Champaign Cty Circuit Court
101 East Main
Urbana, IL 61801

## CHRISTIAN COUNTY
Circuit Court Clerk
Courthouse Square
PO Box 617
Taylorville, IL 62568

## CLARK COUNTY
Circuit Court Clerk
Clark County Circuit Court
PO Box 187
Marshall, IL 62441

## CLAY COUNTY
Circuit Court Clerk
Clay County Circuit Court
PO Box 100
Louisville, IL 62858

## CLINTON COUNTY
Circuit Court Clerk
Clinton County Circuit Court
PO Box 407
Carlyle, IL 62231

## COLES COUNTY
Circuit Court Clerk
Coles County Circuit Court
PO Box 48
Charleston, IL 61920

## COOK COUNTY
Circuit Court Clerk
Law Division, Room 801
50 West Washington
Chicago, IL 60602

## COOK COUNTY
Circuit Court Clerk
Daley Center, Room 601
50 West Washington
Chicago, IL 60602

**CRAWFORD COUNTY**
Circuit Court Clerk
Crawford County Circuit Court
PO Box 222
Robinson, IL 62454

**CUMBERLAND COUNTY**
Circuit Court Clerk
Cumberland Cty Circuit Court
PO Box 145
Toledo, IL 62468

**DE KALB COUNTY**
Circuit Court Clerk
De Kalb County Courthouse
133 West State Street
Sycamore, IL 60178

**DE WITT COUNTY**
Circuit Court Clerk
De Witt County Circuit Court
PO Box 439
Clinton, IL 61727

**DOUGLAS COUNTY**
Circuit Court Clerk
Douglas County Circuit Court
PO Box 50
Tuscola, IL 61953

**DU PAGE COUNTY**
Circuit Court Clerk
Du Page County Circuit Court
PO Box 707
Wheaton, IL 60189-0707

**EDGAR COUNTY**
Circuit Court Clerk
Edgar County Courthouse
115 West Court Street, Rm M
Paris, IL 61944

**EDWARDS COUNTY**
Circuit Court Clerk
Edwards County Courthouse
50 Main Street
Albion, IL 62806

**EFFINGHAM COUNTY**
Circuit Court Clerk
Effingham Cty Circuit Court
PO Box 586
Effingham,IL 62401

**FAYETTE COUNTY**
Circuit Court Clerk
Fayette County Circuit Court
221 South 7th
Vandalia, IL 62471

**FORD COUNTY**
Circuit Court Clerk
Ford County Circuit Court
PO Box 80
Paxton, IL 60957

**FRANKLIN COUNTY**
Circuit Court Clerk
Franklin County Courthouse
Courthouse Square
Benton, IL 62812

## FULTON COUNTY
Circuit Court Clerk
Fulton County Circuit Court
PO Box 152
Lewistown, IL 61542

## GALLATIN COUNTY
Circuit Court Clerk
Gallatin County Circuit Court
PO Box 503
Shawneetown, IL 62984

## GREENE COUNTY
Circuit Court Clerk
Greene County Circuit Court
519 North Main
Carrollton, IL 62016

## GRUNDY COUNTY
Circuit Court Clerk
Grundy County Circuit Court
PO Box 707
Morris, IL 60450

## HAMILTON COUNTY
Circuit Court Clerk
Hamilton County Courthouse
Courthouse Square
McLeansboro, IL 62859

## HANCOCK COUNTY
Circuit Court Clerk
Hancock County Circuit Court
PO Box 189
Carthage, IL 62321

## HARDIN COUNTY
Circuit Court Clerk
Hardin County Circuit Court
PO Box 308
Elizabethtown, IL 62931

## HENDERSON COUNTY
Circuit Court Clerk
Henderson County Courthouse
Courthouse Square
Oquawka, IL 61469

## HENRY COUNTY
Circuit Court Clerk
Henry County Circuit Court
PO Box 9
Cambridge, IL 61238

## IROQUOIS COUNTY
Circuit Court Clerk
Iroquois County Courthouse
550 South 10th
Watseka, IL 60970

## JACKSON COUNTY
Circuit Court Clerk
Jackson County Courthouse
Courthouse Square
Murphysboro, IL 62966

## JASPER COUNTY
Circuit Court Clerk
Jasper County Circuit Court
100 West Jourdan
Newton, IL 62448

## JEFFERSON COUNTY
Circuit Court Clerk
Jefferson Cty Circuit Court
PO Box 1266
Mount Vernon, IL 62864

## JERSEY COUNTY
Circuit Court Clerk
Jersey County Circuit Court
201 West Pearl
Jerseyville, IL 62052

## JO DAVIESS COUNTY
Circuit Court Clerk
Jo Daviess Cty Circuit Court
330 North Bench
Galena, IL 61036

## JOHNSON COUNTY
Circuit Court Clerk
Johnson County Circuit Court
PO Box 517
Vienna, IL 62995

## KANE COUNTY
Circuit Court Clerk
Kane County Circuit Court
PO Box 112
Geneva, IL 60134

## KANKAKEE COUNTY
Circuit Court Clerk
Kankakee County Circuit Court
450 East Court Street
Kankakee, IL 60901

## KENDALL COUNTY
Circuit Court Clerk
Kendall County Circuit Court
PO Drawer M
Yorkville, IL 60560

## KNOX COUNTY
Circuit Court Clerk
Knox County Courthouse
Courthouse Square
Galesburg, IL 61401

## LA SALLE COUNTY
Circuit Court Clerk
La Salle County Circuit Court
119 W. Madison
Ottawa, IL 61350

## LAKE COUNTY
Circuit Court Clerk
18 N. County Street
Rm C-104
Waukegan, IL 60085

## LAWRENCE COUNTY
Circuit Court Clerk
Lawrence County Circuit Court
Courthouse Square
Lawrenceville, IL 62439

## LEE COUNTY
Circuit Court Clerk
Lee County Circuit Court
PO Box 325
Dixon, IL 61021

## LIVINGSTON COUNTY
Circuit Court Clerk
Livingston County Circuit Court
PO Box 320
Pontiac, IL 61764

## LOGAN COUNTY
Circuit Court Clerk
Logan County Courthouse
601 Broadway
Lincoln, IL 62656-0158

## MACON COUNTY
Circuit Court Clerk
Macon County Circuit Court
253 East Wood Street
Decatur, IL 62523

## MACOUPIN COUNTY
Circuit Court Clerk
Macoupin County Circuit Court
PO Box 197
Carlinville, IL 62626

## MADISON COUNTY
Circuit Court Clerk
Madison County Courthouse
155 North Main
Edwardsville, IL 62025

## MARION COUNTY
Circuit Court Clerk
Main and Broadway
PO Box 130
Salem, IL 62881

## MARSHALL COUNTY
Circuit Court Clerk
122 North Prairie
Box 98
Lacon,IL 61540

## MASON COUNTY
Circuit Court Clerk
Mason County Circuit Court
PO Box 446
Havana, IL 62644

## MASSAC COUNTY
Circuit Court Clerk
Massac County Circuit Court
PO Box 152
Metropolis, IL 62960

## MCDONOUGH COUNTY
Circuit Court Clerk
McDonough County Circuit Court
McDonough County Courthouse
Macomb, IL 61455

## MCHENRY COUNTY
Circuit Court Clerk
McHenry County Circuit Court
2200 North Seminary Ave
Woodstock, IL 60098

## MCLEAN COUNTY
Circuit Court Clerk
McLean County Circuit Court
104 West Front, Rm 303
Bloomington, IL 61701

## MENARD COUNTY
Circuit Court Clerk
Menard County Circuit Court
PO Box 466
Petersburg, IL 62675

## MERCER COUNTY
Circuit Court Clerk
Mercer County Circuit Court
PO Box 175
Aledo, IL 61231

## MONROE COUNTY
Circuit Court Clerk
Monroe County Courthouse
Main Street
Waterloo, IL 62298

## MONTGOMERY COUNTY
Circuit Court Clerk
Montgomery Cty Circuit Court
PO Box C
Hillsboro, IL 62049

## MORGAN COUNTY
Circuit Court Clerk
Morgan County Circuit Court
300 West State Street
Jacksonville, IL 62650

## MOULTRIE COUNTY
Circuit Court Clerk
Moultrie Cty Circuit Court
Moultrie County Courthouse
Sullivan, IL 61951

## OGLE COUNTY
Circuit Court Clerk
Ogle County Circuit Court
PO Box 337
Oregon, IL 61061

## PEORIA COUNTY
Circuit Court Clerk
Peoria County Courthouse
324 Main Street, Rm G-22
Peoria, IL 61602

## PERRY COUNTY
Circuit Court Clerk
#1 Public Square
PO Box 217
Pinckneyville, IL 62274

## PIATT COUNTY
Circuit Court Clerk
Piatt County Circuit Court
PO Box 288
Monticello, IL 61856

## PIKE COUNTY
Circuit Court Clerk
Pike County Circuit Court
Courthouse
Pittsfield, IL 62363

## POPE COUNTY
Circuit Court Clerk
Pope County Circuit Court
PO Box 502
Golconda, IL 62938

## PULASKI COUNTY
Circuit Court Clerk
Pulaski County Circuit Court
PO Box 88
Mound City, IL 62963

## PUTNAM COUNTY
Circuit Court Clerk
Putnam County Circuit Court
PO Box 207
Hennepin, IL 61327

## RANDOLPH COUNTY
Circuit Court Clerk
Randolph Cty Circuit Court
1 Taylor Street
Chester, IL 62233

## RICHLAND COUNTY
Circuit Court Clerk
Richland County Courthouse
103 West Main, Rm 21
Olney, IL 62450

## ROCK ISLAND COUNTY
Circuit Court Clerk
Rock Island Cty Circuit Court
PO Box 5230
Rock Island, IL 61204-5230

## SALINE COUNTY
Circuit Court Clerk
Saline County Courthouse
Courthouse Square
Harrisburg, IL 62946

## SANGAMON COUNTY
Circuit Court Clerk
Sangamon County Building
200 South 9th Street, Rm 405
Springfield, IL 62701

## SCHUYLER COUNTY
Circuit Court Clerk
Schuyler County Courthouse
PO Box 189
Rushville, IL 62681

## SCOTT COUNTY
Circuit Court Clerk
Scott County Courthouse
35 East Market Street
Winchester, IL 62694

## SHELBY COUNTY
Circuit Court Clerk
Shelby County Circuit Court
PO Box 469
Shelbyville, IL 62565

## STARK COUNTY
Circuit Court Clerk
Stark County Courthouse
Courthouse Square
Toulon, IL 61483

## STEPHENSON COUNTY
Circuit Court Clerk
Stephenson County Courthouse
15 North Galena
Freeport, IL 61032

## ST. CLAIR COUNTY
Circuit Court Clerk
St. Clair County Circuit Court
10 Public Square
Belleville, IL 62220

## TAZEWELL COUNTY
Circuit Court Clerk
Tazewell County Circuit Court
PO Box 69
Pekin, IL 61554

## UNION COUNTY
Circuit Court Clerk
309 W. Market Street
PO Box 360
Jonesboro, IL 62952

## VERMILION COUNTY
Circuit Court Clerk
Vermilion County Circuit Court
7 North Vermilion Street
Danville, IL 61832

## WABASH COUNTY
Circuit Court Clerk
Wabash County Circuit Court
PO Box 1057
Mt. Carmel, IL 62863

## WARREN COUNTY
Circuit Court Clerk
Warren County Courthouse
Public Square
Monmouth, IL 61462

## WASHINGTON COUNTY
Circuit Court Clerk
Washington County Courthouse
101 East Street Louis Street
Nashville, IL 62263

## WAYNE COUNTY
Circuit Court Clerk
Wayne County Circuit Court
PO Box 43
Fairfield, IL 62837

## WHITE COUNTY
Circuit Court Clerk
White County Circuit Court
PO Box 310
Carmi, IL 62821

## WHITESIDE COUNTY
Circuit Court Clerk
Whiteside County Courthouse
Courthouse Square
Morrison, IL 61270

## WILL COUNTY
Circuit Court Clerk
Will County Courthouse
14 West Jefferson, Rm 212
Joliet, IL 60431

## WILLIAMSON COUNTY
Circuit Court Clerk
Williamson Cty Circuit Court
200 Jefferson
Marion, IL 62959

## WINNEBAGO COUNTY
Circuit Court Clerk
400 W. State Street
Rm 236
Rockford, IL 61101

## WOODFORD COUNTY
Circuit Court Clerk
Woodford County Courthouse
PO Box 284
Eureka, IL 61530

# INDIANA

## ADAMS COUNTY
Court Clerk
Adams County Courthouse
South 2nd Street
Decatur, IN 46733

## ALLEN COUNTY
Court Clerk
Allen County Courthouse
Rm 200
Ft. Wayne, IN 46802

## BARTHOLOMEW COUNTY
Bartholomew County Court
Courthouse
PO Box 924
Columbus, IN 47202-0924

## BENTON COUNTY
Court Clerk
Benton County Court
700 East 5th Street
Fowler, IN 47944

## BLACKFORD COUNTY
Court Clerk
Blackford County Court
110 West Washington Street
Hartford City, IN 47348

## BOONE COUNTY
Court Clerk
Boone County Court
1 Courthouse Square
Lebanon, IN 46052

## BROWN COUNTY
Court Clerk
Brown County Court
PO Box 85
Nashville, IN 47448

## CARROLL COUNTY
Court Clerk
Carroll County Courthouse
2nd Floor
Delphi, IN 46923

## CASS COUNTY
Court Clerk
Cass County Court
200 Court Park
Logansport, IN 46947

## CLARK COUNTY
Court Clerk
Clark County Court
501 East Court Ave
Jeffersonville, IN 47130

## CLAY COUNTY
Court Clerk
Clay County Court
PO Box 33
Brazil, IN 47834

## CLINTON COUNTY
Court Clerk
Clinton County Courthouse
265 Courthouse Square
Frankfort, IN 46041-1993

## CRAWFORD COUNTY
Court Clerk
Crawford County Court
PO Box 375
English, IN 47118

## DAVIESS COUNTY
Court Clerk
Daviess County Court
200 East Walnut
Washington, IN 47501

## DE KALB COUNTY
Court Clerk
De Kalb County Court
Main Street and 7th St
Auburn, IN 46706

## DEARBORN COUNTY
Court Clerk
Dearborn County Courthouse
West High Street
Lawrenceburg, IN 47025

## DECATUR COUNTY
Court Clerk
Decatur County Court
150 Courthouse Square,#1
Greensburg, IN 47240

## DELAWARE COUNTY
Court Clerk
Delaware County Court
100 West Main
Muncie, IN 47308

## DUBOIS COUNTY
Court Clerk
Dubois County Courthouse
Courthouse Square
Jasper, IN 47546

## ELKHART COUNTY
Court Clerk
Elkhart County Court
315 South 2nd Street
Elkhart, IN 46516

## FAYETTE COUNTY
Court Clerk
Fayette County Court
401 Central
Connersville, IN 47331-0607

## FLOYD COUNTY
Court Clerk
Floyd County Court
311 West 1st Street, Rm 244
New Albany, IN 47150

## FOUNTAIN COUNTY
Court Clerk
Fountain County Court
PO Box 183
Covington, IN 47932

## FRANKLIN COUNTY
Court Clerk
Franklin County Court
459 Main Street
Brookville, IN 47012

## FULTON COUNTY
Court Clerk
Fulton County Court
815 Main Street
Rochester, IN 46975

## GIBSON COUNTY
Court Clerk
Gibson County Courthouse
Courthouse Square
Princeton, IN 47670

## GRANT COUNTY
Court Clerk
Grant County Courthouse
101 East 4th Street
Marion, IN 46952

## GREENE COUNTY
Court Clerk
Greene County Court
PO Box 229
Bloomfield, IN 47424

## HAMILTON COUNTY
Court Clerk
Hamilton County Courthouse
Courthouse Square
Noblesville, IN 46060

## HANCOCK COUNTY
Court Clerk
Hancock County Court
9 East Main Street, Rm 201
Greenfield, IN 46140

## HARRISON COUNTY
Court Clerk
Harrison County Court
300 North Capitol
Corydon, IN 47112

## HENDRICKS COUNTY
Court Clerk
Hendricks County Court
PO Box 599
Danville, IN 46122

## HENRY COUNTY
Court Clerk
Henry County Court
PO Box B
New Castle, IN 47362

## HOWARD COUNTY
Court Clerk
Howard County Courthouse
PO Box 9004
Kokomo, IN 46904

**Adoption Searches Made Easier**

## HUNTINGTON COUNTY
Court Clerk
Huntington County Courthouse
Rm 201
Huntington, IN 46750

## JACKSON COUNTY
Court Clerk
Jackson County Court
PO Box 122
Brownstown, IN 47220

## JASPER COUNTY
Court Clerk
Jasper County Courthouse
PO Box 10
Rensselaer, IN 47978

## JAY COUNTY
Court Clerk
Jay County Courthouse
Courthouse Square
Portland, IN 47371

## JEFFERSON COUNTY
Court Clerk
Jefferson County Courthouse
Government Center
Madison, IN 47250

## JENNINGS COUNTY
Court Clerk
Jennings County Courthouse
Courthouse Square
Vemon, IN 47282

## JOHNSON COUNTY
Court Clerk
Johnson County Courthouse
PO Box 368
Franklin, IN 46131

## KNOX COUNTY
Court Clerk
Knox County Court
PO Box 906
Vincennes, IN 47591

## KOSCIUSKO COUNTY
Court Clerk
Koscuisko County Court
121 North Lake
Warsaw, IN 46580

## LA PORTE COUNTY
Court Clerk
La Porte County Court
Lincolnway
La Porte, IN 46350

## LAGRANGE COUNTY
Court Clerk
LaGrange County Courthouse
105 North Detroit Street
La Grange, IN 46761

## LAKE COUNTY
Court Clerk
Lake County Courthouse
2293 North Main Street
Crown Point, IN 46307

## LAWRENCE COUNTY
Court Clerk
Lawrence County Courthouse
Judicial Complex
Bedford, IN 47421

## MADISON COUNTY
Court Clerk
Madison County Court
16 East 9th
Anderson, IN 46015

## MARION COUNTY
Indianapolis-Marion County
Repository, Rm E-G7
50 North Alabama ST
Indianapolis, IN 46204

## MARSHALL COUNTY
Court Clerk
Marshall County Court
211 Madison Street
Plymouth, IN 46563

## MARTIN COUNTY
Court Clerk
Martin County Court
PO Box 120
Shoals, IN 47581

## MIAMI COUNTY
Court Clerk
Miami County Court
PO Box 184
Peru, IN 46970

## MONROE COUNTY
Court Clerk
Monroe County Court
301 North College
Bloomington, IN 47402

## MONTGOMERY COUNTY
Court Clerk
Montgomery County Court
PO Box 768
Crawfordsville, IN 47933

## MORGAN COUNTY
Court Clerk
Morgan County Court
PO Box 1556
Martinsville, IN 46151

## NEWTON COUNTY
Court Clerk
Newton Cty Courthouse Square
PO Box 49
Kentland, IN 47951

## NOBLE COUNTY
Court Clerk
Noble County Court
101 North Orange Street
Albion, IN 46701

## OHIO COUNTY
Court Clerk
Ohio County Court
PO Box 185
Rising Sun, IN 47040

## ORANGE COUNTY
Court Clerk
Orange County Courthouse
Court Street
Paoli, IN 47454

## OWEN COUNTY
Court Clerk
Owen County Courthouse
PO Box 146
Spencer, IN 47460

## PARKE COUNTY
Court Clerk
Parke County Court
116 West High, Rm 204
Rockville, IN 47872

## PERRY COUNTY
Court Clerk
Perry County Courthouse
Courthouse Square
Cannelton, IN 47520

## PIKE COUNTY
Court Clerk
Pike County Courthouse
Judicial Complex
Petersburg, IN 47567

## PORTER COUNTY
Court Clerk
Porter County Court
157 South Franklin
Valparaiso, IN 46383

## POSEY COUNTY
Court Clerk
Posey County Court
300 Main Street
Mount Vernon, IN 47620-1897

## PULASKI COUNTY
Court Clerk
Pulaski County Courthouse
112 East Main Street, Room 230
Winamac, IN 46996

## PUTNAM COUNTY
Court Clerk
Putnam County Courthouse
PO Box 546
Greencastle, IN 46135

## RANDOLPH COUNTY
Court Clerk
Randolph County Courthouse
PO Box 230
Winchester, IN 47394-0230

## RIPLEY COUNTY
Court Clerk
Ripley County Court
Tyson and Washington Street
Versaille, IN 47042

## RUSH COUNTY
Court Clerk
Rush County Court
PO Box 429
Rushville, IN 46173

## SCOTT COUNTY
Court Clerk
Scott County Courthouse
Courthouse Square
Scottsburg, IN 47170

## SHELBY COUNTY
Court Clerk
Shelby County Court
407 South Harrison
Shelbyville, IN 46176

## SPENCER COUNTY
Court Clerk
Spencer County Court
PO Box 12
Rockport, IN 47635

## STARKE COUNTY
Court Clerk
Starke County Courthouse
Courthouse Square
Knox, IN 46534

## STEUBEN COUNTY
Court Clerk
Steuben County Court
PO Box 327
Angola, IN 46703

## ST. JOSEPH COUNTY
Court Clerk
St. Joseph County Court
101 South Main Street
South Bend, IN 46601

## SULLIVAN COUNTY
Court Clerk
Sullivan County Court
100 Courthouse Sq.,#304
Sullivan, IN 47882

## SWITZERLAND COUNTY
Court Clerk
Switzerland County Court
212 West Main
Vevay, IN 47043

## TIPPECANOE COUNTY
Court Clerk
Tippecanoe Cty Courthouse
PO Box 1665
Lafayette, IN 47902

## TIPTON COUNTY
Court Clerk
Tipton County Court
PO Box 244
Tipton, IN 46072

## UNION COUNTY
Court Clerk
Union County Court
26 West Union Street, Rm 105
Liberty, IN 47353

## VANDERBURGH COUNTY
Court Clerk
Vanderburgh County Court
Courts Building, Rm 216
Evansville, IN 47732-3356

## VERMILLION COUNTY
Court Clerk
Vermillion County Court
PO Box 8
Newport, IN 47966

## VIGO COUNTY
Court Clerk
Vigo County Courthouse,
PO Box 8449
Terre Haute, IN 47808-8449

## WABASH COUNTY
Court Clerk
Wabash County Courthouse
One West Hill
Wabash, IN 46992

## WARREN COUNTY
Court Clerk
Warren County Courthouse
125 North Monroe, Rm 11
Williamsport, IN 47993

## WARRICK COUNTY
Court Clerk
Warrick County Courthouse
Government Center
Boonville, IN 47601

## WASHINGTON COUNTY
Court Clerk
Washington County Courthouse
Courthouse Square
Salem, IN 47167

## WAYNE COUNTY
Court Clerk
Wayne County Court
PO Box 1172
Richmond, IN 47375

## WELLS COUNTY
Court Clerk
Wells County Court
102 Market Street W
Bluffton, IN 46714

## WHITE COUNTY
Court Clerk
White County Courthouse
PO Box 350
Monticello, IN 47960

## WHITLEY COUNTY
Court Clerk
Whitley County Courthouse
101 West Van Buren, Rm 10
Columbia City, IN 46725

# KANSAS

## ALLEN COUNTY
District Court Clerk
Allen County District Court
PO Box 660
Iola, KS 66749

## ANDERSON COUNTY
District Court Clerk
Anderson Cty District Court
PO Box 305
Garnett, KS 66032

## ATCHISON COUNTY
District Court Clerk
Atchison Cty District Court
PO Box 408
Atchison, KS 66002

## BARBER COUNTY
District Court Clerk
Barber County District Court
PO Box 329
Medicine Lodge, KS 67104

## BARTON COUNTY
District Court Clerk
Barton County District Court
1400 North Main, Rm 306
Great Bend, KS 67530-4098

## BOURBON COUNTY
District Court Clerk
Bourbon Cty District Court
PO Box 868
Ft Scott, KS 66701

## BROWN COUNTY
District Court Clerk
Brown County Courthouse
PO Box 417
Hiawatha, KS 66434

## BUTLER COUNTY
District Court Clerk
Butler County District Court
PO Box 1367
El Dorado, KS 67042

## CHASE COUNTY
District Court Clerk
Chase County District Court
PO Box 207
Cottonwood Falls, KS 66845

## CHAUTAUQUA COUNTY
District Court Clerk
Chautauqua Cty District Court
215 North Chautauqua
Sedan, KS 67361

## CHEROKEE COUNTY
District Court Clerk
Cherokee Cty District Court
PO Box 189
Columbus, KS 66725

## CHEYENNE COUNTY
District Court Clerk
Cheyenne County District Court
PO Box 646
St. Francis, KS 67756

## CLARK COUNTY
District Court Clerk
Clark County District Court
PO Box 790
Ashland, KS 67831

## CLAY COUNTY
District Court Clerk
Clay County District Court
PO Box 203
Clay Center, KS 67432

## CLOUD COUNTY
District Court Clerk
Cloud County District Court
811 Washington
Concordia, KS 66901

## COFFEY COUNTY
District Court Clerk
Coffey County District Court
PO Box 330
Burlington, KS 66839

## COMANCHE COUNTY
District Court Clerk
Comanche County District Court
PO Box 722
Coldwater, KS 67029

## COWLEY COUNTY
District Court Clerk
Cowley County District Court
311 East 9th
Winfield, KS 67156

## CRAWFORD COUNTY
District Court Clerk
Crawford County District Court
PO Box 1348
Pittsburg, KS 66762

## DECATUR COUNTY
District Court Clerk
Decatur County District Court
PO Box 89
Oberlin, KS 67749

## DICKINSON COUNTY
District Court Clerk
Dickinson County District Court
PO Box 127
Abilene, KS 67410

## DONIPHAN COUNTY
District Court Clerk
Doniphan County District Court
PO Box 295
Troy, KS 66087

## DOUGLAS COUNTY
District Court Clerk
Douglas County District Court
111 East 11th
Lawrence, KS 66044

## EDWARDS COUNTY
District Court Clerk
Edwards County District Court
PO Box 232
Kinsley, KS 67547

## ELK COUNTY
District Court Clerk
Elk County District Court
PO Box 306
Howard, KS 67349

## ELLIS COUNTY
District Court Clerk
Ellis County District Court
PO Box 8
Hays, KS 67601

## ELLSWORTH COUNTY
District Court Clerk
Ellsworth Cty District Court
215 North Kansas
Ellsworth, KS 67439-3118

## FINNEY COUNTY
District Court Clerk
Finney County District Court
PO Box 798
Garden City, KS 67846

## FORD COUNTY
District Court Clerk
Ford County District Court
PO Box 197
Dodge City, KS 67801

## FRANKLIN COUNTY
District Court Clerk
Franklin Cty District Court
PO Box P
Ottawa, KS 66067

## GEARY COUNTY
District Court Clerk
Geary County District Court
PO Box 1147
Junction City, KS 66441

## GOVE COUNTY
District Court Clerk
Gove County District Court
PO Box 97
Gove, KS 67736

## GRAHAM COUNTY
District Court Clerk
Graham County District Court
410 North Pomeroy
Hill City, KS 67642

## GRANT COUNTY
District Court Clerk
Grant County District Court
108 South Glenn
Ulysses, KS 67880

## GRAY COUNTY
District Court Clerk
Gray County District Court
PO Box 487
Cimarron, KS 67835

## GREELEY COUNTY
District Court Clerk
Greeley County District Court
PO Box 516
Tribune, KS 67879

## GREENWOOD COUNTY
District Court Clerk
Greenwood Cty District Court
311 North Main
Eureka, KS 67045

## HAMILTON COUNTY
District Court Clerk
Hamilton County District Court
PO Box 745
Syracuse, KS 67878

**Adoption Searches Made Easier**

## HARPER COUNTY
District Court Clerk
Harper County District Court
PO Box 467
Anthony, KS 67003

## HARVEY COUNTY
District Court Clerk
Harvey County District Court
PO Box 665
Newton, KS 67114

## HASKELL COUNTY
District Court Clerk
Haskell County District Court
PO Box 146
Sublette, KS 67877

## HODGEMAN COUNTY
District Court Clerk
Hodgeman County District Court
PO Box 187
Jetmore, KS 67854

## JACKSON COUNTY
District Court Clerk
Jackson County District Court
Jackson County Courthouse
Holton, KS 66436

## JEFFERSON COUNTY
District Court Clerk
Jefferson Cty District Court
PO Box 312
Oskaloosa, KS 66066

## JEWELL COUNTY
District Court Clerk
Jewell County District Court
307 North Commercial
Mankato, KS 66956

## JOHNSON COUNTY
District Court Clerk
Johnson County District Court
PO Box 1600
Olathe, KS 66061

## KEARNY COUNTY
District Court Clerk
Kearny County District Court
PO Box 64
Lakin, KS 67860

## KINGMAN COUNTY
District Court Clerk
Kingman County District Court
PO Box 495
Kingman, KS 67068

## KIOWA COUNTY
District Court Clerk
Kiowa County District Court
211 East Florida
Greensburg, KS 67054

## LABETTE COUNTY
District Court Clerk
Labette Cty District Court
Labette County Courthouse
Oswego, KS 67356

## LANE COUNTY
District Court Clerk
Lane County District Court
PO Box 188
Dighton, KS 67839

## LEAVENWORTH COUNTY
District Court Clerk
Leavenworth Cty District Court
4th and Walnut
Leavenworth, KS 66048

## LINCOLN COUNTY
District Court Clerk
Lincoln County District Court
216 East Lincoln
Lincoln, KS 67455

## LINN COUNTY
District Court Clerk
Linn County District Court
PO Box B
Mound City, KS 66056

## LOGAN COUNTY
District Court Clerk
Logan County District Court
710 West 2nd Street
Oakley, KS 67748

## LYON COUNTY
District Court Clerk
Lyon County District Court
402 Commercial
Emporia, KS 66801

## MARION COUNTY
District Court Clerk
Marion Cty District Court
Box 298
Marion, KS 66861

## MARSHALL COUNTY
District Court Clerk
Marshall Cty District Court
PO Box 86
Marysville, KS 66508

## MCPHERSON COUNTY
District Court Clerk
McPherson Cty District Court
PO Box 1106
McPherson, KS 67460

## MEADE COUNTY
District Court Clerk
Meade County District Court
PO Box 623
Meade, KS 67864

## MIAMI COUNTY
District Court Clerk
Miami County District Court
PO Box 187
Paola, KS 66071

## MITCHELL COUNTY
District Court Clerk
Mitchell Cty District Court
115 South Hersey
Beloit, KS 67420

**Adoption Searches Made Easier**

## MONTGOMERY COUNTY
District Court Clerk
Montgomery Cty District Court,
PO Box 768
Independence, KS 67301

## MORRIS COUNTY
District Court Clerk
Morris County District Court
Morris County Courthouse
Council Grove, KS 66846

## MORTON COUNTY
District Court Clerk
Morton Cty DistrSict Court
PO Box 825
Elkhart, KS 67950

## NEMAHA COUNTY
District Court Clerk
Nemaha County District Court
PO Box 213
Seneca, KS 66538

## NEOSHO COUNTY
District Court Clerk
Neosho County District Court
101 South Lincoln
Chanute, KS 66720

## NESS COUNTY
District Court Clerk
Ness County District Court
PO Box 445
Ness City, KS 67560

## NORTON COUNTY
District Court Clerk
Norton County District Court
PO Box 70
Norton, KS 67654

## OSAGE COUNTY
District Court Clerk
Osage County District Court
PO Box 549
Lyndon, KS 66451

## OSBORNE COUNTY
District Court Clerk
Osborne County District Court
Osborne County Courthouse
Osborne, KS 67473

## OTTAWA COUNTY
District Court Clerk
Ottawa County District Court
307 North Concord
Minneapolis, KS 67467

## PAWNEE COUNTY
District Court Clerk
Pawnee County District Court
PO Box 270
Larned, KS 67550

## PHILLIPS COUNTY
District Court Clerk
Phillips Cty District Court
Phillips County Courthouse
Phillipsburg, KS 67661

## POTTAWATOMIE COUNTY
District Court Clerk
Pottawatomie Cty District Court
PO Box 129
Westmoreland, KS 66549

## PRATT COUNTY
District Court Clerk
Pratt County District Court
PO Box 984
Pratt, KS 67124

## RAWLINS COUNTY
District Court Clerk
Rawlins County District Court
PO Box 257
Atwood, KS 67730

## RENO COUNTY
District Court Clerk
Reno County District Court
206 West 1st
Hutchinson, KS 67501

## REPUBLIC COUNTY
District Court Clerk
Republic County District Court
PO Box 8
Belleville, KS 66935

## RICE COUNTY
District Court Clerk
Rice County District Court
101 West Commercial
Lyons, KS 67554

## RILEY COUNTY
District Court Clerk
Riley County District Court
100 Courthouse Plaza
Manhattan, KS 66502

## ROOKS COUNTY
District Court Clerk
Rooks County District Court
PO Box 531
Stockton, KS 67669

## RUSH COUNTY
District Court Clerk
Rush County District Court
PO Box 387
La Crosse, KS 67548

## RUSSELL COUNTY
District Court Clerk
Russell County District Court
PO Box 876
Russell, KS 67665

## SALINE COUNTY
District Court Clerk
Saline County District Court
300 West Ash
Salina, KS 67402-1756

## SCOTT COUNTY
District Court Clerk
Scott County District Court
303 Court
Scott City, KS 67871

**Adoption Searches Made Easier**

## SEDGWICK COUNTY
Disttict Court Clerk
Sedgwick Cty District Court
525 North Main, Rm 714
Wichita, KS 67203

## SEWARD COUNTY
District Court Clerk
Seward County District Court
415 North Washington
Liberal, KS 67901

## SHAWNEE COUNTY
District Court Clerk
Shawnee County District Court
200 SE 7th
Topeka, KS 66603

## SHERIDAN COUNTY
District Court Clerk
Sheridan County District Court
PO Box 753
Hoxie, KS 67740

## SHERMAN COUNTY
District Court Clerk
Sherman County District Court
813 Broadway, Rm 201
Goodland, KS 67735

## SMITH COUNTY
District Court Clerk
Smith County District Court
PO Box 273
Smith Center, KS 66967

## STAFFORD COUNTY
District Court Clerk
Stafford County District Court
PO Box 365
St. John, KS 67576

## STANTON COUNTY
District Court Clerk
Stanton County District Court
PO Box 913
Johnson, KS 67855

## STEVENS COUNTY
District Court Clerk
Stevens County District Court
200 East 6th
Hugoton, KS 67951

## SUMNER COUNTY
District Court Clerk
Sumner County District Court
500 North Washington
Wellington, KS 67152

## THOMAS COUNTY
District Court Clerk
Thomas County District Court
PO Box 805
Colby, KS 67701

## TREGO COUNTY
District Court Clerk
Trego County District Court
216 North Main
Wakeeney, KS 67672

**WABAUNSEE COUNTY**
District Court Clerk
Wabaunsee County District Court
215 Kansas
Alma, KS 66401

**WALLACE COUNTY**
District Court Clerk
Wallace County District Court
313 Main
Sharon Springs, KS 67758

**WASHINGTON COUNTY**
District Court Clerk
Washington Cty District Court
Washington County Courthouse
Washington, KS 66968

**WICHITA COUNTY**
District Court Clerk
Wichita County District Court
206 South Main
Leoti, KS 67861

**WILSON COUNTY**
District Court Clerk
Wilson County District Court
600 Madison
Fredonia, KS 66736

**WOODSON COUNTY**
District Court Clerk
Woodson County District Court
105 West Rutledge
Yates Center, KS 66783

**WYANDOTTE COUNTY**
District Court Clerk
Wyandotte Cty District Court
710 North 7th
Kansas City, KS 66101

# KENTUCKY

**ADAIR COUNTY**
Circuit Court Clerk
Adair County Circuit Court
500 Public Square, Ste 6
Columbia, KY 42728

**ALLEN COUNTY**
Circuit Court Clerk
Allen County Courthouse
PO Box 464
Scottsville, KY 42164

**ANDERSON COUNTY**
Circuit Court Clerk
Anderson County Courthouse
151 Main Street
Lawrenceburg, KY 40342

**BALLARD COUNTY**
Circuit Court Clerk
Ballard County Courthouse
PO Box 265
Wickliffe, KY 42087

**BARREN COUNTY**
Circuit Court Clerk
Barren County Circuit Court
102 North Public Square
Glasgow, KY 42142-1359

## BATH COUNTY
Circuit Court Clerk
Bath County Circuit Court
Main Street
Owingsville, KY 40360

## BELL COUNTY
Circuit Court Clerk
Bell County Circuit Court
PO Box 306
Pineville, KY 40977

## BOONE COUNTY
Circuit Court Clerk
2950 Washington
PO Box 480
Burlington, KY 41005

## BOURBON COUNTY
Circuit Court Clerk
Bourbon County Courthouse
PO Box 740
Paris, KY 40361

## BOYD COUNTY
Circuit Court Clerk
2800 Louisa
PO Box 694
Catlettsburg, KY 41129-0694

## BOYLE COUNTY
Circuit Court Clerk
Boyle County Courthouse
321 West Main Street
Danville, KY 40422

## BRACKEN COUNTY
Circuit Court Clerk
Bracken County Courthouse
PO Box 132
Brooksville, KY 41004

## BREATHITT COUNTY
Circuit Court Clerk
Breathitt County Courthouse
1127 Main Street
Jackson, KY 41339

## BRECKINRIDGE COUNTY
Circuit Court Clerk
Breckinridge Cty Courthouse
PO Box 111
Hardinsburg, KY 40143

## BULLITT COUNTY
Circuit Court Clerk
300 Buckinan Street
PO Box 275
Shepherdsville, KY 40165

## BUTLER COUNTY
Circuit Court Clerk
Butler County Courthouse
PO Box 625
Morgantown, KY 42261

## CALDWELL COUNTY
Circuit Court Clerk
Caldwell County Courthouse
100 Market Street, Room 4
Princeton, KY 42445

## CALLOWAY COUNTY
Circuit Court Clerk
Calloway Cty Circuit Court
201 South 4th Street
Murray, KY 42071

## CAMPBELL COUNTY
Circuit Court Clerk
Campbell County Circuit Court
30 West 4th Street
Newport, KY 41071

## CARLISLE COUNTY
Circuit Court Clerk
Carlisle County Courthouse
PO Box 337
Bardwell, KY 42023

## CARROLL COUNTY
Circuit Court Clerk
Carroll Cty Hall of Justice
802 Clay
Carrollton, KY 41008

## CARTER COUNTY
Circuit Court Clerk
Carter County Circuit Court
308 Courthouse
Grayson, KY 41143

## CASEY COUNTY
Circuit Court Clerk
Casey County Courthouse
Government Center
Liberty, KY 42539

## CHRISTIAN COUNTY
Circuit Court Clerk
Christian County Courthouse,
Government Center
Hopkinsville, KY 42240

## CLARK COUNTY
Circuit Court Clerk
Gov James Clark Judicial Center
17 Cleveland Ave
Winchester, KY 40391

## CLAY COUNTY
Circuit Court Clerk
316 Main, Suite 108
PO Box 463
Manchester, KY 40962

## CLINTON COUNTY
Circuit Court Clerk
Clinton County Courthouse
Government Center
Albany, KY 42602

## CRITTENDEN COUNTY
Circuit Court Clerk
Crittenden County Courthouse
107 South Main
Marion, KY 42064

## CUMBERLAND COUNTY
Circuit Court Clerk
600 Public Square
PO Box 384
Burkesville, KY 42717

## DAVIESS COUNTY
Circuit Court Clerk
100 E. 2nd Street
PO Box 477
Owensboro, KY 42302

## EDMONSON COUNTY
Circuit Court Clerk
Courthouse Square
PO Box 130
Brownsville, KY 42210

## ELLIOTT COUNTY
Circuit Court Clerk
Main Street
PO Box 788
Sandy Hook, KY 41171

## ESTILL COUNTY
Circuit Court Clerk
Estill County Courthouse
Government Center
Irvine, KY 40336

## FAYETTE COUNTY
Circuit Court Clerk
215 West Main Street
Courthouse Square
Lexington, KY 40507

## FLEMING COUNTY
Circuit Court Clerk
Fleming County Courthouse
100 Court Square
Flemingsburg, KY 41041

## FLOYD COUNTY
Circuit Court Clerk
Floyd County Circuit Court
PO Box 109
Prestonsburg, KY 41653

## FRANKLIN COUNTY
Circuit Court Clerk
218 Street Clair Street
PO Box 678
Frankfort, KY 40602

## FULTON COUNTY
Circuit Court Clerk
201 Cumberland
PO Box 198
Hickman, KY 42050

## GALLATIN COUNTY
Circuit Court Clerk
100 Main
PO Box 256
Warsaw, KY 41095

## GARRARD COUNTY
Circuit Court Clerk
Courthouse
Public Square Annex
Lancaster, KY 40444

## GRANT COUNTY
Circuit Court Clerk
Grant County Courthouse
101 North Main
Williamstown, KY 41097

## GRAVES COUNTY
Circuit Court Clerk
Graves County Courthouse
114 West Broadway
Mayfield, KY 42066

## GRAYSON COUNTY
Circuit Court Clerk
125 East White Oak
Courthouse Square
Leitchfield, KY 42754

## GREEN COUNTY
Circuit Court Clerk
Courthouse Square
203 W. Court Street
Greensburg, KY 42743

## GREENUP COUNTY
Circuit Court Clerk
Courthouse Annex
Harrison Street
Greenup, KY 41144

## HANCOCK COUNTY
Circuit Court Clerk
Hancock County Courthouse
PO Box 250
Hawesville, KY 42348

## HARDIN COUNTY
Circuit Court Clerk
Hardin County Courthouse
100 Public
Elizabethtown, KY 42701

## HARLAN COUNTY
Circuit Court Clerk
First and Central
PO Box 190
Harlan, KY 40831

## HARRISON COUNTY
Circuit Court Clerk
Main Street
PO Box 10
Cynthiana, KY 41031

## HART COUNTY
Circuit Court Clerk
Hart County Circuit Court
PO Box 548
Munfordville, KY 40601

## HENDERSON COUNTY
Circuit Court Clerk
Henderson County Courthouse
PO Box 675
Henderson, KY 42420

## HENRY COUNTY
Circuit Court Clerk
Henry County Courthouse
PO Box 359
New Castle, KY 40050

## HICKMAN COUNTY
Circuit Court Clerk
Hickman County Circuit Court
110 East Clay
Clinton, KY 42031

## HOPKINS COUNTY
Circuit Court Clerk
Hopkins County Circuit Court
30 South Main
Madisonville, KY 42431

## JACKSON COUNTY
Circuit Court Clerk
Jackson County Circuit Court
PO Box 84
McKee, KY 40447

## JEFFERSON COUNTY
Clerk of Court
Jefferson County Circuit Court
Hall of Justice
Louisville, KY 40202

## JESSAMINE COUNTY
Circuit Court Clerk
Jessamine County Courthouse
Main Street
Nicholasville, KY 40356

## JOHNSON COUNTY
Circuit Court Clerk
Johnson County Circuit Court
PO Box 1405
Paintsville, KY 41240

## KENTON COUNTY
Clerk of Court
Third and Court
PO Box 669
Covington, KY 41012

## KNOTT COUNTY
Circuit Court Clerk
Knott County Courthouse
PO Box 515
Hindman, KY 41822

## KNOX COUNTY
Ciruit Court Clerk
401 Court Square, Ste. 202
PO Box 760
Barbourville, KY 40906

## LARUE COUNTY
Circuit Court Clerk
Larue County Courthouse Annex
209 West High Street
Hodgenville, KY 42748

## LAUREL COUNTY
Circuit Court Clerk
Judicial Annex #2
PO Box 1798
London, KY 40743

## LAWRENCE COUNTY
Circuit Court Clerk
Lawrence Cty Courthouse Annex
PO Box 212
Louisa, KY 41230

## LEE COUNTY
Circuit Court Clerk
Lee County Courthouse,#21
PO Box E
Beattyville, KY 41311

## LESLIE COUNTY
Circuit Court Clerk
Leslie County Courthouse,
Government Center
Hyden, KY 41749

## LETCHER COUNTY
Circuit Court Clerk
Letcher County Courthouse
101 West Main
Whitesburg, KY 41858

## LEWIS COUNTY
Circuit Court Clerk
Lewis County Courthouse
PO Box 70
Vanceburg, KY 41179

## LINCOLN COUNTY
Circuit Court Clerk
Lincoln County Courthouse
102 East Main
Stanford, KY 40484

## LIVINGSTON COUNTY
Circuit Court Clerk
Livingston County Courthouse
PO Box 160
Smithland, KY 42081

## LOGAN COUNTY
Circuit Court Clerk
200 W. 4th
PO Box 420
Russellville, KY 42276-0420

## LYON COUNTY
Circuit Court Clerk
Lyon County Court
PO Box 565
Eddyville, KY 42038

## MADISON COUNTY
Circuit Court Clerk
Madison County Circuit Court
101 West Main
Richmond, KY 40476-0813

## MAGOFFIN COUNTY
Circuit Court Clerk
Magoffin County Courthouse
Government Center
Salyersville, KY 41465

## MARION COUNTY
Circuit Court Clerk
Marion County Courthouse
120 West Main
Lebanon, KY 40033

## MARSHALL COUNTY
Circuit Court Clerk
Marshall County Circuit Court
101 Main Street
Benton, KY 42025

## MARTIN COUNTY
Circuit Court Clerk
Martin County Circuit Court
Court St, PO Box 430
Inez, KY 41224

## MASON COUNTY
Circuit Court Clerk
Mason County Circuit Court
27 West 3rd Street
Maysville, KY 41056

## MCCRACKEN COUNTY
Circuit Court Clerk
McCracken Cty Circuit Court
Government Center
Paducah, KY 42002-1455

## MCCREARY COUNTY
Circuit Court Clerk
McCreary Cty Circuit Court
PO Box 40
Whitley City, KY 42653

## MCLEAN COUNTY
Circuit Court Clerk
McLean County Courthouse
Government Center
Calhoun, KY 42327

## MEADE COUNTY
Circuit Court Clerk
Meade County Courthouse
516 Fairway Dr
Brandenburg, KY 40108

## MENIFEE COUNTY
Circuit Court Clerk
Menifee County Courthouse
Government Center
Frenchburg, KY 40322

## MERCER COUNTY
Circuit Court Clerk
Mercer County Courthouse
Courthouse Square
Harrodsburg, KY 40330

## METCALFE COUNTY
Circuit Court Clerk
Hamilton & Main Streets
PO Box 485
Edmonton, KY 42129

## MONROE COUNTY
Circuit Court Clerk
Monroe County Courthouse
PO Box 245
Tompkinsville, KY 42167

## MONTGOMERY COUNTY
Circuit Court Clerk
Mongomery County Courthouse
1 Court Street
Mount Sterling, KY 40353

## MORGAN COUNTY
Circuit Court Clerk
Morgan County Courthouse
PO Box 85
West Liberty, KY 41472

## MUHLENBERG COUNTY
Circuit Court Clerk
109 East Main Cross
PO Box 776
Greenville, KY 42345

## NELSON COUNTY
Circuit Court Clerk
Courthouse Square
PO Box 845
Bardstown, KY 40004

## NICHOLAS COUNTY
Circuit Court Clerk
Nicholas County Courthouse
PO Box 109
Carlisle, KY 40311

## OHIO COUNTY
Circuit Court Clerk
Community Center
130 Washington Street
Hartford, KY 42347

## OLDHAM COUNTY
Circuit Court Clerk
Oldham County Circuit Court
105 East Jefferson
La Grange, KY 40031

## OWEN COUNTY
Circuit Court Clerk
Owen County Courthouse
PO Box 473
Owenton, KY 40359

## OWSLEY COUNTY
Circuit Court Clerk
Owsley County Courthouse
PO Box 146
Booneville, KY 41314

## PENDLETON COUNTY
Circuit Court Clerk
Courthouse Square
PO Box 69
Falmouth, KY 41040

## PERRY COUNTY
Circuit Court Clerk
Perry County Courthouse
PO Box 743
Hazard, KY 41702

## PIKE COUNTY
Circuit Court Clerk
Hall of Justice, 3rd Floor
89 Division
Pikeville, KY 41501

## POWELL COUNTY
Circuit Court Clerk
Powell County Courthouse
PO Box 562
Stanton, KY 40380

## PULASKI COUNTY
Circuit Court Clerk
Pulaski County Circuit Court
PO Box 664
Somerset, KY 42502

## ROBERTSON COUNTY
Circuit Court Clerk
Robertson County Courthouse
PO Box 63
Mount Olivet, KY 41064

## ROCKCASTLE COUNTY
Circuit Court Clerk
Courthouse Annex, 2nd Floor
PO Box 750
Mount Vernon, KY 40456

## ROWAN COUNTY
Circuit Court Clerk
Rowan County Circuit Court
627 E. Main Street
Morehead, KY 40351

## RUSSELL COUNTY
Circuit Court Clerk
Russell County Circuit Court
410 Monument Square, #203
Jamestown, KY 42629

## SCOTT COUNTY
Circuit Court Clerk
Scott County Courthouse
119 North Hamilton
Georgetown, KY 40324

## SHELBY COUNTY
Circuit Court Clerk
Shelby County Circuit Court
501 Main Street
Shelbyville, KY 40065

## SIMPSON COUNTY
Circuit Court Clerk
Simpson County Courthouse
PO Box 261
Franklin, KY 42134

## SPENCER COUNTY
Circuit Court Clerk
Spencer County Courthouse
PO Box 282
Taylorsville, KY 40071

## TAYLOR COUNTY
Circuit Court Clerk
Taylor County Courthouse
203 North Court Street
Campbellsville, Ky 42718

## TODD COUNTY
Circuit Court Clerk
201 Washington
PO Box 337
Elkton, KY 42220

## TRIGG COUNTY
Circuit Court Clerk
12 Court Street
PO Box 673
Cadiz, KY 42211

## TRIMBLE COUNTY
Circuit Court Clerk
Trimble County Courthouse
PO Box 248
Bedford, KY 40006

## UNION COUNTY
Circuit Court Clerk
Union County Circuit Court
PO Box 59
Morganfield, KY 42437

## WARREN COUNTY
Circuit Court Clerk
925 Center Street
PO Box 2170
Bowling Green, KY 42102

## WASHINGTON COUNTY
Circuit Court Clerk
Washington County Courthouse
PO Box 346
Springfield, KY 40069

## WAYNE COUNTY
Circuit Court Clerk
Wayne County Courthouse
PO Box 816
Monticello, Ky 42533

## WEBSTER COUNTY
Circuit Court Clerk
Highway 41A
PO Box 217
Dixon, KY 42409

## WHITLEY COUNTY
Circuit Court Clerk
Whitley County Courthouse
PO Box 329
Williamsburg, KY 40769-0329

## WOLFE COUNTY
Circuit Court Clerk
Wolfe County Courthouse
PO Box 296
Campton, KY 41301

## WOODFORD COUNTY
Circuit Court Clerk
Woodford County Courthouse
Government Center
Versailles, Ky 40383

# LOUISIANA

## ACADIA PARISH
Clerk of Court
23rd District Court
PO Box 922
Crowley, LA 70526

## ALLEN PARISH
Clerk of Court
33rd District Court
PO Box 248
Oberlin, LA 70655

## ASCENSION PARISH
Clerk of Court
23rd District Court
PO Box 192
Donaldsonville, LA 70346

## ASSUMPTION PARISH
Clerk of Court
23rd District Court
PO Drawer 249
Napoleonville, LA 70390

## AVOYELLES PARISH
Clerk of Court
12th District Court
PO Box 196
Marksville, LA 71351

## BEAUREGARD PARISH
Clerk of Court
36th District Court
PO Box 100
De Ridder, LA 70634

## BIENVILLE PARISH
Clerk of Court
2nd District Court
601 Locust, Rm 100
Arcadia, LA 71001

## BOSSIER PARISH
Clerk of Court
26th District Court
PO Box 369
Benton, LA 71006

## CADDO PARISH
Clerk of Court
1st District Court,
501 Texas Street, Rm 103
Shreveport, LA 71101

## CALCASIEU PARISH
Clerk of Court
14th District Court
PO Box 1030
Lake Charles, LA 70602

## CALDWELL PARISH
Clerk of Court
37th District Court
PO Box 1327
Columbia, LA 71418

## CAMERON PARISH
Clerk of Court
38th District Court
PO Box 549
Cameron, LA 70631

## CATAHOULA PARISH
Clerk of Court
7th District Court
PO Box 198
Harrisonburg, LA 71340

## CLAIBORNE PARISH
Clerk of Court
2nd District Court
PO Box 330
Homer, LA 71040

## CONCORDIA PARISH
Clerk of Court
Concordia Parish
PO Box 790
Vidalia, LA 71373

## DE SOTO PARISH
Clerk of Court
11th District Court
PO Box 1206
Mansfield, LA 71052

## EAST BATON ROUGE
Clerk of Court
19th District Court
PO Box 1991
Baton Rouge, LA 70802

## EAST CARROLL PARISH
Clerk of Court
6th District Court
400 1st Street
Lake Providence, LA 71254

## EAST FELICIANA PARISH
Clerk of Court
East Feliciana Parish
PO Box 595
Clinton, LA 70722

## EVANGELINE PARISH
Clerk of Court
Evangeline Courthouse Bldg
200 Court Street, PO 347
Ville Platte, LA 70586

## FRANKLIN PARISH
Clerk of Court
5th District Court
PO Box 431
Winnsboro, LA 71295

## GRANT PARISH
Clerk of Court
35th District Court
PO Box 264
Colfax, LA 71417

## IBERIA PARISH
Clerk of Court
16th District Court
PO Drawer 12010
New Iberia, LA 70562-2010

## IBERVILLE PARISH
Clerk of Court
18th District Court
PO Box 423
Plaquemine, LA 70764

## JACKSON PARISH
Clerk of Court
2nd District Court
PO Box 730
Jonesboro, LA 71251

## JEFFERSON DAVIS PARISH
Clerk of Court
31st District Court
PO Box 799
Jennings, LA 70546

## JEFFERSON PARISH
Clerk of Courts, Civil Div.
24th District Court
PO Box 10
Gretna, LA 70054-0010

## LA SALLE PARISH
Clerk of Court
28th District Court
PO Box 1372
Jena, LA 71342

## LAFAYETTE PARISH
Clerk of Court
15th District Court
PO Box 2009
Lafayette, LA 70502

## LAFOURCHE PARISH
Clerk of Court
17th District Court
PO Box 818
Thibodaux, LA 70302

## LINCOLN PARISH
Clerk of Court
3rd District Court
PO Box 924
Ruston, LA 71273-0924

## LIVINGSTON PARISH
Clerk of Court
21st District Court
PO Box 1150
Livingston, LA 70754

## MADISON PARISH
Clerk of Court
6th District Court
100 North Cedar
Tallulah, LA 71282

## MOREHOUSE PARISH
Clerk of Court
4th District Court
100 East Madison
Bastrop, LA 71220

## NATCHITOCHES PARISH
Clerk of Court
10th District Court
PO Box 476
Natchitoches, LA 71458

## ORLEANS PARISH
Clerk of Court,Civil Records
Civil Courts Building,#402
421 Loyola Ave
New Orleans, LA 70112

## OUACHITA PARISH
Clerk of Court
4th District Court
PO Box 1862
Monroe, LA 71210-1862

## PLAQUEMINES PARISH
Clerk of Court
25th District Court
PO Box 129
Pointe a LaHache, LA 70082

## POINTE COUPEE PARISH
Clerk of Court
18th District Court
PO Box 38
New Roads, LA 70760

## RAPIDES PARISH
Clerk of Court
9th District Court
PO Box 952
Alexandria, LA 71301

## RED RIVER PARISH
Clerk of Court
39th District Court
PO Box 606
Coushatta, LA 71019

## RICHLAND PARISH

Clerk of Court
5th District Court
100 Julia Street
Rayville, LA 71269

## SABINE PARISH

Clerk of Court
11th District Court
PO Box 419
Many, LA 71449

## ST BERNARD PARISH

Clerk of Court
34th District Court
PO Box 1746
Chalmette, LA 70044

## ST. CHARLES PARISH

Clerk of Court
29th District Court
Hwy 18 and River Rd
Hahnville, LA 70057

## ST. HELENA PARISH

Clerk of Court
21st District Court
PO Box 308
Greensburg, LA 70441

## ST. JAMES PARISH

Clerk of Court
23rd District Court
PO Box 63
Convent, LA 70723

## ST. JOHN THE BAPTIST

Clerk of Court
St. John The Baptist Parish
PO Box 280
Edgard, LA 70049

## ST. LANDRY PARISH

Clerk of Court
27th District Court
PO Box 750
Opelousas, LA 70571

## ST. MARTIN PARISH

Clerk of Court
16th District Court
PO Box 308
St. Martinville, LA 70582

## ST. MARY PARISH

Clerk of Court
16th District Court
PO Drawer 1231
Franklin, LA 70538

## ST. TAMMANY PARISH

Clerk of Court
22nd District Court
PO Box 1090
Covington, LA 70434

## TANGIPAHOA PARISH

Clerk of Court
21st District Court
PO Box 667
Amite, LA 70422

## TENSAS PARISH
Clerk of Court
6th District Court
Courthouse Square
St. Joseph, LA 71366

## TERREBONNE PARISH
Clerk of Court
32nd District Court
PO Box 1569
Houma, LA 70360

## UNION PARISH
Clerk of Court
3rd District Court
Courthouse Bldg
Fannerville, LA 71241

## VERMILION PARISH
Clerk of Court
15th District Court
PO Box 790
Abbeville, LA 70511-0790

## VERNON PARISH
Clerk of Court
30th District Court
PO Box 40
Leesville, LA 71496-0040

## WASHINGTON PARISH
Clerk of Court
22nd District Court
PO Box 607
Franklinton, LA 70438

## WEBSTER PARISH
Clerk of Court
26th District Court
PO Drawer 370
Minden, LA 71055

## W. BATON ROUGE PARISH
Clerk of Court
18th District Court
PO Box 107
Port Allen, LA 70767

## WEST CARROLL PARISH
Clerk of Court
5th District Court
PO Box 1078
Oak Grove, LA 71263

## WEST FELICIANA PARISH
Clerk of Court
20th District Court
PO Box 1843
St. Francisville, LA 70775

## WINN PARISH
Clerk of Court
8th District Court
Courthouse
Winnfield, LA 71483

# MASSACHUSETTS
## BARNSTABLE COUNTY
Clerk of Court
Barnstable County Courthouse
PO Box 425
Barnstable, MA 02630

## BERKSHIRE COUNTY
Superior Court Clerk
Berkshire County Courthouse
76 East Street
Pittsfield, MA 01201

## BRISTOL COUNTY
Superior Court Clerk
Bristol County Courthouse
9 Court Street
Taunton, MA 02780

## DUKES COUNTY
Clerk of Court
Dukes County Courthouse
Main Street
Edgartown, MA 02539

## ESSEX COUNTY
Superior Court Clerk
Essex County Courthouse
34 Federal Street
Salem, MA 01970

## FRANKLIN COUNTY
Superior Court Clerk
Franklin County Courthouse
425 Main Street
Greenfield, MA 01302

## HAMPDEN COUNTY
Clerk of Court
Hampden County Courthouse
50 States Street
Springfield, MA 01102-0559

## HAMPSHIRE COUNTY
Superior Court Clerk
Hampshire County Courthouse
15 Gothis
Northampton, MA 01061

## MIDDLESEX COUNTY
Clerk of Court
Middlesex County Courthouse
40 Thorndike Street
Cambridge, MA 02141

## NANTUCKET COUNTY
Clerk of Court
Nantucket Courthouse
Town and County Bldg
Nantucket, MA 02554

## NORFOLK COUNTY
Superior Court Clerk
Norfolk County Courthouse
650 High Street
Dedham, MA 02026

## PLYMOUTH COUNTY
Superior Court Clerk
Plymouth County Courthouse
72 Belmont Street
Brockton, MA 02401

## SUFFOLK COUNTY
Superior Court Clerk
Suffolk County Courthouse
Old Courthouse
Boston, MA 02102

**WORCESTER COUNTY**
Clerk of Court
Worcester County Courthouse
2 Main Street
Worcester, MA 01608

# MARYLAND

**ALLEGANY COUNTY**
Circuit Court Clerk
4th Judical Circuit Court
Washington Street
Cumberland, MD 21502

**ANNE ARUNDEL COUNTY**
Circuit Court Clerk
5th Judicial Circuit Court
7 Church Circle
Annapolis, MD 21404

**BALTIMORE COUNTY**
Circuit Court Clerk
3rd Judicial Circuit Court
401 Bosley Ave
Towson, MD 21204

**THE CITY OF BALTIMORE**
Circuit Court Clerk,
8th Judicial District
111 North Calvert,Rm 460
Baltimore, MD 21202

**CALVERT COUNTY**
Circuit Court Clerk
7th Judicial District Court
175 Main Street
Prince Frederick, MD 20678

**CAROLINE COUNTY**
Circuit Court Clerk
2nd Judicial Circuit Court
PO Box 458
Denton, MD 21629

**CAROLL COUNTY**
Circuit Court Clerk
5th Judicial Circuit Court
55 North Court Street
Westminster, MD 21158

**CECIL COUNTY**
Circuit Court Clerk
2nd Judicial Circuit Court
126 East Main Street, Rm 108
Elkton, MD 21921

**CHARLES COUNTY**
Circuit Court Clerk
7th Judicial Circuit Court
200 Charles Street
La Plata, MD 20646

**DORCHESTER COUNTY**
Circuit Court Clerk
1st Judicial Circuit Court
206 High Street
Cambridge, MD 21613

**FREDERICK COUNTY**
Circuit Court Clerk
6th Judicial Circuit Court
100 West Patrick Street
Frederick, MD 21701

## GARRETT COUNTY
Circuit Court Clerk
4th Judicial Circuit Court
203 South 4th Street
Oakland, MD 21550

## HARFORD COUNTY
Circuit Court Clerk
3rd Judicial Circuit Court
20 West Courtland Street
Bel Air, MD 21014

## HOWARD COUNTY
Circuit Court Clerk
5th Judicial Circuit Court
8360 Court Ave
Ellicott City, MD 21043

## KENT COUNTY
Circuit Court Clerk
2nd Judicial Circuit Court
103 North Cross Street
Chestertown, MD 21620

## MONTGOMERY COUNTY
Circuit Court Clerk
6th Judicial Circuit Court
50 Courthouse Square
Rockville, MD 20850

## PRINCE GEORGE'S
Clerk of Court
7th Judicial Circuit Court
14735 Main Street, Rm 167M
Upper Marlboro, MD 20772

## QUEEN ANNE'S COUNTY
Circuit Court Clerk
2nd Judicial Circuit Court
Queen Anne's Cty Courthouse
Centreville, MD 21617

## SOMERSET COUNTY
Clerk of Court
1st Judicial Circuit Court
30512 Prince William Street
Princess Anne, MD 21853

## ST. MARY'S COUNTY
Clerk of Court
7th Judicial Circuit Court
1 Courthouse Dr
Leonardtown, MD 20650

## TALBOT COUNTY
Clerk of Court
2nd Judicial Circuit Court
Washington and Federal Streets
Easton, MD 21601

## WASHINGTON COUNTY
Clerk of Court
4th Judicial Circuit Court
95 West Washington
Hagerstown, MD 21741

## WICOMICO COUNTY
Clerk of Court
1st Judicial Circuit Court
101 North Division
Salisbury, MD 21803-0198

**WORCESTER COUNTY**
Clerk of Court
1st Judicial Circuit Court
PO Box 40
Snow Hill, MD 21863

# MAINE

**ANDROSCOGGIN COUNTY**
11th District Court Clerk
Northern Androscoggin County
2 Main Street
Livermore Falls, ME 04254

**ANDROSCOGGIN COUNTY**
8th District Court Clerk
District Court
85 Park Street
Lewiston, ME 04243

**AROOSTOOK COUNTY**
1st District Clerk of Court
District Court
240 Sweden Street
Caribou, ME 04736

**AROOSTOOK COUNTY**
2nd District Clerk of Court
District Court
PO Box 457
Houlton, ME 04730

**CUMBERLAND COUNTY**
9th District Clerk of Court
District Court
142 Federal Street
Portland, ME 04112

**FRANKLIN COUNTY**
12th District Clerk of Court
District Court
25 Main Street
Farmington, ME 04938

**HANCOCK COUNTY**
5th District Clerk of Court
District Court
60 State Street
Ellsworth, ME 04605

**KENNEBEC COUNTY**
7th District Clerk of Court
District Court
145 State Street
Augusta, ME 04330

**KNOX COUNTY**
6th District Court Clerk
District Court
62 Union Street
Rockland, ME 04841

**LINCOLN COUNTY**
6th District Clerk of Court
District Court
High Street
Wiscasset, ME 04578

**OXFORD COUNTY**
11th District Clerk of Court
District Court
26 Western Avenue
South Paris, ME 04281

**PENOBSCOT COUNTY**
3rd District Clerk of Court
District Court
73 Hammond Street
Bangor, ME 04401

**PENOBSCOT COUNTY**
13th District Clerk of Court
District Court
66 Main Street
Lincoln, ME 04457

**PISCATAQUIS COUNTY**
13th District Clerk of Court
District Court
59 East Main Street
Dover-Foxcroft, ME 04426

**SAGADAHOC COUNTY**
6th District Clerk of Court
New Meadow Road
RR #1 Box 310
Bath, ME 04530

**SOMERSET COUNTY**
12th District Clerk of Court
District Court
88 Water Street
Skowhegan, ME 04976

**WALDO COUNTY**
District Court Clerk
Waldo County District Court
PO Box 382
Belfast, ME 04915

**WASHINGTON COUNTY**
4th District Clerk of Court
District Court
47 Court Street
Machias, ME 04654

**YORK COUNTY**
10th District Clerk of Court
District Court
PO Box 95
Springvale, ME 04083

# MICHIGAN

**ALCONA COUNTY**
Clerk of Court
26th Circuit Court
106 5th Street
Harrisville, MI 48740

**ALGER COUNTY**
Clerk of Court
11th Circuit Court
101 Court Street
Munising, MI 49862

**ALLEGAN COUNTY**
Clerk of Court
48th Circuit Court
113 Chestnut Street
Allegan, MI 49010

**ALPENA COUNTY**
Clerk of Court
26th Circuit Court
720 West Chisholm
Alpena, MI 49707

## ANTRIM COUNTY
Clerk of Court
13th Circuit Court
PO Box 520
Bellaire, MI 49615

## ARENAC COUNTY
Clerk of Court
34th Circuit Court
120 North Grove
Standish, MI 48658

## BARAGA COUNTY
Clerk of Court
12th Circuit Court
16 North 3rd
L'Anse, MI 49946

## BARRY COUNTY
Clerk of Court
5th Circuit Court
220 West State Street
Hastings, MI 49058

## BAY COUNTY
Clerk of Court
18th Circuit Court
515 Center Ave
Bay City, MI 48708

## BENZIE COUNTY
Clerk of Court
19th Circuit Court
425 Court Place
Beulah, MI 49617

## BERRIERN COUNTY
Clerk of Court
2nd Circuit Court
811 Port Street
St. Joseph, MI 49085

## BRANCH COUNTY
Clerk of Court
15th Circuit Court
31 Division Street
Coldwater, MI 49036

## CALHOUN COUNTY
Clerk of Court
County Justice Center
161 East Michigan Ave
Battlecreek, MI 49068

## CASS COUNTY
Clerk of Court
43rd Circuit Court
120 North Broadway
Cassopolis, MI 49031-1398

## CHARLEVOIX COUNTY
Clerk of Court
33rd Circuit Court
203 Antrim Street
Charlevoix, MI 49720

## CHEBOYGAN COUNTY
Clerk of Court
53rd Circuit Court
PO Box 70
Cheboygan, MI 49721

## CHIPPEWA COUNTY
Clerk of Court
50th Circuit Court
319 Court Street
Sault Sainte Marie, MI 49783

## CLARE COUNTY
Clerk of Court
55th Circuit Court
225 West Main
Harrison, MI 48625

## CLINTON COUNTY
Clerk of Court
29th Circuit Court
PO Box 69
St. Johns, MI 48879-0069

## CRAWFORD COUNTY
Clerk of Court
46th Circuit Court
200 Michigan Ave
Grayling, MI 49738

## DELTA COUNTY
Clerk of Court
47th Circuit Court
310 Ludington Street
Escanaba, MI 49829

## DICKINSON COUNTY
Clerk of Court
41st Circuit Court
PO Box 609
Iron Mountain, MI 49801

## EATON COUNTY
Clerk of Court
5th Circuit Court
1045 Independence Blvd
Charlotte, MI 48813

## EMMET COUNTY
Clerk of Court
33rd Circuit Court
200 Division Street
Petoskey, MI 49770

## GENESEE COUNTY
Clerk of Court
7th Circuit Court
900 South Saginaw
Flint, MI 48502

## GLADWIN COUNTY
Clerk or Court
Circuit Court
55th Circuit Court
Gladwin, MI 48624

## GOGEBIC COUNTY
Clerk of Court
32nd Circuit Court
200 North Moore
Bessemer, MI 49911

## GRAND TRAVERSE
Clerk of Court
13th Circuit Court
328 Washington Street
Traverse City, MI 49684

## GRATIOT COUNTY
Clerk of Court
29th Circuit Court
PO Box 437
Ithaca, MI 48847

## HILLSDALE COUNTY
Clerk of Court
1st Circuit Court
Courthouse
Hillsdale, MI 49242

## HOUGHTON COUNTY
Clerk of Court
12th Circuit Court
401 East Houghton Ave
Houghton, MI 49931

## HURON COUNTY
Clerk of Court
52nd Circuit Court
250 East Huron Ave
Bad Axe, MI 48413

## INGHAM COUNTY
Clerk of Court
30th Circuit Court
333 South Capitol Ave, Ste C
Lansing, MI 48933

## IONIA COUNTY
Clerk of Court
8th Circuit Court
Government Center
Ionia, MI 48846

## IOSCO COUNTY
Clerk of Court
23rd Circuit Court
PO Box 838
Tawas City, MI 48764

## IRON COUNTY
Clerk of Court
41st Circuit Court
2 South 6th Street
Crystal Falls, MI 49920

## ISABELLA COUNTY
Clerk of Court
21st Circuit Court
County Bldg 200 North Main
Mount Pleasant, MI 48858

## JACKSON COUNTY
Clerk of Court
4th Circuit Court
312 South Jackson Street
Jackson, MI 49201

## KALAMAZOO COUNTY
Clerk of Court
9th Circuit Court
227 West Michigan
Kalamazoo, MI 49007

## KALKASKA COUNTY
Clerk of Court
46th Circuit Court
PO Box 10
Kalkaska, MI 49646

## KENT COUNTY
Clerk of Court
17th Circuit Court
333 Monroe Avenue NW
Grand Rapids, MI 49503

## KEWEENAW COUNTY
Clerk of Court
12th Circuit Court
Unit 1, Box 7
Eagle River, MI 49924

## LAKE COUNTY
Clerk of Court
51 st Circuit Court
PO Box B
Baldwin, MI 49304

## LAPEER COUNTY
Clerk of Court
40th Circuit Court
255 Clay Street
Lapeer, MI 48446

## LEELANAU COUNTY
Clerk of Court
13th Circuit Court
PO Box 467
Leland, MI 49654

## LENAWEE COUNTY
Clerk of Court
39th Circuit Court
425 North Main Street
Adrian, MI 49221

## LIVINGSTON COUNTY
Clerk of Court
44th Circuit Court
210 South Highlander Way
Howell, MI 48843

## LUCE COUNTY
Clerk of Court
11th Circuit Court
County Government Bldg.
Newberry, MI 49868

## MACKINAC COUNTY
Clerk of Court
50th Circuit Court
100 Marley
St. Ignace, MI 49781

## MACOMB COUNTY
Clerk of Court
16th Circuit Court
40 North Main
Mount Clemens, MI 48043

## MANISTEE COUNTY
Clerk of Court
19th Circuit Court
415 3rd Street
Manistee, MI 49660

## MARQUETTE COUNTY
Clerk of Court
25th Circuit Court
Baraga Ave
Marquette, MI 49855

## MASON COUNTY
Clerk of Court
51 Circuit Court
304 East Ludington Ave
Ludington, MI 49431

## MECOSTA COUNTY
Clerk of Court
49th Circuit Court
400 Elm
Big Rapids, MI 49307

## MENOMINEE COUNTY
Clerk of Court
41st Circuit Court
839 10th Ave
Menominee, MI 49858

## MIDLAND COUNTY
Clerk of Court
42nd District Court
301 West Main
Midland, MI 48640

## MISSAUKEE COUNTY
Clerk of Court
28th Circuit Court
Courthouse Bldg.
Lake City, MI 49651

## MONROE COUNTY
Clerk of Court
38th Circuit Court
106 East 1 st Street
Monroe, MI 48161

## MONTCALM COUNTY
Clerk of Court
8th Circuit Court
PO Box 368
Stanton, MI 48888

## MONTMORENCY COUNTY
Clerk of Court
26th Circuit Court
PO Box 415
Atlanta, MI 49709

## MUSKEGON COUNTY
Clerk of Court
Circuit Court
990 Terrace, 6 Fl.
Muskegon, MI 49442

## NEWAYGO COUNTY
Clerk of Court
27th Circuit Court
PO Box 885
White Cloud, MI 49349

## OAKLAND COUNTY
Circuit Court Clerk
6th Circuit Court
1200 North Telegraph Rd
Pontiac, MI 48341

## OCEANA COUNTY
Clerk of Court
27th Circuit Court
PO Box 189
Hart, MI 49420

## OGEMAW COUNTY
Clerk of Court
34th Circuit Court
806 West Houghton Ave
West Branch, MI 48661

## ONTONAGON COUNTY
Clerk of Court
32nd Circuit Court
725 Greenland Rd.
Ontonagon, MI 49953

## OSCEOLA COUNTY
Clerk of Court
49th Circuit Court
301 West Upton Street
Reed City, MI 49677

## OSCODA COUNTY
Clerk of Court
23rd Circuit Court
PO Box 399
Mio, MI 48647

## OTSEGO COUNTY
Clerk of Court
46th Circuit Court
225 West Main Street, Rm 203
Gaylord, MI 49735

## OTTAWA COUNTY
Clerk of Court
20th Circuit Court
414 Washington, Rm 301A
Grand Haven, MI 49417

## PRESQUE ISLE COUNTY
Clerk of Court
26th Circuit Court
PO Box 110
Rogers City, MI 49779

## ROSCOMMON COUNTY
Clerk of Court
34th Circuit Court
PO Box 98
Roscommon, MI 48653

## SAGINAW COUNTY
Clerk of Court
10th Circuit Court
111 South Michigan Ave
Saginaw, MI 48602

## SANILAC COUNTY
Clerk of Court
24th Circuit Court
60 West Sanilac
Sandusky, MI 48471

## SCHOOLCRAFT COUNTY
Clerk of Court
11th Circuit Court
300 Walnut Street
Manistique, MI 49854

## SHIAWASSEE COUNTY
Clerk of Court
35th Circuit Court
Courthouse
Corunna, MI 48817

## ST. CLAIR COUNTY
Clerk of Court
31st Circuit Court
201 McMorran Boulevard
Port Huron, MI 48060

## ST. JOSEPH COUNTY
Clerk of Court
45th Circuit Court
PO Box 189
Centreville, MI 49032

## TUSCOLA COUNTY
Clerk of Court
54th Circuit Courts
440 North State Street
Caro, MI 48723

## VAN BUREN COUNTY
Clerk of Court
36th Circuit Court
212 Paw Paw Street
Paw Paw, MI 49079

## WASHTENAW COUNTY
Clerk of Court
22nd Circuit Court
PO Box 8654
Ann Arbor, MI 48107-8645

## WAYNE COUNTY
Clerk of Court
3rd Circuit Court
201 City County Bldg.
Detroit, MI 48226

## WEXFORD COUNTY
Clerk of Court
28th Circuit Court
Government Center
Cadillac, MI 49601

# MINNESOTA

## AITKIN COUNTY
District Court Administrator
Courthouse West Annex
209 Second Street NW
Aitkin, MN 56431

## ANOKA COUNTY
District Court Administrator
Anoka County Courthouse
325 East Main Street
Anoka, MN 55303

## BECKER COUNTY
District Court Administrator
Becker County Courthouse
Courthouse Square
Detroit Lakes, NW 56501

## BELTRAMI COUNTY
District Court Administrator
Beltrami County Courthouse
PO Box 1008
Bemidji, MN 56601

## BENTON COUNTY
District Court Administrator
Benton County Courthouse
Government Center
Foley, MN 56329

## BIG STONE COUNTY
District Court Administrator
County Court
20 Southeast 2nd Street
Ortonville, MN 56278

## BLUE EARTH COUNTY
District Court Administrator
Blue Earth County Courthouse
204 South 5th Street
Mankato, MN 56001

## BROWN COUNTY
District Court Administrator
Brown County Courthouse
Courthouse Square
New Ulm, MN 56073

## CARLTON COUNTY
District Court Administrator
Carlton County Courthouse
PO Box 190
Carlton, MN 55718

## CARVER COUNTY
District Court Administrator
Carver County Courthouse
600 East 4th Street
Chaska, MN 55318

## CASS COUNTY
District Court Administrator
Cass County Courthouse
PO Box 3000
Walker, MN 56484

## CHIPPEWA COUNTY
District Court Administrator
Chippewa County Courthouse
Courthouse Square
Montevideo, MN 56265

## CHISAGO COUNTY
District Court Administrator
Chisago County Courthouse
PO Box 126
Center City, MN 55012

## CLAY COUNTY
District Court Administrator
County Court
PO Box 280
Moorhead, MN 56560

## CLEARWATER COUNTY
District Court Administrator
County Court
PO Box 127
Bagley, MN 56621

## COOK COUNTY
District Court Administrator
County Court
411 West 2nd Street
Grand Marais, MN 55604

## COTTONWOOD COUNTY
District Court Administrator
County Court
900 3rd Avenue
Windom, MN 56101

## CROW WING COUNTY
District Court Administrator
County Court
Crow Wing County Courthouse
Brainerd, MN 56401

## DAKOTA COUNTY
District Court Administrator
Dakota County Government Ct.
1560 Hwy 55
Hastings, MN 55033

## DODGE COUNTY
District Court Administrator
Dodge County Courthouse
Box 96
Mantorville, MN 55955

## DOUGLAS COUNTY
District Court Administrator
Douglas County Courthouse
305 8th Avenue W
Alexandria, MN 56308

## FARIBAULT COUNTY
District Court Administrator
Faribault County Courthouse
Courthouse Square
Blue Earth, MN 56013

## FILLMORE COUNTY
District Court Administrator
Fillmore County Courthouse
Courthouse Square
Preston, MN 55965

## FREEBORN COUNTY
District Court Administrator
County Court
411 S. Broadway
Albert Lea, MN 56007

## GOODHUE COUNTY
District Court Administrator
Goodhue County Courthouse
Government Center
Red Wing, NW 55066

## GRANT COUNTY
District Court Administrator
Grant County Courthouse
Courthouse Square
Elbow Lake, MN 56531

## HENNEPIN COUNTY
District Court Administrator
Hennepin County Government Ct.
300 South 6th Street, Rm C-1153
Minneapolis, MN 55487

## HOUSTON COUNTY
District Court Administrator
Houston County Courthouse
304 South Marshall
Caledonia, MN 55921

## HUBBARD COUNTY
District Court Administrator
Hubbard County Courthouse
PO Box 72
Park Rapids, MN 56470

## ISANTI COUNTY
District Court Administrator
County Court
237 SW 2nd Avenue
Cambridge, MN 55008

## ITASCA COUNTY
District Court Administrator
Itasca County Courthouse
Courthouse Square
Grand Rapids, MN 55744

## JACKSON COUNTY
District Court Administrator
Jackson County Courthouse
Courthouse Square
Jackson, MN 56143

## KANABEC COUNTY
District Court Administrator
Kanabec County Courthouse
18 North Vine
Mora, MN 55051

## KANDIYOHI COUNTY
District Court Administrator
County Court
PO Box 1337
Willmar, MN 56201

## KITTSON COUNTY
District Court Administrator
Kittson County Courthouse
Box 39
Hallock, MN 56728

## KOOCHICHING COUNTY
District Court Clerk
Koochiching County Courthouse
Courthouse Square
International Falls, MN 56649

## LAC QUI PARLE COUNTY
District Court Administrator
County Court
PO Box 36
Madison, MN 56256

## LAKE COUNTY
District Court Administrator
Lake County Courthouse
601 3rd Ave
Two Harbors, MN 55616

## LAKE OF THE WOODS
District Court Administrator
County Court
PO Box 808
Baudette, MN 56623

## LE SUEUR COUNTY
District Court Administrator
Le Sueur County Courthouse
Box 10
Le Center, MN 56057

## LINCOLN COUNTY
District Court Administrator
County Court
319 N. Rebecca
Ivanhoe, MN 56142

**LYON COUNTY**
District Court Administrator
County Court
607 W. Main
Marshall, MN 56258

**MAHNOMEN COUNTY**
District Court Administrator
Mahnomen County Courthouse
Courthouse Square
Mahnomen, MN 56557

**MARSHALL COUNTY**
District Court Clerk
Marshall County Courthouse
208 East Colvin
Warren, MN 56762

**MARTIN COUNTY**
District Court Administrator
Martin County Courthouse
201 East Lake Ave
Fairmont, MN 56031

**MCLEOD COUNTY**
District Court Administrator
County Court
830 E. 11th
Glencoe, MN 55336

**MEEKER COUNTY**
District Court Administrator
County Court
325 N. Sibley Ave.
Litchfield, MN 55355

**MILLE LACS COUNTY**
District Court Administrator
Mille Lacs County Courthouse
Courthouse Square
Milaca, MN 56353

**MORRISON COUNTY**
District Court Administrator
Morrison County Courthouse
Courthouse Square
Little Falls, MN 56345

**MOWER COUNTY**
District Court Administrator
Mower County Courthouse
201 1st NE
Austin, MN 55912

**MURRAY COUNTY**
District Court Administrator
County Court
Murray County Courts Building
Slayton, MN 56172

**NICOLLET COUNTY**
District Court Clerk
County Court
PO Box 496
St. Peter, MN 56082

**NOBLES COUNTY**
District Court Administrator
Nobles County Courthouse
PO Box 547
Worthington, MN 56187

**NORMAN COUNTY**
District Court Administrator
County Court
16 E. 3rd Avenue
Ada, MN 56510

**OLMSTED COUNTY**
District Court Administrator
Government Center, 5th Floor
151 4th Street SE
Rochester, MN 55904

**OTTER TAIL COUNTY**
District Court Administrator
Otter Tail County Courthouse
PO Box 417
Fergus Falls, MN 56537

**PENNINGTON COUNTY**
District Court Administrator
County Court
PO Box 619
Thief River Falls, MN 56701

**PINE COUNTY**
District Court Administrator
Pine County Courthouse
Courthouse Square
Pine City, MN 55063

**PIPESTONE COUNTY**
District Court Administrator
County Court
PO Box 337
Pipestone, MN 56164

**POLK COUNTY**
District Court Administrator
County Court
PO Box 438
Crookston, MN 56716

**POPE COUNTY**
District Court Administrator
130 E. Minnesota Ave.
PO Box 195
Glenwood, MN 56334

**RAMSEY COUNTY**
District Court Administrator
Ramsey County Courthouse
Rm 1245
St. Paul, MN 55102

**RED LAKE COUNTY**
District Court Administrator
Red Lake County Courthouse
Box 339
Red Lake Falls, MN 56750

**REDWOOD COUNTY**
District Court Administrator
Redwood County Courthouse
PO Box 158
Redwood Falls, MN 56283

**RENVILLE COUNTY**
District Court Administrator
Renville County Courthouse
Courthouse Square
Olivia, MN 56277

## RICE COUNTY
District Court Administrator
Rice County Courthouse
218 NW 3rd Street
Fairbault, MN 55021

## ROCK COUNTY
District Court Administrator
County Court
PO Box 745
Luverne, MN 56156

## ROSEAU COUNTY
District Court Administrator
Roseau County Courthouse
Courthouse Square
Roseau, MN 56751

## SCOTT COUNTY
District Court Clerk
Scott County Courthouse
Government Center
Shakopee, MN 55379

## SHERBURNE COUNTY
District Court Administrator
Sherburne County Courthouse
PO Box 318
Elk River, MN 55330

## SIBLEY COUNTY
District Court Administrator
County Court
PO Box 867
Gaylord, MN 55334

## STEARNS COUNTY
District Court Administrator
County Court
PO Box 1168
St. Cloud, MN 56302

## STEELE COUNTY
District Court Administrator
Steele County Courthouse
PO Box 487
Owatonna, MN 55060

## STEVENS COUNTY
District Court Administrator
Stevens County Courthouse
PO Box 530
Morris, MN 56267

## ST. LOUIS COUNTY
District Court Administrator
County Court
100 North 5th Avenue West #320
Duluth, MN 55802-1294

## SWIFT COUNTY
District Court Administrator
County Court
PO Box 110
Benson, MN 56215

## TODD COUNTY
District Court Administrator
Todd County Courthouse
215 1 st Avenue S
Long Prairie, MN 56347

## TRAVERSE COUNTY
District Court Administrator
Traverse County Courthouse
Courthouse Square
Wheaton, MN 56296

## WABASHA COUNTY
District Court Administrator
Wabasha County Courthouse
Courthouse Square
Wabasha, MN 55981

## WADENA COUNTY
District Court Administrator
Wadena County Courthouse
Courthouse Square
Wadena, MN 56482

## WASECA COUNTY
District Court Administrator
Waseca County Courthouse
Courthouse Square
Waseca, MN 56093

## WASHINGTON COUNTY
District Court Administrator
Washington Cty Gov't Center
14900 61st Street N
Stillwater, MN 55082-0006

## WATONWAN COUNTY
District Court Administrator
Watonwan County Courthouse
Courthouse Square
St. James, MN 56081

## WILKIN COUNTY
District Court Administrator
Wilkin County Courthouse
PO Box 219
Breckenridge, MN 56520

## WINONA COUNTY
District Court Administrator
Winona County Courthouse
Courthouse Square
Winona, MN 55987

## WRIGHT COUNTY
District Court Administrator
Wright County Government Ct.
10 NW 2nd Street
Buffalo, MN 55313

## YELLOW MEDICINE
District Court Administrator
Yellow Medicine Courthouse
Government Center
Granite Falls, MN 56241

# MISSOURI

## ADAIR COUNTY
Clerk of Court
Adair County Circuit Court
PO Box 690
Kirksville, MO 63501

## ANDREW COUNTY
Clerk of Court
Andrew County Circuit Court
PO Box 208
Savannah, MO 64485

## ATCHISON COUNTY
Clerk of Court
Atchison County Circuit Court
PO Box J
Rockport, MO 64482

## AUDRAIN COUNTY
Clerk of Court
Audrain County Circuit Court
Courthouse
Mexico, MO 65265

## BARRY COUNTY
Clerk of Court
Barry County Circuit Court
Barry County Courthouse
Cassville, MO 65625

## BARTON COUNTY
Clerk of Court
Barton County Circuit Court
1007 Broadway
Lamar, MO 64759-1498

## BATES COUNTY
Clerk of Court
Bates County Circuit Court
PO Box 288
Butler, MO 64730

## BENTON COUNTY
Clerk of Court
Benton County Circuit Court
PO Box 37
Warsaw, MO 65355

## BOLLINGER COUNTY
Clerk of Court
Bollinger County Circuit Court
PO Box 12
Marble Hill, MO 63764

## BOONE COUNTY
Clerk of Court
Circuit Court
701 E. Walnut
Columbia, MO 65201

## BUCHANAN COUNTY
Clerk of Courts
Circuit Court
411 Jules Street
St. Joseph, MO 64501

## BUTLER COUNTY
Clerk of Court
Circuit Court, Division 1
Butler County Courthouse
Poplar Bluff, MO 63901

## CALDWELL COUNTY
Clerk of Court
Caldwell Circuit Court
PO Box 86
Kingston, MO 64650

## CALLAWAY COUNTY
Clerk of Court
Callaway Circuit Court
Courthouse
Fulton, MO 65251

## CAMDEN COUNTY
Clerk of Court
Camden Circuit Court
PO Box 930
Camdenton, MO 65020

## CAPE GIRARDEAU
Clerk of Court
Circuit Court
100 Court Street
Jackson, MO 63755

## CARROLL COUNTY
Clerk of Court
Circuit Court
PO Box 245
Carrollton, MO 64633

## CARTER COUNTY
Clerk of Court
Carter County Circuit Court
PO Box 578
Van Buren, MO 63965

## CASS COUNTY
Clerk of Court
Cass County Circuit Court
100 East Wall
Harrisonville, MO 64701

## CEDAR COUNTY
Clerk of Court
Cedar County Circuit Court
PO Box 96
Stockton, MO 65785

## CHARITON COUNTY
Clerk of Court
Circuit Court Clerk
PO Box 112
Keytesville, MO 65261

## CHRISTIAN COUNTY
Clerk of Court
Christian County Circuit Court
PO Box 278
Ozark, MO 65721

## CLARK COUNTY
Clerk of Court
Clark County Circuit Court
111 East Court
Kahoka, MO 63445

## CLAY COUNTY
Clerk of Court
Circuit Court
PO Box 218
Liberty, MO 64068

## CLINTON COUNTY
Clerk of Court
Clinton County Circuit Court
PO Box 275
Plattsburg, MO 64477

## COLE COUNTY
Clerk of Court
Cole County Circuit Court
PO Box 1156
Jefferson City, MO 65102-1156

## COOPER COUNTY
Clerk of Court
Circuit Court
200 Main, Rm 31
Boonville, MO 65233

## CRAWFORD COUNTY
Clerk of Court
Crawford County Circuit Court
PO Box 177
Steelville, MO 65565

## DADE COUNTY
Clerk of Court
Circuit Court
Courthouse
Greenfield, MO 65661

## DALLAS COUNTY
Clerk of Court
Dallas County Circuit Court
PO Box 373
Buffalo, MO 65622

## DAVIESS COUNTY
Clerk of Court
Circuit Court
PO Box 337
Gallatin, MO 64640

## DE KALB COUNTY
Clerk of Court
De Kalb County Circuit Court
PO Box 248
Maysville, MO 64469

## DENT COUNTY
Clerk of Court
Dent County Circuit Court
112 East 5th Street
Salem, MO 65560

## DOUGLAS COUNTY
Clerk of Court
Douglas County Circuit Court
PO Box 655
Ava, MO 65608

## DUNKLIN COUNTY
Clerk of Court
Dunklin County Circuit Court
PO Box 567
Kennett, MO 63857

## FRANKLIN COUNTY
Clerk of Court
Franklin County Circuit Court
PO Box 272
Union, MO 63084

## GASCONADE COUNTY
Clerk of Court
Gasconade County Circuit Court
119 East 1st Street, Rm 6
Hermann, MO 65041-1182

## GENTRY COUNTY
Clerk of Court
Gentry County Circuit Court
PO Box 27
Albany, MO 64402

## GREENE COUNTY
Clerk of Court
Circuit Court
940 Boonville
Springfield, MO 65802

## GRUNDY COUNTY
Clerk of Court
Grundy County Circuit Court
800 Main Street
Trenton, MO 64683

## HARRISON COUNTY
Clerk of Court
Circuit Court
1515 Main
Bethany, MO 64424

## HENRY COUNTY
Clerk of Court
Circuit Court
110 West Franklin
Clinton, MO 64735

## HICKORY COUNTY
Clerk of Court
Hickory County Circuit Court
PO Box 101
Hermitage, MO 65668

## HOLT COUNTY
Clerk of Court
Holt County Circuit Court
PO Box 318
Oregon, MO 64473

## HOWARD COUNTY
Clerk of Court
Howard County Circuit Court
Courthouse
Fayette, MO 65248

## HOWELL COUNTY
Clerk of Court
Howell County Circuit Court
PO Box 1011
West Plains, MO 65775

## IRON COUNTY
Clerk of Court
Iron County Circuit Court
PO Box 24
Ironton, MO 63650

## JACKSON COUNTY
Clerk of Court
Jackson County Circuit Court
1315 Locust
Kansas City, MO 64106

## JASPER COUNTY
Clerk of Court
Circuit Court
Jasper County Courthouse
Carthage, MO 64836

## JEFFERSON COUNTY
Clerk of Court
Jefferson County Circuit Court
PO Box 100
Hillsboro, MO 63050

## JOHNSON COUNTY
Clerk of Court
Circuit Court
Johnson County Courthouse
Warrensburg, MO 64093

## KNOX COUNTY
Clerk of Court
Knox County Circuit Court
PO Box 116
Edina, MO 63537

## LA CLEDE COUNTY
Clerk of Court
La Clede County Circuit Court
204 North Adams Street, #207
Lebanon, MO 65536

## LAFAYETTE COUNTY
Clerk of Court
Lafayette County Circuit Court
PO Box 340
Lexington, MO 64067

## LAWRENCE COUNTY
Clerk of Court
Lawrence County Circuit Court
PO Box 488
Mount Vernon, MO 65712

## LEWIS COUNTY
Clerk of Court
Lewis County Circuit Court
PO Box 97
Monticello, MO 63457

## LINCOLN COUNTY
Clerk of Court
Circuit Court
201 Main Street
Troy, MO 63379

## LINN COUNTY
Clerk of Court
Linn County Circuit Court
309 1/2 N. Main
Brookfield, MO 64628

## LIVINGSTON COUNTY
Clerk of Court
Circuit Court
Courthouse
Chillicothe, MO 64601

## MACON COUNTY
Clerk of Court
Macon County Circuit Court
PO Box 382
Macon, MO 63552

## MADISON COUNTY
Clerk of Court
Madison County Circuit Court
#1 Courthouse Square
Fredericktown, MO 63645

## MARIES COUNTY
Clerk of Court
Maries County Circuit Court
PO Box 213
Vienna, MO 65582

## MARION COUNTY
Clerk of Court
Circuit Court
100 South Main
Palmyra, MO 63461

## MCDONALD COUNTY
Clerk of Court
McDonald County Circuit Court
6th and Main Street
Pineville, MO 64856

## MERCER COUNTY
Clerk of Court
Circuit Court
East Main Street
Princeton, MO 64673

## MILLER COUNTY
Clerk of Court
Miller County Circuit Court
PO Box 11
Tuscumbia, MO 65082

## MISSISSIPPI COUNTY
Clerk of Court
Circuit Court
200 North Main
Charleston, MO 63834

## MONITEAU COUNTY
Clerk of Court
Circuit Court
200 East Main
California, MO 65018

## MONROE COUNTY
Clerk of Court
Monroe County Circuit Court
PO Box 227
Paris, MO 65275

## MONTGOMERY COUNTY
Clerk of Court
Montgomery Circuit Court
211 E. 3rd
Montgomery City, MO 63361

## MORGAN COUNTY
Clerk of Court
Morgan County Circuit Court
100 E. Newton
Versailles, MO 65084

## NEW MADRID COUNTY
Clerk of Court
New Madrid Circuit Court
Government Center
New Madrid, MO 63869

## NEWTON COUNTY
Clerk of Court
Circuit Court
PO Box 130
Neosho, MO 64850

## NODAWAY COUNTY
Clerk of Court
Nodaway County Circuit Court
PO Box 218
Maryville, MO 64468

## OREGON COUNTY
Clerk of Court
Oregon County Circuit Court
PO Box 406
Alton, MO 65606

## OSAGE COUNTY
Clerk of Court
Osage County Circuit Court
PO Box 825
Linn, MO 65051

## OZARK COUNTY
Clerk of Court
Ozark County Circuit Court
PO Box 36
Gainesville, MO 65655

## PEMISCOT COUNTY
Clerk of Court
Circuit Court
Government Center
Caruthersville, MO 63830

## PERRY COUNTY
Clerk of Court
Perry County Circuit Court
15 West Saint Maries, Ste 2
Perryville, MO 63775-1399

## PETTIS COUNTY
Clerk of Court
Pettis County Circuit Court
PO Box 804
Sedalia, MO 65301

## PHELPS COUNTY
Clerk of Court
Circuit Court
200 North Main
Rolla, MO 65401

## PIKE COUNTY
Clerk of Court
Circuit Court
115 West Main
Bowling Green, MO 63334

## PLATTE COUNTY
Clerk of Court
Circuit Court
328 Main Street
Platte City, MO 64079

## POLK COUNTY
Clerk of Court
Polk County Circuit Court
102 E. Broadway, Room 14
Bolivar, MO 65613

## PULASKI COUNTY
Clerk of Court
Circuit Court
301 US Hwy. 44 E
Waynesville, MO 65583

## PUTNAM COUNTY
Clerk of Court
Putnam County Circuit Court
Courthouse, Room 203
Unionville, MO 63565-1659

## RALLS COUNTY
Clerk of Court
Ralls County Circuit Court
PO Box 444
New London, MO 63459

## RANDOLPH COUNTY
Clerk of Court
Randolph County Circuit Court
223 N. Williams
Moberly, MO 65270

## RAY COUNTY
Clerk of Court
Ray County Circuit Court
PO Box 594
Richmond, MO 64085

## REYNOLDS COUNTY
Clerk of Court
Reynolds County Circuit Court
PO Box 76
Centerville, MO 63633

## RIPLEY COUNTY
Clerk of Court
Circuit Court
Government Center
Doniphan, MO 63935

## SALINE COUNTY
Clerk of Court
Saline County Circuit Court
PO Box 597
Marshall, MO 65340

## SCHUYLER COUNTY
Clerk of Court
Schuyler County Circuit Court
PO Box 186
Lancaster, MO 63548

## SCOTLAND COUNTY
Clerk of Court
Scotland County Circuit Court
Courthouse, Room 106
Memphis, MO 63555

## SCOTT COUNTY
Clerk of Court
Scott County Circuit Court
PO Box 277
Benton, MO 63736

## SHANNON COUNTY
Clerk of Court
Shannon County Circuit Court
PO Box 148
Eminence, MO 65466

## SHELBY COUNTY
Clerk of Court
Shelby County Circuit Court
PO Box 176
Shelbyville, MO 63469

## ST. GENEVIEVE COUNTY
Clerk of Court
St. Genevieve Circuit Court
55 South 3rd Street
St. Genevieve, MO 63670

## STODDARD COUNTY
Clerk of Court
Stoddard County Circuit Court
PO Box 30
Bloomfield, MO 63825

## STONE COUNTY
Clerk of Court
Stone County Circuit Court
PO Box 18
Galena, MO 65656

## ST. CHARLES COUNTY
Clerk of Court
Circuit Court
300 North 2nd Street
St. Charles, MO 63301

## ST. CLAIR COUNTY
Clerk of Court
Circuit Court
PO Box 334
Osceola, MO 64776

## ST. FRANCOIS COUNTY
Clerk of Court
St. Francois County Circuit Court
1 N. Washington, 3rd Floor
Farmington, MO 63640

## ST. LOUIS COUNTY
Clerk of Court
St. Louis County Circuit Court
7900 Carondelet
Clayton, MO 63105

## THE CITY OF ST. LOUIS
Clerk of Court
Circuit Court
10 North Tucker
St. Louis, MO 63101

## SULLIVAN COUNTY
Clerk of Court
Circuit Court
Government Center
Milan, MO 63556

## TANEY COUNTY
Clerk of Court
Taney County Circuit Court
PO Box 335
Forsyth, MO 65653

## TEXAS COUNTY
Clerk of Court
Circuit Court
PO Box 237
Houston, MO 65483

## VERNON COUNTY
Clerk of Court
Circuit Court
Vernon County Courthouse
Nevada, MO 64772

## WARREN COUNTY
Clerk of Court
Circuit Court
104 West Main
Warrenton, MO 63383

## WASHINGTON COUNTY
Clerk of Court
Washington County Circuit Court
PO Box 216
Potosi, MO 63664

## WAYNE COUNTY
Clerk of Court
Wayne County Circuit Court
PO Box 187-A
Greenville, MO 63944

## WEBSTER COUNTY
Clerk of Court
Webster County Circuit Court
PO Box 529
Marshfield, MO 65706

## WORTH COUNTY
Clerk of Court
Worth County Circuit Court
PO Box H
Grant City, MO 64456

## WRIGHT COUNTY
Clerk of Court
Wright County Circuit Court
PO Box 39
Hartville, MO 65667

# MISSISSIPPI

## ADAMS COUNTY
Circuit Court Clerk
Adams County Circuit Court
PO Box 1224
Natchez, MS 39121

## ALCORN COUNTY
Circuit Court Clerk
Alcom County Circuit Court
PO Box 430
Corinth, MS 38834

## AMITE COUNTY
Circuit Court Clerk
Amite County Circuit Court
PO Box 312
Liberty, MS 39645

## ATTALA COUNTY
Circuit Court Clerk
Attala County Circuit Court
118 West Washington
Kosciusko, MS 39090

## BENTON COUNTY
Circuit Court Clerk
Benton County Circuit Court
PO Box 262
Ashland, MS 38603

## BOLIVAR COUNTY
Circuit Court Clerk
Bolivar County Circuit Court
PO Box 670
Cleveland, MS 38732-0670

## CALHOUN COUNTY
Circuit Court Clerk
Calhoun County Circuit Court
PO Box 25
Pittsboro, MS 38951

## CARROLL COUNTY
Circuit Court Clerk
Carroll County Circuit Court
PO Box 6
Vaiden, MS 39176

## CHICKASAW COUNTY
Circuit Court Clerk
Chickasaw County Courthouse
PO Box 482
Houston, MS 38851

## CHOCTAW COUNTY
Circuit Court Clerk
Choctaw County Circuit Court
PO Box 34
Ackerman, MS 39735

## CLAIBORNE COUNTY
Circuit Court Clerk
Claiborne County Circuit Court
PO Box 549
Port Gibson, MS 39150

## CLARKE COUNTY
Circuit Court Clerk
Clarke County Circuit Court
PO Box 216
Quitman, MS 39355

## CLAY COUNTY
Circuit Court Clerk
Clay County Circuit Court
PO Box 364
West Point, MS 39773

## COAHOMA COUNTY
Circuit Court Clerk
Coahoma County Circuit Court
PO Box 504
Clarksdale, MS 38614

## COPIAH COUNTY
Circuit Court Clerk
Copiah County Circuit Court
PO Box 467
Hazelhurst, MS 39083

## COVINGTON COUNTY
Circuit Court Clerk
Covington County Circuit Court
PO Box 667
Collins, MS 39428

## DE SOTO COUNTY
Circuit Court Clerk
De Soto County Circuit Court
2535 Hwy 51 S
Hernando, MS 38632

## FORREST COUNTY
Circuit Court Clerk
Forrest County Circuit Court
630 Main
Hattiesburg, MS 39401

## FRANKLIN COUNTY
Circuit Court Clerk
Franklin County Circuit Court
PO Box 267
Meadville, MS 39653

## GEORGE COUNTY
Circuit Court Clerk
George County Circuit Court
Courthouse Square
Lucedale, MS 39452

## GREENE COUNTY
Circuit Court Clerk
Greene County Circuit Court
PO Box 310
Leakesville, MS 39451

## GRENADA COUNTY
Circuit Court Clerk
Grenada County Circuit Court
59 Green Street, Ste 8
Grenada, MS 38901

## HANCOCK COUNTY
Circuit Court Clerk
Hancock County Circuit Court
PO Box 249
Bay Street Louis, MS 39520

## HARRISON COUNTY
Circuit Court Clerk
Harrison County Circuit Court
1801 23rd Ave.
Gulfport, MS 39502

## HINDS COUNTY
Circuit Court Clerk
Hinds County Circuit Court
PO Box 327
Jackson, MS 39205-0327

## HOLMES COUNTY
Circuit Court Clerk
Holmes County Circuit Court
PO Box 265
Lexington, MS 39095

## HUMPHREYS COUNTY
Circuit Court Clerk
Humphreys County Circuit Court
PO Box 696
Belzoni, MS 39038

## ISSAQUENA COUNTY
Circuit Court Clerk
Circuit and Justice Court
PO Box 27
Mayersville, MS 39113

## ITAWAMBA COUNTY
Circuit Court Clerk
Itawamba Circuit Court
201 West Main
Fulton, MS 38843

## JACKSON COUNTY
Circuit Court Clerk
Jackson County Circuit Court
PO Box 998
Pascagoula, MS 39567

## JASPER COUNTY
Circuit Court Clerk
Jasper County Circuit Court
PO Box 447
Bay Springs, MS 39422

## JEFFERSON COUNTY
Circuit Court Clerk
Jefferson County Circuit Court
PO Box 305
Fayette, MS 39069

## JEFFERSON DAVIS
Circuit Court Clerk
Jefferson Davis Circuit Court
PO Box 1082
Prentiss, MS 39474

## JONES COUNTY
Circuit Court Clerk
Jones County Circuit Court
PO Box 1336
Laurel, MS 39440

## KEMPER COUNTY
Circuit Court Clerk
Kemper County Circuit Court
PO Box 130
DeKalb, MS 39328

## LAFAYETTE COUNTY
Circuit Court Clerk
Lafayette County Circuit Court
Courthouse
Oxford, MS 38655

## LAMAR COUNTY
Circuit Court Clerk
Lamar County Circuit Court
PO Box 369
Purvis, MS 39475

## LAUDERDALE COUNTY
Circuit Court Clerk
Lauderdale County Circuit Court
PO Box 1005
Meridian, MS 39302

## LAWRENCE COUNTY
Circuit Court Clerk
Lawrence County Circuit Court
PO Box 1249
Monticello, MS 39654

## LEAKE COUNTY
Circuit Court Clerk
Leake County Circuit Court
PO Box 67
Carthage, MS 39051

## LEE COUNTY
Circuit Court Clerk
Lee County Circuit Court
PO Box 762
Tupelo, MS 38802

## LEFLORE COUNTY
Circuit Court Clerk
Leflore County Circuit Court
PO Box 1953
Greenwood, MS 38930

## LINCOLN COUNTY
Circuit Court Clerk
Lincoln County Circuit Court
PO Box 357
Brookhaven, MS 39601

## LOWNDES COUNTY
Circuit Court Clerk
Lowndes County Circuit Court
PO Box 31
Columbus, MS 39703

## MADISON COUNTY
Circuit Court Clerk
Madison County Circuit Court
PO Box 11
Canton, MS 39046

## MARION COUNTY
Circuit Court Clerk
Marion County Circuit Court
250 Broad Street, Ste #1
Columbia, MS 39429

## MARSHALL COUNTY
Circuit Court Clerk
Marshall County Circuit Court
PO Box 459
Holly Springs, MS 38635

## MONROE COUNTY
Circuit Court Clerk
Monroe County Circuit Court
PO Box 843
Aberdeen, MS 39730

## MONTGOMERY COUNTY
Circuit Court Clerk
Montgomery Circuit Court
PO Box 765
Winona, MS 38967

## NESHOBA COUNTY
Clerk of Court
Neshoba County Courthouse
401 Beacon Street
Philadelphia, MS 39350

## NEWTON COUNTY
Circuit Court Clerk
Newton County Circuit Court
PO Box 447
Decatur, MS 39327

## NOXUBEE COUNTY
Clerk of Court
Noxubee County Circuit Court
505 S. Jefferson Street
Macon, MS 39341

## OKTIBBEHA COUNTY
Circuit Court Clerk
Oktibbeha County Circuit Court
Government Center
Starkville, MS 39759

## PANOLA COUNTY
Circuit Court Clerk
Panola County Circuit Court
PO Box 346
Batesville, MS 38606

## PEARL RIVER COUNTY
Circuit Court Clerk
Pearl River County Circuit Court
Government Center
Poplarville, MS 39470

## PERRY COUNTY
Circuit Court Clerk
Perry County Circuit Court
PO Box 198
New Augusta, MS 39462

## PIKE COUNTY
Circuit Court Clerk
Pike County Circuit Court
PO Box 31
Magnolia, MS 39652

## PONTOTOC COUNTY
Circuit Court Clerk
Pontotoc County Circuit Court
PO Box 428
Pontotoc, MS 38863

## PRENTISS COUNY
Clerk of Court
Circuit and Justice Court
101 North Main
Bonneville, MS 38829

## QUITMAN COUNTY
Circuit Court Clerk
Quitman County Circuit Court
Government Center
Marks, MS 38646

## RANKIN COUNTY
Circuit Court Clerk
Rankin County Circuit Court
PO Drawer 1599
Brandon, MS 39043

## SCOTT COUNTY
Clerk of Courts
Scott County Circuit Court
PO Box 371
Forest, MS 39074

## SHARKEY COUNTY
Circuit Court Clerk
Circuit and Justice Court
PO Box 218
Rolling Fork, MS 39159

## SIMPSON COUNTY
Circuit Court Clerk
Simpson County Circuit Court
PO Box 307
Mendenhall, MS 39114

## SMITH COUNTY
Circuit Court Clerk
Smith County Circuit Court
PO Box 517
Raleigh, MS 39153

## STONE COUNTY
Circuit Court Clerk
Stone County Circuit Court
Government Center
Wiggins, MS 39577

## SUNFLOWER COUNTY
Circuit Court Clerk
Sunflower County Circuit Court
PO Box 576
Indianola, MS 38751

## TALLAHATCHIE COUNTY
Circuit Court Clerk
Tallahatchie County Circuit Court
PO Box 86
Charleston, MS 38921

## TATE COUNTY
Clerk of Court
Tate County Circuit Court
201 Ward Street
Senatobia, MS 38668

## TIPPAH COUNTY
Clerk of Court
Tippah County Circuit Court
Government Center
Ripley, MS 38663

## TISHOMINGO COUNTY
Clerk of Court
Tishomingo County Circuit Court
Government Center
Iuka, MS 38852

## TUNICA COUNTY
Circuit Court Clerk
Tunica County Circuit Court
PO Box 184
Tunica, MS 38676

## UNION COUNTY
Circuit Court Clerk
Union County Circuit Court
PO Box 298
New Albany, MS 38652

## WALTHALL COUNTY
Circuit Court Clerk
Walthall County Circuit Court
200 Ball Ave
Tylertown, MS 39667

## WARREN COUNTY
Circuit Court Clerk
Warren County Circuit Court
PO Box 351
Vicksburg, MS 39180

## WASHINGTON COUNTY
Circuit Court Clerk
Washington County Circuit Court
PO Box 1276
Greenville, MS 38702

## WAYNE COUNTY
Circuit Court Clerk
Wayne County Circuit Court
PO Box 428
Waynesboro, MS 39367

## WEBSTER COUNTY
Circuit Court Clerk
Webster County Circuit Court
PO Box 308
Walthall, MS 39771

## WILKINSON COUNTY
Circuit Court Clerk
Wilkinson County Circuit Court
PO Box 327
Woodville, MS 39669

## WINSTON COUNTY
Circuit Court Clerk
Winston County Circuit Court
PO Box 371
Louisville, MS 39339

## YALOBUSHA COUNTY
Circuit Court Clerk
Yalobusha County Circuit Court
PO Box 431
Water Valley, MS 38965

## YAZOO COUNTY
Circuit Court Clerk
Yazoo County Circuit Court
PO Box 108
Yazoo City, MS 39194

# MONTANA

## BEAVERHEAD COUNTY
Clerk of Court
District and Justice Court
2 South Pacific Street
Dillon, MT 59725

## BIG HORN COUNTY
Clerk of Court
District and Justice Court
PO Drawer H
Hardin, MT 59034

## BLAINE COUNTY
District Court Clerk
District and Justice Court
400 Ohio Street
Chinook, MT 59523

## BROADWATER COUNTY
District Court Clerk
District and Justice Court
515 Broadway
Townsend, MT 59644

## CARBON COUNTY
District Court Clerk
District and Justice Court
PO Box 948
Red Lodge, MT 59068

## CARTER COUNTY
District Court Clerk
District and Justice Court
Ekalaka Route
Ekalaka, MT 59324

## CASCADE COUNTY
District Court Clerk
Courthouse
PO Box 2806
Great Falls, MT 59403

## CHOUTEAU COUNTY
Clerk of Court
District and Justice Court
PO Box 459
Ft. Benton, MT 59442

## CUSTER COUNTY
Clerk of Court
District and Justice Court
1010 Main
Miles City, MT 59301

## DANIELS COUNTY

District Court Clerk
District and Justice Court
PO Box 67
Scobey, MT 59263

## DAWSON COUNTY

Clerk of Court
District and Justice Court
207 West Bell
Glendive, MT 59330

## DEER LODGE COUNTY

Clerk of Court
District and Justice Court
800 South Main
Anaconda, MT 59711

## FALLON COUNTY

District Court Clerk
District and Justice Court
Drawer M
Baker, MT 59313

## FERGUS COUNTY

District Court Clerk
District and Justice Court
PO Box 1074
Lewistown, MT 59457

## FLATHEAD COUNTY

District Court Clerk
District and Justice Court
PO Box 897
Kalispell, MT 59903

## GALLATIN COUNTY

District Court Clerk
District and Justice Court
615 S. 16th, Rm 200
Bozeman, MT 59715

## GARFIELD COUNTY

Clerk of Court
District and Justice Court
PO Box 8
Jordan, MT 59337

## GLACIER COUNTY

Clerk of Court
District and Justice Court
512 East Main Street
Cut Bank, MT 59427

## GOLDEN VALLEY COUNTY

Clerk of Court
District and Justice Court
Box 10
Ryegate, MT 59074

## GRANITE COUNTY

Clerk of Court
District and Justice Court
Government Center
Philipsburg, MT 59858

## HILL COUNTY

Clerk of Court
District and Justice Court
Hill County Courthouse
Havre, MT 59501

## JEFFERSON COUNTY
Clerk of Court
District and Justice Court
PO Box H
Boulder, MT 59632

## JUDITH BASIN COUNTY
District Court Clerk
District and Justice Court
PO Box 307
Stanford, MT 59479

## LAKE COUNTY
Clerk of Court
Lake County Courthouse
106 4th Avenue E
Polson, MT 59860

## LEWIS AND CLARK
District Court Clerk
District and Justice Court
PO Box 158
Helena, MT 59624-0158

## LIBERTY COUNTY
District Court Clerk
District and Justice Court
PO Box 459
Chester, MT 59522

## LINCOLN COUNTY
District Court Clerk
District and Justice Court
512 California Avenue
Libby, MT 59923

## MADISON COUNTY
District Court Clerk
District and Justice Court
PO Box 185
Virginia City, MT 59755

## MCCONE COUNTY
Clerk of Court
District and Justice Court
PO Box 199
Circle, MT 59215

## MEAGHER COUNTY
District Court Clerk
District and Justice Court
PO Box 443
Sulphur Springs, MT 59645

## MINERAL COUNTY
District Court Clerk
District and Justice Court
PO Box 96
Superior, MT 59872

## MISSOULA COUNTY
Clerk of Court
Missoula County Courthouse
200 West Broadway
Missoula, MT 59802

## MUSSELSHELL COUNTY
Clerk of Court
District and Justice Court
PO Box 357
Roundup, MT 59072

## PARK COUNTY
Clerk of Court
District and Justice Court
414 East Callender
Livingston, MT 59047

## PETROLEUM COUNTY
District Court Clerk
District and Justice Court
PO Box 226
Winnett, MT 59087

## PHILLIPS COUNTY
District Court Clerk
District and Justice Court
Box I
Malta, MT 59538

## PONDERA COUNTY
Clerk of Court
District and Justice Court
20 Fourth Avenue SW
Conrad, MT 59425

## POWDER RIVER COUNTY
District Court Clerk
District and Justice Court
Box G
Broadus, MT 59317

## POWELL COUNTY
Clerk of Court
District and Justice Court
409 Missouri Ave
Deer Lodge, MT 59722

## PRAIRIE COUNTY
District Court Clerk
Prairie County Courthouse
PO Box 125
Terry, MT 59349

## RAVALLI COUNTY
District Court Clerk
District and Justice Court
205 Bedford Street
Haniilton, MT 59840

## RICHLAND COUNTY
District Court Clerk
District and Justice Court
201 West Main
Sidney, MT 59270

## ROOSEVELT COUNTY
Clerk of Court
District and Justice Court
Roosevelt County Courthouse
Wolf Point, MT 59201

## ROSEBUD COUNTY
District Court Clerk
District and Justice Court
PO Box 48
Forsyth, MT 59327

## SANDERS COUNTY
Clerk of Court
District and Justice Court
PO Box 519
Thompson Falls, MT 59873

## SHERIDAN COUNTY
Clerk of Court
District and Justice Court
100 West Laurel
Plentywood, MT 59254

## SILVER BOW COUNTY
Clerk of Court
District and Justice Court
155 W. Granite Street
Butte, MT 59701

## STILLWATER COUNTY
District Court Clerk
District and Justice Court
PO Box 367
Columbus, MT 59019

## SWEET GRASS COUNTY
District Court Clerk
District and Justice Court
PO Box 698
Big Timber, MT 59011

## TETON COUNTY
District Court Clerk
District and Justice Court
PO Box 487
Choteau, MT 59422

## TOOLE COUNTY
District Court Clerk
District and Justice Court
PO Box 850
Shelby, MT 59474

## TREASURE COUNTY
District Court Clerk
District and Justice Court
307 Repalje Street
Hysham, MT 59038

## VALLEY COUNTY
District Court Clerk
District and Justice Court
501 Court Square #6
Glasgow, MT 59230

## WHEATLAND COUNTY
District Court Clerk
District and Justice Court
Box 227
Harlowton, MT 59036

## WIBAUX COUNTY
Clerk of Court
District and Justice Court
Government Center
Wibaux, MT 59353

## YELLOWSTONE COUNTY
District Court Clerk
District and Justice Court
PO Box 35030
Billings, MT 59107

# NORTH CAROLINA
## ALAMANCE COUNTY
Clerk of Court
Superior and District Courts
212 West Elm
Graham, NC 27253

## ALEXANDER COUNTY

Clerk of Court
Superior and District Courts
Alexander County Courthouse
Taylorsville, NC 28681

## ALLEGHANY COUNTY

Clerk of Court
Superior and District Courts
PO Box 61
Sparta, NC 28675

## ANSON COUNTY

Clerk of Court
Superior and District Courts
Anson County Courthouse
Wadesboro, NC 28170

## ASHE COUNTY

Clerk of Court
Superior and District Courts
PO Box 95
Jefferson, NC 28640

## AVERY COUNTY

Clerk of Court
Superior and District Courts
PO Box 115
Newland, NC 28657

## BEAUFORT COUNTY

Clerk of Court
Superior and District Courts
112 Second Street
Washington, NC 27889

## BERTIE COUNTY

Clerk of Court
Superior and District Courts
PO Box 370
Windsor, NC 27983

## BLADEN COUNTY

Clerk of Court
Superior and District Courts
PO Box 547
Elizabethtown, NC 28337

## BRUNSWICK COUNTY

Clerk of Court
Superior and District Courts
PO Box 127
Bolivia, NC 28422

## BUNCOMBE COUNTY

Clerk of Court
Superior and District Courts
60 Court Plaza
Asheville, NC 28801-3519

## BURKE COUNTY

Clerk of Court
Superior and District Courts
PO Box 796
Morganton, NC 28655

## CABARRUS COUNTY

Clerk of Court
Superior and District Courts
77 Union Street, South
Concord, NC 28026

## CALDWELL COUNTY
Clerk of Court
Superior and District Courts
208 Main Street NW
Lenoir, NC 28645

## CAMDEN COUNTY
Clerk of Court
Superior and District Courts
117 North 343
Camden, NC 27921

## CARTERET COUNTY
Clerk of Court
Superior and District Courts
Courthouse Square
Beaufort, NC 28516

## CASWELL COUNTY
Clerk of Court
Superior and District Courts
PO Drawer 790
Yanceyville, NC 27379

## CATAWBA COUNTY
Clerk of Court
Superior and District Courts
PO Box 790
Newton, NC 28658

## CHATHAM COUNTY
Clerk of Court
Superior and District Courts
PO Box 368
Pittsboro, NC 27312

## CHEROKEE COUNTY
Clerk of Court
Superior and District Courts
Cherokee County Courthouse
Murphy, NC 28906

## CHOWAN COUNTY
Clerk of Court
Superior and District Courts
PO Box 588
Edenton, NC 27932

## CLAY COUNTY
Clerk of Court
Superior and District Courts
PO Box 506
Hayesville, NC 28904

## CLEVELAND COUNTY
Clerk of Court
Superior and District Courts
100 Justice Pl
Shelby, NC 28150

## COLUMBUS COUNTY
Clerk of Court
Superior and District Courts
Courthouse Square
Whiteville, NC 28472

## CRAVEN COUNTY
Clerk of Court
Superior and District Courts
PO Box 1187
New Bern, NC 28560

## CUMBERLAND COUNTY
Clerk of Court
Superior and District Courts
PO Box 363
Fayetteville, NC 28302

## CURRITUCK COUNTY
Clerk of Court
Superior and District Courts
100 Courthouse Rd
Currituck, NC 27929

## DARE COUNTY
Clerk of Court
Superior and District Courts
PO Box 1849
Manteo, NC 27954

## DAVIDSON COUNTY
Clerk of Court
Superior and District Courts
PO Box 1064
Lexington, NC 27293

## DAVIE COUNTY
Clerk of Court
Superior and District Courts
140 South Main Street
Mocksville, NC 27028

## DUPLIN COUNTY
Clerk of Court
Superior and District Courts
PO Box 188
Kenansville, NC 28349

## DURHAM COUNTY
Clerk of Court
Superior and District Courts
201 East Main
Durham, NC 27702

## EDGECOMBE COUNTY
Clerk of Court
Superior and District Courts
301 Street Andrew
Tarboro, NC 27886

## FORSYTH COUNTY
Clerk of Court
Superior and District Courts
200 North Main
Winston-Salem, NC 27120

## FRANKLIN COUNTY
Clerk of Court
Superior and District Courts
102 South Main Street
Louisburg, NC 27549

## GASTON COUNTY
Clerk of Court
Superior and District Courts
151 South Street
Gastonia, NC 28053

## GATES COUNTY
Clerk of Court
Superior and District Courts
PO Box 31
Galesville, NC 27938

## GRAHAM COUNTY
Clerk of Court
Superior and District Courts
PO Box 1179
Robbinsville, NC 28771

## GRANVILLE COUNTY
Clerk of Court
Superior and District Courts
101 Main Street
Oxford, NC 27565

## GREENE COUNTY
Clerk of Court
Superior and District Courts
PO Box 675
Snow Hill, NC 28580

## GUILFORD COUNTY
Clerk of Court
Superior and District Courts
201 South Eugene Street
Greensboro, NC 27402

## HALIFAX COUNTY
Clerk of Court
Superior and District Courts
PO Box 66
Halifax, NC 27839

## HARNETT COUNTY
Clerk of Court
Superior and District Courts
729 South Main
Lillington, NC 27546

## HAYWOOD COUNTY
Clerk of Court
Superior and District Courts
Haywood County Courthouse
Waynesville, NC 28786

## HENDERSON COUNTY
Clerk of Court
Superior and District Courts
PO Box 965
Hendersonville, NC 28793-0965

## HERTFORD COUNTY
Clerk of Court
Superior and District Courts
King Street
Winton, NC 27986

## HOKE COUNTY
Clerk of Court
Superior and District Courts
304 North Main
Raeford, NC 28376

## HYDE COUNTY
Clerk of Court
Superior and District Courts
PO Box 337
Swanquarter, NC 27885

## IREDELL COUNTY
Clerk of Court
Superior and District Courts
PO Box 186
Statesville, NC 28677

## JACKSON COUNTY

Clerk of Court
Superior and District Courts
Jackson County Courthouse
Sylva, NC 28779

## JOHNSTON COUNTY

Clerk of Court
Superior and District Courts
PO Box 297
Smithfield, NC 27577

## JONES COUNTY

Clerk of Court
Superior and District Courts
PO Box 280
Trenton, NC 28585

## LEE COUNTY

Clerk of Court
Superior and District Courts
1408 South Homer Boulevard
Sanford, NC 27331

## LENOIR COUNTY

Clerk of Court
Superior and District Courts
130 South Queen
Kinston, NC 28502-0068

## LINCOLN COUNTY

Clerk of Court
Superior and District Courts
PO Box 8
Lincolnton, NC 28093

## MACON COUNTY

Clerk of Court
Superior and District Courts
PO Box 288
Franklin, NC 28734

## MADISON COUNTY

Clerk of Court
Superior and District Courts
PO Box 684
Marshall, NC 28753

## MARTIN COUNTY

Clerk of Court
Superior and District Courts
PO Box 807
Williamston, NC 27892

## MCDOWELL COUNTY

Clerk of Court
Superior and District Courts
McDowell County Courthouse
Marion, NC 28752

## MECKLENBURG COUNTY

Clerk of Court
Superior and District Courts
800 East 4th Street
Charlotte, NC 28202

## MITCHELL COUNTY

Clerk of Court
Superior and District Courts
PO Box 402
Bakersville, NC 28705

## MONTGOMERY COUNTY
Clerk of Court
Superior and District Courts
PO Box 527
Troy, NC 27371

## MOORE COUNTY
Clerk of Court
Superior and District Courts
102 Monroe Street
Carthage, NC 28327

## NASH COUNTY
Clerk of Court
Superior and District Courts
PO Box 759
Nashville, NC 27856

## NEW HANOVER COUNTY
Clerk of Court
Superior and District Courts
316 Princess
Wilmington, NC 28402

## NORTHAMPTON COUNTY
Clerk of Court
Superior and District Courts
PO Box 217
Jackson, NC 27845

## ONSLOW COUNTY
Clerk of Court
Superior and District Courts
625 Court Street
Jacksonville, NC 28540

## ORANGE COUNTY
Clerk of Court
Superior and District Courts
106 Margaret Lane
Hillsborough, NC 27278

## PAMLICO COUNTY
Clerk of Court
Superior and District Courts
PO Box 38
Bayboro, NC 28515

## PASQUOTANK COUNTY
Clerk of Court
Superior and District Courts
206 West Main
Elizabeth City, NC 27907

## PENDER COUNTY
Clerk of Court
Superior and District Courts
101 Wright
Burgaw, NC 28425

## PERQUIMANS COUNTY
Clerk of Court
Superior and District Courts
128 North Church
Hertford, NC 27944

## PERSON COUNTY
Clerk of Court
Superior and District Courts
Person County Courthouse
Roxboro, NC 27573

## PITT COUNTY
Clerk of Court
Superior and District Courts
3rd and Washington
Greenville, NC 27834

## POLK COUNTY
Clerk of Court
Superior and District Courts
PO Box 38
Columbus, NC 28722

## RANDOLPH COUNTY
Clerk of Court
Superior and District Courts
145 Worth Street
Asheboro, NC 27204-1925

## RICHMOND COUNTY
Clerk of Court
Superior and District Courts
PO Box 724
Rockingham, NC 28379

## ROBESON COUNTY
Clerk of Court
Superior and District Courts
500 North Elm Street
Lumberton, NC 28358

## ROCKINGHAM COUNTY
Clerk of Court
Superior and District Courts
1086 NC Hwy 65
Wentworth, NC 27375

## ROWAN COUNTY
Clerk of Court
Superior and District Courts
210 North Main
Salisbury, NC 28144

## RUTHERFORD COUNTY
Clerk of Court
Superior and District Courts
PO Box 630
Rutherfordton, NC 28139

## SAMPSON COUNTY
Clerk of Court
Superior and District Courts
Sampson County Courthouse
Clinton, NC 28328

## SCOTLAND COUNTY
Clerk of Court
Superior and District Courts
212 Biggs Street
Laurinburg, NC 28352

## STANLEY COUNTY
Clerk of Court
Superior and District Courts
PO Box 668
Albemarle, NC 28002

## STOKES COUNTY
Clerk of Court
Superior and District Courts
PO Box 256
Danbury, NC 27010

## SURRY COUNTY
Clerk of Court
Superior and District Courts
PO Box 345
Dobson, NC 27017

## SWAIN COUNTY
Clerk of Court
Superior and District Courts
PO Box 1397
Bryson City, NC 28713

## TRANSYLVANIA COUNTY
Clerk of Court
Superior and District Courts
12 East Main
Brevard, NC 28712

## TYRRELL COUNTY
Clerk of Court
Superior and District Courts
PO Box 406
Columbia, NC 27925

## UNION COUNTY
Clerk of Court
Superior and District Courts
500 North Main
Monroe, NC 28110

## VANCE COUNTY
Clerk of Court
Superior and District Courts
122 Young Street
Henderson, NC 27536

## WAKE COUNTY
Clerk of Court
Superior and District Courts
316 Fayetteville Mall
Raleigh, NC 27602

## WARREN COUNTY
Clerk of Court
Superior and District Courts
PO Box 709
Warrenton, NC 27589

## WASHINGTON COUNTY
Clerk of Court
Superior and District Courts
120 Adams Street
Plymouth, NC 27962

## WATAUGA COUNTY
Clerk of Court
Superior and District Courts
403 West King Street
Boone, NC 28607

## WAYNE COUNTY
Clerk of Court
Superior and District Court
PO Box 267
Goldsboro, NC 27530

## WILKES COUNTY
Clerk of Court
Superior and District Courts
Courthouse Square
Wilkesboro, NC 28697

## WILSON COUNTY
Clerk of Court
Superior and District Courts
115 East Nash
Wilson, NC 27893

## YADKIN COUNTY
Clerk of Court
Superior and District Courts
102 East Elm
Yadkinville, NC 27055

## YANCEY COUNTY
Clerk of Court
Superior and District Courts
110 Town Square
Burnsville, NC 28714

# NORTH DAKOTA

## ADAMS COUNTY
Clerk of Court
District and County Courts
PO Box 469
Hettinger, ND 58639

## BARNES COUNTY
County Court Clerk
District and County Court
230 4th Street N.W.
Valley City, ND 58072

## BENSON COUNTY
Clerk of Court
District and County Courts
Box 213
Minnewaukan, ND 58351

## BILLINGS COUNTY
Clerk of Court
District and County Courts
PO Box 138
Medora, ND 58645

## BOTTINEAU COUNTY
Clerk of Court
District and County Courts
314 West 5th Street
Bottineau, ND 58318

## BOWMAN COUNTY
Clerk of Court
District and County Courts
104 West 1st Street
Bowman, ND 58623

## BURKE COUNTY
Clerk of Court
District and County Courts
PO Box 219
Bowbells, ND 58721

## BURLEIGH COUNTY
County Court Clerk
County Court
PO Box 5518
Bismarck, ND 58502

## CASS COUNTY
Clerk of Court
District and County Courts
211 South 9th Street
Fargo, ND 58108

## CAVALIER COUNTY
Clerk of Court
District and County Courts
901 Third Street
Langdon, ND 58249

## DICKEY COUNTY
Clerk of Court
District and County Courts
PO Box 336
Ellendale, ND 58436

## DIVIDE COUNTY
Clerk of Court
District and County Courts
PO Box 68
Crosby, ND 58730

## DUNN COUNTY
Clerk of Court
District and County Courts
PO Box 136
Manning, ND 58642-0136

## EDDY COUNTY
Clerk of Court
District and County Courts
524 Central Ave
New Rockford, ND 58356

## EMMONS COUNTY
Clerk of Court
District and County Courts
PO Box 905
Linton, ND 58552

## FOSTER COUNTY
Clerk of Court
District and County Courts
PO Box 257
Carrington, ND 58421

## GOLDEN VALLEY COUNTY
Clerk of Court
District and County Courts
Box 596
Beach, ND 58621

## GRAND FORKS COUNTY
Clerk of Court
District and County Courts
PO Box 5939
Grand Forks, ND 58206-5939

## GRANT COUNTY
Clerk of Court
District and County Courts
Box 258
Carson, ND 58529

## GRIGGS COUNTY
Clerk of Court
District and County Courts
PO Box 326
Cooperstown, ND 58425

## HETTINGER COUNTY
Clerk of Court
District and County Courts
Box 668
Mott, ND 58646

## KIDDER COUNTY
Clerk of Court
District and County Courts
PO Box 66
Steele, ND 58482

## LA MOURE COUNTY
Clerk of Court
District and County Courts
Box 5
La Moure, ND 58458

## LOGAN COUNTY
Clerk of Court
District and County Courts
PO Box 6
Napoleon, ND 58561-0006

## MCHENRY COUNTY
Clerk of Court
District and County Courts
PO Box 117
Towner, ND 58788

## MCINTOSH COUNTY
Clerk of Court
District and County Courts
PO Box 179
Ashley, ND 58413

## MCKENZIE COUNTY
County Court Clerk
District and County Court
Box 546
Watford City, ND 58854

## MCLEAN COUNTY
Clerk of Court
District and County Courts
PO Box 1108
Washburn, ND 58577

## MERCER COUNTY
Clerk of Court
District and County Courts
PO Box 39
Stanton, ND 58571

## MORTON COUNTY
Clerk of Court
District and County Courts
210 2nd Avenue N.W.
Mandan, ND 58554

## MOUNTRAIL COUNTY
Clerk of Court
District and County Courts
PO Box 69
Stanley, ND 58784

## NELSON COUNTY
Clerk of Court
District and County Courts
PO Box 565
Lakota, ND 58344

## OLIVER COUNTY
Clerk of Court
District and County Courts
Box 125
Center, ND 58530

## PEMBINA COUNTY
Clerk of Court
District and County Courts
PO Box 357
Cavalier, ND 58220

## PIERCE COUNTY
Clerk of Court
District and County Courts
240 SE 2nd Street
Rugby, ND 58368

## RAMSEY COUNTY
Clerk of Court
District and County Courts
524 4th Avenue, #4
Devils Lake, ND 58301

## RANSOM COUNTY
Clerk of Court
District and County Courts
PO Box 626
Lisbon, ND 58054

## RENVILLE COUNTY
Clerk of Court
District and County Courts
PO Box 68
Mohall, ND 58761

## RICHLAND COUNTY
County Court Clerk
County Court
413 3rd Avenue N
Wahpeton, ND 58075

## ROLETTE COUNTY
Clerk of Court
District and County Courts
Box 460
Rolla, ND 58367

## SARGENT COUNTY
Clerk of Court
District and County Courts
645 Main Street
Forman, ND 58032

## SHERIDAN COUNTY
Clerk of Court
District and County Courts
PO Box 668
McClusky, ND 58463

## SIOUX COUNTY
Clerk of Court
District and County Courts
Box L
Fort Yates, ND 58538

## SLOPE COUNTY
Clerk of Court
District and County Courts
PO Box JJ
Amidon, ND 58620

## STARK COUNTY
Clerk of Court
District and County Courts
PO Box 130
Dickinson, ND 58602

## STEELE COUNTY
Clerk of Court
District and County Courts
PO Box 296
Finley, ND 58230

## STUTSMAN COUNTY
Clerk of Court
District and County Courts
511 2nd Avenue SE
Jamestown, ND 58401

## TOWNER COUNTY
Clerk of Court
District and County Courts
Box 517
Cando, ND 58324

## TRAILL COUNTY
Clerk of Court
District and County Courts
Box 805
Hillsboro, ND 58045

## WALSH COUNTY
County Court Clerk
County Court
600 Cooper Ave
Grafton, ND 58237

## WARD COUNTY
Clerk of Court
District and County Courts
315 S.E. 3rd
Minot, ND 58702-5005

## WELLS COUNTY
Clerk of Court
District and County Courts
Box 596
Fessenden, ND 58438

## WILLIAMS COUNTY
Clerk of Court
District and County Courts
PO Box 2047
Williston, ND 58801

# NEBRASKA

## ADAMS COUNTY
County Court Clerk
District and County Court
PO Box 95
Hastings, NE 68902-0095

## ANTELOPE COUNTY
County Court Clerk
District and County Court
501 Main Street
Neligh, NE 68756

## ARTHUR COUNTY
County Court Clerk
District and County Court
PO Box 146
Arthur, NE 69121

## BANNER COUNTY
Clerk of Court
District and County Court
PO Box 67
Harrisburg, NE 69345

**BLAINE COUNTY**
Clerk of Court
District and County Court
PO Box 136
Brewster, NE 68821

**BOONE COUNTY**
Clerk of Court
District and County Court
Government Center
Albion, NE 68620

**BOX BUTTE COUNTY**
County Court Clerk
District and County Court
PO Box 613
Alliance, NE 69301

**BOYD COUNTY**
County Court Clerk
District and County Court
PO Box 396
Butte, NE 68722

**BROWN COUNTY**
Clerk of Court
District and County Court
148 West 4th
Ainsworth, NE 69210

**BUFFALO COUNTY**
Clerk of Court
District and County Court
16th and Central
Kearney, NE 68848

**BURT COUNTY**
Clerk of Court
District and County Court
111 North 13th Street
Tekamah, NE 68061

**BUTLER COUNTY**
County Court Clerk
District and County Court
451 N. 5th Street
David City, NE 68632

**CASS COUNTY**
Clerk of Court
District and County Court
346 Main Street
Plattsmouth, NE 68048-1957

**CEDAR COUNTY**
County Court Clerk
District and County Court
101 W. Broadway
Hartington, NE 68739

**CHASE COUNTY**
Clerk of Court
District and County Court
PO Box 1299
Imperial, NE 69033

**CHERRY COUNTY**
Clerk of Court
District and County Court
365 North Main
Valentine, NE 69201

## CHEYENNE COUNTY
County Court Clerk
District and County Court
1000 10th Ave
Sidney, NE 69162

## CLAY COUNTY
County Court Clerk
District and County Court
PO Box 147
Clay Center, NE 68933

## COLFAX COUNTY
County Court Clerk
District and County Court
411 East 11th Street
Schuyler, NE 68661

## CUMING COUNTY
County Court Clerk
District and County Court
200 South Lincoln
West Point, NE 68788

## CUSTER COUNTY
Clerk of Court
District and County Court
431 South 10th Street
Broken Bow, NE 68822

## DAKOTA COUNTY
County Court Clerk
District and County Court
PO Box 385
Dakota City, NE 68731

## DAWES COUNTY
County Court Clerk
District and County Court
PO Box 806
Chadron, NE 69337

## DAWSON COUNTY
County Court Clerk
District and County Court
700 N. Washington
Lexington, NE 68850

## DEUEL COUNTY
Clerk of Court
District and County Court
PO Box 327
Chappell, NE 69129

## DIXON COUNTY
County Court Clerk
District and County Court
PO Box 497
Ponca, NE 68770

## DODGE COUNTY
County Court Clerk
District and County Court
428 N. Broad Street
Fremont, NE 68025

## DOUGLAS COUNTY
Clerk of Court
District and County Court
1701 Famam
Omaha, NE 68183

## DUNDY COUNTY
County Court Clerk
District and County Court
7th and Chief
Benkelman, NE 69021

## FILLMORE COUNTY
County Court Clerk
District and County Court
PO Box 66
Geneva, NE 68361

## FRANKLIN COUNTY
County Court Clerk
District and County Court
PO Box 174
Franklin, NE 68939

## FRONTIER COUNTY
County Court Clerk
District and County Court
PO Box 38
Stockville, NE 69042

## FURNAS COUNTY
County Court Clerk
District and County Court
PO Box 373
Beaver City, NE 68926

## GAGE COUNTY
County Court Clerk
District and County Court
PO Box 219
Beatrice, NE 68310-0219

## GARDEN COUNTY
County Court Clerk
District and County Court
PO Box 465
Oshkosh, NE 69154

## GARFIELD COUNTY
County Court Clerk
District and County Court
PO Box 431
Burwell, NE 68823

## GOSPER COUNTY
County Court Clerk
District and County Court
PO Box 55
Elwood, NE 68937

## GRANT COUNTY
County Court Clerk
District and County Court
PO Box 97
Hyannis, NE 69350

## GREELEY COUNTY
Clerk of Court
District and County Court
PO Box 287
Greeley, NE 68842

## HALL COUNTY
County Court Clerk
District and County Court
111 W. First
Grand Island, NE 68802

## HAMILTON COUNTY
County Court Clerk
District and County Court
1111 13th Street
Aurora, NE 68818

## HARLAN COUNTY
Clerk of Court
District and County Court
PO Box 379
Alma, NE 68920

## HAYES COUNTY
County Court Clerk
District and County Court
Hayes County Courthouse
Hayes Center, NE 69032

## HITCHCOCK COUNTY
County Court Clerk
District and County Court
PO Box 366
Trenton, NE 69044

## HOLT COUNTY
County Court Clerk
District and County Court
204 N. 4th Street
O'Neill, NE 68763

## HOOKER COUNTY
County Court Clerk
District and County Court
PO Box 263
Mullen, NE 69152

## HOWARD COUNTY
County Court Clerk
District and County Court
PO Box 94
St. Paul, NE 68873

## JEFFERSON COUNTY
Clerk of Court
District and County Court
411 4th Street
Fairbury, NE 68352

## JOHNSON COUNTY
County Court Clerk
District and County Court
PO Box 285
Tecumseh, NE 68450

## KEARNEY COUNTY
County Court Clerk
District and County Court
PO Box 377
Minden, NE 68959

## KEITH COUNTY
County Court Clerk
District and County Court
PO Box 358
Ogallala, NE 69153

## KEYA PAHA COUNTY
County Court Clerk
District and County Court
PO Box 311
Springview, NE 68778

## KIMBALL COUNTY
Clerk of Court
District and County Court
114 East 3rd Street
Kimball, NE 69145

## KNOX COUNTY
County Court Clerk
District and County Court
PO Box 125
Center, NE 68724

## LANCASTER COUNTY
County Court Clerk
District and County Court
555 South 10th Street
Lincoln, NE 68508

## LINCOLN COUNTY
Clerk of Court
District and County Court
301 North Jeffers
North Platte, NE 69103

## LOGAN COUNTY
County Court Clerk
District and County Court
PO Box 202
Stapleton, NE 69163

## LOUP COUNTY
Clerk of Court
District and County Court
PO Box 146
Taylor, NE 68879

## MADISON COUNTY
County Court Clerk
District and County Court
PO Box 230
Madison, NE 68748

## MCPHERSON COUNTY
Clerk of Court
District and Justice Court
PO Box 122
Tryon, NE 69167

## MERRICK COUNTY
County Court Clerk
District and County Court
PO Box 27
Central City, NE 68826

## MORRILL COUNTY
County Court Clerk
District and County Court
PO Box 418
Bridgeport, NE 69336

## NANCE COUNTY
County Court Clerk
District and County Court
PO Box 837
Fullerton, NE 68638

## NEMAHA COUNTY
County Court Clerk
District and County Court
1824 N. Street
Auburn, NE 68305

## NUCKOLLS COUNTY
County Court Clerk
District and County Court
PO Box 372
Nelson, NE 68961

## OTOE COUNTY
County Court Clerk
District and County Court
1021 Central Ave
Nebraska City, NE 68410

## PAWNEE COUNTY
County Court Clerk
District and County Court
PO Box 471
Pawnee City, NE 68420

## PERKINS COUNTY
County Court Clerk
District and County Court
PO Box 222
Grant, NE 69140

## PHELPS COUNTY
County Court Clerk
District and County Court
PO Box 255
Holdrege, NE 68949

## PIERCE COUNTY
County Court Clerk
District and County Court
111 W. Court Street
Pierce, NE 68767

## PLATTE COUNTY
County Court Clerk
District and County Court
PO Box 426
Columbus, NE 68602-0426

## POLK COUNTY
County Court Clerk
District and County Court
PO Box 447
Osceola, NE 68651

## RED WILLOW COUNTY
County Court Clerk
District and County Court
502 Norris Ave.
McCook, NE 69001

## RICHARDSON COUNTY
County Court Clerk
Richardson Courthouse, Rm 205
1700 Stone Street
Falls City, NE 68355

## ROCK COUNTY
County Court Clerk
District and County Court
400 State Street
Bassett, NE 68714

## SALINE COUNT
County Court Clerk
District and County Court
215 S. Court Street
Wilber, NE 68465

**SARPY COUNTY**
County Court Clerk
District and County Court
1210 Golden Gate Drive
Papillion, NE 68046

**SAUNDERS COUNTY**
Clerk of Court
District and County Court
433 North Chestnut
Wahoo, NE 68066

**SCOTTS BLUFF COUNTY**
County Court Clerk
District and County Court
1725 10th Street
Gering, NE 69341

**SEWARD COUNTY**
County Court Clerk
District and County Court
PO Box 37
Seward, NE 68434

**SHERIDAN COUNTY**
County Court Clerk
District and County Court
PO Box 430
Rushville, NE 69360

**SHERMAN COUNTY**
Clerk of Court
District and County Court
630 O. Street
Loup City, NE 68853

**SIOUX COUNTY**
County Court Clerk
District and County Court
PO Box 477
Harrison, NE 69346

**STANTON COUNTY**
County Court Clerk
District and County Court
PO Box 536
Stanton, NE 68779

**THAYER COUNTY**
County Court Clerk
District and County Court
PO Box 94
Hebron, NE 68370

**THOMAS COUNTY**
County Court Clerk
District and County Court
PO Box 233
Thedford, NE 69166

**THURSTON COUNTY**
County Court Clerk
District and County Court
5th and Main
Pender, NE 68047

**VALLEY COUNTY**
Clerk of Court
District and County Court
125 South 15th Street
Ord, NE 68862

## WASHINGTON COUNTY
County Court Clerk
District and County Court
1555 Colfax Street
Blair, NE 68008

## WAYNE COUNTY
Clerk of Court
District and County Court
510 Pearl Street
Wayne, NE 68787

## WEBSTER COUNTY
Clerk of Court
District and County Court
621 North Cedar
Red Cloud, NE 68970

## WHEELER COUNTY
County Court Clerk
District and County Court
PO Box 127
Bartlett, NE 68622

## YORK COUNTY
Clerk of Court
District and County Court
510 Lincoln Ave
York, NE 68467

# NEW HAMPSHIRE

## BELKNAP COUNTY
Superior Court Clerk
Superior Court
64 Court Street
Laconia, NH 03246

## CARROLL COUNTY
Superior Court Clerk
Superior Court
PO Box 157
Ossipee, NH 03864

## CHESHIRE COUNTY
Superior Court Clerk
Superior Court
12 Court Street
Keene, NH 03431

## COOS COUNTY
Superior Court Clerk
Superior Court
148 Main
Lancaster, NH 03584

## GRAFTON COUNTY
Superior Court Clerk
Superior Court
RR1 Box 65
North Haverhill, NH 03774

## HILLSBOROUGH COUNTY
Superior Court Clerk
Superior Court-North
300 Chestnut Street
Manchester, NH 03101

## HILLSBOROUGH COUNTY
Superior Court Clerk
Superior Court-South
30 Spring Street
Nashua, NH 03061-2072

## MERRIMACK COUNTY

Superior Court Clerk
Superior Court
163 N. Main
Concord, NH 03302-2880

## ROCKINGHAM COUNTY

Superior Court Clerk
Superior Court
1 Hampton Road
Exeter, NH 03833

## STRAFFORD COUNTY

Supcrior Court Clerk
Superior Court
PO Box 799
Dover, NH 03820

## SULLIVAN COUNTY

Superior Court Clerk
Superior Court
22 Main Street
Newport, NH 03773

## NEW JERSEY

## ATLANTIC COUNTY

Superior Court Clerk
Atlantic County Courthouse
1201 Baccarat
Atlantic City, NJ 08401

## BERGEN COUNTY

Superior Court Clerk
Bergen County Courthouse
10 Main Street
Hackensack, NJ 07601

## BURLINGTON COUNTY

Superior Court Clerk
Burlington County Courthouse
49 Rancocas Rd
Mount Holly, NJ 08060

## CAMDEN COUNTY

Superior Court Clerk
Camden County Courthouse
101 South 5th Street
Camden, NJ 08103

## CAPE MAY COUNTY

Superior Court Clerk
Cape May Courthouse
#4 Moore Rd
Cape May , NJ 08210

## CUMBERLAND COUNTY

Superior Court Clerk
Cumberland County Courthouse
Broad and Fayette Street
Bridgeton, NJ 08302

## ESSEX COUNTY

Superior Court Clerk
Essex County Courthouse
50 West Market
Newark, NJ 07103

## GLOUCESTER COUNTY

Superior Court Clerk
Gloucester County Courthouse
1 North Broad
Woodbury, NJ 08096

## HUDSON COUNTY
Superior Court Clerk
Hudson County Courthouse
583 Newark Ave
Jersey City, NJ 07306

## HUNTERDON COUNTY
Superior Court Clerk
Hunterdon County Courthouse
71 Main Street
Flemington, NJ 08822

## MERCER COUNTY
Superior Court Clerk
Mercer County Courthouse
209 South Broad Street
Trenton, NJ 08650

## MIDDLESEX COUNTY
Superior Court Clerk
Middlesex County Courthouse
PO Box 2673
New Brunswick, NJ 08903

## MONMOUTH COUNTY
Superior Court Clerk
Monmouth County Courthouse
71 Monument Park
Freehold, NJ 07728

## MORRIS COUNTY
Superior Court Clerk
Morris County Courthouse
#1 Court Street
Morristown, NJ 07960

## OCEAN COUNTY
Superior Court Clerk
Ocean County Courthouse
118 Washington Street
Toms River, NJ 08754

## PASSAIC COUNTY
Superior Court Clerk
Passaic County Courthouse
77 Hamilton Street
Paterson, NJ 07505

## SALEM COUNTY
Superior Court Clerk
Salem County Courthouse
92 Market Street
Salem, NJ 08079

## SOMERSET COUNTY
Superior Court Clerk
Somerset County Courthouse
PO Box 3000
Somerville, NJ 08876

## SUSSEX COUNTY
Superior Court Clerk
Sussex County Judicial Center
43-47 High Street
Newton, NJ 07860

## UNION COUNTY
Superior Court Clerk
Union County Courthouse
PO Box 6073
Elizabeth, NJ 07207-6073

**Adoption Searches Made Easier**

## WARREN COUNTY
Superior Court Clerk
Warren County Courthouse
413 2nd Street
Belvidere, NJ 07823

# NEVADA

## CARSON CITY COUNTY
District Court Clerk
First Judicial District
198 North Carson Street
Carson City, NV 89701

## CHURCHILL COUNTY
District Court Clerk
Third Judicial District
73 North Maine Street
Fallon, NV 89406

## CLARK COUNTY
District Court Clerk
Eighth Judicial District
200 South 3rd Street
Las Vegas, NV 89155

## DOUGLAS COUNTY
District Court Clerk
Ninth Judicial District
1625 8th
Minden, NV 89423

## ELKO COUNTY
District Court Clerk
Fourth Judicial District
Elko Courthouse, Rm 204
Elko, NV 89801

## ESMERALDA COUNTY
District Court Clerk
Fifth Judicial District
PO Box 547
Goldfield, NV 89013

## EUREKA COUNTY
District Court Clerk
Seventh Judicial District
PO Box 677
Eureka, NV 89316

## HUMBOLDT COUNTY
District Court Clerk
Sixth Judicial District
50 West 5th Street
Winnemucca, NV 89445

## LANDER COUNTY
District Court Clerk
Sixth Judicial District
315 South Humboldt
Battle Mountain, NV 89820

## LINCOLN COUNTY
District Court Clerk
Seventh Judicial District
PO Box 90
Pioche, NV 89043

## LYON COUNTY
District Court Clerk
Third Judicial District
PO Box 816
Yerington, NV 89447

## MINERAL COUNTY
District Court Clerk
Fifth Judicial District
105 South A Street
Hawthorne, NV 89415

## NYE COUNTY
District Court Clerk
Fifth Judicial District
PO Box 1031
Tonopah, NV 89049

## PERSHING COUNTY
District Court Clerk
Sixth Judicial District
PO Box 820
Lovelock, NV 89419

## STOREY COUNTY
District Court Clerk
First Judicial District
Storey County Courthouse
Virginia City, NV 89440

## WASHOE COUNTY
District Court Clerk
Second Judicial District
PO Box 11130
Reno, NV 89520

## WHITE PINE COUNTY
District Court Clerk
Seventh Judicial District
PO Box 659
Ely, NV 89301

# NEW YORK

## ALBANY COUNTY
Clerk of Court
Albany County Courthouse
Columbia and Eagle Street
Albany, NY 12207

## ALLEGANY COUNTY
Clerk of Court
Allegany County Courthouse
Belmont, NY 14813

## BRONX COUNTY
Civil Court Clerk
City of New York-Bronx County
851 Grand Concourse
Bronx, NY 10451

## BROOME COUNTY
County Court Clerk
County Office Building
Governmental Plaza
Binghamton, NY 13902

## CATTARAUGUS COUNTY
Clerk of Court
County Courthouse
303 Court Street
Little Valley, NY 14755

## CAYUGA COUNTY
Clerk of Court
County Courthouse
160 Genesee Street
Auburn, NY 13021

## CHAUTAUQUA COUNTY
Clerk of Court
County Courthouse
PO Box 292
Mayville, NY 14757

## CHEMUNG COUNTY
Clerk of Court
County Courthouse
203 Lake
Elmira, NY 14902

## CHENANGO COUNTY
Clerk of Court
County Office Building
5 Court Street
Norwich, NY 13815

## CLINTON COUNTY
Clerk of Court
Government Center
137 Margaret Street
Plattsburgh, NY 12901

## COLUMBIA COUNTY
Clerk of Court
Columbia County Courthouse
Allen Street
Hudson, NY 12534

## CORTLAND COUNTY
Clerk of Court
Cortland County Courthouse
46 Greenbush Street, Ste 301
Cortland, NY 13045

## DELAWARE COUNTY
Clerk of Court
County Courthouse
3 Court Street
Delhi, NY 13753

## DUTCHESS COUNTY
Clerk of Court
County Courthouse
22 Market Street
Poughkeepsie, NY 12601

## ERIE COUNTY
Supreme Court Clerk
County Courthouse
25 Delaware Avenue
Buffalo, NY 14202

## ESSEX COUNTY
Clerk of Court
County Courthouse
Government Center
Elizabethtown, NY 12932

## FRANKLIN COUNTY
Clerk of Court
Franklin County Courthouse
63 West Main Street
Malone, NY 12953

## FULTON COUNT
Clerk of Court
County Courthouse
West Main Street
Johnstown, NY 12095

## GENESEE COUNTY
Clerk of Court
Courthouse
PO Box 379
Batavia, NY 14021

## GREENE COUNTY
Clerk of Court
County Courthouse
PO Box 446
Catskill, NY 12414

## HAMILTON COUNTY
Clerk of Court
Hamilton County Courthouse
PO Box 204
Lake Pleasant, NY 12108

## HERKIMER COUNTY
Clerk of Court
County Courthouse
PO Box 111
Herkimer, NY 13350

## JEFFERSON COUNTY
Clerk of Court
County Courthouse
175 Arsenal Street
Watertown, NY 13601

## KINGS COUNTY
Clerk of Court
Kings County Court
141 Livingston Street, Rm 303
Brooklyn, NY 11201

## LEWIS COUNTY
Clerk of Court
County Courthouse
7660 State Street
Lowville, NY 13367

## LIVINGSTON COUNTY
Clerk of Court
Livingston County Courthouse
Courthouse Square
Geneseo, NY 14454

## MADISON COUNTY
Clerk of Court
County Courthouse
PO Box 668
Wampsville, NY 13163

## MONROE COUNTY
Clerk of Court
Monroe County Office Building
39 West Main Street, Rm 105
Rochester, NY 14614

## MONTGOMERY COUNTY
Clerk of Court
Montgomery County Courthouse
Courthouse Square
Fonda, NY 12068

## NASSAU COUNTY
Court Clerk
First District
99 Main Street
Hempstead, NY 11550

**NASSAU COUNTY**
Clerk of Court
Third District Court
575 Middle Neck Rd
Great Neck, NY 11024

**NASSAU COUNTY**
Clerk of Court
Fourth District Court
87 Bethpage Rd
Hicksville, NY 11801

**NASSAU COUNTY**
Clerk of Court
City Court of Glen Cove
146 Glen Street
Glen Cove, NY 11542

**NASSAU COUNTY**
Clerk of Court
City Court of Long Beach
One West Chester Street
Long Beach, NY 11561

**NEW YORK COUNTY**
Civil Court Clerk
Supreme Court Building
60 Centre Street, Rm 102-B
New York, NY 10013

**NIAGARA COUNTY**
Clerk of Court
County Courthouse
175 Hawley Street-Filing Room
Lockport, NY 14095-0461

**ONEIDA COUNTY**
Clerk of Court
County Courthouse
800 Park Avenue
Utica, NY 13501

**ONONDAGA COUNTY**
Clerk of Court
Courthouse, Room 200
401 Montgomery Street
Syracuse, NY 13202

**ONTARIO COUNTY**
Clerk of Court
Courthouse
25 Pleasant Street
Canandaigua, NY 14424

**ORANGE COUNTY**
Clerk of Court
County Courthouse
255 Main Street
Goshen, NY 10924

**ORLEANS COUNTY**
Clerk of Court
County Courthouse
Courthouse Square
Albion, NY 14411

**OSWEGO COUNTY**
Supreme Court Clerk
County Courthouse
46 E. Bridge Street
Oswego, NY 13126

**OTSEGO COUNTY**
Clerk of Court
County Courthouse
197 Main Street
Cooperstown, NY 13326

**PUTNAM COUNTY**
Clerk of Court
County Courthouse
40 Gleneida Avenue
Carmel, NY 10512

**QUEENS COUNTY**
Civil Court Clerk
Queens County Civil Court
12055 Queens Boulevard
Kew Gardens, NY 11415

**RENSSELAER COUNTY**
County Court Clerk
Rensselaer County Courthouse
2nd and Congress
Troy, NY 12180

**RICHMOND COUNTY**
Civil Court Clerk
County Courthouse
927 Castleton Ave
Staten Island, NY 10310

**ROCKLAND COUNTY**
Supreme Court Clerk
County Courthouse
27 New Hempstead Rd
New City, NY 10956

**SARATOGA COUNTY**
Clerk of Court
County Courthouse
30 McMaster Street
Ballston Spa, NY 12020

**SCHENECTADY COUNTY**
Clerk of Court
County Courthouse
620 State Street
Schenectady, NY 12305

**SCHOHARIE COUNTY**
Clerk of Court
Schoharie County Courthouse
30 Main Street
Schoharie, NY 12157

**SCHUYLER COUNTY**
Clerk of Court
County Courthouse
105 Ninth Street
Watkins Glen, NY 14891

**SENECA COUNTY**
Clerk of Court
County Courthouse
PO Box 638
Waterloo, NY 13165

**STEUBEN COUNTY**
Clerk of Court
County Courthouse
3 Pulteney Square
Bath, NY 14810

## ST. LAWRENCE COUNTY
County Court Clerk
County Courthouse
48 Court Street
Canton, NY 13617-1198

## SUFFOLK COUNTY
Supreme Court Clerk
County Courthouse
310 Center Drive
Riverhead, NY 11901

## SULLIVAN COUNTY
Clerk of Court
County Courthouse
100 North Street
Monticello, NY 12701

## TIOGA COUNTY
Clerk of Court
County Courthouse
16 Court Street
Owego, NY 13827

## TOMPKINS COUNTY
Clerk of Court
County Courthouse
320 N. Tioga Street
Ithaca, NY 14850

## ULSTER COUNTY
Clerk of Court
County Courthouse
Box 1800
Kingston, NY 12401

## WARREN COUNTY
Clerk of Court
Warren County Municipal Center
Government Center
Lake George, NY 12845

## WASHINGTON COUNTY
Clerk of Court
Courthouse
Upper Broadway
Fort Edward, NY 12828

## WAYNE COUNTY
Clerk of Court
County Courthouse
9 Pearl Street
Lyons, NY 14489-0608

## WESTCHESTER COUNTY
Clerk of Court
County Courthouse
110 Grove Street, Rm 330
White Plains, NY 10601

## WYOMING COUNTY
Clerk of Court
County Courthouse
143 N. Main
Warsaw, NY 14569

## YATES COUNTY
Clerk of Court
County Courthouse
110 Court Street
Penn Yan, NY 14527

# OHIO

## ADAMS COUNTY
Clerk of Courts
Court of Common Pleas
110 West Main Street
West Union, OH 45693

## ALLEN COUNTY
Clerk of Court
Court of Common Pleas
301 North Main Street
Lima, OH 45802

## ASHLAND COUNTY
Clerk of Court
Court of Common Pleas
142 West 2nd Street
Ashland, OH 44805

## ASHTABULA COUNTY
Clerk of Court
Court of Common Pleas
25 West Jefferson Street
Jefferson, OH 44047

## ATHENS COUNTY
Clerk of Court
Court of Common Pleas
Athens County Courthouse
Athens, OH 45701

## AUGLAIZE COUNTY
Clerk of Court
Court of Common Pleas
PO Box 1958
Wapakoneta, OH 45895

## BELMONT COUNTY
Clerk of Court
Court of Common Pleas
101 Main Street
St. Clairsville, OH 43950

## BROWN COUNTY
Clerk of Court
Court of Common Pleas
101 South Main
Georgetown, OH 45121

## BUTLER COUNTY
Clerk of Court
Court of Common Pleas
101 High Street
Hamilton, OH 45011

## CARROLL COUNTY
Clerk of Court
Court of Common Pleas
PO Box 367
Carrollton, OH 44615

## CHAMPAIGN COUNTY
Clerk of Court
Court of Common Pleas
214 North Main Street
Urbana, OH 43078

## CLARK COUNTY
Clerk of Courts
Court of Common Pleas
101 North Limestone Street
Springfield, OH 45502

**Adoption Searches Made Easier**

**CLERMONT COUNTY**
Clerk of Court
Court of Common Pleas
270 Main Street
Batavia, OH 45103

**CLINTON COUNTY**
Clerk of Court
Court of Common Pleas
46 South South Street
Wilmington, OH 45177

**COLUMBIANA COUNTY**
Clerk of Court
Court of Common Pleas
105 South Market Street
Lisbon, OH 44432

**COSHOCTON COUNTY**
Clerk of Court
Court of Common Pleas
318 Main Street
Coshocton, OH 43812

**CRAWFORD COUNTY**
Clerk of Court
Court of Common Pleas
112 East Mansfield
Bucyrus, OH 44820

**CUYAHOGA COUNTY**
Clerk of Court
Court of Common Pleas
1200 Ontario Street
Cleveland, OH 44113

**DARKE COUNTY**
Clerk of Court
Court of Common Pleas
Darke County Courthouse
Greenville, OH 45331

**DEFIANCE COUNTY**
Clerk of Court
Court of Common Pleas
221 Clinton
Defiance, OH 43512

**DELAWARE COUNTY**
Clerk of Court
Court of Common Pleas
91 North Sandusky
Delaware, OH 43015

**ERIE COUNTY**
Clerk of Court
Court of Common Pleas
323 Columbus Ave
Sandusky, OH 44870

**FAIRFIELD COUNTY**
Clerk of Court
Court of Common Pleas
224 East Main
Lancaster, OH 43130

**FAYETTE COUNTY**
Clerk of Court
Court of Common Pleas
110 East Court Street
Washington House, OH 43160

## FRANKLIN COUNTY
Clerk of Court
Court of Common Pleas
369 South High Street
Columbus, OH 43215

## FULTON COUNTY
Clerk of Court
Court of Common Pleas
210 South Fulton Street, Rm 203
Wauseon, OH 43567

## GALLIA COUNTY
Clerk of Court
Court of Common Pleas
Government Center
Gallipolis, OH 45631

## GEAUGA COUNTY
Clerk of Court
Court of Common Pleas
Government Center
Chardon, OH 44024

## GREENE COUNTY
Clerk of Court
Court of Common Pleas
45 North Detroit Street
Xenia, OH 45385

## GUERNSEY COUNTY
Clerk of Court
Court of Common Pleas
PO Box 766
Cambridge, OH 43725

## HAMILTON COUNTY
Clerk of Court
Court of Common Pleas
1000 Main Street, Rm 315
Cincinnati, OH 45202

## HANCOCK COUNTY
Clerk of Court
Court of Common Pleas
300 South Main Street
Findlay, OH 45840

## HARDIN COUNTY
Clerk of Court
Court of Common Pleas
1 Courthouse Sq., #310
Kenton, OH 43326

## HARRISON COUNTY
Clerk of Court
Court of Common Pleas
100 West Market
Cadiz, OH 43907

## HENRY COUNTY
Clerk of Court
Court of Common Pleas
660 North Perry
Napoleon, OH 43545

## HIGHLAND COUNTY
Clerk of Court
Court of Common Pleas
PO Box 821
Hillsboro, OH 45133

## HOCKING COUNTY
Clerk of Court
Court of Common Pleas
PO Box 108
Logan, OH 43138

## HOLMES COUNTY
Clerk of Court
Court of Common Pleas
1 East Jackson Street, Ste 306
Millersburg, OH 44654

## HURON COUNTY
Clerk of Court
Court of Common Pleas
2 East Main Street
Norwalk, OH 44857

## JACKSON COUNTY
Clerk of Court
Court of Common Pleas
226 East Main Street
Jackson, OH 45640

## JEFFERSON COUNTY
Clerk of Court
Court of Common Pleas
301 Market Street
Steubenville, OH 43952

## KNOX COUNTY
Clerk of Court
County of Common Pleas
114 East Chestnut Street
Mount Vernon, OH 43050

## LAKE COUNTY
Clerk of Court
Court of Common Pleas
PO Box 490
Painesville, OH 44077

## LAWRENCE COUNTY
Clerk of Court
Court of Common Pleas
PO Box 208
Ironton, OH 45638

## LICKING COUNTY
Clerk of Court
Court of Common Pleas
PO Box 878
Newark, OH 43055-0878

## LOGAN COUNTY
Clerk of Court
Court of Common Pleas
100 South Main
Bellefontaine, OH 43311

## LORAIN COUNTY
Clerk of Court
Court of Common Pleas
308 2nd Street
Elyria, OH 44036

## LUCAS COUNTY
Clerk of Court
Court of Common Pleas
Adams & Erie Street
Toledo, OH 43624

## MADISON COUNTY
Clerk of Court
Court of Common Pleas
1 North Main
London, OH 43140

## MAHONING COUNTY
Clerk of Court
Court of Common Pleas
120 Market Street
Youngstown, OH 44503

## MARION COUNTY
Clerk of Court
Court of Common Pleas
100 North Main
Marion, OH 43302

## MEDINA COUNTY
Clerk of Court
Court of Common Pleas
93 Public Square
Medina, OH 44256

## MEIGS COUNTY
Clerk of Court
Court of Common Pleas
2nd and Court Street
Pomeroy, OH 45769

## MERCER COUNTY
Clerk of Court
Court of Common Pleas
101 North Main
Celina, OH 45822

## MIAMI COUNTY
Clerk of Court
Court of Common Pleas
201 West Main Street
Troy, OH 45373

## MONROE COUNTY
Clerk of Court
Court of Common Pleas
101 North Main Street, Rm 38
Woodsfield, OH 43793

## MONTGOMERY COUNTY
Clerk of Court
Court of Common Pleas
41 North Perry Street, Rm 9
Dayton, OH 45422

## MORGAN COUNTY
Clerk of Court
Court of Common Pleas
19 East Main Street
McConnelsville, OH 43756

## MORROW COUNTY
Clerk of Courts
Court of Common Pleas
48 East High Street
Mount Gilead, OH 43338

## MUSKINGUM COUNTY
Clerk of Court
Court of Common Pleas
401 Main
Zanesville, OH 43702

**NOBLE COUNTY**
Clerk of Court
Court of Common Pleas
350 Courthouse, 3rd Floor
Caldwell, OH 43724

**OTTAWA COUNTY**
Clerk of Court
Court of Common Pleas
315 Madison Street, Rm 304
Port Clinton, OH 43452

**PAULDING COUNTY**
Clerk of Court
Court of Common Pleas
Courthouse, 1st Floor
Paulding, OH 45879

**PERRY COUNTY**
Clerk of Court
Court of Common Pleas
PO Box 67
New Lexington, OH 43764

**PICKAWAY COUNTY**
Clerk of Court
Court of Common Pleas
Courthouse
Circleville, OH 43113

**PIKE COUNTY**
Clerk of Court
Court of Common Pleas
100 East Second Street
Waverly, OH 45690

**PORTAGE COUNTY**
Clerk of Court
Court of Common Pleas
203 West Main
Ravenna, OH 44266

**PREBLE COUNTY**
Clerk of Court
Court of Common Pleas
100 Main Street
Eaton, OH 45320

**PUTNAM COUNTY**
Clerk of Court
Court of Common Pleas
245 East Main Street, Ste 301
Ottawa, OH 45875

**RICHLAND COUNTY**
Clerk of Court
Court of Common Pleas
50 Park Ave
Mansfield, OH 44902

**ROSS COUNTY**
Clerk of Court
Court of Common Pleas
2 North Paint, Ste A
Chillicothe, OH 45601

**SANDUSKY COUNTY**
Clerk of Court
Court of Common Pleas
100 North Park Ave
Fremont, OH 43420

## SCIOTO COUNTY
Clerk of Court
Court of Common Pleas
602 7th Street, Rm 205
Portsmouth, OH 45662

## SENECA COUNTY
Clerk of Court
Court of Common Pleas
103 South Washington
Tiffin, OH 44883

## SHELBY COUNTY
Clerk of Court
Court of Common Pleas
Main and Court Street
Sidney, OH 45365

## STARK COUNTY
Clerk of Court
Court of Common Pleas
110 Central Plaza South
Canton, OH 44702

## SUMMIT COUNTY
Clerk of Court
Court of Common Pleas
53 University Ave.
Akron, OH 44308-1662

## TRUMBULL COUNTY
Clerk of Court
Court of Common Pleas
160 High Street
Warren, OH 44481

## TUSCARAWAS COUNTY
Clerk of Court
Court of Common Pleas
125 East High Ave
New Philadelphia, OH 44663

## UNION COUNTY
Clerk of Court
Court of Common Pleas
215 West 5th Street
Marysville, OH 43040

## VAN WERT COUNTY
Clerk of Court
Court of Common Pleas
East Main Street
Van Wert, OH 45891

## VINTON COUNTY
Clerk of Court
Court of Common Pleas
100 East Main Street
McArthur, OH 45651

## WARREN COUNTY
Clerk of Court
Court of Common Pleas
500 Justice Drive
Lebanon, OH 45036

## WASHINGTON COUNTY
Clerk of Court
Court of Common Pleas
205 Putnam Street
Marietta, OH 45750

## WAYNE COUNTY
Clerk of Court
Court of Common Pleas
PO Box 113
Wooster, OH 44691

## WILLIAMS COUNTY
Clerk of Court
Court of Common Pleas
Courthouse, Third Floor
Bryan, OH 43506

## WOOD COUNTY
Clerk of Court
Court of Common Pleas
PO Box 829
Bowling Green, OH 43402

## WYANDOT COUNTY
Clerk of Court
Court of Common Pleas
Courthouse
Upper Sandusky, OH 43351

# OKLAHOMA

## ADAIR COUNTY
Clerk of Court
District Court
210 West Division
Stilwell, OK 74960

## ALFALFA COUNTY
Clerk of Court
District Court
300 South Grand
Cherokee, OK 73728

## ATOKA COUNTY
Clerk of Court
District Court
200 East Court Street
Atoka, OK 74525

## BEAVER COUNTY
Clerk of Court
District Court
PO Box 237
Beaver, OK 73932

## BECKHAM COUNTY
Clerk of Court
District Court
PO Box 520
Sayre, OK 73662

## BLAINE COUNTY
Clerk of Court
District Court
PO Box 399
Watonga, OK 73772

## BRYAN COUNTY
Clerk of Court
District Court
4th and Evergreen,
Durant, OK 74701

## CADDO COUNTY
Clerk of Court
District Court
Courthouse, PO Box 10
Anadarko, OK 73005

## CANADIAN COUNTY
Clerk of Court
District Court
PO Box 730
El Reno, OK 73036

## CARTER COUNTY
Clerk of Court
District Court
PO Box 37
Ardmore, OK 73402

## CHEROKEE COUNTY
Clerk of Court
District Court
213 West Delaware, Rm 300
Tahlequah, OK 74464

## CHOCTAW COUNTY
Clerk of Court
District Court
300 East Duke
Hugo, OK 74743

## CIMMARRON COUNTY
Clerk of Court
District Court
PO Box 788
Boise City, OK 73933

## CLEVELAND COUNTY
Clerk of Court
District Court
200 South Peters
Norman, OK 73069

## COAL COUNTY
Clerk of Court
District Court
3 North Main
Coalgate, OK 74538

## COMANCHE COUNTY
Clerk of Court
District Court
Courthouse, Rm 504
Lawton, OK 73501

## COTTON COUNTY
Clerk of Court
District Court
301 North Broadway
Walters, OK 73572

## CRAIG COUNTY
Clerk of Court
District Court
301 West Canadian
Vinita, OK 74301

## CREEK COUNTY
Clerk of Court
District Court
222 East Dewey
Sapulpa, OK 74067

## CUSTER COUNTY
Clerk of Court
District Court
PO Box D
Arapaho, OK 73620

## DELAWARE COUNTY
Clerk of Court
District Court
Box 407
Jay, OK 74346

## DEWEY COUNTY
Clerk of Court
District Court
PO Box 278
Taloga, OK 73667

## ELLIS COUNTY
Clerk of Court
District Court
PO Box 217
Arnette, OK 73832

## GARFIELD COUNTY
Clerk of Court
District Court
PO Box 3340
Enid, OK 73702

## GARVIN COUNTY
Clerk of Court
District Court
PO Box 239
Pauls Valley, OK 73075

## GRADY COUNTY
Clerk of Court
District Court
PO Box 605
Chickasha, OK 73023

## GRANT COUNTY
Clerk of Court
District Court
100 East Guthrie
Medford, OK 73759

## GREER COUNTY
Clerk of Court
District Court
PO Box 216
Mangum, OK 73554

## HARMON COUNTY
Clerk of Court
District Court
114 West Hollis
Hollis, OK 73550

## HARPER COUNTY
Clerk of Court
District Court
311 SE 1st
Buffalo, OK 73834

## HASKELL COUNTY
Clerk of Court
District Court
202 East Main
Stigler, OK 74462

## HUGHES COUNTY
Clerk of Court
District Court
PO Box 32
Holdenville, OK 74848

## JACKSON COUNTY
Clerk of Court
District Court
Courthouse, Rm 303
Altus, OK 73521

## JEFFERSON COUNTY
Clerk of Court
District Court
220 North Main, Rm 302
Waurika, OK 73573

## JOHNSTON COUNTY
Clerk of Court
District Court
414 West Main Street, Ste 201
Tishomingo, OK 73460

## KAY COUNTY
Clerk of Court
District Court
PO Box 428
Newkirk, OK 74647

## KINGFISHER COUNTY
Clerk of Court
District Court
PO Box 328
Kingfisher, OK 73750

## KIOWA COUNTY
Clerk of Court
District Court
PO Box 854
Hobart, OK 73651

## LATIMER COUNTY
Clerk of Court
District Court
109 North Central, Rm 202
Wilburton, OK 74578

## LE FLORE COUNTY
Clerk of Court
District Court
100 South Broadway
Poteau, OK 74953

## LINCOLN COUNTY
Clerk of Court
District Court
PO Box 307
Chandler, OK 74834

## LOGAN COUNTY
Clerk of Court
District Court
301 East Harrison
Guthrie, OK 73044

## LOVE COUNTY
Clerk of Court
District Court
405 West Main, Ste 201
Marietta, OK 73448

## MAJOR COUNTY
Clerk of Court
District Court
Courthouse
Fairview, OK 73737

## MARSHALL COUNTY
Clerk of Court
District Court
1 Plaza Square
Madill, OK 73446

## MAYES COUNTY
Clerk of Court
District Court
PO Box 867
Pryor, OK 74362

## MCCLAIN COUNTY
Clerk of Court
District Court
PO Box 631
Purcell, OK 73080

## MCCURTAIN COUNTY
Clerk of Court
District Court
PO Box 1378
Idabel, OK 74745

## MCINTOSH COUNTY
Clerk of Court
District Court
PO Box 426
Eufaula, OK 74432

## MURRAY COUNTY
Clerk of Court
District Court
PO Box 578
Sulphur, OK 73086

## MUSKOGEE COUNTY
Clerk of Court
District Court
PO Box 1350
Muskogee, OK 74402

## NOBLE COUNTY
Clerk of Court
District Court
300 Courthouse Dr, #14
Perry, OK 73077

## NOWATA COUNTY
Clerk of Court
District Court
229 North Maple
Nowata, OK 74048

## OKFUSKEE COUNTY
Clerk of Court
District Court
PO Box 30
Okemah, OK 74859

## OKLAHOMA COUNTY
Clerk of Court
District Court
320 Robert South Kerr Ave
Oklahoma City, OK 73102

## OKMULGEE COUNTY
Clerk of Court
District Court
7th and Seminole
Okmulgee, OK 74447

## OSAGE COUNTY
Clerk of Court
District Court
600 Grandview, Rm 301
Pawhuska, OK 74056-4253

## OTTAWA COUNTY
Clerk of Court
District Court
102 East Central Ave, #300
Miami, OK 74354-7043

## PAWNEE COUNTY
Clerk of Court
District Court
500 Harrison, Rm 300
Pawnee, OK 74058

## PAYNE COUNTY
Clerk of Court
District Court
6th and Husband, Rm 308
Stillwater, OK 74074

## PITTSBURG COUNTY
Clerk of Court
District Court
PO Box 460
McAlester, OK 74502

## PONTOTOC COUNTY
Clerk of Court
District Court
PO Box 427
Ada, OK 74820

## POTTAWATOMIE COUNTY
Clerk of Court
District Court
325 North Broadway
Shawnee, OK 74801

## PUSHMATAHA COUNTY
Clerk of Court
District Court
204 SW 3rd
Antlers, OK 74523

## ROGER MILLS COUNTY
Clerk of Court
District Court
PO Box 409
Cheyenne, OK 73628

## ROGERS COUNTY
Clerk of Court
District Court
PO Box 839
Claremore, OK 74018

## SEMINOLE COUNTY
Clerk of Court
District Court
PO Box 130
Wewoka, OK 74884

## SEQUOYAH COUNTY
Clerk of Court
District Court
Courthouse, Rm 10
Sallisaw, OK 74955

## STEPHENS COUNTY
Clerk of Court
District Court
101 South 11th Street
Duncan, OK 73533

## TEXAS COUNTY
Clerk of Court
District Court
PO Box 1081
Guymon, OK 73942

## TILLMAN COUNTY
Clerk of Court
District Court
10th & Gladstone
Frederick, OK 73542

## TULSA COUNTY
Clerk of Court
District Court
500 South Denver
Tulsa, OK 74103

## WAGONER COUNTY
Clerk of Court
District Court
PO Box 249
Wagoner, OK 74477

## WASHINGTON COUNTY
Clerk of Court
District Court
5th and Johnstone
Bartlesville, OK 74003

## WASHITA COUNTY
Clerk of Court
District Court
PO Box 397
Cordell, OK 73632

## WOODS COUNTY
Clerk of Court
District Court
PO Box 924
Alva, OK 73717

## WOODWARD COUNTY
Clerk of Court
District Court
1600 Main
Woodward, OK 73801

# OREGON

## BAKER COUNTY
Clerk of Court
Circuit and District Court
1995 Third Street
Baker City, OR 97814

## BENTON COUNTY
Clerk of Courts
Circuit and District Court
PO Box 1870
Corvallis, OR 97339

## CLACKAMAS COUNTY
Clerk of Courts
Circuit and District Court
807 Main Street
Oregon City, OR 97045

## CLATSOP COUNTY
Clerk of Court
Clatsop County Circuit Court
PO Box 835
Astoria, OR 97103

## DOUGLAS COUNTY
Clerk of Courts
Circuit and District Court
Justice Bldg, Rm 202
Roseburg, OR 97470

## COLUMBIA COUNTY
Clerk of Courts
Circuit and District Court
Courthouse
St. Helens, OR 97051

## GILLIAM COUNTY
Clerk of Courts
Circuit and District Court
PO Box 622
Condon, OR 97823

## COOS COUNTY
Clerk of Courts
Circuit and District Court
Courthouse
Coquille, OR 97423

## GRANT COUNTY
Clerk of Court
Grant County Circuit Court
PO Box 159
Canyon City, OR 97820

## CROOK COUNTY
Clerk of Courts
Circuit and District Court
Courthouse
Prineville, OR 97754

## HARNEY COUNTY
Clerk of Courts
Circuit and District Court
450 North Buena Vista
Burns, OR 97720

## CURRY COUNTY
Clerk of Courts
Circuit and District Court
PO Box H
Gold Beach, OR 97444

## HOOD RIVER COUNTY
Clerk of Courts
Circuit and District Court
309 State Street
Hood River, OR 97031

## DESCHUTES COUNTY
Clerk of Courts
Circuit and District Court
1100 NW Bond
Bend, OR 97701

## JACKSON COUNTY
Clerk of Courts
Circuit and District Court
100 South Oakdale
Medford, OR 97501

## JEFFERSON COUNTY
Clerk of Courts
Circuit and District Court
75 SE C Street ., 2nd Floor
Madras, OR 97741

## JOEPHINE COUNTY
Clerk of Courts
Circuit and District Court
Government Center
Grants Pass, OR 97526

## KLAMATH COUNTY
Clerk of Courts
Circuit and District Court
316 Main Street
Klamath Falls, OR 97601

## LAKE COUNTY
Clerk of Courts
Circuit and District Court
513 Center Street
Lakeview, OR 97630

## LANE COUNTY
Clerk of Courts
Circuit and District Court
125 East 8th Ave
Eugene, OR 97401

## LINCOLN COUNTY
Clerk of Courts
Circuit and District Court
225 West Olive
Newport, OR 97365

## LINN COUNTY
Clerk of Courts
Circuit and District Court
PO Box 1749
Albany, OR 97321

## MALHEUR COUNTY
Clerk of Courts
Circuit and District Court
251 B Street W
Vale, OR 97918

## MARION COUNTY
Clerk of Courts
Circuit and District Court
100 High Street
Salem, OR 97301

## MORROW COUNTY
Clerk of Courts
Circuit and District Court
PO Box 609
Heppner, OR 97836

## MULNOMAH COUNTY
Clerk of Courts
Circuit and District Court
1021 SW 4th Ave
Portland, OR 97204

## POLK COUNTY
Clerk of Courts
Circuit and District Court
Polk County Courthouse, Rm 301
Dallas, OR 97338

## SHERMAN COUNTY
Clerk of Court
Sherman County Circuit Court
PO Box 402
Moro, OR 97039

## TILLAMOOK COUNTY
Clerk of Courts
Circuit and District Court
201 Laurel Ave
Tillamook, OR 97141

## UMATILLA COUNTY
Trial Court Administrator
Circuit and District Court
PO Box 1307
Pendleton, OR 97801

## UNION COUNTY
Clerk of Court
Circuit and District Courts
1008 K. Ave
La Grande, OR 97850

## WALLOWA COUNTY
Clerk of Courts
Circuit and District Court
101 South River Street, Rm 204
Enterprise, OR 97828

## WASCO COUNTY
Clerk of Courts
Circuit and District Court
Courthouse, 511 Washington
The Dalles, OR 97058

## WASHINGTON COUNTY
Clerk of Court
Washington County Circuit Court
145 NE 2nd
Hillsboro, OR 97124

## WHEELER COUNTY
Clerk of Courts
Circuit and Justice Courts
Courthouse, PO Box 173
Fossil, OR 97830

## YAMHILL COUNTY
Clerk of Courts
Circuit and District Court
5th and Evans, Rm 206
McMinnville, OR 97128

# PENNSYLVANIA

## ADAMS COUNTY
Court of Common Pleas
Courthouse, Rm 103
111-117 Baltimore Street
Gettysburg, PA 17325

## ALLEGHENY COUNTY
Prothonotary
Court of Common Pleas
414 Grant Street
Pittsburgh, PA 15219

## ARMSTRONG COUNTY
Prothonotary
Court of Common Pleas
Courthouse
Kittanning, PA 16201

## BEAVER COUNTY
Prothonotary
Court of Common Pleas
Courthouse, 3rd Street
Beaver, PA 15009

## BEDFORD COUNTY
Prothonotary
Court of Common Pleas
Courthouse
Bedford, PA 15522

## BERKS COUNTY
Prothonotary
Court of Common Pleas
Courthouse, 633 Court Street
Reading, PA 19601

## BLAIR COUNTY
Prothonotary
Court of Common Pleas
423 Allegheny
Hollidaysburg, PA 16648

## BRADFORD COUNTY
Prothonotary
Court of Common Pleas
Courthouse, Main Street
Towanda, PA 18848

## BUCKS COUNTY
Prothonotary
Court of Common Pleas
Courthouse, Main and Court
Doylestown, PA 18901

## BUTLER COUNTY
Prothonotary
Court of Common Pleas
Courthouse, PO Box 1208
Butler, PA 16003-1208

## CAMBRIA COUNTY
Prothonotary
Court of Common Pleas
Courthouse
Ebensburg, PA 15931

## CAMERON COUNTY
Prothonotary
Court of Common Pleas
Courthouse
Emporium, PA 15834

## CARBON COUNTY
Prothonotary
Court of Common Pleas
Courthouse
Jim Thorpe, PA 18229

## CENTRE COUNTY
Prothonotary
Court of Common Pleas
Courthouse
Bellefonte, PA 16823

## CHESTER COUNTY
Prothonotary
Court of Common Pleas
2 North High Street, Ste 2
West Chester, PA 19380

## CLARION COUNTY
Prothonotary
Court of Common Pleas
Courthouse, Main Street
Clarion, PA 16214

## CLEARFIELD COUNTY
Prothonotary
Court of Common Pleas
231 1/2 East Market Street
Clearfield, PA 16830

## CLINTON COUNTY
Prothonotary
Court of Common Pleas
PO Box 630
Lock Haven, PA 17745

## COLUMBIA COUNTY
Prothonotary
Court of Common Pleas
PO Box 380
Bloomsburg, PA 17815

## CRAWFORD COUNTY
Prothonotary
Court of Common Pleas
903 Diamond Park
Meadville, PA 16335

## CUMBERLAND COUNTY
Prothonotary
Court of Common Pleas
One Courthouse Square
Carlisle, PA 17013

## DAUPHIN COUNTY
Prothonotary
Court of Common Pleas
Front and Market Street
Harrisburg, PA 17101

## DELAWARE COUNTY
Prothonotary
Court of Common Pleas
Government Center Bldg
Media, PA 19063

## ELK COUNTY
Prothonotary
Court of Common Pleas
PO Box 237
Ridgway, PA 15853

## ERIE COUNTY
Prothonotary
Court of Common Pleas
140 West 6th Street, Rm 103
Erie, PA 16501

## FAYETTE COUNTY
Prothonotary
Court of Common Pleas
61 East Main Street
Uniontown, PA 15401

## FOREST COUNTY
Prothonotary
Court of Common Pleas
526 Elm Street
Tionesta, PA 16353

## FRANKLIN COUNTY
Prothonotary
Court of Common Pleas
157 Lincoln Way E
Chambersburg, PA 17201

## FULTON COUNTY
Prothonotary
Court of Common Pleas
Courthouse
McConnellsburg, PA 17233

## GREENE COUNTY
Prothonotary
Court of Common Pleas
Courthouse, High Street
Waynesburg, PA 15370

## HUNTINGDON COUNTY
Prothonotary
Court of Common Pleas
Courthouse
Huntingdon, PA 16652

## INDIANA COUNTY
Prothonotary
Court of Common Pleas
825 Philadelphia Street
Indiana, PA 15701

## JEFFERSON COUNTY
Prothonotary
Court of Common Pleas
Courthouse, 200 Main Street
Brookville, PA 15825

## JUNIATA COUNTY
Prothonotary
Court of Common Pleas
Courthouse
Mifflintown, PA 17059

## LACKAWANNA COUNTY
Prothonotary
Court of Common Pleas
Courthouse, 3rd Floor
Scranton, PA 18503

## LANCASTER COUNTY
Prothonotary
Court of Common Pleas
50 North Duke Street
Lancaster, PA 17602

## LAWRENCE COUNTY
Prothonotary
Court of Common Pleas
430 Court Street
New Castle, PA 16101

## LEBANON COUNTY
Prothonotary
Court of Common Pleas
400 South 8th Street, Rm 106
Lebanon, PA 17042

## LEHIGH COUNTY
Prothonotary
Court of Common Pleas
PO Box 1548
Allentown, PA 18105

## LUZERNE COUNTY
Prothonotary
Court of Common Pleas
200 North River Street
Wilkes-Barre, PA 18711

## LYCOMING COUNTY
Prothonotary
Court of Common Pleas
48 West 3rd
Williamsport, PA 17701

## MCKEAN COUNTY
Prothonotary
Court of Common Pleas
PO Box 273
Smithport, PA 16749

## MERCER COUNTY
Prothonotary
Court of Common Pleas
112 Mercer County Courthouse
Mercer, PA 16137

## MIFFLIN COUNTY
Prothonotary
Court of Common Pleas
20 North Wayne Street
Lewistown, PA 17044

## MONROE COUNTY
Prothonotary
Court of Common Pleas
Courthouse
Stroudsburg, PA 18360

## MONTGOMERY COUNTY
Prothonotary
Court of Common Pleas
Airy and Swede Street
Norristown, PA 19404

## MONTOUR COUNTY
Prothonotary
Court of Common Pleas
29 Mill Street
Danville, PA 17821

## NORTHAMPTON COUNTY
Prothonotary
Court of Common Pleas
669 Washington Street
Easton, PA 18042

## NORTHUMBERLAND
Prothonotary
Court of Common Pleas
201 Market Street
Sunbury, PA 17801

## PERRY COUNTY
Prothonotary
Court of Common Pleas
PO Box 325
New Bloomfield, PA 17068

## PHILADELPHIA COUNTY
Prothonotary
Court of Common Pleas
284 City Hall
Philadelphia, PA 19107

## PIKE COUNTY
Prothonotary
Court of Common Pleas
412 Broad Street
Milford, PA 18337

## POTTER COUNTY
Prothonotary
Court of Common Pleas
1 East 2nd Street
Coudersport, PA 16915

## SCHUYLKILL COUNTY
Prothonotary
Court of Common Pleas
401 North 2nd Street
Pottsville, PA 17901

## SNYDER COUNTY
Prothonotary
Court of Common Pleas
Courthouse
Middleburg, PA 17842

## SOMERSET COUNTY
Prothonotary
Court of Common Pleas
Courthouse
Somerset, PA 15501

## SULLIVAN COUNTY
Prothonotary
Court of Common Pleas
Main Street
LaPorte, PA 18626

## SUSQUEHANNA COUNTY
Prothonotary
Court of Common Pleas
Courthouse
Montrose, PA 18801

## TIOGA COUNTY
Prothonotary
Court of Common Pleas
Main Street
Wellsboro, PA 16901

## UNION COUNTY
Prothonotary
Court of Common Pleas
Courthouse
Lewisburg, PA 17837

## VENANGO COUNTY
Prothonotary
Court of Common Pleas
Courthouse
Franklin, PA 16323

## WARREN COUNTY
Prothonotary
Court of Common Pleas
4th and Market Street
Warren, PA 16365

## WASHINGTON COUNTY
Prothonotary
Court of Common Pleas
Courthouse
Washington, PA 15301

**WAYNE COUNTY**
Prothonotary
Court of Common Pleas
925 Court Street
Honesdale, PA 18431

**WESTMORELAND**
Prothonotary
Court of Common Pleas
203 Courthouse Square
Greensburg, PA 15601-1168

**WYOMING COUNTY**
Prothonotary
Court of Common Pleas
One Courthouse Square
Tunkhannock, PA 18657

**YORK COUNTY**
Prothonotary
Court of Common Pleas
Courthouse
York, PA 17401

# RHODE ISLAND

**BRISTOL COUNTY**
Clerk of Court
County Superior Court
250 Benefit Street
Providence,, RI 02903

**KENT COUNTY**
Clerk of Court
Superior and District Court
222 Quaker Ln
Warwick, RI 02886

**NEWPORT COUNTY**
Clerk of Court
Superior and District Court
45 Washington Square
Newport, RI 02840

**PROVIDENCE COUNTY**
Clerk of Court
Superior Court
250 Benefit Street
Providence, RI 02903

**WASHINGTON COUNTY**
Clerk of Court
Superior and District Court
4800 Towerhill Rd
Wakefield, RI 02879

# SOUTH CAROLINA

**ABBEVILLE COUNTY**
Clerk of Court
Abbeville County Circuit Court
Courthouse, Court Square
Abbeville, SC 29620

**AIKEN COUNTY**
Clerk of Court
Aiken County Circuit Court
109 Park Ave
Aiken, SC 29802

**ALLENDALE COUNTY**
Clerk of Court
Allendale County Circuit Court
Courthouse
Allendale, SC 29810

## ANDERSON COUNTY
Clerk of Court
Anderson County Circuit Court
100 South Main Street
Anderson, SC 29622

## BAMBERG COUNTY
Clerk of Court
Bamberg County Circuit Court
110 North Main
Bamberg, SC 29003

## BARNWELL COUNTY
Clerk of Court
Barnwell County Circuit Court
Courthouse, Main Street
Barnwell, SC 29812

## BEAUFORT COUNTY
Clerk of Court
Beaufort County Circuit Court
1000 Ribaut Rd
Beaufort, SC 29901

## BERKELEY COUNTY
Clerk of Court
Berkeley Cty Circuit Court
223 North Live Oak Dr
Moncks Corner, SC 29461

## CALHOUN COUNTY
Clerk of Court
Calhoun County Circuit Court
302 South Huff Dr
St. Matthews, SC 29135

## CHARLESTON COUNTY
Clerk of Court
Charleston Cty Circuit Court
2144 Melbourne Street
Charleston, SC 29402

## CHEROKEE COUNTY
Clerk of Court
Cherokee County Circuit Court
125 Floyd Baker Blvd
Gaffney, SC 29342

## CHESTER COUNTY
Clerk of Court
Chester County Circuit Court
140 Main Street
Chester, SC 29706

## CHESTERFIELD COUNTY
Clerk of Court
Chesterfield County Circuit Court
200 West Main
Chesterfield, SC 29709

## CLARENDON COUNTY
Clerk of Court
Clarendon County Circuit Court
Courthouse, Drawer E
Manning, SC 29102

## COLLETON COUNTY
Clerk of Court
Colleton County Circuit Court
1 Washington Street
Walterboro, SC 29488

## DARLINGTON COUNTY
Clerk of Court
Darlington County Circuit Court
Courthouse, PO Box 498
Darlington, SC 29532

## DILLON COUNTY
Clerk of Court
Dillon County Circuit Court
401 West Main Street
Dillon, SC 29536

## DORCHESTER COUNTY
Clerk of Court
Dorchester Cty Circuit Court
101 Ridge Street
St. George, SC 29477

## EDGEFIELD COUNTY
Clerk of Court
Edgefield Cty Circuit Court
129 Courthouse Square
Edgefield, SC 29824

## FAIRFIELD COUNTY
Clerk of Court
Fairfield County Circuit Court
Courthouse
Winnsboro, SC 29180

## FLORENCE COUNTY
Clerk of Court
Florence County Circuit Court
180 North Irby Street
Florence, SC 29501

## GEORGETOWN COUNTY
Clerk of Court
Georgetown County Circuit Court
715 Prince Street
Georgetown, SC 29442

## GREENVILLE COUNTY
Clerk of Court
Greenville Cty Circuit Court
Courthouse
Greenville, SC 29601

## GREENWOOD COUNTY
Clerk of Court
Greenwood Cty Circuit Court
Courthouse, Rm 114
Greenwood, SC 29646

## HAMPTON COUNTY
Clerk of Court
Hampton County Circuit Court
1 Elm Street
Hampton, SC 29924

## HORRY COUNTY
Clerk of Court
Horry County Circuit Court
1201 Third Ave
Conway, SC 29526

## JASPER COUNTY
Clerk of Court
Jasper County Circuit Court
350 Russell Street
Ridgeland, SC 29936

**KERSHAW COUNTY**
Clerk of Court
Kershaw County Circuit Court
1121 Broad Street, Rm 313
Camden, SC 29020

**LANCASTER COUNTY**
Clerk of Court
Lancaster Cty Circuit Court
116 West Dunlap
Lancaster, SC 29720

**LAURENS COUNTY**
Clerk of Court
Laurens County Circuit Court
Courthouse, PO Box 287
Laurens, SC 29360

**LEE COUNTY**
Clerk of Court
Lee County Circuit Court
Courthouse Square
Bishopville, SC 29010

**LEXINGTON COUNTY**
Clerk of Court
Lexington County Circuit Court
139 East Main, Rm 107
Lexington, SC 29072

**MARION COUNTY**
Clerk of Court
Marion County Circuit Court
100 Court Street
Marion, SC 29571

**MARLBORO COUNTY**
Clerk of Court
Marlboro County Circuit Court
105 Main Street
Bennettsville, SC 29512

**MCCORMICK COUNTY**
Clerk of Court
McCormick Cty Circuit Court
133 South Mine Street
McCormick, SC 29835

**NEWBERRY COUNTY**
Clerk of Court
Newberry County Circuit Court
1226 College Street
Newberry, SC 29108

**OCONEE COUNTY**
Clerk of Court
Oconee County Circuit Court
211 West Main
Walhalla, SC 29691

**ORANGEBURG COUNTY**
Clerk of Court
Orangeburg County Circuit Court
190 Sunnyside Street
Orangeburg, SC 29116

**PICKENS COUNTY**
Clerk of Court
Pickens County Circuit Court
PO Box 215
Pickens, SC 29671

## RICHLAND COUNTY

Clerk of Court
Richland County Circuit Court
1701 Main Street
Columbia, SC 29201

## SALUDA COUNTY

Clerk of Court
Saluda County Circuit Court
Church Street
Saluda, SC 29138

## SPARTANBURG COUNTY

Clerk of Court
Spartanburg Cty Circuit Court
180 Magnolia Street
Spartanburg, SC 29301

## SUMTER COUNTY

Clerk of Court
Sumter County Circuit Court
141 North Main Street
Sumter, SC 29150

## UNION COUNTY

Clerk of Court
Union County Circuit Court
210 West Main
Union, SC 29379

## WILLIAMSBURG COUNTY

Clerk of Court
Williamsburg Cty Circuit Court
125 West Main
Kingstree, SC 29556

## YORK COUNTY

Clerk of Court
York County Circuit Court
PO Box 649
York, SC 29745

# SOUTH DAKOTA

## AURORA COUNTY

Clerk of Court
Aurora County Circuit Court
PO Box 366
Plankinton, SD 57368

## BEADLE COUNTY

Clerk of Court
Beadle County Circuit Court
PO Box 1358
Huron, SD 57350

## BENNETT COUNTY

Clerk of Court
Bennett County Circuit Court
PO Box 281
Martin, SD 57551

## BON HOMME COUNTY

Clerk of Court
Bon Homme Cty Circuit Court
300 West Cherry
Tyndall, SD 57066

## BROOKINGS COUNTY

Clerk of Court
Brookings Cty Circuit Court
314 6th Ave
Brookings, SD 57006

**BROWN COUNTY**
Clerk of Court
Brown County Circuit Court
101 lst Avenue SE
Aberdeen, SD 57401

**BRULE COUNTY**
Clerk of Court
Brule County Circuit Court
300 South Courtland
Chamberlain, SD 57325

**BUFFALO COUNTY**
Clerk of Court
Buffalo County Circuit Court
PO Box 148
Gann Valley, SD 57341

**BUTTE COUNTY**
Clerk of Court
Butte County Circuit Court
PO Box 237
Belle Fourche, SD 57717

**CAMPBELL COUNTY**
Clerk of Court
Campbell County Circuit Court
PO Box 146
Mound City, SD 57646

**CHARLES MIX COUNTY**
Clerk of Court
Charles Mix Cty Circuit Court
PO Box 640
Lake Andes, SD 57356

**CLARK COUNTY**
Clerk of Court
Clark County Circuit Court
PO Box 294
Clark, SD 57225

**CLAY COUNTY**
Clerk of Court
Clay County Circuit Court
PO Box 377
Vermillion, SD 57069

**CODINGTON COUNTY**
Clerk of Court
Codington Cty Circuit Court
PO Box 1054
Watertown, SD 57201

**CORSON COUNTY**
Clerk of Court
Corson County Circuit Court
Courthouse Street, PO Box 175
McIntosh, SD 57641

**CUSTER COUNTY**
Clerk of Court
Custer County Circuit Court
420 Mt Rushmore Rd
Custer, SD 57730

**DAVISON COUNTY**
Clerk of Court
Davison County Circuit Court
PO Box 927
Mitchell, SD 57301

## DAY COUNTY
Clerk of Court
Day County Circuit Court
710 West 1st Street
Webster, SD 57274

## DEUEL COUNTY
Clerk of Court
Deuel County Circuit Court
PO Box 308
Clear Lake, SD 57226

## DEWEY COUNTY
Clerk of Court
Dewey County Circuit Court
PO Box 96
Timber Lake, SD 57656

## DOUGLAS COUNTY
Clerk of Court
Douglas County Circuit Court
PO Box 36
Armour, SD 57313

## EDMUNDS COUNTY
Clerk of Court
Edmunds County Circuit Court
PO Box 384
Ipswich, SD 57451

## FALL RIVER COUNTY
Clerk of Court
Fall River Cty Circuit Court
906 North River Street
Hot Springs, SD 57747

## FAULK COUNTY
Clerk of Court
Faulk County Circuit Court
PO Box 357
Faulkton, SD 57438

## GRANT COUNTY
Clerk of Court
Grant County Circuit Court
PO Box 509
Milbank, SD 57252

## GREGORY COUNTY
Clerk of Court
Gregory County Circuit Court
PO Box 430
Burke, SD 57523

## HAAKON COUNTY
Clerk of Court
Haakon County Circuit Court
PO Box 70
Philip, SD 57567

## HAMLIN COUNTY
Clerk of Court
Hamlin County Circuit Court
PO Box 256
Hayti, SD 57241

## HAND COUNTY
Clerk of Court
Hand County Circuit Court
PO Box 122
Miller, SD 57362

## HANSON COUNTY
Clerk of Court
Hanson County Circuit Court
PO Box 127
Alexandria, SD 57311

## HARDING COUNTY
Clerk of Court
Harding Cty Circuit Court
PO Box 534
Buffalo, SD 57720

## HUGHES COUNTY
Clerk of Court
Hughes County Circuit Court
104 East Capitol
Pierre, SD 57501

## HUTCHINSON COUNTY
Clerk of Court
Hutchinson Cty Circuit Court
PO Box 7
Olivet, SD 57052

## HYDE COUNTY
Clerk of Court
Hyde County Circuit Court
116 Commercial Street
Highmore, SD 57345

## JACKSON COUNTY
Clerk of Court
Jackson County Circuit Court
PO Box 128
Kadoka, SD 57543

## JERAULD COUNTY
Clerk of Court
Jerauld County Circuit Court
Box 435
Wessington Springs, SD 57382

## JONES COUNTY
Clerk of Court
Jones County Circuit Court
PO Box 448
Murdo, SD 57559

## KINGSBURY COUNTY
Clerk of Court
Kingsbury Cty Circuit Court
102 Second Street
DeSmet, SD 57231

## LAKE COUNTY
Clerk of Court
Lake County Circuit Court
200 East Center
Madison, SD 57042

## LAWRENCE COUNTY
Clerk of Court
Lawrence County Circuit Court
PO Box 626
Deadwood, SD 57732

## LINCOLN COUNTY
Clerk of Court
Lincoln County Circuit Court
100 East 5th Street
Canton, SD 57013

## LYMAN COUNTY

Clerk of Court
Lyman County Circuit Court
PO Box 235
Kennebec, SD 57544

## MARSHALL COUNTY

Clerk of Court
Marshall County Circuit Court
PO Box 130
Britton, SD 57430

## MCCOOK COUNTY

Clerk of Court
McCook County Circuit Court
PO Box 504
Salem, SD 57058

## MCPHERSON COUNTY

Clerk of Court
McPherson Cty Circuit Court
PO Box 248
Leola, SD 57456

## MEADE COUNTY

Clerk of Court
Meade County Circuit Court
PO Box 939
Sturgis, SD 57785

## MELLETTE COUNTY

Clerk of Court
Mellette County Circuit Court
PO Box 257
White River, SD 57579

## MINER COUNTY

Clerk of Court
Miner County Circuit Court
PO Box 265
Howard, SD 57349

## MINNEHAHA COUNTY

Clerk of Court
Minnehaha Cty Circuit Court
415 North Dakota Ave
Sioux Falls, SD 57102

## MOODY COUNTY

Clerk of Court
Moody County Circuit Court
101 East Pipestone
Flandreau, SD 57028

## PENNINGTON COUNTY

Clerk of Court
Pennington Cty Circuit Court
315 Street Joseph Street
Rapid City, SD 57709

## PERKINS COUNTY

Clerk of Court
Perkins County Circuit Court
PO Box 426
Bison, SD 57620

## POTTER COUNTY

Clerk of Court
Potter County Circuit Court
201 South Exene
Gettysburg, SD 57442

## ROBERTS COUNTY
Clerk of Court
Roberts County Circuit Court
411 2nd Avenue E
Sisseton, SD 57262

## SANBORN COUNTY
Clerk of Court
Sanborn County Circuit Court
PO Box 56
Woonsocket, SD 59385

## SHANNON COUNTY
Clerk of Court
Shannon County Circuit Court
906 North River
Hot Springs, SD 57747

## SPINK COUNTY
Clerk of Court
Spink County Circuit Court
210 East 7th Ave
Redfield, SD 57469-1299

## STANLEY COUNTY
Clerk of Court
Stanley County Circuit Court
PO Box 758
Fort Pierre, SD 57532

## SULLY COUNTY
Clerk of Court
Sully County Circuit Court
PO Box 188
Onida, SD 57564

## TODD COUNTY
Clerk of Court
Todd County Circuit Court
200 East 3rd Street
Winner, SD 57580

## TRIPP COUNTY
Clerk of Court
Tripp County Circuit Court
200 East 3rd Street
Winner, SD 57580

## TURNER COUNTY
Clerk of Court
Turner County Circuit Court
PO Box 446
Parker, SD 57053

## UNION COUNTY
Clerk of Court
Union County Circuit Court
PO Box 757
Elk Point, SD 57025

## WALWORTH COUNTY
Clerk of Court
Walworth County Circuit Court
PO Box 328
Selby, SD 57472

## YANKTON COUNTY
Clerk of Court
Yankton County Circuit Court
PO Box 155
Yankton, SD 57078

**ZIEBACH COUNTY**
Clerk of Court
Ziebach County Circuit Court
PO Box 306
Dupree, SD 57623

# TENNESSEE

**ANDERSON COUNTY**
Clerk of Court
Circuit and Trial Courts
Courthouse, 100 Main Street
Clinton, TN 37716

**BEDFORD COUNTY**
Clerk of Court
Circuit and General Courts
1 Public Square, Ste 200
Shelbyville, TN 37160

**BENTON COUNTY**
Clerk of Court
Circuit and General Courts
PO Box 466
Camden, TN 38320

**BLEDSOE COUNTY**
Clerk of Court
Circuit and General Courts
Courthouse, PO Box 455
Pikeville, TN 37367

**BLOUNT COUNTY**
Clerk of Court
Circuit and General Courts
391 Court Street
Maryville, TN 37804

**BRADLEY COUNTY**
Clerk of Court
Circuit and General Courts
Government Center
Cleveland, TN 37311

**CAMPBELL COUNTY**
Clerk of Court
Circuit and General Courts
PO Box 26
Jacksboro, TN 37757

**CANNON COUNTY**
Clerk of Courts
Circuit and General Courts
Government Center
Woodbury, TN 37190

**CARROLL COUNTY**
Clerk of Courts
Circuit and General Courts
PO Box 487
Huntingdon, TN 38344

**CARTER COUNTY**
Clerk of Court
Circuit and General Courts
900 East Elk Avenue
Elizabethton, TN 37643

**CHEATHAM COUNTY**
Clerk of Court
Circuit and General Courts
Government Center
Ashland City, TN 37015

## CHESTER COUNTY
Clerk of Court
Circuit and General Courts
PO Box 133
Henderson, TN 38340

## CLAIBORNE COUNTY
Clerk of Court
Circuit and General Courts
PO Box 34
Tazewell, TN 37879

## CLAY COUNTY
Clerk of Court
Circuit and General Courts
PO Box 749
Celina, TN 38551

## COCKE COUNTY
Clerk of Court
Circuit Court
111 Court Ave, Room 201
Newport, TN 37821

## COFFEE COUNTY
Clerk of Court
Circuit and General Courts
PO Box 629
Manchester, TN 37355

## CROCKETT COUNTY
Clerk of Court
Circuit and General Courts
Government Center
Alamo, TN 38001

## CUMBERLAND COUNTY
Clerk of Court
Circuit and General Courts
Courthouse, Box 7
Crossville, TN 38555

## DAVIDSON COUNTY
Clerk of Court
Circuit and Criminal Courts
303 Metro Courthouse
Nashville, TN 37201

## DEKALB COUNTY
Clerk of Court
Circuit and General Courts
Government Center
Smithville, TN 37166

## DECATUR COUNTY
Clerk of Court
Circuit and General Courts
PO Box 488
Decaturville, TN 38329

## DICKSON COUNTY
Clerk of Court
Circuit and General Courts
Court Square, PO Box 220
Charlotte, TN 37036

## DYER COUNTY
Clerk of Court
Circuit and General Courts
PO Box 1360
Dyersburg, TN 38024

## FAYETTE COUNTY
Clerk of Court
Circuit and General Courts
PO Box 670
Somerville, TN 38068

## FENTRESS COUNTY
Clerk of Court
Circuit and General Courts
PO Box 699
Jamestown, TN 38556

## FRANKLIN COUNTY
Clerk of Court
Circuit and General Courts
#1 South Jefferson Street
Winchester, TN 37398

## GIBSON COUNTY
Clerk of Court
Circuit and General Courts
Government Center
Trenton, TN 38382

## GILES COUNTY
Clerk of Court
Circuit and General Courts
Public Square, PO Box 678
Pulaski, TN 38478

## GRAINGER COUNTY
Clerk of Court
Circuit and General Courts
PO Box 157
Rutledge, TN 37861

## GREENE COUNTY
Clerk of Court
Circuit and General Courts
101 South Main, Ste 202
Greeneville, TN 37743

## GRUNDY COUNTY
Clerk of Court
Circuit and General Courts
PO Box 161
Altamont, TN 37301

## HAMBLEN COUNTY
Clerk of Court
Circuit and General Courts
510 Allison Street
Morristown, TN 37814

## HAMILTON COUNTY
Clerk of Court
Circuit Court
500 Courthouse
Chattanooga, TN 37402

## HANCOCK COUNTY
Clerk of Court
Circuit and General Courts
PO Box 347
Sneedville, TN 37869

## HARDEMAN COUNTY
Clerk of Court
Circuit and General Courts
Government Center
Bolivar, TN 38008

## HARDIN COUNTY
Clerk of Court
Circuit and General Courts
601 Main, 2nd Floor
Savannah, TN 38372

## HAWKINS COUNTY
Clerk of Court
Circuit and General Courts
PO Box 9
Rogersville, TN 37857

## HAYWOOD COUNTY
Clerk of Court
Circuit and General Courts
Courthouse
Brownsville, TN 38012

## HENDERSON COUNTY
Clerk of Court
Circuit and General Courts
Government Center
Lexington, TN 38351

## HENRY COUNTY
Clerk of Court
Circuit and General Courts
100 W. Washington Street
Paris, TN 38242

## HICKMAN COUNTY
Clerk of Court
Circuit and General Courts
Government Center
Centerville, TN 37033

## HOUSTON COUNTY
Clerk of Court
Circuit and General Courts
PO Box 403
Erin, TN 37061

## HUMPHREYS COUNTY
Clerk of Court
Circuit and General Courts
Government Center
Waverly, TN 37185

## JACKSON COUNTY
Clerk of Court
Circuit and General Courts
PO Box 205
Gainesboro, TN 38562

## JEFFERSON COUNTY
Clerk of Court
Jefferson Cty Circuit Court
PO Box 671
Dandridge, TN 37725

## JOHNSON COUNTY
Clerk of Court
Circuit and General Courts
PO Box 73
Mountain City, TN 37683

## KNOX COUNTY
Clerk of Court
General Courts
400 Main Street
Knoxville, TN 37902

## LAKE COUNTY
Clerk of Court
Circuit and General Courts
227 Church Street
Tiptonville, TN 38079

## LAUDERDALE COUNTY
Clerk of Court
Circuit and General Courts
Government Center
Ripley, TN 38063

## LAWRENCE COUNTY
Clerk of Court
Circuit and General Courts
NBU #12 Court, 240 West Gaines
Lawrenceburg, TN 38464

## LEWIS COUNTY
Clerk of Court
Circuit and General Courts
Government Center
Hohenwald, TN 38462

## LINCOLN COUNTY
Clerk of Court
Circuit and General Courts
PO Box 78
Fayetteville, TN 37334

## LOUDON COUNTY
Clerk of Court
Circuit and General Courts
PO Box 160
Loudon, TN 37774

## MACON COUNTY
Clerk of Court
Circuit and General Courts
Courthouse, Rm 202
Lafayette, TN 37083

## MADISON COUNTY
Clerk of Court
Circuit and General Courts
Government Center
Jackson, TN 38301

## MARION COUNTY
Clerk of Court
Circuit and General Courts
Courthouse, PO Box 789
Jasper, TN 37347

## MARSHALL COUNTY
Clerk of Court
Circuit and General Courts
Government Center
Lewisburg, TN 37091

## MAURY COUNTY
Clerk of Court
Circuit and General Courts
41 Public Square
Columbia, TN 38401

## MCMINN COUNTY
Clerk of Court
Circuit and General Courts
PO Box 506
Athens, TN 37303

## MCNAIRY COUNTY
Clerk of Court
Circuit and General Courts
Government Center
Selmer, TN 38375

## MEIGS COUNTY
Clerk of Court
Circuit and General Courts
PO Box 205
Decatur, TN 37322

## MONROE COUNTY
Clerk of Court
Circuit and General Courts
105 College Street
Madisonville, TN 37354

## MONTGOMERY COUNTY
Clerk of Court
Circuit and General Courts
120 Commerce Street
Clarksville, TN 37041

## MOORE COUNTY
Clerk of Court
Circuit and General Courts
Government Center
Lynchburg, TN 37352

## MORGAN COUNTY
Clerk of Court
Circuit and General Courts
PO Box 163
Wartburg, TN 37887

## OBION COUNTY
Court Clerk
Circuit and General Courts
Government Center
Union City, TN 38261

## OVERTON COUNTY
Clerk of Court
Circuit and General Courts
Government Center
Livingston, TN 38570

## PERRY COUNTY
Clerk of Court
Circuit and General Courts
PO Box 91
Linden, TN 37096

## PICKETT COUNTY
Clerk of Court
Circuit and General Courts
PO Box 5
Byrdstown, TN 38549

## POLK COUNTY
Clerk of Court
Circuit and General Courts
PO Box 256
Benton, TN 37307

## PUTNAM COUNTY
Clerk of Court
Circuit and General Courts
Courthouse, Rm 9
Cookeville, TN 38501

**RHEA COUNTY**
Clerk of Court
Circuit and General Courts
Government Center
Dayton, TN 37321

**SEVIER COUNTY**
Clerk of Court
Circuit and Trial Courts
125 Court Ave
Sevierville, TN 37862

**ROANE COUNTY**
Clerk of Court
Circuit and General Courts
PO Box 73
Kingston, TN 37763

**SHELBY COUNTY**
Clerk of Court
Circuit and General Court
201 Poplar Ave
Memphis, TN 38103

**ROBERTSON COUNTY**
Clerk of Court
Circuit and General Courts
Courthouse, Rm 200
Springfield, TN 37172

**SMITH COUNTY**
Clerk of Court
Circuit and General Courts
218 Main Street
Carthage, TN 37030

**RUTHERFORD COUNTY**
Clerk of Court
Circuit and General Courts
Judicial Building
Murfreesboro, TN 37130

**STEWART COUNTY**
Clerk of Court
Circuit and General Courts
225 Donaldson Pkwy
Dover, TN 37058

**SCOTT COUNTY**
Clerk of Court
Circuit and General Courts
PO Box 73
Huntsville, TN 37756

**SULLIVAN COUNTY**
Clerk of Court
Circuit and General Courts
140 Blockville Bypass
Blountville, TN 37617

**SEQUATCHIE COUNTY**
Clerk of Court
Circuit and General Courts
PO Box 551
Dunlap, TN 37327

**SUMNER COUNTY**
Clerk of Court
Circuit and General Courts
Public Square, 4th Floor
Gallatin, TN 37066

## TIPTON COUNTY
Clerk of Court
Circuit and General Courts
Justice Complex Bldg
Covington, TN 38019

## TROUSDALE COUNTY
Clerk of Court
Circuit and General Courts
Courthouse, Rm 5
Hartsville, TN 37074

## UNICOI COUNTY
Clerk of Court
Circuit and General Courts
Courthouse, PO Box 376
Erwin, TN 37650

## UNION COUNTY
Clerk of Court
Circuit and General Courts
PO Box 306
Maynardsville, TN 37807

## VAN BUREN COUNTY
Clerk of Court
Circuit and General Courts
PO Box 126
Spencer, TN 38585

## WARREN COUNTY
Clerk of Court
Circuit and General Courts
Government Center
McMinnville, TN 37110

## WASHINGTON COUNTY
Clerk of Court
Law Court
101 East Market Street
Johnson City, TN 37659

## WAYNE COUNTY
Clerk of Court
Circuit and General Courts
PO Box 869
Waynesboro, TN 38485

## WEAKLEY COUNTY
Clerk of Court
Circuit and General Courts
PO Box 11
Dresden, TN 38225

## WHITE COUNTY
Clerk of Court
Circuit and General Courts
Courthouse, Rm 304
Sparta, TN 38583

## WILLIAMSON COUNTY
Clerk of Court
Circuit and General Courts
305 Public Square
Franklin, TN 37064

## WILSON COUNTY
Clerk of Court
Circuit and General Courts
PO Box 1366
Lebanon, TN 37087

# TEXAS

## ANDERSON COUNTY
Clerk of Court
District and County Courts
500 North Church
Palestine, TX 75802-1159

## ANDREWS COUNTY
Clerk of Court
Andrews County Court
PO Box 727
Andrews, TX 79714

## ANGELINA COUNTY
Clerk of Court
District and County Courts
PO Box 908
Lufkin, TX 75902-0908

## ARANSAS COUNTY
Clerk of Court
District and County Courts
301 North Live Oak
Rockport, TX 78382

## ARCHER COUNTY
Clerk of Court
District and County Courts
PO Box 815
Archer City, TX 76351

## ARMSTRONG COUNTY
Clerk of Court
District and County Courts
PO Box 309
Claude, TX 79019

## ATASCOSA COUNTY
Clerk of Court
Atascosa Cty District Court
#52 Courthouse Circle
Jourdanton, TX 78026

## AUSTIN COUNTY
Clerk of Court
District and County Courts
1 East Main
Bellville, TX 77418

## BAILEY COUNTY
Clerk of Court
District and County Courts
300 South 1st
Muleshoe, TX 79347

## BANDERA COUNTY
Clerk of Court
District and County Courts
PO Box 823
Bandera, TX 78003

## BASTROP COUNTY
Clerk of Court
District and County Courts
804 Pecan Street
Bastrop, TX 78602

## BAYLOR COUNTY
Clerk of Court
District and County Courts
PO Box 689
Seymour, TX 76380

**BEE COUNTY**
Clerk of Court
Bee County District Court
PO Box 666
Beeville, TX 78104

**BELL COUNTY**
Clerk of Court
Bell County District Court
104 South Main
Belton, TX 76513

**BEXAR COUNTY**
Clerk of Court
Bexar County District Court
Courthouse, 100 Delorosa
San Antonio, TX 78205

**BLANCO COUNTY**
Clerk of Court
District and County Courts
PO Box 65
Johnson City, TX 78636

**BORDEN COUNTY**
Clerk of Court
District and County Courts
Box 124
Gail, TX 79738

**BOSQUE COUNTY**
Clerk of Court
Bosque County District Court
PO Box 674
Meridian, TX 76665

**BOWIE COUNTY**
Clerk of Court
District and County Courts
PO Box 248
New Boston, TX 75570

**BRAZORIA COUNTY**
Clerk of Court
Brazoria Cty District Court
PO Box 1869
Angelton, TX 77516-1869

**BRAZOS COUNTY**
Clerk of Court
Brazos Cty District Court
PO Box 2208
Bryan, TX 77806

**BREWSTER COUNTY**
Clerk of Court
District and County Courts
PO Drawer 119
Alpine, TX 79831

**BRISCOE COUNTY**
Clerk of Court
District and County Courts
PO Box 375
Silverton, TX 79257

**BROOKS COUNTY**
Clerk of Court
Brooks County District Court
PO Box 534
Falfurrias, TX 78355

## BROWN COUNTY

Clerk of Court
District and County Courts
200 South Broadway
Brownwood, TX 76801

## BURLESON COUNTY

Clerk of Court
District and County Courts
PO Box 179
Caldwell, TX 77836

## BURNET COUNTY

Clerk of Court
District and County Courts
220 South Pierce
Burnet, TX 78611

## CALDWELL COUNTY

Clerk of Court
Caldwell Cty District Court
Main Street, Rm 201
Lockhart, TX 78644

## CALHOUN COUNTY

Clerk of Court
District and County Courts
211 South Ann
Port Lavaca, TX 77979

## CALLAHAN COUNTY

Clerk of Court
Callahan Cty District Court
400 Market Street, Ste 300
Baird, TX 79504

## CAMERON COUNTY

Clerk of Court
Cameron County District Court
974 East Harrison Street
Brownsville, TX 78520

## CAMP COUNTY

Clerk of Court
Camp County District Court
126 Church Street, Rm 203
Pittsburg, TX 75686

## CARSON COUNTY

Clerk of Court
District and County Courts
PO Box 487
Panhandle, TX 79068

## CASS COUNTY

Clerk of Court
Cass County District Court
PO Box 510
Linden, TX 75563

## CASTRO COUNTY

Clerk of Court
District and County Courts
100 East Bedford
Dimmitt, TX 79027

## CHAMBERS COUNTY

Clerk of Court
Chambers County District Court
Drawer NN
Anahuac, TX 77514

**CHEROKEE COUNTY**
Clerk of Court
Cherokee Cty District Court
Drawer C
Rusk, TX 75785

**COLLIN COUNTY**
Clerk of Court
Collin County District Court
PO Box 578
McKinney, TX 75069

**CHILDRESS COUNTY**
Clerk of Court
District and County Courts
Courthouse, Box 4
Childress, TX 79201

**COLLINGSWORTH**
Clerk of Court
District and County Courts
Courthouse, Rm 3
Wellington, TX 79095

**CLAY COUNTY**
Clerk of Court
Clay County District Court
PO Box 554
Henrietta, TX 76365

**COLORADO COUNTY**
Clerk of Court
District and County Courts
Government Center
Columbus, TX 78934

**COCHRAN COUNTY**
Clerk of Court
District and County Courts
Courthouse, Rm 102
Morton, TX 79346

**COMAL COUNTY**
Clerk of Court
Comal County District Court
150 North Seguin, Ste 304
New Braunfels, TX 78130

**COKE COUNTY**
Clerk of Court
District and County Courts
PO Box 150
Robert Lee, TX 76945

**COMANCHE COUNTY**
Clerk of Court
Comanche County District Court
Government Center
Comanche, TX 76442

**COLEMAN COUNTY**
Clerk of Court
Coleman County District Court
PO Box 957
Coleman, TX 76834

**CONCHO COUNTY**
Clerk of Court
District and County Courts
PO Box 98
Paint Rock, TX 76866

## COOKE COUNTY

Clerk of Court
Cooke County District Court
Government Center
Gainesville, TX 76240

## CORYELL COUNTY

Clerk of Court
Coryell County District Court
PO Box 4
Gatesville, TX 76528

## COTTLE COUNTY

Clerk of Court
District and County Courts
PO Box 717
Paducah, TX 79248

## CRANE COUNTY

Clerk of Court
District and County Courts
PO Box 578
Crane, TX 79731

## CROCKETT COUNTY

Clerk of Court
District and County Courts
PO Drawer C
Ozona, TX 76943

## CROSBY COUNTY

Clerk of Court
Crosby County District Court
PO Box 495
Crosbyton, TX 79322

## CULBERSON COUNTY

Clerk of Court
District and County Courts
PO Box 158
Van Horn, TX 79855

## DALLAM COUNTY

Clerk of Court
District and County Courts
PO Box 1352
Dalhart, TX 79022

## DALLAS COUNTY

ATTN: Records Copy Clerk
Dallas County District Court
600 Commerce St
Dallas, TX 75202

## DAWSON COUNTY

Clerk of Court
District and County Courts
Drawer 1268
Lamesa, TX 79331

## DE WITT COUNTY

Clerk of Court
De Witt County District Court
PO Box 845
Cuero, TX 77954

## DEAF SMITH COUNTY

Clerk of Court
District and County Courts
235 East 3rd
Hereford, TX 79045

## DELTA COUNTY
Clerk of Court
District and County Courts
200 West Dallas St
Cooper, TX 75432

## DENTON COUNTY
Clerk of Court
Denton County District Court
PO Box 2146
Denton, TX 76202

## DICKENS COUNTY
Clerk of Court
District and County Courts
PO Box 120
Dickens, TX 79229

## DIMMIT COUNTY
Clerk of Court
District and County Courts
103 North 5th
Carrizo Springs, TX 78834

## DONLEY COUNTY
Clerk of Court
District and County Courts
PO Drawer Z
Clarendon, TX 79226

## DUVAL COUNTY
Clerk of Court
Duval County District Court
400 East Gravis St
San Diego, TX 78384

## EASTLAND COUNTY
Clerk of Court
Eastland Cty District Court
100 West Main St
Eastland, TX 76448

## ECTOR COUNTY
Clerk of Court
Ector County District Court
Courthouse, Rm 301
Odessa, TX 79761

## EDWARDS COUNTY
Clerk of Court
District and County Courts
400 Main
Rocksprings, TX 78880

## EL PASO COUNTY
Clerk of Court
District and County Court
500 E. San Antonio Street,#105
El Paso, TX 79901

## ELLIS COUNTY
Clerk of Court
District and County Courts
101 West Main Street
Waxahachie, TX 75165

## ERATH COUNTY
Clerk of Court
District and County Courts
Government Center
Stephenville, TX 76401

## FALLS COUNTY
Clerk of Court
Falls County District Court
PO Box 229
Marlin, TX 76661

## FANNIN COUNTY
Clerk of Court
District and County Courts
Government Center
Bonham, TX 75418

## FAYETTE COUNTY
Clerk of Court
District and County Courts
Government Center
LaGrange, TX 78945

## FISHER COUNTY
Clerk of Court
Fisher County District Court
PO Box 88
Roby, TX 79543

## FLOYD COUNTY
Clerk of Court
Floyd County District Court
PO Box 67
Floydada, TX 79235

## FOARD COUNTY
Clerk of Court
District and County Courts
PO Box 539
Crowell, TX 79227

## FORT BEND COUNTY
Clerk of Court
Fort Bend County District Court
401 Jackson Street
Richmond, TX 77406-0136

## FRANKLIN COUNTY
Clerk of Court
District and County Courts
Dallas and Kaufman Street
Mount Vernon, TX 75457

## FREESTONE COUNTY
Clerk of Court
Freestone Cty District Court
PO Box 722
Fairfield, TX 75840

## FRIO COUNTY
Clerk of Court
District and County Courts
400 East San Antonio Street
Pearsall, TX 78061

## GAINES COUNTY
Clerk of Court
District and County Courts
Government Center
Seminole, TX 79360

## GALVESTON COUNTY
Clerk of Court
Galveston County District Court
722 Moody, Rm 404
Galveston, TX 77550

## GARZA COUNTY
Clerk of Court
District and County Courts
Government Center
Post, TX 79356

## GILLESPIE COUNTY
Clerk of Court
Gillespie Cty District Court
101 West Main Street, #204
Fredericksburg, TX 78624-3700

## GLASSCOCK COUNTY
Clerk of Court
District and County Courts
Government Center
Garden City, TX 79739

## GOLIAD COUNTY
Clerk of Court
District and County Courts
PO Box 5
Goliad, TX 77963

## GONZALES COUNTY
Clerk of Court
Gonzales Cty District Court
PO Box 34
Gonzales, TX 78629

## GRAY COUNTY
Clerk of Court
Gray County District Court
PO Box 1139
Pampa, TX 79066-1139

## GRAYSON COUNTY
Clerk of Court
District and County Courts
200 South Crockett, Rm 120-A
Sherman, TX 75090

## GREGG COUNTY
Clerk of Court
Gregg County District Court
101 East Methvin, Ste 334
Longview, TX 75606

## GRIMES COUNTY
Clerk of Court
Grimes County District Court
PO Box 234
Anderson, TX 77830

## GUADALUPE COUNTY
Clerk of Court
District and County Courts
101 East Court Street
Seguin, TX 78155

## HALE COUNTY
Clerk of Court
Hale County District Court
Government Center
Plainview, TX 79072

## HALL COUNTY
Clerk of Court
District and County Courts
6th and Main Street
Memphis, TX 79245

## HAMILTON COUNTY
Clerk of Court
District and County Courts
Government Center
Hamilton, TX 76531

## HANSFORD COUNTY
Clerk of Court
District and County Courts
PO Box 397
Speannan, TX 79081

## HARDEMAN COUNTY
Clerk of Court
District and County Courts
PO Box 30
Quanah, TX 79252

## HARDIN COUNTY
Clerk of Court
Hardin County District Court
PO Box 2997
Kountze, TX 77625

## HARRIS COUNTY
Clerk of Court
Harris County District Court
301 Fannin
Houston, TX 77210

## HARRISON COUNTY
Clerk of Court
Harrison Cty District Court
Houston and Wellington Street
Marshall, TX 75670

## HARTLEY COUNTY
Clerk of Court
District and County Courts
PO Box T
Channing, TX 79018

## HASKELL COUNTY
Clerk of Court
Haskell County District Court
PO Box 27
Haskell, TX 79521

## HAYS COUNTY
Clerk of Court
District and County Courts
Government Center
San Marcos, TX 78666

## HEMPHILL COUNTY
Clerk of Court
District and County Courts
PO Box 867
Canadian, TX 79014

## HENDERSON COUNTY
Clerk of Court
Henderson County District Court
Government Center
Athens, TX 75751

## HIDALGO COUNTY
Clerk of Court
Hidalgo County District Court
100 South Closner
Edinburg, TX 78540

**Adoption Searches Made Easier**

## HILL COUNTY
Clerk of Court
District and County Courts
PO Box 634
Hillsboro, TX 76645

## HOCKLEY COUNTY
Clerk of Court
District and County Courts
Courthouse, #16
Levelland, TX 79336

## HOOD COUNTY
Clerk of Court
Hood County District Court
Courthouse, Rm 21
Granbury, TX 76048

## HOPKINS COUNTY
Clerk of Court
Hopkins County District Court
PO Box 391
Sulphur Springs, TX 75482

## HOUSTON COUNTY
Clerk of Court
Houston County District Court
Government Center
Crockett, TX 75835

## HOWARD COUNTY
Clerk of Court
Howard County District Court
PO Box 2138
Big Spring, TX 79721

## HUDSPETH COUNTY
Clerk of Court
District and County Courts
PO Drawer A
Sierra Blanca, TX 79851

## HUNT COUNTY
Clerk of Court
Hunt County District Court
PO Box 1627
Greenville, TX 75401

## HUTCHINSON COUNTY
Clerk of Court
Hutchinson Cty District Court
PO Box 580
Stinnett, TX 79083

## IRION COUNTY
Clerk of Court
District and County Courts
PO Box 736
Mertzon, TX 76941

## JACK COUNTY
Clerk of Court
Jack County District Court
Government Center
Jacksboro, TX 76458

## JACKSON COUNTY
Clerk of Court
District and County Courts
115 West Main
Edna, TX 77957

## JASPER COUNTY
Clerk of Court
Jasper County District Court
202 County Courthouse
Jasper, TX 75951

## JEFF DAVIS COUNTY
Clerk of Court
District and County Courts
PO Box 398
Ft. Davis, TX 79734

## JEFFERSON COUNTY
Clerk of Court
Jefferson Cty District Court
PO Box 3707
Beaumont, TX 77704

## JIM HOGG COUNTY
Clerk of Court
District and County Courts
PO Box 729
Hebbronville, TX 78361

## JIM WELLS COUNTY
Clerk of Court
District and County Courts
PO Drawer 2219
Alice, TX 78333

## JOHNSON COUNTY
Clerk of Court
Johnson County District Court
PO Box 495
Cleburne, TX 76033

## JONES COUNTY
Clerk of Court
District and County Courts
12th and Commercial Street
Anson, TX 79501

## KARNES COUNTY
Clerk of Court
Karnes County District Court
Government Center
Karnes City, TX 78118

## KAUFMAN COUNTY
Clerk of Court
District and County Courts
Government Center
Kaufman, TX 75142

## KENDALL COUNTY
Clerk of Court
Kendall County District Court
204 East San Antonio Street
Boerne, TX 78006

## KENEDY COUNTY
Clerk of Court
District and County Courts
PO Box 1519
Sarita, TX 78385

## KENT COUNTY
Clerk of Court
District and County Courts
PO Box 9
Jayton, TX 79528

## KERR COUNTY
Clerk of Court
Kerr County District Court
Government Center
Kerrville, TX 78028

## KIMBLE COUNTY
Clerk of Court
District and County Courts
501 Main Street
Junction, TX 76849

## KING COUNTY
Clerk of Court
District and County Courts
PO Box 71
Guthrie, TX 79236

## KINNEY COUNTY
Clerk of Court
Kinney County District Court
PO Drawer 9
Bracketville, TX 78832

## KLEBERG COUNTY
Clerk of Court
Kleberg County District Court
PO Box 312
Kingsville, TX 78364-0312

## KNOX COUNTY
Clerk of Court
District and County Courts
PO Box 196
Benjamin, TX 79505

## LA SALLE COUNTY
Clerk of Court
La Salle Cty District Court
PO Box 340
Cotulla, TX 78014

## LAMAR COUNTY
Clerk of Court
Lamar County District Court
Government Center
Paris, TX 75460

## LAMB COUNTY
Clerk of Court
Lamb County District Court
100 6th Street, Rm 212
Littlefield, TX 79339-3366

## LAMPASAS COUNTY
Clerk of Court
District and County Courts
400 South Live Oak Street
Lampasas, TX 76550

## LAVACA COUNTY
Clerk of Court
Lavaca County District Court
PO Box 306
Hallettsville, TX 77964

## LEE COUNTY
Clerk of Court
Lee County District Court
PO Box 176
Giddings, TX 78942

## LEON COUNTY
Clerk of Court
Leon County District Court
PO Box 39
Centerville, TX 75833

## LIBERTY COUNTY
Clerk of Court
Liberty County District Court
1923 Sam Houston, Rm 303
Liberty, TX 77575

## LIMESTONE COUNTY
Clerk of Court
Limestone County District Court
PO Box 230
Groesbeck, TX 76642

## LIPSCOMB COUNTY
Clerk of Court
District and County Courts
PO Box 70
Lipscomb, TX 79056

## LIVE OAK COUNTY
Clerk of Court
Live Oak Cty District Court
301 Houston Street
George West, TX 78022

## LLANO COUNTY
Clerk of Court
Llano County District Court
801 Ford, #209
Llano, TX 78643

## LOVING COUNTY
Clerk of Court
District and County Courts
Box 194
Mentone, TX 79754

## LUBBOCK COUNTY
Clerk of Court
District and County Courts
904 Broadway Street
Lubbock, TX 79408

## LYNN COUNTY
Clerk of Court
Lynn County District Court
PO Box 939
Tahoka, TX 79373

## MADISON COUNTY
Clerk of Court
Madison Cty District Court
Rm 226
Madisonville, TX 77864

## MARION COUNTY
Clerk of Court
Marion County District Court
102 Austin Street
Jefferson, TX 75657

## MARTIN COUNTY
Clerk of Court
District and County Courts
PO Box 906
Stanton, TX 79782

**MASON COUNTY**
Clerk of Court
District and County Courts
PO Box 702
Mason, TX 76856

**MATAGORDA COUNTY**
Clerk of Court
Matagorda County District Court
PO Drawer 188
Bay City, TX 77414

**MAVERICK COUNTY**
Clerk of Court
Maverick Cty District Court
PO Box 3659
Eagle Pass, TX 78853

**MCCULLOCH COUNTY**
Clerk of Court
District and County Courts
Courthouse Square
Brady, TX 76825

**MCLENNAN COUNTY**
Clerk of Court
McLennan County District Court
PO Box 2451
Waco, TX 76703

**MCMULLEN COUNTY**
Clerk of Court
District and County Courts
PO Box 235
Tilden, TX 78072

**MEDINA COUNTY**
Clerk of Court
District and County Courts
Government Center
Hondo, TX 78861

**MENARD COUNTY**
Clerk of Court
District and County Courts
PO Box 1028
Menard, TX 76859

**MIDLAND COUNTY**
Clerk of Court
Midland County District Court
200 West Wall Street, Ste 301
Midland, TX 79701

**MILAM COUNTY**
Clerk of Court
Milam County District Court
PO Box 999
Cameron, TX 76520

**MILLS COUNTY**
Clerk of Court
District and County Courts
PO Box 646
Goldthwaite, TX 76844

**MITCHELL COUNTY**
Clerk of Court
Mitchell County District Court
Government Center
Colorado City, TX 79512

**MONTAGUE COUNTY**
Clerk of Court
Montague County District Court
PO Box 155
Montague, TX 76251

**MONTGOMERY COUNTY**
Clerk of Court
Montgomery Cty District Court
PO Box 2985
Conroe, TX 77305

**MOORE COUNTY**
Clerk of Court
Moore County District Court
715 Dumas Ave, Rm 109
Dumas, TX 79029

**MORRIS COUNTY**
Clerk of Court
Monis County District Court
500 Brodnax
Daingerfield, TX 75638

**MOTLEY COUNTY**
Clerk of Court
District and County Courts
PO Box 66
Matador, TX 79244

**NACOGDOCHES COUNTY**
Clerk of Court
Nacogdoches Cty District Court
101 West Main Street
Nacogdoches, TX 75961

**NAVARRO COUNTY**
Clerk of Court
Navarro County District Court
PO Box 1439
Corsicana, TX 75151-1439

**NEWTON COUNTY**
Clerk of Court
Newton County District Court
PO Box 535
Newton, TX 75966

**NOLAN COUNTY**
Clerk of Court
Nolan County District Court
100 East 3rd Street
Sweetwater, TX 79556

**NUECES COUNTY**
Clerk of Court
Nueces County District Court
PO Box 2987
Corpus Christi, TX 78403

**OCHILTREE COUNTY**
Clerk of Court
Ochiltree County District Court
511 South Main Street
Perryton, TX 79070

**OLDHAM COUNTY**
Clerk of Court
District and County Courts
PO Box 360
Vega, TX 79092

## ORANGE COUNTY
Clerk of Court
Orange County District Court
PO Box 427
Orange, TX 77630

## PALO PINTO COUNTY
Clerk of Court
Palo Pinto County District Court
PO Box 189
Palo Pinto, TX 76484-0189

## PANOLA COUNTY
Clerk of Court
Panola County District Court
Government Center
Carthage, TX 75633

## PARKER COUNTY
Clerk of Court
Parker County District Court
PO Box 340
Weatherford, TX 76086-0340

## PARMER COUNTY
Clerk of Court
Parmer County District Court
PO Box 888
Farwell, TX 79325

## PECOS COUNTY
Clerk of Court
Pecos County District Court
400 South Nelson
Fort Stockton, TX 79735

## POLK COUNTY
Clerk of Court
Polk County District Court
101 West Church Street
Livingston, TX 77351

## POTTER COUNTY
Clerk of Court
Potter County District Court
PO Box 9570
Amarillo, TX 79105

## PRESIDIO COUNTY
Clerk of Court
District and County Courts
PO Box 789
Marfa, TX 79843

## RAINS COUNTY
Clerk of Court
District and County Courts
PO Box 187
Emory, TX 75440

## RANDALL COUNTY
Clerk of Court
Randall County District Court
501 16th Street
Canyon, TX 79015

## REAGAN COUNTY
Clerk of Court
District and County Courts
PO Box 100
Big Lake, TX 76932

## REAL COUNTY

Clerk of Court
District and County Courts
PO Box 656
Leakey, TX 78873

## RED RIVER COUNTY

Clerk of Court
Red River County District Court
400 North Walnut
Clarksville, TX 75426

## REEVES COUNTY

Clerk of Court
Reeves County District Court
PO Box 848
Pecos, TX 79772

## REFUGIO COUNTY

Clerk of Court
Refugio County District Court
PO Box 736
Refugio, TX 78377

## ROBERTS COUNTY

Clerk of Court
District and County Courts
PO Box 477
Miami, TX 79059

## ROBERTSON COUNTY

Clerk of Court
Robertson County District Court
PO Box 250
Franklin, TX 77856

## ROCKWALL COUNTY

Clerk of Court
Rockwall Cty District Court
Government Center
Rockwall, TX 75087

## RUNNELS COUNTY

Clerk of Court
Runnels County District Court
PO Box 166
Ballinger, TX 76821

## RUSK COUNTY

Clerk of Court
Rusk County District Court
115 North Main
Henderson, TX 75652

## SABINE COUNTY

Clerk of Court
Sabine County District Court
PO Box 850
Hemphill, TX 75948

## SAN AUGUSTINE COUNTY

Clerk of Court
San Augustine Cty District Court
Government Center
San Augustine, TX 75972

## SAN JACINTO COUNTY

Clerk of Court
San Jacinto County District Court
PO Box 369
Cold Springs, TX 77331

## SAN PATRICIO COUNTY
Clerk of Court
San Patricio County District Court
PO Box 1084
Sinton, TX 78387

## SAN SABA COUNTY
Clerk of Court
District and County Courts
Government Center
San Saba, TX 76877

## SCHLEICHER COUNTY
Clerk of Court
District and County Courts
PO Drawer 580
El Dorado, TX 76936

## SCURRY COUNTY
Clerk of Court
District and County Courts
Government Center
Snyder, TX 79549

## SHACKELFORD COUNTY
Clerk of Court
District and County Court
PO Box 247
Albany, TX 76430

## SHELBY COUNTY
Clerk of Court
Shelby County District Court
PO Box 1546
Center, TX 75935

## SHERMAN COUNTY
Clerk of Court
District and County Courts
PO Box 270
Stratford, TX 79084

## SMITH COUNTY
Clerk of Court
Smith County District Court
PO Box 1077
Tyler, TX 75710

## SOMERVELL COUNTY
Clerk of Court
District and County Courts
PO Box 1098
Glen Rose, TX 76043

## STARR COUNTY
Clerk of Court
District and County Courts
4th & Britton Avenue
Rio Grande City, TX 78582

## STEPHENS COUNTY
Clerk of Court
District and County Courts
200 West Walker
Breckenridge, TX 76424

## STERLING COUNTY
Clerk of Court
District and County Courts
PO Box 55
Sterling City, TX 76951

## STONEWALL COUNTY

Clerk of Court
District and County Courts
PO Drawer P
Aspermont, TX 79502

## SUTTON COUNTY

Clerk of Court
District and County Courts
300 East Oak, Ste 3
Sonora, TX 76950

## SWISHER COUNTY

Clerk of Court
District and County Courts
Government Center
Tulia, TX 79088

## TARRANT COUNTY

Clerk of Court
Tarrant County District Court
300 West Belknap
Fort Worth, TX 76196-0402

## TAYLOR COUNTY

Clerk of Court
Taylor County District Court
300 Oak Street
Abilene, TX 79602

## TERRELL COUNTY

Clerk of Court
District and County Courts
PO Drawer 410
Sanderson, TX 79848

## TERRY COUNTY

Clerk of Court
Teny County District Court
Government Center
Brownfield, TX 79316

## THROCKMORTON

Clerk of Court
District and County Courts
PO Box 309
Throckmorton, TX 76083

## TITUS COUNTY

Clerk of Court
Titus County District Court
Government Center
Mount Pleasant, TX 75455

## TOM GREEN COUNTY

Clerk of Court
Tom Green County District Court
Government Center
San Angelo, TX 76903

## TRAVIS COUNTY

Clerk of Court
Travis County District Court
PO Box 1748
Austin, TX 78767

## TRINITY COUNTY

Clerk of Court
District and County Courts
PO Box 548
Groveton, TX 75845

## TYLER COUNTY
Clerk of Court
Tyler County District Court
Government Center
Woodville, TX 75979

## UPSHUR COUNTY
Clerk of Court
Upshur County District Court
PO Box 950
Gilmer, TX 75644

## UPTON COUNTY
Clerk of Court
District and County Courts
PO Box 465
Rankin, TX 79778

## UVALDE COUNTY
Clerk of Court
Uvalde County District Court
Government Center
Uvalde, TX 78801

## VAL VERDE COUNTY
Clerk of Court
Val Verde County District Court
PO Box 1544
Del Rio, TX 78841

## VAN ZANDT COUNTY
Clerk of Court
Van Zandt County District Court
121 East Dallas, Rm 302
Canton, TX 75103

## VICTORIA COUNTY
Clerk of Court
Victoria Cty District Court
PO Box 1357
Victoria, TX 77902

## WALKER COUNTY
Clerk of Court
Walker County District Court
1100 University Ave, #301
Huntsville, TX 77340

## WALLER COUNTY
Clerk of Court
District and County Courts
836 Austin Street, Rm 318
Hempstead, TX 77445

## WARD COUNTY
Clerk of Court
Ward County District Court
PO Box 440
Monahans, TX 79756

## WASHINGTON COUNTY
Clerk of Court
Washington County District Court
100 East Main, Ste 304
Brenham, TX 77833

## WEBB COUNTY
Clerk of Court
Webb County District Court
PO Box 667
Laredo, TX 78042-0667

## WHARTON COUNTY

Clerk of Court
Wharton County District Court
PO Drawer 391
Wharton, TX 77488

## WHEELER COUNTY

Clerk of Court
Wheeler County District Court
PO Box 528
Wheeler, TX 79096

## WICHITA COUNTY

Clerk of Court
Wichita County District Court
PO Box 718
Wichita Falls, TX 76307

## WILBARGER COUNTY

Clerk of Court
Wilbarger Cty District Court
1700 Wilbarger, Rm 33
Vernon, TX 76384

## WILLACY COUNTY

Clerk of Court
Willacy County District Court
Government Center
Raymondville, TX 78580

## WILLIAMSON COUNTY

Clerk of Court
Williamson Cty District Court
PO Box 24
Georgetown, TX 78627

## WILSON COUNTY

Clerk of Court
Wilson County District Court
PO Box 812
Floresville, TX 78114

## WINKLER COUNTY

Clerk of Court
Winkler County District Court
100 East Winkler
Kermit, TX 79745

## WISE COUNTY

Clerk of Court
Wise County District Court
101 1/2 Trinity Street
Decatur, TX 76234

## WOOD COUNTY

Clerk of Court
Wood County District Court
PO Box 488
Quitman, TX 75783

## YOAKUM COUNTY

Clerk of Court
Yoakum County District Court
PO Box 899
Plains, TX 79355

## YOUNG COUNTY

Clerk of Court
Young County District Court
516 4th Street, Rm 201
Graham, TX 76046

**ZAPATA COUNTY**
Clerk of Court
District and County Courts
7th and Hidalgo
Zapata, TX 78076

**ZAVALA COUNTY**
Clerk of Court
Zavala County District Court
PO Box 704
Crystal City, TX 78839

# UTAH

**BEAVER COUNTY**
Clerk of Court
5th District Court,
105 East Center
Beaver, UT 84713

**BOX ELDER COUNTY**
Clerk of Court
1st District Court,
1 South Main
Brigham City, UT 84302

**CACHE COUNTY**
Clerk of Court
1st District and Circuit Court
140 North 100 West
Logan, UT 84321

**CARBON COUNTY**
Clerk of Court
7th District Court,
149 East 100 South
Price, UT 84501

**DAGGETT COUNTY**
Clerk of Court
8th District Court,
95 North 1st West
Manila, UT 84046

**DAVIS COUNTY**
Clerk of Court
2nd District Court,
PO Box 769
Farmington, UT 84025

**DUCHESNE COUNTY**
Clerk of Court
8th District Court,
Drawer 270
Duchesne, UT 84021

**EMERY COUNTY**
Clerk of Court
7th District Court,
PO Box 907
Castle Dale, UT 84513

**GARFIELD COUNTY**
Clerk of Court
6th District Court,
55 South Main
Panguitch, UT 84759

**GRAND COUNTY**
Clerk of Court
7th District Court,
125 East Center
Moab, UT 84532

## IRON COUNTY
Clerk of Court
5th District Court,
40 North & 100 East
Cedar City, UT 84720

## JUAB COUNTY
Clerk of Court
4th District and Circuit Court
160 North Main
Nephi, UT 84648

## KANE COUNTY
Clerk of Court
6th District Court
76 North Main
Kanab, UT 84741

## MILLARD COUNTY
Clerk of Court
4th District Court
765 South Hwy 99
Fillmore, UT 84631

## MORGAN COUNTY
Clerk of Court
2nd District Court
48 West Young Street
Morgan, UT 84050

## PIUTE COUNTY
Clerk of Court
6th District Court
Piute County PO Box 99
Junction, UT 84740

## RICH COUNTY
Clerk of Court
1st District Court
20 South Main
Randolph, UT 84064

## SALT LAKE COUNTY
Clerk of Court
3rd District Court
240 East 4th South, #205
Salt Lake City, UT 84111

## SAN JUAN COUNTY
Clerk of Court
7th District Court
297 South Main
Monticello, UT 84535

## SANPETE COUNTY
Clerk of Court
6th District Court
160 North Main
Manti, UT 84642

## SEVIER COUNTY
Clerk of Court
6th District Court
250 North Main
Richfield, UT 84701

## SUMMIT COUNTY
Clerk of Court
3rd District Court
60 North Main
Coalville, UT 84017

## TOOELE COUNTY
Clerk of Court
3rd District Court
47 South Main
Tooele, UT 84074

## UINTAH COUNTY
Clerk of Court
8th District Court
147 East Main
Vernal, UT 84078

## UTAH COUNTY
Clerk of Court
4th District Court
125 North 100 West
Provo, UT 84603

## WASATCH COUNTY
Clerk of Court
4th District Court
25 North Main
Heber City, UT 84032

## WASHINGTON COUNTY
Clerk of Court
5th District Court
220 North 200 East
St. George, UT 84770

## WAYNE COUNTY
Clerk of Court
6th District Court,
Wayne County 18 South Main
Loa, UT 84747

## WEBER COUNTY
Clerk of Court
2nd District Court
2549 Washington Boulevard
Ogden, UT 84401

# VIRGINIA

## ACCOMACK COUNTY
Clerk of Court
Accomack County Circuit Court
PO Box 126
Accomack, VA 23301

## ALBEMARLE COUNTY
Clerk of Court
Circuit and General District Court
501 East Jefferson Street
Charlottesville, VA 22902-5176

## THE CITY OF ALEXANDRIA
Clerk of Court
Circuit and General District Court
520 King Street
Alexandria, VA 22314

## ALLEGHANY COUNTY
Clerk of Court
Alleghany County Circuit Court
266 West Main
Covington, VA 24426

## AMELIA COUNTY
Clerk of Court
Amelia County Circuit Court
PO Box 237
Amelia, VA 23002

## AMHERST COUNTY
Clerk of Court
Amherst County Circuit Court
PO Box 462
Amherst, VA 24521

## APPOMATTOX COUNTY
Clerk of Court
Appomattox County Circuit Court
Circuit Court Bldg
Appomattox, VA 24522

## ARLINGTON COUNTY
Clerk of Court
Arlington County Circuit Court
1436 North Courthouse Rd, #101
Arlington, VA 22201

## AUGUSTA COUNTY
Clerk of Court
Augusta County Circuit Court
PO Box 689
Staunton, VA 24401

## BATH COUNTY
Clerk of Court
Bath County Circuit Court
Courthouse Hill, PO Box 180
Warm Springs, VA 24484

## BEDFORD COUNTY
Clerk of Court
Bedford County Circuit Court
Main and Court Street
Bedford, VA 24523

## BLAND COUNTY
Clerk of Court
Bland County Circuit Court
PO Box 295
Bland, VA 24315

## BOTETOURT COUNTY
Clerk of Court
Botetourt Cty Circuit Court
PO Box 219
Fincastle, VA 24090

## THE CITY OF BRISTOL
Clerk of Court
Bristol Circuit Court
497 Cumberland Street
Bristol, VA 24201

## BRUNSWICK COUNTY
Clerk of Court
Circuit Court
216 Main Street
Lawrenceville, VA 23868

## BUCHANAN COUNTY
Clerk of Court
Circuit Court
PO Box 929
Grundy, VA 24614

## BUCKINGHAM COUNTY
Clerk of Court
Buckingham County Circuit Court
PO Box 107
Buckingham, VA 23921

## THE CITY OF BUENA VISTA
Clerk of Courts
Circuit Court
2039 Sycamore Ave
Buena Vista, VA 24416

## CAMPBELL COUNTY
Clerk of Court
Campbell County Circuit Court
PO Box 7
Rustburg, VA 24588

## CAROLINE COUNTY
Clerk of Court
Caroline County Circuit Court
PO Box 309
Bowling Green, VA 22427

## CARROLL COUNTY
Clerk of Court
Carroll County Circuit Court
PO Box 218
Hillsville, VA 24343

## CHARLES CITY COUNTY
Clerk of Court
Charles City County Circuit Court
PO Box 86
Charles City, VA 23030-0086

## CHARLOTTE COUNTY
Clerk of Court
Charlotte County Circuit Court
PO Box 38
Charlotte Courthouse, VA 23923

## CHARLOTTESVILLE
Clerk of Court
Charlottesville Circuit Court
315 East High Street
Charlottesville, VA 22901

## THE CITY OF CHESAPEAKE
Clerk of Court
Chesapeake Circuit Court
PO Box 15205
Chesapeake, VA 23320

## CHESTERFIELD COUNTY
Clerk of Court
Chesterfield Cty Circuit Court
PO Box 125
Chesterfield, VA 23832

## CLARKE COUNTY
Clerk of Court
Circuit Court
102 North Church
Berryville, VA 22611

## CLIFTON FORGE
Clerk of Court
Clifton Forge Circuit Court
PO Box 27
Clifton Forge, VA 24422

## COLONIAL HEIGHTS
Clerk of Court
Circuit Court
401 Temple Ave
Colonial Heights, VA 23834

**CRAIG COUNTY**
Clerk of Court
Craig County Circuit Court
PO Box 185
New Castle, VA 24127

**CULPEPER COUNTY**
Clerk of Court
Circuit Court
135 West Cameron Street
Culpeper, VA 22701

**CUMBERLAND COUNTY**
Clerk of Court
Cumberland Cty Circuit Court
PO Box 8
Cumberland, VA 23040

**THE CITY OF DANVILLE**
Clerk of Court
Circuit Court
212 Lynn Street
Danville, VA 24543

**DICKENSON COUNTY**
Clerk of Court
Dickenson Cty Circuit Court
PO Box 190
Clintwood, VA 24228

**DINWIDDIE COUNTY**
Clerk of Court
Dinwiddie Cty Circuit Court
PO Box 63
Dinwiddie, VA 23841

**ESSEX COUNTY**
Clerk of Court
Essex County Circuit Court
PO Box 445
Tappahannock, VA 22560

**FAIRFAX COUNTY**
Clerk of Court
Circuit Court
4110 Chain Bridge Rd
Fairfax, VA 22030

**THE CITY OF FAIRFAX**
Clerk of Court
Circuit Court
10455 Armstrong
Fairfax, VA 22030

**FALLS CHURCH**
Clerk of Court
General District Court
300 Park Ave
Arlington, VA 22201

**FAUQUIER COUNTY**
Clerk of Court
Fauquier County Circuit Court
40 Culpeper Street
Warrenton, VA 22186

**FLOYD COUNTY**
Clerk of Court
Floyd County Circuit Court
100 East Main Street, Rm 200
Floyd, VA 24091

## FLUVANNA COUNTY
Clerk of Court
Fluvanna County Circuit Court
Court Green and Rt 15
Palmyra, VA 22963

## FRANKLIN COUNTY
Clerk of Court
Franklin County Circuit Court
PO Box 567
Rocky Mount, VA 24151

## FREDERICK COUNTY
Clerk of Court
Circuit Court
5 North Kent Street
Winchester, VA 22601

## FREDERICKSBURY
Clerk of Court
Fredericksburg Circuit Court
815 Princess Anne
Fredericksburg, VA 22404-0359

## THE CITY OF GALAX
Clerk of Court
Galax District Court
PO Box 214
Galax, VA 24333

## GILES COUNTY
Clerk of Court
Giles County Circuit Court
501 Wenonah Ave
Pearisburg, VA 24134

## GLOUCESTER COUNTY
Clerk of Court
Gloucester Cty Circuit Court
Box N
Gloucester, VA 23061

## GOOCHLAND COUNTY
Clerk of Court
Goochland Cty Circuit Court
2938 River Road West
Goochland, VA 23063

## GRAYSON COUNTY
Clerk of Court
Circuit Court
129 Davis Street
Independence, VA 24348

## GREENE COUNTY
Clerk of Court
Greene County Circuit Court
PO Box 386
Standardsville, VA 22973

## GREENSVILLE COUNTY
Clerk of Court
Greensville County Circuit Court
PO Box 631
Emporia, VA 23847

## HALIFAX COUNTY
Clerk of Court
Halifax County Circuit Court
PO Box 729
Halifax, VA 24558

## THE CITY OF HAMPTON
Clerk of Court
Hampton Circuit Court
101 Kingsway
Hampton, VA 23669

## HANOVER COUNTY
Clerk of Court
Hanover County Circuit Court
PO Box 39
Hanover, VA 23069

## HENRICO COUNTY
Clerk of Court
Henrico County Circuit Court
4301 East Parhem Rd.
Richmond, VA 23273

## HENRY COUNTY
Clerk of Court
Henry County Circuit Court
PO Box 1049
Martinsville, VA 24114

## HIGHLAND COUNTY
Clerk of Court
Highland County Circuit Court
PO Box 190
Monterey, VA 24465

## THE CITY OF HOPEWELL
Clerk of Court
Hopewell Circuit Court
100 East Broadway
Hopewell, VA 23860

## ISLE OF WIGHT COUNTY
Clerk of Court
Circuit and General District Court
County Courthouse
Isle of Wight, VA 23397

## JAMES CITY COUNTY
Clerk of Court
James City County Circuit Court
South Henry Street
Williamsburg, VA 23187

## KING AND QUEEN CTY
Clerk of Court
Circuit Court
PO Box 67
King and Queen, VA 23085

## KING GEORGE COUNTY
Clerk of Court
King George Cty Circuit Court
PO Box 105
King George, VA 22485

## KING WILLIAM COUNTY
Clerk of Court
King William Cty Circuit Court
County Courthouse, PO Box 216
King William, VA 23086

## LANCASTER COUNTY
Clerk of Court
Lancaster County Circuit Court
Courthouse Square
Lancaster, VA 22503

## LEE COUNTY
Clerk of Court
Lee County Circuit Court
PO Box 326
Jonesville, VA 24263

## LOUDOUN COUNTY
Clerk of Court
Loudoun County Circuit Court
18 North King Street
Leesburg, VA 22075

## LOUISA COUNTY
Clerk of Court
Louisa County Circuit Court
102 West Main, PO Box 37
Louisa, VA 23093

## LUNENBURG COUNTY
Clerk of Court
Circuit and General District Court
Rt 40 & 49
Lunenberg, VA 23952

## THE CITY OF LYNCHBURG
Clerk of Court
Lynchburg Circuit Court
900 Court Street, PO Box 4
Lynchburg, VA 24505-0004

## MADISON COUNTY
Clerk of Court
Circuit Court
PO Box 470
Madison, VA 22727

## MARTINSVILLE
Clerk of Court
Martinsville Circuit Court
PO Box 1206
Martinsville, VA 24114-1206

## MATHEWS COUNTY
Clerk of Court
Mathews County Circuit Court
PO Box 463
Mathews, VA 23109

## MECKLENBURG COUNTY
Clerk of Court
Mecklenburg Circuit Court
Courthouse, PO Box 530
Boydton, VA 23917

## MIDDLESEX COUNTY
Clerk of Court
Middlesex Cty Circuit Court
Rt 33 & 17, PO Box 158
Saluda, VA 23149

## MONTGOMERY COUNTY
Clerk of Court
Montgomery Cty Circuit Court
1 East Main, PO Box 209
Christiansburg, VA 24073

## NELSON COUNTY
Clerk of Court
Nelson County Circuit Court
PO Box 10
Lovingston, VA 22949

## NEW KENT COUNTY
Clerk of Court
New Kent County Circuit Court
1201 Courthouse Circle
New Kent, VA 23124

## NEWPORT NEWS
Clerk of Court
Newport News Circuit Court
2500 Washington Ave
Newport News, VA 23607

## THE CITY OF NORFOLK
Clerk of Court
Norfolk Circuit Court
100 Street Paul Blvd
Norfolk, VA 23510

## NORTHAMPTON COUNTY
Clerk of Court
Northampton Cty Circuit Court
16404 Courthouse Rd
Eastville, VA 23347

## NORTHUMBERLAND
Clerk of Court
Northumberland Cty Circuit Court
PO Box 217
Heathsville, VA 22473

## NOTTOWAY COUNTY
Clerk of Court
Nottoway County Circuit Court
PO Box 25
Nottoway, VA 23955

## ORANGE COUNTY
Clerk of Court
Orange County Circuit Court
PO Box 230
Orange, VA 22960

## PAGE COUNTY
Clerk of Court
Page County Circuit Court
116 South Court Street
Luray, VA 22835

## PATRICK COUNTY
Clerk of Court
Patrick County Circuit Court
Blue Ridge and Main Street
Stuart, VA 24171

## THE CITY OF PETERSBURG
Clerk of Court
Petersburg Circuit Court
Courthouse Hill
Petersburg, VA 23803

## PITTSYLVANIA COUNTY
Clerk of Court
Pittsylvania Cty Circuit Court
1 South Main, PO Drawer 31
Chatham, VA 24531

## PORTSMOUTH
Clerk of Court
Portsmouth Circuit Court
601 Crawford Street
Portsmouth, VA 23705

**POWHATAN COUNTY**
Clerk of Court
Powhatan Cty Circuit Court
PO Box 37
Powhatan, VA 23139

**PRINCE EDWARD COUNTY**
Clerk of Court
Prince Edward Cty Circuit Court
PO Box 304
Farinville, VA 23901

**PRINCE GEORGE COUNTY**
Clerk of Court
Prince George Cty Circuit Court
PO Box 98
Prince George, VA 23875

**PRINCE WILLIAM COUNTY**
Clerk of Court
Circuit Court
9311 Lee Ave
Manassas, VA 22110

**PULASKI COUNTY**
Clerk of Court
Pulaski County Circuit Court
1055 East Main
Pulaski, VA 24301

**THE CITY OF RADFORD**
Clerk of Court
Radford Circuit Court
619 Second Street
Radford, VA 24141

**RAPPAHANNOCK COUNTY**
Clerk of Court
Rappahannock Cty Circuit Court
PO Box 116
Washington, VA 22747

**RICHMOND COUNTY**
Clerk of Court
Circuit Court
PO Box 1000
Warsaw, VA 22572

**THE CITY OF RICHMOND**
Clerk of Court
Richmond Circuit Court
800 East Marshall
Richmond, VA 23219

**ROANOKE COUNTY**
Clerk of Court
Roanokc County Circuit Court
305 East Main
Salem, VA 24153

**THE CITY OF ROANOKE**
Clerk of Court
Roanoke Circuit Court
315 West Church Avenue
Roanoke, VA 24016

**ROCKBRIDGE COUNTY**
Clerk of Court
Rockbridge Cty Circuit Court
2 South Main, Courthouse Square
Lexington, VA 24450

## ROCKINGHAM COUNTY
Clerk of Court
Circuit Court
Court Square
Harrisonburg, VA 22801

## RUSSELL COUNTY
Clerk of Court
Russell County Circuit Court
PO Box 435
Lebanon, VA 24266

## THE CITY OF SALEM
Clerk of Court
Salem Circuit Court
2 East Calhoun
Salem, VA 24153

## SCOTT COUNTY
Clerk of Courts
Circuit Court
104 East Jackson Street
Gate City, VA 24251

## SHENANDOAH COUNTY
Clerk of Court
Shenandoah Cty Circuit Court
112 South Main, PO Box 406
Woodstock, VA 22664

## SMYTH COUNTY
Clerk of Court
Smyth County Circuit Court
PO Box 1025
Marion, VA 24354

## SOUTHAMPTON COUNTY
Clerk of Court
Southampton Cty Circuit Court
22350 Main Street, PO Box 190
Courtland, VA 23837

## SPOTSYLVANIA COUNTY
Clerk of Court
Spotsylvania Cty Circuit Court
9101 Courthouse Rd
Spotsylvania, VA 22553

## STAFFORD COUNTY
Clerk of Court
Circuit Court
1300 Courthouse Rd
Stafford, VA 22554

## THE CITY OF STAUNTON
Clerk of Court
Staunton Circuit Court
21 North New Street
Staunton, VA 24401

## THE CITY OF SUFFOLK
Clerk of Court
Suffolk Circuit Court
441 Market Street
Suffolk, VA 23439

## SURRY COUNTY
Clerk of Court
Surry County Circuit Court
28 Colonial Trail E
Surry, VA 23883

## SUSSEX COUNTY
Clerk of Court
Sussex County Circuit Court
Courthouse, PO Box 1337
Sussex, VA 23884

## TAZEWELL COUNTY
Clerk of Court
Tazewell County Circuit Court
101 Main, PO Box 968
Tazewell, VA 24651

## VIRGINIA BEACH
Clerk of Court
Princess Ann Station
2401 Courthouse Boulevard
Virginia Beach, VA 23456

## WARREN COUNTY
Clerk of Court
Circuit Court
1 East Main Street
Front Royal, VA 22630

## WASHINGTON COUNTY
Clerk of Court
Circuit Court
Court Street
Abingdon, VA 24210

## WAYNESBORO
Clerk of Court
Waynesboro Circuit Court
250 South Wayne, PO Box 210
Waynesboro, VA 22980

## WESTMORELAND
Clerk of Court
Westmoreland Cty Circuit Court
PO Box 307
Montross, VA 22520

## WISE COUNTY
Clerk of Court
Wise County Circuit Court
PO Box 1248
Wise, VA 24293

## WYTHE COUNTY
Clerk of Courts
Circuit Court
225 South 4th Street
Wytheville, VA 24382

## YORK COUNTY
Clerk of Court
York County Circuit Court
PO Box 371
Yorktown, VA 23690

# VERMONT

## ADDISON COUNTY
Clerk of Court
District and Superior Courts
5 Court Street
Middlebury, VT 05753

## BENNINGTON COUNTY
Clerk of Court
Bennington Cty Superior Court
PO Box 4157
Bennington, VT 05201

## CALEDONIA COUNTY
Clerk of Court
Caledonia County Superior Court
PO Box 4129
St. Johnsbury, VT 05819-4129

## CHITTENDEN COUNTY
Clerk of Court
Chittenden County Superior Court
175 Main
Burlington, VT 05401

## ESSEX COUNTY
Clerk of Court
District and Superior Courts
PO Box 75
Guildhall, VT 05905

## FRANKLIN COUNTY
Clerk of Court
Franklin Cty Superior Court
PO Box 808
St. Albans, VT 05478

## GRAND ISLE COUNTY
Clerk of Court
District and Superior Courts
PO Box 7
North Hero, VT 05474

## LAMOILLE COUNTY
Clerk of Court
Lamoille Cty Superior Court
PO Box 490
Hyde Park, VT 05655

## ORANGE COUNTY
Clerk of Court
District and Superior Courts
RR 1, Box 30
Chelsea, VT 05038

## ORLEANS COUNTY
Clerk of Court
Orleans County Superior Court
83 Main Street
Newport, VT 05855

## RUTLAND COUNTY
Clerk of Court
Rutland County Superior Court
83 Center Street
Rutland, VT 05702-4017

## WASHINGTON COUNTY
Clerk of Court
Washington Cty Superior Court
PO Box 426
Montpelier, VT 05602

## WINDHAM COUNTY
Clerk of Court
Windham County Superior Court
PO Box 207
Newfane, VT 05345

## WINDSOR COUNTY
Clerk of Court
Windsor County Superior Court
12 The Green, PO Box 428
Woodstock, VT 05091

# WASHINGTON

## ADAMS COUNTY
Clerk of Court
Adams County Superior Court
PO Box 187
Ritzville, WA 99169

## ASOTIN COUNTY
Clerk of Court
Asotin County Superior Court
PO Box 159
Asotin, WA 99402

## BENTON COUNTY
Clerk of Court
Benton County Superior Court
7320 West Quinault
Kennewick, WA 99336

## CHELAN COUNTY
Clerk of Court
Chelan County Superior Court
Box 3025
Wenatchee, WA 98807

## CLALLAM COUNTY
Clerk of Court
Superior and District Courts
223 East 4th Street
Port Angeles, WA 98362

## CLARK COUNTY
Clerk of Court
Clark County Superior Court
PO Box 5000
Vancouver, WA 98668

## COLUMBIA COUNTY
Clerk of Court
Superior and District Court
341 East Main Street
Dayton, WA 99328

## COWLITZ COUNTY
Clerk of Court
Cowlitz County Superior Court
312 SW First Ave
Kelso, WA 98626

## DOUGLAS COUNTY
Clerk of Court
Douglas County Superior Court
PO Box 516
Waterville, WA 98858

## FERRY COUNTY
Clerk of Court
Superior and District Courts
PO Box 302
Republic, WA 99166

## FRANKLIN COUNTY
Clerk of Court
Superior and District Court
1016 North 4th Street
Pasco, WA 99301

## GARFIELD COUNTY
Clerk of Court
Garfield County Superior Court
Box 915
Pomeroy, WA 99347

## GRANT COUNTY
Clerk of Court
Superior and District Courts
PO Box 37
Ephrata, WA 98823

## GRAYS HARBOR COUNTY
Clerk of Court
Grays Superior Court
PO Box 711
Montesano, WA 98563

## ISLAND COUNTY
Clerk of Court
Island County Superior Court
6th and Main, PO Box 5000
Coupeville, WA 98239

## JEFFERSON COUNTY
Clerk of Court
Superior and District Courts
PO Box 1220
Port Townsend, WA 98368

## KING COUNTY
Clerk of Court
Superior and District Courts
516 3rd Ave
Seattle, WA 98104

## KITSAP COUNTY
Clerk of Court
Superior and District Courts
614 Division Street
Port Orchard, WA 98366

## KITTITAS COUNTY
Clerk of Court
Kittitas Cty Superior Court
205 West 5th, Room 210
Ellensburg, WA 98926

## KLICKITAT COUNTY
Clerk of Court
Klickitat County Superior Court
205 South Columbus Avenue
Goldendale, WA 98620

## LEWIS COUNTY
Clerk of Court
Lewis County Superior Court
360 NW North Street
Chehalis, WA 98532-1900

## LINCOLN COUNTY
Clerk of Court
Lincoln County Superior Court
Box 369
Davenport, WA 99122

## MASON COUNTY
Clerk of Court
Mason County Superior Court
PO Box 340
Shelton, WA 98584

## OKANOGAN COUNTY
Clerk of Court
Okanogan Cty Superior Court
PO Box 72
Okanogan, WA 98840

## PACIFIC COUNTY
Clerk of Court
Pacific County Superior Court
PO Box 67
South Bend, WA 98586

## PEND OREILLE COUNTY
Clerk of Court
Superior and District Court
PO Box 5000
Newport, WA 99156-5020

## PIERCE COUNTY
Clerk of Court
Pierce County Superior Court
930 Tacoma Avenue S, Rm 110
Tacoma, WA 98402

## SAN JUAN COUNTY
Clerk of Court
San Juan County Superior Court
350 Court Street, #7
Friday Harbor, WA 98250

## SKAGIT COUNTY
Clerk of Court
Skagit County Superior Court
PO Box 837
Mount Vernon, WA 98273

## SKAMANIA COUNTY
Clerk of Court
Superior and District Courts
PO Box 790
Stevenson, WA 98648

## SNOHOMISH COUNTY
Clerk of Court
Snohomish Superior Court
3000 Rockefeller, Rm 246
Everett, WA 98201

## SPOKANE COUNTY
Clerk of Court
Spokane County Superior Court
West 1116 Broadway, Rm 300
Spokane, WA 99260-0090

## STEVENS COUNTY
Clerk of Court
Stevens County Superior Court
PO Box 350
Colville, WA 99114-0350

## THURSTON COUNTY
Clerk of Court
Superior and District Court
2000 Lakeridge Dr,SW Bldg #2
Olympia, WA 98502

## WAHKIAKUM COUNTY
Clerk of Court
Wahkiakum Superior Court
PO Box 116
Cathlamet, WA 98612

## WALLA WALLA COUNTY
Clerk of Court
Walla Walla Cty Superior Court
PO Box 836
Walla Walla, WA 99362

## WHATCOM COUNTY
Clerk of Court
Superior and District Court
311 Grand Ave
Bellingham, WA 98227

## WHITMAN COUNTY
Clerk of Court
Whitman County Superior Court
North 404 Main Street
Colfax, WA 99111

## YAKIMA COUNTY
Clerk of Court
Yakima County Superior Court
128 North 2nd Street
Yakima, WA 98901

# WISCONSIN

## ADAMS COUNTY
Clerk of Court
Circuit Court
PO Box 220
Friendship, WI 53934

## ASHLAND COUNTY
Clerk of Court
Circuit Court
201 West Main, Rm 307
Ashland, WI 54806

## BARRON COUNTY
Clerk of Court
Circuit Court
330 East LaSalle
Barron, WI 54812

## BAYFIELD COUNTY
Clerk of Court
Circuit Court
117 East 5th
Washburn, WI 54891

## BROWN COUNTY
Clerk of Court
Circuit Court
PO Box 23600
Green Bay, WI 54305-3600

## BUFFALO COUNTY
Clerk of Court
Circuit Court
407 South 2nd
Alma, WI 54610

## BURNETT COUNTY
Clerk of Court
Circuit Court
7410 County Road K
Siren, WI 54872

## CALUMET COUNTY
Clerk of Court
Circuit Court
206 Court Street
Chilton, WI 53014

## CHIPPEWA COUNTY
Clerk of Court
Circuit Court
711 North Bridge Street
Chippewa Falls, WI 54729

## CLARK COUNTY
Clerk of Court
Circuit Court
517 Court Street
Neillsville, WI 54456

## COLUMBIA COUNTY
Clerk of Court
Circuit Court
PO Box 405
Portage, WI 53901

## CRAWFORD COUNTY
Clerk of Court
Circuit Court
220 North Beaumont Rd
Prairie Du Chien, WI 53821

## DANE COUNTY
Clerk of Court
Circuit Court
Dane County Courthouse
Madison, WI 53709

## DODGE COUNTY
Clerk of Court
Circuit Court
105 North Main
Juneau, WI 53039

## DOOR COUNTY
Clerk of Court
Circuit Court
PO Box 670
Sturgeon Bay, WI 54235

## DOUGLAS COUNTY
Clerk of Court
Circuit Court
1313 Belknap Street
Superior, WI 54880

## DUNN COUNTY
Clerk of Court
Circuit Court
800 Wilson Ave
Menomonie, WI 54751

## EAU CLAIRE COUNTY
Clerk of Court
Circuit Court
721 Oxford Ave
Eau Claire, WI 54703

## FLORENCE COUNTY
Clerk of Court
Circuit Court
PO Box 410
Florence, WI 54121

## FOND du LAC COUNTY
Clerk of Court
Circuit Court
PO Box 1355
Fond du Lac, WI 54936-1355

## FOREST COUNTY
Clerk of Court
Circuit Court
200 East Madison
Crandon, WI 54520

## GRANT COUNTY
Clerk of Court
Circuit Court
PO Box 46
Lancaster, WI 53813

## GREEN COUNTY
Clerk of Court
Circuit Court
1016 16th Ave
Monroe, WI 53566

## GREEN LAKE COUNTY
Clerk of Court
Circuit Court
492 Hill Street
Green Lake, WI 54941

## IOWA COUNTY
Clerk of Court
Circuit Court
222 North Iowa Street
Dodgeville, WI 53533

## IRON COUNTY
Clerk of Court
Circuit Court
300 Taconite Street
Hurley, WI 54534

## JACKSON COUNTY
Clerk of Court
Circuit Court
307 Main Street
Black River Falls, WI 54615

## JEFFERSON COUNTY
Clerk of Court
Circuit Court
320 South Main Street
Jefferson, WI 53549

## JUNEAU COUNTY
Clerk of Court
Circuit Court
220 East State Street
Mouston, WI 53948

## KENOSHA COUNTY
Clerk of Court
Circuit Court
912 56th Street
Kenosha, WI 53140

## KEWAUNEE COUNTY
Clerk of Court
Circuit Court
613 Dodge Street
Kewaunee, WI 54216

## LA CROSSE COUNTY
Clerk of Court
Circuit Court
400 North 4th Street
La Crosse, WI 54601

## LAFAYETTE COUNTY
Clerk of Court
Circuit Court
626 Main Street
Darlington, WI 53530

## LANGLADE COUNTY
Clerk of Court
Circuit Court
800 Clermont Street
Antigo, WI 54409

## LINCOLN COUNTY
Clerk of Court
Circuit Court
Government Center
Merrill, WI 54452

## MANITOWOC COUNTY
Clerk of Court
Circuit Court
PO Box 2000
Manitowoc, WI 54220

## MARATHON COUNTY
Clerk of Court
Circuit Court
500 Forrest Street
Wausau, WI 54403

## MARINETTE COUNTY
Clerk of Court
Circuit Court
PO Box 320
Marinette, WI 54143

## MARQUETTE COUNTY
Clerk of Court
Circuit Court
PO Box 187
Montello, WI 53949

## MENOMINEE COUNTY
Clerk of Court
Circuit Court
Courthouse Rd
Keshena, WI 54135

## MILWAUKEE COUNTY
Clerk of Court
Circuit Court
901 North 9th Street
Milwaukee, WI 53233

## MONROE COUNTY
Clerk of Court
Circuit Court
PO Box 186
Sparta, WI 54656

## OCONTO COUNTY
Clerk of Court
Circuit Court
300 Washington Street
Oconto, WI 54153

## ONEIDA COUNTY
Clerk of Court
Circuit Court
PO Box 400
Rhinelander, WI 54501

## OUTAGAMIE COUNTY
Clerk of Court
Circuit Court
320 South Walnut Street
Appleton, WI 54911

**OZAUKEE COUNTY**
Clerk of Court
Circuit Court
1201 South Spring Street
Port Washington, WI 53074

**PEPIN COUNTY**
Clerk of Court
Circuit Court
550 7th Avenue West
Durand, WI 54736

**PIERCE COUNTY**
Clerk of Court
Circuit Court
PO Box 129
Ellsworth, WI 54011

**POLK COUNTY**
Clerk of Court
Circuit Court
100 Polk Plaza, Hwy 46
Balsam Lake, WI 54810

**PORTAGE COUNTY**
Clerk of Court
Circuit Court
1516 Church Street
Stevens Point, WI 54481

**PRICE COUNTY**
Clerk of Court
Circuit Court
Courthouse, Hwy 13
Phillips, WI 54555

**RACINE COUNTY**
Clerk of Court
Circuit Court
717 Wisconsin Ave
Racine, WI 53403

**RICHLAND COUNTY**
Clerk of Court
Circuit Court
PO Box 655
Richland Center, WI 53581

**ROCK COUNTY**
Clerk of Court
Circuit Court
51 South Main
Janesville, WI 53545

**ROCK COUNTY**
Clerk of Court
Circuit Court
250 Garden Lane
Beloit, WI 53511

**RUSK COUNTY**
Clerk of Court
Circuit Court
311 Miner Avenue E
Ladysmith, WI 54848

**SAUK COUNTY**
Clerk of Court
Circuit Court
PO Box 449
Baraboo, WI 53913

## SAWYER COUNTY
Clerk of Court
Circuit Court
PO Box 508
Hayward, WI 54843

## SHAWANO COUNTY
Clerk of Court
Circuit Court
311 North Main, Rm 206
Shawano, WI 54166

## SHEBOYGAN COUNTY
Clerk of Court
Circuit Court
615 North 6th Street
Sheboygan, WI 53081

## ST. CROIX COUNTY
Clerk of Court
Circuit Court
1101 Carmichael Road
Hudson, WI 54016

## TAYLOR COUNTY
Clerk of Court
Circuit Court
PO Box 97
Medford, WI 54451

## TREMPEALEAU COUNTY
Clerk of Court
Circuit Court
Main Street
Whitchall, WI 54773

## VERNON COUNTY
Clerk of Court
Circuit Court
PO Box 426
Viroqua, WI 54665

## VILAS COUNTY
Clerk of Court
Circuit Court
PO Box 369
Eagle River, WI 54521

## WALWORTH COUNTY
Clerk of Court
Circuit Court
PO Box 1001
Elkhom, WI 53121

## WASHBURN COUNTY
Clerk of Court
Circuit Court
PO Box 339
Shell Lake, WI 54871

## WASHINGTON COUNTY
Clerk of Court
Circuit Court
PO Box 1986
West Bend, WI 53095

## WAUKESHA COUNTY
Clerk of Court
Circuit Court
515 Westmoreland
Waukesha, WI 53188

## WAUPACA COUNTY
Clerk of Court
Circuit Court
PO Box 354
Waupaca, WI 54981

## WAUSHARA COUNTY
Clerk of Court
Circuit Court
PO Box 507
Wautoma, WI 54982

## WINNEBAGO COUNTY
Clerk of Court
Circuit Court
415 Jackson Drive
Oshkosh, WI 54903

## WOOD COUNTY
Clerk of Court
Circuit Court
400 Market Street
Wisconsin Rapids, WI 54494

## WEST VIRGINIA

## BARBOUR COUNTY
Clerk of Court
Barbour County Circuit Court
8 North Main Street
Philippi, WV 26416

## BERKELEY COUNTY
Clerk of Court
Berkeley County Circuit Court
100 West King Street
Martinsburg, WV 25401

## BOONE COUNTY
Clerk of Courts
Boone County Circuit Court
200 State Street
Madison, WV 25130

## BRAXTON COUNTY
Clerk of Court
Braxton County Circuit Court
Government Center
Sutton, WV 26601

## BROOKE COUNTY
Clerk of Court
Brooke County Circuit Court
632 Main, PO Box 474
Wellsburg, WV 26070

## CABELL COUNTY
Clerk of Court
Cabell County Circuit Court
PO Box 545
Huntington, WV 25711

## CALHOUN COUNTY
Clerk of Court
Calhoun County Circuit Court
PO Box 266
Grantsville, WV 26147

## CLAY COUNTY
Clerk of Court
Clay County Circuit Court
207 Main, PO Box 129
Clay, WV 25043

**Adoption Searches Made Easier**

## DODDRIDGE COUNTY

Clerk of Court
Doddridge Cty Circuit Court
118 East Court Street
West Union, WV 26456

## FAYETTE COUNTY

Clerk of Court
Fayette County Circuit Court
100 Court Street
Fayetteville, WV 25840

## GILMER COUNTY

Clerk of Court
Gilmer County Circuit Court
Government Center
Glenville, WV 26351

## GRANT COUNTY

Clerk of Court
Grant County Circuit Court
5 Highland Ave
Petersburg, WV 26847

## GREENBRIER COUNTY

Clerk of Court
Greenbrier Cty Circuit Court
200 North Court Street
Lewisburg, WV 24901

## HAMPSHIRE COUNTY

Clerk of Court
Hampshire Cty Circuit Court
Courthouse, PO Box 343
Romney, WV 26757

## HANCOCK COUNTY

Clerk of Court
Hancock County Circuit Court
102 Court Street, PO Box 428
New Cumberland, WV 26047

## HARDY COUNTY

Clerk of Court
Hardy County Circuit Court
204 Washington
Moorefield, WV 26836

## HARRISON COUNTY

Clerk of Court
Harrison County Circuit Court
301 West Main Street
Clarksburg, WV 26301

## JACKSON COUNTY

Clerk of Court
Jackson County Circuit Court
PO Box 800
Ripley, WV 25271

## JEFFERSON COUNTY

Clerk of Court
Jefferson Cty Circuit Court
PO Box 584
Charles Town, WV 25414

## KANAWHA COUNTY

Clerk of Court
Kanawha County Circuit Court
111 Court Street
Charleston, WV 25328

## LEWIS COUNTY
Clerk of Court
Lewis County Circuit Court
110 Center Ave
Weston, WV 26452

## LINCOLN COUNTY
Clerk of Court
Lincoln County Circuit Court
8000 Court Street
Hamlin, WV 25523

## LOGAN COUNTY
Clerk of Court
Logan County Circuit Court
Government Center
Logan, WV 25601

## MARION COUNTY
Clerk of Court
Marion County Circuit Court
Courthouse, PO Box 1269
Fairmont, WV 26554

## MARSHALL COUNTY
Clerk of Court
Marshall County Circuit Court
Courthouse, 7th Street
Moundsville, WV 26041

## MASON COUNTY
Clerk of Court
Mason County Circuit Court
6th and Viand Street
Point Pleasant, WV 25550

## MCDOWELL COUNTY
Clerk of Court
McDowell County Circuit Court
PO Box 400
Welch, WV 24801

## MERCER COUNTY
Clerk of Court
Mercer County Circuit Court
1501 West Main Street
Princeton, WV 24740-2626

## MINERAL COUNTY
Clerk of Court
Mineral County Circuit Court
150 Armstrong
Keyser, WV 26726

## MINGO COUNTY
Clerk of Court
Mingo County Circuit Court
75 East 2nd, PO Box 435
Williamson, WV 25661

## MONONGALIA COUNTY
Clerk of Court
Monongalia County Circuit Court
243 High Street, Room 110
Morgantown, WV 26505-5500

## MONROE COUNTY
Clerk of Court
Monroe County Circuit Court
PO Box 350
Union, WV 24983

## MORGAN COUNTY
Clerk of Court
Morgan County Circuit Court
202 Fairfax Street
Berkeley Springs, WV 25411

## NICHOLAS COUNTY
Clerk of Court
Nicholas County Circuit Court
700 Main Street
Summersville, WV 26651

## OHIO COUNTY
Clerk of Court
Ohio County Circuit Court
1500 Chapline Street
Wheeling, WV 26003

## PENDLETON COUNTY
Clerk of Court
Pendleton Cty Circuit Court
PO Box 846
Franklin, WV 26807

## PLEASANTS COUNTY
Clerk of Court
Pleasants Cty Circuit Court
301 Court Ln, Room 201
St. Marys, WV 26170

## POCAHONTAS COUNTY
Clerk of Court
Pocahontas County Circuit Court
900 D. 10th Ave
Marlinton, WV 24954

## PRESTON COUNTY
Clerk of Court
Preston County Circuit Court
101 West Main Street
Kingwood, WV 26537

## PUTNAM COUNTY
Clerk of Court
Putnam County Circuit Court
PO Box 906
Winfield, WV 25213

## RALEIGH COUNTY
Clerk of Court
Raleigh County Circuit Court
215 Main Street
Beckley, WV 25801

## RANDOLPH COUNTY
Clerk of Court
Randolph County Circuit Court
Government Center
Elkins, WV 26241

## RITCHIE COUNTY
Clerk of Court
Ritchie County Circuit Court
115 East Main Street
Harrisville, WV 26362

## ROANE COUNTY
Clerk of Court
Roane County Circuit Court
200 Main, PO Box 122
Spencer, WV 25276

## SUMMERS COUNTY
Clerk of Court
Summers County Circuit Court
102 Bellangee, PO Box 1058
Hinton, WV 25951

## TAYLOR COUNTY
Clerk of Court
Taylor County Circuit Court
214 West Main Street, Room 104
Grafton, WV 26354

## TUCKER COUNTY
Clerk of Court
Tucker County Circuit Court
215 First Street
Parsons, WV 26287

## TYLER COUNTY
Clerk of Court
Tyler County Circuit Court
Main Street, PO Box 8
Middlebourne, WV 26149

## UPSHUR COUNTY
Clerk of Court
Upshur County Circuit Court
40 West Main Street
Buckhannon, WV 26201

## WAYNE COUNTY
Clerk of Court
Wayne County Circuit Court
PO Box 38
Wayne, WV 25570

## WEBSTER COUNTY
Clerk of Court
Webster County Circuit Court
2 Court Square, Room 4
Webster Springs, WV 26288

## WETZEL COUNTY
Clerk of Court
Wetzel County Circuit Court
PO Box 263
New Martinsville, WV 26155

## WIRT COUNTY
Clerk of Court
Wirt County Circuit Court
PO Box 465
Elizabeth, WV 26143

## WOOD COUNTY
Clerk of Court
Wood County Circuit Court
#2 Government Square
Parkersburg, WV 26101

## WYOMING COUNTY
Clerk of Court
Wyoming County Circuit Court
PO Box 190
Pineville, WV 24874

# WYOMING

## ALBANY COUNTY
Clerk of Courts
2nd Judicial District Court
525 Grand
Laramie, WY 82070

## BIG HORN COUNTY
Clerk of Court
5th Judicial District Court
PO Box 670
Basin, WY 82410

## CAMPBELL COUNTY
Clerk of Courts
6th Judicial District Court
500 South Gillette Ave
Gillette, WY 82716

## CARBON COUNTY
Clerk of Court
2nd Judicial District Court
PO Box 67
Rawlins, WY 82301

## CONVERSE COUNTY
Clerk of Courts
8th Judicial District Court
107 North 5th
Douglas, WY 82633

## CROOK COUNTY
Clerk of Court
6th Judicial District Court
309 Cleveland
Sundance, WY 82729

## FREMONT COUNTY
Clerk of Courts
9th Judicial District Court
450 North 2nd
Lander, WY 82520

## GOSHEN COUNTY
Clerk of Courts
8th Judicial District Court
2123 East A Street
Torrington, WY 82240

## HOT SPRINGS COUNTY
Clerk of Courts
5th Judicial District Court
415 Arapaho
Thermopolis, WY 82443

## JOHNSON COUNTY
Clerk of Court
4th Judicial District Court
76 North Main
Buffalo, WY 82834

## LARAMIE COUNTY
Clerk of Court
1st Judicial District Court
1902 Carey, PO Box 787
Cheyenne, WY 82003

## LINCOLN COUNTY
Clerk of Court
3rd Judicial District Court
925 Sage Ave
Kemmerer, WY 83101

## NATRONA COUNTY
Clerk of Court
7th Judicial District Court
200 North Center, PO Box 3120
Casper, WY 82602

## NIOBRARA COUNTY
Clerk of Court
8th Judicial District Court
PO Box 1318
Lusk, WY 82225

## PARK COUNTY
Clerk of Courts
5th Judicial District Court
1002 Sheridan
Cody, WY 82414

## PLATTE COUNTY
Clerk of Court
8th Judicial District Court
Courthouse, PO Box 158
Wheatland, WY 82201

## SHERIDAN COUNTY
Clerk of Courts
4th Judicial District Court
224 South Main
Sheridan, WY 82801

## SUBLETTE COUNTY
Clerk of Court
9th Judicial District Court
21 South Tyler
Pinedale, WY 82941

## SWEETWATER COUNTY
Clerk of Court
3rd Judicial District Court
80 West Flaming Gorge
Green River, WY 82935

## TETON COUNTY
Clerk of Court
9th Judicial District Court
180 King Street, PO Box 4460
Jackson, WY 83001

## UINTA COUNTY
Clerk of Court
3rd Judicial District Court
Government Center
Evanston, WY 82931

## WASHAKIE COUNTY
Clerk of Courts
5th Judicial District Court
10th and Big Horn
Worland, WY 82401

## WESTON COUNTY
Clerk of Court
6th Judicial District Court
1 West Main
Newcastle, WY 82701

**Adoption Searches Made Easier**

# 5

# *Professional Researchers*

**1.**　　Most people who are searching will find at one point or another that they require the help of a professional researcher. The following is a partial list of reasons why the help of a professional researcher might become manditory during the course of your search:

**a.** A searcher needs to research a birth index which is housed in a state archive that is distant from the searcher's home.

**b.** A searcher needs to research a specific Docket Appearance Calendar or Minute Book in a county court which is distant from the searcher's home.

**c.** A searcher needs to research the in-house library of a certain newspaper where legal notices pertaining to the searcher's adoption were normally placed. The newspaper's location is distant from the searcher's home.

**d.** A county library has a microfiche collection of original birth certificates that might include the searcher's original certificate. The library is located in another state which is distant from the searcher's home.

**e.** A professional researcher has been able to collect and index medical records from a hospital that the searcher believes he/she was born in. The only source to these records is the professional researcher who owns the records.

**f.** A searcher needs to look at specific church records to confirm a birth, marriage, death, baptism, or confirmation. A professional researcher who normally works in this area can quickly locate and provide the records required.

**g**. Some professional researchers have access to very specialized computerized data basis which can be extremely useful in extracting needed information quickly and accurately.

**h**. A document which is pertinent to your search such as a birth certificate is located in a non-english speaking foreign country. The help of a professional researcher might be required to find the document and have it translated.

There are many other circumstances that arise that require the assistance of a professional researcher to help move the search forward. The question then becomes where do you find them and how do you know if they are competent.

**2.** One of the best sources for obtaining the name of a good professional researcher is a library. Most professional researchers spend a good deal of their time in libraries and they normally develop a working relationship with the librarians. Librarians might also be willing to do research during their off hours or the library might have a research service established.

For example a searcher living in New York City requires research to be done in Tucson, Arizona and does not personally know of a good professional researcher who lives there. The easiest approach is for the searcher to go to their local library and use a reference book entitled *American Library Directory* published by R.R. Bowker. This two volume work has a detailed listing of all of the libraries in the United States, Canada, and Mexico. This listing generally includes the name, address, telephone, fax, and Internet address (if available) of the library plus size and type of collections, special interests, and names of staff. By looking up the library in Tucson the following information becomes available:

*TUCSON-PIMA LIBRARY 101 N Stone Ave,*
*PO Box 27470, 85726-7470. Tel 520-791-4391.*
*FAX 520-791-3213. Dir Liz Rodriguez Miller;*
*Dep Dir Barbara J Murray; Asst Dir Patrick Corella*

Another excellent source for professional researchers are the state archives. Due to the wealth of research data stored and categorized in most state archives it becomes a facility that researchers use repeatedly. These researchers are known to the staff of the archives and an archivist may be able to recommend a person that he/she considers competent and reliable. In some states the archive can provide in-house professional research assistance for an hourly fee.

Licensed private investigators who are listed in the yellow pages are another possible source. These professionals are accustomed to doing investigative work and most are capable of doing research.

The staffs of local Historical Societies and Genealogical Clubs are another exceptional source for finding good professional researchers or even excellent amateur researchers willing to do research for a fee. Their address may be found in another reference book found in most libraries entitled THE GENEALOGIST'S ADDRESS BOOK published by Genealogical Publishing Co., Inc.

Law students at a local law school are another excellent source. These people are not professional researchers but they are intelligent and normally know their way around a library. By calling the law school and speaking with an administrator it is possible to find a student with the time and need for extra money to research the information the searcher requires.

3.　　　An enormous amount of important information is available to the searcher today by accessing specialized computer databases. It is essential that the modern searcher is aware that these effective and highly accurate sources of information exist and that they can be employed where the circumstances of the case permit. Much of the following text has been taken from YOU, TOO, CAN FIND ANYBODY.

### *Social Security Death Master File*
I will explain how the Master Death File is accessed because it will prove to be one of the most time-saving and cost-effective techniques you will use.

The Social Security Administration releases an updated list every months that contains the names of all persons who have died. The information that is available to the public is:

1. *Social Security Number;*
2. *First and last name;*
3. *Date of birth;*
4. *Date of death;*
5. *Zip Code of exact place of death;*
6. *Zip Code where lump sum Death Payment was made.*

The total number of persons listed in the Death Master File is currently 59 million. The list includes deaths since 1937.

Several companies have bought the magnetic tapes that the Social Security Administration makes available for sale that contain the Master Death File. They have spent $32,000 to convert the tapes over to usable computer disks and the quarterly updates cost $1,700.

The various ways the Master Death File can be accessed are:

1. *By name only;*
2. *By name and date of birth;*
3. *By Social Security Number;*
4. *By name and date of death;*
5. *By first name only with date of birth.*

If the subject I am trying to find has been missing for more than several years, I will order a check of the Master Death File. If the subject does appear, then I will order a copy of the death certificate to give to the client as proof that the subject is deceased. Case closed.

The most important use of the Death Master File is to quickly and with a minimum of information find the death record of a parent. If I believe

that the parent of the subject has died I will request a Death Master File record be run on their name. Even though the date of birth, Social Security Number, or even the place of death of the parent is not usually known, a search can be conducted. Of course, a name like John Smith will not yield a good result because of the long list that will be produced. But if you have the year of birth, then the field can be narrowed down considerably.

When I review the Death Master File record of a parent, I look up the zip code that states the place of death. I will order a death certificate and then contact the funeral home that is listed. The funeral home's records will indicate the next of kin, which may be your subject. Even if your subject is not listed, the home address and telephone number of the spouse or other family members will be contained in the funeral home's records. The close relatives may be questioned regarding the location of the subject.

Since you now have the place of death of the parent, you may want to contact the probate court of jurisdiction. If the parent had died intestate (no will), there will be a file that contains much information, including the names and addresses of all persons that were paid monies by the probate court for the estate.

If your subject was an offspring, he/she will be entitled to part of the estate. The subject's address will be listed along with the amount of money they received. If the subject was not located when the distribution of the estate took place, then the subject's entitlement will be held in escrow. Take a very close look at the file because buried in the voluminous folder may be paperwork indicating that your subject had been found by a professional heir finder and monies were dispersed to the subject. The subject's address will be listed on the green return receipt that the court had used to ensure proper delivery of the check.

On many occasions, I have ordered from the Probate Court a copy of the check that was cashed or deposited by the subject. Many times the subject will have their driver license number listed on the back of the check because they were required to show identification when cashing the check. At the very least, you will know what city the subject's bank is in.

## The information that is contained on the
## Death Master File is as follows:

| St | Soc Sec Num | Last Name | First Name | Birth Date | Death Date | Resi | Zip1 | Zip2 |
| --- | ------------------- | -------------- | ---------------- | -------------- | ---------------- | ----- | ----- | ------ |

**St** - This indicates what state the subject lived in when they applied for a Social Security Number.

**Soc Sec Num** - Social Security Number

**Last Name** - The name that the death benefits list as an account holder.

**First Name** - Walt would be Walter, Larry would be Lawrence, and Bob would be Robert if this is the formal name used by the decedent when they applied for their Social Security Number but the name Harry could very well be Harry instead of Harold if this is what was written on the original application.

**Birth Date** - The full birth date is usually printed on the Death Master File.

**Death Date** - The exact day is sometimes missing from the Master Death File but the month and year are usually available.

**Resi** - This represents the residence and indicates in which state death occurred.

**Zip 1** - Indicates the Zip Code area in which the death occurred.

**Zip 2** - Indicates the Zip Code that the lump sum Death payment was mailed to.

The following sample records of well-known persons will be used to illustrate different information that may or may not appear on the Death Master Record.

| St | Soc Sec Num | Last Name | First Name | Birth Date | Death Date | Resi | Zip1 | Zip2 |
|---|---|---|---|---|---|---|---|---|
| CA | 563-66-4692 | ASTAIRE | ANN | 12/22/1878 | 07/00/1975 | (CA) | 91202 | |
| **CA** | **568-05-4206** | **ASTAIRE** | **FRED** | **05/10/1899** | **06/00/1987** | **(CA)** | **90213** | |
| ME | 004-12-2305 | ASTAIRE | THEODORE | 08/12/1913 | 09/00/1979 | (CT) | 06503 | 06511 |

06503 CT New Haven .....    06511 CT New Haven .....  90213 CA Beverly Hills
91202 CA Glendale .....

The record for the last name Astaire will show that certain names will not produce a lengthy list which will make your search that much easier. Since 1962, only three people with the name Astaire have died.

| St | Soc SecNum | Last Name | First Name | Birth Date | Death Date | Resi | Zip1 | Zip2 |
|---|---|---|---|---|---|---|---|---|
| MD | 215-09-2405 | DISNEY | WALTER | 03/21/1878 | 08/00/1967 | (MD) | 21228 | |
| IL | 342-10-3698 | DISNEY | WALTER | 10/17/1890 | 05/00/1973 | (IL) | 61734 | |
| DC | 577-07-8270 | DISNEY | WALTER | 05/31/1894 | 01/00/1979 | (MD) | 61734 | |
| NY | 110-12-1395 | DISNEY | WALTER | 09/09/1899 | 06/00/1983 | (FL) | 33062 | |
| **KY** | **402-07-4149** | **DISNEY** | **WALTER** | **12/05/1901** | **12/00/1966** | **( )** | **00000** | |
| TN | 413-09-3359 | DISNEY | WALTER | 03/20/1908 | 10/00/1972 | (TN) | 37311 | |
| VA | 228-10-8454 | DISNEY | WALTER | 09/24/1908 | 03/00/1978 | (KY) | 40391 | 24277 |
| KY | 401-24-1418 | DISNEY | WALTER | 09/11/1921 | 03/00/1972 | (KY) | 40272 | |
| TN | 408-76-5315 | DISNEY | WALTER | 04/20/1947 | 09/00/1985 | (TN) | 37714 | |

20782 MD Hyatsville .....    21228 MD Baltimore .....  24277 VA Pennington Gap .....
38062 FL Pompano Beach..... 37311 TN Cleveland .....   37714 TN Caryville .....
40272 KY Louisville ......   40391 KY Winchester ..... 40906 KY Barbourville .....
61734 IL Delaven .......

The above list contains all the Walter Disneys that have died since 1962. When you have a record that does not indicate a place of death then look at the beginning of the record. The Social Security Number of the highlighted Walter Disney shows that this individual applied for his number in California. This would be where you would start a search for a will that will show the distribution of his assets. If this was the father of your subject, in this hypothetical sample, his will would be a good record to review for the address of your subject.

| St | Soc Sec Num | Last Name | First Name | Birth Date | Death Date | Resi | Zip1 | Zip2 |
|----|-------------|-----------|------------|------------|------------|------|------|------|
| PA | 164-09-9984 | EISENHOWER | DAVID | 10/05/1898 | 02/00/1983 | (PA) | 19124 | 33526 |
| PA | 815-30-5818 | EISENHOWER | DAVID | 12/25/1914 | 12/00/1978 | (PA) | 18102 | |
| PA | 204-40-5790 | EISENHOWER | DESSIE | 07/29/1881 | 05/00/1970 | (PA) | 17044 | |
| PA | 205-20-0582 | EISENHOWER | DOLORES | 11/01/1906 | 08/00/1972 | (PA) | 17834 | |
| PA | 182-36-0274 | EISENHOWER | DOROTHY | 10/05/1885 | 12/00/1975 | (PA) | 19026 | |
| PA | 203-20-9135 | EISENHOWER | DOROTHY | 09/27/1899 | 06/00/1979 | (PA) | 17751 | 17745 |
| PA | 208-18-5794 | EISENHOWER | DOROTHY | 10/08/1904 | 12/00/1981 | (PA) | 19607 | |
| PA | 209-20-7686 | EISENHOWER | DOROTHY | 06/17/1927 | 11/00/1987 | (PA) | 18201 | |
| OK | 440-12-7856 | EISENHOWER | DOWELL | 10/16/1903 | 09/00/1966 | (TX) | 78401 | |
| **CA** | **572-64-0315** | **EISENHOWER** | **DWIGHT** | **10/14/1890** | **03/00/1969** | **(PA)** | **17325** | |

| | | | |
|---|---|---|---|
| 10504 NY Armonk ..... | 17044 PA Lewistown ..... | 17325 PA Gettysburg ..... |
| 17745 PA Lock Haven ..... | 17751 PA Mill Hall ..... | 17834 PA Kulpmont ..... |
| 18102 PA Allentown ..... | 18201 PA Hazletown ..... | 19026 PA Drexel Hill ..... |
| 19124 PA Philadelphia ..... | 19607 PA Shillington ..... | 33526 FL Dade City ..... |
| 78401 TX Corpus Christi ..... | | |

Every Eisenhower with the first name initial D was requested. If you are not sure of the exact first name of the person you are searching for in the Death Master File list, you may want to use this technique of not giving a first name, but just the first initial of the first name. After you receive the list, then you will be able to review other information and determine the correct decedent. The year of death, state of death, and the issuing state of Social Security Number would have helped find the subject of the search in this hypothetical case.

| St | Soc Sec Num | Last Name | First Name | Birth Date | Death Date | Resi | Zip1 | Zip2 |
|----|-------------|-----------|------------|------------|------------|------|------|------|
| KY | 402-03-2297 | TRUMAN | HARRY | 10/16/1884 | 10/00/1966 | (KY) | 41015 | |
| **MO** | **488-40-6969** | **TRUMAN** | **HARRY** | **05/08/1884** | **12/00/1972** | **(MO)** | **64050** | |
| PA | 170-03-8745 | TRUMAN | HARRY | 05/15/1866 | 03/00/1973 | (PA) | 15223 | |
| MI | 386-01-1149 | TRUMAN | HARRY | 08/08/1887 | 07/00/1963 | (MI) | 00000 | |
| KY | 402-20-8745 | TRUMAN | HARRY | 01/27/1890 | 03/00/1978 | (KY) | 40205 | |
| WA | 535-20-7745 | TRUMAN | HARRY | 10/30/1896 | 05/00/1965 | (WA) | 98611 | 98532 |
| PA | 178-05-8291 | TRUMAN | HARRY | 07/04/1897 | 10/00/1965 | (PA) | 00000 | |
| MI | 367-26-8037 | TRUMAN | HARRY | 03/12/1901 | 11/00/1978 | (OH) | 43023 | |
| AZ | 527-01-2253 | TRUMAN | HARRY | 02/17/1905 | 02/00/1968 | (CA) | 95258 | |
| NY | 119-26-6047 | TRUMAN | HARRY | 08/19/1905 | 02/00/1985 | (IN) | 47130 | |

| | | |
|---|---|---|
| 15223 PA Pittsburgh ..... | 40205 KY Louisville ..... | 41015 KY Covington ..... |
| 43023 OH Granville ..... | 47130 IN Jeffersonville ..... | 49415 MI Fruitport ..... |
| 64050 MO Independence ..... | 92646 CA Huntington Beach ..... | 95258 CA Woodbridge .... |
| 98532 WA Chehalis ...... | 98611 WA Castle Rock | |

**Adoption Searches Made Easier**

| St | Soc Sec Num | Last Name | First Name | Birth Date | Death Date | Resi | Zip1 | Zip2 |
| ----- | ------------------ | ------------ | ------------- | ------------ | -------------- | ------ | -------- | -------- |
| **MO** | **495-50-5300** | **TRUMAN** | **BESS** | **02/13/1885** | **10/00/1982** | **(MO)** | **64050** | |
| WV | 234-80-3101 | TRUMAN | BESSIE | 04/18/1889 | 12/30/1989 | (WV) | 25276 | |
| IN | 305-70-2063 | TRUMAN | BESSIE | 08/07/1889 | 09/00/1983 | (IN) | 46806 | |
| OR | 542-22-6633 | TRUMAN | BESSIE | 01/15/1893 | 07/00/1976 | (OR) | 97034 | |
| OK | 445-32-1574 | TRUMAN | BESSIE | 10/05/1936 | 11/00/1969 | (OK) | 73502 | |

25276 WV Spencer .....   46806 IN Fort Wayne .....   64050 MO Independence .....
73502 OK Lawtow .....   97034 OR Lake Oswego .....

The two Truman Master Death Records were ordered by name only. There are numerous decedents with the name Harry Truman but if you knew that the person you were searching for was from Missouri, then you would have isolated the focus of your search easily.

You will notice that there is only one Bess Truman that has died since 1962. In this case, you did not need to know what area the person was from.

| St | Soc Sec Num | Last Name | First Name | Birth Date | Death Date | Resi | Zip1 | Zip2 |
| ---- | ------------------ | ------------ | ------------- | ------------ | -------------- | ------- | -------- | ------- |
| TN | 408-50-1182 | PRESLEY | EARL | 07/09/1930 | 03/00/1985 | (TN) | 38555 | |
| GA | 256-48-7374 | PRESLEY | EARL | 05/08/1936 | 02/00/1987 | (GA) | 31904 | |
| MS | 428-58-7758 | PRESLEY | EDDIE | 05/25/1934 | 05/00/1983 | (MS) | 39501 | |
| WV | 232-58-9834 | PRESLEY | EDWARD | 01/11/1930 | 03/00/1983 | ( ) | 24830 | |
| AL | 424-52-7031 | PRESLEY | EDWARD | 07/22/1937 | 03/00/1980 | (AL) | 36256 | |
| TN | 409-64-5512 | PRESLEY | ELMER | 08/06/1940 | 09/22/1990 | ( ) | 38134 | |
| **TN** | **409-52-2002** | **PRESLEY** | **ELVIS** | **01/08/1935** | **08/16/1977** | **( )** | | **38116** |
| MS | 425-11-0453 | PRESLEY | ELVIS | 10/24/1957 | 04/00/1987 | (MS) | 38858 | |
| TX | 455-46-8412 | PRESLEY | ERNEST | 12/24/1930 | 03/00/1979 | ( ) | 76179 | |

24830 WV Elbert      .....        31904 GA Columbus.....    36256 AL Daviston.....
38116 TN Memphis .....        38134 TN Memphis.....    38555 TN Crossville.....
38858 MS Nettleton .....        39501 MS Gulfport.....    76179 TX Saginaw.....

The above record is a result of a request for all persons with the last name Presley and the first name containing the letter E as the first letter. You will notice that in this case, the highlighted Presley does not show a place of death under Zip Code 1, but Zip Code 2 indicates where the lump sum Social Security was sent. For each space on a death master file record there may be no information entered. You can see that there are several death date, Resi, Zip1, and Zip 2 spaces that have no information.

The Master Death File is responsible for the successful resolution of more missing person cases than any other source. There is no quicker or more precise method for ascertaining someone's death. It has been a great tool to use for the past several years. The Social Security Administration will not accept any requests for Death Master File inquiries. I use a company in Miami that charges $45.00 for each name search. This fee covers a list of up to one hundred duplicate names returned for each name requested. The fee for over one hundred duplicate names is $30.00 per hundred.

*Research Investigative Services, Inc.*
*12864 Biscayne Blvd. Suite 101*
*Miami, Florida 33181-2007*

Research Investigative Services, Inc. does not advertise as its clients are investigative firms, such as mine, corporations, and government and they keep their telephone number unlisted. However, orders are accepted from the public for the items mentioned here. In fact, you may remember Pam Casey of Northern California was reunited with her sister after 42 years on *The Maury Povich Show*, on December 3, 1992. She along with three other families on that particular program had obtained the needed information by using Research Investigative Services, Inc.

## 4.    NATIONWIDE TELEPHONE SEARCH

Research Investigative Services, Inc. has an excellent system for nationwide examination of listed telephone numbers. They charge $40 for the first hundred names and $25 for every increment of one hundred names thereafter. Research Investigative Services, Inc. will run a name such as Robert Hamilton and the system will respond with every Robert Hamilton who has a **listed** telephone number, plus the address. In some cases, the name will appear with an address and just an area code, indicating an unlisted number, but now you have a location for this person.

This system is of tremendous assistance in cases where people have been missing for a period of time. Many times a subject will move to

a different part of the country. After the subject feels comfortable that the search for them is over, they will resume listing their telephone number as they move back into the mainstream of life. Another use for the nationwide examination of a telephone number to a particular name is to find relatives. I recently ran the name Joseph Culligan and came up with many people with my name. Several were directly related to me from two generations ago.

## 5. SOCIAL SECURITY NUMBER ADDRESS UPDATE REPORT

Another service that Research Investigative Services, Inc. provides is the Social Security Address Update Report. If you have gleaned your subject's Social Security Number from your research, you may submit a request for a search to be conducted on this number.

Any address that the subject had used for any dealings with certain businesses, governments, credit card companies and other entities may be given. This system is perfectly legal because no credit information is released. Research Investigative Services, Inc. charges a fee of $35.00 dollars and is the only company I know of that will not charge a fee if the computer search fails to return at least one address.

## 6. NON-IDENTIFYING INFORMATION ANALYSIS

Research Investigative Services, Inc., having access to many highly sophisticated databases as well as a staff of researchers, can professionally analize any non-identifying information a searcher may receive from a state agency, public or private adoption service, or any other source. The benefit of this service is having an experienced investigator review the information that might reveal a clue that an inexperienced amateur might overlook. For example let us suppose that a searcher's non-identifying information discloses that the birthmother's name is Kura, an American citizen of Turkish ancestry, 19 years of age at the time she gave birth. This normally insignificant information may lead a professional investigator to the identity of the birthmother by using a database not normally available to the public.

Another instance of non-identifying information perhaps being revealing is when the occupation of a subject is given. If for example they list the birthfather as an electrician. That occupation may require a license issued by the state in which the birthfather lived and worked which may identify him.

There are any number of facts and circumstances revealed in non-identifying information that may help unlock the door and reveal pertinent facts. Research Investigative Services, Inc. will review non-identifying information and issue a report of their findings for a fee of $75.00 dollars.

## SEARCHING PATH ANALYSIS

Research Investigative Services, Inc.'s professional researchers will review all the information pertaining to the adoption that a searcher has available. During the review process the investigators will determine whether or not there are other avenues to pursue to gather additional useful information. After the investigators are satisfied that all possible information is available they will recommend by way of written report the steps they would go through if they were conducting the search. The searcher may then use this professional plan in conducting their search. The fee for this analysis is $175.00 dollars.

## ADDITIONAL SERVICES

I do not believe in hourly charges for searches because I have heard of many horror stories (and I am sure you have too) in which people have been charged for many hours of time plus expenses and received nothing for their money except the response from the searcher or investigator saying he\she needs more and more money to complete the search. Research Investigative Services, Inc. has had many requests for searches from the public. You may write to Research Investigative Services, Inc. to have a representative contact you. An adoption search will be done on a **NO TRACE/NO CHARGE** basis for the fee of $2,900 (twenty nine hundred dollars) while a missing person search will be done on a **NO**

**TRACE/NO CHARGE** basis for the fee of $900 (nine hundred dollars), The guarantee of finding the person you are looking for or be charged nothing may make it worth the expense.

# *Notes*

**Adoption Searches Made Easier**

# Genealogical and Historical Societies 6

In many instances, searchers are required to do investigative work in locations far from their home. For example, a searcher presently lives in California but they were adopted out in New Jersey. The records that hold the answers to their questions are located at the court of jurisdiction which is located in New Jersey.

If the searcher is required to go to New Jersey to do the necessary examination of the records it will be a costly and time consuming process. The expense of transportation, food, and lodging may be prohibitive and the time required to locate and review the necessary records may not be available to the average person trying to live a normal life with family and career responsibilities.

The best way to overcome these obstacles is to find qualified researchers in the location where you require them. Some of the best sources for qualified people are state, regional and local genealogical and historical societies.

Genealogical societies are comprised of people who are interested in tracing the historical roots of their families as far back in time as the available evidence will allow them to go. They normally deal with many of the same type of records we have been discussing and are accustomed to doing research in the locale they live in. The permanent staff member(s) of the society are usually experienced researcher(s) that might be willing to do private research for an hourly fee. If they are not willing to do the research themselves they almost always know of some knowledgable and dependable person who they will be willing to recommend. This is an

excellent source for obtaining skilled researchers that are familiar with the subject matter and records involved as well as with the locale in which these records exist.

Historical societies are normally interested in the historical development of an area. Their area of interest may be local, regional, or statewide. The professional staff are normally researcher(s) that deal with many of the same records we have been discussing. They also have a detailed knowledge of the locale in which the society is located and consequently are also an excellent source of skilled and knowledgable researchers. The permanent staff might be willing to do the necessary research on an hourly fee basis or will normally be able to recommend someone who is capable of doing the research.

I have included a list of state genealogical and historical societies at the end of this chapter. These statewide societies may be able to do the research required or they may recommend a regional or local organization that will be better able to satisfy the request.

As I have mentioned before another excellent source of state, regional, and local genealogical and historical societies is a book entitled THE GENEALOGIST'S ADDRESS BOOK published by Genealogical Publishing Co. Inc. This reference book, which probably can be found in your local library, contains valuable source information including libraries, archives, and genealogical and historical societies in the United States by state, regional, and local addresses.

# State Genealogical Societies

## ALABAMA
Alabama Genealogical Society
800 Lakeshore Drive
Birmingham, AL 35229

## ALASKA
Alaska Genealogical Society
7030 Dickerson Drive
Anchorage, AK 99504

## ARIZONA
Family History Society
PO Box 310
Glendale, AZ 85311

## ARKANSAS
Arkansas Genealogical Society
PO Box 908
Hot Springs, AR 71902-0908

## CALIFORNIA
California Genealogical Society
PO Box 77105
San Francisco, CA 94107-0105

## COLORADO
Colorado Genealogical Society
PO Box 9218
Denver, CO 80209-0218

## CONNECTICUT
Society of Genealogists Inc.
PO Box 435
Glastonbury, CT 06033-0435

## DELAWARE
Delaware Genealogical Society
505 Market Street Mall
Wilmington, DE 19801-3901

## FLORIDA
Society for Genealogical Research
8461 54th Street, North
Pinellas Park, FL 33565

## GEORGIA
Georgia Genealogical Society
PO Box 54575
Atlanta, GA 30308-0575

## HAWAII
Genealogical Society
478 South King Street
Honolulu, HI 96813

## IDAHO
Idaho Genealogical Society, Inc.
4620 Overland Road, #204
Boise, ID 83705-2867

## ILLINOIS
Illinois Genealogical Society
PO Box 10195
Springfield, IL 62791-0195

## INDIANA
Indiana Genealogical Society,
PO Box 10507
Fort Wayne, IN 46852-0507

## IOWA
Iowa Genealogical Society
6000 Douglas
Des Moines, IA 50322-7735

## KANSAS
Council of Genealogical Societies
PO Box 3858
Topeka, KS 66604-6858

## KENTUCKY
Kentucky Genealogical Society
PO Box 153
Frankfort, KY 40602

## LOUISIANA
Louisiana Genealogical Society
PO Box 3454
Baton Rouge, LA 70821

## MAINE
Maine Genealogical Society
PO Box 221
Farmington, ME 04938-0221

## MARYLAND
Maryland Genealogical Society
201 West Monument Street
Baltimore, MD 21201

## MASSACHUSETTS
Society of Genealogists
PO Box 215
Ashland, MA 01721-0215

## MICHIGAN
Michigan Genealogical Council
PO Box 80953
Lansing, MI 48908-0953

## MINNESOTA
Minnesota Genealogical Society
PO Box 16069
Saint Paul, MN 55116-0069

## MISSISSIPPI
Genealogical Asso. of Mississippi
618 Avalon Road
Jackson, MS 39206

## MISSOURI
Missouri Genealogical Association
PO Box 833
Columbia, MO 65205-0833

## MONTANA
Montana Genealogical Society
PO Box 555
Chester, MT 59522

## NEBRASKA
Nebraska Genealogical Society
PO Box 5608
Lincoln, NE 68508

## NEVADA
Nevada Genealogical Society
PO Box 20666
Reno, NV 89515

**NEW HAMPSHIRE**
Society of Genealogists
PO Box 633
Exeter, NH 03833-0633

**NEW JERSEY**
Genealogical Society of N. J.
PO Box 1291
New Brunswick, NJ 08903

**NEW MEXICO**
Genealogical Society
PO Box 8283
Albuquerque, NM 87198-8283

**NEW YORK**
Genealogical Society
122 East 58th Street
New York, NY 10022-1939

**NORTH CAROLINA**
Genealogical Society
PO Box 1492
Raleigh, NC 27602

**OHIO**
Genealogical Society
34 Sturges Avenue
Mansfield, OH 44906-0625

**OKLAHOMA**
Oklahoma Genealogical Society
PO Box 12986
Oklahoma City, OK 73157-2986

**OREGON**
Oregon Genealogical Society
PO Box 10306
Eugene, OR 97440-2306

**PENNSYLVANIA**
Genealogical Society of Penn.
1300 Locust Street
Philadelphia, PA 19107-5699

**RHODE ISLAND**
Genealogical Society
13 Countryside Drive
Cumberland, RI 02864-2601

**SOUTH CAROLINA**
Genealogical Society
PO Box 16355
Greenville, SC 29606

**SOUTH DAKOTA**
Genealogical Society
Rt. 2, Box 10
Burke, SD 57523

**TENNESSEE**
Tennessee Genealogical Society
PO Box 111249
Memphis, TN 38111-1249

**TEXAS**
Texas State Genealogical Society
2507 Tannehill
Houston, TX 77008-3052

## UTAH
Utah Genealogical Society
PO Box 1144
Salt Lake City, UT 84110

## VERMONT
Genealogical Society
Main Street
Pittsford, VT 05763

## VIRGINIA
Virginia Genealogical Society
5001 West Broad Street, # 115
Richmond, VA 23230-3023

## WASHINGTON
Washington Genealogical Society
PO Box 1422
Olympia, WA 98507

## WEST VIRGINIA
Genealogical Society
5238 Elk River Road, North
Elkview, WV 25071

## WISCONSIN
Genealogical Council, Inc.
Rt. 3, Box 253
Black River Falls, WI 54615

# Historical Societies

## ALABAMA
Alabama Historical Association
P.O. Box 870380
Tuscaloosa, Al 35498-0380

## ALASKA
Alaska Historical Society
524 West Fourth Avenue
Anchorage, AK 99510-0299

## ARIZONA
Arizona Historical Society
949 East Second Street
Tucson, AZ 85719

## ARKANSAS
Arkansas Historical Association
U. of AR., Old Main, #416
Fayetteville, AR 72701

## CALIFORNIA
California Historical Society
2099 Pacific Avenue
San Francisco, CA 94109-2235

## COLORADO
Colorado Historical Society
1300 Broadway
Denver, Co 80203-2137

## CONNECTICUT
Connecticut Historical Society
1 Elizabeth St. at Asylum Avenue
Hartford, CT 06105

## DELAWARE
Historical Society of Delaware
505 Market Street
Wilmington, DE 19801

## DISTRICT OF COLUMBIA
Columbia Historical Society
1307 New Hampshire Ave. N.W.
Washington, DC 20036

## FLORIDA
Florida Historical Society
4204 Fowler Avenue
Tampa, FL 33687-0197

## GEORGIA
Georgia Historical Society
501 Whittaker Street
Savannah, GA 31499

## HAWAII
Hawaiian Historical Society
560 Kawaiahao Street
Honolulu, HI 96813

## IDAHO
Idaho State Historical Society
450 North Fourth Street
Boise, ID 83702

## ILLINOIS
Illinois State Historical Society
Old State Capitol
Springfield, IL 62701

## INDIANA
Indiana Historical Society
315 West Ohio Street
Indianapolis, IN 46202

## IOWA
State Historical Society of Iowa
600 E. Locust, Capitol Complex
Des Moines, IA 50319

## KANSAS
Kansas State Historical Society
120 West Tenth Street
Topeka, KS 66612

## KENTUCKY
Kentucky Historical Society
300 Broadway
Frankfort, KY 40602-2108

## LOUISIANA
Louisiana Historical Society
Maritime Building
New Orleans, LA 70130

## MAINE
Maine Historical Society
485 Congress Street
Portland, ME 04101

## MARYLAND
Maryland Historical Society
201 West Monument Street
Baltimore, MD 21201

## MASSACHUSETTS
Massachusetts Historical Society
1154 Boylston Street
Boston, MA 02215

## MICHIGAN
Historical Society of Michigan
2117 Washtenaw Avenue
Ann Arbor, MI 48104

## MINNESOTA
Minnesota Historical Society
345 Kellogg Boulevard, West
Saint Paul, MN 55102-1906

## MISSISSIPPI
Mississippi Historical Society
PO Box 571
Jackson, MS 39205-0571

## MISSOURI
Missouri Historical Society
Jefferson Memorial Building
Saint Louis, MO 63112-1099

## MONTANA
Montana Historical Society
225 North Roberts Street
Helena, MT 59620

## NEBRASKA
Nebraska Historical Society
PO Box 82554
Lincoln, NE 68501-2554

## NEVADA
Nevada Historical Society
1650 North Virginia Street
Reno, NV 89503

## NEW HAMPSHIRE
Historical Society
30 Park Street
Concord, NH 03301

## NEW JERSEY
New Jersey Historical Comm.
20 West State Street CN 305
Trenton, NJ 08625-0305

## NEW MEXICO
New Mexico Historical Society
PO Box 1912
Santa Fe, NM 87504-1912

## NEW YORK
New York Historical Association
PO Box 800
Cooperstown, NY 13326

## NORTH CAROLINA
Historical Societies Federation
109 East Jones Street
Raleigh, NC 27601

## NORTH DAKOTA
Historical Society North Dakota
612 East Boulevard Avenue
Bismarck, ND 58505

## OHIO
Ohio Historical Society
1982 Velma Avenue
Columbus, OH 43211-2497

## OKLAHOMA
Oklahoma Historical Society
2100 North Lincoln Boulevard
Oklahoma City, OK 73105

## OREGON
Oregon Historical Society
1200 S.W. Park Avenue
Portland, OR 97205

## PENNSYLVANIA
Historical Society of Pennsylvania
1300 Locust Street
Philadelphia, PA 19107-5699

## RHODE ISLAND
Rhode Island Historical Society
110 Benevolent Street
Providence, RI 02906

## SOUTH CAROLINA
South Carolina Historical Society
100 Meeting Street
Charleston, SC 29401

## SOUTH DAKOTA
South Dakota Historical Society
900 Governors Drive
Pierre, SD 57501-2217

## TENNESSEE

Tennessee Historical Society
300 Capital Boulevard
Nashville, TN 37243-0084

## TEXAS

Texas State Historical Association
2306 SRH, University Station
Austin, TX 78712

## UTAH

Utah State Historical Society
300 Rio Grande
Salt Lake City, UT 84101-1182

## VERMONT

Vermont Historical Society
109 State Street
Montpelier, VT 05609-0901

## VIRGINIA

Virginia Historical Society
PO Box 7311
Richmond, VA 23211-0311

## WASHINGTON

Washington Historical Society
315 North Stadium Way
Tacoma, WA 98403

## WEST VIRGINIA

West Virginia Historical Society
1900 Kanawha Boulevard East
Charleston, WV 25305-0300

## WISCONSIN

Historical Society of Wisconsin
816 State Street
Madison, WI 53706

## WYOMING

Wyoming State Historical Society
2301 Central Avenue
Cheyenne, WY 82002

# 7

# Libraries

1. Libraries store vast amounts of historical and reference information that can be extremely useful in determining the names, places, and dates that can solve an adoption mystery. Some but not all of the useful information that may be found in a library are:

## a. OLD NEWSPAPERS ON MICROFICHE, MICROFILM OR CD-ROM

1) If a searcher knows the county and state of the court of jurisdiction, the library in that county may be used to search for a legal notice(s) that might have been published prior to the granting of a Petition For Adoption or the Final Adoption Decree to the adoptive parents by the court. Libraries normally have a historical collection of the county newspaper(s) going back for decades on microfiche, microfilm or CD-ROM.

2) The same historical collection of county newspaper(s), stored on the library's microfiche, microfilm or CD-ROM collection, might have published an obituary notice(s) that might reveal important facts pertaining to a particular adoption case.

## b. SCHOOL YEARBOOKS

Many public libraries maintain a historical collection of yearbooks from every high school and junior high school in the county. These yearbooks can be extremely useful if a searcher suspects a certain student of being a birthparent. For example, a female student suspected of being a birthmother appears in the high school yearbook during her junior year but obviously missing from the yearbook during her senior year. This is an indication that she may not have

attended school in order to have the baby and she may warrant further background investigation.

### c. TELEPHONE DIRECTORIES

Libraries normally have a collection of telephone directories for the county, perhaps the entire state, sometimes a section of the country, and in bigger libraries the entire country. These directories can be either the white or yellow pages or both. With modern technology some libraries with user computer systems have telephone directories on CD-ROM.

Some libraries also maintain a historical collection of telephone directories. These directories can be of great value if a searcher is looking for a person who previously lived in the area.

Another useful reference that a library might also have is a crisscross telephone directory. This directory may be extremely useful when an investigator has only a street address and is searching for a telephone number because the directory is organized by street address instead of by name.

### d. LEGAL SECTION

Most libraries have copies of the current state statutes and local laws. Some libraries, including government and private law libraries, maintain historical sets of state statutes and local laws which may be very helpful to searchers trying to determine what the adoption laws were during a specific previous year.

### e. GENEALOGICAL SECTION

Many libraries have a genealogical section where they house various historical records and indices that are of interest to genealogists, professional researchers, private investigators and amateur searchers. This section might include a historical collection of the county's birth indexes, county court records, church records, and many other official and private records that have historical significance to the local area.

## f. THE LIBRARIANS

One of the most valuable resources of the library are the librarians themselves. These highly trained individuals are expert in determining what information is stored, where it is housed and how to best retrieve it. Many librarians have developed an expertise in a specific area such as reference, law, or genealogy and their assistance can be invaluable. They are normally acquainted with the professional researchers in the area and their recommendations can be invaluable. Unfortunately most people do not realize how valuable an information source these professionals are and consequently do not avail themselves of their expertise. Lastly, a librarian who has worked in the same library for a number of years may have firsthand knowledge about particular people and events that may prove extremely important. Tapping into the normally friendly and intelligent librarian resource can be an important asset for a creative investigator.

# LIBRARIES

## ALABAMA
Harwell Goodwin Davis Library
800 Lakeshore Drive
Birmingham, AL 35229

## ALASKA
Alaska State Library
State Office Building, 8th Floor
Juneau, Ak 99801

## ARIZONA
Arizona Department of Library
1700 West Washington
Phoenix, AZ 85007

## ARKANSAS
Arkansas State Library
1 Capitol Mall
Little Rock, AR 72201

## CALIFORNIA
Los Angeles Public Library
630 West Fifth Street
Los Angeles, CA 90071

## COLORADO
Denver Public Library
1357 Broadway
Denver, CO 80203-2165

## CONNECTICUT
Connecticut State Library
231 Capitol Avenue
Hartford, CT 06106

## DELAWARE
Delaware Division of Libraries
43 South Dupont Highway
Dover, DE 19901

## DISTRICT OF COLUMBIA
N. S. D. A. R. Library
1776 D Street, NW
Washington, DC 20006-5392

Genealogical Room LJ20
Library of Congress
10 First Street, SE
Washington, DC 20540-5554

## FLORIDA
Burdick Ancestry Library
2317 Riverbluff Parkway, #249
Sarasota, FL 34231-5032

## GEORGIA
Genealogical Center Library
PO Box 71343
Marietta, GA 30007-1343

## HAWAII
Hawaii State Library
478 South King Street
Honolulu, HI 95813

## IDAHO
Heritage Hall Museum
HC 62, Box 41
Dubois, ID 83423

## ILLINOIS
Newberry Library
60 West Walton Street
Chicago, Il 60610

## INDIANA
Allen County Public Library
900 Webster Street
Fort Wayne, IN 46802

## IOWA
Carnegie-Stout Public Library
360 West 11th Street
Dubuque, IA 52001

## KANSAS
Kansas State Library
Third Floor, Statehouse
Topeka. KS 66612

## KENTUCKY
Kentucky State Libraries
300 Coffee Tree Road
Frankfort, KY 40602-0537

## LOUISIANA
State Library of Louisiana
760 North Third Steet
Baton Rouge, LA 70821

## MAINE
Maine State Library
State House Station, Number 64
Augusta, ME 04333

## MARYLAND
Maryland State Archives
350 Rowe Boulevard
Annapolis, MD 21401

## MASSACHUSETTS
The Genealogical Society
99-101 Newbury Street
Boston, MA 02116

## MICHIGAN
Detroit Public Library
5201 Woodward Avenue
Detroit, MI 48202

## MINNESOTA
Minnesota Historical Society
345 Kellogg Boulevard West
Saint Paul, MN 55102-1906

## MISSISSIPPI
Historic Trails Library
Rt. 1, Box 373
Philadelphia, MS 39350-9762

## MISSOURI
Mid-Continent Public Library
15616 East 24 Highway
Independence, MO 64050

Saint Louis Public Library
History and Genealogical Dept.
1301 Olive Street
Saint Louis, MO 63103

Tree Trackers Library
HCR-01 Box 1210
Eagle Rock, MO 65641

## MONTANA
Montana State Library
1515 East Sixth Avenue
Helena, MT 59620

## NEBRASKA
W. Dale Clark Library
215 South 15th Street
Omaha, NE 68102

## NEVADA
Nevada State Library
100 Stewart Street
Carson City, NV 89710

## NEW HAMPSHIRE
Division of Records
71 South Fruit Street
Concord, NH 03301-2410

## NEW JERSEY
New Jersey State Library
Genealogy Section, CN 520
Trenton, NJ 08625-0520

## NEW MEXICO
New Mexico State Library
325 Don Gaspar Avenue
Santa Fe, NM 87503

## NEW YORK
The New York Public Library
Fifth Avenue and 42nd Street
New York, NY 10018

## NORTH CAROLINA
State Library of North Carolina
109 East Jones Street
Raleigh, NC 27601-2807

## NORTH DAKOTA
Historical Research Library
612 Boulevard Avenue
Bismarck, ND 58505

## OHIO
Cleveland Public Library
325 Superior Avenue
Cleveland, OH 44114-1271

Historical Society
10825 East Boulevard
Cleveland, OH 44106-1788

## OKLAHOMA
Oklahoma Dept.of Libraries
200 NE 18th Street
Oklahoma City, OK 73105

## OREGON
Oregon State Library
Winter and Court Street, NE
Salem, OR 97310

## PENNSYLVANIA
State Library of Pennsylvania
PO Box 1601
Harrisburg, PA 17105

## RHODE ISLAND
Rhode Island State Library
337 Westminster Street
Providence, RI 02903

## SOUTH CAROLINA
South Carolina State Library
1500 Senate Street
Columbia, SC 29211

## SOUTH DAKOTA
South Dakota State Library
800 Governors Drive
Pierre, SD 57501-2294

## TENNESSEE
Tennessee State Library
403 Seventh Avenue, North
Nashville, TN 37243-0312

## TEXAS
Dallas Public Library
1515 Young Street
Dallas, TX 75201

Houston Public Library
5300 Caroline
Houston, TX 77004-6896

Genealogical Library
Rt. 1 Box 405
Kountze, TX 77625

Univ. of Texas at Austin Library
Sid Richardson Hall, 2101
Austin, TX 78713

## UTAH

Genealogical Society of Utah
35 North West Temple
Salt Lake City, UT 84150

## VERMONT

Vermont Dept. of Libraries
109 State Street
Montpelier, VT 05609-0601

## VIRGINIA

National Genealogical Society
4527 17th Street, North
Arlington, VA 22207-2399

## WASHINGTON

Seattle Public Library
1000 Fourth Avenue
Seattle, WA 98104

## WEST VIRGINIA

Archives and History Section
1900 Kanawha Boulevard East
Charleston, WV 25305-0300

## WISCONSIN

Historical Society of Wisconsin
816 State Street
Madison, WI 53706

## WYOMING

Wyoming State Library
2301 Capitol Avenue
Cheyenne, WY 82002

# _Notes_

**Adoption Searches Made Easier**

# 8

# *Government Agencies*

## 1. THE BUREAU OF VITAL STATISTICS

Each state has a centralized office in the state capitol that receives, stores, maintains, and disperses vital information on citizens and residents. This information may include but is not limited to the following:

**a. Original Certificates of Birth** - The certificate issued at birth or shortly thereafter which normally includes the time and place of birth, the name(s) of the birthparent(s), the name and sex of the infant and the name of the attending physician.

**b. Amended Certificate of Birth** - This certificate is authorized by the court of jurisdiction and is issued after the Final Adoption Decree is issued. It alters the original certificate of birth so as to eliminate the name of the birthparent(s) and substitutes the name of the adoptive parents. It may also alter the time and place of birth as well as the original name of the infant.

**c. Death Certificate** - This certificate may be issued by a medical professional such as a physician or coroner at the time of a person's death or shortly thereafter. The certificate may include a full legal description of the deceased, the time and place of death, the reason for the death, and the name of the medical authority issuing the certificate.

**d. Marriage License and Application** - These forms identify two people who have decide to enter a legal union for life. Normally the

forms require a great deal of background information on each of the participants that may include their names, ages, sex, present addresses, family backgrounds, blood-types, education, social security numbers, and a host of other valuable and identifying information.

**e. Divorce Records** - These forms identify two people who were legally married and have decided to an absolute legal dissolution of their marriage. Normally the forms include the individuals names, ages, sex, addresses at the time of the Final Divorce Decree, social security numbers, terms of settlement of jointly-owned property, child custody arrangements, and a host of other background and valuable information.

The information held by the Bureau of Vital Statistics may be valuable to the searcher. In addition city and county bureau of vital statistics still exist and they normally feed current information to the state bureau. The local bureaus of vital statistics hold duplicate and sometimes older records than the state equivalent and sometimes these records are easier to obtain.

## 2.    STATE DEPARTMENT OF SOCIAL SERVICES

Most states have a central bureau located in the state capitol whose responsibility it is to maintain records on all adoptions that are either originated, completed, or both in the state. The records that these bureaus collect, categorize, and disperse are as follows:

**a. Original Certificate of Birth** - The certificate issued at birth or shortly thereafter which normally includes the time and place of birth, the name(s) of the birthparent(s), the name and sex of the infant and the name of the attending physician.

**b. Amended Certificate of Birth** - This certificate is authorized by the court of jurisdiction and is issued after the Final Adoption Decree is issued. It alters the original certificate of birth so as to eliminate

the name of the birthparent(s) and substitutes the name of the adoptive parents. It may also alter the time and place of birth as well as the original name of the infant.

**c. Relinquishment, Consent to Adopt, Surrender** - These are the legal documents that transfer the rights and responsibilities of parenthood from the birthparents to another legal guardian who is appointed by the court. These papers must be signed by at least one birthparent prior to 1972 (after 1972 the birthfather's signature was also required as decided in the precedent setting case of Stanley vs Illinois). The information generally contained in these documents are the birthparents' names, addresses, age, the baby's name, time and place of birth, and the name of the legal guardian appointed by the court.

**d. Petition to Adopt** - "*an application made to a court ex parte, or where there are no parties in opposition, praying for the exercise of judicial powers of the court in relation to some matter which is not the subject of a suit or action, or for authority to do some act which requires the sanction of the court; as for the appointment of a guardian, for a child without parents.*" This adoption petition is typically an intermediate step (interlocutory) that normally allows for a one year probationary period before a Final Adoption Decree is granted. The petition will normally have the original name of the infant, the name of the birthparent(s), the names of the would be adoptive parents or guardians (petitioners), the name of the judge who heard the petition, the name of the attorney who represented the petitioner, and the name of the caseworker who works for the state adoption agency or the state department of health (in the case of a private adoption). Clearly this is a very important document packed with meaningful information.

**e. Home Study Report** - A study conducted by the adoption agency placing the child or the state department of health which is overseeing the child's welfare. The caseworker is charged with the responsibility of investigating the living standard and family values of the proposed

adoptive parents or foster parents. The court will normally review the caseworker's report to be certain the child is being placed in a wholesome environment. The information found in the home study report usually includes the original name of the child, the name of the potential adoptive parents or foster parents, the name of judge, identifies the name of the placing agency or agent, and the name of the caseworker.

**f. Final Adoption Decree** - is "one which fully and finally disposes of the whole litigation, determining all questions raised by the case, and leaving nothing that requires further judicial action." Normally the information recorded in this decree will include the original name of the child, the name of the adoptive or foster parents, the name of the judge, the name of the attorney who represented the petitioners, the name of the caseworker, the name of the state agency or third party agent involved in the adoption, and possibly the name(s) of the birthparent(s).

**3.    PUBLIC OR PRIVATE PLACING AGENCY**
A public placing agency is a department of a state government charged with the responsibility of protecting the rights of minors surrendered for adoption, finding and placing the child in a wholesome environment, and filing and maintaining the various records connected with an adoption.

A private placing agency is licensed to operate by a state government and is responsible to protecting the rights of minors surrendered for adoption, finding and placing the child in a wholesome environment, and filing and maintaining the various records connected with an adoption.

Some of the documents in an adoption agency's case file may include:

1. *Original Certificate of Birth*
2. *Amended Certificate of Birth*
3. *Relinquishment, Surrender, or Consent to Adopt document(s)*
4. *Petition to Adopt*
5. *Final Adoption Decree*
6. *Background Information on Birthfamily*
7. *Medical Information on Birthfamily*
8. *Home Study Report on Adoptive or Foster Parents*
9. *Foster Care Information*

# STATE BUREAUS OF VITAL STATISTICS

## ALABAMA
Alabama Dept.of Public Health
PO Box 5625
Montgomery, AL 36130-5625

## ALASKA
Bureau of Vital Statistics
P.O. Box 110675
Juneau, AK 99811-0675

## ARIZONA
Office of Vital Records
P.O. Box 3887
Phoenix, AZ 85030-3887

## ARKANSAS
Division of Vital Records
4815 West Markham Street
Little Rock, AR 72205-3867

## CALIFORNIA
Office of Vital Statistics
P O Box 730241
Sacramento, CA 94244-0241

## COLORADO
Vital Records Section
4300 Cherry Creek Drive South
Denver, CO 80222-1530

## CONNECTICUT
Vital Records Unit
150 Washington Street
Hartford, CT 06106

## DELAWARE
Office of Vital Statistics
P.O. Box 637
Dover, DE 19903-0637

## DISTRICT OF COLUMBIA
Vital Records Branch
613 G Street, N.W.
Washington, DC 20001

## FLORIDA
Vital Statistics
P.O. Box 210
Jacksonville, FL 32231-0042

## GEORGIA
Vital Records Service
47 Trinity Ave. S.W., # 27-H
Atlanta, GA 30334-1201

## HAWAII
Vital Records Section
P.O. Box 3378
Honolulu, HI 96801

## IDAHO
Bureau of Vital Statistics
P O Box 83720
Boise, ID 83720-0036

## ILLINOIS
Division of Vital Records
605 West Jefferson Street
Springfield, IL 62702-5097

## INDIANA
Indiana State Dept. of Health
1330 West Michigan Street
Indianapolis, IN 46206-1964

## IOWA
Vital Records Section
Lucas State Office Bldg.
Des Moines, IA 50319-0075

## KANSAS
Office of Vital Statistics
900 S.W. Jackson, #151
Topeka, KS 66612-2221

## KENTUCKY
Office of Vital Records
275 East Main Street
Frankfort, KY 40621-0001

## LOUISIANNA
Vital Records Registry
P.O. Box 60630
New Orleans, LA 70160-0630

## MAINE
Office of Vital Statistics
State House, Station 11
Augusta, ME 04333-0011

## MARYLAND
Division of Vital Records
P.O. Box 68760
Baltimore, MD 21215-0020

## MASSACHUSETTS
Registry of Vital Records
150 Tremont St., Rm. B-3
Boston, MA 02111-1197

## MICHIGAN
Office of State Registrar
P.O. Box 30195
Lansing, MI 48909

## MINNESOTA
Vital Statistics Registration
P.O. Box 9441
Minneapolis, MN 55440-9441

## MISSISSIPPI
Vital Records Office
P.O. Box 1700
Jackson, MS 39215-1700

## MISSOURI
Bureau of Vital Records
P.O. Box 570
Jefferson City, MO 65102-0570

## MONTANA
Bureau of Records & Statistics
1400 Broadway
Helena, MT 59620-0901

## NEBRASKA
Bureau of Vital Statistics
P.O. Box 95007
Lincoln, NE 68509-5007

## NEVADA
Section of Vital Statistics
505 East King Street, Rm 102
Carson City, NV 89710-4761

## NEW HAMPSHIRE
Bureau of Vital Records
6 Hazen Drive
Concord, NH 03301-6527

## NEW JERSEY
Bureau of Vital Records
State Registrar-CN370
Trenton, NJ 08625-0370

## NEW MEXICO
Vital Statistics Office
P.O. Box 26110
Santa Fe, NM 87504-6110

## NEW YORK CITY
Division of Vital Records
125 Worth Street
New York City, NY 10007

## NEW YORK STATE
Bureau of Vital Records
Corning Tower Room 321
Albany, NY 12237-0023

## NORTH CAROLINA
Vital Records Branch
P.O. Box 27687
Raleigh, NC 27611

## NORTH DAKOTA
Division of Vital Records
600 East Boulevard Avenue
Bismarck, ND 58505

## OHIO
Division of Vital Statistics
PO Box 15098
Columbus, OH 43215-0098

## OKLAHOMA
Division of Vital Records
P.O. Box 53551
Oklahoma City, OK 73152-3551

## OREGON
Vital Statistics Section
P.O. Box 14050
Portland, OR 97214-0050

## PENNSYLVANIA
Division of Vital Records
P.O. Box 1528
New Castle, PA 16103-1528

## RHODE ISLAND
Division of Vital Statistics
3 Capitol Hill, Room #101
Providence, RI 02908-5097

## SOUTH CAROLINA
Office of Vital Records
2600 Bull Street
Columbia, SC 29201-1797

## SOUTH DAKOTA
Center for Health Statistics
445 East Capitol Bldg.
Pierre, SD 57501-3185

## TENNESSEE
Vital Records Office
Cordell Hull Building C3-324
Nashville, TN 37247-0350

## TEXAS
Bureau of Vital Statistics
1100 West 49th Street
Austin, TX 78756-3191

## UTAH
Bureau of Health Statistics
P.O. Box 16700
Salt Lake City, UT 84116-0700

## VERMONT
Vital Records Unit
P.O. Box 70
Burlington, VT 05402-0070

## VIRGINIA
Division of Vital Records
P.O. Box 100
Richmond, VA 23208-1000

## WASHINGTON
Vital Records
P.O. Box 9709
Olympia, WA 98507-9709

## WEST VIRGINIA
Vital Registration Office
Capitol Complex, Bldg. 3 # 516
Charleston, WV 25305

## WISCONSIN
Section of Vital Statistics
P.O. Box 309
Madison, WI 53701-0309

## WYOMING
Vital Recors Services
Hathaway Bldg.
Cheyenne, WY 82002

# STATE ADOPTION AGENCIES

**ALABAMA**
Office of Adoption
50 N. Ripley Street
Montgomery, AL 36130

**ALASKA**
Family & Youth Services
PO Box 110630
Juneau, AK 99811-0630

**ARIZONA**
Dept. of Economic Security
PO Box 6123
Phoenix, AZ 85005

**ARKANSAS**
Children & Family Services
PO Box 1437, Slot 808
Little Rock, AR 72203-1437

**CALIFORNIA**
Department of Social Services
744 P Street, M.S. 19-31
Sacramento, CA 95814

**COLORADO**
Dept.of Human Services
1575 Sherman Street
Denver, CO 80203-1714

**CONNECTICUT**
Children and Family Services
Undercliff Road
Meriden, Ct 06451

**DELAWARE**
Division of Family Services
1825 Falkland Rd
Wilmington, DE 19805-1195

**FLORIDA**
Department of HRS
1317 Winewood Boulevard
Tallahassee, FL 32399-0700

**GEORGIA**
Adoption Reunion Registry
2 Peachtree Street, NW # 400
Atlanta, GA 30303-3917

**HAWAII**
Adoption Records Unit
PO Box 3498
Honolulu, HI 96811-3498

**IDAHO**
Dept. of Health & Welfare
PO Box 83720, 3rd Fl
Boise, ID 83720-0036

**ILLINOIS**
Children and Family Specialist
406 East Monroe Street
Springfield, IL 62701-1498

**INDIANA**
Adoption History Program
PO Box 1964
Indianapolis, IN 46206-1964

## IOWA
Department of Human Services
Hoover Office Bldg. 5th Floor
Des Moines, IA 50319

## KANSAS
Youth and Adult Services
300 S.W. Oakley St.-West Hall
Topeka, KS 66606

## KENTUCKY
Adult Adoptees
275 East Main St. 6th Fl. West
Frankfort, KY 40621

## LOUISIANA
Office of Community Services
PO Box 3318
Baton Rouge, LA 70821

## MAINE
Department of Human Services
221 State House, Station 11
Augusta, ME 04333

## MARYLAND
Adoption Registry
311 West Saratoga Street
Baltimore, MD 21201

## MASSACHUSETTS
Department of Social Services
24 Farnsworth Street
Boston, MA 02210

## MICHIGAN
Adoption Services Division
PO Box 30037
Lansing, MI 48909

## MINNESOTA
Department of Human Services
444 La Fayette Road
St. Paul, MN 55155-3831

## MISSISSIPPI
Adoption Unit
PO Box 352
Jackson, MS 39205

## MISSOURI
Division of Family Services
PO Box 88
Jefferson City, MO 65103-0088

## MONTANA
Department of Family Services
PO Box 8005
Helena, MT 59604

## NEBRASKA
Department of Social Services
PO Box 95026
Lincoln, NE 68509

## NEVADA
Child and Family Services
6171 W. Charleston Blvd., # 15
Las Vegas, NV 89102

## NEW HAMPSHIRE
Adoption Unit
6 Hazen Drive
Concord, NH 03301

## NEW JERSEY
Adoption Unit
CN 717 - 50 East State Street
Trenton, NJ 08625-0717

## NEW MEXICO
Children, Youth & Family Dept.
PO Drawer 5160
Sante Fe, NM 87502

## NEW YORK
Adoption Information Registry
Empire State Plaza
Albany, NY 12237-0023

## NORTH CAROLINA
Dept. of Human Resources
325 North Salisbury Street
Raleigh, NC 27603

## NORTH DAKOTA
Department of Human Services
600 East Boulevard
Bismarck, ND 58505

## OHIO
Adoption Services Section
65 East State Street, 5th Floor
Columbus, OH 43215

## OKLAHOMA
Department of Human Services
PO Box 25352
Oklahoma City, OK 73125

## OREGON
Adoption Registry
500 Summer Street NE, 2 Fl. S.
Salem, OR 97310-1017

## PENNSYLVANIA
Department of Public Welfare
PO Box 2675
Harrisburg, PA 17105-2675

## RHODE ISLAND
Adoption Services
610 Mt. Pleasant Ave. Bldg. 2
Providence, RI 02908-1935

## SOUTH CAROLINA
Department of Social Services
PO Box 1520
Columbia, SC 29202-1520

## SOUTH DAKOTA
Child Protective Services
700 Governors Drive
Pierre, SD 57501-2291

## TENNESSEE
Adoption Unit, 14th Floor
400 Dearderick Street
Nashville, TN 37248-9000

## TEXAS
Central Adoption Registry
PO Box 149030
Austin, TX 78714-9030

## UTAH
Bureau of Vital Records
288 North 1460 West
Salt Lake City, UT 84116-0700

## VERMONT
Social and Rehabilitation Serv.
103 South Main Street
Waterbury, VT 05671

## VIRGINIA
Virginia Social Services
730 East Broad Street
Richmond, VA 23219-1849

## WASHINGTON
Children & Family Services
Mail Stop: PO Box 45713
Olympia, WA 98504-5713

## WEST VIRGINIA
Voluntary Adoption Registry
PO Box 2942
Charleston, WV 25330-2942

## WISCONSIN
Health & Social Services
PO Box 7851
Madison, WI 53707-7851

## WYOMING
Division of Youth Services
321 Hathaway Building, # 317
Cheyenne, WY 82002-0710

# *9*

# *Search Patterns*

This is the most significant chapter in the entire book because it will help you decide how to conduct your search depending on the information available to you. It will point you in the right direction and make certain that you do not go down the wrong path. It will save you an enormous amount of time and energy. It will force you to analyze the facts you have and make you think like an investigator. This chapter is the equivalent to a road map of your search and if you follow it you should come to your desired destination.

## 1.    SEARCH PATTERNS OF THE ADOPTEE

### *1st Case:*

An adoptee has no information except that the adoptive parents told the adoptee where (which county and state) the adoption was finalized (adoption decree granted).

1. The adoptee or a hired professional researcher goes to the court of jurisdiction, where the petition to adopt and the final adoption decree were granted, to find the docket appearance book and the minute book.

2. If these books are presently stored in the courthouse they may be examined because they are public information.

3. If these books are not stored in the courthouse, determine where they are being stored. They may be in the county library, transferred to microfiche and stored in a nearby annex, or stored in the county or state archive.

4. If these books are found they might yield the following information:

> a) *name of one or more of the birthparents;*
> b) *name of judge who heard this case;*
> c) *date and name of court where proceedings took place;*
> d) *name of caseworker that did homestudy on adoptive parents;*
> e) *name of attorney that represented adoptive parents;*
> f) *name of agency (public or private) or third party (lawyer, doctor, foster parent, legal guardian, etc. that adoptee was surrendered to:*
> h) *the name of the couple trying to legally adopt the child.*

With the name of one birthparent the adoptee can use the search techniques described in YOU, TOO, CAN FIND ANYBODY to find the present location of the missing birthparent.

### *2nd Case:*

The docket appearance book or the minute book are not available for examination. The searcher should attempt to locate the county newspaper(s) that specialized in publishing legal notices at the time of the adoption. If the legal notice pertaining to the adoption is found it might reveal the following information:

1. *birthparent(s) name;*
2. *adoptee's name prior to final decree of adoption;*
3. *date, time and place of hearing;*
4. *name of caseworker assigned to the case:*
5. *name of couple trying to legally adopt the child.*

With the name of one birthparent the adoptee can use the search techniques described in YOU, TOO, CAN FIND ANYBODY to find the present location of the missing birthparent.

### 3rd Case:

If the docket appearance book, the minute book, and the legal notice are not available, the searcher should attempt to locate the birth index for the year of the adoptee's birth. This birth index may be located at the county library, county board of vital statistics, town clerk's office, state bureau of vital statistics, or state archives. If the birth index is located and is available to the public it may produce the following information:

1. *name of birthparent(s)*
2. *date of birth*
3. *location of birth (city, county)*
4. *Bureau of Vital Statistics file number*

With the name of one birthparent the adoptee can use the search techniques described in YOU, TOO, CAN FIND ANYBODY to find the present location of the missing birthparent.

### 4th Case:

Let's backtrack for a moment and create the worst possible scenario, the adoptee searcher has absolutely no information whatsoever. The adoptive parents are completely hostile to the adoptee's intended search and totally refuse to cooperate. Given this grim set of circumstances where would the adoptee start?

The adoptee has been asked when filling out various applications and official documents such as driver's license permit, school records, job applications, social security card application form, etc. where and when he/she was born. Even if the adoptee has only the inaccurate information given on an amended birth certificate the adoptee has that much. What I would do is write to Bureau of Vital Statistics in the state that issued the amended birth certificate and request my original birth certificate (the one that has my birthparent(s) name on it). If the state honors your request than half your search is over because you have the name of at least one birthparent. Chances are excellent however that the state will deny this request because of

the adoption. In that case I would write back to the Bureau and ask for the name of the court of jurisdiction on the grounds that I would like to file a petition to open the adoption file for "humanitarian" or "medical" reasons. As an adoptee you are well within your legal rights to make this petition and therefore the name of the court of jurisdiction must be supplied. If the Bureau of Vital Statistics refuses this request go to the state attorney's office. They know the law and they may be able to assist you free of charge. Once you have the name of the court of jurisdiction follow the steps starting with case 1.

### 5th Case:

Let's assume that the adoptive parents are supportive of the adoptee's search and are willing to cooperate in every possible way to reach a successful conclusion. In this case the adoptive parents may petition the court to obtain copies of their petition to adopt as well as their final decree of adoption. The adoptive parents are normally legally entitled to these two forms which they signed during the adoption process. The name of at least the birthmother is normally found on these forms which would make the search that much easier to complete.

Another valuable source of information that might be easily accessible to the adoptive parents are the documents in the file of the attorney that they hired to represent them in court during the adoption process. The attorney's file should have a copy of the surrender, relinquishment, or consent decree signed by the birthparent(s), the petition to adopt, the final adoption decree, among other papers like an original birth certificate, and possibly hospital records. These are the same documents that are in the sealed court records pertaining to the adoption and will yield all of the information necessary to locate the present whereabouts of the birthparent(s) in most instances.

### 6th Case:

Another source of information that might unintentionally reveal the identity of birthparents is non-identifying information

supplied by a public or private adoption agency. Many times a social worker reveals facts about a birthparent or their family that are solid clues and may quickly lead to uncovering the identity of a birthparent. A good example of this is the letter from Chaplin Spencer (pages 3-8) which states that the birthfather's family was quite large and they lived in a state park in Connecticut. That is a very solid clue in that it is possible to go to Connecticut and visit all the large state parks and inquire about a park attendant who lived there for a number of years with a large family. I'm sure older towns people such as a priest, police officer, politician, barber would remember the name of such a family (see example ). The point is non-identifying information very often is very identifying.

The previous six cases are just some of the more common ways that an adoptee can trace their roots successfully. The legal paper trail that was generated by the adoption process is the searcher's key back to the beginning. Understanding the adoption process that the birthparent(s) went through, have a working knowledge of the state statutes and procedures that were used at the time of the adoptee's birth, and carefully tracing the paper trail back to the courthouse, library, archive is generally the formula to success. Once an adoptee has the name of a birthparent(s) and some background information including a birthdate the process of finding their present location is relatively easy in most cases. These techniques are discussed at length in YOU, TOO, CAN FIND ANYBODY.

## 2.  THE SEARCH PATTERNS OF THE BIRTHPARENT

Birthparent(s) to an adoption normally only agree to surrender or relinquish their legal parental rights and responsibilities. They do not agree to terminate their legal rights to due process under law. What this means is birthparent(s) automatically retain certain rights which they are entitled to exercise. One of these rights is to acquire a copy of the original birth certificate because the birthparent probably was the legal guardian of the child at the time of birth and shortly thereafter. Other legal prerogatives normally retained by the

birthparent(s) include the option to request and obtain medical and historical hospital records if they still exist and a copy of the consent to adopt agreement signed by the birthparent(s) shortly after the birth of the child. These retained legal rights are some of the keys that can be used to unlock the adoption secrets held by the state.

A searching birthparent(s) should request a copy of the original birth certificate from the Bureau of Vital Statistics (or their counterpart) in the state where the birth occurred. Sometimes the request is granted but more often than not, because it involves an adoption, the request is denied. The birthparent(s) has the legal right to petition the court of jurisdiction where the final adoption decree was granted for a copy of the birth certificate. This is exactly what the searcher is trying to accomplish because when the state furnishes the location of the court the searcher will have a legal paper trail to follow.

A method a searcher may use to ascertain the location of the court of jurisdiction from the proper authorities is to simply request the information. Many times the bureaucrat will view this request as non-identifying information and simply hand over the information.

Another possible reason a searcher may request the name of the court of jurisdiction from the state would be to begin some type of legal action such as a petition to open the sealed file based on a medical, humanitarian, or birthright issue. These are all valid grounds for a legal action and because due process can not be denied, the name of the court should be forthcoming from the proper authorities.

There are many techniques an imaginative searcher may use to obtain the needed information and it requires a generous mixture of research, creativity, and bulldog-like perseverance to achieve the desired results.

*1st Case:*
      The birthparent(s) has been given the location of the court of jurisdiction that finalized the adoption (that granted the final adoption decree).

1. The searcher or a hired professional researcher goes to the court of jurisdiction, where the petition to adopt and the final adoption decree were granted, to find and examine the docket appearance book and the minute book.

2. If these books are presently stored in the courthouse they may be examined because they are public information.

3. If these books are not stored in the courthouse try to determine where they are being stored. They may be in the county library, transferred to microfiche and stored in a nearby annex, or stored in the county or state archive.

4. If these books are found they may yield the following information:

        *a) name of one or more of the birthparents;*
        *b) name of judge who heard this case;*
        *c) date and name of court where proceedings took place;*
        *d) name of caseworker that did homestudy on adoptive*
            *parents;*
        *e) name of attorney that represented adoptive parents;*
        *f) name of agency (public or private) or third party*
            *(lawyer, doctor, foster parent, legal guardian, etc.*
            *that adoptee was surrendered to:*
        *h) the name of the couple trying to legally adopt the child.*

      With the name of one of the adoptive parents the birthparent(s) can use search techniques to find the present location of the birthchild and/or the adoptive parents.

## 2nd Case:

The docket appearance book or the minute book are not available for examination. The searcher should attempt to locate the county newspaper(s) that specialized in publishing legal notices at the time of the adoption. If the legal notice pertaining to the adoption is found it may reveal the following information:

1. *birthparent(s) name;*
2. *adoptee's name prior to final decree of adoption;*
3. *date, time and place of hearing;*
4. *name of caseworker assigned to the case:*
5. *name of couple trying to legally adopt the child.*

With the name of the adoptive parents the searcher can use the search techniques in YOU, TOO, CAN FIND ANYBODY to find the present location of the birthchild and/or the adoptive parent.

## 3rd Case:

If the docket appearance book and the minute book are not available and the searcher has not been able to locate a legal notice then the searcher should request non-identifying information from the agency (public or private) that supervised the adoption procedure. Many time a caseworker reveals information which when properly analyzed becomes an important clue which may lead to the identity of the adoptee or adoptive parents. (see Chaplin Spencer, page 3-8).

## 4th Case:

The worst possible situation for a searching birthparent is if the docket appearance book, the minute book, and the legal notice are not available and non-identifying information has not yielded any significant clues. Even under this unusual adverse set of circumstances there is still another road that a searcher may employ.

At this point it is normally necessary to take a more inactive approach in the search. File a Waiver of Confidentiality and a Disclosure Agreement with the state or private agency that have your

adoption records. This Waiver of Confidentiality legally allows the agency to release identifying information to your birthchild should the child contact the agency for such information. This approach is more frustrating because it requires patience while waiting for the birthchild to contact the same agency but it can be successful and should not be overlooked.

## 3.    SEARCH PATTERNS OF THE ADOPTIVE PARENTS

The easiest search under normal circumstances is that of the adoptive parents searching for the birthparent(s). The reason this is generally true is that the adoptive parents have easy access to the name of at least one of the birthparent(s).

During the adoption process, assuming that it was legally conducted, the adoptive parents signed a Petition to Adopt and a Final Adoption Decree. Generally the name of the birthmother (and possibly the birthfather) are included on each of these documents.

If the adoptive parents discarded or misplaced these documents normally they may be easily replaced by petitioning the court of jurisdiction (where the adoption was finalized) or by contacting the attorney that represented the adoptive parents during the adoption process. The attorney normally keeps an archive of the cases he has represented and will probably be able to furnish the documents you are requesting. Since the Petition to Adopt and the Final Adoption Decree are documents that the adoptive parents signed they are legal entitled to a copy and the court will generally be agreeable to releasing them.

If the adoption documents do not reveal the name(s) of the birthparent(s) the adoptive parents should attempt to locate the birth index for the year of the adoptee's birth. This birth index may be located at the county library, county board of vital statistics, town clerk's office, state bureau of vital statistics, or state archives. If the birth index is located and is available to the public it can produce the

following information:
1. *name of birthparent(s);*
2. *date of birth;*
3. *location of birth (city, county);*
4. *Bureau of Vital Statistics file number.*

Once the name of the birthparent(s) is known the adoptive parents can start the search by employing the techniques described in YOU, TOO, CAN FIND ANYBODY.

## 4.   <u>SEARCH PATTERNS FOR SIBLINGS</u>

The difficulty with sibling searches is that they arise from a number of different circumstances, and the route of the search is determined by the amount of information known. For example, a sibling may be:

1. *born to the same mother and father but at an earlier or later time;*
2. *born to the same mother but a different father;*
3. *born to the same father but different mother;*
4. *adopted out at exactly the same time as sibling;*
5. *adopted out at any earlier or later time;*
6. *not adopted out at all.*

The starting point for the search is determined by the information that is available to the sibling. The following cases are some of the possibilities, however it should be remembered that most paths normally lead to the court of jurisdiction (where the Final Adoption Decree was granted) assuming that it was a legal adoption.

1. The sibling was born either earlier or later than the sibling that was adopted out. The searching sibling who lived with the birthparents has been given the following information:
   a) *The date and place of birth of the adopted out child;*
   b) *The name of the agency the child was relinquished to.*

Searching sibling(s) should request a copy of the original birth certificate from the Bureau of Vital Statistics (or their counterpart) in the state where the birth occurred. Sometimes the request is granted but more often than not, because it involves an adoption, the request is denied. The sibling(s) has the legal right to petition the court of jurisdiction where the final adoption decree was granted for a copy of the birth certificate. This is exactly what the searcher is trying to accomplish because when the state furnishes the location of the court the searcher will have a legal paper trail to follow.

Another method a searcher may use to ascertain the location of the court of jurisdiction from the proper authorities is to simply request the information. Many times the bureaucrat will view this request as non-identifying information and simply hand over the information.

Additional reasons a searcher may request the name of the court of jurisdiction from the state would be to begin some type of legal action such as a petition to open the sealed file based on a medical, humanitarian, or birth right issue. These are all valid grounds for a legal action and because due process can not be denied, the name of the court should be forthcoming from the proper authorities.

As I've mentioned before in this chapter there are many techniques an imaginative searcher may use to obtain the needed information and it requires a generous mixture of research, creativity, and bulldog-like perseverance to achieve the desired results.

### *1st Case:*
The sibling(s) has been given the location of the court of jurisdiction that finalized the adoption (that granted the Final Adoption Decree).

1. The searcher or a hired professional researcher goes to the court of jurisdiction, where the petition to adopt and the final adoption decree were granted, to find and examine the Docket Appearance Book and

the Minute Book.

2. If these books are presently stored in the courthouse they may be examined because they are public information.

3. If these books are not stored in the courthouse try to determine where they are being stored. They may be in the county library, transferred to microfiche or microfilm and stored in a nearby annex, or stored in the county or state archive.

4. If these books are found they may yield the following information:

> a) *name of one or more of the birthparents;*
> b) *name of judge who heard this case;*
> c) *date and name of court where proceedings took place;*
> d) *name of caseworker that did homestudy on adoptive parents;*
> e) *name of attorney that represented adoptive parents;*
> f) *name of agency (public or private) or third party (lawyer, doctor, foster parent, legal guardian, etc. that adoptee was surrendered to:*
> h) *the name of the couple trying to legally adopt the child.*

With the name of one of the adoptive parents the sibling(s) can use the search techniques described in YOU, TOO, CAN FIND ANYBODY to find the present location of the birthchild and/or the adoptive parents.

### 2nd Case:

The docket appearance book or the minute book are not available for examination. The searcher should attempt to locate the county newspaper(s) that specialized in publishing legal notices at the time of the adoption. If the legal notice pertaining to the adoption is found it may reveal the following information:

1. *birthparent(s) name;*
2. *adoptee's name prior to final decree of adoption;*
3. *date, time and place of hearing;*
4. *name of caseworker assigned to the case:*
5. *name of couple trying to legally adopt the child.*

With the name of the adoptive parents the searcher can use the search techniques described in YOU, TOO, CAN FIND ANYBODY to find the present location of the birthchild and/or the adoptive parent.

### *3rd Case:*

If the docket appearance book and the minute book are not available and the searcher has not been able to locate a legal notice then the searcher should request non-identifying information from the agency (public or private) that supervised the adoption procedure. Many times a caseworker reveals information which properly analyzed becomes an important clue that may lead to the identity of the adoptee or adoptive parents.

### *4th Case:*

The worst possible situation for a searching sibling is if the docket appearance book, the minute book, and the legal notice are not available and non-identifying information has not yielded any significant clues. Even under this unusual adverse set of circumstances there is still another road that a searcher may employ.

At this point it is normally necessary to take a more indirect approach in the search. File a Waiver of Confidentiality and a Disclosure Agreement with the state or private agency that have your adoption records. This Waiver of Confidentiality legally allows the agency to release identifying information to the sibling should the sibling contact the agency for such information.

Another type of search is when a sibling was adopted out. The searching sibling has had no contact with the birthparents and is

aware at this point that siblings exist.

This is another case of an adoptee's search for birthparents (see page 9-1 SEARCH PATTERNS FOR ADOPTEE'S). When the sibling's search for the birthparent(s) is successful the searcher might discover that a siblings exist. With the information that might be available from birthparents the searcher may continue to search for the sibling.

# *10*

# *State Archives*

In many cases the records most important to a successful adoption search are stored in the state archives. It is here that one may find old birth indexes, old county courthouse records, documents, telephone directories, school yearbooks, newspapers, and a host of other dated material that may contain important clues and strong evidence. It is essential that every searcher become familiar with the resources, services and location of their state archive.

Typically the various departments and courts of county and local governments send their records to the state archives for safe keeping after a certain period of time has passed. Each area has their own policy as to which records will be sent, the age of the record to be sent, and whether or not the record is the original or a copy. The most common historical records of interest to an adoption searcher that may be found in state archives are:

**1. Birth Index** - list of all the births in the city, county, or state for a certain length of time, generally one year. The births are normally listed by last name in an ascending alphabetical order, or by date of birth in a chronological order.

**2. Death Index** - list of all the deaths in the city, county, or state for a certain length of time, generally one year. The deaths are normally listed by last name in an ascending alphabetical order, or by date of death in a chronological order.

**3. Marriages and Divorces Index** - list of all marriages and divorces in the city, county, or state for a certain length of time, generally one

year. The marriage and divorces are normally listed by last name in an ascending alphabetical order, or by date of marriage or divorce in a chronological order.

**4. Old County Court Records** - The records that are of interest to adoption searchers include Relinquishment, Surrender, or Consent to Adopt Decrees, Petitions to Adopt, Final Adoption Decrees, Original and Amended Birth Certificates.

**5. Old Newspapers** - may contain legal notices, obituaries, announcements, or news stories that open doors in an adoption search.

**6. Old Telephone Directories** - can be useful when trying to locate someone from years past that has moved.

**7. Old School Yearbooks** - can be an excellent source of identifying information. Often the yearbook can be used to contact classmates and teachers as well as a subject.

A searcher may be compelled to do research at a state archive which is distant from home. Due to time or distant constraints the searcher might find it cost effective to hire a researcher who lives near the state archive. Another valuable service available from most state archives is to either provide a professional researchers for an hourly fee or be able to recommend competent local professional researcher that have registered with the archive or are personally known by the archivists.

### LOCAL AND COUNTY ARCHIVES

A number of dated documents that are important to a searcher may be found on the local or county level. The Town and County Clerk Office may contain old birth, death, marriage, or divorce records. The County Clerk's Office may store old Docket Appearance or Minute Books. The County Library may have an extensive collection of old local newspapers which house legal notices. The possible list of sources of information is quite large and a searcher needs to be

creative and open-minded in their thinking. A possible interesting aspect of local archivists and record- keepers is that it may be easier to obtain information from them than their counterparts on a state level. A town or county clerk may by mistake or by sympathetic design give a searcher a document that the searcher is not normally entitled to such as an original birth certificate. In many instances the record keeping on a local level is more lax and errors are more likely to occur. If a searcher has a choice between a state or local source of information I would recommend trying the local source first.

# STATE ARCHIVES

**ALABAMA**
Dept.of Archives and History
624 Washington Avenue
Montgomery, AL 36130-0100

**ALASKA**
Alaska Collection and Archives
4101 University Drive
Anchorage, AK 99508

Division of Archives
141 Willoughby
Junean, AK 99801-1720

**ARIZONA**
Department of Archives
1700 West Washington
Phoenix, AZ 85007

**ARKANSAS**
History Commission
1 Capitol Mall, 2nd Floor
Little Rock, AR 72201

**CALIFORNIA**
The California State Archives
1020 O Street
Sacramento, CA 95814

**COLORADO**
Division of Archives
1313 Sherman Street
Denver, CO 80203

**CONNECTICUT**
The Connecticut State Archives
231 Capitol Avenue
Hartford, CT 06115

**DELAWARE**
Delaware State Archives
P. O. Box 1401
Dover, DE 19901

**DISTRICT OF COLUMBIA**
District of Columbia Archives
1300 Naylor Court, N.W.
Washington, DC 20001-4225

## FLORIDA
Florida State Archives
500 South Bronough Street
Tallahassee, FL 32399-0250

## GEORGIA
Department of Archives
330 Capitol Ave., S.E.
Atlanta, GA 30334

## HAWAII
Hawaii State Archives
478 South King Street
Honolulu, HI 96813

## IDAHO
Idaho State Archives
450 North Fourth Street
Boise, ID 83702

## ILLINOIS
Archives Building
Capital Complex
Springfield, IL 62756

## INDIANA
Indiana State Archives
140 North Senate Avenue # 117
Indianapolis, IN 46204

## IOWA
State Archives of Iowa
600 East Locust,
Des Moines, IA 50319

## KANSAS
State Archives
Third Floor State House
Topeka, KS 66612

## KENTUCKY
Kentucky State Archives
P. O. Box 537
Frankfurt, KY 40602-0537

## LOUISIANA
State Archives & Records
3851 Essen Lane
Baton Rouge, LA 70804-9125

## MAINE
Maine State Archives
State House Station, #84
Augusta, ME 04333

## MARYLAND
Maryland State Archives
350 Rowe Boulevard
Annapolis, MD 21401

## MASSACHUSETTS
Archives of the Commonwealth
220 Morrissey Boulevard
Boston, MA 02125

## MICHIGAN
State of Archives of Michigan
717 West Allegan Street
Lansing, MI 48919

## MINNESOTA
Minnesota Historical Society
345 Kellogg Boulevard, West
Saint Paul, MN 55102-1906

## MISSISSIPPI
Department of Archives
P.O. Box 571
Jackson, MS 39205-0571

## MISSOURI
Missouri State Archives
P.O. Box 778
Jefferson City, MO 65102

## MONTANA
Montana State Archives
225 North Roberts Street
Helena, MT 59620

## NEBRASKA
State Archives Division
P.O. Box 82554
Lincoln, NE 68501-2554

## NEVADA
Nevada State Archives
100 Stewart Street
Carson City, NV 89710

## NEW HAMPSHIRE
Division of Archives
71 South Fruit Street
Concord, NH 03301-2410

## NEW JERSEY
New Jersey State Archives
185 West State Street CN 307
Trenton, NJ 08625-0307

## NEW MEXICO
New Mexico Archives
404 Montezuma Street
Santa Fe, NM 87501

## NEW YORK
New York State Archives
11 D 40 Cultural Education Ctr.
Albany, NY 12230

## NORTH CAROLINA
North Carolina State Archives
109 East Jones Street
Raleigh, NC 27601-2807

## NORTH DAKOTA
North Dakota State Archives
612 East Boulevard Avenue
Bismarck, ND 58505

## OHIO
Archives - Library Division
1982 Velma Avenue
Columbus, OH 43211-2497

## OKLAHOMA
Office of Archives & Records
200 N.E. 18th Street
Oklahoma City, OK 73105

## OREGON
Archives Division
800 Summer Street, N.E.
Salem, OR 97310

## PENNSYLVANIA
Pennsylvania State Archives
P.O. Box 1026
Harrisburg, PA 17108-1026

## RHODE ISLAND
Rhode Island State Archives
337 Westminster Street
Providence, RI 02903

## SOUTH CAROLINA
Dept. of Archives & History
1430 Senate Street
Columbia, SC 29211-1669

## SOUTH DAKOTA
South Dakota Archives
900 Governors Drive
Pierre, SD 57501-2217

## TENNESSEE
Tennessee State Archives
403 Seventh Avenue, North
Nashville, TN 37243-0312

## TEXAS
Texas State Library
Capitol Station, Box 12927
Austin, TX 78711

## UTAH
Utah State Archives
State Capitol
Salt Lake City, UT 84114

## VERMONT
Vermont State Archives
26 Terrace Street
Montpelier, VT 05609-1103

## VIRGINIA
Virginia State Archives
11th Street at Capitol Square
Richmond, VA 23219-3491

## WASHINGTON STATE
Washington State Archives
1120 Washington St., SE
Olympia, WA 98504-0238

## WEST VIRGINIA
West Virginia Archives
1900 Kanawha Boulevard East
Charleston, WV 25305-0300

## WISCONSIN
Historical Society of Wisconsin
816 State Street
Madison, WI 53706

## WYOMING
Wyoming State Archives
2301 Central Avenue, 3rd Floor
Cheyenne, WY 82002

# *11*

# *Attorneys*

The adoption process is a legal procedure wherein birthparent(s) consents to relinquish or surrender their legal rights and responsibilities as a parent to another legal guardian and an individual or couple agree to take permanent custody of a child(ren) and raise that child(ren) as their own.

The steps to be followed in a legal adoption are rigidly described and governed by state statute. The court of jurisdiction is responsible for the child's welfare and will oversee and sanction the adoption procedure.

Attorneys play an important role throughout the adoption procedure. They may act as a third party thereby arranging the adoption of a child from the birthparent(s) to the adoptive parents. They may represent and counsel a private agency during an adoption procedure. They may work for the state government and represent the public agency during the adoption. Attorneys always represent the prospective adoptive parents during the various stages of the adoption procedures and normally they write and present to the court the Petition to Adopt and Final Adoption Decree.

Under ordinary circumstances in the majority of States in the United States and the Provinces of Canada, the court records pertaining to an adoption case are normally sealed and unavailable. The file of the adoption retained by the attorney who represented the adoptive parents normally includes the Original Birth Certificate, the Amended Birth Certificate, the Consent to Adopt, the Petition to Adopt, and the Final Adoption Decree. This is virtually the same

information as in the official, sealed court records but these records are not sealed. If the searcher determines the identity of the attorney who represented the adoptive parents he/she may ask the attorney or the heirs to open or surrender the file. If this occurs the searcher will have all the names, dates and facts relevant to the adoption.

### *THE LAST RESORT*

A lawyer may be able to succesfully petition the court to open sealed adoption files. If a searcher decides to hire an attorney, the searcher should be certain that the attorney has been practicing in the court of jurisdiction for a long time and is very familiar with the law as well as the judges that administer the law.

# State Bar Associations

## ALABAMA

Alabama State Bar
Post Office Box 671
Montgomery, AL 36101
Tel: (205) 269-1515

## ALASKA

Alaska Bar Association
Post Office Box 279
Anchorage, AK 99510
Tel: (907) 272-7496

## ARIZONA

State Bar of Arizona
234 North Central
Phoenix, AZ 85004
Tel: (602) 252-4804

## ARKANSAS

Arkansas Bar Association
400 West Markham
Little Rock, AR 72201
Tel: (501) 375-4605

## CALIFORNIA

State Bar of California
555 Franklin Street
San Francisco, CA 94102
Tel: (415) 561-8200

## COLORADO

Colorado Bar Association
250 West 14th Street
Denver, CO 80204
Tel: (303) 629-6873

## CONNECTICUT

Connecticut Bar Association
15 Lewis Street
Hartford, CT 06103
Tel: (203) 249-9141

## DELAWARE

Delaware State Bar Association
820 North French Street
Wilmington, DE 19801
Tel: (302) 658-5278

## DISTRICT OF COLUMBIA

The District of Columbia Bar
1426 H Street NW
Washington, D.C. 20005
Tel: (202) 638-1500

## FLORIDA

The Florida Bar Association
650 Apalachee Parkway
Tallahassee, FL 32301
Tel: (904) 561-5600

## GEORGIA

State Bar of Georgia
84 Peachtree Street
Atlanta, GA 30303
Tel: (404) 522-6255

## HAWAII

Hawaii State Bar
820 Mililani
Honolulu, HI 96813
Tel: (808) 537-1868

## IDAHO

Idaho State Bar
Post Office Box 895
Boise, ID 83701
Tel: (208) 342-8958

## ILLINOIS

Illinois Bar Center
424 South 2nd Streeet
Springfield, IL 62701
Tel: (217) 525-1760

## INDIANA

Indiana State Bar Association
230 East Ohio Street
Indianapolis, IN 42604
Tel: (317) 639-5465

## IOWA

Iowa State Bar Association
1101 Fleming Building
Des Moines, IA 50309
Tel: (515) 243-3179

## KANSAS

Kansas Bar Association
Post Office Box 1037
Topeka, KS 66601
Tel: (913) 234-5696

## KENTUCKY

Kentucky Bar Association
West Main at Kentucky River
Frankfort, KY 40601
Tel: (502) 564-3795

## LOUISIANA

Louisiana State Bar Association
210 O'Keefe Avenue
New Orleans, LA 70112
Tel: (504) 566-1600

## MAINE

Maine State Bar Association
Post Office Box 788
August, ME 04330
Tel: (207) 622-7523

## MARYLAND

Maryland State Bar Association
207 East Redwood Street
Baltimore, MD 21202
Tel: (301) 685-7878

## MASSACHUSETTS

Massachusetts Bar Association
One Center Plaza
Boston, MA 02108
Tel: (617) 523-4529

## MICHIGAN

State Bar of Michigan
306 Townsend Street
Lansing, MI 48933
Tel: (517) 372-9030

## MINNESOTA

Minnesota State Bar Assoc.
430 Marquette Avenue
Minneapolis, MN 55402
Tel: (612) 335-1183

## MISSISSIPPI

Mississippi State Bar
Post Office Box 2168
Jackson, MS 39205
Tel: (601) 948-4471

## MISSOURI

The Missouri Bar
Post Office Box 119
Jefferson City, MO 65102
Tel: (314) 635-4128

## MONTANA

State Bar of Montana
Post Office Box 4669
Helena, MT 59604
Tel: (406) 442-7660

## NEBRASKA

Nebraska State Bar Association
206 South 13th Street
Lincoln, NB 65808
Tel: (402) 475-7091

## NEVADA

State Bar of Nevada
834 Willow Street
Reno, NV 89501
Tel: (702) 329-4100

## NEW HAMPSHIRE

New Hampshire Bar Assoc.
18 Centre Street
Concord, NH 03301
Tel: (603) 224-6942

## NEW JERSEY

New Jersey State Bar Assoc.
172 West State Street
Trenton, NJ 08608
Tel: (609) 394-1101

## NEW MEXICO

State Bar of New Mexico
Post Office Box 25883
Albuquerque, NM 87125
Tel: (505) 842-6132

## NEW YORK

New York State Bar Association
One Elk Street
Albany, NY 12207
Tel: (518) 463-3200

## NORTH CAROLINA

North Carolina State Bar
Post Office Box 25908
Raleigh, NC 27611
Tel: (919) 828-4620

## NORTH DAKOTA

State Bar Assoc. of N. Dakota
Post Office Box 2136
Bismarck, ND 58502
Tel: (701) 255-1404

## OHIO

Ohio State Bar Association
33 West 11th Avenue
Columbus, OH 42301
Tel: (614) 421-2121

## OKLAHOMA

Oklahoma Bar Association
Post Office Box 53036
Oklahoma City, OK 73152
Tel: (405) 524-2365

## OREGON

Oregon State Bar
1776 S.W. Madison
Portland, OR 97205
Tel: (503) 224-4280

## PENNSYLVANIA

Pennsylvania Bar Association
Post Office Box 186
Harrisburg, PA 17108
Tel: (717) 238-6715

## PUERTO RICO

Bar Association of Puerto Rico
Box 1900
San Juan, PR 00903
Tel: (809) 721-3358

## RHODE ISLAND

Rhode Island Bar Association
1804 Industrial Bank Building
Providence, RI 02903
Tel: (401) 421-5740

## SOUTH CAROLINA

South Carolina Bar Association
Post Office Box 11039
Columbia, SC 29211
Tel: (803) 799-6653

## SOUTH DAKOTA

State Bar of South Dakota
222 East Capitol
Pierre, SD 57501
Tel: (605) 224-7554

## TENNESSEE

Tennessee Bar Association
3622 West End Avenue
Nashville, TN 37205
Tel: (615) 383-7421

## TEXAS

State Bar of Texas
Post Office Box 12487
Austin, TX 78711
Tel: (512) 475-4200

## UTAH

Utah State Bar
425 East First South
Salt Lake City, UT 84111
Tel: (801) 531-9077

## VERMONT

Vermont Bar Association
Post Office Box 100
Montpelier, VT 05602
Tel: (802) 223-2020

## VIRGINIA

Virginia State Bar
700 East Main Street
Richmond, VA 23219
Tel: (804) 786-2061

## WASHINGTON

Washington State Bar Assoc.
505 Madison
Seattle, WA  98104
Tel: (206) 622-6054

## WEST VIRGINIA

West Virginia State Bar
2006 Kanawha Boulevard
Charleston, WV  25311
Tel: (304) 346-8414

## WISCONSIN

State Bar of Wisconsin
Post Office Box 7158
Madison, WI  53707
Tel: (608) 257-3838

## WYOMING

Wyoming State Bar
Post Office Box 109
Cheyenne, WY  82003
Tel: (307) 632-9061

# County Bar Associations

## ALABAMA

### BIRMINGHAM
BIRMINGHAM BAR ASSOC.
109 North 20th Street
Birmingham, Alabama 35203
Tel: (205) 251-8006

### HUNTSVILLE
HUNTSVILLE BAR ASSOC.
205 East Side Square
Huntsville, Alabama 35801
Tel: (205) 532-1585

### MOBILE
MOBILE BAR ASSOCIATION
Post Office Drawer 2005
Mobile, Alabama 36652
Tel: (205) 433-9790

## ARIZONA

### PHOENIX
MARICOPA BAR ASSOC.
303 East Palm Lane
Phoenix, Arizona 85004
Tel: (602) 257-4200

### TUCSON
PIMA COUNTY BAR ASSOC.
177 North Church, #101
Tucson, Arizona 85701
Tel: (602) 623-8258

## CALIFORNIA

### BAKERSFIELD
KERN BAR ASSOCIATION
1400 Chester Avenue, Suite P
Bakersfield, California 93301
Tel: (805) 327-3995

### BEVERLY HILLS
BEVERLY HILL BAR ASSOC.
300 South Beverly Drive,
Beverly Hills, CA 90212
Tel: (310) 553-6644

### BURBANK
BURBANK BAR ASSOC.
222 East Olive Avenue
Burbank, California 91502
Tel: (818) 843-0931

### CHICO
BUTTE BAR ASSOCIATION
341 Broadway, Suite 309
Chico, California 95928
Tel: (916) 891-6808

### CHULA VISTA
SOUTH BAY BAR ASSOC.
230 Glover Avenue, Suite I
Chula Vista, California 91910
Tel: (619) 422-5377

## CONCORD
CONTRA COSTA BAR ASSO.
1001 Galaxy Way, Suite 103
Concord, California 94520
Tel: (510) 686-6900

## LONG BEACH
LONG BEACH BAR ASSOC.
11 Golden Shore No. 230
Long Beach, California 90802
Tel: (213) 432-5913

## ENCINO
FERNANDO BAR ASSOC.
5435 Balboa Boulevard, #205
Encino, California 91316
Tel: (818) 995-6665

## LOS ANGELES
LAWYERS CLUB OF L.A.
700 South Flower Street,#1512
Los Angeles, California 90071
Tel: (213) 624-2525

## EUREKA
HUMBOLDT BAR ASSOC.
Post Office Box 187
Eureka, California 95501
Tel: (707) 445-2652

LOS ANGELES BAR ASSOC.
617 South Olive Street
Los Angeles, California 90014
Tel: (213) 627-2727

## FRESNO
FRESNO BAR ASSOCIATION
420 T.W. Patterson Building
Fresno, California 93721
Tel: (209) 264-0137

## MODESTO
STANISLAUS BAR ASSOC.
Post Office Box 763
Modesto, California 95353
Tel: (209) 523-7853

## GLENDALE
GLENDALE BAR ASSOC.
512 East Wilson Avenue, #307
Glendale, California 91206
Tel: (818) 956-1633

## MONTEREY
MONTEREY BAR ASSOC.
411 Pacific Street, Suite 308
Monterey, California 93940
Tel: (408) 375-1693

## HAYWARD
ALAMEDA BAR ASSOC.
570 B Street
Hayward, California 94541
Tel: (415) 582-0091

## OAKLAND
ALAMEDA BAR ASSOC.
360 22nd Street, Suite 800
Oakland, California 94612
Tel: (415) 893-7160

| PALO ALTO | SACRAMENTO |
|---|---|
| PALO ALTO BAR ASSOC. | SACRAMENTO BAR ASSOC. |
| 405 Sherman Avenue | 901 H Street, Suite 101 |
| Palo Alto, California 94306 | Sacramento, California 95814 |
| Tel: (415) 326-8322 | Tel: (916) 448-1087 |

PASADENA
PASADENA BAR ASSOC.
234 East Colorado Blvd, #110
Pasadena, California 91101
Tel: (818) 795-5641

SAN BERNARDINO
BERNARDINO BAR ASSOC.
150 West Fifth Street,#104
San Bernardino, CA 92401
Tel: (714) 888-6791

POMONA
BAR ASSOC. L.A. COUNTY
c/o Box 380
Pomona, California 91769
Tel: (818) 967-3115

SAN DIEGO
SAN DIEGO BAR ASSOC.
1333 7th Avenue, Suite 200
San Diego, California 92101
Tel: (619) 231-0781

RANCHO CUCAMONGA
BERNARDINO BAR ASSOC.
10722 Arrow Route, Suite 214
Rancho Cucamonga, CA 91730
Tel: (909) 363-4230

SAN FRANCISCO
BAR ASSOC. OF S. F.
685 Market Street, Suite 700
San Francisco, CA 94105
Tel: (415) 764-1600

REDWOOD CITY
SAN MATEO BAR ASSOC.
303 Bradford Street, #A
Redwood City, CA 94063
Tel: (909) 363-4230

LAWYERS' CLUB OF S. F.
685 Market Street, Suite 750
San Francisco, CA 94105
Tel: (415) 882-9150

RIVERSIDE
RIVERSIDE BAR ASSOC.
3612 Seventh Street
Riverside, California 92501
Tel: (909) 682-1015

SAN JOSE
SANTA CLARA BAR ASSOC.
Four North Second Street, #400
San Jose, California 95113
Tel: (408) 287-2557

## SAN RAFAEL
MARIN BAR ASSOCIATION
1010 B Street, Suite 325
San Rafael, California 94901
Tel: (415) 453-8181

## SANTA ANA
ORANGE BAR ASSOC.
601 Civic Center Drive, West
Santa Ana, CA 92701-4002
Tel: (714) 541-OCBA

## SANTA BARBARA
BAR ASSOCIATION
1111 Garden Street, Suite 106
Santa Barbara, CA 93101
Tel: (805) 962-3443

## SANTA CRUZ
SANTA CRUZ BAR ASSOC.
340 Soquel Avenue, Suite 209
Santa Cruz, California 95062
Tel: (408) 423-5031

## SANTA MONICA
BAR ASSOCIATION
1707 Fourth Street, #209
Santa Monica, California 90401
Tel: (213) 394-6979

## STOCKTON
SAN JOAQUIN BAR ASSOC.
6 South El Dorado Street, #504
Stockton, California 95202
Tel: (209) 948-4620

## SUNNYVALE
SUNNYVALE BAR ASSOC.
510 South Mathilda Ave, #9
Sunnyvale, California 94086
Tel: (408) 736-2520

## TORRANCE
BAR ASSOCIATION
Post Office Box 3825
Torrance, California 90510
Tel: (310) 320-4295

## VENTURA
VENTURA BAR ASSOC.
4475 Market Street, #B
Ventura, California 93003
Tel: (805) 653-5252

## VISALIA
TULARE COUNTY ASSOC.
208 West Main Street
Visalia, California 93291
Tel: (209) 732-2513

## VISTA
BAR ASSOC. OF SAN DIEGO
Post Office Box 2802
Vista, California 92085

## **COLORADO**
### COLORADO SPRINGS
EL PASO BAR ASSOCIATION
19 North Tejon Street, #200
Colorado Springs, CO 80903
Tel: (719) 473-9700

## DENVER
DENVER BAR ASSOC.
1900 Grant Street, Suite 950
Denver, Colorado 80203-4309
Tel: (303) 860-1115

## FORT COLLINS
LARIMER BAR ASSOC.
107 Cameron Drive
Fort Collins, Colorado 80525
Tel: (303) 226-1122

## GRAND JUNCTION
MESA BAR ASSOCIATION
2808 North Ave, #400, Box 398
Grand Junction, CO 81502
Tel: (303) 242-7322

## CONNECTICUT
### BRIDGEPORT
BRIDGEPORT BAR ASSOC.
360 Fairfield Avenue
Bridgeport, CT 06610-0035
Tel: (203) 335-4116

## HARTFORD
HARTFORD BAR ASSOC.
61 Hungerford Streert
Hartford, Connecticut 06106
Tel: (203) 525-8106

## NEW HAVEN
NEW HAVEN BAR ASSOC.
Post Office Box 1441
New Haven, Connecticut 06506
Tel: (203) 562-9652

## WATERBURY
WATERBURY BAR ASSOC.
P.O. Box 1767
Waterbury, Connecticut 06721
Tel: (203) 753-1938

## YANTIC
NEW LONDON BAR ASSOC.
P.O. Box 97
Yantic, Connecticut 06389
Tel: (203) 889-9384

## FLORIDA
### ALTAMONTE SPRINGS
SEMINOLE BAR ASSOC.
370 Whooping Loop Ln., #1184
Altamonte Springs, FL 32701
Tel: (407) 834-0530

## CLEARWATER
BAR ASSOCIATION
314 South Missouri Ave,#107
Clearwater, Florida 34616
Tel: (813) 461-4869

## DAYTONA BEACH
VOLUSIA BAR ASSOC.
Post Office Drawer 15050
Daytona Beach, Florida 32115
Tel: (904) 253-9471

## FORT LAUDERDALE
BROWARD BAR ASSOC.
1051 Southeast Third Avenue
Fort Lauderdale, Florida 33316
Tel: (954) 764-8040

## FORT MYERS
LEE COUNTY BAR ASSOC.
Post Office Box 1387
Fort Myers, Florida 33902
Tel: (813) 334-0047

## JACKSONVILLE
BAR ASSOCIATION
1200 Gulf Life Drive, #830
Jacksonville, FL 32207-9092
Tel: (804) 399-4486

## LAKELAND
POLK BAR ASSOCIATION
820 South Florida Ave, #206
Lakeland, Florida 33801
Tel: (813) 686-8215

## MELBOURNE
BREVARD BAR ASSOC.
1600 Sarno Road, Suite V3
Melbourne, Florida 32935
Tel: (407) 242-1922

## MIAMI
DADE BAR ASSOCIATION
123 Northwest First Avenue
Miami, Florida 33128
Tel: (305) 371-2220

## NAPLES
COLLIER BAR ASSOC.
3301 E. Tamiami Trail
Naples, Florida 33962
Tel: (813) 775-3939

## ORLANDO
ORANGE BAR ASSOC.
880 North Orange Ave, #100
Orlando, Florida 32801
Tel: (305) 422-4551

## PENSACOLA
SANTA ROSA BAR ASSOC.
24 West Government St, #275
Pensacola, Florida 32501
Tel: (904) 434-8135

## SAINT PETERSBURG
BAR ASSOCIATION
Post Office Box 7538
Saint Petersburg, FL 33734
Tel: (813) 823-7474

## SARASOTA
SARASOTA BAR ASSOC.
2000 Main Street, Room 305
Sarasota, Florida 34237
Tel: (813) 366-6703

## TALLAHASSEE
BAR ASSOCIATION
Post Office Box 813
Tallahassee, Florida 32302
Tel: (904) 222-3292

## TAMPA
BAR ASSOCIATION
315 Madison, Suite 1010
Tampa, Florida 33602
Tel: (813) 226-6431

WEST PALM BEACH
PALM BEACH BAR ASSOC.
1601 Belvedere Rd, #302 East
West Palm Beach, Fl 33406
Tel: (407) 687-2800

COUNCIL OF LAWYERS
220 South State St, Suite 800
Chicago, Illinois 60604
Tel: (312) 427-0710

## GEORGIA
### ATLANTA
ATLANTA BAR ASSOC.
Equitable Building, Suite 2500
Atlanta, Georgia 30303
Tel: (404) 521-0781

WOMEN'S BAR ASSOC.
309 West Washington, #900
Chicago, Illinois 60606
Tel: (312) 541-0048

### MARIETTA
COBB BAR ASSOCIATION
30 Waddell Street, Suite 601
Marietta, Georgia 30090

### FOREST PARK
BAR ASSOCIATION
320 Circle Avenue
Forest Park, Illinois 60130
Tel: (708) 366-1122

### SAVANNAH
SAVANNAH BAR ASSOC.
10 Whitaker Street, 2nd Floor
Savannah, Georgia 31412
Tel: (912) 236-9344

### GENEVA
KANE BAR ASSOCIATION
Post Office Box 571
Geneva, Illinois 60134
Tel: (708) 232-6416

## ILLINOIS
### ARLINGTON HEIGHTS
BAR ASSOCIATION
515 East Golf Road, #100-101
Arlington Heights,IL60005
Tel: (708) 290-8070

### JOLIET
WILL BAR ASSOCIATION
16 Wm. Van Buren, Third Floor
Joliet, Illinois 60431
Tel: (815) 726-0383

### CHICAGO
CHICAGO BAR ASSOC.
321 South Plymouth Court
Chicago, Illinois 60604
Tel: (312) 554-2000

### PEORIA
PEORIA BAR ASSOCIATION
1618 First Financial Plaza
Peoria, Illinois 61602
Tel:(309) 674-6049

## ROCKFORD
WINNEBAGO BAR ASSOC.
321 West State St, #300
Rockford, Illinois 61101
Tel: (815) 964-4992

## WAUKEGAN
LAKE BAR ASSOCIATION
7 North County Street
Waukegan, Illinois 60085
Tel: (708) 244-3143

## WHEATON
DU PAGE BAR ASSOC.
126 South County Farm Road
Wheaton, Illinois 60187
Tel: (708) 653-7779

## INDIANA
### CROWN POINT
LAKE BAR ASSOCIATION
2293 North Main Street
Crown Point Indiana 46307
Tel: (219) 738-1905/06

### EVANSVILLE
EVANSVILLE BAR ASSOC.
123 Northwest Fourth St, #18
Evansville, Indiana 47708
Tel: (812) 426-1712

### HAMMOND
HAMMOND BAR ASSOC.
232 Russell Street
Hammond, Indiana 46320
Tel: (219) 932-2787

## INDIANAPOLIS
INDIANAPOLIS BAR ASSOC.
10 West Market St, Suite 440
Indianapolis, Indiana 46204
Tel: (317) 269-2000

## MUNCIE
MUNCIE BAR ASSOCIATION
330 East Main St, Suite Four
Muncie, Indiana 47305
Tel: (317) 288-0207

## SOUTH BEND
ST. JOSEPH BAR ASSOC.
101 South Main Street
South Bend, Indiana 46601
Tel: (219) 235-9657

## IOWA
### SIOUX CITY
WOODBURY BAR ASSOC.
Woodbury County Courthouse
Sioux City, Iowa 51101
Tel: (712) 279-6609

## KANSAS
### KANSAS CITY
WYANDOTTE BAR ASSOC.
710 North Seventh Street
Kansas City, Kansas 66101

### TOPEKA
TOPEKA BAR ASSOCIATION
Post Office Box 1399
Topeka, Kansas 66601
Tel: (913) 233-3945

## WICHITA
WICHITA BAR ASSOC.
301 North Main, Suite 700
Wichita, Kansas 67202
Tel: (316) 263-2251

## KENTUCKY
### HIGHLAND HEIGHTS
KENTUCKY BAR ASSOC.
301 Nunn Hall Dr.
Highland Heights, KY 41076
Tel: (606) 781-1300

### LEXINGTON
FAYETTE BAR ASSOC.
122 North Broadway
Lexington, Kentucky 40507

### LOUISVILLE
LOUISVILLE BAR ASSOC.
707 West Main Street
Louisville, Kentucky 40202
Tel: (502) 583-5314

## LOUISIANA
### BATON ROUGE
BAR ASSOCIATION
309 North Boulevard
Baton Rouge, Louisiana 70802
Tel: (504) 344-4803

### LAFAYETTE
LAFAYETTE BAR ASSOC.
Post Office Box 2194
Lafayette, LA 70502-2194
Tel: (318) 237-4700

## NEW ORLEANS
BAR ASSOCIATION
228 Saint Charles Ave. #1233
New Orleans, Louisiana 70130
Tel: (504) 525-7432

### SHREVEPORT
BAR ASSOCIATION
Post Office Box 470
Shreveport, Louisiana 71101

## MAINE
### PORTLAND
BAR ASSOCIATION
P.O. Box 15216
Portland, Maine 04101
Tel: (207) 774-0317

## MARYLAND
### ANNAPOLIS
BAR ASSOCIATION
P.O. Box 161
Annapolis, Maryland 21404
Tel: (410) 280-6950

### BALTIMORE
BAR ASSOC OF BALTIMORE
111 North Calvert St., #627
Baltimore, Maryland 21202
Tel: (410) 539-5936

### ELLICOTT CITY
HOWARD BAR ASSOC.
8360 Court Avenue
Ellicott City, Maryland 21043
Tel: (301) 465-2721

## ROCKVILLE
BAR ASSOCIATION
27 West Jefferson Street
Rockville, Maryland 20850
Tel: (303) 424-3454

## TOWSON
BALTIMORE BAR ASSOC.
401 Bosley Avenue
Towson, Maryland 21204
Tel: (410) 337-9103

## UPPER MARLBORO
BAR ASSOCIATION.
14330 Old Marlborough Pike
Upper Marlboro, MD 20772
Tel: (301) 952-1442

## MASSACHUSETTS
## BOSTON
BOSTON BAR ASSOC.
16 Beacon Street
Boston, Massachusetts 02108
Tel: (617) 742-0615

## CAMBRIDGE
MIDDLESEX BAR ASSOC.
40 Thorndike Street
Cambridge, MA 02141
Tel: (617) 494-4150

## HINGHAM
BAR ASSOCIATION
115 North Street
Hingham, Massachusetts 02043
Tel: (617) 749-9922

## NEW BEDFORD
BRISTOL BAR ASSOC.
448 County Street
New Bedford, MA 02740
Tel: (617) 990-1303

## NORTHAMPTON
HAMPSHIRE BAR ASSOC.
15 Gothic Street
Northampton, MA 01060
Tel: (413) 586-8729

## QUINCY
BAR ASSOC. OF NORFOLK
15 Cottage Avenue, Suite 206
Quincy, Massachusetts 02169
Tel: (617) 471-9693

## SPRINGFIELD
HAMPDEN BAR ASSOC.
50 State Street, Room 137
Springfield, MA 01103
Tel: (413) 732-4648

## WORCESTER
WORCESTER BAR ASSOC.
19 Norwich Street
Worcester, MA 01608
Tel: (508) 752-1311

## MICHIGAN
## ANN ARBOR
WASHTENAW BAR ASSOC.
Post Office Box 8645
Ann Arbor, Michigan 48107
Tel: (313) 996-3229

## DEARBORN
DEARBORN BAR ASSOC.
P.O. Box 2313
Dearborn, Michigan 43123
Tel: (313) 565-6711

## LIVONIA
LIVONIA BAR ASSOC.
33900 Schoolcraft
Livonia, Michigan 48150
Tel: (313) 427-8900

## DETROIT
DETROIT BAR ASSOC.
2380 Penobscot Building
Detroit, Michigan 48226
Tel: (313) 961-6120

## MOUNT CLEMENS
MACOMB BAR ASSOC.
Macomb Court Bldg, #435
Mount Clemens, MI 48043
Tel: (313) 468-2940

## FLINT
GENESEE BAR ASSOC.
653 South Saginaw Street,#100
Flint, Michigan 48502
Tel: (313) 232-6000

## PONTIAC
OAKLAND BAR ASSOC.
1200 North Telegraph
Pontiac, Michigan 48341-0406
Tel: (313) 338-2100

## GRAND RAPIDS
BAR ASSOCIATION
200 Monroe, Suite 400
Grand Rapids, Michigan 49503
Tel: (616) 454-5550

## SAGINAW
SAGINAW BAR ASSOC.
111 South Michigan
Saginaw, Michigan 48604

## KALAMAZOO
KALAMAZOO BAR ASSOC.
227 West Michigan Avenue
Kalamazoo, Michigan 49007
Tel: (616) 384-8257

## SAINT JOSEPH
BERRIEN BAR ASSOC.
901 Port Street
Saint Joseph, Michigan 49085
Tel: (616) 473-4251

## LANSING
INGHAM BAR ASSOC.
City Hall, Room 9, 2nd Fl
Lansing, Michigan 48933
Tel: (517) 482-8816

## MINNESOTA
## MINNEAPOLIS
HENNEPIN BAR ASSOC.
514 Nicollet Mall, Suite 350
Minneapolis, Minnesota 55402
Tel: (612) 340-0022

SAINT PAUL
RAMSEY BAR ASSOC.
332 Minnesota Street, # E1312
Saint Paul, Minnesota 55101
Tel: (612) 222-0846

**MISSISSIPPI**
JACKSON
HINDS BAR ASSOCIATION
151 East Griffith Street
Jackson, Mississippi 39201
Tel: (601) 969-6097

**MISSOURI**
CLAYTON
SAINT LOUIS BAR ASSOC.
25 North Brentwood Boulevard
Clayton, Missouri 63105
Tel: (314) 726-5189

KANSAS CITY
KANSAS CITY BAR ASSOC.
1125 Grand, Fourth Floor
Kansas City, Missouri 64106
Tel: (816) 474-4322

LAWYERS ASSOCIATION
106 West 11th Street, #1121
Kansas City, Missouri 64105
Tel: (816) 474-6444

SAINT LOUIS
BAR ASSOC. OF ST LOUIS
One Metropolitan Sq., #1400
Saint Louis, Missouri 63102
Tel: (314) 421-4134

LAWYERS ASSOCIATION
25 North Brentwood Boulevard
Saint Louis, Missouri 63105
Tel: (314) 862-0136

SPRINGFIELD
SPRINGFIELD BAR ASSOC.
333 Park Central East,#1010
Springfield, Missouri 65806
Tel: (417) 831-2783

**NEBRASKA**
OMAHA
OMAHA BAR ASSOCIATION
2133 California
Omaha, Nebraska 68178
Tel: (402) 342-3786

**NEW JERSEY**
ATLANTIC CITY
ATLANTIC BAR ASSOC.
1201 Bacharach Boulevard
Atlantic City, NJ 08401
TEl: (609) 345-3544

CAMDEN
CAMDEN BAR ASSOC.
Post Office Box 1027
Camden, New Jersey 08101
Tel: (609) 964-3420

CAPE MAY COURTHOUSE
CAPE MAY BAR ASSOC.
Post Office Box 425
Cape May, NJ 08210
Tel: (609) 463-0313

ELIZABETH
UNION BAR ASSOCIATION
Courthouse, 3rd Floor
Elizabeth, New Jersey 07207
Tel: (201) 363-4715

MOUNT HOLLY
BURLINGTON BAR ASSOC.
117 High Street
Mount Holly, New Jersey 08060
Tel: (609) 261-4542

FREEHOLD
MONMOUTH BAR ASSOC.
Court House
Freehold, New Jersey 07728
Tel: (201) 431-5544

NEW BRUNSWICK
MIDDLESEX BAR ASSOC.
Courthouse, 2nd Fl. JFK Square
New Brunswick, NJ 08901
Tel: (908) 828-0053

HACKENSACK
BERGEN BAR ASSOC.
61 Hudson Street
Hackensack, New Jersey 07601
Tel: (201) 488-0032

NEWARK
ESSEX BAR ASSOCIATION
1111 Raymond Boulevard
Newark, New Jersey 07102
Tel: (201) 622-6207

JERSEY CITY
HUDSON BAR ASSOC.
583 Newark Avenue
Jersey City, New Jersey 07306
Tel: (201) 798-2727

PATERSON
PASSAIC BAR ASSOC.
Court House, Hamilton Street
Paterson, New Jersey 07505
Tel: (201) 345-4585

MERCERVILLE
MERCER BAR ASSOC.
2333 Whitehorse Rd
Mercerville, New Jersey 08619
Tel: (609) 890-6200

SOMERVILLE
SOMERSET BAR ASSOC.
Post Office Box 1095
Somerville, New Jersey 08876
Tel: (908) 685-2323

MORRISTOWN
MORRIS BAR ASSOCIATION
Ten Park Place, Room 308
Morristown, New Jersey 07960
Tel: (201) 267-6089

TOMS RIVER
OCEAN BAR ASSOCIATION
Washington and Hooper Avenue
Toms River, New Jersey 08753
Tel: (908) 240-3666

## VINELAND
SALEM BAR ASSOCIATION
538 Landis Avenue CN1501
Vineland, New Jersey 08360
Tel: (609) 935-3559

## WOODBURY
GLOUCESTER BAR ASSOC.
Post Office Box 338
Woodbury, New Jersey 08096

## NEW MEXICO
### ALBUQUERQUE
BAR ASSOCIATION
400 Gold, Southwest, Suite 620
Albuquerque, NM 87102
Tel: (505) 243-2615

## NEW YORK
### ALBANY
ALBANY BAR ASSOC.
Albany Cty Court House, #315
Albany, New York 12207
Tel: (518) 445-7691

## BINHAMTON
BROOME BAR ASSOC.
71 State Street
Binhamton, New York 13901
Tel: (607) 723-6331

## BRONX
BRONX BAR ASSOCIATION
851 Grand Concourse
Bronx, New York 10451
Tel: (212) 293-5600

## BROOKLYN
BROOKLYN BAR ASSOC.
123 Remsen Street
Brooklyn, New York 11201
Tel: (718) 624-0675

## BUFFALO
BAR ASSOCIATION
1450 Statler Towers
Buffalo, New York 14202

## CARMEL
PUTNAM BAR ASSOC.
Post Office Box 44
Carmel, New York 10512
Tel: (914) 225-4904

## GOSHEN
ORANGE BAR ASSOC.
Route 17M, Post Office Box 88
Goshen, New York 10924
Tel: (914) 294-8222

## HAUPPAUGE
SUFFOLK BAR ASSOC.
560 Wheeler Road
Hauppauge, New York 11788
Tel: (516) 234-5511

## ILION
HERKIMER BAR ASSOC.
Post Office Box 420
Ilion, New York 13357-04420
Tel: (315) 895-7771

JAMAICA
QUEENS BAR ASSOCIATION
90-35 148th Street
Jamaica, New York 11435
Tel: (718) 291-4500

N. Y. C. LAWYERS' ASSOC.
14 Vesey Street
New York, New York 10007
Tel: (212) 267-6646

MINEOLA
BAR ASSOCIATION
15th and West Streets
Mineola, New York 11501
Tel: (516) 747-4070

TRIAL LAWYERS ASSOC.
132 Nassau Street
New York, New York 10038
Tel: (212) 349-5890

MONTICELLO
SULLIVAN BAR ASSOC.
P.O. Box 979
Monticello, New York 12701
Tel: (914) 794-2426

NIAGARA FALLS
BAR ASSOCIATION
730 Main Street
Niagara Falls, New York 14301
Tel: (716) 282-1242

NEW CITY
ROCKLAND BAR ASSOC.
120 North Main Street
New City, New York 10956
Tel: (914) 634-2149

POUGHKEEPSIE
DUTCHESS BAR ASSOC.
Post Office Box 4865
Poughkeepsie, New York 12602
Tel: (914) 473-2488

NEW YORK
THE BAR OF NEW YORK
42 West 44th Street
New York, New York 10036
Tel: (212) 382-6600

ROCHESTER
MONROE BAR ASSOC.
One Exchange Street, 5th Floor
Rochester, New York 14614
Tel: (716) 546-1817

STATEN ISLAND
GAY BAR ASSOCIATION
799 Broadway, Room 340
New York, New York 10003
Tel: (212) 353-9118

RICHMOND BAR ASSOC.
2012 Victory Boulevard
Staten Island, New York 10314
Tel: (718) 442-4500

## SYRACUSE
ONONDAGA BAR ASSOC.
1000 State Tower Building
Syracuse, New York 13202
Tel: (315) 471-2667

## TROY
RENSSELAER BAR ASSOC.
297 River Street
Troy, New York 12180
Tel: (518) 272-7229

## UTICA
ONEIDA BAR ASSOCIATION
304 Mayro Building
Utica, New York 13501
Tel: (315) 724-4901

## WHITE PLAINS
BAR ASSOCIATION
300 Hamilton Ave., Suite 400
White Plains, New York 10601
Tel: (914) 761-3707

## NORTH CAROLINA
### CHARLOTTE
MECKLENBURG BAR
737 East Boulevard
Charlotte, NC 28203
Tel: (704) 375-8624

### GREENSBORO
GREENSBORO BAR ASSOC.
Post Office Box 1825
Greensboro, NC 27402
Tel: (910) 378-0300

## RALEIGH
WAKE BAR ASSOCIATION
Post Office Box 10625
Raleigh, North Carolina 27605
Tel: (919) 677-9903

## OHIO
### AKRON
AKRON BAR ASSOCIATION
90 South High Street
Akron, Ohio 44308
Tel: (216) 253-5007

### BATAVIA
CLERMONT BAR ASSOC.
25 North Second Street
Batavia, Ohio 45103
Tel: (513) 732-2050

### CANTON
STARK BAR ASSOCIATION
116 Cleveland Avenue N.,#309
Canton, Ohio 44702-1727
Tel: (216) 453-0685

### CINCINNATI
CINCINNATI BAR ASSOC.
25 Seventh Street, 8th FL
Cincinnati, Ohio 45202
Tel: (513) 381-8213

### CLEVELAND
CLEVELAND BAR ASSOC.
113 St. Clair Avenue Northeast
Cleveland, Ohio 44114-1253
Tel: (216) 696-3525

CUYAHOGA BAR ASSOC.
1228 Euclid Avenue, #370
Cleveland, Ohio 44115-1831
Tel: (216) 621-5112

PAINESVILLE
LAKE BAR ASSOCIATION
47 North Park Place, 3rd Fl.
Painesville, Ohio 44077
Tel: (216) 357-2639

COLUMBUS
COLUMBUS BAR ASSOC.
175 South Third Street
Columbus, Ohio 43215
Tel: (614) 221-4112

PARMA
PARMA BAR ASSOCIATION
5700 Pearl Road
Parma, Ohio 44129
Tel: (216) 886-3000

DAYTON
DAYTON BAR ASSOC.
600 One First National Plaza
Dayton, Ohio 45402-1501
Tel: (513) 222-7902

RAVENNA
PORTAGE BAR ASSOC.
Post Office Box 128
Ravenna, Ohio 44266
Tel: (216) 296-6357

ELYRIA
LORAIN BAR ASSOCIATION
401 Broad Street, #202
Elyria, Ohio 44035
Tel: (216) 323-8416

TOLEDO
TOLEDO BAR ASSOC.
311 North Superior
Toledo, Ohio 43604
Tel: (419) 242-9363

HAMILTON
BUTLER BAR ASSOCIATION
118 South 2nd Street
Hamilton, Ohio 45011
Tel: (513) 896-6671

WARREN
TRUMBULL BAR ASSOC.
Post Office Box 4222
Warren, Ohio 44482
Tel: (216) 675-2415

MARIETTA
WASHINGTON BAR ASSOC.
322 Third Street
Marietta, Ohio 45750
Tel: (614) 374-2629

YOUNGSTOWN
MAHONING BAR ASSOC.
29 East Front Street
Youngstown, Ohio 44503
Tel: (216) 746-2933

## OKLAHOMA

### NORMAN
CLEVELAND BAR ASSOC.
Eutaula and Peters
Norman, Oklahoma 73069
Tel: (405) 360-0912

### OKLAHOMA CITY
OKLAHOMA BAR ASSOC.
119 North Robinson, Suite 240
Oklahoma City, OK 73102
Tel: (405) 236-8421

### TULSA
TULSA BAR ASSOCIATION
1446 South Boston
Tulsa, Oklahoma 74119
Tel: (918) 584-5243

## OREGON
### PORTLAND
MULTNOMAH BAR ASSOC.
711 Southwest Alder, Suite 311
Portland, Oregon 97205
Tel: (503) 222-3275

## PENNSYLVANIA
### ALLENTOWN
BAR ASSOC. OF LEHIGH
114 Walnut Street
Allentown, Pennsylvania 18102
Tel: (215) 433-6204

## PENNSYLVANIA

### CHAMBERSBURG
FRANKLIN BAR ASSOC.
P.O. Box 866
Chambersburg, PA 17201
Tel: (717) 264-6494

### DOYLESTOWN
BUCKS BAR ASSOCIATION
Post Office Box 300
Doylestown, PA 18901
Tel: (215) 348-9413

### EASTON
BAR ASSOCIATION
155 South Ninth Street
Easton, Pennsylvania 18042
Tel: (215) 258-6333

### ERIE
ERIE BAR ASSOCIATION
302 West 9th Street
Erie, Pennsylvania 16502
Tel: (814) 459-3111

### GREENSBURG
BAR ASSOCIATION
129 North Pennsylvania Avenue
Greensburg, PA 15601
Tel: (412) 834-6730

## HARRISBURG
DAUPHIN BAR ASSOC.
213 North Front Street
Harrisburg, Pennsylvania 17101
Tel: (717) 232-7536

## PITTSBURGH
ALLEGHENY BAR ASSOC.
436 Seventh Avenue, #400
Pittsburgh, Pennsylvania 15219
Tel: (412) 261-6161

## LANCASTER
LANCASTER BAR ASSOC.
28 East Orange Street
Lancaster, Pennsylvania 17602
Tel: (717) 393-0737

## READING
BERKS BAR ASSOCIATION
Post Office Box 1058
Reading, Pennsylvania 19603
Tel: (215) 375-4591

## MEADVILLE
CRAWFORD BAR ASSOC.
Crawford County Courthouse
Meadville, Pennsylvania 16335
Tel: (814) 336-1151

## SCRANTON
BAR ASSOCIATION
204 Wyoming Ave., Suite 205
Scranton, Pennsylvania 18503
Tel: (717) 969-9161

## MEDIA
DELAWARE BAR ASSOC.
Post Office Box 466
Media, Pennsylvania 19063
Tel: (215) 566-6627

## UNIONTOWN
FAYETTE BAR ASSOC.
61 East Main Street
Uniontown, PA 15401
Tel: (412) 430-1227

## NORRISTOWN
BAR ASSOCIATION
Post Office Box 268
Norristown, PA 19404
Tel: (215) 279-9660

## WASHINGTON
WASHINGTON BAR ASSOC.
523 Washington Trust Building
Washington, PA 15301
Tel: (412) 225-6710

## PHILADELPHIA
BAR ASSOCIATION
1101 Market Street, 11th Floor
Philadelphia, PA 19107-1159
Tel: (215) 238-6300

## WEST CHESTER
CHESTER BAR ASSOC.
15 West Gay Street
West Chester, PA 19380
Tel: (215) 692-1889

#### WILKES-BARRE
LUZERNE BAR ASSOC.
Courthouse, Room 23
Wilkes-Barre, PA 18711

#### YORK
YORK BAR ASSOCIATION
137 East Market Street
York, Pennsylvania 17401

## SOUTH CAROLINA
### CHARLESTON
CHARLESTON BAR ASSOC.
P.O. Box 858
Charleston, SC 29401
Tel: (803) 723-2000

### COLUMBIA
RICHLAND BAR ASSOC.
Post Office Box 394
Columbia, SC 29202
Tel: (803) 779-2650

## SOUTH DAKOTA
### ABERDEEN
BROWN BAR ASSOCIATION
415 South Main Street,
Aberdeen, South Dakota 57401

## TENNESSEE
### CHATTANOOGA
BAR ASSOCIATION
700 James Building
Chattanooga, Tennessee 37402
Tel: (615) 266-5950

#### KNOXVILLE
BAR ASSOCIATION
P.O. Box 2027
Knoxville, Tennessee 37901

#### MEMPHIS
MEMPHIS BAR ASSOC.
One Commerce Square, #1190
Memphis, Tennessee 38103
Tel: (901) 527-3573

#### NASHVILLE
NASHVILLE BAR ASSOC.
221 Fourth Ave. N., Suite 400
Nashville, TN 37219-2100
Tel: (615) 242-9272

## TEXAS
### AUSTIN
TRAVIS BAR ASSOCIATION
700 Lavaca, Suite 602
Austin, Texas 78701
Tel: (512) 472-0279

#### BEAUMONT
JEFFERSON BAR ASSOC.
1001 Pearl Street, Room 328
Beaumont Texas 77701
Tel: (409) 835-8647

#### CORPUS CHRISTI
BAR ASSOCIATION
901 Leopard, Suite 312
Corpus Christi, Texas 78401
Tel: (512) 883-4022

## DALLAS
DALLAS BAR ASSOCIATION
2101 Ross Avenue
Dallas, Texas 75201
Tel: (214) 969-7066

## ARLINGTON
ARLINGTON BAR ASSOC.
1400 N. Court House R.d., #501
Arlington, Virginia 22201
Tel: (703) 358-3390

## EL PASO
EL PASO BAR ASSOCIATION
500 East San Antonio, L-115
El Paso, Texas 79901
Tel: (915) 532-7052

## FAIRFAX
FAIRFAX BAR ASSOC.
4110 Chain Bridge Road
Fairfax, Virginia 22030
Tel: (703) 273-9784

## HOUSTON
HOUSTON BAR ASSOC.
1001 Fannin, Suite 1300
Houston, Texas 77002-6708
Tel: (713) 759-1133

## NORFOLK
NORFOLK BAR ASSOC.
999 Waterside Drive, #1330
Norfolk, Virginia 23510
Tel: (804) 622-3152

## SAN ANTONIO
SAN ANTONIO BAR ASSOC.
Bexar Cty Courthouse, 5 Fl.
San Antonio, Texas 78205
Tel: (512) 227-8822

## RICHMOND
BAR ASSOC. OF RICHMOND
Post Office Box 1213
Richmond, Virginia 23209
Tel: (804) 780-0700

## WICHITA FALLS
WICHITA BAR ASSOC.
Post Office Box 1388
Wichita Falls, Texas 76307
Tel: (817) 322-8401

## ROANOKE
ROANOKE BAR ASSOC.
720 Shenandoah Building
Roanoke, Virginia 24011
Tel: (703) 344-8722

## VIRGINIA
## ALEXANDRIA
BAR ASSOCIATION
520 King Street, Room 202
Alexandria, Virginia 22314
Tel: (703) 548-1106

## VIRGINIA BEACH
VIRGINIA BEACH BAR
ASSOCIATION
Municipal Center
Virginia Beach, Virginia 23456
Tel: (804) 486-3249

# WASHINGTON

### SEATTLE
KING COUNTY BAR ASSOC.
600 Bank of California Bldg
Seattle, Washington 98164
Tel: (206) 624-9365

### SPOKANE
SPOKANE BAR ASSOC.
West 1116 Broadway, # 404
Spokane, Washington 99260
Tel: (509) 456-6032

### TACOMA
BAR ASSOCIATION
930 Tacoma Ave. S., Room 137
Tacoma, Washington 98402
Tel: (206) 383-3432

# WISCONSIN
### MILWAUKEE
MILWAUKEE BAR ASSOC.
533 East Wells Street
Milwaukee, Wisconsin 53202
Tel: (414) 274-6760

# *Notes*

Adoption Searches Made Easier

# Appendix

# City-County Directory

| City | County |
|------|--------|
| ABBEBILLE | Henry |
| ABERNANT | Tuscaloosa |
| ADAMSVILLE | Jefferson |
| ADDISON | Winston |
| ADGER | Jefferson |
| AKRON | Hale |
| ALABASTER | Shelby |
| ALBERTA | Wilcox |
| ALBERTVILLE | Marshall |
| ALEXANDER CITY | Tallapoosa |
| ALEXANDRIA | Calhoun |
| ALICEVILLE | Pickens |
| ALLEN | Clarke |
| ALLGOOD | Blount |
| ALMA | Clarke |
| ALPINE | Talladega |
| ALTON | Jefferson |
| ALTOONA | Etowah |
| ANDALUSIA | Covington |
| ANDERSON | Lauderdale |
| ANNEMANIE | Wilcox |
| ANNISTON | Calhoun |
| ARAB | Marshall |
| ARDMORE | Limestone |
| ARITON | Dale |
| ARLEY | Winston |
| ARLINGTON | Wilcox |
| ASHFORD | Houston |
| ASHLAND | Clay |
| ASHVILLE | Saint Clair |
| ATHENS | Limestone |
| ATMORE | Escambia |
| ATTALLA | Etowah |
| AUBURN | Lee |
| AUTAUGAVILLE | Autauga |
| AXIS | Mobile |
| BAILEYTON | Cullman |
| BANKS | Pike |
| BANKSTON | Fayette |
| BAY MINETTE | Baldwin |
| BAYOU LA BATRE | Mobile |
| BEAR CREEK | Marion |
| BEATRICE | Monroe |
| BEAVERTON | Lamar |
| BELK | Fayette |
| BELLAMY | Sumter |
| BELLE MINA | Limestone |
| BELLWOOD | Geneva |
| BERRY | Fayette |
| BESSEMER | Jefferson |
| BIGBEE | Washington |
| BILLINGSLEY | Autauga |
| BIRMINGHAM | Jefferson |
| BLACK | Geneva |
| BLOUNTSVILLE | Blount |
| BLUE MOUNTAIN | Calhoun |
| BLUFF PARK | Jefferson |
| BOAZ | Marshall |
| BOLIGEE | Greene |
| BOLINGER | Choctaw |
| BON AIR | Talladega |
| BON SECOUR | Baldwin |
| BOOTH | Autauga |
| BOYKIN | Wilcox |
| BRANTLEY | Crenshaw |
| BREMEN | Cullman |
| BRENT | Bibb |
| BREWTON | Escambia |
| BRIDGEPORT | Jackson |
| BRIERFIELD | Bibb |
| BRILLIANT | Marion |
| BROOKLEY FIELD | Mobile |
| BROOKLYN | Conecuh |
| BROOKSIDE | Jefferson |
| BROOKWOOD | Tuscaloosa |
| BROWNSBORO | Madison |
| BRUNDIDGE | Pike |
| BRYANT | Jackson |
| BUCKS | Mobile |
| BUHL | Tuscaloosa |
| BURNT CORN | Monroe |
| BURNWELL | Walker |
| BUTLER | Choctaw |
| BYNUM | Calhoun |
| CALERA | Shelby |
| CALVERT | Washington |
| CAMDEN | Wilcox |
| CAMPBELL | Fayette |
| CAMP HILL | Tallapoosa |
| CAPSHAW | Limestone |
| CARBON HILL | Walker |
| CARDIFF | Jefferson |
| CARLTON | Clarke |
| CARROLLTON | Pickens |
| CASTLEBERRY | Conecuh |
| CATHERINE | Wilcox |
| CEDAR BLUFF | Cherokee |
| CENTRE | Cherokee |
| CENTREVILLE | Bibb |
| CHANCELLOR | Geneva |
| CHAPMAN | Butler |

| | | | |
|---|---|---|---|
| CHATOM | Washington | DEER PARK | Washington |
| CHELSEA | Shelby | DELMAR | Winston |
| CHEROKEE | Colbert | DELTA | Clay |
| CHILDERSBURG | Talladega | DEMOPOLIS | Marengo |
| CHOCCOLOCCO | Calhoun | DETROIT | Lamar |
| CHUNCHULA | Mobile | DICKINSON | Clarke |
| CITRONELLE | Mobile | DIXIANA | Jefferson |
| CLANTON | Chilton | DIXONS MILLS | Marengo |
| CLAY | Jefferson | DOCENA | Jefferson |
| CLAYTON | Barbour | DOLOMITE | Jefferson |
| CLEVELAND | Blount | DORA | Walker |
| CLINTON | Greene | DOTHAN | Houston |
| CLIO | Barbour | DOUBLE SPRINGS | Winston |
| CLOPTON | Dale | DOUGLAS | Marshall |
| CLOVERDALE | Lauderdale | DOZIER | Crenshaw |
| COALING | Tuscaloosa | DUNCANVILLE | Tuscaloosa |
| CODEN | Mobfle | DUTTON | Jackson |
| COFFEE SPRINGS | Geneva | EASTABOGA | Calhoun |
| COFFEEVILLE | Clarke | EAST BREWTON | Escambia |
| COKER | Tuscaloosa | EASTBROOK | Montgomery |
| COLLINSVILLE | DeKalb | EASTDALE | Montgomery |
| COLUMBIA | Houston | EAST GADSDEN | Etowah |
| COLUMBIANA | Shelby | EAST LAKE-ROEBUCK | Jefferson |
| COOK SPRINGS | Saint Clair | EAST SIDE | Tuscaloosa |
| COOSADA | Elmore | EAST TALLASSEE | Tallapoosa |
| COOSA PINES | Talladega | ECHOLA | Tuscaloosa |
| CORDOVA | Walker | ECLECTIC | Elmore |
| COTTONDALE | Tuscaloos | EDWARDSVILLE | Cleburne |
| COTTONTON | Russell | EIGHT MILE | Mobile |
| COTTONWOOD | Houston | ELBA | Coffee |
| COURTLAND | Lawrence | ELBERTA | Baldwin |
| COWARTS | Houston | ELDRIDGE | Walker |
| COY | Wilcox | ELKMONT | Limestone |
| CRAGFORD | Clay | ELMORE | Elmore |
| CRANE HILL | Cullman | ELROD | Tuscaloosa |
| CREOLA | Mobile | ELTING | Florence |
| CROMWELL | Choctaw | EMELLE | Sumter |
| CROPWELL | Saint Clair | EMPIRE | Walker |
| CROSSVILLE | DeKalb | ENSLEY | Jefferson |
| CUBA | Sumter | ENTERPRISE | Coffee |
| CULLIMAN | Culliman | EPES | Sumter |
| CUSSETA | Chambers | EQUALITY | Coosa |
| DADEVILLE | Tallapoosa | ESTILLFORK | Jackson |
| DALEVILLE | Dale | ETHELSVILLE | Pickens |
| DANVILLE | Morgan | EUFAULA | Barbour |
| DAPHNE | Baldwin | EUTAW | Greene |
| DAUPHIN ISLAND | Mobile | EVA | Morgan |
| DAVISTON | Tallapoosa | EVERGREEN | Conecuh |
| DAWSON | DeKalb | EXCEL | Monroe |
| DAYTON | Marengo | FACKLER | Jackson |
| DE ARMANVILLE | Calhoun | FAIRFIELD | Jefferson |
| DEATSVILLE | Elmore | FAIRHOPE | Baldwin |
| DECATUR | Morgan | FAIRVIEW | Jefferson |

| | | | |
|---|---|---|---|
| FALKVILLE | Morgan | GORDON | Houston |
| FAUNSDALE | Marengo | GOSHEN | Pike |
| FAYETTE | Fayette | GRADY | Montgomery |
| FITZPATRICK | Bullock | GRAHAM | Randolph |
| FIVE POINTS | Chambers | GRAND BAY | Mobile |
| FIVE POINTS | Madison | GRANT | Marshall |
| FLAT ROCK | Jackson | GRAYSVILLE | Jefferson |
| FLOMATON | Escambia | GREEN LANTERN | Montgomery |
| FLORALA | Covington | GREEN POND | Bibb |
| FLORENCE | Lauderdale | GREENSBORO | Hale |
| FOLEY | Baldwin | GREEN SPRINGS | Jefferson |
| FORESTDALE | Jefferson | GREENVILLE | Butler |
| FOREST HOME | Butler | GROVE HILL | Clarke |
| FORKLAND | Greene | GROVEOAK | DeKalb |
| FORT DAVIS | Macon | GUIN | Marion |
| FORT DEPOSIT | Lowndes | GULF SHORES | Baldwin |
| FORT MC CLELLAN | Calhoun | GUNTERSVILLE | Marshall |
| FORT MITCHELL | Russell | GURLEY | Madison |
| FORT MORGAN | Baldwin | HACKLEBURG | Marion |
| FORT PAYNE | DeKalb | HALEYVILLE | Winston |
| FORT RUCKER | Dale | HAMILTON | Marion |
| FOSTERS | Tuscaloosa | HANCEVILLE | Cullman |
| FRANKLIN | Monroe | HARDAWAY | Macon |
| FRANVILLE | Washington | HARPERSVILLE | Shelby |
| FRISCO CITY | Monroe | HARTFORD | Geneva |
| FRUITDALE | Washington | HARTSELLE | Morgan |
| FRUITHURST | Cleburne | HARVEST | Madison |
| FULTON | Clarke | HATCHECHUBBEE | Russell |
| FULTONDALE | Jefferson | HAVANA | Hale |
| FURMAN | Wilcox | HAYDEN | Blount |
| FYFFE | DeKalb | HAYNEVILLE | Lowndes |
| GADSDEN | Etowah | HAYSLAND | Madison |
| GAINESTOWN | Clarke | HAZEL GREEN | Madison |
| GAINESVILLE | Sumter | HEADLAND | Henry |
| GALLANT | Etowah | HEFLIN | Cleburne |
| GALLERIA | Jefferson | HELENA | Shelby |
| GALLION | Hale | HENAGAR | DeKalb |
| GANTT | Covington | HIGDON | Jackson |
| GARDEN CITY | Cullman | HIGHLAND HOME | Crenshaw |
| GARDENDALE | Jefferson | HILLSBORO | Lawrence |
| GAYLESVILLE | Cherokee | HODGES | Franklin |
| GENEVA | Geneva | HOKES BLUFF | Etowah |
| GEORGIANA | Butler | HOLLINS | Clay |
| GERALDINE | DeKalb | HOLLY POND | Cullman |
| GILBERTOWN | Choctaw | HOLLYTREE | Jackson |
| GLEN ALLEN | Fayette | HOLLYWOOD | Jackson |
| GLENCOE | Etowah | HOLT | Tuscaloosa |
| GLENWOOD | Crenshaw | HOLY TRINITY | Russell |
| GOLDEN SPRINGS | Calhoun | HOMEWOOD | Jefferson |
| GOODSPRINGS | Walker | HONORAVILLE | Crenshaw |
| GOODWATER | Coosa | HOOVER | Jefferson |
| GOODWAY | Monroe | HOPE HULL | Montgomery |
| GORDO | Pickens | HORTON | Marshall |

| | | | |
|---|---|---|---|
| HOUSTON | Winston | LIVINGSTON | Sumter |
| HUEYTOWN | Jefferson | LOACHAPOKA | Lee |
| HUNTSVILLE | Madison | LOCKHART | Covington |
| HURTSBORO | Russell | LOCUST FORK | Blount |
| HUXFORD | Escambia | LOGAN | Cullman |
| HYTOP | Scottsboro | LOOP | Mobile |
| IDER | DeKalb | LOUISVILLE | Barbour |
| INDIAN SPRINGS | Shelby | LOWER PEACH TREE | Wilcox |
| IRONSIDE | Jefferson | LOWNDESBORO | Lowndes |
| IRVINGTON | Mobile | LOXLEY | Baldwin |
| JACHIN | Choctaw | LUVERNE | Crenshaw |
| JACK | Coffee | LYNN | Winston |
| JACKSON | Clarke | MADISON | Madison |
| JACKSONS GAP | Tallapoosa | MAGAZINE | Mobile |
| JACKSONVILLE | Calhoun | MAGNOLIA | Marengo |
| JASPER | Walker | MAGNOLIA SPRINGS | Baldwin |
| JEFFERSON | Marengo | MALCOLM | Washington |
| JEMISON | Chilton | MALVERN | Geneva |
| JONES | Autauga | MAPLESVILLE | Chilton |
| JOPPA | Cullman | MARBURY | Autauga |
| KANSAS | Walker | MARGARET | Saint Clair |
| KELLERMAN | Tuscaloosa | MARION | Perry |
| KELLYTON | Coosa | MARION JUNCTION | Dallas |
| KENNEDY | Lamar | MASTIN LAKE | Madison |
| KENT | Elmore | MATHEWS | Montgomery |
| KEYSTONE | Shelby | MAXWELL AFB | Montgomery |
| KILLEN | Lauderdale | MAYLENE | Shelby |
| KIMBERLY | Jefferson | MEADOWBROOK | Jefferson |
| KINSTON | Coffee | MCCALLA | Jefferson |
| KNOXVILLE | Greene | MCCULLOUGH | Escambia |
| LACEYS SPRING | Morgan | MCFARLAND | Tuscaloosa |
| LAFAYETTE | Chambers | MCINTOSH | Washington |
| LAGOON PARK | Montgomery | MCKENZIE | Butler |
| LAMISON | Wilcox | MCSHAN | Pickens |
| LANETT | Chambers | MCWILLIAMS | Wilcox |
| LANGSTON | Jackson | MEGAREL | Monroe |
| LAPINE | Montgomery | MELVIN | Choctaw |
| LAVACA | Choctaw | MENTONE | DeKalb |
| LAWLEY | Bibb | MERIDIANVILLE | Madison |
| LEEDS | Jefferson | MEXIA | Monroe |
| LEESBURG | Cherokee | MIDFIELD | Jefferson |
| LEIGHTON | Colbert | MIDLAND CITY | Dale |
| LENOX | Conecuh | MIDTOWN | Mobile |
| LEROY | Washington | MIDWAY | Bullock |
| LESTER | Limestone | MILLBROOK | Elmore |
| LETOHATCHEE | Lowndes | MILLERS FERRY | Wilcox |
| LEXINGTON | Lauderdale | MILLERVILLE | Clay |
| LILLLAN | Baldwin | MILLPORT | Lamar |
| LINCOLN | Talladega | MILLRY | Washington |
| LINDEN | Marengo | MINTER | Dallas |
| LINEVILLE | Clay | MOBILE | Mobile |
| LISMAN | Choctaw | MONROEVILLE | Monroe |
| LITTLE RIVER | Baldwin | MONTEVALLO | Shelby |

| | | | |
|---|---|---|---|
| MONTGOMERY | Montgomery | PANSEY | Houston |
| MONTROSE | Baldwin | PARRISH | Walker |
| MOODY | Saint Clair | PELHAM | Shelby |
| MOORESVILLE | Limestone | PELL CITY | Saint Clair |
| MORRIS | Jefferson | PENNINGTON | Choctaw |
| MORVIN | Clarke | PERDIDO | Baldwin |
| MOULTON | Lawrence | PERDUE HILL | Monroe |
| MOUNDVILLE | Hale | PETERMAN | Monroe |
| MOUNTAIN BROOK | Jefferson | PETERSON | Tuscaloosa |
| MOUNT HOPE | Lawrence | PETERSVILLE | Florence |
| MOUNT MEIGS | Montgomery | PETREY | Crenshaw |
| MOUNT OLIVE | Jefferson | PHENIX CITY | Russell |
| MOUNT VERNON | Mobile | PHIL CAMPBELL | Franklin |
| MULGA | Jefferson | PIEDMONT | Calhoun |
| MUNFORD | Talladega | PIKE ROAD | Montgomery |
| MUSCADINE | Cleburne | PINCKARD | Dale |
| MUSCLE SHOALS | Sheffield | PINE APPLE | Wilcox |
| MYRTLEWOOD | Marengo | PINE HILL | Wilcox |
| NANAFALIA | Marengo | PINE LEVEL | Montgomery |
| NAPIER FIELD | Houston | PINSON | Jefferson |
| NATURAL BRIDGE | Winston | PISGAH | Jackson |
| NAUVOO | Walker | PITTSVIEW | Russell |
| NEEDHAM | Choctaw | PLANTERSVILLE | Dallas |
| NEWBERN | Hale | PLAZA DE MALAGA | Mobile |
| NEW BROCKTON | Coffee | PLEASANT GROVE | Jefferson |
| NEW CASTLE | Jefferson | POINT CLEAR | Baldwin |
| NEWELL | Randolph | PRAIRIE | Wilcox |
| NEW HOPE | Madison | PRATTVILLE | Autauga |
| NEW MARKET | Madison | PRICHARD | Mobile |
| NEW SITE | Tallapoosa | PRINCETON | Jackson |
| NEWTON | Dale | PULASKI PIKE | Madison |
| NEWVILLE | Henry | QUINTON | Walker |
| NORMAL | Madison | RAGLAND | Saint Clair |
| NORTH BIRMINGHAM | Jefferson | RAINBOW CITY | Etowah |
| NORTH FLORENCE | Lauderdale | RAINSVILLE | DeKalb |
| NORTHPORT | Tuscaloosa | RALPH | Tuscaloosa |
| NORTHSIDE | Houston | RAMER | Montgomery |
| NOTASULGA | Macon | RANBURNE | Cleburne |
| OAK HILL | Wilcox | RANDOLPH | Bibb |
| OAKMAN | Walker | RANGE | Conecah |
| ODENVILLE | Saint Clair | RED BAY | Franklin |
| OHATCHEE | Calhoun | RED LEVEL | Covington |
| ONEONTA | Blount | REFORM | Pickens |
| OPELIKA | Lee | REGENCY | Florence |
| OPP | Covington | REMLAP | Blount |
| ORANGE BEACH | Baldwin | REPTON | Conecuh |
| ORRVILLE | Dallas | RIVER FALLS | Covington |
| OWENS CROSS ROADS | Madison | RIVERSIDE | Saint Clair |
| OXFORD | Calhoun | RIVERVIEW | Chambers |
| OZARK | Dale | ROANOKE | Randolph |
| PAINT ROCK | Jackson | ROBERTSDALE | Baldwin |
| PALMERDALE | Jefferson | ROCKFORD | Coosa |
| PANOLA | Sumter | ROCKMILLS | Randolph |

**Adoption Searches Made Easier**

| | | | |
|---|---|---|---|
| ROEBUCK | Jefferson | STEVENSON | Jackson |
| ROGERSVILLE | Lauderdale | STEWART | Hale |
| RUSSELLVILLE | Franklin | STOCKTON | Baldwin |
| RUTLEDGE | Crenshaw | SULLIGENT | Lamar |
| RYLAND | Madison | SUMITON | Walker |
| SAFFORD | Dallas | SUMMERDALE | Baldwin |
| SAGINAW | Shelby | SUNFLOWER | Washington |
| SAINT ELMO | Mobile | SWEET WATER | Marengo |
| SAINT STEPHENS | Washington | SYCAMORE | Talladega |
| SALEM | Lee | SYLACAUGA | Talladega |
| SALITPA | Clarke | SYLVANIA | DeKalb |
| SAMANTHA | Tuscaloosa | TALLADEGA | Talladega |
| SAMSON | Geneva | TALLASSEE | Elmore |
| SARALAND | Mobile | TALLASSEE | Tallapoosa |
| SARDIS | Dallas | TANNER | Limestone |
| SATSUMA | Mobile | TARRANT | Jefferson |
| SAWYERVILLE | Hale | TAYLOR | Dothan |
| SAYRE | Jefferson | THEODORE | Mobile |
| SCOTTSBORO | Jackson | THOMASTON | Marengo |
| SEALE | Russell | THOMASVILLE | Clarke |
| SECTION | Jackson | THORSBY | Chilton |
| SELMA | Dallas | TIBBIE | Washington |
| SEMINOLE | Baldwin | TILLMANS CORNER | Mobile |
| SEMMES | Mobile | TITUS | Elmore |
| SHAKESPEARE | Montgomery | TONEY | Madison |
| SHANNON | Jefferson | TOWN CREEK | Lawrence |
| SHEFFIELD | Colbert | TOWNE WEST | Mobile |
| SHELBY | Shelby | TOWNLEY | Walker |
| SHOAL CREEK | Jefferson | TOXEY | Choctaw |
| SHORTER | Macon | TRAFFORD | Jefferson |
| SHORTERVILLE | Henry | TRENTON | Jackson |
| SILAS | Choctaw | TRIANA | Madison |
| SILURIA | Shelby | TRINITY | Morgan |
| SILVERHILL | Baldwin | TROY | Pike |
| SIPSEY | Walker | TRUSSVILLE | Jefferson |
| SKIPPERVILLE | Dale | TUSCALOOSA | Tuscaloosa |
| SLOCOMB | Geneva | TUSCUMBIA | Colbert |
| SMITHS | Lee | TUSKEGEE | Macon |
| SNEAD | Etowah | TUSKEGEE INSTITUTE | Macon |
| SNOW HILL | Wilcox | TYLER | Dallas |
| SOMERVILLE | Morgan | UNION GROVE | Marshall |
| SOUTH HIGHLAND | Jefferson | UNION SPRINGS | Bullock |
| SOUTHSIDE | Etowah | UNIONTOWN | Peny |
| SPANISH FORT | Baldwin | UNIVERSITY | Tuscaloosa |
| SPRING GARDEN | Cherokee | UNIVERSITY OF AL | Mobile |
| SPRING HILL | Mobile | URIAH | Monroe |
| SPRINGVILLE | Saint Clair | VALHERMOSO SPRINGS | Morgan |
| SPROTT | Perry | VALLEY | Chambers |
| SPRUCE PINE | Franklin | VALLEY HEAD | DeKalb |
| STANTON | Chilton | VANCE | Tuscaloosa |
| STAPLETON | Baldwin | VANDIVER | Shelby |
| STEELE | Saint Clair | VERBENA | Chilton |
| STERRETT | Shelby | VERNON | Lamar |

| | | | |
|---|---|---|---|
| VESTAVIA HILLS | Jefferson | ANCHOR POINT | Kenai Peninsula |
| VETERANS HOSPITAL | Tuscaloosa | ANDERSON | Denali |
| VINA | Franklin | ANGOON | Skagway-Yakutat |
| VINCENT | Shelby | ANIAK | Bethel |
| VINEGAR BEND | Washington | ANVIK | Yukon Koyukuk |
| VINEMONT | Cullman | ARTIC VILLAGE | Yukon Koyukuk |
| VREDENBURGH | Monroe | ATKA | Aleutian Islands |
| WADLEY | Randolph | ATMAUTLUAK | Bethel |
| WAGARVILLE | Washington | ATQUSUK | North Slope |
| WALKER SPRINGS | Clarke | AUKE BAY | Juneau |
| WALNUT GROVE | Etowah | BADGER | Fairbanks |
| WARD | Sumter | BARROW | North Slope |
| WARRIOR | Jefferson | BEAVER | Yukon Koyukuk |
| WATERLOO | Lauderdale | BETHEL | Bethel |
| WATSON | Jefferson | BETTLES FIELD | Yukon Koyukuk |
| WATTSVILLE | Saint Clair | BIG LAKE | Mantanuska Susitna |
| WAVERLY | Lee | BORDER | Tok |
| WEAVER | Calhoun | BRENTWOOD | Wasilla |
| WEBB | Houston | BREVIG MISSION | Nome |
| WEDOWEE | Randolph | BUCKLAND | Northwest Artic |
| WELLINGTON | Calhoun | CANTWELL | Yukon Koyukuk |
| WEOGUFKA | Coosa | CENTRAL | Yukon Koyukuk |
| WEST | Madison | CHALKYITSIK | Yukon Koyukuk |
| WEST BLOCTON | Bibb | CHEFORNAK | Bethel |
| WEST END | Jefferson | CHENEGA BAY | Cordova |
| WEST GREENE | Greene | CHEVAK | Wade Hampton |
| WESTOVER | Shelby | CHICKALOON | Sutton |
| WEST SIDE | Montgoxnery | CHICKEN | Southeast Fairbanks |
| WETUMPKA | Elmore | CHIGNIK | Lake And Peninsula |
| WHATLEY | Clarke | CHIGNIK LAGOON | Lane And Peninsula |
| WHITESBURG | Madison | CHIGNIK LAKE | Lane And Peninsula |
| WILMER | Mobile | CHINIAK | Kudiak |
| WILSONVILLE | Shelby | CHITINA | Valdez Cordova |
| WILTON | Shelby | CHUGIAK | Anchorage |
| WINFIELD | Marion | CIRCLE | Yukon Koyukuk |
| WING | Covington | CLAM GULCH | Kenai Peninsula |
| WOODLAND | Randolph | CLARKS POINT | Dillingham |
| WOODLAWN | Jefferson | CLEAR | Yukon Koyukuk |
| WOODSTOCK | Bibb | COFFMAN COVE | Prince of Wales |
| WOODVILLE | Jackson | COLD BAY | Aleutian East |
| WYLAM | Jefferson | COLDFOOT | Fairbanks |
| YORK | Sumter | COLLEGE | Fairbanks |
| **ALASKA** | | COOPER LANDING | Kenai Peninsula |
| AKHIOK | Kodiak | COPPER CENTER | Valdez-Cordova |
| AKIACHAK | Bethel | CORDOVA | Valdez-Cordova |
| AKIAK | Bethel | CRAIG | Prince of Wales |
| AKUTAN | Aleutians East | CROOKED CREEK | Bethel |
| ALAKANUK | Wade Hampton | DEERING | Northwest Artic |
| ALEKNAGIK | Dillingham | DELTA JUNCTION | Southeast Fairbanks |
| ALLAKAKET | Yukon Koyukuk | DENALI NATL PARK | Yukon |
| AMBLER | Northwest Arctic | DILLINGHAM | Dillingham |
| ANAKTUVUK PASS | North Slope | DOT LAKE | Delta Junction |
| ANCHORAGE | Anchorage | DOUGIAS | Juneau |

| | | | |
|---|---|---|---|
| DUTCH HARBOR | Aleutian Islands | KASIGLUK | Bethel |
| EAGLE | Southeast Fairbanks | KASILOF | Kenai Peninsula |
| EAGLE RIVER | Anchorage | KENIA | Kenai Peninsula |
| EASTCHESTER | Anchorage | KETCHIKAN | Ketchikan Gateway |
| EEK | Bethel | KIANA | Northwest Arctic |
| EGEGIK | Lake And Peninsula | KING COVE | Aleutian Islands |
| EIELSON AFB | Fairbanks North | KING SALMON | Bristol Bay |
| EKWOK | Dillingham | KIPNUK | Bethel |
| ELFIN COVE | Skagway-Yakutat | KIVALINA | Northwest Arctic |
| ELIM | Nome | KLAWOCK | Prince of Wales |
| ELMENDORF AFB | Anchorage | KNIK | Wasilla |
| EMMONAK | Wade Hampton | KOBUK | Northwest Arctic |
| ENGLISH BAY | Homer | KODIAK | Kodiak Island |
| ESTER | Fairbanks North | KOKHANOK | Iliamna |
| FAIRBANKS | Fairbanks North | KOLIGANEK | Dillingham |
| FALSE PASS | Aleutian Islands | KONGIGANAK | Bethel |
| FLAT | Yukon Koyukuk | KOTLIK | Wade Hampton |
| FORT RICHARDSON | Anchorage | KOTZEBUE | Northwest Arctic |
| FORT WAINWRIGHT | Fairbanks North | KOYUK | Nome |
| FORT YUKON | Yukon Koyukuk | KOYUKUK | Yukon Koyukuk |
| FRITZ CREEK | Homer | KWETHLUK | Bethel |
| GAKONA | Valdez-Cordova | KWIGILLINGOK | Bethel |
| GALENA | Yukon Koyukuk | LAKE MINCHUMINA | Yukon Koyukuk |
| GAMBELL | Nome | LAKE OTIS | Anchorage |
| GIRDWOOD | Anchorage | LARSEN BAY | Kodiak Island |
| GLENNALLEN | Valdez-Cordova | LEVELOCK | Lake And Peninsula |
| GOLOVIN | Nome | LITTLE DIOMEDE | Nome |
| GOODNEWS BAY | Bethel | LOWER KALSKAG | Bethel |
| GRAYLING | Yukon Koyukuk | MANLEY HOT SPRINGS | Yukon Koyukuk |
| GUSTAVUS | Skagway-Yakutat | MANOKOTAK | Dillingham |
| HAINES | Haines | MARSHALL | Wade Hampton |
| HALIBUT COVE | Homer | MCGRATH | Yukon Koyukuk |
| HEALY | Denali | MEADOW LAKE | Wasilla |
| HOLY CROSS | Yukon Koyukuk | MEKORYUK | Bethel |
| HOMER | Kenai Peninsula | MENDENHALL | Juneau |
| HOONAH | Skagway-Yakutat | METLAKATIA | Prince of Wales |
| HOOPER BAY | Wade Hampton | MEYERS CHUCK | Prince of Wales |
| HOPE | Kenai Peninsula | MINTO | Yukon Koyukuk |
| HOUSTON | Matanuska Susitna | MOOSE PASS | Kenai Peninsula |
| HUFFMAN | Anchorage | MOUNTAIN VILLAGE | Wade Hampton |
| HUGHES | Yukon Koyukuk | MULDOON | Anchorage |
| HUSLIA | Yukon Koyukuk | NAKNEK | Bristol Bay |
| HYDABURG | Prince of Wales | NAPASKIAK | Bethel |
| HYDER | Prince of Wales | NELSON LAGOON | Cold Bay |
| IGIUGIG | King Salmon | NENANA | Yukon Koyukuk |
| ILIAMNA | Lake And Peninsula | NEW STUYAHOK | Dillingham |
| INDIAN | Anchorage | NEWTOK | Bethel |
| JUNEAU | Juneau | NIGHTMUTE | Bethel |
| KAKE | Wrangell-tersburg | NIKISKI | Kenai Peninsula |
| KAKTOVIK | North Slope | NIKOLAEVSK | Anchor Point |
| KALSKAG | Bethel | NIKOLAI | Yukon Koyukuk |
| KALTAG | Yukon Koyukuk | NIKOLSKI | Aleutian Islands |
| KARLUK | Kodiak Island | NINILCHIK | Kenai Peninsula |

| | | | |
|---|---|---|---|
| NOATAK | Northwest Arctic | SITKA | Sitka |
| NOME | Nome | SKAGWAY | Skagway-Yakutat |
| NONDALTON | Lake And Peninsula | SKWENTNA | Matanuska-Susitna |
| NOORVIK | Northwest Arctic | SIANA | Gakona |
| NORTH POLE | Fairbanks North | SLEETMUTE | Bethel |
| NORTHWAY | Southeast Fairbanks | SOLDOTNA | Kenai Peninsula |
| NUIGSUT | North Slope | SOUTH NAKNEK | Bristol Bay |
| NULATO | Yukon Koyukuk | SPENARD | Anchorage |
| NUNAPITCHUK | Bethel | STEBBINS | Nome |
| NYAC | Bethel | STEESE | Fairbanks |
| OLD HARBOR | Kodiak Island | STERLING | Kenai Peninsula |
| OUZINKIE | Kodiak Island | STEVENS VILLAGE | Yukon Koyukuk |
| PALMER | Matanuska-Susitna | STONY RIVER | Aniak |
| PAXSON | Delta Junction | SUTTON | Matanuska Susitna |
| PEDRO BAY | Lake And Peninsula | TAKOTINA | Yukon |
| PELICAN | Skagway-Yakutat | THORNE BAY | Prince of Wales |
| PERRYVILLE | Lake And Peninsula | TALKEETNA | Matanuska-Susitna |
| PETERSBURG | Wrangell-Petersburg | TANANA | Yukon Koyukuk |
| PILOT POINT | Dillingham | TELLER | Nome |
| PILOT STATION | Wade Hampton | TENAKEE SPRINGS | Skagway-Yakutat |
| PIONEER | Sitka | TOGIAK | Dillingham |
| PLATINUM | Bethel | TOK | Southeast Fairbanks |
| POINT BAKER | Prince of Wales | TOKSCOK BAY | Bethel |
| POINT HOPE | North Slope | TRAPPER CREEK | Matansuka Susitna |
| POINT LAY | North Slope | TULUKSAK | Bethel |
| PORT ALSWORTH | Lake And Peninsula | TUNTUTULIAK | Bethel |
| PORT GRAHAM | Homer | TUNUNAK | Bethel |
| PORT HEIDEN | Lake And Peninsula | TWIN HILLS | Dillingham |
| PORT LIONS | Kodiak Island | TWO RIVERS | Fairbanks North |
| PRUDHOE BAY | North Slope | TYONEK | Kenai Peninsula |
| QUINHAGAK | Bethel | UNALAKLEET | Nome |
| RAMPART | Yukon Koyukuk | UNALASKA | Aleutian Islands |
| RED DEVIL | Bethel | VALDEZ | Valdez-Cordova |
| RUBY | Yukon Koyukuk | VENETIE | Yukon Koyukuk |
| RUSSIAN JACK | Anchorage | WAINWRIGHT | North Slope |
| RUSSIAN MISSION | Wade Hampton | WALES | Nome |
| SAINT GEORGE ISLAND | Aleutian Islands | WARD COVE | Ketchikan Gateway |
| SAINT MARYS | Wade Hampton | WASILLA | Matanuska-Susitna |
| SAINT MICHAEL | Nome | WHITE MOUNTAIN | Nome |
| SAINT PAUL ISLAND | Aleutian Islands | WILLOW | Matanuska-Susitna |
| SALCHA | Fairbanks North | WHITTIER | Valdez Cordova |
| SAND LAKE | Anchorage | WRANGELL | Wrangell-Petersburg |
| SAND POINT | Aleutain East | YAKUTAT | Skagway-Yakutat |
| SAVOONGA | Nome | **ARIZONA** | |
| SCAMMON BAY | Wade Hampton | AGUILA | Maricopa |
| SELAWIK | Northwest Arctic | AHWATUKEE | Maricopa |
| SELDOVIA | Kenai Peninsula | AJO | Pima |
| SEWARD | Kenai Peninsula | ALPINE | Apache |
| SHAGELUK | Yukon Koyukuk | APACHE JUNCTION | Pinal |
| SHAKTOOLIK | Nome | ARCADIA | Maricopa |
| SHELDON POINT | Wade Hampton | ARIVACA | Pima |
| SHISHMAREF | Nome | ARIZONA ST UNIV | Maricopa |
| SHUNGNAK | Northwest Arctic | ARLINGTON | Maricopa |

**Adoption Searches Made Easier**

| | | | |
|---|---|---|---|
| ARROWHEAD | Maricopa | FLORENCE | Pinal |
| ASH FORK | Yavapai | FORT APACHE | Navajo |
| AVONDALE | Maricopa | FORT DEFIANCE | Apache |
| BAGDAD | Yavapai | FORT GRANT | Graham |
| BENSON | Cochise | FORT HUACHUCA | Cochise |
| BISBEE | Cochise | FORT LOWELL | Pima |
| BLACK CANYON CITY | Yavapai | FORT MOHAVE | Mohave |
| BLUE | Greenlee | FOUNTAIN HILLS | Maricopa |
| BOUSE | LaPaz | FORT THOMAS | Graham |
| BOWIE | Cochise | FREDONIA | Conconino |
| BUCKEYE | Maricopa | GADSDEN | Yuma |
| BULLHEAD CITY | Mohave | GANADO | Apache |
| BYLAS | Graham | GIIA BEND | Maricopa |
| CACTUS | Maricopa | GILBERT | Maricopa |
| CAMERON | Coconino | GLENDALE | Maricopa |
| CAMP VERDE | Yavapai | GLOBE | Gila |
| CASA GRANDE | Pinal | GOODYEAR | Maricopa |
| CASHION | Maricopa | GRAND CANYON | Coconino |
| CAVE CREEK | Maricopa | GREEN VALLEY | Pima |
| CENTRAL | Graham | GREER | Apache |
| CHAMBERS | Apache | HAYDEN | Gila |
| CHANDLER | Maricopa | HEBER | Navajo |
| CHANDLER HEIGHTS | Maricopa | HEREFORD | Cochise |
| CHAPARRAL | Maricopa | HIGLEY | Maricopa |
| CHINLE | Apache | HOLBROOK | Navajo |
| CHINO VALLEY | Yavapai | HOTEVILLA | Navajo |
| CHLORIDE | Mohave | HOUCK | Apache |
| CLARKDALE | Yavapai | HUACHUCA CITY | Cochise |
| CLAYPOOL | Gila | HUMBOLDT | Yavapai |
| CLAY SPRINGS | Navajo | JEROME | Yavapai |
| CLIFTON | Greenlee | JOSEPH CITY | Navajo |
| COCHISE | Cochise | KAYENTA | Navajo |
| COLORADO CITY | Mohave | KEAMS CANYON | Navajo |
| CONCHO | Apache | KEARNY | Pinal |
| CONGRESS | Yavapai | KINGMAN | Mohave |
| COOLIDGE | Pinal | KIRKLAND | Yavapai |
| CORNVILLE | Yavapai | KYKOTSMOVI VILLAGE | Navajo |
| CORTARO | Pima | LAKE HAVASU CITY | Mohave |
| COTTONWOOD | Yavapai | LAKESIDE | Navajo |
| CROMN KING | Yavapai | LAVEEN | Maricopa |
| DATELAND | Yuma | LEUPP | Coconino |
| DAVIS MONTHAN AFB | Pima | LITCHFIELD PARK | Maricopa |
| DEWEY | Yavapai | LITTLEFIELD | Mohave |
| DOUGLAS | Cochise | LUKE AFB | Maricopa |
| DRAGOON | Cochise | LUKEVILLE | Pima |
| DUNCAN | Greenlee | LUPTON | Apache |
| EAGAR | Apache | MANNOTH | Pinal |
| EHRENBERG | LaPaz | MANY FARMS | Apache |
| ELFRIDA | Cochise | MARANA | Pima |
| ELGIN | Santa Cruz | MARBLE CANYON | Coconino |
| EL MIRAGE | Maricopa | MARICOPA | Pinal |
| ELOY | Pinal | MARINE CORPS AIR STA | Yuma |
| FLAGSTAFF | Coconino | MARTINEZ LAKE | Yuma |

| | | | |
|---|---|---|---|
| MARYVALE | Maricopa | PRESCOTT VALLEY | Yavapai |
| MAYER | Yavapai | QUARTZSITE | La Paz |
| MCDOWELL | Maricopa | QUEEN CREEK | Maricopa |
| MCNARY | Apache | QUEEN VALLEY | Pinal |
| MCNEAL | Cochise | RED ROCK | Pinal |
| MEADVIEW | Mohave | RED VALLEY | Apache |
| MESA | Maricopa | RILLITO | Pima |
| MIAMI | Gila | RIMROCK | Yavapai |
| MISSION | Pima | RINCON | Pima |
| MOHAVE VALLEY | Mohave | RIO RICO | Cochise |
| MORENCI | Greenlee | RIO SALADO | Maricopa |
| MORMON LAKE | Coconino | RIO VERDE | Maricopa |
| MORRISTOWN | Maricopa | RIVIERA | Mohave |
| MOUNTAIN VIEW | Maricopa | ROLL | Yuma |
| MOUNT LEMMON | Pima | ROOSEVELT | Gila |
| MUNDS PARK | Coconino | SACATON | Maricopa |
| NACO | Cochise | SAFFORD | Graham |
| NAVAJO | Apache | SAHUARITA | Pima |
| NAZLINI | Apache | SAINT DAVID | Cochise |
| NOGALES | Cochise | SAINT JOHNS | Apache |
| NUTRIOSO | Apache | SAINT MICHAELS | Apache |
| OATMAN | Apache | SALOME | La Paz |
| ORACLE | Pinal | SAN CARLOS | Gila |
| OVERGAARD | Navajo | SANDERS | Apache |
| PAGE | Coconino | SAN LUIS | Yuma |
| PALO VERDE | Maricopa | SAN MANUEL | Pinal |
| PAPAGO | Scottsdale | SAN SIMON | Cochise |
| PARADISE VALLEY | Maricopa | SASABE | Pima |
| PARKER | La Paz | SAWMILL | Apache |
| PARKS | Coconino | SCOTTSDALE | Maricopa |
| PATAGONIA | Santa Cruz | SECOND MESA | Navajo |
| PAULDEN | Yavapai | SEDONA | Coconino |
| PAYSON | Gila | SELIGMAN | Yavapai |
| PEACH SPRINGS | Mohave | SELLS | Pima |
| PEARCE | Cochise | SHAW BUTTE | Maricopa |
| PEORIA | Maricopa | SHERWOOD | Maricopa |
| PERIDOT | Gila | SHONTO | Navajo |
| PETRIFIED FOREST NAT'L PK | Apache | SHOW LOW | Navajo |
| PHOENIX | Maricopa | SIERRA ADOBE | Maricopa |
| PICACHO | Pinal | SIERRA VISTA | Cochise |
| PIMA | Graham | SKULL VALLEY | Yavapai |
| PINE | Gila | SNOWFLAKE | Navajo |
| PINEDALE | Navajo | SOLOMAN | Graham |
| PINETOP | Navajo | SOMERTON | Yuma |
| PINON | Navajo | SONOITA | Pima |
| PIONEER | Maricopa | SPRINGERVILLE | Apache |
| PIRTLEVILLE | Cochise | STANFIELD | Pinal |
| PISINEMO | Pima | STRAWBERRY | Gila |
| POLACCA | Navajo | SUN CITY | Maricopa |
| POMERENE | Cochise | SUN CITY WEST | Maricopa |
| PORTAL | Cochise | SUNNYSLOPE | Maricopa |
| POSTON | La Paz | SUN VALLEY | Navajo |
| PRESCOTT | Yavapai | SUPAI | Coconino |

| | | | |
|---|---|---|---|
| SUPERIOR | Pinal | YUMA PROVING GROUND | Yuma |
| SURPRISE | Maricopa | **ARKANSAS** | |
| TACNA | Maricopa | ADONA | Perry |
| TAYLOR | Navajo | AGNOS | Sharp |
| TEEC NOS POS | Apache | ALBERT PIKE | Garland |
| TEMPE | Maricopa | ALCO | Stone |
| THATCHER | Graham | ALEXANDER | Pulaski |
| TOLLESON | Maricopa | ALICIA | Lawrence |
| TOMBSTONE | Cochise | ALIX | Franklin |
| TONALEA | Coconino | ALLEENE | Little River |
| TONOPAH | Maricopa | ALMA | Crawford |
| TONTO BASIN | Gila | ALMYRA | Arkansas |
| TOPAWA | Pima | ALPENA | Boone |
| TOPOCK | Mohave | ALPINE | Clark |
| TORTILLA FLAT | Maricopa | ALTHEIMER | Jefferson |
| TSALLE | Apache | ALTUS | Franklin |
| TUBAC | Santa Cruz | AMAGON | Jackson |
| TUBA CITY | Coconino | AMITY | Clark |
| TUCSON | Pima | ANTOINE | Pike |
| TUMACACORI | Santa Cruz | APPLETON | Pope |
| TUSAYAN | Coconino | ARKADELPHIA | Clark |
| UNIV OF AZ | Pima | ARKANSAS CITY | Desha |
| VAIL | Pima | ARMOREL | Mississippi |
| VALLENTINE | Mohave | ASHDOWN | Pulaski |
| VALLEY FARMS | Pinal | ASHER | Pulaski |
| VERNON | Apache | ASH FLAT | Sharp |
| VILLAGE OF OAK CREEK | Yavapi | ATKINS | Pope |
| WADDELL | Maricopa | AUBREY | Lee |
| WARREN | Cochise | AUGUSTA | Woodruff |
| WELTON | Yuma | AUSTIN | Lonoke |
| WENDEN | La Paz | AVOCA | Benton |
| WESTRIDGE | Maricopa | BALCH | Jackson |
| WEST SEDONA | Yavapai | BALD KNOB | White |
| WHIPPLE | Yavapai | BANKS | Bradley |
| WHITE MOUNTAIN LAKE | Navajo | BARBER | Logan |
| WHITERIVER | Navajo | BARLING | Sebastian |
| WHY | Pima | BARTON | Phillips |
| WICKENBURG | Maricopa | BASELINE | Pulaski |
| WIKIEUP | Mohave | BASS | Newton |
| WILCOX | Graham | BASSETT | Mississippi |
| WILLIAMS | Coconino | BATESVILLE | Independence |
| WILLIAMS AFB | Maricopa | BAUXITE | Saline |
| WILLOW BEACH | Mohave | BAY | Craighead |
| WINDOW ROCK | Apache | BEARDEN | Ouachita |
| WINKLEMAN | Gila | BEAVER | Carroll |
| WINSLOW | Navajo | BEEBE | White |
| WITTMANN | Maricopa | BEE BRANCH | Van Buren |
| WOODRUFF | Navajo | BEECH GROVE | Greene |
| YARNELL | Yavapai | BEEDEVILLE | Jackson |
| YOUNG | Gila | BEIRNE | Clark |
| YOUNGTOWN | Maricopa | BELLEVILLE | Yell |
| YUCCA | Mohave | BEN LOMOND | Sevier |
| YUMA | Yuma | BENTON | Saline |

| | | | |
|---|---|---|---|
| BENTONVILLE | Benton | CARTHAGE | Dallas |
| BERGMAN | Boone | CASA | Perry |
| BERRYVILLE | Carroll | CASH | Craighead |
| BEXAR | Fulton | CASSCOE | Arkansas |
| BIGELOW | Perry | CAVE CITY | Sharp |
| BIG FLAT | Baxter | CAVE SPRINGS | Benton |
| BIGGERS | Randolph | CECIL | Franklin |
| BIRDEYE | Cross | CEDARVILLE | Crawford |
| BISCOE | Prairie | CENTER HILL | Greene |
| BISMARCK | Hot Spring | CENTER RIDGE | Conway |
| BLACK OAK | Craighead | CENTERTON | Benton |
| BLACK ROCK | Lawrence | CENTERVILLE | Yell |
| BLACKWELL | Conway | CENTRAL CITY | Garland |
| BLAKELY | Garland | CHARLESTON | Franklin |
| BLEVINS | Hempstead | CHARLOTTE | Independence |
| BLUE MOUNTAIN | Logan | CHEROKEE VILIAGE | Sharp |
| BLUFF CITY | Nevada | CHATFIELD | Crittenden |
| BLUFFTON | Yell | CHERRY VALLEY | Cross |
| BLYTHEVILLE | Mississippi | CHESTER | Crawford |
| BLYTHEVILLE AFB | Mississippi | CHIDESTER | Ouachita |
| BOARD CAMP | Polk | CHOCTAW | Van Buren |
| BOLES | Scott | CLARENDON | Monroe |
| BONNERDALE | Hot Spring | CLARKEDALE | Crittenden |
| BONO | Craighead | CLARKRIDGE | Baxter |
| BOONEVILLE | Logan | CLARKSVILLE | Johnson |
| BOSWELL | Izard | CLEVELAND | Conway |
| BRADFIDRD | White | CLINTON | Van Buren |
| BRADLEY | Lafayette | COAL HILL | Johnson |
| BRADY | Pulaski | COLLEGE CITY | Lawrence |
| BRANCH | Franklin | COLLEGE STATION | Pulaski |
| BRICKEYS | Lee | COLT | Saint Francis |
| BRIGGSVILLE | Yell | COLUMBUS | Hempstead |
| BRINKLEY | Monroe | COMBS | Madison |
| BROCKWELL | Izard | COMPTON | Newton |
| BROOKLAND | Craighead | CONCORD | Cleburne |
| BRUNO | Marion | CONWAY | Faulkner |
| BRYANT | Saline | CORD | Independence |
| BUCKNER | Lafayette | CORNING | Clay |
| BULL SHOALS | Marion | COTTER | Baxter |
| BURDETTE | Mississippi | COTTON PLANT | Woodruff |
| BUSCH | Carroll | COVE | Polk |
| BYRON | Fulton | COY | Lonoke |
| CABOT | Lonoke | COZAHOME | Searcy |
| CADDO GAP | Montgomery | CRAWFORDSVILLE | Crittenden |
| CALDWELL | Saint Francis | CROCKETTS BLUFF | Arkansas |
| CALE | Nevada | CROSSETT | Ashley |
| CALICO ROCK | Izard | CRUMROD | Phillips |
| CALION | Union | CULLENDALE | Ouachita |
| CAMDEN | Ouachita | CURTIS | Clark |
| CAMP | Fulton | CUSHMAN | Independence |
| CANEHILL | Washington | DAMASCUS | Faulkner |
| CARAWAY | Craighead | DANVILLE | Yell |
| CARLISLE | Lonoke | DARDANELLE | Yell |

| | | | |
|---|---|---|---|
| DATTO | Clay | FLIPPIN | Marion |
| DECATUR | Benton | FLORAL | Independence |
| DEER | Newton | FORDYCE | Dallas |
| DELAPLAINE | Greene | FOREMAN | little River |
| DELAWARE | Logan | FORREST CITY | Saint Francis |
| DELIGHT | Pike | FORT SMITH | Sebastian |
| DELL | Mississippi | FOUKE | Miller |
| DENNARD | Van Buren | FOUNTAIN HILL | Ashley |
| DEQUEEN | Sevier | FOX | Stone |
| DERM0T | Chicot | FRANKLIN | Izard |
| DES ARC | Prairie | FRENCHMANS BAYOU | Mississippi |
| DESHA | Independence | FRIENDSHIP | Hot Spring |
| DEVALLS BLUFF | Prairie | FULTON | Hempstead |
| DEWITT | Arkansas | GAMALIEL | Baxter |
| DIAMOND CITY | Boone | GARFIELD | Benton |
| DIAMONDHEAD | Garland | GARLAND CITY | Miller |
| DIAZ | Jackson | GARNER | White |
| DIERKS | Howard | GASSVILLE | Baxter |
| DODDRIDGE | Miller | GATEWAY | Benton |
| DOGPATCH | Newton | GENOA | Miller |
| DOLPH | Izard | GENTRY | Benton |
| DONALDSON | Hot Spring | GEPP | Fulton |
| DOVER | Pope | GILBERT | Searcy |
| DRASCO | Cleburne | GILLETT | Arkansas |
| DRIVER | Mississippi | GILLHAM | Sevier |
| DUMAS | Desha | GILMORE | Crittenden |
| DYER | Crawford | GLENCOE | Fulton |
| DYESS | Mississippi | GLENWOOD | Pike |
| EARLE | Crittenden | GOODWIN | Saint Francis |
| EDGEMONT | Cleburne | GOSHEN | Washington |
| EDMONDSON | Crittenden | GOSNELL | Mississippi |
| EGYPT | Craighead | GOULD | Lincoln |
| ELAINE | Phillips | GRADY | Lincoln |
| EL DORADO | Union | GRANNIS | Polk |
| ELIZABETH | Fulton | GRAPEVINE | Grant |
| ELKINS | Washington | GRAVELLY | Yell |
| ELM SPRINGS | Washington | GRAVEL RIDGE | Pulaski |
| EL PASO | White | GRAVETTE | Benton |
| EMERSON | Columbia | GREENBRIER | Faulkner |
| EMMET | Nevada | GREEN FOREST | Carroll |
| ENGLAND | Lonoke | GREENLAND | Washington |
| ENOIA | Faulkner | GREENWAY | Clay |
| ETHEL | Arkansas | GREENWOOD | Sebastian |
| ETOWAH | Mississippi | GREGORY | Woodruff |
| EUDORA | Chicot | GRIFFITHVILLE | White |
| EUREKA SPRINGS | Carroll | GRUBBS | Jackson |
| EVANSVILLE | Washington | GUION | Izard |
| EVENING SHADE | Sharp | GURDON | Clark |
| EVERTON | Boone | GUY | Faulkner |
| FARMINGTON | Washington | HACKETT | Sebastian |
| FAYETTEVILLE | Washington | HAGARVILLE | Johnson |
| FERNDALE | Pulaski | HAMBURG | Ashley |
| FISHER | Poinsett | HAMPTON | Calhoun |

| | | | |
|---|---|---|---|
| HANOVER | Stone | JACKSONPORT | Jackson |
| HARDY | Sharp | JACKSONVILLE | Pulaski |
| HARRELL | Calhoun | JASPER | Newton |
| HARRIET | Searcy | JEFFERSON | Jefferson |
| HARRISBURG | Poinsett | JENNIE | Chicot |
| HARRISON | Boone | JERSEY | Bradley |
| HARTFORD | Sebastian | JERUSALEM | Conway |
| HARTMAN | Johnson | JESSIEVILLE | Garland |
| HARVEY | Scott | JOHNSON | Washington |
| HASTY | Newton | JOINER | Mississippi |
| HATFIELD | Polk | JONESBORO | Craighead |
| HATTIEVILLE | Conway | JONES MILLS | Hot Spring |
| HATTON | Polk | JORDAN | Izard |
| HAVANA | Yell | JUDSONIA | White |
| HAYNES | Lee | JUNCTION CITY | Union |
| HAZEN | Prairie | KEISER | Mississippi |
| HEBER SPRINGS | Cleburne | KENSETT | White |
| HECTOR | Pope | KEO | Lonoke |
| HELENA | Phillips | KINGSLAND | Cleveland |
| HENDERSON | Baxter | KINGSTON | Madison |
| HENDERSON COLLEGE | Clark | KIRBY | Pike |
| HENDRIX COLLEGE | Faulkner | KNOBEL | Clay |
| HENSLEY | Pulaski | KNOXVILLE | Johnson |
| HERMITAGE | Bradley | LACROSSE | Izard |
| HETH | Saint Francis | LAGRANGE | Lee |
| HICKORY PIAINS | Prairie | LAKE CATHERINE | Garland |
| HICKORY RIDGE | Cross | LAKE CITY | Craighead |
| HIGDEN | Cleburne | LAKEVIEW | Baxter |
| HIGGINSON | White | LAKE VILLAGE | Chicot |
| HILLCREST | Pulaski | LAMAR | Johnson |
| HINDSVILLE | Madison | LAMBROOK | Phillips |
| HIWASSE | Benton | LANEBURG | Nevada |
| HOLLY GROVE | Monroe | LANGLEY | Pike |
| HOPE | Hempstead | LAVACA | Sebastian |
| HORATIO | Sevier | LAWSON | Union |
| HORSESHOE BEND | Izard | LEACHVILLE | Mississippi |
| HOLLYFIELD | Hot Spring | LEAD HILL | Boone |
| NATIONAL PARK | Garland | LEOLA | Grant |
| HOUSTON | Perry | LEPANTO | Poinsett |
| HOWELL | Woodruff | LESLIE | Searcy |
| HOXIE | Lawrence | LETONA | White |
| HUGHES | Saint Francis | LEWISVILLE | Lafayette |
| HUMNOKE | Lonoke | LEXA | Phillips |
| HUMPHREY | Arkansas | LINCOLN | Washington |
| HUNT | Johnson | LITTLE FLOCK | Benton |
| HUNTER | Woodruff | LITTLE ROCK | Pulaski |
| HUNTINGTON | Sebastian | LOCKESBURG | Sevier |
| HUNTSVILLE | Madison | LOCUST GROVE | Independence |
| HUTTIG | Union | LONDON | Pope |
| IDA | Cleburne | LONOKE | Lonoke |
| IMBODEN | Lawrence | LONSDALE | Garland |
| INDIANDALE | Garland | LOUANN | Ouachita |
| IVAN | Dallas | LOWELL | Benton |

| | | | |
|---|---|---|---|
| LUXORA | Mississippi | MULBERRY | Crawford |
| LYNN | Lawrence | MURFREESBORO | Pike |
| MABELVALE | Pulaski | NAIL | Newton |
| MADISON | Saint Francis | NASHVILLE | Howard |
| MAGAZINE | Logan | NATURAL DAM | Crawford |
| MAGNESS | Independence | NEWARK | Independence |
| MAGNOLIA | Columbia | NEW BLAINE | Logan |
| MALVERN | Hot Spring | NEW EDINBURG | Cleveland |
| MAMMOUTH SPRING | Fulton | NEWHOPE | Pike |
| MANILA | Mississippi | NEWPORT | Jackson |
| MANSFIELD | Scott | NORFORK | Baxter |
| MARCELLA | Stone | NORMAN | Montgomery |
| MARIANNA | Lee | NORPHLET | Union |
| MARION | Crittenden | NORTH LITTLE ROCK | Pulaski |
| MARKED TREE | Poinsett | OAK GROVE | Carroll |
| MARMADUKE | Greene | OAKLAND | Marion |
| MARSHALL | Searcy | OARK | Johnson |
| MARVELL | Phillips | ODEN | Montgomery |
| MAYFLOWER | Faulkner | OGDEN | Pulaski |
| MAYNARD | Randolph | OIL TROUGH | Independence |
| MAYSVILLE | Benton | O'KEAN | Randolph |
| MCCASKILL | Hempstead | OKOLONA | Clark |
| MCCRORY | Woodruff | OLA | Yell |
| MCDOUGAL | Clay | OMAHA | Boone |
| MCGEHEE | Desha | ONEIDA | Phillips |
| MCNEIL | Columbia | ONIA | Stone |
| MCRAE | White | OSCEOLA | Mississippi |
| MELBOURNE | Izard | OUACHITA COLLEGE | Clark |
| MELLWOOD | Phillips | OXFORD | Izard |
| MENA | Polk | OZAN | Hempstead |
| MENIFEE | Conway | OZARK | Franklin |
| MIDLAND | Sebastian | OZONE | Johnson |
| MIDWAY | Baxter | PALESTINE | Saint Francis |
| MINERAL SPRINGS | Howard | PANGBURN | White |
| MINTURN | Lawrence | PARAGOULD | Greene |
| MOKO | Fulton | PARIS | Logan |
| MONETTE | Craighead | PARKDALE | Ashley |
| MONROE | Monroe | PARKIN | Cross |
| MONTICELLO | Drew | PARKS | Scott |
| MONTROSE | Ashley | PARON | Saline |
| MORO | Lee | PARTHENON | Newton |
| MORRILTON | Conway | PATTERSON | Woodruff |
| MORROW | Washington | PEACH ORCHARD | Clay |
| MOSCOW | Jefferson | PEARCY | Garland |
| MOUNTAINBURG | Crawford | PEA RIDGE | Benton |
| MOUNTAIN HOME | Baxter | PEEL | Marion |
| MOUNTAIN PINE | Garland | PELSOR | Pope |
| MOUNTAIN VIEW | Stone | PENCIL BLUFF | Montgomery |
| MOUNT HOLLY | Union | PERRY | Perry |
| MOUNT IDA | Montgomery | PERRYTOWN | Hempstead |
| MOUNT JUDEA | Newton | PERRYVILLE | Perry |
| MOUNT PLEASANT | Izard | PETTIGREW | Madison |
| MOUNT VERNON | Faulkner | PICKENS | Desha |

| | | | |
|---|---|---|---|
| PIGGOTT | Clay | SAINT PAUL | Madison |
| PINDALL | Searcy | SALADO | Independence |
| PINE BLUFF | Jefferson | SALEM | Fulton |
| PINE RIDGE | Montgomery | SARATOGA | Howard |
| PINEVILLE | Izard | SCOTLAND | Van Buren |
| PLAINVIEW | Yell | SCOTT | Pulaski |
| PLEASANT GROVE | Stone | SCRANTON | Logan |
| PLEASANT PLAINS | Independence | SEARCY | White |
| PLUMERVILLE | Conway | SEDGWICK | Lawrence |
| POCAHONTAS | Randolph | SHERIDAN | Grant |
| POLLARD | Clay | SHERRILL | Jefferson |
| PONCA | Newton | SHIRLEY | Van Buren |
| POPLAR GROVE | Phillips | SIDNEY | Sharp |
| PORTIA | Lawrence | SILOAM SPRINGS | Benton |
| PORTLAND | Ashley | SIMS | Montgomery |
| POTTSVILLE | Pope | SMACKOVER | Union |
| POUGHKEEPSIE | Sharp | SMITHVILLE | Lawrence |
| POWHATAN | Lawrence | SNOW LAKE | Desha |
| POYEN | Grant | SOLGOHACHIA | Conway |
| PRAIRIE GROVE | Washington | SPARKMAN | Dallas |
| PRATTSVILLE | Grant | SPRINGDALE | Washington |
| PRESCOTT | Nevada | SPRINGFIELD | Conway |
| PRIM | Cleburne | SPRINGTOWN | Benton |
| PROCTOR | Crittenden | STAMPS | Lafayette |
| PYATT | Marion | STAR CITY | Lincoln |
| QUITMAN | Cleburne | STATE UNIVERSITY | Craighead |
| RATCLIFF | Logan | STEPHENS | Ouachita |
| RAVENDEN | Lawrence | STEPROCK | White |
| RAVENDEN SPRINGS | Randolph | STORY | Montgomery |
| RECTOR | Clay | STRAWBERRY | Lawrence |
| REDFIELD | Jefferson | STRONG | Union |
| REYDELL | Jefferson | STURKIE | Fulton |
| REYNO | Randolph | STTUTGART | Arkansas |
| RISON | Cleveland | SUBAICO | Logan |
| RIVERVALE | Poinsett | SUCCESS | Clay |
| ROE | Monroe | SULPHUR ROCK | Independence |
| ROGERS | Benton | SULPHUR SPRINGS | Benton |
| ROLAND | Pulaski | SUMMERS | Washington |
| ROMANCE | White | SUMMIT | Marion |
| ROSE BUD | White | SWEET HOME | Pulaski |
| ROSIE | Independence | SWIFTON | Jackson |
| ROSSTON | Nevada | TAYLOR | Columbia |
| ROUND POND | Saint Francis | THIDA | Independence |
| ROVER | Yell | THORNTON | Calhoun |
| ROYAL | Garland | TICHNOR | Arkansas |
| RUDY | Crawford | TILLAR | Drew |
| RUSSELL | White | TILLY | Pope |
| RUSSELLVILLE | Pope | TIMBO | Stone |
| SAFFELL | Lawrence | TOMATO | Mississippi |
| SAGE | Izard | TONTITOWN | Washington |
| SAINT CHARLES | Arkansas | TRASKWOOD | Saline |
| SAINT FRANCIS | Clay | TRUMANN | Poinsett |
| SAINT JOE | Searcy | TUCKER | Jefferson |

| | | | |
|---|---|---|---|
| TUCKERMAN | Jackson | WILSON | Mississippi |
| TUMBLING SHOALS | Cleburne | WILTON | Little River |
| TUPELO | Jackson | WINCHESTER | Drew |
| TURNER | Phillips | WINSLOW | Washington |
| TURRELL | Crittenden | WINTHROP | Little River |
| TWIST | Cross | WISEMAN | Izard |
| TYRONZA | Poinsett | WITTER | Madison |
| ULM | Praine | WITTS SPRINGS | Searcy |
| UMPIRE | Howard | WOODSON | Pulaski |
| UNIONTOWN | Crawford | WOOSTER | Faulkner |
| UNIV OF AR FAYETTEVILLE | Washington | WRIGHT | Jefferson |
| UNIV OF AR MONTICELLO | Drew | WRIGHTSVILLE | Pulaski |
| UNIV OF CENTRAL AR | Faulkner | WYNNE | Cross |
| UNIV OF SOUTHERN AR | Columbia | YELLVILLE | Marion |
| VALLEY SPRINGS | Boone | YORKTOWN | Lincoln |
| VAN BUREN | Crawford | ZION | Izard |
| VANDERVOORT | Polk | **CALIFORNIA** ▰▰▰▰ | |
| VANNDALE | Cross | ACAMPO | San Joaquin |
| VENDOR | Newton | ACTON | Los Angeles |
| VILLAGE | Columbia | ADELANTO | San Bernardino |
| VILONIA | Faulkner | ADIN | Modoc |
| VIOLA | Fulton | AGOURA HILLS | Los Angeles |
| VIOLET HILL | Izard | AGUANGA | Riverside |
| WABASH | Phillips | AHWAHNEE | Madera |
| WABBESEKA | Jefferson | ALAMEDA | Alameda |
| WALCOTT | Greene | ALAMO | Contra Costa |
| WALDENBURG | Poinsett | ALBION | Mendocino |
| WALDO | Columbia | ALDERPOINT | Humboldt |
| WALDRON | Scott | ALHAMBRA | Los Angeles |
| WALNUT RIDGE | Lawrence | ALLEGHANY | Sierra |
| WARD | Lonoke | ALPAUGH | Tulare |
| WARREN | Bradley | ALPINE | San Diego |
| WASHINGTON | Hempstead | ALTA | Placer |
| WATSON | Desha | ALTADENA | Los Angeles |
| WAVELAND | Yell | ALTA LOMA | San Bernardino |
| WEINER | Poinsett | ALTURAS | Modoc |
| WESLEY | Madison | ALVISO | Santa Clara |
| WESTERN GROVE | Newton | AMADOR CITY | Amador |
| WEST FORK | Washington | AMBOY | San Bernardino |
| WEST HELENA | Phillips | ANAHEIM | Orange |
| WEST MEMPHIS | Crittenden | ANDERSON | Shasta |
| WEST POINT | White | ANGELS CAMP | Calaveras |
| WEST RIDGE | Mississippi | ANGELUS OAKS | San Bernardino |
| WHEATLEY | Saint Francis | ANGWIN | Napa |
| WHEELER | Washington | ANNAPOLIS | Sonoma |
| WHELEN SPRINGS | Clark | ANTIOCH | Contra Costa |
| WICKES | Polk | ANZA | Riverside |
| WIDEMAN | Izard | APPLEGATE | Placer |
| WIDENER | Saint Francis | APPLE VALLEY | San Bernardino |
| WILBURN | Cleburne | APTOS | Santa Cruz |
| WILLISVILLE | Nevada | ARBUCKLE | Colusa |
| WILMAR | Drew | ARCADIA | Los Angeles |
| WILMOT | Ashley | ARCATA | Humboldt |

| | | | |
|---|---|---|---|
| ARMONA | Kings | BLOOMINGTON | San Bernardino |
| ARNOLD | Calaveras | BLUE JAY | San Bernardino |
| AROMAS | Monterey | BLUE LAKE | Humboldt |
| ARROYO GRANDE | San Luis Obispo | BLYTHE | Riverside |
| ARTESIA | Los Angeles | BODEGA | Sonoma |
| ARTOIS | Glenn | BODFISH | Kern |
| ARVIN | Kern | BOLINAS | Marin |
| ATASCADERO | San Luis Obispo | BOLSA | Orange |
| ATWATER | Merced | BONITA | San Diego |
| ATWOOD | Orange | BONSALL | San Diego |
| AUBERRY | Fresno | BOONSVILLE | Mendocino |
| AUBURN | Placer | BORON | Kern |
| AVALON | Los Angeles | BORREGO SPRINGS | San Diego |
| AVENAL | Kings | BOULDER CREEK | Santa Cruz |
| AVERY | Calaveras | BOULEVARD | San Diego |
| AVILA BEACH | San Luis Obispo | BOYES HOT SPRINGS | Sonoma |
| AZASA | Los Angeles | BRADLEY | Monterey |
| BAKER | San Bernardino | BRAWLEY | Imperial |
| BAKERSFIELD | Kern | BREA | Orange |
| BALDWIN PARK | Los Angeles | BRENTWOOD | Contra Costa |
| BALLICO | Merced | BRIDGEPORT | Mono |
| BANGOR | Butte | BRIDGEVILLE | Humboldt |
| BANNING | Riverside | BRISBANE | San Mateo |
| BARD | Imperial | BROADWAY | Sacramento |
| BARSTOW | San Bernardino | BRODERICK | Yolo |
| BASS LAKE | Madera | BROOKDALE | Santa Cruz |
| BAYSIDE | Humboldt | BROOKS | Yolo |
| BEAUMONT | Riverside | BROWNS VALLEY | Yuba |
| BELL | Los Angeles | BROWNSVILLE | Yuba |
| BELLA VISTA | Shasta | BRYN MAWR | San Bernardino |
| BELLFLOWER | Los Angeles | BUELLTON | Santa Barbara |
| BELMONT | San Mateo | BUENA PARK | Orange |
| BELVEDERE-TIBURON | Marin | BURBANK | Los Angeles |
| BENICIA | Solano | BURLINGAME | San Mateo |
| BEN LOMOND | Santa Cruz | BURNEY | Shasta |
| BERKELEY | Alameda | BURNT RANCH | Trinity |
| BERRY CREEK | Butte | BURSON | Calaveras |
| BETHEL ISLAND | Contra Costa | BUTTE CITY | Glenn |
| BEVERLY HILLS | Los Angeles | BUTTONWILLOW | Kern |
| BIEBER | Lassen | BYRON | Contra Costa |
| BIG BAR | Trinity | CABAZON | Riverside |
| BIG BEAR CITY | San Bernardino | CADIZ | San Bernardino |
| BIG BEND | Shasta | CALEXICO | Imperial |
| BIG CREEK | Fresno | CALIENTE | Kern |
| BIGGS | Butte | CALIMESA | Riverside |
| BIG OAK FLAT | Tuolumne | CALIPATRIA | Imperial |
| BIG PINE | Inyo | CALISTOGA | Napa |
| BIG SUR | Monterey | CALLAHAN | Siskiyou |
| BIOLA | Fresno | CAMARILLO | Ventura |
| BIRDS LANDING | Solano | CAMBRIA | San Luis Obispo |
| BISHOP | Inyo | CAMINO | El Dorado |
| BLAIRSDEN | Plumas | CAMPBELL | Santa Clara |
| BLOCKSBURG | Humboldt | CAMP MEEKER | Sonoma |

| | | | |
|---|---|---|---|
| CAMPO | San Diego | CLOVERDALE | Sonoma |
| CAMPTONVILLE | Yuba | CLOVIS | Fresno |
| CANBY | Modoc | COACHELLA | Riverside |
| CANOGA PARK | Los Angeles | COALINGA | Fresno |
| CANTUA CREEK | Fresno | COARSEGOLD | Madera |
| CANYON | Contra Costa | COBB | Lake |
| CANYONDOM | Plumas | COLEVILLE | Mono |
| CAPITOLA | Santa Cruz | COLFAX | Placer |
| CARDIFF BY THE SEA | San Diego | COLLEGE CITY | Colusa |
| CARLOTTA | Humboldt | COLOMA | El Dorado |
| CARLSBAD | San Diego | COLTON | San Bernardino |
| CARMEL | Monterey | COLUMBIA | Tuolumne |
| CARMELL VALLEY | Monterey | COLUSA | Colusa |
| CARMICHAEL | Sacramento | COMPTCHE | Mendocino |
| CARNELIAN BAY | Placer | COMPTON | Los Angeles |
| CARPINTERIA | Santa Barbara | CONCORD | Contra Costa |
| CARUTHERS | Fresno | COOL | El Dorado |
| CASMALIA | Santa Barbara | COPPEROPOLIS | Calaveras |
| CASSEL | Shasta | CORCORAN | Kings |
| CASTELLA | Shasta | CORNING | Tehama |
| CASTROVILLE | Monterey | CORONA | Riverside |
| CATHEYS VALLEY | Mariposa | CORONA DEL MAR | Orange |
| CATHEDRAL CITY | Riverside | CORTE MADERA | Marin |
| CAYUCOS | San Luis Obispo | COSTA MESA | Orange |
| CAZABERO | Sonoma | COTATI | Sonoma |
| CEDAR GLEN | San Bernardino | COTTONWOOD | Shasta |
| CEDAR RIDGE | Nevada | COULTERVILLE | Mariposa |
| CEDARVILLE | Modoc | COURTLAND | Sacramento |
| CENTRAL VALLEY | Shasta | COVELO | Mendocino |
| CERES | Stanislaus | COVINA | Los Angeles |
| CHALLENGE | Yuba | CRESCENT CITY | Del Norte |
| CHATSWORTH | Los Angeles | CRESCENT MILLS | Plumas |
| CHESTER | Plumas | CRESSEY | Merced |
| CHICAGO PARK | Nevada | CRESTLINE | San Bernardino |
| CHICO | Butte | CRESTON | San Luis Obispo |
| CHILCOOT | Plumas | CREST PARK | San Bernardino |
| CHINESE CAMP | Tuolumne | CROCKETT | Contra Costa |
| CHINO | San Bernardino | CROWS LANDING | Stanislaus |
| CHOLAME | San Luis Obispo | RANCHO CUCAMONGA | San Bernardino |
| CHOWCHILLA | Madera | CULVER CITY | Los Angeles |
| CHUALAR | Monterey | CUPERTINO | Santa Clara |
| CHULA VISTA | San Diego | CUTLER | Tulare |
| CIMA | San Bernardino | CUYAMA | Santa Barbara |
| CITRUS HEIGHTS | Sacramento | CYPRESS | Orange |
| CLAREMONT | Los Angeles | DAGGETT | San Bernardino |
| CLARKSBURG | Yolo | DALY CITY | San Mateo |
| CLAYTON | Contra Costa | DANA POINT | Orange |
| CLEARLAKE | Lake | DANVILLE | Contra Costa |
| CLEARLAKE OAKS | Lake | DARWIN | Inyo |
| CLEARLAKE PARK | Lake | DAVENPORT | Santa Cruz |
| CLEMENTS | San Joaquin | DAVIS | Yolo |
| CLIO | Plumas | DAVIS CREEK | Modoc |
| CLIPPER MILLS | Butte | DEATH VALLEY | Inyo |

| | | | |
|---|---|---|---|
| DELANO | Kern | ELVERTA | Sacramento |
| DELHI | Merced | EMPIRE | Stanislaus |
| DEL MAR | San Diego | ENCINITAS | San Diego |
| DEL REY | Fresno | ESCALON | San Joaquin |
| DENAIR | Stanislaus | ESCONDIDO | San Diego |
| DESCANSO | San Diego | ESPARTO | Yolo |
| DESERT CENTER | Riverside | ESSEX | San Bernardino |
| DESERT HOT SPRINGS | Riverside | ETIWANDA | San Bernardino |
| DIABLO | Contra Costa | ETNA | Siskiyou |
| DIAMOND SPRINGS | El Dorado | EUREKA | Humboldt |
| DI GIORGIO | Kern | EXETER | Tulare |
| DILLON BEACH | Marin | FAIRFAX | Marin |
| DINUBA | Tulare | FAIRFIELD | Solano |
| DIXON | Solano | FAIR OAKS | Sacramento |
| DOBBINS | Yuba | FALLBROOK | San Diego |
| DORRIS | Siskiyou | FALL RIVER MILLS | Shasta |
| DOS PALOS | Merced | FARMERSVILLE | Tulare |
| DOUGLAS CITY | Trinity | FARMINGTON | San Joaquin |
| DOWNEY | Los Angeles | FAWNSKIN | San Bernardino |
| DOWNIEVILLE | Sierra | FELLOWS | Kern |
| DOYLE | Lassen | FELTON | Santa Cruz |
| DUARTE | Los Angeles | FERNDALE | Humboldt |
| DUCOR | Tulare | FIDDLETOWN | Amador |
| DULZURA | San Diego | FIELDS LANDING | Humboldt |
| DUNCANS MILLS | Sonoma | FILLMORE | Ventura |
| DUNLAP | Fresno | FINELY | Lake |
| DUNNIGAN | Yolo | FIREBAUGH | Fresno |
| DUNSMUIR | Siskiyou | FISH CAMP | Mariposa |
| DURHAM | Butte | FIVE POINTS | Fresno |
| DUTCH FLAT | Placer | FLORISTON | Nevada |
| EAGLEVILLE | Modoc | FOLSOM | Sacramento |
| EARLIMART | Tulare | FONTANA | San Bernardino |
| EARP | San Bernardino | FORBESTOWN | Butte |
| EAST NICOLAUS | Sutter | FOREST FALLS | San Bernardino |
| EDISON | Kern | FOREST KNOLLS | Marin |
| EDWARDS | Kern | FORESTVILLE | Sonoma |
| EDWARDS AFB | Kern | FORKS OF SALMON | Siskiyou |
| EL CAJON | San Diego | FORT BIDWELL | Modoc |
| EL CENTRO | Imperial | FORT BRAGG | Mendocino |
| EL CERRITO | Contra Costa | FORT DICK | Del Norte |
| EL DORADO | El Dorado | FORT IRWIN | San Bernardino |
| ELDRIDGE | Sonoma | FORT JONES | Siskiyou |
| EL GRANADA | San Mateo | FORT MACARTHUR | Los Angeles |
| ELK | Mendocino | FORT ORD | Monterey |
| ELK CREEK | Glenn | FORT SUTTER | Sacramento |
| ELK GROVE | Sacramento | FORTUNA | Humboldt |
| ELMIRA | Solano | FOWLER | Fresno |
| EL MONTE | Los Angeles | FRANKLIN | Napa |
| EL NIDO | Merced | FRAZIER PARK | Kern |
| EL PORTAL | Mariposa | FREEDOM | Santa Cruz |
| EL SEGUNDO | Los Angeles | FREMONT | Alameda |
| EL TORO | Orange | FRENCH CAMP | San Joaquin |
| EL VERANO | Sonoma | FRENCH GULCH | Shasta |

| | | | |
|---|---|---|---|
| FRESNO | Fresno | HAWTHORNE | Los Angeles |
| FRIANT | Fresno | HAYFORK | Trinity |
| FULLERTON | Orange | HAYWARD | Alameda |
| FULTON | Sonoma | HEALDSBURG | Sonoma |
| GALT | Sacramento | HEBER | Imperial |
| GARBERVILLE | Humboldt | HELENDALE | San Bernardino |
| GARDENA | Los Angeles | HELM | Fresno |
| GARDEN GROVE | Orange | HEMET | Riverside |
| GARDEN VALLEY | El Dorado | HERALD | Sacramento |
| GASQUET | Del Norte | HERLONG | Lassen |
| GAZELLE | Siskiyau | HESPERIA | San Bernardino |
| GEORGETOWN | El Dorado | HICKMAN | Stanislaus |
| GERBER | Tehama | HIGHLAND | San Bernardino |
| GEYSERVILLE | Sonoma | HILMAR | Merced |
| GILROY | Santa Clara | HINKLEY | San Bernardino |
| GLENCOE | Calaveras | HOLLISTER | San Benito |
| GLENDALE | Los Angeles | HOLT | San Joaquin |
| GLENDORA | Los Angeles | HOLTVILLE | Imperial |
| GLEN ELLEN | Sonoma | HOMELAND | Riverside |
| GLENHAVEN | Lake | HOMEWOOD | Placer |
| GLENN | Glenn | HONEYDEW | Humboldt |
| GLENNVILLE | Kern | HOOD | Sacramento |
| GOLD RUN | Placer | HOOPA | Humboldt |
| GONZALES | Monterey | HOPLAND | Mendocino |
| GOODYEARS BAR | Sierra | HORNBROOK | Siskiyou |
| GOSHEN | Tulare | HORNITOS | Mariposa |
| GRASS VALLEY | Nevada | HORSE CREEK | Siskiyou |
| GRATON | Sonoma | HUGHSON | Stanislaus |
| GREENFIELD | Monterey | HUNTINGTON BEACH | Orange |
| GREEN VALLEY LAKE | San Bernardino | HUNTINGTON PARK | Los Angeles |
| GREENVIEW | Siskiyou | HURON | Fresno |
| GREENWOOD | El Dorado | HYMAPOM | Trinity |
| GRENADA | Siskiyou | HYDESVILLE | Humboldt |
| GRIDLEY | Butte | IDYLLWILD | Riverside |
| GRIMES | Colusa | IGO | Shasta |
| GRIZZLEY FLATS | El Dorado | IMPERIAL | Imperial |
| GROVELAND | Tuolumne | IMPERIAL BEACH | San Diego |
| GROVER CITY | San Luis Obispo | INDEPENDENCE | Inyo |
| GUADALUPE | Santa Barbara | INDIO | Riverside |
| GUALALA | Mendocino | INGLEWOOD | Los Angeles |
| GUASTI | San Bernardino | INVERNESS | Marin |
| GUATAY | San Diego | INYOKERN | Kern |
| GUERNEVILLE | Sonoma | IONE | Amador |
| GUINDA | Yolo | ISLETON | Sacramento |
| GUSTINE | Merred | IVANHOE | Tulare |
| HALF MOON BAY | San Mateo | JACKSON | Amador |
| HAMILTON CITY | Glenn | JACUMBA | San Diego |
| HANFORD | Kings | JAMESTOWN | Tuolumne |
| HAPPY CAMP | Siskiyou | JAMUL | San Diego |
| HARBAR CITY | Los Angeles | JANESVILLE | Lassen |
| HARMONY | San Luis Obispo | JENNER | Sonoma |
| HAT CREEK | Shasta | JOHANNESBURG | Kern |
| HATHAWAY PINES | Calaveras | JOLON | Monterey |

| | | | |
|---|---|---|---|
| JOSHUA TREE | San Bernardino | LAVERNE | Los Angeles |
| JULIAN | San Diego | LAWNDALE | Los Angeles |
| JUNCTION CITY | Trinity | LAYTONVILLE | Mendocino |
| JUNE LAKE | Mono | LEBEC | Kern |
| KEELER | Inyo | LEE VINING | Mono |
| KEENE | Kern | LEGGETT | Mendocino |
| KELSEYVILLE | Lake | LE GRAND | Merced |
| KELSO | San Bernardino | LEMONCOVE | Tulare |
| KENSINGTON | Berkeley | LEMON GROVE | San Diego |
| KENTFIELD | Marin | LEMOORE | Kings |
| KENWOOD | Sonoma | LEWISTON | Trinity |
| KERMAN | Fresno | LIKELY | Modoc |
| KERNVILLE | Kern | LINCOLN | Placer |
| KETTLEMAN CITY | Kings | LINDEN | San Joaquin |
| KEYES | Stanislaus | LINDSAY | Tulare |
| KING CITY | Monterey | LITCHFIELD | Lassen |
| KINGS BEACH | Placer | LITTLE NORWAY | El Dorado |
| KINGSBURG | Fresno | LITTLE RIVER | Mendocino |
| KLAMATH | Del Norte | LIVE ROCK | Los Angeles |
| KNEELAND | Humboldt | LIVE OAK | Sutter |
| KNIGHTSEN | Contra Costa | LIVERMORE | Alameda |
| KNIGHTS LANDING | Yolo | LIVINGSTON | Merced |
| KORBEL | Humboldt | LLANO | Los Angeles |
| KYBURZ | El Dorado | LOCKEFORD | San Joaquin |
| LACANADA-FLINTRIDGE | Los Angeles | LOCKWOOD | Monterey |
| LA COSTA | Los Angeles | LODI | San Joaquin |
| LA CRESCENTA | Los Angeles | LOLETA | Humboldt |
| LAFAYETTE | Contra Costa | LOMA LINDA | San Bernardino |
| LAGRANGE | Stanislaus | LOMA MAR | San Mateo |
| LAGUNA BEACH | Orange | LOMITA | Los Angeles |
| LAGUNITAS | Marin | LOMPOC | Santa Barbara |
| LAHABRA | Orange | LONE PINE | Inyo |
| LAHONDA | San Mateo | LONG BARN | Tuolumne |
| LAJOLLA | San Diego | LONG BEACH | Los Angeles |
| LAKE ARROWHEAD | San Bernardino | LOOKOUT | Modoc |
| LAKE CITY | Modoc | LOOMIS | Placer |
| LAKE ELSINORE | Riverside | LOS ALAMITOS | Orange |
| LAKEHEAD | Shasta | LOS ALAMOS | Santa Barbara |
| LAKE HUGHES | Los Angeles | LOS ALTOS | Santa Clara |
| LAKE ISABELLA | Kern | LOS ANGELES | Los Angeles |
| LAKEPORT | Lake | LOS BANOS | Merced |
| LAKESIDE | San Diego | LOS GATOS | Santa Clara |
| LAKEVIEW | Riverside | LOS MOLINOS | Tehama |
| LAKEWOOD | Los Angeles | LOS OLIVOS | Santa Barbara |
| LAMESA | San Diego | LOST HILLS | Kern |
| LAMIRADA | Los Angeles | LOTUS | El Dorado |
| LAMONT | Kern | LOWER LAKE | Lake |
| LANCASTER | Los Angeles | LOYALTON | Sierra |
| LAPUENTE | Los Angeles | LUCERNE | Lake |
| LAQUINTA | Riverside | LUCERNE VALLEY | San Bernardino |
| LARKSPUR | Marin | LYNWOOD | Los Angeles |
| LATHROP | San Joaquin | LYTLE CREEK | San Bernardino |
| LATON | Fresno | MCARTHLTR | Shasta |

| | | | |
|---|---|---|---|
| MCCLOUD | Siskiyou | MONTARA | San Mateo |
| MCFARLAND | Kern | MONTCLAIR | San Bernardino |
| MCKITTRICK | Kern | MONTEBELLO | Los Angeles |
| MACDOEL | Siskiyou | MONTEREY | Monterey |
| MADELINE | Lassen | MONTEREY PARK | Los Angeles |
| MADERA | Madera | MONTE RIO | Sonoma |
| MADISON | Yolo | MONTGOMERY CREEK | Shasta |
| MAD RIVER | Trinity | MONTROSE | Los Angeles |
| MAGALIA | Butte | MOORPARK | Ventura |
| MALIBU | Los Angeles | MORAGA | Contra Costa |
| MAMMOUTH LAKES | Mono | MORENO VALLEY | Riverside |
| MANCHESTER | Mendocino | MORRO BAY | San Luis Obispo |
| MANHATTAN BEACH | Los Angeles | MOSS BEACH | San Mateo |
| MANTECA | San Joaquin | MOSS LANDING | Monterey |
| MANTON | Tehama | MOUNTAIN CENTER | Riverside |
| MARICOPA | Kern | MOUNTAIN RANCH | Calaveras |
| MARINA | Monterey | MOUNTAIN VIEW | Santa Clara |
| MARIPOSA | Mariposa | MOUNT HERMON | Santa Clara |
| MARINA | Monterey | MOUNT LAGUNA | San Diego |
| MARIPOSA | Mariposa | MOUNT SHASTA | Siskiyou |
| MARKLEEVILLE | Alpine | MOUNT AUKUM | El Dorado |
| MARSHALL | Marin | MOUNT BALDY | San Bernardino |
| MARTINEZ | Contra Costa | MURPHYS | Calaveras |
| MARYSVILLE | Yuba | MURRIETA | Riverside |
| MAXWELL | Colusa | MYERS FLAT | Humboldt |
| MEADOW VALLEY | Plumes | NAPA | Napa |
| MEADOW VISTA | Placer | NATIONAL CITY | San Diego |
| MECCA | Riverside | NEEDLES | San Bernardino |
| MENDOCINO | Mendocino | NESTOR | San Diego |
| MENDOTA | Fresno | NEVADA CITY | Nevada |
| MENLO PARK | San Mateo | NEW ALMADEN | Santa Clara |
| MENTONE | San Bernardino | NEWARK | Alameda |
| MERCED | Merced | NEWBERRY SPRINGS | San Bernardino |
| MERIDIAN | Sutter | NEWCASTLE | Placer |
| MIDDLETOWN | Lake | NEW CUYAMA | Santa Barbara |
| MIDPINES | Mariposa | NEWMAN | Stanislaus |
| MIDWAY CITY | Orange | NEWPORT BEACH | Orange |
| MILFORD | Lassen | NICASIO | Marin |
| MILLBRAE | San Mateo | NICE | Lake |
| MILL VALLEY | Marin | NICOLAUS | Sutter |
| MILLVILLE | Shasta | NILAND | Imperial |
| MILPITAS | Santa Clara | NIPOMO | San Luis Obispo |
| MINERAL | Tehama | NORCO | Riverside |
| MIRA LOMA | Riverside | NORDEN | Nevada |
| MIRAMONTE | Fresno | NORTH FORK | Madera |
| MIRANDA | Humboldt | NORTH HIGHLANDS | Sacramento |
| MI-WUK VILLAGE | Tuolumne | NORTH HOLLYWOOD | Los Angeles |
| MOCCASIN | Tuolumne | NORTH PALM SPRINGS | Riverside |
| MODESTO | Stanislaus | NORTHRIDGE | Los Angeles |
| MOJAVE | Kern | NORTH SAN JUAN | Nevada |
| MOKELUMNE HILL | Calaveras | NORWALK | Los Angeles |
| MONROVIA | Los Angeles | NOVATO | Marin |
| MONTAGUE | Siskiyou | NUBIEBER | Lassen |

| | | | |
|---|---|---|---|
| NUEVO | Riverside | PASKENTA | Tehama |
| OAKDALE | Stanislaus | PASO ROBLES | San Luis Obispo |
| OAKHURST | Madera | PATTERSON | Stanislaus |
| OAKLAND | Alameda | PATTON | San Bernardino |
| OAKLEY | Contra Costa | PAUMA VALLEY | San Diego |
| OAK RUN | Shasta | PEARBLOSSOM | Los Angeles |
| OAK VIEW | Ventura | PEBBLE BEACH | Monterey |
| OAKVILLE | Napa | PENNGROVE | Sonoma |
| OCCIDENTAL | Sonoma | PENRYN | Placer |
| OCEANO | San Luis Obispo | PERRIS | Riverside |
| OCEANSIDE | San Diego | PESCADERO | San Mateo |
| OCOTILLO | Imperial | PETALUMA | Sonoma |
| OJAI | Ventura | PETROLIA | Humboldt |
| OLANCHA | Inyo | PHELAN | San Bernardino |
| OLD STATION | Shasta | PHILLIPSVILLE | Humboldt |
| OLEMA | Marin | PHILO | Mendocino |
| OLIVEHURST | Yuba | PICO RIVERA | Los Angeles |
| O'NEALS | Madera | PIEDRA | Fresno |
| ONTARIO | San Bernardino | PIERCY | Mendocino |
| ONYX | Kern | PILOT HILL | El Dorado |
| ORANGE | Orange | PINECREST | Tuolumne |
| ORANGE COVE | Fresno | PINE GROVE | Amador |
| ORANGEVALE | Sacramento | PINE VALLEY | San Diego |
| OREGON HOUSE | Yuba | PINOLE | Contra Costa |
| ORICK | Humboldt | PINON HILLS | San Bernardino |
| ORINDA | Contra Costa | PIONEER | Amador |
| ORLAND | Glenn | PIONEERTOWN | San Luis Obispo |
| ORLEANS | Humboldt | PIRU | Ventura |
| ORO GRANDE | San Bernardino | PISMO BEACH | San Luis Obispo |
| OROSI | Tulare | PITTSBURG | Contra Costa |
| OROVILLE | Butte | PIXLEY | Tulare |
| OXNARD | Ventura | PLACENTIA | Orange |
| PACIFICA | San Mateo | PLACERVILLE | El Dorado |
| PACIFIC GROVE | Monterey | PLANADA | Merced |
| PACIFIC HOUSE | El Dorado | PLATINA | Shasta |
| PACIFIC PALISADES | Los Angeles | PLEASANT GROVE | Sutter |
| PACOIMA | Los Angeles | PLEASANTON | Alameda |
| PAICINES | Los Angeles | PLYMOUTH | Amador |
| PALA | San Diego | POINT ARENA | Mendocino |
| PALERMO | Butte | POINT REYES STATION | Marin |
| PALMDALE | Los Angeles | POLLOCK PINES | El Dorado |
| PALM DESERT | Riverside | POMONA | Los Angeles |
| PALM SPRINGS | Riverside | POPE VALLEY | Napa |
| PALO ALTO | Santa Clara | PORT COSTA | Contra Costa |
| PALO CEDRO | Shasta | PORTERVILLE | Tulare |
| PALOMAR MOUNTAIN | San Diego | PORT HUENEME | Ventura |
| PALOS VERDES PENINSUIA | Los Angeles | PORTOLA | Plumas |
| PALO VERDE | Imperial | POSEY | Tulare |
| PARADISE | Butte | POTRERO | San Diego |
| PARAMOUNT | Los Angeles | POTTER VALLEY | Mendocino |
| PARKER DAM | San Bernardino | POWAY | San Diego |
| PARLIER | Fresno | PRATHER | Fresno |
| PASADENA | Los Angeles | PRINCETON | Colusa |

**Adoption Searches Made Easier**

| | | | |
|---|---|---|---|
| PROBERTA | Tehama | SALIDA | Stanislaus |
| QUINCY | Plumas | SALINAS | Monterey |
| RACKERBY | Yuba | SALYER | Trinity |
| RAIL ROAD FLAT | Calaveras | SAMOA | Humboldt |
| RAISIN | Fresno | SAN ANDREAS | Calaveras |
| RAMONA | San Diego | SAN ANSELMO | Marin |
| RANCHO CORDOVA | Sacramento | SAN ARDO | Monterey |
| RANCHO MIRAGE | Riverside | SAN BERNARDINO | San Bernardino |
| RANCHO SANTA FE | San Diego | SAN BRUNO | San Mateo |
| RAVENDALE | Lassen | SAN CARLOS | San Mateo |
| RAYMOND | Madera | SAN CLEMENTE | Orange |
| RED BLUFF | Tehama | SAN DIEGO | San Diego |
| REDCREST | Humboldt | SAN DIMAS | Los Angeles |
| REDDING | Shasta | SAN FERNANDO | Los Angeles |
| REDLANDS | San Bernardino | SAN FRANCISCO | San Francisco |
| REDONDO BEACH | Los Angeles | SAN GABRIEL | Los Angeles |
| REDWAY | Humboldt | SANGER | Fresno |
| REDWOOD CITY | San Mateo | SAN GERONIMO | Marin |
| REDWOOD ESTATES | Santa Clara | SAN GREGORIO | San Mateo |
| REDWOOD VALLEY | Mendocino | SAN JACINTO | Riverside |
| REEDLEY | Fresno | SAN JOAQUIN | Riverside |
| RESCUE | El Dorado | SAN JOSE | Santa Clara |
| RESEDA | Los Angeles | SAN JUAN BAUTISTA | SanBenito |
| RIALTO | San Bernardino | SAN JUAN CAPISTRANO | Orange |
| RICHGROVE | Tulare | SAN LEANDRO | Alameda |
| RICHMOND | Contra Costa | SAN LORENZO | Alameda |
| RICHVALE | Butte | SAN LUCAS | Monterey |
| RIDGECREST | Kern | SAN LUIS OBISPO | SanLuis Obispo |
| RIMFOREST | San Bernardino | SAN LUIS REY | San Diego |
| RIO DELL | Humboldt | SAN MARCOS | San Diego |
| RIO LINDA | Sacramento | SAN MARTIN | Santa Clara |
| RIO OSO | Sutter | SAN MATEO | San Mateo |
| RIO VISTA | Solano | SAN MIGUEL | San Luis Obispo |
| RIPLEY | Riverside | SAN PEDRO | Los Angeles |
| RIPON | San Joaquin | SAN QUENTIN | Marin |
| RIVERBANK | Stanislaus | SAN RAFAEL | Marin |
| RIVERDALE | Fresno | SAN RAMON | Contra Costa |
| RIVER PINES | Amador | SAN SIMEON | San Luis Obispo |
| RIVERSIDE | Riverside | SANTA ANA | Orange |
| ROBBINS | Sutter | SANTA BARBARA | Santa Barbara |
| ROCKLIN | Placer | SANTA CLARA | Santa Clara |
| RODEO | Contra Costa | SANTA CRUZ | Santa Cruz |
| ROSAMOND | Kern | SANTA FE SPRINGS | Los Angeles |
| ROSEMEAD | Los Angeles | SANTA MARGARITA | San Luis Obispo |
| ROSEVILLE | Placer | SANTA MARIA | Santa Barbara |
| ROSS | Marin | SANTA MONICA | Los Angeles |
| ROUGH AND READY | Nevada | SANTA PAULA | Ventura |
| ROUND MOUNTAIN | Shasta | SANTA RITA PARK | Merced |
| RUNNING SPRINGS | San Bernardino | SANTA ROSA | Sonoma |
| RUTHERFORD | Napa | SANTA YNEZ | Santa Barbara |
| RYDE | Sacramento | SANTA YSABEL | San Diego |
| SACRAMENTO | Sacramento | SANTEE | San Diego |
| SAINT HELENA | Napa | SARATOGA | Santa Clara |

| | | | |
|---|---|---|---|
| SATTLEY | Sierra | STOCKTON | San Joaquin |
| SAUGUS | Los Angeles | STONYFORD | Colusa |
| SAUSALITO | Marin | STRATFORD | Kings |
| SCOTIA | Humboldt | STRATHMORE | Tulare |
| SCOTT BAR | Siskiyou | STRAWBERRY VALLEY | Yuba |
| SEAL BEACH | Orange | SUISUN CITY | Solano |
| SEASIDE | Monterey | SULTANA | Tulare |
| SEBASTOPOL | Sonoma | SUMMERLAND | SantaBarbara |
| SEELEY | Imperial | SUMMIT CITY | Shasta |
| SEIAD VALLEY | Siskiyou | SUN CITY | Riverside |
| SELMA | Fresno | SUNLAND | Los Angeles |
| SEQUOIA NATIONAL PARK | Tulare | SUNNYVALE | Santa Clara |
| SHAFTER | Kern | SUNOL | Alameda |
| SHANDON | San Luis Obispo | SUNSET BEACH | Orange |
| SHASTA | Shasta | SUN VALLEY | Los Angeles |
| SHAVER LAKE | Fresno | SURFSIDE | Orange |
| SHERIDAN | Placer | SUSANVILLE | Lassen |
| SHINGLE SPRINGS | El Dorado | SUTTER | Sutter |
| SHINGLETOWN | Shasta | SUTTER CREEK | Amador |
| SHOSHONE | Inyo | TAFT | Kern |
| SIERRA CITY | Sierra | TAHOE CITY | Placer |
| SIERRA MADRE | Los Angeles | TAHOE VISTA | Placer |
| SIERRAVILLE | Sierra | TALMAGE | Mendocino |
| SILVERADO | Orange | TARZANA | Los Angeles |
| SIMI VALLEY | Ventura | TAYLORSVILLE | Plumas |
| SKYFOREST | San Bernardino | TECATE | San Diego |
| SLOUGHHOUSE | Sacramento | TECOPA | Inyo |
| SMARTVILLE | Yuba | TEHACHAPI | Kern |
| SMITH RIVER | Del Norte | TEHAMA | Tehama |
| SNELLING | Merced | TEMECUIA | Riverside |
| SODA SPRINGS | Nevada | TEMPLE CITY | Los Angeles |
| SOLANA BEACH | San Diego | TEMPLETON | San Luis Obispo |
| SOLEDAD | Monterey | TERMO | Lassen |
| SOLVANG | Santa Barbara | TERRA BELLA | Tulare |
| SOMERSET | El Dorado | THERMAL | Riverside |
| SOMIS | Ventura | THORNTON | San Joaquin |
| SONOMA | Sonoma | THOUSAND OAKS | Ventura |
| SONORA | Tuolumne | THOUSAND PALMS | Riverside |
| SOQUEL | Santa Cruz | THREE RIVERS | Tulare |
| SOULSBYVILLE | Tuolumne | TIPTON | Tulare |
| SOUTH DOS PALOS | Merced | TOLLHOUSE | Fresno |
| SOUTH GATE | Los Angeles | TOMALES | Marin |
| SOUTH LAKE TAHOE | El Dorado | TOPANGA | Los Angeles |
| SOUTH PASADENA | Los Angeles | TOPAZ | Mono |
| SOUTH SAN FRANCISO | San Mateo | TORRANCE | Los Angeles |
| SPRING VALLEY | San Diego | TRABUCO CANYON | Orange |
| SPRINGVILLE | Tulare | TRACY | San Joaquin |
| STANDISH | Lassen | TRANQUILLITY | Fresno |
| STANTON | Orange | TRAVER | Tulare |
| STEVINSON | Merced | TRES PINOS | San Benito |
| STEWARTS POINT | Sonoma | TRINIDAD | Humboldt |
| STINSON BEACH | Marin | TRINITY CENTER | Trinity |
| STIRLING CITY | Butte | TRONA | San Bernardino |

| | | | |
|---|---|---|---|
| TRUCKEE | Nevada | WESTMINSTER | Orange |
| TUJUNGA | Los Angeles | WESTMORLAND | Imperial |
| TULARE | Tulare | WEST POINT | Calaveras |
| TULELAKE | Siskiyou | WEST SACRAMENTO | Yolo |
| TUOLUMNE | Tuolumne | WESTWOOD | Lassen |
| TUPMAN | Kern | WHEATLAND | Yuba |
| TURLOCK | Stanislaus | WHISKEYTOWN | Shasta |
| TUSTIN | Orange | WHITETHORN | Humboldt |
| TWAIN | Plumas | WHITE WATER | Riverside |
| TWAIN HARTE | Tuolumne | WHITMORE | Shasta |
| TWENTYNINE PALMS | San Bernardino | WHITTIER | Los Angeles |
| TWIN BRIDGES | El Dorado | WILDOMAR | Riverside |
| TWIN PEAKS | San Bernardino | WILLIAMS | Colusa |
| UKIAH | Mendocino | WILLITS | Mendocino |
| UNION CITY | Alameda | WILLOW CREEK | Humboldt |
| UPLAND | San Bernardino | WILLOWS | Glenn |
| UPPER LAKE | Lake | WILLMINGTON | Los Angeles |
| VACAVILLE | Solano | WILSEYVILLE | Calaveras |
| VALLECITO | Calaveras | WILTON | Sacramento |
| VALLEJO | Solano | WINCHESTER | Riverside |
| VALLEY CENTER | San Diego | WINDSOR | Sonoma |
| VALLEY FORD | Sonoma | WINTERHAVEN | Imperial |
| VALLEY HOME | Stanislaus | WINTERS | Yolo |
| VALLEY SPRINGS | Calaveras | WINTON | Merced |
| VAN NUYS | Los Angeles | WOFFORD HEIGHTS | Kern |
| VENICE | Los Angeles | WOODACRE | Marin |
| VENTURA | Ventura | WOODBRIDGE | San Joaquin |
| VERDUGO CITY | Los Angeles | WOODLAKE | Tulare |
| VICTOR | San Joaquin | WOODLAND HILLS | Los Angeles |
| VICTIORVILLE | San Bernardino | WOODY | Kern |
| VILIA GRANDE | Sonoma | WRIGHTWOOD | San Bernardino |
| VINA | Tehama | YERMO | San Bernardino |
| VINEBURG | Sonoma | YETTEM | Tulare |
| VINTON | Plumas | YOLO | Yolo |
| VISALIA | Tulare | YORBA LINDA | Orange |
| VISTA | San Diego | YORKVILLE | Mendocino |
| VOLCANO | Amador | YOSEMITE NATIONAL PARK | Mariposa |
| WALLACE | Calaveras | YOUNTVILLE | Napa |
| WALNUT | Los Angeles | YREKA | Siskiyou |
| WALNUT CREEK | Contra Costa | YUBA CITY | Sutter |
| WALNUT GROVE | Sacramento | YUCAIPA | San Bernardino |
| WARNER SPRINGS | San Diego | YUCCA VALLEY | San Bernardino |
| WASCO | Kern | ZAMORA | Yolo |
| WASHINGTON | Nevada | ZENIA | Trintiy |
| WATERFORD | Stanislaus | **COLORADO** | |
| WATSONVILLE | Santa Cruz | ADAM CITY | Adams |
| WEAVERVILLE | Trinity | ADAMS ST COLL | Alamosa |
| WEED | Siskiyou | AGAGE | Elbert |
| WEIMAR | Placer | AGUILAR | Las Animas |
| WELDON | Kern | AKRON | Washington |
| WEOTT | Humboldt | ALAMOSA | Alamosa |
| WEST COVINA | Los Angeles | ALCOTT | Denver |
| WESTLEY | Stanislaus | ALLENSPARK | Boulder |

| | | | |
|---|---|---|---|
| ALMA | Park | CADDOA | Bent |
| ALMONT | Gunnison | CAHONE | Dolores |
| ALTURA | Adams | CALHAN | El Paso |
| AMHERST | Phillips | CAMPO | Baca |
| ANTARES | El Paso | CANYON CITY | Fremont |
| ANTON | Washington | CAPULIN | Conejos |
| ANTONITO | Conejos | CARBONDALE | Garfield |
| ARAPAHOE | Cheyenne | CARR | Weld |
| ARAPAHOE EAST | Arapahoe | CASCADE | El Paso |
| ARBOLES | Archuleta | CASTLE ROCK | Douglas |
| ARBOR VILLAGE | Jefferson | CEDAREDGE | Delta |
| ARLINGTON | Kiowa | CENTER | Rio Grande |
| ARRIBA | Lincoln | CENTRAL CITY | Gilpin |
| ARVADA | Jefferson | CHAMA | Costilla |
| ASPEN | Pitkin | CHERAW | Otero |
| ATWOOD | Logan | CHERRY CREEK | Denver |
| AULT | Weld | CHERRY HILLS VILLAGE | Arapahoe |
| AURORA | Adams | CHEYENNE WELLS | Cheyenne |
| AUSTIN | Delta | CHIMNEY ROCK | Archuleta |
| AVON | Eagle | CHIPITA PARK | El Paso |
| AVONDALE | Pueblo | CHIVINGTON | Kiowa |
| BAILEY | Park | CHROMO | Archuleta |
| BASALT | Eagle | CIMARRON | Montrose |
| BAYFIELD | La Plata | CLARK | Routt |
| BEAR VALLEY | Denver | CLIFTON | Mesa |
| BEDROCK | Montrose | CLIMAX | Lake |
| BELLVUE | Larimer | COAL CREEK | Fremont |
| BELMONT | Pueblo | COALDALE | Fremont |
| BENNETT | Adams | COALMONT | Jackson |
| BERTHOUD | Larimer | COKEDALE | Las Animas |
| BETHUNE | Kit Carson | COLBRAN | Mesa |
| BEULAH | Pueblo | COLLEGE HEIGHTS | La Plata |
| BLACK HAWK | Gilpin | COLORADO CITY | Pueble |
| BLANCO | Costilla | COLORADO SPRINGS | El Paso |
| BONCARBO | Las Animas | COLORADO ST UNIV | Larimer |
| BOND | Eagle | COLUMBINE HILLS | Arapahoe |
| BOONE | Pueblo | COLUMBINE VALLEY | Arapahoe |
| BOULDER | Boulder | COMMERCE CITY | Adams |
| BOW MAR | Arapahoe | COMO | Park |
| BOYERO | Lincoln | CONEJOS | Conejos |
| BRANDON | Kiowa | CONIFER | Jefferson |
| BRANSON | Las Animas | COPE | Washington |
| BRECKENRIDGE | Summit | COPPER MOUNTAIN | Sununit |
| BRIGGSDALE | Weld | CORTEZ | Montezuma |
| BRIGHTON | Adams | CORY | Delta |
| BRISTON | Prowers | COTOPAXI | Fremont |
| BROOMFIELD | Boulder | COWDREY | Jackson |
| BRUSH | Morgan | CRAIG | Moffat |
| BUENA VISTA | Chaffee | CRAWFORD | Delta |
| BUFFALO CREEK | Jefferson | CREEDE | Mineral |
| BURLINGTON | Kit Carson | CRESTED BUTTE | Gunnison |
| BURNS | Eagle | CRESTONE | Saguache |
| BYERS | Arapahoe | CRIPPLE CREEK | Teller |

| | | | |
|---|---|---|---|
| CROOK | Logan | FLORISSANT | Teller |
| CROWLEY | Crowley | FORT CARSON | El Paso |
| CUCHARA | Huerfano | FORT COLLINS | Larimer |
| DACONA | Weld | FORT GARLAND | Costilla |
| DE BEQUE | Mesa | FORT LUPTON | Weld |
| DECKERS | Sedalia | FORT LYON | Bent |
| DEER TRAIL | Arapahoe | FORT MORGAN | Morgan |
| DELHI | Las Animas | FOUNTAIN | El Paso |
| DEL NORTE | Rio Grande | FOWLER | Otero |
| DELTA | Delta | FOXTON | Jefferson |
| DENVER | Denver | FRANKTOWN | Douglas |
| DEORA | Las Animas | FRASER | Grand |
| DILLON | Summit | FREDERICK | Weld |
| DINOSAUR | Moffat | FRISCO | Summit |
| DIVIDE | Teller | FRUITA | Mesa |
| DOLORES | Montezuma | FRUITVALE | Mesa |
| DOVE CREEK | Dolores | GALETON | Weld |
| DOYLEVILLE | Gunnison | GARCIA | Costilla |
| DRAKE | Larimer | GARDEN CITY | Greeley |
| DUMONT | Clear Creek | GARDNER | Huerfano |
| DUPONT | Adams | GARFIELD | Chaffee |
| DURANGO | La Plata | GATEWAY | Mesa |
| EADS | Kiowa | GATEWAY | Adams |
| EAGLE | Eagle | GENOA | Lincoln |
| EASTLAKE | Adams | GEORGETOWN | Clear Creek |
| EAST QUINCY | Denver | GILCREST | Weld |
| EATON | Weld | GILL | Weld |
| ECKERT | Delta | GILMAN | Eagle |
| ECKLEY | Yuma | GLADE PARK | Mesa |
| EDEGEWATER | Denver | GLENDALE | Denver |
| EDWARDS | Eagle | GLEN HAVEN | Larimer |
| EGNAR | San Miguel | GLENWOOD SPRINGS | Garfield |
| ELBERT | Elbert | GOLDEN | Jefferson |
| ELDORADO SPRINGS | Boulder | GRANADA | Prowers |
| ELIZABETH | Elbert | GRANBY | Grand |
| EL JEBEL | Eagle | GRAND JUNCTION | Mesa |
| ELK SPRINGS | Moffat | GRAND LAKE | Grand |
| EL RANCHO | Jefferson | GRANITE | Chaffee |
| EMPIRE | Clear Creek | GRANT | Park |
| ENGLEWOOD | Arapahoe | GREELEY | Weld |
| ERIE | Boulder | GREEN MOUNTAIN FALLS | El Paso |
| ESTES PARK | Larimer | GREENWOOD VILLAGE | Arapahoe |
| EVANS | Weld | GROVER | Weld |
| EVERGREEN | Jefferson | GUFFEY | Park |
| FAIRPLAY | Park | GULNARE | Las Animas |
| FALCON AIR STATION | El Paso | GUNNISON | Gunnison |
| FARISITA | Huerfano | GYPSUM | Eagle |
| FIRESTONE | Weld | HALE | Yuma |
| FITZSIMONS AMC | Adams | HAMILTON | Moffat |
| FLAGLER | Kit Carson | HARTMAN | Prowers |
| FLEMING | Logan | HARTSEL | Park |
| FLETCHER | Adams | HASTY | Bent |
| FLORENCE | Fremont | HASWELL | Kiowa |

| | | | |
|---|---|---|---|
| HAXTUN | Phillips | LAKE GEORGE | Park |
| HAYDEN | Routt | LAKEWOOD | Jefferson |
| HENDERSON | Adams | LAMAR | Prowers |
| HEREFORD | Weld | LAPORTE | Larimer |
| HESPERUS | La Plata | LARKSPUR | Douglas |
| HIGHLANDS RANCH | Arapahoe | LASALLE | Weld |
| HIGH MAR | Boulder | LAS ANIMAS | Bent |
| HILLROSE | Morgan | LAVETA | Huerfano |
| HILLSIDE | Fremont | LAZEAR | Delta |
| HOEHNE | Las Animas | LEADVILLE | Lake |
| HOFFMAN HEIGHTS | Adams | LEWIS | Montezuma |
| HOLLY | Prowers | LIMON | Lincoln |
| HOLYOKE | Phillips | LINDON | Washington |
| HOOPER | Alamosa | LITTLETON | Arapahoe |
| HOTCHKISS | Delta | LIVERMORE | Larimer |
| HOT SULPHUR SPRINGS | Grand | LOCHBUI | Adams |
| HOWARD | Freemont | LOG LANE VILLAGE | Morgan |
| HOYT | Morgan | LOMA | Mesa |
| HUDSON | Weld | LONGMONT | Boulder |
| HUGO | Lincoln | LOUISVILLE | Boulder |
| HYGEINE | Boulder | LOUVIERS | Douglas |
| IDAHO SPRINGS | Clear Creek | LOVELAND | Larimer |
| IDALIA | Yuma | LOWRY AFB | Denver |
| IDLEDALE | Jefferson | LUCERNE | Weld |
| IGNACIO | La Plata | LYCAN | Baca |
| ILIFF | Logan | LYONS | Larimer |
| INDIAN HILLS | Jefferson | MACK | Mesa |
| INDIAN TREE | Jefferson | MAHER | Delta |
| IVYWILD | El Paso | MANASSA | Conejos |
| JAMESTOWN | Boulder | MANCOS | Montezuma |
| JANSEN | Las Animas | MANITOU SPRINGS | El Paso |
| JAROSO | Costilla | MANZANOLA | Otero |
| JEFFERSON | Park | MARBLE | Garfield |
| JOES | Yuma | MARVEL | La Plata |
| JOHNSTOWN | Weld | MASONVILLE | Larimer |
| JULESBURG | Sedgwick | MATHESON | Elbert |
| KARVAL | Lincoln | MAYBELL | Moffat |
| KEENESBURG | Weld | MC CLAVE | Bent |
| KERSEY | Weld | MC COY | Eagle |
| KEYSTONE | Summit | MEAD | Weld |
| KIM | Las Animas | MEEKER | Rio Blanco |
| KIOWA | Elbert | MEREDITH | Pitkin |
| KIRK | Yuma | MERINO | Logan |
| KIT CARSON | Cheyenne | MESA | Mesa |
| KITTREDGE | Jefferson | MESA VERDE PARK | Montezuma |
| KREMMLING | Grand | MESITA | Costilla |
| KUTCH | El Paso | MILLIKEN | Weld |
| LAFAYETTE | Boulder | MINTURN | Eagle |
| LA GARITA | Rio Grande | MODEL | Las Animas |
| LAIRD | Yuma | MOFFAT | Saguache |
| LAJARA | Conejos | MOLINA | Mesa |
| LAJUNTA | Otero | MONARCH | Chaffee |
| LAKE CITY | Hinsdale | MONTEBELLO | Denver |

| | | | |
|---|---|---|---|
| MONTCLAIR | Denver | PINECLIFFE | Boulder |
| MONTE VISTA | Rio Grande | PITKIN | Gunnison |
| MONTROSE | Montrose | PLACERVILLE | San Miguel |
| MONUMENT | El Paso | PLATTEVILLE | Weld |
| MORRISON | Jefferson | PLEASANT VIEW | Montezuma |
| MOSCA | Alamosa | PONCHA SPRINGS | Chaffee |
| MOUNTAIN VIEW | Denver | POWDERHORN | Gunnison |
| MOUNT CRESTED BUTTE | Gunnison | PRITCHETT | Baca |
| NATHROP | Chaffee | PRYOR | Huerfano |
| NATURITA | Montrose | PUEBLO | Pueblo |
| NEDERLAND | Boulder | PUEBLO WEST | Pueblo |
| NEW CASTLE | Garfield | PURGATORY | Durango |
| NEW RAYMER | Weld | RAMAH | El Paso |
| NINAVIEW | Las Animas | RAND | Jackson |
| NIWOT | Boulder | RANGELY | Rio Blanco |
| NORTH AVONDALE | Pueblo | RED CLIFF | Eagle |
| NORTH END | El Paso | RED FEATHER LAKES | Larimer |
| NORTHGLENN | Denver | REDSTONE | Carbondale |
| NORTH PECOS | Denver | REDVALE | Montrose |
| NORWOOD | San Miguel | RED WING | Huerfano |
| NUCLA | Montrose | RICO | Dolores |
| NUNN | Weld | RIDGWAY | Ouray |
| OAK CREEK | Routt | RIFLE | Garfield |
| OHIO | Gunnison | ROCKRIMMON | El Paso |
| OLATHE | Montrose | ROCKVALE | Fremont |
| OLNEY SPRINGS | Crowley | ROCKY FORD | Otero |
| OPHIR | San Miguel | ROGGEN | Weld |
| ORCHARD | Morgan | ROLLINSVILLE | Gilpin |
| ORDWAY | Crowley | ROMEO | Conejos |
| OTIS | Washington | ROSITA | Westcliffe |
| OURAY | Ouray | RUSH | El Paso |
| OVID | Sedgwick | RYE | Pueblo |
| PADRONI | Logan | SAGUACHE | Saguache |
| PAGOSA JUNCTION | Archuleta | SALIDA | Chaffee |
| PAGOSA SPRINGS | Archuleta | SAN ACACIO | Coutilla |
| PALISADE | Mesa | SANFORD | Conejos |
| PALMER LAKE | El Paso | SAN LUIS | Costilla |
| PAOLI | Phillips | SAN PABLO | Costilla |
| PAONIA | Delta | SANTA FE | Denver |
| PARACHUTE | Garfield | SAPINERO | Gunnison |
| PARADOX | Montrose | SARGENTS | Saguache |
| PARKDALE | Fremont | SECURITY | El Paso |
| PARKER | Douglas | SEDALIA | Douglas |
| PARK HILL | Denver | SEDGWICK | Sedgwick |
| PARLIN | Gunnison | SEGUNDO | Las Animas |
| PARSHALL | Grand | SEIBERT | Kit Carson |
| PEETZ | Logan | SEVERANCE | Weld |
| PENROSE | Fremont | SHAWNEE | Park |
| PETERSON AFB | El Paso | SHERIDAN | Arapahoe |
| PEYTON | El Paso | SHERIDAN LAKE | Kiowa |
| PHIPPSBURG | Routt | SILT | Garfield |
| PIERCE | Weld | SILVER CLIFF | Custer |
| PINE | Jefferson | SILVER PLUME | Clear Creek |

| | | | |
|---|---|---|---|
| SILVERTHORNE | Summit | VICTOR | Teller |
| SILVERTON | San Juan | VILAS | Baca |
| SIMLA | Elbert | VILIA GROVE | Saguache |
| SLATER | Moffat | VILLEGREEN | Las Animas |
| SLICK ROCK | San Miguel | VIRGINIA DALE | Larimer |
| SMOKY HILL | Adams | VONA | Kit Carson |
| SNOWMASS | Pitkin | WALDEN | Jackson |
| SNYDER | Morgan | WALSENBURG | Huerfano |
| SOMERSET | Gunnison | WALSH | Baca |
| SOPRIS | Las Animas | WARD | Boulder |
| SOUTH DENVER | Denver | WATKINS | Adams |
| SOUTH FORK | Rio Grande | WATTENBURG | Weld |
| SOUTHGLENN | Arapahoe | WELDONA | Morgan |
| SOUTH TRENTON | Denver | WELLINGTON | Larimer |
| SPRINGFIELD | Baca | WELLSHIRE | Denver |
| STARKVILLE | Las Animas | WESTCLIFFE | Custer |
| STEAMBOAT SPRINGS | Routt | WEST END | El Paso |
| STERLING | Logan | WESTERN STATE COLLEGE | Gunnison |
| STOCKYARDS | Denver | WESTMINSTER | Jefferson |
| STONEHAM | Weld | WESTMINSTER | Boulder |
| STONINGTON | Baca | WESTON | Las Animas |
| STRASBURG | Adams | WESTWOOD | Denver |
| STRATTON | Kit Carson | WETMORE | Custer |
| SUGAR CITY | Crowley | WHEAT RIDGE | Jefferson |
| SUNNYSIDE | Denver | WHITEWATER | Mesa |
| SUNSET | Pueblo | WIGGINS | Morgan |
| SWINK | Otero | WILD HORSE | Cheyenne |
| TABERNASH | Grand | WILEY | Prowers |
| TELLURIDE | San Miguel | WILLARD | Logan |
| TEMPLETON | El Paso | WINDSOR | Weld |
| TEXAS CREEK | Fremont | WINTER PARK | Grand |
| THATCHER | Las Animas | WOLCOTT | Eagle |
| THORTON | Denver | WOODLAND PARK | Teller |
| TIMNATH | Larinier | WOODROW | Washington |
| TIMPAS | Otero | WOOD CREEK | Pitkin |
| TOPONAS | Routt | WRAY | Yuma |
| TOWAOC | Montezuma | YAMPA | Routt |
| TOWNER | Kiowa | YELLOW JACKET | Montezuma |
| TRINCHERA | Las Animas | YODER | El Paso |
| TRINIDAD | Las Animas | YUMA | Yuma |
| TWIN LAKES | Lake | **CONNECTICUT** | |
| TWO BUTTES | Baca | ANDOVER | Tolland |
| TYRONE | Las Animas | ANSONIA | New Haven |
| USAF ACADEMY | El Paso | ASHFORD | Windham |
| UNIVERSITY OF CO | Boulder | AVON | Hartford |
| UNIVERSITY PARK | Denver | BARKHAMSTED | Litchfield |
| UNIVERSITY OF DENVER | Denver | BEACON FALLS | New Haven |
| UNIVERSITY OF NO. CO | Weld | BERLIN | Hartford |
| UTLEYVILLE | Baca | BETHANY | New Haven |
| VAIL | Eagle | BETHEL | Fairfield |
| VALDEZ | Segundo | BETHLEHEM | Litchfield |
| VALMONT | Boulder | BLOOMFIELD | Hartford |
| VERNON | Yuma | BOLTON | Tolland |

| Town | County | Town | County |
|---|---|---|---|
| BOZRAH | Tolland | LEBANON | New London |
| BRANFORD | New Haven | LEDYARD | New London |
| BRIDGEPORT | Fairfield | LISBON | New London |
| BRIDGEWATER | Litchfield | LITCHFIELD | Litchfield |
| BRISTOL | Hartford | LYME | New London |
| BROOKFIELD | Fairfield | MADISON | New Haven |
| BROOKLYN | Windham | MANCHESTER | Hartford |
| BURLINGTON | Hartford | MANSFIELD | Tolland |
| CANAAN | Litchfield | MARLBOROUGH | Hartford |
| CANTEBURY | Windham | MERIDEN | New Haven |
| CANTON | Hartford | MIDDLEBURY | New Haven |
| CHAPLIN | Windham | MIDDLEFIELD | Middlesex |
| CHESIRE | New Haven | MIDDLETOWN | Middlesex |
| CHESTER | Middlesex | MILFORD | New Haven |
| CLINTON | Middlesex | MONROE | Fairfield |
| COLCHESTER | New London | MONTVILLE | New London |
| COLEBROOK | Litchfield | MORRIS | Litchfield |
| COLUMBIA | Tolland | NAUGATUCK | New Haven |
| CORNWELL | Litchfield | NEW BRITAIN | Hartford |
| COVENTRY | Tolland | NEW CANAAN | Fairfield |
| CROMWELL | Middlesex | NEW FAIRFIELD | Fairfield |
| DANBURY | Fairfield | NEW HARTFIELD | Litchfield |
| DARIEN | Fairfield | NEW HAVEN | New Haven |
| DEEP RIVER | Middlesex | NEWINGTON | Hartford |
| DERBY | New Haven | NEW LONDON | New London |
| DURHAM | Middlesex | NEW MILFORD | Litchfield |
| EASTFORD | Windham | NEWTOWN | Fairfield |
| EAST GRANBY | Hartford | NORFOLK | Litchfield |
| EAST HADDAM | Middlesex | NORTH BRANFORD | New Haven |
| EAST HAMPTON | Middlesex | NORTH CANAAN | Litchfield |
| EAST HARTFORD | Hartford | NORTH HAVEN | New Haven |
| EAST HAVEN | New Haven | NORTH STONINGTON | New London |
| EAST LYME | New London | NORWALK | Fairfield |
| FAIRFIELD | Fairfield | NORWICH | New London |
| FARMINGTON | Hartford | OLD LYME | New London |
| FRANKLIN | New London | OLD SAYBROOK | Middlesex |
| GLASTONBURY | Hartfield | ORANGE | New Haven |
| GOSHEN | Litchfield | OXFORD | New Haven |
| GRANBY | Hartford | PLAINFIELD | Windham |
| GREENWICH | Fairfield | PLAINVILLE | Hartford |
| GRISWOLD | New London | PLYMOUTH | Litchfield |
| GROTON | New London | POMFRET | Windham |
| GUILFORD | New Haven | PORTLAND | Middlesex |
| HADDAM | Middlesex | PRESTON | New London |
| HAMDEN | New Haven | PROSPECT | New Haven |
| HAMPTON | Windham | PUTNAM | Windham |
| HARTFORD | Hartford | REDDING | Fairfield |
| HARTLAND | Litchfield | RIDGEFIELD | Fairfield |
| HARWINTON | Litchfield | ROCKY HILL | Hartford |
| HEBRON | Tolland | ROXBURY | Litchfield |
| KENT | Litchfield | SALEM | New London |
| KILLINGLY | Windham | SALISBURY | Litchfield |
| KILLINGWORTH | Middlesex | SCOTLAND | Windham |

| | |
|---|---|
| SEYMOUR | New Haven |
| SHARON | Litchfield |
| SHERMAN | Fairfield |
| SHELTON | Fairfield |
| SIMSBURY | Hartford |
| SOMERS | Tolland |
| SOUTHBURY | New Haven |
| SOUTHINGTON | Hartford |
| SOUTH WINDSOR | Hartford |
| SPRAGUE | New London |
| STAFFORD | Tolland |
| STAMFORD | Fairfield |
| STERLING | Windham |
| STONINGTON | New London |
| STRATFORD | Fairfield |
| SUFFIELD | Hartford |
| THOMASTON | Litchfield |
| THOMPSON | Windham |
| TOLLAND | Tolland |
| TORRINGTON | Litchfield |
| TRUMBULL | Fairfield |
| UNION | Tolland |
| VERNON | Tolland |
| VOLUNTOWN | New London |
| WALLINGFORD | New Haven |
| WARREN | Litchfield |
| WASHINGTON | Litchfield |
| WATERBURY | New Haven |
| WATERFORD | New London |
| WATERTOWN | Litchfield |
| WESTBROOK | Middlesex |
| WEST HARTFORD | Harford |
| WEST HAVEN | New Haven |
| WESTON | Fairfield |
| WESTPORT | Fairfield |
| WETHERSFIELD | Hartford |
| WILLINGTON | Tolland |
| WILTON | Fairfield |
| WINCHESTER CENTER | Litchfield |
| WINDHAM | Windham |
| WINDSOR | Hartford |
| WINDSOR LOCKS | Hartford |
| WINSTED | Litchfield |
| WOLCOTT | Litchfield |
| WOODBRIDGE | New Haven |
| WOODBURY | Litchfield |
| WOODSTOCK | Windham |

## DELAWARE

| | |
|---|---|
| AFTON | New Castle |
| ARDEN | New Castle |
| ASHLEY | New Castle |
| AVALON | New Castle |
| BAYVILLE | Sussex |
| BEAR | New Castle |
| BELLEMOOR | New Castle |
| BELLTOWN | Sussex |
| BETHANY BEACH | Sussex |
| BETHEL | Sussex |
| BLADES | Sussex |
| BOWERS | Kent |
| BRIDGEVILLE | Sussex |
| CAMDEN | Kent |
| CANNON | Sussex |
| CAPITOL PARK | Kent |
| CARRCROFT | New Castle |
| CARTER | Kent |
| CASTLE HILLS | New Castle |
| CHESWOLD | Kent |
| CLARKSVILLE | Sussex |
| CLAYMONT | New Castle |
| CLAYTON | Kent |
| COLONIAL HEIGHTS | New Castle |
| CRANSTON HEIGHTS | New Castle |
| DAGSBORO | Sussex |
| DELAWARE CITY | New Castle |
| DELMAR | Sussex |
| DOVER | Kent |
| DOVER AFB | Kent |
| DRUMMOND NORTH | New Castle |
| EBERTON | Kent |
| EDEN PARK | New Castle |
| EDGEMORE | New Castle |
| ELLENDALE | Sussex |
| ELMHURST | New Castle |
| ELSMERE | New Castle |
| FAIRFAX | New Castle |
| FARMINGTON | Kent |
| FEDERAL | New Castle |
| FELTON | Kent |
| FENWICK ISLAND | Sussex |
| FOREST BROOK GLEN | New Castle |
| FOUR SEASONS | New Castle |
| FRANKFORD | Sussex |
| FREDERICA | Kent |
| GARFIELD PARK | New Castle |
| GEORGETOWN | Sussex |
| GLASCOW | New Castle |
| GLENDALE | New Castle |
| GLENVILLE | New Castle |
| GREENVILLE | New Castle |
| GREENWOOD | Sussex |
| HARBESON | Sussex |
| HARRINGTON | Kent |
| HARTLY | Kent |
| HOCKESSIN | New Castle |
| HOLLY OAK | New Castle |

| | | | |
|---|---|---|---|
| HOUSTON | Kent | ALTAMONTE SPRINGS | Seminole |
| INDIAN FIELD | New Castle | ALTHA | Calhoun |
| KENTON | Kent | ALTOONA | Lake |
| KIRKWOOD | New Castle | ALTURAS | Polk |
| LAUREL | Sussex | ALVA | Lee |
| LEBANON | Kent | AMELIA ISLAND | Nassau |
| LEIPSIC | Kent | ANNA MARIA | Manatee |
| LEWES | Sussex | ANTHONY | Marion |
| LINCOLN | Sussex | APAIACHICOLA | Franklin |
| LITTLE CREEK | Kent | APOLLO BEACH | Hillsborough |
| MAGNOLIA | Kent | APOPKA | Orange |
| MANOR | New Castle | ARCADIA | De Soto |
| MARSHALLTON | New Castle | ARCHER | Alachua |
| MIDDLETOWN | New Castle | ARGYLE | Walton |
| MILFORD | Sussex | ARIPEKA | Pasco |
| MILLSBORO | Sussex | ARLINGTON | Duval |
| MILLVILLE | Sussex | ASTATUIA | Lake |
| MILTON | Sussex | ASTOR | Lake |
| MONTCHANIN | New Castle | ATLANTIC | Palm Beach |
| NASSAU | Sussex | ATLANTIC BEACH | Duval |
| NEWARK | New Castle | AUBURNDALE | Polk |
| NEW CASTLE | New Castle | AVENTURA | Dade |
| OCEAN VIEW | Sussex | AVON PARK | Highlands |
| ODESSA | New Castle | AZALEA PARK | Orange |
| PORT PENN | New Castle | BABSON PARK | Polk |
| REHOBOTH BEACH | Sussex | BAGDAD | Santa Rosa |
| ROCKLAND | New Castle | BAKER | Okaloosa |
| ROSELLE | New Castle | BALDWIN | Duval |
| SAINT GEORGES | New Castle | BAL HARBOUR | Dade |
| SANDTOWN | Kent | BALM | Hillsborough |
| SCOTTFIELD | New Castle | BARBERVILLE | Volusia |
| SEABREEZE | Sussex | BAREFOOT BAY | Indian River |
| SEAFORD | Sussex | BARRY UNIVERSITY | Dade |
| SELBYVILLE | Sussex | BARTOW | Polk |
| SMYRNA | Kent | BASCOM | Jackson |
| STANTON | New Castle | BASINGER | Okeechobee |
| STAR HILL | Kent | BAYONET POINT | Pasco |
| TALLEYVILLE | New Castle | BAY PINES | Pinellas |
| TOWNSEND | New Castle | BAY POINT | Bay |
| VARLANO | New Castle | BAY VISTA | Dade |
| VIOLA | Kent | BEACON LIGHT | Broward |
| WELSHIRE | New Castle | BELL | Gilchrist |
| WILMINGTON | New Castle | BELLE GLADE | Palm Beach |
| WOODBROOK | New Castle | BELLEVIEW | Marion |
| WOODSIDE | Kent | BEULAH | Escambia |
| WYOMING | Kent | BEVERLY HILLS | Citrus |
| YORKLYN | New Castle | BIG PINE KEY | Monroe |
| **FLORIDA** | | BISCAYNE ONE | Dade |
| ALACHUA | Alachua | BLOUNTSTOWN | Calhoun |
| ALFORD | Jackson | BLUEWATER BAY | Okaloosa |
| ALLANDALE | Volusia | BOCA GRANDE | Lee |
| ALLAPATTAH | Dade | BOCA RATON | Palm Beach |
| ALOMA | Orange | BOKEELIA | Lee |

| | | | |
|---|---|---|---|
| BONIFAY | Holmes | CITRA | Marion |
| BONITA SPRINGS | Lee | CITY OF SUNRISE | Broward |
| BOSTWICK | Putnam | CLARCONA | Orange |
| BOWLING GREEN | Hardee | CLARKSVILLE | Calhoun |
| BOYNTON BEACH | Palm Beach | CLEARWATER | Pinellas |
| BRADEN RIVER | Manatee | CLEARWATER BEACH | Pinellas |
| BRADENTON | Manatee | CLERMONT | Lake |
| BRADENTON BEACH | Sarasota | CLEWISTON | Hendry |
| BRADLEY | Polk | COCOA | Brevard |
| BRANDON | Hillsborough | COCOA BEACH | Brevard |
| BRANFORD | Suwanee | COCONUT CREEK | Broward |
| BRENT | Escambia | COCONUT GROVE | Dade |
| BRIGHT | Dade | COLEE | Broward |
| BRINY BREEZES | Palm Beach | COLEMAN | Sumter |
| BRISTON | Liberty | COLLEGE PARK | Orange |
| BRONSON | Levy | COLONIALTOWN | Orange |
| BROOKER | Bradford | COOPER CITY | Broward |
| BROOKSVILLE | Hernando | COPELAND | Collier |
| BRUCE | Holmes | CORAL GABLES | Dade |
| BRYANT | Palm Beach | CORAL RIDGE | Broward |
| BRYCEVILLE | Nassau | CORAL SPRINGS | Broward |
| BUENA VENTURA LAKES | Osceola | CORDOVA | Escambia |
| BUENA VISTA | Dade | CORTEZ | Manatee |
| BUNNELL | Flagler | COTTONDALE | Jackson |
| BUSHNELL | Sumter | COUNTRYSIDE | Marion |
| CALLAHAN | Nassau | COVE | Bay |
| CALLAWAY | Bay | COYTOWN | Orange |
| CAMPBELLTON | Jackson | CRAWFORDVILLE | Wakulla |
| CANAL POINT | Palm Beach | CRESCENT CITY | Putnam |
| CANDLER | Marion | CRESTVIEW | Okalooga |
| CANTONMENT | Escambia | CROSS CITY | Dixie |
| CAPE CANAVERAL | Brevard | CROSSROADS | Pinellas |
| CAPE CORAL | Lee | CRYSTAL BEACH | Pinellas |
| CAPTIVA | Lee | CRYSTAL RIVER | Citrus |
| CAROL CITY | Dade | CRYSTAL SPRINGS | Pasco |
| CARRABELLE | Franklin | CYPRESS | Jackson |
| CARROLLWOOD | Hillsborough | CYPRESS | Broward |
| CARVER | Duval | CYPRESS GARDENS | Polk |
| CARYVILLE | Washington | DADE CITY | Pasco |
| CASSADAGA | Volusia | DANIA | Broward |
| CASSELBERRY | Seminole | DAVENPORT | Polk |
| CEDAR KEY | Levy | DAVIE | Broward |
| CEDAR SHORES | Marion | DAY | Lafayette |
| CECIL FIELD NAS | Duval | DAYTONA BEACH | Volusia |
| CENTER HILL | Sumter | DAYTONA BEACH SHORES | Volusia |
| CENTERVILLE | Leon | DE BARRY | Volusia |
| CENTURY | Escambia | DEERFIELD BEACH | Broward |
| CHATTAHOOCHEE | Gadsden | De FUNIAK SPRINGS | Walton |
| CHIEFLAND | Levy | De LAND | Volusia |
| CHIPLEY | Washington | De LEON SPRINGS | Volusia |
| CHOKOLOSKEE | Collier | DELRAY BEACH | Palm Beach |
| CHRISTMAS | Orange | DELTONA | Volusia |
| CHULUOTA | Seminole | DESTIN | Okaloosa |

| | | | |
|---|---|---|---|
| DINSMORE | Duval | FLAGLER BEACH | Flagler |
| DIPLOMAT MALL | Hallandale | FLAMINGO | Dade |
| DIXIEIAND | Polk | FLORAHOME | Putnam |
| DIXIE VILLAGE | Orange | FLORAL CITY | Citrus |
| DOCTORS INLET | Clay | FLORENCE VILLA | Polk |
| DONA VISTA | Lake | FLORIDA A&M UNIV | Leon |
| DOVER | Hillsborough | FLORIDA CITY | Dade |
| DOVER SHORES | Orange | FLORIDA STATE UNIV | Leon |
| DOWLING PARK | Suwannee | FOREST CITY | Seminole |
| DUNDEE | Polk | FOREST HILLS | Hillsborough |
| DUNEDIN | Pinellas | FORT LAUDERDALE | Broward |
| DUNNELLON | Marion | FORT McCOY | Marion |
| DURANT | Hillsborough | FORT MEADE | Polk |
| EAGLE LAKE | Polk | FORT MYERS | Lee |
| EARLETON | Alachua | FORT MYERS BEACH | Lee |
| EASTGATE | Orange | FORT OGDEN | DeSoto |
| EAST HILL | Escambia | FORT PIERCE | Saint Lucie |
| EASTLAKE WEIR | Marion | FORT WALTON BEACH | Okaloosa |
| EAST PALATKA | Putnam | FORT WHITE | Columbia |
| EASTPOINT | Franklin | FOUNTAIN | Bay |
| EAST SIDE | Seminole | FREEPORT | Walton |
| EATON PARK | Polk | FROSTPROOF | Polk |
| EATONVILLE | Maitland | FRUITLAND PARK | Lake |
| EAU GALLIE | Brevard | GAINESVILLE | Alachua |
| EBRO | Washington | GENEVA | Seminole |
| EDGAR | Putnam | GEORGETOWN | Putnam |
| EDGEWATER | Volusia | GIBSONIA | Polk |
| EDISON CENTER | Dade | GIBSONTON | Hillsborough |
| EGLIN A F B | Okaloosa | GLEN SAINT MARY | Baker |
| ELFERS | Pasco | GLENWOOD | Volusia |
| EL JOBEAN | Charlotte | GOLDEN GATE | Collier |
| ELKTON | Saint Johns | GOLDENROD | Seminole |
| ELLETON | Manatee | GONZALEZ | Escambia |
| ELOISE | Polk | GOODLAND | Collier |
| ENGLEWOOD | Sarasota | GOTHA | Orange |
| ENSLEY | Eacambia | GOULDS | Dade |
| ENTERPRISE | Orange City | GRACEVILLE | Jackson |
| ESTERO | Lee | GRAHAM | Bradford |
| ESTO | Holmes | GRANDIN | Putnam |
| EUCLID | Pinellas | GRAND ISIAND | Lake |
| EUSTIS | Lake | GRAND RIDGE | Jackson |
| EVERGLADES CITY | Collier | GRANT | Brevard |
| EVINSTON | Alachua | GRATIGNY | Dade |
| FAIRFIELD | Marion | GREEN COVE SPRINGS | Clay |
| FAIRVILLA | Orange | GREENSBORO | Gadsden |
| FEDHAVEN | Polk | GREENVILLE | Madison |
| FELDA | Hendry | GREENWOOD | Jackson |
| FELLSMERE | Indian River | GRENELEFE | Polk |
| FERNANDINA BEACH | Nassau | GRETNA | Gadsden |
| FERNDALE | Lake | GROVEIAND | Lake |
| FIVE POINTS | Brevard | GULF BREEZE | Santa Rosa |
| FLAGLER | Monroe | GULD GATE | Sarasota |
| FLAGLER | Dade | GULF HAMMOCK | Levy |

| | | | |
|---|---|---|---|
| HAINES CITY | Polk | INTERBAY | Hillsborough |
| HALIANDALE | Broward | INTERCESSION CITY | Osceola |
| HAMILTON | Broward | INTERLACHEN | Putnam |
| HAMPTON | Brafford | INVERNESS | Citrus |
| HARBOR OAKS | Volusia | ISLAMORADA | Monroe |
| HAROLD | Santa Rosa | ISLAND GROVE | Alachua |
| HASTINGS | Saint Johns | ISTACHATTA | Hernando |
| HAVANA | Gadsden | IVES DAIRY | Dade |
| HAWTHORNE | Alachua | JACKSONVILLE | Duval |
| HEATHROW | Seminole | JACKSONVILLE BEACH | Duval |
| HERNANDO | Citrus | JACKSONVILLE NAS | Duval |
| HERNDON | Orange | JASPER | Hamilton |
| HERSCHEL | Duval | JAY | Santa Rosa |
| HIALEAH | Dade | JENNINGS | Hamilton |
| HIALEAH GARDENS | Dade | JENSEN BEACH | Martin |
| HIALEAH LAKES | Dade | JUPITER | Palm Beach |
| HIAWASSEE | Orange | KATHLEEN | Polk |
| HIGHLAND BEACH | Palm Beach | KENANSVILLE | Osceola |
| HIGHLAND CITY | Polk | KENDALL | Dade |
| HIGH SPRINGS | Alachua | KENNEDY SPACE CTR | Orange |
| HILLDALE | Hillsborough | KEY BISCAYNE | Dade |
| HILLIARD | Nassau | KEY COLONY BEACH | Monroe |
| HOBE SOUND | Martin | KEY LARGO | Monroe |
| HOLDER | Citrus | KEYSTONE HEIGHTS | Clay |
| HOLIDAY | Pasco | KEY WEST | Monroe |
| HOLLISTER | Putnam | KILLARNEY | Osceola |
| HOLLYHILL | Volusia | KINARD | Calhoun |
| HOLLYWOOD | Broward | KISSIMMEE | Osceola |
| HOLLYWOOD HILLS | Broward | LABELLE | Hendry |
| HOLMES BEACH | Manatee | LACOOCHEE | Pasco |
| HOLT | Okaloosa | LACROSSE | Alachua |
| HOMELAND | Polk | LADY LAKE | Lake |
| HOMESTEAD | Dade | LAGUNA BEACH | Bay |
| HOMESTEAD AFB | Dade | LAKE ALFRED | Polk |
| HOMOSASSA | Citrus | LAKE BUENA VISTA | Orange |
| HOMOSASSA SPRINGS | Citrus | LAKE BUTLER | Union |
| HORSESHOE BEACH | Dixie | LAKE CITY | Columbia |
| HOSFORD | Liberty | LAKE COMO | Putnam |
| HOWEY IN THE HILLS | Lake | LAKE FOREST | Duval |
| HUDSON | Pasco | LAKE GENEVA | Clay |
| HUNT CLUB | Orange | LAKE HAMILTON | Polk |
| HURLBURT FIELD | Okaloosa | LAKE HARBOR | Palm Beach |
| HUTCHINSON ISLAND | Martin | LAKE HELEN | Volusia |
| IMMOKALEE | Collier | LAKE JEM | Orange |
| INDIANALANTIC | Brevard | LAKELAND | Polk |
| INDIAN HARBOR BEACH | Brevard | LAKE MARY | Seminole |
| INDIAN LAKE ESTATES | Polk | LAKE MONROE | Seminole |
| INDIAN RIVER CITY | Brevard | LAKE PANASOFFKEE | Sumter |
| INDIAN RIVER SHORES | Indian River | LAKE PARK | West Palm Beach |
| INDIAN ROCKS BEACH | Pinellas | LAKE PLACID | Highlands |
| INDIANTOWN | Martin | LAKE SHORE | Duval |
| INGLIS | Levy | LAKE WALES | Polk |
| INNERARITY POINT | Escambia | LAKE WORTH | Palm Beach |

| | | | |
|---|---|---|---|
| LAMONT | Jefferson | MAYPORT | Duval |
| LANARK VILLAGE | Franklin | MAYPORT NAVAL STA | Duval |
| LAND O'LAKES | Pasco | MAYO | Lafayette |
| LANTANA | Lake Worth | MC ALPIN | Suwannee |
| LARGO | Pinellas | MC DAVID | Escambia |
| LAUREL | Sarasota | MCINTOSH | Marion |
| LAUREL HILL | Okaloosa | MELBOURNE | Brevard |
| LAWTEY | Bradford | MELBOURNE BEACH | Brevard |
| LECANTO | Citrus | MELROSE | Putnam |
| LEE | Madison | MERRITT ISLAND | Brevard |
| LEESBURG | Lake | MEXICO BEACH | Bay |
| LEHIGH ACRES | Lee | MIAMI | Dade |
| LEON | Leon | MICANOPY | Alachua |
| LIGHTHOUSE POINT | Broward | MICCOSUKEC | Leon |
| LITHIA | Hillsborough | MIDDLEBURG | Clay |
| LITTLE RIVER | Dade | MIDWAY | Gadsden |
| LIVE OAK | Suwannee | MILLIGAN | Okaloosa |
| LLOYD | Jefferson | MILTON | Santa Rosa |
| LOCHLOOSA | Alachua | MIMS | Brevard |
| LOCKHART | Orange | MINNEOLA | Lake |
| LONG KEY | Monroe | MIRACLE MILE | Lee |
| LONGBOAT KEY | Manatee | MIRAMAR | Broward |
| LONGWOOD | Seminole | MOLINO | Escambia |
| LORIDA | Highlands | MONTICELLO | Jefferson |
| LOUGHMAN | Polk | MONTVERDE | Lake |
| LOWELL | Marion | MOORE HAVEN | Glades |
| LOXAHATCHEE | Palm Beach | MORRISTON | Levy |
| LUDLAM | Dade | MOSSY HEAD | Walton |
| LULU | Columbia | MOUNT DORA | Lake |
| LUTZ | Hillsborough | MOUNT PLEASANT | Gadsden |
| LYNN HAVEN | Bay | MULBERRY | Polk |
| MACCLENNY | Baker | MURDOCK | Punta Gorda |
| MAC DILL AFB | Hillsborough | MURRY HILL | Duval |
| MADEIRA BEACH | Pinellas | MYAKKA CITY | Manatee |
| MADISON | Madison | MYRTLE GROVE | Escambia |
| MAINLAND | Volusia | NALCREST | Polk |
| MAITLAND | Orange | NAPLES | Collier |
| MALABAR | Brevard | NARANJA | Dade |
| MALONE | Jackson | NAVAL AIR STA | Escambia |
| MANASOTA | Manatee | NAVAL COASTAL SYST LAB | Bay |
| MANDARIN | Duval | NAVAL HOSP | Escambia |
| MANGO | Hillsborough | NAVAL TRAINING CTR | Orange |
| MAPLE LEAF | Charlotte | NAVARRE | Santa Rosa |
| MARATHON | Monroe | NEWBERRY | Alachua |
| MARCO | Collier | NEW PORT RICHEY | Pasco |
| MARGATE | Broward | NEW RIVER | Broward |
| MARIANNA | Jackson | NEW SMYRNA BEACH | Volusia |
| MARION OAKS | Oscala | NICEVILLE | Okaloosa |
| MARY ESTHER | Okaloosa | NICHOLS | Polk |
| MASARYKTOWN | Hernando | NOBLES | Escambia |
| MASCOTRE | Lake | NOBLETON | Hernando |
| MATLACHA | Lee | NOCATEE | DeSoto |
| MAXVILLE | Duval | NOKOMIS | Sarasota |

| | | | |
|---|---|---|---|
| NOMA | Holmes | PAISLEY | Lake |
| NORLAND | Dade | PALATKA | Putnam |
| NORTH BABCOCK | Brevard | PALMA SOLA | Manatee |
| NORTH BAY VILLAGE | Dade | PALM BAY | Brevard |
| NORTH CORAL SPRINGS | Broward | PALM BEACH | Palm Beach |
| NORTH FORT MYERS | Fort Meyers | PALM BEACH GARDENS | Palm Beach |
| NORTH JACKSONVILLE | Duval | PALM CITY | Martin |
| NORTH LAUDERDALE | Broward | PALM COAST | Flagler |
| NORTH MIAMI | Dade | PALMDALE | Glades |
| NORTH MIAMI BEACH | Dade | PALMETTO | Manatee |
| NORTH PALM BEACH | Palm Beach | PALM HARBOR | Pinellas |
| NORTH PORT | Sarasota | PALM SPRINGS NORTH | Dade |
| NORTHWOOD | West Palm Beach | PALM VILLAGE | Dade |
| OAKCREST | Marion | PANACEA | Wakulla |
| OAK HILL | Volusia | PANAMA CITY | Bay |
| OAKLAND | Orange | PANAMA CITY BEACH | Bay |
| OAKLAND PARK | Broward | PARK AVENUE | Leon |
| O'BRIEN | Suwannee | PARKER | Bay |
| OCALA | Marion | PARRISH | Manatee |
| OCEAN VIEW | Dade | PASS-A-GRILLE BEACH | Pinellas |
| OCHOPEE | Collier | PARTICK AFB | Brevard |
| OCOEE | Orange | PAXTON | Walton |
| ODESSA | Hillsborough | PELLICAN LAKE | Palm Beach |
| OJUS | Dade | PEMBROKE PINES | Broward |
| OKAHUMPKA | Lake | PENINSULA | Dayton Beach |
| OKALOOSA ISLAND | Fort Walton Beach | PENINSUIA | Hillsborough |
| OKEECHOBEE | Okeechobee | PENNEY FARMS | Clay |
| OKLAWAHA | Marion | PENSACOLA | Escambia |
| OLDSMAR | Pinellas | PERRINE | Dade |
| OLD TOWN | Dixie | PERRY | Taylor |
| OLUSTEE | Baker | PIERSON | Volusia |
| OLYMPIA HEIGHTS | Dade | PINE CASTLE | Orange |
| ONA | Hardee | PINE HILLS | Orange |
| ONECO | Manatee | PINELAND | Lee |
| OPA-LOCKA | Dade | PINELLAS PARK | Pinellas |
| OPEN AIR | Pinellas | PINE RIDGE | Broward |
| ORANGE BLOSSUM | Orange | PINETTA | Madison |
| ORANGE CITY | Volusia | PLACIDA | Charlotte |
| ORANGE LAKE | Marion | PLANTATION | Broward |
| ORANGE PARK | Clay | PLANT CITY | Hillsborough |
| ORANGE SPRINGS | Marion | PLYMOUTH | Orange |
| ORLANDO | Orange | POINCINAL | Osceola |
| ORLO VISTA | Orange | POINT ST. JOHN | Cocoa |
| ORMOND BEACH | Volusia | POINT ST. LUCIE | Saint Lucie |
| OSPREY | Sarasota | POINT WASHINGTON | Walton |
| OSTEEN | Volusia | POLK CITY | Polk |
| OTTER CREEK | Levy | POMONA PARK | Putnam |
| OVERSTREET | Gulf | POMPANO BEACH | Broward |
| OVIEDO | Seminole | PONCE | Dade |
| OXFORD | Sumter | PONCE DELEON | Holmes |
| OZONA | Pinellas | PONTE VEDRA BEACH | Saint Johns |
| PACE | Santa Rosa | PORT CHARLOTTE | Charlotte |
| PAHOKEE | Palm Beach | PORT EVERGLADES | Broward |

| | | | |
|---|---|---|---|
| PORT ORANGE | Volusia | SAUFLEY FIELD | Escambia |
| PORT RICHEY | Pasco | SCOTTSMOOR | Brevard |
| PORT SAINT JOE | Gulf | SEASIDE | Walton |
| PORT SALERNO | Martin | SEBASTIAN | Indian River |
| PORT TAMPA CITY | Hillsborough | SEBRING | Highlands |
| POTTSBURG | Duval | SEFFNER | Hillsborough |
| PRINCETON | Dade | SEMINOLE | Pinellas |
| PRODUCE | Hillsborough | SEMINOLE HEIGHTS | Hillsborough |
| PROSPECT | Broward | SEVILLE | Volusia |
| PUNTA GORDA | Charlotte | SHADY GROVE | Taylor |
| PUTNAM HALL | Putnam | SHALIMAR | Okaloosa |
| QUAIL HEIGHTS | Dade | SHARPES | Brevard |
| QUINCY | Gadsden | SHENANDOAH | Dade |
| RAIFORD | Union | SILVER SPRINGS | Marion |
| RAINBOW LAKES | Marion | SILVER SPRINGS SHORES | Marion |
| RED BAY | Holmes | SINGER ISLAND | Palm Beach |
| REDDICK | Marion | SNAPPER CREEK | Dade |
| REGENCY | Duval | SNEADS | Jackson |
| RIDGE MANOR | Pasco | SOPCHOPPY | Wakulla |
| RIVER RANCH | Polk | SORRENTO | Lake |
| RIVERSIDE | Dade | SOUTH BAY | Palm Beach |
| RIVERVIEW | Hillsborough | SOUTHBORO | West Palm Beach |
| RIVIERA BEACH | Palm Beach | SOUTH DAYTON | Volusia |
| ROCKLEDGE | Brevard | SOUTH DIXIE | Dade |
| ROSELAND | Indian River | SOUTH FLORIDA | Broward |
| ROTUNDA WEST | Charlotte | SOUTHGATE | Sarasota |
| ROYAL OAKS | Orange | SOUTH JACKSONVILLE | Duval |
| RUBONIA | Manatee | SOUTH MIAMI | Dade |
| RUSKIN | Hillsborough | SOUTHPORT | Bay |
| SAFETY HARBOR | Pinellas | SOUTHSIDE | Broward |
| SAINT ANDREWS | Bay | SOUTHSIDE | Polk |
| SAINT AUGUSTINE | Saint Johns | SPARR | Marion |
| SAINT CLOUD | Osceola | SPRINGFIELD | Bay |
| SAINT GEORGE ISLAND | Franklin | SPRING HILL | Hernando |
| SAINT JAMES CITY | Lee | STARKE | Bradford |
| SAINT LEO | Pasco | STEINHATCHEE | Taylor |
| SAINT MARKS | Wakulla | STUART | Martin |
| SAINT PETERSBURG | Pinellas | SULPHUR SPRINGS | Hillsborough |
| SAINT PETERSBURG BEACH | Pinellas | SUMANTRA | Liberty |
| SALEM | Taylor | SUMMERFIELD | Marion |
| SALT SPRING | Marion | SUMMERLAND KEY | Monroe |
| SAMPLE SQUARE | Broward | SUMTERVILLE | Sumter |
| SAN ANTONIO | Pasco | SUN CITY | Hillsborough |
| SANDERSON | Baker | SUN CITY CENTER | Hillsborough |
| SANDESTIN | Okaloosa | SUNNILAND | Dade |
| SAND LAKE | Orange | SUNNYSIDE | Bay |
| SANFORD | Seminole | SUNRISE | Broward |
| SANIBEL | Lee | SUNSET | Dade |
| SAN MATEO | Putnam | SUNTREE | Brevard |
| SANTA FE | Alachua | SURFSIDE | Dade |
| SANTA ROSA BEACH | Walton | SUWANNEE | Dixie |
| SARASOTA | Sarasota | SYDNEY | Hillsborough |
| SATSUMA | Putnam | TALLAHASSEE | Leon |

| | | | |
|---|---|---|---|
| TALLEVAST | Manatee | WEST ATLANTIC | Broward |
| TAMARAC | Broward | WEST BAY | Bay |
| TAMIAMI | Dade | WEST CORAL SPRINGS | Broward |
| TAMPA | Hillsborough | WEST DADE | Dade |
| TANGERINE | Orange | WEST END | Jackson |
| TARPON SPRINGS | Pinellas | WEST HOLLYWOOD | Broward |
| TAVARES | Lake | WEST KENDALL | Dade |
| TAVERNIER | Monroe | WEST LANTANA | Palm Beach |
| TELOGIA | Liberty | WEST MELBOURNE | Brevard |
| TEMPLE TERRACE | Hillsborough | WEST PALM BEACH | Palm Beach |
| TEQUESTA | Palm Beach | WEST PALMETTO PARK | Boca Raton |
| TERRA CEIA | Manatee | WEST PANAMA CITY BEACH | Bay |
| THONOTOSASSA | Hillsborough | WESTSIDE | Marion |
| TICE | Lee | WESTSIDE CROSSING | Orange |
| TIERRA VERDE | Pinellas | WEST TAMPA | Hillsborough |
| TIGER POINT | Gulf Breeze | WESTVILLE | Holmes |
| TITUSVILLE | Brevard | WEWAHITCHKA | Gulf |
| TRENTON | Gilchrist | WHITE CITY | Gulf |
| TRILBY | Pasco | WHITE HOUSE | Duval |
| TROPIC | Indian River | WHITE SPRINGS | Hamilton |
| TUSKAWILLA | Seminole | WHITING FIELD | Santa Rosa |
| TYNDALL AFB | Bay | WILDWOOD | Sumter |
| ULETA | Dade | WILLIAMSBURG | Orange |
| UNION PARK | Orange | WILLISTON | Levy |
| UNIVERSITY | Alachua | WIMAUMA | Hillsborough |
| UNIV OF MIAMI | Dade | WINDERMERE | Orange |
| UNIV OF WEST FL | Escambia | WINTER BEACH | Indian River |
| UMATILLA | Lake | WINTER GARDEN | Orange |
| VALPARAISO | Okaloosa | WINTER HAVEN | Polk |
| VALRICO | Hillsborough | WINTER PARK | Orange |
| VENICE | Sarasota | WINTER SPRINGS | Seminole |
| VENTURO | Orange | WOODLAND | Boca Raton |
| VENUS | Highlands | WOODMONT | Broward |
| VERNON | Washington | WOODVILLE | Leon |
| VERO BEACH | Indian River | WORTHINGTON SPRINGS | Union |
| VILLAGE | Broward | YALAHA | Lake |
| VILIAGE GREEN | Rockledge | YANKEETOWN | Levy |
| WABASSO | Indian River | YBAR | Hillsborough |
| WACISSA | Jefferson | YOUNGSTOWN | Bay |
| WAKULLA SPRINGS | Wakulla | YULEE | Nassau |
| WALDO | Alachua | ZELLWOOD | Orange |
| WALNUT HILL | Escambia | ZEPHYRHILLS | Pasco |
| WARM MINERAL SPRINGS | Venice | ZOLFO SPRINGS | Hardee |
| WARRINGTON | Escambia | **GEORGIA** | |
| WAUCHULA | Hardee | ABAC | Tift |
| WAUSAU | Washington | ABBEVILLE | Wilcox |
| WAVERLY | Polk | ACWORTH | Cobb |
| WEBSTER | Sumter | ADAIRSVILLE | Bartow |
| WEIRSDALE | Marion | ADEL | Cook |
| WELAKA | Putnam | ADRIAN | Emanuel |
| WELLBORN | Suwannee | AGNES SCOTT COLLEGE | DeKalb |
| WESLEY CHAPEL | Pasco | AILEY | Montgomery |
| WESLEY MANOR | Duval | ALAMO | Wheeler |

| | | | |
|---|---|---|---|
| ALAPAHA | Berrien | BOGART | Clarke |
| ALBANY | Dougherty | BOLINGBROKE | Monroe |
| ALLENHURST | Liberty | BONAIRE | Houston |
| ALLENTOWN | Wilkinson | BONEVILLE | McDuffie |
| ALMA | Bacon | BOSTON | Thomas |
| ALPHARETTA | Fulton | BOSTWICK | Morgan |
| ALSTON | Montgomery | BOWDON | Carroll |
| ALTO | Banks | BOWDON JUNCTION | Carroll |
| AMBROSE | Coffee | BOWERSVILLE | Hart |
| AMERICUS | Sumter | BOWMAN | Elbert |
| ANDERSONVILLE | Sumter | BOX SPRINGS | Talbot |
| APPLING | Columbia | BRASELTON | Jackson |
| ARABI | Crisp | BREMEN | Carroll |
| ARAGON | Polk | BRIARCLIFF | Fulton |
| ARGYLE | Clinch | BRINSON | Decatur |
| ARLINGTON | Calhoun | BRISTOL | Pierce |
| ARMUCHEE | Floyd | BRONWOOD | Terrell |
| ARNOLDSVILLE | Oglethorpe | BROOKFIELD | Tift |
| ASHBURN | Turner | BROOKLET | Bulloch |
| ATHENS | Clarke | BROOKS | Fayette |
| ATLANTA | Fulton | BROXTON | Coffee |
| ATLANTA | DeKalb | BRUNSWICK | Glynn |
| ATRAPULGUS | Decatur | BUCHANAN | Haralson |
| AUBURN | Barrow | BUCKHEAD | Morgan |
| AUGUSTA | Richmond | BUENA VISTA | Marion |
| AUSTELL | Cobb | BUFORD | Gwinnett |
| AVERA | Jefferson | BUTLER | Taylor |
| AVONDALE ESTATES | DeKalb | BYROMVILLE | Dooly |
| AXSON | Atkinson | BYRON | Peach |
| BACONTON | Mitchell | CADWELL | Laurens |
| BAINBRIDGE | Decatur | CAIRO | Grady |
| BAKER VILLAGE | Muscogee | CALHOUN | Gordon |
| BALDWIN | Banks | CALVARY | Grady |
| BALL GROUND | Cherokee | CAMAK | Warren |
| BARNESVILLE | Lamar | CAMILLA | Mitchell |
| BARNEY | Brooks | CANON | Franklin |
| BARRETT PKWY | Cobb | CANOCCHEE | Emanuel |
| BARTOW | Jefferson | CARL | Barrow |
| BARWICK | Brooks | CARLTON | Madison |
| BAXLEY | Appling | CARNESVILLE | Franklin |
| BEALLWOOD | Muscogee | CARROLLTON | Carroll |
| BENEVOLENCE | Randolph | CARTERSVILLE | Bartow |
| BERLIN | Colquitt | CASSVILLE | Bartow |
| BETHLEHEM | Barrow | CATAULA | Harris |
| BIBB CITY | Muscogee | CAVE SPRING | Berrien |
| BISHOP | Oconee | CECIL | Cook |
| BLACKSHEAR | Pierce | CEDAR SPRINGS | Early |
| BLAIRSVILLE | Union | CEDARTOWN | Polk |
| BLAKELY | Early | CHATSWORTH | Murray |
| BLOOMINGDALE | Chatham | CHAUNCEY | Dodge |
| BLUE RIDGE | Fannin | CHERRYLOG | Gilmer |
| BLUFFTON | Clay | CHESTER | Dodge |
| BLYTHE | Richmond | CHESTNUT MOUNTAIN | Hall |

| Place | County | Place | County |
|---|---|---|---|
| CHICKAMAUGA | Walker | DAVISBORO | Washington |
| CHULA | Tift | DAWSON | Terrell |
| CISCO | Murray | DAWSONVILLE | Lumpkin |
| CLARKDALE | Cobb | DE SOTO | Sumter |
| CLARKESVILLE | Habersham | DEARING | McDuffie |
| CLARKSTON | DeKalb | DECATUR | DeKalb |
| CLAXTON | Evans | DEMOREST | Habersham |
| CLAYTON | Rabun | DENTON | Jeff Davis |
| CLERMONT | Hall | DEWY ROSE | Elbert |
| CLEVELAND | White | DEXTER | Laurens |
| CLIMAX | Decatur | DILLARD | Rabun |
| CLINCHFIELD | Houston | DIXIE | Brooks |
| CLYO | Effingham | DOBBINS AFB | Cobb |
| COBB | Sumter | DOERUN | Colquitt |
| COBBTOWN | Candler | DONALSONVILLE | Seminole |
| COCHRAN | Bleckley | DOUGLAS | Coffee |
| COGDELL | Clinch | DOUGLASVILLE | Douglas |
| COHUTTA | Whitfield | DOVER | Screven |
| COLBERT | Madison | DRY BRANCH | Twiggs |
| COLEMAN | Randolph | DU PONT | Clinch |
| COLLINS | Tattnall | DUBLIN | Laurens |
| COLQUITT | Miller | DUDLEY | Laurens |
| COLUMBUS | Muscogee | DULUTH | Gwinnett |
| COMER | Madison | DUNWOODY | DeKalb |
| COMMERCE | Jackson | EASTANOLLEE | Stephens |
| CONCORD | Pike | EAST ATLANTA | Fulton |
| CONCORD SQUARE | Cobb | EAST DUBLIN | Dublin |
| CONLEY | Clayton | EAST ELLIJAY | Gilmer |
| CONYERS | Rockdale | EAST GEORGE | Charlton |
| COLLIDGE | Thomas | EASTMAN | Dodge |
| COOSA | Floyd | EAST MARYS | Camden |
| CORDELE | Crisp | EATONTON | Putnam |
| CORNELIA | Habersham | EDEN | Effingham |
| COTTON | Mitchell | EDISON | Calhoun |
| COURT SQUARE | Laurens | ELBERTON | Elbert |
| COVINGTON | Newton | ELKO | Houston |
| CRANDALL | Murray | ELLABELL | Bryan |
| CRAWFORD | Oglethorpe | ELLAVILLE | Schley |
| CRAWFORDVILLE | Taliaferro | ELLENTON | Colquitt |
| CRESCENT | McIntosh | ELLENWOOD | DeKalb |
| CULLODEN | Monroe | ELLERSLIE | Harris |
| CUMMING | Forsyth | ELLIJAY | Gilmer |
| CUSSETA | Chattahoochee | EMBRY HILLS | Fulton |
| CUTHBERT | Randolph | EMERSON | Bartow |
| DACULA | Gwinnett | EMORY UNIV | Fulton |
| DAHLONEGA | Lumpkin | ENIGMA | Berrien |
| DAISY | Evans | EPWORTH | Fannin |
| DALLAS | Paulding | ESOM HILL | Berrien |
| DALTON | Whitfield | ETON | Murray |
| DAMASCUS | Early | EVANS | Columbia |
| DANIELSVILLE | Madison | EXPERIMENT | Spalding |
| DANVILLE | Twiggs | FAIRBURN | Fulton |
| DARIEN | McIntosh | FAIRMOUNT | Gordon |

| | | | |
|---|---|---|---|
| FARGO | Clinch | HARDWICK | Baldwin |
| FARMINGTON | Oconee | HARLEM | McDuffie |
| FAYETTEVILLE | Fayette | HARRISON | Washington |
| FELTON | Haralson | HARTSFIELD | Colquitt |
| FITZGERALD | Irwin | HARTWELL | Hart |
| FLEMING | Liberty | HAWKINSVILLE | Pulaski |
| FLINTSTONE | Walker | HAZLEHURST | Jeff Davis |
| FLOVILLA | Butts | HELEN | White |
| FLOWERY BRANCH | Hall | HELENA | Telfair |
| FOLKSTON | Charlton | HEPHZIBAH | Richmond |
| FOREST PARK | Clayton | HIAWASSEE | Towns |
| FORSYTH | Monroe | HIGH SHOALS | Morgan |
| FORT BENNING | Muscogee | HILLSBORO | Jasper |
| FORT GAINES | Clay | HINESVILLE | Bryan |
| FORT OGLETHORPE | Catoosa | HIRAM | Paulding |
| FORT VALLEY | Peach | HOBOKEN | Brantley |
| FORTSON | Muscogee | HOGANSVILLE | Troup |
| FOWLSTOWN | Decatur | HOLLY SPRINGS | Cherokee |
| FRANKLIN | Heard | HOMER | Banks |
| FRANKLIN SPRINGS | Franklin | HOMERVILLE | Clinch |
| FUNSTON | Colquitt | HORTENSE | Brantley |
| GAINESVILLE | Hall | HOSCHTON | Jackson |
| GARFIELD | Emanuel | HOWARD | Taylor |
| GAY | Meriwether | HULL | Madison |
| GENEVA | Talbot | IDEAL | Macon |
| GEORGETOWN | Quitman | ILA | Madison |
| GEORGIA SOUTHERN | Bulloch | IRON CITY | Seminole |
| GA SOUTHWESTERN COLL | Sumter | IRWINTON | Wilkinson |
| GEORGIA UNIV | Clarke | IRWINVILLE | Irwin |
| GIBSON | Glascock | JACKSON | Butts |
| GILLSVILLE | Banks | JACKSONVILLE | Telfair |
| GIRARD | Burke | JAKIN | Early |
| GLENNVILLE | Tattnall | JASPER | Dawson |
| GLENWOOD | Wheeler | JEFFERSON | Jackson |
| GOOD HOPE | Walton | JEFFERSONVILLE | Twiggs |
| GORDON | Wilkinson | JENKINSBURG | Butts |
| GRACEWOOD | Richmond | JERSEY | Walton |
| GRANTVILLE | Coweta | JESUP | Wayne |
| GRAY | Jones | JEWELL | Warren |
| GRAYSON | Gwinnett | JONESBORO | Clayton |
| GRAYSVILLE | Catoosa | JULIETTE | Monroe |
| GREENSBORO | Greene | JUNCTION CITY | Talbot |
| GREENVILLE | Meriwether | KATHLEEN | Houston |
| GRESHAM ROAD | Cobb | KENNESAW | Cobb |
| GRIFFIN | Spalding | KEYSVILLE | Burke |
| GROVETOWN | Columbia | KINGSLAND | Camden |
| GUYTON | Effingham | KINGSTON | Bartow |
| HADDOCK | Jones | KITE | Johnson |
| HAGAN | Evans | KNOXVILLE | Crawford |
| HAHIRA | Lowndes | LA FAYETTE | Walker |
| HAMILTON | Harris | LA GRANGE | Troup |
| HAMPTON | Henry | LAKE PARK | Lowndes |
| HARALSON | Coweta | LAKELAND | Lanier |

| | | | |
|---|---|---|---|
| LAKEMONT | Rabun | MIDLAND | Muscogee |
| LAVONIA | Franklin | MIDVILLE | Emanuel |
| LAWRENCEVILLE | Gwinnett | MIDWAY | Liberty |
| LEARY | Calhoun | MILAN | Telfair |
| LEBANON | Cherokee | MILLEDGEVILLE | Baldwin |
| LEESBURG | Lee | MILLEN | Jenkins |
| LENOX | Cook | MILLWOOD | Ware |
| LESLIE | Sumter | MILNER | Lamar |
| LEXINGTON | Oglethorpe | MINERAL BLUFF | Fannin |
| LILBURN | Gwinnett | MITCHELL | Glascock |
| LILLY | Dooly | MOLENA | Upson |
| LINCOLNTON | Lincoln | MONROE | Walton |
| LINDALE | Floyd | MONTEZUMA | Dooly |
| LITHIA SPRINGS | Douglas | MONTICELLO | Jasper |
| LITHONIA | DeKalb | MONTROSE | Laurens |
| LIZELLA | Bibb | MOODY AFB | Valdasta |
| LOCUST GROVE | Henry | MORELAND | Coweta |
| LOGANVILLE | Gwinnett | MORGAN | Calhoun |
| LOOKOUT MOUNTAIN | Walker | MORGANTON | Fannin |
| LOUISVILLE | Jefferson | MORRIS | Quitman |
| LOUVALE | Stewart | MORROW | Clayton |
| LOVEJOY | Clayton | MORVEN | Brooks |
| LUDOWICI | Long | MOULTRIE | Colquitt |
| LULA | Banks | MOUNTAIN CITY | Rabun |
| LUMBER CITY | Telfair | MURRAYVILLE | Hall |
| LUMPKIN | Stewart | MUSELLA | Crawford |
| LUTHERSVILLE | Meriwether | MYSTIC | Irwin |
| LYERLY | Chattooga | NAHUNTA | Brantley |
| LYONS | Toombs | NASHVILLE | Berrien |
| MABLETON | Cobb | NAYLOR | Lowndes |
| MACON | Bibb | NELSON | Cherokee |
| MADISON | Morgan | NEWBORN | Newton |
| MANCHESTER | Meriwether | NEWINGTON | Effingham |
| MANOR | Ware | NEWNAN | Coweta |
| MANSFIELD | Jasper | NEWTON | Baker |
| MARBLE HILL | Pickens | NICHOLLS | Ware |
| MARIETTA | Cobb | NICHOLSON | Jackson |
| MARSHALLVILLE | Macon | NORCROSS | Gwinnett |
| MARTIN | Stephens | NORMAN PARK | Colquitt |
| MAUK | Taylor | NORRISTOWN | Emanuel |
| MAYSVILLE | Jackson | NORWOOD | Warren |
| MC CAYSVILLE | Fannin | NUNEZ | Emanuel |
| MC DONOUGH | Henry | OAKFIELD | Worth |
| MC INTYRE | Wilkinson | OAKMAN | Gordon |
| MC RAE | Telfair | OAKWOOD | Hall |
| MEANSVILLE | Pike | OCHLOCKNEE | Thomas |
| MEIGS | Thomas | OCILLA | Erwin |
| MELDRIM | Effingham | OCONEE | Washington |
| MENLO | Chattooga | ODUM | Wayne |
| MERIDIAN | McIntosh | OFFERMAN | Pierce |
| MERSHON | Bacon | OGLETHORPE | Macon |
| MESENA | Warren | OLIVER | Screven |
| METTER | Candler | OMAHA | Stewart |

| | | | |
|---|---|---|---|
| OMEGA | Tift | ROBERTA | Crawford |
| ORCHARD HILL | Spalding | ROCHELLE | Wilcox |
| OXFORD | Newton | ROCKLEDGE | Laurens |
| PALMETTO | Fulton | ROCKMART | Polk |
| PARROTT | Terrell | ROCK SPRING | Walker |
| PATTERSON | Pierce | ROCKY FACE | Whitfield |
| PAVO | Thomas | ROCKY FORD | Screven |
| PEARSON | Atkinson | ROME | Floyd |
| PELHAM | Mitchell | ROOPVILLE | Carroll |
| PEMBROKE | Bryan | ROSSVILLE | Walker |
| PENDERGRASS | Jackson | ROSWELL | Fulton |
| PERKINS | Jenkins | ROYSTON | Franklin |
| PERRY | Houston | RUPERT | Taylor |
| PINE LAKE | DeKalb | RUTLEDGE | Morgan |
| PINE LOG | Rydal | RYDAL | Bartow |
| PINE MOUNTAIN | Harris | SAINT GEORGE | Charlton |
| PINE MOUNTAIN VALLEY | Harris | SAINT MARYS | Camden |
| PINEHURST | Dooly | SALE CITY | Mitchell |
| PINEVIEW | Wilcox | SANDERSVILLE | Washington |
| PITTS | Wilcox | SAPELO ISLAND | McIntosh |
| PLAINFIELD | Dodge | SARDIS | Burke |
| PLAINS | Sumter | SARGENT | Coweta |
| PLAINVILLE | Gordon | SASSER | Terrell |
| POOLER | Chatham | SAUTEE-NACOOCHEE | White |
| PORTAL | Bulloch | SAVANNAH | Chatham |
| PORTERDALE | Newton | SCOTLAND | Telfair |
| POULAN | Worth | SCOTTDALE | DeKalb |
| POWDER SPRINGS | Cobb | SCREVEN | Wayne |
| PRESTON | Webster | SEA ISLAND | Glynn |
| PULASKI | Candler | SENOIA | Coweta |
| PUTNEY | Dougherty | SEVILLE | Wilcox |
| QUITMAN | Brooks | SHADY DALE | Jasper |
| RABUN GAP | Rabun | SHANNON | Floyd |
| RANGER | Gordon | SHARON | Taliaferro |
| RAY CITY | Berrien | SHARPSBURG | Coweta |
| RAYLE | Taliaferro | SHELLMAN | Randolph |
| REBECCA | Turner | SHILOH | Harris |
| RED OAK | Fulton | SILOAM | Greene |
| REDAN | DeKalb | SILVER CREEK | Floyd |
| REGISTER | Bulloch | SMARR | Monroe |
| REIDSVILLE | Tattnall | SMITHVILLE | Lee |
| RENTZ | Laurens | SMYRNA | Cobb |
| RESACA | Gordon | SNELLVILLE | Gwinnett |
| REX | Clayton | SOCIAL CIRCLE | Walton |
| REYNOLDS | Taylor | SOPERTON | Treutlen |
| RHINE | Dodge | SPARKS | Cook |
| RICEBORO | Liberty | SPARTA | Hancock |
| RICHLAND | Stewart | SPRINGFIELD | Effingham |
| RICHMOND HILL | Bryan | STAPLETON | Jefferson |
| RINCON | Effingham | STATENVILLE | Echols |
| RINGGOLD | Catoosa | STATESBORO | Bulloch |
| RISING FAWN | Dade | STATHAM | Barrow |
| RIVERDALE | Clayton | STEPHENS | Oglethorpe |

| | | | |
|---|---|---|---|
| STILLMORE | Emanuel | VANNA | Hart |
| STILLWELL | Effingham | VARNELL | Whitfield |
| STOCKBRIDGE | Henry | VIDALIA | Toombs |
| STOCKTON | Lanier | VIENNA | Dooly |
| STONE MOUNTAIN | DeKalb | VILLA RICA | Carroll |
| STOVALL | Meriwether | WACO | Haralson |
| SUCHES | Union | WADLEY | Jefferson |
| SUGAR VALLEY | Gordon | WALESKA | Cherokee |
| SUMMERVILLE | Chattooga | WALTHOURVILLE | Liberty |
| SUMNER | Worth | WARESBORO | Ware |
| SUNNY SIDE | Spalding | WARM SPRINGS | Meriwether |
| SURRENCY | Appling | WARNER ROBINS | Houston |
| SUWANEE | Gwinnett | WARRENTON | Warren |
| SWAINSBORO | Emanuel | WARTHEN | Washington |
| SYCAMORE | Turner | WARWICK | Worth |
| SYLVANIA | Screven | WASHINGTON | Wilkes |
| SYLVESTER | Worth | WATKINSVILLE | Oconee |
| TALBOTRON | Talbot | WAVERLY | Camden |
| TALKING ROCK | Pickens | WAVERLY HALL | Harris |
| TALLAPOOSA | Haralson | WAYCROSS | Ware |
| TALLULAH FALLS | Rabun | WAYNESBORO | Burke |
| TALMO | Jackson | WAYNESVILLE | Brantley |
| TARRYTOWN | Montgomery | WEST GREEN | Coffee |
| TATE | Pickens | WESTON | Webster |
| TAYLORSVILLE | Bartow | WEST POINT | Troup |
| TEMPLE | Carroll | WHIGHAM | Grady |
| TENNGA | Murray | WHITE | Bartow |
| TENNILLE | Washington | WHITE OAK | Camden |
| THE ROCK | Upson | WHITE PLAINS | Greene |
| THOMASTON | McDuffie | WHITESBURG | Carroll |
| THOMASVILLE | Thomas | WILDWOOD | Dade |
| THOMSON | McDuffie | WILEY | Rabun |
| TIFTON | Tift | WILLACOOCHEE | Atkinson |
| TIGER | Rabun | WILLIAMSON | Pike |
| TIGNALL | Wilkes | WINDER | Barrow |
| TOCCOA | Stephens | WINSTON | Douglas |
| TOOMSBORO | Wilkinson | WINTERVILLE | Clarke |
| TOWNSEND | McIntosh | WOODBINE | Camden |
| TRENTON | Dade | WOOODBURY | Meriwether |
| TRION | Chattooga | WOODLAND | Talbot |
| TUCKER | DeKalb | WOODSTOCK | Cherokee |
| TUNNEL HILL | Whitfield | WRAY | Irwin |
| TURIN | Coweta | WRENS | Jefferson |
| TURNERVILLE | Habersham | WRIGHTSVILLE | Johnson |
| TWIN CITY | Emanuel | YATESVILLE | Upson |
| TYBEE ISLAND | Chatham | YOUNG HARRIS | Towns |
| TYRONE | Fayette | ZEBULON | Pike |
| TY TY | Tift | **HAWAII** | |
| UNADILLA | Dooly | AHUIMANO | Honolulu |
| UNION CITY | Fulton | AIEA | Honolulu |
| UNION POINT | Greene | AIKAHI | Honolulu |
| UVALDA | Montgomery | AINA HAINA | Honolulu |
| VALDOSTA | Lowndes | ALA MOANA | Honolulu |

| | | | |
|---|---|---|---|
| ANAHOLA | Kauai | KOLOA | Kauai |
| ANDRADE | Honolulu | KUALAPUU | Maui |
| BARBERS POINT | Honolulu | KUKUIHAELE | Hawaii |
| BYU | Honolulu | KUKUIULA | Kauai |
| CAPTAIN COOK | Hawaii | KULA | Maui |
| CHAMINADE | Honolulu | KUNIA | Honolulu |
| CHINATOWN | Hoholulu | KURTISTOWN | Hawaii |
| ELEELE | Kauai | LAHAINA | Maui |
| ENCHANTED LAKES | Hoholulu | LAIE | Honolulu |
| EWA BEACH | Honolulu | LANAI CITY | Maui |
| FORD ISLAND | Honolulu | LAUPAHOEHOE | Hawaii |
| FORT SHAFTER | Honolulu | LAWAI | Kauai |
| GIBSON | Honolulu | LIHUE | Kauai |
| HAIKU | Maui | MAALAEA | Maui |
| HAKALAU | Hawaii | MAKAHA | Honolulu |
| HALAWA HEIGHTS | Honolulu | MAKAKILO CITY | Honolulu |
| HALEIWA | Honolulu | MAKAPALA | Hawaii |
| HALIIMAILE | Maui | MAKAWAO | Maui |
| HANA | Maui | MAKAWELI | Kauai |
| HANALEI | Kauai | MAKIKI | Hoholulu |
| HANAMAULU | Kauai | MANOA | Honolulu |
| HANAPEPE | Kauai | MAUNALOA | Maui |
| HAUULA | Honolulu | MAUNAWILI | Honolulu |
| HAWAII NATIONAL PARK | Hawaii | MILILANI | Honolulu |
| HAWI | Hawaii | MOILIILI | Honolulu |
| HEEIA | Honolulu | MOKAPU | Honolulu |
| HILO | Hawaii | MOUNTAIN VIEW | Hawaii |
| HOLUALOA | Hawaii | NAALEHU | Hawaii |
| HONALUNAU | Hawaii | NANAKULI | Honolulu |
| HONAKAA | Hawaii | NAPILI | Maui |
| HONOLULU | Honolulu | NINOLE | Hawaii |
| HONOMU | Hawaii | OLOMANA | Honolulu |
| HOOLEHUA | Maui | OLOWALU | Maui |
| KAAAWA | Honolulu | OMAO | Kauai |
| KAHUKU | Honolulu | OOKALA | Hawaii |
| KAHULUI | Maui | PAAUHAU | Hawaii |
| KAILUA | Honolulu | PAAUILO | Hawaii |
| KAILUA KONA | Hawaii | PAHALA | Hawaii |
| KALAHEO | Kauai | PAHOA | Hawaii |
| KALAUPAPA | Maui | PAIA | Maui |
| KAMUELA | Hawaii | PAPAALOA | Hawaii |
| KANEOHE | Honolulu | PAPAIKOU | Hawaii |
| KAPAA | Kauai | PEARL CITY | Honolulu |
| KAPAAU | Hawaii | PEARL RIDGE | Honolulu |
| KAUMAKANI | Kauai | PEPEEKEO | Hawaii |
| KAUNAKAKAI | Maui | PRINCEVILLE | Kauai |
| KEAAU | Hawaii | PUHI | Kauai |
| KEALAKEKUA | Hawaii | PUKALANI | Maui |
| KEALIA | Kauai | PUUNENE | Maui |
| KEKAHA | Kauai | ROYAL HAWAIIAN | Honolulu |
| KIHEI | Maui | SPRECKELSVILLE | Maui |
| KILAUEA | Kauai | SUNSET BEACH | Honolulu |
| KOKOMO | Maui | TIMBER TOWN | Honolulu |

| | | | |
|---|---|---|---|
| UNION MILL | Hawaii | CHALLIS | Custer |
| UNIVERSITY | Honolulu | CHESTER | Fremont |
| VOLCANO | Hawaii | CLARK FORK | Bonner |
| WAHIAWA | Honolulu | CLARKIA | Shoshone |
| WAIALUA | Honolulu | CLAYTON | Custer |
| WAIANAE | Honolulu | CLIFTON | Franklin |
| WAILUKU | Maui | COBALT | Lemhi |
| WAIMANALO | Honolulu | COCOLALLA | Bonner |
| WAIMEA | Kauai | COUER D ALENE | Kootenai |
| WAIPAHU | Honolulu | COLBURN | Bonner |
| WAKE ISLAND | Honolulu | CONDA | Caribou |
| WHARF | Maui | COOLIN | Bonner |
| WHITMORE VILLAGE | Honolulu | CORRAL | Camas |
| **IDAHO** | | COTTONWOOD | Idaho |
| ABDEREEN | Bingham | COUNCIL | Adams |
| ACEQUIA | Minidoka | CRAIGMONT | Lewis |
| AHASHKA | Clearwater | CULDESAC | Nez Perce |
| ALBION | Cassia | DARLINGTON | Butte |
| ALMO | Cassia | DAYTON | Franklin |
| AMERICAN FALLS | Power | DEARY | Latah |
| ARBON | Power | DECLO | Cassia |
| ARCO | Butte | DESMET | Benewah |
| ARIMO | Bannock | DIETRICH | Lincoln |
| ASHTON | Fremont | DINGLE | Bear Lake |
| ATHOL | Kootenai | DIXIE | Idaho |
| ATLANTA | Elmore | DONNELLY | Valley |
| ATOMIC CITY | Bingham | DOVER | Bonner |
| AVERY | Shoshone | DOWNEY | Bannock |
| BANCROFT | Caribou | DRIGGS | Teton |
| BANKS | Boise | DUBOIS | Clark |
| BASALT | Bingham | EAGLE | Ada |
| BAYVIEW | Kootenai | EASTPORT | Boundary |
| BELLEVUE | Blaine | EDEN | Jerome |
| BERN BEAR | Lame | ELBA | Cassia |
| BLACKFOOT | Bingham | ELK CITY | Idaho |
| BLANCHARD | Bonner | ELK HORN | Blaine |
| BLISS | Gooding | ELK RIVER | Clearwater |
| BLOOMINGTON | Bear Lake | ELLIS | Custer |
| BOISE | Ada | EMMETT | Gem |
| BONNERS FERRY | Boundary | FAIRFIELD | Camas |
| BOVILL | Latah | FELT | Teton |
| BRUNEAU | Owyhee | FENN | Idaho |
| BUHL | Twin Falls | FERDINAND | Idaho |
| BURLEY | Cassia | FERNWOOD | Benewah |
| CALDER | Shoshone | FILER | Twin Falls |
| CALDWELL | Canyon | FIRTH | Bingham |
| CAMBRIDGE | Washington | FISH HAVEN | Bear Lake |
| CAREY | Blame | FORT HALL | Bingham |
| CAREYWOOD | Bonner | FRANKLIN | Franklin |
| CARMEN | Lemhi | FRUITLAND | Payette |
| CASCADE | Valley | FRUITVALE | Adams |
| CASTLEFLORD | Twin Falls | GARDEN CITY | Ada |
| CATALDO | Kootenai | GARDEN VALLEY | Boise |

**Adoption Searches Made Easier**

| | | | |
|---|---|---|---|
| GENESEE | Latah | LAVA HOT SPRINGS | Bannock |
| GENEVA | Bear Lake | LEADORE | Lemhi |
| GEORGETOWN | Bear Lake | LEMHI | Lemhi |
| GIBBONSVILLE | Lemhi | LENORE | Nez Perce |
| GLENNS FERRY | Elmore | LETHA | Gem |
| GOODING | Gooding | LEWISTON | Nez Perce |
| GRACE | Caribou | LEWISVILLE | Jefferson |
| GRAND VIEW | Owyhee | LOMAN | Boise |
| GRANGEVILLE | Idaho | LUCILE | Idaho |
| GRASMERE | Owyee | MACKAY | Custer |
| GREENCREEK | Idaho | MACKS INN | Fremont |
| GREENLEAF | Canyon | MALAD CITY | Oneida |
| HAGERMAN | Gooding | MALTA | Cassia |
| HAILEY | Blaine | MARSING | Owyhee |
| HAMER | Jefferson | MAY | Lemhi |
| HAMMETT | Elmore | MCCALL | Valley |
| HANSEN | Twin Falls | MCCAMMON | Bannock |
| HARRISON | Kootenai | MEDIMONT | Kootenai |
| HARVARD | Latah | MELBA | Canyon |
| HAYDEN | Kootenai | MENAN | Jefferson |
| HAYDEN LAKE | Hayden | MERIDIAN | Ada |
| HAZELTON | Jerome | MESA | Adams |
| HEYBURN | Minidoka | MIDDLETON | Canyon |
| HILL CITY | Camas | MIDVALE | Washington |
| HOLBROOK | Oneida | MINIDOKA | Minidoka |
| HOMEDALE | Owyhee | MONTEVIEW | Jefferson |
| HOPE | Bonner | MONTOUR | Gem |
| HORSESHOE BEND | Boise | MONTPELIER | Bear Lake |
| HOWE | Butte | MOORE | Butte |
| HOUSTON | Canyon | MORELAND | Bingham |
| IDAHO CITY | Boise | MOSCOW | Latah |
| IDAHO FALLS | Bonneville | MOUNTAIN HOME | Elmore |
| INDIAN VALLEYU | Adams | MOUNTAIN HOME AFB | Elmore |
| INKOM | Bannock | MOYLE SPRINGS | Boundary |
| IONA | Bonneville | MULLAN | Shoshone |
| IRWIN | Bonneville | MURPHY | Owyhee |
| ISLAND PARK | Fremont | MURRAY | Shoshone |
| JEROME | Jerome | MURTAUGH | Twin Falls |
| JUILAETTA | Latah | NAMPA | Canyon |
| KAMIAH | Lewis | NAPLES | Boundary |
| KELLOGG | Shoshone | NEWDALE | Fremont |
| KENDRICK | Latah | NEW MEADOWS | Adams |
| KETCHUM | Blaine | NEW PLYMOUTH | Payette |
| KEUTERVILLE | Idaho | NEZPERCE | Lewis |
| KIMBERLY | Twin Falls | NORDMAN | Bonner |
| KING HILL | Elmore | NORTH FORK | Lemhi |
| KINGSTON | Shoshone | NOTUS | Canyon |
| KOOSKIA | Idaho | OAKLEY | Cassia |
| KOOTENAL | Bonner | OBSIDIAN | Blaine |
| KUNA | Ada | OLA | Gem |
| LACLEDE | Bonner | OLD TOWN | Bonner |
| LAKE FORK | Valley | OREANA | Owyhee |
| LAPWAY | Nez Perce | OROFINO | Clearwater |

| | | | |
|---|---|---|---|
| OSBURN | Shoshone | SPENCER | Clark |
| OVID | Bear Lake | SPIRIT LAKE | Kootenai |
| PALISADES | Bonneville | SPRINGFIELD | Bingham |
| PARIS | Bear Lake | SQUIRREL | Fremont |
| PARKER | Fremont | STANLEY | Custer |
| PARMA | Canyon | STAR | Ada |
| PATTERSON | Lemhi | STERLING | Bingham |
| PAUL | Minidoka | STITES | Idaho |
| PAYETTE | Payette | STONE | Oneida |
| PECK | Nez Perce | SUGAR CITY | Madison |
| PICABO | Blaine | SUN VALLEY | Blaine |
| PIERCE | Clearwater | SWANLAKE | Bannock |
| PINEHURST | Shoshone | SWAN VALLEY | Bonneville |
| PINGREE | Bingham | SWEET | Gem |
| PLACERVILLE | Boise | TENDOY | Lemhi |
| PLUMMER | Benewah | TENSED | Benewah |
| POCATELLO | Bannock | TERRETON | Jefferson |
| POLLOCK | Idaho | TETON | Fremont |
| PONDERAY | Bonner | TETONIA | Teton |
| PORTHILL | Boundary | THATCHER | Franklin |
| POST FALLS | Kootenai | TROY | Latah |
| POTLACH | Latah | TWIN FALLS | Twin Falls |
| PRESTON | Franklin | UCON | Bonneville |
| PRIEST RIVER | Bonner | VICTOR | Teton |
| PRINCETON | Latah | VIOLA | Latah |
| RATHDRUM | Kootenai | WALLACE | Shoshone |
| REUBENS | Lewis | WARREN | Idaho |
| REXBURG | Madison | WAYAN | Caribou |
| RICHFIELD | Lincoln | WEIPPE | Clearwater |
| RIDDLE | Owyhee | WEISER | Washington |
| RIGBY | Jefferson | WENDELL | Gooding |
| RIGGINS | Idaho | WESTON | Franklin |
| RIRIE | Jefferson | WHITE BIRD | Idaho |
| ROBERTS | Jefferson | WILDER | Canyon |
| ROCKLAND | Power | WINCHESTER | Lewis |
| ROGERSON | Twin Falls | WORLEY | Kootenai |
| RUPERT | Minidoka | YELLOW PINE | Valley |
| SAGLE | Bonner | **ILLINOIS** | |
| SAINT ANTHONY | Fremont | ABBOTT PARK | Cook |
| SAINT CHARLES | Bear Lake | ABINGDON | Knox |
| SAINT MARIES | Benewah | ADAIR | McDonough |
| SALMON | Lemhi | ADDIEVILLE | Washington |
| SAMUELS | Bonner | ADDISON | DuPage |
| SANDPOINT | Bonner | ADRIAN | Hancock |
| SANTA | Benewah | AKIN | Franklin |
| SHELLEY | Bingham | ALBANY | Whiteside |
| SHOSHONE | Lincoln | ALBERS | Clinton |
| SHOUP | Lemhi | ALBION | Edwards |
| SILVERTON | Shoshone | ALDEN | McHenry |
| SMELTERVILLE | Shoshone | ALEDO | Mercer |
| SMITHS FERRY | Valley | ALEXANDER | Morgan |
| SODA SPRINGS | Caribou | ALEXIS | Mercer |
| SPALDING | Nez Perce | ALGONQUIN | McHenry |

| | | | |
|---|---|---|---|
| ALHAMBRA | Madison | ATWATER | Macoupin |
| ALLEN | Mason | ATWOOD | Douglas |
| ALLENDALE | Wabash | AUBURN | Sangamon |
| ALLEN GROVE | Mason | AUBURN PARK | Cook |
| ALLERTON | Vermilion | AUGUSTA | Hancock |
| ALMA | Marion | AURORA | DuPage |
| ALORTON | Saint Clair | AUSTIN | Cook |
| ALPHA | Henry | AVA | Jackson |
| ALSEY | Scott | AVISTON | Clinton |
| ALSIP | Cook | AVON | Fulton |
| ALTAMONT | Effingham | BADER | Browning |
| ALTON | Madison | BAILEYVILLE | Ogle |
| ALTONA | Knox | BALDWIN | Randolph |
| ALTO PASS | Union | BARCLAY | Sherman |
| ALVIN | Vermilion | BARDOLPH | McDonough |
| AMBOY | Lee | BARNHILL | Wayne |
| AMOCO | Cook | BARR | Macoupin |
| ANCHOR | McLean | BARRINGTON | Lake |
| ANCONA | Livingston | BARRY | Pike |
| ANDALUSIA | Rock Island | BARSTOW | Rock Island |
| ANDOVER | Henry | BARTELSO | Clinton |
| ANDREW | Sangamon | BARTLETT | Cook |
| ANNA | Union | BARTONVILLE | Peoria |
| ANNAPOLIS | Crawford | BASCO | Hancock |
| ANNAWAN | Henry | BATCHTOWN | Calhoun |
| ANTIOCH | Lake | BATES | New Berlin |
| APPLE RIVER | Jo Daviess | BATH | Mason |
| ARCADIA | Jacksonville | BAYLIS | Pike |
| ARCHER | Sangamon | BEARDSTOWN | Cass |
| ARCOLA | Douglas | BEARSDALE | Decatur |
| ARENZVILLE | Cass | BEASON | Logan |
| ARGENTA | Macon | BEAVERVILLE | Iroquois |
| ARGO | Cook | BECKEMEYER | Clinton |
| ARGONNE | Lemont | BEDFORD PARK | Cook |
| ARLINGTON | Bureau | BEECHER | Will |
| ARLINGTON HEIGHTS | Cook | BEECHER CITY | Effingham |
| ARMINGTON | Tazewell | BELKNAP | Johnson |
| ARMSTRONG | Vermilion | BELLE RIVE | Jefferson |
| ARNOLD | Jacksonville | BELLEVILLE | Saint Clair |
| ARROWSMITH | McLean | BELLFLOWER | McLean |
| ARTHUR | Douglas | BELLMONT | Wabash |
| ASHBURN | Cook | BELLWOOD | Cook |
| ASHKUM | Iroquois | BELVIDERE | Boone |
| ASHLAND | Cass | BEMENT | Piatt |
| ASHLEY | Washington | BENLD | Macoupin |
| ASHMORE | Coles | BENSENVILLE | DuPage |
| ASHTON | Lee | BENSON | Woodford |
| ASSUMPTION | Christian | BENTON | Franklin |
| ASTORIA | Fulton | BERKELEY | Cook |
| ATHENS | Menard | BERLIN | Sangamon |
| ATKINSON | Henry | BERRY | Sangamon |
| ATLANTA | Logan | BERWICK | Warren |
| ATTERBURY | Petersburg | BERWYN | Cook |

| | | | |
|---|---|---|---|
| BETHALTO | Madison | BROWNING | Schuyler |
| BETHANY | Moultrie | BROWNS | Edwards |
| BIBLE GROVE | Louisville | BROWNSTOWN | Fayette |
| BIGGS | Easton | BRUNSWICK | Findlay |
| BIGGSVILLE | Henderson | BRUSSELS | Calhoun |
| BIG ROCK | Kane | BRYANT | Fulton |
| BINGHAM | Fayette | BUCKHART | Mechanicsburg |
| BIRDS | Lawrence | BUCKINGHAM | Kankakee |
| BISHOP HILL | Henry | BUCKLEY | Iroquois |
| BISMARK | Vermilion | BUCKNER | Franklin |
| BISSELL | Springfield | BUDA | Bureau |
| BLACKLAND | Macon | BUFFALO | Sangamon |
| BLACKSTONE | Livingston | BUFFALO PRAIRIE | Rock Island |
| BLANDINSVILLE | McDonough | BULPITT | Christian |
| BLOOMINGDALE | DuPage | BUNCOMBE | Johnson |
| BLOOMINGTON | McLean | BUNKER HILL | Macoupin |
| BLUE ISLAND | Cook | BUREAU | Bureau |
| BLUE MOUND | Macon | BURLINGTON | Kane |
| BLUFF CITY | Browning | BURNSIDE | Hancock |
| BLUFFS | Scott | BURNT PRAIRIE | White |
| BLUFF SPRINGS | Cass | BUSHNELL | McDonough |
| BLUFORD | Jefferson | BUTLER | Montgomery |
| BOLES | Johnson | BYRON | Ogle |
| BOLINGBROOK | Will | CABERY | Kankakee |
| BOLIVIA | Mechanicsburg | CACHE | Alexander |
| BONDVILLE | Champaign | CAHOKIA | St. Clair |
| BONE GAP | Edwards | CAIRO | Alexander |
| BONFIELD | Kankakee | CALEDONIA | Boone |
| BONNIE | Jefferson | CALHOUN | Richland |
| BOODY | Macon | CALUMENT CITY | Cook |
| BOURBONNAIS | Kankakee | CAMARGO | Douglas |
| BOWEN | Hancock | CAMBRIA | Williamson |
| BRACEVILLE | Grundy | CAMBRIDGE | Henry |
| BRADFORD | Stark | CAMDEN | Schuyler |
| BRADFORDTON | Springfield | CAMERON | Warren |
| BRADLEY | Kankakee | CAMPBELL HILL | Jackson |
| BRAIDWOOD | Will | CAMP GROVE | Marshall |
| BRECKENRIDGE | Rochester | CAMP POINT | Adams |
| BREESE | Clinton | CAMPUS | Livingston |
| BRIDGEPORT | Lawrence | CANTON | Fulton |
| BRIDGEVIEW | Oak Lawn | CANTRALL | Sangamon |
| BRIGHTON | Macoupin | CAPRON | Boone |
| BRIMFIELD | Peoria | CARBON CLIFF | Rock Island |
| BRISTOL | Kendall | CARBONDALE | Jackson |
| BROADLANDS | Champaign | CARLINVILLE | Macoupin |
| BROADVIEW | Maywood | CARLOCK | McLean |
| BROADWAY | Rockford | CARLYE | Clinton |
| BROADWELL | Elkhart | CARMAN | Henderson |
| BROCTON | Edgar | CARMI | White |
| BROOKFIELD | Cook | CARPENTERSVILLE | Kane |
| BROOKPORT | Massac | CARRIER MILLS | Saline |
| BROUGHTON | Hamilton | CARROLLTON | Greene |
| BROAWFIELD | Golconda | CARTERVILLE | Williamson |

| | | | |
|---|---|---|---|
| CARTHAGE | Hancock | COLLINSVILLE | Madison |
| CARY | McHenry | COLLISON | Vermilion |
| CASEY | Clark | COLMAR | McDonough |
| CASEYVILLE | Saint Clair | COLONA | Henry |
| CASTLETON | Stark | COLP | Williamson |
| CATLIN | Vermilion | COLUMBIA | Monroe |
| CAVE IN ROCK | Hardin | COLUMBUS | Adams |
| CEDAR POINT | LaSalle | COLUSA | Hancock |
| CEDARVILLE | Stephenson | COMPTON | Lee |
| CENTRALIA | Marion | CONCORD | Morgan |
| CERRO GORDO | Piatt | CONGERVILLE | Morgan |
| CHADWICK | Carroll | COOKSVILLE | McLean |
| CHAMBERSBURG | Pike | CORDOVA | Rock Island |
| CHAMPAIGN | Champaign | CORNELL | Livingston |
| CHANA | Ogle | CORNLAND | Logan |
| CHANDLERVILLE | Cass | CORTLAND | DeKalb |
| CHANNAHON | Will | COTTAGE HILLS | Madison |
| CHAPIN | Morgan | COULTERVILLE | Randolph |
| CHARLESTON | Coles | COWDEN | Shelby |
| CHATHAM | Sangamon | CREAL SPRINGS | Williamson |
| CHATSWORTH | Livingston | CRESCENT CITY | Iroquois |
| CHEBANSE | Iroquois | CRESTON | Ogle |
| CHENOA | McLean | CRETE | Will |
| CHERRY | Bureau | CROPSEY | McLean |
| CHERRY VALLEY | Winnebago | CROSSVILLE | White |
| CHESTER | Randolph | CRYSTAL LAKE | McHenry |
| CHESTERFIELD | Macoupin | CUBA | Fulton |
| CHESTNUT | Logan | CULLOM | Livingston |
| CHICAGO | Cook | CUSTER PARK | Will |
| CHICAGO HEIGHTS | Cook | CUTLER | Perry |
| CHICAGO RIDGE | Cook | CYPRESS | Johnson |
| CHILLICOTHE | Peoria | DAHINDA | Knox |
| CHRISMAN | Edgar | DAHLGREN | Hamilton |
| CHRISTOPHER | Franklin | DAKOTA | Stephenson |
| CISCO | Piatt | DALE | Hamilton |
| CISNE | Wayne | DALLAS CITY | Hancock |
| CISSNA PARK | Iroquois | DALTON CITY | Moultrie |
| CLARE | DeKalb | DALZELL | Bureau |
| CLAREMONT | Richland | DANA | LaSalle |
| CLARENDON HILLS | DuPage | DANFORTH | Iroquois |
| CLAY CITY | Clay | DANVERS | McLean |
| CLAYTON | Adams | DANVILLE | Vermillion |
| CLAYTONVILLE | Iroquois | DAVIS | Stephenson |
| CLIFTON | Iroquois | DAVIS JUNCTION | Ogle |
| CLINTON | DeWitt | DAWSON | Sangamon |
| COAL CITY | Grundy | DECATUR | Macon |
| COAL VALLEY | Rock Island | DEER CREEK | Tazewell |
| COATSBURG | Adams | DEERFIELD | Lake |
| COBDEN | Union | DEER GROVE | Whiteside |
| COELLO | Franklin | DEKALB | DeKalb |
| COFFEEN | Montgomery | DELAND | Piatt |
| COLCHESTER | McDonough | DELAVAN | Tazewell |
| COLFAX | McLean | DENNISON | Clark |

| | | | |
|---|---|---|---|
| DEPUE | Bureau | EDINBURG | Christian |
| DESOTO | Jackson | EDWARDS | Peoria |
| DES PLAINES | Cook | EDWARDSVILLE | Madison |
| DETROIT | Pike | EFFINGHAM | Effingham |
| DEWEY | Champaign | ELBURN | Kane |
| DEWITT | Dewitt | ELCO | Alexander |
| DIETERICH | Effingham | ELDENA | Lee |
| DIVERNON | Sangamon | ELDORADO | Saline |
| DIX | Jefferson | ELDRED | Greene |
| DIXON | Lee | ELEROY | Stephenson |
| DOLTON | Cook | ELGIN | Kane |
| DONGOLA | Union | ELIZABETH | Jo Daviess |
| DONNELLSON | Montgomery | ELIZABETHTOWN | Hardin |
| DONOVAN | Iroquois | ELK GROVE VILLAGE | Cook |
| DORCHESTER | Macoupin | ELKHART | Logan |
| DORSEY | Madison | ELKVILLE | Jackson |
| DOVER | Bureau | ELLERY | Edwards |
| DOW | Jersey | ELLIOTT | Ford |
| DOWELL | Jackson | ELLIS GROVE | Randolph |
| DOWNERS GROVE | DuPage | ELLISVILLE | Fulton |
| DOWNS | McLean | ELLSWORTH | McLean |
| DUBOIS | Washington | ELMHURST | DuPage |
| DUNDAS | Richland | ELMWOOD | Peoria |
| DUNDEE | Kane | EL PASO | Woodford |
| DUNFERMLINE | Fulton | ELSAH | Jersey |
| DUNLAP | Peoria | ELVASTON | Hancock |
| DUPO | Saint Clair | ELWIN | Macon |
| DU QUOIN | Perry | ELWOOD | Will |
| DURAND | Winnebago | EMDEN | Logan |
| DWIGHT | Livingston | EMINGTON | Livingston |
| EAGERVILLE | Macoupin | EMMA | White |
| EARLVILLE | LaSalle | ENERGY | Williamson |
| EAST ALTON | Madison | ENFIELD | White |
| EAST ANNE | Kankakee | EOLA | DuPage |
| EAST AUGUSTINE | Knox | EQUALITY | Gallatin |
| EAST CARONDELET | Saint Clair | ERIE | Whiteside |
| EAST CHARLES | Kane | ESMOND | DeKalb |
| EAST DAVID | Fulton | ESSEX | Kankakee |
| EAST DUBUQUE | Jo Daviess | EUREKA | Woodford |
| EAST ELMO | Fayette | EVANSTON | Cook |
| EAST FRANCISVILLE | Lawrence | EVANSVILLE | Randolph |
| EAST GALESBURG | Knox | EWING | Franklin |
| EAST JACOB | Madison | FAIRBURY | Livingston |
| EAST JOSEPH | Champaign | FAIRFIELD | Wayne |
| EAST LIBORY | St. Clair | FAIRMOUNT | Vermillion |
| EAST LYNN | Vermilion | FAIRVIEW | Fulton |
| EAST MOLINE | Rock Island | FARINA | Fayette |
| EAST PETER | Fayette | FARMER CITY | DeWitt |
| EASTON | Mason | FARMERSVILLE | Montgomery |
| EAST SAINT LOUIS | Saint Clair | FARMINGTON | Fulton |
| EDDYVILLE | Pope | FENTON | Whiteside |
| EDELSTEIN | Peoria | FERRIS | Hancock |
| EDGEWOOD | Effingham | FIATT | Fulton |

| | | | |
|---|---|---|---|
| FIDELITY | Jersey | GIRARD | Macoupin |
| FIELDON | Jersey | GLADSTONE | Henderson |
| FILLMORE | Montgomery | GLASFORD | Peoria |
| FINDLAY | Shelby | GLENARM | Sangamon |
| FISHER | Champaign | GLEN CARBON | Madison |
| FITHIAN | Vermilion | GLENCOE | Cook |
| FLANAGAN | Livingston | GLEN ELLYN | DuPage |
| FLAT ROCK | Crawford | GLENDALE HEIGHTS | DuPage |
| FLORA | Clay | GLENVIEW | Cook |
| FLOSSMOOR | Cook | GLENWOOD | Cook |
| FOOSLAND | Champaign | GODFREY | Madison |
| FOREST CITY | Mason | GOLCONDA | Pope |
| FOREST PARK | Cook | GOLDEN | Adams |
| FORREST | Livingston | GOLDEN EAGLE | Calhoun |
| FORRESTON | Ogle | GOLDENGATE | Wayne |
| FORSYTH | Macon | GOLF | Cook |
| FORT SHERIDAN | Lake | GOODFIELD | Woodford |
| FOWLER | Adams | GOOD HOPE | McDonough |
| FOX LAKE | Lake | GOODWINE | Iroquois |
| FOX RIVER GROVE | McHenry | GOREVILLE | Johnson |
| FRANKFORT | Will | GORHAM | Jackson |
| FRANKFORT HEIGHTS | Franklin | GRAFTON | Jersey |
| FRANKLIN | Morgan | GRAND CHAIN | Pulaski |
| FRANKLIN GROVE | Lee | GRAND RIDGE | LaSalle |
| FRANKLIN PARK | Cook | GRAND TOWER | Jackson |
| FREDERICK | Schuyler | GRANITE CITY | Madison |
| FREEBURG | Saint Clair | GRANT PARK | Kankakee |
| FREEMAN SPUR | Williamson | GRANTSBURG | Johnson |
| FREEPORT | Stephenson | GRANVILLE | Putnam |
| FULTON | Whiteside | GRAYMONT | Livingston |
| FULTS | Monroe | GRAYSLAKE | Lake |
| GALATIA | Saline | GRAYVILLE | White |
| GALENA | Jo Daviess | GREENFIELD | Greene |
| GALESBURG | Knox | GREENUP | Cumberland |
| GALT | Whiteside | GREEN VALLEY | Tazewell |
| GALVA | Henry | GREENVIEW | Menard |
| GARDEN PRAIRIE | Boone | GREENVILLE | Bond |
| GARDNER | Grundy | GRIDLEY | McLean |
| GAYS | Moultrie | GRIGGSVILLE | Pike |
| GEFF | Wayne | GROVELAND | Tazewell |
| GENESEO | Henry | GURNEE | Lake |
| GENEVA | Kane | HAGERSTOWN | Fayette |
| GENOA | DeKalb | HAMBURG | Calhoun |
| GEORGETOWN | Vermilion | HAMEL | Madison |
| GERLAW | Warren | HAMILTON | Hancock |
| GERMANTOWN | Clinton | HAMLETSBURG | Pope |
| GERMAN VALLEY | Stephenson | HAMMOND | Piatt |
| GIBSON CITY | Ford | HAMPSHIRE | Kane |
| GIFFORD | Champaign | HAMPTON | Rock Island |
| GILBERTS | Kane | HANNA CITY | Peoria |
| GILLESPIE | Macoupin | HANOVER | Jo Daviess |
| GILMAN | Iroquois | HARCO | Saline |
| GILSON | Knox | HARDIN | Calhoun |

| | | | |
|---|---|---|---|
| HARMON | Lee | HUTSONVILLE | Crawford |
| HARRISBURG | Saline | ILINOTS CITY | Rock Island |
| HARRISTOWN | Macon | ILLIOPOLIS | Sangamon |
| HARTFORD | Madison | INA | Jefferson |
| HARTSBURG | Logan | INDIANOLA | Vermilion |
| HARVARD | McHenry | INDUSTRY | McDonough |
| HARVEL | Montgomery | INGLESIDE | Lake |
| HARVEY | Cook | INGRAHAM | Clay |
| HAVANA | Mason | IOLA | Clay |
| HAZEL CREST | Cook | IPAVA | Fulton |
| HEBRON | McHenry | IROQUOIS | Iroquois |
| HECKER | Monroe | IRVING | Montgomery |
| HENDERSON | Knox | IRVINGTON | Washington |
| HENNEPIN | Putnam | ISLAND LAKE | Lake |
| HENNING | Vermilion | ITASCA | DuPage |
| HENRY | Marshall | IUKA | Marion |
| HERALD | White | IVESDALE | Champaign |
| HEROD | Pope | JACKSONVILLE | Morgan |
| HERRICK | Shelby | JACOB | Jackson |
| HERRIN | Williamson | JANESVILLE | Cumberland |
| HERSCHER | Kankakee | JERSEYVILLE | Jersey |
| HETTICK | Macoupin | JEWETT | Cumberland |
| HEYWORTH | McLean | JOHNSONVILLE | Wayne |
| HIDALGO | Jasper | JOHNSTON CITY | Williamson |
| HIGHLAND | Madison | JOLIET | Will |
| HIGHLAND PARK | Lake | JONESBORO | Union |
| HIGHWOOD | Lake | JOPPA | Massac |
| HILLSBORO | Montgomery | JOY | Mercer |
| HILLSDALE | Rock Island | JUNCTION | Gallatin |
| HILLVIEW | Greene | KAMPSVILLE | Calhoun |
| HINCKLEY | DeKalb | KANE | Greene |
| HINDSBORO | Douglas | KANESVILLE | Kane |
| HINES | Cook | KANKAKEE | Kankakee |
| HINSDALE | DuPage | KANSAS | Edgar |
| HOFFMAN | Clinton | KARBERS RIDGE | Hardin |
| HOFFMAN ESTATES | Cook | KARNAK | Pulaski |
| HOLCOMB | Ogle | KASBEER | Bureau |
| HOLDER | McLean | KEENES | Wayne |
| HOMER | Champaign | KEESBURG | Wabash |
| HOMEWOOD | Cook | KEITHSBURG | Mercer |
| HOOPESTON | Vermilion | KELL | Marion |
| HOOPPOLE | Henry | KEMPTON | Ford |
| HOPEDALE | Tazewell | KENILWORTH | Cook |
| HOPKINS PARK | Kankakee | KENNEY | DeWitt |
| HOYLETON | Washington | KENT | Stephenson |
| HUDSON | McLean | KEWANEE | Henry |
| HUEY | Clinton | KEYESPORT | Clinton |
| HULL | Pike | KILBOURNE | Mason |
| HUMBOLDT | Coles | KINCAID | Christian |
| HUME | Edgar | KINDERHOOK | Pike |
| HUNTLEY | McHenry | KINGSTON | DeKalb |
| HUNTSVILLE | Schuyler | KINGSTON MINES | Peoria |
| HURST | Williamson | KINMUNDY | Marion |

| | | | |
|---|---|---|---|
| KINSMAN | Grundy | LIVINGSTON | Madison |
| KIRKLAND | DeKalb | LOAMI | Sangamon |
| KIRKWOOD | Warren | LOCKPORT | Will |
| KNOXVILLE | Knox | LODA | Iroquois |
| LACON | Marshall | LOGAN | Franklin |
| LADD | Bureau | LOMAX | Henderson |
| LAFAYETTE | Stark | LOMBARD | DuPage |
| LAFOX | Kane | LONDON MILLS | Fulton |
| LAGRANGE | Cook | LONG POINT | Livingston |
| LAHARPE | Hancock | LONGVIEW | Champaign |
| LAKE BLUFF | Lake | LOOGOOTEE | Fayette |
| LAKE FOREST | Lake | LORAINE | Adams |
| LAKE FORK | Logan | LOSTANT | LaSalle |
| LAKE VILLA | Lake | LOUISVILLE | Clay |
| LAKEWOOD | Shelby | LOVEJOY | Saint Clair |
| LAKE ZURICH | Lake | LOVINGTON | Moultrie |
| LAMOILLE | Bureau | LOWDER | Sangamon |
| LANARK | Carroll | LOWPOINT | Woodford |
| LANCASTER | Wabash | LUDLOW | Champaign |
| LANE | DeWitt | LYNDON | Whiteside |
| LANSING | Cook | LYNN CENTER | Henry |
| LAPLACE | Piatt | LYONS | Cook |
| LAPRAIRIE | Adams | MCCLURE | Alexander |
| LAROSE | Marshall | MCCONNELL | Stephenson |
| LASALLE | LaSalle | MCHENRY | McHenry |
| LATHAM | Logan | MCLEAN | McLean |
| LAURA | Peoria | MCLEANSBORO | Hamilton |
| LAWNDALE | Logan | MCNABB | Putnam |
| LAWRENCEVILLE | Lawrence | MACEDONIA | Hamilton |
| LEAF RIVER | Ogle | MACKINAW | Tazewell |
| LEBANON | Saint Clair | MACOMB | McDonough |
| LEE | Lee | MACON | Macon |
| LEE CENTER | Lee | MADISON | Madison |
| LELAND | LaSalle | MAEYSTOWN | Monroe |
| LEMONT | Cook | MAGNOLIA | Putnam |
| LENA | Stephenson | MAHOMET | Champaign |
| LENZBURG | Saint Clair | MAKANDA | Jackson |
| LEONORE | LaSalle | MALDEN | Bureau |
| LERNA | Coles | MALTA | DeKalb |
| LE ROY | McLean | MANCHESTER | Scott |
| LEWISTOWN | Fulton | MANHATTAN | Will |
| LEXINGTON | McLean | MANITO | Mason |
| LIBERTY | Adams | MANLIUS | Bureau |
| LIBERTYVILLE | Lake | MANSFIELD | Piatt |
| LIMA | Adams | MANTENO | Kankakee |
| LINCOLN | Logan | MANVILLE | Livingston |
| LINDENWOOD | Ogle | MAPLE PARK | Kane |
| LISLE | DuPage | MAPLETON | Peoria |
| LITCHFIELD | Montgomery | MAQUON | Knox |
| LITERBERRY | Morgan | MARENGO | McHenry |
| LITTLETON | Schuyler | MARIETTA | Fulton |
| LITTLE YORK | Warren | MARINE | Madison |
| LIVERPOOL | Fulton | MARION | Williamson |

| | | | |
|---|---|---|---|
| MARISSA | Saint Clair | MOMENCE | Kankakee |
| MARK | Putnam | MONEE | Will |
| MAROA | Macon | MONMOUTH | Warren |
| MARSEILLES | LaSalle | MONROE CENTER | Ogle |
| MARSHALL | Clark | MONTGOMERY | Kane |
| MARTINSVILLE | Clark | MONTICELLO | Piatt |
| MARTINTON | Iroquois | MONTROSE | Effingham |
| MARYVILLE | Madison | MOOSEHEART | Kane |
| MASCOUTAH | Saint Clair | MORO | Madison |
| MASON | Effingham | MORRIS | Grundy |
| MASON CITY | Mason | MORRISON | Whiteside |
| MATHERVILLE | Mercer | MORRISVILLE | Christian |
| MATTESON | Cook | MORTON | Tazewell |
| MATTOON | Coles | MORTON GROVE | Cook |
| MAUNIE | White | MOSSVILLE | Peoria |
| MAYWOOD | Coook | MOUND CITY | Pulaski |
| MAZON | Grundy | MOUNDS | Pulaski |
| MECHANICSBURG | Sangamon | MOUNT AUBURN | Christian |
| MEDIA | Henderson | MOUNT CARMEL | Wabash |
| MEDINAH | DuPage | MOUNT CARROLL | Carroll |
| MEDORA | Macoupin | MOUNT ERIE | Wayne |
| MELROSE PARK | Cook | MOUNT MORRIS | Ogle |
| MELVIN | Ford | MOUNT OLIVE | Macoupin |
| MENARD | Randolph | MOUNT PROSPECT | Cook |
| MENDON | Adams | MOUNT PULASKI | Logan |
| MENDOTA | LaSalle | MOUNT STERLING | Brown |
| MEPPEN | Calhoun | MOUNT VERNON | Jefferson |
| MEREDOSIA | Morgan | MOUNT ZION | Macon |
| MERNA | McLean | MOWEAQUA | Shelby |
| METAMORA | Woodford | MOZIER | Calhoun |
| METCALF | Edgar | MUDDY | Saline |
| METROOLIS | Massac | MULBERRY GROVE | Bond |
| MICHAEL | Calhoun | MULKEYTOWN | Franklin |
| MIDDLETOWN | Logan | MUNCIE | Vermilion |
| MIDLOTHIAN | Cook | MUNDELEIN | Lake |
| MILAN | Rock Island | MURDOCK | Douglas |
| MILFORD | Iroquois | MURPHYSBORO | Jackson |
| MILLBROOK | Kendall | MURRAYVILLE | Morgan |
| MILLCREEK | Union | NACHUSA | Lee |
| MILLEDGEVILLE | Carroll | NAPERVILLE | DuPage |
| MILLER CITY | Alexander | NASHVILLE | Washington |
| MILLINGTON | Kendall | NASON | Jefferson |
| MILL SHOALS | White | NATIONAL STOCK YARDS | Saint Clair |
| MILLSTADT | Saint Clair | NAUVOO | Hancock |
| MILMINE | Piatt | NEBO | Pike |
| MILTON | Pike | NEOGA | Cumberland |
| MINERAL | Bureau | NEPONSET | Bureau |
| MINIER | Tazewell | NEWARK | Kendall |
| MINONK | Woodford | NEW ATHENS | Saint Clair |
| MINOOKA | Grundy | NEW BADEN | Clinton |
| MODESTO | Macoupin | NEW BEDFORD | Bureau |
| MOKENA | Will | NEW BERLIN | Sangamon |
| MOLINE | Rock Island | NEW BOSTON | Mercer |

**Adoption Searches Made Easier**

| | | | |
|---|---|---|---|
| NEW BURNSIDE | Johnson | ORANGEVILLE | Stephson |
| NEW CANTON | Pike | ORAVILLE | Jackson |
| NEW DOUGLAS | Madison | OREANA | Macon |
| NEW HAVEN | Gallatin | OREGON | Ogle |
| NEW HOLLAND | Logan | ORIENT | Franklin |
| NEW LENOX | Will | ORION | Henry |
| NEWMAN | Douglas | ORLAND PARK | Cook |
| NEW MEMPHIS | Clinton | OSCO | Henry |
| NEW SALEM | Pike | OSWEGO | Kendall |
| NEWTON | Jasper | OTTAWA | LaSalle |
| NEW WINDSOR | Mercer | OWANECO | Christian |
| NIANTIC | Macon | OZARK | Johnson |
| NILWOOD | Macoupin | PALATINE | Cook |
| NIOTA | Hancock | PALESTINE | Crawford |
| NOBLE | Richland | PALMER | Christian |
| NOKOMIS | Montgomery | PALMYRA | Macoupin |
| NORA | Jo Daviess | PALOMA | Adams |
| NORMAL | McLean | PALOS HEIGHTS | Cook |
| NORRIS | Fulton | PALOS PARK | Cook |
| NORRIS CITY | White | PANA | Christian |
| NORTH AURORA | Kane | PANAMA | Montgomery |
| NORTH FLAKE | Cook | PAPINEAU | Iroquois |
| NORTHBROOK | Cook | PARIS | Edgar |
| NORTH CHICAGO | Lake | PARKERSBURG | Richland |
| NORTH HENDERSON | Mercer | PARK FOREST | Cook |
| OAKDALE | Washington | PARK RIDGE | Cook |
| OAKFORD | Menard | PATOKA | Marion |
| OAK FOREST | Cook | PATTERSON | Greene |
| OAKLAND | Coles | PAWNEE | Sangamon |
| OAK LAWN | Cook | PAW PAW | Lee |
| OAKLEY | Macon | PAXTON | Ford |
| OAK PARK | Cook | PAYSON | Adams |
| OAKWOOD | Vermilion | PEARL | Pike |
| OBLONG | Crawford | PEARL CITY | Stephenson |
| OCONEE | Shelby | PECATONICA | Winnebago |
| ODELL | Livingston | PEKIN | Tazewell |
| ODIN | Marion | PENFIELD | Champaign |
| O'FALLON | Saint Clair | PEORIA | Peoria |
| OGDEN | Champaign | PEOTONE | Will |
| OGLESBY | LaSalle | PERCY | Randolph |
| OHIO | Bureau | PERKS | Pulaski |
| OHLMAN | Montgomery | PERRY | Pike |
| OKAWVILLE | Washington | PERU | LaSalle |
| OLIVE BRANCH | Alexander | PESOTUM | Champaign |
| OLMSTED | Pulaski | PETERSBURG | Menard |
| OLNEY | Richland | PHILO | Champaign |
| OLYMPIA FIELDS | Cook | PIASA | Macoupin |
| OMAHA | Gallatin | PIERRON | Bond |
| ONARGA | Iroquois | PINCKNEYVILLE | Perry |
| ONEIDA | Knox | PIPER CITY | Ford |
| OPDYKE | Jefferson | PITTSBURG | Williamson |
| OPHEIM | Henry | PITTSFIELD | Pike |
| OQUAWKA | Henderson | PLAINFIELD | Will |

| | | | |
|---|---|---|---|
| PLAINVIEW | Macoupin | ROANOKE | Woodford |
| PLAINVILLE | Adams | ROBBINS | Cook |
| PLANO | Kendall | ROBERTS | Ford |
| PLATO CENTER | Kane | ROBINSON | Crawford |
| PLEASANT HILL | Pike | ROCHELLE | Ogle |
| PLEASANT PLAINS | Sagamon | ROCHESTER | Sangamon |
| PLYMOUTH | Hancock | ROCKBRIDGE | Greene |
| POCAHONTAS | Bond | ROCK CITY | Stephenson |
| POLO | Ogle | ROCK FALLS | Whiteside |
| POMONA | Jackson | ROCKFORD | Winnebago |
| PONTIAC | Livingston | ROCK ISLAND | Rock Island |
| POPLAR GROVE | Boone | ROCKPORT | Pike |
| PORT BYRON | Rock Island | ROCKTON | Winnebago |
| POSEN | Cook | ROCKWOOD | Randolph |
| POTOMAC | Vermilion | ROLLING MEADOWS | Cook |
| PRAIRIE CITY | McDonough | ROME | Peoria |
| PRAIRIE DU ROCHER | Randolph | ROODHOUSE | Greene |
| PRAIRIE VIEW | Lake | ROSAMOND | Christian |
| PREEMPTION | Mercer | ROSCOE | Winnebago |
| PRINCETON | Bureau | ROSELLE | DuPage |
| PRINCEVILLE | Peoria | ROSEVILLE | Warren |
| PROPHETSTOWN | Whiteside | ROSICLARE | Hardin |
| PROSPECT HEIGHTS | Cook | ROSSVILLE | Vermilion |
| PULASKI | Pulaski | ROUND LAKE | Lake |
| PUTNAM | Putnam | ROXANA | Madison |
| QUINCY | Adams | ROYAL | Champaign |
| RADOM | Washington | ROYALTON | Franklin |
| RALEIGH | Saline | RUSHVILLE | Schuyler |
| RAMSEY | Fayette | RUSSELL | Lake |
| RANKIN | Vermilion | RUTLAND | LaSalle |
| RANSOM | LaSalle | SADORUS | Champaign |
| RANTOUL | Champaign | SAILOR SPRINGS | Clay |
| RAPIDS CITY | Rock Island | SAINT ANNE | Kankakee |
| RARITAN | Henderson | SAINT AUGUSTINE | Knox |
| RAYMOND | Montgomery | SAINT CHARLES | Kane |
| RED BUD | Randolph | SAINT DAVID | Fulton |
| REDDICK | Kankakee | SAINT ELMO | Fayette |
| REDMON | Edgar | SAINTE MARIE | Jasper |
| RENAULT | Monroe | SAINT FRANCISVILLE | Lawrence |
| REYNOLDS | Rock Island | SAINT JACOB | Madison |
| RICHMOND | McHenry | SAINT JOSEPH | Champaign |
| RICHTON PARK | Cook | SAINT LIBORY | Saint Clair |
| RICHVIEW | Washington | SAINT PETER | Fayette |
| RIDGE FARM | Vermilion | SALEM | Marion |
| RIDGEWAY | Gallatin | SANDOVAL | Marion |
| RIDOTT | Stephenson | SANDWICH | DeKalb |
| RINARD | Wayne | SAN JOSE | Mason |
| RINGWOOD | McHenry | SAUNEMIN | Livingston |
| RIO | Knox | SAVANNA | Carroll |
| RIVER FORREST | Cook | SAVOY | Champaign |
| RIVER GROVE | Cook | SAWYERVILLE | Macoupin |
| RIVERSIDE | Cook | SAYBROOK | McLean |
| RIVERTON | Sangamon | SCALES MOUND | Jo Daviess |

| | | | |
|---|---|---|---|
| SCHAUMBERG | Cook | SOUTH PEKIN | Tazewell |
| SCHELLER | Jefferson | SOUTH PROSPECT | Cook |
| SCHILLER PARK | Cook | SOUTH PULASKI | Logan |
| SCIOTO MILLS | Stephenson | SOUTH ROXANA | Madison |
| SCOTT AFB | St. Clark | SOUTH STERLING | Brown |
| SCOTTVILLE | Macoupin | SOUTH VERNON | Jefferson |
| SEATON | Mercer | SOUTH WILMINGTON | Grundy |
| SEATONVILLE | Bureau | SOUTH ZION | Macon |
| SECOR | Woodford | SPARLAND | Marshall |
| SENECA | LaSalle | SPARTA | Randolph |
| SERENA | LaSalle | SPEER | Stark |
| SESSER | Franklin | SPRINGERTON | White |
| SEWARD | Winnebago | SPRINGFIELD | Sangamon |
| SEYMOUR | Champaign | SPRING GROVE | McHenry |
| SHABBONA | DeKalb | SPRING VALLEY | Bureau |
| SHANNON | Carroll | STANDARD | Putnam |
| SHATTUC | Clinton | STANDARD CITY | Macoupin |
| SHAWNEETOWN | Gallatin | STANFORD | McLean |
| SHEFFIELD | Bureau | STAUTON | Macoupin |
| SHELBYVILLE | Shelby | STEELEVILLE | Randolph |
| SHELDON | Iroquois | STEGER | Cook |
| SHERIDAN | LaSalle | STERLING | Whiteside |
| SHERMAN | Sangamon | STEWARD | Lee |
| SHERRARD | Mercer | STEWARDSON | Shelby |
| SHIPMAN | Macoupin | STILLMAN VALLEY | Ogle |
| SHIRLAND | Winnebago | STOCKLAND | Iroquois |
| SHIRLEY | McLean | STOCKTON | Jo Daviess |
| SHOBONIER | Fayette | STONEFORT | Saline |
| SHUMWAY | Effingham | STONINGTON | Christian |
| SIBLEY | Ford | STOY | Crawford |
| SIDELL | Vermilion | STRASBURG | Shelby |
| SIDNEY | Champaign | STRAWN | Livingston |
| SIGEL | Shelby | STREAMWOOD | Cook |
| SILVIS | Rock Island | STREATOR | LaSalle |
| SIMPSON | Johnson | STRONGHURST | Henderson |
| SIMS | Wayne | SUBLETTE | Lee |
| SKOKIE | Cook | SUGAR GROVE | Kane |
| SMITHBORO | Bond | SULLIVAN | Moultrie |
| SMITHFIELD | Fulton | SUMMERFIELD | Saint Clair |
| SMITHSHIRE | Warren | SUMMER HILL | Pike |
| SMITHTON | Saint Clair | SUMMIT-ARGO | Cook |
| SOLON MILLS | McHenry | SUMNER | Lawrence |
| SOMONAUK | DeKalb | SUTTER | Hancock |
| SORENTO | Bond | SWANWICK | Perry |
| SOUTH AUBURN | Christian | SYCAMORE | DeKalb |
| SOUTH BELIOT | Winnebago | TABLE GROVE | Fulton |
| SOUTH CARMEL | Wabash | TALLULA | Menard |
| SOUTH CARROLL | Carroll | TAMAROA | Perry |
| SOUTH ELGIN | Kane | TAMMS | Alexander |
| SOUTH ERIE | Wayne | TAMPICO | Whiteside |
| SOUTH HOLLAND | Cook | TAYLOR RIDGE | Rock Island |
| SOUTH MORRIS | Ogle | TAYLOR SPRINGS | Montgomery |
| SOUTH OLIVE | Macoupin | TAYLORVILLE | Christian |

| | | | |
|---|---|---|---|
| TECHNY | Cook | VERSAILLES | Brown |
| TENNESSEE | McDonough | VICTORIA | Knox |
| TEUTOPOLIS | Effingham | VIENNA | Johnson |
| TEXICO | Jefferson | VILLA GROVE | Douglas |
| THAWVILLE | Iroquois | VILLA PARK | DuPage |
| THAYER | Sangamon | VILLA RIDGE | Pulaski |
| THEBES | Alexander | VIOLA | Mercer |
| THOMASBORO | Champaign | VIRDEN | Macoupin |
| THOMPSONVILLE | Franklin | VIRGIL | Kane |
| THOMSON | Carroll | VIRGINIA | Cass |
| THORNTON | Cook | WADSWORTH | Lake |
| TILDEN | Randolph | WAGGONER | Montgomery |
| TILTON | Vermillion | WALNUT | Bureau |
| TIMEWELL | Brown | WALNUT HILL | Marion |
| TINLEY PARK | Cook | WALSH | Randolph |
| TISKILWA | Bureau | WALSHVILLE | Montgomery |
| TOLEDO | Cumberland | WALTONVILLE | Jefferson |
| TOLONO | Champaign | WAPELLA | DeWitt |
| TOLUCA | Marshall | WARREN | Jo Daviess |
| TONICA | LaSalle | WARRENSBURG | Macon |
| TOPEKA | Mason | WARRENVILLE | DuPage |
| TOULON | Stark | WARSAW | Hancock |
| TOVEY | Christian | WASCO | Kane |
| TOWANDA | McLean | WASHBURN | Woodford |
| TOWER HILL | Shelby | WASHINGTON | Tazewell |
| TREMONT | Tazewell | WATAGA | Knox |
| TRENTON | Clinton | WATERLOO | Monroe |
| TRILLA | Coles | WATERMAN | DeKalb |
| TRIUMPH | LaSalle | WATSEKA | Iroquois |
| TRIVOLI | Peoria | WATSON | Effingham |
| TROY | Madison | WAUCONDA | Lake |
| TROY GROVE | LaSalle | WAUKEGAN | Lake |
| TUNNEL HILL | Johnson | WAVERLY | Morgan |
| TUSCOLA | Douglas | WAYNE | DuPage |
| ULLIN | Pulaski | WAYNE CITY | Wayne |
| UNION | McHenry | WAYNESVILLE | DeWitt |
| UNION HILL | Kankakee | WEDRON | LaSalle |
| UNITY | Alexander | WELDON | DeWitt |
| URBANA | Champaign | WELLINGTON | Iroquois |
| URSA | Adams | WENONA | Marshall |
| UTICA | LaSalle | WEST BROOKLYN | Lee |
| VALIER | Franklin | WEST CHICAGO | DuPage |
| VALMEYER | Monroe | WESTERN SPRINGS | Cook |
| VANDALIA | Fayette | WESTERVELT | Shelby |
| VAN ORIN | Bureau | WESTFIELD | Clark |
| VARNA | Marshall | WEST FRANKFORT | Franklin |
| VENICE | Madison | WEST LIBERTY | Jasper |
| VERGENNES | Jackson | WESTMONT | DuPage |
| VERMILION | Edgar | WEST POINT | Hancock |
| VERMONT | Fulton | WEST SALEM | Edwards |
| VERNON | Marion | WEST UNION | Clark |
| VERNON HILLS | Lake | WESTVILLE | Vermilion |
| VERONA | Grundy | WEST YORK | Crawford |

| | | | |
|---|---|---|---|
| WHEATON | DuPage | AMBOY | Miami |
| WHEELER | Jasper | AMO | Hendricks |
| WHEELING | Cook | ANDERSON | Madison |
| WHITE HALL | Greene | ANDREWS | Huntington |
| WHITE HEALTH | Piatt | ANGOLA | Steuben |
| WHITTINGTON | Franklin | ARCADIA | Hamilton |
| WILLIAMSFIELD | Knox | ARCOLA | Allen |
| WILLIAMSVILLE | Sangamon | ARGOS | Marshall |
| WILLISVILLE | Perry | ARLINGTON | Rush |
| WILLOW HILL | Jasper | ASHLEY | DeKalb |
| WILLOW SPRINGS | Cook | ATHENS | Fulton |
| WILMETTE | Cook | ATLANTA | Hamilton |
| WILMINGTON | Will | ATTICA | Fountian |
| WILSONVILLE | Macoupin | ATWOOD | Kosciusko |
| WINCHESTER | Scott | AUBURN | DeKalb |
| WINDSOR | Shelby | AURORA | Dearborn |
| WINFIELD | DuPage | AUSTIN | Scott |
| WINNEBAGO | Winnebago | AVILLA | Noble |
| WINNETKA | Cook | AVOCA | Lawrence |
| WINSLOW | Stephenson | BACON | Marion |
| WINTHROP HARBOR | Lake | BAINBRIDGE | Putnam |
| WITT | Montgomery | BARGERSVILLE | Johnson |
| WOLF LAKE | Union | BATESVILLE | Ripley |
| WONDER LAKE | McHenry | BATH | Franklin |
| WOOD DALE | DuPage | BATTLE GROUND | Tippecanoe |
| WOODHULL | Henry | BEDFORD | Lawrence |
| WOODLAND | Iroquois | BEECH GROVE | Marion |
| WOODLAWN | Jefferson | BELLMORE | Parke |
| WOOD RIVER | Madison | BENNINGTON | Switzerland |
| WOODSON | Morgan | BENTONVILLE | Fayette |
| WOODSTOCK | McHenry | BERNE | Adams |
| WOOSUNG | Ogle | BETHLEHEM | Clark |
| WORDEN | Madison | BEVERLY SHORES | Porter |
| WORTH | Cook | BICKNELL | Knox |
| WRIGHTS | Greene | BIPPUS | Huntington |
| WYANET | Bureau | BIRDSEYE | Dubois |
| WYOMING | Stark | BLANFORD | Vermillion |
| XENIA | Clay | BLOOMFIELD | Greene |
| YALE | Jasper | BLOOMINGDALE | Parke |
| YATES CITY | Knox | BLOOMINGTON | Monroe |
| YORKVILLE | Kendall | BLUFFTON | Wells |
| ZEIGLER | Franklin | BOGGSTOWN | Shelby |
| ZION | Lake | BOONE GROVE | Porter |
| **INDIANA** | | BOONVILLE | Warrick |
| ACTON | Marion | BORDEN | Clark |
| ADAMS | Greensburg | BOSTON | Wayne |
| ADVANCE | Boone | BOSWELL | Benton |
| AKRON | Fulton | BOURBON | Marshall |
| ALAMO | Montgomery | BOWLING GREEN | Clay |
| ALBANY | Delaware | BRADFORD | Harrison |
| ALBION | Noble | BRANCHVILLE | Perry |
| ALEXANDRIA | Madison | BRAZIL | Clay |
| AMBIA | Benton | BRIDGEPORT | Marion |

| | | | |
|---|---|---|---|
| BREMEN | Marshall | CHALMERS | White |
| BRIDGETON | Parke | CHANDLER | Warrick |
| BRIMFIELD | Noble | CHARLESTOWN | Clark |
| BRINGHURST | Carroll | CHARLOTTESVILLE | Hancock |
| BRISTOL | Elkhart | CHESTERTON | Porter |
| BROSTOW | Perry | CHESTERFIELD | Anderson |
| BROAD RIPPLE | Marion | CHIPPEWA | St. Joseph |
| BROOK | Newton | CHRISNEY | Spencer |
| BROOKLYN | Morgan | CHURUBUSCO | Whitley |
| BROOKSTON | White | CICERO | Hamilton |
| BROOKVILLE | Franklin | CLARKSBURG | Decatur |
| BROWNSBURG | Hendricks | CLARKS HILL | Tippecanoe |
| BROWNSTOWN | Jackson | CLAY CITY | Clay |
| BROWNSVILLE | Union | CLAYPOOL | Kosciusko |
| BRUCEVILLE | Knox | CLAYTON | Hendricks |
| BRUNSWICK | Lake | CLEAR CREEK | Monroe |
| BRYANT | Jay | CLIFFORD | Bartholomew |
| BUCK CREEK | Tippecanoe | CLINTON | Vermillion |
| BUCKSKIN | Gibson | CLOVERDALE | Putnam |
| BUFFALO | White | COAL CITY | Owen |
| BUFFALOVILLE | Lamar | COALMONT | Clay |
| BUFFINGTON | Lake | COATESVILLE | Hendricks |
| BUNKER HILL | Miami | COLBURN | Tippecanoe |
| BURKET | Kosciusko | COLFAX | Clinton |
| BURLINGTON | Carroll | COLLEGEVILLE | Jasper |
| BURNETTSVILLE | White | COLUMBIA CITY | Whitley |
| BURNEY | Decatur | COLUMBUS | Bartholomew |
| BURR OAK | Culver | COMMISKEY | Jennings |
| BURROWS | Carroll | CONNERSVILLE | Fayette |
| BUTLER | DeKalb | CONVERSE | Miami |
| BUTLERVILLE | Jennings | CORTLAND | Jackson |
| CAMBRIDGE CITY | Wayne | CORUNNA | DeKalb |
| CAMBY | Marion | CORY | Clay |
| CAMDEN | Carroll | CORYDON | Harrison |
| CAMPBELLSBURG | Washington | COVINGTON | Fountain |
| CANAAN | Jefferson | CRAIGVILLE | Wells |
| CANNELBURG | Daviess | CRANDALL | Harrison |
| CANNELTON | Perry | CRANE | Martin |
| CARBON | Clay | CRANE NAVAL DEPOT | Martin |
| CARLISLE | Sullivan | CRAWFORDSVILLE | Montgomery |
| CARMEL | Hamilton | CROMWELL | Noble |
| CARTERSBURG | Hendricks | CROSS PLAINS | Ripley |
| CARTHAGE | Rush | CROTHERSVILLE | Jackson |
| CATES | Fountain | CROWN POINT | Lake |
| CAYUGA | Vermillion | CULVER | Marshall |
| CEDAR GROVE | Franklin | CUTLER | Carroll |
| CEDAR LAKE | Lake | CYNTHIANA | Posey |
| CELESTINE | Dubois | DALE | Spencer |
| CENTENNIAL | Allen | DALEVILLE | Delaware |
| CENTERPOINT | Clay | DARLINGTON | Montgomery |
| CENTERTON | Morgan | DAYTON | Tippecanoe |
| CENTERVILLE | Wayne | DECATUR | Adams |
| CENTRAL | Harrison | DECKER | Knox |

| | | | |
|---|---|---|---|
| DEEDSVILLE | Miami | FARMLAND | Randolph |
| DELONG | Fulton | FERDINAND | Dubois |
| DELPHI | Carroll | FILLMORE | Putnam |
| DEMOTTE | Jasper | FINLY | Hancock |
| DENHAM | Pulaski | FISHERS | Hamilton |
| DENVER | Miami | FLAT ROCK | Shelby |
| DEPAUW | Harrison | FLORA | Carroll |
| DEPUTY | Jefferson | FLORENCE | Switzerland |
| DERBY | Perry | FLOYDS KNOBS | Floyd |
| DIAMOND VALLEY | Vanderburgh | FOLSOMVILLE | Warrick |
| DILLSBORO | Dearborn | FONTANET | Vigo |
| DONALDSON | Marshall | FOREST | Clinton |
| DUBLIN | Wayne | FORT BRANCH | Gibson |
| DUBOIS | Dubois | FORT RITNER | Lawrence |
| DUGGER | Sullivan | FORTVILLE | Hancock |
| DUNKIRK | Jay | FORT WAYNE | Allen |
| DUNREITH | Henry | FOUNTAIN CITY | Wayne |
| DUPPONT | Jefferson | FOUNTAINTOWN | Shelby |
| DYER | Lake | FOWLER | Benton |
| EARL PARK | Benton | FOWLERTON | Grant |
| EAST ANTHONY | Dubois | FRANCESVILLE | Pulaski |
| EAST BERNICE | Vermillion | FRANCISCO | Gibson |
| EAST CHICAGO | Lake | FRANKFORT | Clinton |
| EAST CROIX | Perry | FRANKLIN | Johnson |
| EAST ENTERPRISE | Switzerland | FRANKTON | Madison |
| EAST JOE | DeKalb | FREDERICKSBURG | Washington |
| EAST JOHN | Lake | FREEDOM | Owen |
| EAST MEINRAD | Spencer | FREELANDVILLE | Knox |
| EAST PAUL | Decatur | FREETOWN | Jackson |
| EATON | Delaware | FREMONT | Steuben |
| ECKERTY | Crawford | FRENCH LICK | Orange |
| ECONOMY | Wayne | FRIENDSHIP | Ripley |
| EDINBERGH | Johnson | FULDA | Spencer |
| EDWARDSPORT | Knox | FULTON | Fulton |
| ELBERFELD | Warrick | GALVESTON | Cass |
| ELIZABETH | Harrison | GARRETT | DeKalb |
| ELIZABETHTOWN | Bartholomew | GARY | Lake |
| ELKHART | Elkhart | GAS CITY | Grant |
| ELLETTSVILLE | Monroe | GASTON | Delaware |
| ELNORA | Daviess | GENEVA | Adams |
| ELWOOD | Madison | GENTRYVILLE | Spencer |
| EMINENCE | Morgan | GEORGETOWN | Floyd |
| EMISON | Knox | GLENWOOD | Fayette |
| ENGLISH | Crawford | GOLDSMITH | Tipton |
| ETNA GREEN | Kosciusko | GOODLAND | Newton |
| EVANSTON | Spencer | GOSHEN | Elkhart |
| EVANSVILLE | Vanderburgh | GOSPORT | Owen |
| FAIRBANKS | Sullivan | GRABILL | Allen |
| FAIRLAND | Shelby | GRANDVIEW | Sullivan |
| FAIRMOUNT | Grant | GRANGER | Saint Joseph |
| FAIR OAKS | Jasper | GRANTSBURG | Crawford |
| FALMOUTH | Rush | GRASS CREEK | Fulton |
| FARMERSBURG | Sullivan | GRAYSVILLE | Sullivan |

| | | | |
|---|---|---|---|
| GREENCASTLE | Putnam | IDAVILLE | White |
| GREENFIELD | Hancock | INDIANAPOLIS | Marion |
| GREENSBORO | Henry | INDIAN SPRINGS | Martin |
| GREENSBURG | Decantur | INGALLS | Madison |
| GREENS FORK | Wayne | INGLEFIELD | Vanderburgh |
| GREENTOWN | Howard | IRELAND | Dubois |
| GREENVILLE | Floyd | JAMESTOWN | Boone |
| GREENWOOD | Johnson | JASONVILLE | Greene |
| GRIFFIN | Posey | JASPER | Dubois |
| GRIFFITH | Lake | JEFFERSONVILLE | Clark |
| GROVERTOWN | Starke | JONESBORO | Grant |
| GUIILFORD | Dearborn | JONESVILLE | Bartholomew |
| GWYNNEVILLE | Shelby | JUDSON | Parke |
| HAGERTOWN | Wayne | KEMPTON | Tipton |
| HAMILTON | Steuben | KENDALLVILLE | Noble |
| HAMLET | Starke | KENNARD | Henry |
| HAMMOND | Lake | KENTLAND | Newton |
| HANNA | La Porte | KEWANNA | Fulton |
| HANOVER | Jefferson | KEYSTONE | Wells |
| HARDINSBURG | Washington | KIMMELL | Noble |
| HARLAN | Allen | KINGMAN | Fountain |
| HARMONY | Clay | KINGSBURY | La Porte |
| WEST HARRISON | Dearborn | KINGSFORD HEIGHTS | La Porte |
| HARRODSBURG | Monroe | KIRKLIN | Clinton |
| HARTFORD CITY | Blackford | KNIGHTSTOWN | Henry |
| HARTSVILLE | Bartholomew | KNIGHTSVILLE | Clay |
| HATFIELD | Spencer | KNOX | Starke |
| HAUBSTADT | Gibson | KOKOMO | Howard |
| HAYDEN | Jennings | KOLEEN | Greene |
| HAZELTON | Gibson | KOUTS | Porter |
| HEBRON | Porter | KURTZ | Jackson |
| HELMER | Steuben | LACONIA | Harrison |
| HELMSBURG | Brown | LACROSSE | La Porte |
| HELTONVILLE | Lawrence | LADOGA | Montgomery |
| HEMLOCK | Howard | LAFAYETTE | Tippecanoe |
| HENRYVILLE | Clark | LAFONTAINE | Wabash |
| HILLISBURG | Clinton | LAGRANGE | LaGrange |
| HILLSBORO | Fountain | LAGRO | Wabash |
| HILLSDALE | Vermillion | LAKE CICOTT | Cass |
| HOAGLAND | Allen | LAKETON | Wabash |
| HOBART | Lake | LAKE VILLAGE | Newton |
| HOBBS | Tipton | LAKEVILLE | Saint Joseph |
| HOLLAND | Dubois | LAMAR | Spencer |
| HOLTON | Ripley | LANDESS | Grant |
| HOMER | Rush | LANESVILLE | Harrison |
| HOPE | Bartholomew | LAOTTO | Noble |
| HOWE | LaGrange | LAPAZ | Marshall |
| HUDSON | Steuben | LAPEL | Madison |
| HUNTERTOWN | Allen | LAPORTE | La Porte |
| HUNTINGBURG | Dubois | LARWILL | Whitley |
| HUNTINGTON | Huntington | LAUREL | Franklin |
| HURON | Lawrence | LAWRENCEBURG | Dearborn |
| HYMERA | Sullivan | LEAVENWORTH | Crawford |

| | | | |
|---|---|---|---|
| LEBANON | Boone | METAMORA | Franklin |
| LEESBURG | Kosciuko | MEXICO | Miami |
| LEITERS FORD | Fulton | MIAMI | Miami |
| LEO | Allen | MICHIGAN CITY | La Porte |
| LEOPOLD | Perry | MICHIGANTOWN | Clinton |
| LEROY | Lake | MIDDLEBURY | Elkhart |
| LEWIS | Vigo | MIDDLETOWN | Henry |
| LEWISVILLE | Henry | MIDLAND | Greene |
| LEXINGTON | Scott | MILAN | Ripley |
| LIBERTY | Union | MILFORD | Kosciusko |
| LIBERTY CENTER | Wells | MILL CREEK | La Porte |
| LIBERTY MILLS | Wabash | MILLERSBURG | Elkhart |
| LIGONIER | Noble | MILHOUSEN | Decatur |
| LINCOLN CITY | Spencer | MILLTOWN | Crawford |
| LINDEN | Montgomery | MILROY | Rush |
| LINN GROVE | Adams | MILTON | Wayne |
| LINTON | Greene | MISHAWAKA | Saint Joseph |
| LITTLE YORK | Washington | MITCHELL | Lawrence |
| LIZTON | Hendricks | MODOC | Randolph |
| LOGANSPORT | Cass | MONGO | LaGrange |
| LOOGOOTEE | Martin | MONON | White |
| LOSANTVILLE | Randolph | MONROE | Adams |
| LOWELL | Lake | MONROE CITY | Knox |
| LUCERNE | Cass | MONROEVILLE | Allen |
| LYNN | Randolph | MONROVIA | Morgan |
| LYNNVILLE | Warrick | MONTEREY | Pulaski |
| LYONS | Greene | MONTEZUMA | Parke |
| MCCORDSVILLE | Hancock | MONTGOMERY | Daviess |
| MACKEY | Gibson | MONTICELLO | White |
| MACY | Miami | MONTMORENCI | Tippecanoe |
| MADISON | Jefferson | MONTPELIER | Blackford |
| MAGNET | Perry | MOORELAND | Henry |
| MANILLA | Rush | MOORES HILL | Dearborn |
| MARENGO | Crawford | MORRESVILLE | Morgan |
| MARIAH HILL | Spencer | MORGANTOWN | Morgan |
| MARION | Grant | MOROCCO | Newton |
| MARKLE | Huntington | MORRIS | Ripley |
| MARKLEVILLE | Madison | MORRISTOWN | Shelby |
| MARSHALL | Parke | MOUNT AYR | Newton |
| MARSHFIELD | Warren | MOUNT PLEASANT | Perry |
| MARTINSVILLE | Morgan | MOUNT SAINT FRANCIS | Floyd |
| MARYSVILLE | Clark | MOUNT SUMMIT | Henry |
| MATTHEWS | Grant | MOUNT VERNON | Posey |
| MAUCKPORT | Harrison | MULBERRY | Clinton |
| MAXWELL | Hancock | MUNCIE | Delaware |
| MAYS | Rush | NABB | Clark |
| MECCA | Parke | NAPOLEON | Ripley |
| MEDARYVILLE | Pulaski | NAPPPANEE | Elkhart |
| MEDORA | Jackson | NASHVILLE | Brown |
| MELLOTT | Fountain | NEBRASKA | Jennings |
| MEMPHIS | Clark | NEEDHAM | Johnson |
| MENTONE | Kosciusko | NEW ALBANY | Floyd |
| MEROM | Sullivan | NEWBERRY | Greene |

| | | | |
|---|---|---|---|
| NEWBURGH | Warrick | PARAGON | Morgan |
| NEW CARLISLE | SaintJoseph | PARIS CROSSING | Jennings |
| NEW CASTLE | Henry | PARKER CITY | Randolph |
| NEW GOSHEN | Vigo | PATOKA | Gibson |
| NEW HARMONY | Posey | PATRICKSBURG | Owen |
| NEW HAVEN | Allen | PATRIOT | Switzerland |
| NEW LISBON | Henry | PAXTON | Sullivan |
| NEW MARKET | Montgomery | PEKIN | Washington |
| NEW MIDDLETOWN | Harrison | PENCE | Warren |
| NEW PALESTINE | Hancock | PENDLETON | Madison |
| NEW PARIS | Elkhart | PENNVILLE | Jay |
| NEW POINT | Decatur | PERRYSVILLE | Vermillion |
| NEWPORT | Vermillion | PERSHING | Wayne |
| NEW RICHMOND | Montgomery | PERU | Miami |
| NEW ROSS | Montgomery | PETERSBURG | Pike |
| NEW SALISBURY | Harrison | PETROLEUM | Wells |
| NEWTOWN | Fountain | PIERCETON | Kosciusko |
| NEW TRENTON | Franklin | PIERCEVILLE | Ripley |
| NEW WASHINGTON | Clark | PIMENTO | Vigo |
| NEW WAVERLY | Cass | PINE VILLAGE | Warren |
| NINEVEH | Johnson | PITTSBORO | Hendricks |
| NOBLESVILLE | Hamilton | PLAINFIELD | Hendricks |
| NORMAN | Jackson | PLAINVILLE | Daviess |
| NORTH JUDSON | Starke | PLEASANT LAKE | Steuben |
| NORTH LIBERTY | St Joseph | PLEASANT MILLS | Adams |
| NORTH MANCHESTER | Wabash | PLYMOUTH | Marshall |
| NORTH SALEM | Hendricks | POLAND | Clay |
| NORTH VERNON | Jennings | PONETO | Wells |
| NORTH WEBSTER | Kosciusko | PORTAGE | Porter |
| NORTE DAME | St Joseph | PORTLAND | Jay |
| OAKFORD | Howard | POSEYVILLE | Posey |
| OAKLAND CITY | Gibson | PRAIRIE CREEK | Vigo |
| OAKTOWN | Knox | PRAIRIETON | Vigo |
| OAKVILLE | Delaware | PREBLE | Adams |
| ODON | Daviess | PRINCETON | Gibson |
| OLDENBURG | Franklin | PUTNAMVILLE | Putnam |
| ONWARD | Cass | QUINCY | Owen |
| OOLITIC | Lawrence | RAGSDALE | Knox |
| ORA | Starke | RAMSEY | Harrison |
| ORESTES | Madison | REDKEY | Jay |
| ORLAND | Steuben | REELSVILLE | Putnbam |
| ORLEANS | Orange | REMINGTON | Jasper |
| OSCEOLA | Saint Joseph | RENSSELAER | Jasper |
| OSGOOD | Ripley | REYNOLDS | White |
| OSSIAN | Wells | RICHLAND | Spencer |
| OTISCO | Clark | RIDGEVILLE | Randolph |
| OTTERBEIN | Benton | RILEY | Vigo |
| OTWELL | Pike | RISING SUN | Ohio |
| OWENSBURG | Greene | ROACHDALE | Putnam |
| OWENSVILLE | Gibson | ROANN | Wabash |
| OXFORD | Benton | ROANOKE | Huntington |
| PALMYRA | Harrison | ROCHESTER | Fulton |
| PAOLI | Orange | ROCKFIELD | Carroll |

| | | | |
|---|---|---|---|
| ROCKPORT | Spencer | SOMERSET | Wabash |
| ROCKVILLE | Parke | SOMERVILLE | Gibson |
| ROLLING PRAIRIE | La Porte | SOUTH AYR | Newton |
| ROME | Perry | SOUTH BEND | Saint Joseph |
| ROME CITY | Noble | SOUTH MILFORD | LaGrange |
| ROMNEY | Tippecanoe | SOUTH PLEASANT | Perry |
| ROSEDALE | Parke | SOUTH SAINT FRANCIS | Floyd |
| ROSELAWN | Newton | SOUTH SUMMIT | Henry |
| ROSSVILLE | Clinton | SOUTH VERNON | Posey |
| ROYAL CENTER | Cass | SOUTH WHITLEY | Whitley |
| RUSHVILLE | Rush | SPENCER | Owen |
| RUSSELLVILLE | Putnam | SPENCERVILLE | DeKalb |
| RUSSIAVILLE | Howard | SPICELAND | Henry |
| SAINT ANTHONY | Dubois | SPRINGPORT | Henry |
| SAINT BERNICE | Vermillion | SPRINGVILLE | Lawrence |
| SAINT CROIX | Perry | SPURGEON | Pike |
| SAINT JOE | DeKalb | STANFORD | Monroe |
| SAINT JOHN | Lake | STAR CITY | Pulaski |
| SAINT MARY-OF-THE-WOODS | Vigo | STATE LINE | Warren |
| SAINT MEINRAD | Spencer | STAUNTON | Clay |
| SAINT PAUL | Decatur | STENDAL | Pike |
| SALAMONIA | Jay | STEWARTSVILLE | Posey |
| SALEM | Washington | STILEVILLE | Hendricks |
| SANDBORN | Knox | STILLWELL | La Porte |
| SANDFORD | Vigo | STINESVILLE | Monroe |
| SAN PIERRE | Starke | STOCKWELL | Tippecanoe |
| SANTA CLAUS | Spencer | STRAUGHN | Henry |
| SARATOGA | Randolph | STROH | LaGrange |
| SCHERERVILLE | Lake | SULLIVAN | Sullivan |
| SCHNEIDER | Lake | SULPHUR | Crawford |
| SCIPIO | Jennings | SULPHUR SPRINGS | Henry |
| SCOTLAND | Greene | SUMAVA RESORTS | Newton |
| SCOTTSBURG | Scott | SUMMITVILLE | Madison |
| SEDALIA | Clinton | SUNMAN | Ripley |
| SEELYVILLE | Vigo | SWAYZEE | Grant |
| SELLERSBURG | Clark | SWEETSER | Grant |
| SELMA | Delaware | SWITZ CITY | Greene |
| SERVIA | Wabash | SYARACUSE | Kosciusko |
| SEYMOUR | Jackson | TALBOT | Benton |
| SHARPSVILLE | Tipton | TANGIER | Parke |
| SHELBURN | Sullivan | TASWELL | Crawford |
| SHELBY | Lake | TAYLORSVILLE | Bartholomew |
| SHELBYVILLE | Shelby | TEFFT | Jasper |
| SHEPARDSVILLE | Vigo | TELL CITY | Perry |
| SHERIDAN | Hamilton | TENNYSON | Warrick |
| SHIPSHEWANA | LaGrange | TERRE HAUTE | Vigo |
| SHIRLEY | Henry | THAYER | Newton |
| SHOALS | Martin | THORNTOWN | Boone |
| SIDNEY | Kosciusko | TIPPECANOE | Marshall |
| SILVER LAKE | Kosciusko | TIPTON | Tipton |
| SIMS | Grant | TOBINSPORT | Perry |
| SMITHVILLE | Monroe | TOPEKA | LaGrange |
| SOLSBERRY | Greene | TRAFALGAR | Johnson |

| | | | |
|---|---|---|---|
| TROY | Perry | WHITING | Lake |
| TUNNELTON | Lawrence | WILKINGSON | Hancock |
| TWELVE MILE | Cass | WILLIAMS | Lawrence |
| TYNER | Marshall | WILLIAMSBURG | Wayne |
| UNION CITY | Randolph | WILLLAMSPORT | Warren |
| UNION MILLS | La Porte | WILLOW BRANCH | Hancock |
| UNIONDALE | Wells | WINAMAC | Pulaski |
| UNIONVILLE | Monroe | WINCHESTER | Randolph |
| UNIVERSAL | Vermillion | WINDFALL | Tipton |
| UPLAND | Grant | WINGATE | Montgomery |
| URBANA | Wabash | WINONA LAKE | Kosciusko |
| VALLONIA | Jackson | WINSLOW | Pike |
| VALPARAISO | Porter | WOLCOTT | White |
| VAN BUREN | Grant | WOLCOTTVILLE | LaGrange |
| VEEDERSBURG | Fountain | WOLFLAKE | Noble |
| VELPEN | Pike | WOODBURN | Allen |
| VERNON | Jennings | WORTHINGTON | Greene |
| VERSAILLES | Ripley | WYATT | St Joseph |
| VEVAY | Switzerland | YEOMAN | Carroll |
| VINCENNES | Knox | YODER | Allen |
| WABASH | Wabash | YORKTOWN | Delaware |
| WADESVILLE | Posey | YOUNG AMERICA | Cass |
| WAKARUSA | Elkhart | ZANESVILLE | Allen |
| WALDRON | Shelby | ZIONSVILLE | Boone |
| WALKERTON | Saint Joseph | **IOWA** | |
| WALLACE | Fountain | ACKLEY | Hardin |
| WALTON | Cass | ACKWORTH | Warren |
| WANATAH | La Porte | ADAIR | Adair |
| WARREN | Huntington | ADEL | Dallas |
| WARSAW | Kosciusko | AFTON | Union |
| WASHINGTON | Daviess | AGENCY | Wapello |
| WATERLOO | DeKalb | AINSWORTH | Washington |
| WAVELAND | Montgomery | AKRON | Plymouth |
| WAWAKA | Noble | ALBERT CITY | Buena Vista |
| WAYNETOWN | Montgomery | ALBIA | Monroe |
| WEBSTER | Wayne | ALBION | Marshall |
| WEST BADEN SPRINGS | Orange | ALBURNETT | Linn |
| WESTFIELD | Hamilton | ALDEN | Hardin |
| WEST FORK | Crawford | ALEXANDER | Franklin |
| WEST HARRISON | Dearborn | ALGONA | Kossuth |
| WEST LEBANON | Warren | ALLEMAN | Polk |
| WEST MIDDLETON | Howard | ALLERTON | Wayne |
| WEST NEWTON | Marion | ALLISON | Butler |
| WESTPHALIA | Knox | ALTA | Buena Vista |
| WESTPOINT | Tippecanoe | ALTA VISTA | Chickasaw |
| WESTPORT | Decatur | ALTON | Sioux |
| WEST TERRE HAUTE | Vigo | ALTOONA | Polk |
| WESTVILLE | La Porte | ALVORD | Lyon |
| WHEATFIELD | Jasper | AMANA | Iowa |
| WHEATLAND | Knox | AMES | Story |
| WHEELER | Porter | ANAMOSA | Jones |
| WHITELAND | Johnson | ANDOVER | Clinton |
| WHITESTOWN | Boone | ANDREW | Jackson |

| | | | |
|---|---|---|---|
| ANITA | Cass | BIRMINGHAM | Van Buren |
| ANKENY | Polk | BLAIRSBURG | Hamilton |
| ANTON | Woodbury | BLAIRSTOWN | Benton |
| APLINGTON | Butler | BLAKESBURG | Wapello |
| ARCADIA | Carroll | BLANCHARD | Page |
| ARCHER | O'Brien | BLENCOE | Monona |
| AREDALE | Butler | BLOCKTON | Taylor |
| ARGYLE | Lee | BLOOMFIELD | Davis |
| ARION | Crawford | BLUE GRASS | Scott |
| ARISPE | Union | BODE | Humboldt |
| ARLINGTON | Fayette | BONAPARTE | Van Buren |
| ARMSTRONG | Enunett | BONDURANT | Polk |
| ARNOLDS PARK | Dickinson | BOONE | Boone |
| ARTHUR | Ida | BONNEVILLE | Dallas |
| ASHTON | Osceola | BOUTON | Dallas |
| ASPINWALL | Crawford | BOXHOLM | Boone |
| ATALISSA | Muscatine | BOYDEN | Sioux |
| ATKINS | Benton | BRADDYVILLE | Page |
| ATLANTIC | Cass | BRADFORD | Franklin |
| AUBURN | Sac | BRADGATE | Humboldt |
| AUDUBON | Audubon | BRANDON | Buchanan |
| AURELIA | Cherokee | BRAYTON | Audubon |
| AURORA | Buchanan | BREDA | Carroll |
| AUSTINVILLE | Butler | BRIDGEWATER | Adair |
| AVOCA | Pottawattamie | BRIGHTON | Washington |
| AYRSHIRE | Palo Alto | BRISTOW | Butler |
| BADGER | Webster | BRITT | Hancock |
| BAGLEY | Guthrie | BRONSON | Woodbury |
| BALDWIN | Jackson | BROOKLYN | Poweshiek |
| BANCROFT | Kossuth | BRUNSVILLE | Plymouth |
| BARNES CITY | Mahaska | BRYANT | Clinton |
| BARNUM | Webster | BUCKEYE | Hardin |
| BARTLETT | Fremont | BUCKINGHAM | Tama |
| BATAVIA | Jefferson | BUFFALO | Scott |
| BATTLE CREEK | Ida | BUFFALO CENTER | Winnebago |
| BAXTER | Jasper | BURLINGTON | Des Moines |
| BAYARD | Guthrie | BURNSIDE | Webster |
| BEACON | Mahaska | BURR OAK | Winneshiek |
| BEACONSFIELD | Ringgold | BURT | Kossuth |
| BEAMAN | Grundy | BUSSEY | Marion |
| BEAVER | Boone | CALAMUS | Clinton |
| BEAVERDALE | Polk | CALLENDER | Webster |
| BEDFORD | Taylor | CALMAR | Winneshiek |
| BELLE PLAINE | Benton | CALUMET | O'Brien |
| BELLEVUE | Jackson | CAMANCHE | Clinton |
| BELLMOND | Wright | CAMBRIDGE | Story |
| BENNETT | Cedar | CANTRIL | Van Buren |
| BENTON | Ringgold | CARBON | Adams |
| BERNARD | Dubuque | CARLISLE | Warren |
| BERWICK | Polk | CARNARVON | Sac |
| BETTENDORF | Scott | CARPENTER | Mitchell |
| BEVINGTON | Madison | CARROLL | Carroll |
| BIG ROCK | Scott | CARSON | Pottawattamie |

| | | | |
|---|---|---|---|
| CASCADE | Dubuque | CORALVILLE | Johnson |
| CASEY | Guthrie | CORNING | Adams |
| CASTALIA | Winneshiek | CORRECTIONVILLE | Woodbury |
| CASTANA | Monona | CORWITH | Hancock |
| CEDAR | Mahaska | CORYDON | Wayne |
| CEDAR FALLS | Black Hawk | COULTER | Franklin |
| CEDAR RAPIDS | Linn | COUNCIL BLUFFS | Pottawattamie |
| CENTER JUNCTION | Jones | CRAIG | Plymouth |
| CENTER POINT | Linn | CRAWFORDSVILLE | Washington |
| CENTERVILLE | Appanoose | CRESCENT | Pottawattamie |
| CENTRAL | Scott | CRESCO | Howard |
| CENTRAL CITY | Linn | CRESTON | Union |
| CENTRAL COLLEGE | Marion | CROMWELL | Union |
| CHAPIN | Franklin | CRYSTAL LAKE | Hancock |
| CHARITON | Lucas | CUMBERLAND | Cass |
| CHARLES CITY | Floyd | CUMMING | Warren |
| CHARLOTTE | Clinton | CURLEW | Palo Alto |
| CHARTER OAK | Crawford | CUSHING | Woodbury |
| CHELSEA | Tama | CYLINDER | Palo Alto |
| CHEROKEE | Cherokee | DAKOTA CITY | Humboldt |
| CHESTER | Howard | DALLAS | Marion |
| CHILLICOTHE | Wapello | DALLAS CENTER | Dallas |
| CHURDAN | Greene | DANA | Greene |
| CINCINNATI | Appanoose | DANBURY | Woodbury |
| CLARE | Webster | DANVILLE | Des Moines |
| CLARENCE | Cedar | DAVENPORT | Scott |
| CLARINDA | Page | DAVIS CITY | Decatur |
| CLARION | Wright | DAWSON | Dallas |
| CLARKSVILLE | Butler | DAYTON | Webster |
| CLEARFIELD | Woodbury | DECATUR | Decatur |
| CLEAR LAKE | Cerro Gordo | DECORAH | Winneshiek |
| CLEGHORN | Cherokee | DEDHAM | Carroll |
| CLEMONS | Marshall | DEEP RIVER | Poweshiek |
| CLERMONT | Fayette | DEFIANCE | Shelby |
| CLIMBING HILL | Woodbury | DELAWARE | Delaware |
| CLINTON | Clinton | DELHI | Delaware |
| CLIO | Wayne | DELMAR | Clinton |
| CLUTIER | Tama | DELOIT | Crawford |
| COGGON | Linn | DELPHOS | Ringgold |
| COIN | Page | DELTA | Keokuk |
| COLESBURG | Delaware | DENISON | Crawford |
| COLFAX | Jasper | DENMARK | Lee |
| COLLEGE SPRINGS | Page | DENVER | Bremer |
| COLLINS | Story | DERBY | Lucas |
| COLO | Story | DES MOINES | Polk |
| COLUMBIA | Marion | DESOTO | Dallas |
| COLUMBUS CITY | Louisa | DEWAR | Black Hawk |
| COLUMBUS JUNCTION | Louisa | DE WITT | Clinton |
| CONESVILLE | Muscatine | DEXTER | Dallas |
| CONRAD | Grundy | DIAGONAL | Ringgold |
| CONROY | Iowa | DICKENS | Clay |
| COON RAPIDS | Carroll | DIKE | Grundy |
| COOPER | Greene | DIXON | Scott |

| | | | |
|---|---|---|---|
| DOLLIVER | Emmett | ESTHERVILLE | Emmet |
| DONAHUE | Scott | EVERLY | Clay |
| DONNELLSON | Lee | EXIRA | Audubon |
| DOON | Lyon | EXLINE | Appanoose |
| DORCHESTER | Allamakee | FAIRBANK | Buchanan |
| DOUDS | Van Buren | FAIRFAX | Linn |
| DOUGHERTY | Cerro Gordo | FAIRFIELD | Jefferson |
| DOW CITY | Crawford | FARLEY | Dubuque |
| DOWS | Wright | FARMERSBURG | Clayton |
| DRAKESVILLE | Davis | FARMINGTON | Van Buren |
| DUBUQUE | Dubuque | FARNHAMVILLE | Calhoun |
| DUMONT | Butler | FARRAGUT | Fremont |
| DUNCOMBE | Webster | FAYETTE | Fayette |
| DUNDEE | Delaware | FENTON | Kossuth |
| DUNKERTON | Black Hawk | FERGUSON | Marshall |
| DUNLAP | Harrison | FERTILE | Worth |
| DURANGO | Dubuque | FESTINA | Winneshiek |
| DURANT | Cedar | FLORIS | Davis |
| DYERSVILLE | Dubuque | FLOYD | Floyd |
| DYSART | Tama | FONDA | Pocahontas |
| EAGLE GROVE | Wright | FONTANELLE | Adair |
| EARLHAM | Madison | FOREST CITY | Winnebago |
| EARLING | Shelby | FORT ATKINSON | Winneshiek |
| EARLVILLE | Delaware | FORT DODGE | Webster |
| EARLY | Sac | FORT MADISON | Lee |
| EAST ANSGAR | Mitchell | FOSTORIA | Clay |
| EAST ANTHONY | Marshall | FREDERICKSBURG | Chickasaw |
| EAST CHARLES | Madison | FREDERIKA | Bremer |
| EAST DONATUS | Jackson | FREMONT | Mahaska |
| EAST LUCAS | Fayette | FRUITIAND | Muscatine |
| EAST MARYS | Warren | GALT | Wright |
| EAST OLAF | Clayton | GALVA | Ida |
| EDDYVILLE | Wapello | GARBER | Clayton |
| EDGEWOOD | Clayton | GARDEN CITY | Hardin |
| ELBERON | Tama | GARDEN GROVE | Decatur |
| ELDON | Wapello | GARNAVILLO | Clayton |
| ELDORA | Hardin | GARNER | Hancock |
| ELDRIDGE | Scott | GARRISON | Benton |
| ELGIN | Fayette | GARWIN | Tama |
| ELKADER | Clayton | GENEVA | Franklin |
| ELKHART | Polk | GEORGE | Lyon |
| ELK HORN | Shelby | GIBSON | Keokuk |
| ELKPORT | Clayton | GILBERT | Story |
| ELLIOTT | Montgomery | GILBERTVILLE | Black Hawk |
| ELLSTON | Ringgold | GILLETT GROVE | Clay |
| ELLSWORTH | Hamilton | GILMAN | Marshall |
| ELMA | Howard | GILMORE CITY | Pocahontas |
| ELWOOD | Clinton | GLADBROOK | Tama |
| ELY | Linn | GLENWOOD | Mills |
| EMERSON | Mills | GLIDDEN | Carroll |
| EMMETSBURG | Palo Alto | GOLDFIELD | Wright |
| EPWORTH | Dubuque | GOODELL | Hancock |
| ESSEX | Page | GOOSE LAKE | Clinton |

| | | | |
|---|---|---|---|
| GOWRIE | Webster | HIGHLANDVILLE | Winneshiek |
| GRAETTINGER | Palo Alto | HILLS | Johnson |
| GRAFTON | Worth | HILLSBORO | Henry |
| GRAND JUNCTION | Greene | HINTON | Plymouth |
| GRAND MOUND | Clinton | HOLLAND | Grundy |
| GRAND RIVER | Decatur | HOLSTEIN | Ida |
| GRANDVIEW | Louisa | HOLY CROSS | Dubuque |
| GRANGER | Dallas | HOMESTEAD | Iowa |
| GRANT | Montgomery | HONEY CREEK | Pottawattamie |
| GRANVILLE | Sioux | HOPKINTON | Delaware |
| GRAVITY | Taylor | HORNICK | Woodbury |
| GRAY | Audubon | HOSPERS | Sioux |
| GREELEY | Delaware | HOUGHTON | Lee |
| GREENE | Butler | HUBBARD | Hardin |
| GREENFIELD | Adair | HUDSON | Black Hawk |
| GREEN ISLAND | Jackson | HULL | Sioux |
| GREEN MOUNTAIN | Marshall | HUMBOLDT | Humboldt |
| GRIMES | Polk | HUMESTON | Wayne |
| GRINNELL | Poweshiek | HUXLEY | Story |
| GRISWOLD | Cass | IDA GROVE | Ida |
| GRUNDY CENTER | Grundy | IMOGENE | Fremont |
| GRUVER | Emmet | INDEPENDENCE | Buchanan |
| GUTHRIE CENTER | Guthrie | INDIANOLA | Warren |
| GUTTENBERG | Clayton | INWOOD | Lyon |
| HALBUR | Fremont | IONIA | Chickasaw |
| HALE | Jones | IOWA CITY | Johnson |
| HAMBURG | Fremont | IOWA FALLS | Hardin |
| HAMILTON | Marion | IRETON | Sioux |
| HAMLIN | Audubon | IRWIN | Shelby |
| HAMPTON | Franklin | JACKSON JUNCTION | Winneshiek |
| HANCOCK | Pottawattamie | JAMAICA | Guthrie |
| HANLONTOWN | Worth | JANESVILLE | Bremer |
| HANSELL | Franklin | JEFFERSON | Greene |
| HARCOURT | Webster | JESUP | Buchanan |
| HARDY | Humboldt | JEWELL | Hamilton |
| HARLAN | Shelby | JOHNSTON | Polk |
| HARPER | Keokuk | JOICE | Worth |
| HARPERS FERRY | Allamakee | JOLLEY | Calhoun |
| HARRIS | Osceola | KALONA | Washington |
| HARTFORD | Warren | KAMRAR | Hamilton |
| HARTLEY | O'Brien | KANAWHA | Hancock |
| HARTWICK | Poweshiek | KELLERTON | Ringgold |
| HARVEY | Marion | KELLEY | Story |
| HASTINGS | Mills | KELLOGG | Jasper |
| HAVELOCK | Pocahontas | KENSETT | Worth |
| HAVERHILL | Marshall | KENT | Union |
| HAWARDEN | Sioux | KEOKUK | Lee |
| HAWKEYE | Fayette | KEOSAUQUA | Van Buren |
| HAYESVILLE | Keokuk | KEOTA | Keokuk |
| HAZLETON | Buchanan | KESLEY | Butler |
| HEDRICK | Keokuk | KESWICK | Keokuk |
| HENDERSON | Mills | KEYSTONE | Benton |
| HIAWATHA | Linn | KILLDUFF | Jasper |

| | | | |
|---|---|---|---|
| KIMBALLTON | Audubon | LITTLE CEDAR | Mitchell |
| KINGSLEY | Plymouth | LITTLE ROCK | Lyon |
| KINROSS | Keokuk | LITTLE SIOUX | Harrison |
| KIRKMAN | Shelby | LIVERMORE | Humboldt |
| KIRKVILLE | Wapello | LOCKRIDGE | Jefferson |
| KIRON | Crawford | LOGAN | Harrison |
| KLEMME | Hancock | LOHRVILLE | Calhoun |
| KNIERIM | Calhoun | LONE ROCK | Kossuth |
| KNOKE | Pocahontas | LONE TREE | Johnson |
| KNOXVILLE | Marion | LONG GROVE | Scott |
| LACONA | Warren | LORIMOR | Union |
| LADORA | Iowa | LOST NATION | Clinton |
| LAKE CITY | Calhoun | LOVILIA | Monroe |
| LAKE MILLS | Winnebago | LOWDEN | Cedar |
| LAKE PARK | Dickinson | LOW MOOR | Clinton |
| LAKE VIEW | Sac | LUANA | Clayton |
| LAKOTA | Kossuth | LUCAS | Lucas |
| LAMONI | Decatur | LUTHER | Boone |
| LAMONT | Buchanan | LU VERNE | Kossuth |
| LAMOTTE | Jackson | LUXEMBURG | Dubuque |
| LANESBORO | Carroll | LUZERNE | Benton |
| LANSING | Allamakee | LYNNVILLE | Jasper |
| LAPORTE CITY | Black Hawk | LYTTON | Sac |
| LARCHWOOD | Lyon | MCCALLSBURG | Story |
| LARRABEE | Cherokee | MCCAUSLAND | Scott |
| LATIMER | Franklin | MCCLELLAND | Pottawattamie |
| LAUREL | Marshall | MCGREGOR | Clayton |
| LAURENS | Pocahontas | MCINTIRE | Mitchell |
| LAWLER | Chickasaw | MACEDONIA | Pottawattamie |
| LAWTON | Woodbury | MACKSBURG | Madison |
| LE CLAIRE | Scott | MADRID | Boone |
| LEDYARD | Kossuth | MALCOM | Poweshiek |
| LE GRAND | Marshall | MALLARD | Palo Alto |
| LEHIGH | Webster | MALOY | Ringgold |
| LEIGHTON | Mahaska | MALVERN | Mills |
| LELAND | Winnebago | MANCHESTER | Delaware |
| LE MARS | Plymouth | MANILLA | Crawford |
| LENOX | Taylor | MANLY | Worth |
| LEON | Decatur | MANNING | Carroll |
| LESTER | Lyon | MANSON | Calhoun |
| LETTS | Louisa | MAPLETON | Monona |
| LEWIS | Cass | MAQUOKETA | Jackson |
| LIBERTY CENTER | Warren | MARATHON | Buena Vista |
| LIBERTYVILLE | Jefferson | MARBLE ROCK | Floyd |
| LIDDERDALE | Carroll | MARCUS | Cherokee |
| LIME SPRINGS | Howard | MARENGO | Iowa |
| LINCOLN | Tama | MARION | Linn |
| LINDEN | Dallas | MARNE | Cass |
| LINEVILLE | Wayne | MARQUETTE | Clayton |
| LINN GROVE | Buena Vista | MARSHALLTOWN | Marshall |
| LISBON | Linn | MARTELLE | Jones |
| LISCOMB | Marshall | MARTENSDALE | Warren |
| LITTLEPORT | Clayton | MARTINSBURG | Keokuk |

| | | | |
|---|---|---|---|
| MASON CITY | Cerro Gordo | MOUNT UNION | Henry |
| MASONVILLE | Delaware | MOUNT VERNON | Linn |
| MATLOK | Sioux | MOVILLE | Woodbury |
| MASSENA | Cass | MURRAY | Clarke |
| MAURICE | Sioux | MUSCATINE | Muscatine |
| MAXWELL | Story | MYSTIC | Appanoose |
| MAYNARD | Fayette | NASHUA | Chickasaw |
| MECHANICSVILLE | Cedar | NEMAHA | Sac |
| MEDIAPOLIS | Des Moines | NEOLA | Pottawattamie |
| MELBOURNE | Marshall | NEVADA | Story |
| MELCHER | Marion | NEW ALBIN | Allamakee |
| MELROSE | Monroe | NEWELL | Buena Vista |
| MELVIN | Osceola | NEWHALL | Benton |
| MENLO | Guthrie | NEW HAMPTON | Chickasaw |
| MERIDEN | Cherokee | NEW HARTFORD | Butler |
| MERRILL | Plymouth | NEW LIBERTY | Scott |
| MESERVEY | Cerro Gordo | NEW LONDON | Henry |
| MIDDLE | Iowa | NEW MARKET | Taylor |
| MIDDLETOWN | Des Moines | NEW PROVIDENCE | Hardin |
| MILES | Jackson | NEW SHARON | Mahaska |
| MILFORD | Dickinson | NEWTON | Jasper |
| MILLERSBURG | Iowa | NEW VIENNA | Dubuque |
| MILLERTON | Wayne | NEW VIRGINIA | Warren |
| MILO | Warren | NICHOLS | Muscatine |
| MILTON | Van Buren | NODAWAY | Adams |
| MINBURN | Dallas | NORA SPRINGS | Floyd |
| MINDEN | Pottawattamie | NORTHBORO | Page |
| MINEOLA | Mills | NORTH BUENA VISTA | Clayton |
| MINGO | Jasper | NORTH ENGLISH | Iowa |
| MISSOURI VALLEY | Harrison | NORTH LIBERTY | Johnson |
| MITCHELLVILLE | Polk | NORTHWOOD | Worth |
| MODALE | Harrison | NORWALK | Warren |
| MONDAMIN | Harrison | NORWAY | Benton |
| MONMOUTH | Jackson | NUMA | Appanoose |
| MONONA | Clayton | OAKDALE | Johnson |
| MONROE | Jasper | OAKLAND | Pottawattamie |
| MONTEZUMA | Poweshiek | OAKVILLE | Louisa |
| MONTICELLO | Jones | OCHEYEDAN | Osceola |
| MONTOUR | Tama | ODEBOLT | Sac |
| MONTPELIER | Muscatine | OELWEIN | Fayette |
| MONTROSE | Lee | OGDEN | Boone |
| MOORHEAD | Monona | OKOBOJI | Dickinson |
| MOORLAND | Webster | OLDS | Henry |
| MORAVIA | Appanoose | OLIN | Jones |
| MORLEY | Jones | OLLIE | Keokuk |
| MORNING SUN | Louisa | ONAWA | Monona |
| MORRISON | Grundy | ONSLOW | Jones |
| MOSCOW | Muscatine | ORAN | Fayette |
| MOULTON | Appanoose | ORANGE CITY | Sioux |
| MOUNT AUBURN | Benton | ORCHARD | Mitchell |
| MOUNT AYR | Ringgold | ORIENT | Adair |
| MOUNT ETNA | Adams | OSAGE | Mitchell |
| MOUNT PLEASANT | Henry | OSCEOLA | Clarke |

| | | | |
|---|---|---|---|
| OSKALOOSA | Mahaska | PROTIVIN | Howard |
| OSSIAN | Winneshiek | PULASKI | Davis |
| OTHO | Webster | QUASQUETON | Buchanan |
| OTLEY | Marion | QUIMBY | Cherokee |
| OTO | Woodbury | RADCLIFFE | Hardin |
| OTTOSEN | Humboldt | RAKE | Winnebago |
| OTTUMWA | Wapello | RALSTON | Carroll |
| OXFORD | Johnson | RANDALIA | Fayette |
| OXFORD JUNCTION | Jones | RANDALL | Hamilton |
| OYENS | Plymouth | RANDOLPH | Fremont |
| PACIFIC JUNCTION | Mills | RAYMOND | Black Hawk |
| PACKWOOD | Jefferson | READLYN | Bremer |
| PALMER | Pocahontas | REASNOR | Jasper |
| PALO | Linn | REDDING | Ringgold |
| PANAMA | Shelby | REDFIELD | Dallas |
| PANORA | Guthrie | RED OAK | Montgomery |
| PARKERSBURG | Butler | REINBECK | Grundy |
| PARNELL | Iowa | REMBRANDT | Buena Vista |
| PATON | Greene | REMSEN | Plymouth |
| PATTERSON | Madison | RENWICK | Humboldt |
| PAULLINA | O'Brien | RHODES | Marshall |
| PELLA | Marion | RICEVILLE | Mitchell |
| PEOSTA | Dubuque | RICHLAND | Keokuk |
| PERCIVAL | Fremont | RICKETTS | Crawford |
| PERRY | Dallas | RIDGEWAY | Winneshiek |
| PERSHING | Marion | RINGSTED | Emmet |
| PERSIA | Harrison | REPPEY | Greene |
| PERU | Madison | RIVERSIDE | Washington |
| PETERSON | Clay | RIVERTON | Fremont |
| PIERSON | Woodbury | ROBINS | Linn |
| PILOT GROVE | Lee | ROCKFORD | Floyd |
| PILOT MOUND | Boone | ROCK RAPIDS | Lyon |
| PISGAH | Harrison | ROCK VALLEY | Sioux |
| PLAINFIELD | Bremer | ROCKWELL | Cerro Gordo |
| PLANO | Appanoose | ROCKWELL CITY | Calhoun |
| PLEASANT VALLEY | Scott | RODMAN | Palo Alto |
| PLEASANTVILLE | Marion | RODNEY | Monona |
| PLOVER | Pocahontas | ROLAND | Story |
| PLYMOUTH | Cerro Gordo | ROLFE | Pocahontas |
| POCAHONTAS | Pocahontas | ROME | Henry |
| POLK CITY | Polk | ROSE HILL | Mahaska |
| POMEROY | Calhoun | ROWAN | Wright |
| POPEJOY | Franklin | ROWLEY | Buchanan |
| PORTSMOUTH | Shelby | ROYAL | Clay |
| POSTVILLE | Allamakee | RUDD | Floyd |
| PRAIRIE CITY | Jasper | RUNNELLS | Polk |
| PRAIRIEBURG | Linn | RUSSELL | Lucas |
| PRESCOTT | Adams | RUTHVEN | Palo Alto |
| PRESTON | Jackson | RUTLAND | Humboldt |
| PRIMGHAR | O'Brien | RYAN | Delaware |
| PRINCETON | Scott | SABULA | Jackson |
| PROLE | Warren | SAC CITY | Sac |
| PROMISE CITY | Wayne | SAINT ANSGAR | Mitchell |

*Appendix*  A-81

| | | | |
|---|---|---|---|
| SAINT ANTHONY | Marshall | SPERRY | Des Moines |
| SAINT CHARLES | Madison | SPILLVILLE | Winneshiek |
| SAINT DONATUS | Jackson | SPIRIT LAKE | Dickinson |
| SAINT LUCAS | Fayette | SPRAGUEVILLE | Jackson |
| SAINT MARYS | Warren | SPRINGBROOK | Jackson |
| SAINT OLAF | Clayton | SPRINGVILLE | Linn |
| SALEM | Henry | STACYVILLE | Mitchell |
| SALIX | Woodbury | STANHOPE | Hamilton |
| SANBORN | O'Brien | STANLEY | Buchanan |
| SCARVILLE | Winnebago | STANTON | Montgomery |
| SCHALLER | Sac | STANWOOD | Cedar |
| SCHELSWIG | Crawford | STATE CENTER | Marshall |
| SCOTCH GROVE | Jones | STEAMBOAT ROCK | Hardin |
| SCRANTON | Greene | STOCKPORT | Van Buren |
| SEARSBORO | Poweshiek | STOCKTON | Muscatine |
| SELMA | Van Buren | STORM LAKE | Buena Vista |
| SERGEANT BLUFF | Woodbury | STORY CITY | Story |
| SEYMOUR | Wayne | STOUT | Grundy |
| SHAMBAUGH | Page | STRATFORD | Hamilton |
| SHANNON CITY | Union | STRAWBERRY POINT | Clayton |
| SHARPSBURG | Taylor | STRUBLE | Plymouth |
| SHEFFIELD | Franklin | STUART | Guthrie |
| SHELBY | Shelby | SULLY | Jasper |
| SHELDAHL | Polk | SUMNER | Bremer |
| SHELDON | O'Brien | SUPERIOR | Dickinson |
| SHELL ROCK | Butler | SUTHERLAND | O'Brien |
| SHELLSBURG | Benton | SWALEDALE | Cerro Gordo |
| SHENANDOAH | Page | SWAN | Marion |
| SHERRILL | Dubuque | SWEA CITY | Kossuth |
| SIBLEY | Osceola | SWEDESBURG | Henry |
| SIDNEY | Fremont | SWISHER | Johnson |
| SIGOURNEY | Keokuk | TABOR | Fremont |
| SILVER CITY | Mills | TAINTOR | Mahaska |
| SIOUX CENTER | Sioux | TAMA | Tama |
| SIOUX CITY | Woodbury | TEEDS GROVE | Clinton |
| SIOUX RAPIDS | Buena Vista | TEMPLETON | Carroll |
| SLATER | Story | TENNANT | Shelby |
| SLOAN | Woodbury | TERRIL | Dickinson |
| SMITHLAND | Woodbury | THAYER | Union |
| SOLDIER | Monona | THOMPSON | Winnebago |
| SOLON | Johnson | THOR | Humboldt |
| SOMERS | Calhoun | THORNBURG | Keokuk |
| SOUTH AMANA | Iowa | THORNTON | Cerro Gordo |
| SOUTH AUBURN | Benton | THURMAN | Fremont |
| SOUTH AYR | Ringgold | TIFFIN | Johnson |
| SOUTH DES MOINES | Polk | TINGLEY | Ringgold |
| SOUTH ENGLISH | Keokuk | TIPTON | Cedar |
| SOUTH ETNA | Adams | TITONKA | Kossuth |
| SOUTH PLEASANT | Henry | TODDVILLE | Linn |
| SOUTH STERLING | Van Buren | TOLEDO | Tama |
| SOUTH UNION | Henry | TORONTO | Clinton |
| SOUTH VERNON | Linn | TRACY | Marion |
| SPENCER | Clay | TRAER | Tama |

| | | | |
|---|---|---|---|
| TREYNOR | Pottawattamie | WELTON | Clinton |
| TRIPOLI | Bremer | WESLEY | Kossuth |
| TROY MILLS | Linn | WEST AMANA | Iowa |
| TRUESDALE | Buena Vista | WEST BEND | Palo Alto |
| TRURO | Madison | WEST BRANCH | Cedar |
| TURIN | Monona | WEST BURLINGTON | Des Moines |
| UDELL | Appanoose | WEST CHESTER | Washington |
| UNDERWOOD | Pottawattamie | WEST DES MOINES | Polk |
| UNION | Hardin | WEST DES MOINES | Des Moines |
| UNIONVILLE | Appanoose | WESTFIELD | Plymouth |
| UNIVERSITY PARK | Mahaska | WESTGATE | Fayette |
| UNIVERSITY PLACE | Des Moines | WEST GROVE | Davis |
| URBANA | Benton | WEST LIBERTY | Muscatine |
| URBANDALE | Des Moines | WESTPHALIA | Shelby |
| UTE | Monona | WEST POINT | Lee |
| VAIL | Crawford | WESTSIDE | Crawford |
| VAN HORNE | Benton | WEST SUBURBAN | Des Moines |
| VAN METER | Dallas | WEST UNION | Fayette |
| VAN WERT | Decatur | WEVER | Lee |
| VARINA | Pocahontas | WHAT CHEER | Keokuk |
| VENTURA | Cerro Gordo | WHEATLAND | Clinton |
| VICTOR | Iowa | WHITING | Monona |
| VILLISCA | Montgomery | WHITTEMORE | Kossuth |
| VINCENT | Webster | WHITTEN | Hardin |
| VINING | Tama | WILLIAM PENN COLLEGE | Mahaska |
| VINTON | Benton | WILLIAMS | Hamilton |
| VIOLA | Linn | WILLIAMSBURG | Iowa |
| VOLGA | Clayton | WILLIAMSON | Lucas |
| WADENA | Fayette | WILTON | Muscatine |
| WALCOTT | Scott | WINFIELD | Henry |
| WALFORD | Benton | WINTERSET | Madison |
| WALKER | Linn | WINTHROP | Buchanan |
| WALLINGFORD | Emmet | WIOTA | Cass |
| WALL LAKE | Sac | WODEN | Hancock |
| WALNUT | Pottawattamie | WOODBINE | Harrison |
| WAPELLO | Louisa | WOODBURN | Clarke |
| WASHBURN | Black Hawk | WOODWARD | Dallas |
| WASHINGTON | Washington | WOOLSTOCK | Wright |
| WASHTA | Cherokee | WORTHINGTON | Dubuque |
| WATERLOO | Black Hawk | WYOMING | Jones |
| WATERVILLE | Allamakee | YALE | Guthrie |
| WATKINS | Benton | YARMOUTH | Des Moines |
| WAUCOMA | Fayette | YETTER | Auburn |
| WAUKEE | Dallas | YORKTOWN | Page |
| WAUKON | Allamakee | ZEARING | Story |
| WAVERLY | Bremer | ZWINGLE | Dubuque |
| WAYLAND | Henry | **KANSAS** | |
| WEBB | Clay | ABBYVILLE | Reno |
| WEBSTER | Keokuk | ABILENE | Dickinson |
| WEBSTER CITY | Hamilton | ADMIRE | Lyon |
| WELDON | Decatur | AGENDA | Republic |
| WELLMAN | Washington | AGRA | Phillips |
| WELLSBURG | Grundy | ALAMOTA | Lane |

| | | | |
|---|---|---|---|
| ALBERT | Barton | BELMONT | Kingman |
| ALDEN | Rice | BELOIT | Mitchell |
| ALEXANDER | Rush | BELPRE | Edwards |
| ALLEN | Lyon | BELVIDERE | Kiowa |
| ANGOLA | Coffey | BELVUE | Pottawatomie |
| ALMA | Wabaunsee | BENDENA | Doniphan |
| ALMENA | Norton | BENEDICT | Wilson |
| ALTAMONT | Labette | BENNINGTON | Ottawa |
| ALTA VISTA | Wabaunsee | BENTLEY | Sedgewick |
| ALTON | Osborne | BENTON | Butler |
| ALTOONA | Wilson | BERN | Nemaha |
| AMERICUS | Lyon | BERRYTON | Shawnee |
| AMES | Cloud | BEVERLY | Lincoln |
| ANDALE | Sedgwick | BIRD CITY | Cheyenne |
| ANDOVER | Butler | BISON | Rush |
| ANTELOPE | Lincolnville | BLOOM | Ford |
| ANTHONY | Harper | BLUE MOUND | Linn |
| ANTONIO | Hays | BLUE RAPIDS | Marshall |
| ARCADIA | Crawford | BLUE VALLEY | Johnson |
| ARGENTINE | Wyandotte | BLUFF CITY | Harper |
| ARGONIA | Sumner | BOGUE | Graham |
| ARKANSAS CITY | Cowley | BONNER SPRINGS | Wyandotte |
| ARLINGTON | Reno | BREMEN | Marshall |
| ARMA | Crawford | BREWSTER | Thomas |
| ARNOLD | Ness | BRONSON | Bourbon |
| ASHLAND | Clark | BROOKRIDGE | Johnson |
| ASSARIA | Saline | BROOKVILLE | Saline |
| ATCHISON | Atchison | BROWNELL | Ness |
| ATHOL | Smith | BUCKLIN | Ford |
| ATLANTA | Cowley | BUCYRUS | Miami |
| ATTICA | Harper | BUFFALO | Wilson |
| ATWOOD | Rawlins | BUHLER | Reno |
| AUBURN | Shawnee | BUNKER HILL | Russell |
| AUGUSTA | Butler | BURDEN | Cowley |
| AURORA | Cloud | BURDETT | Pawnee |
| AXTELL | Marshall | BURDICK | Morris |
| BAILEYVILLE | Nemaha | BURLINGAME | Osage |
| BALDWIN CITY | Douglas | BURLINGTON | Coffey |
| BARNARD | Lincoln | BURNS | Marion |
| BARNES | Washington | BURR OAK | Jewell |
| BARTLETT | Labette | BURRTON | Harvey |
| BASEHOR | Leavenworth | BUSHONG | Allen |
| BAVARIA | Salina | BUSHTON | Rice |
| BAXTER SPRINGS | Cherokee | BYERS | Pratt |
| BAZINE | Ness | CALDWELL | Sumner |
| BEATTIE | Marshall | CAMBRIDGE | Cowley |
| BEAUMONT | Butler | CANEY | Montgomery |
| BEAVER | Barton | CANTON | McPherson |
| BEELER | Ness | CARBONDALE | Osage |
| BEL AIRE | Wichita | CARLTON | Dickinson |
| BELLAIRE | Lebanon | CARLYLE | Iola |
| BELLE PLAINE | Sumner | CARONA | Cherokee |
| BELLEVILLE | Republic | CASSODAY | Butler |

**Adoption Searches Made Easier**

| | | | |
|---|---|---|---|
| CATHARINE | Ellis | DAMAR | Rooks |
| CAWKER CITY | Mitchell | DANVILLE | Harper |
| CEDAR | Smith | DEARING | Montgomery |
| CEDAR POINT | Chase | DEERFIELD | Kearny |
| CEDAR VALE | Chautauqua | DELANO | Wichita |
| CENTERVILLE | Linn | DELAVAN | Morris |
| CENTRALIA | Nemaha | DELIA | Jackson |
| CHANUTE | Neosho | DELPHOS | Ottawa |
| CHAPMAN | Dickinson | DENISON | Jackson |
| CHASE | Rice | DENNIS | Labette |
| CHAUTAUQUA | Chautauqua | DENSMORE | Norton |
| CHENEY | Sedgwick | DENTON | Doniphan |
| CHEROKEE | Crawford | DERBY | Sedgwick |
| CHERRYVALE | Montgomery | DE SOTO | Johnson |
| CHETOPA | Labette | DEXTER | Cowley |
| CHISHOLM | Wichita | DIGHTON | Lane |
| CIMARRON | Gray | DODGE CITY | Ford |
| CIRCLEVILLE | Jackson | DORRANCE | Russell |
| CLAFLIN | Barton | DOUGLASS | Butler |
| CLAY CENTER | Clay | DOVER | Shawnee |
| CLAYTON | Norton | DOWNS | Osborne |
| CLEARVIEW CITY | Johnson | DRESDEN | Decatur |
| CLEARWATER | Sedgwick | DULUTH | Pottawatomie |
| CLEMENTS | Chase | DUNLAP | Morris |
| CLIFTON | Washington | DURHAM | Marion |
| CLIMAX | Greenwood | DWIGHT | Morris |
| CLYDE | Cloud | EASTBOROUGH | Wichita |
| COATS | Pratt | EASTON | Leavenworth |
| CODELL | Rooks | EDGERTON | Johnson |
| COFFEYVILLE | Montgomery | EDMOND | Norton |
| COLBY | Thomas | EDNA | Labette |
| COLDWATER | Comanche | EDSON | Sherman |
| COLLYER | Trego | EDWARDSVILLE | Wyandotte |
| COLONY | Anderson | EFFINGHAM | Atchison |
| COLUMBUS | Cherokee | ELBING | Butler |
| COLWICH | Sedgwick | EL DORADO | Butler |
| CONCORDIA | Cloud | ELK CITY | Montgomery |
| CONWAY | McPherson | ELK FALLS | Elk |
| CONWAY SPRINGS | Sumner | ELKHART | Morton |
| COOLIDGE | Hamilton | ELLINWOOD | Barton |
| COPELAND | Gray | ELLIS | Ellis |
| CORBIN | Sumner | ELLSWORTH | Ellsworth |
| CORNING | Nemaha | ELMDALE | Chase |
| CORPORATE HILLS | Wichita | ELSMORE | Allen |
| COTTONWOOD FALLS | Chase | ELWOOD | Doniphan |
| COUNCIL GROVE | Morris | EMMETT | Pottawatomie |
| COURTLAND | Republic | EMPORIA | Lyon |
| COYVILLE | Wilson | ENGLEWOOD | Clark |
| CRESTLINE | Cherokee | ENSIGN | Gray |
| CUBA | Republic | ENTERPRISE | Dickinson |
| CULVER | Ottawa | ERIE | Neosho |
| CUMMINGS | Atchison | EBSON | Jewell |
| CUNNINGHAM | Kingman | ESKRIDGE | Wabaunsee |

| | | | |
|---|---|---|---|
| EUDORA | Douglas | GREAT BEND | Barton |
| EUREKA | Greenwood | GREELEY | Anderson |
| EVEREST | Brown | GREEN | Clay |
| FAIRFAX | Wyandotte | GREENLEAF | Washington |
| FAIRVIEW | Brown | GREENSBURG | Kiowa |
| FAIRWAY | Johnson | GREENWICH | Wichita |
| FALL RIVER | Greenwood | GRENOLA | Elk |
| FALUN | Saline | GRIDLEY | Coffey |
| FARLINGTON | Crawford | GRINNELL | Gove |
| FLORENCE | Marion | GYPSUM | Saline |
| FONTANA | Miami | HADDAM | Washington |
| FORD | Ford | HALLOWELL | Cherokee |
| FORMOSA | Jewell | RAISTEAD | Harvey |
| FORT DODGE | Ford | HAMILTON | Greenwood |
| FORT LEAVENWORTH | Leavenworth | HANOVER | Washington |
| FORT RILEY | Geary | HANSTON | Hodgeman |
| FORT SCOTT | Bourbon | HARDTNER | Barber |
| FOSTORIA | Pottawatomie | HARLAN | Smith |
| FOWLER | Meade | HARPER | Harper |
| FRANKFORT | Marshall | HARTFORD | Lyon |
| FRANKLIN | Crawford | HARVEYVILLE | Wabaunsee |
| FREDONIA | Wilson | HAVANA | Montgomery |
| FREEPORT | Harper | HAVEN | Reno |
| FRIEND | Finney | HAVENSVILLE | Pottawatomie |
| FRONTENAC | Crawford | HAVILAND | Kiowa |
| FULTON | Bourbon | HAYS | Ellis |
| GAGE CENTER | Topeka | HAYSVILLE | Sedgwick |
| GALENA | Cherokee | HAZELTON | Barber |
| GALESBURG | Neosho | HEALY | Lane |
| GALVA | McPherson | HEPLER | Crawford |
| GARDEN CITY | Finney | HERINGTON | Dickinson |
| GARDEN PLAIN | Sedgwick | HERKIMER | Marshall |
| GARDNER | Johnson | HERNDON | Rawlins |
| GARFIELD | Pawnee | HESSTON | Harvey |
| GARLAND | Bourbon | HIATTVILLE | Bourbon |
| GARNETT | Anderson | HIAWATHA | Brown |
| GAS | Allen | HICREST | Shawnee |
| GAYLORD | Smith | HIGHLAND | Doniphan |
| GEM | Thomas | HILL CITY | Graham |
| GENESEO | Rice | HILLSBORO | Marion |
| GEUDA SPRINGS | Sumner | HILLSDALE | Miami |
| GIRARD | Crawford | HOISINGTON | Barton |
| GLADE | Phillips | HOLCOMB | Finney |
| GLASCO | Cloud | HOLLENBERG | Washington |
| GLEN ELDER | Mitchell | HOLTON | Jackson |
| GODDARD | Sedgwick | HOLYROOD | Ellsworth |
| GOESSEL | Marion | HOME | Marshall |
| GOFF | Nemaha | HOPE | Dickinson |
| GOODLAND | Sherman | HORTON | Brown |
| GORHAM | Russell | HOWARD | Elk |
| GOVE | Gove | HOXIE | Sheridan |
| GRAINFIELD | Gove | HOYT | Jackson |
| GRANTVILLE | Jefferson | HUDSON | Stafford |

**Adoption Searches Made Easier**

| | | | |
|---|---|---|---|
| HUGOTON | Stevens | LEAWOOD | Johnson |
| HUMBOLDT | Allen | LEBANON | Smith |
| HUNTER | Mitchell | LEBO | Coffey |
| HURON | Atchison | LECOMPTON | Douglas |
| HUTCHINSON | Reno | LEHIGH | Marion |
| INDEPENDENCE | Montgomery | LENEXA | Johnson |
| INDIAN CREEK | Johnson | LENORA | Norton |
| INDIAN SPRING | Wyandotte | LEON | Butler |
| INGALLS | Gray | LEONARDVILLE | Riley |
| INMAN | McPherson | LEOTI | Wichita |
| IOLA | Allen | LE ROY | Coffey |
| IONIA | Jewell | LEVANT | Thomas |
| ISABEL | Barber | LEWIS | Edwards |
| IUKA | Pratt | LIBERAL | Seward |
| JAMESTOWN | Cloud | LIBERTY | Montgomery |
| JAYHAWK | Lawrence | LIEBENTHAL | Rush |
| JENNINGS | Decatur | LINCOLN | Lincoln |
| JETMORE | Hodgeman | LINCOLNVILLE | Marion |
| JEWELL | Jewell | LINDSBORG | McPherson |
| JOHNSON | Stanton | LINN | Washington |
| JUNCTION CITY | Geary | LINWOOD | Leavenworth |
| KALVESTA | Finney | LITTLE RIVER | Rice |
| KANOPOLIS | Ellsworth | LOGAN | Phillips |
| KANORADO | Sherman | LONGFORD | Clay |
| KANSAS CITY | Wyandotte | LONG ISLAND | Phillips |
| KECHI | Sedgwick | LONGTON | Elk |
| KELLY | Seneca | LORRAINE | Ellsworth |
| KENDALL | Hamilton | LOST SPRINGS | Marion |
| KENSINGTON | Smith | LOUISBURG | Miami |
| KINCAID | Anderson | LOUISVILLE | Pottawatomie |
| KINGMAN | Kingman | LUCAS | Russell |
| KINGSDOWN | Ford | LUDELL | Rawlins |
| KINSLEY | Edwards | LURAY | Russell |
| KIOWA | Barber | LYNDON | Osage |
| KIRWIN | Phillips | LYONS | Rice |
| KISMET | Seward | MACKSVILLE | Stafford |
| LA CROSSE | Rush | MADISON | Greenwood |
| LA CYGNE | Linn | MAHASKA | Washington |
| LA HARPE | Allen | MAIZE | Sedgwick |
| LAKE CITY | Barber | MANCHESTER | Dickinson |
| LAKE OF THE FOREST | Wyandotte | MANHATTEN | Riley |
| LAKE QUIVIRA | Wyandotte | MANKATO | Jewell |
| LAKIN | Kearny | MANTER | Stanton |
| LAMONT | Greenwood | MAPLE CITY | Cowley |
| LANCASTER | Atchison | MAPLE HILL | Wabaunsee |
| LANE | Franklin | MAPLETON | Bourbon |
| LANGDON | Reno | MARIENTHAL | Wichita |
| LANSING | Leavenworth | MARION | Marion |
| LARNED | Pawnee | MARQUETTE | McPherson |
| LATHAM | Butler | MARYSVILLE | Marshall |
| LAWRENCE | Douglas | MATFIELD GREEN | Chase |
| LAWTON | Weir | MAYETTA | Jackson |
| LEAVENWORTH | Leavenworth | MAYFIELD | Sumner |

| | | | |
|---|---|---|---|
| McCONNEL AFB | Wichita | NEOSHO FALLS | Woodson |
| McCRACKEN | Rush | NEOSHO RAPIDS | Lyon |
| McCUNE | Crawford | NESS CITY | Ness |
| McDONALD | Rawlins | NETAWAKA | Jackson |
| McLOUTH | Jefferson | NEW ALBANY | Wilson |
| McPHERSON | McPherson | NEW ALMELO | Norton |
| MEADE | Meade | NEW CAMBRIA | Saline |
| MEDICINE LODGE | Barber | NEWTON | Harvey |
| MEDORA | Hutchinson | NICKERSON | Reno |
| MELVERN | Osage | NIOTAZE | Chautauqua |
| MENLO | Thomas | NORCATUR | Decatur |
| MENTOR | Saline | NORTH NEWTON | Harvey |
| MERIDEN | Jefferson | NORTH TOPEKA | Shawnee |
| MERRIAM | Johnson | NORTH WICHITA | Wichita |
| MIDLAND | Wichita | NORTON | Norton |
| MILAN | Sumner | NORTONVILLE | Jefferson |
| MILDRED | Anderson | NORWAY | Republic |
| MILFORD | Geary | NORWICH | Kingman |
| MILTON | Sumner | OAKHILL | Clay |
| MILTONVALE | Cloud | OAKLEY | Logan |
| MINNEAPOLIS | Ottawa | OBERLIN | Decatur |
| MINNEOLA | Clark | ODIN | Barton |
| MISSION | Johnson | OFFERLE | Edwards |
| MISSION WOODS | Johnson | OGALLAH | Trego |
| MODOC | Scott | OGDEN | Riley |
| MOLINE | Elk | OKETO | Marshall |
| MONTEZUMA | Gray | OLATHE | Johnson |
| MONUMENT | Logan | OLMITZ | Barton |
| MORAN | Allen | OLPE | Lyon |
| MORGANVILLE | Clay | OLSBURG | Pottawatomie |
| MORLAND | Graham | ONAGA | Pottawatomie |
| MORRILL | Brown | ONEIDA | Nemaha |
| MORROWVILLE | Washington | OPOLIS | Crawford |
| MOSCOW | Stevens | OSAGE CITY | Osage |
| MOUND CITY | Linn | OSAWATOMIE | Miami |
| MOUNDRIDGE | McPherson | OSBORNE | Osborne |
| MOUND VALLEY | Labette | OSKALOOSA | Jefferson |
| MOUNT HOPE | Sedgwick | OSWEGO | Labette |
| MULBERRY | Crawford | OTIS | Rush |
| MULLINVILLE | Kiowa | OTTAWA | Franklin |
| MULVANE | Sumner | OVERBROOK | Osage |
| MUNCIE | Wyandotte | OVERLAND PARK | Johnson |
| MUNDEN | Republic | OXFORD | Sumner |
| MUNGER | Wichita | OZAWKIE | Jefferson |
| MURDOCK | Kingman | PACKERS | Wyandotte |
| MUSCOTAH | Atchison | PALCO | Rooks |
| NARKA | Republic | PALMER | Washington |
| NASHVILLE | Kingman | PAOLA | Miami |
| NATOMA | Osborne | PARADISE | Russell |
| NAVARRE | Dickinson | PARK | Gove |
| NEAL | Greenwood | PARK CITY | Wichita |
| NEKOMA | Rush | PARKER | Linn |
| NEODESHA | Wilson | PARSONS | Labette |

**Adoption Searches Made Easier**

| | | | |
|---|---|---|---|
| PARTRIDGE | Reno | RIVERTON | Cherokee |
| PAULINE | Shawnee | ROBINSON | Brown |
| PAWNEE ROCK | Barton | ROCK | Cowley |
| PAXICO | Wabaunsee | ROELAND PARK | Johnson |
| PEABODY | Marion | ROLLA | Morton |
| PECK | Sedgwick | ROSALIA | Butler |
| PENALOSA | Cunningham | ROSEDALE | Wyandotte |
| PENOKEE | Graham | ROSE HILL | Butler |
| PERRY | Jefferson | ROSSVILLE | Shawnee |
| PERU | Chautauqua | ROXBURY | McPherson |
| PFEIFER | Ellis | ROZEL | Pawnee |
| PHILLIPSBURG | Phillips | RUSH CENTER | Rush |
| PIEDMONT | Greenwood | RUSSELL | Russell |
| PIERCEVILLE | Finney | RUSSELL SPRINGS | Logan |
| PIQUA | Woodson | SABETHA | Nemaha |
| PITTSBURG | Crawford | SAINT FRANCIS | Cheyenne |
| PLAINS | Meade | SAINT GEORGE | Pottawatomie |
| PLAINVILLE | Rooks | SAINT JOHN | Stafford |
| PLEASANTON | Linn | SAINT MARYS | Pottawatomie |
| PLEVNA | Reno | SAINT PAUL | Neosho |
| POMOMA | Franklin | SALINA | Saline |
| PORTIS | Osborne | SATANTA | Haskell |
| POTTER | Atchison | SAVONBURG | Allen |
| POTWIN | Butler | SAWYER | Pratt |
| POWHATTAN | Brown | SCAMMON | Cherokee |
| PRAIRIE VIEW | Phillips | SCANDIA | Republic |
| PRAIRIE VILLAGE | Johnson | SCHOENEHEN | Ellis |
| PRATT | Pratt | SCOTT CITY | Scott |
| PRESCOTT | Linn | SCOTTSVILLE | Mitchell |
| PRESTON | Pratt | SCRANTON | Osage |
| PRETTY PRAIRIE | Reno | SEDAN | Chautauqua |
| PRINCETON | Franklin | SEDGWICK | Harvey |
| PROTECTION | Comanche | SELDEN | Sheridan |
| QUENEMO | Osage | SENECA | Nemaha |
| QUINTER | Gove | SEVERANCE | Doniphan |
| RADIUM | Larned | SEVERY | Greenwood |
| RADLEY | Crawford | SEWARD | Stafford |
| RAGO | Kingman | SHARON | Barber |
| RAMONA | Marion | SHARON SPRINGS | Wallace |
| RANDALL | Jewell | SHAWNEE | Johnson |
| RANDOLPH | Riley | SHAWNEE MISSION | Johnson |
| RANSOM | Ness | SHIELDS | Lane |
| RANTOUL | Franklin | SILVER LAKE | Shawnee |
| RAYMOND | Rice | SIMPSON | Mitchell |
| READING | Lyon | SMITH CENTER | Smith |
| REDFIED | Bourbon | SMOLAN | Saline |
| REPUBLIC | Republic | SOLDIER | Jackson |
| RESERVE | Brown | SOLOMON | Dickinson |
| REXFORD | Thomas | SOUTH HAVEN | Sumner |
| RICE | Cloud | SOUTH HUTCHINSON | Reno |
| RICHFIELD | Morton | SPEARVILLE | Ford |
| RICHMOND | Franklin | SPIVEY | Kingman |
| RILEY | Riley | SPRING HILL | Johnson |

| | | | |
|---|---|---|---|
| STAFFORD | Stafford | WALDO | Russell |
| STANLEY | Johnson | WALDRON | Harper |
| STARK | Neosho | WALKER | Ellis |
| STATE HOUSE | Shawnee | WALLACE | Wallace |
| STERLING | Rice | WALNUT | Crawford |
| STILWELL | Johnson | WALTON | Harvey |
| STOCKTON | Rooks | WAMEGO | Pottatomie |
| STRAWN | Coffey | WASHINGTON | Washington |
| STRONG CITY | Chase | WATERVILLE | Marshall |
| STUDLEY | Sheridan | WATHENA | Doniphan |
| STUTTGART | Phillips | WAVERLY | Coffey |
| SUBLETTE | Haskell | WEBBER | Jewell |
| SUMMERFIELD | Marshall | WEIR | Cherokee |
| SUN CITY | Barber | WELDA | Anderson |
| SUSANK | Barton | WELLINGTON | Sumner |
| SYCAMORE | Montgomery | WELLS | Ottawa |
| SYLVAN GROVE | Lincoln | WELLSVILLE | Franklin |
| SYLVIA | Reno | WESKAN | Wallace |
| SYRACUSE | Hamilton | WESTFALL | Lincoln |
| TALMAGE | Dickinson | WEST MINERAL | Cherokee |
| TAMPA | Marion | WESTMORELAND | Pottawatomie |
| TECUMSEH | Shawnee | WESTPHALIA | Anderson |
| TESCOTT | Ottawa | WESTWOOD | Johnson |
| THAYER | Neosho | WESTWOOD HILLS | Johnson |
| TIMKEN | Rush | WETMORE | Nemaha |
| TIPTON | Mitchell | WHEATON | Pottawatomie |
| TONGANOXIE | Leavenworth | WHEELER | Cheyenne |
| TOPEKA | Shawnee | WHITE CITY | Morris |
| TORONTO | Woodson | WHITE CLOUD | Doniphan |
| TOWANDA | Butler | WHITEWATER | Butler |
| TREECE | Cherokee | WHITING | Jackson |
| TRIBUNE | Greeley | WICHITA | Sedgwick |
| TROY | Doniphan | WILLIAMSBURG | Franklin |
| TURON | Reno | WILLIS | Brown |
| TYRO | Montgomery | WILMORE | Comanche |
| UDALL | Cowley | WILSEY | Morris |
| ULYSSES | Grant | WILSON | Ellsworth |
| UNIONTOWN | Bourbon | WINCHESTER | Jefferson |
| UNIVERSITY | Crawford | WINDOM | McPherson |
| UNIVERSITY OF KS | Lawrence | WINFIELD | Cowley |
| UTICA | Ness | WINIFRED | Frankfort |
| VALLEY CENTER | Sedgwick | WINONA | Logan |
| VALLEY FALLS | Jefferson | WOODBINE | Dickinson |
| VASSAR | Osage | WOODSTON | Rooks |
| VERMILLION | Marshall | WRIGHT | Ford |
| VICTORIA | Ellis | WYANDOTTE WEST | Wyandotte |
| VIOLA | Sedgwick | YATES CENTER | Woodson |
| VIRGIL | Greenwood | YODER | Reno |
| VLIETS | Marshall | ZENDA | Kingman |
| WADSWORTH | Leavenworth | ZURICH | Rooks |
| WAKARUSA | Shawnee | **KENTUCKY** | |
| WA KEENEY | Trego | AARON | Clinton |
| WAKEFIELD | Clay | ABERDEEN | Butler |

| | | | |
|---|---|---|---|
| ACORN | Pulaski | BEAR BRANCH | Leslie |
| ADAIRVILLE | Logan | BEARVILLE | Knott |
| ADAMS | Lawrence | BEATTYVILLE | Lee |
| ADOLPHUS | Allen | BEAUMONT | Metcalfe |
| AFLEX | Pike | BEAUTY | Martin |
| AGES | Harlan | BEAVER | Floyd |
| ALBANY | Clinton | BEAVER DAM | Ohio |
| ALCALDE | Pulaski | BEDFORD | Trimble |
| ALEXANDRIA | Campbell | BEECH CREEK | Muhlenberg |
| ALLEGRE | Todd | BEECH GROVE | McLean |
| ALLEN | Floyd | BEECHMONT | Muhlenberg |
| ALLENSVILLE | Todd | BEECHMONT | Jefferson |
| ALLOCK | Perry | BEE SPRING | Edmonson |
| ALMO | Calloway | BELCHER | Pike |
| ALPHA | Clinton | BELFRY | Pike |
| ALTRO | Breathitt | BELLEVUE | Campbell |
| ALVATON | Warren | BELTON | Muhlenberg |
| AMBURGEY | Knott | BENHAM | Harlan |
| ANCHORAGE | Jefferson | BENTON | Marshall |
| ANCO | Knott | BEREA | Madison |
| ANNVILLE | Jackson | BERRY | Harrison |
| ARGILLITE | Greenup | BETHANNA | Magoffin |
| ARGO | Pike | BETHANY | Wolfe |
| ARJAY | Bell | BETHEL | Bath |
| ARLINGTON | Carlisle | BETHELRIDGE | Casey |
| ARTEMUS | Knox | BETHLEHEM | Henry |
| ARY | Perry | BETSY LAYNE | Floyd |
| ASHCAMP | Pike | BEULAH HEIGHTS | McCreary |
| ASHER | Leslie | BEVERLY | Bell |
| ASHLAND | Boyd | BEVINSVILLE | Floyd |
| AUBURN | Logan | BIG CLIFTY | Grayson |
| AUGUSTA | Bracken | BIG CREEK | Clay |
| AUSTIN | Barren | BIGGS | Pike |
| AUXIER | Floyd | BIGHILL | Madison |
| AVAWAM | Perry | BIG LAUREL | Harlan |
| AVONDALE | McCracken | BIG ROCK | Leslie |
| AXTEL | Breckinridge | BIG SPRING | Breckenridge |
| BAGDAD | Shelby | BIMBLE | Knox |
| BAILEYS SWITCH | Knox | BLACKEY | Letcher |
| BAKERTON | Cumberland | BLACKFORD | Webster |
| BANDANA | Ballard | BLAINE | Lawrence |
| BANNER | Floyd | BLAIRS MILL | Morgan |
| BARBOURVILLE | Knox | BLANDVILLE | Ballard |
| BARDSTOWN | Nelson | BLAZE | Morgan |
| BARDWELL | Carlisle | BLEDSOE | Harlan |
| BARLOW | Ballard | BLOOMFIELD | Nelson |
| BARNETTS CREEK | Johnson | BLUE DIAMOND | Perry |
| BASKETT | Henderson | BLUE GRASS | Lexington |
| BATTLETOWN | Meade | BLUEHOLE | Clay |
| BAUGHMAN | Knox | BLUE RIVER | Floyd |
| BAXTER | Harlan | BOAZ | Graves |
| BAXTER | Jefferson | BOND | Jackson |
| BAYS | Breathitt | BONDVILLE | Mercer |

| | | | |
|---|---|---|---|
| BONNIEVILLE | Hart | CALIFORNIA | Campbell |
| BONNYMAN | Perry | CALLAWAY | Bell |
| BOONEVILLE | Owsley | CALVERT CITY | Marshall |
| BOONS CAMP | Johnson | CALVIN | Bell |
| BOSTON | Nelson | CAMPBELLSBURG | Henry |
| BOW | Cumberland | CAMPBELLSVILLE | Taylor |
| BOWEN | Powell | CAMP DIX | Lewis |
| BOWLING GREEN | Warren | CAMPTON | Wolfe |
| BRADFORDSVILLE | Marion | CANADA | Pike |
| BRANDENBURG | Meade | CANE VALLEY | Adair |
| BREEDING | Adair | CANEY | Morgan |
| BREMEN | Muhlenberg | CANEYVILLE | Grayson |
| BRIDGE STREET | McCracken | CANMER | Hart |
| BRIGHT SHADE | Clay | CANNEL CITY | Morgan |
| BRINKLEY | Knott | CANNON | Knox |
| BROAD BOTTOM | Pike | CANNONSBURG | Boyd |
| BRODHEAD | Rockcastle | CANOE | Breathitt |
| BRONSTON | Pulaski | CANTON | Trigg |
| BROOKLYN | Butler | CARCASSONNE | Letcher |
| BROOKS | Bullitt | CARLISLE | Nicholas |
| BROOKSIDE | Harlan | CARPENTER | Knox |
| BROOKSVILLE | Bracken | CARRIE | Knott |
| BROWDER | Muhlenberg | CARROLLTON | Carroll |
| BROWNS FORK | Perry | CARTER | Carter |
| BROWNSVILLE | Edmonson | CARVER | Magoffin |
| BRUIN | Elliott | CASEY CREEK | Adair |
| BRYANTS STORE | Knox | CATLETTSBURG | Boyd |
| BRYANTSVILLE | Garrard | CAVE CITY | Barren |
| BUCKHORN | Perry | CAWOOD | Harlan |
| BUCKINGHAM | Floyd | CECILIA | Hardin |
| BUCKNER | Oldham | CENTER | Metcalfe |
| BUECHEL | Jefferson | CENTERTOWN | Ohio |
| BUFFALO | Larue | CENTRAL CITY | Muhlenberg |
| BULAN | Perry | CERULEAN | Trigg |
| BURDINE | Letcher | CHAPLIN | Nelson |
| BURGIN | Mercer | CHAPPELL | Leslie |
| BURKE | Elliott | CHAVIES | Perry |
| BURKESVILLE | Cumberland | CHENOA | Bell |
| BURKHART | Wolfe | CHEROKEE | Jefferson |
| BURLINGTON | Boone | CHESTNUTBURG | Clay |
| BURNA | Livingston | CHEVROLET | Harlan |
| BURNING FORK | Magoffin | CINDA | Leslie |
| BURNSIDE | Pulaski | CISCO | Magoffin |
| BURNWELL | Pike | CLARKSON | Grayson |
| BUSH | Laurel | CLAY | Webster |
| BUSKIRK | Morgan | CLAY CITY | Powell |
| BUSY | Perry | CLAYHOLE | Breathitt |
| BUTLER | Pendleton | CLEARFIELD | Rowan |
| BUTTERFLY | Perry | CLEATON | Muhlenberg |
| BYBEE | Madison | CLERMONT | Bullitt |
| BYPRO | Floyd | CLIFFORD | Lawrence |
| CADIZ | Trigg | CLIFTY | Todd |
| CALHOUN | McLean | CLIMAX | Rockcastle |

| | | | |
|---|---|---|---|
| CLINTON | Fulton | CUTSHIN | Leslie |
| CLOSPLINT | Harlan | CUTUNO | Magoffin |
| CLOVER BOTTOM | Jackson | CYNTHIANA | Harrison |
| CLOVERPORT | Breckinridge | CYRUS | Magoffin |
| COALGOOD | Harlan | DABOLT | Jackson |
| COBHILL | Estill | DAISY | Perry |
| COLDIRON | Harlan | DANA | Floyd |
| COLD SPRINGS | Campbell | DANVILLE | Boyle |
| COLLEGE | Madison | DARFORK | Perry |
| COLLEGE HEIGHTS | Warren | DAVELLA | Martin |
| COLLEGE HILL | Madison | DAVID | Floyd |
| COLUMBIA | Adair | DAVISPORT | Martin |
| COLUMBUS | Hickman | DAWSON SPRINGS | Hopkins |
| COMBS | Perry | DAYHOIT | Harlan |
| CONCORD | Lewis | DAYSVILLE | Logan |
| CONFLUENCE | Leslie | DAYTON | Campbell |
| CONLEY | Magoffin | DEANE | Letcher |
| CONSTANCE | Boone | DEATSVILLE | Nelson |
| CONSTANTINE | Breckinridge | DEBORD | Martin |
| CONWAY | Rockcastle | DECOY | Knott |
| COOPERSVILLE | Wayne | DEFOE | Henry |
| CORBIN | Whitley | DELPHIA | Perry |
| CORINTH | Grant | DELTA | Wayne |
| CORNETTSVILLE | Perry | DEMA | Knott |
| CORNISHVILLE | Mercer | DEMOCRAT | Letcher |
| CORYDON | Henderson | DE MOSSVILLE | Pendleton |
| COTTLE | Morgan | DENNISTON | Menifee |
| COVINGTON | Kenton | DENTON | Carter |
| COXS CREEK | Nelson | DENVER | Johnson |
| CRAB ORCHARD | Lincoln | DEPOY | Muhlenberg |
| CRANKS | Harlan | DEWITT | Knox |
| CRAYNE | Crittenden | DEXTER | Calloway |
| CRAYNOR | Floyd | DICE | Perry |
| CRESTWOOD | Oldham | DINGUS | Morgan |
| CRITTENDEN | Grant | DISPUTANTA | Rockcastle |
| CROCKETT | Morgan | DIXIE | Kenton |
| CROFTON | Christian | DIXON | Webster |
| CROMONA | Letcher | DIZNEY | Harlan |
| CROMWWELL | Ohio | DONGOLA | Letcher |
| CROPPER | Henry | DORTON | Pike |
| CROWN | Letcher | DOVER | Mason |
| CRUMMIES | Harlan | DRAFFIN | Pike |
| CRUTCHFIELD | Fulton | DRAKE | Warren |
| CRYSTAL | Estill | DRAKESBORO | Muhlenberg |
| CUBAGE | Bell | DREYFUS | Madison |
| CUB RUN | Hart | DRIFT | Floyd |
| CULVER | Elliott | DRY CREEK | Knott |
| CUMBERLAND | Harlan | DRYHILL | Leslie |
| CUMBERLAND COLLEGE | Whitley | DRY RIDGE | Grant |
| CUNDIFF | Adair | DUBRE | Cumberland |
| CUMMINGHAM | Carlisle | DUCO | Magoffin |
| CURDSVILLE | Daviess | DUNBAR | Butler |
| CUSTER | Breckinridge | DUNDEE | Ohio |

| | | | |
|---|---|---|---|
| DUNMOR | Muhlenberg | FAIRDALE | Jefferson |
| DUNNVILLE | Casey | FAIRFIELD | Nelson |
| DWALE | Floyd | FAIRPLAY | Adair |
| DWARF | Perry | FAIRVIEW | Christian |
| DYCUSBURG | Crittenden | FALCON | Magoffin |
| EARLINGTON | Hopkins | FALL ROCK | Clay |
| EAST BERNSTADT | Laurel | FALLSBURG | Lawrence |
| EASTERN | Floyd | FALLS OF ROUGH | Grayson |
| EAST MCDOWELL | Floyd | FALMOUTH | Pendleton |
| EAST POINT | Johnson | FANCY FARM | Graves |
| EASTVIEW | Hardin | FARLER | Perry |
| EASTWOOD | Jefferson | FARMERS | Rowan |
| EBERLE | Jackson | FARMINGTON | Graves |
| ECHOLS | Ohio | FAUBUSH | Pulaski |
| EDDYVILLE | Lyon | FEDSCREEK | Pike |
| EDMONTON | Metcalfe | FERGUSON | Pulaski |
| EDNA | Magoffin | FERN CREEK | Jefferson |
| EGYPT | Jackson | FILLMORE | Lee |
| EIGHTY EIGHT | Barren | FINCHVILLE | Shelby |
| EKRON | Meade | FINLEY | Taylor |
| ELAMTON | Morgan | FIREBRICK | Lewis |
| ELIAS | Jackson | FISHERVILLE | Jefferson |
| ELIHU | Pulaski | FISHTRAP | Pike |
| ELIZABETHTOWN | Hardin | FISTY | Knott |
| ELIZAVILLE | Letcher | FLAT | Wolfe |
| ELKATAWA | Jackson | FLAT FORK | Magoffin |
| ELKFORK | Morgan | FLATGAP | Johnson |
| ELK HORN | Taylor | FLAT LICK | Knox |
| ELKHORN CITY | Pike | FLATWOODS | Greenup |
| ELKTON | Todd | FLEMING | Letcher |
| ELLIOTTVILLE | Rowan | FLEMINGSBURG | Letcher |
| ELMROCK | Floyd | FLORENCE | Boone |
| ELNA | Johnson | FOGERTOWN | Clay |
| ELSIE | Magoffin | FONDE | Bell |
| EMERSON | Lewis | FORAKER | Magoffin |
| EMINENCE | Henry | FORD | Clark |
| EMLYN | Whitley | FORDS BRANCH | Pike |
| EMMA | Floyd | FORDSVILLE | Ohio |
| EMMALENA | Knott | FOREST HILLS | Pike |
| ENDICOIT | Floyd | FORT CAMPBELL | Christian |
| EOLIA | Letcher | FORT KNOX | Hardin |
| ERILINE | Clay | FORT THOMAS | Campbell |
| ERIANGER | Kenton | FOUNTAIN RUN | Monroe |
| ERMINE | Letcher | FOURMILE | Bell |
| ESSIE | Leslie | FOXTOWN | Jackson |
| ESTILL | Floyd | FRAKES | Bell |
| ETOILE | Barren | FRANKFORT | Franklin |
| ETTY | Pike | FRANKLIN | Simpson |
| EUBANK | Pulaski | FRAZER | Wayne |
| EVARTS | Harlan | FREDONIA | Caldwell |
| EVER | Magoffin | FREDVILLE | Magoffin |
| EWING | Letcher | FREEBURN | Pike |
| EZEL | Morgan | FRENCHBURG | Menifee |

| | | | |
|---|---|---|---|
| FREW | Leslie | GRETHEL | Floyd |
| FRITZ | Magoffin | GUAGE | Jackson |
| FROZEN CREEK | Jackson | GUERRANT | Jackson |
| FUGET | Johnson | GULNARE | Pike |
| FULTON | Fulton | GULSTON | Harlan |
| FULTZ | Grayson | GUNLOCK | Magoffin |
| GALVESTON | Floyd | GUSTON | Meade |
| GAMALIEL | Monroe | GUTHRIE | Todd |
| GAPVILLE | Magoffin | GYPSY | Magoffin |
| GARDENSIDE | Fayette | HADDIX | Breathitt |
| GARFIELD | Breckinridge | HADLEY | Warren |
| GARNER | Knott | HAGER | Magoffin |
| GARRARD | Clay | HAGERHILL | Johnson |
| GARRETT | Floyd | HALDEMAN | Rowan |
| GARRISON | Lewis | HALFWAY | Allen |
| GAUSDALE | Knox | HALL | Letcher |
| GAYS CREEK | Perry | HALLIE | Letcher |
| GEORGETOWN | Scott | HALO | Floyd |
| GERMANTOWN | Bracken | HAMLIN | Calloway |
| GHENT | Carroll | HAMPTON | Livingston |
| GILLFORD | Magoffin | HANSON | Hopkins |
| GILBERTSVILLE | Marshall | HAPPY | Perry |
| GILLMORE | Wolfe | HARDBURLY | Perry |
| GILLY | Letcher | HARDIN | Marshall |
| GIRDLER | Knox | HARDINSBURG | Breckinridge |
| GLASGOW | Barren | HARDSHELL | Breathitt |
| GLENCOE | Gallatin | HARDY | Pike |
| GLENDALE | Hardin | HARDYVILLE | Hart |
| GLEN DEAN | Grayson | HARLAN | Harlan |
| GLENS FORK | Adair | HARNED | Breckinridge |
| GLENVIEW | Jefferson | HAROLD | Floyd |
| GOLDEN POND | Trigg | HARPER | Magoffin |
| GOODY | Pike | HARRODSBURG | Mercer |
| GOOSE ROCK | Clay | HARRODS CREEK | Jefferson |
| GORDON | Letcher | HARTFORD | Ohio |
| GOSHEN | Oldham | HATTON | Frankfort |
| GRACEY | Christian | HAWESVILLE | Hancock |
| GRADYVILLE | Adair | HAZARD | Perry |
| GRAHAM | Muhlenberg | HAZEL | Calloway |
| GRAHN | Carter | HAZEL GREEN | Wolfe |
| GRAND RIVERS | Livingston | HEAD OF GRASSY | Lewis |
| GRASSY CREEK | Morgan | HEBRON | Boone |
| GRATZ | Owen | HEIDELBERG | Lee |
| GRAVEL SWITCH | Marion | HEIDRICK | Knox |
| GRAY | Knox | HELECHAWA | Wolfe |
| GRAY HAWK | Jackson | HELLIER | Pike |
| GRAYS KNOB | Harlan | HELTON | Leslie |
| GRAYSON | Carter | HENDERSON | Henderson |
| GREEN HALL | Owsley | HENDRICKS | Magoffin |
| GREEN ROAD | Knox | HENRY CLAY | Fayette |
| GREENSBURG | Green | HENSHAW | Union |
| GREENUP | Greenup | HERD | Jackson |
| GREENVILLE | Muhlenberg | HERNDON | Christian |

| | | | |
|---|---|---|---|
| HESTAND | Monroe | IVYTON | Magoffin |
| HICKMAN | Fulton | JABEZ | Pulaski |
| HICKORY | Graves | JACKHORN | Letcher |
| HIGH BRIDGE | Jessamine | JACKSON | Breathitt |
| HI HAT | Floyd | JACOBS | Carter |
| HIGH POINT | Jefferson | JAMBOREE | Pike |
| HILLSBORO | Letcher | JAMESTOWN | Russell |
| HIMA | Clay | JARVIS | Knox |
| HIMYAR | Knox | JEFF | Perry |
| HINDMAN | Knott | JEFFERSONTOWN | Jefferson |
| HINKLE | Knox | JEFFERSONVILLE | Montgomery |
| HIPPO | Floyd | JENKINS | Letcher |
| HISEVILLE | Barren | JEREMIAH | Letcher |
| HISLE | Jackson | JETSON | Butler |
| HITCHINS | Carter | JINKS | Estill |
| HITE | Martin | JOB | Martin |
| HODE | Martin | JOHNETTA | Rockcastle |
| HODGENVILLE | Larue | JOHNS RUN | Carter |
| HOLLAND | Allen | JONANCY | Pike |
| HOLLYBUSH | Knott | JONESVILLE | Grant |
| HOLLYHILL | McCreary | JONICAN | Pike |
| HOLMES MILL | Harlan | JUNCTION CITY | Boyle |
| HONAKER | Floyd | KALIOPI | Leslie |
| HOPE | Montgomery | KAYJAY | Knox |
| HOPKINSVILLE | Christian | KEATON | Johnson |
| HORSE BRANCH | Ohio | KEAVY | Laurel |
| HORSE CAVE | Hart | KEENE | Jessamine |
| HOSKINSTON | Leslie | KEITH | Harlan |
| HOWARDSTOWN | Nelson | KENTON | Kenton |
| HUDDY | Pike | KENVIR | Harlan |
| HUDSON | Breckinridge | KERBY KNOB | Jackson |
| HUEYSVILLE | Floyd | KETTLE | Cumberland |
| HUFF | Edmonson | KETTLE ISLAND | Bell |
| HULEN | Bell | KEVIL | Ballard |
| HUNTER | Floyd | KIMPER | Pike |
| HUNTSVILLE | Butler | KINGS MOUNTAIN | Lincoln |
| HUSTONVILLE | Lincoln | KIRKSEY | Calloway |
| HYDEN | Leslie | KITE | Knott |
| INDEPENDENCE | Kenton | KITTS | Harlan |
| INDEX | Morgan | KNIFLEY | Adair |
| INEZ | Martin | KNOB LICK | Metcalfe |
| INGLE | Pulaski | KONA | Letcher |
| INGRAM | Bell | KOREA | Menifee |
| INSKO | Morgan | KRYPTON | Perry |
| IROQUOIS | Jefferson | KUTTAWA | Lyon |
| IRVINE | Estill | KYROCK | Edmonson |
| IRVINGTON | Breckinridge | LACENTER | Ballard |
| ISLAND | McLean | LACKEY | Floyd |
| ISLAND CITY | Owsley | LAFAYETTE | Christian |
| ISOM | Letcher | LAGRANGE | Oldham |
| ISONVILLE | Elliott | LAMB | Monroe |
| IUKA | Livingston | LAMBRIC | Breathitt |
| IVEL | Floyd | LAMERO | Rockcastle |

| | | | |
|---|---|---|---|
| LANCASTER | Clay | LOVELACEVILLE | Ballard |
| LANGLEY | Floyd | LOVELY | Martin |
| LARKSLANE | Garner | LOWES | Graves |
| LATONIA | Kenton | LOWMANSVILLE | Lawrence |
| LAURA | Martin | LOYALL | Harlan |
| LAWRENCEBURG | Anderson | LUCAS | Barren |
| LAWTON | Carter | LUDLOW | Kenton |
| LEANDER | Johnson | LYNCH | Harlan |
| LEATHERWOOD | Perry | LYNDON | Jefferson |
| LEBANON | Marion | LYNN | Greenup |
| LEBANON JUNCTION | Bullitt | LYNNVILLE | Graves |
| LEBURN | Knott | LYTTEN | Elliott |
| LEDBETTER | Livingston | MACEO | Daviess |
| LEE CITY | Wolfe | MACKVILLE | Washington |
| LEECO | Lee | MADISONVILLE | Hopkins |
| LEITCHFIELD | Grayson | MAGGARD | Magoffin |
| LEJUNIOR | Harlan | MAGNOLIA | Larue |
| LENOX | Morgan | MAJESTIC | Pike |
| LEROSE | Owsley | MALLIE | Knott |
| LETCHER | Letcher | MALONE | Morgan |
| LEWISBURG | Logan | MALEONETON | Greenup |
| LEWIS CREEK | Harlan | MAMMOTH CAVE | Edmonson |
| LEWISPORT | Hancock | MAMMOTH CAVE NAT'L PARK | Edmonson |
| LEXINGTON | Fayette | MANCHESTER | Clay |
| LIBERTY | Casey | MANILA | Johnson |
| LIBERTY ROAD | Fayette | MANITOU | Hopkins |
| LICKBURG | Magoffin | MANNSVILLE | Taylor |
| LICK CREEK | Pike | MANTON | Floyd |
| LIGON | Floyd | MAPLE MOUNT | Daviess |
| LILY | Laurel | MARCUM | Clay |
| LINDSEYVILLE | Edmonson | MARIBA | Menifee |
| LINEFORK | Letcher | MARION | Crittenden |
| LITTCARR | Knott | MARROWBONE | Cumberland |
| LITTLE | Breathitt | MARSHALLVILLE | Magoffin |
| LITTLE SANDY | Elliott | MARSHES SIDING | McCreary |
| LIVERMORE | McLean | MARTHA | Lawrence |
| LIVINGSTON | Rockcastle | MARTIN | Floyd |
| LLOYD | Greenup | MARY ALICE | Harlan |
| LOAD | Greenup | MARYDELL | Laurel |
| LOCKPORT | Henry | MASHFORK | Magoffin |
| LOCUST HILL | Breckinridge | MASON | Grant |
| LOGANSPORT | Butler | MASONIC HOME | Jefferson |
| LOGVILLE | Magoffin | MATTHEW | Morgan |
| LOLA | Livingston | MAUD | Washington |
| LONDON | Laurel | MAULDEN | Jackson |
| LONE | Lee | MAYFIELD | Graves |
| LONE OAK | McCracken | MAYKING | Letcher |
| LOOKOUT | Pike | MAYS LICK | Mason |
| LORETTO | Marion | MAYSVILLE | Mason |
| LOST CREEK | Breathitt | MAYTOWN | Wolfe |
| LOUELLEN | Harlan | MAYTOW | Floyd |
| LOUISA | Lawrence | MAZIE | Lawrence |
| LOUISVILLE | Jefferson | McANDREWS | Pike |

| | | | |
|---|---|---|---|
| McCARR | Pike | MOUNT SHERMAN | Larue |
| McCOMBS | Pike | MOUNT STERLING | Montgomery |
| McDANIELS | Breckinridge | MOUNT VERNON | Rockcastle |
| McDOWELL | Floyd | MOUNT WASHINGTON | Bullitt |
| McHENRY | Ohio | MOUSIE | Knott |
| McKEE | Jackson | MOUTHCARD | Pike |
| McKINNEY | Lincoln | MOZELLE | Leslie |
| McQUADY | Breckinridge | MULDRAUGH | Meade |
| McROBERTS | Letcher | MUNFORDVILLE | Hart |
| McVEIGH | Pike | MURRAY | Calloway |
| MEALLY | Johnson | MUSES MILLS | Letcher |
| MEANS | Menifee | MYRA | Pike |
| MELBER | McCracken | NANCY | Pulaski |
| MELBOURNE | Campbell | NAPFOR | Perry |
| MELVIN | Floyd | NAPLES | Boyd |
| META | Pike | NARROWS | Ohio |
| MIDDLEBURG | Casey | NAZARETH | Nelson |
| MIDDLESBORO | Bell | NEAFUS | Grayson |
| MIDDLETOWN | Jefferson | NEBO | Hopkins |
| MIDWAY | Woodford | NED | Breathitt |
| MILBURN | Carlisle | NELSE | Pike |
| MILLERSBURG | Bourbon | NEON | Letcher |
| MILLS | Knox | NERINX | Marion |
| MILL SPRINGS | Wayne | NEVISDALE | Whitley |
| MILLSTONE | Letcher | NEW CASTLE | Henry |
| MILLTOWN | Adair | NEW CONCORD | Calloway |
| MILLWOOD | Grayson | NEWFOUNDLAND | Elliott |
| MILO | Martin | NEWGARDEN | Hardin |
| MILTON | Trimble | NEW HAVEN | Nelson |
| MIMA | Morgan | NEW HOPE | Nelson |
| MINERVA | Mason | NEW LIBERTY | Owen |
| MINNIE | Floyd | NEWPORT | Campbell |
| MIRACLE | Bell | NEW ZION | Jackson |
| MISTLETOE | Owsley | NICHOLASVILLE | Jessamine |
| MITCHELLSBURG | Boyle | NIPPA | Johnson |
| MIZE | Morgan | NOCTOR | Breathitt |
| MONTICELLO | Wayne | NORTH MIDDLETOWN | Bourbon |
| MONTPELIER | Adair | NORTONVILLE | Hopkins |
| MOOLEYVILLE | Breckinridge | OAK GROVE | Christian |
| MOON | Morgan | OAKLAND | Warren |
| MOOREFIELD | Nicholas | OAKVILLE | Logan |
| MOORES CREEK | Jackson | OFFUTT | Johnson |
| MOORMAN | Muhlenberg | OIL SPRINGS | Johnson |
| MOREHEAD | Rowan | OLATON | Ohio |
| MORGANFIELD | Union | OLD LANDING | Lee |
| MORGANTOWN | Butler | OKOLONA | Jefferson |
| MORNING VIEW | Kenton | OLDTOWN | Greenup |
| MORRILL | Jackson | OLIVE HILL | Carter |
| MORRIS FORK | Owsley | OLLIE | Edmonson |
| MORTONS GAP | Hopkins | OLMSTEAD | Logan |
| MOUNT EDEN | Spencer | OLYMPIA | Bath |
| MOUNT HERMON | Monroe | OMAHA | Knott |
| MOUNT OLIVER | Robertson | ONEIDA | Clay |

| | | | |
|---|---|---|---|
| OPHIR | Morgan | POMEROYTON | Menifee |
| ORKNEY | Floyd | POOLE | Webster |
| ORLANDO | Rockcastle | PORT ROYAL | Henry |
| OSCALOOSA | Letcher | POWDERLY | Muhlenberg |
| OVEN FORK | Letcher | PREMIUM | Letcher |
| OWENSBORO | Daviess | PRESTON | Bath |
| OWENTON | Owen | PRESTONSBURG | Floyd |
| OWINGSVILLE | Bath | PRICE | Floyd |
| PADUCAH | McCracken | PRIMROSE | Lee |
| PAINT LICK | Garrard | PRINCETON | Caldwell |
| PAINTSVILLE | Johnson | PRINTER | Floyd |
| PARIS | Bourbon | PROSPECT | Jefferson |
| PARK CITY | Barren | PROVIDENCE | Webster |
| PARKERS LAKE | McCreary | PROVO | Butler |
| PARKSVILLE | Boyle | PRYSE | Estill |
| PARROT | Jackson | PUEBLO | Wayne |
| PARTRIDGE | Letcher | PUNCHEON | Kite |
| PATHFORK | Harlan | PUTNEY | Harlan |
| PATSEY | Stanton | PYRAMID | Floyd |
| PAW PAW | Pike | QUALITY | Butler |
| PAYNE GAP | Letcher | QUICKSAND | Breathitt |
| PAYNEVILLE | Meade | QUINCY | Lewis |
| PEBWORTH | Oweley | RABBIT HASH | Boone |
| PELLVILLE | Hancock | RACCOON | Pike |
| PEMBROKE | Christian | RACELAND | Russell |
| PENDLETON | Henry | RADCLIFF | Hardin |
| PENROD | Muhlenberg | RANSOM | Pike |
| PEOPLES | Jackson | RAVEN | Knott |
| PERRY PARK | Owen | RAVENA | Estill |
| PERRYVILLE | Boyle | RAYWICK | Marion |
| PETERSBURG | Boone | REDBUSH | Johnson |
| PEWEE VALLEY | Oldham | REDFOX | Knott |
| PEYTONSBURG | Cumberland | REED | Henderson |
| PHELPS | Pike | REEDYVILLE | Edmonson |
| PHILPOT | Daviess | REGINA | Pike |
| PHYLLIS | Pike | REIDLAND | McCracken |
| PIKEVILLE | Pike | RELIEF | Morgan |
| PILGRIM | Martin | RENFRO VALLEY | Rockcastle |
| PINE GROVE | Clark | REVELO | McCreary |
| PINE KNOT | McCreary | REYNOLDS STATION | Ohio |
| PINE RIDGE | Wolfe | RHODELIA | Meade |
| PINE TOP | Knott | RICETOWN | Owsley |
| PINEVILLE | Bell | RICEVILLE | Johnson |
| PINSONFORK | Pike | RICHARDSON | Lawrence |
| PIPPA PASSES | Knott | RICHARDSVILLE | Warren |
| PISO | Pike | RICHMOND | Madison |
| PITTSBURG | Laurel | RINEYVILLE | Hardin |
| PLAINVIEW | Jefferson | RISNER | Martin |
| PLANK | Clay | RITNER | Wayne |
| PLEASUREVILLE | Henry | RIVER | Johnson |
| PLUMMERS LANDING | Letcher | RIVERFRONT | Jefferson |
| PLUM SPRINGS | Warren | RIVERSIDE | Warren |
| POINTER | Paluski | ROARK | Leslie |

| | | | |
|---|---|---|---|
| ROBARDS | Henderson | SCIENCE HILL | Pulaski |
| ROBINSON CREEK | Pike | SCOTTSVILLE | Allen |
| ROCHESTER | Butler | SCRANTON | Menifee |
| ROCKFIELD | Warren | SCUDDY | Perry |
| ROCKHOLDS | Whitley | SEBASTIANS BRANCH | Breathitt |
| ROCKHOUSE | Pike | SEBREE | Webster |
| ROCKPORT | Ohio | SECO | Letcher |
| ROCKYBRANCH | Wayne | SEDALIA | Graves |
| ROCKY HILL | Edmonson | SEITZ | Magoffin |
| ROGERS | Wolfe | SENTERVILLE | Pike |
| ROSINE | Ohio | SE REE | Breckinridge |
| ROSSLYN | Stanton | SERGENT | Letcher |
| ROUNDHILL | Edmonson | SEXTONS CREEK | Clay |
| ROUSE | Kenton | SHARON GROVE | Todd |
| ROUSSEAU | Breathitt | SHARPSBURG | Bath |
| ROWDY | Perry | SHELBIANA | Pike |
| ROWLETTS | Hart | SHELBY | Jefferson |
| ROXANA | Letcher | SHELBY GAP | Pike |
| ROYALTON | Magoffin | SHELBYVILLE | Shelby |
| RUMSEY | McLean | SHEPHERDSVILLE | Bullitt |
| RUSH | Boyd | SHIVELY | Jefferson |
| RUSSELL | Greenup | SHOPVILLE | Pulaski |
| RUSSELL SPRINGS | Russell | SIDNEY | Pike |
| RUSSELLVILLE | Logan | SILER | Whitley |
| RUTH | Pulaski | SILVER GROVE | Campbell |
| SACRAMENTO | McLean | SILVERHILL | Morgan |
| SADIEVILLE | Scott | SIMPSONVILLE | Shelby |
| SADLER | Grayson | SITKA | Johnson |
| SAINT CATHARINE | Washington | SIZEROCK | Leslie |
| SAINT CHARLES | Hopkins | SKYLINE | Letcher |
| SAINT FRANCIS | Marion | SLADE | Powell |
| SAINT HELENS | Lee | SLAUGHTERS | Webster |
| SAINT JOSEPH | Daviess | SLEMP | Perry |
| SAINT MARY | Marion | SLOANS VALLEY | Pulaski |
| SAINT MATTHEWS | Jefferson | SMILAX | Leslie |
| SAINT PAUL | Lewis | SMITH | Harlan |
| SALDEE | Breathitt | SMITHFIELD | Henry |
| SALEM | Livingston | SMITHLAND | Livingston |
| SALT GUM | Knox | SMITH MILLS | Henderson |
| SALT LICK | Bath | SMITHS CREEK | Carter |
| SALVISA | Mercer | SMITHS GROVE | Warren |
| SALYERSVILLE | Magoffin | SOFT SHELL | Knott |
| SAMPLE | Breckinridge | SOLDIER | Carter |
| SAMUELS | Nelson | SOMERSET | Pulaski |
| SANDERS | Carroll | SONORA | Hardin |
| SANDGAP | Jackson | SOUTH | Grayson |
| SANDY HOOK | Elliott | SOUTH CARROLLTON | Muhlenberg |
| SARDIS | Mason | SOUTHGATE | Campbell |
| SASSAFRAS | Knott | SOUTH PORTSMOUTH | Greenup |
| SASSER | London | SOUTH SHORE | Greenup |
| SAUL | Perry | SOUTH UNION | Logan |
| SAWYER | McCreary | SPARTA | Gallatin |
| SCALF | Knox | SPEIGHT | Pike |

| | | | |
|---|---|---|---|
| SPENCE | Campbell | THEALKA | Johnson |
| SPOTTSVILLE | Henderson | THELMA | Johnson |
| SPRINGFIELD | Washington | THORNTON | Letcher |
| SPRING LICK | Grayson | THOUSANDSTICKS | Leslie |
| SPURLOCK | Clay | THREEFORKS | Martin |
| STAB | Pulaski | TILINE | Livingston |
| STACY FORK | Morgan | TINA | Knott |
| STAFFORDSVILLE | Johnson | TINSLEY | Bell |
| STAMBAUGH | Johnson | TINYTOWN | Todd |
| STAMPING GROUND | Scott | TOLER | Pike |
| STANFORD | Lincoln | TOLLESBORO | Lewis |
| STANLEY | Daviess | TOLU | Crittenden |
| STANTON | Powell | TOMAHAWK | Martin |
| STANVILLE | Floyd | TOMPKINSVILLE | Monroe |
| STARK | Elliott | TOPMOST | Knott |
| STEARNS | McCreary | TOTZ | Harlan |
| STEELE | Pike | TRAM | Floyd |
| STEFF | Grayson | TRAPPIST | Nelson |
| STELLA | Magoffin | TRENTON | Todd |
| STEPHENS | Elliott | TROSPER | Knox |
| STEPHENSBURG | Hardin | TURKEY CREEK | Pike |
| STEPHENSPORT | Breckinridge | TURNERS STATION | Henry |
| STEUBENVILLE | Wayne | TUTOR KEY | Johnson |
| STINNETT | Leslie | T OVILLE | Monroe |
| STONE | Pike | TYNER | Jackson |
| STONEY FORK | Bell | TYPO | Perry |
| STOPOVER | Pike | ULYSSES | Lawrence |
| STRUNK | McCreary | UNION | Boone |
| STURGIS | Union | UNION STAR | Breckinridge |
| SUBLETT | Magoffin | UNIONTOWN | Union |
| SUBTLE | Edmonson | UPPER TYGART | Carter |
| SUDITH | Bath | UPTON | Hardin |
| SULLIVAN | Union | UTICA | Daviess |
| SULPHUR | Henry | VADA | Lee |
| SULPHERWELL | Edmonson | VANCEBURG | Lewis |
| SUMMER SHADE | Metcalfe | VANCLEVE | Breathitt |
| SUMMERSVILLE | Green | VAN LEAR | Johnson |
| SUMMIT | Hardin | VARNEY | Pike |
| SUMMIT | Boyd | VERONA | Boone |
| SUNFISH | Edmonson | VERSAILLES | Woodford |
| SUNNYBROOK | Wayne | VERTREES | Hardin |
| SWAMP BRANCH | Johnson | VEST | Knott |
| SWAMPTON | Magoffin | VICCO | Perry |
| SWEEDEN | Edmonson | VINCENT | Owsley |
| SYMBOL | Laurel | VINE GROVE | Hardin |
| SYMSONIA | Graves | VIPER | Perry |
| TALBERT | Breathitt | VIRGIE | Pike |
| TALCUM | Knott | VOLGA | Johnson |
| TALLEGA | Lee | WACO | Madison |
| TATEVILLE | Pulaski | WADDY | Shelby |
| TAYLORSVILLE | Spencer | WALKER | Knox |
| TEABERRY | Floyd | WALLINGFORD | Letcher |
| TEDDERS | Knox | WALLINS CREEK | Harlan |

| | | | |
|---|---|---|---|
| WALNUT GROVE | Pulaski | WIND CAVE | Jackson |
| WALTON | Boone | WINDSOR | Russell |
| WANETA | Jackson | WINDY | Wayne |
| WARBRANCH | Leslie | WINGO | Graves |
| WARFIELD | Martin | WINSTON | Estill |
| WARSAW | Gallatin | WITTENSVILLE | Johnson |
| WASHINGTON | Mason | WOLF COAL | Breathitt |
| WATER VALLEY | Graves | WOODBINE | Knox |
| WATERVIEW | Cumberland | WOODBURN | Warren |
| WAVERLY | Union | WOODBURY | Butler |
| WAX | Grayson | WOODMAN | Pike |
| WAYLAND | Floyd | WOOLLUM | Knox |
| WAYNESBURG | Lincoln | WOOTON | Leslie |
| WEBBVILLE | Lawrence | WORTHINGTON | Greenup |
| WEBSTER | Breckinridge | WORTHVILLE | Carroll |
| WEEKSBURY | Floyd | YEADDISS | Leslie |
| WELCHS CREEK | Butler | YERKES | Perry |
| WELLINGTON | Menifee | YOSEMITE | Casey |
| WENDOVER | Leslie | ZACARIAH | Lee |
| WESTBEND | Powell | ZOE | Lee |
| WEST LIBERTY | Morgan | **LOUISIANA** | |
| WEST LOUISVILLE | Daviess | ABBEVILLE | Vermilion |
| WEST PADUCAH | McCracken | ABITA SPRINGS | St Tammany |
| WEST POINT | Hardin | ACME | Concordia |
| WESTPORT | Oldham | ADDIS | West Baton Rouge |
| WEST PRESTONSBURG | Floyd | AIMWELL | Catahoula |
| WEST VAN LEAR | Johnson | AKERS | Tangipahoa |
| WESTVIEW | Breckinridge | ALBANY | Livingston |
| WESTWOOD | Boyd | ALEXANDRIA | Rapides |
| WHEATCROFT | Webster | ALTO | Richland |
| WHEATLEY | Owen | AMA | St Charles |
| WHEELERSBURG | Magoffin | AMELIA | St Mary |
| WHEELWRIGHT | Floyd | AMITE | Tangipahoa |
| WHICK | Breathitt | ANACOCO | Vernon |
| WHITEHOUSE | Johnson | ANGIE | Washington |
| WHITE MILLS | Hardin | ANGOLA | West Feliciana |
| WHITE OAK | Morgan | ARABI | St Bernard |
| WHITE PLAINS | Hopkins | ARCADIA | Bienville |
| WHITESBURG | Letcher | ARCHIBALD | Richland |
| WHITESVILLE | Daviess | ARNAUDVILLE | St Landry |
| WHITLEY CITY | McCreary | ASHLAND | Natchitoches |
| WIBORG | McCreary | ATHENS | Claiborne |
| WICKLIFFE | Ballard | ATLANTA | Winn |
| WIDECREEK | Breathitt | AUDUBON | East Baton Rouge |
| WILDIE | Rockcastle | AVERY ISLAND | Iberia |
| WILLARD | Carter | AVONDALE | Jefferson |
| WILLIAMSBURG | Whitley | BAKER | East Baton Rouge |
| WILLIAMSPORT | Johnson | BALDWIN | St Mary |
| WILLIAMSTOWN | Grant | BALL | Rapides |
| WILLISBURG | Washington | BARTARIA | Jefferson |
| WILLOW SHADE | Metcalfe | BARKSDALE AFB | Caddo |
| WILMORE | Jessamine | BASILE | Evangeline |
| WINCHESTER | Clark | BASKIN | Franklin |

| | | | |
|---|---|---|---|
| BASTROP | Morehouse | CARVILLE | Iberville |
| BATCHELOR | Point Coupee | CASPLANA | Caddo |
| BATON ROUGE | East Baton Rouge | CASTOR | Bienville |
| BAYOU GOULA | Iberville | CECILLIA | St Martin |
| BELCHER | Caddo | CENTENARY | Caddo |
| BELL CITY | Calcasieu | CENTER POINT | Avoyelles |
| BELLE CHASSE | Plaquemines | CENTERVILLE | St Mary |
| BELLE ROSE | Assumption | CHALMETTE | St Bernard |
| BELMONT | Sabine | CHARENTON | St Mary |
| BENTLEY | Grant | CHASE | Franklin |
| BENTON | Bossier | CHATAIGNIER | Evangeline |
| BERNICE | Union | CHATHAM | Jackson |
| BERWICK | St Mary | CHAUVIN | Terrebonne |
| BETHANY | Caddo | CHEF MENTEUR | Orleans |
| BIENVILLE | Bienville | CHENEYVILLE | Rapides |
| BIG BEND | Avoyelles | CHESTNUT | Bienville |
| BLANCHARD | Caddo | CHOPIN | Natchitoches |
| BLANKS | Pointe Coupee | CHOUDRANT | Lincoln |
| BLUEBONNET | East Baton Rouge | CHURCH POINT | Acadia |
| BOGALUSA | Washington | CLARENCE | Natchitoches |
| BONITA | Morehouse | CLARKS | Caldwell |
| BOOTHVILLE | Plaquemines | CLAYTON | Concordia |
| BORDELONVILLE | Avoyelles | CLINTON | East Feliciana |
| BOSSIER CITY | Bossier | CLOUTIERVILLE | Natchitoches |
| BOURG | Terrebonne | COLFAX | Grant |
| BOUTTE | St Charles | COLLINSTON | Morehouse |
| BOYCE | Rapides | COLUMBIA | Caldwell |
| BRAITHWAITE | Plaquemines | COMMERCE PARK | East Baton Rouge |
| BRANCH | Acadia | CONVENT | St James |
| BREAUX BRIDGE | St Martin | CONVERSE | Sabine |
| BRIDGE CITY | Jefferson | COTTONPORT | Avoyelles |
| BRITTANY | Ascension | COTTON VALLEY | Webster |
| BROADVIEW | East Baton Rouge | COUSHATTA | Red River |
| BROUSSARD | Lafayette | COVINGTON | St Tammany |
| BRUSLY | West Baton Rouge | COW ISLAND | Verniillion |
| BRYCELAND | Bienville | CREOLE | Cameron |
| BUCKEYE | Rapides | CRESTON | Natchitoches |
| BUECHE | West Baton Rouge | CROWLEY | Acadia |
| BUNKIE | Avoyelles | CROWVILLE | Franklin |
| BURAS | Plaquermines | CULLEN | Webster |
| BURNSIDE | Ascension | CUT OFF | Lafourche |
| BUSH | St Tammany | CYPRESS | Natchitoches |
| BUTTE LAROSE | St Martin | DARROW | Ascension |
| BYWATER | Orleans | DAVANT | Plaquemines |
| CADE | St Martin | DELCAMBRE | Vermillion |
| CALHOUN | Ouachita | DELHI | Richland |
| CALVIN | Winn | DELTA | Madison |
| CAMERON | Cameron | DENHAM SPRINGS | Livingston |
| CAMPTI | Natchitoches | DEQUINCY | Calcasieu |
| CANKTON | St Landry | DERIDDER | Beauregard |
| CARENCRO | Lafayette | DERRY | Natchitoches |
| CARLISLE | Plaquemines | DES ALLEMANDS | St Charles |
| CARROLLTON | Orleans | DESTREHAN | St Charles |

| | | | |
|---|---|---|---|
| DEVILLE | Rapides | FOREST | West Carroll |
| DIXIE | Caddo | FOREST HILL | Rapides |
| DODSON | Winn | FORKED ISLAND | Vermillion |
| DONALDSONVILLE | Ascension | FORT NECESSITY | Franklin |
| DONNER | Terrebonne | FORT POLK | Vernon |
| DOWNSVILLE | Union | FRANKLIN | St Mary |
| DOYLINE | Webster | FRANKLINTON | Washington |
| DRUSILLA | East Baton Rouge | FRENCH SETTLEMENT | Livingston |
| DRY CREEK | Beauregard | FRIERSON | De Soto |
| DRY PRONG | Grant | FROGMORE | Concordia |
| DUBACH | Lincoln | FULLERTON | Vernon |
| DUBBERLY | Webster | GALLIANO | Lafourche |
| DULAC | Terrebonne | GALVEZ | Ascension |
| DUPLESSIS | Ascension | GARDEN CITY | St Mary |
| DUPONT | Avoyelles | GARDNER | Rapides |
| DUSON | Lafayette | GARYVILLE | St John The Baptist |
| EAST POINT | Red River | GATEWAY | East Baton Rouge |
| ECHO | Rapides | GEISMAR | Ascension |
| EDGARD | St. John The Baptist | GENTILLY | Orleans |
| EFFIE | Avoyelles | GEORGETOWN | Grant |
| EGAN | Acadia | GHEENS | Lafourche |
| ELIZABETH | Allen | GIBSLAND | Bienville |
| ELMER | Rapides | GIBSON | Terrebonne |
| ELN GROVE | Bossier | GILBERT | Franklin |
| ELMWOOD | Orleans | GILLIAM | Caddo |
| ELTON | Jefferson Davis | GIRARD | Richland |
| EMPIRE | Plaquemines | GLENMORA | Rapides |
| ENTERPRISE | Catahoula | GLOSTE | De Soto |
| EOLA | Avoyelles | GLYNN | Pointe Coupee |
| EPPS | West Carroll | GOLDEN MEADOW | Lafourche |
| ERATH | Vermillion | GOLDONNA | Natchitoches |
| EROS | Jackson | GONZALES | Ascension |
| ERWINVILLE | West Baton Rouge | GORUM | Natchitoches |
| ESTHERWOOD | Acadia | GOUDEAU | Avoyelles |
| ETHER | East Feliciana | GRAMBLING | Lincoln |
| EUNICE | St Landry | GRAMERCY | St James |
| EVANGELINE | Acadia | GRAND CANE | De Soto |
| EVANS | Vernon | GRAND CHENIER | Cameron |
| EVERGREEN | Avoyelles | GRAND COTEAU | St Landry |
| EXTENSION | Franklin | GRAND ISLE | Jefferson |
| FAIRBANKS | Ouachita | GRANT | Allen |
| FARMERVILLE | Union | GRAY | Terrebonne |
| FENTON | Jefferson Davis | GRAYSON | Caldwell |
| FERRIDAY | Concordia | GREENSBURG | St Helena |
| FIELDS | Beauregard | GREENWELL SPRINGS | East Baton Rouge |
| FISHER | Sabine | GREENWOOD | Caddo |
| FLATWOODS | Rapides | GREENWOOD | East Baton Rouge |
| FLORA | Natchitoches | GRETNA | Jefferson |
| FLORIEN | Sabine | GROSSE TETE | Iberville |
| FLUKER | Tangipahoa | GUEYDAN | Vermillion |
| FOLSOM | St Tammany | HACKBERRY | Cameron |
| FORBING | Caddo | HAHNVILLE | St Charles |
| FORDOCHE | Pointe Coupee | HALL SUMMIT | Red River |

| | | | |
|---|---|---|---|
| HAMBURG | Avoyelles | KURTHWOOD | Vernon |
| HAMMOND | Tangipahoa | LABADIEVILLE | Assumption |
| HARAHAN | Orleans | LABARRE | Pointe Coupee |
| HARMON | Red River | LACAMP | Vernon |
| HARRISONBURG | Catahoula | LACASSINE | Jefferson Davis |
| HARVEY | Jefferson | LACOMBE | St Tamznany |
| HAUGHTON | Bossier | LAFAYETTE | Lafayette |
| HAYES | Calcasieu | LAFAYETTE SQUARE | Orleans |
| HAYNESVILLE | Claiborne | LAFITTE | Jefferson |
| HEBERT | Caldwell | LAKE ARTHUR | Jefferson Davis |
| HEFLIN | Webster | LAKE CHARLES | Calcasieu |
| HESSMER | Avoyelles | LAKE FOREST | Orleans |
| HESTER | St James | LAKELAND | Pointe Coupee |
| HICKS | Vernon | LAKE PROVIDENCE | East Carroll |
| HINESTON | Rapides | LAKEVIEW | Orleans |
| HODGE | Jackson | LA PLACE | St. John The Baptist |
| HOLDEN | Livingston | LAROSE | Lafourche |
| HOMER | Claiborne | LARTO | Catahoula |
| HORNBECK | Vernon | LAWTELL | St Landry |
| HOSSTON | Caddo | LEANDER | Vernon |
| HOUMA | Terrebonne | LEBEAU | St Landry |
| HUSSER | Tangipahoa | LEBLANC | Allen |
| IDA | Caddo | LECOMPTE | Rapides |
| INDEPENDENCE | St Helena | LEESVILLE | Vernon |
| INNIS | Pointe Coupee | LE MOYEN | Saint landry |
| INTRACOASTAL CITY | Vermillion | LENA | Rapides |
| IOTA | Acadia | LEONVILLE | St Landry |
| IOWA | Calcasieu | LETTSWORTH | Pointe Coupee |
| ISTROUMA | East Baton Rouge | LIBUSE | Rapides |
| JACKSON | East Feliciana | LILLIE | Union |
| JAMESTOWN | Bienville | LISBON | Claiborne |
| JARREAU | Pointe Coupee | LIVINGSTON | Livingston |
| JEANERETTE | Iberia | LIVONIA | Pointe Coupee |
| JEFFERSON | Orleans | LOCKPORT | Lafourche |
| JENA | La Salle | LOGANSPORT | De Soto |
| JENNINGS | Jefferson Davis | LONGLEAF | Rapides |
| JEWELLA | Caddo | LONGVILLE | Beauregard |
| JIGGER | Franklin | LORANGER | Tangipahoa |
| JONES | Morehouse | LOREAUVILLE | Iberia |
| JONESBORO | Jackson | LOTTIE | Pointe Coupee |
| JONESVILLE | Catahoula | LULING | St Charles |
| JOYCE | Winn | LUCHER | St James |
| KAPLAN | Vermillion | LYDIA | Iberia |
| KEATCHIE | De Soto | LYNBROOK | Caddo |
| KEITHVILLE | Caddo | MADISONVILLE | St Tammany |
| KELLY | Caldwell | MAMOU | Evangeline |
| KENNER | Jefferson | MANDEVILLE | St Tammany |
| KENTWOOD | Tangipahoa | MANGHAM | Richland |
| KILBOURNE | West Carroll | MANSFIELD | De Soto |
| KILLONA | St Charles | MANSURA | Avoyelles |
| KINDER | Allen | MANY | Sabine |
| KRAEMER | Lafourche | MARINGOULIN | Iberville |
| KROTZ SPRINGS | St Landry | MARION | Union |

| Place | Parish | Place | Parish |
|---|---|---|---|
| MARKSVILLE | Avoyelles | NOBLE | Sabine |
| MARRERO | Jefferson | NORCO | St Charles |
| MARTHAVILLE | Natchitoches | NORTH KENNER | Jefferson |
| MATHEWS | Lafourche | NORTHSIDE | Ouachita |
| MAUREPAS | Livingston | NORWOOD | East Feliciana |
| MAURICE | Vermillion | OAKDALE | Allen |
| MCNEESE ST. UNIV | Calcasieu | OAK GROVE | West Carroll |
| MELDER | Rapides | OAK RIDGE | Morehouse |
| MELROSE | Natchitoches | OBERLIN | Allen |
| MELVILLE | St Landry | OIL CENTER | Lafayette |
| MERAUX | St Bernard | OIL CITY | Caddo |
| MERMENTAU | Acadia | OLD HAMMOND | East Baton Rouge |
| MER ROUGE | Morehouse | OLLA | La Salle |
| MERRYVILLE | Beauregard | OPELOUSAS | St Landry |
| METAIRIE | Jefferson | OSCAR | Pointe Coupee |
| MICHOUD | Orleans | OTIS | Rapides |
| MID CITY | Orleans | PAINCOURTVILLE | Assumption |
| MIDLAND | Acadia | PALMETTO | St Landry |
| MILTON | Lafayette | PARADIS | St Charles |
| MINDEN | Webster | PARK MANOR | Jefferson |
| MIRA | Caddo | PARKS | St Martin |
| MITCHELL | Converse | PATTERSON | St Mary |
| MITTIE | Allen | PAULINA | St James |
| MODESTE | Ascension | PEARL RIVER | St Tammany |
| MOISANT AIRPORT | Orleans | PELICAN | De Soto |
| MONROE | Ouachita | PERRY | Vermillion |
| MONTEGUT | Terrebonne | PIERRE PART | Assumption |
| MONTEREY | Concordia | PILOTTONW | Plaquemines |
| MONTGOMERY | Grant | PINE GROVE | St Helena |
| MOORINGSPORT | Caddo | PINE PRAIRIE | Evangeline |
| MORA | Natchitoches | PINEVILLE | Rapides |
| MOREAUVILLE | Avoyelles | PIONEER | West Carroll |
| MORGAN CITY | St Mary | PITKIN | Vernon |
| MORGANZA | Point Coupee | PLAIN DEALING | Bossier |
| MORNINGSIDE | Caddo | PLAQUEMINE | Iberville |
| MORROW | St Landry | PLATTENVILLE | Assumption |
| MORSE | Acadia | PLAUCHEVILLE | Avoyelles |
| MOSS BLUFF | Calcasieu | PLEASANT HILL | Sabine |
| MOUND | Tallulah | POINT CLAIR | Iberville |
| MOUNT AIRY | St. John The Baptist | POINTE A LA HACHE | Plaquemines |
| MOUNT HERMON | Washington | POLLOCK | Grant |
| NAPOLEONVILLE | Assumption | PONCHATOULA | Tangipahoa |
| NATALBANY | Tangipahoa | PORT ALLEN | West Baton Rouge |
| NATCHEZ | Natchitoches | PORT BARRE | St Landry |
| NATCHITOCHES | Natchitoches | PORT SULPHUR | Plaquemines |
| NEGREET | Sabine | PORT VINCENT | Livingston |
| NEWELLTON | Tensas | POWHATAN | Natchitoches |
| NEW IBERTIA | Iberia | PRAIRIEVILLE | Ascension |
| NEWLLANO | Vernon | PRIDE | East Baton Rouge |
| NEW ORLEANS | Orleans | PRINCETON | Bossier |
| NEW ROADS | Pointe Coupee | PROVENCAL | Natchitoches |
| NEW SARPY | St Charles | QUITMAN | Jackson |
| NICHOLLS UNIVERSITY | Lafourche | RACELAND | Lafourche |

| | | | |
|---|---|---|---|
| RAGLEY | Beauregard | SOUTH PARK | Rapides |
| RAYNE | Acadia | SOUTH PARK | Caddo |
| RAYVILLE | Richland | SOUTHSIDE | Lafayette |
| REDDELL | Evangeline | SPEARSVILLE | Union |
| REEVES | Allen | SPENCER | Ouachita |
| RESERVE | St John The Baptist | SPRINGFIELD | Livingston |
| RHINEHART | Catahoula | SPRINGHILL | Webster |
| RICHWOOD | Ouachita | STARKS | Calcasieu |
| RINGGOLD | Bienville | START | Richland |
| ROANOKE | Jefferson Davis | STERLINGTON | Ouachita |
| ROBELINE | Natchitoches | STONEWALL | De Soto |
| ROBERT | Tangipahoa | SUGARTOWN | Beauregard |
| ROSESSA | Caddo | SULPHUR | Calcasieu |
| ROSA | St Landry | SUMMERFIELD | Claiborne |
| ROSEDALE | Iberville | SUN | St Tammany |
| ROSELAND | Tangipahoa | SUNSET | St Landry |
| ROSEPINE | Vernon | SUNSHINE | Iberville |
| ROUGON | Pointe Coupee | SWARTZ | Ouachita |
| RUBY | Rapides | TALISHEEK | St Tammany |
| RUSTON | Lincoln | TALLULAH | Madison |
| SAINT AMANT | Ascension | TANGIPAHOA | Tangipahoa |
| SAINT BENEDICT | StTammany | TAYLOR | Bienville |
| SAINT BERNARD | St Bernard | TEMPLE | Vernon |
| SAINT FRANCISVILLE | West Feliciana | TERRY | West Carroll |
| SAINT GABRIEL | Iberville | TERRYTOWN | Jefferson |
| SAINT JAMES | St James | THE BLUFFS | Jackson |
| SAINT JOSEPH | Tensas | THERIOT | Terrebonne |
| SAINT LANDRY | Evangeline | THIBODAUX | Lafourche |
| SAINT MARTINVILLE | St Martin | TICKFAW | Tangipahoa |
| SAINT MAURICE | Winn | TIOGA | Rapides |
| SAINT ROSE | St Charles | TORBET | Pointe Coupee |
| SAINT TAMMANY | St Tammany | TOWER PARK | Vernon |
| SALINE | Bienville | TRANSYLVANIA | East Carroll |
| SAREPTA | Webster | TREES | Caddo |
| SCHRIEVER | Terrebonne | TROUT | La Salle |
| SCOTLANDVILLE | East Baton Rouge | TULLOS | La Salle |
| SCOTT | Lafayette | TUNICA | West Feliciana |
| SHONGALOO | Webster | TURKEY CREEK | Evangeline |
| SIBLEY | Webster | UNCLE SAM | St James |
| SICILY ISLAND | Catahoula | UNIV OF SOUTHWESTERNLA | Lafayette |
| SIEPER | Rapides | URANIA | La Salle |
| SIKES | Winn | VACHERIE | St James |
| SIMMESPORT | Avoyelles | VARNADO | Washington |
| SIMPSON | Vernon | VENICE | Plaquemines |
| SIMSBORO | Lincoln | VENTRESS | Pointe Coupee |
| SINGER | Beauregard | VERDA | Grant |
| SLAGLE | Vernon | VICK | Avoyelles |
| SLAUGHTER | East Feliciana | VIDALIA | Concordia |
| SLIDELL | St Tammany | VIEUX CARRE | Orleans |
| SONDHEIMER | East Carroll | VILLAGE PLACE | Livingston |
| SORRENTO | Ascension | VILLE PLATTE | Evangeline |
| SOUTHEASTERN UNIVERSITY | Tangipahoa | VINTON | Calcasieu |
| SOUTHFIELD | Caddo | VIOLET | St Bernard |

| | | | |
|---|---|---|---|
| VIVIAN | Caddo | BENEDICTA | Aroostook |
| WAKEFIELD | West Feliciana | BERNARD | Hancock |
| WALKER | Livingston | BERWICK | York |
| WARDEN | Richland | BETHEL | Oxford |
| WASHINGTON | St Landry | BIDDEFORD | York |
| WATERPROOF | Tensas | BODDEFORD POOL | York |
| WATSON | Livingston | BINGHAM | Somerset |
| WAVERLY | Richland | BIRCH HARBOR | Hancock |
| WELSH | Jefferson Davis | BIRCH ISLAND | Cumberland |
| WESTLAKE | Calcasieu | BLAINE | Aroostook |
| WEST MONROE | Ouachita | BLUE HILL | Hancock |
| WESTSIDE | Alexandria | BLUE HILL FALLS | Hancock |
| WEST SLIDELL | St Tammany | BOOTHBAY | Lincoln |
| WESTWEGO | Jefferson | BOOTHBAY HARBOR | Lincoln |
| WEYANOKE | West Feliciana | BOWDOINHAM | Sagadahoc |
| WHITE CASTLE | Iberville | BRADFORD | Penobscot |
| WHITEHALL | Avoyelles | BRADLEY | Penobscot |
| WILDSVILLE | Concordia | BREWER | Penobscot |
| WILSON | East Feliciana | BRIDGEWATER | Aroostook |
| WINNFIELD | Winn | BRIDGTON | Cumberland |
| WINNSBORO | Franklin | BRISTOL | Lincoln |
| WISNER | Franklin | BROOKLIN | Hancock |
| WOODLAWN | Baton Rouge | BROOKS | Waldo |
| WOODWORTH | Rapides | BROOKSVILLE | Hancock |
| YOUNGSVILLE | Lafayette | BROOKTON | Washington |
| ZACHARY | East Baton Rouge | BROWNFIELD | Oxford |
| ZWOLLE | Sabine | BROWNVILLE | Piscataquis |
| **MAINE** | | BROWNVILLE JCT. | Piscataquis |
| ABBOTT VILLAGE | Piscataquis | BRUNSWICK | Cumberland |
| ACTON | York | BRYANT POND | Oxford |
| ADDISON | Washington | BUCKFIELD | Oxford |
| ALBION | Kennebec | BUCKS HARBOR | Washington |
| ALFRED | York | BUCKSPORT | Hancock |
| ALNA | Lincoln | BURLINGTON | Penobscot |
| ANDOVER | Oxford | BURNHAM | Waldo |
| ANSON | Somerset | BUSTINS ISLAND | Cumberland |
| ASHLAND | Aroostook | CALAIS | Washington |
| ATHENS | Somerset | CAMBRIDGE | Somerset |
| ATLANTIC | Hancock | CAMDEN | Knox |
| AUBURN | Androscoggin | CANAAN | Somerset |
| AUGUSTA | Kennebec | CANTON | Oxford |
| AURORA | Hancock | CAPE COTTAGE | Cumberland |
| BAILEY ISLAND | Cumberland | CAPE ELIZABETH | Cumberland |
| BANGOR | Penobscot | CAPE NEDDICK | York |
| BAR HARBOR | Hancock | CAPE PORPOISE | York |
| BAR MILLS | York | CAPITOL ISLAND | Lincoln |
| BASS HARBOR | Hancock | CARATUNK | Somerset |
| BATH | Sagadahoc | CARDVILLE | Penobscot |
| BAYVILLE | Lincoln | CARIBOU | Aroostook |
| BEALS | Washington | CARMEL | Penobscot |
| BELFAST | Waldo | CASCO | Cumberland |
| BELGRADE | Kennebec | CASTINE | Hancock |
| BELGRADE LAKES | Kennebec | CENTER LOVELL | Oxford |

| | | | |
|---|---|---|---|
| CHAMBERLAIN | Lincoln | EAST POLAND | Androscoggin |
| CHARLESTON | Penobscot | EASTPORT | Washington |
| CHEBEAGUE ISLAND | Cumberland | EAST SEBAGO | Cumberland |
| CHERRYFIELD | Washington | EAST STONEHAM | Oxford |
| CHINA | Kennebec | EAST VASSALBORO | Kennebec |
| CLAYTON LAKE | Aroonstock | EAST WATERBORO | York |
| CLIFF ISLAND | Cumberland | EAST WATERFORD | Oxford |
| CLINTON | Kennebec | EAST WILTON | Franklin |
| COLBY COLLEGE | Kennebec | EAST WINTHROP | Kennebec |
| COLUMBIA FALLS | Washington | EDGECOMB | Lincoln |
| COOPERS MILLS | Lincoln | ELIOT | York |
| COREA | Hancock | ELLSWORTH | Hancock |
| CORINNA | Penobscot | EMERY MILLS | York |
| CORNISH | York | ENFIELD | Penobscot |
| COSTIGAN | Penobscot | ESTCOURT STATION | Aroostook |
| CRANBERRY ISLES | Hancock | ETNA | Penobscot |
| CROUSEVILLE | Aroostook | EUSTIS | Franklin |
| CUMBERLAND CENTER | Cumberland | EXETER | Penobscot |
| CUNDYS HARBOR | Cumberland | FAIRFIELD | Somerset |
| CUSHING | Knox | FALMOUTH | Cumberland |
| CUTLER | Washington | FARMINGDALE | Kennebec |
| DAMARISCOTTA | Lincoln | FARMINGTON | Franklin |
| DANFORTH | Washington | FARMINGTON FALLS | Franklin |
| DANVILLE | Androscoggin | FIVE ISLANDS | Sagadahoc |
| DEER ISLE | Hancock | FORT FAIRFIELD | Aroostook |
| DENMARK | Oxford | FORT KENT | Aroostook |
| DENNYSVILLE | Washington | FORT KENT MILLS | Aroostock |
| DETROIT | Somerset | FRANKFORT | Waldo |
| DEXTER | Penobscot | FRANKLIN | Hancock |
| DIAMOND ISLAND | Cumberland | FREEDOM | Waldo |
| DIXFIELD | Oxford | FREEPORT | Cumberland |
| DIXMONT | Penobscot | FRENCHBORO | Hancock |
| DOVER-FOXCROFT | Piscataquis | FRENCHVILLE | Aroostook |
| DRESDEN | Lincoln | FRIENDSHIP | Knox |
| DRYDEN | Franklin | FRYE | Oxford |
| EAGLE LAKE | Aroostook | FRYEBURG | Oxford |
| EAST ANDOVER | Oxford | GARDINER | Kennebec |
| EAST BALDWIN | Cumberland | GARLAND | Penobscot |
| EAST BLUE HILL | Hancock | GEORGETOWN | Sagadahoc |
| EAST BOOTHBAY | Lincoln | GLEN COVE | Knox |
| EAST CORINTH | Penobscot | GORHAM | Cumberland |
| EAST DIXFIELD | Franklin | GOULDSBORO | Hancock |
| EAST EDDINGTON | Penobscot | GRAND ISLE | Aroostook |
| EAST HOLDEN | Penobscot | GRAND LAKE STREAM | Washington |
| EAST LEBANON | York | GRAY | Cumberland |
| EAST LIVERMORE | Androscoggin | GREAT DIAMOND ISLAND | Cumberland |
| EAST MACHIAS | Washington | GREENE | Androscoggin |
| EAST MILLINOCKET | Penobscot | GREENVILLE | Piscataquis |
| EAST NEWPORT | Penobscot | GREENVILLE JUNCTION | Piscataquis |
| EASTON | Aroostook | GROVE | Washington |
| EAST ORLAND | Hancock | GUILFORD | Piscataquis |
| EAST PARSONFIELD | York | HALLOWELL | Kennebec |
| EAST PERU | Oxford | HAMPDEN | Penobscot |

| | | | |
|---|---|---|---|
| HANCOCK | Hancock | LISBON FALLS | Androscoggin |
| HANOVER | Oxford | LITCHFIELD | Kennebec |
| HARBOR ISLAND | Cumberland | LITTLE DEER ISLE | Hancock |
| HARBORSIDE | Hancock | LITTLE DIAMOND ISLAND | Cumberland |
| HARMONY | Somerset | LIVERMORE FALLS | Androscoggin |
| HARRINGTON | Washington | LOCKE MILLS | Oxford |
| HARRISON | Cumberland | LONG ISLAND | Cumberland |
| HARTLAND | Somerset | LORING AFB | Aroostock |
| HAYNESVILLE | Aroostook | LOVELL | Oxford |
| HEBRON | Oxford | LUBEC | Washington |
| HINCKLEY | Somerset | MACHIAS | Wasington |
| HIRAM | Oxford | MACHIASPORT | Washington |
| HOLLIS CENTER | York | MAC MAHAN | Sagadahoc |
| HOPE | Knox | MADAWASKA | Aroostook |
| HOULTON | Aroostook | MADISON | Somerset |
| HOWLAND | Penobscot | MANCHESTER | Kennebec |
| HUDSON | Penobscot | MANSET | Hancock |
| HULLS COVE | Hancock | MAPLETON | Aroostook |
| ISLAND FALLS | Aroostook | MAPLEWOOD | York |
| ISLE-AU-HAUT | Knox | MARS HILL | Aroostook |
| ISLESBORO | Waldo | MASARDIS | Aroostock |
| ISLESFORD | Hancock | MATINICUS | Knox |
| JACKMAN | Somerset | MAITAWAMKEAG | Penobscot |
| JAY | Franklin | MECHANIC FALLS | Androscoggin |
| JEFFERSON | Lincoln | MEDDYBEMPS | Washington |
| JONESBORO | Washington | MEDOMAK | Lincoln |
| JONESPORT | Washington | MEDWAY | Penobscot |
| KENDUSKEAG | Penobscot | MEREPOINT | Cumberland |
| KENNEBUNK | York | MEXICO | Oxford |
| KENNEBUNKPORT | York | MILBRIDGE | Washington |
| KENTS HILL | Kennebec | MILFORD | Penobscot |
| KEZAR FALLS | York | MILLINOCKET | Penobscot |
| KINGFIELD | Franklin | MILLTOWN | Washington |
| KINGMAN | Penobscot | MILO | Piscataquis |
| KITTERY | York | MINOT | Androscoggin |
| KITTERY POINT | York | MINTURN | Hancock |
| LAGRANGE | Penobscot | MONHEGAN | Lincoln |
| LAMBERT LAKE | Washington | MONMOUTH | Kennebec |
| LEE | Penobscot | MONROE | Waldo |
| LEEDS | Androscoggin | MONSON | Piscataquis |
| LEVANT | Penobscot | MONTICELLO | Aroostook |
| LEWISTON | Androscoggin | MOODY | York |
| LIBERTY | Waldo | MORRILL | Waldo |
| LILLE | Aroostook | MOUNT DESERT | Hancock |
| LIMERICK | York | MOUNT VERNON | Kennebec |
| LIMESTONE | Aroostook | NAPLES | Cumberland |
| LIMINGTON | York | NAVAL AIR STATION | Cumberland |
| LINCOLN | Penobscot | NEWAGEN | Lincoln |
| LINCOLN CENTER | Penobscot | NEWCASTLE | Lincoln |
| LINCOLNVILLE | Waldo | NEWFIELD | York |
| LINCOLNVILLE CENTER | Waldo | NEW GLOUCESTER | Cumberland |
| LISBON | Androscoggin | NEW HARBOR | Lincoln |
| LISBON CENTER | Androscoggin | NEW LIMERICK | Aroostook |

| | | | |
|---|---|---|---|
| NEWPORT | Penobscot | PEMBROKE | Washington |
| NEW PORTLAND | Somerset | PENOBSCOT | Hancock |
| NEWRY | Oxford | PERHAM | Aroostook |
| NEW SHARON | Franklin | PERRY | Washington |
| NEW SWEDEN | Aroostook | PERU | Oxford |
| NEW VINEYARD | Franklin | PHILLIPS | Franklin |
| NOBLEBORO | Lincoln | PHIPPSBURG | Sagadahoc |
| NORRIDGEWOCK | Somerset | PITTSFIELD | Somerset |
| NORTH AMITY | Aroostook | PLAISTED | Aroostook |
| NORTH ANSON | Somerset | PLYMOUTH | Penobscot |
| NORTH BERWICK | York | POLAND | Androscoggin |
| NORTH BRIDGTON | Cumberland | POLAND SPRING | Androscoggin |
| NORTH BROOKLIN | Hancock | POND COVE | Cumberland |
| NORTHEAST HARBOR | Hancock | PORTAGE | Aroostook |
| NORTH EDGECOMB | Lincoln | PORT CLYDE | Knox |
| NORTH FRYEBURG | Oxford | PORTER | Oxford |
| NORTH HAVEN | Knox | PORTLAND | Cumberland |
| NORTH JAY | Franklin | POWNAL | Cumberland |
| NORTH MONMOUTH | Kennebec | PRESQUE ISLE | Aroostook |
| NORTH NEW PORTLAND | Somerset | PRINCETON | Washington |
| NORTH SHAPLEIGH | York | PROSPECT HARBOR | Hancock |
| NORTH SULLIVAN | Hancock | PROUTS NECK | Scarborough |
| NORTH TURNER | Androscoggin | QUIMBY | Aroostook |
| NORTH VASSALBORO | Kennebec | RANDOLPH | Kennebec |
| NORTH WATERBORO | York | RANGELEY | Franklin |
| NORTH WATERFORD | Oxford | RAYMOND | Cumberland |
| NORTH WHITEFIELD | Lincoln | READFIELD | Kennebec |
| NORWAY | Oxford | RICHMOND | Sagadahoc |
| OAKFIELD | Aroostook | ROBBINSTON | Washington |
| OAKLAND | Kennebec | ROCKLAND | Knox |
| OCEAN PARK | York | ROCKPORT | Knox |
| OGUNQUIT | York | ROCKWOOD | Somerset |
| OLAMON | Penobscot | ROUND POND | Lincoln |
| OLD ORCHARD BEACH | York | ROXBURY | Oxford |
| OLD TOWN | Penobscot | RUMFORD | Oxford |
| OQUOSSOC | Franklin | RUMFORD CENTER | Oxford |
| ORIENT | Aroostook | RUMFORD POINT | Oxford |
| ORLAND | Hancock | SABATTUS | Androscoggin |
| ORONO | Penobscot | SACO | York |
| ORRINGTON | Penobscot | SAINT AGATHA | Aroostook |
| ORRS ISLAND | Cumberland | SAINT ALBANS | Somerset |
| OTTER CREEK | Hancock | SAINT DAVID | Aroostook |
| OWLS HEAD | Knox | SAINT FRANCIS | Aroostook |
| OXBOW | Aroostook | SAINT GEORGE | Knox |
| OXFORD | Oxford | SALSBURY COVE | Hancock |
| PALERMO | Waldo | SANDY POINT | Waldo |
| PALMYRA | Somerset | SANFORD | York |
| PARIS | Oxford | SANGERVILLE | Piscataquis |
| PASSADUMKEAG | Penobscot | SARGENTVILLE | Hancock |
| PATTEN | Penobscot | SCARBOROUGH | Cumberland |
| PEAKS ISLAND | Cumberland | SEAL COVE | Hancock |
| PEJEPSCOT | Sagadahoc | SEAL HARBOR | Hancock |
| PEMAQUID | Lincoln | SEARSMONT | Waldo |

| | | | |
|---|---|---|---|
| SEARSPORT | Waldo | SWANS ISLAND | Hancock |
| SEBAGO LAKE | Cumberland | TEMPLE | Franklin |
| SEBASCO ESTATES | Sagadahoc | TENANTS HARBOR | Knox |
| SEBEC | Piscataquis | THOMASTON | Knox |
| SEBEC LAKE | Guildord | THORNDIKE | Waldo |
| SEBOEIS | Penobscot | TOPSFIELD | Washington |
| SEDGWICK | Hancock | TOPSHAM | Sagadahoc |
| SHAPLEIGH | York | TREVETT | Lincoln |
| SHAWMUT | Somerset | TROY | Waldo |
| SHERIDAN | Aroostook | TURNER | Androscoggin |
| SHERMAN MILLS | Aroostook | TURNER CENTER | Androscoggin |
| SHERMAN STATION | Penobscot | UNION | Knox |
| SHIRLEY MILLS | Piscataquis | UNITY | Waldo |
| SINCLAIR | Aroostook | UPPER FRENCHVILLE | Arrostook |
| SKOWHEGAN | Somerset | VAN BUREN | Aroostook |
| SMALL POINT | Sagadahoc | VANCEBORO | Washington |
| SMITHFIELD | Somerset | VASSALBORO | Kennebec |
| SMYRNA MILLS | Aroostook | VIENNA | Kennebec |
| SOLDIER POND | Aroostook | VINAHLAVEN | Knox |
| SOLON | Somerset | WALDOBORO | Lincoln |
| SORRENTO | Hancock | WALPOLE | Lincoln |
| SOUTH BERWICK | York | WARREN | Knox |
| SOUTH BRISTON | Lincoln | WASHBURN | Aroostook |
| SOUTH CASCO | Cumberland | WASHINGTON | Knox |
| SOUTH CHINA | Kennebec | WATERBORO | York |
| SOUTH FREEPORT | Cumberland | WATERFORD | Oxford |
| SOUTH GARDINER | Kennebec | WATERVILLE | Kennebec |
| SOUTH GOULDSBORO | Hancock | WAYNE | Kennebec |
| SOUTH HARPSWELL | Cumberland | WEEKS MILLS | Kennebec |
| SOUTH HIRAM | Oxford | WELD | Franklin |
| SOUTH PARIS | Oxford | WELLS | York |
| SOUTH PORTLAND | Cumberland | WEST BALDWIN | Cumberland |
| SOUTH THOMASTON | Knox | WEST BETHEL | Oxford |
| SOUTH WATERFORD | Oxford | WEST BOOTHBAY HARBOR | Lincoln |
| SOUTHWEST HARBOR | Hancock | WEST BOWDOIN | Sagadahoc |
| SOUTH WINDHAM | Cumberland | WESTBROOK | Cumberland |
| SPRINGFIELD | Penobscot | WEST BUXTON | York |
| SPRINGVALE | York | WEST ENFIELD | Penobscot |
| SPRUCE HEAD | Knox | WEST FARMINGTON | Franklin |
| SQUIRREL ISLAND | Lincoln | WESTFIELD | Aroostook |
| STACYVILLE | Penobscot | WEST FORKS | Somerset |
| STANDISH | Cumberland | WEST KENNEBUNK | York |
| STEEP FALLS | Cumberland | WEST MINOT | Androscoggin |
| STETSON | Penobscot | WEST NEWFIELD | York |
| STEUBEN | Washington | WEST PARIS | Oxford |
| STILLWATER | Penobscot | WEST POLAND | Androscoggin |
| STOCKHOLM | Aroostook | WEST ROCKPORT | Knox |
| STOCKTON SPRINGS | Waldo | WEST SOUTHPORT | Lincoln |
| STOINGTON | Knox | WEST SULLIVAN | Hancock |
| STRATTON | Franklin | WEST SUMNER | Oxford |
| STRONG | Franklin | WEST TREMONT | Hancock |
| SUNSET | Hancock | WHITEFIELD | Lincoln |
| SURRY | Hancock | WHITING | Washington |

| | |
|---|---|
| WHITNEYVILLE | Washington |
| WILTON | Franklin |
| WINDHAM | Cumberland |
| WINDSOR | Kennebec |
| WINN | Penobscot |
| WINTER HARBOR | Hancock |
| WINTERPORT | Waldo |
| WINTERVILLE | Aroostook |
| WINTHROP | Kennebec |
| WISCASSET | Lincoln |
| WOODLAND | Washington |
| WOOLWICH | Sagadahoc |
| WYTOPITLOCK | Aroostook |
| YARMOUTH | Cumberland |
| YORK | York |
| YORK BEACH | York |
| YORK HARBOR | York |

## MARYLAND

| | |
|---|---|
| ABELL | St Mary's |
| ABERDEEN | Harford |
| ABERDEEN PROVINGGROUND | Harford |
| ABINGTON | Harford |
| ACCIDENT | Garrett |
| ACCOKEEK | Prince George's |
| ADAMSDOWN | Frederick |
| ADELPHI | Prince George's |
| ALLEN | Wicominco |
| AMERICAN CITIES | Howard |
| ANNAPOLIS | Anne Arundel |
| ANNAPOLIS JUNCTION | Howard |
| AQUASCO | Prince George's |
| ARLINGTON | Baltimore |
| ARNOLD | Anne Arundel |
| ASHTON | Montgomery |
| ASPEN HILL | Montgomery |
| AVENUE | St Mary's |
| BALTIMORE | Baltimore |
| BARCLAY | Queen Anne's |
| BARNESVILLE | Montgomery |
| BARSTOW | Calvert |
| BARTON | Allegany |
| BEALLSVILLE | Montgomery |
| BEL AIR | Harford |
| BEL ALTON | Charles |
| BELCAMP | Harford |
| BELTSVILLE | Prince George's |
| BENEDICT | Charles |
| BENSON | Harford |
| BENTLEY SPRINGS | Baltimore |
| BERLIN | Worcester |
| BERWYN HEIGHTS | Prince George's |
| BETHESDA | Montgomery |
| BETHELEHEM | Caroline |

| | |
|---|---|
| BELTERTON | Kent |
| BIG POOL | Washington |
| PIB SPRING | Washington |
| BISHOPVILLE | Worcester |
| BITTINGER | Garrett |
| BIVALVE | Wicomico |
| BLADENSBURG | Prince George's |
| BLAIR | Montgomery |
| BLOOMINGTON | Garrett |
| BOONSBORO | Washington |
| BORING | Baltimore |
| BOWIE | Prince George's |
| BOYDS | Montgomery |
| MOZMAN | Talbot |
| BRADDOCK HEIGHTS | Frederick |
| BRADSHAW | Baltimore |
| BRANDYWINE | Prince George's |
| BRENTWOOD | Prince George's |
| BRINKLOW | Montgomery |
| BROOKEVILLE | Montgomery |
| BROOKLANDVILLE | Baltimore |
| BROOKLYN CURTIS BAY | Anne Arundel |
| BROOMES ISLAND | Calvert |
| BROVWNSVILLE | Washington |
| BRUNSWICK | Frederick |
| BRYANS ROAD | Charles |
| BRYANTOWN | Charles |
| BUCKEYSTOWN | Frederick |
| BURKITTSVILLE | Frederick |
| BURTONSVILLE | Montgomery |
| BUSHWOOD | St Mary's |
| BUTLER | Baltimore |
| CABIN JOHN | Montgomery |
| CALIFORNIA | St Mary's |
| CALLAWAY | St Mary's |
| CALVERT | Baltimore |
| CAMBRIDGE | Dorcester |
| CAMP SPRINGS | Prince George's |
| CAPE SAINT CLAIRE | Anne Arundel |
| CAPITAL HEIGHTS | Prince George's |
| CARDIFF | Harford |
| CARROLL | Baltimore |
| CARROLLTON | Carroll |
| CASCADE | Washington |
| CATONSVILLE | Baltimore |
| CAVETOWN | Washington |
| CECILTON | Cecil |
| CENTREVILLE | Queen Anne's |
| CHANCE | Somerset |
| CHAPTICO | St Mary's |
| CHARLESTOWN | Cecil |
| CHARLOTTE HELL | StMary's |
| CHASE | Baltimore |

| | | | |
|---|---|---|---|
| CHELTENHAM | Prince George's | DICKERSON | Montgomery |
| CHESAPEAKE BEACH | Calvert | DISTRICT HEIGHTS | Prince George's |
| CHESAPEAKE CITY | Cecil | DOUBS | Frederick |
| CHESTER | Queen Anne's | DOWELL | Calvert |
| CHESTERTOWN | Kent | DRAYDEN | St Mary's |
| CHEVERLY | Prince George's | DRUID | Baltimore |
| CHEVY CHASE | Montgomery | DUNKIRK | Calvert |
| CHEWSVILLE | Washington | EARLEVILLE | Cecil |
| CHILDS | Cecil | EAST NEW MARKET | Dorcester |
| CHILLUM | Prince George's | EASTON | Talbot |
| CHURCH CREEK | Dorcester | EASTPORT | Anne Arundel |
| CHURCH HILL | Queen Anne's | ECKHART MINES | Allegany |
| CHURCHTON | Anne Arundel | EDEN | Somerset |
| CHURCHVILLE | Harford | EDGEWATER | Anne Arundel |
| CLAIBORNE | Talbot | EDGEWOOD | Harford |
| CLARKSBURG | Montgomery | ELDERSBURG | Carroll |
| CLARKSVILLE | Howard | ELK MILLS | Cecil |
| CLEAR SPRING | Washington | ELKTON | Cecil |
| CLEMENTS | St Mary's | ELLERSLIE | Allegany |
| CLINTON | Prince George's | ELLICOTT CITY | Howard |
| COBB ISLAND | Charles | ELLICOTT MILLS | Howard |
| COCKEYSVILLE HUNTVALLEY | Baltimore | EMMITSBURG | Frederick |
| COLESVILLE | Montgomery | ESSEX | Baltimore |
| COLLEGE PARK | Prince George's | EUDOWOOD | Baltimore |
| COLORA | Cecil | EWELL | Somerset |
| COLTONS POINT | St Mary's | FAIR PLAY | Washington |
| COLUMBIA | Howard | FALLSTON | Harford |
| COMPTON | St Mary's | FAULKNER | Charles |
| CONOWINGO | Cecil | FEDERALSBURG | Caroline |
| COOKSVILLE | Howard | FERNDALE | Anne Arundel |
| CORDOVA | Talbot | FINKSBURG | Carroll |
| CORRIGANVILLE | Allegany | FISHING CREEK | Dorcester |
| CRAPO | Dorcester | FLINTSTONE | Allegany |
| CRELLIN | Garrett | FORREST HILL | Harford |
| CRISFIELD | Somerset | FORESTVILLE | Prince George's |
| CROCHERON | Dorcester | FORK | Baltimore |
| CROFTON | Anne Arundel | FORT DETRICK | Frederick |
| CROWNSVILLE | Anne Arundel | FORT GEORGE G. MEADE | Anne Arundel |
| CRUMPTON | Queen Anne's | FORT HOWARD | Baltimore |
| CUMBERLAND | Allegany | FORT RITCHIE | Washington |
| DAMASCUS | Montgomery | FORT WASHINGTON | Prince George's |
| DAMERON | St Mary's | FOWBELSBURG | Carroll |
| DAMES QUARTER | Somerset | FRANKLIN | Baltimore |
| DANIELS | Howard | FREDERICK | Frederick |
| DARLINGTON | Harford | FREELAND | Baltimore |
| DAVIDSONVILLE | Anne Arundel | FRIENDSHIP | Anne Arundel |
| DAYTON | Howard | FRIENDSHIP HEIGHTS | Montgomery |
| DEALE | Anne Arundel | FRIENDSVILLE | Garrett |
| DEER PARK | Garrett | FROSTBURG | Allegany |
| DELMAR | Wicomico | FRUITLAND | Wicomico |
| DENTON | Caroline | FULTON | Howard |
| DETOUR | Carroll | FUNKSTOWN | Washington |
| DIAMOND FARMS | Montgomery | GAITHER | Carroll |

| | | | |
|---|---|---|---|
| GAITHERSBURG | Montgomery | ILCHESTER | Howard |
| GELENA | Kent | INDIAN HEAD | Charles |
| GALESVILLE | Anne Arundel | INGLESIDE | Queen Anne's |
| GAMBRILLS | Anne Arundel | IRONSIDES | Charles |
| GAPLAND | Washington | ISSUE | Charles |
| GARRETT PARK | Montgomery | JACKSONVILLE | Baltimore |
| GARRISON | Baltimore | JARRETTSVILLE | Harford |
| GEORGETOWN | Cecil | JEFFERSON | Frederick |
| GERMANTOWN | Montgomery | JENNINGS | Garrett |
| GIBSON ISLAND | Anne Arundel | JESSUP | Anne Arundel |
| GIRDLETREE | Worcester | JOPPA | Harford |
| GLENARDEN | Prince George's | KEEDYSVILLE | Washington |
| GLEN ARM | Baltimore | KENILWORTH | Prince George's |
| GLEN BURNIE | Anne Arundel | KENNEDYVILLE | Kent |
| GLENCOE | Baltimore | KENSINGTON | Montgomery |
| GLEN ECHO | Montgomery | KEYMAR | Carroll |
| GLENELG | Howard | KINGSVILLE | Baltimore |
| GLENN DALE | Prince George's | KITZMILLER | Garrett |
| GLENWOOD | Howard | KNOXVILLE | Frederick |
| GLYNDON | Baltimore | LADIESBURG | Frederick |
| GOLDSBORO | Caroline | LAKE SHORE | Anne Arundel |
| GOLTS | Kent | LANHAM SEABROOK | Prince George's |
| GOVANS | Baltimore | LA PLATA | Charles |
| GRACEHAM | Frederick | LAUREL | Prince George's |
| GRANITE | Howard | LAVALE | Allegany |
| GRANTSVILLE | Garrett | LAYTONSVILLE | Montgomery |
| GRASONVILLE | Queen Anne's | LEONARDTOWN | St Mary's |
| GREAT MILLS | St Mary's | LEWISTOWN | Frederick |
| GREENBELT | Prince George's | LEXINGTON PARK | St Mary's |
| GREENMOUNT | Baltimore | LIBERTYTOWN | St Mary's |
| GREENSBORO | Caroline | LIME KILN | Frederick |
| GUNPOWDER | Harford | LINEBORO | Carroll |
| GWYNN OAK | Baltimore | LINKWOOD | Dorchester |
| HAGERSTOWN | Washington | LINTHICUM HEIGHTS | Anne Arundel |
| HALETHORPE | Baltimore | LINWOOD | Carroll |
| HAMPSTEAD | Baltimore | LISBON | Howard |
| HARMANS | Anne Arundel | LITTLE ORLEANS | Allegany |
| HARWOOD | Anne Arundel | LONACONING | Allegany |
| HAVRE DE GRACE | Harford | LONG GREEN | Baltimore |
| HEBRON | Wicomico | LOTHIAN | Anne Arundel |
| HELEN | St Mary's | LOVEVILLE | St Mary's |
| HENDERSON | Caroline | LUKE | Allegany |
| HENRYTOWN | Carroll | LUSBY | Calvert |
| HIGHLAND | Howard | LUTHERVILLE | Lutherville |
| HILLSBORO | Caroline | LYNCH | Kent |
| HOLLYWOOD | St Mary's | MADDOX | St Mary's |
| HUGHESVILLE | Charles | MADISON | Dorchester |
| HUNTINGTOWN | Calvert | MAGNOLIA | Harford |
| HURLICK | Dorcester | MANCHESTER | Carroll |
| HUTTON | Garrett | MANOKIN | Somerset |
| HYATTSVILLE | Prince George's | MARBURY | Charles |
| HYDES | Baltimore | MARDELA SPRINGS | Wicomico |
| IJAMSVILLE | Frederick | MARION STATION | Somerset |

| | | | |
|---|---|---|---|
| MARKET CENTER | Baltimore | OELLA | Howard |
| MARRIOTTSVILLE | Howard | OLDTOWN | Allegany |
| MARYDEL | Caroline | OLNEY | Montgomery |
| MARYLAND LINE | Baltimore | OWINGS | Calvert |
| MASSEY | Kent | OWINGS MILLS | Baltimore |
| MAUGANSVILLE | Washington | OXFORD | Talbot |
| MAYO | Anne Arundel | OXON HILL | Prince George's |
| MCCOOLE | Allegany | PARK HALL | St Mary's |
| MCDANIEL | Talbot | PARKTON | Baltimore |
| MC HENRY | Garrett | PARSONBURG | Wicomico |
| MECHANICSVILLE | St Mary's | PASADENA | Anne Arundel |
| MIDDLEBURG | Carroll | PATAPSCO | Finksburg |
| MIDDLETOWN | Frederick | PATTERSON | Baltimore |
| MIDLAND | Allegany | PATUXENT RIVER | St Mary's |
| MIDLOTHIAN | Allegany | PERRY HALL | Baltimore |
| MILLERS | Carroll | PERRYMAN | Harford |
| MILLERSVILLE | Anne Arundel | PERRY POINT | Cecil |
| MILLINGTON | Kent | PERRYVILLE | Cecil |
| MITCHELLVILLE | Prince George's | PHOENIX | Baltimore |
| MONKTON | Baltimore | PIKE | Montgomery |
| MONROVIA | Frederick | PIKESVILLE | Baltimore |
| MONTEGO | Worcester | PINEY POINT | St Mary's |
| MORGANZA | St Mary's | PINTO | Allegany |
| MOUNTAIN LAKE PARK | Garrett | PISGAH | Charles |
| MOUNT AIRY | Carroll | PITTSVILLE | Wicomico |
| MOUNT RANIER | Prince George's | POCOMOKE CITY | Worcester |
| MOUNT SAVAGE | Allegany | POINT OF ROCKS | Frederick |
| MOUNT VICTORIA | Charles | POMFRET | Charles |
| MOUNT WASHINGTON | Baltimore | POOLESVILLE | Montgomery |
| MOUNT WILSON | Baltimore | PORT DEPOSIT | Cecil |
| MYERSVILLE | Frederick | PORT REPUBLIC | Calvert |
| NANJEMOY | Charles | PORT TOBACCO | Charles |
| NANTICOKA | Wicomico | POTOMAC | Montgomery |
| NAVAL ACADEMY | Anne Arundel | PRESTON | Caroline |
| NEAVITT | Talbot | PRICE | Queen Anne's |
| NEWARK | Worcester | PRINCE FREDERICK | Calvert |
| NEWBURG | Charles | PRINCESS ANNE | Somerset |
| NEWCOMB | Talbot | PYLESVILLE | Harford |
| NEW MARKET | Frederick | QUANTICO | Wicomico |
| NEW MIDWAY | Frederick | QUEEN ANNE | Talbot |
| NEW WINDSOR | Carroll | QUEENSTOWN | Queen Anne's |
| NIKEP | Allegany | RANDALLSTOWN | Baltimore |
| NORTH BEACH | Calvert | RAWLINGS | Allegany |
| NORTH COLLEGE PARK | Prince George's | REHOBETH | Somerset |
| NORTH EAST | Cecil | REISTERSTOWN | Baltimore |
| NORTHERN | Washington | RHODESDALE | Dorchester |
| NORTH OCEAN CITY | Worcester | RHODES POINT | Somerset |
| NORTH POTOMAS | Montgomery | RIDERWOOD | Baltimore |
| NORTHWOOD | Baltimore | RIDGE | St Mary's |
| NOTTINGHAM | Baltimore | RIDGELY | Caroline |
| OAKLAND | Garrett | RISING SUN | Cecil |
| OCEAN CITY | Worcester | RISON | Charles |
| ODENTON | Anne Arundel | RIVA | Anne Arundel |

| | | | |
|---|---|---|---|
| RIVERDALE | Prince George's | TAYLORS ISLAND | Dorchester |
| RIVIERA BEACH | Anne Arundel | TEMPLE HILLS | Prince George's |
| ROCK HALL | Kent | TEMPLEVILLE | Caroline |
| ROCK POINT | Charles | THURMONT | Frederick |
| ROCKS | Haxford | TILGHMAN | Talbot |
| ROCKVILLE | Montgomery | TIMONIUM | Baltimore |
| ROCKY RIDGE | Frederick | TODDVILLE | Dorchester |
| ROHRERSVILLE | Washington | TOWSON | Baltimore |
| ROLAND PARK | Baltimore | TRACYS LANDING | Anne Arundel |
| ROSEDALE | Baltimore | TRAPPE | Talbot |
| ROYAL OAK | Talbot | TUSCARORA | Frederick |
| SABILLASVILLE | Frederick | TWINBROOK | Montgomery |
| SAINT INIGOES | St Mary's | TYASKIN | Wicomico |
| SAINT JAMES | Frederick | TYLERTON | Somerset |
| SAINT LEONARD | Calvert | UNION BRIDGE | Carroll |
| SAINT MARYS CITY | St Mary's | UNIONTOWN | Westminster |
| SAINT MICHAELS | Talbot | UNIONVILLE | Frederick |
| SALISBURY | Wicomico | UNIONVILLE | Union Bridge |
| SANDY SPRING | Montgomery | UPPERCO | Baltimore |
| SANG RUN | Garrett | UPPER FAIRMOUNT | Somerset |
| SAVAGE | Howard | UPPER FALLS | Baltimore |
| SCOTLAND | St Mary's | UPPER HILL | Somerset |
| SECRETARY | Dorchester | UPPER MARLBORO | Prince George's |
| SEVERN | Anne Arundel | VALLEY LEE | St Mary's |
| SEVERNA PARK | Anne Arundel | VIENNA | Dorchester |
| SHADY SIDE | Anne Arundel | WALBROOK | Baltimore |
| SHALIMAR | Garrett | WALDORF | Charles |
| SHARPSBURG | Washington | WALKERSVILLE | Frederick |
| SHARPTOWN | Wicomico | WARWICK | Cecil |
| SHERWOOD | Talbot | WASHINGTON GROVE | Montgomery |
| SHERWOOD FOREST | Anne Arundel | WAVERLY ROLAND PARK | Baltimore |
| SHOWELL | Worcester | WELCOME | Charles |
| SILVER SPRING | Montgomery | WENONA | Somerset |
| SIMPSONVILLE | Howard | WEST BETHESDA | Montgomery |
| SMITHSBURG | Washington | WEST BOWIE | Prince George's |
| SNOW HILL | Worcester | WESTERNPORT | Allegany |
| SOLOMONS | Calvert | WEST FRIENDSHIP | Howard |
| SPARKS GLENCOE | Baltimore | WEST HYATTSVILLE | Hyattsville |
| SPENCERVILLE | Montgomery | WESTMINSTER | Carroll |
| SPRING GAP | Allegany | WESTOVER | Somerset |
| STEVENSON | Baltimore | WEST RIVER | Anne Arundel |
| STEVENSVILLE | Queen Anne's | WHALEYSVILLE | Worcester |
| STILL POND | Kent | WHEATON | Montgomery |
| STOCKTON | Worcester | WHITEFORD | Harford |
| STREET | Harford | WHITE HALL | Harford |
| SUDLERSVILLE | Queen Anne's | WHITE MARSH | Baltimore |
| SUITLAND | Prince George's | WHITE PLAINS | Charles |
| SUNDERLAND | Calvert | WILLARDS | Wicomico |
| SWANTON | Garrett | WILLIAMSBURG | Dorchester |
| SYKESVILLE | Carroll | WILLIAMSPORT | Washington |
| TAKOMA PARK | Montgomery | WINGATE | Dorchester |
| TALL TIMBERS | St Mary's | WITTMAN | Talbot |
| TANEYTOWN | Carroll | WOODBINE | Carroll |

| | |
|---|---|
| WOODMOOR | Montgomery |
| WOODSBORO | Frederick |
| WOODSTOCK | Howard |
| WOOLFORD | Dorchester |
| WORTON | Kent |
| WYE MILLS | Talbot |
| **MASSACHUSETTS** | |
| ABINGTON | Plymouth |
| ACCORD | Plymouth |
| ACTON | Middlesex |
| ACUSHNET | Bristol |
| ADAMS | Berkshire |
| AGAWAM | Hampden |
| ALLERTON | Plymouth |
| ALISTON | Suffolk |
| AMESBURY | Essex |
| AMHERST | Hampshire |
| ANDOVER | Essex |
| ARLINGTON | Middlesex |
| ARLINGTON HEIGHTS | Middlesex |
| ASHBURNHAM | Worcester |
| ASHBY | Middlesex |
| ASHFIELD | Franklin |
| ASHLAND | Middlesex |
| ASHLEY FALLS | Berkshire |
| ASSONET | Bristol |
| ASTOR | Suffolk |
| ATHOL | Worcester |
| ATTLEBORO | Bristol |
| ATTLEBORO FALLS | Bristol |
| AUBURN | Worcester |
| AUBURNDALE | Middlesex |
| AVON | Norfolk |
| AYER | Middlesex |
| BABSON PARK | Norfolk |
| BALDWINVILLE | Worcester |
| BALLARDVILLE | Essex |
| BARNSTABLE | Barnstable |
| BARRE | Worcester |
| BEACH | Suffolk |
| BECKET | Berkshire |
| BEDFORD | Middlesex |
| BELCHERTOWN | Hampshire |
| BELLINGHAM | Norfolk |
| BELMONT | Middlesex |
| BERKELEY | Bristol |
| BERKSHIRE | Berkshire |
| BERLIN | Worcester |
| BERNARDSTON | Franklin |
| BEVERLY | Essex |
| BEVERLY FARMS | Essex |
| BILLERICA | Middlesex |
| BLACKSTONE | Worcester |

| | |
|---|---|
| BLANDFORD | Hampden |
| BOLTON | Worcester |
| BONDSVILLE | Hampden |
| BOSTON | Suffolk |
| BOSTON COLLEGE | Middlesex |
| BOSTON UNIV | Suffolk |
| BOURNE | Barnstable |
| BOXBORO | Middlesex |
| BOXFORD | Essex |
| BOYLSTON | Worchester |
| BRADFORD | Essex |
| BRAINTREE | Norfolk |
| BRIGHTON | Suffolk |
| BRIGHTWOOD | Hampden |
| BROOKLINE | Norfolk |
| BROOKLINE VILLAGE | Norfolk |
| BRANT ROCK | Plymouth |
| BREWSTER | Barnstable |
| BRIDGEWATER | Plymouth |
| BRIMFIELD | Hampden |
| BROCKTON | Plymouth |
| BROOKFIELD | Worcester |
| BRYANTVILLE | Plymouth |
| BUCKLAND | Franklin |
| BURLINGTON | Middlesex |
| BUZZARDS BAY | Barnstable |
| BYFIELD | Essex |
| CAMBRIDGE | Middlesex |
| CANTON | Norfolk |
| CARLISLE | Middlesex |
| CARVER | Plymouth |
| CATAUMET | Barnstable |
| CATHEDRAL | Suffolk |
| CENTER STATION | Plymouth |
| CENTERVILLE | Barnstable |
| CHARLEMONT | Franklin |
| CHARLESTON | Suffolk |
| CHARLTON | Worcester |
| CHARLTON CITY | Worcester |
| CHARLTON DEPOT | Worcester |
| CHARTLEY | Bristol |
| CHATHAM | Barnstable |
| CHELMSFORD | Middlesex |
| CHELSEA | Suffolk |
| CHERRY VALLEY | Worcester |
| CHESHIRE | Berkshire |
| CHESTER | Hampden |
| CHESTERFIELD | Hampshire |
| CHESTNUT HILL | Middlesex |
| CHICOPEE | Hampden |
| CHICOPEE CENTER | Hampden |
| CHILMARK | Dukes |
| CLARKSBURG | Berkshire |

| | | | |
|---|---|---|---|
| CLINTON | Worcester | EAST WEYMOUTH | Norfolk |
| COCHITUATE | Middlesex | EDGARTOWN | Dukes |
| COHASSET | Norfolk | ELMWOOD | Plymouth |
| COLRAIN | Franklin | ERVING | Franklin |
| CONCORD | Middlesex | ESSEX | Essex |
| CONWAY | Franklin | EVERETT | Middlesex |
| COTUIT | Barnstable | FAIRHAVEN | Bristol |
| CRAIGVILLE | Barnstable | FALL RIVER | Bristol |
| CUMMAQUID | Barnstable | FALMOUTH | Barnstable |
| CUMMINGTON | Hampshire | FAYVILLE | Worcester |
| CUSHMAN | Hampshire | FEEDING HILLS | Hampden |
| CUTTYHUNK | Dukes | FISKDALE | Worcester |
| DALTON | Berkshire | FITCHBURG | Worcester |
| DANVERS | Essex | FLINT | Bristol |
| DARTMOUTH | Bristol | FLORENCE | Hampshire |
| DEDHAM | Norfolk | FLORIDA | Berkshire |
| DEERFIELD | Franklin | FORESTDALE | Barnstable |
| DENNIS | Barnstable | FOREST PARK | Hampden |
| DENNIS PORT | Barnstable | FORGE VILLAGE | Middlesex |
| DIGHTON | Bristol | FORT DEVENS | Middlesex |
| DORCHESTER | Suffolk | FOXBORO | Norfolk |
| DOVER | Norfolk | FRAMINGHAM | Middlesex |
| DRACUT | Middlesex | FRANKLIN | Norfolk |
| DRURY | Berkshire | GARDNER | Worcester |
| DUDLEY | Worcester | GEORGETOWN | Essex |
| DUDLEY HILL | Worcester | GILBERTVILLE | Worcester |
| DUNSTABLE | Middlesex | GLENDALE | Berkshire |
| DUXBURY | Plymouth | GLOUCESTER | Essex |
| EAST ARLINGTON | Middlesex | GOSHEN | Hampshire |
| EAST BOSTON | Suffolk | GRAFTON | Worcester |
| EAST BRIDGEWATER | Plymouth | GRANBY | Hampshire |
| EAST BROOKFIELD | Worcester | GRANVILLE | Hampden |
| EAST CAMBRIDGE | Middlesex | GREAT BARRINGTON | Berkshire |
| EAST DEDHAM | Norfolk | GREENBUSH | Plymouth |
| EAST DENNIS | Barnstable | GREENDALE | Worcester |
| EAST DOUGLAS | Worcester | GREENFIELD | Franklin |
| EAST FALMOUTH | Barnstable | GREEN HARBOR | Plymouth |
| EAST FREETOWN | Bristol | GROTON | Middlesex |
| EASTHAM | Barnstable | GROVE HALL | Suffolk |
| EASTHAMPTON | Hampshire | GROVELAND | Essex |
| EAST LONGMEADOW | Hampden | HADLEY | Hampshire |
| EAST LYNN | Essex | HALIFAX | Plymouth |
| EAST MANSFIELD | Bristol | HAMILTON | Essex |
| EASTON | Bristol | HAMPDEN | Hampden |
| EAST ORLEANS | Barnstable | HANCOCK | Berkshire |
| EAST OTIS | Berkshire | HANOVER | Plymouth |
| EAST PRINCETON | Worcester | HANSCOM AFB | Middlesex |
| EAST SANDWICH | Barnstable | HANSON | Plymouth |
| EAST TAUNTON | Bristol | HARDWICK | Worcester |
| EAST TEMPLETON | Worcester | HARVARD | Worcester |
| EAST WALPOLE | Norfolk | HARVARD SQUARE | Middlesex |
| EAST WAREHAM | Plymouth | HARWICH | Barnstable |
| EAST WATERTOWN | Middlesex | HARWICH PORT | Barnstable |

*Appendix*

| | | | |
|---|---|---|---|
| HARWOOD | Middlesex | LONGMEADOW | Hampden |
| HATFIELD | Hampshire | LOWELL | Middlesex |
| HATHORNE | Essex | LUDLOW | Hampden |
| HAVERHILL | Essex | LUNDS CORNER | Bristol |
| HAWLEY | Franklm | LUNENBURG | Worcester |
| HAYDENVILLE | Hampshire | LYNN | Essex |
| HEATH | Franklin | LYNNFIELD | Essex |
| HIGHLAND | Hampden | MAGNOLIA | Essex |
| HINGHAM | Plymouth | MALDEN | Middlesex |
| HINSDALE | Berkshire | MANCHAUG | Worcester |
| HOLBROOK | Norfolk | MANCHESTER | Essex |
| HOLDEN | Worcester | MANOMET | Plymouth |
| HOLLAND | Hampden | MANSFIELD | Bristol |
| HOLLISTON | Middlesex | MARBLEHEAD | Essex |
| HOLYOKE | Hampden | MARION | Plymouth |
| HOPEDALE | Worcester | MARLBOROUGH | Middlesex |
| HOPKINTON | Middlesex | MARSHFIELD | Plymouth |
| HOUSATONIC | Berkshire | MARSHFIELD HILLS | Plymouth |
| HUBBARDSTON | Worcester | MARSTONS MILLS | Barnstable |
| HUDSON | Middlesex | MASHPEE | Barnstable |
| HULL | Plymouth | MATTAPAN | Suffolk |
| HUMAROCK | Plymouth | MATTAPOISETT | Plymouth |
| HUNTINGTON | Hampshire | MAYNARD | Middlesex |
| HYANNIS | Barnstable | MEDFIELD | Norfolk |
| HYANNIS PORT | Barnstable | MEDFORD | Middlesex |
| HYDE PARK | Suffolk | MEDWAY | Norfolk |
| INDIAN ORCHARD | Hampden | MELROSE | Middlesex |
| INMAN SQUARE | Middlesex | MENDON | Worcester |
| IPSWICH | Essex | MENEMSHA | Dukes |
| ISLINGTON | Norfolk | MERRIMAC | Essex |
| JAMAICA PLAIN | Suffolk | METHUEN | Essex |
| JEFFERSON | Worcester | MIDDLEBORO | Plymouth |
| KEARNEY SQUARE | Middlesex | MIDDLEFIELD | Hampshire |
| KENDALL SQUARE | Middlesex | MIDDLETON | Essex |
| KENMORE | Suffolk | MILFORD | Worcester |
| KINGSTON | Plymouth | MILLBURY | Worcester |
| LAKE PLEASANT | Franklin | MILLERS FALLS | Franklin |
| LAKEVILLE | Plymouth | MILLIS | Norfolk |
| LANCASTER | Worcester | MILL RIVER | Berkshire |
| LANESBORO | Berkshire | MILLVILLE | Worcester |
| LAWRENCE | Essex | MILTON | Norfolk |
| LEE | Berkshire | MILTON VILLAGE | Norfolk |
| LEEDS | Hampshire | MINOT | Plymouth |
| LEICESTER | Worcester | M I T | Middlesex |
| LENOX | Berkshire | MONPONSETT | Plymouth |
| LENOX DALE | Berkshire | MONROE BRIDGE | Franklin |
| LEOMINSTER | Worcester | MONSON | Hampden |
| LEVERETT | Franklin | MONTAQUE | Franklin |
| LEXINGTON | Middlesex | MONTEREY | Berkshire |
| LEYDEN | Franklin | MONTGOMERY | Hampden |
| LINCOLN | Middlesex | MONUMENT BEACH | Barnstable |
| LINWOOD | Worcester | MOUNT HERMON | Franklin |
| LTTLETON | Middlesex | MOUNT TOM | Hampshire |

| | | | |
|---|---|---|---|
| NABNASSET | Middlesex | OSTERVILLE | Barnstable |
| NAHANT | Essex | OTIS | Berkshire |
| NANTUCKET | Nantucket | OTIS AFB | Barnstable |
| NATICK | Middlesex | OXFORD | Worcester |
| NEEDHAM | Norfolk | PALMER | Hampden |
| NEEDHAM HEIGHTS | Norfolk | PAXTON | Worcester |
| NEW ASHFORD | Berkshire | PEABODY | Essex |
| NEW BEDFORD | Bristol | PELHAM | Hampshire |
| NEW BRAINTREE | Worcester | PEMBROKE | Plymouth |
| NEWEBURYPORT | Essex | PEPPERELL | Middlesex |
| NEW SALEM | Franklin | PERU | Berkshire |
| NEW SEABURY | Barnstable | PETERSHAM | Worcester |
| NEWTON | Middlesex | PHILLIPSTON | Worcester |
| NORFOLK | Norfolk | PIGEON COVE | Essex |
| NORTH ABINGTON | Plymouth | PINEHURST | Middlesex |
| NORTH ADAMS | Berkshire | PITTSFIELD | Berkshire |
| NORTHAMPTON | Hampshire | PLAINFIELD | Hampshire |
| NORTH ATTLEBORO | Bristol | PLAINVILLE | Bristol |
| NORTH BILLERICA | Middlesex | PLYMOUTH | Plymouth |
| NORTHBOROUGH | Worcester | PLYMPTON | Plymouth |
| NORTHBRIDGE | Worcester | POCASSET | Barnstable |
| NORTH BROOKFIELD | Worcester | PRIDES CROSSING | Essex |
| NORTH CARVER | Plymouth | PRINCETON | Worcester |
| NORTH CHATHAM | Barnstable | PROVINCETOWN | Barnstable |
| NORTH CHELMSFORD | Middlesex | QUINCY | Norfolk |
| NORTH DARTMOUTH | Bristol | PORTER SQUARE | Middlesex |
| NORTH DIGHTON | Bristol | RANDOLPH | Norfolk |
| NORTH EASTHAM | Barnstable | RAYNHAM | Bristol |
| NORTH EASTON | Bristol | RAYNHAM CENTER | Bristol |
| NORTH FALMOUTH | Barnstable | READING | Middlesex |
| NORTHFIELD | Franklin | READVILLE | Suffolk |
| NORTH GRAFTON | Worcester | REHOBOTH | Bristol |
| NORTH HATFIELD | Hampshire | REVERE | Suffolk |
| NORTH MARSHFIELD | Plymouth | RICHMOND | Berkshire |
| NORTH OXFORD | Worcester | RIVERDALE | Essex |
| NORTH PEMBROOK | Plymouth | ROCHDALE | Worcester |
| NORTH QUINCY | Norfolk | ROCHESTER | Plymouth |
| NORTH READING | Middlesex | ROCKLAND | Plymouth |
| NORTH TRURO | Barnstable | ROCKPORT | Essex |
| NORTH UXBRIDGE | Worcester | ROSLINDALE | Suffolk |
| NORTH WALTHAM | Middlesex | ROWE | Franklin |
| NORTH WEYMOUTH | Norfolk | ROWLEY | Essex |
| NORTON | Bristol | ROXBURY | Suffolk |
| NORWELL | Plymouth | ROYALSTON | Worcester |
| NORWOOD | Norfolk | RUSSELL | Hampden |
| NUTTING LAKE | Middlesex | RUTLAND | Worcester |
| OAK BLUFFS | Dukes | SAGAMORE | Barnstable |
| OAKDALE | Worcester | SAGAMORE BEACH | Barnstable |
| OAKHAM | Worcester | SALEM | Essex |
| OCEAN BLUFF | Plymouth | SALISBURY | Essex |
| ONSET | Plymouth | SALISBURY BEACH | Essex |
| ORANGE | Franklin | SANDISFIELD | Berkshire |
| ORLEANS | Barnstable | SANDWICH | Barnstable |

| | | | |
|---|---|---|---|
| SAUGUS | Essex | SUTTEN | Worcester |
| SAVOY | Berkshire | SWANSEA | Bristol |
| SAXONVILLE | Middlesex | TAUNTON | Bristol |
| SCITUATE | Plymouth | TEMPLETON | Worcester |
| SEEKONK | Bristol | TEWKSBURY | Middlesex |
| SHARON | Norfolk | THORNDIKE | Hampden |
| SHATTUCK | Franklin | THREE RIVERS | Hampden |
| SHEFFIELD | Berkshire | TOLLAND | Hampton |
| SHELBURNE FALLS | Franklin | TOPSFIELD | Essex |
| SHELDONVILLE | Norfolk | TOWNSEND | Middlesex |
| SHERBORN | Middlesex | TRURO | Barnstable |
| SHIRLEY | Middlesex | TUFTS UNIV | Middlesex |
| SHIRLEY CENTER | Middlesex | TURNERS FALLS | Franklin |
| SHREWSBURY | Worcester | TYNGSBORO | Middlesex |
| SHUTESBURY | Franklin | UXBRIDGE | Worcester |
| SILVER BEACH | Barnstable | VINEYARD HAVEN | Dukes |
| SOMERSET | Bristol | WABAN | Middlesex |
| SOMERVILLE | Middlesex | WAKEFIELD | Middlesex |
| SOUTHHAMPTON | Hampshire | WALES | Hampden |
| SOUTH BARRE | Worcester | WALPOLE | Norfolk |
| SOUTH BERLIN | Worcester | WALTHAM | Middlesex |
| SOUTHBOROUGH | Worcester | WARD HILL | Essex |
| SOUTHBRIDGE | Worcester | WARE | Hampshire |
| SOUTH CARVER | Plymouth | WAREHAM | Plymouth |
| SOUTH CHATHAM | Barnstable | WARREN | Worcester |
| SOUTH DEERFIELD | Franklin | WARWICK | Franklin |
| SOUTH DENNIS | Barnstable | WATERTOWN | Middlesex |
| SOUTH EASTON | Bristol | WAYLAND | Middlesex |
| SOUTH EGREMONT | Berkshire | WEBSTER | Worcester |
| SOUTHFIELD | Berkshire | WELLESLEY | Norfolk |
| SOUTH GRAFTON | Worcester | WELLFLEET | Barnstable |
| SOUTH HADLEY | Hampshire | WENDELL | Franklin |
| SOUTH HAMILTON | Essex | WENDELL DEPOT | Franklin |
| SOUTH HARWICH | Barnstable | WENHAM | Essex |
| SOUTH LANCASTER | Worcester | WEST BARNSTABLE | Barnstable |
| SOUTH LEE | Berkshire | WESTBOROUGH | Worcester |
| SOUTH ORLEANS | Barnstable | WEST BOXFORD | Essex |
| SOUTH WALPOLE | Norfolk | WEST BOYLSTON | Worcester |
| SOUTH WELPLEET | Barnstable | WEST BRIDGEWATER | Plymouth |
| SOUTH WEYMOUTH | Norfolk | WEST BROOKFIELD | Worcester |
| SOUTHWICK | Hampden | WEST CHATHAM | Barnstable |
| SOUTH YARMOUTH | Barnstable | WEST CHESTERFIELD | Hampshire |
| SPENCER | Worcester | WEST CONCORD | Middlesex |
| SPRINGFIELD | Hampden | WEST DENNIS | Barnstable |
| STERLING | Worcester | WEST FALMOUTH | Barnstable |
| STILL RIVER | Worcester | WESTFIELD | Hampden |
| STOCKBRIDGE | Berkshire | WESTFORD | Middlesex |
| STONEHAM | Middlesex | WEST GROTON | Middlesex |
| STOUGHTON | Norfolk | WEST HANOVER | Plymouth |
| STOW | Middlesex | WEST HARWICH | Barnstable |
| STURBRIDGE | Worcester | WEST HATFIELD | Hampshire |
| SUDBURY | Middlesex | WEST HYANNISPORT | Barnstable |
| SUNDERLAND | Franklin | WEST NEWTON | Middlesex |

| WESTON | Middlesex | ALLEN PARK | Wayne |
|---|---|---|---|
| WESTMINSTER | Worcester | ALLENTOWN | St Clair |
| WEST NEWBURY | Essex | ALLOUEZ | Keweenaw |
| WESTPORT | Bristol | ALMA | Gratiot |
| WESTPORT POINT | Bristol | ALMONT | Alpena |
| WEST SPRINGFIELD | Hampden | ALPENA | Alpena |
| WEST STOCKBRIDGE | Berkshire | ALPHA | Iron |
| WEST TISBURY | Dukes | ALTO | Kent |
| WEST UPTON | Worcester | AMASA | Iron |
| WEST WAREHAM | Plymouth | ANCHORVILLE | St Clair |
| WEST WARREN | Worcester | ANN ARBOR | Weashtenaw |
| WESTWOOD | Norfolk | APPLEGATE | Sanilac Isle |
| WEYMOUTH | Norfolk | ARCADE | Ann Arbor |
| WHATELY | Franklin | ARCADIA | Manistee |
| WHEELWRIGHT | Worcester | ARGYLE | Sanilac Isle |
| WHITE HORSE BEACH | Plymouth | ARMADA | Macomb |
| WHITINSVILLE | Worcester | ARNOLD | Marquette |
| WHITMAN | Plymouth | ASHLEY | Gratiot |
| WILBRAHAM | Hampden | ATHENS | Calhoun |
| WILKINSONVILLE | Worcester | ATLANTA | Montmorency |
| WILLIAMSBURG | Hampshire | ATLANTIC MINE | Houghton |
| WILLIAMSTOWN | Berkshire | ATLAS | Genesee |
| WILMINGTON | Middlesex | ATTICA | Lapeer |
| WINCHENDON | Worcester | AUBURN | Bay |
| WINCHENDON SPRINGS | Worcester | AUBURN HILLS | Oakland |
| WINCHESTER | Middlesex | AU GRES | Arenac |
| WINDSOR | Berkshire | AUGUSTA | Kalamazoo |
| WINTHROP | Suffolk | AU TRAIN | Alger |
| WOBURN | Middlesex | AVOCA | St Clair |
| WOODVILLE | Middlesex | AZALIA | Monroe |
| WORCESTER | Worcester | BAD AXE | Huron |
| WORONOCO | Hampden | BAILEY | Muskegon |
| WORTHINGTON | Hampshire | BALDWIN | Lake |
| WRENTHAM | Norfolk | BANCROFT | Shiawassee |
| YARMOUTH PORT | Barnstable | BANGOR | Van Buren |
| **MICHIGAN** | | BANNISTER | Gratiot |
| ACME | Grand Traverse | BARAGA | Baraga |
| ADA | Kent | BARBEAU | Chippewa |
| ADDISON | Lenawee | BARK RIVER | Delta |
| ADDISON TOWNSHIP | Oakland | BARODA | Berrien |
| ADRIAN | Lenawee | BARRYTON | Mecosta |
| AFTON | Cheboygan | BARTON CITY | Alcona |
| AHMEEK | Keweenaw | BATH | Clinton |
| AKRON | Tuscola | BATTLE CREEK | Calhoun |
| ALANSON | Emmet | BAY CITY | Bay |
| ALBA | Antrim | BAY PORT | Huron |
| ALBION | Calhoun | BAYSHORE | Charlevoix |
| ALDEN | Antrim | BAY VIEW | Emmet |
| ALGER | Arenac | BEAR LAKE | Manistee |
| ALGONAC | St Clair | BEAVERTON | Gladwin |
| ALLEGAN | Allegan | BEDFORD | Calhoun |
| ALLEN | Hillsdale | BEECHWOOD | Iron |
| ALLENDALE | Ottawa | BELDING | Ionia |

| | | | |
|---|---|---|---|
| BELLAIRE | Antrim | BRUNSWICK | Newaygo |
| BELLVILLE | Wayne | BRUTUS | Emmet |
| BELLEVUE | Eaton | BUCHANAN | Berrien |
| BELMONT | Kent | BUCKLEY | Wexford |
| BENTLEY | Gladwin | BURLINGTON | Calhoun |
| BENTON HARBOR | Berrien | BURNIPS | Allegan |
| BENZONIA | Benzie | BURR OAK | St Joseph |
| BERGLAND | Ontonagon | BURT | Saginaw |
| BERKLEY | Oakland | BURT LAKE | Cheboygan |
| BERRIEN CENTER | Berrien | BURTON | Genesee |
| BERRIEN SPRINGS | Berrien | BYRON | Shiawassee |
| BERVILLE | St. Clair | BYRON CENTER | Kent |
| BESSEMER | Gogebic | CADILLAC | Wexford |
| BEULAH | Benzie | CADMUS | Lenawee |
| BEVERLY HILLS | Oakland | CALEDONIA | Kent |
| BIG BAY | Marquette | CALUMET | Houghton |
| BIG RAPIDS | Mecosta | CAMDEN | Hillsdale |
| BINGHAM FARMS | Oakland | CANNONSBURG | Kent |
| BIRCH RUN | Saginaw | CONTON | Wayne |
| BIRMINGHAM | Oakland | CAPAC | St Clair |
| BITELY | Newaygo | CARLAND | Shiawassee |
| BLACK RIVER | Alcona | CARLETON | Monroe |
| BLANCHARD | Isabella | CARNEY | Menominee |
| BLISSFIELD | Lenawee | CARO | Tuscola |
| BLOOMFIELD | Oakland | CARP LAKE | Emmet |
| BLOOMFIELD HILLS | Oakland | CARROLTON | Saginaw |
| BLOOMFIELD TOWNSHIP | Oakland | CARSON CITY | Montcalm |
| BLOOMFIELD VILLAGE | Oakland | CARSONVILLE | Sanilac Isle |
| BLOOMINGDALE | Van Buren | CASEVILLE | Huron |
| BOON | Wexford | CASNOVIA | Muskegon |
| BOYNE CITY | Charlevoix | CASPIAN | Iron |
| BOYNE FALLS | Charlevoix | CASS CITY | Tuscola |
| BRADLEY | Allegan | CASSOPOLIS | Cass |
| BRAMPTON | Gladstone | CEDAR | Leelanau |
| BRANCH | Lake | CEDAR LAKE | Montcalm |
| BRANT | Saginaw | CEDAR RIVER | Menominee |
| BRECKENRIDGE | Gratiot | CEDAR SPRINGS | Kent |
| BREEDSVILLE | Van Buren | CEDARVILLE | Mackinac |
| BRETHREN | Manistee | CEMENT CITY | Hillsdale |
| BRIDGEPORT | Saginaw | CENTER LINE | Macomb |
| BRIDGEWATER | Washtenaw | CENTRAL LAKE | Antrim |
| BRIDGMAN | Berrien | CENTRAL MI UNIV. | Isabella |
| BRIGHTMOOR | Wayne | CENTREVILLE | St Joseph |
| BRIGHTON | Livingston | CERESCO | Calhoun |
| BRIMLEY | Chippewa | CHAMPION | Marquette |
| BRITTON | Lenawee | CHANNING | Dickinson |
| BROCKWAY | St. Clair | CHARLEVOIX | Charlevoix |
| BROHMAN | Newaygo | CHARLOTTE | Eaton |
| BRONSON | Branch | CHASE | Lake |
| BROOKLYN | Jackson | CHASSELL | Houghton |
| BROWN CITY | Sanilac Isle | CHATHAM | Alger |
| BRUCE CROSSING | Ontonagon | CHEBOYGAN | Cheboygan |
| BRUCE TOWNSHIP | Macomb | CHELSEA | Washtenaw |

| City | County | City | County |
|---|---|---|---|
| CHESANING | Saginaw | DALTON | Muskegon |
| CHIPPEWA LAKE | Mecosta | DANSVILLE | Ingham |
| CHRISTMAS | Alger | DAVISBURG | Oakland |
| CLARE | Clare | DAVISON | Genesee |
| CLARKLAKE | Jackson | DEARBORN | Wayne |
| CLARKSTON | Oakland | DEARBORN HEIGHTS | Wayne |
| CLARKSVILLE | Ionia | DECATUR | Van Buren |
| CLAWSON | Oakland | DECKER | Sanilac Isle |
| CLAYTON | Unawee | DECKERVILLE | Sanilac Isle |
| CLAY TOWNSHIP | Algonac | DEERFIELD | Lenawee |
| CLIFFORD | Lapeer | DEERTON | Alger |
| CLIMAX | Kalamazoo | DEFORD | Tuscola |
| CLINTON | Lenawee | DELTA BRANCH | Lansing |
| CLIO | Genesee | DELTON | Barry |
| CLOVERDALE | Barry | DE TOUR VILLAGE | Chippewa |
| CODY | Genessee | DETROIT | Wayne |
| COHOCTAH | Livingston | DEWITT | Clinton |
| COLDWATER | Branch | DEXTER | Washtenaw |
| COLEMAN | Midland | DIMONDALE | Eaton |
| COLLEGE PARK | Wayne | DODGEVILLE | Houghton |
| COLLEGE PARK | Oakland | DOLLAR BAY | Houghton |
| COLOMA | Berrien | DORR | Allegan |
| COLON | St Joseph | DOUGLAS | Allegan |
| COLUMBIAVILLE | Lapeer | DOWAGIAC | Cass |
| COMINS | Oscoda | DOWLING | Barry |
| COMMERCE TOWNSHIP | Oakland | DRAYTON PLAINS | Oakland |
| COMMERCE TOWNSHIP | Lake | DRUMMOND ISLAND | Chippewa |
| COMSTOCK | Kalamazoo | DRYDEN | Lapeer |
| COMSTOCK PARK | Kent | DUNDEE | Monroe |
| CONCORD | Jackson | DURAND | Shiawassee |
| CONKLIN | Ottawa | DUTTON | Kent |
| CONSTANTINE | St Joseph | EAGLE | Clinton |
| CONWAY | Emmet | EAGLE HARBOR | Keweenaw |
| COOKS | Schoolcraft | EAGLE RIVER | Keweenaw |
| COOPERSVILLE | Ottawa | EAST DETROIT | Macomb |
| COPEMISH | Manistee | EAST JORDAN | Charlevoix |
| COPPER CITY | Houghton | EASTLAKE | Manistee |
| COPPER HARBOR | Keweenaw | EAST LANSING | Ingham |
| CORAL | Montcalm | EAST LEROY | Calhoun |
| CORNELL | Delta | EASTPORT | Antrim |
| CORUNNA | Shiawassee | EASTSIDE CARRIER | Saginaw |
| COURT | Kalamazoo | EAST TAWAS | Iosco |
| COVERT | Van Buren | EATON RAPIDS | Eaton |
| COVINGTON | Baraga | EAU CLAIR | Berrien |
| CROSS VILLAGE | Emmet | EBEN JUNCTION | Alger |
| CROSWELL | Sanilac Isle | ECKERMAN | Chippewa |
| CRYSTAL | Montcalm | ECORSE | Wayne |
| CRYSTAL FALLS | Iron | EDENVILLE | Midland |
| CURRAN | Alcona | EDMORE | Montcalm |
| CURTIS | Mackinac | EDWARDSBURG | Cass |
| CUSTER | Mason | ELBERTA | Benzie |
| DAFTER | Chippewa | ELK RAPIDS | Antrim |
| DAGGETT | Menominee | ELKTON | Huron |

| | | | |
|---|---|---|---|
| ELLSWORTH | Antrim | FREEMONT | Newaygo |
| ELM HALL | Gratiot | FRONTIER | Hillsdale |
| ELMIRA | Otsego | FRUITPORT | Muskegon |
| ELOISE | Wayne | FULTON | Kalamazoo |
| ELSIE | Clinton | GAASTRA | Iron |
| ELWELL | Gratiot | GAGETOWN | Tuscola |
| EMMETT | St Clair | GAINES | Genesee |
| EMPIRE | Leelanau | GALESBURG | Kalamazoo |
| ENGADINE | Mackinac | GALIEN | Berrien |
| ERIE | Monroe | GARDEN | Delta |
| ESCANABA | Delta | GARDEN CITY | Wayne |
| ESSEXVILLE | Bay | GAY | Houghton |
| EUREKA | Clinton | GAYLORD | Otsego |
| EVART | Osceola | GENESEE | Genesee |
| EWEN | Ontonagon | GERMFASK | Schoolcraft |
| FAIRGROVE | Tuscola | GIBRALTAR | Wayne |
| FAIR HAVEN | St Clair | GILFORD | Tuscola |
| FAIRVIEW | Oscoda | GLADSTONE | Delta |
| FALMOUTH | Missaukee | GLADWIN | Gladwin |
| FARMINGTON | Oakland | GLEN ARBOR | Leelanau |
| FARMINGTON HILLS | Farmington | GLENN | Allegan |
| FARWELL | Clare | GLENNIE | Alcona |
| FELCH | Dickinson | GOBLES | Van Buren |
| FENKELL | Wayne | GOETZVILLE | Chippewa |
| FENNVILLE | Allegan | GOODELLS | St Clair |
| FENTON | Genesee | GOOD HART | Emmet |
| FENWICK | Montcalm | GOODRICH | Genesee |
| FERNDALE | Oakland | GOULD CITY | Mackinac |
| FERRYSBURG | Ottawa | GOWEN | Montcalm |
| FIBRE | Chippewa | GRAND BLANC | Genesee |
| FIFE LAKE | Grand Traverse | GRAND HAVEN | Ottawa |
| FILER CITY | Manistee | GRAND JUNCTION | Van Buren |
| FILION | Huron | GRAND LEDGE | Eaton |
| FLAT ROCK | Wayne | GRAND MARAIS | Alger |
| FLINT | Genesee | GRAND RAPIDS | Kent |
| FLUSHING | Genesee | GRAND RIVER | Wayne |
| FORESTVILLE | Sanilac Isle | GRANDVILLE | Kent |
| FORT DEARBORN | Dearborn | GRANT | Newaygo |
| FOSTER CITY | Dickinson | GRASS LAKE | Jackson |
| FOSTORIA | Tuscola | GRATIOT | Wayne |
| FOUNTAIN | Mason | GRAWN | Grand Traverse |
| FOWLER | Clinton | GRAYLING | Crawford |
| FOWLERVILLE | Livingston | GREENBUSH | Alcona |
| FOX CREEK | Wayne | GREENLAND | Ontonagon |
| FRANDOR | Ingham | GREENVILLE | Montcalm |
| FRANKENMUTH | Saginaw | GREGORY | Livingston |
| FRANKFORT | Benzie | GROSSE ILE | Wayne |
| FRANKLIN | Oakland | GROSSE POINTE | Wayne |
| FRASER | Macomb | GROSSE POINT | Harper |
| FREDERIC | Crawford | GULLIVER | Schoolcraft |
| FREELAND | Saginaw | GWINN | Marquette |
| FREEPORT | Barry | HADLEY | Lapee |
| FREE SOIL | Mason | HALE | Iosco |

| | | | |
|---|---|---|---|
| HAMBURG | Livingston | HUBBELL | Houghton |
| HAMILTON | Allegan | HUDSON | Lenawee |
| HAMTRAMCK | Wayne | HUDSONVILLE | Ottawa |
| HANCOCK | Houghton | HULBERT | Chippewa |
| HANOVER | Jackson | HUNTINGTON WOODS | Oakland |
| HARBERT | Berrien | IDA | Monroe |
| HARBOR BEACH | Huron | IDLEWILD | Lake |
| HARBOR POINT | Harbor | IMLAY CITY | Lapeer |
| HARBOR SPRINGS | Emmet | INDEPENDENCE TOWNSHIP | Clarkston |
| HARDWOOD | Delta | INDIAN RIVER | Cheboygan |
| HARPER | Wayne | INGALLS | Menominee |
| HARPER WOODS | Wayne | INKSTER | Wayne |
| HARRIETTA | Wexford | INTERLOCHEN | Grand Traverse |
| HARRIS | Menominee | IONIA | Ionia |
| HARRISON | Clare | IRA | St. Clair |
| HARRISVILLE | Alcona | IRON MOUNTAIN | Dickinson |
| HARSENS ISLAND | St Clair | IRON RIVER | Iron |
| HART | Oceana | IRONS | Lake |
| HARTFORD | Van Buren | IRONWOOD | Gogebic |
| HARTLAND | Oakland | ISHPEMING | Marquette |
| HASLETT | Ingham | ITHACA | Gratiot |
| HASTINGS | Barry | JACKSON | Jackson |
| HAWKS | Presque Isle | JAMESTOWN | Ottawa |
| HAZEL PARK | Oakland | JASPER | Lenawee |
| HEMLOCK | Saginaw | JEDDO | St Clair |
| HENDERSON | Shiawassee | JEFFERSON | Wayne |
| HERMANSVILLE | Menominee | JENISON | Ottawa |
| HERRON | Alpena | JEROME | Hillsdale |
| HERSEY | Osceola | JOHANNESBURG | Otsego |
| HESPERIA | Oceana | JONES | Cass |
| HESSEL | Mackinac | JONESVILLE | Hillsdale |
| HICKORY CORNERS | Barry | JOYFIELD | Wayne |
| HIGGINS LAKE | Roscommon | KALAMAZOO | Kalamazoo |
| HIGHLAND | Oakland | KALEVA | Manistee |
| HIGHLAND PARK | Wayne | KALKASKA | Kalkaska |
| HILLMAN | Montmorency | KARLIN | Grand Traverse |
| HILLSDALE | Hillsdale | KAWKAWLIN | Bay |
| HOLLAND | Ottawa | KEARSARGE | Houghton |
| HOLLY | Oakland | KEEGO HARBOR | Oakland |
| HOLT | Ingham | KENDALL | Van Buren |
| HOLTON | Muskegon | KENSINGTON | Wayne |
| HOMER | Calhoun | KENT CITY | Kent |
| HONOR | Benzie | KENTON | Houghton |
| HOPE | Midland | KENTWOOD | Kent |
| HOPKINS | Allegan | KEWADIN | Antrim |
| HORTON | Jackson | KINDE | Huron |
| HOUGHTON | Houghton | KINGSLEY | Grand Traverse |
| HOUGHTON LAKE | Roscommon | KINGSTON | Tuscola |
| HOUGHTON LAKE HEIGHTS | Roscommon | KINROSS | Chippewa |
| HOWARD CITY | Montcalm | K.I. SAWYER AFT | Marquette |
| HOWELL | Livingston | LACHINE | Alpena |
| HUBBARD LAKE | Alpena | LACOTA | Van Buren |
| HUBBARDSTON | Ionia | LAINGSBURG | Shiawassee |

| | | | |
|---|---|---|---|
| LAKE | Clare | LYONS | Ionia |
| LAKE ANGELUS | Oakland | MACATAWA | Ottawa |
| LAKE ANN | Benzie | MACKINAC ISLAND | Mackinac |
| LAKE CITY | Missaukee | MACKINAW CITY | Cheboygan |
| LAKE GEORGE | Clare | MACOMB TOWNSHIP | Mount Clemens |
| LAKELAND | Livingston | MADISON HEIGHTS | Oakland |
| LAKE LEELANAU | Leelanau | MANCELONA | Antrim |
| LAKE LINDEN | Houghton | MANCHESTER | Washtenaw |
| LAKE ODESSA | Ionia | MANISTEE | Manistee |
| LAKE ORION | Oakland | MANISTIQUE | Schoolcraft |
| LAKESIDE | Berrien | MANITOU BEACH | Lenawee |
| LAKEVIEW | Montcalm | MANTON | Wexford |
| LAKEVILLE | Oakland | MAPLE | Wayne |
| LAMBERTVILLE | Monroe | MAPLE CITY | Leelanau |
| LAMONT | Ottawa | MAPLE RAPIDS | Clinton |
| LANSE | Baraga | MARCELLUS | Cass |
| LANSING | Ingham | MARENISCO | Gogebic |
| LAPEER | Lapeer | MARINE CITY | St Clair |
| LA SALLE | Monroe | MARION | Osceola |
| LAURIUM | Calumet | MARLETTE | Sanilac Isle |
| LAWRENCE | Van Buren | MARNE | Ottawa |
| LAWTON | Van Buren | MARQUETTE | Marquette |
| LEDYARD | Grand Rapids | MARSHALL | Calhoun |
| LELAND | Leelanau | MARTIN | Allegan |
| LENNON | Genesee | MARYSVILLE | St Clair |
| LOENARD | Oakland | MASON | Ingham |
| LEONIDAS | St Joseph | MASS CITY | Ontonagon |
| LE ROY | Osceola | MATTAWAN | Van Buren |
| LESLIE | Ingham | MAYBEE | Monroe |
| LEVERING | Emmet | MAYFIELD | Grand Traverse |
| LEWISTON | Montmorency | MAYVILLE | Tuscola |
| LEXINGTON | Sanilac Isle | McBAIN | Missaukee |
| LIBERTY | Weashtenaw | McBRIDES | Montcalm |
| LIMESTONE | Chatham | McMILLAN | Luce |
| LINCOLN | Alcona | MEARS | Oceana |
| LINCOLN PARK | Wayne | MECOSTA | Mecosta |
| LINDEN | Genesee | MELVIN | Sanilac Isle |
| LINWOOD | Bay | MELVINDALE | Wayne |
| LINWOOD | Wayne | MEMPHIS | Macomb |
| LITCHFIELD | Hillsdale | MENDON | St Joseph |
| LITTLE LAKE | Marquette | MENOMINEE | Menominee |
| LIVERNOIS | Wayne | MERRILL | Saginaw |
| LIVONIA | Wayne | MERRITT | Missaukee |
| LONG LAKE | Iosco | MESICK | Wexford |
| LORETTO | Dickinson | METAMORA | Lapeer |
| LOWELL | Kent | MICHIGAMME | Marquette |
| LUDINGTON | Mason | MICHIGAN CENTER | Jackson |
| LUM | Lapeer | MIDDLEBELT | Romulus |
| LUNA PIER | Monroe | MIDDLETON | Gratiot |
| LUPTON | Ogemaw | MIDDLEVILLE | Barry |
| LUTHER | Lake | MIDLAND | Midland |
| LUZERNE | Osmda | MIKADO | Aloona |
| LYNN | Yale | MILAN | Washtenaw |

| | | | |
|---|---|---|---|
| MILFORD | Oakland | NILES | Berrien |
| MILLBROOK | Mecosta | NISULA | Houghton |
| MILLERSBURG | Presque Isle | NORTH ADAMS | Hillsdale |
| MILLINGTON | Tuscola | NORTH BRANCH | Lapeer |
| MINDEN CITY | Sanilac Isle | NORTHLAND | Marquette |
| MIO | Oscoda | NORTHPORT | Leelanau |
| MOHAWK | Keweenaw | NORTH STAR | Gratiot |
| MOLINE | Allegan | NORTH STREET | St Clair |
| MONROE | Monroe | NORTHVILLE | Wayne |
| MONTAGUE | Muskegon | NORVELL | Jackson |
| MONTGOMERY | Branch | NORWAY | Dickinson |
| MONTROSE | Genesee | NOTTAWA | St Joseph |
| MOORESTOWN | Lake City | NOVI | Oakland |
| MORAN | Mackinac | NUNICA | Ottawa |
| MORENCI | Lenawee | OAK GROVE | Livingston |
| MORLEY | Mecosta | OAKLEY | Saginaw |
| MORRICE | Shiawassee | ODEN | Emmet |
| MOSCOW | Hillsdale | OKEMOS | Ingham |
| MOSHERVILLE | Hillsdale | OLD MISSION | Grand Traverse |
| MOTT PARK | Genessee | OLIVET | Eaton |
| MOUNT CLEMENS | Macomb | OMENA | Leelanau |
| MOUNT ELLIOTT | Wayne | OMER | Arenac |
| MOUNT MORRIS | Genesee | ONAWAY | Presque Isle |
| MOUNT PLEASANT | Isabella | ONEKAMA | Manistee |
| MUIR | Ionia | ONONDAGA | Ingham |
| MULLETT LAKE | Cheboygan | ONSTED | Lenawee |
| MULLIKEN | Eaton | ONTONAGON | Ontonagon |
| MUNGER | Bay | ORCHARD LAKE | Oakland |
| MUNISING | Alger | ORLEANS | Ionia |
| MUNITH | Jackson | ORTONVILLE | Oakland |
| MUSKEGON | Muskegon | OSCODA | Iosco |
| MUSKEGON HEIGHTS | Muskegon | OSHTEMO | Kalamazoo |
| MUSSEY | St. Clair | OSSEO | Hillsdale |
| NADEAU | Menominee | OSSINEKE | Alpena |
| NARMA | Delta | OTISVILLE | Genesee |
| NAPOLEON | Jackson | OTSEGO | Allegan |
| NASHVILLE | Barry | OTTAWA LAKE | Monroe |
| NATIONAL CITY | Iosco | OTTER LAKE | Lapeer |
| NAUBINWAY | Mackinac | OVID | Clinton |
| NAZARETH | Kalamazoo | OWENDALE | Huron |
| NEGAUNEE | Marquette | OWOSSO | Shiawassee |
| NEWAYGO | Newaygo | OXFORD | Oakland |
| NEW BALTIMORE | Macomb | PAINESDALE | Houghton |
| NEWBERRY | Luce | PALMER | Marquette |
| NEW BOSTON | Wayne | PALMS | Sanilac Isle |
| NEW BUFFALO | Berrien | PALMYRA | Lenawee |
| NEW ERA | Oceana | PALO | Ionia |
| NEW HAVEN | Macomb | PARADISE | Chippewa |
| NEW HUDSON | Oakland | PARIS | Mecosta |
| NEW LOTHROP | Shiawassee | PARMA | Jackson |
| NEW RICHMOND | Allegan | PAW PAW | Van Buren |
| NEW TROY | Berrien | PEARL BEACH | St Clair |
| NEWPORT | Monroe | PECK | Sanilac Isle |

| | | | |
|---|---|---|---|
| PELKIE | Baraga | RICHVILLE | Tuscola |
| PELLSTON | Emmet | RIDGEWAY | Lenawee |
| PENTWATER | Oceana | RIGA | Lenawee |
| PERKINS | Delta | RIVERDALE | Gratiot |
| PERRINTON | Gratiot | RIVERSIDE | Berrien |
| PERRONVILLE | Menominee | RIVES JUNCTION | Jackson |
| PERRY | Shiawassee | ROCHESTER | Oakland |
| PETERSBURG | Monroe | ROCK | Delta |
| PETOSKEY | Emmet | ROCKFORD | Kent |
| PEWAMO | Ionia | ROCKLAND | Ontonagon |
| PICKFORD | Chippewa | ROCKWOOD | Wayne |
| PIERSON | Montcalm | RODNEY | Mecosta |
| PIGEON | Huron | ROGERS CITY | Presque Isle |
| PINCKNEY | Livingston | ROLLIN | Lenawee |
| PINCONNING | Bay | ROMEO | Macomb |
| PITTSFORD | Hillsdale | ROMULUS | Wayne |
| PLAINWELL | Allegan | ROSCOMMON | Roscommon |
| PLEASANT LAKE | Jackson | ROSEBUSH | Isabella |
| PLYMOUTH | Wayne | ROSE CITY | Ogemaw |
| POINTE AUX PINS | Mackinac | ROSEVILLE | Macomb |
| POMPEII | Gratiot | ROTHBURY | Oceana |
| PONTIAC | Oakland | ROYAL OAK | Oakland |
| PORTAGE | Kalamozoo | RUDYARD | Chippewa |
| PORT AUSTIN | Huron | RUTH | Huron |
| PORT HOPE | Huron | SAGINAW | Saginaw |
| PORT HURON | St Clair | SAGOLA | Dickinson |
| PORTLAND | Ionia | SAINT CHARLES | Saginaw |
| PORT SANILAC | Sanilac Isle | SAINT HELEN | Roscommon |
| POSEN | Preque Isle | SAINT IGNACE | Mackinac |
| POTTERVILLE | Eaton | SAINT JAMES | Charlevoix |
| POWERS | Menominee | SAINT JOHNS | Clinton |
| PRATTVILLE | Hillsdale | SAINT JOSEPH | Berrien |
| PRESCOTT | Ogemaw | SAINT LOUIS | Gratiot |
| PRESQUE ISLE | Presque Isle | SALINE | Washtenaw |
| PRINCETON | Marquette | SAMARIA | Monroe |
| PRUDENVILLE | Roscommon | SAND CREEK | Lenawee |
| PULLMAN | Allegan | SAND LAKE | Kent |
| QUINCY | Branch | SANDUSKY | Sanilac Isle |
| QUINNESEC | Dickinson | SANFORD | Midland |
| RACO | Chippewa | SARANAC | Ionia |
| RALPH | Dickinson | SAUGATUCK | Allegan |
| RAMSAY | Gogebic | SAULT SAINTE MARIE | Chippewa |
| RAPID CITY | Kalkaska | SAWYER | Berrien |
| RAPID RIVER | Delta | SCHOOLCRAFT | Kalamazoo |
| RAVENNA | Muskegon | SCOTTS | Kalamazoo |
| READING | Hillsdale | SCOTTVILLE | Mason |
| REED CITY | Osceola | SEARS | Osceola |
| REESE | Tuscola | SEBEWAING | Huron |
| REMUS | Mecosta | SENECA | Lenawee |
| REPUBLIC | Marquette | SENEY | Schoolcraft |
| RHODES | Gladwin | SHAFTSBURG | Shiawassee |
| RICHLAND | Kalamazoo | SHELBY | Oceana |
| RICHMOND | Macomb | SHELBYVILLE | Allegan |

| | | | |
|---|---|---|---|
| SHEPHERD | Isabella | TEMPERANCE | Monroe |
| SHERIDAN | Montcalm | THOMPSONVILLE | Benzie |
| SHERWOOD | Branch | THREE OAKS | Berrien |
| SHINGLETON | Alger | THREE RIVERS | St Joseph |
| SIDNAW | Houghton | TIPTON | Lenawee |
| SIDNEY | Montcalm | TIOVOLA | Houghton |
| SILVERWOOD | Tuscola | TOPINABEE | Cheboygan |
| SIX LAKES | Montcalm | TOWER | Cheboygan |
| SKANDIA | Marquette | TRAUNIK | Alger |
| SKANEE | Baraga | TRAVERSE CITY | Grand Traverse |
| SMITHS CREEK | St Clair | TRENARY | Alger |
| SMYRNA | Ionia | TRENTON | Wayne |
| SNOVER | Sanilac Isle | TROUT CREEK | Ontonagon |
| SODUS | Berrien | TROUT LAKE | Chippewa |
| SOMERSET | Hillsdale | TROY | Oakland |
| SOMERSET CENTER | Hillsdale | TRUFANT | Montcalm |
| SOUTH BOARDMAN | Kalkaska | TURNER | Arenac |
| SOUTH BRANCH | Ogemaw | TUSTIN | Osceola |
| SOUTH CLEMENS | Macomb | TWINING | Arenac |
| SOUTHFIELD | Oakland | TWIN LAKE | Muskegon |
| SOUTH HAVEN | Van Buren | UBLY | Huron |
| SOUTH LYON | Oakland | UNION CITY | Branch |
| SOUTH MORRIS | Genesee | UNION LAKE | Oakland |
| SOUTH PLEASANT | Isabella | UNION PIER | Berrien |
| SOUTH RANGE | Houghton | UNIONVILLE | Tuscola |
| SOUTH ROCKWOOD | Monroe | UTICA | Macomb |
| SPALDING | Menominee | VANDALIA | Cass |
| SPARTA | Kent | VANDERBILT | Otsego |
| SPRING ARBOR | Jackson | VASSAR | Tuscola |
| SPRING LAKE | Ottawa | VERMONTVILLE | Eaton |
| SPRINGPORT | Jackson | VERNON | Shiawassee |
| SPRUCE | Alcona | VESTABURG | Montcalm |
| STALWART | Chippewa | VICKSBURG | Kalamazoo |
| STAMBAUGH | Iron | VULCAN | Dickinson |
| STANDISH | Arenac | WAKEFIELD | Gogebic |
| STANTON | Montcalm | WALDRON | Hillsdale |
| STANWOOD | Meocosta | WALLHALLA | Mason |
| SAINT CLAIR | St Clair | WALKERVILLE | Oceana |
| SAINT CLAIR SHORES | Macomb | WALLACE | Menominee |
| STEPHENSON | Menominee | WALLED LAKE | Oakland |
| STERLING | Arenac | WALLOON LAKE | Charlevoix |
| STERLING HEIGHTS | MaComb | WARREN | Macomb |
| STEVENSVILLE | Berrien | WASHINGTON | Macomb |
| STOCKBRIDGE | Ingham | WATERFORD | Oakland |
| STURGIS | St Joseph | WATERS | Otsego |
| SUMNER | Gratiot | WATERSMEET | Gogebic |
| SUNFIELD | Eaton | WATERVLIET | Berrien |
| SUTTONS BAY | Leelanau | WATTON | Baraga |
| SWARTZ CREEK | Genesee | WAYLAND | Allegan |
| TAWAS CITY | Iosco | WAYNE | Wayne |
| TAYLOR | Wayne | WEBBERVILLE | Ingham |
| TECUMSEH | Lenawee | WEIDMAN | Isabella |
| TEKONSHA | Calboun | WELLS | Delta |

| | | | |
|---|---|---|---|
| WELLSTON | Manistee | ANNANDALE | Wright |
| WEST BLOOMFIELD | Oakland | ANOKA | Anoka |
| WEST BRANCH | Ogemaw | APPLETON | Swift |
| WEST OLIVE | Ottawa | ARCO | Lincoln |
| WESTON | Lenawee | ARGYLE | Marshall |
| WESTPHALIA | Clinton | ARLINGTON | Sibley |
| WETMORE | Alger | ASHBY | Grant |
| WHEELER | Gratiot | ASKOV | Pine |
| WHITE CLOUD | Newaygo | ATWATER | Kandiyohi |
| WHITEHALL | Muskegon | AUDUBON | Becker |
| WHITE PIGEON | St Joseph | AURORA | St Louis |
| WHITE PINE | Ontonagon | AUSTIN | Mower |
| WHITMORE LAKE | Washtenaw | AVOCA | Murray |
| WHITTAKER | Washtenaw | AVON | Stearns |
| WHITTEMORE | Iosco | BABBITT | St Louis |
| WILLIAMSBURG | Grand Traverse | BACKUS | Cass |
| WILLIAMSTON | Ingham | BADGER | Roseau |
| WILLIS | Washtenaw | BAGLEY | Clearwater |
| WILSON | Menominee | BAKER | Clay |
| WINN | Isabella | BALATON | Lyon |
| WIXOM | Oakland | BARNESVILLE | Clay |
| WOLVERINE | Cheboygan | BARNUM | Carlton |
| WOODLAND | Barry | BARRETT | Grant |
| WYANDOTTE | Wayne | BATTLE LAKE | Otter Tail |
| WYOMING | Kent | BAUDETTE | Lake Of The Woods |
| YALE | St Clair | BAYPORT | Washington |
| YPSILANTI | Washtenaw | BEARDSLEY | Big Stone |
| ZEELAND | Ottawa | BEAVER BAY | Lake |
| **MINNESOTA** | | BEAVER CREEK | Rock |
| ADA | Norman | BECKER | Sherburne |
| ADAMS | Mower | BEJOU | Mahnomen |
| ADOLPH | St Louis | BELGRADE | Stearns |
| ADRIAN | Nobles | BELLE PLAINE | Scott |
| AFTON | Washington | BELLINGHAM | Lac Qui Parle |
| AH-GWAH-CHING | Cass | BELTRAMI | Polk |
| AITKIN | Aitkin | BELVIEW | Redwood |
| AKELEY | Hubbard | BEMIDJI | Beltrami |
| ALBANY | Stearns | BENA | Cass |
| ALBERTA | Stevens | BENEDICT | Hubbard |
| ALBERT LEA | Freeborn | BENSON | Swift |
| ALBERTVILLE | Wright | BEROUN | Pine |
| ALBORN | St Louis | BERTHA | Todd |
| ALDEN | Freeborn | BETHEL | Anoka |
| ALDRICH | Wadena | BIGELOW | Nobles |
| ALEXANDRIA | Douglas | BIG FALLS | Koochiching |
| ALPHA | Jackson | BIGFORK | Itasca |
| ALTURA | Winona | BIG LAKE | Sherburne |
| ALVARADO | Marshall | BINGHAM LAKE | Cottonwood |
| AMBOY | Blue Earth | BIRCHDALE | Koochiching |
| AMIRET | Lyon | BIRD ISLAND | Renville |
| ANGLE INLET | Lake Of The Woods | BIWABIK | St Louis |
| ANGORA | St Louis | BIACKDUCK | Beltrami |
| ANGUS | Polk | BLOMKEST | Kandiyohi |

| | | | |
|---|---|---|---|
| BLOOMING PRAIRIE | Steele | CHAMPLIN | Hennepin |
| BLUE EARTH | Faribault | CHANDLER | Murray |
| BLUFFTON | Otter Tail | CHANHASSEN | Carver |
| BOCK | Mille Lacs | CHASKA | Carver |
| BORUP | Norman | CHATFIELD | Fillmore |
| BOVEY | Itasca | CHISAGO CITY | Chisago |
| BOWLUS | Morrison | CHISHOLM | St Louis |
| BOWSTRING | Itasca | CHOKIO | Stevens |
| BOYD | Lac Qui Parle | CIRCLE PINES | Anoka |
| BOY RIVER | Cass | CLARA CITY | Chippewa |
| BRAHAM | Isanti | CLAREMONT | Dodge |
| BRAINERD | Crow Wing | CLARISSA | Todd |
| BRANDON | Douglas | CLARKFIELD | Yellow Medicine |
| BRECKENRIDGE | Wilkin | CLARKS GROVE | Freeborn |
| BREWSTER | Nobles | CLEARBROOK | Clearwater |
| BRICELYN | Faribault | CLEAR LAKE | Sherburne |
| BRIMSON | St Louis | CLEARWATER | Wright |
| BRITT | St Louis | CLEMENTS | Redwood |
| BROOK PARK | Pine | CLEVELAND | Le Sueur |
| BROOKS | Red Lake | CLIMAX | Polk |
| BROOKSTON | St Louis | CLINTON | Big Stone |
| BROOTEN | Stearns | CLITHERALL | Otter Tail |
| BROWERVILLE | Todd | CLONTARF | Swift |
| BROWNSDALE | Mower | CLOQUET | Carlton |
| BROWNS VALLEY | Traverse | COHASSET | Itasca |
| BROWNSVILLE | Houston | COKATO | Wright |
| BROWNTON | McLeod | COLD SPRING | Stearns |
| BRUNO | Pine | COLERAINE | Itasca |
| BUCKMAN | Morrison | COLLEGEVILLE | Stearns |
| BUFFALO | Wright | COLOGNE | Carver |
| BUFFALO LAKE | Renville | COMFREY | Brown |
| BUHL | St Louis | COMSTOCK | Clay |
| BURNSVILLE | Dakoka | CONGER | Freeborn |
| BURTRUM | Todd | COOK | St Louis |
| BUTTERFIELD | Watonwan | CORRELL | Big Stone |
| BYRON | Olmsted | COSMOS | Meeker |
| CALEDONIA | Houston | COTTAGE GROVE | Washington |
| CALLAWAY | Becker | COTTON | St Louis |
| CALUMET | Itasca | COTTONWOOD | Lyon |
| CAMBRIDGE | Isanti | COURTLAND | Nicollet |
| CAMPBELL | Wilken | CRANE LAKE | St Louis |
| CANBY | Yellow Medicine | CROMWELL | Carlton |
| CANNON FALLS | Goodhue | CROOKSTON | Polk |
| CANTON | Fillmore | CROSBY | Crow Wing |
| CANYON | St Louis | CROSSLAKE | Crow Wing |
| CARLOS | Douglas | CRYSTAL BAY | Hennepin |
| CARLTON | Carlton | CULVER | St Louis |
| CARVER | Carver | CURRIE | Murray |
| CASS LAKE | Cass | CUSHING | Morrison |
| CASTLE ROCK | Dakota | CYRUS | Pope |
| CEDAR | Anoka | DAKOTA | Winona |
| CENTER CITY | Chisago | DALBO | Isanti |
| CEYLON | Martin | DALTON | Otter Tail |

| | | | |
|---|---|---|---|
| DANUBE | Renville | EDGERTON | Pipestone |
| DANVERS | Swift | EFFIE | Itasca |
| DARFUR | Watonwan | EITZEN | Houston |
| DARWIN | Meeker | ELBOW LAKE | Grant |
| DASSEL | Meeker | ELGIN | Wabasha |
| DAWSON | Lac Qui Parle | ELKO | Scott |
| DAYTON | Hennepin | ELK RIVER | Sherburne |
| DEER CREEK | Otter Tail | ELKTON | Mower |
| DEER RIVER | Itasca | ELLENDALE | Steele |
| DEERWOOD | Crow Wing | ELLSWORTH | Nobles |
| DEGRAFF | Swift | ELMORE | Faribault |
| DELANO | Wright | ELROSA | Stearns |
| DELAVAN | Faribault | ELY | St Louis |
| DELFT | Cottonwood | ELYSAIN | Le Sueur |
| DENHAM | Pine | EMBARRASS | St Louis |
| DENNISON | Goodhue | EMILY | Crow Wing |
| DENT | Otter Tail | EMMONS | Freeborn |
| DETROIT LAKES | Becker | ERHARD | Otter Tail |
| DEXTER | Mower | ERSKINE | Polk |
| DILWORTH | Clay | ESKO | Carlton |
| DODGE CENTER | Dodge | ESSIG | Brown |
| DONALDSON | Kittson | EUCLID | Polk |
| DONNELLY | Stevens | EVAN | Brown |
| DORAN | Wilkin | EVANSVILLE | Douglas |
| DOVER | Olmsted | EVELETH | St Louis |
| DOVRAY | Murray | EXCELSIOR | Hennepin |
| DULUTH | St Louis | EYOTA | Olmsted |
| DUMONT | Traverse | FAIRFAX | Renville |
| DUNDAS | Rice | FAIRMONT | Martin |
| DUNDEE | Nobles | FARIBAULT | Rice |
| DUNNELL | Martin | FARMINGTON | Dakota |
| EAGLE BEND | Todd | FARWELL | Pope |
| EAGLE LAKE | Blue Earth | FEDERAL DAM | Cass |
| EAST BONIFACIUS | Hennepin | FELTON | Clay |
| EAST CHARLES | Winona | FERGUS FALLS | Otter Tail |
| EAST CLAIR | Blue Earth | FERTILE | Polk |
| EAST CLOUD | Stearns | FIFTY LAKES | Crow Wing |
| EAST FRANCIS | Anoka | FINLAND | Lake |
| EAST GRAND FORKS | Polk | FINLAYSON | Pine |
| EAST HILAIRE | Pennington | FISHER | Polk |
| EAST JAMES | Watonwan | FLENSBURG | Morrison |
| EAST JOSPEH | Stearns | FLOM | Norman |
| EAST LEO | Yellow Medicine | FLOODWOOD | St Louis |
| EAST MARTIN | Stearns | FLORENCE | Lyon |
| EAST MICHAEL | Wright | FOLEY | Benton |
| EAST PAUL | Dakota | FORBES | St Louis |
| EAST PAUL PARK | Washington | FOREST LAKE | Washington |
| EAST PETER | Nicollet | FORESTON | Mille Lacs |
| EAST VINCENT | Kittson | FORT RIPLEY | Crow Wing |
| EASTON | Faribault | FOSSTON | Polk |
| ECHO | Yellow Medicine | FOUNTAIN | Fillmore |
| EDEN PRAIRIE | Hennepin | FOXHOME | Wilken |
| EDEN VALLEY | Meeker | FRANKLIN | Renville |

| | | | |
|---|---|---|---|
| FRAZEE | Becker | HAMPTON | Dakota |
| FREEBORN | Freeborn | HANCOCK | Stevens |
| FREEPORT | Stearns | HANLEY FALLS | Yellow Medicine |
| FRONTENAC | Goodhue | HANOVER | Wright |
| FROST | Faribault | HANSKA | Brown |
| FULDA | Murray | HARDWICK | Rock |
| GARDEN CITY | Blue Earth | HARMONY | Fillmore |
| GARFIELD | Douglas | HARRIS | Chisago |
| GARRISON | Crow Wing | HARTLAND | Freeborn |
| GARVIN | Lyon | HASTINGS | Dakota |
| GARY | Norman | HATFIELD | Pipestone |
| GATZKE | Marshall | HAWICK | Kandiyohi |
| GAYLORD | Sibley | HAWLEY | Clay |
| GENEVA | Freeborn | HAYFIELD | Dodge |
| GEORGETOWN | Clay | HAYWARD | Freeborn |
| GHEEN | St Louis | HAZEL RUN | Yellow Medicine |
| GHENT | Lyon | HECTOR | Renville |
| GIBBON | Sibley | HENDERSON | Sibley |
| GILBERT | St Louis | HENDRICKS | Lincoln |
| GILMAN | Benton | HENDRUM | Norman |
| GLENCOE | McLeod | HENNING | Otter Tail |
| GLENVILLE | Freeborn | HERMAN | Grant |
| GLENWOOD | Pope | HERON LAKE | Jackson |
| GLYNDON | Clay | HEWITT | Todd |
| GONVICK | Clearwater | HIBBING | St Louis |
| GOODHUE | Goodhue | HILL CITY | Aitkin |
| GOODLAND | Itasca | HILLMAN | Morrison |
| GOODRIDGE | Pennington | HILLS | Rock |
| GOOD THUNDER | Blue Earth | HINCKLEY | Pine |
| GRACEVILLE | Big Stone | HINES | Beltrami |
| GRANADA | Martin | HITTERDAL | Clay |
| GRAND MARAIS | Cook | HOFFMAN | Grant |
| GRAND MEADOW | Mower | HOKAH | Houston |
| GRAND PORTAGE | Cook | HOLDINGFORD | Stearns |
| GRAND RAPIDS | Itasca | HOLLAND | Pipestone |
| GRANDY | Isanti | HOLLANDALE | Freeborn |
| GRANGER | Fillmore | HOLLOWAY | Swift |
| GRANITE FALLS | Yellow Medicine | HOLMES CITY | Douglas |
| GRASSTON | Kanabec | HOLYOKE | Carlton |
| GREENBUSH | Roseau | HOPE | Steele |
| GREEN ISLE | Sibley | HOPKINS | Hennepin |
| GREENWALD | Stearns | HOUSTON | Houston |
| GREY EAGLE | Todd | HOVLAND | Cook |
| GROVE CITY | Meeker | HOWARD LAKE | Wright |
| GRYGLA | Marshall | HOYT LAKES | St Louis |
| GULLY | Polk | HUGO | Washington |
| HACKENSACK | Cass | HUMBOLDT | Kittson |
| HADLEY | Murray | HUNTLEY | Faribault |
| HALLOCK | Kittson | HUTCHINSON | McLeod |
| HALMA | Kittson | IHLEN | Pipestone |
| HALSTAD | Norman | INTERNATIONAL FALLS | Koochiching |
| HAMBURG | Carver | IONA | Murray |
| HAMEL | Hennepin | IRON | St Louis |

| | | | |
|---|---|---|---|
| IRONTON | Crow Wing | LAMBERTON | Redwood |
| ISANTI | Isanti | LANCASTER | Kittson |
| ISLE | Mille Lacs | LANESBORO | Fillmore |
| IVANHOE | Lincoln | LANSING | Mower |
| JACKSON | Jackson | LAPORTE | Hubbard |
| JACOBSON | Aitkin | LASALLE | Watonwan |
| JANESVILLE | Waseca | LASTRUP | Morrison |
| JASPER | Pipestone | LE CENTER | Le Sueur |
| JEFFERS | Cottonwood | LENGBY | Polk |
| JENKINS | Crow Wing | LEONARD | Clearwater |
| JOHNSON | Big Stone | LEOTA | Nobles |
| JORDAN | Scott | LE ROY | Mower |
| KANARANZI | Rock | LESTER PRAIRIE | McLead |
| KANDIYOHI | Kandiyohi | LE SUEUR | Le Sueur |
| KARLSTAD | Kittson | LEWISTON | Winona |
| KASOTA | Le Sueur | LEWISVILLE | Watonwan |
| KASSON | Dodge | LINDSTROM | Chisago |
| KEEWATIN | Itasca | LISMORE | Nobles |
| KELLIHER | Beltrami | LITCHFIELD | Meeker |
| KELLOGG | Wabasha | LITTLE FALLS | Morrison |
| KELLY LAKE | St Louis | LITTLEFORK | Koochiching |
| KELSEY | St Louis | LITTLE SAUK | Todd |
| KENNEDY | Kittson | LOMAN | Koochiching |
| KENNETH | Rock | LONDON | Freeborn |
| KENSINGTON | Douglas | LONG LAKE | Hennepin |
| KENT | Wilkin | LONG PRAIRIE | Todd |
| KENYON | Goodhue | LONGVILLE | Cass |
| KERKHOVEN | Swift | LONSDALE | Rice |
| KERRICK | Pine | LORETTO | Hennepin |
| KETTLE RIVER | Carlton | LOUISBURG | Lac Qui Parle |
| KIESTER | Faribault | LOWRY | Pope |
| KILKENNY | Le Sueur | LUCAN | Redwood |
| KIMBALL | Stearns | LUTSEN | Cook |
| KINGSTON | Meeker | LUVERNE | Rock |
| KINNEY | St Louis | LYLE | Mower |
| KNIFE RIVER | Lake | LYND | Lyon |
| LACRESCENT | Houston | MCGRATH | Aitkin |
| LAFAYETTE | Nicollet | MCGREGOR | Aitkin |
| LASALLE | Watonwan | MCINTOSH | Polk |
| LAKE BENTON | Lincoln | MCKINLEY | St Louis |
| LAKE BRONSON | Kittson | MABEL | Fillmore |
| LAKE CITY | Wabasha | MADELIA | Watonwan |
| LAKE CRYSTAL | Blue Earth | MADISON | Lac Qui Parle |
| LAKE ELMO | Washington | MADISON LAKE | Blue Earth |
| LAKEFIELD | Jackson | MAGNOLIA | Rock |
| LAKE GEORGE | Hubbard | MAHNOMEN | Mahnomen |
| LAKE HUBERT | Crow Wing | MAHTOWA | Carlton |
| LAKE ITASCA | Clearwater | MAKINEN | St Louis |
| LAKELAND | Washington | MANCHESTER | Freeborn |
| LAKE LILLIAN | Kandiyohi | MANHATTEN BEACH | Crow Wing |
| LAKE PARK | Becker | MANKATO | Blue Earth |
| LAKEVILLE | Dakota | MANTORVILLE | Dodge |
| LAKE WILSON | Murray | MAPLE LAKE | Wright |

| | | | |
|---|---|---|---|
| MAPLE PLAIN | Hennepin | NELSON | Douglas |
| MAPLETON | Blue Earth | NERSTRAND | Rice |
| MARBLE | Itasca | NEVIS | Hubbard |
| MARCELL | Itasca | NEW AUBURN | Sibley |
| MARIETTA | Lac Qui Parle | NEWFOLDEN | Marshall |
| MARINE ON SAINT CROIX | Washington | NEW GERMANY | Carver |
| MARKVILLE | Pine | NEW LONDON | Kandiyohi |
| MARSHALL | Lyon | NEW MARKET | Scott |
| MAX | Itasca | NEW MUNICH | Stearns |
| MAYER | Carver | NEWPORT | Washington |
| MAYNARD | Chippewa | NEW PRAGUE | Le Sueur |
| MAZEPPA | Wabasha | NEW RICHLAND | Waseca |
| MEADOWLANDS | St Louis | NEW ULM | Brown |
| MEDFORD | Steele | NEW YORK MILLS | Otter Tail |
| MELROSE | Stearns | NICOLLET | Nicollet |
| MENAHGA | Wadena | NIELSVILLE | Polk |
| MENTOR | Polk | NISSWA | Crow Wing |
| MERIDEN | Steele | NORCROSS | Grant |
| MERRIFIELD | Crow Wing | NORTH BRANCH | Chisago |
| MIDDLE RIVER | Marshall | NORTHFIELD | Rice |
| MILACA | Mille Lacs | NORTHOME | Koochiching |
| MILAN | Chippewa | NORWOOD | Carver |
| MILLVILLE | Wabasha | NOYES | Kittson |
| MILROY | Redwood | OAK ISLAND | Lake Of The Woods |
| MILTONA | Douglas | OAKLAND | Freeborn |
| MINNEAPOLIS | Hennepin | OAK PARK | Benton |
| MINNEOTA | Lyon | OAK PARK HEIGHTS | Washington |
| MINNESOTA CITY | Winona | ODESSA | Big Stone |
| MINNESOTA LAKE | Faribault | ODIN | Watonwan |
| MINNETONKA | Hennepin | OGEMA | Becker |
| MINNETONKA BEACH | Hennepin | OGILVIE | Kanabec |
| MIZPAH | Koodchiching | OKABENA | Jackson |
| MONTEVIDEO | Chippewa | OKLEE | Red Lake |
| MONTGOMERY | Le Sueur | OLIVIA | Renville |
| MONTICELLO | Wright | ONAMIA | Mille Lacs |
| MONTROSE | Wright | ORMSBY | Watonwan |
| MOORHEAD | Clay | ORONOCO | Olmsted |
| MOOSE LAKE | Carlton | ORR | St Louis |
| MORA | Kanabec | ORTONVILLE | Big Stone |
| MORGAN | Redwood | OSAGE | Becker |
| MORRIS | Stevens | OSAKIS | Douglas |
| MORRISTOWN | Rice | OSLO | Marshall |
| MORTON | Renville | OSSEO | Hennepin |
| MOTLEY | Morrison | OSTRANDER | Fillmore |
| MOUND | Hennepin | OTISCO | Waseca |
| MOUNTAIN IRON | St Louis | OTTER TAIL | Otter Tail |
| MOUNTAIN LAKE | Cottonwood | OUTING | Cass |
| MURDOCK | Swift | OWATONNA | Steele |
| MYRTLE | Freeborn | PALISADE | Aitkin |
| NASHUA | Wilkin | PARKERS PRAIRIE | Otter Tail |
| NASHWAUK | Itasca | PARK RAPIDS | Hubbard |
| NASSAU | Lac Qui Parle | PARKVILLE | St Louis |
| NAYTAHWAUSH | Mahnomen | PAYNESVILLE | Stearns |

| | | | |
|---|---|---|---|
| PEASE | Mille Lacs | RICE | Benton |
| PELICAN RAPIDS | Otter Tail | RICHFIELD | Hennepin |
| PEMBERTON | Blue Earth | RICHMOND | Stearns |
| PENCER | Roseau | RICHVILLE | Otter Tail |
| PENGILLY | Itasca | RICHWOOD | Becker |
| PENNINGTON | Beltrami | RIVERVIEW | Ramsey |
| PENNOCK | Kandiyohi | ROBINSDALE | Hennepin |
| PEQUOT LAKES | Crow Wing | ROCHERT | Becker |
| PERHAM | Otter Tail | ROCHESTER | Olmsted |
| PERLEY | Norman | ROCK CREEK | Pine |
| PETERSON | Fillmore | ROCKFORD | Wright |
| PIERZ | Morrison | ROCKVILLE | Stearns |
| PILLAGER | Cass | ROGERS | Hennepin |
| PINE CITY | Pine | ROLLAG | Hawley |
| PINE ISLAND | Goodhue | ROLLINGSTONE | Winona |
| PINE RIVER | Cass | ROOSEVELT | Roseau |
| PINE SPRINGS | Saint Paul | ROSCOE | Stearns |
| PINEWOOD | Beltrami | ROSEAU | Roseau |
| PIONEER | Ramsey | ROSE CREEK | Mower |
| PIPESTONE | Pipestone | ROSEMOUNT | Dakota |
| PITT | Lake Of The Woods | ROSEVILLE | Ramsey |
| PLAINVIEW | Wabasha | ROSS | Roseau |
| PLATO | McLeod | ROTHSAY | Wilkin |
| PLUMMER | Red Lake | ROUND LAKE | Nobles |
| PLYMOUTH | Hennepin | ROYALTON | Morrison |
| PONEMAH | Beltrami | RUSH CITY | Chisago |
| PONSFORD | Becker | RUSHFORD | Fillmore |
| PORTER | Yellow Medicine | RUSHMORE | Nobles |
| PRESTON | Fillmore | RUSSELL | Lyon |
| PRINCETON | Mille Lacs | RUTHTON | Pipestone |
| PRINSBURG | Kandiyohi | RUTLEDGE | Pine |
| PRIOR LAKE | Scott | SABIN | Clay |
| PROCTOR | St. Louis | SACRED HEART | Renville |
| PUPOSKY | Beltrami | SAGINAW | St Louis |
| QUAMBA | Pine | SAINT BONIFACIUS | Hennepin |
| RACINE | Mower | SAINT CHARLES | Winona |
| RADIUM | Warren | SAINT CLAIR | Blue Earth |
| RAMSEY | Anoka | SAINT CLOUD | Stearns |
| RANDALL | Morrison | SAINT FRANCIS | Anoka |
| RANDOLPH | Dakota | SAINT HILAIRE | Pennington |
| RANIER | Koochiching | SAINT JAMES | Watonwan |
| RAY | Koochiching | SAINT JOSEPH | Stearns |
| RAYMOND | Kandiyohi | SAINT LEO | Yellow Medicine |
| READING | Nobles | SAINT LOUIS PARK | Hennepin |
| READS LANDING | Wabasha | SAINT MARTIN | Stearns |
| REDBY | Beltrami | SAINT MICHAEL | Wright |
| RED LAKE | Beltrami | SAINT PAUL | Ramsey |
| RED LAKE FALLS | Red Lake | SAINT PAUL PARK | Washington |
| RED WING | Goodhue | SAINT PETER | Nicollet |
| REDWOOD FALLS | Redwood | SAINT VINCENT | Kittson |
| REMER | Cass | SALOL | Roseau |
| RENVILLE | Renville | SANBORN | Redwood |
| REVERE | Redwood | SANDSTONE | Pine |

| | | | |
|---|---|---|---|
| SANTIAGO | Sherburne | SUNFISH LAKE | St. Paul |
| SARGEANT | Mower | SVEA | Kandiyohi |
| SARTELL | Stearns | SWAN RIVER | Itasca |
| SAUK CENTRE | Stearns | SWANVILLE | Morrison |
| SAUK RAPIDS | Benton | SWATARA | Aitkin |
| SAUM | Beltrami | SWIFT | Roseau |
| SAVAGE | Scott | TACONITE | Itasca |
| SAWYER | Carlton | TALMOON | Itasca |
| SCANDIA | Washington | TAMARACK | Aitkin |
| SCHROEDER | Cook | TAOPI | Mower |
| SEAFORTH | Redwood | TAUNTON | Lyon |
| SEARLES | Brown | TAYLORS FALLS | Chisago |
| SEBEKA | Wadena | TENNEY | Tintah |
| SEDAN | Pope | TENSTRIKE | Beltrami |
| SHAFER | Chisago | THEILMAN | Wabasha |
| SHAKOPEE | Scott | THIEF RIVER FALLS | Pennington |
| SHELLY | Norman | TINTAH | Traverse |
| SHERBURN | Martin | TOFTE | Cook |
| SHEVLIN | Clearwater | TOGO | Itasca |
| SHOREVIEW | Ramsey | TOIVOIA | St Louis |
| SIDE LAKE | St Louis | TOWER | St Louis |
| SILVER BAY | Lake | TRACY | Lyon |
| SILVER CREEK | Wright | TRAIL | Polk |
| SILVER LAKE | McLeod | TRIMONT | Martin |
| SLAYTON | Murray | TROSKY | Pipestone |
| SLEEPY EYE | Brown | TRUMAN | Martin |
| SOLWAY | Beltrami | TWIG | St Louis |
| SOUDAN | St Louis | TWIN CITIES | Rammy |
| SOUTH HAVEN | Wright | TWIN LAKES | Freeborn |
| SOUTH INT'L FALLS | Koochiching | TWIN VALLEY | Norman |
| SOUTH SAINT PAUL | Dakota | TWO HARBORS | Lake |
| SPICER | Kandiyohi | TYLER | Lincoln |
| SPRINGFIELD | Brown | ULEN | Clay |
| SPRING GROVE | Houston | UNDERWOOD | Otter Tail |
| SPRING LAKE | Itasca | UPSALA | Morrison |
| SPRING PARK | Hennepin | UTICA | Winona |
| SPRING VALLEY | Fillmore | VADNAIS HEIGHTS | Ramsey |
| SQUAW LAKE | Itasca | VERDI | Lincoln |
| STACY | Chisago | VERGAS | Otter Tail |
| STANCHFIELD | Isanti | VERMILLION | Dakota |
| STAPLES | Todd | VERNDALE | Wadena |
| STARBUCK | Pope | VERNON CENTER | Blue Earth |
| STEEN | Rock | VESTA | Redwood |
| STEPHEN | Marshall | VICTORIA | Carver |
| STEWART | McLeod | VIKING | Marshall |
| STEWARTVILLE | Olmsted | VILLARD | Pope |
| STILLWATER | Washington | VINING | Otter Tail |
| STOCKTON | Winona | VIRGINIA | St Louis |
| STORDEN | Cottonwood | WABASHA | Wabasha |
| STRANDQUIST | Marshall | WABASSO | Redwood |
| STRATHCONA | Roseau | WACONIA | Carver |
| STURGEON LAKE | Pine | WADENA | Wadena |
| SUNBURG | Kandiyohi | WAHKON | Mille Lacs |

| | | | |
|---|---|---|---|
| WAITE PARK | Stearns | WOLF LAKE | Becker |
| WALDORF | Waseca | WOLVERTON | Wilkin |
| WALKER | Cass | WOODBURY | Ramsey |
| WALNUT GROVE | Redwood | WOOD LAKE | Yellow Medicine |
| WALTERS | Faribault | WOODSTOCK | Pipestone |
| WALTHAM | Mower | WORTHINGTON | Nobles |
| WANAMINGO | Goodhue | WRENSHALL | Carlton |
| WANDA | Redwood | WRIGHT | Carlton |
| WANNASKA | Roseau | WYKOFF | Fillmore |
| WARBA | Itasca | WYOMING | Chisago |
| WARREN | Marshall | YOUNG AMERICA | Carver |
| WARROAD | Roseau | ZIM | St Louis |
| WARSAW | Rice | ZIMMERMAN | Sherburne |
| WASECA | Waseca | ZUMBRO FALLS | Wabasha |
| WASKISH | Beltrami | ZUMBROTA | Goodhue |
| WATERTOWN | Carver | **MISSISSIPPI** | |
| WATERVILLE | Le Sueur | ABBEVILLE | Lafayette |
| WATKINS | Meeker | ABERDEEN | Monroe |
| WATSON | Chippewa | ACKERMAN | Choctaw |
| WAUBUN | Mahnomen | ALGOMA | Pontotoc |
| WAVERLY | Wright | ALLIGATOR | Bolivar |
| WAWINA | Itasca | AMORY | Monroe |
| WAYZATA | Hennepin | ANGUILLA | Sharkey |
| WEBSTER | Rice | ARCOLA | Washington |
| WELCH | Goodhue | ARKABUTLA | Tate |
| WELCOME | Martin | ARTESIA | Lowndes |
| WELLS | Faribault | ASHLAND | Benton |
| WENDELL | Grant | AVALON | Carroll |
| WESTBROOK | Cottonwood | AVON | Washington |
| WEST CONCORD | Dodge | BAILEY | Lauderdale |
| WEST DULUTH | St. Louis | BALDWYN | Prentiss |
| WEST ST. PAUL | Ramsey | BANNER | Calhoun |
| WEST UNION | Todd | BASSFIELD | Jefferson Davis |
| WHALAN | Fillmore | BATESVILLE | Panola |
| WHEATON | Traverse | BAY SAINT LOUIS | Hancock |
| WHIPHOLT | Cass | BAY SPRINGS | Jasper |
| WHITE BEAR LAKE | Ramsey | BEAUMONT | Perry |
| WHITE EARTH | Becker | BECKER | Monroe |
| WILDER | Jackson | BELDEN | Lee |
| WILLERNIE | Washington | BELEN | Quitman |
| WILLLAMS | Lake Of The Woods | BELLE FONTAINE | Webster |
| WILLMAR | Kandiyohi | BELMONT | Tishomigo |
| WILLOW RIVER | Pine | BELZONI | Humphreys |
| WILMONT | Nobles | BENOIT | Bolivar |
| WILTON | Beltrami | BENTON | Yazoo |
| WINDOM | Cottonwood | BENTONIA | Yazoo |
| WINGER | Polk | BEULAH | Bolivar |
| WINNEBAGO | Faribault | BIGBEE VALLEY | Noxubee |
| WINONA | Winona | BIG CREEK | Calhoun |
| WINSTED | McLeod | BILOXI | Harrison |
| WINTHROP | Sibley | BLUE MOUNTAIN | Tippah |
| WINTON | St Louis | BLUE SPRINGS | Union |
| WIRT | Itasca | BOGUE CHITTO | Lincoln |

| | | | |
|---|---|---|---|
| BOLTON | Hinds | DALEVILLE | Lauderdale |
| BOONEVILLE | Prentiss | DARLING | Quitman |
| BOYLE | Bolivar | DECATUR | Newton |
| BRANDON | Rankin | DEKALB | Kemper |
| BRAXTON | Simpson | DELTA CITY | Sharkey |
| BROOKHAVEN | Lincoln | DENNIS | Tishomingo |
| BROOKLYN | Forrest | DERMA | Calhoun |
| BROOKSVILLE | Noxubee | D'LO | Simpson |
| BRUCE | Calhoun | DODDSVILLE | Sunflower |
| BUCKATUNNA | Wayne | DREW | Sunflower |
| BUDE | Franklin | DUBLIN | Coahoma |
| BURNSVILLE | Tishomingo | DUCK HILL | Montgomery |
| BYHALIA | Marshall | DUMAS | Tippah |
| CALEDONIA | Lowndes | DUNCAN | Bolivar |
| CALHOUN CITY | Calhoun | DUNDEE | Tunica |
| CAMDEN | Madison | DURANT | Holmes |
| CANTON | Madison | EASTABUCHIE | Jones |
| CARRIERE | Pearl River | EBENEZER | Holmes |
| CARROLLTON | Carroll | ECRU | Pontotoc |
| CARSON | Jefferson Davis | EDWARDS | Hinds |
| CARTHAGE | Leake | ELLIOTT | Grenada |
| CARY | Sharkey | ELLISVILLE | Jones |
| CASCILLA | Tallahatchie | ENID | Tallahatchie |
| CEDARBLUFF | Clay | ENTERPRISE | Clarke |
| CENTREVILLE | Wilkinson | ESCATAWPA | Jackson |
| CHARLESTON | Tallahatchie | ETHEL | Attala |
| CHATAWA | Pike | ETTA | Union |
| CHATHAM | Washington | EUPORA | Webster |
| CHUNKY | Newton | FALCON | Quitman |
| CHURCH HILL | Jefferson | FALKNER | Tippah |
| CLARA | Wayne | FARRELL | Coahoma |
| CLARKSDALE | Coahoma | FAYETTE | Jefferson |
| CLERMONT HARBOR | Hancock | FERNWOOD | Pike |
| CLEVELAND | Bolivar | FLORA | Madison |
| CLINTON | Hinds | FLORENCE | Rankin |
| COAHOMA | Coahoma | FOREST | Scott |
| COFFEEVILLE | Yalobusha | FORKVILLE | Scott |
| COILA | Carroll | FOXWORTH | Marion |
| COLDWATER | Tate | FRENCH CAMP | Choctaw |
| COLLINS | Covington | FRIARS POINT | Coahoma |
| COLLINSVILLE | Lauderdale | FULTON | Itawamba |
| COLUMBIA | Marion | GALLMAN | Copiah |
| COLUMBUS | Lowndes | GARMAN | Monroe |
| COMO | Panola | GAUTIER | Jackson |
| CONEHATTA | Newton | GEORGETOWN | Copiah |
| CORINTH | Alcorn | GLEN | Alcorn |
| COURTLAND | Panola | GLEN ALLEN | Washington |
| CRAWFORD | Lowndes | GLENDORA | Tallahatchie |
| CRENSHAW | Panola | GLOSTER | Amite |
| CROSBY | Amite | GOLDEN | Tishomingo |
| CROWDER | Quitman | GOODMAN | Holmes |
| CRUGER | Holmes | GORE SPRINGS | Grenada |
| CRYSTAL SPRINGS | Copiah | GRACE | Issaquena |

| | | | |
|---|---|---|---|
| GREENVILLE | Washington | LEXINGTON | Holmes |
| GREENWOOD | Leflore | LIBERTY | Amite |
| GREENWOOD SPRINGS | Monroe | LITTLE ROCK | Newton |
| GRENADA | Grenada | LONG BEACH | Harrison |
| GULFPORT | Harrison | LORMAN | Jefferson |
| GUNNISON | Bolivar | LOUIN | Jasper |
| GUNTOWN | Lee | LOUISE | Humphreys |
| HAMILTON | Monroe | LOUISVILLE | Winston |
| HARPERVILLE | Scott | LUCEDALE | George |
| HARRISTON | Jefferson | LUDLOW | Scott |
| HARRISVILLE | Simpson | LULA | Coahoma |
| HATTIESBURG | Forrest | LUMBERTON | Lamar |
| HAZLEHURST | Copiah | LYON | Coahoma |
| HEIDELBERG | Jasper | MCADAMS | Attala |
| HERMANVILLE | Claiborne | MCCALL CREEK | Franklin |
| HERNADO | DeSoto | MCCARLEY | Carroll |
| HICKORY | Newton | MCCOMB | Pike |
| HICKORY FLAT | Benton | MCCONDY | Chickasaw |
| HILLSBORO | Scott | MCCOOL | Attala |
| HOLCOMB | Grenada | MCHENRY | Stone |
| HOLLANDALE | Washington | MCLAIN | Greene |
| HOLLY BLUFF | Yazoo | MCNEILL | Pearl River |
| HOLLY RIDGE | Sunflower | MABEN | Oktibbeha |
| HOLLY SPRINGS | Marshall | MACON | Noxubee |
| HORN LAKE | DeSoto | MADDEN | Leake |
| HOULKA | Chickasaw | MADISON | Madison |
| HOUSTON | Chickasaw | MAGEE | Simpson |
| HURLEY | Jackson | MAGNOLIA | Pike |
| INDEPENDENCE | Tate | MANTACHIE | Itawamba |
| INDIANOLA | Sunflower | MANTEE | Webster |
| INVERNESS | Sunflower | MARIETTA | Prentiss |
| ISOLA | Humphreys | MARION | Lauderdale |
| ITTA BENA | Leflore | MARKS | Quitman |
| IUKA | Tishomingo | MATHISTON | Webster |
| JACKSON | Hinds | MAYERSVILLE | Issaquena |
| JAYESS | Lawrence | MAYHEW | Lowndes |
| JONESTOWN | Coahoma | MEADVILLE | Franklin |
| KILMICHAEL | Montgomery | MENDENHALL | Simpson |
| KILN | Hancock | MERIDIAN | Lauderdale |
| KOKOMO | Marion | MERIGOLD | Bolivar |
| KOSCIUSKO | Attala | METCALFE | Washington |
| LAKE | Scott | MICHIGAN CITY | Benton |
| LAKE CORMORANT | DeSoto | MIDNIGHT | Humphreys |
| LAKESHORE | Hancock | MINERAL WELLS | DeSoto |
| LAMAR | Benton | MINTER CITY | Leflore |
| LAMBERT | Quitman | MISSISSIPPI STATE | Okibbeha |
| LAMONT | Bolivar | MIZE | Smith |
| LAUDERDALE | Lauderdale | MONEY | Leflore |
| LAUREL | Jones | MONTICELLO | Lawrence |
| LAWRENCE | Newton | MONTPELIER | Clay |
| LEAKSVILLE | Greene | MOOREVILLE | Lee |
| LELAND | Washington | MOORHEAD | Sunflower |
| LENA | Leake | MORGAN CITY | Leflore |

| | | | |
|---|---|---|---|
| MORGANTOWN | Marion | PORTERVILLE | Kemper |
| MORTON | Scott | PORT GIBSON | Claiborne |
| MOSELLE | Jones | POTTS CAMP | Marshall |
| MOSS | Jasper | PRAIRIE | Monroe |
| MOUND BAYOU | Bolivar | PRAIRIE POINT | Noxubee |
| MOUNT OLIVE | Covington | PRENTISS | Jefferson Davis |
| MYRTLE | Union | PRESTON | Kemper |
| NATCHEZ | Adams | PUCKETT | Rankin |
| NEELY | Greene | PULASKI | Scott |
| NESBIT | DeSoto | PURVIS | Lamar |
| NETTLETON | Lee | QUITMAN | Clarke |
| NEW ALBANY | Union | RALEIGH | Smith |
| NEW AUGUSTA | Perry | RANDOLPH | Pontotoc |
| NEWHEBRON | Lawrence | RAYMOND | Hinds |
| NEW SITE | Prentiss | RED BANKS | Marshall |
| NEWTON | Newton | REDWOOD | Warren |
| NICHOLSON | Pearl River | REFORM | Choctaw |
| NITTA YUMA | Sharkey | RENA LARA | Coahoma |
| NORTH CARROLLTON | Carroll | RICH | Coahoma |
| NOXAPATER | Winston | RICHTON | Perry |
| OAKLAND | Yalobusha | RIDGELAND | Madison |
| OAK VALE | Lawrence | RIENZI | Alcorn |
| OCEAN SPRINGS | Jackson | RIPLEY | Tippah |
| OKOLONA | Chickasaw | ROBINSONVILLE | Tunica |
| OLIVE BRANCH | DeSoto | ROLLING FORK | Sharkey |
| OSYKA | Pike | ROME | Sunflower |
| OVETT | Jones | ROSEDALE | Bolivar |
| OXFORD | Lafayette | ROSE HILL | Jasper |
| PACE | Bolivar | ROXIE | Franklin |
| PACHUTA | Clarke | RULEVILLE | Sunflower |
| PANTHER BURN | Sharkey | RUTH | Lincoln |
| PARIS | Lafayette | SALLIS | Attala |
| PASCAGOULA | Jackson | SALTILLO | Lee |
| PASS CHRISTIAN | Harrison | SANDERSVILLE | Jones |
| PATTISON | Claiborne | SANDHILL | Rankin |
| PAULDING | Jasper | SANDY HOOK | Marion |
| PEARLINGTON | Hancock | SARAH | Tate |
| PELAHATCHIE | Rankin | SARDIS | Panola |
| PERKINSTON | Stone | SAREPTA | Calhoun |
| PETAL | Forest | SATARTIA | Yazoo |
| PHEBA | Clay | SAUCIER | Harrison |
| PHILADEPHIA | Neshoba | SAVAGE | Tate |
| PHILLIPP | Tallahatchie | SCHLATER | Leflore |
| PICAYUNE | Pearl River | SCOBEY | Yalobusha |
| PICKENS | Holmes | SCOOBA | Kemper |
| PINEY WOODS | Rankin | SCOTT | Bolivar |
| PINOLA | Simpson | SEBASTOPOL | Scott |
| PITTSBORO | Calhoun | SEMINARY | Covington |
| PLANTERSVILLE | Lee | SENATOBIA | Tate |
| PLEASANT GROVE | Panola | SHANNON | Lee |
| PONTOTOC | Pontotoc | SHARON | Madison |
| POPE | Panola | SHAW | Bolivar |
| POPLARVILLE | Pearl River | SHELBY | Bolivar |

| | | | |
|---|---|---|---|
| SHERARD | Coahoma | TUNICA | Tunica |
| SHERMAN | Pontotoc | TUPELO | Lee |
| SHUBUTA | Clarke | TUTWILER | Tallahatchie |
| SHUQUALAK | Noxubee | TYLERTOWN | Walthall |
| SIBLEY | Adams | UNION | Newton |
| SIDON | Leflore | UNION CHURCH | Jefferson |
| SILVER CITY | Humphreys | UNIVERSITY | Lafayette |
| SILVER CREEK | Lawrence | UTICA | Hinds |
| SKENE | Bolivar | VAIDEN | Carroll |
| SIATE SPRING | Calhoun | VALLEY PARK | Issaquena |
| SLEDGE | Quitman | VANCE | Quitman |
| SMITHDALE | Amite | VAN VLEET | Chickasaw |
| SMITHVILLE | Monroe | VARDAMAN | Calhoun |
| SONTAG | Lawrence | VAUGHAN | Yazoo |
| SOSO | Jones | VERONA | Lee |
| SOUTH OLIVE | Covington | VICKSBURG | Warren |
| SOUTH PLEASANT | Marshall | VICTORIA | Marshall |
| SOUTHAVEN | DeSoto | VOSSBURG | Jasper |
| STAR | Rankin | WALLS | DeSoto |
| STARKVILLE | Oktibbeha | WALNUT | Tippah |
| STATE LINE | Greene | WALNUT GROVE | Leake |
| STEENS | Lowndes | WALTHALL | Webster |
| STEWART | Montgomery | WASHINGTON | Adams |
| STONEVILLE | Washington | WATERFORD | Marshall |
| STONEWALL | Clarke | WATER VALLEY | Yalobusha |
| STRINGER | Jasper | WAVELAND | Hancock |
| STURGIS | Oktibbeha | WAYNESBORO | Wayne |
| SUMMIT | Pike | WAYSIDE | Washington |
| SUMNER | Tallahatchie | WEBB | Tallahatchie |
| SUMRALL | Lamar | WEIR | Choctaw |
| SUNFLOWER | Sunflower | WESSON | Copiah |
| SWAN LAKE | Tallahatchie | WEST | Holmes |
| SWIFTWON | Leflore | WEST POINT | Clay |
| TAYLOR | Lafayette | WHEELER | Prentiss |
| TAYLORSVILLE | Smith | WHITFIELD | Rankin |
| TCHULA | Homles | WIGGINS | Stone |
| TERRY | Hinds | WINONA | Montgomery |
| THAXTON | Pontotoc | WINSTONVILLE | Bolivar |
| THOMASTOWN | Leake | WINTERVILLE | Washington |
| THORNTON | Holmes | WOODLAND | Chickasaw |
| TIE PLANT | Grenada | WOODVILLE | Wilkinson |
| TILLATOBA | Yalobusha | YAZOO CITY | Yazoo |
| TINSLEY | Yazoo | **MISSOURI** | |
| TIPLERSVILLE | Tippah | ADRIAN | Bates |
| TIPPO | Tallahatchie | ADVANCE | Stoddard |
| TISHOMINGO | Tishomingo | AFFTON | St Louis |
| TOCCUPOLA | Pontotoc | AGENCY | Buchanan |
| TOOMSUBA | Lauderdale | ALBA | Jasper |
| TOUGALOO | Hinds | ALBANY | Gentry |
| TREBLOC | Chickasaw | ALDRICH | Polk |
| TREMONT | Itawamba | ALEXANDRIA | Clark |
| TRIBBETT | Washington | ALLENDALE | Worth |
| TULA | Lafayette | ALLENTON | St Louis |

| | | | |
|---|---|---|---|
| ALMA | Lafayette | BERNIE | Stoddard |
| ALTAMONT | Daviess | BERTRAND | Mississippi |
| ALTENBURG | Perry | BETHANY | Harrison |
| ALTON | Oregon | BETHEL | Shelby |
| AMAZONIA | Andrew | BEULAH | Phelps |
| AMITY | DeKalb | BEVIER | Macon |
| AMORET | Bates | BIGELOW | Holt |
| AMSTERDAM | Bates | BILLINGS | Christian |
| ANABEL | MaoDn | BIRCH TREE | Shannon |
| ANDERSON | McDonald | BISMARCK | St. Francois |
| ANNADA | Pike | BIXBY | Iron |
| ANNAPOLIS | Iron | BLACK | Reyonds |
| ANNISTON | Mississippi | BLACKBURN | Saline |
| ANTIOCH | Jackson | BLACKWATER | Cooper |
| APPLETON CITY | St. Clair | BLACKWELL | St. Francois |
| ARAB | Bollinger | BLAIRSTOWN | Henry |
| ARBELA | Scotland | BLAND | Gasconade |
| ARBYRD | Dunklin | BLODGETT | Scott |
| ARCADIA | Iron | BLOOMFIELD | Stoddard |
| ARCHIE | Cass | BLOOMSDALE | St. Genevieve |
| ARCOLA | Dade | BLUE EYE | Stone |
| ARGYLE | Osage | BLUE SPRINGS | Jackson |
| ARMSTRONG | Howard | BLYTHEDALE | Harrison |
| ARNOLD | Jefferson | BOGARD | Carroll |
| ARROW ROCK | Saline | BOIS D ARC | Greene |
| ASBURY | Jasper | BOLCKOW | Andrew |
| ASHBURN | Pike | BOLIVAR | Polk |
| ASH GROVE | Greene | BONNE TERRE | St. Francois |
| ASHLAND | Boone | BONNOTS MILL | Osage |
| ATLANTA | Macon | BOONVILLE | Cooper |
| AUGUSTA | St. Charles | BOSS | Dent |
| AURORA | Lawrence | BOSWORTH | Carroll |
| AUXVASSE | Callaway | BOURBON | Crawford |
| AVA | Douglas | BOWLING GREEN | Pike |
| AVILLA | Jasper | BRADLEYVILLE | Taney |
| BAKERSFIELD | Ozark | BRAGGADOCIO | Pemiscot |
| BALLWIN | St. Louis | BRAGG CITY | Pemiscot |
| BARING | Knox | BRANDSVILLE | Howell |
| BARNARD | Nodaway | BRANSON | Taney |
| BARNETT | Morgan | BRASHEAR | Adair |
| BARNHART | Jefferson | BRAYMER | Caldwell |
| BATES CITY | Lafayette | BRAZEAU | Perry |
| BEAUFORT | Franklin | BRECKENRIDGE | Caldwell |
| BELGRADE | Washington | BRIAR | Ripley |
| BELL CITY | Stoddard | BRIGHTON | Polk |
| BELLE | Maries | BRINKTOWN | Maries |
| BELLEVIEW | Iron | BRIXEY | Ozark |
| BELLFLOWER | Montgomery | BRONAUGH | Vernon |
| BELTON | Cass | BROOKFIELD | Linn |
| BENDAVIS | Texas | BROOKLINE STATION | Greene |
| BENTON | Scott | BROSELEY | Butler |
| BENTON CITY | Audrain | BROWNING | Linn |
| BERGER | Franklin | BROWNWOOD | Stoddard |

| | | | |
|---|---|---|---|
| BRUMLEY | Miller | CHARLESTON | Mississippi |
| BRUNER | Christian | CHERRYVILLE | Crawford |
| BRUNSWICK | Chariton | CHESTERFIELD | St. Louis |
| BUCKLIN | Linn | CHESTNUTRIDGE | Christian |
| BUCKNER | Jackson | CHILHOWEE | Johnson |
| BUCYRUS | Texas | CHILLICOTHE | Livingston |
| BUFFALO | Dallas | CHULA | Livingston |
| BUNCETON | Cooper | CLARENCE | Shelby |
| BUNKER | Reynolds | CLARK | Randolph |
| BURFORDVILLE | Cape Girardeau | CLARKSBURG | Moniteau |
| BURLINGTON JUNCTION | Nodaway | CLARKSDALE | DeKalb |
| BUTLER | Bates | CLARKSVILLE | Pike |
| BUTTERFIELD | Barry | CLARKTON | Dunklin |
| CABOOL | Texas | CLEARMONT | Nodaway |
| CADET | Washington | CLEVELAND | Cass |
| CAINSVILLE | Harrison | CLEVER | Christian |
| CAIRO | Randolph | CLIFTON HILL | Randolph |
| CALADONIA | Washington | CLIMAX SPRINGS | Camden |
| CALHOUN | Henry | CLINTON | Henry |
| CALIFORNIA | Moniteau | CLUBB | Wayne |
| CALLAO | Macon | CLYDE | Nodaway |
| CAMDEN | Ray | COATSVILLE | Schuyler |
| CAMDEN POINT | Platte | COFFEY | Daviess |
| CAMDENTON | Camden | COLE CAMP | Benton |
| CAMERON | Clinton | COLLINS | St. Clair |
| CAMPBELL | Dunklin | COLUMBIA | Boone |
| CANALOU | New Madrid | COMMERCE | Scott |
| CANTON | Lewis | CONCEPTION | Nodaway |
| CAPE FAIR | Stone | CONCEPTION JUNCTION | Nodaway |
| CAPE GIRARDEAU | Cape Girardeau | CONCORDIA | Lafayette |
| CAPLINGER MILLS | Cedar | CONRAN | New Madrid |
| CARDWELL | Dunklin | CONWAY | Laclede |
| CARL JUNCTION | Jasper | COOK STATION | Crawford |
| CARROLLTON | Carroll | COOTER | Pemiscot |
| CARTERVILLE | Jasper | CORDER | Lafayette |
| CARTHAGE | Jasper | COSBY | Andrew |
| CARUTHERSVILLE | Pemiscot | COTTLEVILLE | St. Charles |
| CASCADE | Wayne | COUCH | Oregon |
| CASSVILLE | Barry | COURTOIS | Washington |
| CATAWISSA | Franklin | COWGILL | Caldwell |
| CATRON | New Madrid | CRAIG | Holt |
| CAULFIELD | Howell | CRANE | Stone |
| CEDAR CITY | Callaway | CREIGHTON | Cass |
| CEDARCREEK | Taney | CRESCENT | St. Louis |
| CEDAR HILL | Jefferson | CROCKER | Pulaski |
| CENTER | Ralls | CROSS TIMBERS | Hickory |
| CENTERTOWN | Coles | CRYSTAL CITY | Jefferson |
| CENTERVIEW | Johnson | CUBA | Crawford |
| CENTERVILLE | Reynolds | CURRYVILLE | Pike |
| CENTRALIA | Boone | DADEVILLE | Dade |
| CHADWICK | Christian | DAISY | Cape Girardeau |
| CHAFFEE | Scott | DALTON | Chariton |
| CHAMOIS | Osage | DARLINGTON | Gentry |

| City | County | City | County |
|---|---|---|---|
| DAVISVILLE | Crawford | EDGERTON | Platte |
| DAWN | Livingston | EDINA | Knox |
| DEARBORN | Platte | EDWARDS | Benton |
| DEEPWATER | Henry | ELDON | Miller |
| DEERFIELD | Vernon | EL DORADO SPRINGS | Cedar |
| DEERING | Pemiscot | ELDRIDGE | Laclede |
| DEFIANCE | St. Charles | ELK CREEK | Texas |
| DEKALB | Buchanan | ELKLAND | Webster |
| DELTA | Cape Girardeau | ELLINGTON | Reynolds |
| DENVER | Worth | ELLSINORE | Carter |
| DES ARC | Iron | ELMER | Macon |
| DESOTO | Jefferson | ELMO | Nodaway |
| DEVILS ELBOW | Pulaski | ELSBERRY | Lincoln |
| DEWITT | Carroll | EMDEN | Shelby |
| DEXTER | Stoddard | EMINENCE | Shannon |
| DIAMOND | Newton | EMMA | Saline |
| DIGGINS | Webster | EOLIA | Pike |
| DITTMER | Jefferson | ESSEX | Stoddard |
| DIXON | Pulaski | ETHEL | Macon |
| DOE RUN | St. Francois | ETTERVILLE | Miller |
| DONIPHAN | Ripley | EUDORA | Polk |
| DORA | Ozark | EUGENE | Cole |
| DOVER | Lafayette | EUNICE | Texas |
| DOWNING | Schuyler | EUREKA | St. Louis |
| DREXEL | Cass | EVERTON | Dade |
| DRURY | Douglas | EWING | Lewis |
| DUDLEY | Stoddard | EXCELLO | Macon |
| DUENWEG | Jasper | EXCELSIOR SPRINGS | Clay |
| DUGGINSVILLE | Ozark | EXETER | Barry |
| DUKE | Phelps | FAGUS | Butler |
| DUNNEGAN | Polk | FAIRDEALING | Ripley |
| DURHAM | Lewis | FAIRFAX | Atchison |
| DUTCHTOWN | Cape Girardeau | FAIR GROVE | Greene |
| DUTZOW | Warren | FAIR PLAY | Polk |
| EAGLE ROCK | Barry | FAIRVIEW | Newton |
| EAGLEVILLE | Harrison | FALCON | Laclede |
| EAST ALBANS | Franklin | FARBER | Audrain |
| EAST ANN | St. Louis | FARLEY | Platte |
| EAST CATHERINE | Linn | FARMINGTON | St. Francois |
| EAST CHARLES | St. Charles | FARRAR | Perry |
| EAST CLAIR | Franklin | FAUCETT | Buchanan |
| EAST ELIZABETH | Miller | FAYETTE | Howard |
| EAST JAMES | Phelps | FENTON | St. Louis |
| EAST JOSEPH | Buchanon | FESTUS | Jefferson |
| EAST LOUIS | St. Louis | FILLMORE | Andrew |
| EAST LYNNE | Cass | FISK | Butler |
| EAST MARYS | Perry | FLAT RIVER | St. Francois |
| EAST PATRICK | Clark | FLEMINGTON | Polk |
| EAST PETERS | St. Charles | FLETCHER | Jefferson |
| EAST THOMAS | Cole | FLINTHILL | St. Charles |
| EASTON | Buchanan | FLORENCE | Morgan |
| EAST PRAIRIE | Mississippi | FLORISSANT | St. Louis |
| EDGAR SPRINGS | Phelps | FOLEY | Lincoln |

| | | | |
|---|---|---|---|
| FORDLAND | Webster | GRANGER | Scotland |
| FOREST CITY | Holt | GRANT CITY | Worth |
| FORISTELL | St. Charles | GRASSY | Bollinger |
| FORSYTH | Taney | GRAVOIS MILLS | Morgan |
| FORT LEONARD WOOD | Pulaski | GRAYRIDGE | Stoddard |
| FORTUNA | Moniteau | GRAY SUMMIT | Franklin |
| FOSTER | Bates | GREEN CASTLE | Sullivan |
| FRANKCLAY | St. Francois | GREEN CITY | Sullivan |
| FRANKFORD | Pike | GREENFIELD | Dade |
| FRANKLIN | Howard | GREEN RIDGE | Pettis |
| FREDERICKTOWN | Madison | GREENTOP | Schuyler |
| FREEBURG | Osage | GREENVILLE | Wayne |
| FREEMAN | Cass | GREENWOOD | Jackson |
| FREISTATT | Lawrence | GROVER | SL Louis |
| FREMONT | Carter | GROVESPRING | Wright |
| FRENCH VILLAGE | St. Francois | GRUBVILLE | Jefferson |
| FROHNA | Perry | GUILFORD | Nodaway |
| FULTON | Callaway | HALE | Carroll |
| GAINESVILLE | Ozark | HALF WAY | Polk |
| GALENA | Stone | HALLSVILLE | Boone |
| GALLATIN | Daviess | HALLTOWN | Lawrence |
| GALT | Grundy | HAMILTON | Caldwell |
| GARDEN CITY | Cass | HANNIBAL | Marion |
| GARRISON | Christian | HARDENVILLE | Ozark |
| GASCONADE | Gasconade | HARDIN | Ray |
| GATEWOOD | Ripley | HARRISBURG | Boone |
| GENTRY | Gentry | HARRISONVILLE | Cass |
| GERALD | Franklin | HARTSBURG | Boone |
| GIBBS | Adair | HARTSHORN | Texas |
| GIBSON | Dunklin | HARTVILLE | Wright |
| GIDEON | New Madrid | HARVIELL | Butler |
| GILLIAM | Saline | HARWOOD | Vernon |
| GILMAN CITY | Harrison | HAWK POINT | Lincoln |
| GIPSY | Bollinger | HAYTI | Pemiscot |
| GLASGOW | Howard | HAZELWOOD | St. Louis |
| GLENALLEN | Bollinger | HELENA | Andrew |
| GLENCOE | St. Louis | HEMATITE | Jefferson |
| GLENWOOD | Schuyler | HENLEY | Cole |
| GLOVER | Iron | HENRIETTA | Ray |
| GOBLER | Pemiscot | HERCULANEUM | Jefferson |
| GOLDEN | Barry | HERMANN | Gasconade |
| GOLDEN CITY | Barton | HERMITAGE | Hickory |
| GOODMAN | McDonald | HIGBEE | Randolph |
| GOODSON | Polk | HIGGINSVILLE | Lafayette |
| GORDONVILLE | Cape Girardeau | HIGH HILL | Montgomery |
| GORIN | Scotland | HIGH POINT | Moniteau |
| GOWER | Clinton | HIGHLANDVILLE | Christian |
| GRAFF | Wright | HIGH RIDGE | Jefferson |
| GRAHAM | Nodaway | HILLSBORO | Jefferson |
| GRAIN VALLEY | Jackson | HIRAM | Wayne |
| GRANBY | Newton | HOLCOMB | Dunklin |
| GRANDIN | Carter | HOLDEN | Johnson |
| GRANDVIEW | Jackson | HOLLAND | Pemiscot |

| City | County | City | County |
|---|---|---|---|
| HOLIDAY | Monroe | KINGSVILLE | Johnson |
| HOLLISTER | Taney | KIRBYVILLE | Taney |
| HOLT | Clay | KIRKSVILLE | Adair |
| HOLTS SUMMIT | Callaway | KISSEE MILLS | Taney |
| HOPKINS | Nodaway | KNOB LICK | St. Francois |
| HORNERSVILLE | Dunkin | KNOB NOSTER | Johnson |
| HORTON | Veron | KNOX CITY | Knox |
| HOUSE SPRINGS | Jefferson | KOELTZTOWN | Osage |
| HOUSTON | Texas | KOSHKONONG | Oregon |
| HOUSTONIA | Pettis | LABADIE | Franklin |
| HUGGINS | Texas | LABELLE | Lewis |
| HUGHESVILLE | Pettis | LACLEDE | Linn |
| HUMANSVILLE | Polk | LADDONIA | Audrain |
| HUME | Bates | LAGRANGE | Lewis |
| HUMPHREYS | Sullivan | LAKE OZARK | Miller |
| HUNNEWELL | Shelby | LAKE SPRING | Dent |
| HUNTSVILLE | Randolph | LAKE ST. LOUIS | St. Charles |
| HURDLAND | Knox | LAMAR | Barton |
| HURLEY | Stone | LAMONTE | Pettis |
| IBERIA | Miller | LAMPE | Stone |
| IMPERIAL | Jefferson | LANAGAN | McDonald |
| INDEPENDENCE | Jackson | LANCASTER | Schuyler |
| IONIA | Benton | LAPLATA | Macon |
| IRONDALE | Washington | LAQUEY | Pulaski |
| IRONTON | Iron | LAREDO | Grundy |
| ISABELLA | Ozark | LARUSSELL | Jasper |
| JACKSON | Cape Girardeau | LATHAM | Moniteau |
| JACKSONVILLE | Randolph | LATHROP | Clinton |
| JADWIN | Dent | LATOUR | Johnson |
| JAMESON | Daviess | LAWSON | Ray |
| JAMESPORT | Daviess | LEADWOOD | St. Francois |
| JAMESTOWN | Moniteau | LEASBURG | Crawford |
| JANE | McDonald | LABANON | Laclede |
| JASPER | Jasper | LACOMA | Dent |
| JEFFERSON CITY | Cole | LEES SUMMIT | Jackson |
| JERICO SPRINGS | Cole | LEETON | Johnson |
| JEROME | Phelps | LENOX | Dent |
| JONESBURG | Montgomery | LENTNER | Shelby |
| JOPLIN | Jasper | LEONARD | Shelby |
| KAHOKA | Clark | LEOPOLD | Bollinger |
| KAISER | Miller | LESLIE | Franklin |
| KANSAS CITY | Jackson | LESTERVILLE | Reynolds |
| KEARNEY | Clay | LEVASY | Jackson |
| KELSO | Scott | LEWISTOWN | Lewis |
| KENNETT | Dunklin | LEXINGTON | Lafayette |
| KEWANEE | New Madrid | LIBERAL | Barton |
| KEYTESVILLE | Chariton | LIBERTY | Clay |
| KIDDER | Caldwell | LICKING | Texas |
| KIMBERLING CITY | Stone | LIGUORI | Jefferson |
| KIMMSWICK | Jefferson | LILBOURN | New Madrid |
| KING CITY | Gentry | LINCOLN | Benton |
| KINGDOM CITY | Callaway | LINN | Osage |
| KINGSTON | Caldwell | LINN CREEK | Camden |

| | | | |
|---|---|---|---|
| LINNEUS | Linn | MENFRO | Perry |
| LIVONIA | Putnam | MERCER | Mercer |
| LOCKWOOD | Dade | META | Osage |
| LODI | Wayne | METZ | Vernon |
| LOHMAN | Cole | MEXICO | Audrain |
| LONEDELL | Franklin | MIAMI | Saline |
| LONE JACK | Jackson | MIDDLE BROOK | Iron |
| LONG LANE | Dallas | MIDDLETOWN | Montgomery |
| LOOSE CREEK | Osage | MILAN | Sullivan |
| LOUISBURG | Dallas | MILLER | Lawrence |
| LOUISIANA | Pike | MILLERSVILLE | Cape Girardeau |
| LOWNDES | Wayne | MILLS SPRING | Wayne |
| LOWRY CITY | St. Clair | MILO | Vernon |
| LUCERNE | Putnam | MINDENMINES | Barton |
| LUDLOW | Livingston | MINE LAMOTTE | Madison |
| LUEBBERING | Franklin | MINERAL POINT | Washington |
| LURAY | Clark | MISSOURI CITY | Clay |
| LUTESVILE | Bollinger | MOBERLY | Randolph |
| LYNCHBURG | Laclede | MOKANE | Callaway |
| MCBRIDE | Perry | MONETT | Barry |
| MCCLURG | Taney | MONROE CITY | Monroe |
| MCFALL | Gentry | MONTGOMERY CITY | Montgomery |
| MCGEE | Wayne | MONTICELLO | Lewis |
| MCGIRK | Moniteau | MONTIER | Shannon |
| MCKITTERICK | Montgomery | MONTREAL | Camden |
| MACKS CREEK | Camdon | MONTROSE | Henry |
| MACOMB | Wright | MOODY | Howell |
| MACON | Macon | MOORESVILLE | Polk |
| MADISON | Monroe | MORA | Benton |
| MAITLAND | Holt | MOREHOUSE | New Madrid |
| MALDEN | Dunklin | MORLEY | Scott |
| MALTA BEND | Saline | MORRISON | Gasconade |
| MANSFIELD | Wright | MORRISVILLE | Livingston |
| MAPAVILE | Jefferson | MORA | Benton |
| MARBLE HILL | Bollinger | MOREHOUSE | New Madrid |
| MARCELINE | Linn | MORLEY | Scott |
| MARIONVILLE | Lawrence | MORRISON | Gasconade |
| MARQUAND | Madison | MORRISVILLE | Polk |
| MARSHALL | Saline | MORSE MILL | Jefferson |
| MARSHFIELD | Webster | MOSBY | Clay |
| MARSTON | New Madrid | MOSCOW MILLS | Lincoln |
| MARTHASVILLE | Warren | MOUND CITY | Holt |
| MARTINSBURG | Audrain | MOUNDVILLE | Vernon |
| MARTINSVILLE | Harrison | MOUNTAIN GROVE | Wright |
| MARYLAND HEIGHS | St. Louis | MOUNTAIN VIEW | Howell |
| MARYVILLE | Nodaway | MOUNT VERNON | Lawrence |
| MATTHEWS | New Madrid | MYRTLE | Oregon |
| MAYSVILLE | DeKalb | NAPOLEON | Lafayette |
| MAYVIEW | Lafayette | NAYLOR | Ripley |
| MAYWOOD | Lewis | NEBO | LaClede |
| MEADVILLE | Linn | NECK CITY | Jasper |
| MEMPHIS | Scotland | NEELYVILLE | Butler |
| MENDON | Chariton | NELSON | Saline |

| | | | |
|---|---|---|---|
| NEOSHO | Newton | PASCOLA | Pemiscot |
| NEVADA | Vernon | PATTERSON | Wayne |
| NEWARK | Knox | PATTON | Bollinger |
| NEW BLOOMFIELD | Callaway | PATTONSBURG | Daviess |
| NEW BOSTON | Linn | PAYNESVILLE | Pike |
| NEWBURG | Phelps | PEACE VALLEY | Howell |
| NEW CAMBRIA | Macon | PECULIAR | Cass |
| NEW FLORENCE | Montgomery | PERKINS | Scott |
| NEW FRANKLIN | Howard | PERRY | Ralls |
| NEW HAMPTON | Harrison | PERRYVILLE | Perry |
| NEW HARTFORD | Pike | PEVELY | Jefferson |
| NEW HAVEN | Franklin | PHILADELPHIA | Marion |
| NEW LONDON | Ralls | PHILLIPSBURG | Laclede |
| NEW MADRID | New Madrid | PICKERING | Nodaway |
| NEW MELLE | St. Charles | PIEDMONT | Wayne |
| NEW OFFENBURG | St. Genevieve | PIERCE CITY | Lawrence |
| NEWTOWN | Sullivan | PILOT GROVE | Cooper |
| NEW WELLS | Cape Girardeau | PILOT KNOB | Iron |
| NIANGUA | Webster | PINEVILLE | McDonald |
| NIXA | Christian | PITTSBURG | Hickory |
| NOBLE | Ozark | PLATO | Texas |
| NOEL | McDonald | PLATTE CITY | Platte |
| NORBORNE | Carroll | PLATTSBURG | Clinton |
| NORWOOD | Wright | PLEASANT HILL | Cass |
| NOTTINGHILL | Ozark | PLEASANT HOPE | Polk |
| NOVELTY | Knox | PLEVNA | Knox |
| NOVINGER | Adair | POCAHONTAS | Cape Girardeau |
| OAK GROVE | Jackson | POINT LOOKOUT | Taney |
| OAK RIDGE | Cape Girardeau | POLK | Polk |
| ODESSA | Lafayette | POLLOCK | Sullivan |
| O'FALLON | St. Charles | POLO | Caldwell |
| OLD APPLETON | Cape Girardeau | POMONA | Howell |
| OLDFIELD | Christian | PONCE DELEON | Stone |
| OLD MONROE | Lincoln | PONTIAC | Ozark |
| OLEAN | Miller | POPLAR BLUFF | Butler |
| OLNEY | Lincoln | PORTAGE DES SIOUX | St. Charles |
| ORAN | Scott | PORTAGEVILLE | New Madrid |
| OREGON | Holt | PORTLAND | Callaway |
| ORONOGO | Jasper | POTOSI | Washington |
| ORRICK | Ray | POTTERSVILLE | Howell |
| OSAGE BEACH | Camden | POWELL | McDonald |
| OSBORN | DeKalb | POWERSITE | Taney |
| OSCEOLA | St. Clair | POWERSVILLE | Putnam |
| OTTERVILLE | Cooper | POYNOR | Ripley |
| OWENSVILLE | Gasconade | PRAIRIE HOME | Cooper |
| OXLY | Ripley | PRESTON | Hickory |
| OZARK | Christian | PRINCETON | Mercer |
| PACIFIC | Franklin | PROTEM | Taney |
| PAINTON | Stoddard | PURCELL | Jasper |
| PALMYRA | Marion | PURDIN | Linn |
| PARIS | Monroe | PURDY | Barry |
| PARMA | New Madrid | PUXICO | Stoddard |
| PARNELL | Nodaway | QUEEN CITY | Schuyler |

| | | | |
|---|---|---|---|
| QUINCY | Hickory | SAINT CLAIR | Franklin |
| QUITMAN | Nodaway | SAINTE GENEVIEVE | St. Genevieve |
| QULIN | Butler | SAINT ELIZABETH | Miller |
| RACINE | Newton | SAINT JAMES | Phelps |
| RAVENWOOD | Nodaway | SAINT JOSEPH | Buchanan |
| RAYMONDVILLE | Texas | ST. LOUIS | Independent City |
| RAYMORE | Cass | SAINT MARY'S | St. Genevieve |
| RAYVILLE | Ray | SAINT PATRICK | Clark |
| REA | Andrew | SAINT PETERS | St. Charles |
| REDFORD | Reynolds | SAINT THOMAS | Cole |
| REEDS | Jasper | SALEM | Dent |
| REEDS SPRING | Stone | SALISBURY | Chariton |
| RENICK | Randolph | SANTA FE | Monroe |
| REPUBLIC | Greene | SARCOXIE | Jasper |
| REVERE | Clark | SAVANNAH | Andrew |
| REYNOLDS | Reynolds | SAVERTON | Ralls |
| RHINELAND | Montgomery | SCHELL CITY | Vernon |
| RICHARDS | Vernon | SCOTT CITY | Scott |
| RICH HILL | Bates | SEDALIA | Pettis |
| RICHLAND | Pulaski | SEDGEWICKVILLE | Bollinger |
| RICHMOND | Ray | SELIGMAN | Barry |
| RICHWOODS | Washington | SENATH | Dunklin |
| RIDGEDALE | Taney | SENECA | Newton |
| RIDGEWAY | Harrison | SEYMOUR | Webster |
| RISCO | New Madrid | SHELBINA | Shelby |
| RIVES | Dunklin | SHELBYVILLE | Shelby |
| ROACH | Camden | SHELDON | Vernon |
| ROBERTSVILLE | Franklin | SHELL KNOB | Barry |
| ROBY | Texas | SHERIDAN | Worth |
| ROCHEPORT | Boone | SHOOK | Wayne |
| ROCKAWAY BEACH | Taney | SIBLEY | Jackson |
| ROCKBRIDGE | Ozark | SIKESTON | Scott |
| ROCK PORT | Atchinson | SILEX | Lincoln |
| ROCKVILLE | Bates | SILVA | Wayne |
| ROCKY COMFORT | McDonald | SKIDMORE | Nodaway |
| ROCKY MOUNT | Morgan | SLATER | Saline |
| ROGERSVILLE | Webster | SMITHTON | Pettis |
| ROLLA | Phelps | SMITHVILLE | Clay |
| ROMBAUER | Butler | SOLO | Texas |
| ROSCOE | St. Clair | SOUDER | Ozark |
| ROSEBUD | Gasconade | SOUTH FORK | Howell |
| ROSENDALE | Andrew | SOUTH GREENFIELD | Dade |
| ROTHVILLE | Chariton | SOUTH STERLING | Gasconde |
| RUETER | Taney | SOUTH VERNON | Lawrence |
| RUSH HILL | Audrain | SOUTH WEST CITY | McDonald |
| RUSHVILLE | Buchanan | SPARTA | Christian |
| RUSSELLVILLE | Cole | SPICKARD | Grundy |
| RUTLEDGE | Scotland | SPOKANE | Christian |
| SAGINAW | Newton | SPRINGFIELD | Greene |
| SAINT ALBANS | Franklin | SQUIRES | Douglas |
| SAINT ANN | St. Louis | STANBERRY | Gentry |
| SAINT CATHARINE | Linn | STANTON | Franklin |
| SAINT CHARLES | St. Charles | STARK CITY | Newton |

| | | | |
|---|---|---|---|
| STEEDMAN | Callaway | UNIONTOWN | Perry |
| STEELE | Pemiscot | UNIONVILLE | Putnam |
| STEELVILLE | Crawford | URBANA | Dallas |
| STEFFENVILLE | Lewis | URICH | Henry |
| STELLA | Newton | UTICA | Livingston |
| STEWARTSVILLE | DeKalb | VALLES MINES | Jefferson |
| STOCKTON | Cedar | VALLEY PARK | St. Louis |
| STOTTS CITY | Lawrence | VAN BUREN | Carter |
| STOUTLAND | Camden | VANDALIA | Audrain |
| STOUTSVILLE | Monroe | VANDUSER | Scott |
| STOVER | Morgan | VANZANT | Douglas |
| STRAFFORD | Greene | VERONA | Lawrence |
| STRASBURG | Cass | VERSAILLES | Morgan |
| STURDIVANT | Bollinger | VIBURNUM | Iron |
| STURGEON | Boone | VICHY | Maries |
| SUCCESS | Texas | VIENNA | Maries |
| SULLIVAN | Franklin | VILLA RIDGE | Franklin |
| SULPHUR SPRINGS | Jefferson | VULCAN | Iron |
| SUMMERSVILLE | Texas | WACO | Jasper |
| SUMNER | Chariton | WAKENDA | Carroll |
| SUNRISE BEACH | Camden | WALDRON | Platte |
| SWEDEBORG | Pulaski | WALKER | Vernon |
| SWEET SPRINGS | Saline | WALNUT GROVE | Greene |
| SYRACUSE | Morgan | WALNUT SHADE | Taney |
| TALLAPOOSA | New Madrid | WAPPAPELLO | Wayne |
| TANEYVILLE | Taney | WARDELL | Pemiscot |
| TARKIO | Atchison | WARRENSBURG | Johnson |
| TAYLOR | Marion | WARRENTON | Warren |
| TEBBETTS | Callaway | WARSAW | Benton |
| TECUMSEH | Ozark | WASHBURN | Barry |
| TERESITA | Shannon | WASHINGTON | Franklin |
| THAYER | Oregon | WASOLA | Ozark |
| THEODOSIA | Ozark | WAVERLY | Lafayette |
| THOMPSON | Audrain | WAYLAND | Clark |
| THORNFIELD | Ozark | WAYNESVILLE | Pulaski |
| TIFF | Washington | WEATHERBY | DeKalb |
| TIFF CITY | McDonald | WEAUBLEAU | Hickory |
| TINA | Carroll | WEBB CITY | Jasper |
| TIPTON | Moniteau | WELLINGTON | Lafayette |
| TRELOAR | Warren | WELLSVILLE | Montgomery |
| TRENTON | Grundy | WENTWORTH | Newton |
| TRIMBLE | Clinton | WENTZVILLE | St. Charles |
| TRIPLETT | Chaziton | WESCO | Crawford |
| TROY | Lincoln | WEST ALTON | St. Charles |
| TRUXTON | Lincoln | WESTBORO | Atchison |
| TUNAS | Dallas | WESTON | Platte |
| TURNERS | Greene | WESTPHALIA | Osage |
| TURNEY | Clinton | WEST PLAINS | Howell |
| TUSCUMBIA | Miller | WHEATLAND | Hickory |
| UDALL | Ozark | WHEATON | Barry |
| ULMAN | Miller | WHEELING | Livingston |
| UNION | Franklin | WHITEMAN AFB | Johnson |
| UNION STAR | DeKalb | WHITEOAK | Dunklin |

| | | | |
|---|---|---|---|
| WHITESIDE | Lincoln | BILLINGS HEIGHTS | Yellowstone |
| WHITEWATER | Cape Girardeau | BIRNEY | Rosebud |
| WILLARD | Greene | BLACK EAGLE | Cascade |
| WILLIAMSBURG | Callaway | BLOOMFIELD | Dawson |
| WILLIAMSTOWN | Lewis | BONNER | Missoula |
| WILLIAMSVILLE | Wayne | BOULDER | Jefferson |
| WILLOW SPRINGS | Howell | BOX ELDER | Hill |
| WINDSOR | Henry | BOYES | Carter |
| WINDYVILLE | Dallas | BOZEMAN | Gallatin |
| WINFIELD | Lincoln | BRADY | Pondera |
| WINIGAN | Sulivan | BRIDGER | Carbon |
| WINONA | Shannon | BROADUS | Powder River |
| WINSTON | Daviess | BROADVIEW | Yellowstone |
| WITTENBERG | Perry | BROCKTON | Roosevelt |
| WOLF ISLAND | Mississippi | BROCKWAY | McCone |
| WOOLDRIDGE | Cooper | BROWNING | Glacier |
| WORTH | Worth | BRUSETT | Garfield |
| WORTHINGTON | Putnam | BUFFALO | Fergus |
| WRIGHT CITY | Warren | BUSBY | Big Horn |
| WYACONDA | Clark | BUTTE | Silver Bow |
| WYATT | Mississippi | BYNUM | Teton |
| YUKON | Texas | CAMERON | Madison |
| ZALMA | Bollinger | CANYON CREEK | Lewis and Clark |
| ZANONI | Ozark | CAPITOL | Carter |
| **MONTANA** | | CARDWELL | Jefferson |
| ABSAROKEE | Stillwater | CARLYLE | Wilbaux |
| ACTON | Yellowstone | CARTER | Chouteau |
| ALBERTON | Mineral | CASCADE | Cascade |
| ALDER | Madison | CAT CREEK | Petroleum |
| ALZADA | Carter | CENTENNIAL | Yellowstone |
| ANACONDA | Deer Lodge | CHARLO | Lake |
| ANGELA | Rosebud | CHESTER | Liberty |
| ANTELOPE | Sheridan | CHINOOK | Blain |
| ARLEE | Lake | CHOTEAU | Teton |
| ASHLAND | Rosebud | CHRISTINA | Fergus |
| AUGUSTA | Lewis and Clark | CLINTON | Missoula |
| AVON | Powell | CLYDE PARK | Park |
| BABB | Glacier | COFFEE CREEK | Fergus |
| BAINVILLE | Roosevelt | COHAGEN | Garfield |
| BAKER | Fallon | COLSTRIP | Rosebud |
| BALLANTINE | Yellowstone | COLUMBIA FALLS | Flathead |
| BASIN | Jefferson | COLUMBUS | Stillwater |
| BEARCREEK | Carbon | CONDON | Missoula |
| BELFRY | Carbon | CONNER | Ravalli |
| BELGRADE | Gallatin | CONRAD | Pondera |
| BELT | Cascade | COOKE CITY | Park |
| BIDDLE | Powder River | CORVALLIS | Ravalli |
| BIG ARM | Lake | CORWIN SPRINGS | Park |
| BIGFORK | Flathead | CRANE | Richland |
| BIGHORN | Treasure | CRESTON | Flathead |
| BIG SANDY | Chouteau | CROW AGENCY | Big Horn |
| BIG TIMBER | Sweet Grass | CULBERTSON | Roosevelt |
| BILLINGS | Yellowstone | CUSTER | Yellowstone |

| | | | |
|---|---|---|---|
| CUT BANK | Glacier | GLEN | Beaverhead |
| DAGMAR | Sheridan | GLENDIVE | Dawson |
| DARBY | Ravalli | GLENTANA | Valley |
| DAYTON | Lake | GOLDCREEK | Powell |
| DE BORGIA | Mineral | GRANTSDALE | Ravalli |
| DECKER | Big Horn | GRASS RANGE | Fergus |
| DEER LODGE | Powell | GREAT FALLS | Cascade |
| DELL | Beaverhead | GREENOUGH | Missoula |
| DENTON | Fergus | GREYCLIFF | Sweet Grass |
| DILLON | Beaverhead | HALL | Granite |
| DIVIDE | Silver Bow | HAMILTON | Ravalli |
| DIXON | Sanders | HAMMOND | Carter |
| DODSON | Phillips | HARDIN | Big Horn |
| DRUMMOND | Granite | HARLEM | Blaine |
| DUPUYER | Pondera | HARLOWTON | Wheatland |
| DUTTON | Teton | HARRISON | Madison |
| EAST GLACIER PARK | Glacier | HATHAWAY | Rosebud |
| EAST HELENA | Lewis and Clark | HAUGAN | Mineral |
| EDGAR | Carbon | HAVRE | Hill |
| EKALAKA | Carter | HAYS | Blaine |
| ELLISTON | Powell | HEART BUTTE | Ponderosa |
| ELMO | Lake | HELENA | Lewis and Clark |
| EMIGRANT | Park | HALLGATE | Missoula |
| ENNIS | Madison | HELMVILLE | Powell |
| ESSEX | Flathead | HERON | Sanders |
| ETHRIDGE | Toole | HIGHWOOD | Chouteau |
| EUREKA | Lincoln | HILGER | Fergus |
| EVERGREEN | Flathead | HINGHAM | Hill |
| FAIRFIELD | Teton | HINDSDALE | Valley |
| FAIRVIEW | Richland | HOBSON | Judith Basin |
| FALLON | Prairie | HOGELAND | Blaine |
| FISHTAIL | Stillwater | HOMESTEAD | Sheridan |
| FLAXVILLE | Daniels | HOT SPRINGS | Sanders |
| FLORENCE | Ravalli | HUNTLEY | Yellowstone |
| FORESTGROVE | Fergus | HYSHAM | Treasure |
| FORSYTH | Rosebud | INGOMAR | Rosebud |
| FORT BENTON | Chouteau | INVERNESS | Hill |
| FORT HARRISON | Lewis and Clark | ISMAY | Custer |
| FORTINE | Lincoln | JACKSON | Beaverhead |
| FORT PECK | Valley | JEFFERSON CITY | Jefferson |
| FORT SHAW | Cascade | JOLIET | Carbon |
| FRAZER | Valley | JOPLIN | Liberty |
| FRENCHTOWN | Missoula | JORDAN | Garfield |
| FROID | Roosevelt | JUDITH GAP | Wheatland |
| FROMBERG | Carbon | KALISPELL | Flathead |
| GALATA | Toole | KEVIN | Toole |
| GALLATIN GATEWAY | Gallatin | KILA | Flathead |
| GARDINER | Park | KINSEY | Custer |
| GARRYOWEN | Big Horn | KREMLIN | Hill |
| GERALDINE | Chouteau | LAKE MCDONALD | Flathead |
| GEYSER | Judith Basin | LAKESIDE | Flathead |
| GILFORD | Hill | LAMBERT | Richland |
| GLASGOLW | Valley | LAME DEER | Rosebud |

| | | | |
|---|---|---|---|
| LARSLAN | Valley | OLNEY | Flathead |
| LAST CHANCE | Lewis and Clark | OPHEIM | Valley |
| LAUREL | Yellowstone | OTTER | Powder River |
| LAVINA | Golden Valley | OUTLOOK | Sheridan |
| LEDGER | Pondera | OVANDO | Powell |
| LEWISTOWN | Fergus | PABLO | Lake |
| LIBBY | Lincoln | PARADISE | Sanders |
| LIMA | Beaverhead | PARK CITY | Stillwater |
| LINCOLN | Lewis and Clark | PEERLESS | Daniels |
| LINDSAY | Dawson | PENDROY | Teton |
| LIVINGSTON | Park | PHILIPSBURG | Granite |
| LLOYD | Blaine | PINESDALE | Lake |
| LODGE GRASS | Big Horn | PIONEER | Yellowstone |
| LOLO | Missola | PLAINS | Sanders |
| LOMA | Chouteau | PLENTYWOOD | Sheridan |
| LONEPINE | Sanders | PLEVNA | Fallon |
| LORING | Phillips | POLARIS | Beaverhead |
| LOTHAIR | Liberty | POLEBRIDGE | Flathead |
| LUSTRE | Valley | POLSON | Lake |
| LUTHER | Carbon | POMPEYS PILLAR | Yellowstone |
| MALMSTROM AFB | Cascade | PONY | Madison |
| MALTA | Phillips | POPLAR | Roosevelt |
| MANHATTAN | Gallatin | POWER | Teton |
| MARION | Flathead | PRAY | Park |
| MARTIN CITY | Flathead | PROCTOR | Lake |
| MARTINSDALE | Meagher | PRYOR | Big Horn |
| MARYSVILLE | Lewis and Clark | RADERSBURG | Broadwater |
| MCALLISTER | Madison | RAMSAY | Silver Bow |
| MCCABE | Roosevelt | RAPELJE | Stillwater |
| MCLEOD | Sweet Grass | RAYMOND | Sheridan |
| MEDICINE LAKE | Sheridan | RAYNESFORD | Judith Basin |
| MELROSE | Silver Bow | RED LODGE | Carbon |
| MELSTONE | Musselshell | REDSTONE | Sheridan |
| MELVILLE | Sweet Grass | REEDPOINT | Stillwater |
| MILES CITY | Custer | RESERVE | Sheridan |
| MILL IRON | Carter | REXFORD | Lincoln |
| MILLSTOWN | Missoula | RICHEY | Dawson |
| MISSOULA | Missoula | RICHLAND | Valley |
| MOCCASIN | Judith Basin | RINGLING | Meagher |
| MOIESE | Lake | ROBERTS | Carbon |
| MOLT | Stillwater | ROLLINS | Lake |
| MONARCH | Cascade | RONAN | Lake |
| MONTANT CITY | Jefferson | ROSCOE | Carbon |
| MOORE | Fergus | ROSEBUD | Rosebud |
| MUSSELSHELL | Musselshell | ROUNDUP | Musselshell |
| NASHUA | Valley | ROY | Fergus |
| NEIHART | Cascade | RUDYARD | Hill |
| NIARADA | Sanders | RYEGATE | Golden Valley |
| NORRIS | Madison | SACO | Phillips |
| NOXON | Sanders | SAINT IGNATIUS | Lake |
| NYE | Stillwater | SAINT MARIE | Valley |
| OILMONT | Toole | SAINT MARY | Glacier |
| OLIVE | Powder River | SAINT REGIS | Mineral |

| | | | |
|---|---|---|---|
| SAINT XAVIER | Big Horn | VIRGINIA CITY | Madison |
| SALTESE | Mineral | VOLBORG | Custer |
| SAND COULEE | Cascade | WAGNER | Phillips |
| SANDERS | Treasure | WALKERVILLE | Silver Bow |
| SAND SPRINGS | Garfield | WARMSPRINGS | Deer Valley |
| SANTA RITA | Galacier | WESTBY | Sheridan |
| SAVAGE | Richland | WEST GLACIER | Flathead |
| SCOBEY | Daniels | WEST YELLOWSTONE | Gallatin |
| SEELEY LAKE | Missola | WHITEFISH | Flathead |
| SHAWMUT | Wheatland | WHITEHALL | Jefferson |
| SHELBY | Toole | WHITE SULPHUR SPRINGS | Meagher |
| SHEPHERD | Yellowstone | WHITETAIL | Daniels |
| SHERIDAN | Madison | WHITEWATER | Phillips |
| SHONKIN | Chouteau | WHITLASH | Liberty |
| SIDNEY | Richland | WIBAUX | Wibaux |
| SILESIA | Carbon | WILLARD | Fallon |
| SILVERGATE | Park | WILLOW CREEK | Gallatin |
| SILVER STAR | Madison | WILSALL | Park |
| SIMMS | Cascade | WINIFRED | Fergus |
| SOMERS | Flathead | WINNETT | Petroleum |
| SONNETTE | Powder River | WINSTON | Broadwater |
| SOUTHGATE | Missoula | WISDOM | Beaverhead |
| SPRINGDALE | Park | WISE RIVER | Beaverhead |
| STANFORD | Judith Basin | WOLF CREEK | Lewis and Clark |
| STEVENSVILLE | Ravalli | WOLF POINT | Roosevelt |
| STOCKETT | Cascade | WORDEN | Yellowstone |
| STRYKER | Lincoln | WYOLA | Big Horn |
| SULA | Ravalli | YELLOWTAIL | Big Horn |
| SUMATRA | Rosebud | ZORTMAN | Phillips |
| SUNBURST | Toole | ZURICH | Blaine |
| SUN RIVER | Cascade | **NEBRASKA** | |
| SUPERIOR | Mineral | ADAMS | Gage |
| SWAN LAKE | Flathead | AINSWORTH | Brown |
| SWEETGRASS | Toole | ALBION | Boone |
| TEIGEN | Petroleum | ALDA | Hall |
| TERRY | Prairei | ALEXANDRIA | Thayer |
| THOMPSON FALLS | Sanders | ALLEN | Dixon |
| THREE FORKS | Gallatin | ALLIANCE | Box Butte |
| TOSTON | Broadwater | ALMA | Harlan |
| TOWNSEND | Broadwater | ALVO | Cass |
| TREGO | Lincoln | AMELIA | Holt |
| TROUT CREEK | Sanders | AMHERST | Buffalo |
| TROY | Lincoln | ANGORA | Morrill |
| TURNER | Blaine | ANSELMO | Custer |
| TWIN BRIDGES | Madison | ANSLEY | Custer |
| TWODOT | Wheatland | ARAPAHOE | Furnas |
| ULM | Cascade | ARCADIA | Valley |
| UTICA | Judith Basin | ARCHER | Merrick |
| VALIER | Pondera | ARLINGTON | Washington |
| VANDALIA | Valley | ARNOLD | Custer |
| VAUGHN | Cascade | ARTHUR | Arthur |
| VICTOR | Ravalli | ASHBY | Grant |
| VIDA | McCone | ASHLAND | Saunders |

| | | | |
|---|---|---|---|
| ASHTON | Sherman | BRULE | Keith |
| ATKINSON | Holt | BRUNING | Thayer |
| ATLANTA | Phelps | BRUNO | Butler |
| AUBURN | Nemaha | BRUNSWICK | Antelope |
| AURORA | Hamilton | BURCHARD | Pawnee |
| AVOCA | Cass | BURR | Otoe |
| AXTELL | Kearney | BURWELL | Garfield |
| AYR | Adams | BUSHNELL | Kimball |
| BANCROFT | Cuming | BUTTE | Boyd |
| BARNESTON | Gage | BYRON | Thayer |
| BARTLETT | Wheeler | CAIRO | Hall |
| BARTLEY | Red Willow | CALLAWAY | Custer |
| BASSETT | Rock | CAMBRIDGE | Furnas |
| BATTLE CREEK | Madison | CAMPBELL | Franklin |
| BAYARD | Morrill | CARLETON | Thayer |
| BEATRICE | Gage | CARROLL | Wayne |
| BEAVER CITY | Furnas | CEDAR BLUFFS | Saunders |
| BEAVER CROSSING | Seward | CEDAR CREEK | Cass |
| BEE | Seward | CEDAR RAPIDS | Boone |
| BEEMER | Cuming | CENTER | Knox |
| BELDEN | Cedar | CENTRAL CITY | Merrick |
| BELGRADE | Nance | CERESCO | Saunders |
| BELLEVUE | Sarpy | CHADRON | Dawes |
| BELLWOOD | Butler | CHAMBERS | Holt |
| BELVIDERE | Thayer | CHAMPION | Chase |
| BENEDICT | York | CHAPMAN | Merrick |
| BENKELMAN | Dundy | CHAPPEL | Deuel |
| BENNET | Lancaster | CHESTER | Thayer |
| BENNINGTON | Douglas | CLARKS | Merrick |
| BERTRAND | Phelps | CLARKSON | Colfax |
| BERWYN | Custer | CLATONIA | Gage |
| BIG SPRINGS | Deuel | CLAY CENTER | Clay |
| BINGHAM | Sheridan | CLEARWATER | Antelope |
| BLADEN | Webster | CODY | Cherry |
| BLAIR | Washington | COLERIDGE | Cedar |
| BLOOMFIELD | Knox | COLON | Saunders |
| BLOOMINGTON | Franklin | COLUMBUS | Platte |
| BLUE HILL | Webster | COMSTOCK | Custer |
| BLUE SPRINGS | Gage | CONCORD | Dixon |
| BOELUS | Howard | COOK | Johnson |
| BOONE | Boone | CORDOVA | Seward |
| BOYS TOWN | Douglas | CORNLEA | Platte |
| BRADSHAW | York | CORTLAND | Gage |
| BRADY | Lincoln | COTESFIELD | Howard |
| BRAINARD | Butler | COZAD | Dawson |
| BREWSTER | Blaine | CRAB ORCHARD | Johnson |
| BRIDGEPORT | Morrill | CRAIG | Burt |
| BRISTOW | Boyd | CRAWFORD | Dawes |
| BROADWATER | Morrill | CREIGHTON | Knox |
| BROCK | Nemaha | CRESTON | Platte |
| BROKEN BOW | Custer | CRETE | Saline |
| BROWNLEE | Cherry | CROFTON | Knox |
| BROWNVILLE | Nemaha | CROOKSTON | Cherry |

| | | | |
|---|---|---|---|
| CULBERTSON | Hitchcock | FALLS CITY | Richardson |
| CURTIS | Frontier | FARNAM | Dawson |
| DAKOTA CITY | Dakota | FARWELL | Howard |
| DALTON | Cheyenne | FILLEY | Gage |
| DANBURY | Red Willow | FIRTH | Lancaster |
| DANNEBROG | Howard | FORDYCE | Cedar |
| DAVENPORT | Thayer | FORT CALHOUN | Washington |
| DAVEY | Lancaster | FOSTER | Pierce |
| DAVID CITY | Butler | FRANKLIN | Franklin |
| DAWSON | Richardson | FREMONT | Dodge |
| DAYKIN | Jefferson | FRIEND | Saline |
| DECATUR | Burt | FULLERTON | Nance |
| DENTON | Lancaster | FUNK | Phelps |
| DESHLER | Thayer | GARLAND | Seward |
| DEWEESE | Clay | GENEVA | Fillmore |
| DEWITT | Saline | GENOA | Nance |
| DILLER | Jefferson | GERING | Scotts Bluff |
| DIX | Kimball | GIBBON | Buffalo |
| DIXON | Dixon | GILTNER | Hamilton |
| DODGE | Dodge | GLENVIL | Clay |
| DONIPHAN | Hall | GOEHNER | Seward |
| DORCHESTER | Saline | GORDON | Sheridan |
| DOUGLAS | Otoe | GOTHENBURG | Dawson |
| DU BOIS | Pawnee | GRAFTON | Fillmore |
| DUNBAR | Otoe | GRAND ISLAND | Hall |
| DUNCAN | Platte | GRANT | Perkins |
| DUNNING | Blaine | GREELEY | Greeley |
| DWIGHT | Butler | GREENWOOD | Cass |
| EAGLE | Cass | GRESHAM | York |
| EDDYVILLE | Dawson | GRETNA | Sarpy |
| EDGAR | Clay | GUIDE ROCK | Webster |
| EDISON | Furnas | GURLEY | Cheyenne |
| ELBA | Howard | HAIGLER | Dundy |
| ELGIN | Antelope | HALLAM | Lancaster |
| ELK CREEK | Johnson | HALSEY | Thomas |
| ELKHORN | Douglas | HAMLET | Hayes |
| ELLSWORTH | Sheridan | HAMPTON | Hamilton |
| ELM CREEK | Buffalo | HARDY | Nuckolls |
| ELMWOOD | Cass | HARRISBURG | Banner |
| ELSIE | Perkins | HARRISON | Sioux |
| ELSMERE | Cherry | HARTINGTON | Cedar |
| ELWOOD | Gosper | HARVARD | Clay |
| EMERSON | Dakota | HASTINGS | Adams |
| EMMET | Holt | HAYES CENTER | Hayes |
| ENDERS | Chase | HAY SPRINGS | Sheridan |
| ENDICOTT | Jefferson | HAZARD | Sherman |
| ERICSON | Wheeler | HEARTWELL | Kearney |
| EUSTIS | Frontier | HEBRON | Thayer |
| EWING | Holt | HEMINGFORD | Box Butte |
| EXETER | Fillmore | HENDERSON | York |
| FAIRBURY | Jefferson | HERMAN | Washington |
| FAIRFIELD | Clay | HERSHEY | Lincoln |
| FAIRMONT | Fillmore | HICKMAN | Lancaster |

| | | | |
|---|---|---|---|
| HILDRETH | Franklin | LORTON | Otoe |
| HOLBROOK | Furnas | LOUISVILLE | Cass |
| HOLDREGE | Phelps | LOUP CITY | Sherman |
| HOLMESVILLE | Gage | LYMAN | Scotts Bluff |
| HOLSTEIN | Adams | LYNCH | Boyd |
| HOMER | Dakota | LYONS | Burt |
| HOOPER | Dodge | MACY | Thurston |
| HORDVILLE | Hamilton | MADISON | Madison |
| HOSKINS | Wayne | MADRID | Perkins |
| HOWELLS | Colfax | MAGNET | Cedar |
| HUBBARD | Dakota | MALCOLM | Lancaster |
| HUBBELL | Thayer | MALMO | Saunders |
| HUMBOLT | Richardson | MANLEY | Cass |
| HUMPHREY | Platte | MARQUETTE | Hamilton |
| HUNTLEY | Harlan | MARSLAND | Dawes |
| HUYANNIS | Grant | MARTELL | Lancaster |
| IMPERIAL | Chase | MASKELL | Dixon |
| INAVALE | Webster | MASON CITY | Custer |
| INDIANOLA | Red Willow | MAX | Dundy |
| INLAND | Clay | MAXWELL | Lincoln |
| INMAN | Holt | MAYWOOD | Frontier |
| ITHACA | Saunders | MC COOK | Red Willow |
| JACKSON | Dakota | MC COOL JUNCTION | York |
| JANSEN | Jefferson | MCGREW | Scotts Bluff |
| JOHNSON | Nemaha | MC LEAN | Pierce |
| JOHNSTOWN | Brown | MEAD | Saunders |
| JULIAN | Nemaha | MEADOW GROVE | Madison |
| JUNIATA | Adams | MELBETA | Scotts Bluff |
| KEARNEY | Buffalo | MEMPHIS | Saunders |
| KENESAW | Adams | MERNA | Custer |
| KENNARD | Washington | MERRIMAN | Cherry |
| KEYSTONE | Keith | MILFORD | Seward |
| KILGORE | Cherry | MILLER | Buffalo |
| KIMBALL | Kimball | MILLIGAN | Fillmore |
| LAKESIDE | Sheridan | MILLS | Keya Paha |
| LAMAR | Chase | MINATARE | Scotts Bluff |
| LAUREL | Cedar | MINDEN | Kearney |
| LAWRENCE | Nuckolls | MITCHELL | Scotts Bluff |
| LEBANON | Red Willow | MONROE | Platte |
| LEIGH | Colfax | MOOREFIELD | Frontier |
| LEMOYNE | Keith | MORRILL | Scotts Bluff |
| LEWELLEN | Garden | MORSE BLUFF | Saunders |
| LEWISTON | Pawnee | MULLEN | Hooker |
| LEXINGTON | Dawson | MURDOCK | Cass |
| LIBERTY | Gage | MURRAY | Cass |
| LINCOLN | Lancaster | NAPER | Boyd |
| LINDSAY | Platte | NAPONEE | Franklin |
| LINWOOD | Butler | NEBRASKA CITY | Otoe |
| LISCO | Garden | NEHAWKA | Cass |
| LITCHFIELD | Sherman | NELIGH | Antelope |
| LODGEPOLE | Cheyenne | NELSON | Nuckolls |
| LONG PINE | Brown | NEMAHA | Nemaha |
| LOOMIS | Phelps | NENZEL | Cherry |

| | | | |
|---|---|---|---|
| NEWCASTLE | Dixon | PLEASANT DALE | Seward |
| NEWMAN GROVE | Madison | PLEASANTON | Buffalo |
| NEWPORT | Keya Paha | PLYMOUTH | Jefferson |
| NICKERSON | Dodge | POLK | Polk |
| NIOBRARA | Knox | PONCA | Dixon |
| NORA | Nuckolls | POOLE | Buffalo |
| NORFOLK | Madison | POTTER | Cheyenne |
| NORMAN | Kearney | PRAGUE | Saunders |
| NORTH BEND | Dodge | PRIMROSE | Boone |
| NORTH LOUP | Valley | PROSSER | Adams |
| NORTH PLATTE | Lincoln | PURDUM | Blaine |
| OAK | Nuckolls | RALSTON | Douglas |
| OAKDALE | Antelope | RANDOLPH | Cedar |
| OAKLAND | Burt | RAVENNA | Buffalo |
| OBERT | Cedar | RAYMOND | Lancaster |
| OCONTO | Custer | RED CLOUD | Webster |
| OCTAVIA | Butler | REPUBLICAN CITY | Harlan |
| ODELL | Gage | REYNOLDS | Jefferson |
| ODESSA | Buffalo | RICHFIELD | Sarpy |
| OFFUTT AFB | Sarpy | RISING CITY | Butler |
| OGALLALA | Keith | RIVERDALE | Buffalo |
| OHIOWA | Fillmore | RIVERTON | Franklin |
| OMAHA | Douglas | ROCA | Lancaster |
| ONEILL | Holt | ROCKVILLE | Sherman |
| ONG | Clay | ROGERS | Colfax |
| ORCHARD | Antelope | ROSALIE | Thurston |
| ORD | Valley | ROSELAND | Adams |
| ORLEANS | Harlan | ROYAL | Antelope |
| OSCEOLA | Polk | RULO | Richardson |
| OSHKOSH | Garden | RUSHVILLE | Sheridan |
| OSMOND | Pierce | RUSKIN | Nuckolls |
| OTOE | Otoe | SADDLE CREEK | Douglas |
| OVERTON | Dawson | SAINT EDWARD | Boone |
| OXFORD | Furnas | SAINT HELENA | Cedar |
| PAGE | Holt | SAINT LIBORY | Howard |
| PALISADE | Hitchcock | SAINT MARY | Johnson |
| PALMER | Merrick | SAINT PAUL | Howard |
| PALMYRA | Otoe | SALEM | Richardson |
| PANAMA | Lancaster | SARGENT | Custer |
| PAPILLION | Sarpy | SARONVILLE | Clay |
| PARKS | Dundy | SCHUYLER | Colfax |
| PAWNEE CITY | Pawnee | SCOTIA | Greeley |
| PAXTON | Keith | SCOTTSBLUFF | Scotts Bluff |
| PENDER | Thurston | SCRIBNER | Dodge |
| PERU | Nemaha | SENECA | Thomas |
| PETERSBURG | Boone | SEWARD | Seward |
| PHILLIPS | Hamilton | SHELBY | Polk |
| PICKRELL | Gage | SHELTON | Buffalo |
| PIERCE | Pierce | SHICKLEY | Fillmore |
| PILGER | Stanton | SHUBERT | Richardson |
| PLAINVIEW | Antelope | SIDNEY | Cheyenne |
| PLATTE CENTER | Platte | SILVER CREEK | Merrick |
| PLATTSMOUTH | Cass | SMITHFIELD | Gasper |

| | | | |
|---|---|---|---|
| SNYDER | Dodge | VERDIGRE | Knox |
| SOUTH BEND | Cass | VERDON | Richardson |
| SOUTH OMAHA | Douglas | WACO | York |
| SOUTH SIOUX CITY | Dakota | WAHOO | Saunders |
| SPALDING | Greeley | WAKEFIELD | Dixon |
| SPENCER | Boyd | WALLACE | Lincoln |
| SPRAGUE | Lancaster | WALTHILL | Thurston |
| SPRINGFIELD | Sarpy | WALTON | Lancaster |
| SPRINGVIEW | Keys Paha | WASHINGTON | Washington |
| STAMFORD | Harlan | WATERBURY | Dixon |
| STANTON | Stanton | WATERLOO | Douglas |
| STAPLEHURST | Seward | WAUNETA | Chase |
| STAPLETON | Logan | WAUSA | Knox |
| STEELE CITY | Jefferson | WAVERLY | Lancaster |
| STEINAUER | Pawnee | WAYNE | Wayne |
| STELLA | Richardson | WEBB PLAZA | Grand Island |
| STERLING | Johnson | WEEPING WATER | Cass |
| STOCKVILLE | Frontier | WEISSERT | Custer |
| STRANG | Fillmore | WELLFLEET | Lincoln |
| STRATTON | Hitchcock | WESTERN | Saline |
| STROMSBURG | Polk | WESTERVILLE | Custer |
| STUART | Holt | WEST OMAHA | Omaha |
| SUMNER | Dawson | WESTON | Saunders |
| SUPERIOR | Nuckolls | WEST POINT | Cuming |
| SURPRISE | Butler | WHITECLAY | Sheridan |
| SUTHERLAND | Lincoln | WHITMAN | Grant |
| SUTTON | Clay | WHITNEY | Dawes |
| SWANTON | Sabne | WILBER | Saline |
| SYRACUSE | Otoe | WILOX | Kearney |
| TABLE ROCK | Pawnee | WILLOW ISLAND | Dawson |
| TALMAGE | Otoe | WILSONVILLE | Furnas |
| TAYLOR | Loup | WINNEBAGO | Thurston |
| TECUMSEH | Johnson | WINNETOON | Knox |
| TEKAMAH | Burt | WINSIDE | Wayne |
| THEDFORD | Thomas | WINSLOW | Dodge |
| THURSTON | Thurston | WISNER | Cuming |
| TILDEN | Antelope | WOLBACK | Greeley |
| TOBIAS | Saline | WOOD LAKE | Cherry |
| TRENTON | Hitchcock | WOOD RIVER | Hall |
| TRUMBULL | Clay | WYMORE | Gage |
| TRYON | McPherson | WYNOT | Cedar |
| UEHLING | Dodge | YORK | York |
| ULYSSES | Butler | YUTAN | Saunders |
| UNADILLA | Otoe | **NEVADA** | |
| UNION | Cass | ALAMO | Lincoln |
| VIRGINIA | Gage | AMARGOSA VALLEY | Nye |
| UPLAND | Franklin | AUSTIN | Lander |
| UTICA | Seward | BAKER | White Pine |
| VALENTINE | Cherry | BATTLE MOUNTAIN | Lander |
| VALLEY | Douglas | BEAM | Nye |
| VALPARAISO | Saunders | BEOWAWE | Eureka |
| VENANGO | Perkins | BLUE DIAMOND | Clark |
| VERDEL | Knox | BONANZA | Clark |

| | | | |
|---|---|---|---|
| BOULDER CITY | Clark | MANHATTAN | Nye |
| BUNKERVILLE | Clark | McDERMITT | Humboldt |
| CALIENTE | Lincoln | McGILL | White Pine |
| CARLIN | Elko | MERCURY | Nye |
| CARSON CITY | Carson City | MESQUITE | Clark |
| COTTONWOOD COVE | Clark | MINA | Mineral |
| CRESCENT VALLEY | Eureka | MINDEN | Douglas |
| CRYSTAL BAY | Washoe | MOAPA | Clark |
| DAYTON | Lyon | MONTELLO | Elko |
| DEETH | Elko | MOUNDHOUSE | Carson |
| DENIO | Humboldt | MOUNTAIN CITY | Elko |
| DUCKWATER | White Pine | NIXON | Washoe |
| DYER | Esmeralda | NORTH LAS VEGAS | Clark |
| EAST ELY | White Pine | OASIS | Elko |
| EAST LAS VEGAS | Clark | OROVADA | Humboldt |
| ELKO | Elko | OVERTON | Clark |
| ELY | White Pine | OWYHEE | Elko |
| EMPIRE | Washoe | PAHRUMP | Nye |
| EUREKA | Eureka | PANACA | Lincoln |
| FALLON | Churchill | PARADISE VALLEY | Humboldt |
| FALLON NAS | Churchill | PARADISE VALLEY | Clark |
| FERNLEY | Lyon | PIOCHE | Lincoln |
| GABBS | Nye | RED ROCK VISTA | Clark |
| GALENA | Washoe | RENO | Washoe |
| GARDNERVILLE | Douglas | ROUND MOUNTAIN | Nye |
| GARSIDE | Clark | RUBY VALLEY | Nye |
| GENOA | Douglas | RUTH | White Pine |
| GERLACH | Washoe | SANDY VALLEY | Clark |
| GLENBROOK | Douglas | SCHURZ | Mineral |
| GOLCONDA | Humboldt | SEARCHLIGHT | Clark |
| GOLDFIELD | Esmeralda | SIERRA | Washoe |
| GOODSPRINGS | Clark | SILVER CITY | Lyon |
| GREEN VALLEY | Clark | SILVERPEAK | Esmeralda |
| HALLECK | Elko | SILVER SPRINGS | Lyon |
| HAWTHORNE | Mineral | SMITH | Lyon |
| HENDERSON | Clark | SPARKS | Washoe |
| HIKO | Lincoln | SUN VALLEY | Washoe |
| HUNTRIDGE | Clark | SPRING VALLEY | Clark |
| IMLAY | Pershing | STATELINE | Douglas |
| INCLINE VILLAGE | Washoe | STEAMBOAT | Washoe |
| INDIAN SPRINGS | Clark | SUN VALLEY | Washoe |
| JACKPOT | Elko | TONOPAH | Nye |
| JARBIDGE | Elko | TUSCARARA | Elko |
| JEAN | Clark | UNIONVILLE | Pershing |
| JIGGS | Elko | UNIVERSITY | Washoe |
| LAMOILLO | Elko | UNIVERSITY | Clark |
| LAS VEGAS | Clark | VALMY | Humboldt |
| LAUGHLIN | Clark | VERDI | Washoe |
| LEE | Clark | VIRGINIA CITY | Storey |
| LOGANDALE | Clark | WADSWORTH | Washoe |
| LOVELOCK | Pershing | WASHINGTON | Washoe |
| LUND | White Pine | WELLINGTON | Lyon |
| LUNING | Mineral | WELLS | Elko |

| | | | |
|---|---|---|---|
| WENDOVER | Elko | DANBURY | Merrimack |
| WINNEMUCCA | Humboldt | DANVILLE | Rockingham |
| YERINGTON | Lyon | DEERFIELD | Rockingham |
| ZEPHYR COVE | Douglas | DERRY | Rockingham |
| **NEW HAMPSHIRE** | | DOVER | Strafford |
| ACWORTH | Sullivan | DREWSVILLE | Cheshire |
| ALLENSTOWN | Merrimack | DUBLIN | Cheshire |
| ALSTEAD | Cheshire | DURHAM | Strafford |
| ALTON | Belknap | EAST ANDOVER | Merrimack |
| ALTON BAY | Belknap | EAST CANDIA | Rockingham |
| AMHERST | Hillsborough | EAST DERRY | Rockingham |
| ANDOVER | Merrimack | EAST HAMPSTEAD | Rockingham |
| ANTRIM | Hillsborough | EAST HEBRON | Grafton |
| ASHLAND | Grafton | EAST KINGSTON | Rockingham |
| ASHUELOT | Cheshire | EAST LEMPSTER | Sullivan |
| ATKINSON | Rockingham | EAST SWANZEY | Cheshire |
| AUBURN | Rockingham | EAST WAKEFIELD | Carroll |
| BARNSTEAD | Belknap | ELKINS | Merrimack |
| BARRINGTON | Strafford | ENFIELD | Grafton |
| BARTLETT | Carroll | ENFIELD CENTER | Grafton |
| BATH | Grafton | EPPING | Rockingham |
| BEDFORD | Hillsborough | EPSOM | Merrimack |
| BEEBE RIVER | Grafton | ERROL | Coos |
| BELMONT | Belknap | ETNA | Grafton |
| BENNINGTON | Hillsborough | EXETER | Rockingham |
| BERLIN | Coos | FARMINGTON | Strafford |
| BETHLEHEM | Grafton | FITZWILLIAM | Cheshire |
| BOSCAWEN | Merrimack | FRANCESTOWN | Hillsborough |
| BOW | Merrimack | FRANCONIA | Grafton |
| BRADFORD | Merrimack | FRANKLIN | Merrimack |
| BRISTOL | Grafton | FREEDOM | Carroll |
| BROOKLINE | Hillsborough | FREMONT | Rockingham |
| CAMPTON | Grafton | GEORGES MILLS | Sullivan |
| CANAAN | Grafton | GILMANTON | Belknap |
| CANDIA | Rockingham | GILMANTON IRON WORKS | Belknap |
| CANTERBURY | Merrimack | GILSUM | Cheshire |
| CENTER BARNSTEAD | Belknap | GLEN | Carroll |
| CENTER CONWAY | Carroll | GLENCLIFF | Grafton |
| CENTER HARBOR | Belknap | GOFFSTOWN | Hillsborough |
| CENTER OSSIPEE | Carroll | GORHAM | Coos |
| CENTER SANDWICH | Carroll | GOSHEN | Sullivan |
| CENTER STRAFFORD | Strafford | GRAFTON | Grafton |
| CHARLESTOWN | Sullivan | GRANTHAM | Sullivan |
| CHESTER | Rockingham | GREENFIELD | Hillsborough |
| CHESTERFIELD | Cheshire | GREENLAND | Rockingham |
| CHOCORUA | Carroll | GREENVILLE | Hillsborough |
| CLAREMONT | Sullivan | GROVETON | Coos |
| COLEBROOK | Coos | GUILD | Sullivan |
| CONCORD | Merrimack | HAMPSTEAD | Rockingham |
| CONTOOCOOK | Merrimack | HAMPTON | Rockingham |
| CONWAY | Carroll | HAMPTON FALLS | Rockingham |
| CORNISH | Sullivan | HANCOCK | Hillsborough |
| CORNISH FLAT | Sullivan | HANOVER | Grafton |

| | | | |
|---|---|---|---|
| HARRISVILLE | Cheshire | NEWBURY | Merrimack |
| HAVERHILL | Grafton | NEW CASTLE | Rockingham |
| HEBRON | Grafton | NEW DURHAM | Strafford |
| HENNIKER | Merrimack | NEWFIELDS | Rockingham |
| HILL | Merrimack | NEW HAMPTON | Belknap |
| HILLSBOROUGH | Hillsborough | NEW IPSWICH | Hillsborough |
| HINSDALE | Cheshire | NEW LONDON | Merrimack |
| HOLDERNESS | Grafton | NEWMARKET | Rockingham |
| HOLLIS | Hillsborough | NEWPORT | Sullivan |
| HOOKSETT | Merrimack | NEWTON | Rockingham |
| HOPKINTON | Merrimack | NEWTON JUNCTION | Rockingham |
| HUDSON | Hillsborough | NORTH CONWAY | Carroll |
| INTERVALE | Carroll | NORTH HAMPTON | Rockingham |
| JACKSON | Carroll | NORTH HAVERHILL | Grafton |
| JAFFREY | Cheshire | NORTH SALEM | Rockingham |
| JEFFERSON | Coos | NORTH SANDWICH | Carroll |
| KEARSARGE | Carroll | NORTH STRATFORD | Coos |
| KEENE | Cheshire | NORTH SUTTON | Merrimack |
| KINGSTON | Rockingham | NORTHWOOD | Rockingham |
| LACONIA | Belknap | NORTH WOODSTOCK | Grafton |
| LANCASTER | Coos | NOTTINGHAM | Rockingham |
| LEBANON | Grafton | ORFORD | Grafton |
| LEMPSTER | Sullivan | OSSIPEE | Carroll |
| LINCOLN | Grafton | PELHAM | Hillsborough |
| LISBON | Grafton | PETERBOROUGH | Hillsborough |
| LITTLETON | Grafton | PIERMONT | Grafton |
| LOCHMERE | Belknap | PIKE | Grafton |
| LONDONDERRY | Rockingham | PITTSBURG | Coos |
| LYME | Grafton | PITTSFIELD | Merrimack |
| LYME CENTER | Grafton | PlAINSFIELD | Sullivan |
| LYNDEBOROUGH | Hillsborough | PLAISTOW | Rockingham |
| MADISON | Carroll | PLYMOUTH | Grafton |
| MANCHESTER | Hillsborough | PORTSMOUTH | Rockingham |
| MARLBOROUGH | Cheshire | POTTER PLACE | Merrimack |
| MARLOW | Cheshire | RAYMOND | Rockingham |
| MEADOWS | Coos | RINDGE | Cheshire |
| MELVIN VILLAGE | Carroll | ROCHESTER | Strafford |
| MEREDITH | Belknap | ROLLINSFORD | Strafford |
| MERIDEN | Sullivan | RUMNEY | Grafton |
| MERRIMACK | Hillsborough | RYE | Rockingham |
| MILAN | Coos | RYE BEACH | Rockingham |
| MILFORD | Hillsborough | SALEM | Rockingham |
| MILTON | Strafford | SALISBURY | Merrimack |
| MILTON MILLS | Strafford | SANBORNTON | Belknap |
| MIRROR LAKE | Carroll | SANBORNVILLE | Carroll |
| MONROE | Grafton | SANDOWN | Rockingham |
| MONT VERNON | Hillsborough | SILVER LAKE | Carroll |
| MOULTONBORO | Carroll | SOMERSWORTH | Strafford |
| MOUNT SUNAPEE | Merrimack | SOUTH DANVILLE | Rockingham |
| MOUNT WASHINGTON | Coos | SOUTH EFFINGHAM | Carroll |
| MUNSONVILLE | Cheshire | LYNDEBOROUGH | Hillsborough |
| NASHUA | Hillsborough | SOUTH NEWBURY | Merrimack |
| NEW BOSTON | Hillsborough | SOUTH SUTTON | Merrimack |

| | | | |
|---|---|---|---|
| SOUTH TAMWORTH | Carroll | ATCO | Camden |
| SPOFFORD | Cheshire | ATLANTIC CITY | Atlantic |
| STODDARD | Cheshire | ATLANTIC HIGHLANDS | Monmouth |
| STRAFFORD | Strafford | AUDUBON | Camden |
| STRATHAM | Rockingham | AUGUSTA | Sussex |
| SUNAPEE | Sullivan | AVLON | Cape May |
| SUNCOOK | Merrimack | AVENEL | Middlesex |
| TAMWORTH | Carroll | AVON BY THE SEA | Monmouth |
| TEMPLE | Hillsborough | BAPISTOWN | Hunterdon |
| TILTON | Belknap | BARNEGAT | Ocean |
| TROY | Cheshire | BARNEGAT LIGHT | Ocean |
| TWIN MOUNTAIN | Coos | BARRINGTON | Camden |
| UNION | Carroll | BASKING RIDGE | Somerset |
| WALPOLE | Cheshire | BATSTO | Atlantic |
| WARNER | Merrimack | BAY HEAD | Ocean |
| WARREN | Grafton | BAYONNE | Hudson |
| WASHINGTON | Sullivan | BAYVILLE | Ocean |
| WEARE | Hillsborough | BAYWAY | Union |
| WENTWORTH | Grafton | BEACH HAVEN | Ocean |
| WEST CHESTERFIELD | Cheshire | BEACHWOOD | Ocean |
| WESTMORELAND | Cheshire | BEDMINSTER | Somerset |
| WEST NOTTINGHAM | Rockingham | BELFORD | Monmouth |
| WEST OSSIPEE | Carroll | BELL MEAD | Somerset |
| WEST PETERBOROUGH | Hillsborough | BELLEVILLE | Essex |
| WEST SPRINGFIELD | Sullivan | BELLMAWR | Camden |
| WEST STEWARTSTOWN | Coos | BELMAR | Monmouth |
| WEST SWANZEY | Cheshire | BELVIDERE | Warren |
| WHITEFIELD | Coos | BERGEN | Hudson |
| WILMOT FLAT | Merrimack | BERGENFIELD | Bergen |
| WILTON | Hillsborough | BERGENLINE | Hudson |
| WINCHESTER | Cheshire | BERGEN POINT | Hudson |
| WINDHAM | Rockingham | BERKELEY HEIGHTS | Union |
| WINNISQUAM | Belknap | BERLIN | Camden |
| WOLFEBORO | Carroll | BERNARDSVILLE | Somerset |
| WOLFEBORO FALLS | Carroll | BEVERLY | Burlington |
| WONALANCET | Carroll | BIRMINGHAM | Burlington |
| WOODSVILLE | Grafton | BLACKWOOD | Camden |
| **NEW JERSEY** | | BLACKWOOD TERRACE | Gloucester |
| ABSECON | Atlantic | BLAIRSTOWN | Warren |
| ADELPHIA | Monmouth | BLAWENBURG | Somerset |
| ALLAMUCHY | Warren | BLOOMFIELD | Essex |
| ALLENDALE | Bergen | BLOOMINGDALE | Passaic |
| ALLENHURST | Monmouth | BLOOMSBURY | Hunterdon |
| ALLENTOWN | Monmouth | BOGOTA | Bergen |
| ALLENWOOD | Monmouth | BOONTON | Morris |
| ALLOWAY | Salem | BORDENTOWN | Burlington |
| ALLWOOD | Passaic | BOUND BROOK | Somerset |
| ALPHA | Warren | BRADLEY BEACH | Monmouth |
| ALPINE | Bergen | BRAINY BORO | Middlesex |
| AMPERE | Essex | BRANCHVILLE | Sussex |
| ANDOVER | Sussex | BRICK | Ocean |
| ANNANDALE | Hunterdon | BRIDGEPORT | Gloucester |
| ASBURY | Warren | BRIDGETON | Cumberland |

| | | | |
|---|---|---|---|
| BRIDGEWATER | Somerset | COLUMBUS | Burlington |
| BRIELLE | Monmouth | COOKSTOWN | Burlington |
| BRIGANTINE | Atlantic | CRANBURY | Middlesex |
| BROADWAY | Warren | CRANFORD | Union |
| BROOKDALE | Essex | CREAMRIDGE | Monmouth |
| BROOKSIDE | Morris | CRESSKILL | Bergen |
| BROWNS MILLS | Burlington | CROSSWICKS | Burlington |
| BROWNTOWN | Middlesex | DAYTON | Middlesex |
| BUDD LAKE | Morris | DEAL | Monmouth |
| BUENA | Atlantic | DEEPWATER | Salem |
| BURLINGTON | Burlington | DEERFIELD STREET | Cumberland |
| BUTLER | Morris | DELAIR | Camden |
| BUTTZVILLE | Warren | DELANCO | Burlington |
| CALDWELL | Essex | DELAWANNA | Passaic |
| CALIFON | Hunterdon | DELAWARE | Warren |
| CAMDEN | Camden | DELMONT | Cumberland |
| CAMPBELLS JUNCTION | Monmouth | DELRAN | Riverside |
| CAPE MAY | Cape May | DEMAREST | Bergen |
| CAPE MAY POINT | Cape May | DENNISVILLE | Cape May |
| CARLSTADT | Bergen | DENVILLE | Morris |
| CARNEYS POINT | Salem | DEPTFORD | Gloucester |
| CARTERET | Middlesex | DIVIDING CREEK | Cumberland |
| CASSVILLE | Hudson | DODDTOWN | Essex |
| CEDAR BROOK | Camden | DORCHESTER | Cumberland |
| CEDAR GROVE | Essex | DOROTHY | Atlantic |
| CEDAR KNOLLS | Morris | DOVER | Morris |
| CEDARVILLE | Cumberland | DUMONT | Bergen |
| CHAMBERSBURG | Mercer | DUNDEE | Passaic |
| CHANGEWATER | Warren | DUNELLEN | Middlesex |
| CHATHAM | Morris | EAST BRUNSWICK | Middlesex |
| CHATSWORTH | Burlington | EAST CAMDEN | Camden |
| CHERRY HILL | Camden | EAST HANOVER | Morris |
| CHESTER | Morris | EAST KEANSBURG | Monmouth |
| CHESTNUT | Union | EAST ORANGE | Essex |
| CINNAMINSON | Burlington | EAST RUTHERFORD | Bergen |
| CIRCLE | Mercer | EATONTOWN | Monmouth |
| CLARK | Union | EDGEWATER | Bergen |
| CLARKSBORO | Gloucester | EDISON | Middlesex |
| CLARKSBURG | Monnwuth | EGG HARBOR CITY | Atlantic |
| CLAYTON | Gloucester | ELBERON | Monmouth |
| CLEMENTON | Camden | ELIZABETH | Union |
| CLIFF PARK | Bergen | ELIZABETHPORT | Union |
| CLIFFSIDE PARK | Bergen | ELLISBURG | Camden |
| CLIFFWOOD | Monmouth | ELMER | Salem |
| CLIFTON | Passaic | ELMORA | Union |
| CLINTON | Hunterdon | ELMWOOD PARK | Bergen |
| CLOSTER | Bergen | ELWOOD | Atlantic |
| COAST GUARD BASE | Cape May | EMERSON | Bergen |
| COLLINGSWOOD | Camden | ENGLEWOOD | Bergen |
| COLOGNE | Atlantic | ENGLEWOOD CLIFFS | Bergen |
| COLONIA | Middlesex | ENGLISHTOWN | Monmouth |
| COLTS NECK | Monmouth | ERNSTON | Middlesex |
| COLUMBIA | Warren | ESSEX FELLS | Essex |

| | | | |
|---|---|---|---|
| ESTELL MANOR | Atlantic | GREYSTONE PARK | Morris Plains |
| EWAN | Gloucester | GROVE | Essex |
| FAIRFIELD | Essex | GUTTENBERG | Hudson |
| FAIR HAVEN | Monmouth | HACKENSACK | Berpn |
| FAIR LAWN | Bergen | HACKETTSTOWN | Warren |
| FAIRTON | Cumberland | HADDONFIELD | Camden |
| FAIRVIEW | Bergen | HADDON HEIGHTS | Camden |
| FANWOOD | Union | HAINESPORT | Burlington |
| FAR HILLS | Somerset | HALEDON | Passaic |
| FARMINGDALE | Monmouth | HAMBURG | Sussex |
| FIVE CORNERS | Hudson | HAMMONTON | Atlantic |
| FLAGTOWN | Somerset | HAMPTON | Hunterdon |
| FLANDERS | Morris | HANCOCKS BRIDGE | Salem |
| FLEMINGTON | Hunterdon | HARRINGTON PARK | Bergen |
| FLORENCE | Burlington | HARRISON | Hudson |
| FLORHAM PARK | Morris | HARRISONVILE | Gloucester |
| FORDS | Middlesex | HARVEY CEDARS | Ocean |
| FORKED RIVER | Ocean | HASBROUCK HEIGHTS | Bergen |
| FORT DIX | Mercer | HASKELL | Passaic |
| FORTESCUE | Cumberland | HAWORTH | Bergen |
| FORT HANCOCK | Monmouth | HAWTHORNE | Passaic |
| FORT LEE | Bergen | HAZLET | Monmouth |
| FORT MONMOUTH | Monmouth | HEISLERVILLE | Cumberland |
| FRANKLIN | Sussex | HELMETTA | Middlesex |
| FRANKLIN LAKES | Bergen | HEWITT | Passaic |
| FRANKLIN PARK | Somerset | HIBERNIA | Morris |
| FRANKLINVILLE | Gloucester | HIGH BRIDGE | Hunterdon |
| FREDON TOWNSHIP | Sussex | HIGHLAND LAKES | Sussex |
| FREEHOLD | Monmouth | HIGHLAND PARK | Middlesex |
| FRENCHTOWN | Hunterdon | HIGHLANDS | Monmouth |
| GARFIELD | Bergen | HIGHTSTOWN | Mercer |
| GARWOOD | Union | HILLCREST | Passaic |
| GIBBSBORO | Camden | HILLSDALE | Bergen |
| GIBBSTOWN | Gloucester | HILLSIDE | Union |
| GILLETTE | Morris | HOBOKEN | Hudson |
| GLADSTONE | Somerset | HO HO KUS | Bergen |
| GLASSBORO | Gloucester | HOLMDEL | Monmouth |
| GLASSER | Sussex | HOPATCONG | Sussex |
| GLENDORA | Camden | HOPE | Warren |
| GLEN GARDNER | Hunterdon | HOPEWELL | Mercer |
| GLEN RIDGE | Essex | HOWELL | Monmouth |
| GLENWOOD | Sussex | HUDSON CITY | Hudson |
| GLOUCESTER CITY | Camden | HUDSON HEIGHTS | Hudson |
| GOSHEN | Cape May | IMLAYSTOWN | Monmouth |
| GRASSELLI | Union | INDUSTRIAL HILLSIDE | Bergen |
| GREAT MEADOWS | Warren | IRONBOUND | Essex |
| GREEN BROOK | Middlesex | IRONIA | Morris |
| GREEN CREEK | Cape May | IRVINGTON | Essex |
| GREENDELL | Sussex | ISELIN | Middlesex |
| GREEN VILLAGE | Morris | ISLAND HEIGHTS | Ocean |
| GREENVILLE | Hudson | JACKSON | Ocean |
| GREENWICH | Cumberland | JAMESBURG | Middlesex |
| GRENLOCH | Gloumftr | JERSEY CITY | Hudson |

| | | | |
|---|---|---|---|
| JOBSTOWN | Burlington | MADISON | Morris |
| JOHNSONBURG | Warren | MAGNOLIA | Camden |
| JOURNAL SQUARE | Hudson | MAHWAH | Bergen |
| JULIUSTOWN | Burlington | MALAGA | Gloucester |
| KEANSBURG | Monmouth | MANAHAWKIN | Ocean |
| KEARNY | Hudson | MANASQUAN | Monmouth |
| KEASBEY | Middlesex | MANTOLOKING | Ocean |
| KENDALL PARK | Middlesex | MANTUA | Gloucester |
| KENILWORTH | Union | MANVILLE | Somerset |
| KENVIL | Morris | MAPLECREST | Essex |
| KEYPORT | Monmouth | MAPLE SHADE | Burlington |
| KINGSTON | Somerset | MAPLEWOOD | Essex |
| KINNELON | Morris | MARGATE CITY | Atlantic |
| KIRKWOOD VOORHEES | Camden | MARLBORO | Monmouth |
| LAFAYETTE | Sussex | MARLTON | Burlington |
| LAKE HIAWATHA | Morris | MARMORA | Cape May |
| LAKE HOPATCONG | Morris | MARTINSVILLE | Somerset |
| LAKEHURST | Ocean | MATAWAN | Monmouth |
| LAKEWOOD | Ocean | MAURICETOWN | Cumberland |
| LAMBERTVILLE | Hunterdon | MAYS LANDING | Atlantic |
| LANDING | Morris | MAYWOOD | Bergen |
| LANDISVILLE | Atlantic | MCAFFE | Sussex |
| LANOKA HARBOR | Ocean | MCGUIRE AFB | Mercer |
| LAUREL SPRINGS | Camden | MEADOWS | Hudson |
| LAURENCE HARBOR | Middlesex | MEADOWVIEW | Hudson |
| LAVALLETTE | Ocean | MEDFORD | Burlington |
| LAWNSIDE | Camden | MEDFORD LAKES | Burlington |
| LEONIA | Bergen | MENDHAM | Morris |
| LAYTON | Sussex | MENLO PARK | Middlesex |
| LEBANON | Hunterdon | MERCERVILLE | Mercer |
| LEDGEWOOD | Morris | MERCHANTVILLE | Camden |
| LEEDS POINT | Atlantic | METUCHEN | Middlesex |
| LEESBURG | Cumberland | MICKLETON | Gloucester |
| LEONARDO | Monmouth | MIDDLESEX | Middlesex |
| LIBERTY CORNER | Somerset | MIDDLETOWN | Monmouth |
| LINCOLN PARK | Morris | MIDDLEVILLE | Sussex |
| LINCROFT | Monmouth | MIDLAND PARK | Bergen |
| LINDEN | Union | MILFORD | Hunterdon |
| LINWOOD | Atlantic | MILLBURN | Essex |
| LITTLE FALLS | Passaic | MILLINGTON | Morris |
| LITTLE FERRY | Bergen | MILLTOWN | Middlesex |
| LITTLE SILVER | Monmouth | MILLVILLE | Cumberland |
| LITTLE YORK | Hunterdon | MILMAY | Atlantic |
| LIVINGSTON | Essex | MINOTOLA | Atlantic |
| LODI | Bergen | MIZPAH | Atlantic |
| LONG BEACH | Ocean | MONITOR | Hudson |
| LONG BRANCH | Monmouth | MONMOUTH BEACH | Monmouth |
| LONG PORT | Atlantic | MONMOUTH JUNCTION | Middlesex |
| LONG VALLEY | Morris | MONROEVILLE | Salem |
| LUMBERTON | Burlington | MONTCLAIR | Essex |
| LYNDHURST | Bergen | MONTVALE | Bergen |
| LYONS | Somerset | MONTVILLE | Morris |
| MCAFEE | Sussex | MOONACHIE | Bergen |

| | | | |
|---|---|---|---|
| MOORESTOWN | Burlington | OAK RIDGE | Passaic |
| MORGANVILLE | Monmouth | OCEAN CITY | Cape May |
| MORRIS PLAINS | Morris | OCEAN GATE | Ocean |
| MORRISTOWN | Morris | OCEAN GROVE | Monmouth |
| MOUNTAIN LAKES | Morris | OCEANPORT | Monmouth |
| MOUNTAINSIDE | Bergen | OCEAN VIEW | Cape May |
| MOUNT ARLINGTON | Morris | OCEANVILLE | Atlantic |
| MOUNT EPHRAIM | Camden | OGDENSBURG | Sussex |
| MOUNT FREEDOM | Morris | OLD BRIDGE | Middlesex |
| MOUNT HOLLY | Burlington | OLD TAPPAN | Westwood |
| MOUNT LAUREL | Burlington | OLDWICK | Hunterdon |
| MOUNT ROYAL | Gloucester | ORADELL | Bergen |
| MOUNT TABOR | Morris | ORANGE | Essex |
| MUHLENBERG | Somerset | OSBORNVILLE | Ocean |
| MULLICA HILL | Gloucester | OUTWATER | Bergen |
| MYSTIC ISLANDS | Ocean | OVERBROOK | Essex |
| NATIONAL PARK | Gloucester | OXFORD | Warren |
| NAVESINK | Monmouth | PACKANACK LAKE | Passaic |
| NEPTUNE | Monmouth | PALISADE | Bergen |
| NEPTUNE CITY | Monmouth | PALISADES PARK | Bergen |
| NESHANIC STATION | Somerset | PALMER SQUARE | Mercer |
| NETCONG | Morris | PALMYRA | Burlington |
| NETHERWOOD | Somerset | PAMRAPO | Hudson |
| NEWARK | Essex | PARAMUS | Bergen |
| NEW BRUNSWICK | Middlesex | PARK RIDGE | Bergen |
| NEW EGYPT | Ocean | PARLIN | Middlesex |
| NEWFIELD | Gloucester | PARSIPPANY | Morris |
| NEWFOUNDLAND | Passaic | PASSAIC | Passaic |
| NEW GRETNA | Burlington | PASSAIC PARK | Passaic |
| NEW LISBON | Burlington | PATERSON | Passaic |
| NEW MILFORD | Bergen | PATTENBURG | Warren |
| NEWPORT | Cumberland | PAULSBORO | Gloucester |
| NEW PROVIDENCE | Union | PEAPACK | Somerset |
| NEWTON | Sussex | PEDRICKTOWN | Salem |
| NEWTONVILLE | Atlantic | PEMBERTON | Burlington |
| NEW VERNON | Morris | PENNINGTON | Mercer |
| NIXON | Middlesex | PENNSAUKEN | Camden |
| NORMA | Salem | PENNSGROVE | Salem |
| NORMANDY BEACH | Ocean | PENNSVILLE | Salem |
| NORTH ARLINGTON | Bergen | PEQUANNOCK | Morris |
| NORTH BERGEN | Hudson | PERRINEVILLE | Monmouth |
| NORTH BRUNSWICK | Middlesex | PERTH AMBOY | Middlesex |
| NORTH CAPE MAY | Cape May | PHILLIPSBURG | Warren |
| NORTH CENTER | Essex | PICATINNY ARSENAL | Morris |
| NORTH ELIZABETH | Union | PINE BEACH | Ocean |
| NORTHFIELD | Atlantic | PINE BROOK | Morris |
| NORTH WILDWOOD | Cape May | PISCATAWAY | Middlesex |
| NORTHVALE | Bergen | PITMAN | Gloucester |
| NORWOOD | Bergen | PITTSTOWN | Hunterdon |
| NUTLEY | Essex | PLAINFIELD | Union |
| OAKHURST | Monmouth | PLAINSBORO | Middlesex |
| OAKLAND | Bergen | PLEASANTVILLE | Atlantic |
| OAKLYN | Camden | PLUCKEMIN | Somerset |

| | | | |
|---|---|---|---|
| POINT PLEASANT BEACH | Ocean | SECAUCUS | Hudson |
| POMONA | Atlantic | SERGEANTSVILLE | Hunterdon |
| POMPTON LAKES | Passaic | SEWAREN | Middlesex |
| POMPTON PLAINS | Morris | SEWELL | Gloucester |
| PORT ELIZABETH | Cumberland | SHILOH | Cumberland |
| PORT MONMOUTH | Monmouth | SHORT HILLS | Essex |
| PORT MURRAY | Warren | SICKLERVILLE | Camden |
| PORT NORRIS | Cumberland | SKILLMAN | Sonierset |
| PORT READING | Middlesex | SOMERDALE | Camden |
| PORT REPUBLIC | Atlantic | SOMERSET | Sonierset |
| POTTERSVILLE | Somerset | SOMERS POINT | Atlantic |
| PRINCETON | Mercer | SOMERVILLE | Somerset |
| PRINCTON JUNCTION | Mercer | SOUTH AMBOY | Middlesex |
| PUAKERTOWN | Hunterdon | SOUTH ARLINGTON | Morris |
| QUINTON | Salem | SOUTH BOUND BROOK | Somerset |
| RAHWAY | Union | SOUTH DENNIS | Cape May |
| RAMSEY | Bergen | SOUTH EPHRAIM | Camden |
| RANCOCAS | Burlington | SOUTH FREEDON | Morris |
| RARITAN | Somerset | SOUTH HOLLY | Burlington |
| READINGTON | Hunterdon | SOUTH LAUREL | Burlington |
| RED BANK | Monmouth | SOUTH ORANGE | Essex |
| RICHLAND | Atlantic | SOUTH PLAINFIELD | Middlesex |
| RICHWOOD | Gloucester | SOUTH RIVER | Middlesex |
| RIDGEFIELD | Bergen | SOUTH ROYAL | Gloucester |
| RIDGEFIELD PARK | Bergen | SOUTH SEAVILLE | Cape May |
| RIDGEWOOD | Bergen | SOUTH TABOR | Morris |
| RINGOES | Hunterdon | SPARTA | Sussex |
| RINGWOOD | Passaic | SPOTSWOOD | Middlesex |
| RIO GRANDE | Cape May | SPRINGFIELD | Union |
| RIVERDALE | Morris | SPRING LAKE | Monmouth |
| RIVER EDGE | Bergen | STANHOPE | Sussex |
| RIVERSIDE | Burlington | STANTON | Hunterdon |
| RIVERTON | Burlington | STEWARTSVILLE | Warren |
| ROCHELLE PARK | Bergen | STILLWATER | Sussex |
| ROCKAWAY | Morris | STIRLING | Morris |
| ROCKY HILL | Somerset | STOCKHOLM | Sussex |
| ROEBLING | Burlington | STOCKTON | Hunterdon |
| ROOSEVELT | Monmouth | STONE HARBOR | Cape May |
| ROSELAND | Essex | STRATFORD | Camden |
| ROSELLE | Union | STRATHMERE | Cape May |
| ROSEMONT | Hunterdon | SUCCASUNNA | Morris |
| ROSENHAYN | Cumberland | SUMMIT | Union |
| RUMSON | Monmouth | SUSSEX | Sussex |
| RUNNEMEDE | Camden | SWARTSWOOD | Sussex |
| RUTHERFORD | Bergen | SWEDESBORO | Gloucester |
| SADDLE RIVER | Bergen | MOUNT TABOR | Morris |
| SALEM | Salem | TEANECK | Bergen |
| SAYREVILLE | Middlesex | TENAFLY | Bergen |
| SCHOOLEYS MOUNTAIN | Morris | TENNENT | Moninouth |
| SCOTCH PLAINS | Union | THOROFARE | Gloucester |
| SEA GIRTH | Momnouth | THREE BRIDGES | Hunterdon |
| SEA ISLE CITY | Cape May | TITUSVILLE | Mercer |
| SEASIDE PARK | Ocean | TOMS RIVER | Ocean |

| | | | |
|---|---|---|---|
| TOWACO | Morris | ALAMOGORDO | Ortero |
| TOTOWA | Passaic | ALBUQUERQUE | Bernalillo |
| TRANQUILITY | Sussex | ALCALDE | Rio Arriba |
| TRENTON | Mercer | ALTO | Lincoln |
| TUCKAHOE | Cape May | AMALIA | Taos |
| TUCKERTON | Ocean | AMISTAD | Union |
| UNION | Union | ANIMAS | Hidalgo |
| UNION CITY | Hudson | ANTHONY | Dona Ana |
| VAUXHALL | Union | ANTON CHICO | Guadalupe |
| VERNON | Sussex | ARAGON | Catron |
| VIENNA | Warren | ARENAS VALLEY | Grant |
| VILLAS | Cape May | ARREY | Sierra |
| VINCENTOWN | Burlington | ARROYO HONDO | Taos |
| VINELAND | Cumberland | ARROYO SECO | Taos |
| WALDWICK | Bergen | ARTESIA | Eddy |
| WALLPACK CENTER | Sussex | AZTEC | San Juan |
| WANAQUE | Passaic | BARD | Quay |
| WARETOWN | Ocean | BAYARD | Grant |
| WASHINGTON | Warren | BELEN | Valencia |
| WATERFORD WORKS | Camden | BELLVIEW | Curry |
| WAYNE | Passaic | BENT | Otero |
| WENONAH | Gloucester | BERNALILLO | Sandoval |
| WEST BERLIN | Camden | BINGHAM | Socorro |
| WEST CREEK | Ocean | BLANCO | San Juan |
| WESTFIELD | Union | BLOOMFIELD | San Juan |
| WEST LONG BRANCH | Monmouth | BLUEWATER | Cibola |
| WEST MILFORD | Passaic | BOSQUE | Valencia |
| WEST NEW YORK | Hudson | BROADVIEW | Curry |
| WESTVILLE | Gloucester | BUCKHORN | Grant |
| WESTWOOD | Bergen | BUENA VISTA | Mora |
| WHARTON | Morris | BUEYEROS | Harding |
| WHIPPANY | Morris | CABALLO | Sierra |
| WHITEHOUSE | Hunterdon | CANJILON | Rio Arriba |
| WHITE HOUSE STATION | Hunterdon | CANONES | Rio Arriba |
| WHITESBORO | Cape May | CAPITAN | Lincoln |
| WICKATUNK | Monmouth | CAPROCK | Lea |
| WILDWOOD | Cape May | CAPULIN | Union |
| WILLIAMSTOWN | Gloucester | CARLSBAD | Eddy |
| WILLINGBORO | Burlington | CARRIZOZO | Lincoln |
| WINDSOR | Mercer | CARSON | Taos |
| WINSLOW | Camden | CASA BLANCA | Cibola |
| WOODBINE | Cape May | CAUSEY | Roosevelt |
| WOODBRIDGE | Middlesex | CEBOLLA | Rio Arriba |
| WOODBURY | Gloucester | CEDAR CREST | Bernalillo |
| WOODBURY HEIGHTS | Gloucester | CEDARVALE | Torrance |
| WOODSTOWN | Salem | CENTRAL | Grant |
| WRIGHTSTOWN | Burlington | CERRILLOS | Santa Fe |
| WYCKOFF | Bergen | CERRO | Taos |
| YARDVILLE | Mercer | CHACON | Mora |
| ZAREPATH | Somerset | CHAMA | Rio Arriba |
| **NEW MEXICO** | | CHAMBERINO | Dona Ana |
| ABIQUIU | Rio Arriba | CHAMISAL | Taos |
| ALAMO | Socorro | CHIMAYO | Rio Arriba |

| | | | |
|---|---|---|---|
| CHURCH ROCK | McKinley | FORT SUMNER | DeBaca |
| CIMARRON | Colfax | FORT WINGGATE | McKinley |
| CLAUNCH | Socorro | FRUITLAND | San Juan |
| CLAYTON | Union | GALLINA | Rio Arriba |
| CLEVELAND | Mora | GALLUP | McKinley |
| CLIFF | Grant | GARFIELD | Dona Ana |
| CLOUDCROFT | Otero | GARITA | San Miguel |
| CLOVIS | Curry | GILA | Grant |
| COLUMBUS | Luna | GLADSTONE | Union |
| CONTINENTAL DIVIDE | McKinley | GLENCOE | Lincoln |
| CORDOVA | Rio Arriba | GLENRIO | Quay |
| CORONA | Lincoln | GLENWOOD | Catron |
| CORRALES | Sandoval | GLORIETA | Santa Fe |
| COSTILLA | Taos | GONZALES RANCH | San Miguel |
| COYOTE | Rio Arriba | GRADY | Curry |
| CROSSROADS | Lea | GRANTS | Cibola |
| CROWNPOINT | McKinley | GRENVILLE | Union |
| CUBA | Sandoval | GUADALUPITA | Mora |
| CUBERO | Cibola | HACHITA | Grant |
| CUCHILLO | Sierra | HAGERMAN | Chaves |
| CUERVO | Guadalupe | HANOVER | Grant |
| DATIL | Catron | HATCH | Dona Ana |
| DEMING | Luna | HIGH ROLLS MOUNTAIN PARK | Otero |
| DERRY | Sierra | HILLSBORO | Sierra |
| DES MOINES | Union | HOBBS | Lea |
| DEXTER | Chaves | HOLLOMAN AIR FORCE BASE | Otero |
| DIXON | Rio Arriba | HOLMAN | Mora |
| DONA ANA | Dona Ana | HONDO | Lincoln |
| DORA | Roosevelt | HOPE | Eddy |
| DULCE | Rio Arriba | HOUSE | Quay |
| DURAN | Torrance | HURLEY | Grant |
| EAGLE NEST | Colfax | ISLETA | Bernalillo |
| EAST VRAIN | Curry | JAL | Lea |
| EDGEWOOD | Santa Fe | JAMESTOWN | McKinley |
| ELEPHANT BUTTE | Sierra | JARALES | Valencia |
| ELIDA | Roosevelt | JEMEZ PUEBLO | Sandoval |
| EL PRADO | Taos | JEMEZ SPRINGS | Sandoval |
| EL RITO | Rio Arriba | KENNA | Roosevelt |
| EMBUDO | Rio Arriba | KIRTLAND | San Juan |
| ENCINO | Torrance | LAGUNA | Cibola |
| ESPANOLA | Rio Arriba | LAJARA | Sandoval |
| ESTANCIA | Torrance | LAJOYA | Socorro |
| EUNICE | Lea | LAKE ARTHUR | Chaves |
| FAIRACRES | Dona Ana | LAKEWOOD | Eddy |
| FARMINGTON | San Juan | LAGUNA | Bernalillo |
| FAYWOOD | Grant | LALOMA | Guadalupe |
| FENCE LAKE | Cibola | LALUZ | Otero |
| FIVE POINTS | Bernalillo | LAMADERA | Rio Arriba |
| FLORA VISTA | San Juan | LAMESA | Dona Ana |
| FLOYD | Roosevelt | LAPLATA | San Juan |
| FLYING H | Chaves | LAS CRUCES | Dona Ana |
| FOLSOM | Union | LAS TABLAS | Rio Arriba |
| FORT STANTON | Lincoln | LAS VEGAS | San Miguel |

| | | | |
|---|---|---|---|
| LEDOUX | Mora | OROGRANDE | Otero |
| LEMITAR | Socorro | PAGUATE | Cibola |
| LINCOLN | Lincoln | PECOS | San Miguel |
| LINDRITH | Rio Arriba | PENA BLANCA | Sandoval |
| LOCO HILLS | Eddy | PENASCO | Taos |
| LOGAN | Quay | PEP | Roosevelt |
| LORDSBURG | Hidalgo | PERALTA | Valencia |
| LOS ALAMOS | Los Alamos | PETACA | Rio Arriba |
| LOS LUNAS | Valencia | PICACHO | Lincoln |
| LOS OJOS | Rio Arriba | PIE TOWN | Catron |
| LOVING | Eddy | PINON | Otero |
| LOVINGTON | Lea | PLACITAS | Sandoval |
| LUMBERTON | Rio Arriba | POLVADERA | Socorro |
| LUNA | Catron | PONDEROSA | Sandoval |
| MCALISTER | Quay | PORTALES | Roosevelt |
| MCDONALD | Lea | PREWITT | McKinley |
| MCINTOCH | Torrance | QUAY | Quay |
| MAGDALENA | Socorro | QUEMADO | Catron |
| MALAGA | Eddy | QUESTA | Taos |
| MALJAMAR | Lea | RADIUM SPRINGS | Dona Ana |
| MAXWELL | Colfax | RAINSVILLE | Mora |
| MAYHILL | Otero | RAMAH | McKinley |
| MEDANALES | Rio Arriba | RANCHOS DE TAOS | Taos |
| MELROSE | Curry | RATON | Colfax |
| MESCALERO | Otero | RED RIVER | Taos |
| MESILLA | Dona Ana | REHOBOTH | McKinley |
| MESILLA PARK | Dona Ana | RESERVE | Catron |
| MESQUITE | Dona Ana | RIBERA | San Miguel |
| MEXICAN SPRINGS | McKinley | RINCON | Dona Ana |
| MILLS | Harding | ROCIADA | San Miguel |
| MILNESAND | Roosevelt | RODEO | Hidalgo |
| MIMBRES | Grant | ROGERS | Roosevelt |
| MONTEZUMA | San Miguel | ROSWELL | Chaves |
| MONTICELLO | Sierra | ROWE | San Miguel |
| MONUMENT | Lea | ROY | Harding |
| MORA | Mora | RUIDOSO | Lincoln |
| MORIARTY | Torrance | RUIDOSO DOWNS | Lincoln |
| MOSQUERO | Harding | RUTHERON | Rio Arriba |
| MOUNTAINAIR | Torrance | SACRAMENTO | Otero |
| MOUNT DORA | Union | SAINT VRAIN | Curry |
| MULE CREEK | Grant | SALEM | Dona Ana |
| NAGEEZI | San Juan | SAN ACACIA | Socorro |
| NARA VISA | Quay | SAN ANTONIO | Socorro |
| NAVAJO DAM | San Juan | SAN CRISTOBAL | Taos |
| NEWCOMB | San Juan | SANDIA PARK | Bernalillo |
| NEWKIRK | Guadalupe | SAN FIDEL | Cibola |
| NEW LAGUNA | Cibola | SAN JON | Quay |
| NOGAL | Lincoln | SAN JOSE | San Miguel |
| OCATE | Mora | SAN JUAN PUEBLO | Rio Arriba |
| OIL CENTER | Lea | SAN MATEO | Cibola |
| OJO CALIENTE | Taos | SAN MIGUEL | Dona Ana |
| OJO SARCO | Rio Arriba | SANOSTEE | San Juan |
| ORGAN | Dona Ana | SAN PATRICIO | Lincoln |

| | | | |
|---|---|---|---|
| SAN RAFAEL | Cibola | WILLARD | Torrance |
| SANTA CRUZ | Santa Fe | WILLIAMSBURG | Sierra |
| SANTA FE | Santa Fe | WINSTON | Sierra |
| SANTA ROSA | Guadalupe | YESO | DeBaca |
| SANTO DOMINGO PUEBLO | Sandoval | YOUNGSVILLE | Rio Arriba |
| SAN YSIDRO | Sandoval | ZOLLOMAN AFB | Otero |
| SEBOYETA | Cibola | ZUNI | McKinley |
| SEDAN | Union | **NEW YORK** | |
| SENA | San Miguel | ACCORD | Ulster |
| SENECA | Union | ACRA | Greene |
| SERAFINA | San Miguel | ADAMS | Jefferson |
| SHIPROCK | San Juan | ADAMS BASIN | Monroe |
| SILVER CITY | Grant | ADAMS CENTER | Jefferson |
| SOCORRO | Socorro | ADDISON | Steuben |
| SOLANO | Harding | ADIRONDACK | Warren |
| SPRINGER | Colfax | AFTON | Chenango |
| STEAD | Union | AKRON | Erie |
| SUNLAND PARK | Dona Ana | ALABAMA | Genesee |
| SUNSPOT | Otero | ALBANY | Albany |
| TAIBAN | DeBaca | ALBERTSON | Nassau |
| TAOS | Taos | ALBION | Orleans |
| TATUM | Lea | ALCOVE | Albany |
| TERERRO | San Miguel | ALDEN | Erie |
| TESUQUE | Santa Fe | ALDER CREEK | Oneida |
| TEXICO | Curry | ALEXANDER | Genesee |
| THOREAU | McKinley | ALEXANDRIA BAY | Jefferson |
| TIERRA AMARILLA | Rio Arriba | ALFRED | Allegany |
| TIJERAS | Bernalillo | ALFRED STATION | Allegany |
| TINNIE | Lincoln | ALLEGANY | Cattaraugus |
| TORATCHI | McKinley | ALLENTOWN | Allegany |
| TOME | Valencia | ALMA | Allegany |
| TORREON | Torrance | ALMOND | Allegany |
| TRAMPAS | Taos | ALPINE | Schuyler |
| TREMENTINA | San Miguel | ALPLAUS | Schenectady |
| TRES PIEDRAS | Taos | ALTAMONT | Albany |
| TRUTH OR CONSEQUENCES | Sierra | ALTMAR | Oswego |
| TUCUMCARI | Quay | ALTON | Wayne |
| TULAROSA | Otero | ALTONA | Clinton |
| TYRONE | Grant | AMAGANSETT | Suffolk |
| UTE PARK | Colfax | AMAWALK | Westchester |
| VADITO | Taos | AMENIA | Dutchess |
| VALDEZ | Taos | AMITYVILLE | Suffolk |
| VALLECITOS | Rio Arriba | AMSTERDAM | Montgomery |
| VANADIUM | Grant | ANCRAM | Columbia |
| VAUGHN | Guadalupe | ANCRAMDALE | Columbia |
| VEGUITA | Socorro | ANDES | Delaware |
| VELARDE | Rio Arriba | ANDOVER | Allegany |
| VILLANUEVA | San Miguel | ANGELICA | Allegany |
| WAGON MOUND | Mora | ANGOLA | Erie |
| WATERFLOW | San Juan | ANNANDALE ON HUDSON | Dutchess |
| WATROUS | Mora | ANSONIA | New York |
| WEED | Otero | ANTWERP | Jefferson |
| WHITES CITY | Eddy | APALACHIN | Tioga |

| | | | |
|---|---|---|---|
| APPLETON | Niagara | BEAVER DAMS | Schuyler |
| APULIA STATION | Onondaga | BEAVER FALLS | Lewis |
| AQUEBOGUE | Suffolk | BEDFORD | Westchester |
| ARCADE | Wyoming | BEDFORD HILLS | Westchester |
| ARDEN | Orange | BELFAST | Allegany |
| ARDSLEY | Westchester | BELLEVILLE | Jefferson |
| ARDSLEY-ON-HUDSON | Westchester | BELLMORE | Nassau |
| ARGYLE | Washington | BELLONA | Yates |
| ARKPORT | Steuben | BELLPORT | Suffolk |
| ARKVILLE | Delaware | BELLVALE | Orange |
| ARMONK | Westchester | BELMONT | Allegany |
| ASHLAND | Greene | BEMUS POINT | Chautauqua |
| ASHVILLE | Chautauqua | BERGEN | Genesee |
| ATHENS | Greene | BERKSHIRE | Tioga |
| ATHOL | Warren | BERLIN | Rensselaer |
| ATHOL SPRINGS | Erie | BERNE | Albany |
| ATLANTA | Steuben | BERNHARDS BAY | Oswego |
| ATLANTIC BEACH | Nassau | BETHEL | Sullivan |
| ATTACA | Wyoming | BETHPAGE | Nassau |
| AUBURN | Cayuga | BIBLE SCHOOL PARK | Broome |
| AURORA | Cayuga | BIG FLATS | Chemung |
| AU SABLE CHASM | Clinton | BIG INDIAN | Ulster |
| AU SABLE FORKS | Essex | BILLINGS | Dutchess |
| AUSTERLITZ | Columbia | BINGHAMTON | Broome |
| AVA | Oneida | BLACK CREEK | Allegany |
| AVERILL PARK | Rensselaer | BLACK RIVER | Jefferson |
| AVOCA | Steuben | BLASDELL | Erie |
| AVON | Livingston | BLAUVELT | Rockland |
| BABYLON | Suffolk | BLISS | Wyoming |
| BAINBRIDGE | Chenango | BLODGETT MILLS | Cortland |
| BAKERS MILLS | Warren | BLOOMINGBURG | Sullivan |
| BALDWIN | Nassau | BLOOMINGDALE | Essex |
| BALDWIN PLACE | Putnam | BLOOMING GROVE | Orange |
| BALDWINSVILLE | Onondaga | BLOOMINTON | Ulster |
| BALLSTON LAKE | Saratoga | BLOOMVILLE | Delaware |
| BALLSTON SPA | Saratoga | BLOSSVALE | Oneida |
| BALMAT | Saint Lawrence | BLUE MOUNTAIN LAKE | Hamilton |
| BANGALL | Dutchess | BLUE POINT | Suffolk |
| BARKER | Niagara | BOHEMIA | Suffolk |
| BARNES CORNERS | Lewis | BOICEVILLE | Ulster |
| BARNEVELD | Oneida | BOLIVAR | Allegany |
| BARRYTOWN | Dutcheas | BOLTON LANDING | Warren |
| BARRYVILLE | Sullivan | BOMBAY | Franklin |
| BARTON | Tioga | BOONVILLE | Oneida |
| BASOM | Genesee | BOSTON | Erie |
| BATAVIA | Genesee | BOUCKVILLE | Madison |
| BATH | Steuben | BOVINA CENTER | Delaware |
| BAYPORT | Suffolk | BOWMANSVILLE | Erie |
| BAY SHORE | Suffolk | BRADFORD | Steuben |
| BAYVILLE | Nassau | BRAINARD | Rensselaer |
| BEACON | Dutchess | BRAINARDSVILLE | Franklin |
| BEAR MOUNTAIN | Rockland | BRANCHPORT | Yates |
| BEARSVILLE | Ulster | BRANT | Erie |

| | | | |
|---|---|---|---|
| BRANTINGHAM | Lewis | CANASTOTA | Madison |
| BRANT LAKE | Warren | CANDOR | Tioga |
| BRASHER FALLS | Saint Lawrence | CANEADEA | Allegany |
| BREESPORT | Chemung | CANISTEO | Steuben |
| BRENTWOOD | Suffolk | CANTON | Saint Lawrence |
| BREWERTON | Onondaga | CAPE VINCENT | Jefferson |
| BREWSTER | Putnam | CARLE PLACE | Nassau |
| BRIARCLIFF MANOR | Westchester | CARLISLE | Schoharie |
| BRIDGEHAMPTON | Suffolk | CARMEL | Putnam |
| BRIDGEPORT | Madison | CAROGA LAKE | Fulton |
| BRIDGEWATER | Oneida | CARTHAGE | Jefferson |
| BRIER HILL | Saint Lawrence | CASSADAGA | Chautauqua |
| BRIGHTWATERS | Suffolk | CASSVILLE | Oneida |
| BROADALBIN | Fulton | CASTILE | Wyoming |
| BROCKPORT | Monroe | CASTLE CREEK | Broome |
| BROCTON | Chautauqua | CASTLE POINT | Dutchess |
| BRONX | Bronx | CASTLETON ON HUDSON | Rensselaer |
| BROOKFIELD | Madison | CASTORLAND | Lewis |
| BROOKHAVEN | Suffolk | CATHEDRAL | New York |
| BROOKLYN | Kings | CATO | Cayuga |
| BROOKTONDALE | Tompkins | CATSKILL | Greene |
| BROOKVIEW | Rensselaer | CATTARAUGUS | Cattaraugus |
| BROWNVILLE | Jefferson | CAYUGA | Cayuga |
| BRUSHTON | Franklin | CAYUTA | Schuyler |
| BUCHANAN | Westchester | CAZENOVIA | Madison |
| BUFFALO | Erie | CEDARHURST | Nassau |
| BULLVILLE | Orange | CELORON | Chautauqua |
| BURDETT | Schuyler | CEMENTON | Greene |
| BURKE | Franklin | CENTEREACH | Suffolk |
| BURLINGHAM | Sullivan | CENTER MORICHES | Suffolk |
| BURLINGTON FLATS | Otsego | CENTERPORT | Suffolk |
| BURNT HILLS | Saratoga | CENTERVILLE | Allegany |
| BURT | Niagara | CENTRAL BRIDGE | Schoharie |
| BUSKIRK | Rensselaer | CENTRAL ISLIP | Suffolk |
| BYRON | Genesee | CENTRAL SQUARE | Oswego |
| CADYVILLE | Clinton | CENTRAL VALLEY | Orange |
| CAIRO | Greene | CERES | Allegany |
| CALCIUM | Jefferson | CHADWICKS | Oneida |
| CALEDONIA | Livingston | CHAFFEE | Erie |
| CALLICOON | Sullivan | CHAMPLAIN | Clinton |
| CALLICOON CENTER | Sullivan | CHAPPAQUA | Westchester |
| CALVERTON | Suffolk | CHARLOTTEVILLE | Schoharie |
| CAMBRIDGE | Washington | CHASE MILLS | Saint Lawrence |
| CAMDEN | Oneida | CHATEAUGAY | Franklin |
| CAMERON | Steuben | CHATHAM | Columbia |
| CAMERON MILLS | Steuben | CHAUMONT | Jefferson |
| CAMILLUS | Onondaga | CHAUTAUQUA | Chautauqua |
| CAMPBELL | Steuben | CHAZY | Clinton |
| CAMPBELL HALL | Orange | CHELSEA | Dutchess |
| CANAAN | Columbia | CHEMUNG | Chemung |
| CANAJOHARIE | Montgomery | CHENANGO BRIDGE | Broome |
| CANANDAIGUA | Ontario | CHENANGO FORKS | Broome |
| CANASERAGA | Allegany | CHERRY CREEK | Chautauqua |

| | | | |
|---|---|---|---|
| CHERRY PLAIN | Rensselaer | COLUMBIA | Herkimer |
| CHERRY VALLEY | Otsego | COLLTMBIAVILLE | Columbia |
| CHESTER | Orange | COMMACK | Suffolk |
| CHESTERTOWN | Warren | COMSTOCK | Washington |
| CHICHESTER | Ulster | CONESUS | Livingston |
| CHILDWOLD | Saint Lawrence | CONEWANGO VALLEY | Cattaraugus |
| CHIPPEWA BAY | Saint Lawrence | CONGERS | Rockland |
| CHITTENANGO | Madison | CONKLIN | Broome |
| CHURCHVILLE | Monroe | CONNELLY | Ulster |
| CHURUBUSCO | Clinton | CONSTABLE | Franklin |
| CICERO | Onondaga | CONSTABLEVILLE | Lewis |
| CINCINNATUS | Cortland | CONSTANTIA | Oswego |
| CIRCLEVILLE | Orange | COOKS FALLS | Delaware |
| CLARENCE | Erie | COOPERS PLAINS | Steuben |
| CLARENCE CENTER | Erie | COOPERSTOWN | Otsego |
| CLARENDON | Orleans | COPAKE | Columbia |
| CLARK MILLS | Oneida | COPAKE FALLS | Columbia |
| CLARKSON | Monroe | COPENHAGEN | Lewis |
| CLARKSVILLE | Albany | COPIAGUE | Suffolk |
| CLARYVILLE | Sullivan | CORAM | Suffolk |
| CLAVERACK | Columbia | CORBETTSVILLE | Broome |
| CLAY | Onondaga | CORFU | Genesee |
| CLAYTON | Jefferson | CORINTH | Saratoga |
| CLAYVILLE | Oneida | CORNING | Steuben |
| CLEMONS | Washington | CORNWALL | Orange |
| CLEVELAND | Oswego | CORNWALL ON HUDSON | Orange |
| CLEVERDALE | Warren | CORNWALLVILLE | Greene |
| CLIFTON | Monroe | CORTLAND | Cortland |
| CLIFTON PARK | Saratoga | COSSAYUNA | Washington |
| CLIFTON SPRINGS | Ontario | COTTEKILL | Ulster |
| CLIMAX | Greene | COWLESVILLE | Wyoming |
| CLINTON | Oneida | COXSACKIE | Greene |
| CLINTON CORNERS | Dutchess | CRAGSMOOR | Ulster |
| CLINTONDALE | Ulster | CRANBERRY LAKE | Saint Lawrence |
| CLOCKVILLE | Madison | CRARYVILLE | Columbia |
| CLYDE | Wayne | CRITTENDEN | Erie |
| CLYMER | Chautauqua | CROGHAN | Lewis |
| COBLESKILL | Schoharie | CROMPOND | Westchester |
| COCHECTON | Sullivan | CROPSEYVILLE | Rensselaer |
| COCHECTON CENTER | Sullivan | CROSS RIVER | Westchester |
| COEYMANS | Albany | CROTON FALLS | Westchester |
| COEYMANS HOLLOW | Albany | CROTON-ON-HUDSON | Westchester |
| COHOCTON | Steuben | CROWN POINT | Essex |
| COHOES | Albany | CUBA | Allegany |
| COLCHESTER | Delaware | CUDDEBACKVILLE | Orange |
| COLD BROOK | Herkimer | CUTCHOGUE | Suffolk |
| COLDEN | Erie | CUYLER | Cortland |
| COLD SPRING | Putnam | DALE | Wyoming |
| COLD SPRING HARBOR | Suffolk | DALTON | Livingston |
| COLLIERSVILLE | Otsego | DANNEMORA | Clinton |
| COLLINS | Erie | DANSVILLE | Livingston |
| COLLINS CENTER | Erie | DANDEE | Herkimer |
| COLTON | Saint Lawrence | DARIEN CENTER | Genesee |

| | | | |
|---|---|---|---|
| DAVENPORT | Delaware | EAST DURHAM | Greene |
| DAVENPORT CENTER | Delaware | EAST FREETOWN | Cortland |
| DAYTON | Cattarougus | EAST GREENBUSH | Rensselaer |
| DEANSBORO | Oneida | EAST GREENWICH | Washington |
| DEER PARK | Suffolk | EAST HAMPTON | Suffolk |
| DEER RIVER | Lewis | EAST HOMER | Cortland |
| DEFERIET | Jefferson | EAST ISLIP | Suffolk |
| DEKALB JUNCTION | Saint Lawrence | EAST JAMES | Suffolk |
| DELANCEY | Delaware | EAST JEWETT | Greene |
| DELANSON | Schenectady | EAST JOHNSVILLE | Fulton |
| DELEVAN | Cattaraugus | EAST MARION | Suffolk |
| DELHI | Delaware | EAST MEADOW | Nassau |
| DELMAR | Albany | EAST MEREDITH | Delaware |
| DELPHI FALLS | Onondaga | EAST MORICHES | Suffolk |
| DENMARK | Lewis | EAST NASSAU | Rensselaer |
| DENVER | Delaware | EAST NORTHPORT | Suffolk |
| DEPAUVILLE | Jefferson | EAST NORWICH | Nassau |
| DEPEW | Erie | EAST OTTO | Cattaraugus |
| DE PEYSER | St. Lawrence | EAST PALMYRA | Wayne |
| DEPEYSTER | Saint Lawrence | EAST PEMBROKE | Genesee |
| DEPOSIT | Broome | EAST PHARSALIA | Chenango |
| DERBY | Erie | EASTPORT | Suffolk |
| DE RUYTER | Madison | EAST QUOGUE | Suffolk |
| DERUYTER | Madison | EAST RANDOLPH | Cattaraugus |
| DEWITTVILLE | Chautauqua | EAST ROCHESTER | Monroe |
| DEXTER | Jefferson | EAST ROCKAWAY | Nassau |
| DIAMOND POINT | Warren | EAST SCHODACK | Rensselaer |
| DICKINSON CENTER | Franklin | EAST SETAUKET | Suffolk |
| DOBBS FERRY | Westchester | EAST SPRINGFIELD | Otsego |
| DOLGEVILLE | Herkimer | EAST SYRACUSE | Onondaga |
| DORLOO | Schoharie | EAST WILLIAMSON | Wayne |
| DOVER PLAINS | Dutchess | EAST WORCESTER | Otsego |
| DOWNSVILLE | Delaware | EATON | Madison |
| DRESDEN | Yates | EDDYVILLE | Ulster |
| DRYDEN | Tompkins | EDEN | Erie |
| DUANESBURG | Schenectady | EDMESTON | Otsego |
| DUNDEE | Yates | EDWARDS | Saint Lawrence |
| DUNKIRK | Chautauqua | ELBA | Genesee |
| DURHAM | Greene | ELBRIDGE | Onondaga |
| DURHAMVILLE | Oneida | ELDRED | Sullivan |
| EAGLE BAY | Herkimer | ELIZABETHTOWN | Essex |
| EAGLE BRIDGE | Rensselaer | ELIZAVILLE | Columbia |
| EAGLE HARBOR | Orleans | ELKA PARK | Greene |
| EARLTON | Greene | ELLENBURG | Clinton |
| EARLVILLE | Madison | ELLENBURG CENTER | Clinton |
| EAST AMHERST | Erie | ELLENBURG DEPOT | Clinton |
| EAST AURORA | Erie | ELLENVILLE | Ulster |
| EAST BERNE | Albany | ELLICOTTVILLE | Cattaraugus |
| EAST BETHANY | Genesee | ELLINGTON | Chautauqua |
| EAST BLOOMFIELD | Ontario | ELLISBURG | Jefferson |
| EAST BRANCH | Delaware | ELMA | Erie |
| EAST CHATHAM | Columbia | ELMIRA | Chemung |
| EAST CONCORD | Erie | ELMSFORD | Westchester |

| | | | |
|---|---|---|---|
| ENDICOTT | Broome | FRANKLIN SQUARE | Nassau |
| ERIEVILLE | Madison | FRANKLINVILLE | Cattaraugus |
| ERIN | Chemung | FREDONIA | Chautauqua |
| ESOPUS | Ulster | FREEDOM | Cattaraugus |
| ESPERANCE | Schoharie | FREEHOLD | Greene |
| ESSEX | Essex | FREEPORT | Nassau |
| ETNA | Tompkins | FREEVILLE | Tompkins |
| EVANS MILLS | Jefferson | FREMONT CENTER | Sullivan |
| FABIUS | Onondaga | FREWSBURG | Chautauqua |
| FAIRFIELD | Herkimer | FRIENDSHIP | Allegany |
| FAIR HAVEN | Cayuga | FULTON | Oswego |
| FAIRPORT | Monroe | FULTONHAM | Schoharie |
| FALCONER | Chautauqua | FULTONVILLE | Montgomery |
| FALLSBURG | Sullivan | GABRIELS | Franklin |
| FANCHER | Orleans | GAINESVILLE | Wyoming |
| FARMERSVILLE STATION | Cattaraugus | GALLUPVILLE | Schoharie |
| FARMINGDALE | Nassau | GALWAY | Saratoga |
| FARMINGVILLE | Suffolk | GANSEVOORT | Saratoga |
| FARNHAM | Erie | GARDEN CITY | Nassau |
| FAR ROCKAWAY | Queens | GARDINER | Ulster |
| FAYETTE | Seneca | GARNERVILLE | Rockland |
| FAYETTEVILLE | Onandaga | GARRATTSVILLE | Otsego |
| FELTS MILLS | Jefferson | GARRISON | Putnam |
| FERNDALE | Sullivan | GASPORT | Niagara |
| FEURA BUSH | Albany | GENESO | Livingston |
| FILLMORE | Allegany | GENEVA | Ontario |
| FINDLEY LAKE | Chautauqua | GENOA | Cayuga |
| FINE | Saint Lawrence | GEORGETOWN | Madison |
| FINEVIEW | Jefferson | GERMAN FLATTS | Herkimer |
| FISHERS | Ontario | GERMANTOWN | Columbia |
| FISHER ISLAND | Suffolk | GERRY | Chautauqua |
| FISHER LANDING | Jefferson | GETZVILLE | Erie |
| FISHKILL | Dutchess | GHENT | Columbia |
| FISHS EDDY | Delaware | GILBERSVILLE | Otsego |
| FLEISCHMANNS | Delaware | GILBOA | Schoharie |
| FLORAL PARK | Nassau | GLASCO | Ulster |
| FLORIDA | Orange | GLEN AUBREY | Broome |
| FLUSHING | Queens | GLEN COVE | Nassau |
| FLY CREEK | Otsego | GLENFIELD | Lewis |
| FONDA | Montgomery | GLENFORD | Ulster |
| FORESTPORT | Oneida | GLENHAM | Dutchess |
| FORESTVILLE | Chautauqua | GLEN HEAD | Nassau |
| FORT ANN | Washington | GLENMONT | Albany |
| FORT COVINGTON | Franklin | GLENS FALLS | Warren |
| FORT EDWARD | Washington | GLEN SPEY | Sullivan |
| FORT HUNTER | Montgomery | GLEN WILD | Sullivan |
| FORT JOHNSON | Montgomery | GLENWOOD | Erie |
| FORT MONTGOMERY | Orange | GLENWOOD LANDING | Nassau |
| FORT PLAIN | Montgomery | GLOVERSVILLE | Fulton |
| FOSTERDALE | Sullivan | GODEFFROY | Orange |
| FRANKFORT | Herkimer | GOLDENS BRIDGE | Westchester |
| FRANKLIN | Delaware | GORHAM | Ontario |
| FRANKLIN SPRINGS | Onedia | GOSHEN | Orange |

| | | | |
|---|---|---|---|
| GOUVERNEUR | Saint Lawrence | HARRIMAN | Orange |
| GOWANDA | Cattaraugus | HARRIS | Sullivan |
| GRAFTON | Rensselaer | HARRISON | Westchester |
| GRAHAMSVILLE | Sullivan | HARRISVILLE | Lewis |
| GRAND GORGE | Delaware | HARTFORD | Washington |
| GRAND ISLAND | Erie | HARTSDALE | Westchester |
| GRANITE SPRINGS | Westchester | HARTWICK | Otsego |
| GRANVILLE | Washington | HARTWICK SEMINARY | Otsego |
| GREAT BEND | Jefferson | HASTINGS | Oswego |
| GREAT NECK | Nassau | HAUPPAGE | Suffolk |
| GREAT RIVER | Suffolk | HAVERSTRAW | Rockland |
| GREAT VALLEY | Cattaraugus | HAWTHORNE | Westchester |
| GREENE | Chenango | HECTOR | Schuyler |
| GREENFIELD CENTER | Saratoga | HELENA | Saint Lawrence |
| GREENFIELD PARK | Ulster | HELMUTH | Erie |
| GREENHURST | Chautauqua | HEMLOCK | Livingston |
| GREENLAWN | Suffolk | HEMPSTEAD | Nassau |
| GREENPORT | Suffolk | HENDERSON | Jefferson |
| GREENVALE | Nassau | HENDERSON HARBOR | Jefferson |
| GREENVILLE | Greene | HENRIETTA | Monroe |
| GREENWICH | Washington | HENSONVILLE | Greene |
| GREENWOOD | Steuben | HERKIMER | Herkimer |
| GREENWOOD LAKE | Orange | HERMON | Saint Lawrence |
| GREIG | Lewis | HERRINGS | Jefferson |
| GROTON | Tompkins | HEUVELTON | Saint Lawrence |
| GROVELAND | Livingston | HEWLETT | Nassau |
| GUILDERLAND | Albany | HICKSVILLE | Nassau |
| GUILDERLAND CENTER | Albany | HIGH FALLS | Ulster |
| GUILFORD | Chenango | HIGHLAND | Ulster |
| HADLEY | Saratoga | HIGHLAND FALLS | Orange |
| HAGAMAN | Montgomery | HIGHLAND LAKE | Sullivan |
| HAGUE | Warren | HIGHLAND MILLS | Orange |
| HAILESBORO | Saint Lawrence | HIGHMOUNT | Ulster |
| HAINES FALLS | Greene | HILLBURN | Rockland |
| HALCOTTSVILLE | Delaware | HILLSDALE | Columbia |
| HALL | Ontario | HILTON | Monroe |
| HAMBURG | Eire | HIMROD | Yates |
| HAMDEN | Delaware | HINCKLEY | Oneida |
| HAMILTON | Madison | HINSDALE | Cattaraugus |
| HAMLIN | Monroe | HOBART | Delaware |
| HAMMOND | Saint Lawrence | HOFFMEISTER | Hamilton |
| HAMMONDSPORT | Steuben | HOGANSBURG | Franklin |
| HAMPTON | Washington | HOLBROOK | Suffolk |
| HAMPTON BAYS | Suffolk | HOLCOMB | Ontario |
| HANCOCK | Delaware | HOLLAND | Erie |
| HANKINS | Sullivan | HOLLAND PATENT | Oneida |
| HANNACROIX | Greene | HOLLEY | Orleans |
| HANNAWA FALLS | Saint Lawrence | HOLLOWVILLE | Columbia |
| HANNIBAL | Oswego | HOLMES | Dutchess |
| HARFORD | Cortland | HOLMESVILLE | Chenango |
| HARFORD MILLS | Cortland | HOLTSVILLE | Suffolk |
| HARPERSFIELD | Delaware | HOMER | Cortland |
| HARPURSVILLE | Broome | HONEOYE | Ontario |

| | | | |
|---|---|---|---|
| HONEOYE FALLS | Monroe | JOHNSVILLE | Rensselaer |
| HOOSICK | Rensselaer | JOHNSTOWN | Fulton |
| HOOSICK FALLS | Rensselaer | JORDAN | Onondaga |
| HOPEWELL JUNCTION | Dutchess | JORDANVILLE | Herkimer |
| HORNELL | Steuben | KANONA | Steuben |
| HORSEHEADS | Chemung | KATONAH | Westchester |
| HORTONVILLE | Sullivan | KATTSKILL BAY | Warren |
| HOUGHTON | Allegany | KAUNEONGA LAKE | Sullivan |
| HOWELLS | Orange | KEENE | Essex |
| HOWES CAVE | Schoharie | KEENE VALLEY | Essex |
| HUBBARDVILLE | Madison | KEESEVILLE | Essex |
| HUDSON | Columbia | KELLY CORNERS | Delaware |
| HUDSON FALLS | Washington | KENDALL | Orleans |
| HUGHSONVILLE | Dutchess | KENNEDY | Chautauqua |
| HUGUENOT | Orange | KENOZA LAKE | Sullivan |
| HULETTS LANDING | Washington | KENT | Orleans |
| HUME | Allegany | KERHONKSON | Ulster |
| HUNT | Livingston | KEUKA PARK | Yates |
| HUNTER | Greene | KIAMESHA LAKE | Sullivan |
| HUNTINGTON | Suffolk | KILLAWOG | Broome |
| HUNTINGTON STATION | Suffolk | KILL BUCK | Cattaraugus |
| HURLEY | Ulster | KINDERHOOK | Columbia |
| HURLEYVILLE | Sullivan | KING FERRY | Cayuga |
| HYDE PARK | Dutchess | KINGS PARK | Suffolk |
| ILLION | Herkimer | KINGSTON | Ulster |
| INDIAN LAKE | Hamilton | KIRKVILLE | Onondaga |
| INDUSTRY | Monroe | KIRKWOOD | Broome |
| INLET | Hamilton | KNAPP CREEK | Cattaraugus |
| INTERLAKEN | Seneca | KNOWLESVILLE | Orleans |
| IONIA | Ontario | KNOX | Albany |
| IRVING | Chautauqua | KNOXBORO | Oneida |
| IRVINGTON | Westchester | KORTRIGHT | Delaware |
| ISLAND PARK | Nassau | LACONA | Oswego |
| ISLIP | Suffolk | LAFARGEVILLE | Jefferson |
| ISLIP TERRACE | Suffolk | LAFAYETTE | Onondaga |
| ITHACA | Tompkins | LAGRANGEVILLE | Dutchess |
| JACKSONVILLE | Tompkins | LAKE CLEAR | Franklin |
| JAMAICA | Queens | LAKE GEORGE | Warren |
| JAMESPORT | Suffolk | LAKE GROVE | Suffolk |
| JAMESTOWN | Chautauqua | LAKE HILL | Ulster |
| JAMESVILLE | Onondaga | LAKE HUNTINGTON | Sullivan |
| JASPER | Steuben | LAKE KATRINE | Ulster |
| JAVA CENTER | Wyoming | LAKE LUZERNE | Warren |
| JAVA VILLAGE | Wyoming | LAKEMONT | Yates |
| JAY | Essex | LAKE PEEKSKILL | Putnam |
| JEFFERSON | Schoharie | LAKE PLACID | Essex |
| JEFFERSON VALLEY | Westchester | LAKE PLEASANT | Hamilton |
| JEFFERSONVILLE | Sullivan | LAKE VIEW | Erie |
| JERICHO | Nassau | LAKEVILLE | Livingston |
| JEWETT | Greene | LAKEWOOD | Chautauqua |
| JOHNSBURG | Warren | LANCASTER | Erie |
| JOHNSON | Orange | LANESVILLE | Greene |
| JOHNSON CITY | Broome | LARCHMONT | Westchester |

| | | | |
|---|---|---|---|
| LATHAM | Albany | LOWVILLE | Lewis |
| LAUREL | Suffolk | LYCOMING | Oswego |
| LAURENS | Otsego | LYNBROOK | Nassau |
| LAWRENCE | Nassau | LYNDONVILLE | Orleans |
| LAWRENCEVILLE | Saint Lawrence | LYON MOUNTAIN | Clinton |
| LAWTONS | Erie | LYONS | Wayne |
| LAWYERSVILLE | Schoharie | LYONS FALLS | Lewis |
| LEBANON | Madison | LYSANDER | Onondaga |
| LEBANON SPRINGS | Columbia | MCCONNELLSVILLE | Oneida |
| LEE CENTER | Oneida | MCDONOUGH | Chenango |
| LEEDS | Greene | MCGRAW | Cortland |
| LEICESTER | Livingston | MCLEAN | Tompkins |
| LEON | Cattaraugus | MACEDON | Wayne |
| LEONARDSVILLE | Madison | MACHIAS | Cattaraugus |
| LE ROY | Genesee | MADISON | Madison |
| LEVITTOWN | Nassau | MADRID | Saint Lawrence |
| LEWBEACH | Sullivan | MAHOPAC | Putnam |
| LEWIS | Essex | MAHOPAC FALLS | Putnam |
| LEWISTON | Niagara | MAINE | Broome |
| LEXINGTON | Greene | MALDEN BRIDGE | Columbia |
| LIBERTY | Sullivan | MALDEN ON HUDSON | Ulster |
| LILY DALE | Chautauqua | MALLORY | Oswego |
| LIMA | Livingston | MALONE | Franklin |
| LIMERICK | Jefferson | MALVERNE | Nassau |
| LIMESTONE | Cattaraugus | MAMARONECK | Westchester |
| LINCOLNDALE | Westchester | MANCHESTER | Ontario |
| LINDENHURST | Suffolk | MANHASSET | Nassau |
| LINDLEY | Steuben | MANHEIN | Herkimer |
| LINWOOD | Livingston | MANLIUS | Onondaga |
| LISBON | Saint Lawrence | MANNSVILLE | Jefferson |
| LISLE | Broome | MANORVILLE | Suffolk |
| LITCHFIELD | Herkimer | MAPLECREST | Greene |
| LITTLE FALLS | Herkimer | MAPLE SPRINGS | Chautauqua |
| LITTLE GENESEE | Allegany | MAPLE VIEW | Oswego |
| LITTLE VALLEY | Cattaraugus | MARATHON | Cortland |
| LITTLE YORK | Cortland | MARCELLUS | Onondaga |
| LIVERPOOL | Onondaga | MARCY | Oneida |
| LIVINGSTON | Columbia | MARGARETVILLE | Delaware |
| LIVINGSTON MANOR | Sullivan | MARIETTA | Onondaga |
| LIVONIA | Livingston | MARILLA | Erie |
| LIVONIA CENTER | Livingston | MARION | Wayne |
| LOCK SHELDRAKE | Sullivan | MARLBORO | Ulster |
| LOCKE | Cayuga | MARTINSBURG | Lewis |
| LOCKPORT | Niagara | MARTVILLE | Cayuga |
| LOCKWOOD | Tioga | MARYKNOLL | Westchester |
| LOCUST VALLY | Nassau | MARYLAND | Otsego |
| LODI | Seneca | MASONVILLE | Delaware |
| LONG BEACH | Nassau | MASSAPEQUA | Nassau |
| LONG EDDY | Sullivan | MASSAPEQUA PARK | Nassau |
| LONG ISLAND CITY | Queens | MASSENA | Saint Lawrence |
| LONG LAKE | Hamilton | MASTIC | Suffolk |
| LORRAINE | Jefferson | MASTIC BEACH | Suffolk |
| LOWMAN | Chemung | MATTITUCK | Suffolk |

| | | | |
|---|---|---|---|
| MAYBROOK | Orange | MOOERS | Clinton |
| MAYFIELD | Fulton | MOOERS FORKS | Clinton |
| MAYVILLE | Chautauqua | MORAVIA | Cayuga |
| MECHANICVILLE | Saratoga | MORIAH | Essex |
| MECKLENBURG | Schuyler | MORIAH CENTER | Essex |
| MEDFORD | Suffolk | MORICHES | Suffolk |
| MEDINA | Orleans | MORRIS | Otsego |
| MEDUSA | Albany | MORRISONVILLE | Clinton |
| MELLENVILLE | Columbia | MORRISTOWN | Saint Lawrence |
| MELROSE | Rensselaer | MORRISVILLE | Madison |
| MEMPHIS | Onondaga | MORTON | Orleans |
| MENDON | Monroe | MOTTVILLE | Onondaga |
| MEREDITH | Delaware | MOUNTAIN DALE | Sullivan |
| MERIDALE | Delaware | MOUNTAINVILLE | Orange |
| MERIDAN | Cayuga | MOUNT KISCO | Westchester |
| MERRICK | Nassau | MOUNT MARION | Ulster |
| MEXICO | Oswego | MOUNT MORRIS | Livingston |
| MIDDLEBURGH | Schoharie | MOUNT SINAI | Suffolk |
| MIDDLE FALLS | Washington | MOUNT TREMPER | Ulster |
| MIDDLE GRANVILL | Washington | MOUNT UPTON | Chenango |
| MIDDLE GROVE | Saratoga | MOUNT VERNON | Westchester |
| MIDDLE ISLAND | Suffolk | MOUNT VISION | Otsego |
| MIDDLEPORT | Niagara | MUMFORD | Monroe |
| MIDDLESEX | Yates | MUNNSVILLE | Madison |
| MIDDLETOWN | Orange | NANUET | Rockland |
| MIDDLEVILLE | Herkimer | NAPANOCH | Ulster |
| MILFORD | Otsego | NAPLES | Ontario |
| MILLBROOK | Dutchess | NARROWSBURG | Sullivan |
| MILLER PLACE | Suffolk | NASSAU | Rensselaer |
| MILLERTON | Dutchess | NATURAL BRIDGE | Jefferson |
| MILL NECK | Nassau | NEDROW | Onondaga |
| MILLPORT | Chemung | NELLISTON | Montgomery |
| MILLWOOD | Westchester | NESCONSET | Suffolk |
| MILTON | Ulster | NEVERSINK | Sullivan |
| MINEOLA | Nassau | NEWARK | Wayne |
| MINERNA | Essex | NEWARK VALLEY | Tioga |
| MINETTO | Oswego | NEW BALTIMORE | Greene |
| MINEVILLE | Essex | NEW BERLIN | Chenango |
| MINOA | Onondaga | NEW BREMEN | Lewis |
| MODEL CITY | Niagara | NEWBURGH | Orange |
| MODENA | Ulster | NEW CITY | Rockland |
| MOHAWK | Herkimer | NEWCOMB | Essex |
| MOHEGAN LAKE | Westchester | NEWFANE | Niagara |
| MOIRA | Franklin | NEWFIELD | Tompkins |
| MONGAUP VALLEY | Sullivan | NEW HAMBURG | Dutchess |
| MONROE | Orange | NEW HAMPTON | Orange |
| MONSEY | Rockland | NEW HARTFORD | Oneida |
| MONTAUK | Suffolk | NEW HAVEN | Oswego |
| MONTEZUMA | Cayuga | NEW HYDE PARK | Nassau |
| MONTGOMERY | Orange | NEW KINGSTON | Delaware |
| MONTICELLO | Sullivan | NEW LEBANON | Columbia |
| MONTOUR FALLS | Schuyler | NEW LEBANON CENTER | Columbia |
| MONTROSE | Westchester | NEW LISBON | Otsego |

| | | | |
|---|---|---|---|
| NEW MILFORD | Orange | NUNDA | Livingston |
| NEW PALTZ | Ulster | NYACK | Rockland |
| NEWPORT | Herkimer | OAKDALE | Suffolk |
| NEW ROCHELLE | Westchester | OAKFIELD | Genesee |
| NEW RUSSIA | Essex | OAK HILL | Greene |
| NEW SCOTLAND | Albany | OAKS CORNERS | Ontario |
| NEW SUFFOLK | Suffolk | OBERNBURG | Sullivan |
| NEWTON FALLS | Saint Lawrence | OCEAN BEACH | Suffolk |
| NEWTONVILLE | Albany | ODESSA | Schuyler |
| NEW WOOKDSTOCK | Madison | OGDENSBURG | Saint Lawrence |
| NEW YORK | New York | OHIO | Herkimer |
| NEW YORK MILLS | Oneida | OLCOTT | Niagara |
| NIAGARA FALLS | Niagara | OLD BETHPAGE | Nassau |
| NIAGARA UNIVERSITY | Niagara | OLD CHATHAM | Columbia |
| NICHOLS | Tioga | OLD FORGE | Herkimer |
| NICHOLVILLE | Saint Lawrence | OLEAN | Cattaraugus |
| NINEVEH | Broome | OLIVEBRIDGE | Ulster |
| NIOBE | Chautauqua | OLIVEREA | Ulster |
| NIVERVILLE | Chautauqua | OLMSTEDVILLE | Essex |
| NORFOLK | Saint Lawrence | ONCHIOTA | Franklin |
| NORTH BABYLON | Suffolk | ONEIDA | Madison |
| NORTH BANGOR | Franklin | ONEONTA | Otsego |
| NORTH BAY | Oneida | ONTARIO | Wayne |
| NORTH BLENHEIM | Schoharie | ONTARIO CENTER | Wayne |
| NORTH BOSTON | Erie | ORAN | Onondaga |
| NORTH BRANCH | Sullivan | ORANGEBURG | Rockland |
| NORTH BROOKFIELD | Madison | ORCHARD PARK | Erie |
| NORTH CHATHAM | Columbia | ORIENT | Suffolk |
| NORTH CHILI | Monroe | ORISKANY | Oneida |
| NORTH CLYMER | Chautauqua | ORISKANY FALLS | Oneida |
| NORTH COHOCTON | Steuben | ORWELL | Oswego |
| NORTH COLLINS | Erie | OSSINING | Westchester |
| NORTH CREEK | Warren | OSWEGATCHIE | Saint Lawrence |
| NORTH EVANS | Erie | OSWEGO | Oswego |
| NORTH GRANVILLE | Washington | OTEGO | Otsego |
| NORTH GREECE | Monroe | OTISVILLE | Orange |
| NORTH HOOSICK | Rensselaer | OTSELIC | Chenango |
| NORTH HUDSON | Essex | OTTO | Cattaraugus |
| NORTH JAVA | Wyoming | OUAQUAGA | Broome |
| NORTH LAWRENCE | Saint Lawrence | OVID | Seneca |
| NORTH NORWICH | Chenango | OWASCO | Cayuga |
| NORTH PITCHER | Chenango | OWEGO | Tioga |
| NORTHPORT | Suffolk | OWLS HEAD | Franklin |
| NORTH RIVER | Warren | OXFORD | Chenango |
| NORTH ROSE | Wayne | OYSTER BAY | Nassau |
| NORTH SALEM | Westcheswr | PAINTED POST | Steuben |
| NORTH TONAWANDA | Niagara | PALATINE BRIDGE | Montgomery |
| NORTHVILLE | Fulton | PALENVILLE | Greene |
| NORTH WESTERN | Oneida | PALISADES | Rockland |
| NORTON HILL | Greene | PALMYRA | Wayne |
| NORWAY | Herkimer | PANAMA | Chautauqua |
| NORWICH | Chenango | PARIS | Oneida |
| NORWOOD | Saint Lawrence | PARISH | Oswego |

| | | | |
|---|---|---|---|
| PARISHVILLE | Saint Lawrence | POND EDDY | Sullivan |
| PARKSVILLE | Sullivan | POOLVILLE | Madison |
| PATCHOGUE | Suffolk | POPLAR RIDGE | Cayuga |
| PATTERSON | Putnam | PORTAGEVILLE | Wyoming |
| PATTERSONVILLE | Schenectady | PORT BYRON | Cayuga |
| PAUL SMITHS | Franklin | PORT CHESTER | Westchester |
| PAVILION | Genesee | PORT CRANE | Broome |
| PAWLING | Dutcheas | PORTER CORNERS | Saratoga |
| PEARL RIVER | Rockland | PORT EWEN | Ulster |
| PECONIC | Suffolk | PORT GIBSON | Ontario |
| PEEKSKILL | Westchester | PORT HENRY | Essex |
| PENFIELD | Monroe | PORT JEFFERSON STATION | Suffolk |
| PENNELLVILLE | Oswego | PORT JERVIS | Orange |
| PENN YAN | Yates | PORT KENT | Essex |
| PERKINSVILLE | Steuben | PORTLAND | Chautauqua |
| PERRY | Wyoming | PORTLANDVILLE | Otsego |
| PERRYSBURG | Cattaraugus | PORT LEYDEN | Lewis |
| PERRWILLE | Madison | PORTVILLE | Cattaraugus |
| PERU | Clinton | PORT WASHINGTON | Nassau |
| PETERBORO | Madison | POTSDAM | Saint Lawrence |
| PETERSBURG | Rensselaer | POTTERSVILLE | Warren |
| PHELPS | Ontario | POUGHKEEPIE | Dutchess |
| PHILADEPHIA | Jefferson | POUGHQUAG | Dutchess |
| PHILLIPSPORT | Sullivan | POUND RIDGE | Westchester |
| PHILMONT | Columbia | PRATTSBURG | Steuben |
| PHOENICIA | Ulster | PRATTS HOLLOW | Madison |
| PHOENEK | Oswego | PRATTSVILLE | Greene |
| PIERCEFIELD | Saint Lawrence | PREBLE | Cortland |
| PIERMONT | Rockland | PRESTON HOLLOW | Albany |
| PIERREPONT MANOR | Jefferson | PROSPECT | Oneida |
| PIFFARD | Livingston | PULASKI | Oswep |
| PIKE | Wyoming | PULTENEY | Steuben |
| PINE BUSH | Orange | PULTNEYVILLE | Wayne |
| PINE CITY | Chemung | PURCHASE | Westchester |
| PINE HILL | Ulster | PURDYS | Westchester |
| PINE ISLAND | Orange | PURLING | Greene |
| PINE PLAINS | Dutchess | PUTNAM STATION | Washington |
| PINE VALLEY | Chemung | PUTNAM VALLEY | Putnam |
| PISECO | Hamilton | PYRITES | Saint Lawrence |
| PITCHER | Chenango | QUAKER STREET | Schenectady |
| PITTSFORD | Monroe | QUEENS BURG | Warren |
| PLAINVILLE | Onondaga | QUOGUE | Suffolk |
| PLATTEKILL | Ulster | RAINBOW LAKE | Franklin |
| PLATTSBURGH | Clinton | RANDOLPH | Cattaraugus |
| PLEASANT VALLEY | Dutchess | RANSOMVILLE | Niagara |
| PLEASANTVILLE | Westchester | RAQUETTE LAKE | Hamilton |
| PLESSIS | Jefferson | RAVENA | Albany |
| PLYMOUTH | Chenango | RAY BROOK | Essex |
| POESTENKILL | Rensselaer | RAYMONDVILLE | Saint Lawrence |
| POINT LOOKOUT | Nassau | READING CENTER | Schuyler |
| POLAND | Herkimer | RED CREEK | Wayne |
| POMANA | Rockland | REDFIELD | Oswego |
| POMPEY | Onondaga | REDFORD | Clinton |

| | | | |
|---|---|---|---|
| RED HOOK | Dutchess | RUSSIA | Herkimer |
| REDWOOD | Jefferson | RYE | Westchester |
| REMSEN | Oneida | SABAEL | Hamilton |
| REMSENBURG | Suffolk | SACKETS HARBOR | Jefferson |
| RENSSELAER | Rensselaer | SAGAPONACK | Suffolk |
| RENSSELAER FALLS | Saint Lawrence | SAG HARBOR | Suffolk |
| RENSSELAERVILLE | Albany | SAINT BONAVENTURE | Cattaraugus |
| RETSOF | Livingston | SAINT JAMES | Suffolk |
| REXFORD | Saratoga | SAINT JOHNSVILLE | Montgomery |
| REXVILLE | Steuben | SAINT REGIS FALLS | Franklin |
| RHINEBECK | Dutchess | SALAMANCA | Cattaraugus |
| RHINECLIFF | Dutchess | SALEM | Washington |
| RICHBURG | Allegany | SALISBURY CENTER | Herkimer |
| RICHFIELD SPRINGS | Otsego | SALISBURY MILLS | Orange |
| RICHFORD | Tioga | SALT POINT | Dutchess |
| RICHLAND | Oswego | SANBORN | Niagara |
| RICHMONDVILLE | Schoharie | SAND LAKE | Rensselaer |
| RICHVILLE | Saint Lawrence | SANDUSKY | Cattaraugus |
| RIDGE | Suffolk | SANDY CREEK | Oswego |
| RIFTON | Ulster | SANGERFIELD | Oneida |
| RIPARIUS | Warren | SANITARIA SPRINGS | Broome |
| RIPLEY | Chautauqua | SARANAC | Clinton |
| RIVERHEAD | Suffolk | SARANAC LAKE | Franklin |
| ROCHESTER | Monroe | SARATOGA SPRINGS | Saratoga |
| ROCK CITY FALLS | Saratoga | SARDINIA | Erie |
| ROCK HILL | Sullivan | SAUGERTIES | Ulster |
| ROCK STREAM | Yates | SAUQUOIT | Oneida |
| ROCK TAVERN | Orange | SAVANNAH | Wayne |
| ROCKVILLE CENTRE | Nassau | SAVONA | Steuben |
| ROCKY POINT | Suffolk | SAYVILLE | Suffolk |
| RODMAN | Jefferson | SCARSDALE | Westchester |
| ROME | Oneida | SCHAGHTICOKE | Rensselaer |
| ROMULUS | Seneca | SCHENECTADY | Schenectady |
| RONKONKOMA | Suffolk | SCHENEVUS | Otsego |
| ROOSEVELT | Nassau | SCHODACK LANDING | Rensselaer |
| ROOSEVELTOWN | Saint Lawrence | SCHOHARIE | Schoharie |
| ROSCOE | Sullivan | SCHROON LAKE | Essex |
| ROSE | Wayne | SCHUYLER | Herkimer |
| ROSEBOOM | Otsego | SCHUYLER FALLS | Clinton |
| ROSENDALE | Ulster | SCHUYLER LAKE | Otsego |
| ROSLYN | Nassau | SCHUYLERVILLE | Saratoga |
| ROSLYN HEIGHTS | Nassau | SCIO | Allegany |
| ROSSBURG | Allegany | SCIPIO CENTER | Cayuga |
| ROTTERDAM JUNCTION | Schenectady | SCOTTSVILLE | Monroe |
| ROUND LAKE | Saratoga | SEA CLIFF | Nassau |
| ROUND TOP | Greene | SEAFORD | Nassau |
| ROUSES POINT | Clinton | SELDEN | Suffolk |
| ROXBURY | Delaware | SELKIRK | Albany |
| RUBY | Ulster | SENECA CASTLE | Ontario |
| RUSH | Monroe | SENECA FALLS | Seneca |
| RUSHFORD | Allegany | SENNETT | Cayuga |
| RUSHVILLE | Yates | SEVERANCE | Essex |
| RUSSELL | Saint Lawrence | SHADY | Ulster |

| | | | |
|---|---|---|---|
| SHANDAKEN | Ulster | SOUTHFIELDS | Orange |
| SHARON SPRINGS | Schoharie | SOUTH JAMESPORT | Suffolk |
| SHEDS | Madison | SOUTH KORTRIGHT | Delaware |
| SHELTER ISLAND | Suffolk | SOUTH LIMA | Livingston |
| SHELTER ISLAND HEIGHTS | Suffolk | SOUTH MARION | Ulster |
| SHENOROCK | Westcheser | SOUTH MORRIS | Livingston |
| SHERBURNE | Chenango | SOUTH NEW BERLIN | Chenango |
| SHERIDAN | Chautauqua | SOUTHOLD | Suffolk |
| SHERMAN | Chautauqua | SOUTH OTSELIC | Chenango |
| SHERRILL | Oneida | SOUTH PLYMOUTH | Chenango |
| SHINHOPPLE | Delaware | SOUTH RUTLAND | Jefferson |
| SHIRLEY | Suffolk | SOUTH SALEM | Westchester |
| SHOKAN | Ulster | SOUTH SCHODACK | Rensselaer |
| SHOREHAM | Suffolk | SOUTH SCHROON | Essex |
| SHORTSVILLE | Ontario | SOUTH SINAI | Suffolk |
| SHRUB OAK | Westchester | SOUTH TREMPER | Ulster |
| SHUSHAN | Washington | SOUTH UPTON | Chenango |
| SIDNEY | Delaware | SOUTH VERNON | Westchester |
| SIDNEY CENTER | Delaware | SOUTH VISION | Otsego |
| SILVER BAY | Warren | SOUTH WALES | Erie |
| SILVER CREEK | Chautauqua | SOUTH WESTERLO | Albany |
| SILVER LAKE | Wyoming | SPARKILL | Rockland |
| SILVER SPRINGS | Wyoming | SPARROW BUSH | Orange |
| SINCLAIRVILLE | Chautauqua | SPECULATOR | Hamilton |
| SKANEATELES | Onondaga | SPENCER | Tioga |
| SKANEATELES FALLS | Onondaga | SPENCERPORT | Monroe |
| SLATE HILL | Orange | SPENCERTOWN | Columbia |
| SLATERVILLE SPRINGS | Tompkins | SPEONK | Suffolk |
| SLINGERLANDS | Albany | SPRAKERS | Montgomery |
| SLOANSVILLE | Schoharie | SPRING BROOK | Erie |
| SLOATSBURG | Rockland | SPRINGFIELD CENTER | Otsego |
| SMALLWOOD | Sullivan | SPRING GLEN | Ulster |
| SMITHBORO | Tioga | SPRING VALLEY | Rockland |
| SMITHTOWN | Suffolk | SPRINGVILLE | Erie |
| SMITHVILLE | Jefferson | SPRINGWATER | Livingston |
| SMITHVILLE FLATS | Chenango | STAATSBURG | Dutchess |
| SMYRNA | Chenango | STAFFORD | Genesee |
| SODUS | Wayne | STAMFORD | Delaware |
| SODUS CENTER | Wayne | STANFORDVILLE | Dutchess |
| SODUS POINT | Wayne | STANLEY | Ontario |
| SOLSVILLE | Madison | STAR LAKE | Saint Lawrence |
| SOMERS | Westchester | STARK | Herkimer |
| SONYEA | Livingston | STATEN ISLAND | Richmond |
| SOUND BEACH | Suffolk | STEAMBURG | Cattaraugus |
| SOUTHHAMPTON | Suffolk | STELLA NIAGARA | Niagara |
| SOUTH BETHLEHEM | Albany | STEPHENTOWN | Rensselaer |
| SOUTH BUTLER | Wayne | STERLING | Cayuga |
| SOUTH BYRON | Genesee | STERLING FOREST | Orange |
| SOUTH CAIRO | Greene | STILLWATER | Saratoga |
| SOUTH COLTON | Saint Lawrence | STITTVILLE | Oneida |
| SOUTH DAYTON | Cattaraugus | STOCKPORT | Columbia |
| SOUTH EDMESTON | Otsego | STOCKTON | Chautauqua |
| SOUTH FALLSBURG | Sullivan | STONE RIDGE | Ulster |

**Adoption Searches Made Easier**

| | | | |
|---|---|---|---|
| STONY BROOK | Suffolk | TULLY | Onondaga |
| STONY CREEK | Warren | TUNNEL | Broome |
| STONY POINT | Rockland | TUPPER LAKE | Franklin |
| STORMVILLE | Dutchess | TURIN | Lewis |
| STOTTVILLE | Columbia | TUSCARORA | Livingston |
| STOW | Chautauqua | TUXEDO PARK | Orange |
| STRATFORD | Fulton | TWELVE CORNERS | Monroe |
| STRYKERSVILLE | Wyoming | TYRONE | Schuyler |
| STUYVESANT | Columbia | ULSTER PARK | Ulster |
| STUYVESANT FALLS | Columbia | UNADILLA | Otsego |
| SUFFERN | Rockland | UNIONDALE | Nassau |
| SUGAR LOAF | Orange | UNION HILL | Monroe |
| SUMMIT | Schoharie | UNION SPRINGS | Cayuga |
| SUMMITVILLE | Sullivan | UNIONVILLE | Orange |
| SURPRISE | Greene | UPPERJAY | Essex |
| SWAIN | Allegany | UPTON | Suffolk |
| SWAN LAKE | Sullivan | UTICA | Oneida |
| SWORMVILLE | Erie | VAILS GATE | Orange |
| SYLVAN BEACH | Oneida | VALATIE | Columbia |
| SYOSSET | Nassau | VALHALLA | Westchester |
| SYRACUSE | Onondaga | VALLEY COTTAGE | Rockland |
| TABERG | Oneida | VALLEY FALLS | Rensselaer |
| TALLMAN | Rockland | VALLEY STREAM | Nassau |
| TANNERSVILLE | Greene | VALOIS | Schuyler |
| TAPPAN | Rockland | VAN BRUNT | Kings |
| TARRYTOWN | Westchester | VAN BUREN POINT | Chautauqua |
| THENDARA | Herkimer | VAN COLT | Kings |
| THERESA | Jefferson | VAN ETTEN | Chemung |
| THIELLS | Rockland | VAN HORNESVILLE | Herkimer |
| THOMPSON RIDGE | Orange | VARYSBURG | Wyoming |
| THOMPSONVILLE | Sullivan | VENICE CENTER | Cayuga |
| THORNWOOD | Westchester | VERBANK | Dutchess |
| THOUSAND ISLAND PARK | Jefferson | VERMONTVILLE | Franklin |
| THREE MILE BAY | Jefferson | VERNON | Oneida |
| TICONDEROGA | Essex | VERNON CENTER | Oneida |
| TILLSON | Ulster | VERONA | Oneida |
| TIMES SQUARE | New York | VERONA BEACH | Oneida |
| TIOGA CENTER | Tioga | VERPLANCK | Westchester |
| TIVOLI | Dutchess | VERSAILLES | Cattaraugus |
| TOMPKINS COVE | Rockland | VESTAL | Broome |
| TOMPKINS | Delaware | VICTOR | Ontario |
| TONAWANDA | Erie | VICTORY MILLS | Saratoga |
| TOTTENVILLE | Richmond | VOORHEESVILLE | Albany |
| TRANSMEADOW | Queens | WACCABUT | Westchester |
| TREADWELL | Delaware | WADDINGTON | Saint Lawrence |
| TRIBES MILL | Montgomery | WADHAMS | Essex |
| TROUPSBURG | Steuben | WADING RIVER | Suffolk |
| TROUT CREEK | Delaware | WADSWORTH | Livingston |
| TROY | Rensselaer | WAINSCOTT | Suffolk |
| TRUMANSBURG | Tompkins | WAKEFIELD | New York |
| TRUXTON | Cortland | WALDEN | Orange |
| TUCKAHOE | Westchester | WALES CENTER | Erie |
| TUDOR | New York | WALKER VALLEY | Ulster |

| | | | |
|---|---|---|---|
| WALTON | Delaware | WESTERNVILLE | Oneida |
| WALWORTH | Wayne | WEST EXETER | Otsego |
| WAMPSVILLE | Madison | WEST FALLS | Erie |
| WANAKENA | Saint Lawrence | WESTFIELD | Chautauqua |
| WANTAGH | Nassau | WESTFORD | Otsego |
| WAPPINGERS FALLS | Dutchess | WEST FULTON | Schoharie |
| WARDS ISLAND | New York | WESTGATE | Monroe |
| WARNERS | Onondaga | WESTHAMPTON | Suffolk |
| WARNERVILLE | Schoharie | WESTHAMPTON BEACH | Suffolk |
| WARREN | Herkimer | WEST HAVERSTRAW | Rockland |
| WARRENSBURG | Warren | WEST HEMPSTEAD | Nassau |
| WARSAW | Wyoming | WEST HENRIETTA | Monroe |
| WARWICK | Orange | WEST HURLEY | Ulster |
| WASHINGTON MILLS | Oneida | WEST ISLIP | Suffolk |
| WASHINGTONVILLE | Orange | WEST KILL | Greene |
| WASSAIC | Dutchess | WEST LEBANON | Columbia |
| WATERFORD | Saratoga | WEST LEYDEN | Lewis |
| WATERLOO | Seneca | WEST MONROE | Oswego |
| WATER MILL | Suffolk | WESTMORELAND | Oneida |
| WATERPORT | Orleans | WEST NYACK | Rockland |
| WATERTOWN | Jefferson | WEST ONEONTA | Otsego |
| WATERVILLE | Oneida | WESTONS MILLS | Cattaraugus |
| WATERVLIET | Albany | WEST PARK | Ulster |
| WATKINS GLEN | Schuyler | WEST POINT | Orange |
| WAVERLY | Tioga | WESTPORT | Essex |
| WAWARSUBG | Ulster | WEST RIDGE | Monroe |
| WAYLAND | Steuben | WEST RUSH | Monroe |
| WAYNE | Schuyler | WEST SAND LAKE | Rensselaer |
| WEBB | Herkimer | WEST SAYVILLE | Suffolk |
| WEBSTER | Monroe | WEST SENECA | Erie |
| WEBSTER CROSSING | Livingston | WEST SHOKAN | Ulster |
| WEEDSPORT | Cayuga | WEST STOCKHOLM | Saint Lawrence |
| WELLS | Haniilton | WESTTOWN | Orange |
| WELLS BRIDGE | Otsego | WEST VALLEY | Cattaraugus |
| WELLSBURG | Chemung | WEST WINFIELD | Herkimer |
| WELLSVILLE | Allegany | WEVERTOWN | Warren |
| WEST BABYLON | Suffolk | WHALLONSBURG | Essex |
| WEST BANGOR | Franklin | WHEATLEY HEIGHTS | Suffolk |
| WEST BLOOMFIELD | Ontario | WHIPPLEVILLE | Franklin |
| WEST BRENTWOOD | Brentwood | WHITE CREEK | Washington |
| WESTBROOKVILLE | Sullivan | WHITEHALL | Washington |
| WEST BURLINGTON | Otsego | WHITE LAKE | Sullivan |
| WESTBURY | Nassau | WHITE PLAINS | Westchester |
| WEST CAMP | Ulster | WHITESBORO | Oneida |
| WEST CHAZY | Clinton | WHITE SULPHUR SPRINGS | Sullivan |
| WEST CLARKSVILLE | Allegany | WHITESVILLE | Allegany |
| WEST COPAKE | Columbia | WHITNEY POINT | Broome |
| WESTDALE | Oneida | WILLARD | Seneca |
| WEST DANBY | Tompkins | WILLET | Cortland |
| WEST DAVENPORT | Delaware | WILLIAMSBRIDGE | NewYork |
| WEST EATON | Madison | WILLIAMSBURG | Kings |
| WEST EDMESTON | Otsego | WILLIAMSON | Wayne |
| WESTERLO | Albany | WILLIAMSTOWN | Oswego |

**Adoption Searches Made Easier**

| | | | |
|---|---|---|---|
| WILLISTON PARK | Nassau | AQUONE | Macon |
| WILLOW | Ulster | ARAPAHOE | Pamlico |
| WILLSBORO | Essex | ARARAT | Surry |
| WILLSEYVILLE | Tioga | ARCHDALE | Guilford |
| WILMINGTON | Essex | ARDEN | Buncombe |
| WILSON | Niagara | ARDMORE | Forsyth |
| WINDHAM | Greene | ARROWWOOD | Mecklenburg |
| WINDSOR | Broome | ASH | Brunswick |
| WINFIELD | Herkimer | ASHEBORO | Randolph |
| WINGDALE | Dutchess | ASHEVILLE | Buncombe |
| WINTHROP | Saint Lawrence | ATKINSON | Pender |
| WITHERBEE | Essex | ATLANTIC | Carteret |
| WOLCOTT | Wayne | ATLANTIC BEACH | Carteret |
| WOODBOURNE | Sullivan | AULANDER | Bertie |
| WOODBURY | Nassau | AURORA | Beaufort |
| WOODGATE | Oneida | AUTRYVILLE | Sampson |
| WOODHULL | Steuben | AVON | Dare |
| WOODLAWN | New York | AYDEN | Pitt |
| WOODMERE | Nassau | AYDLETT | Currituck |
| WOODRIDGE | Sullivan | AZALEA | New Hanover |
| WOODSTOCK | Ulster | BADIN | Stanly |
| WOODVILLE | Jefferson | BAHAMA | Durham |
| WORCESTER | Otsego | BAILEY | Nash |
| WURTSBORO | Sullivan | BAKERSVILLE | Mitchell |
| WYANDANCH | Suffolk | BALFOUR | Henderson |
| WYNANTSKILL | Rensselaer | BALSAM | Jackson |
| WYOMING | Wyoming | BALSAM GROVE | Transylvania |
| YAPHANK | Suffolk | BANNER ELK | Avery |
| YONKERS | Westchester | BARBER | Rowan |
| YORK | Livingston | BARCO | Currituck |
| YORKSHIRE | Cattaraugus | BARIUM SPRINGS | Iredell |
| YORKTOWN HEIGHTS | Westchester | BARNARDSVILLE | Buncombe |
| YORKVILLE | Oneida | BARNESVILLE | Robeson |
| YOUNGSTOWN | Niagara | BARTON COLLEGE | Wilson |
| YOUNGSVILLE | Sullivan | BAT CAVE | Henderson |
| YULAN | Sullivan | BATH | Beaufort |
| **NORTH CAROLINA** ▓▓▓ | | BATTLEBORO | Nash |
| ABERDEEN | Moore | BAYBORO | Pamlico |
| ADVANCE | Davie | BEAR CREEK | Chatham |
| AHOSKIE | Hertford | BEAUFORT | Carteret |
| ALAMANCE | Alamance | BELEWS CREEK | Forsyth |
| ALAMANCE SQUARE | Guilford | BELHAVEN | Beaufort |
| ALBEMARLE | Stanly | BELLARTHUR | Pitt |
| ALBERTSON | Duplin | BELMONT | Gaston |
| ALEXANDER | Buncombe | BELVIDERE | Perquimans |
| ALEXIS | Gaston | BENNETT | Chatham |
| ALLIANCE | Pamlico | BENSON | Johnston |
| ALMOND | Swain | BERKELEY | Wayne |
| ALTAMAHAW | Alamance | BESSEMER CITY | Gaston |
| ANDREWS | Cherokee | BETHANIA | Forsyth |
| ANGIER | Harnett | BETHEL | Pitt |
| ANSONVILLE | Anson | BETHLEHEM | Catawba |
| APEX | Wake | BEULAVILLE | Duplin |

| | | | |
|---|---|---|---|
| BILTMORE | Buncome | CASTLE HAYNE | New Hanover |
| BISCOE | Montgomery | CATAWBA | Catawba |
| BLACK CREEK | Wilson | CEDAR FALLS | Randolph |
| BLACK MOUNTAIN | Buncombe | CEDAR GROVE | Orange |
| BLADENBORO | Bladen | CEDAR ISLAND | Carteret |
| BLANCH | Caswell | CEDAR MOUNTAIN | Transylvania |
| BLOUNTS CREEK | Beaufort | CENTER CITY | Forsyth |
| BLOWING ROCK | Watauga | CENTURY | Wake |
| BOILING SPRINGS | Cleveland | CERRO GORDO | Columbus |
| BOLIVIA | Brunswick | CHADBOURN | Columbus |
| BOLTON | Columbus | CHAPEL HILL | Orange |
| BONLEE | Chatham | CHARLOTTE | Mecklenburg |
| BOOMER | Wilkes | CHEROKEE | Swain |
| BOONE | Watauga | CHERRY POINT | Craven |
| BOONVILLE | Yadkin | CHERRYVILLE | Gaston |
| BOSTIC | Rutherford | CHIMNEY ROCK | Rutherford |
| BOWDENS | Duplin | CHINA GROVE | Rowan |
| BRASSTOWN | Clay | CHINQUAPIN | Duplin |
| BRENTWOOD | Wake | CHOCOWINITY | Beaufort |
| BREVARD | Transylvania | CLAREMONT | Catawba |
| BRIDGETON | Craven | CLARENDON | Columbus |
| BROADWAY | Lee | CLARKTON | Bladen |
| BROWNS SUMMIT | Guilford | CLAYTON | Johnston |
| BRUNSWICK | Columbus | CLEMMONS | Forsyth |
| BRYSON CITY | Swain | CLEVELAND | Rowan |
| BUIES CREEK | Harnett | CLIFFSIDE | Rutherford |
| BULLOCK | Granville | CLIMAX | Guilford |
| BUNN | Franklin | CLINTON | Sampson |
| BUNNLEVEL | Harnett | CLYDE | Haywood |
| BURGAW | Pender | COATS | Harnett |
| BURLINGTON | Alamance | COFIELD | Hertford |
| BURNSVILLE | Yancey | COINJOCK | Currituck |
| BUTNER | Granville | COLERAIN | Bertie |
| BUTTERS | Bladen | COLERIDGE | Randolph |
| BUXTON | Dare | COLFAX | Guilford |
| BYNUM | Chatham | COLLEGE | Durham |
| CALABASH | Brunswick | COLLETTSVILLE | Caldwell |
| CALYPSO | Duplin | COLON | Lee |
| CAMDEN | Camden | COLONNADE | Mecklenburg |
| CAMERON | Moore | COLUMBIA | Tyrell |
| CAMERON VILLAGE | Wake | COLUMBUS | Polk |
| CAMP LEJEUNE | Onslow | COMFORT | Jones |
| CANDLER | Buncombe | COMO | Hertford |
| CANDOR | Montgomery | CONCORD | Cabarrus |
| CANTON | Haywood | CONETOE | Edgecombe |
| CAROLEEN | Rutherford | CONNELLYS SPRINGS | Burke |
| CAROLINA BEACH | New Hanover | CONOVER | Catawba |
| CARRBORO | Orange | CONWAY | Northampton |
| CARTHAGE | Moore | COOLEEMEE | Davie |
| CARY | Wake | CORAPEAKE | Gates |
| CASAR | Cleveland | CORDOVA | Richmond |
| CASHIERS | Jackson | CORNELIUS | Mecklenburg |
| CASTALIA | Nash | COROLIA | Currituck |

| | | | |
|---|---|---|---|
| COTSWOLD | Mecklenburg | ELLERBE | Richmond |
| COUNCIL | Bladen | ELM CITY | Wilson |
| COVE CITY | Craven | ELON COLLEGE | Alamance |
| CRABTREE VALLEY | Wake | EMERALD ISLE | Carteret |
| CRAMERTON | Gaston | ENFIELD | Halifax |
| CRANBERRY | Avery | ENGELHARD | Hyde |
| CREEDMOOR | Granville | ENKA | Buncombe |
| CRESTON | Ashe | ENNICE | Alleghany |
| CRESWELL | Washington | ERNUL | Craven |
| CROSSNORE | Avery | ERWIN | Harnett |
| CROUSE | Lincoln | ETHER | Monogomery |
| CRUMPLER | Ashe | ETOWAH | Henderson |
| CULBERSON | Cherokee | EURE | Gates |
| CULLOWHEE | Jackson | EVERETTS | Martin |
| CUMBERLAND | Cumberland | EVERGREEN | Columbus |
| CUMNOCK | Lee | FAIR BLUFF | Columbus |
| CURRIE | Pender | FAIRFIELD | Hyde |
| CURRITUCK | Currituck | FAIRMONT | Robeson |
| DALLAS | Gaston | FAIRVIEW | Buncombe |
| DANA | Henderson | FAISON | Duplin |
| DANBURY | Stokes | FAITH | Rowan |
| DAVIDSON | Mecklenburg | FALCON | Cumberland |
| DAVIS | Carteret | FALKLAND | Pitt |
| DEEP GAP | Watauga | FALLSTON | Cleveland |
| DEEP RUN | Lenoir | FARMVILLE | Pitt |
| DELCO | Columbus | FAYETTEVILLE | Cumberland |
| DENTON | Davidson | FERGUSON | Wilkes |
| DENVER | Lincoln | FLAT ROCK | Henderson |
| DILLSBORO | Jackson | FLEETWOOD | Ashe |
| DOBSON | Surry | FLETCHER | Henderson |
| DOVER | Craven | FONTANA DAM | Graham |
| DREXEL | Burke | FOREST CITY | Rutherford |
| DUBLIN | Bladen | FOUNTAIN | Pitt |
| DUDLEY | Wayne | FOUR OAKS | Johnston |
| DUNN | Harnett | FRANKLIN | Macon |
| DURHAM | Durham | FRANKLINTON | Franklin |
| EAGLE ROCK | Wake | FRANKLINVILLE | Randolph |
| EAGLE SPRINGS | Moore | FREMONT | Wayne |
| EARL | Cleveland | FRISCO | Dare |
| EAST BEND | Yadkin | FUQUAY-VARINA | Wake |
| EAST FLAT ROCK | Henderson | GARLAND | Sampson |
| EASE LAKE | Dare | GARNER | Wake |
| EAST SPENCER | Rowan | GARYSBURG | Northampton |
| EDEN | Rockingham | GASTON | Northampton |
| EDENTON | Chowan | GASTONIA | Gaston |
| EDNEYVILLE | Henderson | GATES | Gates |
| EDWARD | Beaufort | GATESVILLE | Gates |
| EFLAND | Orange | GEORGE | Northampton |
| ELIZABETH CITY | Pasquotank | GERMANTON | Stokes |
| ELIZABETHTOWN | Bladen | GERTON | Henderson |
| ELKIN | Surry | GIBSON | Scotland |
| ELK PARK | Avery | GIBSONVILLE | Guiford |
| ELLENBORO | Rutherford | GLADE VALLEY | Alleghany |

| | | | |
|---|---|---|---|
| GLEN ALPINE | Burke | HIGHFALLS | Moore |
| GLENDALE SPRINGS | Ashe | HIGHLANDS | Macon |
| GLENDON | Moore | HIGH POINT | Guilford |
| GLENVILLE | Jackson | HIGH SHOALS | Gaston |
| GLENWOOD | McDowell | HILDEBRAN | Burke |
| GLOUCESTER | Carteret | HILLSBOROUGH | Orange |
| GODWIN | Cumberland | HOBBSVILLE | Gates |
| GOLD HILL | Rowan | HOBGOOD | Halifax |
| GOLDSBORO | Wayne | HOBUCKEN | Pamlico |
| GOLDSTON | Chatham | HOFFMAN | Richmond |
| GRAHAM | Alamance | HOLLISTER | Halifax |
| GRANDY | Currituck | HOLLY RIDGE | Onslow |
| GRANITE FALLS | Caldwell | HOLLY SPRINGS | Wake |
| GRANITE QUARRY | Rowan | HOOKERTON | Greene |
| GRANTHAM | Wayne | HOPE MILLS | Cumberland |
| GRANTSBORO | Pamlico | HORSE SHOE | Henderson |
| GRASSY CREEK | Ashe | HOT SPRINGS | Madison |
| GRAYSON | Ashe | HUBERT | Onslow |
| GREENMOUNTAIN | Yancey | HUDSON | Caldwell |
| GREENSBORO | Guilford | HUNTERVILLE | Mecklenburg |
| GREENVILLE | Pitt | HURDLE MILLS | Person |
| GRIFTON | Pitt | HUSK | Ashe |
| GRIMESLAND | Pitt | ICARD | Burke |
| GROVER | Cleveland | INDIAN TRAIL | Union |
| GULF | Chatham | INGOLD | Sampson |
| GUMBERRY | Northhampton | IRON STATION | Lincoln |
| HALIFAX | Halifax | IVANHOE | Sampson |
| HALLSBORO | Columbus | JACKSON | Northampton |
| HAMILTON | Martin | JACKSON PARK | Cabarrus |
| HAMLET | Richmond | JACKSON SPRINGS | Moore |
| HAMPSTEAD | Pender | JACKSONVILLE | Onslow |
| HAMPTONVILLE | Yadkin | JAMESTOWN | Guilford |
| HARBINGER | Currituck | JAMESVILLE | Martin |
| HARKERS ISLAND | Carteret | JARVISBURG | Currituck |
| HARMONY | Iredell | JEFFERSON | Ashe |
| HARRELLS | Sampson | JONAS RIDGE | Burke |
| HARRELLVILLE | Hertford | JONESVILLE | Yadkin |
| HARRIS | Rutherford | JULION | Guilford |
| HARRISBURG | Cabarrus | KANNAPOLIS | Cabarus |
| HASSELL | Martin | KELFORD | Bertie |
| HATTERAS | Dare | KELLY | Bladen |
| HAVELOCK | Craven | KENANSVILLE | Duplin |
| HAW RIVER | Alamance | KENLY | Johnston |
| HAYESVILLE | Clay | KERNERSVILLE | Forsyth |
| HAYS | Wildes | KILL DEVIL HILLS | Dare |
| HAZELWOOD | Haywood | KING | Stokes |
| HENDERSON | Vance | KINGS MOUNTAIN | Cleveland |
| HENDERSONVILLE | Henderson | KINSTON | Lenoir |
| HENRICO | Northampton | KIPLING | Harnett |
| HENRIETTA | Rutherford | KITTRELL | Vance |
| HERTFORD | Perquimans | KITTY HAWK | Dare |
| HICKORY | Catawba | KNIGHTDALE | Wake |
| HIDDENITE | Alexander | KNOTS ISLAND | Currituck |

| | | | |
|---|---|---|---|
| KURE BEACH | New Hanover | MADISON | Rockingham |
| LAGRANGE | Lenoir | MAGGIE VALLEY | Haywood |
| LAKE JUNALUSKA | Haywood | MAGNOLIA | Duplin |
| LAKE LURE | Rutherford | MAIDEN | Catawba |
| LAKE TOXAWAY | Transylvania | MAMERS | Harnett |
| LAKEVIEW | Moore | MANNS HARBOR | Dare |
| LAKE WACCAMAW | Columbus | MANSON | Warren |
| LANDIS | Rowan | MANTEO | Dare |
| LANSING | Ashe | MAPLE | Currituck |
| LASKER | Northampton | MAPLE HILL | Pender |
| LATTIMOR | Cleveland | MARBLE | Cherokee |
| LAUREL HILL | Scotland | MARGARETTSVILLE | Northampton |
| LAUREL SPRINGS | Alleghany | MARIETTA | Robeson |
| LAURINBURG | Scotland | MARION | McDowell |
| LAWNDALE | Cleveland | MARSHALL | Madison |
| LAWSONVILLE | Stokes | MARSHALLBERG | Carteret |
| LEASBURG | Caswell | MARS HILL | Madison |
| LEICESTER | Buncombe | MARSHVILLE | Union |
| LELAND | Brunswick | MARSTON | Richmond |
| LEMON SPRINGS | Lee | MATTHEWS | Mecklenburg |
| LENOIR | Caldwell | MAURY | Greene |
| LEWISTON WOODVILLE | Bertie | MAXTON | Robeson |
| LEWISVILLE | Forsyth | MAYODAN | Rockingham |
| LEXINGTON | Davidson | MAYSVILLE | Jones |
| LIBERTY | Randolph | MEBANE | Alamance |
| LILESVILLE | Anson | MERRITT | Pamlico |
| LILLINGTON | Harnett | MERRY HILL | Bertie |
| LLNCOLNTON | Lincoln | MICAVILLE | Yancey |
| LINDEN | Cumberland | MICRO | Johnston |
| LINVILLE | Avery | MIDDLEBURG | Vance |
| LINVILLE FALLS | Burke | MIDDLESEX | Nash |
| LINWOOD | Davidson | MIDLAND | Cabarrus |
| LITTLE SWITZERLAND | McDowell | MIDWAY | Cabarrus |
| LITTLETON | Halifax | MIDWAY PARK | Onslow |
| LOCUST | Stanly | MILLERS CREEK | Wilkes |
| LONGISLAND | Catawba | MILL SPRING | Polk |
| LONGWOOD | Brunswick | MILTON | Caswell |
| LOUISBURG | Franklin | MILWAUKEE | Northampton |
| LOWELL | Gaston | MINERAL SPRINGS | Union |
| LOWGAP | Surry | MINNEAPOLIS | Avery |
| LOWLAND | Pamlico | MINT HILL | Mecklenburg |
| LUCAMA | Wilson | MISENHEIMER | Stanly |
| LUMBER BRIDGE | Robeson | MOCKSVILLE | Davie |
| LUMBERTON | Robeson | MONCURE | Chatham |
| LYNN | Polk | MONROE | Union |
| MCADENVILLE | Gaston | MONTEZUMA | Avery |
| MCCAIN | Hoke | MONTREAT | Buncombe |
| MCCUTCHEON FIELD | Onslow | MOORESBORO | Cleveland |
| MCFARLAN | Anson | MOORESVILLE | Wake |
| MCGRADY | Wilkes | MORAVIAN FALLS | Wilkes |
| MCLEANSVILLE | Guilford | MOREHEAD CITY | Carteret |
| MACCLESFIELD | Edgecombe | MORGANTON | Burke |
| MACON | Warren | MORRISVILLE | Wake |

| | | | |
|---|---|---|---|
| MORVEN | Anson | PARMELE | Martin |
| MOUNTAIN HOME | Henderson | PATTERSON | Caldwell |
| MOUNT AIRY | Surry | PAW CREEK | Mecklenburg |
| MOUNT GILEAD | Montgomery | PEACHLAND | Anson |
| MOUNT HOLLY | Gaston | PELHAM | Caswell |
| MOUNT MOURNE | Iredell | PEMBROKE | Robeson |
| MOUNT OLIVE | Wayne | PENDLETON | Northampton |
| MOUNT PLEASANT | Cabarrus | PENLAND | Mitchell |
| MOUNT ULLA | Rowan | PENROSE | Transylvania |
| MOYOCK | Currituck | PFAFFTOWN | Forsyth |
| MURFREESBORO | Hertford | PIKEVILLE | Wayne |
| MURPHY | Cherokee | PILOT MOUNTAIN | Surry |
| NAGS HEAD | Dare | PINEBLUFF | Moore |
| NAKINA | Columbus | PINE HALL | Stokes |
| NAPLES | Henderson | PINEHURST | Moore |
| NASHVILLE | Nash | PINE LEVEL | Johnston |
| NEBO | McDowell | PINEOLA | Avery |
| NEW BERN | Craven | PINETOPS | Edgecombe |
| NEWELL | Mecklenburg | PINETOWN | Beaufort |
| NEWHILL | Wake | PINEVILLE | Mecklenburg |
| NEWLAND | Avery | PINEY CREEK | Alleghany |
| NEW LONDON | Stanly | PINK HILL | Lenoir |
| NEWPORT | Carteret | PINNACLE | Stokes |
| NEWTON | Catawba | PISGAH FOREST | Transylvania |
| NEWTON GROVE | Sampson | PITTSBORO | Chatham |
| NORLINA | Warren | PLEASANT GARDEN | Guilford |
| NORMAN | Richmond | PLEASANT HILL | Northampton |
| NORTH BURLINGTON | Alamance | PLUMTREE | Avery |
| NORTH CARY | Wake | PLYMOUTH | Washington |
| NORTH CHARLOTTE | Mecklenburg | POINT HARBOR | Currituck |
| NORTH DURHAM | Durham | POLKTON | Anson |
| NORTHGATE | Durham | POLKVILLE | Cleveland |
| NORTH HILLS | Wake | POLLOCKSVILLE | Jones |
| NORTH RIDGE | Wake | POPE AFB | Cumberland |
| NORTH ROXBORO | Person | POPLAR BRANCH | Currituck |
| NORTHSIDE | Granville | POTECASI | Northampton |
| NORTH TRYON | Mecklenburg | POWELLS POINT | Currituck |
| NORTH WILKESBORO | Wilkes | POWELLSVILLE | Bertie |
| NORWOOD | Stanly | PRINCETON | Johnston |
| OAKBORO | Stanly | PROCTORVILLE | Robeson |
| OAK CITY | Martin | PROSPECT HILL | Caswell |
| OAK RIDGE | Guilford | PROVIDENCE | Caswell |
| OCRACOKE | Hyde | PURLEAR | Wilkes |
| OLD FORT | McDowell | RAEFORD | Hoke |
| OLIN | Iredell | RALEIGH | Wake |
| OLIVIA | Harnett | RAMSEUR | Randolph |
| ORIENTAL | Pamlico | RANDLEMAN | Randolph |
| ORRUM | Robeson | RED OAK | Nash |
| OTTO | Macon | RED SPRINGS | Robeson |
| OXFORD | Granville | REIDSVILLE | Rockingham |
| PALMYRA | Halifax | RESEARCH TRIANGLE PARK | Durham |
| PANTEGO | Beaufort | REX | Robeson |
| PARKTON | Robeson | RHODHISS | Caldwell |

**Adoption Searches Made Easier**

| | | | |
|---|---|---|---|
| RICHFIELD | Stanly | SEVEN SPRINGS | Wayne |
| RICHLANDS | Onslow | SEVERN | Northampton |
| RICH SQUARE | Northampton | SEYMOUR JOHNSON AFB | Wayne |
| RIDGECREST | Buncombe | SHALLOTTE | Brunswick |
| RIDGEWAY | Warren | SHANNON | Robeson |
| RIEGELWOOD | Columbus | SHARPSBURG | Nash |
| ROANOKE RAPIDS | Halifax | SHAWBORO | Currituck |
| ROARING GAP | Alleghany | SHELBY | Cleveland |
| ROARING RIVER | Wilkes | SHERRILLS FORD | Catawba |
| ROBBINS | Moore | SHILOH | Camden |
| ROBBINSVILLE | Graham | SILLER CITY | Chatham |
| ROBERSONVILLE | Martin | SILOAM | Surry |
| ROCKINGHAM | Richmond | SIMPSON | Pitt |
| ROCKWELL | Rowan | SIMS | Wilson |
| ROCKY MOUNT | Edgecombe | SKYLAND | Buncombe |
| ROCKY POINT | Pender | SMITHFIELD | Johnston |
| RODANTHE | Dare | SMYRNA | Carteret |
| RODUCO | Gates | SNEADS FERRY | Onslow |
| ROLESVILLE | Wake | SNOW CAMP | Alamance |
| RONDA | Wilkes | SNOW HILL | Green |
| ROPER | Washington | SOPHIA | Randolph |
| ROSEBORO | Sampson | SOUTHERN PINES | Moore |
| ROSE HILL | Duplin | SOUTHERN SHORES | Dare |
| ROSMAN | Transylvania | SOUTH MILLS | Camden |
| ROUGEMONT | Durham | SOUTHMONT | Davidson |
| ROWLAND | Robeson | SOUTHPORT | Brunswick |
| ROXBORO | Person | SPARTA | Alleghany |
| ROXOBEL | Bertie | SPEED | Edgecombe |
| RUFFIN | Rockingham | SPENCER | Rowan |
| RURAL HALL | Forsyth | SPROALE | Rutherford |
| RUTHERFORD COLLEGE | Burke | SPRING HOPE | Nash |
| SAINT PAULS | Robeson | SPRING LAKE | Cumberland |
| SALEMBURG | Sampson | SPURCE PINE | Mitchell |
| SALISBURY | Rowan | STALEY | Randolph |
| SALTER PATH | Carteret | STANFIELD | Stanly |
| SALUDA | Polk | STANLEY | Gaston |
| SALVO | Dare | STANTONSBURG | Wilson |
| SANDY RIDGE | Stokes | STAR | Montgomery |
| SANFORD | Lee | STATE ROAD | Surry |
| SAPPHIRE | Transylvania | STATESVILLE | Iredell |
| SARATOGA | Wilson | STEDMAN | Cumberland |
| SAXAPAHAW | Alamance | STELLA | Carteret |
| SCALY MOUNTAIN | Macon | STEM | Granville |
| SCOTLAND NECK | Halifax | STOKES | Pitt |
| SCOTTS | Iredell | STOKESDALE | Guilford |
| SCOTTVILLE | Ashe | STONEVILLE | Rockingham |
| SCRANTON | Hyde | STONEWALL | Pamlico |
| SEABOARD | Northampton | STONY POINT | Alexander |
| SEAGROVE | Randolph | STOVALL | Granville |
| SEALEVEL | Carteret | STUMPY POINT | Dare |
| SEDALIA | Guilford | SUGAR GROVE | Watauga |
| SELMA | Johnston | SUMMERFIELD | Guilford |
| SEMORA | Caswell | SUNBURY | Gates |

| | | | |
|---|---|---|---|
| SUNSET BEACH | Brunswick | WALLACE | Duplin |
| SUPPLY | Brunswick | WALLBURG | Davidson |
| SWANNANOA | Buncombe | WALNUT | Marshall |
| SWANQUARTER | Hyde | WALNUT COVE | Stokes |
| SWANSBORO | Onslow | WALSTONBURG | Greene |
| SWEPSONVILLE | Alamance | WANCHESE | Dare |
| SYLVA | Jackson | WARNE | Clay |
| TABOR CITY | Columbus | WARRENSVILLE | Ashe |
| TAPOCO | Graham | WARRENTON | Warren |
| TARBORO | Edgecombe | WARSAW | Duplin |
| TAR HEEL | Bladen | WASHINGTON | Beaufort |
| TAYLORSVILLE | Alexander | WATHA | Pender |
| TEACHEY | Duplin | WAVES | Dare |
| TERRELL | Catawba | WAXHAW | Union |
| THOMASVILLE | Davidson | WAYNESVILLE | Haywood |
| THURMOND | Wilkes | WEAVERVILLE | Buncombe |
| TILLERY | Halifax | WEBSTER | Jackson |
| TIMBERLAKE | Person | WEDDINGTON | Mecklenburg |
| TOAST | Surry | WELCOME | Davidson |
| TOBACCOVILLE | Forsyth | WELDON | Halifax |
| TODD | Ashe | WENDELL | Wake |
| TOPTON | Cherokee | WENTWORTH | Rockingham |
| TOWNSVILLE | Vance | WEST ASHEVILLE | Buncombe |
| TRAPHILL | Wilkes | WEST DURHAM | Durham |
| TRENTON | Jones | WEST NEWBERN | Craven |
| TRINITY | Randolph | WESTRIDGE | Nash |
| TRIPLETT | Watauga | WEST ROCKY MOUNT | Nash |
| TROUTMAN | Iredell | WEST STATESVILLE | Iredell |
| TROY | Montgomery | WEST END | Moore |
| TRYON | Polk | WESTFIELD | Surry |
| TUCKASEGEE | Jackson | WEST JEFFERSON | Ashe |
| TURKEY | Sampson | WHITAKERS | Nash |
| TURNERSBURG | Iredell | WHITEHEAD | Alleghany |
| TUXEDO | Henderson | WHITE OAK | Bladen |
| TYNER | Chowan | WHITE PLAINS | Surry |
| UNAKA | Cherokee | WHITEVILLE | Columbus |
| UNION GROVE | Iredell | WHITNEL | Caldwell |
| UNION MILLS | Rutherford | WHITSETT | Guilford |
| VALDESE | Burke | WHITTIER | Jackson |
| VALE | Lincoln | WILBAR | Wilkes |
| VALLE CRUCIS | Watauga | WILKESBORO | Wilkes |
| VANCEBORO | Craven | WILLARD | Pender |
| VANDERMERE | Pamlico | WILLIAMSTON | Martin |
| VASS | Moore | WILLISTON | Carteret |
| VAUGHAN | Warren | WILLOW SPRING | Wake |
| VILAS | Watauga | WILMAR PARK | Cabarrus |
| WACO | Cleveland | WILMINGTON | New Hanover |
| WADE | Cumberland | WILSON | Wilson |
| WADESBORO | Anson | WILSONS MILLS | Johnston |
| WAGRAM | Scotland | WINDSOR | Bertie |
| WAKE FOREST | Wake | WINFALL | Perquimans |
| WAKULLA | Robeson | WINGATE | Union |
| WALKERTOWN | Forsyth | WINNABOW | Brunswick |

| | | | |
|---|---|---|---|
| WINSTON-SALEM | Forsyth | BENEDICT | McLean |
| WINTERVILLE | Pitt | BERLIN | LaMoure |
| WINTON | Hertford | BERTHOLD | Ward |
| WISE | Warren | BEULAH | Mercer |
| WOODARD | Wilson | BINFORD | Griggs |
| WOODLAND | Northampton | BISBEE | Towner |
| WOODLEAF | Rowan | BISMARCK | Burleigh |
| WRIGHTSVILLE BEACH | New Hanover | BLAISDELL | Mountrail |
| YADKINVILLE | Yadkin | BORDULAC | Foster |
| YANCEYVILLE | Caswell | BOTTINEAU | Bottineau |
| YOUNGSVILLE | Franklin | BOWBELLS | Burke |
| ZEBULON | Wake | BOWDON | Wells |
| ZIONVILLE | Watauga | BOWMAN | Bowman |
| ZIRCONIA | Henderson | BRADDOCK | Emmons |
| **NORTH DAKOTA** | | BRINSMADE | Benson |
| ABERCROMBIE | Richland | BROCKET | Ramsey |
| ABSARAKA | Cass | BUCHANAN | Stutsman |
| ADAMS | Walsh | BUFFALO | Cass |
| AGATE | Rolette | BURLINGTON | Ward |
| ALAMO | Williams | BUTTE | McLean |
| ALEXANDER | McKenzie | BUXTON | Traill |
| ALFRED | LaMoure | CALEDONIA | Traill |
| ALICE | Cass | CALIO | Cavalier |
| ALKABO | Divide | CALVIN | Cavalier |
| ALMONT | Morton | CANDO | Towner |
| ALSEN | Cavalier | CANNONBALL | Sioux |
| AMBROSE | Divide | CARPIO | Ward |
| AMENIA | Cass | CARRINGTON | Foster |
| AMIDON | Slope | CARSON | Grant |
| ANAMOOSE | McHenry | CARTWRIGHT | McKenzie |
| ANETA | Nelson | CASSELTON | Cass |
| ANTLER | Bottineau | CATHAY | Wells |
| ARDOCH | Walsh | CAVALIER | Pembina |
| ARENA | Burleigh | CAYUGA | Sargent |
| ARGUSVILLE | Cass | CENTER | Oliver |
| ARNEGARD | McKenzie | CHASELEY | Wells |
| ARTHUR | Cass | CHRISTINE | Richland |
| ARVILLA | Grand Forks | CHURCHS FERRY | Ramsey |
| ASHELY | McIntosh | CLEVELAND | Stutsman |
| AYR | Cass | CLIFFORD | Traill |
| BACKOO | Pembina | COGSWELL | Sargent |
| BALDWIN | Burleigh | COLEHARBOT | McLean |
| BALFOUR | McHenry | COLFAX | Richland |
| BALTA | Pierce | COLUMBUS | Burke |
| BANTRY | McHenry | COOPERSTOWN | Griggs |
| BARNEY | Richland | COTEAU | Burke |
| BARTON | Pierce | COURTENAY | Stuttsman |
| BATHGATE | Pembina | CRARY | Raxnsey |
| BATTLEVIEW | Burke | CROSBY | Divide |
| BEACH | Golden Valley | CRYSTAL | Pembina |
| BELCOURT | Rolette | CRYSTAL SPRINGS | Kidder |
| BELDEN | Mountrail | CUMMINGS | Traill |
| BELFIELD | Stark | DAVENPORT | Cass |

| | | | |
|---|---|---|---|
| DAWSON | Kidder | FOXHOLM | Ward |
| DAZEY | Barnes | FREDONIA | Logan |
| DEERING | McHenry | FULLERTON | Dickey |
| DENBIGH | McHenry | GACKLE | Logan |
| DENHOFF | Sheridan | GALESBURG | Traill |
| DES LACS | Ward | GARDENIA | Bottineau |
| DEVILS LAKE | Ramsey | GARDNER | Cass |
| DICKEY | LaMoure | GARRISON | MclAan |
| DICKINSON | Stark | GENESEO | Sargent |
| DODGE | Dunn | GILBY | Grand Forks |
| DONNYBROOK | Ward | GLADSTONE | Pembina |
| DOUGLAS | Ward | GLENBURN | Renville |
| DOYON | Ramsey | GLENFIELD | Foster |
| DRAKE | McHenry | GLEN ULLIN | Morton |
| DRAYTON | Pembina | GOLDEN VALLEY | Mercer |
| DRISCOLL | Burleigh | GOLVA | Golden Valley |
| DUNN CENTER | Dunn | GOODRICH | Sheridan |
| DUNSEITH | Rolette | GRACE CITY | Foster |
| EAST ANTHONY | Morton | GRAFTON | Walsh |
| EAST JOHN | Rolette | GRAND FORKS | Grand Forks |
| EAST MICHAEL | Benson | GRANDIN | Cars |
| EAST THOMAS | Pembina | GRANVILLE | McHenry |
| ECKELSON | Barnes | GRASSY BUTTE | McKenzie |
| EDGELEY | La Moure | GREAT BEND | Richland |
| EDINBURG | Walsh | GRENORA | Williams |
| EDMORE | Ramsey | GUELPH | Dickey |
| EGELAND | Towner | GWINNER | Sargent |
| ELGIN | Grant | HAGUE | Emmons |
| ELLENDALE | Dickey | HALLIDAY | Dunn |
| EMERADO | Grand Forks | HAMBERG | Wells |
| ENDERLIN | Ransom | HAMILTON | Pembina |
| EPPING | Williams | HAMPDEN | Ramsey |
| ERIE | Cass | HANKINSON | Richland |
| ESMOND | Benson | HANNAFORD | Griggs |
| FAIRDALE | Walsb | HANNAH | Cavalier |
| FAIRFIELD | Billings | HARVEY | Wells |
| FAIRMOUNT | Richland | HARWOOD | Cass |
| FARGO | Cass | HATTON | Traill |
| FESSENDEN | Wells | HAVANA | Sargent |
| FILLMORE | Benson | HAYNES | Adams |
| FINGAL | Barnes | HAZELTON | Emmons |
| FINLEY | Steele | HAZEN | Mercer |
| FLASHER | Morton | HEATON | Wells |
| FLAXTON | Burke | HEBRON | Morton |
| FORBES | Dickey | HEIMDAL | Wells |
| FORDVILLE | Walsh | HENSEL | Pembina |
| FOREST RIVER | Walsh | HENSLER | Oliver |
| FORMAN | Sargent | HETTINGER | Adams |
| FORT RANSOM | Ransom | HILLSBORO | Traill |
| FORT RICE | Morton | HOOPLE | Walsh |
| FORT TOTTEN | Benson | HOPE | Steele |
| FORTUNA | Divide | HORACE | Cass |
| FORT YATES | Sioux | HUNTER | Cass |

| | | | |
|---|---|---|---|
| HURDSFIELD | Wells | MANVEL | Grand Forks |
| INKSTER | Grand Forks | MAPLETON | Cass |
| JAMESTOWN | Stutsman | MARION | LaMoure |
| JESSIE | Griggs | MARSHALL | Dunn |
| JOHNSTOWN | Grand Forks | MARTIN | Sheridan |
| JOLIETTE | Pembina | MAX | McLean |
| JUD | LaMoure | MAXBASS | Bottineau |
| KARLSRUHE | McHenry | MAYVILLE | Traill |
| KATHRYN | Barnes | MEDINA | Stutsman |
| KEENE | McKenzie | MEDORA | Billings |
| KENMARE | Ward | MEKINOCK | Grand Forks |
| KENSAL | Stutsman | MENOKEN | Burleigh |
| KIEF | McHenry | MERCER | McLean |
| KILLDEER | Dunn | MERRICOURT | Dickey |
| KINDRED | Cass | MICHIGAN | Nelson |
| KINTYRE | Emmons | MILNOR | Sargent |
| KLOTEN | Nelson | MILTON | Cavalier |
| KNOX | Benson | MINNEWAUKAN | Benson |
| KRAMER | Bottineau | MINOT | Ward |
| KULM | LaMoure | MINTO | Walsh |
| LAKOTA | Nelson | MOFFIT | Burleigh |
| LAMOURE | LaMoure | MOHALL | Renville |
| LANDA | Bottineau | MONANGO | Dickey |
| LANGDON | Cavalier | MONTPELIER | Stutsman |
| LANKIN | Walsh | MOORETON | Richland |
| LANSFORD | Bottineau | MOTT | Hettinger |
| LARIMORE | Grand Forks | MOUNTAIN | Pembina |
| LAWTON | Ramsey | MUNICH | Cavalier |
| LEEL | Rogers | MYLO | Rolette |
| LEEDS | Benson | NAPOLEON | Logan |
| LEFOR | Stark | NASH | Walsh |
| LEHR | McIntosh | NECHE | Pembina |
| LEITH | Grant | NEKOMA | Cavalier |
| LEONARD | Cass | NEWBURG | Bottineau |
| LIDGERWOOD | Richland | NEW ENGLAND | Hettinger |
| LIGNITE | Burke | NEW HRADEC | Dunn |
| LINTON | Emmons | NEW LEIPZIG | Grant |
| LISBON | Ransom | NEW ROCKFORD | Eddy |
| LITCHVILLE | Barnes | NEW SALEM | Morton |
| LUVERNE | Steele | NEW TOWN | Mountrail |
| MCCANNA | Grand Forks | NIAGARA | Grand Forks |
| MCCLUSKY | Sheridan | NOME | Barnes |
| MCGREGOR | Williams | NOONAN | Divide |
| MCHENRY | Foster | NORTHWOOD | Grand Forks |
| MCLEOD | Ransom | NORTONVILLE | LaMoure |
| MCVILLE | Nelson | NORWICH | McHenry |
| MADDOCK | Benson | OAKES | Dickey |
| MAKOTI | Ward | OBERON | Benson |
| MANDAN | Morton | ORISKA | Barnes |
| MANDAREE | McKenzie | ORRIN | Pierce |
| MANFRED | Wells | OSNABROCK | Cavalier |
| MANNING | Dunn | OVERLY | Bottineau |
| MANTADOR | Richland | PAGE | Cass |

| | | | |
|---|---|---|---|
| PALERMO | Mountrail | SOURIS | Bottineau |
| PARK RIVER | Walsh | SOUTH HEART | Stark |
| PARSHALL | Mountrail | SPRITWOOD | Stutsman |
| PEKIN | Nelson | SPRING BROOK | Williams |
| PEMBINA | Pembina | STANLEY | Mountrail |
| PENN | Ramsey | STANTON | Mercer |
| PERTH | Towner | STARKWEATHER | Ramsey |
| PETERSBURG | Nelson | STEELE | Kidder |
| PETTIBONE | Kidder | STERLING | Burleigh |
| PILLSBURY | Barnes | STRASBURG | Emmons |
| PINGREE | Stutsman | STREETER | Stutsman |
| PISEK | Walsh | SURREY | Ward |
| PLAZA | Mountrail | SUTTON | Griggs |
| PORTAL | Burke | SYKESTON | Wells |
| PORTLAND | Traill | TAPPEN | Kidder |
| POWERS LAKE | Burke | TAYLOR | Stark |
| RALEIGH | Grant | THOMPSON | Grand Forks |
| RAY | Williams | TIOGA | Williams |
| REEDER | Adams | TOKIO | Benson |
| REGAN | Burleigh | TOLLEY | Renville |
| REGENT | Hettinger | TOLNA | Nelson |
| REYNOLDS | Grand Forks | TOWER CITY | Cass |
| RHAME | Bowman | TOWNER | McHenry |
| RICHARDTON | Stark | TRENTON | Williams |
| RIVERDALE | McLean | TROTTERS | Golden Valley |
| ROBINSON | Kidder | TUTTLE | Kidder |
| ROCKLAKE | Towner | TURTLE LAKE | McLean |
| ROGERS | Barnes | UNDERWOOD | McLean |
| ROLETTE | Rolette | UNION | Cavalier |
| ROLLA | Rolette | UPHAM | McHenry |
| ROSEGLEN | McLean | VALLEY CITY | Barnes |
| ROSS | Mountrail | VELVA | McHenry |
| RUGBY | Pierce | VENTURIA | McIntosh |
| RUSO | McLean | VERONA | LaMoure |
| RUTLAND | Sargent | VOLTAIRE | McHenry |
| RYDER | Ward | WAHPETON | Ricland |
| SAINT JOHN | Rolette | WALCOTT | Richland |
| SAINT MICHAEL | Benson | WALES | Cavalier |
| SAINT THOMAS | Pembina | WALHALIA | Pembina |
| SANBORN | Barnes | WARWICK | Benson |
| SAN HAVEN | Rollette | WASHBURN | McLean |
| SARLES | Cavalier | WATFORD CITY | McKenzie |
| SAWYER | Ward | WEBSTER | Ramsey |
| SCRANTON | Bowman | WEST FARGO | Cass |
| SELFRIDGE | Sioux | WESTHOPE | Bottineau |
| SELZ | Pierce | WHEATLAND | Cass |
| SENTINEL BUTTE | Golden Valley | WHITE EARTH | Mountrail |
| SHARON | Steele | WILDROSE | Williams |
| SHELDON | Ransom | WILLISTON | Williams |
| SHERWOOD | Renville | WILLOW CITY | Bottineau |
| SHEYENNE | Eddy | WILTON | McLean |
| SHIELDS | Grant | WIMBLEDON | Barnes |
| SOLEN | Sioux | WING | Burleigh |

| | | | |
|---|---|---|---|
| WISHEK | McIntosh | ATWATER | Portage |
| WOLFORD | Pierce | AUGUSTA | Carroll |
| WOODWORTH | Stutsman | AURORA | Portage |
| WYNDMERE | Richland | AUSTINBURG | Ashtabula |
| YORK | Benson | AUSTINTOWN | Mahoning |
| YPSILANTI | Stutsman | AVA | Noble |
| ZAHL | Williams | AVON | Lorain |
| ZAP | Mercer | AVONDALE | Hamilton |
| ZEELAND | McIntosh | AVON LAKE | Lorain |
| **OHIO** | | BAINBRIDGE | Ross |
| ABERDEEN | Brown | BAKERSVILLE | Coshocton |
| ADA | Hardin | BALTIC | Tuscarawas |
| ADAMS MILLS | Muskingum | BALTIMORE | Fairfield |
| ADAMSVILLE | Muskingum | BANNOCK | Belmont |
| ADDYSTON | Hamilton | BARBERTON | Summit |
| ADELPHI | Ross | BARLOW | Washington |
| ADENA | Jefferson | BARNESVILLE | Belmont |
| ADRIAN | Seneca | BARTLETT | Washington |
| AKRON | Summit | BARTON | Belmont |
| ALBANY | Athens | BASCOM | Seneca |
| ALEXANDRIA | Licking | BATAVIA | Clermont |
| ALGER | Hardin | BATH | Summit |
| ALLEDONIA | Belmont | BAY VILLAGE | Cuyahoga |
| ALLENSVILLE | McArthur | BEACH CITY | Stark |
| ALLIANCE | Stark | BEACHLAND | Cuyahoga |
| ALPHA | Greene | BEACHWOOD | Cuyahoga |
| ALVADA | Seneca | BEALLSVILLE | Monroe |
| ALVORDTON | Williams | BEAVER | Pike |
| AMANDA | Fairfield | BEAVER CREEK | Montgomery |
| AMELIA | Clermont | BEAVERDAM | Allen |
| AMESVILLE | Athens | BEDFORD | Cuyahoga |
| AMHERST | Lorain | BEECHWOLD | Franklin |
| AMLIN | Franklin | BELLAIRE | Belmont |
| AMSDEN | Seneca | BELLBROOK | Greene |
| AMSTERDAM | Jefferson | BELLE CENTER | Logan |
| ANDERSON | Hamilton | BELLEFONTAINE | Logan |
| ANDOVER | Ashtabula | BELLE VALLEY | Noble |
| ANNA | Shelby | BELLEVUE | Huron |
| ANSONIA | Darke | BELLVILLE | Richland |
| ANTIOCH | Monroe | BELMONT | Belmont |
| ANTWERP | Paulding | BELMORE | Putnam |
| APPLE CREEK | Wayne | BELOIT | Mahoning |
| ARCADIA | Hancock | BELPRE | Washington |
| ARCANUM | Darke | BENTON RIDGE | Hancock |
| ARCHBOLD | Fulton | BENTONVILLE | Adams |
| ARLINGTON | Hancock | BEREA | Cuyahoga |
| ARMSTRONG MILLS | Belmont | BERGHOLZ | Jefferson |
| ASHLAND | Ashland | BERKEY | Lucas |
| ASHLEY | Delaware | BERLIN | Holmes |
| ASHTABULA | Ashtabula | BERLIN CENTER | Mahoning |
| ASHVILLE | Pickaway | BERLIN HEIGHTS | Erie |
| ATHENS | Athens | BETHEL | Clermont |
| ATTICA | Seneca | BETHESDA | Belmont |

| | | | |
|---|---|---|---|
| BETTSVILLE | Seneca | BURBANK | Wayne |
| BEVERLY | Washington | BURGHILL | Trumbull |
| BEXLEY | Franklin | BURGOON | Sandusky |
| BIDWELL | Gallia | BURKETTSVILLE | Mercer |
| BIG PRAIRIE | Holmes | BURNET WOODS | Hamilton |
| BIRMINGHAM | Erie | BURTON | Geauga |
| BLACKLICK | Franklin | BUSCH | Franklin |
| BLADENSBURG | Knox | BUTLER | Richland |
| BLAINE | Belmont | BYESVILLE | Guernsey |
| BLAKESLEE | Williams | CABLE | Champaign |
| BLANCHESTER | Clinton | CADIZ | Harrison |
| BLISSFIELD | Coshocton | CAIRO | Allen |
| BLOOMDALE | Wood | CALCUTTA | Columbiana |
| BLOOMINGBURG | Fayette | CALDWELL | Noble |
| BLOOMINGDALE | Jefferson | CALEDONIA | Marion |
| BLOOMVILLE | Seneca | CAMBRIDGE | Guernsey |
| BLUE CREEK | Adams | CAMDEN | Preble |
| BLUE ROCK | Muskingum | CAMERON | Monroe |
| BLUFFTON | Allen | CAMPBELL | Mahoning |
| BOARDMAN | Mahoning | CAMP DENNISON | Hamilton |
| BOLIVAR | Tuscarawas | CANAL FULTON | Stark |
| BONO | Ottawa | CANAL WINCHESTER | Franklin |
| BOTKINS | Shelby | CANFIELD | Mahoning |
| BOURNEVILLE | Ross | CANTON | Stark |
| BOWERSTON | Harrison | CARBONDALE | Athens |
| BOWERSVILLE | Greene | CARBON HILL | Hocking |
| BOWLING GREEN | Wood | CARDINGTON | Morrow |
| BRADFORD | Miami | CAREY | Wyandot |
| BRADNER | Wood | CARROLL | Fairfield |
| BRADY LAKE | Portage | CARROLLTON | Carroll |
| BREMEN | Fairfield | CARROTHERS | Seneca |
| BREWSTER | Stark | CASSTOWN | Miami |
| BRICE | Franklin | CASTALIA | Erie |
| BRIDGEPORT | Belmont | CASTINE | Darke |
| BRIGGS | Cuyahoga | CATAWBA | Clark |
| BRILLIANT | Jefferson | CECIL | Paulding |
| BRINKHAVEN | Knox | CEDARVILLE | Greene |
| BRISTOLVILLE | Trumbull | CELINA | Mercer |
| BROADVIEW HEIGHTS | Cuyahoga | CENTERBURG | Knox |
| BROADWAY | Union | CENTERVILLE | Montgomery |
| BROOKFIELD | Trumbull | CENTRAL | Lucas |
| BROOKLYN | Cuyahoga | CHAGRIN FALLS | Cuyahoga |
| BROOKPARK | Cuyahoga | CHANDLERSVILLE | Muskingum |
| BROOKVILLE | Montgomery | CHARDON | Geauga |
| BROANSVILLE | Licking | CHARM | Holmes |
| BRUNSWICK | Medina | CHATFIELD | Crawford |
| BRYAN | Williams | CHAUNCY | Athens |
| BUCHTEL | Athens | CHERRY FORK | Adams |
| BUCKEYE LAKE | Licking | CHESAPEAKE | Lawrence |
| BUCKLAND | Auglaize | CHESHIRE | Gallia |
| BUCYRUS | Crawford | CHESTER | Meigs |
| BUFFALO | Guernsey | CHESTERHILL | Morgan |
| BUFORD | Highland | CHESTERLAND | Geauga |

| | | | |
|---|---|---|---|
| CHESTERVILLE | Morrow | CRESTLINE | Crawford |
| CHICKASAW | Mercer | CRESTON | Wayne |
| CHILLICOTHE | Ross | CRIDERSVILLE | Allen |
| CHILO | Clermont | CROOKSVILLE | Perry |
| CHIPPEWA LAKE | Medina | CROTON | Licking |
| CHRISTIANSBURG | Champaign | CROWN CITY | Gallia |
| CHRISTOPHER COLUMBUS | Franklin | CUBA | Clinton |
| CINCINNATI | Hamilton | CUMBERLAND | Guernsey |
| CIRCLEVILLE | Pickaway | CUMMINSVILLE | Hamilton |
| CLARINGTON | Monroe | CURTICE | Ottawa |
| CLARKSBURG | Ross | CUSTAR | Wood |
| CLARKSVILLE | Clinton | CUTLER | Washington |
| CLAY CENTER | Ottawa | CUYAHOGA FALLS | Summit |
| CLAYSVILLE | Guernsey | CYGNET | Wood |
| CLAYTON | Montgomery | CYNTHIANA | Pike |
| CLEVELAND | Cuyahoga | DABEL | Montgomery |
| CLEVELAND HEIGHTS | Cuyahoga | DALTON | Wayne |
| CLEVES | Hamilton | DAMASCUS | Mahoning |
| CLIFTON | Greene | DANVILLE | Knox |
| CLINTON | Summit | DAY HEIGHTS | Clermont |
| CLINTONVILLE | Franklin | DAYTON | Montgomery |
| CLOVERDALE | Putnam | DAYTON VIEW | Montgomery |
| CLYDE | Sandusky | DECATUR | Brown |
| COAL RUN | Washington | DEERFIELD | Portage |
| COALTON | Jackson | DEERSVILLE | Harrison |
| COLDWATER | Mercer | DEFIANCE | Defiance |
| COLERAIN | Belmont | DEGRAFF | Logan |
| COLLEGE CORNER | Butler | DELAWARE | Delaware |
| COLLEGE HILLS | Hamilton | DELLROY | Carroll |
| COLLINS | Huron | DELPHOS | Allen |
| COLLINSVILLE | Butler | DELTA | Fulton |
| COLLINWOOD | Cuyahoga | DENNISON | Tuscarawas |
| COLTON | Henry | DERBY | Pickaway |
| COLUMBIANA | Columbiana | DERWENT | Guernsey |
| COLUMBIA STATION | Lorain | DESHLER | Henry |
| COLUMBUS | Franklin | DEXTER | Meigs |
| COLUMBUS GROVE | Putnam | DEXTER CITY | Noble |
| COMMERCIAL POINT | Pickaway | DIAMOND | Portage |
| CONESVILLE | Coshocton | DILLONVALE | Jefferson |
| CONNEAUT | Ashtabula | DOLA | Hardin |
| CONOVER | Miami | DONNELSVILLE | Clark |
| CONTINENTAL | Putnam | DORSET | Ashtabula |
| CONVOY | Van Wert | DOVER | Tuscarawas |
| COOLVILLE | Athens | DOYLESTOWN | Wayne |
| COPLEY | Summit | DRESDEN | Muskingum |
| CORNERSBURG | Mahoning | DUBLIN | Franklin |
| CORNING | Perry | DUNBRIDGE | Wood |
| CORRYVILLE | Hamilton | DUNCAN FALLS | Muskingum |
| CORTLAND | Trumbull | DUNDEE | Tuscarawas |
| COSHOCTON | Coshocton | DUNKIRK | Hardin |
| COVINGTON | Miami | DUPONT | Putnam |
| CRANWOOD | Cuyahoga | EAST AKRON | Summit |
| CREOLA | Vinton | EAST CANTON | Stark |

| | | | |
|---|---|---|---|
| EAST CLARIDON | Geauga | FLY | Monroe |
| EAST CLEVELAND | Cuyahoga | FOREST | Hardin |
| EAST FULTONHAM | Muskingum | FOREST PARK | Montgomery |
| EASTLAND | Franklin | FORT JENNINGS | Putnam |
| EAST LIBERTY | Logan | FORT LORAMIE | Shelby |
| EAST LIVERPOOL | Columbiana | FORT RECOVERY | Mercer |
| EAST ORWELL | Ashtabula | FORT SENECA | Seneca |
| EAST PALESTINE | Columbiana | FOSTORIA | Seneca |
| EAST ROCHESTER | Columbiana | FOUNTAIN SQUARE | Hamilton |
| EAST SIDE | Mahoning | FOWLER | Trumbull |
| EAST SPARTA | Stark | FRANKFORT | Ross |
| EAST SPRINGFIELD | Jefferson | FRANKLIN | Warren |
| EATON | Preble | FRANKLIN FURNACE | Scioto |
| EDGERTON | Williams | FRANKLIN PARK | Lucas |
| EDGEWATER | Cuyahoga | FRAZEYSBURG | Muskingum |
| EDISON | Morrow | FREDERICKSBURG | Wayne |
| EDON | Williams | FREDERICKTOWN | Knox |
| ELDORADO | Preble | FREEPORT | Harrison |
| ELGIN | Van Wert | FREMONT | Sandusky |
| ELIDA | Allen | FRESNO | Coshocton |
| ELKTON | Columbiana | FRIENDSHIP | Scioto |
| ELLET | Summit | FULTON | Morrow |
| ELLISTON | Ottawa | FULTONHAM | Muskingum |
| ELLSWORTH | Mahoning | GAHANNA | Franklin |
| ELMORE | Ottawa | GALENA | Delaware |
| ELYRIA | Lorain | GALION | Crawford |
| EMPIRE | Jefferson | GALLIPOLIS | Gallia |
| ENGLEWOOD | Montgomery | GALLOWAY | Franklin |
| ENON | Clark | GAMBIER | Knox |
| ERIEVIEW | Cuyahoga | GARFIELD HEIGHTS | Cuyahoga |
| ETNA | Licking | GARRETTSVILLE | Portage |
| EUCLID | Cuyahoga | GATES MILLS | Cuyahoga |
| EVANSPORT | Defiance | GENEVA | Ashtabula |
| FAIRBORN | Greene | GENOA | Ottawa |
| FAIRFIELD | Butler | GEORGETOWN | Brown |
| FAIRLAWN | Summit | GERMANTOWN | Montgomery |
| FAIRPOINT | Belmont | GETTYSBURG | Darke |
| FAIRVIEW | Guernsey | GIBSONBURG | Erie |
| FAIRVIEW PARK | Cuyahoga | GILBOA | Putnam |
| FARMDALE | Trumbull | GIRARD | Trumbull |
| FARMER | Defiance | GLANDORF | Putnam |
| FARMERSVILLE | Montgomery | GLENCOE | Belmont |
| FAYETTE | Fulton | GLENFORD | Perry |
| FAYETTEVILLE | Brown | GLENMONT | Holmes |
| FEESBURG | Brown | GLOUSTER | Athens |
| FELICITY | Clermont | GNADENHUTTEN | Tuscarawas |
| FINDLAY | Hancock | GOMER | Allen |
| FIRESTONE PARK | Summit | GORDON | Darke |
| FIVE POINTS | Summit | GOSHEN | Clermont |
| FLAT ROCK | Seneca | GRAFTON | Lorain |
| FLEMING | Washington | GRAND RAPIDS | Wood |
| FLETCHER | Miami | GRAND RIVER | Lake |
| FLUSHING | Belmont | GRANVILLE | Licking |

| | | | |
|---|---|---|---|
| GRATIOT | Licking | HICKSVILLE | Defiance |
| GRATIS | Preble | HIGGINSPORT | Brown |
| GRAYSVILLE | Monroe | HIGHLAND | Highland |
| GRAYTOWN | Ottawa | HILLIARD | Franklin |
| GREEN CAMP | Marion | HILLSBORO | Highland |
| GREENFIELD | Highland | HINCKLEY | Medina |
| GREENFORD | Mahoning | HIRAM | Portage |
| GREENSBURG | Summit | HOCKINGPORT | Athens |
| GREEN SPRINGS | Seneca | HOLGATE | Henry |
| GREENTOWN | Stark | HOLLAND | Lucas |
| GREENVILLE | Darke | HOLLANSBURG | Darke |
| GREENWICH | Huron | HOLLOWAY | Belmont |
| GROVE CITY | Franklin | HOLMESVILLE | Holmes |
| GROVEPORT | Franklin | HOMER | Licking |
| GROVER HILL | Paulding | HOMERVILLE | Medina |
| GUERNE | Wayne | HOMEWORTH | Columbiana |
| GUSTAVUS | Trumball | HOOKER | Fairfield |
| GUYSVILLE | Athens | HOOVEN | Hamilton |
| GYPSUM | Ottawa | HOPEDALE | Harrison |
| HALLSVILLE | Ross | HOPEWELL | Muskingum |
| HAMBDEN | Geauga | HOUSTON | Shelby |
| HAMDEN | Vinton | HOWARD | Knox |
| HAMERSVILLE | Brown | HOYTVILLE | Wood |
| HAMILTON | Butler | HUBBARD | Trumbull |
| HAMLER | Henry | HUDSON | Summit |
| HAMLET | Clermont | HUE | Vinton |
| HANNONDSVILLE | Jefferson | HUNTINGTON | Lorain |
| HANNIBAL | Monroe | HUNTSBURG | Geauga |
| HANOVERTON | Columbiana | HUNTSVILLE | Logan |
| HARBOR VIEW | Lucas | HURON | Erie |
| HARLEM SPRINGS | Carroll | IBERIA | Morrow |
| HARPSTER | Wyandot | IDAHO | Pike |
| HARRIETSVILLE | Noble | IRONDALE | Jefferson |
| HARRISBURG | Franklin | IRONTON | Lawrence |
| HARRISON | Hamilton | IRWIN | Union |
| HARRISVILLE | Harrison | ISLE SAINT GEORGE | Ottawa |
| HARROD | Allen | JACKSON | Jackson |
| HARTFORD | Trumbull | JACKSON CENTER | Shelby |
| HARTVILLE | Stark | JACKSTONTOWN | Licking |
| HARVEYSBURG | Warren | JACKSONVILLE | Athens |
| HASKINS | Wood | JACOBSBURG | Belmont |
| HAVERHILL | Scioto | JAMESTOWN | Greene |
| HAVILAND | Paulding | JASPER | Pike |
| HAYDENVILLE | Hocking | JEFFERSON | Ashtabula |
| HAYESVILLE | Ashland | JEFFERSONVILLE | Fayette |
| HEATH | Licking | JELLOWAY | Knox |
| HEBRON | Licking | JEROMESVILLE | Ashland |
| HECIA | Lawrence | JERRY CITY | Wood |
| HELENA | Sandusky | JERUSALEM | Monroe |
| HEMLOCK | Perry | JEWELL | Defiance |
| HENDRYSBURG | Belmont | JOHNSTON | Trumball |
| HEPBURN | Hardin | JEWETT | Harrison |
| HESSVILLE | Sandusky | JOHNSTOWN | Licking |

| | | | |
|---|---|---|---|
| JONES CORNER | Adams | LEIPSIC | Putnam |
| JUNCTION CITY | Perry | LEMOYNE | Wood |
| KALIDA | Putnam | LEVANNA | Brown |
| KANSAS | Seneca | LEWISBURG | Preble |
| KEENE | Coshocton | LEWIS CENTER | Delaware |
| KELEYS ISLAND | Erie | LEWISTOWN | Logan |
| KENSINGTON | Columbiana | LEWISVILLE | Monroe |
| KENT | Portage | LIBERTY CENTER | Henry |
| KENTON | Hardin | LIMA | Allen |
| KERR | Gallia | LIMAVILLE | Stark |
| KETTERING | Montgomery | LINDALE | Clermont |
| KETTLERSVILLE | Shelby | LINDSEY | Sandusky |
| KIDRON | Wayne | LISBON | Columbiana |
| KIEFERVILLE | Putnam | LITCHFIELD | Medina |
| KILBOURNE | Delaware | LITHOPOLIS | Fairfield |
| KILLBUCK | Holmes | LITTLE HOCKING | Washington |
| KILLBOLTON | Guernsey | LOCKBOURNE | Franklin |
| KINGS MILLS | Warren | LOCUST GROVE | Adams |
| KINGSTON | Ross | LODI | Medina |
| KINGSVILLE | Ashtabula | LOGAN | Hocking |
| KINNIKINNICK | Ross | LONDON | Madison |
| KINSMAN | Trumbull | LONDONDERRY | Ross |
| KIPLING | Guernsey | LONG BOTTOM | Meigs |
| KIPTON | Lorain | LONGLEY | Seneca |
| KIRBY | Wyandot | LORAIN | Lorain |
| KIRKERSVILLE | Licking | LORE CITY | Guernsey |
| KITTS HILL | Lawrence | LOUDONVILLE | Ashland |
| KUNKLE | Williams | LOUISVILLE | Stark |
| LACARNE | Ottawa | LOVELAND | Hamilton |
| LAFAYETTE | Allen | LOWELL | Washington |
| LAFFERTY | Belmont | LOWELLVILLE | Mahoning |
| LAGRANGE | Lorain | LOWER SALEM | Washington |
| LAINGS | Monroe | LUCAS | Richland |
| LAKE MILTON | Mahoning | LUCASVILLE | Scioto |
| LAKEMORE | Summit | LUCKEY | Wood |
| LAKESIDE-MARBLEHEAD | Ottawa | LUDLOW FALLS | Miami |
| LAKEVIEW | Logan | LURAY | Fairfield |
| LAKEVILLE | Holmes | LYNCHBURG | Highland |
| LAKEWOOD | Cuyahoga | LYNX | Adams |
| LANCASTER | Fairfield | LYONS | Fulton |
| LANGSVILLE | Meigs | LYRA | Scioto |
| LANSING | Belmont | MABEE | Jackson |
| LARUE | Marion | MACEDONIA | Summit |
| LATHAM | Pike | MACKSBURG | Washington |
| LATTY | Paulding | MADERIA | Hamilton |
| LAURA | Miami | MADISON | Lake |
| LAURELVILLE | Hocking | MAGNETIC SPRINGS | Union |
| LEAVITTSBURG | Trumbull | MAGNOLIA | Stark |
| LEBANON | Warren | MAINEVILLE | Warren |
| LEESBURG | Highland | MALAGA | Monroe |
| LEES CREEK | Clinton | MALINTA | Henry |
| LEESVILLE | Carroll | MALTA | Morgan |
| LEETONIA | Columbiana | MALVERN | Carroll |

| | | | |
|---|---|---|---|
| MANCHETER | Adams | MIDDLEBURY | Van Wert |
| MANSFIELD | Richland | MIDDLEFIELD | Geauga |
| MANURA | Portage | MIDDLE POINT | Van Wert |
| MAPLE HEIGHTS | Cuyahoga | MIDDLEPORT | Van Wert |
| MAPLEWOOD | Shelby | MIDDLETOWN | Butler |
| MARATHON | Clermont | MIDLAND | Clinton |
| MARENGO | Morrow | MIDVALE | Tuscarawas |
| MARIA STEIN | Mercer | MILAN | Erie |
| MARIEMONT | Clermont | MILFORD | Clermont |
| MARIETTA | Washington | MILFORD CENTER | Union |
| MARION | Marion | MILLBURY | Wood |
| MARK CENTER | Defiance | MILLEDGEVILLE | Fayette |
| MARSHALL | Highland | MILLER CITY | Putnam |
| MARSHALLVILLE | Wayne | MILLERSBURG | Holmes |
| MARTEL | Marion | MILLERSPORT | Fairfield |
| MARTIN | Ottawa | MILLFIELD | Athens |
| MARTINSBURG | Knox | MILLVILLE | Butler |
| MARTINS FERRY | Belmont | MILLWOOD | Knox |
| MARTINSVILLE | Clinton | MILTON CENTER | Wood |
| MARYSVILLE | Union | MINERAL CITY | Tuscarawas |
| MASON | Warren | MINERAL RIDGE | Trumbull |
| MASSILLON | Stark | MINERVA | Stark |
| MASURY | Trumbull | MINFORD | Scioto |
| MAUMEE | Lucas | MINGO | Champaign |
| MAXIMO | Stark | MINGO JUNCTION | Jefferson |
| MAYNARD | Belmont | MINSTER | Auglaize |
| MCARTHUR | Vinton | MOGADORE | Summit |
| MCCLURE | Henry | MONCLOVA | Lucas |
| MCCOMB | Hancock | MONROE | Butler |
| MCCONNELSVILLE | Morgan | MONROEVILLE | Huron |
| MCCUTCHENVILLE | Wyandot | MONTEZUMA | Mercer |
| MCDERMOTT | Scioto | MONTGOMERY | Hamilton |
| MCDONALD | Trumbull | MONTPELIER | Williams |
| MCCUFFEY | Hardin | MONTVILLE | Geauga |
| MECHANICSBURG | Champaign | MOORVILLE | Geauga |
| MECHANICSTOWN | Carroll | MOOREFIELD | Harrison |
| MEDINA | Medina | MORELAND | Wayne |
| MEDWAY | Clark | MORNING SUN | Preble |
| MEEKER | Marion | MORRAL | Marion |
| MELMORE | Seneca | MORRISTOWN | Belmont |
| MELROSE | Paulding | MORROW | Warren |
| MENDON | Mercer | MOSCOW | Clermont |
| MENTOR | Lake | MOUNT BLANCHARD | Hancock |
| MERCER | Mercer | MOUNT CORY | Hancock |
| MERMILL | Wood | MOUNT EATON | Wayne |
| MESOPOTAMIA | Trumbull | MOUNT GILEAD | Morrow |
| METAMORA | Fulton | MOUNT HOPE | Holmes |
| MIAMISBURG | Montgomery | MOUNT LIBERTY | Knox |
| MIAMITOWN | Hamilton | MOUNT OLIVE | Clermont |
| MIAMIVILLE | Clermont | MOUNT ORAB | Brown |
| MIDDLE BASS | Ottawa | MOUNT PERRY | Perry |
| MIDDLEBRANCH | Stark | MOUNT PLEASANT | Jefferson |
| MIDDLEBURG | Logan | MOUNT SAINT JOSEPH | Hamilton |

| | | | |
|---|---|---|---|
| MOUNT STERLING | Madison | NEW STRAITSVILLE | Perry |
| MOUNT VERNON | Knox | NEWTON FALLS | Trumbull |
| MOUNT VICTORY | Hardin | NEWTONSVILLE | Clermont |
| MOWRYSTOWN | Highland | NEW VIENNA | Clinton |
| MOXAHALA | Perry | NEW WASHINGTON | Crawford |
| MONROE FALLS | Summit | NEW WATERFORD | Columbiana |
| MULBERRY | Clermont | NEY | Defiance |
| MURRAY CITY | Hocking | NILES | Trumbull |
| NANKIN | Ashland | NORTH BALITOMRE | Wood |
| NAPOLEON | Henry | NORTH BEND | Hamilton |
| NASHPORT | Muskingum | NORTH BENTON | Mahoning |
| NASHVILLE | Holmes | NORTH BLOOMFIELD | Trumbull |
| NAVARRE | Stark | NORTH FAIRFIELD | Huron |
| NEAPOLIS | Lucas | NORTHFIELD | Summit |
| NEFFS | Belmont | NORTH GEORGETOWN | Columbiana |
| NEGLEY | Columbiana | NORTH HAMPTON | Clark |
| NELSONVILLE | Athens | NORTH JACKSON | Mahoning |
| NEVADA | Wyandot | NORTH KINGSVILLE | Ashtabula |
| NEVILLE | Clermont | NORTH LAWRENCE | Stark |
| NEW ALBANY | Franklin | NORTH LEWISBURG | Champaign |
| NEWARK | Licking | NORTH LIMA | Mahoning |
| NEW ATHENS | Harrison | NORTH OLMSTED | Cuyahoga |
| NEW BAVARIA | Henry | NORTH ROBINSON | Crawford |
| NEW BLOOMINGTON | Marion | NORTH STAR | Darke |
| NEW BOSTON | Scioto | NORTHUP | Gallia |
| NEW BREMEN | Auglaize | NORWALK | Huron |
| NEWBURY | Geauga | NORWICH | Muskingum |
| NEW CARLISLE | Clark | NOVA | Ashland |
| NEWCOMERSTOWN | Tuscarawas | NOVELTY | Geauga |
| NEW CONCORD | Muskingum | OAK HARBOR | Ottawa |
| NEW DOVER | Union | OAK HILL | Jackson |
| NEW GARDEN | Columbiana | OAKWOOD | Paulding |
| NEW HAMPSHIRE | Auglaize | OBERLIN | Lorain |
| NEW HAVEN | Huron | OCEOLA | Crawford |
| NEW HOLLAND | Pickaway | OHIO CITY | Van Wert |
| NEW KNOXVILLE | Auglaize | OKEANA | Butler |
| NEW LEBANON | Montgomery | OKOLONA | Henry |
| NEW LEXINGTON | Perry | OLD FORT | Seneca |
| NEW LONDON | Huron | OLD WASHINGTON | Guernsey |
| NEW LYME | Ashtabula | ONTARIO | Richland |
| NEW MADISON | Darke | ORANGEVILLE | Trumbull |
| NEW MARKET | Highland | OREGONIA | Warren |
| NEW MARSHFIELD | Athens | ORIENT | Pickaway |
| NEW MATAMORAS | Washington | ORRVILLE | Wayne |
| NEW MIDDLETOWN | Mahoning | ORWELL | Ashtabula |
| NEW PARIS | Preble | OSGOOD | Drake |
| NEW PHILADELPHIA | Tuscarawas | OSTRANDER | Delaware |
| NEW PLYMOUTH | Vinton | OTTAWA | Putnam |
| NEWPORT | Washington | OTTOVILLE | Putnam |
| NEW RICHMOND | Clermont | OTWAY | Scioto |
| NEW RIEGEL | Seneca | OVERPECK | Butler |
| NEW RUMLEY | Harrison | OWENSVILLE | Clermont |
| NEW SPRINGFIELD | Mahoning | OXFORD | Butler |

| | | | |
|---|---|---|---|
| PAINESVILLE | Lake | QUAKER CITY | Guernsey |
| PALESTINE | Drake | QUINCY | Logan |
| PANDORA | Putnam | RACINE | Meigs |
| PARIS | Stark | RADCLIFF | Vinton |
| PARKMAN | Geauga | RADNOR | Delaware |
| PATASKALA | Licking | RANDOLPH | Portage |
| PATROIT | Gallia | RARDEN | Scioto |
| PAULDING | Paulding | RAVENNA | Portage |
| PAYNE | Paulding | RAWSON | Hancock |
| PEDRO | Lawrence | RAY | Vinton |
| PEEBLES | Adams | RAYLAND | Jefferson |
| PEMBERTON | Shelby | RAYMOND | Union |
| PEMBERVILLE | Wood | REEDSVILLE | Meigs |
| PENINSULA | Summit | REESVILLE | Clinton |
| PENNSVILLE | Morgan | RENO | Washington |
| PERRY | Lake | REPUBLIC | Seneca |
| PERRYSBURG | Wood | REYNOLDSBURG | Franklin |
| PERRYSVILLE | Ashland | RICHFIELD | Summit |
| PETERSBURG | Mahoning | RICHMOND | Jefferson |
| PETTISVILLE | Fulton | RICHMOND DALE | Ross |
| PHILLIPSBURG | Montgomery | RICHWOOD | Union |
| PHILO | Muskingum | RIDGEVILLE CORNERS | Henry |
| PICKERINGTON | Fairfield | RIDGEWAY | Hardin |
| PIEDMONT | Harrison | RINARD MILLS | Monroe |
| PIERPONT | Ashtabula | RIO GRANDE | Gallia |
| PIKETON | Pike | RIPLEY | Brown |
| PINEY FORK | Jefferson | RISINGSUN | Wood |
| PIONEER | Williams | RITTMAN | Wayne |
| PIQUA | Miami | ROBERTSVILLE | Stark |
| PITSBURG | Drake | ROCKBRIDGE | Hocking |
| PLAIN CITY | Madison | ROCK CAMP | Lawrence |
| PLAINFIELD | Coshocton | ROCK CREEK | Ashtabula |
| PLEASANT CITY | Guernsey | ROCKFORD | Mercer |
| PLEASANT HILL | Miami | ROCKY RIDGE | Ottawa |
| PLEASANT PLAIN | Warren | ROGERS | Columbiana |
| PLEASANTVILLE | Fairfield | ROME | Ashtabula |
| PLYMOUTH | Richland | ROOTSTOWN | Portage |
| POLAND | Mahoning | ROSEVILLE | Muskingum |
| POLK | Ashland | ROSEWOOD | Champaign |
| POMEROY | Meigs | ROSS | Butler |
| PORTAGE | Wood | ROSSBURG | Darke |
| PORT CLINTON | Ottawa | ROUNDHEAD | Hardin |
| PORT JEFFERSON | Shelby | RUDOLPH | Wood |
| PORT WILLIAM | Clinton | RUSHSYLVANIA | Logan |
| PORTLAND | Meigs | RUSHVILLE | Fairfield |
| PORTSMOUGH | Scioto | RUSSELLS POINT | Logan |
| PORT WASHINGTON | Tuscarawas | RUSSELLVILLE | Brown |
| POTSDAM | Miami | RUSSIA | Shelby |
| POWELL | Delaware | RUTLAND | Meigs |
| POWHATAN POINT | Belmont | SABINA | Clinton |
| PROCTORVILLE | Lawrence | SAINT HENRY | Mercer |
| PROSPECT | Marion | SAINT JOHNS | Auglaize |
| PUT-IN-BAY | Ottawa | SAINT LOUISVILLE | Licking |

| | | | |
|---|---|---|---|
| SAINT MARYS | Auglaize | SOUTH SAINT JOSEPH | Hamilton |
| SAINT PARIS | Champaign | SOUTH SALEM | Ross |
| SALEM | Columbiana | SOUTH SOLON | Madison |
| SALESVILLE | Guernsey | SOUTH STERLING | Madison |
| SALMVILLE | Columbiana | SOUTH VERNON | Knox |
| SANDUSKY | Erie | SOUTH VICTORY | Hardin |
| SANDYVILLE | Tuscarawas | SOUTH VIENNA | Clark |
| SARAHSVILLE | Noble | SOUTH WEBSTER | Scioto |
| SARDINIA | Brown | SPARTA | Morrow |
| SARDIS | Monroe | SPENCER | Medina |
| SAVANNAH | Ashland | SPENCERVILLE | Allen |
| SCIO | Harrison | SPRINGBORO | Warren |
| SCIOTO FURNACE | Scioto | SPRINGFIELD | Clark |
| SCOTT | Van Wert | SPRING VALLEY | Greene |
| SCOTTOWN | Lawrence | STAFFORD | Monroe |
| SEAMAN | Adams | SAINT CLAIRSVILLE | Belmont |
| SEBRING | Mahoning | STERLING | Wayne |
| SEDALIA | Madison | STEUBENVILLE | Jefferson |
| SENECAVILLE | Guernsey | STEWART | Athens |
| SEVEN MILE | Butler | STEWARTSVILLE | Belmont |
| SEVILLE | Medina | STILLWATER | Tuscarawas |
| SHADE | Athens | STOCKDALE | Pike |
| SHADYSIDE | Belmont | STOCKPORT | Morgan |
| SHANDON | Butler | STONE CREEK | Tuscarawas |
| SHARON CENTER | Medina | STONY RIDGE | Wood |
| SHAUCK | Morrow | STOUT | Adams |
| SHAWNEE | Perry | STOUTSVILLE | Fairfield |
| SHELBY | Richland | STRASBURG | Tuscarawas |
| SHERRODSVILLE | Carroll | STRATTON | Jefferson |
| SHERWOOD | Defiance | STREETSBORO | Portage |
| SHILOH | Richland | STRUTHERS | Mahoning |
| SHORT CREEK | Harrison | STRYKER | Williams |
| SHREVE | Wayne | SUGARCREEK | Tuscarawas |
| SIDNEY | Shelby | SUGAR GROVE | Fairfield |
| SINKING SPRING | Highland | SULLIVAN | Ashland |
| SMITHFIELD | Jefferson | SULPHUR SPRINGS | Crawford |
| SOMERDALE | Tuscarawas | SUMMERFIELD | Noble |
| SOMERSET | Perry | SUMMIT STATION | Licking |
| SOMERVILLE | Butler | SUMMITVILLE | Columbiana |
| SONORA | Muskingum | SUNBURY | Delaware |
| SOUTH BLANCHARD | Hancock | SWANTON | Fulton |
| SOUTH CHARLESTON | Clark | SYCAMORE | Wyandot |
| SOUTH CORY | Hancock | SYLVANIA | Lucas |
| SOUTH EATON | Wayne | SYRACUSE | Meigs |
| SOUTH GILEAD | Morrow | TALLMADGE | Summit |
| SOUTH HOPE | Holmes | TARLTON | Pickaway |
| SOUTHINGTON | Trumbull | TERRACE PARK | Hamilton |
| SOUTH LEBANON | Warren | THE PLAINS | Athens |
| SOUTH LIBERTY | Knox | THOMPSON | Geauga |
| SOUTH ORAB | Brown | THORNVILLE | Perry |
| SOUTH PERRY | Perry | THURMAN | Gallia |
| SOUTH PLEASANT | Jefferson | THURSTON | Fairfield |
| SOUTH POINT | Lawrence | TIFFIN | Seneca |

| | | | |
|---|---|---|---|
| TILTONSVILLE | Jefferson | WASHINGTONVILLE | Columbiana |
| TIPP CITY | Miami | WATERFORD | Washington |
| TIPPECANOE | Harrison | WATERLOO | Lawrence |
| TIRO | Crawford | WATERTOWN | Washington |
| TOLEDO | Lucas | WATERVILLE | Lucas |
| TONTOGANY | Wood | WAUSEON | Fulton |
| TORCH | Athens | WAVERLY | Pike |
| TORONTO | Jefferson | WAYLAND | Portage |
| TREMONT CITY | Clarke | WAYNE | Wood |
| TRENTON | Butler | WAYNESBURG | Stark |
| TRIMBLE | Athens | WAYNESFIELD | Auglaize |
| TRINWAY | Muskingum | WAYNESVILLE | Warren |
| TROY | Miami | WELLINGTON | Lorain |
| TUPPERS PLAINS | Meigs | WELLSTON | Jackson |
| TUSCARAWAS | Tuscarawas | WELLSVILLE | Columbiana |
| TWINSBURG | Summit | WEST ALEXANDRIA | Preble |
| UHRICHSVILLE | Tuscarawas | WEST CHESTER | Butler |
| UNION FURNACE | Hocking | WEST ELKTON | Preble |
| UNIONPORT | Jefferson | WESTERVILLE | Franklin |
| UNIONTOWN | Stark | WEST FARMINGTON | Trumbull |
| UNIONVILLE | Ashtabula | WESTFIELD CENTER | Medina |
| UNIONVILLE CENTER | Union | WEST JEFFERSON | Madison |
| UNIOPOLIS | Auglaize | WEST LAFAYETTE | Coshocton |
| UPPER SANDUSKY | Wyandot | WEST LIBERTY | Logan |
| URBANA | Champaign | WEST MANCHESTER | Preble |
| UTICA | Licking | WEST MANSFIELD | Logan |
| VALLEY CITY | Medin | WEST MILLGROVE | Wood |
| VAN BUREN | Hancock | WEST MILTON | Miami |
| VANDALIA | Montgomery | WESTON | Wood |
| VANLUE | Hancock | WEST POINT | Columbiana |
| VAN WERT | Van Wert | WEST RUSHVILLE | Fairfield |
| VAUGHNSVILLE | Putnam | WEST SALEM | Wayne |
| VENEDOCIA | Van Wert | WEST UNION | Adams |
| VERMILION | Erie | WEST UNITY | Williams |
| VERONA | Preble | WESTVILLE | Champaign |
| VERSAILLES | Darke | WHARTON | Wyandot |
| VICKERY | Sandusky | WHEELERSBURG | Scioto |
| VIENNA | Trumbull | WHIPPLE | Washington |
| VINCENT | Washington | WHITE COTTAGE | Muskingum |
| VINTON | Gallia | WHITEHOUSE | Lucas |
| WADSWORTH | Medina | WICKLIFFE | Lake |
| WAKEFIELD | Pike | WILBERFORCE | Greene |
| WAKEMAN | Huron | WILKESVILLE | Vinton |
| WALBRIDGE | Wood | WILLARD | Huron |
| WALDO | Marion | WILLIAMSBURG | Clemont |
| WALHONDING | Coshocton | WILLIAMSFIELD | Ashtabula |
| WALNUT CREEK | Holmes | WILLIAMSPORT | Pickaway |
| WAPAKONETA | Auglaize | WILLIAMSTOWN | Hancock |
| WARNER | Washington | WILLISTON | Ottawa |
| WARNOCK | Belmont | WILOUGHBY | Lake |
| WARREN | Trumbull | WILLOW WOOD | Lawrence |
| WARSAW | Coshoction | WILLSHIRE | Van Wert |
| WASHINGTON COURTHOUSE | Fayette | WILMINGTON | Clinton |

*Appendix*

| | | | |
|---|---|---|---|
| WILMOT | Stark | AVANT | Osage |
| WINCHESTER | Adams | BACHE | Pittsburg |
| WINDHAM | Portage | BALKO | Beaver |
| WINDSOR | Ashtabula | BARNSDALL | Osage |
| WINESBURG | Holmes | BARTLESVILLE | Washington |
| WINGETT RUN | Washington | BATTIEST | McCurtain |
| WINONA | Columbiana | BEAVER | Beaver |
| WOLF RUN | Jefferson | BEGGS | Okmulgee |
| WOODSFIELD | Monroe | BENNINGTON | Bryan |
| WOODSTOCK | Champaign | BESSIE | Washita |
| WOODSVILLE | Sandusky | BETHANY | Oklahoma |
| WOOSTER | Wayne | BETHEL | McCurtain |
| WREN | Van Wert | BIG CABIN | Craig |
| XENIA | Greene | BILLINGS | Noble |
| YELLOW SPRINGS | Greene | BINGER | Caddo |
| YORKSHIRE | Darke | BISON | Garfield |
| YORKVILLE | Jefferson | BIXBY | Tulsa |
| YOUNGSTOWN | Mahoning | BLACKWELL | Kay |
| ZALESKI | Vinton | BLAIR | Jackson |
| ZANESFIELD | Logan | BLANCHARD | McClain |
| ZANESVILLE | Muskingum | BLANCO | Pittsburg |
| ZOAR | Tuscarawas | BLOCKER | Pittsburg |
| **OKLAHOMA** | | BLUEJACKET | Craig |
| ACHILLE | Bryan | BOISE CITY | Cimarron |
| ADA | Pontotoc | BOKCHITO | Bryan |
| ADAIR | Mayes | BOKOSHE | LeFlore |
| ADAMS | Texas | BOLEY | Okfuskee |
| ADDINGTON | Jefferson | BOSWELL | Choctaw |
| AFTON | Ottawa | BOWLEGS | Seminole |
| AGRA | Lincoln | BOYNTON | Muskogee |
| ALBANY | Bryan | BRADLEY | Grady |
| ALBERT | Caddo | BRAGGS | Muskogee |
| ALBION | Pushmataha | BRAMAN | Kay |
| ALDERSON | Pittsburg | BRISTOW | Creek |
| ALEX | Grady | BROKEN ARROW | Tulsa |
| ALINE | Alfalfa | BROKEN BOW | McCurtain |
| ALLEN | Pontotoc | BROMIDE | Johnson |
| ALTUS | Jackson | BUFFALO | Harper |
| ALVA | Woods | BUNCH | Adair |
| AMBER | Grady | BURBANK | Osage |
| AMES | Major | BURLINGTON | Alfalfa |
| AMORITA | Alfalfa | BURNEYVILLE | Love |
| ANADARKO | Caddo | BURNS FLAT | Washita |
| ANTLERS | Pushmataha | BUTLER | Custer |
| APACHE | Caddo | BYARS | McClain |
| ARAPAHO | Custer | BYRON | Alfalfa |
| ARCADIA | Oklahoma | CACHE | Comanche |
| ARDMORE | Carter | CADDO | Bryan |
| ARKOMA | LeFlore | CALERA | Bryan |
| ARNETT | Ellis | CALUMET | Canadian |
| ASHER | Pottawatomie | CALVIN | Hughes |
| ATOKA | Atoka | CAMARGO | Dewey |
| ATWOOD | Hughes | CAMERON | LeFlore |

**Adoption Searches Made Easier**

| | | | |
|---|---|---|---|
| CANADIAN | Pittsburg | COYLE | Logan |
| CANEY | Atoka | CRAWFORD | Roger Mills |
| CANTON | Blaine | CRESCENT | Logan |
| CANUTE | Washita | CROMWELL | Seminole |
| CAPRON | Woods | CROWDER | Pittsburg |
| CARDIN | Ottawa | CUSHING | Payne |
| CARMEN | Alfalfa | CUSTER CITY | Custer |
| CARNEGIE | Caddo | CYRIL | Caddo |
| CARNEY | Lincoln | DACOMA | Woods |
| CARRIER | Garfleld | DAISY | Atoka |
| CARTER | Beckham | DALE | Pottawatomie |
| CARTWRIGHT | Bryan | DAVENPORT | Lincoln |
| CASHION | Kingfisher | DAVIDSON | Tillman |
| CASTLE | Okfuskee | DAVIS | Murray |
| CATOOSA | Rogers | DEER CREEK | Grant |
| CEMENT | Caddo | DELAWARE | Nowata |
| CENTRAHOMA | Coal | DEPEW | Creek |
| CENTRALIA | Craig | DEVOL | Cotton |
| CHANDLER | Lincoln | DEWAR | Okmulgee |
| CHATTANOOGA | Comanche | DEWEY | Washington |
| CHECOTAH | McIntosh | DIBBLE | McClain |
| CHELSEA | Rogers | DILL CITY | Washita |
| CHEROKEE | Alfalfa | DISNEY | Mayes |
| CHESTER | Major | DOUGHERTY | Murray |
| CHEYENNE | Roger Mills | DOUGLAS | Garfield |
| CHICKASHA | Grady | DOVER | Kingfisher |
| CHOCTAW | Oklahoma | DRUMMOND | Garfield |
| CHOUTEAU | Mayes | DRUMRIGHT | Creek |
| CLAREMORE | Rogers | DUKE | Jackson |
| CLARITA | Coal | DUNCAN | Stephens |
| CLAYTON | Pushmataha | DURANT | Bryan |
| CLEARVIEW | Okfuskee | DURHAM | Roger Mills |
| CLEO SPRINGS | Major | DUSTIN | Hughes |
| CLEVELAND | Pawnee | EAST LOUIS | Pottawatomie |
| CLINTON | Custer | EAGLETOWN | McCurtain |
| COALGATE | Coal | EAKLY | Caddo |
| COLBERT | Bryan | EARLSBORO | Pottawatomie |
| COLCORD | Delaware | EDMOND | Oklahoma |
| COLEMAN | Johnston | ELDORADO | Jackson |
| COLLINSVILLE | Tulsa | ELGIN | Comanche |
| COLONY | Washita | ELK CITY | Beckham |
| COMANCHE | Stephens | ELMA | Jackson |
| COMMERCE | Ottawa | ELMORE CITY | Garvin |
| CONCHO | Canadian | ELMWOOD | Beaver |
| CONNERVILLE | Johnston | EL RENO | Canadian |
| COOKSON | Cherokee | ENID | Garfield |
| COPAN | Washington | ERICK | Beckham |
| CORDELL | Washita | EUCHA | Delaware |
| CORN | Washita | EUFAULA | McIntosh |
| COUNCIL HILL | Muskogee | FAIRFAX | Osage |
| COUNTYLINE | Stephens | FAIRLAND | Ottawa |
| COVINGTON | Garfield | FAIRMONT | Garfield |
| COWETA | Wagoner | FAIRVIEW | Major |

| | | | |
|---|---|---|---|
| FANSHAWE | Le Flore | HARTSHORNE | Pittsburg |
| FARGO | Ellis | HASKELL | Muskogee |
| FAXON | Comanche | HASTINGS | Jefferson |
| FAY | Dewey | HAWORTH | McCurtain |
| FELT | Cimarron | HAYWOOD | Pittsburg |
| FINLEY | Pushmataha | HEADRICK | Jackson |
| FITTSTOWN | Pontotoc | HEALDTON | Carter |
| FITZHUGH | Pontotoc | HEAVENER | LeFlore |
| FLETCHER | Corrunanche | HELENA | Alfalfa |
| FORGAN | Beaver | HENDRIX | Bryan |
| FORT COBB | Caddo | HENNEPIN | Garvin |
| FORT GIBSON | Muskogee | HENNESSEY | Kingfisher |
| FORT SUPPLY | Woodward | HENRYETTA | Okmulgee |
| FORT TOWSON | Choctaw | HILLSDALE | Garfield |
| FOSS | Washita | HINTON | Caddo |
| FOSTER | Garvin | HITCHCOCK | Blaine |
| FOX | Carter | HITCHITA | McIntosh |
| FOYIL | Rogers | HOBART | Koiwa |
| FRANCIS | Pontotoc | HODGEN | Le Flore |
| FREDERICK | Tillman | HOLDENVILLE | Hughes |
| FREEDOM | Woods | HOLLIS | Harmon |
| GAGE | Ellis | HOLLISTER | Tillman |
| GANS | Sequoyah | HOMINY | Osage |
| GARBER | Garfield | HONOBIA | Pushmataha |
| GARVIN | McCurtain | HOOKER | Texas |
| GATE | Beaver | HOPETON | Woods |
| GEARY | Blaine | HOWE | Le Flore |
| GENE AUTRY | Carter | HOYT | Haskell |
| GERONIMO | Comanche | HUGO | Choctaw |
| GLENCOE | Payne | HULBERT | Cherokee |
| GLENPOOL | Tulsa | HUNTER | Garfield |
| GOLDEN | McCurtain | HYDRO | Caddo |
| GOLTRY | Alfalfa | IDABEL | McCurtain |
| GOODWELL | Texas | INDIAHOMA | Comanche |
| GORE | Sequoyah | INDIANOLA | Pittsburg |
| GOTEBO | Kiowa | INOLA | Rogers |
| GOULD | Harmon | ISABELLA | Major |
| GOWEN | Latimer | JAY | Delaware |
| GRACEMONT | Caddo | JENKS | Tulsa |
| GRAHAM | Carter | JENNINGS | Pawnee |
| GRANDFIELD | Tillman | JET | Alfalfa |
| GRANITE | Greer | JONES | Oklahoma |
| GRANT | Choctaw | KANSAS | Delaware |
| GREENFIELD | Blaine | KAW CITY | Kay |
| GROVE | Delaware | KELLYVILLE | Creek |
| GUTHRIE | Logan | KEMP | Bryan |
| GUYMON | Texas | KENEFIC | Bryan |
| HAILEYVILLE | Pittsburg | KENTON | Cimarron |
| HALLETT | Pawnee | KEOTA | Haskell |
| HAMMON | Roger Mills | KETCHUM | Craig |
| HANNA | Mclintosh | KEYES | Cimarron |
| HARDESTY | Texas | KIEFER | Creek |
| HARRAH | Oklahoma | KINGFISHER | Kingfisher |

| | | | |
|---|---|---|---|
| KINGSTON | Marshall | MAUD | Pottawatomie |
| KINTA | Haskell | MAY | Harper |
| KIOWA | Pittsburg | MAYSVILLE | Garvin |
| KNOWLES | Beaver | MEAD | Bryan |
| KONAWA | Seminole | MEDFORD | Grant |
| KREBS | Pittsburg | MEDICINE PARK | Comanche |
| KREMLIN | Garfield | MEEKER | Lincoln |
| LAHOMA | Garfield | MENO | Major |
| LAMAR | Hughes | MERIDIAN | Logan |
| LAMONT | Grant | MIAMI | Ottawa |
| LANE | Atoka | MILBURN | Johnston |
| LANGLEY | Mayes | MILFAY | Creek |
| LANGSTON | Logan | MILL CREEK | Johnston |
| LAVERNE | Harper | MILLERTON | McCurtain |
| LAWTON | Comanche | MINCO | Grady |
| LEBANON | Marshall | MOFFETT | Sequoyah |
| LEEDEY | Dewey | MONROE | Le Flore |
| LEFLORE | Le Flore | MOODYS | Cherokee |
| LEHIGH | Coal | MOORELAND | Woodward |
| LENAPAH | Nowata | MORRIS | Okmulgee |
| LEON | Love | MORRISON | Noble |
| LEONARD | Tulsa | MOUNDS | Creek |
| LEQUIRE | Haskell | MOUNTAIN PARK | Kiowa |
| LEXINGTON | Cleveland | MOUNTAIN VIEW | Kiowa |
| LINDSAY | Garvin | MOYERS | Pushmataha |
| LOCO | Stephens | MULDROW | Sequoyah |
| LOCUST GROVE | Mayes | MULHALL | Logan |
| LOGAN | Beaver | MUSE | Le Flore |
| LONE GROVE | Carter | MUSKOGEE | Muskogee |
| LONE WOLF | Koiwa | MUSTANG | Canadian |
| LONGDALE | Blaine | MUTUAL | Woodward |
| LOOKEBA | Caddo | NARDIN | Kay |
| LOVELAND | Tillman | NASH | Grant |
| LOYAL | Kingsfisher | NASHOBA | Pushmataba |
| LUCIEN | Noble | NEWALLA | Oklahoma |
| LUTHER | Oklahoma | NEWCASTLE | McClain |
| MCALESTER | Pittsburg | NEWKIRK | Kay |
| MCCURTAIN | Haskell | NICOMA PARK | Oklahoma |
| MCLOUD | Pottawatomie | NINNEKAH | Grady |
| MACOMB | Pottawatomie | NOBLE | Cleveland |
| MADILL | Marshall | NORMAN | Cleveland |
| MANCHESTER | Grant | NORTH MIAMI | Ottawa |
| MANGUM | Greer | NOWATA | Nowata |
| MANITOU | Tillman | OAKHURST | Tulsa |
| MANNFORD | Creek | OAKLAND | Marshall |
| MANNSVILLE | Johnston | OAKS | Delaware |
| MARAMEC | Pawnee | OAKWOOD | Dewey |
| MARBLE CITY | Sequoyah | OCHELATA | Washington |
| MARIETTA | Love | OILTON | Creek |
| MARLAND | Noble | OKARCHE | Kingfisher |
| MARLOW | Stephens | OKAY | Wagoner |
| MARSHALL | Logan | OKEENE | Blaine |
| MARTHA | Jackson | OKEMAH | Okfuskee |

| | | | |
|---|---|---|---|
| OKLAHOMA CITY | Oklahoma | RED ROCK | Noble |
| OKMULGEE | Okmulgee | REED | Greer |
| OKTAHA | Muskogee | RENTIESVILLE | McIntosh |
| OLUSTEE | Jackson | REYDON | Roger Mills |
| OMEGA | Kingfisher | RINGLING | Jefferson |
| OOLOGAH | Rogers | RINGOLD | McCurtain |
| OPTIMA | Texas | RINGWOOD | Major |
| ORLANDO | Logan | RIPLEY | Payne |
| OSAGE | Osage | ROCKY | Washita |
| OVERBROOK | Lover | ROFF | Pontotoc |
| OWASSO | Tulsa | ROLAND | Sequoyah |
| PADEN | Okfuskee | ROOSEVELT | Kiowa |
| PANAMA | Le Flore | ROSE | Mayes |
| PANOLA | Latimer | ROSSTON | Harper |
| PAOLI | Garvin | RUFE | McCurtain |
| PARK HILL | Cherokee | RUSH SPRINGS | Grady |
| PAULS VALLEY | Garvin | RYAN | Jefferson |
| PAWHUSKA | Osage | SAINT LOUIS | Pottawatomie |
| PAWNEE | Pawnee | SALINA | Mayes |
| PEGGS | Cherokee | SALLISAW | Sequoyah |
| PERKINS | Payne | SAND SPRINGS | Tulsa |
| PERNELL | Garvin | SAPULPA | Creek |
| PERRY | Noble | SASAKWA | Seminole |
| PHAROAH | Okfuskee | SAVANNA | Pittsburg |
| PICHER | Ottawa | SAWYER | Choctaw |
| PICKENS | McCurtain | SAYRE | Beckham |
| PIEDMONT | Canadian | SCHULTER | Okmulgee |
| PITTSBURG | Pittsburg | SEILING | Dewey |
| PLATTER | Bryan | SEMINOLE | Seminole |
| POCASSET | Grady | SENTINEL | Washita |
| PONCA CITY | Kay | SHADY POINT | Le Flore |
| POND CREEK | Grant | SHAMROCK | Creek |
| PONTOTA | Johnston | SHARON | Woodward |
| PORTER | Wagoner | SHATTUCK | Ellis |
| PORUM | Muskogee | SHAWNEE | Pottawatomie |
| POTEAU | Le Flore | SHIDLER | Osage |
| PRAGUE | Lincoln | SKIATOOK | Tulsa |
| PRESTON | Okmulgee | SLICK | Creek |
| PROCTOR | Adair | SMITHVILLE | McCurtain |
| PRUE | Osage | SNOW | Pushmataha |
| PRYOR | Mayes | SNYDER | Kiowa |
| PURCELL | McClain | SOPER | Choctaw |
| PUTNAM | Dewey | SOUTHARD | Blaine |
| QUAPAW | Ottawa | SOUTH COFFEYVILLE | Nowata |
| QUINTON | Pittsburg | SPARKS | Lincoln |
| RALSTON | Pawnee | SPAVINAW | Mayes |
| RAMONA | Washington | SPENCER | Oklahoma |
| RANDLETT | Cotton | SPENCERVILLE | Choctaw |
| RATLIFF CITY | Carter | SPERRY | Tulsa |
| RATTAN | Pushmataha | SPIRO | Le Flore |
| RAVIA | Johnston | SPRINGER | Carter |
| REDBIRD | Wagoner | STERLING | Comanche |
| RED OAK | Latimer | STIDHAM | McIntosh |

| | | | |
|---|---|---|---|
| STIGLER | Haskell | WANETTE | Pottawatomie |
| STILLWATER | Payne | WANN | Nowata |
| STILWELL | Adair | WAPANUCKA | Johnston |
| STONEWALL | Pontotoc | WARDVILLE | Atoka |
| STRANG | Mayes | WARNER | Muskogee |
| STRATFORD | Garvin | WARR ACRES | Oklahoma |
| STRINGTOWN | Atoka | WASHINGTON | McClain |
| STROUD | Lincoln | WASHITA | Caddo |
| STUART | Hughes | WATONGA | Blaine |
| SULPHUR | Murray | WATSON | McCurtain |
| SWEETWATER | Roger Mills | WATTS | Adair |
| SWINK | Choctaw | WAURIKA | Jefferson |
| TAFT | Muskogee | WAYNE | McClain |
| TAHLEQUAH | Cherokee | WAYNOKA | Woods |
| TALALA | Rogers | WEATHERFORD | Custer |
| TALIHINA | Le Flore | WEBBERS FALLS | Muskogee |
| TALOGA | Dewey | WELCH | Craig |
| TATUMS | Carter | WELEETKA | Okfuskee |
| TECUMSEH | Pottawatomie | WELLING | Cherokee |
| TEMPLE | Cotton | WELLSTON | Lincoln |
| TERLTON | Pawnee | WELTY | Okfuskee |
| TERRAL | Jefferson | WEST PARK | Oklahoma |
| TEXHOMA | Texas | WESTVILLE | Adair |
| TEXOLA | Beckham | WETUMKA | Hughes |
| THACKERVILLE | Love | WEWOKA | Seminole |
| THOMAS | Custer | WHEATLAND | Oklahoma |
| TIPTON | Tillman | WHITEFIELD | Haskell |
| TISHOMINGO | Johnston | WHITESBORO | Le Flore |
| TONKAWA | Kay | WILBURTON | Latimer |
| TRYON | Lincoln | WILLOW | Greer |
| TULLAHASSE | Wagoner | WILSON | Carter |
| TULSA | Tulsa | WISTER | Le Flore |
| TUPELO | Coal | WOODWARD | Woodward |
| TURPIN | Beaver | WRIGHT CITY | McCurtain |
| TUSKOHOMA | Pushmataha | WYANDOTTE | Ottawa |
| TUSSY | Carter | WYNNEWOOD | Garvin |
| TUTTLE | Grady | WYNONA | Osage |
| TWIN OAKS | Delaware | YALE | Payne |
| TYRONE | Texas | YUKON | Canadian |
| UNION CITY | Canadian | **OREGON** | |
| VALLIANT | McCurtain | ADAMS | Umatilla |
| VELMA | Stephens | ADEL | Lake |
| VERA | Washington | ADRIAN | Malheur |
| VERDEN | Grady | AGNESS | Curry |
| VERNON | McIntosh | ALBANY | Linn |
| VIAN | Sequoyah | ALLEGANY | Coos |
| VICI | Dewey | ALOHA | Washington |
| VINITA | Craig | ALSEA | Benton |
| VINSON | Harmon | ALVADORE | Lane |
| WAGONER | Wagoner | AMITY | Yamhill |
| WAINWRIGHT | Muskogee | ANTELOPE | Wasco |
| WAKITA | Grant | APPLEGATE | Jackson |
| WALTERS | Cotton | ARCH CAPE | Clatsop |

| | | | |
|---|---|---|---|
| ARLINGTON | Gilliam | CAYUSE | Umatilla |
| AROCK | Malheur | CEDAR HILLS | Washington |
| ASHLAND | Jackson | CEDAR MILL | Washington |
| ASHWOOD | Jefferson | CENTRAL POINT | Jackson |
| ASTORIA | Clatsop | CHARLESTON | Coos |
| ATHENA | Umatilla | CHEMULT | Klamath |
| AUMSVILLE | Marion | CHESHIRE | Lane |
| AURORA | Marion | CHILOQUIN | Klamath |
| AZALEA | Douglas | CLACKAMAS | Clackamas |
| BAKER CITY | Baker | CLATSKANIE | Columbia |
| BANDON | Coos | CLOVERDALE | Tillamook |
| BANKS | Washington | COBURG | Lane |
| BATES | Grant | COLTON | Clackamas |
| BAY CITY | Tillamook | COLUMBIA CITY | Columbia |
| BEATTY | Klamath | CONDON | Gilliam |
| BEAVER | Tillamook | COOS BAY | Coos |
| BEAVERCREEK | Clackamas | COQUILLE | Coos |
| BEAVERTON | Washington | CORBETT | Multnomah |
| BEND | Deschutes | CORNELIUS | Washington |
| BIRKENFELD | Columbia | CORVALLIS | Benton |
| BLACHLY | Lane | COTTAGE GROVE | Lane |
| BLACK BUTTE RANCH | Deschutes | COVE | Union |
| BLODGETT | Benton | CRABTREE | Linn |
| BLUE RIVER | Lane | CRANE | Harney |
| BLY | Klamath | CRATER LAKE | Klammath |
| BOARDMAN | Morrow | CRAWFORDSVILLE | Linn |
| BONANZA | Klamath | CRESCENT | Klamath |
| BONNEVILLE | Hood River | CRESCENT LAKE | Klamath |
| BORING | Clackamas | CRESTON | Multnomah |
| BRIDAL VEIL | Multnomah | CRESWELL | Lane |
| BRIDGEPORT | Baker | CROOKED RIVER RANCH | Deschutes |
| BRIGHTWOOD | Clackamas | CULP CREEK | Lane |
| BROADBENT | Coos | CULVER | Jefferson |
| BROGAN | Malheur | CURTIN | Douglas |
| BROOKINGS | Curry | DAIRY | Klamath |
| BROOKLYN | Multnomah | DAIRY | Lane |
| BROOKS | Marion | DALE | Umatilla |
| BROTHERS | Deschutes | DALLAS | Polk |
| BROWNSVILLE | Linn | DAYS CREEK | Douglas |
| BURNS | Harney | DAYTON | Yamhill |
| BUTTE FALLS | Jackson | DAYVILLE | Grant |
| BUXTON | Washington | DEADWOOD | Lane |
| CAMAS VALLEY | Douglas | DEER ISLAND | Columbia |
| CAMP SHERMAN | Jefferson | DEPOE BAY | Lincoln |
| CANBY | Clackamas | DETROIT | Marion |
| CANNON BEACH | Clatsop | DEXTER | Lane |
| CANYON CITY | Grant | DIAMOND | Harney |
| CANYONVILLE | Douglas | DIAMOND LAKE | Klamath |
| CARLTON | Yamhill | DILLARD | Douglas |
| CASCADE LOCKS | Hood River | DONALD | Marion |
| CASCADE SUMMIT | Hood River | DORENA | Lane |
| CASCADIA | Linn | DOWNTOWN | Deschutes |
| CAVE JUNCTION | Josephine | DRAIN | Douglas |

| | | | |
|---|---|---|---|
| DREWSEY | Harney | HALFWAY | Baker |
| DUFUR | Wasco | HALSEY | Linn |
| DUNDEE | Yamhill | HAMMOND | Clatsop |
| DURKEE | Baker | HARBOR | Curry |
| EAGLE CREEK | Clackamas | HARPER | Malheur |
| EAGLE POINT | Jackson | HARRISBURG | Linn |
| EAST PORTLAND | Multnomah | HEBO | Tillamook |
| EASTSIDE | Coos | HELIX | Umatilla |
| ECHO | Umatilla | HEPPNER | Morrow |
| EDDYVILLE | Lincoln | HEREFORD | Baker |
| ELGIN | Union | HERMISTON | Umatilla |
| ELKTON | Douglas | HILLSBORO | Washington |
| ELMIRA | Lane | HINES | Harney |
| EMPIRE | Coos | HOLLADAY PARK | Multnomah |
| ENTERPRISE | Wallowa | HOLLYWOOD | Marion |
| ESTACADA | Clackamas | HOOD RIVER | Hood River |
| EUGENE | Lane | HUBBARD | Marion |
| FAIRVIEW | Multnomah | HUNTINGTON | Baker |
| FALL CREEK | Lane | IDANHA | Marion |
| FALLS CITY | Polk | IDLEYLD PARK | Douglas |
| FIELDS | Harney | IMBLER | Union |
| FLORENCE | Lane | IMNAHA | Wallowa |
| FOREST GROVE | Washington | INDEPENDENCE | Polk |
| FOREST PARK | Multnomah | IONE | Morrow |
| FORT KLAMATH | Klamath | IRONSIDE | Malheur |
| FORT ROCK | Lake | IRRIGON | Morrow |
| FOSSIL | Wheeler | JACKSONVILLE | Jackson |
| FOSTER | Linn | JAMIESON | Malheur |
| FOX | Grant | JASPER | Lane |
| FRENCHGLEN | Harney | JEFFERSON | Marion |
| FRIEND | Wasco | JOHN DAY | Grant |
| GALES CREEK | Washington | JORDAN VALLEY | Malheur |
| GARDINER | Douglas | JOSEPH | Wallowa |
| GARIBALDI | Tillamook | JUNCTION CITY | Lane |
| GASTON | Washington | JUNTURA | Malheur |
| GATES | Marion | KEIZER | Marion |
| GEARHART | Clatsop | KEIZER | Salem |
| GERVAIS | Marion | KENO | Klamath |
| GILCHRIST | Klamath | KENT | Sherman |
| GLADSTONE | Clackamas | KENTON | Multnomah |
| GLENDALE | Douglas | KERBY | Josephine |
| GLENEDEN BEACH | Lincoln | KIMBERLY | Grant |
| GLENWOOD | Washington | KING CITY | Washington |
| GLIDE | Douglas | KINZUA | Wheeler |
| GOLD BEACH | Curry | KLAMATH FALLS | Klamath |
| GOLD HILL | Jackson | LAFAYETTE | Yamhill |
| GOVERNMENT CAMP | Clackamas | LA GRANDE | Union |
| GRAND RONDE | Polk | LAKE GROVE | Clackamas |
| GRANTS PASS | Josephine | LAKE OSWEGO | Clackamas |
| GRASS VALLEY | Sherman | LAKESIDE | Coos |
| GREENLEAF | Lane | LAKEVIEW | Lake |
| GRESHAM | Multnomah | LANGLOIS | Curry |
| HAINES | Baker | LA PINE | Deschutes |

| | | | |
|---|---|---|---|
| LAWEN | Harney | NAHALEM | Tillamook |
| LEABURG | Lane | NEOTSU | Lincoln |
| LEBANON | Linn | NETARTS | Tillamook |
| LENTS | Multnomah | NEWBERG | Yamhill |
| LEXINGTON | Morrow | NEW PINE CREEK | Lake |
| LINCOLN CITY | Lincoln | NEWPORT | Lincoln |
| LOGSDEN | Lincoln | NORTH BEND | Coos |
| LONG CREEK | Grant | NORTH PLAINS | Washington |
| LORANE | Lane | NORTH POWDER | Union |
| LOSTINE | Wallowa | NORTH ROSEBURG | Douglas |
| LOWELL | Lane | NORWAY | Coos |
| LYONS | Linn | NOTI | Lane |
| MADRAS | Jefferson | NYSSA | Malheur |
| MALIN | Klamath | OAK GROVE | Clackamas |
| MANNING | Washington | OAKLAND | Douglas |
| MANZANITA | Tillamook | OAKRIDGE | Lane |
| MAPLETON | Lane | O'BRIEN | Josephine |
| MARCOLA | Lane | OCEANSIDE | Tillamook |
| MARION | Marion | ODELL | Hood River |
| MARYLHURST | Clackamas | ONTARIO | Malheur |
| MAUPIN | Wasco | OPHIR | Curry |
| MAYVILLE | Wheeler | OREGON CITY | Clackamas |
| MCMINNVILLE | Yamhill | ORETECH | Klamath |
| MCKENZIE BRIDGE | Lane | OTIS | Lincoln |
| MCMINNVILLE | Yamhill | OTTER ROCK | Lincoln |
| MCNARY | Umatilla | OXBOW | Baker |
| MEACHAM | Umatilla | PACIFIC CITY | Tillamook |
| MEDFORD | Jackson | PAISLEY | Lake |
| MEDICAL SPRINGS | Baker | PARKROSE | Multnomah |
| MEHAMA | Marion | PAULINA | Crook |
| MERLIN | Josephine | PENDLETON | Umatilla |
| MERRILL | Klamath | PHILOMATH | Benton |
| MIDLAND | Klamath | PHOENIX | Jackson |
| MIDWAY | Multnomah | PIEDMONT | Multnomah |
| MIKKALO | Gilliam | PILOT ROCK | Umatilla |
| MILL CITY | Linn | PIONEER | Multnomah |
| MILTON-FREEWATER | Umatilla | PISTOL RIVER | Curry |
| MILWAUKIE | Multnomah | PLEASANT HILL | Lane |
| MITCHELL | Wheeler | PLUSH | Lake |
| MOLALLA | Clackamas | PONY VILLAGE | Coos |
| MONMOUTH | Polk | PORTLAND | Multnomah |
| MONROE | Benton | PORT ORFORD | Curry |
| MONUMENT | Grant | POST | Crook |
| MORO | Sherman | POWELL BUTTE | Crook |
| MOSIER | Wasco | POWERS | Coos |
| MOUNT ANGEL | Marion | PRAIRIE CITY | Grant |
| MOUNT HOOD-PARYDALE | Hood River | PRINCETON | Harney |
| MOUNT VERNON | Grant | PRINEVILLE | Crook |
| MULINO | Clackamas | PRINGLE PARK | Marion |
| MULTNOMAH | Multnomah | PROSPECT | Jackson |
| MURPHY | Josephine | RAINIER | Columbia |
| MYRTLE CREEK | Douglas | REDMOND | Deschutes |
| MYRTLE POINT | Coos | REEDSPORT | Douglas |

| | | | |
|---|---|---|---|
| REMOTE | Coos | SWISSHOME | Lane |
| RHODODENDRON | Clackamas | TALENT | Jackson |
| RICHLAND | Baker | TANGENT | Linn |
| RICKREALL | Polk | TENMILE | Douglas |
| RIDDLE | Douglas | TERREBONNE | Deschutes |
| RILEY | Harney | THE DALLES | Wasco |
| RITTER | Grant | THURSTON | Lane |
| RIVERSIDE | Malheur | TIDEWATER | Lincoln |
| ROCKAWAY | Tillamook | TIGARD | Washington |
| ROGUE RIVER | Jackson | TILLAMOOK | Tillamook |
| ROSEBURG | Douglas | TILLER | Douglas |
| ROSE CITY PARK | Multnomah | TIMBER | Washington |
| ROSE LODGE | Lincoln | TOLEDO | Lincoln |
| RUFUS | Sherman | TOLOVANA PARK | Clatsop |
| SAINT HELENS | Columbia | TRAIL | Jackson |
| SAINT JOHNS | Multnomah | TROUTDALE | Multnomah |
| SAINT PAUL | Marion | TUALATIN | Washington |
| SALEM | Marion | TURNER | Marion |
| SANDY | Clackamas | TYGH VALLEY | Wasco |
| SCAPPOOSE | Columbia | UKIAH | Umatilla |
| SCIO | Linn | UMATILLA | Umatilla |
| SCOTTSBURG | Douglas | UMPQUA | Douglas |
| SCOTTS MILLS | Marion | UNION | Union |
| SEAL ROCK | Lincoln | UNITY | Baker |
| SEASIDE | Clatsop | UNIVERSITY | Lane |
| SELLWOOD MORELAND | Multnomah | UNIVERSITY | Multnomah |
| SELMA | Josephine | VALE | Malheur |
| SENECA | Grant | VENETA | Lane |
| SHADY COVE | Jackson | VERNONIA | Columbia |
| SHANIKO | Wasco | VIDA | Lane |
| SHEDD | Linn | VISTA | Marion |
| SHERIDAN | Yamhill | WALDPORT | Lincoln |
| SHERWOOD | Washington | WALLOWA | Wallowa |
| SILETZ | Lincoln | WALTERVILLE | Lane |
| SILVER LAKE | Lake | WALTON | Lane |
| SILVERTON | Marion | WAMIC | Wasco |
| SISTERS | Deschutes | WARM SPRINGS | Jefferson |
| SIXES | Curry | WARREN | Columbia |
| SOUTH BEACH | Lincoln | WARRENTON | Clatsop |
| SOUTHSIDE | Lane | WASCO | Sherman |
| SPRAGUE RIVER | Klamath | WASHINGTON PARK ZOO | Multnomah |
| SPRAY | Wheeler | WEDDERBURN | Curry |
| SPRINGFIELD | Lane | WELCHES | Clackamas |
| STANFIELD | Umatilla | WESTFALL | Malheur |
| STAYTON | Marion | WESTFIR | Lane |
| SUBLIMITY | Marion | WESTLAKE | Lane |
| SUMMER LAKE | Lake | WEST LINN | Clackamas |
| SUMMERVILLE | Union | WEST MAIN | Jackson |
| SUMPTER | Baker | WESTON | Umatilla |
| SUNNY VALLEY | Josephine | WESTPORT | Columbia |
| SUNRIVER | Deschutes | WEST SALEM | Marion |
| SUTHERLIN | Douglas | WEST SIDE | Lane |
| SWEET HOME | Linn | WEST SLOPE | Multnomah |

| | | | |
|---|---|---|---|
| WEST STAYTON | Marion | AMITY | Washington |
| WHEELER | Tillamook | ANALOMINK | Monroe |
| WHITE CITY | Jackson | ANDREAS | Schuylkill |
| WILBUR | Douglas | ANITA | Jefferson |
| WILDERVILLE | Joesphine | ANNVILLE | Lebanon |
| WILLAMINA | Yamhill | ANTES FORT | Lycoming |
| WILLIAMS | Josephine | APOLLO | Armstrong |
| WILSONVILLE | Clackamas | AQUASHICOLA | Carbon |
| WINCHESTER | Douglas | ARCADIA | Indiana |
| WINCHESTER BAY | Douglas | ARCHBALD | Lackawanna |
| WINSTON | Douglas | ARCOLA | Montgomery |
| WOLF CREEK | Josephine | ARDARA | Westmoreland |
| WOODBURN | Marion | ARDMORE | Montgomery |
| YACHATS | Lincoln | ARENDTSVILLE | Adams |
| YAMHILL | Yamhill | ARISTES | Columbia |
| YONCALLA | Douglas | ARMAGH | Indiana |
| ZIGZAG | Clackamas | ARMBRUST | Westmoreland |
| **PENNSYLVANIA** | | ARNOT | Tioga |
| AARONSBURG | Centre | ARONA | Westmoreland |
| ABBOTTSTOWN | Adams | ARTEMAS | Bedford |
| ABINGTON | Westmoreland | ASHFIELD | Carbon |
| ACME | Westmoreland | ASHLAND | Schuylkill |
| ACOSTA | Somerset | ASHLEY | Luzeme |
| ADAH | Fayette | ASHVILLE | Cambria |
| ADAMSBURG | Wstmoreland | ASPERS | Adams |
| ADAMSTOWN | Lancaster | ATGLEN | Chester |
| ADAMSVILLE | Crawford | ATHENS | Bradford |
| ADDISON | Somerset | ATLANTIC | Crawford |
| ADRIAN | Armstrong | ATLASBURG | Washington |
| AIRVILLE | York | AUBURN | Schuylkill |
| AKRON | Lancaster | AULTMAN | Indiana |
| ALBA | Bradford | AUSTIN | Potter |
| ALBION | Erie | AVELLA | Washington |
| ALBRIGHTSVILLE | Carbon | AVIS | Clinton |
| ALBURTIS | Lehigh | AVOCA | Luzerne |
| ALEPPO | Greene | AVONDALE | Chester |
| ALEXANDRIA | Huntingdon | AVONMORE | Westmoreland |
| ALIQUIPPA | Beaver | BADEN | Beaver |
| ALLEGHENY | Allegheny | BAINBRIDGE | Lancaster |
| ALLENPORT | Washington | BAIRFORD | Allegheny |
| ALLENSVILLE | Mifflin | BAKERS SUMMIT | Bedford |
| ALLENTOWN | Lehigh | BAKERSTOWN | Allegheny |
| ALLENWOOD | Union | BALA-CYNWYD | Montgomery |
| ALLISON | Fayette | BALLY | Berks |
| ALLISON PARK | Allegheny | BANGOR | Northhampton |
| ALLPORT | Clearfield | BARKING | Westmoreland |
| ALTOONA | Blair | BARNESBORO | Cambria |
| ALUM BANK | Bedford | BARNESVILLE | Schuylkill |
| ALVERDA | Indiana | BARREE | Huntingdon |
| ALVERTON | Westmoreland | BART | Lancaster |
| AMBERSON | Franklin | BARTO | Berks |
| AMBLER | Montgomery | BARTONSVILLE | Monroe |
| AMBRIDGE | Beaver | BATH | Northampton |

| | | | |
|---|---|---|---|
| BAUSMAN | Lancaster | BLANDBURG | Cambria |
| BEACH HAVEN | Luzerne | BLANDON | Berks |
| BEACH LAKE | Wayne | BLOOMING GLEN | Bucks |
| BEALLSVILLE | Washington | BLOOMSBURG | Columbia |
| BEAR CREEK | Luzerne | BLOSSBURG | Tioga |
| BEAR LAKE | Warren | BLUE BALL | Lancaster |
| BEAVER | Beaver | BLUE BELL | Montgomery |
| BEAVERDALE | Cambria | BLUE RIDGE SUMMIT | Franklin |
| BEAVER FALLS | Beaver | BOALSBURG | Centre |
| BEAVER MEADOWS | Carbon | BOBTOWN | Greene |
| BEAVER SPRINGS | Snyder | BOILING SPRINGS | Cumberland |
| BEAVERTOWN | Snyder | BOLIVAR | Westmoreland |
| BECCARIA | Clearfield | BON AIRE | Butler |
| BECHTELSVILLE | Berks | BOOTHWYN | Delaware |
| BEDFORD | Bedford | BOSTON | Allegheny |
| BEDMINSTER | Bucks | BOSWELL | Somerset |
| BEECH CREEK | Clinton | BOVARD | Westmoreland |
| BEL AIR | Cambria | BOWERS | Berks |
| BELLEFONTE | Centre | BOWMANSDALE | Cumberland |
| BELLE VERNON | Fayette | BOWMANSTOWN | Carbon |
| BELLEVILLE | Mifflin | BOWMANSVILLE | Lancaster |
| BELLEVUE | Allegheny | BOYERS | Butler |
| BELLWOOD | Blair | BOYERTOWN | Berks |
| BELSANO | Cambria | BOYNTON | Somerset |
| BENDERSVILLE | Adams | BRACKENRIDGE | Allegheny |
| BENEZETT | Elk | BRACKNEY | Susquehanna |
| BENSALEM | Bucks | BRADDOCK | Allegheny |
| BENTLYVILLE | Washington | BRADENVILLE | Westmoreland |
| BENTON | Columbia | BRADFORD | McKean |
| BERKELEY HILLS | Allegheny | BRADFORDWOODS | Allegheny |
| BERLIN | Somerset | BRADY | Clearfield |
| BERNVILLE | Berks | BRANCH DALE | Schuylkill |
| BERRYSBURG | Dauphin | BRANCHTON | Butler |
| BERWICK | Columbia | BRANDAMORE | Chester |
| BERWYN | Chester | BRANDY CAMP | Elk |
| BESSEMER | Lawrence | BRAVE | Greene |
| BETHEL | Berks | BREEZEWOOD | Bedford |
| BETHEL PARK | Allegheny | BREINIGSVILLE | Lehigh |
| BETHLEHEM | Northampton | BRENTWOOD | Allegheny |
| BETHTON | Montgomery | BRIDESBURG | Philadelphia |
| BEYER | Indiana | BRIDGEVILLE | Allegheny |
| BIGLER | Clearfield | BRIER HILL | Fayette |
| BIGLERVILLE | Adams | BRISBIN | Clearfield |
| BIG RUN | Jefferson | BRISTOL | Bucks |
| BIRCHRUNVILLE | Chester | BROAD TOP | Huntingdon |
| BIRD IN HAND | Lancaster | BROCKPORT | Elk |
| BIRDSBORO | Berks | BROCKTON | Schuylkill |
| BLACK LICK | Indiana | BROCKWAY | Jefferson |
| BLAIN | Perry | BRODBECKS | York |
| BLAIRS MILLS | Huntingdon | BRODHEADSVILLE | Monroe |
| BLAIRSVILLE | Indiana | BROGUE | York |
| BLAKESLEE | Monroe | BROOKHAVEN | Chester |
| BLANCHARD | Centre | BROOKLINE | Allegheny |

*Appendix*

| | | | |
|---|---|---|---|
| BROOKLYN | Susquehanna | CASSANDRA | Cambria |
| BROOKVILLE | Jefferson | CASSVILLE | Huntingdon |
| BROOMALL | Delaware | CASTANEA | Clinton |
| BROWNFIELD | Fayette | CASTE VILLAGE | Allegheny |
| BROWNSTOWN | Lancaster | CASTLE SHANNON | Allegheny |
| BROWNSVILLE | Fayette | CASTOR | Allegheny |
| BRUIN | Butler | CATASAUQUA | Lehigh |
| BRUSH VALLEY | Indiana | CATAWISSA | Columbia |
| BRYN ATHYN | Montgomery | CECIL | Washington |
| BRYN MAWR | Montgomery | CEDAR CLIFF | Cumberland |
| BUCK HILL FALLS | Monroe | CEDARHURST | Allegheny |
| BUCKINGHAM | Bucks | CEDAR RUN | Lycoming |
| BUENA VISTA | Allegheny | CEDARS | Montgomery |
| BUFFALO MILLS | Bedford | CENTER CITY | Lycoming |
| BUHL | Mercer | CENTERPORT | Berks |
| BULGER | Washington | CENTER VALLEY | Lehigh |
| BUNOLA | Allegheny | CENTERVILLE | Crawford |
| BURGETTSTOWN | Washington | CENTRAL CITY | Somerset |
| BURLINGTON | Bradford | CENTRAL HIGHLANDS | Allegheny |
| BURNHAM | Mifflin | CENTRALIA | Columbia |
| BURNSIDE | Clearfield | CENTRE HALL | Centre |
| BURNT CABINS | Fulton | CHADDS FORD | Delaware |
| BUSHKILL | Pike | CHALFONT | Bucks |
| BUSTLETON | Philadelphia | CHALKHILL | Fayette |
| BUTLER | Butler | CHAMBERSBURG | Franklin |
| BYRNEDALE | Elk | CHAMBERSVILLE | Indiana |
| CABOT | Butler | CHAMPION | Westmoreland |
| CADOGAN | Armstrong | CHANDLERS VALLEY | Warren |
| CAIRNBROOK | Somerset | CHARLEROI | Washington |
| CALIFORNIA | Washington | CHATHAM | Chester |
| CALLENSBURG | Clarion | CHELTENHAM | Montgomery |
| CALLERY | Butler | CHERRY TREE | Indiana |
| CALUMET | Westmoreland | CHERRYVILLE | Northampton |
| CALVIN | Huntingdon | CHESTER | Delaware |
| CAMBRA | Luzerne | CHESTER HEIGHTS | Delaware |
| CAMBRIDGE SPRINGS | Crawford | CHESTER SPRINGS | Chester |
| CAMMAL | Lycoming | CHESTNUT RIDGE | Fayette |
| CAMPBELLTOWN | Lebanon | CHEST SPRINGS | Cambria |
| CAMP HILL | Cumberland | CHESEICK | Allegheny |
| CAMPTOWN | Bradford | CHEYNEY | Delaware |
| CANADENSIS | Monroe | CHICORA | Butler |
| CANONSBURG | Washington | CHINCHILLA | Lackawanna |
| CANTON | Bradford | CHRISTIANA | Lancaster |
| CARBONDALE | Lackawanna | CLAIRTON | Allegheny |
| CARDALE | Fayette | CLARENCE | Centre |
| CARLISLE | Cumberland | CLARENDON | Warren |
| CARLTON | Mercer | CLARIDGE | Westmoreland |
| CARMICHAFLS | Greene | CLARINGTON | Forest |
| CARNEGIE | Allegheny | CLARION | Clarion |
| CARROLLTOWN | Cambria | CLARK | Mercer |
| CARSON | Allegheny | CLARKSBURG | Indiana |
| CARVERSVILLE | Bucks | CLARKS MILLS | Mercer |
| CASHTOWN | Adams | CLARKS SUMMIT | Lackawanna |

| | | | |
|---|---|---|---|
| CLARKSVILLE | Greene | COURTNEY | Washington |
| CLAYSBURG | Blair | COVINGTON | Tioga |
| CLEARFIELD | Clearfield | COWANESQUE | Tioga |
| CLEARVILLE | Bedford | COWANSVILLE | Armstrong |
| CLIFFORD | Susquehanna | CRABTREE | Westmoreland |
| CLIFTON HEIGHTS | Delaware | CRAIGSVILLE | Armstrong |
| CLIMAX | Armstrong | CRALEY | York |
| CLINTON | Allegheny | CRANBERRY | Venango |
| CLINTONVILLE | Venango | CRANESVILLE | Erie |
| CLUNE | Indiana | CREAMERY | Montgomery |
| CLYMER | Indiana | CREEKSIDE | Indiana |
| COAL CENTER | Washington | CREIGHTON | Allegheny |
| COALDALE | Schuylkill | CRESCO | Monroe |
| COALPORT | Clearfield | CRESSON | Cambria |
| COATESVILLE | Chester | CRESSONA | Schuylkill |
| COBURN | Centre | CROFT | Clearfield |
| COCHRANTON | Crawford | CROSBY | McKean |
| COCHRANVILLE | Chester | CROSS FORK | Potter |
| COCOLAMUS | Juniata | CROWN | Clarion |
| CODORUS | York | CRUCIBLE | Greene |
| COGAN STATION | Lycoming | CRYSTAL SPRING | Fulton |
| COKEBURG | Washington | CUDDY | Allegheny |
| COLEBROOK | Lebanon | CURLLSVILLE | Clarion |
| COLLEGEVILLE | Montgomery | CURRY RUN | Clearfield |
| COLMAR | Montgomery | CURRYVILLE | Blair |
| COLUMBIA | Lancaster | CURTISVILLE | Allegheny |
| COLUMBIA CROSS ROADS | Bradford | CURWENSVILLE | Clearfield |
| COLUMBUS | Warren | CUSTER CITY | McKean |
| COLVER | Cambria | CYCLONE | McKean |
| COMBOLA | Schuylkill | DAGUS MINES | Elk |
| COMMODORE | Indiana | DAISYTOWN | Washington |
| CONCORD | Franklin | DALLAS | Luzerne |
| CONCORDVILLE | Delaware | DALLASTOWN | York |
| CONESTOGA | Lancaster | DALMATIA | Northumberland |
| CONFLUENCE | Somerset | DALTON | Lackawanna |
| CONNEAUT LAKE | Crawford | DAMASCUS | Wayne |
| CONNEAUTVILLE | Crawford | DANBORO | Bucks |
| CONNELLSVILLE | Fayette | DANIELSVILLE | Northampton |
| ONNOQUENESSING | Butler | DANVILLE | Montour |
| CONSHOHOCKEN | Montgomery | DARBY | Delaware |
| CONWAY | Beaver | DARLINGTON | Beaver |
| CONYNGHAM | Luzerne | DARRAGH | Westmoreland |
| COOKSBURG | Forest | DAUPHIN | Dauphin |
| COOPERSBURG | Lehigh | DAVIDSVILLE | Somerset |
| COOPERSTOWN | Venango | DAWSON | Fayette |
| COPLAY | Lehigh | DAYTON | Armstrong |
| CORAL | Indiana | DEFIANCE | Bedford |
| CORAPOLIS | Allegheny | DELANCEY | Jefferson |
| CORNWALL | Lebanon | DELANO | Schuylkill |
| CORRY | Erie | DELAWARE WATER GAP | Monroe |
| CORSICA | Jefferson | DELMONT | Westmoreland |
| COUDERSPORT | Potter | DELTA | York |
| COULTERS | Allegheny | DENBO | Washington |

| | | | |
|---|---|---|---|
| DENVER | Lancaster | EAST CLAIR | Schuylkill |
| DERRICK CITY | McKean | EAST EARL | Lancaster |
| DERRY | Westmoreland | EAST FREEDOM | Blair |
| DEVAULT | Chester | EAST GREENVILLE | Montgomery |
| DEVON | Chester | EAST HICKORY | Forest |
| DEWART | Northumberland | EAST JOHNS | Luzerne |
| DEYOUNG | Elk | EAST MARYS | Elk |
| DICKERSON RUN | Fayette | EAST MCKEESPORT | Allegheny |
| DICKINSON | Cumberland | EAST MICHAEL | Cambria |
| DILLINER | Greene | EAST MILLSBORO | Fayette |
| DILLSBURG | York | EASTON | Northampton |
| DILLTOWN | Indiana | EAST PETERSBURG | Lancaster |
| DIMOCK | Susquehanna | EAST PITTSBURGH | Al legheny |
| DINGMANS FERRY | Pike | EAST PROSPECT | York |
| DISTANT | Armstrong | EAST SMETHPORT | McKean |
| DIXONVILLE | Indiana | EAST SMITHFIELD | Bradford |
| DONEGAL | Westmoreland | EAST SPRINGFIELD | Erie |
| DONORA | Washington | EAST STROUDSBURG | Monroe |
| DORNSIFE | Northumberland | EAST TEXAS | Lehigh |
| DOUGLASSVILLE | Berks | EAST THOMAS | Franklin |
| DOVER | York | EAST VANDERGRIFT | estmoreland |
| DOWNINGTOWN | Chester | EAST WATERFORD | Juniata |
| DOYLESTOWN | Buck | EAU CLAIRE | Butler |
| DRAVASBURG | Allegheny | EBENSBURG | Cambria |
| DREXEL HILL | Delaware | EBERVALE | Luzerne |
| DRIFTING | Clearfield | EDGEMONT | Delaware |
| DRIFTON | Luzerne | EDINBORO | Erie |
| DRIFTWOOD | Cameron | EDINBURG | Lawrence |
| DRUMMORE | liancmWr | EDMON | Armstrong |
| DRUMS | Luzerne | EFFORT | Monroe |
| DRY RUN | Franklin | EIGHTY FOUR | Washington |
| DUBLIN | Bucks | ELCO | Washington |
| DU BOIS | Clearfield | ELDERSVILLE | Washington |
| DUDLEY | Huntingdon | ELDERTON | Armstrong |
| DUKE CENTER | McKean | ELDRED | McKean |
| DUNBAR | Fayette | ELGIN | Erie |
| DUNCANNON | Perry | ELIZABETH | Allegheny |
| DUNCANSVILLE | Blair | ELIZABETHTOWN | Lancaster |
| DUNLEBY | Washington | ELIZABETHVILLE | Dauphin |
| DUNLO | Cambria | ELKLAND | Tioga |
| DUQUESNE | Allegheny | ELLIOTTSBURG | Perry |
| DURHAM | Bucks | ELLSWORTH | Washington |
| DUSHORE | Sullivan | ELLWOOD CITY | Lawrence |
| DYSART | Cambria | ELM | Lancaster |
| EAGLES MERE | Sullivan | ELMHURST | Lackawanna |
| EAGLESVILLE | Montgomery | ELMORA | Cambria |
| EARLINGTON | Montgomery | ELRAMA | Washington |
| EARLVILLE | Berks | ELTON | Cambria |
| EAST BENEDICT | Cambria | ELVERSON | Chester |
| EAST BERLIN | Adams | ELYSBURG | Northumberland |
| EAST BONIFACE | Cambria | EMEIGH | Cambria |
| EAST BRADY | Clarion | EMIGSVILLE | York |
| EAST BUTLER | Butler | EMLENTON | Venango |

| | | | |
|---|---|---|---|
| EMMAUS | Lehigh | FORCE | Elk |
| EMPORIUM | Cameron | FORD CITY | Armstrong |
| ENDEAVOR | Forest | FORD CLIFF | Armstrong |
| ENOLA | Cumberland | FOREST CITY | Susquehanna |
| ENON VALLEY | Lawrence | FOREST GROVE | Bucks |
| ENTRIKEN | Huntingdon | FORESTVILLE | Butler |
| EPHRATA | Lancaster | FORKSVILLE | Sullivan |
| EQUINUNK | Wayne | FORT HILL | Somerset |
| ERIE | Erie | FORT LOUDON | Frankin |
| ERWINNA | Bucks | FORT WASHINGTON | Montgomery |
| ESSINGTON | Delware | FOUNTAINVILLE | Bucks |
| ETTERS | York | FOXBURG | Clarion |
| EVANS CITY | Butler | FRACKVILLE | Schuylkill |
| EVANSVILLE | Berks | FRANKLIN | Venango |
| EVERETT | Bedford | FRANKLINTOWN | York |
| EVERSON | Fayette | FREDERICK | Montgomery |
| EXCELSIOR | Northumberland | FREDERICKSBURG | ebanon |
| EXPORT | Westmoreland | FREDERICKTOWN | Washington |
| EXTON | Chester | FREDONIA | Mercer |
| FACTORYVILLE | Wyoming | FREEBURG | Snyder |
| FAIRBANK | Fayette | FREEDOM | Beaver |
| FAIRCHANCE | Fayette | FREELAND | Luzerne |
| FAIRFIELD | Adams | FREEPORT | Armstrong |
| FAIRHOPE | Somerset | FRENCHVILLE | Clearfield |
| FAIRLESS HILLS | Bucks | FRIEDENS | Somerset |
| FAIRMOUNT CITY | Clarion | FRIEDENSBURG | Schuylkill |
| FAIRVIEW | Erie | FRIENDSVILLE | Susquehanna |
| FALLENTIMBER | Cambria | FRYBURG | Clarion |
| FALLS | Wyoming | FURLONG | Bucks |
| FALLS CREEK | Jefferson | GAINES | Tioga |
| FANNETTSBURG | Franklin | GALETON | Potter |
| FARMINGTON | Fayette | GALILEE | Wayne |
| FARRANDSVILLE | Clinton | GALLITZIN | Cambria |
| FARRELL | Mercer | GAP | Lancaster |
| FAWN GROVE | York | GARARDS FORT | Greene |
| FAYETTE CITY | Fayette | GARDENVILLE | Bucks |
| FAYETTEVILLE | Franklin | GARDNERS | Adams |
| FELTON | York | GARLAND | Warren |
| FENELTON | Butler | GARRETT | Somerset |
| FERNDALE | Bucks | GASTONVILLE | Washington |
| FINLEYVILLE | Washington | GIEGERTOWN | Berks |
| FISHER | Clarion | GENESEE | Potter |
| FISHERTOWN | Bedford | GEORGETOWN | Beaver |
| FLEETVILLE | Lackawanna | GERMANSVILLE | Lehigh |
| FLEETWOOD | Berks | GETTYSBURG | Adams |
| FLEMING | Centre | GIBBON GLADE | Fayette |
| FLINTON | Cambria | GIBSON | Susquehanna |
| FLOURTOWN | Montgomery | GIBSONIA | Allegheny |
| FOGELSVILLE | Lehigh | GIFFORD | McKean |
| FOLCROFT | Delaware | GILBERT | Monroe |
| FOLSOM | Delaware | GILBERTON | Schuylkill |
| FOMBELL | Beaver | GILBERTSVILLE | Montgomery |
| FORBES ROAD | Westmoreland | GILLETT | Bradford |

| | | | |
|---|---|---|---|
| GIPSY | Indiana | HAMILTON | Jefferson |
| GIRARD | Erie | HAMLIN | Wayne |
| GIRARDVILLE | Schuylkill | HANNASTOWN | Westmoreland |
| GLADWYNE | Montgomery | HANOVER | York |
| GLASGOW | Cambria | HARBORCREED | Erie |
| GLASSPORT | Allegheny | HARFORD | Susquehanna |
| GLEN CAMPBELL | Indiana | HARLEIGH | Luzeme |
| GLENCOE | Somerset | HARLEYSVILLE | Montogomery |
| GLEN LYON | Luzerne | HARMONSBURG | Crawford |
| GLEN MILLS | Delaware | HARMONY | Butler |
| GLENMOORE | Chester | HARRISBURG | Dauphin |
| GLENOLDEN | Deleware | HARRISON CITY | Westmoreland |
| GLEN ROCK | York | HARRISVILLE | Butler |
| GLENSHAW | Allegheny | HARTLETON | Union |
| GLENSIDE | Montgomery | HARTSTOWN | Crawford |
| GLENVILLE | York | HARVEYS LAKE | Luzerne |
| GLENWILLARD | Allegheny | HARWICK | Allegheny |
| GOODVILLE | Lancaster | HASTINGS | Cambria |
| GORDON | Schuylkill | HATBORO | Montgomery |
| GORDONVILLE | Lancaster | HATFIELD | Montgomery |
| GOULDSBORO | Wayne | HAVERFORD | Montgomery |
| GOWEN CITY | Northumberland | HAWK RUN | Clearfield |
| GRADYVILLE | Delaware | HAWLEY | Wayne |
| GRAMPIAN | Clearfield | HAWTHORN | Clarion |
| GRAND VALLEY | Warren | HAZEL HURST | McKean |
| GRANTHAM | Cumberland | HAZLETON | Luzerne |
| GRANTVILLE | Dauphin | HEGINS | Schuylkill |
| GRANVILLE | Mifflin | HEILWOOD | Indiana |
| GRANVILLE SUMMIT | Bradford | HELFENSTEIN | Schuykill |
| GRAPEVILLE | Westmoreland | HELLERTOWN | Northampton |
| GRASSFLAT | Clearfield | HENDERSONVILLE | Washington |
| GRATZ | Dauphin | HENRYVILLE | Monroe |
| GRAY | Somerset | HEREFORD | Berks |
| GRAYSVILLE | Greene | HERMAN | Butler |
| GREAT BEND | Susquehanna | HERMINIE | Westmoreland |
| GREELEY | Pike | HERNDON | Northumberland |
| GREENCASTLE | Franklin | HERRICK CENTER | Susquehanna |
| GREEN LANE | Montgomery | HERSHEY | Dauphin |
| GREENOCK | Allegheny | HESSTON | Huntingdon |
| GREENPARK | Perry | HIBBS | Fayette |
| GREENSBORO | Greene | HICKORY | Washington |
| GREENSBURG | Westmoreland | HIGHSPIRE | Dauphin |
| GREENTOWN | Pike | HILLER | Fayette |
| GREENVILLE | Clearfield | HILLIARDS | Butler |
| GRINDSTONE | Fayette | HILLSDALE | Indiana |
| GROVE CITY | Mercer | HISSGROVE | Sullivan |
| GROVER | Bradford | HILLSVILLE | Lawrence |
| GUYS MILLS | Crawford | HILLTOWN | Bucks |
| GWYNEDD VALLEY | Montgomery | HOLBROOK | Greene |
| HADLEY | Mercer | HOLICONG | Bucks |
| HALIFAX | Dauphin | HOLLIDAYSBURG | Blair |
| HALLSTEAD | Susquehanna | HOLLSOPPLE | Somerset |
| HAMBURG | Berks | HOLMES | Delaware |

| | | | |
|---|---|---|---|
| HOLTWOOD | Lancaster | JAMES CREEK | Huntingdon |
| HOME | Indiana | JAMESTOWN | Mercer |
| HOMER CITY | Indiana | JAMISON | Bucks |
| HOMESTEAD | Allegheny | JEANNETTE | Westmoreland |
| HONESDALE | Wayne | JEFFERSON | Greene |
| HONEY BROOK | Chester | JENKINTOWN | Montgomery |
| HONEY GROVE | Juniata | JENNERSTOWN | Somerset |
| HOOKSTOWN | Beaver | JERMYN | Lackawanna |
| HOOVERSVILLE | Somerset | JEROME | Somerset |
| HOP BOTTOM | Susquehanna | JERSEY MILLS | Lycoming |
| HOPELAND | Lancaster | JERSEY SHORE | Lycoming |
| HOPEWELL | Bedford | JESSUP | Lackawanna |
| HOPWOOD | Fayette | JIM THORPE | Carbon |
| HORSHAM | Montgomery | JOFFRE | Washington |
| HOSTETTER | Westmoreland | JOHNSONBURG | Elk |
| HOUSTON | Washington | JOHNSTOWN | Cambria |
| HOUTZDALE | Clearfield | JONES MILLS | Westmoreland |
| HOWARD | Centre | JONESTOWN | Lebanon |
| HUEY | Clarion | JOSEPHINE | Indiana |
| HUGHESVILLE | Lycoming | JULIAN | Centre |
| HUMMELSTOWN | Dauphin | JUNEAU | Indiana |
| HUMMELS WHARF | Snyder | JUNEDALE | Carbon |
| HUNKER | Westmoreland | KANE | McKean |
| HUNLOCK CREEK | Luzerne | KANTNER | Somerset |
| HUNTINGDON | Huntingdon | KARNS CITY | Butler |
| HUNTINGDON VALLEY | Montgomery | KARTHAUS | Clearfield |
| HUNTINGTON MILLS | Luzerne | KASKA | Schuylkill |
| HUSTONTOWN | Fulton | KEISTERVILLE | Fayette |
| HUTCHINSON | Westmoreland | KELAYRES | Schuylkill |
| HYDE | Clearfield | KELTON | Chester |
| HYDE PARK | Westmoreland | KEMBLESVILLE | Chester |
| HYDETOWN | Crawford | KEMPTON | Berks |
| HYNDMAN | Bedford | KENNERDELL | Venango |
| ICKESBURG | Perry | KENNETT SQUARE | Chester |
| IDAVILLE | Adams | KENT | Indiana |
| IMLER | Bedford | KERSEY | Elk |
| IMMACULATA | Chester | KIMBERTON | Chester |
| IMPERIAL | Allegheny | KINGSLEY | Susquehanna |
| INDIANA | Indiana | KINTNERSVILLE | Bucks |
| INDIAN HEAD | Fayette | KINZERS | Lancaster |
| INDIANOLA | Allegheny | KIRKWOOD | Lancaster |
| INDUSTRY | Beaver | KITTANNING | Armstrong |
| INGOMAR | Allegheny | KLEINFELTERSVILLE | Lebanon |
| INTERCOURSE | Lancaster | KLINGERSTOWN | Schuylkill |
| IRISHTOWN | Clearfield | KNOX | Clarion |
| IRVINE | Warren | KNOX DALE | Jefferson |
| IRVONA | Clearfield | KNOXVILLE | Tioga |
| IRWIN | Westmoreland | KOPPEL | Beaver |
| ISABELLA | Fayette | KOSSUTH | Clarion |
| JACKSON | Susquehanna | KREAMER | Snyder |
| JACKSON CENTER | Mercer | KRESGEVILLE | Monroe |
| JACOBS CREEK | Westmoreland | KULPMONT | Northumberland |
| JAMES CITY | Elk | KULPSVILLE | Montgomery |

| | | | |
|---|---|---|---|
| KUNKLETOWN | Monroe | LEHINGTON | Carbon |
| KUTZTOWN | Berks | LEHMAN | Luzerne |
| KYLERTOWN | Clearfield | LEISENRING | Fayette |
| LABELLE | Fayette | LEMASTERS | Franklin |
| LACEYVILLE | Wyoming | LEMONT FURNACE | Fayette |
| LACKAWAXEN | Pike | LEMOYNE | Cumberland |
| LAFAYETTE HILL | Montgomery | LENHARTSVILLE | Burks |
| LAHASKA | Bucks | LENNI | Delaware |
| LAIRDSVILLE | Lycoming | LEOLA | Lancaster |
| LAJOSE | Clearfield | LE RAYSVILLE | Bradford |
| LAKE ARIEL | Wayne | LE ROY | Bradford |
| LAKE CITY | Erie | LEVITTOWN | Bucks |
| LAKE COMO | Wayne | LEWISBERRY | York |
| LAKE HARMONY | Carbon | LEWISBURG | Union |
| LAKE LYNN | Fayette | LEWIS RUN | McKean |
| LAKE WINOLA | Wyoming | LEVISTOWN | Mifflin |
| LAKEWOOD | Wayne | LEWISVILLE | Chester |
| LAMAR | Clinton | LIBERTY | Tioga |
| LAMARTINE | Clarion | LIBRARY | Allegheny |
| LAMPETER | Lancaster | LICKINGVILLE | Clarion |
| LANCASTER | Lancaster | LIGONIER | Westmoreland |
| LANDENBERG | Chester | LILLY | Cambria |
| LANDINGVILLE | Schuylkill | LIMEKILN | Berks |
| LANDISBURG | Perry | LIMEPORT | Lehigh |
| LANDISVILLE | Lancaster | LIMESTONE | Clarion |
| LANESBORO | Susquehanna | LINCOLN UNIVERSITY | Chester |
| LANGELOTH | Washington | LINDEN | Lycoming |
| LANGHORNE | Bucks | LINE LEXINGTON | Bucks |
| LANSDALE | Montgomery | LINESVILLE | Crawford |
| LANSDOWNE | Delaware | LISTIE | Somerset |
| LANSE | Clearfield | LITITZ | Lancaster |
| LANSFORD | Carbon | LITTLE MARSH | Tioga |
| LAPLUME | Lackawanna | LITTLE MEADOWS | Susquehanna |
| LAPORTE | Sullivan | LITTLESTOWN | Adams |
| LAMIMER | Westmoreland | LIVERPOOL | Perry |
| LATROBE | Westmoreland | LLEWELLNY | Schuylkill |
| LATTIMER MINES | Luzerne | LOCK HAVEN | Clinton |
| LAUGHLINTOWN | Westmoreland | LOCUSTDALE | Schuylkill |
| LAURELTON | Union | LOCUST GAP | Northumberland |
| LAURYS STATION | Lehigh | LOGANTON | Clinton |
| LAVELLE | Schuylkill | LOGANVILLE | York |
| LAWN | Lebanon | LONG POND | Monroe |
| LAWRENCE | Washington | LOPEZ | Sullivan |
| LAWRENCEVILLE | Tioga | LORETTO | Cambria |
| LAWTON | Susquehanna | LOST CREEK | Schuylkill |
| LEBANON | Lebanon | LOWBER | Westmoreland |
| LECK KILL | Northumberland | LOYALHANNA | Westmoreland |
| LECKRONE | Fayette | LOYSBURG | Bedford |
| LEDERACH | Montgomery | LOYSVILLE | Perry |
| LEECHBURG | Armstrong | LUCERNEMINES | Indiana |
| LEEPER | Clarion | LUCINDA | Clarion |
| LEESPORT | Berks | LUDLOW | McKean |
| LEETSDALE | Allegheny | LURGAN | Franklin |

| | | | |
|---|---|---|---|
| LUTHERSBURG | Clearfield | MARLIN | Schuylkill |
| LUXOR | Westmoreland | MARS | Butler |
| LYKENS | Dauphin | MARSHALLS CREEK | Monroe |
| LYNDELL | Chester | MARSTELLER | Cambria |
| LYNDORA | Butler | MARTIN | Fayette |
| LYON STATION | Berks | MARTINSBURG | Blair |
| MCADOO | Schuylkill | MARTINS CREEK | Northampton |
| MCALISTERVILLE | Juniata | MARY D | Schuylkill |
| MCCLELLANDTOWN | Fayette | MARYSVILLE | Perry |
| MCCLURE | Snyder | MASONTOWN | Fayette |
| MCCONNELLSBURG | Fulton | MATAMORAS | Pike |
| MCCONNELLSTOWN | Huntingdon | MATHER | Greene |
| MCDONALD | Washington | MATTAWANA | Mifflin |
| MCELHATTAN | Clinton | MAXATAWNY | Berks |
| MCEWENSVILLE | Northumberland | MAYPORT | Clarion |
| MCGRANN | Armstrong | MAYTOWN | Lancaster |
| MCINTYRE | Indiana | MEADOW LANDS | Washington |
| MCKEAN | Erie | MEADVILLE | Crawford |
| MCKEESPORT | Allegheny | MECHANIESBURG | Cumberland |
| MCKEES ROCKS | Allegheny | MECHANIESVILLE | Bucks |
| MCENIGHTSTOWN | Adams | MEDIA | Delaware |
| MCSHERRYSTOWN | Adams | MEHOOPANY | Wyoming |
| MCVEYTOWN | Mifflin | MELCROFT | Fayette |
| MACKEYVILLE | Clinton | MENDENHALL | Chester |
| MACUNGIE | Lehigh | MENTCLE | Indiana |
| MADERA | Clearfield | MERCER | Mercer |
| MADISON | Westmoreland | MERCERSBURG | Franklin |
| MADISONBURG | Centre | MERION STATION | Montgomery |
| MAHAFFEY | Clearfield | MERRITTSTOWN | Fayette |
| MAHANOY CITY | Schuylkill | MERTZTOWN | Berks |
| MAHANOY PLANE | Schuylkill | MESHOPPEN | Wyoming |
| MAINESBURG | Tioga | MEXICO | Juniata |
| MAINLAND | Montgomery | MEYERSDALE | Somerset |
| MALVERN | Chester | MIDDLEBURG | Snyder |
| MAMMOTH | Westmoreland | MIDDLEBURY CENTER | Tioga |
| MANCHESTER | York | MIDDLEPORT | Schuylkill |
| MANHEIM | Lancaster | MIDDLETOWN | Dauphin |
| MANNS CHOICE | Bedford | MIDLAND | Beaver |
| MANOR | Westmoreland | MIDWAY | Washington |
| MANORVILLE | Armstrong | MIFFLIN | Juniata |
| MANSFIELD | Tioga | MIFFLINBURG | Union |
| MAPLETON DEPOT | Huntingdon | MIFFLINTOWN | Juniata |
| MARBLE | Clarion | MIFFLLINVILLE | Columbia |
| MARCHAND | Indiana | MILAN | Bradford |
| MARCUS HOOK | Delaware | MILANVILLE | Wayne |
| MARIANNA | Washington | MILDRED | Sullivan |
| MARIENVILLE | Forest | MILESBLRRG | Centre |
| MARIETTA | Lancaster | MILFORD | Pike |
| MARION | Franklin | MILFORD SQUARE | Bucks |
| MARION CENTER | Indiana | MILL CREEK | Huntingdon |
| MARION HEIGHTS | Northumberland | MILLERSBURG | Dauphin |
| MARKLETON | Somerset | MILLERSTOWN | Perry |
| MARKLEYSBURG | Fayette | MILLERSVBILLE | Lancaster |

| | | | |
|---|---|---|---|
| MILLERTON | Tioga | MOUNT PLEASANT | Westmoreland |
| MILL HALL | Clinton | MOUNT POCONO | Monroe |
| MILLHEIM | Centre | MOUNT UNION | Huntingdon |
| MILLMONT | Union | MOUNTVILLE | Lancaster |
| MILLRIFT | Pike | MOUNT WOLF | York |
| MILL RUN | Fayette | MUIR | Schuylkill |
| MILLS | Potter | MUNCY | Lycoming |
| MILLSBORO | Washington | MUNCY VALLEY | Sullivan |
| MILL VILLAGE | Erie | MUNSON | Clearfield |
| MILLVILLE | Columbia | MURRIYSVILLE | Westmoreland |
| MILNESVILLE | Luzerne | MUSE | Washington |
| MILROY | Mifflin | MYERSTOWN | Lebanon |
| MILTON | Northumberland | NANTICOKE | Luzerne |
| MINERAL POINT | Cambria | NANTY GLO | Cambria |
| MINERAL SPRINGS | Clearfield | NARBERTH | Montgomery |
| MINERSVILLE | Schuylkill | NARVON | Lancaster |
| MINGOVILLE | Centre | NATRONA HEIGHTS | Allegheny |
| MINISINK HILLS | Monroe | NAZARETH | Northampton |
| MIQUON | Montgomery | NEEDMORE | Fulton |
| MODENA | Chester | NEELYTON | Huntingdon |
| MOHNTON | Berks | NEFFS | Lehigh |
| MOHRSVILLE | Berks | NELSON | Tioga |
| MONACA | Beaver | NEMACOLIN | Greene |
| MONESSEN | Westmoreland | NESCOPECK | Luzeme |
| MONOCACY STATION | Berks | NESQUEHONING | Carbon |
| MONONGAHELA | ashington | NEW ALBANY | Braadford |
| MONROETON | Bradford | NEW ALEXANDRIA | Westmoreland |
| MONT ALTO | Franklin | NEW BALTIMORE | Somerset |
| MONTANDON | Northumberland | NEW BEDFORD | Lawrence |
| MONTGOMERY | Lycoming | NEW BERLIN | Union |
| MONTGOMERYVILLE | Montgomery | NEW BERLINVILLE | Berks |
| MONTOURSVILLE | ycoming | NEW BETHLEHEM | Clarion |
| MONTROSE | Susquehanna | NEW BLOOMFIELD | Perry |
| MORANN | Clearfield | NEW BRIGHTON | Beaver |
| MORGAN | Allegheny | NEW BUFFALO | Perry |
| MORGANTOWN | Berks | NEWBURG | Cumberland |
| MORRIS | Tioga | NEW CASTLE | Lawrence |
| MORRISDALE | Clearfield | NEW CUMBERLAND | Cumberland |
| MORRIS RUN | Tioga | NEW DERRY | Westmoreland |
| MORRISVILLE | Bucks | NEW EAGLE | Washington |
| MORTON | Delaware | NEWELL | Fayette |
| MOSCOW | Lackawanna | NEW ENTERPRISE | Bedford |
| MOSHANNON | Centre | NEW FLORENCE | Westmoreland |
| MOUNT AETNA | Berks | NEWFOUNDLAND | Wayne |
| MOUNTAINHOME | Monroe | NEW FREEDOM | York |
| MOUNT BETHEL | Northhampton | NEW FREEPORT | Greene |
| MOUNT BRADDOCK | Fayette | NEW GALILEE | Beaver |
| MOUNT CARMEL | Northumberland | NEW GENEVA | Fayette |
| MOUNT GRETNA | Lebanon | NEW GERMANTOWN | Perry |
| MOUNT HOLLY SPRINGS | Cumberland | NEW HOLLAND | Lancaster |
| MOUNT JEWETT | McKean | NEW HOPE | Bucks |
| MOUNT JOY | Lancaster | NEW KENSINGTON | Westmoreland |
| MOUNT MORRIS | Greene | NEW KINGSTOWN | Cumberland |

| | | | |
|---|---|---|---|
| NEW LONDON | Chester | OLIVEBURG | Jefferson |
| NEWMANSTOWN | Lebanon | OLIVER | Fayette |
| NEW MILFORD | Susquehanna | LOYPHANT | Lackawanna |
| NEW MILLPORT | Clearfield | ONEIDA | Schuylkill |
| NEW OXFORD | Adams | ONO | Lebanon |
| NEW PARIS | Bedford | ORANGEVILLE | Columbia |
| NEW PARK | York | ORBISONIA | Huntingdon |
| NEW PHILADELPHIA | Schuylkill | OREFIELD | Lehigh |
| NEWPORT | Perry | ORELAND | Montgomery |
| NEW PROVIDENCE | Lancaster | ORRSTOWN | Franklin |
| NEW RINGGOLD | Schuylkill | ORRTANNA | Adams |
| NEWRY | Blair | ORSON | Wayne |
| NEW SALEM | Fayette | ORWIGSBURG | Schuylkill |
| NEW STANTON | Washington | OSCEOLA | Tioga |
| NEWTON HAMILTON | Mifflin | OSCEOLA MILLS | Clearfield |
| NEWTOWN | Bucks | OSTERBURG | Bedford |
| NEWTOWN SQUARE | Delaware | OTTSVILLE | Buck |
| NEW TRIPOLI | Lehigh | OXFORD | Chester |
| NEWVILLE | Cumberland | PALM | Montgomery |
| NEW WILMINGTON | Lawrence | PALMERTON | Carbon |
| NICHOLSON | Wyoming | PALMYRA | Lebanon |
| NICKTOWN | Cambria | PAOLI | Chester |
| NIVEVEH | Greene | PARADISE | Lancaster |
| NISBET | Lycoming | PARDEESVILLE | Luzerne |
| NORMALVILLE | Fayette | PARKER | Armstrong |
| NORRISTOWN | Montgomery | PARKER FORD | Chester |
| NORTHAMPTON | Northampton | PARKESBURG | Chester |
| NORTH APOLLO | Armstrong | PARRYVILLE | Carbon |
| NORTH BEND | Clinton | PATTON | Cambria |
| NORTH EAST | Erie | PAUPACK | Pike |
| NORTH SPRINGFIELD | Erie | PAXINOS | Northumberland |
| NORTHUMBERLAND | Northumberland | PAXTONVILLE | Synder |
| NORTH VERSAILLES | Allegheny | PEACH BOTTOM | Lancaster |
| NORTH WALES | Montgomery | PECKVILLE | Lackawanna |
| NORTH WASHINGTON | Butler | PEN ARGYL | Northampton |
| NORVELT | Westmoreland | PENFIELD | Clearfield |
| NORWOOD | Delaware | PENN | Westmoreland |
| NOTTINGHAM | Chester | PENN RUN | Indiana |
| NOXEN | Wyoming | PENNS CREEK | Snyder |
| NUANGOLA | Luzeme | PENNS PARK | Bucks |
| NUMIDIA | Columbia | PENNSYLVANIA FURNACE | Huntingdon |
| NU MINE | Armstrong | PENRYN | Lancaster |
| NURENBERG | Schuylkill | PEQUEA | Lancaster |
| OAKDALE | Allegheny | PERKASIE | Bucks |
| OAKLAND MILLS | Juniata | PERKIOMENVILLE | Montgomery |
| OAKMONT | Allegheny | PERRYOPOLIS | Fayette |
| OAK RIDGE | Armstrong | PETERSBURG | Huntingdon |
| OAKS | Montgomery | PETROLIA | Butler |
| OHIOPYLE | Fayette | PHILADELPHIA | Philadelphia |
| OIL CITY | Venango | PHILIPSBURG | Centre |
| OLANTA | Clearfield | PHOENIXVILLE | Chester |
| OLD ZIONSSVILLE | Lehigh | PICTURE ROCKS | Lycoming |
| OLEY | Berks | PILLOW | Dauphin |

| | | | |
|---|---|---|---|
| PINE BANK | Greene | QUARRYVILLE | Lancaster |
| PINE FORGE | Berks | QUECREEK | Somerset |
| PINE GROVE | Schuylkill | QUEEN | Bedford |
| PINE GROVE MILLS | Centre | QUINCY | Franklin |
| PINEVILLE | Bucks | RAILROAD | York |
| PIPERSVILLE | Bucks | RALSTON | Lycoming |
| PITMAN | Schuylkill | RAMEY | Clearfield |
| PITTSBURGH | Allegheny | RANSOM | Lackawanna |
| PITTSFIELD | Warren | RAVINE | Schuylkill |
| PITTSTON | Luzerne | REA | Washington |
| PLAINFIELD | Cumberland | READING | Berks |
| PLEASANT HALL | Franklin | REAMSTOWN | Lancaster |
| PLEASANT MOUNT | Wayne | REBERSBURG | Centre |
| PLEASANT UNITY | Westmoreland | REBUCK | Northumberland |
| PLEASANTVILLE | Venango | RECTOR | Westmoreland |
| PLUMSTEADVILLE | Bucks | RED HILL | Montgomery |
| PLUMVILLE | Indiana | RED LION | York |
| PLYMOUTH | Luzerne | REEDERS | Monroe |
| PLYMOUTH MEETING | Montgomery | REEDSVILLE | Mifflin |
| POCONO LAKE | Monroe | REFTON | Lancaster |
| POCONO LAKE PRESERVE | Monroe | REHRERSBURG | Berks |
| POCONO MANOR | Monroe | REINHOLDS | Lancaster |
| POCONO PINES | Monroe | RENFREW | Butler |
| POCONO SUMMIT | Monroe | RENO | Venango |
| POCOPSON | Chester | RENOVO | Clinton |
| POINT MARION | Fayette | REPUBLIC | Fayette |
| POINT PLEASANT | Bucks | REVERE | Bucks |
| POLK | Venango | REVLOC | Cambria |
| POMEROY | Chester | REW | McKean |
| PORTAGE | Cambria | REXMONT | Lebanon |
| PORT ALLEGANY | McKean | REYNOLDSVILLE | Jefferson |
| PORT CARBON | Schuylkill | RHEEMS | Lancaster |
| PORT CLINTON | Schuylkill | RICES LANDING | Greene |
| PORTERSVILLE | Butler | RICEVILLE | Crawford |
| PORTLAND | Northampton | RICHEYVILLE | Washington |
| PORT MATILDA | Centre | RICHFIELD | Juniata |
| PORT ROYAL | Juniata | RICHLAND | Lebanon |
| PORT TREVORTON | Snyder | RICHLANDTOWN | Bucks |
| POTTS GROVE | Northumberland | RIDDLESBURG | Bedford |
| POTTSTOWN | Montgomery | RIDGEWAY | Elk |
| POTTSVILLE | Schuylkill | RIDLEY PARK | Delaware |
| POYNTELLE | Wayne | RIEGELSVILLE | Bucks |
| PRESTO | Allegheny | RILLTON | Westmoreland |
| PRESTON PARK | Wayne | RIMERSBURG | Clarion |
| PRINCEDALE | Westmoreland | RINGGOLD | Jefferson |
| PROMPTON | Wayne | RINGTOWN | Schuylkill |
| PROSPECT | Butler | RIVERSIDE | Northumberland |
| PROSPECT PARK | Delaware | RIZFORD | McKean |
| PROSPERTITY | Washington | ROARING BRANCH | Tioga |
| PULASKI | Lawrence | ROARING SPRING | Blair |
| PUNXSUTAWNEY | Jefferson | ROBERTSDALE | Huntingdon |
| QUAKAKE | Schuylkill | ROBESONIA | Berks |
| QUAKERTOWN | Bucks | ROBINSON | Indiana |

| | | | |
|---|---|---|---|
| ROCHESTER | Beaver | SAYLORSBURG | Monroe |
| ROCHESTER MILLS | Indiana | SAYRE | Bradford |
| ROCK GLEN | Luzerne | SCENERY HILL | Washington |
| ROCKHILL FURNANCE | Huntingdon | SCHAEFFERSTOWN | Lebanon |
| ROCKTON | Clearfield | SCHELLSBURG | Bedford |
| ROCKWOOD | Somerset | SCHENLEY | Armstrong |
| ROGERSVILLE | Greene | SCHNECKSVILLE | Lehigh |
| ROME | Bradford | SCHUYLIKLL HAVEN | Schuylkill |
| RONCO | Fayette | SCIOTA | Monroe |
| RONKS | Lancaster | SCOTLAND | Franklin |
| ROSCOE | Washington | SCOTRUN | Monroe |
| ROSSITER | Indiana | SCOTTDALE | Westmoreland |
| ROSSVILLE | York | SCRANTON | Lackawanna |
| ROULETTE | Potter | SEANOR | Somerset |
| ROUSEVILLE | Venango | SELINSGROVE | Snyder |
| ROUZERVILLE | Franklin | SELLERSVILLE | Bucks |
| ROWLAND | Pike | SELTZER | Schuylkill |
| ROXBURY | Franklin | SEMINOLE | Armstrong |
| ROYERSFORD | Montgomery | SENECA | Benango |
| RUFFS DALE | Westmoreland | SEVEN VALLEYS | York |
| RURAL RIDGE | Allegheny | SEWARD | Westmoreland |
| RURAL VALLEY | Armstrong | SEWICKLEY | Allegheny |
| RUSHLAND | Bucks | SHADE GAP | Huntingdon |
| RUSHVILLE | Susquehanna | SHADY GROVE | Franklin |
| RUSSELL | Warren | SHAMOKIN | Northumberland |
| RUSSELTON | Allegheny | SHAMOKIN DAM | Snyder |
| SABINSVILLE | Tioga | SHANKSVILLE | Mercer |
| SACRAMENTO | Schuylkill | SHARTLESVILLE | Berks |
| SADSBURYVILLE | Chester | SHAWANESE | Luzerne |
| SAEGERTOWN | Crawford | SHAWNEE ON DELAWARE | onroe |
| SAGAMORE | Armstrong | SHAWVILLE | Clearfield |
| SAINT BENEDICT | Cambria | SHEAKLEYVIIE | Mercer |
| SAINT BONIFACE | Cambria | SHEFFIELD | Warren |
| SAINT CLAIR | Schuylkill | SHELOCTA | Indiana |
| SAINT JOHNS | Luzerne | SHENANDOAH | Schuylkill |
| SAINT MARYS | Elk | SHEPPTON | Schuylkill |
| SAINT MICHAEL | Cambria | SHERMANS DALE | Perry |
| SAINT PETERS | Chester | SHICKSHINNY | Luzerne |
| SAINT PETERSBURG | Clarion | SHINGLEHOUSE | Potter |
| SAINT THOMAS | Franklin | SHIPPENSBURG | Cumberland |
| SALFORD | Montgomery | SHIPPENVILLE | Clarion |
| SALFORDVILLE | Montgomery | SHIPPINGPORT | Beaver |
| SALINA | Westmoreland | SHIRLEYSBURG | Huntingdon |
| SALISBURY | Somerset | SHOEMAKERSVILLE | Berks |
| SALIX | Cambria | SHOHOLA | Pike |
| SALTILLO | Huntingdon | SHREWSBURY | York |
| SALTSBURG | Indiana | SHUNK | Sullivan |
| SANDY | Clearfield | SIDMAN | Cambria |
| SANDY LAKE | Mercer | SIGEL | Jefferson |
| SARVER | Butler | SILVERDALE | Bucks |
| SASSAMANSVILLE | Montgomery | SILVER SPRING | Lancaster |
| SAXONBURG | Butler | SINNAMAHONING | Cameron |
| SAXTON | Bedford | SIPESVILLE | Somerset |

| | | | |
|---|---|---|---|
| SIX MILE RUN | Bedford | SPRING CITY | Chester |
| SKIPPACK | Montgomery | SPRING CREEK | Warren |
| SKYTOP | Monroe | SPRINGDALE | Allegheny |
| SLATEDALE | Lehigh | SPRING GLEN | Schuylkill |
| SLATE RUN | Lycoming | SPRING GROVE | York |
| SLATINGTON | Lehigh | SPRING MILLS | Centre |
| SLICKVILLE | Westmoreland | SPRING MOUNT | Montgomery |
| SLIGO | Clarion | SPRING RUN | Franklin |
| SLIPPERY ROCK | Butler | SPRINGS | Somerset |
| SLOVAN | Washington | SPRINGTOWN | Bucks |
| SMETHPORT | McKean | SPRINGVILLE | Susquehanna |
| SMICKSBURG | Indiana | SPROUL | Blair |
| SMITHFIELD | Fayette | SPRUCE CREEK | Huntingdon |
| SMITHMILL | Clearfield | STAHLSTOWN | Westmoreland |
| SMITHTON | Westmoreland | STARFORD | Indiana |
| SMOCK | Fayette | STAR JUNCTION | Fayette |
| SMOKERUN | Clearfield | STARLIGHT | Wayne |
| SMOKETOWN | Lancaster | STARRUCCA | Wayne |
| SNOW SHOE | Centre | STATE COLLEGE | Centre |
| SNYDERSBURG | Clarion | STATE LINE | Franklin |
| SOLEBURY | Bucks | STEELVILLE | Chester |
| SOMERSET | Somerset | STERLING | Wayne |
| SOUDERSBURG | Lancaster | STEVENS | Lancaster |
| SOUDERTON | Montgomery | STEVENSVILLE | Bradford |
| SOUTHAMPTON | Bucks | STEWARTSTOWN | York |
| SOUTH AETNA | Berks | STILLWATER | Columbia |
| SOUTH BETHEL | Northhampton | STOCKDALE | Washington |
| SOUTH BRADDOCK | Fayette | STOCKERTOWN | Northampton |
| SOUTH CANAAN | Wayne | STONEBORO | Mercer |
| SOUTH CARMEL | Northumberland | STONY RUN | Berks |
| SOUTH FORK | Cambria | STOYSTOWN | Somerset |
| SOUTH GIBSON | Susqauehanna | STRABANE | Washington |
| SOUTH GRETNA | Lebanon | STRASBURG | Lancaster |
| SOUTH HEIGHTS | Beaver | STRATTANVILLE | Clarion |
| SOUTH HOLLY SPRINGS | Cumberland | STRAUSSTOWN | Berks |
| SOUTH JEWETT | McKean | STROUDSBURG | Monroe |
| SOUTH JOY | Lancaster | STUMP CREEK | Jefferson |
| SOUTH MONTROSE | Susquehanna | STURGEON | Allegheny |
| SOUTH MOUNTAIN | Franklin | SUGARGROVE | Warren |
| SOUTH PLEASANT | Westmoreland | SUGARLOAF | Luzerne |
| SOUTH PLEASANT MILLS | Snyder | SUGAR RUN | Bradford |
| SOUTH STERLING | Wayne | SUMMERDALE | Cumberland |
| SOUTH UNION | Huntingdon | SUMMERHILL | Cambria |
| SOUTH WILLIAMSPORT | Lycoming | SUMMERVILLE | Jefferson |
| SOUTH WOLF | York | SUMMIT HILL | Carbon |
| SOUTHVIEW | Washington | SUMMIT STATION | Schuylkill |
| SOUTHWEST | Westmoreland | SUMNEYTOWN | Montgomery |
| SPANGLER | Cambria | SUNBURY | Northumberland |
| SPARTANSBURG | Crawford | SUPLEE | Chester |
| SPINNERSTOWN | Bucks | SUSQUEHANNA | Susquehanna |
| SPRAGGS | Greene | SUTERSVILLE | Westmoreland |
| SPRINGBORO | Crawford | SWARTHMORE | Delaware |
| SPRING CHURCH | Armstrong | SWEET VALLEY | Luzerne |

| | | | |
|---|---|---|---|
| SWENGEL | Union | TURKEY CITY | Clarion |
| SWIFTWATER | Monroe | TURTLE CREEK | Allegheny |
| SYBERTSVILLE | Luzerne | TURTLEPOINT | McKean |
| SYCAMORE | Greene | TUSCARORA | Schuylkill |
| SYKESVILLE | Jefferson | TWIN RICKS | Cambria |
| SYLVANIA | Bradford | TYLER HILL | Wayne |
| TAFTON | Pike | TYLERSBURG | Clarion |
| TALMAGE | Lancaster | TYLERSPORT | Montgomery |
| TAMAQUA | Schuylkill | TYLERSVILLE | Clinton |
| TANNERSVILLE | Monroe | TYRONE | Blair |
| TARENTUM | Allegheny | ULEDI | Fayette |
| TARRS | Westmoreland | ULSTER | Bradford |
| TATAMY | Northhampton | ULYSSES | Potter |
| TAYLORSTOWN | Washington | UNION CITY | Erie |
| TELFORD | Montgomery | UNION DALE | Susquehanna |
| TEMPLE | Berks | UNIONTOWN | Fayette |
| TEMPLETON | Armstrong | UNIONVILLE | Chester |
| TERRE HILL | Lancaster | UNITED | Westmoreland |
| THOMASVILLE | York | UNITYVILLE | Lycoming |
| THOMPSON | Susquehanna | UPPER BLACK EDDY | Bucks |
| THOMPSONTOWN | Juniata | UPPER DARBY | Delaware |
| THORNTON | Delaware | UPPERSTRASBURG | Franklin |
| THREE SPRINGS | Huntingdon | URSINA | Somerset |
| TIDIOUTE | Warren | UTICA | Venango |
| TIMBLIN | Jefferson | UWCHLAND | Chester |
| TIOGA | Tioga | VALENCIA | Butler |
| TIONA | Warren | VALIER | Jefferson |
| TIONESTA | Forest | VALLEY FORGE | Chester |
| TIPTON | Blair | VALLEY VIEW | Schuylkill |
| TIRE HILL | Somerset | VANDERBILT | Fayette |
| TITUSVILLE | Crawford | VANDERGRIFT | Westmoreland |
| TOBYHANNA | Monroe | VAN VOORHIS | Washington |
| TODD | Huntingdon | VENANGO | Crawford |
| TOPTON | Berks | VENETIA | Washington |
| TORRANCE | Westmoreland | VENUS | Venango |
| TOUGHKENAMON | Chester | VERONA | Allegheny |
| TOWANDA | Bradford | VESTABURG | Washington |
| TOWER CITY | Schuylkill | VICKSBURG | Union |
| TOWNVILLE | Crawford | VILLA MARIA | Lawrence |
| TRAFFORD | Westmoreland | VILLANOVA | Delaware |
| TRANSFER | Mercer | VINTONDALE | Cambria |
| TREICHLERS | Northampton | VIRGINVILLE | Berks |
| TREMONT | Schuylkill | VOLANT | Lawrence |
| TRESCKOW | Carbon | VOWINCKEL | Clarion |
| TREVORTON | Northumberland | WAGONTOWN | Chester |
| TREXLERTOWN | Lehigh | WALLACETON | Clearfield |
| TROUT RUN | Lycoming | WALNUT BOTTOM | Cumberland |
| TROUTVILLE | Clearfield | WALSTON | Jefferson |
| TROXELVILLE | Snyder | WALTERSBURG | Fayette |
| TROY | Bradford | WAMPUN | Lawrence |
| TRUMBAUERSVILLE | Bucks | WAPWALLOPEN | Luzerne |
| TUNKHANNOCK | Wyoming | WARFORDSBURG | Fulton |
| TURBOTVILLE | Northumberland | WARMINSTER | Bucks |

| | | | |
|---|---|---|---|
| WARREN | Warren | WEST WILLOW | Lancaster |
| WARREN CENTER | Bradford | WEXFORD | Allegheny |
| WARRENDALE | Allegheny | WHEATLAND | Mercer |
| WARRINGTON | Bucks | WHITE | Fayette |
| WARRIORS MARK | Huntington | WHITE DEER | Union |
| WASINGTON | Washington | WHITEHALL | Lehigh |
| WASHINGTON BORO | Lancaster | WHITE HAVEN | Luzerne |
| WASHINGTON CROSSING | Bucks | WHITE MILLS | Wayne |
| WASHINGTONVILLE | Montour | WHITNEY | Westmoreland |
| WATERFALL | Fulton | WHITSETT | Fayette |
| WATERFORD | Erie | WICKHAVEN | Fayette |
| WATERVILLE | Lycoming | WICONISCO | Dauphin |
| WATSONTOWN | Northumberland | WIDNOON | Armstrong |
| WATTSBURG | Erie | WILBURTON | Columbia |
| WAVERLY | Lackawanna | WILCOX | Elk |
| WAYMART | Wayne | WILDWOOD | Allegheny |
| WAYNE | Delaware | WILKES-BARRE | Luzerne |
| WAYNESBORO | Franklin | WILLIAMSBURG | Blair |
| WAYNESBURG | Greene | WILLIAMSON | Franklin |
| WEATHERLY | Carbon | WILLIAMSPORT | Lycoming |
| WEBSTER | Westmoreland | WILLIAMSTOWN | Dauphin |
| WEEDVILLE | Elk | WILLOW GROVE | ontgomery |
| WEIKET | Union | WILLOW HILL | Franklin |
| WELLSBORO | Tioga | WILLOW STREET | Lancaster |
| WELLS TANNERY | Fulton | WILMERDING | Allegheny |
| WELLSVILLE | York | WILMORE | Cambria |
| WENDEL | Westmoreland | WINBURNE | Clearfield |
| WERNERSVILLE | Berks | WINDBER | Somerset |
| WEST ALLEXANDER | Washington | WINDGAP | Northampton |
| WEST CHESTER | Chester | WIND RIDGE | Greene |
| WEST DECATUR | Clearfield | WINDSOR | York |
| WEST ELIZABETH | Allegheny | WINFIELD | Union |
| WESTFIELD | Tioga | WITMER | Lancaster |
| WEST FINLEY | Washington | WOMELSDORF | Berks |
| WEST GROVE | Chester | WOOD | Huntingdon |
| WEST HICKORY | Forest | WOODBURY | Bedford |
| WESTLAND | Washington | WOODLAND | Clearfield |
| WEST LEBANON | Indiana | WOODLYN | Delaware |
| WEST LEISENRING | Fayette | WOODWARD | Centre |
| WEST MIDDLESEX | Mercer | WOOLRICH | Clinton |
| WEST MIDDLETOWN | Washington | WORCESTER | Montgomery |
| WEST MILTON | Union | WORTHINGTON | Armstrong |
| WESTMORELAND CITY | Westmoreland | WORTHVILLE | Jefferson |
| WEST NEWTON | Westmoreland | WOXALL | Montgomery |
| WESTON | Luzerne | WRIGHTSVILLE | York |
| WESTOVE | Clearfield | WYALUSING | Bradford |
| WEST PITTSBURG | Lawrence | WYANA | Westmoreland |
| WEST POINT | Montgomery | WYCOMBE | Bucks |
| WESTPORT | Clinton | WYNCOTE | Montgomery |
| WEST SALISBURY | Somerset | WYNNEWOOD | Montgomery |
| WEST SPRINGFILED | Erie | WYSOX | Bradford |
| WEST SUNBURY | Butler | YATESBORO | Armstrong |
| WESTTOWN | Chester | YEAGERTOWN | Mifflin |

| | | | |
|---|---|---|---|
| YORK | York | GLENDALE | Providence |
| YOUR HAVEN | York | GREENE | Kent |
| YOUR NEW SALEM | York | GREENVILLE | Providence |
| YOUR SPRINGS | Adams | HARMONY | Providence |
| YOUNGSTOWN | Westmoreland | HARRISVILLE | Providence |
| YOUNGSVILLE | Warren | HOPE | Providence |
| YOUNGWOOD | Westmoreland | HOPE VALLEY | Washington |
| YUKON | Westmoreland | HOPKINTON | Washington |
| ZELIENOPLE | Butler | JAMESTOWN | Newport |
| ZIEGLERVILLE | Montgomery | JOHNSTON | Providence |
| ZION GROVE | Schuylkill | KEYNON | Washington |
| ZIONHILL | Bucks | KINGSTON | Washington |
| ZIONSVILLE | Lehigh | LINCOLN | Providence |
| ZULLINGER | Franklin | LITTLE COMPTON | Newport |
| **RHODE ISLAND** ▆▆▆▆▆ | | MANVILLE | Providence |
| ADAMSVILLE | Newport | MAPLEVILLE | Providence |
| ALBION | Providence | MIDDLETOWN | Newport |
| ANNEX | Providence | MISQUAMICUT | Washington |
| ASHAWAY | Washington | NARRAGANSETT | Washington |
| ASHTON | Providence | NEWPORT | Newport |
| BARRINGTON | Bristol | NORTH | Providence |
| BLOCK ISLAND | Newport | NORTH KINGSTOWN | Washington |
| BRADFORD | Washington | NORTH SCITUATE | Providence |
| BRISTOL | Bristol | OAKLAND | Providence |
| BROADWAY | Newport | OLNEYVILLE | Providence |
| BROWN | Providence | PASCOAG | Providence |
| CAROLINA | Washington | PAWTUCKET | Providence |
| CENTERDALE | Providence | PEACE DALE | Washington |
| CENTRAL FALLS | Providence | PILGRIM | Kent |
| CHARLESTOWN | Washington | PORTSMOUTH | Newport |
| CHEPACHET | Providence | PROVIDENCE | Providence |
| CLAYVILLE | Providence | PRUDENCE ISLAND | Newport |
| CODDINGTON POINT | Newport | RIVERSIDE | Providence |
| CONIMICUT | Kent | ROCKVILLE | Washington |
| COVENTRY | Kent | RUMFORD | Providence |
| CRANSTON | Providence | SAUNDERSTOWN | Washington |
| CUMBERLAND | Providence | SHANNOCK | Washington |
| CUMBERLAND HILL | Providence | SLATERSVILLE | Providence |
| DARLINGTON | Providence | SLOCUM | Washington |
| DAVISVILLE | Washington | TIVERTON | Newport |
| EAST GREENWICH | Kent | VALLEY FALLS | Providence |
| EAST PROVIDENCE | Providence | WAKEFIELD | Washington |
| EAST SIDE | Providence | WALNUT HILL | Providence |
| EDGEWOOD | Providence | WARREN | Bristol |
| ELMWOOD | Providence | WARWICK | Kent |
| ECHOHEAG | Washington | WARWICK NECK | Kent |
| ESMOND | Providence | WATCH HILL | Washington |
| EXETER | Washington | WEEKAPAUG | Washington |
| FISKEVILLE | Providence | WESTERLY | Washington |
| FORESTDALE | Providence | WEST GREENWICH | Kent |
| FOSTER | Providence | WEST KINGSTON | Washington |
| FRIAR | Providence | WEST WARWICK | Kent |
| GARDEN CITY | Providence | WEYBOSSET HILL | Providence |

| | | | |
|---|---|---|---|
| WILDES CORNER | Kent | CAMERON | Calhoun |
| WOOD RIVER JCT | Washington | CAMPOBELLO | Spartanburg |
| WOONSOCKET | Providence | CANADYS | Colleton |
| WYOMING | Washington | CARLISLE | Union |
| **SOUTH CAROLINA** | | CASSATT | Kershaw |
| ABBEVILLE | Abbeville | CATAWBA | York |
| ADAMS RUN | Charleston | CATEECHEE | Pickens |
| AIKEN | Aiken | CAYCE | Lexington |
| ALCOLU | Clarendon | CEDAR SPRINGS | Spartanburg |
| ALLENDALE | Allendale | CENTENARY | Marion |
| ALVIN | Berkeley | CENTRAL | Pickens |
| ANDERSON | Anderson | CHAPIN | Lexington |
| ANDREWS | Georgetown | CHAPPELLS | Newberry |
| ARCADIA | Spartanburg | CHARLESTON | Charleston |
| ASHLEY RIVER | Charleston | CHARLESTON AFB | Charleston |
| AWENDAW | Charleston | CHERAW | Chesterfield |
| AYNOR | Horry | CHEROKEE FALLS | Cherokee |
| BALLENTINE | Richland | CHERRY GROVE | Horry |
| BAMBERG | Bamberg | CHERRY GROVE BEACH | Horry |
| BARNWELL | Barnwell | CHESNEE | Spartanburg |
| BARESBURG | Lexington | CHESTER | Chester |
| BATH | Aiken | CHESTERFIELD | Chesterfield |
| BEAUFORT | Beaufort | CLARKS HILL | McCormick |
| BEECH ISLAND | Aiken | CLEARWATER | Aiken |
| BELTON | Anderson | CLEMSON | Pickens |
| BENNETTSVILLE | Marlboro | CLEMSON UNIV | Pickens |
| BEREA | Greenville | CLEVELAND | Greenville |
| BETHEL | York | CLIFTON | Spartanburg |
| BETHERA | Berkeley | CLINTON | Laurens |
| BETHUNE | Kershaw | CLIO | Marlboro |
| BISHOPVILLE | Lee | CLOVER | York |
| BLACKSBURG | Cherokee | COLUMBIA | Richland |
| BLACKSTOCK | Chester | CONESTEE | Greenville |
| BLACKVILLE | Barnwell | CONVERSE | Spartanburg |
| BLAIR | Fairfield | CONWAY | Horry |
| BLENHEIM | Marlboro | COOSAWHATCHIE | Jasper |
| BLUFFYON | Beaufort | COPE | Orangeburg |
| BLYTHEWOOD | Richland | CORDESVILLE | Berkeley |
| BOILING SPRINGS | Spartanburg | CORDOVA | Orangeburg |
| BONNEAU | Berkeley | COTTAGEVILLE | Colleton |
| BORDEN | Sumter | COWARD | Florence |
| BOWLING GREEN | York | COWPENS | Spartanburg |
| BOWMAN | Orangeburg | CROCKETVILLE | Hampton |
| BRADLEY | Greenwood | CROSS | Berkeley |
| BRANCHVILLE | Orangeburg | CROSS ANCHOR | Spartanburg |
| BRANWOOD | Greenville | CROSS HILL | Laurens |
| BRUNSON | Hampton | DALE | Beaufort |
| BUCKSPORT | Horry | DALZELL | Sumter |
| BUFFALO | Union | DARLINGTON | Darlington |
| BURTON | Beaufort | DAUFUSKIE ISLAND | Beaufort |
| CADES | Williamsburg | DAVIS STATION | Clarendon |
| CALHOUN FALLS | Abbeville | DENMARK | Bamberg |
| CAMDEN | Kershaw | DILLON | Dillon |

| | | | |
|---|---|---|---|
| DONALDS | Abbeville | GOOSE CREEK | Berkeley |
| DORCHESTER | Dorchester | GRAMLING | Spartanburg |
| DRAYTON | Spartanburg | GRANITEVILLE | Aiken |
| DUE WEST | Abbeville | GRAY COURT | Laurens |
| DUNCAN | Spartanburg | GREAT FALLS | Chester |
| DUNES | Horry | GREELEYVILLE | Williamsburg |
| DUTCH FORK | Richland | GREEN POND | Colleton |
| EARLY BRANCH | Hampton | GREEN SEA | Horry |
| EASLEY | Pickens | GREENVILLE | Greenville |
| EAST BAY | Charleston | GREENWOOD | Greenwood |
| EASTOVER | Richland | GREER | Greenville |
| EAU CLAIRE | Richland | GRESHAM | Marion |
| EDGEFIELD | Edgefield | GROVER | Dorchester |
| EDGEMOOR | Chester | HAMER | Dillon |
| EDISTO ISLAND | Charleston | HAMPTON | Hampton |
| EFFINGHAM | Florence | HANAHAN | Charleston |
| EHRHARDT | Bamberg | HARBISON | Richland |
| ELGIN | Kershaw | HARDEEVILLE | Jasper |
| ELKO | Barnwell | HARLEYVILLE | Dorchester |
| ELLIOTT | Lee | HARRIS | Greenwood |
| ELLOREE | Orangeburg | HARTSVILLE | Darlington |
| ENOREE | Spartanburg | HEATH SPRINGS | Lancaster |
| ESTILL | Hampton | HEMINGWAY | Williamsburg |
| EUTAWVILLE | Orangeburg | HICKORY GROVE | York |
| FAIRFAX | Allendale | HILDA | Barnwell |
| FAIRFOREST | Spartanburg | HILCREST | Spartanburg |
| FAIR PLAY | Oconee | HILTON HEAD ISLAND | Beaufort |
| FINGERVILLE | Spartanburg | HODGES | Greenwood |
| FIVE POINTS | Richland | HOLLY HILL | Orangeburg |
| FLORENCE | Florence | HOLLYWOOD | Charleston |
| FLOYD DALE | Dillon | HONEA PATH | Anderson |
| FOLLY BEACH | Charleston | HOPKINS | Richland |
| FOREST ACRES | Richland | HORATIO | Sumter |
| FORK | Dillon | HUGER | Berkeley |
| FORT JACKSON | Richland | INMAN | Spartanburg |
| FORT LAWN | Chester | IRMO | Lexington |
| FORT MILL | York | ISLANDTON | Colleton |
| FORT MOTTE | Calhoun | ISLE OF PALMS | Charleston |
| FOUNTAIN INN | Greenville | IVA | Anderson |
| FROGMORE | Beaufort | JACKSON | Aiken |
| FURMAN | Hampton | JACKSONBORO | Colleton |
| GABLE | Clarendon | JAMES ISLAND | Charleston |
| GADSDEN | Richland | JAMESTOWN | Berkeley |
| GAFFNEY | Cherokee | JEFFERSON | Chesterfield |
| GALIVANTS FERRY | Horry | JENKINSVILLE | Fairfield |
| GARNETT | Hampton | JERICHO | Charleston |
| GASTON | Lexington | JOANNA | Laurens |
| GEORGETOWN | Georgetown | JOHNS ISLAND | Charleston |
| GIFFORD | Hampton | JOHNSONVILLE | Florence |
| GILBERT | Lexington | JOHNSTON | Edgefield |
| GLENDALE | Spartanburg | JONESVILLE | Union |
| GLEN SPRINGS | Spartanburg | KELTON | Union |
| GLOVERVILLE | Aiken | KERSHAW | Lancaster |

| | | | |
|---|---|---|---|
| KINARDS | Newberry | MINTURN | Dillon |
| KINGS CREEK | Cherokee | MODOC | McCormick |
| KINGSTREE | Williamsburg | MONCKS CORNER | Berkeley |
| KLINE | Barnwell | MONETTA | Saluda |
| LADSON | Charleston | MONTICELLO | Fairfield |
| LAFRANCE | Anderson | MONTMORENCI | Aiken |
| LAKE CITY | Florence | MOORE | Spartanburg |
| LAKE VIEW | Dillon | MOUNTAIN REST | Oconee |
| LAKE WYLIE | York | MOUNT CARMEL | McCormick |
| LAMAR | Darlington | MOUNT CROGHAN | Chesterfield |
| LANCASTER | Lancaster | MOUNT HOLLY | Berkeley |
| LANDO | Chester | MOUNT PLEASANT | Charleston |
| LANDRUM | Spartanburg | MOUNTVILLE | Laurens |
| LANE | Williamsburg | MULLINS | Marion |
| LANGLEY | Aiken | MURRELLS INLET | Georgetown |
| LATTA | Dillon | MYRTLE BEACH | Horry |
| LAURENS | Laurens | NEESES | Orangeburg |
| LEESBURG | Richland | NESMITH | Williamsburg |
| LEESVILLE | Lexington | NEWBERRY | Newberry |
| LEXINGTON | Lexington | NEW ELLENTON | Aiken |
| LIBERTY | Pickens | NEWRY | Oconee |
| LIBERTY HILL | Kershaw | NEW ZION | Clarendon |
| LITTLE MOUNTAIN | Newberry | NICHOLS | Horry |
| LITTLE RIVER | Horry | NINETY SIX | Greenwood |
| LITTLE ROCK | Dillon | NORRIS | Pickens |
| LIVINGSTON | Orangeburg | NORTH | Orangeburg |
| LOBECO | Beaufort | NORTH AGUSTA | Aiken |
| LOCKHART | Union | NORTH ANDERSON | Anderson |
| LODGE | Colleton | NORTH CHARLESTON | Charleston |
| LONE STAR | Calhoun | NORTHEAST | Richland |
| LONG CREEK | Oconee | NORTH GATE | Horry |
| LONGS | Horry | NORTH MYRTLE BEACH | Horry |
| LORIS | Horry | NORTHSIDE | Greenwood |
| LOWNDESVILLE | Abbeville | NORWAY | Orangeburg |
| LUGOFF | Kershaw | OAKLEY | Berkeley |
| LURAY | Hampton | OLANTA | Florence |
| LYDIA | Darlington | OLAR | Bamberg |
| LYMAN | Spartanburg | ORA | Laurens |
| LYNCHBURG | Lee | ORANGEBURG | Orangeburg |
| MANNING | Clarendon | ORCHARD PARK | Greenville |
| MARIETTA | Greenville | OSWEGO | Sumter |
| MARION | Marion | PACOLET | Spartanburg |
| MARTIN | Allendale | PACOLET MILLS | Spartanburg |
| MAULDIN | Greenville | PAGELAND | Chesterfield |
| MAYESVILLE | Sumter | PAMPLICO | Florence |
| MAYO | Spartanburg | PARK PLACE | Greenville |
| McBEE | Chesterfield | PARKSVILLE | McCormick |
| McCLELLANVILLE | Charleston | PATRICK | Chesterfield |
| McCOLL | Marlboro | PAULINE | Spartanburg |
| McCONNELLS | York | PAWLEYS ISLAND | Georgetown |
| McCORMICK | McCormick | PEAK | Newberry |
| MEGGETT | Charleston | PELHAM | Greenville |
| MILEY | Hampton | PELION | Lexington |

| | | | |
|---|---|---|---|
| PELZER | Anderson | SCOTIA | Hampton |
| PENDLETON | Anderson | SCRANTON | Florence |
| PERRY | Aiken | SEABROOK | Georgetown |
| PICKENS | Pickens | SELLERS | Marion |
| PIEDMONT | Greenville | SENECA | Oconee |
| PINEHAVEN | Charleston | SHARON | York |
| PINELAND | Jasper | SHAW AFB | Sumter |
| PINEVILLE | Berkeley | SHELDON | Beaufort |
| PINEWOOD | Sumter | SHOALS JUNCTION | Abbeville |
| PINEWOOD | Spartanburg | SILVERSTREET | Newberry |
| PINOPOLIS | Berkeley | SIMPSONVILLE | Greenville |
| PLEASANTBURG | Greenville | SIX MILE | Pickens |
| PLUM BRANCH | McCormick | SLATER | Greenville |
| POMARIA | Newberry | SMOAKS | Colleton |
| PORT ROYAL | Beaufort | SMYRNA | York |
| POSTON | Florence | SOCASTEE | Horry |
| POWDERSVILLE | Greenville | SOCIETY HILL | Darlington |
| PROSPERITY | Newberry | SOUTH ANDERSON | Anderson |
| QUINBY | Florence | SOUTH PARK | Florence |
| RAINS | Marion | SPARTANBURG | Spartanburg |
| RAVENEL | Charleston | SPRINGFIELD | Orangeburg |
| REEVESVILLE | Dorchester | STARR | Anderson |
| REIDVILLE | Spartanburg | STARTEX | Spartanburg |
| REMBERT | Sumter | STATE PARK | Richland |
| RICHBURG | Chester | ST. HELENA ISLAND | Beaufort |
| RICHLAND | Oconee | SULLIVANS ISLAND | Charleston |
| RIDGELAND | Jasper | SUMMERALL | Aiken |
| RIDGE SPRING | Saluda | SUMMERTON | Clarendon |
| RIDGEVILLE | Dorchester | SUMMERVILLE | Dorchester |
| RIDGEWAY | Fairfield | SUMTER | Sumter |
| RIMINI | Clarendon | SUNSET | Pickens |
| RION | Fairfield | SURFSIDE BEACH | Horry |
| RITTER | Colleton | SWANSEA | Lexington |
| RIVER HILLS | York | SYCAMORE | Allendale |
| ROCK HILL | York | TAMASEE | Oconee |
| ROEBUCK | Spartanburg | TATUM | Marlboro |
| ROUND O | Colleton | TAYLORS | Greenville |
| ROWESVILLE | Orangeburg | TEGA CITY | York |
| RUBY | Chesterfield | TIGERVILLE | Greenville |
| RUFFIN | Colleton | TILLMAN | Jasper |
| RUSSELLVILLE | Berkeley | TIMMONSVILLE | Florence |
| SAINT ANDREWS | Charleston | TOWNVILLE | Anderson |
| SAINT CHARLES | Sumter | TRAVELERS REST | Greenville |
| SAINT GEORGE | Dorchester | TRENTON | Edgefield |
| SAINT MATTHEWS | Calhoun | TRIO | Williamsburg |
| ST STEPHEN | Berkeley | TROY | Greenwood |
| SALEM | Oconee | TURBEVILLE | Clarendon |
| SALLEY | Aiken | ULMER | Allendale |
| SALTERS | Williamsburg | UNA | Spartanburg |
| SALUDA | Saluda | UNION | Union |
| SANDY SPRINGS | Anderson | VALLEY FALLS | Spartanburg |
| SANTEE | Orangeburg | VANCE | Orangeburg |
| SARDINIA | Clarendon | VAN WYCK | Lancaster |

| | | | |
|---|---|---|---|
| VARNVILLE | Hampton | ARTAS | McPherson |
| VAUCLUSE | Aiken | ARTESIAN | Sanborn |
| WADMALAW ISLAND | Charleston | ASHTON | Spink |
| WAGENER | Aiken | ASTORIA | Deuel |
| WALHALLA | Oconee | ATHOL | Spink |
| WALLACE | Marlboro | AURORA | Brookings |
| WALTERBORO | Colleton | AVON | Bon Homme |
| WANDO | Berkeley | BADGER | Kingsbury |
| WARD | Saluda | BALTIC | Minnehaha |
| WARE SHOALS | Greenwood | BANCROFT | Kingsbury |
| WARRENVILLE | Aiken | BARNARD | Brown |
| WATERLOO | Laurens | BATESLAND | Shannon |
| WEDGEFIELD | Sumter | BATH | Brown |
| WELLFORD | Spartanburg | BELLE FOURCHE | Butte |
| WEST COLUMBIA | Lexington | BELVIDERE | Jackson |
| WESTGATE | Spartanburg | BEMIS | Deuel |
| WESTMINSTER | Oconee | BERESFORD | Union |
| WEST UNION | Oconee | BIG STONE CITY | Grant |
| WESTVILLE | Kershaw | BISON | Perkins |
| WHITE OAK | Fairfield | BLACK HAWK | Meade |
| WHITE ROCK | Richland | BLUNT | Hughes |
| WHITE STONE | Spartanburg | BONESTEEL | Gregory |
| WHITMIRE | Newberry | BOWDLE | Edmunds |
| WILLIAMS | Colleton | BOX ELDER | Pennington |
| WILLIAMSTON | Anderson | BRADLEY | Clark |
| WILLINGTON | McCormick | BRANDON | Minnehaha |
| WILLISTON | Barnwell | BRANDT | Deuel |
| WINDSOR | Aiken | BRENTFORD | Spink |
| WINDY HILL | Horry | BRIDGEWATER | McCook |
| WINNSBORO | Fairfield | BRISTOL | Day |
| WINTHROP COLLEGE | York | BRITTON | Marshall |
| WISACKEY | Lee | BROOKINGS | Brookings |
| WOODRUFF | Spartanburg | BRUCE | Brookings |
| YEMASSEE | Hampton | BRYANT | Hamlin |
| YONGES ISLAND | Charleston | BUFFALO | Harding |
| YORK | York | BUFFALO GAP | Custer |
| **SOUTH DAKOTA** | | BUFFALO RIDGE | Minnehaha |
| ABERDEEN | Brown | BULLHEAD | Corson |
| ACADEMY | Charles Mix | BURBANK | Clay |
| AGAR | Sully | BURKE | Gregory |
| AGENCY VILLAGE | Roberts | BUTLER | Day |
| ALASKA | WaLworth | CAMP CROOK | Harding |
| ALBEE | Grant | CANISTOTA | McCook |
| ALCESTER | Union | CANOVA | Miner |
| ALEXANDRIA | Hanson | CANTON | Lincoln |
| ALLEN | Bennett | CAPUTA | Pennington |
| ALPENA | Jerauld | CARPENTER | Clark |
| ALTAMONT | Deuel | CARTER | Tripp |
| AMHERST | Marshall | CARTHAGE | Miner |
| ANDOVER | Day | CASTLEWOOD | Hamlin |
| ARDMORE | Fall River | CAVOUR | Beadle |
| ARLINGTON | Kingsbury | CEDARBUTTE | Mellette |
| ARMOUR | Douglas | CENTERVILLE | Turner |

| City | County | City | County |
|---|---|---|---|
| CHAMBERLAIN | Brule | ETHAN | Davison |
| CHANCELLOR | Turner | EUREKA | McPherson |
| CHERRY CREEK | Zieback | FAIRBURN | Custer |
| CHESTER | Lake | FAIRFAX | Gregory |
| CLAIRE CITY | Roberts | FAIRVIEW | Lincoln |
| CLAREMONT | Brown | FAITH | Meade |
| CLARK | Clark | FARMER | Hanson |
| CLEARFIELD | Tripp | FAULKTON | Faulk |
| CLEAR LAKE | Deuel | FEDORA | Miner |
| COLMAN | Moody | FERNEY | Brown |
| COLOME | Tripp | FIRESTEEL | Dewey |
| COLTON | Minnehaha | FLANDREAU | Moody |
| COLUMBIA | Brown | FLORENCE | Codington |
| CONDE | Spink | FORESTBURG | Sanborn |
| CORONA | Roberts | FORT MEADE | Meade |
| CORSICA | Douglas | FORT PIERRE | Stanley |
| CORSON | Minnehaha | FORT THOMPSON | Buffalo |
| COTTONWOOD | Pennington | FRANKFORT | Spink |
| CRAZY HORSE | Custer | FREDERICK | Brown |
| CREIGHTON | Pennington | FREEMAN | Hutchinson |
| CRESBARD | Faulk | FRUITDALE | Butte |
| CROCKER | Clark | FULTON | Hanson |
| CROOKS | Minnehaha | GANN VALLEY | Buffalo |
| CUSTER | Custer | GARDEN CITY | Clark |
| DAKOTA DUNES | Union | GARRETSON | Minnehaha |
| DALLAS | Gregory | GARY | Deuel |
| DANTE | Charles Mix | GAYVILLE | Yankton |
| DAVIS | Turner | GEDDES | Charles Mix |
| DEADWOOD | Lawrence | GETTYSBURG | Potter |
| DELL RAPIDS | Minnehaha | GLAD VALLEY | Ziebach |
| DELMONT | Douglas | GLENCROSS | Dewey |
| DEMPSTER | Hamlin | GLENHAM | Walworth |
| DENBY | Shannon | GOODWIN | Deuel |
| DESMET | Kingsbury | GREGORY | Gregory |
| DIMOCK | Hutchinson | GRENVILLE | Day |
| DIXON | Gregory | GROTON | Brown |
| DOLAND | Spink | HAMILL | Tripp |
| DOLTON | Turner | HARRISBURG | Lincoln |
| DOWNTOWN | Brown | HARRISON | Douglas |
| DRAPER | Jones | HARROLD | Hughes |
| DUPREE | Ziebach | HARTFORD | Minnehaha |
| EAGLE BUTTE | Dewey | HAYES | Stanley |
| EDEN | Marshall | HAYTI | Hamlin |
| EDGEMONT | Fall River | HAZEL | Hamlin |
| EGAN | Moody | HECLA | Brown |
| ELK POINT | Union | HENRY | Codington |
| ELKTON | Brookings | HEREFORD | Meade |
| ELLSWORTH AFB | Meade | HERMOSA | Custer |
| ELM SPRINGS | Meade | HERREID | Campbell |
| EMERY | Hanson | HERRICK | Gregory |
| ENNING | Meade | HETLAND | Kingsbury |
| ERWIN | Kingsbury | HIGHMORE | Hyde |
| ESTELLINE | Hamlin | HILL CITY | Pennington |

| | | | |
|---|---|---|---|
| HITCHCOCK | Beadle | LUCAS | Gregory |
| HOLABIRD | Hyde | LUDLOW | Harding |
| HOSMER | Edmunds | LYONS | Minnehaha |
| HOT SPRINGS | Fall River | MADISON | Lake |
| HOUGHTON | Brown | MAHTO | Corson |
| HOVEN | Potter | MANDERSON | Shannon |
| HOWARD | Miner | MANSFIELD | Spink |
| HOWES | Meade | MARCUS | Meade |
| HUDSON | Lincoln | MARION | Turner |
| HUMBOLDT | Minnehaha | MARTIN | Bennett |
| HURLEY | Turner | MARTY | Charles Mix |
| HURON | Beadle | MARVIN | Grant |
| IDEAL | Tripp | McCOOK LAKE | Union |
| INTERIOR | Jackson | McINTOSH | Corson |
| IONA | Lyman | McLAUGHLIN | Corson |
| IPSWICH | Edmunds | MEADOW | Perkins |
| IRENE | Clay | MECKLING | Clay |
| IROQUOIS | Kingsbury | MELLETTE | Spink |
| ISABEL | Dewey | MENNO | Hutchinson |
| JAVA | Walworth | MIDLAND | Haakon |
| JEFFERSON | Union | MILBANK | Grant |
| KADOKA | Jackson | MILESVILLE | Haakon |
| KAYLOR | Hutchinson | MILLBORO | Tripp |
| KELDRON | Corson | MILLER | Hand |
| KENNEBEC | Lyman | MINA | Edmunds |
| KEYAPAHA | Tripp | MIRANDA | Faulk |
| KEYSTONE | Pennington | MISSION | Todd |
| KIMBALL | Brule | MISSION HILL | Yankton |
| KRANZBURG | Codington | MISSION RIDGE | Stanley |
| KYLE | Shannon | MITCHELL | Davison |
| LABOLT | Grant | MOBRIDGE | Walworth |
| LAKE ANDES | Charles Mix | MONROE | Turner |
| LAKE CITY | Marshall | MONTROSE | McCook |
| LAKE NORDEN | Hamlin | MORRISTOWN | Corson |
| LAKE PRESTON | Kingsbury | MOUND CITY | Campbell |
| LANE | Jerauld | MOUNT VERNON | Davison |
| LANGFORD | Marshall | MUD BUTTE | Meade |
| LANTRY | Dewey | MURDO | Jones |
| LA PLANT | Dewey | NEMO | Lawrence |
| LEAD | Lawrence | NEW EFFINGTON | Roberts |
| LEBANON | Potter | NEWELL | Butte |
| LEMMON | Perkins | NEW HOLLAND | Douglas |
| LENNOX | Lincoln | NEW UNDERWOOD | Pennington |
| LEOLA | McPherson | NISLAND | Butte |
| LESTERVILLE | Yankton | NORBECK | Faulk |
| LETCHER | Sanborn | NORRIS | Mellette |
| LILY | Day | NORTH SIOUX CITY | Union |
| LITTLE EAGLE | Corson | NORTHVILLE | Spink |
| LODGEPOLE | Perkins | NUNDA | Lake |
| LONGLAKE | McPherson | OACOMA | Lyman |
| LONG VALLEY | Jackson | OELRICHS | Fall River |
| LOOMIS | Davison | OGLALA | Shannon |
| LOWER BRULE | Lyman | OKATON | Jones |

| | | | |
|---|---|---|---|
| OKREEK | Todd | ROSWELL | Miner |
| OLDHAM | Kingsbury | ROWENA | Minnehaha |
| OLIVET | Hutchinson | RUTLAND | Lake |
| ONAKA | Faulk | SAINT CHARLES | Gregory |
| ONIDA | Sully | SAINT FRANCIS | Todd |
| OPAL | Meade | SAINT LAWRENCE | Hand |
| ORAL | Fall River | SAINT ONGE | Lawrence |
| ORIENT | Faulk | SALEM | McCook |
| ORTLEY | Roberts | SCENIC | Pennington |
| OTTUMWA | Haakon | SCOTLAND | Bon Homme |
| OWANKA | Pennington | SELBY | Walworth |
| PARADE | Dewey | SENECA | Faulk |
| PARKER | Turner | SHADEHILL | Perkins |
| PARKSTON | Hutchinson | SHERMAN | Minnehaha |
| PARMELEE | Todd | SILVER CITY | Pennington |
| PEEVER | Roberts | SINAI | Brookings |
| PHILIP | Haakon | SIOUX FALLS | Minnehaha |
| PICKSTOWN | Charles Mix | SISSETON | Roberts |
| PIEDMONT | Meade | SKY RANCH | Harding |
| PIERPONT | Day | SMITHWICK | Fall River |
| PIERRE | Hughes | SOUTH SHORE | Codington |
| PINE RIDGE | Shannon | SPEARFISH | Lawrence |
| PLAINVIEW | Meade | SPENCER | McCook |
| PLANKINTON | Aurora | SPRINGFIELD | Bon Homme |
| PLATTE | Charles Mix | STEPHAN | Hyde |
| POLLOCK | `Campbell | STICKNEY | Aurora |
| PORCUPINE | Shannon | STOCKHOLM | Grant |
| PRAIRIE CITY | Perkins | STONEVILLE | Union Center |
| PRESHO | Lyman | STRANDBURG | Grant |
| PRINGLE | Custer | STRATFORD | Brown |
| PROVO | Fall River | STURGIS | Meade |
| PUKWANA | Brule | SUMMIT | Roberts |
| QUINN | Pennington | TABOR | Bon Homme |
| RALPH | Harding | TEA | Lincoln |
| RAMONA | Lake | TIMBER LAKE | Dewey |
| RAPID CITY | Pennington | TOLSTOY | Potter |
| RAVINIA | Charles Mix | TORONTO | Deuel |
| RAYMOND | Clark | TRAIL CITY | Corson |
| REDFIELD | Spink | TRENT | Moody |
| REDIG | Harding | TRIPP | Hutchinson |
| REDOWL | Meade | TULARE | Spink |
| REE HEIGHTS | Hand | TURTON | Spink |
| RELIANCE | Lyman | TUTHILL | Bennett |
| RENNER | Minnehaha | TWIN BROOKS | Grant |
| REVA | Harding | TYNDALL | Bon Homme |
| REVILLO | Grant | UNION CENTER | Meade |
| RIDGEVIEW | Dewey | UTICA | Yankton |
| ROCHFORD | Pennington | VALE | Butte |
| ROCKHAM | Faulk | VALLEY SPRINGS | Minnehaha |
| ROSCOE | Edmunds | VEBLEN | Marshall |
| ROSEBUD | Todd | VERDON | Spink |
| ROSHOLT | Roberts | VERMILLION | Clay |
| ROSLYN | Day | VETAL | Bennett |

| | | | |
|---|---|---|---|
| VIBORG | Nmer | ALAMO | Crockett |
| VIENNA | Clark | ALCOA | Blount |
| VIRGIL | Beadle | ALEXANDRIA | DeKalb |
| VIVIAN | Lyman | ALGOOD | Putnam |
| VOLGA | Brookings | ALLARDT | Fentress |
| VIOLIN | Yankton | ALLONS | Overton |
| WAGNER | Charles Mix | ALLRED | Overton |
| WAKONDA | Clay | ALPINE | Overton |
| WAKPALA | Corson | ALTAMONT | Grundy |
| WALKER | Walworth | ANDERSONVILLE | Anderson |
| WALL | Pennington | ANTIOCH | Davidson |
| WALLACE | Codington | APISON | Hamilton |
| WANBLEE | Jackson | ARCADE | Davidson |
| WARD | Moody | ARDMORE | Lincoln |
| WARNER | Brown | ARLINGTON | Shelby |
| WASTA | Pennington | ARNOLD AFB | Coffee |
| WATAUGA | Corson | ARRINGTON | Williamson |
| WATERTOWN | Codington | ARTHUR | Claiborne |
| WAUBAY | Day | ASHLAND CITY | Cheatham |
| WAVERLY | Codington | ATHENS | McMinn |
| WEBSTER | Day | ATOKA | Tipton |
| WECOTA | Faulk | ATWOOD | Carroll |
| WENTWORTH | Lake | AUBURNTOWN | Cannon |
| WESSINGTON | Beadle | BAILEYTON | Greene |
| WESSINGTON SPRINGS | Jerauld | BAKEWELL | Hamilton |
| WESTERN MALL | Minnehaha | BANEBERRY | Jefferson |
| WESTPORT | Brown | BAPTIST | Davidson |
| WEWELA | Tripp | BARTLETT | Shelby |
| WHITE | Brookings | BATH SPRINGS | Decatur |
| WHITEHORSE | Dewey | BAXTER | Putnam |
| WHITE LAKE | Aurora | BEAN STATION | Grainger |
| WHITE OWL | Meade | BEECH BLUFF | Madison |
| WHITE RIVER | Mellette | BEECHGROVE | Coffee |
| WHITEWOOD | Lawrence | BEERSHEBA SPRINGS | Grundy |
| WILLOW LAKE | Clark | BELFAST | Marshall |
| WILMOT | Roberts | BELL BUCKLE | Bedford |
| WINFRED | Lake | BELLE MEADE | Davidson |
| WINNER | Tripp | BELLEVUE | Davidson |
| WITTEN | Tripp | BELLS | Crockett |
| WOLSEY | Beadle | BELVIDERE | Franklin |
| WOOD | Mellette | BEMIS | Jackson |
| WOONSOCKET | Sanborn | BENTON | Polk |
| WORTHING | Lincoln | BETHEL SPRINGS | McNairy |
| WOUNDED KNEE | Shannon | BETHPAGE | Sumner |
| YALE | Beadle | BIG ROCK | Stewart |
| YANKTON | Yankton | BIG SANDY | Benton |
| ZELL | Faulk | BINGHAMTON | Shelby |
| ZEONA | Perkins | BIRCHWOOD | Hamilton |
| **TENNESSEE** | | BLAINE | Grainger |
| ACKLEN | Davidson | BLOOMINGDALE | Sullivan |
| ADAMS | Robertson | BLOOMINGTON SPRINGS | Putnam |
| ADAMSVILLE | McNairy | BLOUNTVILLE | Sullivan |
| AFTON | Greene | BLUFF CITY | Sullivan |

| | | | |
|---|---|---|---|
| BOGOTA | Dyer | CLARKSVILLE | Montgomery |
| BOLIVAR | Hardeman | CLEVELAND | Bradley |
| BON AQUA | Hickman | CLIFTON | Wayne |
| BONE CAVE | Warren | CLINTON | Anderson |
| BRADEN | Fayette | COALFIELD | Morgan |
| BRADFORD | Gibson | COALMONT | Grundy |
| BRADYVILLE | Cannon | COKERCREEK | Monroe |
| BRAINERD | Hamilton | COLLEGEDALE | Hamilton |
| BRENTWOOD | Williamson | COLLEGE GROVE | Williamson |
| BRICEVILLE | Anderson | COLLIERVILLE | Shelby |
| BRIGHTON | Tipton | COLLINWOOD | Wayne |
| BRISTOL | Sullivan | COLONIAL | Shelby |
| BROADWAY | Davidson | COLONIAL HEIGHTS | Sullivan |
| BROWNSVILLE | Haywood | COLUMBIA | Maury |
| BRUCETON | Carroll | COMO | Henry |
| BRUNSWICK | Shelby | CONASAUGA | Polk |
| BRUSH CREEK | Smith | CONCORD FARRAGUT | Knox |
| BUCHANAN | Henry | COOKEVILLE | Putnam |
| BUENA VISTA | Carroll | COPPERHILL | Polk |
| BUFFALO VALLEY | Putnam | CORDOVA | Shelby |
| BULLS GAP | Hawkins | CORNERSVILLE | Marshall |
| BUMPUS MILLS | Stewart | CORRYTON | Knox |
| BURLINGTON | Knox | COSBY | Cocke |
| BURLISON | Tipton | COTTAGE GROVE | Henry |
| BURNS | Dickson | COTTONTOWN | Sumner |
| BUTLER | Johnson | COUNCE | Hardin |
| BYBEE | Cocke | COVINGTON | Tipton |
| BYRDSTOWN | Pickett | COWAN | Franklin |
| CALHOUN | McMinn | CRAB ORCHARD | Cumberland |
| CAMDEN | Benton | CRAWFORD | Overton |
| CAMPAIGN | Warren | CROCKETT MILLS | Crockett |
| CARROLL REECE | Johnson | CROSS PLAINS | Robertson |
| CARTHAGE | Smith | CROSSVILLE | Cumberland |
| CARYVILLE | Campbell | CRUMP | Hardin |
| CASTALIAN SPRINGS | Sumner | CULLEOKA | Maury |
| CEDAR GROVE | Carroll | CUMBERLAND CITY | Stewart |
| CEDAR HILL | Robertson | CUMBERLAND FURNACE | Dickson |
| CELINA | Clay | CUMBERLAND GAP | Claiborne |
| CENTERVILLE | Hickman | CUNNINGHAM | Montgomery |
| CHAPEL HILL | Marshall | CYPRESS INN | Wayne |
| CHAPMANSBORO | Cheatham | DANDRIDGE | Jefferson |
| CHARLESTON | Bradley | DARDEN | Henderson |
| CHARLOTE | Dickson | DAYTON | Rhea |
| CHATTANOOGA | Hamilton | DECATUR | Meigs |
| CHESTNUT MOUND | Smith | DECATURVILLE | Decatur |
| CHEWALLA | McNairy | DECHERD | Franklin |
| CHICKAMAUGA | Hamilton | DEER LODGE | Morgan |
| CHRISTIANA | Rutherford | DEFEATED | Smith |
| CHUCKEY | Greene | DELANO | Polk |
| CHURCH HILL | Hawkins | DELLROSE | Lincoln |
| CLAIRFIELD | Claiborne | DEL RIO | Cocke |
| CLARKRANGE | Fentress | DENMARK | Madison |
| CLARKSBURG | Carroll | DENVER | Humphreys |

| | | | |
|---|---|---|---|
| DEVONIA | Anderson | FIVE POINTS | Lawrence |
| DICKEL | Coffee | FLAG POND | Union |
| DICKSON | Dickson | FLATWOODS | Perry |
| DIXON SPRINGS | Smith | FLINTVILLE | Lincoln |
| DONELSON | Davidson | FORT PILLOW | Lauderdale |
| DOVER | Stewart | FOSTERVILLE | Rutherford |
| DOWELLTOWN | DeKalb | FOUNTAIN CITY | Knox |
| DOYLE | White | FOWLKES | Dyer |
| DRESDEN | Weakley | FRANKEWING | Lincoln |
| DRUMMONDS | Tipton | FRANKLIN | Williamson |
| DUCK RIVER | Hickman | FRAYSER | Shelby |
| DUCKTOWN | Polk | FRIENDSHIP | Crockett |
| DUFF | Campbell | FRIENDSVILLE | Blount |
| DUKEDOM | Weakley | FRUITVALE | Crockett |
| DUNLAP | Sequatchie | GADSDEN | Crockett |
| DYER | Gibson | GAINESBORO | Jackson |
| DYERSBURG | Dyer | GALLATIN | Sumner |
| EADS | Shelby | GALLAWAY | Fayette |
| EAGAN | Claiborne | GASSAWAY | DeKalb |
| EAGLEVILLE | Rutherford | GATES | Lauderdale |
| EAST CHATANOOGA | Hamilton | GATLINBURG | Sevier |
| EAST LAKE | Hamilton | GEORGETOWN | Meigs |
| EAST RIDGE | Hamilton | GEORGE W. LEE | Shelby |
| EASTSIDE | Sullivan | GERMANTOWN | Shelby |
| EATON | Gibson | GIBSON | Gibson |
| EIDSON | Hawkins | GLADEVILLE | Wilson |
| ELBRIDGE | Obion | GLEASON | Weakley |
| ELGIN | Scott | GLENVIEW | Davidson |
| ELIZABETHTON | Carter | GOODLETTSVILLE | Davidson |
| ELKTON | Giles | GOODSPRING | Giles |
| ELLENDALE | Shelby | GORDONSVILLE | Smith |
| ELMWOOD | Smith | GRAND JUNCTION | Hardeman |
| ELORA | Lincoln | GRANDVIEW | Rhea |
| ENGLEWOOD | McMinn | GRANVILLE | Jackson |
| ENVILLE | Chester | GRAY | Washington |
| ERIN | Houston | GRAYSVILLE | Rhea |
| ERLANGER | Hamilton | GREENBACK | Loudon |
| ERWIN | Union | GREENBRIER | Robertson |
| ESTES KEFAUVER | Johnson | GREENEVILLE | Greene |
| ESTILL SPRINGS | Franklin | GREENFIELD | Weakley |
| ETHRIDGE | Lawrence | GREEN HILLS | Davidson |
| ETOWAH | McMinn | GRIMSLEY | Fentress |
| EVA | Benton | GRUETLI-LAAGER | Grundy |
| EVENSVILLE | Rhea | GUILD | Marion |
| FAIRFIELD GLADE | Cumberland | GUYS | McNairy |
| FAIRVIEW | Williamson | HALLS | Lauderdale |
| FALL BRANCH | Washington | HAMPSHIRE | Maury |
| FARNER | Polk | HAMPTON | Carter |
| FARRAGUT | Knox | HARRIMAN | Roane |
| FAYETTEVILLE | Lincoln | HARRISON | Hamilton |
| FEDERAL RESERVE | Davidson | HARROGATE | Claiborne |
| FINGER | McNairy | HARTFORD | Cocke |
| FINLEY | Dyer | HARTSVILLE | Trousdale |

| | | | |
|---|---|---|---|
| HEISKELL | Knox | KIMBERLIN HEIGHTS | Knox |
| HELENWOOD | Scott | KIMMINS | Lewis |
| HENDERSON | Chester | KINGSPORT | Sullivan |
| HENDERSONVILLE | Sumner | KINGSTON | Roane |
| HENNING | Lauderdale | KINGSTON SPRINGS | Cheatham |
| HENRY | Henry | KNOXVILLE | Knox |
| HERMITAGE | Davidson | KNOXVILLE COLLEGE | Knox |
| HICKMAN | Smith | KODAK | Sevier |
| HICKORY HILL | Shelby | KYLES FORD | Hancock |
| HICKORY VALLEY | Hardeman | LACONIA | Fayette |
| HICKORY WITHE | Fayette | LAFAYETTE | Macon |
| HIGHLAND HEIGHTS | Shelby | LA FOLLETTE | Campbell |
| HIGHLAND PARK | Hamilton | LA GRANGE | Fayette |
| HILHAM | Clay | LAKE CITY | Anderson |
| HILLDALE | Montgomery | LAMAR | Shelby |
| HILLSBORO | Coffee | LANCASTER | Smith |
| HIWASSEE COLLEGE | Monroe | LANCING | Morgan |
| HIXSON | Hamilton | LASCASSAS | Rutherford |
| HOHENWALD | Lewis | LAUREL BLOOMERY | Johnson |
| HOLIDAY CITY | Shelby | LA VERGNE | Rutherford |
| HOLLADAY | Benton | LAVINIA | Carroll |
| HOLLOW ROCK | Carroll | LAWRENCEBURG | Lawrence |
| HOLLYWOOD | Shelby | LEBANON | Wilson |
| HORNBEAK | Obion | LEE COLLEGE | Bradley |
| HORNSBY | Hardeman | LENOIR CITY | London |
| HUMBOLDT | Gibson | LENOX | Dyer |
| HUNTINGDON | Carroll | LEOMA | Lawrence |
| HUNTLAND | Franklin | LEWISBURG | Marshall |
| HUNTSVILLE | Scott | LEXINGTON | Henderson |
| HURON | Henderson | LIBERTY | DeKalb |
| HURRICANE MILLS | Humphreys | LIMESTONE | Washington |
| IDLEWILD | Gibson | LINDEN | Perry |
| IGA | Henry | LIVINGSTON | Overton |
| INDIAN MOUND | Stewart | LOBELVILLE | Perry |
| IRON CITY | Lawrence | LONE MOUNTAIN | Claiborne |
| ISABELLA | Polk | LONSDALE | Knox |
| JACKSBORO | Campbell | LOOKOUT MOUNTAIN | Hamilton |
| JACKS CREEK | Cheater | LORETTO | Lawrence |
| JACKSON | Madison | LOUDON | London |
| JACKSON SQUARE | Anderson | LOUISVILLE | Blount |
| JAMESTOWN | Fentress | LOWLAND | Hamblen |
| JASPER | Marion | LUPTON CITY | Hamilton |
| JEFFERSON CITY | Jefferson | LURAY | Henderson |
| JELLICO | Campbell | LUTTRELL | Union |
| JERE BAXTER | Davidson | LUTTS | Wayne |
| JUELTON | Davidson | LYLES | Hickman |
| JOHNSON BIBLE COLLEGE | Knox | LYNCHBURG | Moore |
| JOHNSON CITY | Washington | LYNN GARDEN | Sullivan |
| JONESBOROUGH | Washington | LYNNVILLE | Giles |
| KARNS | Knox | MACON | Fayette |
| KELSO | Lincoln | MADISON | Davidson |
| KENTON | Obion | MADISONVILLE | Monroe |
| KIMBALL | Marion | MALLORY | Shelby |

| | | | |
|---|---|---|---|
| MANCHESTER | Coffee | NAS MEMPHIS | Shelby |
| MANSFIELD | Henry | NEWBERN | Dyer |
| MARTIN | Weakley | NEWCOMB | Campbell |
| MARYVILLE | Blount | NEW JOHNSONVILLE | Humphreys |
| MARYVILLE COLLEGE | Blount | NEW MARKET | Jefferson |
| MASCOT | Knox | NEWPORT | Cocke |
| MASON | Tipton | NEW PROVIDENCE | Montgomery |
| MAURY CITY | Crockett | NEW TAZEWELL | Claiborne |
| MAYNARDVILLE | Union | NIOTA | McMinn |
| MCDONALD | Bradley | NOLENSVILLE | Williamson |
| MCEWEN | Humphreys | NORENE | Wilson |
| MCKENZIE | Carroll | NORMANDY | Bedford |
| MCLEMORESVILLE | Carroll | NORRIS | Anderson |
| MCMINWILLE | Warren | NORTH CHATANOOGA | Hamilton |
| MEDINA | Gibson | NORWOOD | Knox |
| MEDON | Madison | NUNNELLY | Hickman |
| MELROSE | Davidson | OAKDALE | Morgan |
| MEMPHIS | Shelby | OAKFIELD | Madison |
| MERCER | Madison | OAKLAND | Fayette |
| MICHIE | McNairy | OAK RIDGE | Anderson |
| MIDDLETON | Hardeman | OBION | Obion |
| MIDWAY | Greene | OCOEE | Polk |
| MILAN | Gibson | OLDFORT | Polk |
| MILLEDGEVILLE | McNairy | OLD HICKORY | Davidson |
| MILLINGTON | Shelby | OLIVEHILL | Hardin |
| MILTON | Rutherford | OLIVER SPRINGS | Morgan |
| MINOR HILL | Giles | ONEIDA | Scott |
| MISTON | Dyer | ONLY | Hickman |
| MITCHELLVILLE | Sumner | OOLTEWAH | Hamilton |
| MOHAWK | Greene | ORLINDA | Robertson |
| MONOVILLE | Smith | OZONE | Cumberland |
| MONROE | Overton | PALL MALL | Fentress |
| MONTEAGLE | Grundy | PALMER | Grundy |
| MONTEREY | Putnam | PALMERSVILLE | Weakley |
| MOORESBURG | Hawkins | PALMYRA | Montgomery |
| MORLEY | Campbell | PARIS | Henry |
| MORRIS CHAPEL | Hardin | PARKWAY | Blount |
| MORRISON | Warren | PARKWAY VILLAGE | Shelby |
| MORRISTOWN | Hamblen | PARROTTSVILLE | Cocke |
| MOSCOW | Fayette | PARSONS | Dercatur |
| MOSHEIM | Greene | PEGRAM | Cheatham |
| MOSS | Clay | PELHAM | Grundy |
| MOUNTAIN CITY | Johnson | PETERSBURG | Lincoln |
| MOUNTAIN HOME | Washington | PETROS | Morgan |
| MOUNT CARMEL | Hawkins | PHILADELPHIA | Loudon |
| MOUNT JULIET | Wilson | PICKWICK DAM | Hardin |
| MOUNT PLEASANT | Maury | PIGEON FORGE | Sevier |
| MOUNT VERNON | Monroe | PIKEVILLE | Bledsoe |
| MULBERRY | Lincoln | PINEY FLATTS | Sullivan |
| MUNFORD | Tipton | PINSON | Madison |
| MURFREESBORO | Rutherford | PIONEER | Campbell |
| MURRAY-LAKE HILLS | Hamilton | PLEASANT HILL | Cumberland |
| NASHVILLE | Davidson | PLEASANT SHADE | Smith |

| | | | |
|---|---|---|---|
| PLEASANT VIEW | Cheatham | SCOTTS HILL | Henderson |
| PLEASANTVILLE | Hickman | SELMER | McNairy |
| POCAHONTAS | Harcleman | SEQUATCHIE | Marion |
| PORTLAND | Sumner | SEVIERVILLE | Sevier |
| POSTELLE | Polk | SEWANEE | Franklin |
| POWDER SPRINGS | Grainger | SEYMOUR | Sevier |
| POWELL | Knox | SHADY VALLEY | Johnson |
| PRIMM SPRINGS | Hickman | SHARON | Weakley |
| PROSPECT | Giles | SHARPS CHAPEL | Union |
| PRUDEN | Claiborne | SHAWANEE | Claiborne |
| PULASKI | Giles | SHELBY CENTER | Shelby |
| PURYEAR | Henry | SHELBYVILLE | Bedford |
| QUEBECK | White | SHERWOOD | Franklin |
| RALEIGH | Shelby | SHILOH | Hardin |
| RAMER | McNairy | SIGNAL MOUNTAIN | Hamilton |
| RAVENSCROFT | White | SILERTON | Hardeman |
| READYVILLE | Cannon | SILVER POINT | Putnam |
| REAGAN | Henderson | SLAYDEN | Dickson |
| RED BANK | Hamilton | SMARTT | Warren |
| RED BOILING SPRINGS | Macon | SMITHVILLE | DeKalb |
| RELIANCE | Polk | SMYRNA | Rutherford |
| RICEVILLE | McMinn | SNEEDVILLE | Hancock |
| RICKMAN | Overton | SODDY-DAISY | Hamilton |
| RIDDLETON | Smith | SOMERVILLE | Fayette |
| RIDGEFIELDS | Sullivan | SOUTH FULTON | Obion |
| RIDGELY | Lake | SOUTH KNOXVILLE | Knox |
| RIDGETOP | Robertson | SOUTH PITTSBURG | Marion |
| RIPLEY | Lauderdale | SOUTHSIDE | Montgomery |
| RIVERSIDE | Shelby | SPARTA | White |
| RIVES | Obion | SPEEDWELL | Claiborne |
| ROAN MOUNTAIN | Carter | SPENCER | Van Buren |
| ROBBINS | Scott | SPRING CITY | Rhea |
| ROCKFORD | Blount | SPRING CREEK | Madison |
| ROCK ISLAND | Warren | SPRINGFIELD | Robertson |
| ROCKVALE | Rutherford | SPRING HILL | Maury |
| ROCKWOOD | Roane | SPRINGVILLE | Henry |
| ROGERSVILLE | Hawkins | STANTON | Haywood |
| ROSSVILLE | Fayette | STANTONVILLE | McNairy |
| ROYAL | Bedford | STEWART | Houston |
| RUGBY | Scott | STRAWBERRY PLAINS | Jefferson |
| RUSSELLVILLE | Hamblen | SUGAR TREE | Decatur |
| RUTHERFORD | Gibson | SUMMERTOWN | Lawrence |
| RUTLEDGE | Grainger | SUMMITVILLE | Coffee |
| SAINT ANDREWS | Franklin | SUNBRIGHT | Morgan |
| SAINT BETHELEHEM | Montgomery | SURGIONSVILLE | Hawkins |
| SAINT JOSEPH | Lawrence | SWEETWATER | Monroe |
| SALE CREEK | Hamilton | TAFT | Lincoln |
| SALTILLO | Hardin | TALBOTT | Hamblen |
| SAMBURG | Obion | TALLASSEE | Blount |
| SANTA FE | Maury | TATE SPRINGS | Grainger |
| SARDIS | Henderson | TAZEWELL | Claiborne |
| SAULSBURY | Hardeman | TELFORD | Washington |
| SAVANNAH | Hardin | TELLICO PLAINS | Monroe |

| | | | |
|---|---|---|---|
| TEN MILE | Meigs | WINCHESTER | Franklin |
| TENNESEE RIDGE | Houston | WINFIELD | Scott |
| THOMPSONS STATION | Williamson | WINONA | Scott |
| THORN HILL | Grainger | WOODBINE | Davidson |
| TIGRETT | Dyer | WOODBURY | Cannon |
| TIPTON | Tipton | WOODLAND MILLS | Obion |
| TIPTONVILLE | Lake | WOODLAWN | Montgomery |
| TOONE | Hardeman | WRIGLEY | Hickman |
| TOWNSEND | Blount | WYNNBURG | Lake |
| TRACY CITY | Grundy | YORKVILLE | Gibson |
| TRADE | Johnson | YUMA | Carroll |
| TREADWAY | Hancock | **TEXAS** | |
| TRENTON | Gibson | ABBOTT | Hill |
| TREZEVANT | Carroll | ABERNATHY | Hale |
| TRIMBLE | Dyer | ABILENE COOK | Taylor |
| TROY | Obion | ACE | Polk |
| TULLAHOMA | Coffee | ACKERLY | Dawson |
| TURTLETOWN | Polk | ADDISON | Dallas |
| TUSCULUM COLLEGE | Greene | ADKINS | Bexar |
| UNICOI | Union | ADRIAN | Oldham |
| UNION CITY | Obion | AFTON | Dickens |
| UNIONVILLE | Bedford | AGUA DULCE | Nueces |
| VANLEER | Dickson | AIKEN | Floyd |
| VIOLA | Warren | AIRLAWN | Dallas |
| VONORE | Monroe | ALAMO | Hidalgo |
| WALLAND | Blount | ALAMO HEIGHTS | Bexar |
| WALLING | White | ALANREED | Gray |
| WARTBURG | Morgan | ALBA | Wood |
| WARTRACE | Bedford | ALBANY | Shackelford |
| WASHBURN | Grainger | ALBERT | Gillespie |
| WASHINGTON COLLEGE | Washington | ALEDO | Parker |
| WATAUGA | Carter | ALICE | Jim Wells |
| WATERTOWN | Wilson | ALIEF | Harris |
| WATTS BAR DAM | Rhea | ALLEN | Collin |
| WAVERLY | Humphreys | ALLEYTON | Colorado |
| WAYNESBORO | Wayne | ALLISON | Wheeler |
| WESTMORELAND | Sumner | ALMEDA | Harris |
| WESTPOINT | Lawrence | ALPINE | Brewster |
| WESTPORT | Carroll | ALTAIR | Colorado |
| WHITE | Shelby | ALTO | Cherokee |
| WHITE BLUFF | Dickson | ALVARADO | Johnson |
| WHITE HOUSE | Robertson | ALVIN | Brazoria |
| WHITE PINE | Jefferson | ALVORD | Wise |
| WHITESBURG | Hamblen | AMARILLO | Potter |
| WHITES CREEK | Davidson | AMHERST | Lamb |
| WHITESIDE | Marion | ANAHUAC | Chambers |
| WHITEVILLE | Hardeman | ANDERSON | Grimes |
| WHITLEYVILLE | Jackson | ANDREWS | Andrews |
| WHITWELL | Marion | ANGLETON | Brazoria |
| WILDER | Fentress | ANNA | Collin |
| WILDERSVILLE | Henderson | ANNONA | Red River |
| WILLIAMSPORT | Maury | ANSON | Jones |
| WILLISTON | Fayette | ANTELOPE | Jack |

| | | | |
|---|---|---|---|
| ANTHONY | El Paso | BAYSIDE | Refugio |
| ANTON | Hockley | BAYTOWN | Harris |
| APPLE SPRINGS | Trinity | BAYVIEW | Cameron |
| AQUILLA | Hill | BEACON HILL | Bexar |
| ARANSAS PASS | San Patricio | BEAR CREEK | Harris |
| ARCHER CITY | Archer | BEASLEY | Fort Bend |
| ARGYLE | Denton | BEAUMONT | Jefferson |
| ARLINGTON | Tarrant | BEBE | Gonzales |
| ARLINGTON HEIGHTS | Tarrant | BECKVILLE | Panola |
| ARMSTRONG | Kenedy | BEDFORD | Tarrant |
| ARP | Smith | BEDIAS | Grimes |
| ART | Mason | BEE HOUSE | Coryell |
| ARTESIA WELLS | La Salle | BEEVILLE | Bee |
| ARTHUR CITY | Lamar | BELLAIRE | Harris |
| ASHERTON | Dimmit | BELLEVUE | Clay |
| ASPERMONT | Stonewall | BELLS | Grayson |
| ATASCOSA | Bexar | BELLVILLE | Austin |
| ATHENS | Henderson | BELMONT | Gonzales |
| ATLANTA | Cass | BELTON | Bell |
| AUBREY | Denton | BEN ARNOLD | Milam |
| AUSTIN | Travis | BENAVIDES | Duval |
| AUSTWELL | Refugio | BEND | San Saba |
| AVALON | Ellis | BEN FRANKLIN | Delta |
| AVERY | Red River | BENJAMIN | Knox |
| AVINGER | Cass | BEN WHEELER | Van Zandt |
| AXTEL | McLennan | BERCLAIR | Goliad |
| AZALEA | Smith | BERTRAM | Burnet |
| AZLE | Tarrant | BEST | Reagan |
| BACLIFF | Galveston | BIG BEND NATIONAL PARK | Brewster |
| BAGWELL | Red River | BIGFOOT | Frio |
| BAILEY | Fannin | BIG LAKE | Reagan |
| BAIRD | Callahan | BIG SANDY | Upshur |
| BALCH SPRINGS | Dallas | BIG SPRING | Howard |
| BALCONES | Travis | BIG WELLS | Dimmit |
| BALLINGER | Runnels | BIROME | Hill |
| BALMORHEA | Reeves | BISHOP | Nueces |
| BANDERA | Bandera | BIVINS | Cass |
| BANGS | Brown | BLACKWELL | Nolan |
| BANQUETTE | Nueces | BLANCO | Blanco |
| BARDWELL | Ellis | BLANKET | Brown |
| BARKER | Harris | BLEDSOE | Cochran |
| BARKSDALE | Edwards | BLEIBLERVILLE | Austin |
| BARNHART | Irion | BLESSING | Matagorda |
| BARRY | Navarro | BLOOMBURG | Cass |
| BARSTOW | Ward | BLOOMING GROVE | Navarro |
| BARTLETT | Bell | BLOOMINGTON | Victoria |
| BARTON CREEK | Travis | BLOSSOM | Lamar |
| BASIN | Brewster | BLUEGROVE | Clay |
| BASTROP | Bastrop | BLUE RIDGE | Collin |
| BATESVILLE | Zavala | BLUFF DALE | Erath |
| BATSON | Hardin | BLUFFTON | Llano |
| BAY CITY | Matagorda | BLUM | Hill |
| BAYLOR UNIV | McLennan | BOERNE | Kendall |

| | | | |
|---|---|---|---|
| BOGATA | Red River | BUSHLAND | Potter |
| BOLING | Wharton | BYERS | Clay |
| BONHAM | Fannin | BYNUM | Hill |
| BON WIER | Newton | CACTUS | Moore |
| BOOKER | Lipscomb | CADDO | Stephens |
| BORGER | Hutchinson | CADDO MILLS | Hunt |
| BOSTON | Bowie | CALDWELL | Burleson |
| BOVINA | Parmer | CALL | Newton |
| BOWIE | Montague | CALLIHAM | McMullen |
| BOYD | Wise | CALVERT | Robertson |
| BOYS RANCH | Oldham | CAMDEN | Polk |
| BRACKELLE | Kinney | CAMERON | Milam |
| BRADY | McCulloch | CAMPBELL | Hunt |
| BRANDON | Hill | CAMPBELLTON | Atascosa |
| BRASHEAR | Hopkins | CAMP WOOD | Real |
| BRAZORIA | Brazoria | CANADIAN | Hemphill |
| BRECKENRIDGE | Stephens | CANTON | Van Zandt |
| BREMOND | Robertson | CANUTILLO | El Paso |
| BRENHAM | Washington | CANYON | Randall |
| BRIDGE CITY | Orange | CANYON CREEK | Dallas |
| BRIDGEPORT | Wise | CANYON LAKE | Comal |
| BRIGGS | Burnet | CARBON | Eastland |
| BRISCOE | Wheeler | CAREY | Childress |
| BROADDUS | San Augustine | CARLSBAD | Tom Green |
| BRONSON | Sabine | CARLTON | Hamilton |
| BRONTE | Coke | CARMINE | Fayette |
| BROOKELAND | Sabine | CARRIZO SPRINGS | Dimmit |
| BROOKESMITH | Brown | CARROLLTON | Dallas |
| BROOKSHIRE | Waller | CARSWELL AFB | Tarrant |
| BROOKSTON | Lamar | CARTA VALLEY | Edwards |
| BROWNFIELD | Terry | CARTHAGE | Panola |
| BROWNSBORO | Henderson | CASON | Morris |
| BROWNSVILLE | Cameron | CASTELL | Llano |
| BROWNWOOD | Brown | CASTROVILLE | Medina |
| BRUCEVILLE | McLennan | CATARINA | Dimmit |
| BRUNI | Webb | CAT SPRINGS | Austin |
| BRYAN | Brazos | CAYUGA | Anderson |
| BRYSON | Jack | CEDAR CREEK | Bastrop |
| BUCHANAN DAM | Llano | CEDAR HILL | Dallas |
| BUCKHOLTS | Milam | CEDAR LANE | Matagorda |
| BUDA | Hays | CEDAR PARK | Williamson |
| BUFFALO | Leon | CEE VEE | Cottle |
| BUFFALO GAP | Taylor | CELESTE | Hunt |
| BULA | Bailey | CELINA | Collin |
| BULLARD | Smith | CENTER | Shelby |
| BUNA | Jasper | CENTER POINT | Kerr |
| BURKBURNETT | Wichita | CENTERVILLE | Leon |
| BURKETT | Coleman | CENTRALIA | Trinity |
| BURKEVILLE | Newton | CHALK | Cottle |
| BURLESON | Johnson | CHANDLER | Henderson |
| BURLINGTON | Milam | CHANNELVIEW | Harris |
| BURNET | Burnet | CHANNING | Hartley |
| BURTON | Washington | CHAPMAN RANCH | Nueces |

| | | | |
|---|---|---|---|
| CHAPPELL HILL | Washington | COOLIDGE | Limestone |
| CHARLOTTE | Atascosa | COOPER | Delta |
| CHATFIELD | Navarro | COPEVILLE | Collin |
| CHEAPSIDE | Gonzales | COPPELL | Dallas |
| CHEROKEE | San Saba | COPPERAS COVE | Coryell |
| CHERRY CREEK | Travis | CORPUS CHRISTI | Nueces |
| CHESTER | Tyler | CORRIGAN | Polk |
| CHICO | Wise | CORSICANA | Navarro |
| CHICOTA | Lamar | COST | Gonzales |
| CHILDRESS | Childress | COTTON CENTER | Hale |
| CHILLICOTHE | Hardeman | COTULLA | LaSalle |
| CHILTON | Falls | COUPLAND | Williamson |
| CHINA | Jefferson | COVINGTON | Hill |
| CHINA SPRINGS | McLennan | COYANOSA | Pecos |
| CHINERO | Nacogdoches | CRANDALL | Kaufman |
| CHRIESMAN | Burleson | CRANE | Crane |
| CHRISTENE | Atascosa | CRANFILLS GAP | Bosque |
| CHRISTOVAL | Tom Green | CRAWFORD | McLennan |
| CIBOLO | Guadalupe | CRESSON | Hood |
| CISCO | Eastland | CROCKETT | Houston |
| CLARENDON | Donley | CROSBY | Harris |
| CLARKSVILLE | Red River | CROSBYTON | Crosby |
| CLAUDE | Armstrong | CROSS PLAINS | Callahan |
| CLAYTON | Panola | CROWELL | Foard |
| CLEBURNE | Johnson | CROWLEY | Tarrant |
| CLEVELAND | Liberty | CRYSTAL BEACH | Galveston |
| CLIFTON | Bosque | CRYSTAL CITY | Zavala |
| CLINT | El Paso | CUERO | DeWitt |
| CLUTE | Brazoria | CUMBY | Hopkins |
| CLYDE | Callahan | CUNEY | Cherokee |
| COAHOMA | Howard | CUNNINGHAM | Lamar |
| COLDSPRING | San Jacinto | CUSHING | Nacogdoches |
| COLEMAN | Coleman | CYPRESS | Harris |
| COLLEGEPORT | Matagorda | DAINGERFIELD | Morris |
| COLLEGE STATION | Brazos | DAISETTA | Liberty |
| COLLEYVILLE | Tarrant | DALE | Caldwell |
| COLLINSVILLE | Grayson | DALHART | Dallam |
| COLMESNEIL | Tyler | DALLARDSVILLE | Polk |
| COLORADO CITY | Mitchell | DALLAS | Dallas |
| COLUMBUS | Colorado | DAMON | Brazoria |
| COMANCHE | Comanche | DANBURY | Brazoria |
| COMBES | Cameron | DANCIGER | Brazoria |
| COMFORT | Kendall | DANEVANG | Wharton |
| COMMERCE | Hunt | DARROUZETT | Lipscomb |
| COMO | Hopkins | DAVILLA | Milam |
| COMSTOCK | Val Verde | DAWN | Deaf Smith |
| CONCAN | Uvalde | DAWSON | Navarro |
| CONCEPCION | Duval | DAYTON | Liberty |
| CONCORD | Leon | DEANVILLE | * Burleson |
| CONE | Crosby | De BERRY | Panola |
| CONROE | Montgomery | DECATUR | Wise |
| CONVERSE | Bexar | DEER PARK | Harris |
| COOKVILLE | Titus | De KALB | Bowie |

| | | | |
|---|---|---|---|
| De LEON | Comanche | EASTLAND | Eastland |
| DELL CITY | Hudspeth | EASTON | Gregg |
| DELMITA | Starr | ECTOR | Fannin |
| DEL RIO | Val Verde | EDCOUCH | Hidalgo |
| DEL VALLE | Travis | EDDY | McLennan |
| DENISON | Grayson | EDEN | Concho |
| DENNIS | Parker | EDGEWOOD | Van Zandt |
| DENTON | Denton | EDINBURG | Hidalgo |
| DENVER CITY | Yoakum | EDMONSON | Hale |
| DEPORT | Lamar | EDNA | Jackson |
| DERMOTT | Scurry | EDROY | San Patricio |
| DESDEMONA | Eastland | EGYPT | Wharton |
| DESOTO | Dallas | ELBERT | Throckmorton |
| DETROIT | Red River | EL CAMPO | Wharton |
| DEVERS | Liberty | EL DORADO | Schleicher |
| DEVINE | Medina | ELECTRA | Wichita |
| DEWEYVILLE | Newton | ELGIN | Bastrop |
| D'HANIS | Medina | ELIASVILLE | Young |
| DIANA | Upshur | EL INDIO | Maverick |
| DIBOLL | Angelina | ELKHART | Anderson |
| DICKENS | Dickens | ELLINGER | Fayette |
| DICKINSON | Galveston | ELMATON | Matagorda |
| DIKE | Hopkins | ELMENDORF | Bexar |
| DILLEY | Frio | ELM MOTT | McLennan |
| DIME BOX | Lee | ELMO | Kaufman |
| DIMMIT | Castro | EL PASO | El Paso |
| DOBBIN | Montgomery | ELSA | Hidalgo |
| DODD CITY | Fannin | ELYSIAN FIELDS | Harrison |
| DODGE | Walker | EMORY | Rains |
| DODSON | Collingsworth | ENCINAL | LaSalle |
| DONIE | Freestone | ENCINO | Brooks |
| DONNA | Hidalgo | ENERGY | Comanche |
| DOOLE | McCulloch | ENLOE | Delta |
| DOSS | Gillespie | ENNIS | Ellis |
| DOUCETTE | Tyler | ENOCHS | Bailey |
| DOUGHERTY | Floyd | EOLA | Concho |
| DOUGLASS | Nacogdoches | ERA | Cooke |
| DOUGLASSVILLE | Cass | ESTELLINE | Hall |
| DRIFTWOOD | Hays | ETOILE | Nacogdoches |
| DRIPPING SPRINGS | Hays | EULESS | Tarrant |
| DRISCOLL | Nueces | EUSTACE | Henderson |
| DRYDEN | Terrell | EVADALE | Jasper |
| DUBLIN | Erath | EVANT | Coryell |
| DUFFAU | Erath | FABENS | El Paso |
| DUMAS | Moore | FAIRFIELD | Freestone |
| DUMONT | King | FALCON HEIGHTS | Starr |
| DUNCANVILLE | Dallas | FALFURRIAS | Brooks |
| DUNN | Scurry | FALLS CITY | Karnes |
| DYESS AFB | Taylor | FANNIN | Goliad |
| EAGLE LAKE | Colorado | FARMERSVILLE | Collin |
| EAGLE PASS | Maverick | FARMSWORTH | Ochiltree |
| EARTH | Lamb | FARWELL | Parmer |
| EAST BERNARD | Wharton | FASHING | Atascosa |

| | | | |
|---|---|---|---|
| FATE | Rockwell | GARDENDALE | Ector |
| FAYETTEVILLE | Fayette | GARLAND | Dallas |
| FENTRESS | Caldwell | GARRISON | Nacogdoches |
| FERRIS | Ellis | GARWOOD | Colorado |
| FIELDTON | Lamb | GARY | Panola |
| FIFE | McCulloch | GATESVILLE | Coryell |
| FISHER | Comal | GAUSE | Milam |
| FIVE POINTS | El Paso | GENEVA | Sabine |
| FLAT | Coryell | GEORGETOWN | Williamson |
| FLATONIA | Fayette | GEORGE WEST | Live Oak |
| FLINT | Smith | GERONIMO | Gaudalupe |
| FLOMOT | Motley | GIDDINGS | Lee |
| FLORENCE | Williamson | GILCHRIST | Galveston |
| FLORESVILLE | Wilson | GILLETT | Karnes |
| FLOYDADA | Floyd | GILMER | Upshur |
| FLUVANNA | Scurry | GIRARD | Kent |
| FLYNN | Leon | GIRVIN | Pecos |
| FOLLETT | Lipscomb | GLADEWATER | Gregg |
| FORESTBURG | Montague | GLEN FLORA | Wharton |
| FORNEY | Kaufman | GLEN ROSE | Somervell |
| FORRESTON | Ellis | GOBER | Fannin |
| FORSAN | Howard | GODLEY | Johnson |
| FORT DAVIS | Jeff Davis | GOLDEN | Wood |
| FORT HANCOCK | Hudspeth | GOLDSBORO | Coleman |
| FORT McKAVETT | Menard | GOLDSMITH | Ector |
| FORT STOCKTON | Pecos | GOLDTHWAITE | Mills |
| FORT WORTH | Tarrant | GOLIAD | Goliad |
| FOWLERTON | LaSalle | GONZALES | Gonzales |
| FRANCITAS | Jackson | GOODLAND | Bailey |
| FRANKLIN | Robertson | GOODRICH | Polk |
| FRANKSTON | Anderson | GORDON | Palo Pinto |
| FRED | Tyler | GORDONVILLE | Grayson |
| FREDERICKSBURG | Gillespie | GOREE | Knox |
| FREDONIA | Mason | GORMAN | Eastland |
| FREEPORT | Brazoria | GRAFORD | Palo Pinto |
| FREER | Duval | GRAHAM | Young |
| FRESNO | Fort Bend | GRANBURY | Hood |
| FRIENDSWOOD | Galveston | GRANDFALLS | Ward |
| FRIONA | Parmer | GRAND PRAIRE | Dallas |
| FRISCO | Collin | GRAND SALINE | Van Zandt |
| FRITCH | Hutchinson | GRANDVIEW | Johnson |
| FROST | Navarro | GRANGER | Williamson |
| FRUITVALE | Van Zandt | GRAPELAND | Houston |
| FULSHEAR | Fort Bend | GRAPEVINE | Tarrant |
| FULTON | Aransas | GREENVILLE | Hunt |
| GAIL | Borden | GREENWOOD | Wise |
| GAINESVILLE | Cooke | GREGORY | San Patricio |
| GALENA PARK | Harris | GROESBECK | Limestone |
| GALLATIN | Cherokee | GROOM | Carson |
| GALVESTON | Galveston | GROVES | Jefferson |
| GANADO | Jackson | GROVETON | Trinity |
| GARCIASVILLE | Starr | GRULLA | Starr |
| GARDEN CITY | Glasscock | GRUVER | Hansford |

| | | | |
|---|---|---|---|
| GUERRA | Jim Hogg | HOLLIDAY | Archer |
| GUNTER | Grayson | HONDO | Medina |
| GUSTINE | Comanche | HONEY GROVE | Fannin |
| GUTHRIE | King | HOOKS | Bowie |
| GUY | Fort Bend | HORSESHOE BAY | Burnet |
| HACKBERRY | Bexar | HOUSTON | Harris |
| HALE CENTER | Hale | HOWE | Grayson |
| HALLETTSVILLE | Lavaca | HUBBARD | Hill |
| HALLSVILLE | Harrison | HUFFMAN | Harris |
| HAMILTON | Hamilton | HUGHES SPRINGS | Cass |
| HAMLIN | Jones | HULL | Liberty |
| HAMSHIRE | Jefferson | HUMBLE | Harris |
| HANKAMER | Chambers | HUNGERFORD | Wharton |
| HAPPY | Swisher | HUNT | Kerr |
| HARDIN | Liberty | HUNTINGTON | Angelina |
| HARGIN | Hidalgo | HUNTSVILLE | Walker |
| HARLETON | Harrison | HURST | Tarrant |
| HARLINGEN | Cameron | HUTCHINS | Dallas |
| HARPER | Gillespie | HUTTO | Williamson |
| HARROLD | Wilbarger | HYE | Blanco |
| HART | Castro | IDALOU | Lubbock |
| HARTLEY | Hartley | IMPERIAL | Pecos |
| HARWOOD | Gonzales | INDUSTRY | Austin |
| HASKELL | Haskell | INEZ | Victoria |
| HASLET | Tarrant | INGLESIDE | San Patricio |
| HASSE | Comanche | INGRAM | Kerr |
| HAWKINS | Wood | IOLA | Grimes |
| HAWLEY | Jones | IOWA PARK | Wichita |
| HEARNE | Robertson | IRA | Scurry |
| HEBBRONVILLE | Jim Hogg | IRAAN | Pecos |
| HEDLEY | Donley | IREDELL | Bosque |
| HEIDENHEIMER | Bell | IRENE | Hill |
| HELOTES | Bexar | IRVING | Dallas |
| HEMPHILL | Sabine | IRVINGTON | Harris |
| HEMPSTEAD | Waller | ITALY | Ellis |
| HENDERSON | Rusk | ITASCA | Hill |
| HENRIETTA | Clay | IVANHOE | Fannin |
| HEREFORD | Deaf Smith | IZORO | Coryell |
| HERMLEIGH | Scurry | JACINTO CITY | Harris |
| HEWITT | McLennan | JACKSBORO | Jack |
| HEXT | Menard | JACKSONVILLE | Cherokee |
| HICO | Hamilton | JARRELL | Williamson |
| HIDALGO | Hidalgo | JASPER | Jasper |
| HIGGINS | Lipscomb | JAYTON | Kent |
| HIGH ISLAND | Galveston | JEFFERSON | Marion |
| HIGHLANDS | Harris | JERMYN | Jack |
| HILLISTER | Tyler | JEWETT | Leon |
| HILLSBORO | Hill | JOAQUIN | Shelby |
| HITCHCOCK | Galveston | JOHNSON CITY | Blanco |
| HOBSON | Karnes | JOINERVILLE | Rusk |
| HOCHHEIM | DeWitt | JONESBORO | Coryell |
| HOCKLEY | Harris | JONESVILLE | Harrison |
| HOLLAND | Bell | JOSEPHINE | Collin |

| | | | |
|---|---|---|---|
| JOSHUA | Johnson | KYLE | Hays |
| JOURDANTON | Atascosa | LA BLANCA | Hidalgo |
| JUDSON | Gregg | LACLAND AFB | Bexar |
| JUNCTION | Kimble | LA COSTE | Medina |
| JUSTICEBURG | Garza | LADONIA | Fannin |
| JUSTIN | Denton | LA FERIA | Cameron |
| KAMAY | Wichita | LA GRANGE | Fayette |
| KARNACK | Harrison | LAIRD HILL | Rusk |
| KARNES CITY | Karnes | LA JOYA | Hidalgo |
| KATEMCY | Mason | LAKE CREEK | Delta |
| KATY | Harris | LAKE DALLAS | Denton |
| KAUFMAN | Kaufman | LAKE JACKSON | Brazoria |
| KEECHI | Buffalo | LAKEVIEW | Hall |
| KEENE | Johnson | LA MARQUE | Galveston |
| KELLER | Tarrant | LAMAR UNIV | Jefferson |
| KELLERVILLE | Mclean | LAMESA | Dawson |
| KELLY AFB | Bexar | LAMPASAS | Lampasas |
| KELTYS | Angelena | LANCASTER | Dallas |
| KEMAH | Galveston | LANE CITY | Wharton |
| KEMP | Kaufman | LANEVILLE | Rusk |
| KEMPNER | Lampasas | LANGTRY | Val Verde |
| KENDALIA | Kendall | LA PORTE | Harris |
| KENDLETON | Fort Bend | LA PRYOR | Zavala |
| KENEDY | Karnes | LAREDO | Webb |
| KENNARD | Houston | LARUE | Henderson |
| KENNEDALE | Tarrant | LA SALLE | Jackson |
| KENNEY | Austin | LASARA | Willacy |
| KERENS | Navarro | LATEXO | Houston |
| KERMIT | Winkler | LAUGHLIN AFB | Val Verde |
| KERRVILLE | Kerr | LA VERNIA | Wilson |
| KILDARE | Cass | LA VILLA | Hidalgo |
| KILGORE | Gregg | LAVON | Collin |
| KILLEEN | Bell | LA WARD | Jackson |
| KINGSBURY | Guadalupe | LAWN | Taylor |
| KINGSLAND | Llano | LAZBUDDIE | Parmer |
| KINGSVILLE | Iceberg | LEADAY | Coleman |
| KINGSVILLE NAVAL | Kleberg | LEAGUE CITY | Galveston |
| KINGWOOD | Harris | LEAKEY | Real |
| KIRBY | Bexar | LEANDER | Williamson |
| KIRBYVILLE | Jasper | LEDBETTER | Fayette |
| KIRKLAND | Childress | LEESBURG | Camp |
| KIRVIN | Freestone | LEESVILLE | Gonzales |
| KLONDIKE | Delta | LEFORS | Gray |
| KNICKERBOCKER | Tom Green | LEGGETT | Polk |
| KNIPPA | Uvalde | LELIA IAKE | Donley |
| KNOTT | Howard | LEMING | Atascosa |
| KNOX CITY | Knox | LENORAH | Martin |
| KOPPERL | Bosque | LEONA | Leon |
| KOSSE | Limestone | LEONARD | Fannin |
| KOUNTZE | Hardin | LEON JUNCTION | Coryell |
| KRESS | Swisher | LEROY | McLennan |
| KRUM | Denton | LEVELLAND | Hockly |
| KURTEN | Brazos | LEWISVILLE | Denton |

| | | | |
|---|---|---|---|
| LEXINGTON | Lee | MACDONA | Bexar |
| LIBERTY | Liberty | MADISONVILLE | Madison |
| LIBERTY HILL | Williamson | MAGNOLIA | Montgomery |
| LILLIAN | Johnson | MAGNOLIA SPRINGS | Jasper |
| LINCOLN | Lee | MALAKOFF | Henderson |
| LINDALE | Smith | MALONE | Hill |
| LINDEN | Cass | MANCHACA | Travis |
| LINDSAY | Cooke | MANOR | Travis |
| LINGLEVILLE | Erath | MANSFIELD | Tarrant |
| LINN | Hidalgo | MANVEL | Brazoria |
| LIPAN | Hood | MAPLE | Bailey |
| LIPSCOMB | Lipscomb | MARATHON | Brewster |
| LISSIE | Wharton | MARBLE FALLS | Burnet |
| LITTLE ELM | Denton | MARFA | Presidio |
| LITTLEFIELD | Lamb | MARIETTA | Cass |
| LITTLE RIVER | Bell | MARION | Guadalupe |
| LIVERPOOL | Brazoria | MARKHAM | Matagorda |
| LIVINGSTON | Polk | MARLIN | Falls |
| LLANO | Llano | MARQUEZ | Leon |
| LOCKHART | Caldwell | MARSHALL | Harrison |
| LOCKNEY | Floyd | MART | McLennan |
| LODI | Marion | MARTINDALE | Caldwell |
| LOHN | McCulloch | MARTINSVILLE | Nacogdoches |
| LOLITA | Jackson | MARYNEAL | Nolan |
| LOMETA | Lampasas | MASON | Mason |
| LONDON | Kimble | MASTERSON | Moore |
| LONE OAK | Hunt | MATADOR | Motley |
| LONE STAR | Morris | MATAGORDA | Matagorda |
| LONG BRANCH | Panola | MATHIS | San Patricio |
| LONG MOTT | Calhoun | MAUD | Bowie |
| LONGVIEW | Gregg | MAURICEVILLE | Orange |
| LOOP | Gaines | MAXWELL | Caldwell |
| LOPENA | Zapata | MAY | Brown |
| LORAINE | Mitchell | MAYDELLE | Cherokee |
| LORENA | McLennan | MAYPEARL | Ellis |
| LORENZO | Crosby | MAYSFIELD | Milam |
| LOS EBANOS | Hidalgo | McADOO | Dickens |
| LOS FRESNOS | Cameron | McALLEN | Hidalgo |
| LOS INDIOS | Cameron | McCAMEY | Upton |
| LOTT | Falls | McCAULLEY | Fisher |
| LOUISE | Wharton | McCOY | Atascosa |
| LOVELADY | Houston | McDADE | Bastrop |
| LOVING | Young | McFADDIN | Victoria |
| LOWAKE | Concho | McGREGOR | McLennan |
| LOZANO | Cameron | McKINNEY | Collin |
| LUBBOCK | Lubbock | McLEAN | Gray |
| LUEDERS | Jones | McLEOD | Cass |
| LUFKIN | Angelina | McNEIL | Travis |
| LULING | Caldwell | McQUEENEY | Guadalupe |
| LYFORD | Willacy | MEADOW | Terry |
| LYONS | Burleson | MEDINA | Bandera |
| LYTLE | Atascosa | MEGARGEL | Archer |
| MABANK | Kaufman | MELISSA | Collin |

| | | | |
|---|---|---|---|
| MELVIN | McCulloch | MOUNT ENTERPRISE | Rusk |
| MEMPHIS | Hall | MOUNT PLEASANT | Tltus |
| MENARD | Menard | MOUNT VERNON | Franklin |
| MENTONE | Loving | MUENSTER | Cooke |
| MERCEDES | Hidalgo | MULDOON | Fayette |
| MERETA | Tom Green | MULESHOE | Bailey |
| MERIDIAN | Bosque | MULLIN | Mills |
| MERIT | Hunt | MUMFORD | Robertson |
| MERKEL | Taylor | MUNDAY | Knox |
| MERTENS | Hill | MURCHISON | Henderson |
| MERTZON | Irion | MYRA | Cooke |
| MESQUITE | Dallas | NACOGDOCHES | Nacogdoches |
| MEXIA | Limestone | NADA | Colorado |
| MEYERSVILLE | De Witt | NAPLES | Morris |
| MIAMI | Roberts | NASH | Bowie |
| MIDFIELD | Matagorda | NATALIA | Medina |
| MIDKIFF | Upton | NAVASCOTA | Grimes |
| MIDLAND | Midland | NAZARETH | Castro |
| MIDLOTHIAN | Ellis | NECHES | Anderson |
| MIDWAY | Madison | NEDERLAND | Jefferson |
| MILAM | Sabine | NEEDVILLE | Fort Bend |
| MILANO | Milam | NEMO | Somervell |
| MILES | Runnels | NEVADA | Collin |
| MILFORD | Ellis | NEWARK | Wise |
| MILLERSVIEW | Concho | NEW BADEN | Robertson |
| MILLICAN | Brazos | NEW BOSTON | Bowie |
| MILLSAP | Parker | NEW BRAUNFELS | Comal |
| MINDEN | Rusk | NEW CANEY | Montgomery |
| MINEOLA | Wood | NEWCASTLE | Young |
| MINERAL WELLS | Palo Pinto | NEW DEAL | Lubbock |
| MINGUS | Palo Pinto | NEWGULF | Wharton |
| MIRANDO CITY | Webb | NEW LONDON | Rusk |
| MISSION | Hidalgo | NEWPORT | Clay |
| MISSOURI CITY | Fort Bend | NEW SUMMERFIELD | Cherokee |
| MOBEETIE | Wheeler | NEWTON | Newton |
| MONAHANS | Ward | NEW ULM | Austin |
| MONROE CITY | Chambers | NEW WAVERLY | Walker |
| MONTAGUE | Montague | NIXON | Gonzales |
| MONTALBA | Anderson | NOCONA | Montague |
| MONT BELVIEU | Chambers | NOLAN | Nolan |
| MONTGOMERY | Montgomery | NOLANVILLE | Bell |
| MOODY | McLennan | NOME | Jefferson |
| MOORE | Frio | NORDHEIM | De Witt |
| MORAN | Shackelford | NORMANGEE | Leon |
| MORGAN | Bosque | NORMANNA | Bee |
| MORGAN MILL | Erath | NORTHFIELD | Motley |
| MORSE | Hansford | NORTH ZULCH | Madison |
| MORTON | Cochran | NORTON | Runnels |
| MOSCOW | Polk | NOTREES | Ector |
| MOULTON | Lavaca | NOVICE | Coleman |
| MOUND | Coryell | NURSERY | Victoria |
| MOUNTAIN HOME | Kerr | OAKHURST | San Jacinto |
| MOUNT CALM | Hill | OAKLAND | Colorado |

| | | | |
|---|---|---|---|
| OAKWOOD | Leon | PECOS | Reeves |
| O'BRIEN | Haskell | PEGGY | Atascosa |
| ODELL | Wilbarger | PENDLETON | Bell |
| ODEM | San Patricio | PENELOPE | Hill |
| ODESSA | Ector | PENITAS | Hidalgo |
| O'DONNELL | Lynn | PENNINGTON | Trinity |
| OGLESBY | Coryell | PENWELL | Ector |
| OILTON | Webb | PEP | Hockley |
| OKLAUNION | Wilbarger | PERRIN | Jack |
| OLDEN | Eastland | PERRY | Falls |
| OLD GLORY | Stonewall | PERRYTON | Ochiltree |
| OLD OCEAN | Brazoria | PETERSBURG | Hale |
| OLMITO | Cameron | PETROLIA | Clay |
| OLNEY | Young | PETTIT | Hockley |
| OLTON | Lamb | PETTUS | Bee |
| OMAHA | Morris | PETTY | Lamar |
| ONALASKA | Polk | PFLUGERVILLE | Travis |
| ORANGE | Orange | PHARR | Hidalgo |
| ORANGEFIELD | Orange | PICKTON | Hopkins |
| ORANGE GROVE | Jim Wells | PIERCE | Wharton |
| ORCHARD | Fort Bend | PILOT POINT | Denton |
| ORE CITY | Upshur | PINEHURST | Montgomery |
| ORLA | Reeves | PINELAND | Sabine |
| OTTINE | Gonzales | PIPE CREEK | Bandera |
| OTTO | Falls | PITTSBURG | Camp |
| OVALO | Taylor | PLACEDO | Victoria |
| OVERTON | Rusk | PLAINS | Yoakum |
| OZONA | Crockett | PLAINVIEW | Hale |
| PADUCAH | Cottle | PLANO | Collin |
| PAIGE | Bastrop | PLANTERSVILLE | Grimes |
| PAINT ROCK | Concho | PLEASANTON | Atascosa |
| PALACIOS | Matagorda | PLEDGER | Matagorda |
| PALESTINE | Anderson | PLUM | Fayette |
| PALMER | Ellis | POINT | Rains |
| PALO PINTO | Palo Pinto | POINTBLANK | San Jacinto |
| PALUXY | Hood | POINT COMFORT | Calhoun |
| PAMPA | Gray | POLLOK | Angelina |
| PANDORA | Wilson | PONDER | Denton |
| PANHANDLE | Carson | PONTOTOC | Mason |
| PANNA MARIA | Karnes | POOLVILLE | Parker |
| PANOLA | Panola | PORT ARANSAS | Nueces |
| PARADISE | Wise | PORT ARTHUR | Jefferson |
| PARIS | Lamar | PORT BOLIVAR | Galveston |
| PASADENA | Harris | PORTER | Montgomery |
| PATTISON | Waller | PORT ISABEL | Cameron |
| PATTONVILLE | Lamar | PORTLAND | San Patricio |
| PAWNEE | Bee | PORT LAVACA | Calhoun |
| PEACOCK | Stonewall | PORT NECHES | Jefferson |
| PEARLAND | Brazoria | PORT O'CONNER | Calhoun |
| PEARSALL | Frio | POST | Garza |
| PEAR VALLEY | McCulloch | POTEET | Atascosa |
| PEASTER | Parker | POTH | Wilson |
| PECAN GAP | Delta | POTTSBORO | Grayson |

| | | | |
|---|---|---|---|
| POTTSVILLE | Hamilton | RIO FRIO | Real |
| POWDERLY | Lamar | RIO GRANDE CITY | Starr |
| POWELL | Navarro | RIO HONDO | Cameron |
| POYNOR | Henderson | RIOMEDINA | Medina |
| PRAIRIE HILL | Limestone | RIO VISTA | Johnson |
| PRAIRIE LEA | Caldwell | RISING STAR | Eastland |
| PRAIRIE VIEW | Waller | RIVERSIDE | Walker |
| PREMONT | Jim Wells | RIVIERA | Kleberg |
| PRESIDIO | Presidio | ROANOKE | Denton |
| PRICE | Rusk | ROARING SPRINGS | Motley |
| PRIDDY | Mills | ROBERT LEE | Coke |
| PRINCETON | Collin | ROBSTOWN | Nueces |
| PROCTOR | Comanche | ROBY | Fisher |
| PROGRESO | Hidalgo | ROCHELLE | McCulloch |
| PROSPER | Collin | ROCHESTER | Haskell |
| PURDON | Navarro | ROCKDALE | Milam |
| PURMELA | Coryell | ROCK ISLAND | Colorado |
| PUTNAM | Callahan | ROCKLAND | Tyler |
| PYOTE | Ward | ROCKPORT | Aransas |
| QUAIL | Collingsworth | ROCKSPRINGS | Edwards |
| QUANAH | Hardeman | ROCKWALL | Rockwall |
| QUEEN CITY | Cass | ROCKWOOD | Coleman |
| QUEMADA | Maverick | ROGERS | Bell |
| QUINLAN | Hunt | ROMA | Starr |
| QUITAQUE | Briscoe | ROMAYOR | Liberty |
| QUITMAN | Wood | ROOSEVELT | Kimble |
| RAINBOW | Somervell | ROPESVILLE | Hockley |
| RALLS | Crosby | ROSANKY | Bastrop |
| RANDOLPH | Fannin | ROSCOE | Nolan |
| RANGER | Eastland | ROSEBUD | Falls |
| RANKIN | Upton | ROSENBERG | Fort Bend |
| RATCLIFF | Houston | ROSHARON | Brazoria |
| RAVENNA | Fannin | ROSS | McLennan |
| RAYMONDVILLE | Willacy | ROSSER | Kaufman |
| RAYWOOD | Liberty | ROSSTON | Cooke |
| REAGAN | Falls | ROTAN | Fisher |
| REALITOS | Duval | ROUND MOUNTAIN | Blanco |
| REDFORD | Presidio | ROUND ROCK | Williamson |
| RED OAK | Ellis | ROUND TOP | Fayette |
| RED ROCK | Bastrop | ROWENA | Runnels |
| RED SPRINGS | Baylor | ROWLETT | Dallas |
| REDWATER | Bowie | ROXTON | Lamar |
| REFUGIO | Refugio | ROYALTY | Ward |
| REKLAW | Cherokee | ROYSE CITY | Rockwall |
| RHOME | Wise | RULE | Haskell |
| RICE | Navarro | RUNGE | Karnes |
| RICHARDS | Grimes | RUSK | Cherokee |
| RICHARDSON | Dallas | RYE | Liberty |
| RICHLAND | Navarro | SABINAL | Uvalde |
| RICHLAND SPRINGS | San Saba | SABINE PASS | Jeferson |
| RICHMOND | Fort Bend | SACUL | Nacogdoches |
| RIESEL | McLennan | SADLER | Grayson |
| RINGGOLD | Montague | SAINT HEDWIG | Bexar |

| | | | |
|---|---|---|---|
| SAINT JO | Montague | SHAFTER | Presidio |
| SALADO | Bell | SHALLOWATER | Lubbock |
| SALINENO | Starr | SHAMROCK | Wheeler |
| SALT FLAT | Hudspeth | SHEFFIELD | Pecos |
| SALTILLO | Hopkins | SHELBYVILLE | Shelby |
| SAMNORWOOD | Collingsworth | SHEPHERD | San Jacinto |
| SAN ANGELO | Tom Green | SHERIDAN | Colorado |
| SAN ANTONIO | Bexar | SHERMAN | Grayson |
| SAN AUGUSTINE | San Augustine | SHINER | Lavaca |
| SAN BENITO | Cameron | SHIRO | Grimes |
| SANDERSON | Terrell | SIDNEY | Comanche |
| SANDIA | Jim Wells | SIERRA BLANCA | Hudspeth |
| SAN DIEGO | Duval | SILSBEE | Hardin |
| SANDY | Blanco | SILVER | Coke |
| SAN ELIZARIO | El Paso | SILVERTON | Briscoe |
| SAN FELIPE | Austin | SIMMS | Bowie |
| SANFORD | Hutchinson | SIMONTON | Fort Bend |
| SANGER | Denton | SINTON | San Patricio |
| SAN ISIDRO | Starr | SKELLYTOWN | Carson |
| SAN JUAN | Hidalgo | SKIDMORE | Bee |
| SAN MARCOS | Hays | SLATON | Lubbock |
| SAN PERLITA | Willacy | SLIDELL | Wise |
| SAN SABA | San Saba | SMILEY | Gonzales |
| SANTA ANNA | Coleman | SMITHVILLE | Bastrop |
| SANTA ELENA | Starr | SMYER | Hockley |
| SANTA FE | Galveston | SNOOK | Burleson |
| SANTA MARIA | Cameron | SNYDER | Scurry |
| SANTA ROSA | Cameron | SOMERSET | Rexar |
| SANTO | Palo Pinto | SOMERVILLE | Burleson |
| SAN YGNACIO | Zapata | SONORA | Sutton |
| SARAGOSA | Reeves | SOUR LAKE | Hardin |
| SARATOGA | Hardin | SOUTH BEND | Young |
| SARITA | Kenedy | SOUTH HOUSTON | Harris |
| SASPAMCO | Wilson | SOUTHMAYD | Grayson |
| SATIN | Falls | SOUTH PLAINS | Floyd |
| SAVOY | Fannin | SPADE | Lamb |
| SCHERTZ | Guadalupe | SPEAKS | Lavaca |
| SCHULENBURG | Fayette | SPEARMAN | Hansford |
| SCHWERTNER | Williamson | SPICEWOOD | Burnet |
| SCOTLAND | Archer | SPLENDORA | Montgomery |
| SCOTTSVILLE | Harrison | SPRING | Harris |
| SCROGGINS | Franklin | SPRING BRANCH | Lamb |
| SCURRY | Kaufman | SPRINGTOWN | Parker |
| SEABROOK | Harris | SPUR | Dickens |
| SEADRIFT | Calhoun | SPURGER | Tyler |
| SEAGOVILLE | Dallas | STAFFORD | Fort Bend |
| SEAGRAVES | Gaines | STAMFORD | Jones |
| SEALY | Austin | STANTON | Martin |
| SEBASTIAN | Willacy | STAPLES | Guadalupe |
| SEGUIN | Guadalupe | STAR | Mills |
| SELMAN CITY | Rusk | STEPHENVILLE | Erath |
| SEMINOLE | Gaines | STERLING CITY | Sterling |
| SEYMOUR | Baylor | STINNETT | Hutchinson |

**Adoption Searches Made Easier**

| | | | |
|---|---|---|---|
| STOCKDALE | Wilson | THROCKMORTON | Throckmorton |
| STONEWALL | Gillespie | TILDEN | McMullen |
| STOWELL | Chambers | TIMPSON | Shelby |
| STRATFORD | Sherman | TIOGA | Grayson |
| STRAAW | Palo Pinto | TIVOLI | Refugio |
| STREETMAN | Freestone | TOKIO | Terry |
| SUBLIME | Lavaca | TOLAR | Hood |
| SUDAN | Lamb | TOMBALL | Harris |
| SUGAR LAND | Fort Bend | TOM BEAN | Grayson |
| SULLIVAN CITY | Hidalgo | TORNILLO | El Paso |
| SULPHUR BLUFF | Hopkins | TOW | Llano |
| SULPHUR SPRINGS | Hopkins | TOYAH | Reeves |
| SUMNER | Lamar | TOYAHVALE | Reeves |
| SUNDOWN | Hockley | TRENT | Taylor |
| SUNRAY | Moore | TRENTON | Fannin |
| SUNSET | Montague | TRINIDAD | Henderson |
| SUTHERLAND SPRINGS | Wilson | TRINITY | Trinity |
| SWEENY | Brazoria | TROUP | Smith |
| SWEET HOME | Lavaca | TROY | Bell |
| SWEETWATER | Nolan | TRUSCOTT | Knox |
| SYLVESTER | Fisher | TULETA | Bee |
| TAFT | San Patricio | TULIA | Swisher |
| TAHOKA | Lynn | TURKEY | Hall |
| TALCO | Titus | TURNERSVILLE | Coryell |
| TALPA | Coleman | TUSCOLA | Taylor |
| TARPLEY | Bandera | TYE | Taylor |
| TARZAN | Martin | TYLER | Smith |
| TATUM | Rusk | TYNAN | Bee |
| TAYLOR | Williamson | UMBARGER | Randall |
| TEAGUE | Freestone | UNIVERSAL CITY | Bexar |
| TEHUACANA | Limestone | UNIVERSITY OF DALLAS | Dallas |
| TELEGRAPH | Kimble | UNIVERSITY OF TEXAS | Tarrant |
| TELEPHONE | Fannin | UNIV OF NORTH TEXAS | Denton |
| TELFERNER | Victoria | UNIV OF TX AT ARLINGTON | Tarrant |
| TELL | Childress | UNIV OF TX AT EL PASO | El Paso |
| TEMPLE | Bell | UTOPIA | Uvalde |
| TENAHA | Shelby | UVALDE | Uvalde |
| TENNESSEE COLONY | Anderson | VALENTINE | Jeff Davis |
| TENNYSON | Coke | VALERA | Coleman |
| TERLINGUA | Brewster | VALLEY MILLS | Bosque |
| TERRELL | Kaufman | VALLEY SPRING | Llano |
| TEXARKANA | Bowie | VALLEY VIEW | Cooke |
| TEXAS CITY | Galveston | VAN | Van Zandt |
| TEXAS WOMENS UNIV | Denton | VAN ALSTYNE | Grayson |
| TEXLINE | Dallas | VANCOURT | Tom Green |
| TEXON | Reagan | VANDERBILT | Jackson |
| THICKET | Hardin | VANDERPOOL | Bandera |
| THOMASTON | De Witt | VAN HORN | Culberson |
| THOMPSONS | Fort Bend | VAN VLECK | Matagorda |
| THORNDALE | Milam | VEGA | Oldham |
| THORNTON | Limestone | VENUS | Johnson |
| THRALL | Williamson | VERA | Knox |
| THREE RIVERS | Live Oak | VERIBEST | Tom Green |

| | | | |
|---|---|---|---|
| VERNON | Wilbarger | WHITHARRAL | Hockley |
| VICTORIA | Victoria | WHITNEY | Hill |
| VIDOR | Orange | WHITSET | Live Oak |
| VILLAGE MILLS | Hardin | WHITT | Parker |
| VOCA | McCulloch | WHON | Coleman |
| VON ORMY | Rexar | WICHITA FALLS | Wichita |
| VOSS | Coleman | WICKETT | Ward |
| VOTAW | Hardin | WIERGATE | Newton |
| WACO | McLennan | WILDORADO | Oldham |
| WADSWORTH | Matagorda | WILLIS | Montgomery |
| WAELDER | Gonzales | WILLOW CITY | Gillespie |
| WAKA | Ochiltree | WILLS POINT | Van Zandt |
| WALBURG | Williamson | WILMER | Dallas |
| WALL | Tom Green | WILSON | Lynn |
| WALLER | Waller | WIMBERLY | Hays |
| WALLIS | Austin | WINCHESTER | Fayette |
| WALLISVILLE | Chambers | WINDOM | Fannin |
| WALNUT SPRINGS | Bosque | WINDHORST | Archer |
| WARDA | Fayette | WINFIELD | Titus |
| WARING | Kendall | WINGATE | Runnels |
| WARREN | Tyler | WINK | Winkler |
| WASHINGTON | Washington | WINNIE | Chambers |
| WASKOM | Harrison | WINNSBORO | Wood |
| WATER VALLEY | Tom Green | WINONA | Smith |
| WAXAHACHIE | Ellis | WINTERS | Runnels |
| WEATHERFORD | Parker | WODEN | Nacogdoches |
| WEBSTER | Harris | WOLFE CITY | Hunt |
| WEESATCHE | Gohad | WOFFORTH | Lubbock |
| WEIMAR | Colorado | WOODLAKE | Trinity |
| WEINERT | Haskell | WOODLAWN | Harrison |
| WEIR | Williamson | WOODSBORO | Refugio |
| WELCH | Dawson | WOODSON | Throckmorton |
| WELLBORN | Brazos | WOODVILLE | Tyler |
| WELLINGTON | Collingsworth | WORTHAM | Freestone |
| WELLMAN | Terry | WRIGHTSBORO | Gonzales |
| WELLS | Cherokee | WYLIE | Collin |
| WESLACO | Hidalgo | YANCY | Medina |
| WEST | McLennan | YANTIS | Wood |
| WESTBROOK | Mitchell | YOAKUM | Lavaca |
| WEST COLUMBIA | Brazoria | YORKTOWN | De Witt |
| WESTHOFF | De Witt | ZAPATA | Zapata |
| WESTMINSTER | Collin | ZAVALLA | Angelina |
| WESTON | Collin | ZEPHYR | Brown |
| WEST POINT | Fayette | **UTAH** | |
| WHARTON | Wharton | ALPINE | Utah |
| WHEELER | Wheeler | ALTA | Salt Lake |
| WHEELOCK | Robertson | ALTAMONT | Duchesne |
| WHITE DEER | Carson | ALTON | Kane |
| WHITEFACE | Cochran | ALTONAH | Duchesne |
| WHITEHOUSE | Smith | AMERICAN FORK | Utah |
| WHITE OAK | Gregg | ANETH | San Juan |
| WHITESBORO | Grayson | ANNABELLA | Sevier |
| WHITEWRIGHT | Grayson | ANTIMONY | Garfield |

| | | | |
|---|---|---|---|
| AURORA | Sevier | EPHRAIM | Sanpete |
| AXTELL | Sanpete | ESCALANTE | Garfield |
| BEAR RIVER CITY | Box Elder | EUREKA | Juab |
| BEAVER | Beaver | FAIRVIEW | Sanpete |
| BERYL | Iron | FARMINGTON | Davis |
| BICKNELL | Wayne | FAYETTE | Sanpete |
| BIG WATER | Kane | FERRON | Emery |
| BINGHAM CANYON | Salt Lake | FIELDING | Box Elder |
| BLANDING | San Juan | FILLMORE | Millard |
| BLUEBELL | Duchesne | FORT DUCHESNE | Uintah |
| BLUFF | San Juan | FOUNTAIN GREEN | Sanpete |
| BOULDER | Garfield | FREMONT | Wayne |
| BOUNTIFUL | Davis | FRUITLAND | Duchesne |
| BRIAN HEAD | Iron | GARDEN CITY | Rich |
| BRIDGELAND | Duchesne | GARLAND | Box Elder |
| BRIGHAM CITY | Box Elder | GARRISON | Millard |
| BRIGHAM YOUNG UNIV | Utah | GLENDALE | Kane |
| BRYCE | Garfield | GLENWOOD | Sevier |
| BRYCE CANYON | Garfield | GOSHEN | Utah |
| BULLFROG | San Juan | GRANTSVILLE | Tooele |
| CACHE JUNCTION | Cache | GREEN RIVER | Emery |
| CANNONVILLE | Garfield | GREENVILLE | Beaver |
| CASTLE DALE | Emery | GREENWICH | Piute |
| CEDAR CITY | Iron | GROUSE CREEK | Box Elder |
| CENTERFIELD | Sanpete | GUNLOCK | Washington |
| CENTERVILLE | Davis | GUNNISON | Sanpete |
| CENTRAL | Washington | GUSHER | Uintah |
| CHESTER | Sanpete | HALLS CROSSING | San Juan |
| CIRCLEVILLE | Piute | HANKSVILLE | Wayne |
| CLARKSTON | Cache | HANNA | Duchesne |
| CLAWSON | Emery | HATCH | Garfield |
| CLEARFIELD | Davis | HEBER CITY | Wasatch |
| CLEVELAND | Emery | HELPER | Carbon |
| COALVILLE | Summit | HENEFER | Summit |
| COLLINSTON | Box Elder | HENRIEVILLE | Garfield |
| CORINNE | Box Elder | HIAWATHA | Carbon |
| CROYDON | Morgan | HILDALE | Washington |
| DAMMERON VALLEY | Washington | HILL AFB | Davis |
| DELTA | Millard | HINCKLEY | Millard |
| DEWEYVILLE | Box Elder | HITE | San Juan |
| DRAPER | Salt Lake | HOLDEN | Millard |
| DUCHESNE | Duchesne | HONEYVILLE | Box Elder |
| DUCK CREEK VILLAGE | Kane | HOOPER | Weber |
| DUGWAY | Tooele | HOWELL | Box Elder |
| DUTCH JOHN | Daggett | HUNTINGTON | Emery |
| EAST CARBON | Carbon | HUNTSVILLE | Weber |
| ECHO | Summit | HURRICANE | Washington |
| EDEN | Weber | HYDE PARK | Cache |
| ELBERTA | Utah | HYRUM | Cache |
| ELMO | Emery | IBAPAH | Tooele |
| ELSINORE | Sevier | IVINS | Washington |
| EMERY | Emery | JENSEN | Uintah |
| ENTERPRISE | Washington | JOSEPH | Sevier |

| | | | |
|---|---|---|---|
| JUNCTION | Piute | MURRAY | Salt Lake |
| KAMAS | Summit | MYTON | Duchesne |
| KANAB | Kane | NEOLA | Duchesne |
| KANARRAVILLE | Iron | NEPHI | Juab |
| KANOSH | Millard | NEWCASTLE | Iron |
| KAYSVILLE | Davis | NEW HARMONY | Washington |
| KEARNS | Salt Lake | NEWTON | Cache |
| KENILWORTH | Carbon | NORTH SALT LAKE | Davis |
| KINGSTON | Piute | OAK CITY | Millard |
| KOOSHAREM | Sevier | OAKLEY | Summit |
| LAKE POWELL | San Juan | OASIS | Millard |
| LAKETOWN | Rich | OGDEN | Weber |
| LAPOINT | Uintah | ORANGEVILLE | Emery |
| LA SAL | San Juan | ORDERVILLE | Kane |
| LA VERKIN | Washington | OREM | Utah |
| LAYTON | Davis | PANGUITCH | Garfield |
| LEAMINGTON | Millard | PARADISE | Cache |
| LEEDS | Washington | PARAGONAH | Iron |
| LEHI | Utah | PARK CITY | Summit |
| LEVAN | Juab | PARK VALLEY | Box Elder |
| LEWISTON | Cache | PAROWAN | Iron |
| LINDON | Utah | PAYSON | Utah |
| LOA | Wayne | PEOA | Summit |
| LOGAN | Cache | PINE VALLEY | Iron |
| LYMAN | Wayne | PLEASANT GROVE | Utah |
| LYNNDYL | Millard | PLYMOUTH | Box Elder |
| MAGNA | Salt Lake | PORTAGE | Box Elder |
| MANILA | Daggett | PRICE | Carbon |
| MANTI | Sanpete | PROVIDENCE | Cache |
| MANTUA | Box Elder | PROVO | Utah |
| MAPLETON | Utah | RANDLETT | Uintah |
| MARYSVALE | Piute | RANDOLPH | Rich |
| MAYFIELD | Sanpete | REDMOND | Sevier |
| MEADOW | Millard | RICHFIELD | Sevier |
| MENDON | Cache | RICHMOND | Cache |
| MEXICAN HAT | San Juan | RIVERSIDE | Box Elder |
| MIDVALE | Salt Lake | RIVERTON | Salt Lake |
| MIDWAY | Wasatch | ROCKVILLE | Washington |
| MILFORD | Beaver | ROOSEVELT | Duchesne |
| MILLVILLE | Cache | ROY | Weber |
| MINERSVILLE | Beaver | RUSH VALLEY | Tooele |
| MOAB | Grand | SAINT GEORGE | Washington |
| MODENA | Iron | SALEM | Utah |
| MONA | Juab | SALINA | Sevier |
| MONROE | Sevier | SALT LAKE CITY | Salt Lake |
| MONTAZUMA CREE | San Juan | SANDY | Salt Lake |
| MONTICELLO | San Juan | SANTA CLARA | Washington |
| MONUMENT VALLEY | San Juan | SANTAQUIN | Utah |
| MORGAN | Morgan | SCIPIO | Millard |
| MORONI | Sanpete | SEVIER | Sevier |
| MOUNTAIN HOME | Duchesne | SIGURD | Sevier |
| MOUNT CARMEL | Kane | SMITHFIELD | Cache |
| MOUNT PLEASANT | Sanpete | SNOWBIRD | Salt Lake |

| | | | |
|---|---|---|---|
| SNOWVILLE | Box Elder | BEEBE PLAIN | Orleans |
| SOUTH SALT LAKE | Salt Lake | BEECHER FALLS | Essex |
| SPANISH FORK | Utah | BELLOWS FALLS | Windham |
| SPRING CITY | Sanpete | BELMONT | Rutland |
| SPRINGDALE | Washington | BELVIDERE CENTER | Lamoille |
| SPRINGVILLE | Utah | BENNINGTON | Bennington |
| STERLING | Sanpete | BENNINGTON COLLEGE | Bennington |
| STOCKTON | Tooele | BENSON | Rutland |
| SUMMIT | Iron | BETHEL | Windsor |
| SUNNYSIDE | Carbon | BOMOSEEN | Rutland |
| SYRACUSE | Davis | BONDVILLE | Bennington |
| TABIONA | Duchesne | BRADFORD | Orange |
| TALMAGE | Duchesne | BRANDON | Rutland |
| TEASDALE | Wayne | BRATTLEBORO | Windham |
| THOMPSON | Grand | BRIDGEWATER | Windsor |
| TOOELE | Tooele | BRIDGEWATER CORNERS | Windsor |
| TOQUERVILLE | Washington | BRIDPORT | Addison |
| TORREY | Wayne | BRISTOL | Addison |
| TREMONTON | Box Elder | BROMLEY MOUNTAIN | Windham |
| TRENTON | Cache | BROOKFIELD | Orange |
| TRIDELL | Uintah | BROWNSVILLE | Windsor |
| TROPIC | Garfield | BURLINGTON | Chittenden |
| TROUT CREEK | Tooele | CABOT | Washington |
| VENICE | Sevier | CALAIS | Washington |
| VERNAL | Uintah | CAMBRIDGE | Lamoille |
| VERNON | Tooele | CAMBRIDGEPORT | Windham |
| VEYO | Washington | CANAAN | Essex |
| VIRGIN | Washington | CASTLETON | Rutland |
| WALES | Sanpete | CAVENDISH | Windsor |
| WALLSBURG | Wasatch | CENTER RUTLAND | Rutland |
| WASHINGTON | Washington | CHAMPLAIN | Chittenden |
| WELLINGTON | Carbon | CHARLOTTE | Chittenden |
| WELLSVILLE | Cache | CHELSEA | Orange |
| WENDOVER | Tooele | CHESTER | Windsor |
| WEST JORDAN | Salt Lake | CHITTENDEN | Rutland |
| WEST VALLEY CITY | Salt Lake | COLCHESTER | Chittenden |
| WHITEROCKS | Uintah | CONCORD | Essex |
| WILLARD | Box Elder | CORINTH | Orange |
| WOODLAND HILLS | Utah | COVENTRY | Orleans |
| WOODRUFF | Rich | CRAFTSBURY | Orleans |
| WOODS CROSS | Davis | CRAFTSBURY COMMON | Orleans |
| ZION NAT'L PARK | Washington | CUTTINGSVILLE | Rutland |
| **VERMONT** | | DANBY | Rutland |
| ADAMANT | Washington | DANVILLE | Caledonia |
| ALBANY | Orleans | DERBY | Orleans |
| ALBURG | Grand Isle | DERBY LINE | Orleans |
| ARLINGTON | Bennington | DORSET | Bennington |
| ASCUTNEY | Windsor | EAST ARLINGTON | Bennington |
| BAKERSFIELD | Franklin | EAST BARRE | Washington |
| BARNARD | Windsor | EAST BERKSHIRE | Franklin |
| BARNET | Caledonia | EAST BURKE | Caledonia |
| BARRE | Washington | EAST CALAIS | Washington |
| BARTON | Orleans | EAST CHARLESTON | Orleans |

| | | | |
|---|---|---|---|
| EAST CORINTH | Orange | JACKSONVILLE | Windham |
| EAST DORSET | Bennington | JAMAICA | Windham |
| EAST DOVER | Windham | JAY PEAK | Orleans |
| EAST FAIRFIELD | Franklin | JEFFERSONVILLE | Lamoille |
| EAST HARDWICK | Caledonia | JERICHO | Chittenden |
| EAST HAVEN | Essex | JERICHO CENTER | Chittenden |
| EAST MIDDLEBURY | Addison | JOHNSON | Lamoille |
| EAST MONTPELIER | Washington | JONESVILLE | Chittenden |
| EAST POULTNEY | Rutland | KILLINGTON | Rutland |
| EAST RANDOLPH | Orange | LEICESTER JUNCTION | Addison |
| EAST RYEGATE | Caledonia | LONDONDERRY | Windham |
| EAST SAINT JOHNSBURY | Caledonia | LOWELL | Orleans |
| EAST THETFORD | Orange | LOWER WATERFORD | Caledonia |
| EAST WALLINGFORD | Rutland | LUDLOW | Windsor |
| EDEN | Lamoille | LUNENBURG | Essex |
| ELY | Orange | LYMAN | Windsor |
| ENOSBURG FALLS | Franklin | LYNDON | Caledonia |
| ESSEX | Chittenden | LYNDON CENTER | Caledonia |
| ESSEX JUNCTION | Chittenden | LYNDONVILLE | Caledonia |
| FAIRFAX | Franklin | McINDOE FALLS | Caledonia |
| FAIRFIELD | Franklin | MANCHESTER | Bennington |
| FAIR HAVEN | Rutland | MANCHESTER CENTER | Bennington |
| FAIRLEE | Orange | MARLBORO | Windham |
| FERRISBURG | Addison | MARSHFIELD | Washington |
| FLORENCE | Rutland | MIDDLEBURY | Addison |
| FOREST DALE | Rutland | MIDDLETOWN SPRINGS | Rutland |
| FRANKLIN | Franklin | MILTON | Chittenden |
| GAYSVILLE | Windsor | MONKTON | Addison |
| GILMAN | Essex | MONTGOMERY | Franklin |
| GLOVER | Orleans | MONTGOMERY CENTER | Franklin |
| GRAFTON | Windham | MONTPELIER | Washington |
| GRANBY | Essex | MORETOWN | Washington |
| GRAND ISLE | Grand Isle | MORGAN | Orleans |
| GRANITEVILLE | Washington | MORGAN CENTER | Orleans |
| GRANVILLE | Addison | MORRISVILLE | Lamoille |
| GREENSBORO | Orleans | MOSCOW | Lamoile |
| GREENSBORO BEND | Orleans | MOUNT HOLLY | Rutland |
| GROTON | Caledonia | NEWBURY | Orange |
| GUILDHALL | Essex | NEWFANE | Windham |
| HANCOCK | Addison | NEW HAVEN | Addison |
| HARDWICK | Caledonia | NEWPORT | Orleans |
| HARTFORD | Windsor | NEWPORT CENTER | Orleans |
| HARTLAND | Windsor | NORTH BENNINGTON | Bennington |
| HARTLAND FOUR CORNERS | Windsor | NORTH CLARENDON | Rutland |
| HIGHGATE CENTER | Franklin | NORTH CONCORD | Essex |
| HIGHGATE SPRINGS | Franklin | NORTH FERRISBURG | Addison |
| HINESBURG | Chittenden | NORTHFIELD | Washington |
| HUNTINGTON | Chittenden | NORTHFIELD FALLS | Washington |
| HYDE PARK | Lamoille | NORTH HARTLAND | Windsor |
| HYDEVILLE | Rutland | NORTH HERO | Grand Isle |
| IRASBURG | Orleans | NORTH HYDE PARK | Lamoille |
| ISLAND POND | Essex | NORTH MONTPELIER | Washington |
| ISLE LAMOTTE | Grand isle | NORTH POMFRET | Windsor |

| | | | |
|---|---|---|---|
| NORTH POWNAL | Bennington | SOUTH HERO | Grand Isle |
| NORTH SPRINGFIELD | Windsor | SOUTH LONDONDERRY | Windham |
| NORTH THETFORD | Orange | SOUTH NEWFANE | Windham |
| NORTH TROY | Orleans | SOUTH POMFRET | Windsor |
| NORTON | Essex | SOUTH ROYALTON | Windsor |
| NORWICH | Windsor | SOUTH RYEGATE | Caledonia |
| NORWICH UNIV | Washington | SOUTH STRAFFORD | Orange |
| ORLEANS | Orleans | SOUTH WOODSTOCK | Windsor |
| ORWELL | Addison | SPRINGFIELD | Windsor |
| PASSUMPSIC | Caledonia | STARKSBORO | Addison |
| PAWLET | Rutland | STOCKBRIDGE | Windsor |
| PEACHAM | Caledonia | STOWE | Lamoille |
| PERKINSVILLE | Windsor | STRAFFORD | Orange |
| PERU | Bennington | SUTTON | Caledonia |
| PITTSFIELD | Rutland | SWANTON | Franklin |
| PITTSFORD | Rutland | TAFTSVILLE | Windsor |
| PLAINFIELD | Washington | THETFORD | Orange |
| PLYMOUTH | Windsor | THETFORD CENTER | Orange |
| POST MILLS | Orange | TOPSHAM | Orange |
| POULTNEY | Rutland | TOWNSHEND | Windham |
| POWNAL | Bennington | TROY | Orleans |
| PROCTOR | Rutland | TUNBRIDGE | Orange |
| PROCTORSVILLE | Windsor | UNDERHILL | Chittenden |
| PUTNEY | Windham | UNDERHILL CENTER | Chittenden |
| QUECHEE | Windsor | VERGENNES | Addison |
| RANDOLPH | Orange | VERNON | Windham |
| RANDOLPH CENTER | Orange | VERSHIRE | Orange |
| READING | Windsor | WAITSFIELD | Washington |
| READSBORO | Bennington | WALLINGFORD | Rutland |
| RICHFORD | Franklin | WARDSBORO | Windham |
| RICHMOND | Chittenden | WARREN | Washington |
| RIPTON | Addison | WASHINGTON | Orange |
| RIVERTON | Washington | WATERBURY | Washington |
| ROCHESTER | Windsor | WATERBURY CENTER | Washington |
| ROXBURY | Washington | WATERVILLE | Lamoille |
| RUPERT | Bennington | WEBSTERVILLE | Washington |
| RUTLAND | Rutland | WELLS | Rutland |
| SAINT ALBANS | Franklin | WELLS RIVER | Orange |
| SAINT ALBANS BAY | Franklin | WEST BRATTLEBORO | Windham |
| SAINT JOHNSBURY | Caledonia | WEST BURKE | Caledonia |
| SAINT JOHNSBURY CENTER | Caledonia | WEST CHARLESTON | Orleans |
| SALISBURY | Addison | WEST DANVILLE | Caledonia |
| SAXTONS RIVER | Windham | WEST DOVER | Windham |
| SHAFTSBURY | Bennington | WEST DUMMERSTON | Windham |
| SHARON | Windsor | WEST FAIRLEE | Orange |
| SHEFFIELD | Caledonia | WESTFIELD | Orleans |
| SHELBURNE | Chittenden | WESTFORD | Chittenden |
| SHELDON | Franklin | WEST HALIFAX | Windham |
| SHELDON SPRINGS | Franklin | WEST HARTFORD | Windsor |
| SHOREHAM | Addison | WESTMINSTER | Windham |
| SOUTH BARRE | Washington | WESTMINSTER STATION | Windham |
| SOUTH BURLINGTON | Rutland | WEST NEWBURY | Orange |
| SOUTH DORSET | Bennington | WESTON | Windsor |

| | | | |
|---|---|---|---|
| WEST PAWLET | Rutland | ARVONIA | Buckingham |
| WEST RUPERT | Bennington | ASHBURN | Loudoun |
| WEST RUTLAND | Rutland | ASHLAND | Hanover |
| WEST TOPSHAM | Orange | ASSAWOMAN | Accomack |
| WEST WARDSBORO | Windham | ATKINS | Smyth |
| WHITE RIVER JUNCTION | Windsor | ATLANTIC | Accomack |
| WHITING | Addison | ATKINS | Smyth |
| WHITINGHAM | Windham | AUGUSTA SPRINGS | Augusta |
| WILDER | Windsor | AUSTINVILLE | Whthe |
| WILLIAMSTOWN | Orange | AXTON | Henry |
| WILLIAMSVILLE | Windham | AYLETT | King William |
| WILLISTON | Chittenden | AYLOR | Madison |
| WILMINGTON | Windham | BACKBAY | Virginia |
| WINDSOR | Windsor | BACOVA | Bath |
| WINOOSKI | Rutland | BANCO | Madison |
| WOLCOTT | Lamoille | BANDY | Tazewell |
| WOODBURY | Washington | BARBOURSVILLE | Orange |
| WOODSTOCK | Windsor | BARHAMSVILLE | New Kent |
| WORCESTER | Washington | BARREN SPRINGS | Wythe |
| **VIRGINIA** | | BASKERVILLE | Mecklenburg |
| ABINGDON | Washington | BASSETT | Henry |
| ACCOMACK | Accomack | BASTIAN | Bland |
| ACHILLES | Gloucester | BASYE | Shenandoah |
| ACREDALE | City of Virginia Beach | BATESVILLE | Albemarle |
| ADVANCE MILLS | Greene | BATTERY PARK | Isle Of Wight |
| AFTON | Nelson | BAVON | Mathews |
| ALBERENE | Albemarle | BAYSIDE | Virginia |
| ALBERTA | Brunswick | BEALETON | Fauquier |
| ALDIE | Loudoun | BEAVERDAM | Hanover |
| ALEXANDRIA | Alexandria City | BEAVERLETT | Mathews |
| ALFONSO | Lancaster | BEDFORD | Bedford City |
| ALLEGHANY | Covington City | BEE | Dickenson |
| ALLISONIA | Pulaski | BELLAMY | Gloucester |
| ALTAVISTA | Campbell | BELLE HAVEN | Accomack |
| ALTON | Halifax | BELLE VIEW | Alexandria City |
| ALUM RIDGE | Floyd | BELLEVUE | Richmond City |
| AMELIA COURT HOUSE | Amelia | BELLSPRING | Pulaski |
| AMHERST | Amherst | BENA | Gloucester |
| AMISSVILLE | Rappahannock | BEN HUR | Lee |
| AMMON | Dinwiddie | BENT MOUNTAIN | Roanoke |
| AMONATE | Tazewell | BENTONVILLE | Warren |
| AMPTHILL | Richmond City | BERGTON | Rockingham |
| ANDERSONVILLE | Buckingham | BERKELEY | Norfolk City |
| ANDOVER | Wise | BERRYVILLE | Clarke |
| ANNANDALE | Fairfax | BIG ISLAND | Bedford |
| APPALACHIA | Wise | BIG ROCK | Buchanan |
| APPOMATTOX | Appomattox | BIG STONE GAP | Wise |
| ARARAT | Patrick | BIRCHLEAF | Dickenson |
| ARCOLA | Loudoun | BIRDSNEST | Northampton |
| ARK | Gloucester | BISHOP | Tazewell |
| ARLINGTON | Arlington | BLACKRIDGE | Mecklenburg |
| AVODA | Madison | BLACKSBURG | Montgomery |
| ARRINGTON | Nelson | BLACKSTONE | Nottoway |

| | | | |
|---|---|---|---|
| BLACKWATER | Lee | CAPE CHARLES | Northampton |
| BLACWATER BRIDGE | Virginia | CAPE HENRY | Virginia |
| BLAIRS | Pittsylvania | CAPEVILLE | Northampton |
| BLAKES | Mathews | CAPRON | Southampton |
| BLAND | Bland | CARDINAL | Mathews |
| BLOXOM | Accomack | CARET | Essex |
| BLUEFIELD | Tazewell | CARROLLTON | Isle Of Wright |
| BLUE GRASS | Highland | CARRSVILLE | Isle Of Wright |
| BLUEMONT | Loudoun | CARSON | Dinwiddie |
| BLUE RIDGE | Botetourt | CARTERSVILLE | Cumberland |
| BOHANNON | Mathews | CASANOVA | Fauquier |
| BOISSEVAIN | Tazewell | CASCADE | Pittsylvania |
| BOLAR | Bath | CASHS CORNER | Orange |
| BON AIR | Richmond City | CASTLETON | Rappahannock |
| BOONES MILL | Franklin | CASTLEWOOD | Russell |
| BOONESVILLE | Greene | CATAWBA | Roanoke |
| BOSTON | Culpeper | CATHARPIN | Prince William |
| BOWERS HILL | Chesapeake | CATLETT | Fauquier |
| BOWLING GREEN | Caroline | CAUTHORNVILLE | King And Queen |
| BOYCE | Clarke | CEDAR BLUFF | Tazewell |
| BOYDTON | Mecklenburg | CENTER CROSS | Essex |
| BRANCHVILLE | Southampton | CENTRAL | Richmond City |
| BRANDY STATION | Culpeper | CENTREVILLE | Fairfax |
| BREAKS | Dickenson | CERES | Bland |
| BREMO BLUFF | Fluvanna | CHAMPLAIN | Essex |
| BRIDGEWATER | Rockingham | CHANCE | Essex |
| BRODNAX | Brunswick | CHANTILLY | Fairfax |
| BROOKE | Stafford | CHARLES CITY | Charles City |
| BROOKNEAL | Campbell | CHARLOTTESVILLE | Charlottesville |
| BROWNSBURG | Rockbridge | CHASE CITY | Mecklenburg |
| BROWNTOWN | Warren | CHATHAM | Pittsylvania |
| BRUCETOWN | Frederick | CHECK | Floyd |
| BRUINGTON | King And Queen | CHERITON | Northampton |
| BUCHANAN | Botetourt | CHESAPEAKE | Chesapeake |
| BUCKINGHAM | Buckingham | CHESTER | Chesterfield |
| BUCKROE BEACH | Hampton City | CHESTERFIELD | Chesterfield |
| BUENA VISTA | Buena Vista City | CHESTER GAP | Rappahannock |
| BUFFALO JUNCTION | Mecklenburg | CHILHOWIE | Smyth |
| BUMPASS | Louisa | CHINCOTEAGUE | Accomack |
| BURGESS | Northumberland | CHRISTCHURCH | Middlesex |
| BURKE | Fairfax | CHRISTIANSBURG | Montgomery |
| BURKES GARDEN | Tazewell | CHURCH ROAD | Dinwiddie |
| BURKEVILLE | Nottoway | CHURCH VIEW | Middlesex |
| BURNLEYS | Orange | CHURCHVILLE | Augusta |
| BURR HILL | Orange | CISMONT | Albemarle |
| BYBEE | Fluvanna | CLAREMONT | Surry |
| CALLANDS | Pittsylvania | CLARKSVILLE | Mecklenburg |
| CALLAO | Northumberland | CLAUDVILLE | Patrick |
| CALLAWAY | Franklin | CLEAR BROOK | Frederick |
| CALVERTON | Fauquier | CLEVELAND | Russell |
| CAMBRIA | Montgomery | CLIFFORD | Amherst |
| CAMPBELL | Albemarle | CLIFTON | Fairfax |
| CANA | Carroll | CLIFTON FORGE | Clifton Forge |

| | | | |
|---|---|---|---|
| CLINCHCO | Dickenson | DANVILLE | Danville City |
| CLINCHPORT | Scott | DARLINGTON HEIGHTS | Prince Edward |
| CLINTWOOD | Dickerson | DAVENPORT | Buchanan |
| CLOVER | Halifax | DAVIS WHARF | Accomack |
| CLOVERDALE | Botetourt | DAYTON | Rockingham |
| CLUSTER SPRINGS | Halifax | DE BREE | Norfolk City |
| COBBS CREEK | Mathews | DEEP CREEK | Chesapeake |
| COBHAM | Albermarle | DEERFIELD | Augusta |
| COEBURN | Wise | DELAPLANE | Fauquier |
| COLEMAN FALLS | Bedford | DELTAVILLE | Middlesex |
| COLES POINT | Westmoreland | DENBIGH | Newport News City |
| COLLINSVILLE | Henry | DENDRON | Surry |
| COLOGNE | Mathews | DEWTT | Dinwiddie |
| COLONIAL BEACH | Westmoreland | DIGGS | Mathews |
| COLONIAL HEIGHTS | Colonial Heights | DILLWYN | Buckingham |
| COLONIAL WILLIAMSBURG | York | DINWIDDIE | Dinwiddie |
| COLUMBIA | Fluvanna | DISPUTANTA | Prince George |
| COMMUNITY | Alexandria | DOE HILL | Highland |
| CONAWAY | Buchanan | DOGUE | King George |
| CONCORD | Campbell | DOLPHIN | Brunswick |
| CONICVILLE | Shenandoah | DORAN | Tazewell |
| COPPER HILL | Floyd | DOSWELL | Hanover |
| CORBIN | Caroline | DRAKES BRANCH | Charlotte |
| COURTLAND | Southampton | DRAPER | Pulaski |
| COVESVILLE | Albemarle | DREWRYVILLE | Southampton |
| COVINGTON | Covington City | DRIVER | Suffolk City |
| CRADDOCKVILLE | Accomack | DRYDEN | Lee |
| CRADOCK | Portsmouth | DRY FORK | Pittsylvania |
| CRAIGSVILLE | Augusta | DUBLIN | Pulaski |
| CREWE | Nottoway | DUFFIELD | Scott |
| CRIDERS | Rockingham | DUGSPUR | Carroll |
| CRIGLERSVILLE | Madison | DUMFRIES | Prince William |
| CRIMORA | Augusta | DUNDAS | Lunenburg |
| CRIPPLE CREEK | Wythe | DUNGANNON | Scott |
| CRITTENDEN | Suffolk City | DUNN LORING | Fairfax |
| CRITZ | Patrick | DUNNSVILLE | Essex |
| CROCKETT | Wythe | DUTTON | Gloucester |
| CROSS JUNCTION | Frederick | DYKE | Greene |
| CROZET | Albemarle | EADS | Arlington |
| CROZIER | Goochland | EAGLE ROCK | Botetourt |
| CRYSTAL CITY | Arlington | EARLYSVILLE | Albemarle |
| CRYSTAL HILL | Halifax | EAST STONE GAP | Wise |
| CULLEN | Charlette | EASTVILLE | Northampton |
| CULPEPER | Culpeper | EBONY | Brunswick |
| CUMBERLAND | Cumberland | EDINBURG | Shenandoah |
| CUNNINGHAM | Fluvanna | EDWARDSVILLE | Northumberland |
| DABNEYS | Louisa | EGGLESTON | Giles |
| DAHLGREN | King George | EHEART | Orange |
| DALE CITY | Prince Williams | ELBERON | Surry |
| DALEVILLE | Botetourt | ELK CREEK | Grayson |
| DAMASCUS | Washington | ELKTON | Rockingham |
| DAM NECK | Virginia Beach | ELKWOOD | Culpeper |
| DANTE | Russell | ELLISTON | Roanoke |

| | | | |
|---|---|---|---|
| EMORY | Washington | FRIES | Grayson |
| EMPORIA | Emporia City | FRONT ROYAL | Warren |
| ENGLESIDE | Alexandria | FULKS RUN | Rockingham |
| ESMONT | Albemarle | GAINESVILLE | Prince William |
| ETLAN | Madison | GALAX | Galax City |
| ETTRICK | Petersburg | GARRISONVILLE | Stafford |
| EVERGREEN | Appomattox | GASBURG | Brunswick |
| EVINGTON | Campbell | GATE CITY | Scott |
| EWING | Franklin | GEORGE WASHINGTON | Alexandria |
| EXETER | Wise | GLADEHILL | Franklin |
| EXMORE | Northampton | GLADE SPRING | Washington |
| FABER | Nelson | GLADSTONE | Nelson |
| FAIRFAX | Faixfax City | GLADYS | Campbell |
| FAIRFIELD | Rockbridge | GLASGOW | Rockridge |
| FAIRLAWN | Radford | GLEN ALLEN | Henrico |
| FALLS CHURCH | Falls Church | GLEN LYN | Giles |
| FALLS MILLS | Tazewell | GLEN WILTON | Botetourt |
| FANCY GAP | Carroll | GLOUCESTER | Gloucester |
| FARMVILLE | Prince Edward | GLOUCESTER POINT | Gloucester |
| FARNHAM | Richmond | GOLDBOND | Giles |
| FENTRESS | Chesapeake | GOLDVEIN | Fauquier |
| FERRUM | Franklin | GOOCHLAND | Goochland |
| FIELDALE | Henry | GOODE | Bedford |
| FIFE | Goochland | GOODVIEW | Bedford |
| FINCASTLE | Botetourt | GORDONSVILLE | Orange |
| FISHERS HILL | Shenandoah | GORE | Frederick |
| FISHERSVILLE | Augusta | GOSHEN | Rockbridge |
| FLEET | Norfolk | GRAVES MILL | Madison |
| FLINT HILL | Rappahannock | GREAT BRIDGE | Cheesapeake |
| FLOYD | Floyd | GREAT FALLS | Fairfax |
| FONESWOOD | Richmond | GREENBACKVILLE | Accomack |
| FORD | Dinwiddie | GREEN BAY | Prince Edward |
| FOREST | Bedford | GREENBUSH | Accomack |
| FOREST HILL | Richmond City | GREEN SPRINGS | Orange |
| FORK UNION | Fluvanna | GREENVILLE | Augusta |
| FORT BELVOIR | Fairfax | GREENWOOD | Albemarle |
| FORT BLACKMORE | Scott | GRETNA | Pittsylvania |
| FORT DEFIANCE | Augusta | GRIMSTEAD | Mathews |
| FORT EUSTIS | Newport News City | GROTTOES | Rockingham |
| FORT HILL | Lynchburg City | GRUNDY | Buchanan |
| FORT LEE | Petersburg City | GUM SPRING | Louisa |
| FORT MITCHELL | Lunenburg | GWYNN | Mathews |
| FORT MYER | Arlington | HACKSNECK | Accomack |
| FORT STORY | Virginia Beach | HADENSVILLE | Goochland |
| FORT VALLEY | Shenandoah | HAGUE | Westmoreland |
| FOSTER | Mathews | HALIFAX | Halifax |
| FOSTERS FALLS | Wythe | HALLIEFORD | Mathews |
| FRANCONIA | Alexandria | HALLWOOD | Accomack |
| FRANKLIN | Franklin City | HAMILTON | Loudoun |
| FRANKTOWN | Northampton | HAMPDEN SYDNEY | Prince Edward |
| FREDERICKSBURG | Spotsylvania | HAMPTON | Hampton City |
| FREEMAN | Brunswick | HANDSOM | Southampton |
| FREE UNION | Albermarle | HANOVER | Hanover |

| | | | |
|---|---|---|---|
| HARBORGON | Accomack | JARRATT | Sussex |
| HARDY | Bedford | JAVA | Pittsylvania |
| HARDYVILLE | Middlesex | JEFFERSON MANOR | Alexandria |
| HARMAN | Buchanan | JEFFERSONTON | Culpeper |
| HARRISONBURG | Harrisonburg City | JENKINS BRIDGE | Accomack |
| HARTFIELD | Middlesex | JERSEY | King George |
| HARTWOOD | Stafford | JETERSVILLE | Amelia |
| HAYES | Gloucester | JEWELL RIDGE | Tazwell |
| HAYMARKET | Prince William | JEWELL VALLEY | TazweH |
| HAYNESVILLE | Richmond | JOLLIFF | Chesapeake |
| HAYSI | Dickenson | JONESVILLE | Lee |
| HAYWOOD | Madison | JORDAN MINES | Allegany |
| HEAD WATERS | Highland | KEELING | Pittsylvania |
| HEATHSVILLE | Northumberland | KEENE | Albemarle |
| HENRY | Franklin | KEEN MOUNTAIN | Buchanan |
| HERNDON | Fairfax | KEEZLETOWN | Rockingham |
| HIDENWOOD | Newport News City | KELLER | Accomack |
| HIGHLAND SPRINGS | Henrico | KENBRIDGE | Lunenburg |
| HIGHTOWN | Highland | KENTS STORE | Fluvanna |
| HILLSVILLE | Carroll | KEOKEE | Lee |
| HILLTOP-OCEANA | Virginia Beach | KESWICK | Albemarle |
| HILTONS | Scott | KEYSVILLE | Charlotte |
| HINTON | Rockingham | KILMARNOCK | Lancaster |
| HIWASSEE | Pulaski | KING GEORGE | King George |
| HOLLINS COLLEGE | Roanoke | KING WILLIAM | King William |
| HONAKER | Russell | KINSALE | Westmoreland |
| HOOD | Madison | LACEY SPRING | Rockingham |
| HOPEWELL | Hopewell City | LACKEY | York |
| HORNTOWN | Accomack | LA CROSSE | Mecklenburg |
| HORSEPEN | Tazewell | LADYSMITH | Caroline |
| HORSEY | Accomack | LAHORE | Orange |
| HOT SPRINGS | Bath | LAKESIDE | Richmond |
| HUDDLESTON | Bedford | LAMSBURG | Carroll |
| HUDGINS | Mathews | LANCASTER | Lancaster |
| HUME | Fauquier | LANEVIEW | Essex |
| HUNTLY | Rappahannock | LANEXA | New Kent |
| HURLEY | Buchanan | LANGLEY AFB | Hampton City |
| HURT | Pittsylvania | LAUREL FORK | Carroll |
| HUSTLE | Essex | LAWRENCEVILLE | Brunswick |
| HYACINTH | Northumberland | LEBANON | Russell |
| INDEPENDENCE | Grayson | LEE MONT | Accomack |
| INDIAN RIVER | Chesapeake | LEESBURG | Loudoun |
| INDIAN VALLEY | Floyd | LEON | Madison |
| IRON GATE | Alleghany | LEWISETTA | Northumberland |
| IRVINGTON | Lancaster | LEXINGTON | Lexington City |
| ISLE OF WRIGHT | Isle Of Wright | LIGHTFOOT | James City |
| IVANHOE | Wythe | LIGNUM | Culpeper |
| IVOR | Southampton | LINCOLN | Loudoun |
| IVY | Albemarle | LINDEN | Warren |
| JAMAICA | Middlesex | LINVILLE | Rockingham |
| JAMES STORE | Floucester | LITTLE PLYMOUTH | King And Queen |
| JAMESTOWN | James City | LIVELY | Lancaster |
| JAMESVILLE | Northampton | LOCUST DALE | Madison |

| | | | |
|---|---|---|---|
| LOCUST GROVE | Orange | MEARS | Accomack |
| LOCUST HILL | Middlesex | MECHANICSVILLE | Hanover |
| LOCUSTVILLE | Accomack | MEHERRIN | Prince Edward |
| LONG ISLAND | Campbell | MELFA | Accomack |
| LORETTO | Essex | MELTON | Gordonsville |
| LORTON | Fairfax | MENDOTA | Washington |
| LOTTSBURG | Northumberland | MEREDITHVILLE | Brunswick |
| LOUISA | Louisa | MERRIFIELD | Fairfax |
| LOVETTSVILLE | Loudoun | MERRY POINT | Lancaster |
| LOVINGSTON | Nelson | MIDDLEBROOK | Augusta |
| LOWESVILLE | Amherst | MIDDLEBURG | Loudoun |
| LOWMOOR | Allegany | MIDDLETOWN | Frederick |
| LOWRY | Bedford | MIDLAND | Fauquier |
| LUNENBURG | Lunenburg | MIDLOTHIAN | Chesterfield |
| LURAY | Page | MILAN | Norfolk City |
| LYNCHBURG | Lynchburg City | MILES | Mathews |
| LYNCH STATION | Campbell | MILFORD | Caroline |
| LYNDHURST | Augusta | MILLBORO | Bath |
| MACHIPONGO | Northampton | MILLBORO SPRING | Millboro |
| MACON | Powhatan | MILLER PARK | Lynchburg City |
| MADISON | Madison | MILLERS TAVERN | Essex |
| MADISON HEIGHTS | Amherst | MILLWOOD | Clarke |
| MADISON MILLS | Madison | MINERAL | Ijouisa |
| MAIDENS | Goochland | MINE RUN | Orange |
| MANAKIN SABOT | Goochland | MINT SPRINGS | Augusta |
| MANASSAS | Manassas City | MISSION HOME | Albemarle |
| MANASSAS PARK | Manassas City | MITCHELLS | Culpeper |
| MANGOHICK | King William | MOBJACK | Mathews |
| MANNBORO | Amelia | MODEST TOWN | Accomack |
| MANQUIN | King William | MOLLUSK | Lancaster |
| MAPPSVILLE | Accomack | MONETA | Bedford |
| MARION | Smyth | MONROE | Amherst |
| MARIONVILLE | Northampton | MONTEBELLO | Nelson |
| MARKHAM | Fauquier | MONTERY | Highland |
| MARSHALL | Fauquier | MONTEVIDO | Rockingham |
| MARTINSVILLE | Martinsville | MONTEZUMA | Dayton |
| MARYUS | Gloucester | MONTICELLO | Charlottesville |
| MASCOT | King And Queen | MONTPELIER | Hanover |
| MASSIES MILL | Nelson | MONTPELIER STATION | Orange |
| MATHEWS | Mathews | MONTROSE HEIGHTS | Richmond City |
| MATTAPONI | King And Queen | MONTROSS | Westmoreland |
| MAURERTOWN | Shenandoah | MONTVALE | Bedford |
| MAVISDALE | Buchanan | MOON | Mathews |
| MAXIE | Buchanan | MORATTICO | Lancaster |
| MAX MEADOWS | Wythe | MORRISVILLE | Fauquier |
| MC CLURE | Dickenson | MOSELEY | Powhattan |
| MC COY | Montgomery | MOUNT CRAWFORD | Rockingham |
| MC DOWELL | Highland | MOUNT HOLLY | Westmoreland |
| MC GAHEYSVILLE | Rockingham | MOUNT JACKSON | Shenandoah |
| MC KENNEY | Dinwiddie | MOUNT SIDNEY | Augusta |
| MC LEAN | Fairfax | MOUNT SOLON | Augusta |
| MEADOWS OF DAN | Patrick | MOUNT VERNON | Fairfax |
| MEADOWVIEW | Washington | MOUTH OF WILSON | Grayson |

| | | | |
|---|---|---|---|
| MUSTOE | Highland | ONANCOCK | Accomack |
| NARROWS | Giles | ONEMO | Mathews |
| NARUNA | Campbell | ONLEY | Accomack |
| NASSAWADOX | Northampton | OPHELIA | Northumberland |
| NATHALIE | Halifax | ORANGE | Orange |
| NATURAL BRIDGE | Rockbridge | ORDINARY | Gloucester |
| NATURAL BRIDGE STATION | Rockbridge | ORISKANY | Botetourt |
| NAVAL AIR STATION | Norfolk City | ORISKNEY SPRINGS | Shenandoah |
| NAVAL AMPHIBIOUS BASE | Norfolk | ORLEAN | Fauquier |
| NAXERA | Gloucester | OYSTER | Northampton |
| NELLYSFORD | Nelson | PAEONIAN SPRINGS | Loudoun |
| NELSON | Mecklenburg | PAINT BANK | Craig |
| NELSONIA | Accomack | PAINTER | Accomack |
| NEWBERN | Pulaski | PALMYRA | Fluvanna |
| NEW CANTON | Buckingham | PAMPLIN | Appomattox |
| NEW CASTLE | Craig | PARK | Waynesboro City |
| NEWCOMBE HALL | Charlottesville | PARKFAIRFAX | Alexandria City |
| NEW CHURCH | Accomack | PARIS | Fauquier |
| NEW HOPE | Augusta | PARKSLEY | Accomack |
| NEWINGTON | Fairfax | PARROTT | Pulaski |
| NEW KENT | New Kent | PARTLOW | Spotsylvania |
| NEW MARKET | Shenadoah | PATRICK SPRINGS | Patrick |
| NEW POINT | Mathews | PATTERSON | Buchanan |
| NEWPORT | Giles | PEARISBURG | Giles |
| NEWPORT NEWS | Independent City | PEMBROKE | Giles |
| NEW RIVER | Pulaski | PENHOOK | Franklin |
| NEWSOMS | Southampton | PENNINGTON GAP | Lee |
| NEWTOWN | King And Queen | PENN LAIRD | Rockingham |
| NICKELSVILLE | Scott | PETERSBURG | Independent City |
| NINDE | King George | PHENIX | Charlotte |
| NOKESVILLE | Prince William | PHILOMONT | Loudoun |
| NOMINI GROVE | Westmoreland | PHOEBUS | Hampton City |
| NORA | Dickerson | PILGRIMS KNOB | Buchanan |
| NORFOLK | Independent City | PILOT | Montogomery |
| NORGE | James City | PINERO | Gloucester |
| NORTH | Mathews | PINEY RIVER | Nelson |
| NORTH GARDEN | Albermarle | PITTSVILLE | Pittsylvania |
| NORTHSIDE | Richmond City | PLAIN VIEW | King And Queen |
| NORTH TAZEWELL | Tazewell | PLEASANT VALLEY | Rockingham |
| NORTON | Independent City | POCAHONTAS | Tazewell |
| NORTONSVILLE | Dyke | POQUOSAN | Hampton City |
| NORWOOD | Nelson | PORT HAYWOOD | Mathews |
| NOTTOWAY | Nottoway | PORTLOCK | Cheseapeake |
| NUTTSVILLE | Lancaster | PORT REPUBLIC | Rockingham |
| OAK HALL | Accomack | PORT ROYAL | Caroline |
| OAKPARK | Madison | PORTSIDE | Portsmouth City |
| OAKTON | Fairfax | PORTSMOUTH | Portsmouth City |
| OAKWOOD | Buchanan | POUND | Wise |
| OCCOQUAN | Prince William | POUNDING MILL | Tazewell |
| OCEANA NAVAL AIR STATION | Virginia | POWHATAN | Powhatan |
| OCEANVIEW | Norfolk City | PRATTS | Madison |
| OILVILLE | Goochland | PRESTON KING | Arlington |
| OLDHAMS | Westmoreland | PRINCE GEORGE | Prince George |

| | | | |
|---|---|---|---|
| PROSPECT | Prince Edward | ROSEDALE | Russell |
| PROVIDENCE FORGE | New Kent | ROSE HILL | Lee |
| PULASKI | Pulaski | ROSELAND | Nelson |
| PUNGOTEAGUE | Accomack | ROUND HILL | Loudoun |
| PURCELLVILLE | Loudoun | ROWE | Buchanan |
| QUANTICO | Prince William | RUBY | Stafford |
| QUICKSBURG | Shenandoah | RUCKERSVILLE | Greene |
| QUINBY | Accomack | RURAL RETREAT | Wythe |
| QUINQUE | Greene | RUSTBURG | Campbell |
| QUINTON | New Kent | RUTHER GLEN | Caroline |
| RACCOON FORD | Culpepper | RUTHVILLE | Charles City |
| RADFORD | Radford City | SAINT CHARLES | Lee |
| RADIANT | Madison | SAINT DAVIDS CHURCH | Shenandoah |
| RANDOLPH | Charlotte | SAINT PAUL | Wise |
| RAPHEU | Rockbridge | SAINT STEPHENS CHURCH | King And Queen |
| RAPIDAN | Culpeper | SALEM | Salem |
| RAPPAHANNOCK ACADEMY | Caroline | SALTVILLE | Smyth |
| RAVEN | Tazewell | SALUDA | Middlesex |
| RAWLINGS | Brunswick | SANDSTON | Henrico |
| RECTORTOWN | Fauquier | SAND HOOK | Goochland |
| REDART | Mathews | SANDY LEVEL | Pittsylvania |
| RED ASH | Tazewell | SANFORD | Accomack |
| RED HOUSE | Charlotte | SAXE | Charlotte |
| RED OAK | Charlotte | SAXIS | Accomack |
| REDWOOD | Franklin | SCHLEY | Gloucester |
| REEDVILLE | Northumberland | SCHUYLER | Nelson |
| REGINA | Lancaster | SCOTTSBURG | Halifax |
| RELIANCE | Warren | SCOTTSVILLE | Albemarle |
| REMINGTON | Fauquier | SEAFORD | York |
| REPUBLICAN GROVE | Halifax | SEALSTON | King George |
| RESCUE | Isle Of Wight | SEAVIEW | Northampton |
| REVA | Culpeper | SEDLEY | Southampton |
| RHOADESVILLE | Orange | SELMA | Alleghany |
| RICE | Prince Edward | SEVEN FOUNTAINS | Shenandoah |
| RICHARDSVILLE | Culpeper | SEVEN MILE FORD | Smyth |
| RICH CREEK | Giles | SEVERN | Gloucester |
| RICHLANDS | Tazewell | SHACKLEFORDS | King And Queen |
| RICHMOND | Richmond City | SHADOW | Mathews |
| RIDGEWAY | Henry | SHADWELL | Albemarle |
| RILEYVILLE | Page | SHANGHAI | King & Queen |
| RINER | Montgomery | SHARPS | Richmond |
| RINGGOLD | Pittsylvania | SHAWSVILLE | Montgomery |
| RIPPLEMEAD | Giles | SHELBY | Madison |
| RIVERTON | Warren | SHENANDOAH | Page |
| RIXEYVILLE | Culpeper | SHILOH | King George |
| ROANOKE | Roanoke City | SHIPMAN | Nelson |
| ROCHELLE | Madison | SINGERS GLEN | Rockingham |
| ROCKBRIDGE BATHS | Rockbridge | SKIPPERS | Greensville |
| ROCKFISH | Nelson | SKIPWITH | Mecklenburg |
| ROCKVILLE | Hanover | SMITHFIELD | Isle Of Wight |
| ROCKY GAP | Bland | SOMERSET | Orange |
| ROCKY MOUNT | Franklin | SOMERVILLE | Fauquier |
| ROLLINS FORK | King George | SOUTH BOSTON | Independent City |

*Appendix*

| | | | |
|---|---|---|---|
| SOUTH HILL | Mecklenburg | THE PLAINS | Fauquier |
| SPARTA | Caroline | THORNBURG | Spotsylvania |
| SPEEDWELL | Wythe | TIMBERVILLE | Rockingham |
| SPENCER | Henry | TIPTOP | Tazewell |
| SPERRYVILLE | Rappahannock | TOANO | James City |
| SPOTSYLVANIA | Spotsylvania | TOMS BROOK | Shenandoah |
| SPOTTSWOOD | Augusta | TOPPING | Middlesex |
| SPOUT SPRING | Appomattox | TOWNSEND | Northampton |
| SPRINGFIELD | Fairfax | TRAMMEL | Dickenson |
| SPRING GROVE | Surry | TRIANGLE | Prince William |
| STAFFORD | Stafford | TROUT DALE | Grayson |
| STAFFORDSVILLE | Giles | TROUTVILLE | Botetourt |
| STANARDSVILLE | Greene | TROY | Fluvanna |
| STANLEY | Page | TURBEVILLE | Halifax |
| STANLEYTOWN | Henry | UNION HALL | Franklin |
| STAR TANNERY | Frederick | UNION LEVEL | Mechlenburg |
| STATE FARM | Goochland | UNIONVILLE | Orange |
| STAUNTON | Independent City | UPPERVILLE | Fauquier |
| STEELES TAVERN | Augusta | URBANNA | Middlesex |
| STEPHENS CITY | Frederick | VALENTINES | Brunseick |
| STEPHENSON | Frederick | VANSANT | Buchanan |
| STERLING | Loudoun | VERNON HILL | Halifax |
| STEVENSBURG | Culpeper | VERONA | Augusta |
| STEVENSVILLE | King And Queen | VESTA | Patrick |
| STONEGA | Wise | VESUVIUS | Rockbridge |
| STONY CREEK | Sussex | VICTORIA | Lunenburg |
| STRASBURG | Shenandoah | VIENNA | Fairfax |
| STRATFORD | Westmoreland | VIEWTOWN | Rappahannock |
| STUART | Patrick | VILLAGE | Richmond |
| SUTARTS DRAFT | Augusta | VILLAMONT | Bedford |
| STUDLEY | Hanover | VINTON | Roanoke |
| SUFFOLK | Independent City | VIRGILINA | Halifax |
| SUGAR GROVE | Smyth | VIRGINIA BEACH | Virginia Beach |
| SUMERDUCK | Fauquier | VOLNEY | Grayson |
| SUPPLY | Essex | WACHAPREAGUE | Accomack |
| SURRY | Surry | WAKE | Middlesex |
| SUSAN | Mathews | WAKEFIELD | Sussex |
| SUSSEX | Sussex | WALKERTON | King And Queen |
| SUTHERLAND | Dinwiddie | WARDTOWN | Northampton |
| SUTHERLIN | Pittsylvania | WARE NECK | Gloucester |
| SWEET BRIAR | Aznherst | WARFIELD | Brunswick |
| SWOOPE | Augusta | WARM SPRINGS | Bath |
| SWORDS CREEK | Russell | WARNER | Middlesex |
| SYRIA | Madison | WARRENTON | Fauquier |
| SYRINGA | Middlesex | WARSAW | Richmond |
| TAMWORTH | Cartersville | WASHINGTON | Rappahannock |
| TANGIER | Accomack | WATERFORD | Loudoun |
| TANNERSVILLE | Tazewell | WATER VIEW | Middlesex |
| TAPPAHANNOCK | Essex | WATTSVILLE | Accomack |
| TASLEY | Accomack | WAVERLY | Sussex |
| TAZEWELL | Tazewell | WAYNESBORO | Independent City |
| TEMPERANCEVILLE | Accomack | WEEMS | Lancaster |
| THAXTON | Bedford | WEIRWOOD | Northampton |

| | | | |
|---|---|---|---|
| CARLSBORG | Clallam | CURTIS | Lewis |
| CARLTON | Okanogan | CUSICK | Pend Oreille |
| CARNATION | King | CUSTER | Whatcom |
| CARROLLS | Cowlitz | DALLESPORT | Klickitat |
| CARSON | Skamania | DANVILLE | Ferry |
| CASCADE PARK | Clark | DARRINGTON | Snohomish |
| CASHMERE | Chelan | DAVENPORT | Lincoln |
| CASTLE ROCK | Cowlitz | DAYTON | Columbia |
| CATHLAMET | Wahkiakum | DEER HARBOR | San Juan |
| CENTERVILLE | Klickitat | DEER PARK | Spokane |
| CENTRAL | Yakima | DEMING | Whatcom |
| CENTRALIA | Lewis | DES MOINES | King |
| CHATTAROY | Spokane | DISHMAN | Spokane |
| CHEHALIS | Lewis | DIXIE | Walla Walla |
| CHELAN | Chelan | DOTY | Lewis |
| CHELAN FALLS | Chelan | DRYDEN | Chelan |
| CHENEY | Spokane | DU PONT | Pierce |
| CHEWELAH | Stevens | DUVALL | King |
| CHIMACUM | Jefferson | EAST OLYMPIA | Thurston |
| CHINOOK | Pacific | EASTON | Kittitas |
| CINEBAR | Lewis | EASTSOUND | San Juan |
| CLALLAM BAY | Clallam | EAST UNION | King |
| CLAREMONT | Snohomish | EAST WENATCHEE | Chelan |
| CLARKSTON | Asotin | EATONVILLE | Pierce |
| CLAYTON | Stevens | EDMONDS | Snohomish |
| CLEARLAKE | Skagit | EDWALL | Lincoln |
| CLE ELUM | Kittitas | ELBE | Pierce |
| CLINTON | Island | ELECTRIC CITY | Grant |
| COLBERT | Spokane | ELK | Spokane |
| COLFAX | Whitman | ELLENSBURG | Kittitas |
| COLLEGE | Whitman | ELMA | Grays Harbor |
| COLLEGE PLACE | Walla Walla | ELMER CITY | Okanogan |
| COLTON | Whitman | ELTOPIA | Franklin |
| COLUMBIA | King | ENDICOTT | Whitman |
| COLUMBIA CENTER | King | ENTIAT | Chelan |
| COLVILLE | Stevens | ENUMCLAW | King |
| CONCONULLY | Okanogan | EPHRATA | Grant |
| CONCRETE | Skagit | ESPANOLA | Spokane |
| CONNELL | Franklin | ETHEL | Lewis |
| CONWAY | Skagit | EVANS | Stevens |
| COOK | Klickitat | EVERETT | Snohomish |
| COPALIS BEACH | Grays Harbor | EVERGREEN | Pierce |
| COPALIS CROSSING | Grays Harbor | EVERSON | Whatcom |
| COSMOPOLIS | Grays Harbor | FACTORIA | King |
| COUGAR | Cowlitz | FAIRCHILD AFB | Spokane |
| COULEE CITY | Grant | FAIRFIELD | Spokane |
| COULEE DAM | Okanogan | FAIRHAVEN | Whatcom |
| COUPEVILLE | Island | FALL CITY | King |
| COWICHE | Yakima | FARMINGTON | Whitman |
| CRESTON | Lincoln | FEDERAL WAY | King |
| CROSSROADS | King | FERNDALE | Whatcom |
| CUNNINGHAM | Adams | FERN HILL | Pierce |
| CURLEW | Ferry | FIFE | Pierce |

| | | | |
|---|---|---|---|
| FIRCREST | Pierce | HUNTERS | Stevens |
| FORD | Stevens | HUSUM | Klickitat |
| FORKS | Clallam | ILWACO | Pacific |
| FORT LEWIS | Pierce | INCHELIUM | Ferry |
| FORT STEILACOOM | Pierce | INDEX | Snohomish |
| FOUR LAKES | Spokane | INDIANOLA | Kitsap |
| FOX ISLAND | Pierce | INTERNATIONAL | King |
| FREELAND | Island | IONE | Pend Oreille |
| FREEMAN | Spokane | ISSAQUAH | King |
| FRIDAY HARBOR | San Juan | JOYCE | Clallam |
| FRUITLAND | Stevens | KAHLOTUS | Franklin |
| GALVIN | Lewis | KALAMA | Cowlitz |
| GARFIELD | Whitman | KAPOWSIN | Pierce |
| GEORGETOWN | King | KELLER | Ferry |
| GIFFORD | Stevens | KELSO | Cowlitz |
| GIG HARBOR | Pierce | KENMORE | King |
| GLACIER | Whatcom | KENNEWICK | ]3enton |
| GLEED | Yakima | KENT | King |
| GLENOMA | Lewis | KETTLE FALLS | Stevens |
| GLENWOOD | Klickitat | KEYPORT | Kitsap |
| GOLD BAR | Snohomish | KINGSTON | Kitsap |
| GOLDENDALE | Klickitat | KIRKLAND | King |
| GOOSE PRAIRIE | Yakima | KITTITAS | Kittitas |
| GRAHAM | Pierce | KLICKITAT | Klickitat |
| GRAND COULEE | Grant | LA CENTER | Clark |
| GRANDVIEW | Yakima | LACEY | Thurston |
| GRANDVIEW | Clallam | LA CONNER | Skagit |
| GRANGER | Yakima | LACROSSE | Whitman |
| GRANITE FALLS | Snohomish | LA GRANDE | Pierce |
| GRAPEVIEW | Mason | LAKEBAY | Pierce |
| GRAYLAND | Grays Harbor | LAKE CITY | King |
| GRAYS RIVER | Wahkiakum | LAKE STEVENS | Snohomish |
| GREENACRES | Spokane | LAKEWOOD | Snohomish |
| GREENBANK | Island | LAKEWOOD CENTER | Pierce |
| GREENWOOD | King | LAMONA | Lincoln |
| HAMILTON | Skagit | LAMONT | Whitman |
| HANSVILLE | Kitsap | LANGLEY | Island |
| HARRAH | Yakima | LA PUSH | Clallam |
| HARRINGTON | Lincoln | LATAH | Spokane |
| HARTLINE | Grant | LAURIER | Ferry |
| HATTON | Adams | LEAVENWORTH | Chelan |
| HAY | Whitman | LEBAM | Pacific |
| HAYS PARK | Spokane | LIBERTY LAKE | Spokane |
| HAZELDELL | Clark | LIBERTY PARK | Spokane |
| HEISSON | Clark | LILLIWAUP | Mason |
| HIGHLANDS | King | LINCOLN | Lincoln |
| HILLYARD | Spokane | LIND | Adams |
| HOBART | King | LITTLEROCK | Thurston |
| HOME | Pierce | LK FOREST PARK | King |
| HOODSPORT | Mason | LONG BEACH | Pacific |
| HOOPER | Whitman | LONG BRANCH | Pierce |
| HOQUIAM | Grays Harbor | LONGVIEW | Cowlitz |
| HUMPTULIPS | Grays Harbor | LOOMIS | Okanogan |

| | | | |
|---|---|---|---|
| LOON LAKE | Stevens | MOXEE CITY | Yakima |
| LOPEZ | San Juan | MUKILETO | Snohomish |
| LOWDEN | Walla Walla | NACHES | Yakima |
| LUMMI ISLAND | Whatcom | NAHCOTTA | Pacific |
| LYLE | Klickitat | NAPAVINE | Lewis |
| LYMAN | Skagit | NASELLE | Pacific |
| LYNDEN | Whatcom | NEAH BAY | Clallam |
| LYNNWOOD | Snohomish | NEILTON | Grays Harbor |
| MABTON | Yakima | NESPELEM | Okanogan |
| MAGNOLIA | King | NEWMAN LAKE | Spokane |
| MALAGA | Chelan | NEWPORT | Pend Oreille |
| MALDEN | Whitman | NINE MILE FALLS | Spokane |
| MALO | Ferry | NOOKSACK | Whatcom |
| MALONE | Grays Harbor | NORDLAND | Jefferson |
| MALOTT | Okanogan | NORTH BEND | King |
| MANCHESTER | Kitsap | NORTH BONNEVILLE | Skamania |
| MANSFIELD | Douglas | NORTHPORT | Stevens |
| MANSON | Chelan | OAKBROOK | Pierce |
| MAPLE FALLS | Whatcom | OAKESDALE | Whitman |
| MAPLE VALLEY | King | OAK HARBOR | Island |
| MARBLEMOUNT | Skagit | OAKVILLE | Grays Harbor |
| MARCUS | Stevens | OCEAN CITY SHORES | Grays Harbor |
| MARLIN | Grant | OCEAN PARK | Pacific |
| MARSHALL | Spokane | ODESSA | Lincoln |
| MARYSVILLE | Snohomish | OKANOGAN | Okanogan |
| MATLOCK | Mason | OLALLA | Kitsap |
| MATTAWA | Adams | OLGA | San Juan |
| MAZAMA | Okanogan | OLYMPIA | Thurston |
| MCCLEARY | Grays Harbor | OMAK | Okanogan |
| MCKENNA | Pierce | ONALASKA | Lewis |
| MCMILLIN | Pierce | ORCAS | San Juan |
| MEAD | Spokane | ORCHARDS | Clark |
| MEDICAL LAKE | Spokane | ORIENT | Ferry |
| MEDINA | King | ORONDO | Douglas |
| MENLO | Pacific | OROVILLE | Okanogan |
| MERCER ISLAND | King | ORTING | Pierce |
| MESA | Franklin | OTHELLO | Adams |
| METALINE | Pend Oreille | OTIS ORCHARDS | Spokane |
| METALINE FALLS | PendOreille | OUTLOOK | Yakima |
| METHOW | Okanogan | OYSTERVILLE | Pacific |
| MICA | Spokane | PACIFIC BEACH | Grays Harbor |
| MIDWAY | King | PACKWOOD | Lewis |
| MILTON | Pierce | PALISADES | Douglas |
| MINERAL | Lewis | PALOUSE | Whitman |
| MOCLIPS | Grays Harbor | PARKER | Yakima |
| MONITOR | Chelan | PARKLAND | Pierce |
| MONROE | Snohomish | PARKWATER | Spokane |
| MONTESANO | Grays Harbor | PASCO | Franklin |
| MORTON | Lewis | PATEROS | Okanogan |
| MOSES LAKE | Grant | PATERSON | Benton |
| MOSSYROCK | Lewis | PE ELL | Lewis |
| MOUNTLAKE TERRACE | Snohomish | PESHASTIN | Chelan |
| MOUNT VERNON | Skagit | PLYMOUTH | Benton |

| | | | |
|---|---|---|---|
| POINT ROBERTS | Whatcom | SELAH | Yakima |
| POMEROY | Garfield | SEQUIM | Clallam |
| PORT ANGELES | Clallam | SHAW ISLAND | San Juan |
| PORT GAMBLE | Kitsap | SHELTON | Mason |
| PORT ORCHARD | Kitsap | SILVANA | Snohomish |
| PORT TOWNSEND | Jefferson | SILVER CREEK | Lewis |
| POULSBO | Kitsap | SILVERDALE | Kitsap |
| PRESCOTT | Walla Walla | SILVERLAKE | Cowlitz |
| PRESTON | King | SKAMOKAWA | Wahkiakum |
| PROSSER | Benton | SKYKOMISH | King |
| PULLMAN | Whitman | SNOHOMISH | Snohomish |
| PUYALLUP | Pierce | SNOQUALMIE | King |
| QUILCENE | Jefferson | SOAP LAKE | Grant |
| QUINCY | Grant | SOUTH BEND | Pacific |
| QUINAULT | Grays Harbor | SOUTH CLE ELUM | Kittitas |
| RAINIER | Thurston | SOUTH COLBY | Kitsap |
| RANDLE | Lewis | SOUTH PRAIRIE | Pierce |
| RAVENSDALE | King | SOUTHWORTH | Kitsap |
| RAYMOND | Pacific | SPANAWAY | Pierce |
| REARDAN | Lincoln | SPANGLE | Spokane |
| REDMOND | King | SPOKANE | Spokane |
| REDONDO | King | SPRAGUE | Lincoln |
| RENTON | King | SPRINGDALE | Stevens |
| REPUBLIC | Ferry | STANWOOD | Snohomish |
| RETSIL | Kitsap | STARBUCK | Columbia |
| RICE | Stevens | STARTUP | Snohomish |
| RICHLAND | Benton | STEHEKIN | Chelan |
| RIDGEFIELD | Clark | STEPTOE | Whitman |
| RITZVILLE | Adams | STEVENSON | Skamania |
| RIVERSIDE | Okanogan | STRATFORD | Grant |
| ROCHESTER | Thurston | SULTAN | Snohomish |
| ROCKFORD | Spokane | SUMAS | Whatcom |
| ROCK ISLAND | Douglas | SUMNER | Pierce |
| ROCKPORT | Skagit | SUNNYSIDE | Yakima |
| ROLLINGBAY | Kitsap | SUQUAMISH | Kitsap |
| RONALD | Kittias | TACOMA | Pierce |
| ROOSEVELT | Klickitat | TAHOLAH | Grays Harbor |
| ROSALIA | Whitman | TAHUYA | Mason |
| ROSBURG | Wahkiakum | TEKOA | Whitman |
| ROSEWOOD | Spokane | TENINO | Thurston |
| ROSLYN | Kittias | TERRACE HEIGHTS | Yakima |
| ROY | Pierce | THORNTON | Whitman |
| ROYAL CITY | Grant | THORP | Kittitas |
| RYDERWOOD | Cowlitz | TIETON | Yakima |
| SAINT JOHN | Whitman | TILLICUM | Pierce |
| SALKUM | Lewis | TOKELAND | Pacific |
| SATSOP | Grays Harbor | TOLEDO | Lewis |
| SEABECK | Kitsap | TONASKET | Okanogan |
| SEAHURST | King | TOPPENISH | Yakima |
| SEATTLE | King | TOTEM LAKE | King |
| SEAVIEW | Pacific | TOUCHET | Walla Walla |
| SEDRO WOOLLEY | Skagit | TOUTLE | Cowlitz |
| SEKIU | Clallam | TRACYTOWN | Kitsap |

| TRENTWOOD | Spokane | ABRAHAM | Raleigh |
|---|---|---|---|
| TROUT LAKE | Klickitat | ACCOVILLE | Logan |
| TUKWILA | King | ADRIAN | Upshur |
| TUMTUM | Stevens | ADVENT | Jackson |
| TWISP | Okanogan | ALBRIGHT | Preston |
| UNDERWOOD | Skamania | ALDERSON | Monroe |
| UNION | Mason | ALEXANDER | Upshur |
| UNION GAP | Yakima | ALGOMA | McDowell |
| UNIONTOWN | Whitman | ALKOL | Lincoln |
| USK | Pend Oreille | ALLEN JUNCTION | Wyoming |
| VADER | Lewis | ALLOY | Fayette |
| VALLEY | Stevens | ALMA | Tyler |
| VALLEYFORD | Spokane | ALPOCA | Wyoming |
| VANCOUVER | Clark | ALUM BRIDGE | Lewis |
| VANTAGE | Kittitas | ALUM CREEK | Kanawha |
| VASHON | King | ALVY | Tyler |
| VAUGHN | Pierce | AMBOY | Preston |
| VERADALE | Spokane | AMEAGLE | Raleigh |
| WAHKIACUS | Klickitat | AMHERSTDALE | Logan |
| WAITSBURG | Walla Walla | AMIGO | Wyoming |
| WALDRON | San Juan | AMMA | Roane |
| WALLA WALLA | Walla Walla | ANAWALT | McDowell |
| WALLINGFORD | King | ANMOORE | Harrison |
| WALLULA | Walla Walla | ANNAMORIAH | Calhoun |
| WAPATO | Yakima | ANSTED | Fayette |
| WARDEN | Grant | ANTHONY | Greenbrier |
| WASHOUGAL | Clark | APPLE GROVE | Mason |
| WASHTUCNA | Adams | ARBOVALE | Pocahontas |
| WATERVILLE | Douglas | ARBUCKLE | Mason |
| WAUCONDA | Okanogan | ARNETT | Raleigh |
| WAUNA | Pierce | ARNOLDSBURG | Calhoun |
| WAVERLY | Spokane | ARTHUR | Grant |
| WEDGEWOOD | King | ARTHURDALE | Preston |
| WELLPINIT | Stevens | ARTIE | Raleigh |
| WENATCHEE | Chelan | ASBURY | Greenbrier |
| WESTPORT | Grays Harbor | ASCO | McDowell |
| WHITE PASS | Yakima | ASHFORD | Boone |
| WHITE SALMON | Klickitat | ASHLAND | McDowell |
| WHITE SWAN | Yakima | ASHTON | Mason |
| WILBUR | Lincoln | ATHENS | Mercer |
| WILKESON | Pierce | AUBURN | Ritchie |
| WILSON CREEK | Grant | AUGUSTA | Hampshire |
| WINLOCK | Lewis | AURORA | Preston |
| WINTHROP | Okanogan | AUTO | Greenbrier |
| WISHRAM | Klickitat | AVONDALE | McDowell |
| WOODINVILLE | King | BAISDEN | Mingo |
| WOODLAND | Cowlitz | BAKER | Hardy |
| WYCOFF | Kitsap | BAKERTON | Jefferson |
| YACOLT | Clark | BALD KNOB | Boone |
| YAKIMA | Yakima | BALDWIN | Gilmer |
| YELM | Thurston | BALLARD | Monroe |
| ZILLAH | Yakima | BALLENGEE | Sununers |
| **WEST VIRGINIA** ▬▬▬ | | BANCROFT | Putnam |

| | | | |
|---|---|---|---|
| BANDYTOWN | Boone | BOOTH | Monongalia |
| BARBOURSVILLE | Cabell | BORDERLAND | Mingo |
| BARNABUS | Logan | BOWDEN | Randolph |
| BARRACKVILLE | Marion | BOZOO | Monroe |
| BARRETT | Boone | BRADLEY | Raleigh |
| BARTLEY | McDowell | BRADSHAW | McDowell |
| BARTOW | Pocahontas | BRAMWELL | Mercer |
| BAYARD | Grant | BRANCHLAND | Lincoln |
| BEARDS FORK | Fayette | BRANDONVILLE | Preston |
| BEAVER | Raleigh | BRANDYWINE | Pendleton |
| BECKLEY | Raleigh | BREEDEN | Mingo |
| BECKWITH | Fayette | BRENTON | Wyoming |
| BEECH BOTTOM | Brooke | BRETZ | Preston |
| BEESON | Mercer | BRIDGEPORT | Harrison |
| BELINGTON | Barbour | BRISTOL | Harrison |
| BELLE | Kanawha | BROADDUS | Barbour |
| BELLEVILLE | Wood | BROHARD | Wirt |
| BELLVIEW | Marion | BROOKS | Summers |
| BELMONT | Pleasants | BROWNTON | Barbour |
| BELVA | Nicholas | BRUCETON MILLS | Preston |
| BENS RUN | Tyler | BRUNO | Logan |
| BENTREE | Clay | BUCKEYE | Pocahontas |
| BENWOOD | Marshall | BUCKHANNON | Upshur |
| BEREA | Ritchie | BUD | Wyoming |
| BERGOO | Webster | BUFFALO | Putnam |
| BERKLEY SPRINGS | Morgan | BUNKER HILL | Berkeley |
| BERWIND | McDowell | BURLINGTON | Mineral |
| BETHANY | Brooke | BURNSVILLE | Braxton |
| BEVERLY | Randolph | BURNWELL | Kanawha |
| BEVERLY HILLS | Cabell | BURTON | Wetzel |
| BICKMORE | Clay | CABIN CREEK | Kanawha |
| BIGBEND | Calhoun | CABINS | Grant |
| BIG CREEK | Logan | CAIRO | Ritchie |
| BIG OTTER | Clay | CALDWELL | Greenbrier |
| BIG RUN | Wetzel | CALVIN | Nicholas |
| BIG SANDY | McDowell | CAMDEN | Lewis |
| BIG SPRINGS | Calhoun | CAMDEN ON GAULEY | Webster |
| BIM | Boone | CAMERON | Marshall |
| BIRCH RIVER | Nicholas | CAMP CREEK | Mercer |
| BLACKSVILLE | Monongalia | CANEBRAKE | McDowell |
| BLAIR | Logan | CANNELTON | Fayette |
| BLANDVILLE | Doddridge | CANVAS | Nicholas |
| BLOOMERY | Hampshire | CAPELS | McDowell |
| BLOOMINGROSE | Boone | CAPON BRIDGE | Hampshire |
| BLOUNT | Kanawha | CAPON SPRINGS | Hampshire |
| BLUE CREEK | Kanawha | CARBON | Kanawha |
| BLUEFIELD | Mercer | CARETTA | McDowell |
| BLUE JAY | Raleigh | CAROLINA | Marion |
| BOB WHITE | Boone | CASCADE | Preston |
| BOGGS | Webster | CASS | Pocahontas |
| BOLT | Raleigh | CASSVILLE | Monongalia |
| BOMONT | Clay | CEDAR GROVE | Kanawha |
| BOOMER | Fayette | CEDARVILLE | Gilmer |

| | | | |
|---|---|---|---|
| CENTER POINT | Doddridge | CRAB ORCHARD | Raleigh |
| CENTRALIA | Braxton | CRAIGSVILLE | Nicholas |
| CENTURY | Barbour | CRANBERRY | Raleigh |
| CEREDO | Wayne | CRAWFORD | Lewis |
| CHAPMANVILLE | Logan | CRAWLEY | Greenbrier |
| CHARLESTON | Kanawha | CRESTON | Wirt |
| CHARLES TOWN | Jefferson | CRICHTON | Greenbrier |
| CHARLTON HEIGHTS | Fayette | CROSS LANES | Kanawha |
| CHARMCO | Greenbrier | CROWN HILL | Kanawha |
| CHATTAROY | Mingo | CRUM | Wayne |
| CHAUNCEY | Logan | CRUMPLER | McDowell |
| CHERRY GROVE | Pendleton | CUCUMBER | McDowell |
| CHESTER | Hancock | CULLODEN | Cabel |
| CHLOE | Calhoun | CURTIN | Webster |
| CIRCLEVILLE | Pendleton | CUZZART | Preston |
| CLARKSBURG | Harrison | CYCLONE | Wyoming |
| CLAY | Clay | DAILEY | Randolph |
| CLEAR CREEK | Raleigh | DALLAS | Marshall |
| CLEAR FORK | Wyoming | DANESE | Fayette |
| CLEM | Braxton | DANIELS | Raleigh |
| CLENDENIN | Kanawha | DANVILLE | Boone |
| CLEVELAND | Upshur | DAVIN | Logan |
| CLIFFTOP | Fayette | DAVIS | Tucker |
| CLIFTON | Mason | DAVISVILLE | Wood |
| CLINTONVILLE | Greenbrier | DAVY | McDowell |
| CLIO | Roane | DAWES | Kanawha |
| CLOTHIER | Logan | DAWMONT | Harrison |
| COAL CITY | Raleigh | DAWSON | Greenbrier |
| COALDALE | Mercer | DECOTA | Kanawha |
| COAL FORK | Kanawha | DEEP WATER | Fayette |
| COAL MOUNTAIN | Wyoming | DEHUE | Logan |
| COALTON | Randolph | DELBARTON | Mingo |
| COALWOOD | McDowell | DELLSLOW | Monongalia |
| COLCORD | Raleigh | DELRAY | Hampshire |
| COLFAX | Marion | DIANA | Webster |
| COLLIERS | Brooke | DILLIE | Clay |
| COMFORT | Boone | DINGESS | Mingo |
| COOL RIDGE | Raleigh | DIXIE | Nicholas |
| COPEN | Braxton | DORCAS | Grant |
| CORA | Logan | DOROTHY | Raleigh |
| CORE | Monongalia | DOTHAN | Fayette |
| CORINNE | Wyoming | DOTT | Mercer |
| CORINTH | Preston | DRENNEN | Nicholas |
| CORLEY | Braxton | DROOP | Pocahontas |
| CORTON | Kanawha | DRYBRANCH | Kanawha |
| COSTA | Boone | DRY CREEK | Raleigh |
| COTTAGEVILLE | Jackson | DRYFORK | Randolph |
| COTTLE | Nicholas | DUCK | Clay |
| COVE | Hancock | DUHRING | Mercer |
| COVE GAP | Wayne | DUNBAR | Kanawha |
| COVEL | Wyoming | DUNCAN | Jackson |
| COWEN | Webster | DUNLOW | Wayne |
| COXS MILLS | Gilmer | DUNMORE | Pocahontas |

| | | | |
|---|---|---|---|
| DURBIN | Pocahontas | FOLLANSBEE | Brooke |
| EARLING | Logan | FOLSOM | Wetzel |
| EAST BANK | Kanawha | FOREST HILL | Summers |
| EAST BECKLEY | Raleigh | FORT ASHBY | Mineral |
| EAST GULF | Raleigh | FORT GAY | Wayne |
| EAST LYNN | Wayne | FORT NEAL | Wood |
| ECCLES | Raleigh | FORT SEYBERT | Pendleton |
| ECKMAN | McDowell | FORT SPRING | Greenbrier |
| EDGARTON | Mingo | FOSTER | Boone |
| EDMOND | Fayette | FOUR STATES | Marion |
| EGLON | Preston | FRAME | Kanawha |
| ELBERT | McDowell | FRAMETOWN | Braxton |
| ELEANOR | Putnam | FRANKFORD | Greenbrier |
| ELGOOD | Mercer | FRANKLIN | Pendleton |
| ELIZABETH | Wirt | FRAZIERS BOTTOM | Putnam |
| ELK GARDEN | Mineral | FREEMAN | Mercer |
| ELKHORN | McDowell | FRENCH CREEK | Upshur |
| ELKINS | Randolph | FRENCHTON | Upshur |
| ELKVIEW | Kanawha | FRIARS HILL | Greenbrier |
| ELLAMORE | Randolph | FRIENDLY | Tyler |
| ELLENBORO | Ritchie | GALLAGHER | Kanawha |
| ELMIRA | Braxton | GALLIPOLIS FERRY | Mason |
| ELTON | Summers | GALLOWAY | Barbour |
| EMMETT | Logan | GANDEEVILLE | Roane |
| ENGLISH | McDowell | GAP MILLS | Monroe |
| ENTERPRISE | Harrison | GARRISON | Boone |
| ERBACON | Webster | GARY | McDowell |
| ESKDALE | Kanawha | GASSAWAY | Braxton |
| ETHEL | Logan | GAULEY BRIDGE | Fayette |
| EUREKA | Pleasants | GAY | Jackson |
| EVANS | Jackson | GEM | Braxton |
| EVERETTVILLE | Monongalia | GENOA | Wayne |
| EXCHANGE | Braxton | GERRARDSTOWN | Berkeley |
| FAIRDALE | Raleigh | GHENT | Raleigh |
| FAIRMONT | Marion | GILBERT | Mingo |
| FAIRVIEW | Marion | GILBOA | Nicholas |
| FALLING ROCK | Kanawha | GILLIAM | McDowell |
| FALLING WATERS | Berkeley | GILMER | Gilmer |
| FALLS MILL | Braxton | GIVEN | Jackson |
| FANROCK | Wyoming | GLACE | Monroe |
| FARMINGTON | Marion | GLADY | Randolph |
| FAYETTEVILLE | Fayette | GLASGOW | Kanawha |
| FENWICK | Nicholas | GLEN | Clay |
| FERRELLSBURG | Lincoln | GLEN DALE | Marshall |
| FILBERT | McDowell | GLEN DANIEL | Raleigh |
| FISHER | Hardy | GLENDON | Braxton |
| FIVE FORKS | Calhoun | GLEN EASTON | Marshall |
| FLAT TOP | Mercer | GLEN FERRIS | Fayette |
| FLATWOODS | Braxton | GLEN FORK | Wyoming |
| FLEMINGTON | Taylor | GLENGARY | Berkeley |
| FLOE | Clay | GLENHAYES | Wayne |
| FLOWER | Gilmer | GLEN JEAN | Fayette |
| FOLA | Clay | GLEN MORGAN | Raleigh |

| | | | |
|---|---|---|---|
| GLEN ROGERS | Wyoming | HENSLEY | McDowell |
| GLENVILLE | Gilmer | HEPZIBAH | Harrison |
| GLEN WHITE | Raleigh | HERNDON | Wyoming |
| GLENWOOD | Mason | HERNSHAW | Kanawha |
| GORDON | Boone | HEWETT | Boone |
| GORMANIA | Grant | HIAWATHA | Mercer |
| GRAFTON | Taylor | HICO | Fayette |
| GRANTSVILLE | Calhoun | HIGH VIEW | Hampshire |
| GRANT TOWN | Marion | HILLSBORO | Pocahontas |
| GRANVILLE | Monogalia | HILLTOP | Fayette |
| GRASSY MEADOWS | Greenbrier | HINES | Greenbrier |
| GREAT CACAPON | Morgan | HINTON | Summers |
| GREEN BANK | Pocahontas | HOLDEN | Logan |
| GREEN SPRING | Hampshire | HOMETOWN | Putnam |
| GREEN SULPHUR SPRINGS | Summers | HORNER | Lewis |
| GREEN VALLEY | Mercer | HUGHESTON | Kanawha |
| GREENVILLE | Monroe | HUNDRED | Wetzel |
| GREENWOOD | Doddridge | HUNTINGTON | Cabell |
| GRIFFITHSVILLE | Lincoln | HURRICANE | Putnam |
| GRIMMS LANDING | Mason | HUTTONSVILLE | Randolph |
| GUARDIAN | Webster | IAEGER | McDowell |
| GYPSY | Harrison | IDAMAY | Marion |
| HACKER VALLEY | Webster | IKES FORK | Wyoming |
| HALLTOWN | Jefferson | INDEPENDENCE | Preston |
| HAMBLETON | Tucker | INDIAN MILLS | Summers |
| HAMLIN | Lincoln | INDORE | Clay |
| HAMPDEN | Mingo | INDUSTRIAL | Harrison |
| HANCOCK | Morgan | INSTITUTE | Kanawha |
| HANDLEY | Kanawha | INWOOD | Berkeley |
| HANOVER | Wyoming | IRELAND | Lewis |
| HANSFORD | Kanawha | ISABAN | McDowell |
| HARMAN | Randolph | ITMANN | Wyoming |
| HARMONY | Roane | IVYDALE | Clay |
| HARPER | Raleigh | JACKSONBURG | Wetzel |
| HARPERS FERRY | Jefferson | JANE LEW | Lewis |
| HARRISON | Clay | JEFFREY | Boone |
| HARRISVILLE | Ritchie | JENKINJONES | McDowell |
| HARTFORD | Mason | JESSE | Wyoming |
| HARTS | Lincoln | JODIE | Fayette |
| HARVEY | Fayette | JOLO | McDowell |
| HAVACO | McDowell | JONBEN | Raleigh |
| HAYWOOD | Harrison | JONES SPRINGS | Hedgeville |
| HAZELGREEN | Ritchie | JORDAN | Fairmont |
| HAZELTON | Preston | JOSEPHINE | Raleigh |
| HEATERS | Braxton | JULIAN | Boone |
| HEBRON | Pleasants | JUMPING BRANCH | Summers |
| HEDGEVILLE | Berkeley | JUNCTION | Hampshire |
| HELEN | Raleigh | JUNIOR | Barbour |
| HELVETIA | Randolph | JUSTICE | Mingo |
| HEMPHILL | McDowell | KANAWHA CITY | Kanawha |
| HENDERSON | Mason | KANAWHA FALLS | Fayette |
| HENDRICKS | Tucker | KANAWHA HEAD | Upshur |
| HENLAWSON | Logan | KASSON | Barbour |

| | | | |
|---|---|---|---|
| KAYFORD | Kanawha | LEWISBURG | Greenbrier |
| KEARNEYSVILLE | Jefferson | LIBERTY | Putnam |
| KEGLEY | Mercer | LIMA | Tyler |
| KELLYSVILLE | Mercer | LINDEN | Roane |
| KENNA | Jackson | LINDSIDE | Monroe |
| KENOVA | Wayne | LINN | Gilmer |
| KENTUCK | Jackson | LITTLE BIRCH | Braxton |
| KERENS | Randolph | LITTLE FALLS | Monongalia |
| KERMIT | Mingo | LITTLETON | Wetzel |
| KESLERS CROSS LANES | Nicholas | LIVERPOOL | Jackson |
| KESSLER | Greenbrier | LIZEMORES | Clay |
| KEYSER | Mineral | LOBATA | Mingo |
| KEYSTONE | McDowell | LOCHGELLY | Fayette |
| KIAHSVILLE | Wayne | LOCKBRIDGE | Summers |
| KIEFFER | Greenbrier | LOCKNEY | Gilmer |
| KILSYTH | Fayette | LOGAN | Logan |
| KIMBALL | McDowell | LONDON | Kanawha |
| KIMBERLY | Fayette | LONGACRE | Fayette |
| KINCAID | Fayette | LONG BRANCH | Fayette |
| KINGMONT | Marion | LOOKOUT | Fayette |
| KINGSTON | Fayette | LOONEYVILLE | Roane |
| KINGWOOD | Preston | LORADO | Logan |
| KIRBY | Hampshire | LORENTZ | Upshur |
| KISTLER | Logan | LOST CITY | Hardy |
| KOPPERSTON | Wyoming | LOST CREEK | Harrison |
| KYLE | Modowell | LOST RIVER | Hardy |
| LAHMANSVILLE | Grant | LUMBERPORT | Harrison |
| LAKE | Logan | LUNDALE | Logan |
| LAKIN | Mason | LYBURN | Logan |
| LANARK | Raleigh | LYNCO | Wyoming |
| LANDVILLE | Logan | MABEN | Wyoming |
| LANHAM | Putnam | MABIE | Randolph |
| LANSING | Fayette | MABSCOTT | Raleigh |
| LASHMEET | Mercer | MAC ARTHUR | Raleigh |
| LAVALETTE | Wayne | MACFARLAN | Ritchie |
| LAWTON | Fayette | MADISON | Boone |
| LAYLAND | Fayette | MAHAN | Fayette |
| LECKIE | McDowell | MAHONE | Ritchie |
| LEET | Lincoln | MAIDSVILLE | Monongalia |
| LEEWOOD | Kanawha | MALDEN | Kanawha |
| LEFT HAND | Roane | MALLORY | Logan |
| LEHEW | Hampshire | MAMMOTH | Kanawha |
| LEIVASY | Nicholas | MAN | Logan |
| LENORE | Mingo | MANHEIM | Preston |
| LEON | Mason | MANNINGTON | Marion |
| LERONA | Mercer | MAPLEWOOD | Fayette |
| LE ROY | Jackson | MARFRANCE | Greenbrier |
| LESAGE | Cabell | MARIANNA | Wyoming |
| LESLIE | Greenbrier | MARLINTON | Pocahontas |
| LESTER | Raleigh | MARTINSBURG | Berkeley |
| LETART | Mason | MARSHALL UNIVERSITY | Cabell |
| LETTER GAP | Gilmer | MASON | Mason |
| LEVELS | Hampshire | MASONTOWN | Preston |

| | | | |
|---|---|---|---|
| MATEWAN | Mingo | MOUNTAIN | Ritchie |
| MATHENY | Wyoming | MOUNT ALTO | Jackson |
| MATHIAS | Hardy | MOUNT CARBON | Fayette |
| MATOAKA | Mercer | MOUNT CLARE | Harrison |
| MAXWELTON | Greenbrier | MOUNT GAY | Logan |
| MAYBEURY | McDowell | MOUNT HOPE | Fayette |
| MAYSEL | Clay | MOUNT LOOKOUT | Nicholas |
| MAYSVILLE | Grant | MOUNT NEBO | Nicholas |
| MCALPIN | Raleigh | MOUNT STORM | Grant |
| MCCOMAS | Mercer | MOUNT ZION | Calhoun |
| MCCONNELL | Logan | MOYERS | Pendleton |
| MCDOWELL | McDowell | MULLENS | Wyoming |
| MCGRAWS | Wyoming | MUNDAY | Wirt |
| MCMECHEN | Marshall | MURRAYSVILLE | Jackson |
| MCWHORTER | Harrison | MYRA | Lincoln |
| MEAD | Raleigh | MYRTLE | Mingo |
| MEADOR | Mingo | NALLEN | FayetW |
| MEADOW BLUFF | Greenbrier | NAOMA | Raleigh |
| MEADOW BRIDGE | Fayette | NAPIER | Braxton |
| MEADOWBROOK | Harrison | NAUGATUCK | Mingo |
| MEADOW CREEK | Suminers | NEBO | Clay |
| MEDLEY | Grant | NELLIS | Boone |
| METZ | Marion | NEMOURS | Mercer |
| MIAMI | Kanawha | NEOLA | Greenbrier |
| MIDDLEBOURNE | Tyler | NETTIE | Nicholas |
| MIDKIFF | Lincoln | NEVILLE | Beckley |
| MIDWAY | Raleigh | NEWBERNE | Gilmer |
| MILAM | Hardy | NEWBURG | Preston |
| MILL CREEK | Randolph | NEW CREEK | Mineral |
| MILL POINT | Pocahontas | NEW CUMBERLAND | Hancock |
| MILLSTONE | Calhoun | NEWELL | Hancock |
| MILLVILLE | Jefferson | NEW ENGLAND | Washington |
| MILLWOOD | Jackson | NEWHALL | McDowell |
| MILTON | Cabell | NEW HAVEN | Mason |
| MINDEN | Fayette | NEW MANCHESTER | Hancock |
| MINERALWELLS | Wood | NEW MARTINSVILLE | Wetzel |
| MINGO | Randolph | NEW MILTON | Doddridge |
| MINNEHAHA SPRINGS | Pocahontas | NEW RICHMOND | Wyoming |
| MINNORA | Calhoun | NEWTON | Roane |
| MOATSVILLE | Barbour | NEWTOWN | Mingo |
| MOHAWK | McDowell | NEWVILLE | Braxton |
| MONAVILLE | Logan | NICUT | Calhoun |
| MONONGAH | Marion | NIMITZ | Summers |
| MONTANA MINES | Marion | NITRO | Kanawha |
| MONTCALM | Mercer | NOBE | Calhoun |
| MONTCOAL | Raleigh | NOLAN | Mingo |
| MONTERVILLE | Randolph | NORMANTOWN | Gilmer |
| MONTGOMERY | Fayette | NORTHFORK | McDowell |
| MONTROSE | Randolph | NORTH MATEWAN | Mingo |
| MOOREFIELD | Hardy | NORTH PARKERSBURG | Good |
| MORGANTOWN | Monongalia | NORTH SPRING | Wyoming |
| MORRISVALE | Lincoln | NORTON | Randolph |
| MOUNDSVILLE | Marshall | NUTTER FORT STONEWOOD | Harrison |

| | | | |
|---|---|---|---|
| OAK HILL | Fayette | POINT PLEASANT | Mason |
| OAKVALE | Mercer | POINTS | Hampshire |
| OCEANA | Wyoming | POND GAP | Kanawha |
| ODD | Raleigh | POOL | Nicholas |
| OHLEY | Kanawha | PORTERS FALLS | Wetzel |
| OLD FIELDS | Hardy | POWELLTON | Fayette |
| OMAR | Logan | POWHATAN | Mcdowell |
| ONA | Cabell | PRATT | Kanawha |
| ONEGO | Pendleton | PREMIER | McDowell |
| ORGAS | Boone | PRENTER | Boone |
| ORLANDO | Lewis | PRICHARD | Wayne |
| ORMA | Calhoun | PRINCE | Fayette |
| OSAGE | Monongalia | PRINCETON | Mercer |
| OTTAWA | Boone | PRINCEWICK | Raleigh |
| OVAPA | Clay | PROCIOUS | Clay |
| PACKSVILLE | Boone | PROCTOR | Marshall |
| PADEN CITY | Wetzel | PROSPERITY | Raleigh |
| PAGE | Fayette | PULLMAN | Ritchie |
| PAGETON | McDowell | PURGITSVILLE | Hampshire |
| PALERMO | Lincoln | PURSGLOVE | Monongalia |
| PALESTINE | Wirt | QUICK | Kanawha |
| PANTHER | McDowell | QUINNIMONT | Fayette |
| PARCOAL | Webster | QUINWOOD | Greenbrier |
| PARKERSBURG | Wood | RACHEL | Marion |
| PARSONS | Tucker | RACINE | Boone |
| PATTERSON CREEK | Mineral | RADNOR | Wayne |
| PAW PAW | Morgan | RAGLAND | Mingo |
| PAX | Fayette | RAINELLE | Greenbrier |
| PAYNESVILLE | McDowell | RALEIGH | Raleigh |
| PEACH CREEK | Logan | RAMAGE | Boone |
| PECKS MILL | Logan | RAMSEY | Fayette |
| PEMBERTON | Raleigh | RANGER | Lincoln |
| PENCE SPRINGS | Summers | RANSON | Jefferson |
| PENNSBORO | Ritchie | RAVENCLIFF | Wyoming |
| PENTRESS | Monongalia | RAVENSWOOD | Jackson |
| PERKINS | Gilmer | RAWL | Mingo |
| PETERSBURG | Grant | RAYSAL | McDowell |
| PETERSTOWN | Monroe | READER | Wetzel |
| PETROLEUM | Ritchie | RED CREEK | Tucker |
| PEYTONA | Boone | RED HOUSE | Putnam |
| PHILIPPI | Barbour | RED JACKET | Mingo |
| PICKAWAY | Monroe | REDSTAR | Fayette |
| PICKENS | Randolph | REEDSVILLE | Preston |
| PIEDMONT | Mineral | REEDY | Roane |
| PIGEON | Clay | RENICK | Greenbrier |
| PINCH | Kanawha | REPLETE | Webster |
| PINE GROVE | Wetzel | REYNOLDSVILLE | Harrison |
| PINEVILLE | Wyoming | RHODELL | Raleigh |
| PINEY VIEW | Raleigh | RICHWOOD | Nicholas |
| PIPESTEM | Summers | RIDGELEY | Mineral |
| PLINY | Putnam | RIDGEVIEW | Boone |
| POCA | Putnam | RIDGEWAY | Berkeley |
| POE | Nicholas | RIFFLE | Braxton |

| | | | |
|---|---|---|---|
| RIG | Hardy | SHARON | Kanawha |
| RIO | Hampshire | SHARPLES | Logan |
| RIPLEY | Jackson | SHENANDOAH JUNCTION | Jefferson |
| RIPPON | Jefferson | SHEPHERDSTOWN | Jefferson |
| RIVERTON | Pendleton | SHERMAN | Jackson |
| RIVESVILLE | Marion | SHINNSTON | Harrison |
| ROANOKE | Lewis | SHIRLEY | Tyler |
| ROBERTSBURG | Putnam | SHOALS | Wayne |
| ROBINETTE | Logan | SHOCK | Gilmer |
| ROBSON | Fayette | SHORT CREED | Brooke |
| ROCK | Mercer | SHREWSBURY | Kanawha |
| ROCK CASTLE | Jackson | SIAS | Linclon |
| ROCK CAVE | Upshur | SIMON | Wyoming |
| ROCK CREEK | Raleigh | SIMPSON | Taylor |
| ROCKPORT | Wood | SINKS GROVE | Monroe |
| ROCK VIEW | Wyoming | SISSONVILLE | Kanawha |
| RODERFIELD | McDowell | SISTERSVILLE | Tyler |
| ROLLYSON | Braxton | SKELTON | Raleigh |
| ROMANCE | Jackson | SKYGUSTY | McDowell |
| ROMNEY | Hampshire | SLAB FORK | Raleigh |
| RONCEVERTE | Greenbrier | SLANESVILLE | Hampshire |
| ROSEDALE | Gilmer | SLATYFORK | Pocahontas |
| ROSEMONT | Taylor | SMITHBURG | Doddridge |
| ROSSMORE | Logan | SMITHERS | Fayette |
| ROWLESBURG | Preston | SMITHFIELD | Wetzel |
| RUNA | Nicholas | SMITHVILLE | Ritchie |
| RUPERT | Greenbrier | SMOOT | Greenbrier |
| RUSSELLVILLE | Fayette | SNOWSHOE | Pocahontas |
| SABINE | Wyoming | SOD | Lincoln |
| SABRATA | Monongalia | SOPHIA | Raleigh |
| SAINT ALBANS | Kanawha | SOUTH CHARLESTON | Kanawha |
| SAINT GEORGE | Tucker | SOUTHSIDE | Mason |
| SAINT MARYS | Pleasants | SPANISHBURG | Mercer |
| SALEM | Harrison | SPELTER | Harrison |
| SALT ROCK | Cabell | SPENCER | Roane |
| SAND FORK | Gilmer | SPRAGUE | Raleigh |
| SAND RIDGE | Calhoun | SPRIGG | Mingo |
| SANDSTONE | Summers | SPRING DALE | Fayette |
| SANDYVILLE | Jackson | SPRINGFIELD | Hampshire |
| SARAH ANN | Logan | SPRING HILL | Charleston |
| SARTON | Monroe | SPURLOCKVILLE | Lincoln |
| SAULSVILLE | Wyoming | SQUIRE | McDowell |
| SAXON | Raleigh | STANAFORD | Raleigh |
| SCARBRO | Fayette | STAR CITY | Monongalia |
| SCHERR | Mineral | STATTS MILLS | Jackson |
| SCOTT DEPOT | Putnam | STEPHENSON | Wyoming |
| SECONDCREEK | Monroe | STICKNEY | Raleigh |
| SEEBERT | Pocahontas | STIRRAT | Logan |
| SELBYVILLE | Upshur | STOLLINGS | Logan |
| SENECA ROCKS | Pendleton | STONEWALL | Kanawha |
| SETH | Boone | STONY BOTTOM | Pocahontas |
| SHADY SPRING | Raleigh | STOUTS MILLS | Gilmer |
| SHANKS | Hampshire | STRANGE CREEK | Braxton |

| | | | |
|---|---|---|---|
| STREETER | Summers | VADIS | Lewis |
| STUMPTOWN | Gilmer | VALLEY BEND | Randolph |
| SUGAR GROVE | Pendleton | VALLEY CHAPEL | Lewis |
| SULLIVAN | Raleigh | VALLEY FORK | Clay |
| SUMERCO | Lincoln | VALLEY GROVE | Ohio |
| SUMMERLEE | Fayette | VALLEY HEAD | Randolph |
| SUMMERSVILLE | Nicholas | VALLSCREEK | McDowell |
| SUMMIT POINT | Jefferson | VAN | Boone |
| SUNDIAL | Raleigh | VARNEY | Mingo |
| SUPERIOR | McDowell | VERDUNVILLE | Logan |
| SURVEYOR | Raleigh | VERNER | Mingo |
| SUTTON | Braxton | VICTOR | Fayette |
| SWEETLAND | Lincoln | VIENNA | Wood |
| SWEET SPRINGS | Monroe | VIVIAN | McDowell |
| SWISS | Nicholas | VOLGA | Barbour |
| SWITCHBACK | McDowell | VULCAN | Mingo |
| SWITZER | Logan | WADESTOWN | Monongalia |
| SYLVESTER | Boone | WAITEVILLE | Monroe |
| TAD | Kanawha | WALKER | Wood |
| TALCOTT | Summers | WALKERSVILLE | Lewis |
| TALLMANSVILLE | Upshur | WALLACE | Harrison |
| TAMS | Raleigh | WALLBACK | Clay |
| TANNER | Gilmer | WALTON | Roane |
| TAPLIN | Logan | WANA | Monongalia |
| TARIFF | Roane | WAR | McDowell |
| TEAYS | Putnam | WARDENSVILLE | Hardy |
| TENNERTON | Upshur | WARRIORMINE | McDowell |
| TERRA ALTA | Preston | WARWOOD | Ohio |
| TERRY | Raleigh | WASHINGTON | Wood |
| TESLA | Braxton | WATSON | Marion |
| THACKER | Mingo | WAVERLY | Wood |
| THOMAS | Tucker | WAYNE | Wayne |
| THORNTON | Taylor | WAYSIDE | Monroe |
| THORPE | McDowell | WEBSTER SPRINGS | Webster |
| THREE CHURCHES | Hampshire | WEIRTON | Hancock |
| THURMOND | Fayette | WELCH | McDowell |
| TIOGA | Nicholas | WELLSBURG | Brooke |
| TOLL GATE | Ritchie | WENDEL | Taylor |
| TORNADO | Kanawha | WEST COLUMBIA | Mason |
| TRIADELPHIA | Ohio | WEST HAMLIN | Lincoln |
| TROUT | Greenbrier | WEST LIBERTY | Ohio |
| TROY | Gilmer | WEST LOGAN | Logan |
| TRUE | Summers | WEST MILFORD | Harrison |
| TUNNELTON | Preston | WESTON | Lewis |
| TURTLE CREEK | Boone | WESTOVER | Monongalia |
| TWILIGHT | Boone | WEST UNION | Doddridge |
| TWIN BRANCH | McDowell | WHARNCLIFFE | Mingo |
| ULER | Roane | WHARTRON | Boone |
| UNEEDA | Boone | WHEELING | Ohio |
| UNGER | Morgan | WHITBY | Raleigh |
| UNION | Monroe | WHITE OAK | Raleigh |
| UPPERGLADE | Webster | WHITE SULPHUR SPRINGS | Greenbrier |
| UPPER TRACT | Pendleton | WHITESVILLE | Boone |

| | | | |
|---|---|---|---|
| WHITMAN | Logan | ALMOND | Portage |
| WHITMER | Randolph | ALTOONA | Eau Claire |
| WHITTAKER | Kanawha | ALVIN | Florence |
| WICK | Tyler | AMBERG | Marinette |
| WIDEN | Clay | AMERY | Polk |
| WILBUR | Tyler | AMHERST | Portage |
| WILCOE | McDowell | AMHERST JUNCTION | Portage |
| WILDCAT | Lewis | ANIWA | Shawano |
| WILEY FORD | Mineral | ANTIGO | Langlade |
| WILEYVILLE | Wetzel | APPLETON | Outagamie |
| WILKINSON | Logan | ARCADIA | Trempealeau |
| WILLIAMSBURG | Greenbrier | ARENA | Iowa |
| WILLIAMS MOUNTAIN | Boone | ARGONNE | Forest |
| WILLIAMSON | Mingo | ARGYLE | Lafayette |
| WILLIAMSTOWN | Wood | ARKANSAW | Pepin |
| WILLOW ISLAND | Pleasants | ARKDALE | Adams |
| WILSIE | Braxton | ARLINGTON | Columbia |
| WILSON | Grant | ARMSTRONG CREEK | Forest |
| WILSONBURG | Harrison | ARPIN | Wood |
| WILSONDALE | Wayne | ASHIPPUN | Dodge |
| WINDING GULF | Raleigh | ASHLAND | Ashland |
| WINDSOR HEIGHTS | Brooke | ASHWAUBENON | Brown |
| WINFIELD | Putnam | ASTICO | Dodge |
| WINIFREDE | Kanawha | ATHELSTANE | Marinette |
| WINONA | Fayette | ATHENS | Marathon |
| WOLFCREEK | Monroe | AUBURNDALE | Wood |
| WOLFE | Mercer | AUGUSTA | Eau Claire |
| WOLF PEN | Wyoming | AVALON | Rock |
| WOLF SUMMIT | Harrison | AVOCA | Iowa |
| WOODVILLE | Lincoln | BABCOCK | Wood |
| WORTH | McDowell | BAGLEY | Grant |
| WORTHINGTON | Marion | BAILEYS HARBOR | Door |
| WYATT | Harrison | BALDWIN | Saint Croix |
| WYCO | Wyoming | BALSAM LAKE | Polk |
| WYMER | Randolph | BANCROFRT | Portage |
| WYOMING | Wyoming | BANGOR | Crosse |
| YAWKEY | Lincoln | BARABOO | Sauk |
| YELLOW SPRING | Hampshire | BARNES | Douglas |
| YOLYN | Logan | BARNEVELD | Iowa |
| YUKON | McDowell | BARRON | Barron |
| **WISCONSIN** | | BARRONETT | Barron |
| ABBOTSFORD | Clark | BASSETT | Kenosha |
| ABRAMS | Oconto | BAY CITY | Pierce |
| ADAMS | Adams | BAYFIELD | Bayfield |
| ADELL | Sheboygan | BAY VIEW | Milwaukee |
| AFTON | Rock | BEAR CREEK | Outagamie |
| ALBANY | Green | BEAVER | Marinette |
| ALGOMA | Kewaunee | BEAVER DAM | Dodge |
| ALLENTON | Washington | BEETOWN | Grant |
| ALLOUEZ | Brown | BELDENVILLE | Pierce |
| ALMA | Buffalo | BELGIUM | Ozaukee |
| ALMA CENTER | Jackson | BELLEVILLE | Dane |
| ALMENA | Barron | BELMONT | Lafayette |

| | | | |
|---|---|---|---|
| BELOIT | Rock | CAMBRIA | Columbia |
| BENTON | Lafayette | CAMBRIDGE | Dane |
| BERLIN | Green Lake | CAMERON | Barron |
| BIG BEND | Waukesha | CAMPBELLSPORT | Fond Du Lac |
| BIG FALLS | Waupaca | CAMP DOUGLAS | Juneau |
| BIRCHWOOD | Washburn | CAMP LAKE | Kenosha |
| BIRNAMWOOD | Shawano | CANTON | Barron |
| BLACK CREEK | Outagamie | CAROLINE | Shawano |
| BLACK EARTH | Dane | CASCADE | Sheboygan |
| BLACK RIVER FALLS | Jackson | CASCO | Kewaunee |
| BLAIR | Trempealeau | CASHTON | Monroe |
| BLANCHARDVILLE | Lafayette | CASSVILLE | Grant |
| BLENKER | Wood | CATARACT | Monroe |
| BLOOMER | Chippewa | CATAWBA | Price |
| BLOOMINGTON | Grant | CATO | Manitowoc |
| BLUE MOUNDS | Dane | CAVOUR | Forest |
| BLUE RIVER | Grant | CAZENOVIA | Richland |
| BONDUEL | Shawano | CECIL | Shawano |
| BOSCOBEL | Grant | CEDARBURG | Ozaukee |
| BOULDER JUNCTION | Vilas | CEDAR GROVE | Sheboygan |
| BOWLER | Shawano | CENTURIA | Polk |
| BOYCEVILLE | Dunn | CHASEBURG | Vernon |
| BOYD | Chippewa | CHELSEA | Taylor |
| BRADLEY | Milwaukee | CHETEK | Barron |
| BRANCH | Manitowoc | CHILI | Clark |
| BRANDON | Fond Du Lac | CHILTON | Calumet |
| BRANTWOOD | Price | CHIPPEWA FALLS | Chippewa |
| BRIGGSVILLE | Marquette | CLAM FALLS | Polk |
| BRILL | Barron | CLAM LAKE | Ashland |
| BRILLION | Calumet | CLAYTON | Polk |
| BRISTOL | Kenosha | CLEAR LAKE | Polk |
| BRODHEAD | Green | CLEVELAND | Manitowoc |
| BROKAW | Marathon | CLINTON | Rock |
| BROOKFIELD | Waukesha | CLINTONVILLE | Waupaca |
| BROOKLYN | Green | CLYMAN | Dodge |
| BROOKS | Adams | COBB | Iowa |
| BROOKWOOD | Dane | COCHRANE | Buffalo |
| BROWNSVILLE | Dodge | COLBY | Clark |
| BROWNTOWN | Green | COLEMAN | Marinette |
| BRUCE | Rusk | COLFAX | Dunn |
| BRULE | Douglas | COLGATE | Washington |
| BRUSSELS | Door | COLLINS | Manitowoc |
| BRYANT | Langlade | COLOMA | Waushara |
| BUFFALO CITY | Buffalo | COLUMBUS | Columbia |
| BURLINGTON | Racine | COMBINED LOCKS | Outagamie |
| BURNETT | Dodge | COMSTOCK | Barron |
| BUTLER | Waukesha | CONOVER | Vilas |
| BUTTE DES MORTS | Winnebago | CONRATH | Rusk |
| BUTTERNUT | Ashland | COON VALLEY | Vernon |
| BYRON | Fond Du Lac | CORNELL | Chippewa |
| CABLE | Bayfield | CORNUCOPIA | Bayfield |
| CADOTT | Chippewa | COTTAGE GROVE | Dane |
| CALEDONIA | Racine | COUDERAY | Sawyer |

| | | | |
|---|---|---|---|
| CRANDON | Forest | ELAND | Shawano |
| CRIVITZ | Marinette | ELCHO | Langlade |
| CROSS PLAINS | Dane | ELDERON | Marathan |
| CUBA CITY | Grant | ELDORADO | Fond Du Lac |
| CUDAHY | Milwaukee | ELEVA | Trempealeau |
| CUMBERLAND | Barron | ELKHART LAKE | Walworth |
| CURTISS | Clark | ELKHORN | Walworth |
| CUSHING | Polk | ELK MOUND | Dunn |
| CUSTER | Portage | ELLISON BAY | Door |
| CUTLER | Juneau | ELLSWORTH | Pierce |
| DAIRYLAND | Burnett | ELM GROVE | Waukesha |
| DALE | Outagamie | ELMWOOD | Pierce |
| DALLAS | Barron | ELROY | Juneau |
| DALTON | Green Lake | ELTON | Langlade |
| DANBURY | Burnett | EMBARRASS | Waupaca |
| DANE | Dane | EMERALD | Saint Croix |
| DARIEN | Walworth | ENDEAVOR | Marquette |
| DARLINGTON | Lafayette | EPHRAIM | Door |
| DEERBROOK | Langlade | ETTRICK | Trempealeau |
| DEERFIELD | Dane | EUREKA | Winnebago |
| DEER PARK | Saint Croix | EVANSVILLE | Rock |
| DEFOREST | Dane | EVERGREEN | Burnett |
| DELAFIELD | Waukesha | EXELAND | Sawyer |
| DELAVAN | Walworth | FAIRCHILD | Eau Claire |
| DELLWOOD | Adams | FAIR WATER | Fond Du Lac |
| DELTA | Bayfield | FALL CREEK | Eau Claire |
| DENMARK | Brown | FALL RIVER | Columbia |
| DEPERE | Brown | FENCE | Florence |
| DESOTO | Vernon | FENNIMORE | Grant |
| DICKEYVILLE | Grant | FERRYVILLE | Crawford |
| DODGE | Trempealeau | FIFIELD | Price |
| DODGEVILLE | Iowa | FISH CREEK | Door |
| DORCHESTER | Clark | FLORENCE | Florence |
| DOUSMAN | Waukesha | FOND DU LAC | Fond Du Lac |
| DOWNING | Dunn | FONTANA | Walworth |
| DOWNSVILLE | Dunn | FOOTVILLE | Rock |
| DOYLESTOWN | Columbia | FOREST JUNCTION | Calumet |
| DRESSER | Polk | FORESTVILLE | Door |
| DRUMMOND | Bayfield | FORT ATKINSON | Jefferson |
| DUNBAR | Marinette | FOUNTAIN CITY | Buffalo |
| DURAND | Pepin | FOXBORO | Douglas |
| EAGLE | Waukesha | FOX LAKE | Dodge |
| EAGLE RIVER | Vilas | FRANCIS CREEK | Manitowoc |
| EASTMAN | Crawford | FRANKLIN | Milwaukee |
| EAST TROY | Walworth | FRANKSVILLE | Racine |
| EAU CLAIRE | Eau Claire | FREDERIC | Polk |
| EAU GALLE | Dunn | FREDONIA | Ozaukee |
| EDEN | Fond Du Lac | FREMONT | Waupaca |
| EDGAR | Marathon | FRIENDSHIP | Adams |
| EDGERTON | Rock | FRIESLAND | Columbia |
| EDGEWATER | Sawyer | GALESVILLE | Trempealeau |
| EDMUND | Iowa | GAYS MILLS | Crawford |
| EGG HARBOR | Door | GENESEE DEPOT | Waukesha |

| | | | |
|---|---|---|---|
| GENOA | Vernon | HERTEL | Burnett |
| GENOA CITY | Walworth | HEWITT | Wood |
| GERMANTOWN | Washington | HIGH BRIDGE | Ashland |
| GILE | Iron | HIGHLAND | Iowa |
| GILLETT | Oconto | HILBERT | Calumet |
| GILMAN | Taylor | HILLDALE | Dane |
| GILMANTON | Buffalo | HILLPOINT | Sauk |
| GLEASON | Lincoln | HILLSBORO | Vernon |
| GLENBEULAH | Sheboygan | HINGHAM | Sheboygan |
| GLEN FLORA | Rusk | HIXTON | Jackson |
| GLEN HAVEN | Grant | HOLCOMBE | Chippewa |
| GLENWOOD CITY | Saint Croix | HOLLANDALE | Iowa |
| GLIDDEN | Ashland | HOLMEN | La Crosse |
| GOODMAN | Marinette | HONEY CREEK | Walworth |
| GORDON | Douglas | HORICON | Dodge |
| GOTHAM | Richland | HORTONVILLE | Outagamie |
| GRAFTON | Ozaukee | HUBERTUS | Washington |
| GRAND MARSH | Adams | HUDSON | Saint Croix |
| GRAND VIEW | Bayfield | HUMBIRD | Clark |
| GRANTON | Clark | HURLEY | Iron |
| GRANTSBURG | Bumett | HUSTISFORD | Dodge |
| GRATIOT | Lafayette | INDEPENDENCE | Trempealeau |
| GREEN BAY | Brown | INGRAM | Rusk |
| GREENBUSH | Sheboygan | IOLA | Waupaca |
| GREENDALE | Milwaukee | IRMA | Lincoln |
| GREENFIELD | Milwaukee | IRON BELT | Iron |
| GREEN LAKE | Green Lake | IRON RIDGE | Dodge |
| GREENLEAF | Brown | IRON RIVER | Bayfield |
| GREEN VALLEY | Shawano | IXONIA | Jefferson |
| GREENWOOD | Clark | JACKSON | Washington |
| GRESHAM | Shawano | JANESVILLE | Rock |
| GURNEY | Iron | JEFFERSON | Jefferson |
| HAGER CITY | Pierce | JIM FALLS | Chippewa |
| HALES CORNERS | Milwaukee | JOHNSON CREEK | Jefferson |
| HAMMOND | Saint Croix | JUDA | Green |
| HANCOCK | Waushara | JUMP RIVER | Taylor |
| HANNIBAL | Taylor | JUNCTION CITY | Portage |
| HANOVER | Rock | JUNEAU | Dodge |
| HARBOR | Milwaukee | KANSASVILLE | Racine |
| HARSHAW | Oneida | KAUKAUNA | Outgamie |
| HARTFORD | Washington | KELLNERSVILLE | Manitowoc |
| HARTLAND | Waukesha | KEMPSTER | Langlade |
| HATLEY | Marathon | KENDALL | Monroe |
| HAUGEN | Barron | KENNAN | Price |
| HAVEN | Sheboygan | KENOSHA | Kenosha |
| HAWKINS | Rusk | KEWASKUM | Washington |
| HAWTHORNE | Douglas | KEWAUNEE | Kewaunee |
| HAYWARD | Sawyer | KIEL | Manitowac |
| HAZEL GREEN | Grant | KIELER | Grant |
| HAZELHURST | Oneida | KIMBERLY | Outagamie |
| HEAFFORD JUNCTION | Lincoln | KING | Waupaca |
| HELENVILLE | Jefferson | KINGSTON | Green Lake |
| HERBSTER | Bayfield | KNAPP | Dunn |

| | | | |
|---|---|---|---|
| KOHLER | Sheboygan | MARENGO | Ashland |
| KRAKOW | Shawano | MARIBEL | Manitowoc |
| LAC DU FLAMBEAU | Vilas | MARINETTE | Marinette |
| LACROSSE | La Crosse | MARION | Waupaca |
| LADYSMITH | Rusk | MARKESAN | Green Lake |
| LAFARGE | Vernon | MARQUETTE | Green Lake |
| LAKE DELTON | Sauk | MARSHALL | Dane |
| LAKE GENEVA | Walworth | MARSHFIELD | Wood |
| LAKE MILLS | Jefferson | MASON | Bayfield |
| LAKE NEBAGAMON | Douglas | MATHER | Juneau |
| LAKE TOMAHAWK | Oneida | MATTOON | Shawano |
| LAKEWOOD | Oconto | MAUSTON | Juneau |
| LANCASTER | Grant | MAYVILLE | Dodge |
| LAND O'LAKES | Vilas | MAZOMANIE | Dane |
| LANNON | Waukesha | MCFARLAND | Dane |
| LAONA | Forest | MCNAUGHTON | Oneida |
| LAPOINTE | Ashland | MEDFORD | Taylor |
| LARSEN | Winnebago | MEDINA | Outagamie |
| LAVALLE | Sauk | MELLEN | Ashland |
| LAYTON PARK | Milwaukee | MELROSE | Jackson |
| LEBANON | Dodge | MELVINA | Monroe |
| LENA | Oconto | MENASHA | Winnebago |
| LEOPOLIS | Shawano | MENOMONEE FALLS | Waukesha |
| LEWIS | Polk | MENOMONIE | Dunn |
| LIMERIDGE | Sauk | MEQUON | Ozaukee |
| LINDEN | Iowa | MERCER | Iron |
| LITTLE CHUTE | Outagamie | MERRILL | Lincoln |
| LITTLE SUAMICO | Oconto | MERRILLAN | Jackson |
| LIVINGSTON | Grant | MERRIMAC | Sauk |
| LODI | Columbia | MERTON | Waukesha |
| LOGANVILLE | Sauk | MID CITY | Milwaukee |
| LOMIRA | Dodge | MIDDLE INLET | Marinette |
| LONE ROCK | Richland | MIDDLETON | Dane |
| LONG LAKE | Florence | MIKANA | Barron |
| LORETTA | Sawyer | MILAN | Marathon |
| LOWELL | Dodge | MILLADORE | Wood |
| LOYAL | Clark | MILLSTON | Jackson |
| LUBLIN | Taylor | MILLTOWN | Polk |
| LUCK | Polk | MILTON | Rock |
| LUXEMBURG | Kewaunee | MILWAUKEE | Milwaukee |
| LYNDON STATION | Juneau | MINDORO | La Crosse |
| LYNXVILLE | Crawford | MINERAL POINT | Iowa |
| LYONS | Walworth | MINOCQUA | Oneida |
| MADISON | Dane | MINONG | Washburn |
| MAIDEN ROCK | Pierce | MISHICOT | Manitowoc |
| MALONE | Fond Du Lac | MODENA | Buffalo |
| MANAWA | Waupaca | MONDOVI | Buffalo |
| MANCHESTER | Green Lake | MONICO | Oneida |
| MANITOWISH WATERS | Vilas | MONONA | Dane |
| MANITOWOC | Manitowoc | MONROE | Green |
| MAPLE | Douglas | MONTELLO | Marquette |
| MAPLEWOOD | Door | MONTFORT | Grant |
| MARATHON | Marathon | MONTICELLO | Green |

| | | | |
|---|---|---|---|
| MONTREAL | Iron | OGEMA | Price |
| MOQUAH | Ashland | OJIBWA | Sawyer |
| MORRISONVILLE | Dane | OKAUCHEE | Waukesha |
| MOSINEE | Marathon | OMRO | Winnebago |
| MOUNTAIN | Oconto | ONALASKA | La Crosse |
| MOUNT CALVARY | Fond Du Lac | ONEIDA | Outagamie |
| MOUNT HOPE | Grant | ONTARIO | Vernon |
| MOUNT HOREB | Dane | OOSTBURG | Sheboygan |
| MOUNT STERLING | Crawford | OREGON | Dane |
| MUKWONAGO | Waukesha | ORFORDVILLE | Rock |
| MUSCADA | Grant | OSCEOLA | Polk |
| MUSKEGO | Waukesha | OSHKOSH | Winnebago |
| NASHOTAH | Waukesha | OSSEO | Trempealeau |
| NAVARINO | Shawano | OWEN | Clark |
| NECEDAH | Juneau | OXFORD | Marquette |
| NEENAH | Winnebago | PACKWAUKEE | Marquette |
| NEILLSVILLE | Clark | PALMYRA | Jefferson |
| NEKOOSA | Wood | PARDEEVILLE | Columbia |
| NELSON | Buffallo | PARK FALLS | Price |
| NELSONVILLE | Portage | PARK LAWN | Milwaukee |
| NEOPIT | Menominee | PATCH GROVE | Grant |
| NEOSHO | Dodge | PEARSON | Langlade |
| NESHKORO | Marquette | PELICAN LAKE | Oneida |
| NEWALD | Forest | PELL LAKE | Walworth |
| NEW AUBURN | Chippewa | PEMBINE | Marinette |
| NEW BERLIN | Waukesha | PENCE | Montreal |
| NEWBURG | Washington | PEPIN | Pepin |
| NEW FRANKEN | Brown | PESHTIGO | Marinette |
| NEW GLARUS | Green | PEWAUKEE | Waukesha |
| NEW HOLSTEIN | Calumet | PHELPS | Vilas |
| NEW LISBON | Jueanu | PHILLIPS | Price |
| NEW LONDON | Outagamie | PHLOX | Langlade |
| NEW MUNSTER | Kenosha | PICKEREL | Langlade |
| NEW POST | Couderay | PICKETT | Winnebago |
| NEW RICHMOND | Saint Croix | PIGEON FALLS | Trempealeau |
| NEWTON | Manitowoc | PINE RIVER | Waushara |
| NIAGARA | Marinette | PITTSVILLE | Wood |
| NICHOLS | Outagamie | PLAIN | Sauk |
| NORTHFIELD | Jackson | PLAINFIELD | Waushara |
| NORTH FREEDOM | Sauk | PLATTEVILLE | Grant |
| NORTH LAKE | Waukesha | PLEASANT PRAIRIE | Kenosha |
| NORTH PRAIRIE | Waukesha | PLOVER | Portage |
| NORTH SHORE | Milwaukee | PLUM CITY | Pierce |
| NORTH WOODS BEACH | Sawyer | PLYMOUTH | Sheboygan |
| NORWALK | Monroe | POPLAR | Douglas |
| OAK CREEK | Milwaukee | PORTAGE | Columbia |
| OAKDALE | Monroe | PORT EDWARDS | Wood |
| OAKFIELD | Fond Du Lac | PORTERFIELD | Marinette |
| OCONOMOWOC | Waukesha | PORT WASHINGTON | Ozaukee |
| OCONTO | Oconto | PORT WING | Bayfield |
| OCONTO FALLS | Oconto | POSKIN | Barron |
| ODANAH | Ashland | POTOSI | Grant |
| OGDENSBURG | Waupaca | POTTER | Calumet |

| | | | |
|---|---|---|---|
| POUND | Marinette | ROTHSCHILD | Marathon |
| POWERS LAKE | Kenosha | ROYALTON | Waupaca |
| POYNETTE | Columbia | RUBICON | Dodge |
| POY SIPPI | Waushara | RUDOLPH | Wood |
| PRAIRIE DU CHIEN | Crawford | SAINT CLOUD | Fond Du Lac |
| PRAIRIE DU SAC | Sauk | SAINT CROIX FALLS | Polk |
| PRAIRIE FARM | Barron | SAINT FRANCIS | Milwaukee |
| PRENTICE | Price | SAINT GERMAIN | Vilas |
| PRESCOTT | Pierce | SAINT JOSPEH | Saint Croix |
| PRESQUE ISLE | Vilas | SAINT NAZIANZ | Manitowoc |
| PRINCETON | Green Lake | SALEM | Kenosha |
| PULASKI | Brown | SALVATORIAN CENTER | Calumet |
| PULCIFER | Oconto | SANBORN | Ashland |
| RACINE | Racine | SAND CREEK | Dunn |
| RADISSON | Sawyer | SARONA | Washburn |
| RANDALL | Burnett | SAUK CITY | Sauk |
| RANDOLPH | Columbia | SAUK VILLE | Ozaukee |
| RANDOM LAKE | Sheboygan | SAXEVILLE | Waushara |
| READFIELD | Waupaca | SAXON | Iron |
| READSTOWN | Vernon | SAYNER | Vilas |
| REDGRANITE | Waushara | SCANDINAVIA | Waupaca |
| REEDSBURG | Sauk | SCHOFIELD | Marathon |
| REEDSVILLE | Manitowoc | SENECA | Crawford |
| REESEVILLE | Dodge | SEQUOIA | Milwaukee |
| REWEY | Iowa | SEXTONVILLE | Richland |
| RHINELANDER | Oneida | SEYMOUR | Outagamie |
| RIB LAKE | Taylor | SHARON | Walworth |
| RICE LAKE | Barron | SHAWANO | Shawano |
| RICHFIELD | Washington | SHEBOYGAN | Sheboygan |
| RICHLAND CENTER | Richland | SHEBOYGAN FALLS | Sheboygan |
| RIDGELAND | Dunn | SHELDON | Rusk |
| RIDGEWAY | Iowa | SHELL LAKE | Washburn |
| RINGLE | Marathon | SHERWOOD | Calumet |
| RIO | Columbia | SHIOCTON | Outagamie |
| RIO CREEK | Kewaunee | SHOREWOOD | Milwaukee |
| RIPON | Fond Du Lac | SHULISBURG | Lafayette |
| RIVER FALLS | Pierce | SILVER LAKE | Kenosha |
| ROBERT | Saint Croix | SINSINAWA | Grant |
| ROCHESTER | Racine | SIREN | Burnett |
| ROCK FALLS | Dunn | SISTER BAY | Door |
| ROCKFIELD | Washington | SLINGER | Washington |
| ROCKLAND | La Crosse | SOBIESKI | Oconto |
| ROOT RIVER | Milwaukee | SOLDIERS GROVE | Crawford |
| ROCK SPRINGS | Sauk | SOLON SPRINGS | Douglas |
| ROSENDALE | Fond Du Lac | SOMERS | Kenosha |
| RIVER FALLS | Pierce | SOMERSET | Saint Croix |
| ROBERTS | Saint Croix | SOUTH BYRON | Dodge |
| ROCHESTER | Racine | SOUTH MILWAUKEE | ilwaukee |
| ROCKFIELD | Washington | SOUTH RANGE | Douglas |
| ROCKLAND | La Crosse | SOUTH SIDE | Dane |
| ROCK SPRINGS | Sauk | SOUTH WAYNE | Lafayette |
| ROSENDALE | Fond Du Lac | SPARTA | Monroe |
| ROSHOLT | Portage | SPENCER | Marathon |

| | | | |
|---|---|---|---|
| SPOONER | Washburn | TWIN LAKES | Kenosha |
| SPRINGBROOK | Washburn | TWO RIVERS | Manitowoc |
| SPRINGFIELD | Walworth | UNDERHILL | Oconto |
| SPRING GREEN | Sauk | UNION CENTER | Juneau |
| SPRING VALLEY | Pierce | UNION GROVE | Racine |
| STANLEY | Chippewa | UNITY | Marathon |
| STARLAKE | Vilas | UNIVERSITY | Madison |
| STAR PRAIRIE | Polk | UPSON | Iron |
| STATE STREET | Racine | VALDERS | Manitowoc |
| STETSONVILLE | Taylor | VAN DYNE | Fond Du Lac |
| STEUBEN | Crawford | VERONA | Dane |
| STEVENS POINT | Portage | VESPER | Wood |
| STILES | Oconto | VICTORY | Vernon |
| STITZER | Grant | VILLARD | Milwaukee |
| STOCKBRIDGE | Calumet | VIOLA | Vernon |
| STOCKHOLM | Pepin | VIROQUA | Vernon |
| STODDARD | Vernon | WABENO | Forest |
| STONE LAKE | Sawyer | WALDO | Sheboygan |
| STOUGHTON | Dane | WALES | Waukesha |
| STRATFORD | Marathon | WALWORTH | Walworth |
| STRUM | Trempealeau | WARRENS | Monroe |
| STURGEON BAY | Door | WASCOTT | Douglas |
| STURTEVANT | Racine | WASHBURN | Bayfield |
| SUAMICO | Brown | WASHINGTON ISLAND | Door |
| SULLIVAN | Jefferson | WASHINGTON SQUARE | Marathon |
| SUMMIT LAKE | Langlade | WATERFORD | Racine |
| SUN PRAIRIE | Dane | WATERLOO | Jefferson |
| SUPERIOR | Douglas | WATERTOWN | Jefferson |
| SURING | Oconto | WAUBEKA | Ozaukee |
| SUSSEX | Waukesha | WAUKAU | Winnebago |
| TAYCHEEDAH | Fond Du Lac | WAUKESHA | Waukesha |
| TAYLOR | Jackson | WAUMANDEE | Buffalo |
| TEUTONIA | Milwaukee | WAUNAKEE | Dane |
| THERESA | Dodge | WAUPACA | Waupaca |
| THIENSVILLE | Ozaukee | WAUPUN | Fond Du Lac |
| THORP | Clark | WAUSAU | Marathon |
| THREE LAKES | Oneida | WAUSAUKEE | Marinette |
| TIFFANY | Rock | WAUTOMA | Waushara |
| TIGERTON | Shawano | WAUWATOSA | Milwaukee |
| TILLEDA | Shawano | WAUZEKA | Crawford |
| TIPLER | Florence | WAYSIDE | Brown |
| TISCH MILLS | Manitowoc | WEBB LAKE | Burnett |
| TOMAH | Monroe | WEBSTER | Burnett |
| TOMAHAWK | Lincoln | WENTWORTH | Douglas |
| TONY | Rusk | WEST ALLIS | Milwaukee |
| TOWNSEND | Oconto | WEST BEND | Washington |
| TREGO | Washburn | WESTBORO | Taylor |
| TREMPEALEAU | Trempealeau | WESTBY | Vernon |
| TREVOR | Kenosha | WESTERN | Milwaukee |
| TRIPOLI | Oneida | WESTFIELD | Marquette |
| TUCKAWAY | Milwaukee | WEST LIMA | Vernon |
| TUNNEL CITY | Monroe | WEST RACINE | Racine |
| TURTLE LAKE | Barron | WEST SALEM | La Crosse |

| Place | County | Place | County |
|---|---|---|---|
| WEYAUWEGA | Waupaca | BEDFORD | Lincoln |
| WEYERHAEUSER | Rusk | BEULAH | Crook |
| WHEELER | Dunn | BIG HORN | Sheridan |
| WHITEHALL | Trempealeau | BIG PINEY | Sublette |
| WHITE LAKE | Langlade | BILL | Converse |
| WHITELAW | Manitowoc | BONDURANT | Sublette |
| WHITEWATER | Walworth | BOSLER | Albany |
| WILD ROSE | Waushara | BOULDER | Sublette |
| WILLARD | Clark | BUFFALO | Johnson |
| WILLIAMS BAY | Walworth | BUFORD | Albany |
| WILMOT | Kenosha | BURLINGTON | Big Horn |
| WILSON | Saint Croix | BURNS | Laramie |
| WILTON | Monroe | BYRON | Big Horn |
| WINCHESTER | Vilas | CARPENTER | Laramie |
| WIND LAKE | Racine | CASPRE | Natrona |
| WINDSOR | Dane | CENTENNIAL | Albany |
| WINNEBAGO | Winnebago | CHEYENNE | Laramie |
| WINNECONNE | Winnebago | CHUGWATER | Platte |
| WINTER | Sawyer | CLEARMONT | Sheridan |
| WISCONSIN DELLS | Columbia | CODY | Park |
| WISCONSIN RAPIDS | Wood | COKEVILLE | Lincoln |
| WITHEE | Clark | COLTER BAY | Teton |
| WITTENBERG | Shawano | CORA | Sublette |
| WONEWOC | Juneau | COWLEY | Big Horn |
| WOOD | Milwaukee | CROWHEART | Fremont |
| WOODFORD | Lafayette | DANIEL | Sublette |
| WOODLAND | Dodge | DAYTON | Sheridan |
| WOODMAN | Grant | DEAVER | Big Horn |
| WOODRUFF | Oneida | DEVILS TOWER | Crook |
| WOODVILLE | Sainte Croix | DIAMONDVILLE | Lincoln |
| WOODWORTH | Kenosha | DIXON | Carbon |
| WRIGHTSTOWN | Brown | DOUGLAS | Converse |
| WYEVILLE | Monroe | DUBOIS | Fremont |
| WYOCENA | Columbia | EDEN | Sweetwater |
| ZACHOW | Shawano | EDGERTON | Natrona |
| ZENDA | Walworth | ELK MOUNTAIN | Carbon |
| **WYOMING** | | EMBLEM | Big Horn |
| ACME | Sheridan | ENCAMPMENT | Carbon |
| AFTON | Lincoln | ETHETE | Fremont |
| AIRPORT | Laramie | ETNA | Lincoln |
| ALADDIN | Crook | EVANSTON | Uinta |
| ALBIN | Laramie | EVANSVILLE | Natrona |
| ALCOVA | Natrona | FAIRVIEW | Lincoln |
| ALPINE | Lincoln | FARSON | Sweetwater |
| ALVA | Crook | F.E. WARREN AFB | Laramie |
| ARAPAHOE | Frermont | FORT BRIDGER | Uinta |
| ARMINGTO | Natrona | FORT LARAMIE | Goshen |
| ARVADA | Sheridan | FORT WASHAKIE | Fremont |
| AUBURN | Lincoln | FOUR CORNERS | Weston |
| BAGGS | Carbon | FOX PARK | Albany |
| BAIROIL | Sweetwater | FRANNIE | Park |
| BANNER | Sheridan | FREEDOM | Lincoln |
| BASIN | Big Horn | FRONTIER | Lincoln |

| | | | |
|---|---|---|---|
| GARRETT | Albany | MCFADDEN | Carbon |
| GAS HILLS | Fremont | MCKINNON | Sweetwater |
| GILLETTE | Campbell | MEDICINE BOW | Carbon |
| GLENDO | Platte | MEETEETSE | Park |
| GLENROCK | Converse | MERIDEN | Laramie |
| GRANGER | Sweetwater | MIDWEST | Natrona |
| GRANITE CANON | Laramie | MILLS | Natrona |
| GRANT VILLAGE | Park | MOORCROFT | Crook |
| GRASS CREEK | Hot Springs | MOOSE | Teton |
| GREEN RIVER | Sweetwater | MORAN | Teton |
| GREYBULL | Big Horn | MORTON | Fremont |
| GROVER | Lincoln | MOUNTAIN VIEW | Uinta |
| GUERNSEY | Platte | NATRONA | Natrona |
| HAMILTON DOME | Hot Springs | NEWCASTLE | Weston |
| HANNA | Carbon | NODE | Niobrara |
| HARTVILLE | Platte | NUMBER ONE | Laramie |
| HAWK SPRINGS | Goshen | OPAL | Lincoln |
| HILAND | Natrona | OSAGE | Weston |
| HILLSDALE | Laramie | OSHOTO | Crook |
| HORSE CREEK | Laramie | OTTO | Big Horn |
| HUDSON | Fremont | PARKMAN | Sheridan |
| HULETT | Crook | PAVILLION | Fremont |
| HUNTLEY | Goshen | PINE BLUFFS | Laramie |
| HYATVILLE | Big Horn | PINEDALE | Sublette |
| IRON MOUNTAIN | Laramie | PINE HAVEN | Crook |
| JACKSON | Teton | POINT OF ROCKS | Sweetwater |
| JAY EM | Goshen | POWDER RIVER | Natrona |
| JEFFREY CITY | Fremont | POWELL | Park |
| JELM | Albany | RALSTON | Park |
| KAYCEE | Johnson | RANCHESTER | Sheridan |
| KEELINE | Niobrara | RAWLINS | Carbon |
| KELLY | Teton | RECLUSE | Campbell |
| KEMMERER | Lincoln | RELIANCE | Sweetwater |
| KINNEAR | Fremont | RIVERTON | Fremont |
| KIRBY | Hot Springs | ROBERTSON | Uinta |
| LA BARGE | Lincoln | ROCK RIVER | Albany |
| LAGRANGE | Goshen | ROCK SPRINGS | Sweetwater |
| LANCE CREEK | Niobrara | ROZET | Carnpbell |
| LANDER | Fremont | RYAN PARK | Carbon |
| LARAMIE | Albany | SADDLESTRING | Johnson |
| LEITER | Sheridan | SAINT STEPHENS | Fremont |
| LINCH | Johnson | SARATOGA | Carbon |
| LINGLE | Goshen | SAVERY | Carbon |
| LITTLE AMERICA | Sweetwater | SHAWNEE | Converse |
| LONETREE | Uinta | SHELL | Big Horn |
| LOST SPRINGS | Converse | SHERIDAN | Sheridan |
| LOVELL | Big Horn | SHIRLEY BASIN | Carbon |
| LUSK | Niobrara | SHOSHONI | Frermnt |
| LYMAN | Uinta | SINCLAIR | Carbon |
| LYSITE | Fremont | SMOOT | Lincoln |
| MANDERSON | Big Horn | SOUTH PASS CITY | Fremont |
| MANVILLE | Niobrara | STORY | Sheridan |
| MARBLETON | Sublette | SUNDANCE | Crook |

| | |
|---|---|
| SUPERIOR | Sweetwater |
| TEN SLEEP | Washakie |
| TETON VILLAGE | Teton |
| THAYNE | Lincoln |
| THERMOPOLIS | Hot Springs |
| TIE SIDING | Albany |
| TORRINGTON | Goshen |
| UNIVERSITY | Laramie |
| UNIVERSITY OF WY | Laramie |
| UPTON | Weston |
| VAN TASSELL | Niobrara |
| VETERAN | Goshen |
| WALCOTT | Carbon |
| WAMSUTTER | Sweetwater |
| WAPITI | Park |
| WESTON | Campbell |
| WHEATLAND | Platte |
| WILSON | Teton |
| WOLF | Sheridan |
| WORLAND | Washakie |
| WRIGHT | Campbell |
| WYARNO | Sheridan |
| YELLOWSTONE NATIONAL PARK | Park |

# County-County Seat List

| County | County Seat | County | County Seat |
|--------|-------------|--------|-------------|
| **ALABAMA** | | Hale | Greensboro |
| Autauga | Prattville | Henry | Abbeville |
| Baldwin | Bay Minette | Houston | Dothan |
| Barbour | Clayton | Jackson | Scottsboro |
| Bibb | Centreville | Jefferson | Birmingham |
| Blount | Oneonta | Lamar | Vernon |
| Bullock | Union Springs | Lauderdale | Florence |
| Butler | Greenville | Lawrence | Moulton |
| Calhoun | Anniston | Lee | Opelika |
| Chambers | Lafayette | Limestone | Athens |
| Cherokee | Centre | Lowndes | Hayneville |
| Chilton | Clanton | Macon | Tuskegee |
| Choctaw | Butler | Madison | Huntsville |
| Clarke | Grove Hill | Marengo | Linden |
| Clay | Ashland | Marion | Hamilton |
| Cleburne | Heflin | Marshall | Guntersville |
| Coffee | Elba | Mobile | Mobile |
| Colbert | Tuscumbia | Monroe | Monroeville |
| Conecuh | Evergreen | Montgomery | Montgomery |
| Coosa | Rockford | Morgan | Decatur |
| Covington | Andalusia | Perry | Marion |
| Crenshaw | Luvern | Pickens | Carrollton |
| Cullman | Cullman | Pike | Troy |
| Dale | Ozark | Randolph | Wedowee |
| Dallas | Selma | Russell | Phenix City |
| DeKalb | Ft Payne | Shelby | Columbiana |
| Elmore | Wetumpka | St Clair | Ashville |
| Escambia | Brewton | Sumter | Livingston |
| Etowah | Gadsden | Talladega | Talladega |
| Fayette | Fayette | Tallapoosa | Dadeville |
| Franklin | Russellville | Tuscaloosa | Tuscaloosa |
| Geneva | Geneva | Walker | Jasper |
| Greene | Eutaw | Washington | Chatom |

| County | County Seat | County | County Seat |
|---|---|---|---|
| Wilcox | Camden | Kenai Peninsula | Kenai |
| Winston | Double Springs | Ketchikan Gateway | Ketchikan |
| | | Kodiak Island | Kodiak |
| | | Lake and Peninsula | King Salmon |
| | | Matanuska-Susitna | Palmer |
| | | North Slope | Barrow |
| | | Northwest Artic | Kotzebue |

# ALASKA

UNIFIED HOME RULE MUNICIPALITIES

City and Borough of Juneau
City and Borough of Sitka
Municipality of Anchorage

| HOME RULE CITIES | BOROUGH |
|---|---|
| Cordova | N/A |
| Fairbanks | Fairbanks North Star |
| Kenai | Kenai Pennisula |
| Ketchikan | Ketchikan Gateway |
| Kodiak | Kodiak Island |
| Nenana | N/A |
| North Pole | Fairbanks North Star |
| Palmer | Matanuska-Susitna |
| Petersburg | N/A |
| Seward | Kenai Pennisula |
| Valdez | N/A |
| Wrangell | N/A |

| BOROUGH | BOROUGH SEAT |
|---|---|
| Aleutains East | Sand Point |
| Bristol Bay | Bristol Bay |
| Denali | Healy-Anderson |
| Fairbanks North Star | Fairbanks |
| Haines | Haines |

# ARIZONA

| | |
|---|---|
| Apache | St. Johns |
| Cochise | Bisbee |
| Coconino | Flagstaff |
| Gila | Globe |
| Graham | Safford |
| Greenlee | Clifton |
| La Paz | Parker |
| Maricopa | Phoenix |
| Mohave | Kingman |
| Navajo | Holbrook |
| Pima | Tucson |
| Pinal | Florence |
| Santa Cruz | Nogales |
| Yavapai | Prescott |
| Yuma | Yuma |

# ARKANSAS

| | |
|---|---|
| Arkansas | DeWitt |
| Ashley | Hamburg |
| Baxter | Mountain |
| Benton | Bentonville |
| Boone | Harrison |
| Bradley | Warren |

| County | County Seat | County | County Seat |
|--------|-------------|--------|-------------|
| Calhoun | Hampton | Logan | Paris |
| Carroll | Berryville | Lonoke | Lonoke |
| Chicot | Lake Village | Madison | Huntsville |
| Clark | Arkadelphia | Marion | Yellville |
| Clay | Piggott | Miller | Texarkana |
| Cleburne | Heber Springs | Mississippi | Blytheville |
| Cleveland | Rison | Monroe | Clarendon |
| Columbia | Magnolia | Montgomery | Mount Ida |
| Conway | Morrilton | | |
| Craighead | Jonesboro | | |

## ARKANSAS

| County | County Seat | County | County Seat |
|--------|-------------|--------|-------------|
| Crawford | Van Buren | Nevada | Prescott |
| Crittenden | Marion | Newton | Jasper |
| Cross | Wynne | Ouachita | Camden |
| Dallas | Fordyce | Perry | Perryville |
| Desha | Arkansas City | Phillips | Helena |
| Drew | Monticello | Pike | Murfreesboro |
| Faulkner | Conway | Poinsett | Harrisburg |
| Franklin | Ozark | Polk | Mena |
| Fulton | Salem | Pope | Russellville |
| Garland | Hot Springs | Prairie | Des Arc |
| Grant | Sheridan | Pulaski | Little Rock |
| Home Greene | Paragould | Randolph | Pocahontas |
| Hempstead | Hope | Saline | Benton |
| Hot Spring | Malvern | Scott | Waldron |
| Howard | Nashville | Searcy | Marshall |
| Independence | Batesville | Sebastian | Ft. Smith |
| Izard | Melbourne | Sevier | De Queen |
| Jackson | Newport | Sharp | Ash Flat |
| Jefferson | Pine Bluff | St.Francis | Forrest City |
| Johnson | Clarksville | Stone | Mountain View |
| Lafayette | Lewisville | Union | El Dorado |
| Lawrence | Walnut Ridge | Van Buren | Clinton |
| Lee | Marianna | Washington | Fayetteville |
| Lincoln | Star City | White | Searcy |
| Little River | Ashdown | Wooodruff | Augusta |

| County | County Seat | County | County Seat |
|---|---|---|---|
| Yell | Danville | Sacramento | Sacramento |
| **C A L I F O R N I A** | | San Benito | Hollister |
| Alameda | Oakland | San Bernardino | San Bernardino |
| Alpine | Markleeville | San Diego | San Diego |
| Amador | Jackson | San Francisco | San Francisco |
| Butte | Oroville | San Joaquin | Stockton |
| Calaveras | San Andreas | San | |
| Colusa | Colusa | Luis Obispo | San Luis Obispo |
| Contra Costa | Martinez | San Mateo | Redwood City |
| Del Norte | Crescent City | Santa Barbara | SantaBarbara |
| El Dorado | Placerville | Santa Clara | San Jose |
| Fresno | Fresno | Santa Cruz | Santa Cruz |
| Glenn | Willows | Shasta | Redding |
| Humboldt | Eureka | Sierra | Downieville |
| Imperial | El Centro | Siskiyou | Yreka |
| Inyo | Independence | Solano | Fairfield |
| Kern | Bakersfield | Sonoma | Santa Rosa |
| Kings | Hanford | Stanislaus | Modesto |
| Lake | Lakeport | Sutter | Yuba City |
| Lassen | Susanville | Tehama | Red Bluff |
| Los Angeles | Los Angeles | Trinity | Weaverville |
| Madera | Madera | Tulare | Visalia |
| Marin | San Rafael | Tuolumne | Sonora |
| Mariposa | Mariposa | Ventura | Ventura |
| Mendocino | Ukiah | Yolo | Woodland |
| Merced | Merced | Yuba | Marysville |
| Modoc | Alturas | | |
| Mono | Bridgeport | **C O L O R A D O** | |
| Monterey | Salinas | Adams | Brighton |
| Napa | Napa | Alamosa | Alamosa |
| Nevada | Nevada City | Arapahoe | Littleton |
| Orange | Santa Ana | Archuleta | Pagosa Springs |
| Placer | Auburn | Baca | Springfield |
| Plumas | Quincy | Bent | Las Aminas |
| Riverside | Riverside | Boulder | Boulder |

| County | County Seat | County | County Seat |
| --- | --- | --- | --- |
| Chaffee | Salida | Montrose | Montrose |
| Cheyenne | Cheyenne Wells | Morgan | Ft Morgan |
| Clear Creek | Georgetown | Otero | La Junta |
| Conejos | Conejos | Ouray | Ouray |
| Costilla | San Luis | Park | Fairplay |
| Crowley | Ordway | Phillips | Holyoke |
| Custer | Westcliffe | Pitkin | Aspen |
| Delta | Delta | Prowers | Lamar |
| Denver | Denver | Pueblo | Pueblo |
| Dolores | Dove Creek | Rio Blanco | Meeker |
| Douglas | Castle Rock | Rio Grande | Del Norte |
| Eagle | Eagle | Routt | Steamboat Springs |
| El Paso | Colorado Springs | Saguache | Saguache |
| Elbert | Kiowa | San Juan | Silverton |
| Fremont | Canon City | San Miguel | Telluride |
| Garfield | GlenwoodSprings | Sedgwick | Julesburg |
| Gilpin | Central City | Summit | Breckenridge |
| Grand | Hot Sulfer Springs | Teller | Cripple Creek |
| Gunnison | Gunnison | Washington | Akron |
| Hinsdale | Lake City | Weld | Greeley |
| Huerfano | Walsenburg | Yuma | Wray |
| Jackson | Walden | | |
| Jefferson | Golden | | |

## CONNECTICUT

| | | | |
| --- | --- | --- | --- |
| Kiowa | Eads | Fairfield | Bridgeport |
| Kit Carson | Burlington | Hartford | Hartford |
| La Plata | Durango | Litchfield | Litchfield |
| Lake | Leadville | Middlesex | Middletown |
| Larimer | Fort Collins | New Haven | New Haven |
| Las Animas | Trinidad | New London | New London |
| Lincoln | Hugo | Tolland | Rockville |
| Logan | Sterling | Windham | Putnam |
| Mesa | Grand Junction | | |
| Mineral | Creede | | |

## DELAWARE

| | | | |
| --- | --- | --- | --- |
| Moffat | Craig | Kent | Dover |
| Montezuma | Cortez | | |

| County | County Seat | County | County Seat |
|---|---|---|---|
| New Castle | Wilmington | Indian River | Vero Beach |
| Sussex | Georgetown | Jackson | Marianna |
| | | Jefferson | Monticello |
| **F L O R I D A** | | Lafayette | Mayo |
| Alachua | Gainesville | Lake | Tavares |
| Baker | Macclenny | Lee | Ft Myers |
| Bay | Panama City | Leon | Tallahassee |
| Bradford | Starke | Levy | Bronson |
| Brevard | Titusville | Liberty | Bristol |
| Broward | Ft Lauderdale | Madison | Madison |
| Calhoun | Blountstown | Manatee | Bradenton |
| Charlotte | Punta Gorda | Marion | Ocala |
| Citrus | Inverness | Martin | Stuart |
| Clay | Green Cove Springs | Monroe | Key West |
| Collier | Naples | Nassau | Fernandina Beach |
| Columbia | Lake City | Okaloosa | Crestview |
| Dade | Miami | Okeechobee | Okeechobee |
| De Soto | Arcadia | Orange | Orlando |
| Dixie | Cross City | Osceola | Kissimmee |
| Duval | Jacksonville | Palm Beach | West Palm Beach |
| Escambia | Pensacola | Pasco | Dade City |
| Flagler | Bunnell | Pinellas | Clearwater |
| Franklin | Apalachicola | Polk | Bartow |
| Gadsden | Quincy | Putnam | Palatka |
| Gilchrist | Trenton | Santa Rosa | Milton |
| Glades | Moore Haven | Sarasota | Sarasota |
| Gulf | Port St Joe | Seminole | Sanford |
| Hamilton | Jasper | St Johns | St Augustine |
| Hardee | Wauchula | St Lucie | Ft Pierce |
| Hendry | La Belle | Sumter | Bushnell |
| Hernando | Brooksville | Suwannee | Live Oak |
| Highlands | Sebring | Taylor | Perry |
| Hillsborough | Tampa | Union | Lake Butler |
| Holmes | Bonifay | Volusia | De Land |

| County | County Seat | County | County Seat |
|---|---|---|---|
| Wakulla | Crawfordville | Clayton | Jonesboro |
| Walton | DeFuniak Springs | Clinch | Homerville |
| Washington | Chipley | Cobb | Marietta |
| | | Coffee | Douglas |

## GEORGIA

| County | County Seat | County | County Seat |
|---|---|---|---|
| | | Colquitt | Moultrie |
| Appling | Baxley | Columbia | Appling |
| Atkinson | Pearson | Cook | Adel |
| Bacon | Alma | Coweta | Newnan |
| Baker | Newton | Crawford | Knoxville |
| Baldwin | Milledgeville | Crisp | Cordele |
| Banks | Homer | Dade | Trenton |
| Barrow | Winder | Dawson | Dawsonville |
| Bartow | Cartersville | Decatur | Bainbridge |
| Ben Hill | Fitzgerald | DeKalb | Decatur |
| Berrien | Nashville | Dodge | Eastman |
| Bibb | Macon | Dooly | Vienna |
| Bleckley | Cochran | Dougherty | Albany |
| Brantley | Nahunta | Douglas | Douglasville |
| Brooks | Quitman | Early | Blakely |
| Bryan | Pembroke | Echols | Statenville |
| Bulloch | Statesboro | Effingham | Springfield |
| Burke | Waynesboro | Elbert | Elberton |
| Butts | Jackson | Emanuel | Swainsboro |
| Calhoun | Morgan | Evans | Claxton |
| Camden | Woodbine | Fannin | Blue Ridge |
| Candler | Metter | Fayette | Fayetteville |
| Carroll | Carrollton | Floyd | Rome |
| Catoosa | Ringgold | Forsyth | Cumming |
| Charlton | Folkston | Franklin | Carnesville |
| Chatham | Savannah | Fulton | Atlanta |
| Chattahoochee | Cusseta | Gilmer | Ellijay |
| Chattooga | Summerville | Glascock | Gibson |
| Cherokee | Canton | Glynn | Brunswick |
| Clarke | Athens | Gordon | Calhoun |
| Clay | Ft Gaines | Grady | Cairo |

| County | County Seat | County | County Seat |
|---|---|---|---|
| Greene | Greensboro | Mitchell | Camilla |
| Gwinnett | Lawrenceville | Monroe | Forsyth |
| Habersham | Clarkesville | Montgomery | Mount Vernon |
| Hall | Gainesville | Morgan | Madison |
| Hancock | Sparta | Murray | Chatsworth |
| Haralson | Buchanan | Muscogee | Columbus |
| Harris | Hamilton | Newton | Covington |
| Hart | Hartwell | Oconee | Watkinsville |
| Heard | Franklin | Oglethorpe | Lexington |
| Henry | McDonough | Paulding | Dallas |
| Houston | Perry | Peach | Ft Valley |
| Irwin | Ocilla | Pickens | Jasper |
| Jackson | Jefferson | Pierce | Blackshear |
| Jasper | Monticello | Pike | Zebulon |
| Jeff Davis | Hazlehurst | Polk | Cedartown |
| Jefferson | Louisville | Pulaski | Hawkinsville |
| Jenkins | Millen | Putnam | Eatonton |
| Johnson | Wrightsville | Quitman | Georgetown |
| Jones | Gray | Rabun | Clayton |
| Lamar | Barnesville | Randolph | Cuthbert |
| Lanier | Lakeland | Richmond | Augusta |
| Laurens | Dublin | Rockdale | Conyers |
| Lee | Leesburg | Schley | Ellaville |
| Liberty | Hinesville | Screven | Sylvania |
| Lincoln | Lincolnton | Seminole | Donalsonville |
| Long | Ludowici | Spalding | Griffin |
| Lowndes | Valdosta | Stephens | Toccoa |
| Lumpkin | Dahlonega | Stewart | Lumpkin |
| Macon | Oglethorpe | Sumter | Americus |
| Madison | Danielsville | Talbot | Talbotton |
| Marion | Buena Vista | Taliaferro | Crawfordville |
| McDuffie | Thomson | Tattnall | Reidsville |
| McIntosh | Darien | Taylor | Butler |
| Meriwether | Greenville | Telfair | McRae |
| Miller | Colquitt | Terrell | Dawson |

| County | County Seat | County | County Seat |
|---|---|---|---|
| Thomas | Thomasville | Bear Lake | Paris |
| Tift | Tifton | Benewah | St Marie's |
| Toombs | Lyons | Bingham | Blackfoot |
| Towns | Hiawassee | Blaine | Hailey |
| Treutlen | Soperton | Boise | Idaho City |
| Troup | La Grange | Bonner | Sandpoint |
| Turner | Ashburn | Bonneville | Idaho Falls |
| Twiggs | Jeffersonville | Boundary | BonnersFerry |
| Union | Blairsville | Butte | Arco |
| Upson | Thomaston | Camas | Fairfield |
| Walker | LaFayette | Canyon | Caldwell |
| Walton | Monroe | Caribou | Soda Springs |
| Ware | Waycross | Cassia | Burley |
| Warren | Warrenton | Clark | Dubois |
| Washington | Sandersville | Clearwater | Orofino |
| Wayne | Jesup | Custer | Challis |
| Webster | Preston | Elmore | Mountain Home |
| Wheeler | Alamo | Franklin | Preston |
| White | Cleveland | Fremont | St Anthony |
| Whitfield | Dalton | Gem | Emmett |
| Wilcox | Abbeville | Gooding | Gooding |
| Wilkes | Washington | Idaho | Grangeville |
| Wilkinson | Irwinton | Jefferson | Rigby |
| Worth | Sylvester | Jerome | Jerome |
| | | Kootenai | Cooeurd'Alene |

# HAWAII

| | | | |
|---|---|---|---|
| | | Latah | Moscow |
| Hawaii | Hilo | Lemhi | Salmon |
| Honolulu | Honolulu | Lewis | Nezperce |
| Kauai | Lihue | | |
| Maui | Wailuku | Lincoln | Shoshone |
| | | Madison | Rexburg |

# IDAHO

| | | Minidoka | Rupert |
|---|---|---|---|
| Ada | Boise | Nez Perce | Lewiston |
| Adams | Council | Oneida | Malad City |
| Bannock | Pocatello | Owyhee | Murphy |

| County | County Seat | County | County Seat |
| --- | --- | --- | --- |
| Payette | Payette | Ford | Paxton |
| Power | American Falls | Franklin | Benton |
| Shoshone | Wallace | Fulton | Lewistown |
| Teton | Driggs | Gallatin | Shawneetown |
| Twin Falls | Twin Falls | Greene | Carrollton |
| Valley | Cascade | Grundy | Morris |
| Washington | Weiser | Hamilton | McLeansboro |
|  |  | Hancock | Carthage |
| **ILLINOIS** |  | Hardin | Elizabethtown |
| Adams | Quincy | Henderson | Oquawka |
| Alexander | Cairo | Henry | Cambridge |
| Bond | Greenville | Iroquois | Watseka |
| Boone | Blevidere | Jackson | Murphysboro |
| Brown | MountSterling | Jasper | Newton |
| Bureau | Princeton | Jefferson | Mount Vernon |
| Calhoun | Hardin | Jersey | Jerseyville |
| Carroll | Mount Carroll | Jo Daviess | Galena |
| Cass | Virginia | Johnson | Vienna |
| Champaign | Urbana | Kane | Geneva |
| Christian | Taylorville | Kankakee | Kankakee |
| Clark | Marshall | Kendall | Yorkville |
| Clay | Louisville | Knox | Galesburg |
| Clinton | Carlyle | Lake | Waukegan |
| Coles | Charleston | LaSalle | Ottawa |
| Cook | Chicago | Lawrence | Lawrenceville |
| Crawford | Robinson | Lee | Dixon |
| Cumberland | Toledo | Livingston | Pontiac |
| DeKalb | Sycamore | Logan | Lincoln |
| DeWitt | Clinton | Macon | Decatur |
| Douglas | Tuscola | Macoupin | Carlinville |
| DuPage | Wheaton | Madison | Edwardsville |
| Edgar | Paris | Marion | Salem |
| Edwards | Albion | Marshall | Lacon |
| Effingham | Effingham | Mason | Havana |
| Fayette | Vandalia | Massac | Metropolis |

**Adoption Searches Made Easier**

| County | County Seat |
|---|---|
| McDonough | Macomb |
| McHenry | Woodstock |
| McLean | Bloomington |
| Menard | Petersburg |
| Mercer | Aledo |
| Monroe | Waterloo |
| Montgomery | Hillsboro |
| Morgan | Jacksonville |
| Moultrie | Sullivan |
| Ogle | Oregon |
| Peoria | Peoria |
| Perry | Pinckneyville |
| Piatt | Monticello |
| Pike | Pittsfield |
| Pope | Golconda |
| Pulaski | Mound City |
| Putnam | Hennepin |
| Randolph | Chester |
| Richland | Olney |
| Rock Island | Rock Island |
| Saline | Harrisburg |
| Sangamon | Springfield |
| Schuyler | Rushville |
| Scott | Winchester |
| Shelby | Shelbyville |
| St Clair | Belleville |
| Stark | Toulon |
| Stephenson | Freeport |
| Tazewell | Pekin |
| Union | Jonesboro |
| Vermillion | Danville |
| Wabash | Mount Carmel |
| Warren | Monmouth |
| Washington | Nashville |
| Wayne | Fairfield |
| White | Carmi |
| Whiteside | Morrison |
| Will | Joliet |
| Williamson | Marion |
| Winnebago | Rockford |
| Woodford | Eureka |

## INDIANA

| County | County Seat |
|---|---|
| Adams | Decatur |
| Allen | Ft Wayne |
| Bartholomew | Columbus |
| Benton | Fowler |
| Blackford | HartfordCity |
| Boone | Lebanon |
| Brown | Nashville |
| Carroll | Delphi |
| Cass | Logansport |
| Clark | Jeffersonville |
| Clay | Brazil |
| Clinton | Frankfort |
| Crawford | English |
| Daviess | Washington |
| Dearborn | Lawrenceburg |
| Decatur | Greensburg |
| DeKalb | Auburn |
| Delaware | Muncie |
| Dubois | Jasper |
| Elkhart | Goshen |
| Fayette | Connersville |
| Floyd | New Albany |
| Fountain | Covington |
| Franklin | Brookville |
| Fulton | Rochester |
| Gibson | Princeton |
| Grant | Marion |

| County | County Seat | County | County Seat |
|---|---|---|---|
| Greene | Bloomfield | Pike | Petersburg |
| Hamilton | Noblesville | Porter | Valparaiso |
| Hancock | Greenfield | Posey | Mount Vernon |
| Harrison | Corydon | Pulaski | Winamac |
| Hendricks | Danville | Putnam | Greencastle |
| Henry | New Castle | Randolph | Winchester |
| Howard | Kokomo | Ripley | Versailles |
| Huntington | Huntington | Rush | Rushville |
| Jackson | Brownstown | Scott | Scottsburg |
| Jasper | Rensselaer | Shelby | Shelbyville |
| Jay | Portland | Spencer | Rockport |
| Jefferson | Madison | Starke | Knox |
| Jennings | Vernon | Steuben | Angola |
| Johnson | Franklin | St Joseph | South Bend |
| Knox | Vincennes | Sullivan | Sullivan |
| Kosciusko | Warsaw | Switzerland | Vevay |
| La Grange | La Grange | Tippecanoe | Lafayette |
| La Porte | La Porte | Tipton | Tipton |
| Lake | Crown Point | Union | Liberty |
| Lawrence | Bedford | Vanderburgh | Evansville |
| Madison | Anderson | Vermillion | Newport |
| Marion | Indianapolis | Vigo | TerreHaute |
| Marshall | Plymouth | Wabash | Wabash |
| Martin | Shoals | Warren | Williamsport |
| Miami | Peru | Warrick | Boonville |
| Monroe | Bloomington | Washington | Salem |
| Montgomery | Crawfordsville | Wayne | Richmond |
| Morgan | Martinville | Wells | Bluffton |
| Newton | Kentland | White | Monticello |
| Noble | Albion | Whitley | Columbia City |
| Ohio | RisingSun | | |
| Orange | Paoli | **I O W A** | |
| Owen | Spencer | Adair | Greenfield |
| Parke | Rockville | Adams | Corning |
| Perry | Cannelton | Allamakee | Waukon |

| County | County Seat | County | County Seat |
|---|---|---|---|
| Appanoose | Centerville | Guthrie | Guthrie Center |
| Audubon | Audubon | Hamilton | Webster City |
| Benton | Vinton | Hancock | Garner |
| Black Hawk | Waterloo | Hardin | Eldora |
| Boone | Boone | Harrison | Logan |
| Bremer | Waverly | Henry | Mount |
| Buchanan | Independence | Howard | Cresco |
| Buena Vista | Storm Lake | Humboldt | Dakota City |
| Butler | Allison | Ida | Ida Grove |
| Calhoun | Rockwell City | Iowa | Marengo |
| Carroll | Carroll | Jackson | Maquoketa |
| Cass | Atlantic | Jasper | Newton |
| Cedar | Tipton | Jefferson | Fairfield |
| CerroGordo | Mason City | Johnson | Iowa City |
| Cherokee | Cherokee | Jones | Anamosa |
| Chickasaw | New Hampton | Keokuk | Sigourney |
| Clarke | Osceola | Kossuth | Algona |
| Clay | Spencer | Lee | Ft Madison |
| Clayton | Elkader | Linn | Cedar Rapids |
| Clinton | Clinton | Louisa | Wapello |
| Crawford | Denison | Lucas | Chariton |
| Dallas | Adel | Lyon | Rock Rapids |
| Davis | Bloomfield | Madison | Winterset |
| Decatur | Leon | Mahaska | Oskaloosa |
| Delaware | Manchester | Marion | Knoxville |
| Des Moines | Burlington | Marshall | Marshalltown |
| Dickinson | Spirit Lake | Mills | Glenwood |
| Dubuque | Dubuque | Mitchell | Osage |
| Emmet | Esterville | Monona | Onawa |
| Fayette | West Union | Monroe | Albia |
| Floyd | Charles City | Montgomery | Red Oak |
| Franklin | Hampton | Muscatine | Muscatine |
| Fremont | Sidney | O'Brien | Primghar |
| Greene | Jefferson | Osceola | Sibley |
| Grundy | Grundy Center | Page | Clarinda |

| County | County Seat | County | County Seat |
|---|---|---|---|
| Palo Alto | Emmetsburg | Butler | El Dorado |
| Plymouth | Le Mars | Chase | Cottonwood Falls |
| Pocahontas | Pocahontas | Chautauqua | Sedan |
| Pleasant Polk | Des Moines | Cherokee | Columbus |
| Pottawattamie | Council Bluffs | Cheyenne | St Francis |
| Poweshiek | Montezuma | Clark | Ashland |
| Ringgold | Mount Ayr | Clay | Clay Center |
| Sac | Sac City | Cloud | Concordia |
| Scott | Davenport | Coffey | Burlington |
| Shelby | Harlan | Comanche | Coldwater |
| Sioux | Orange City | Cowley | Winfield |
| Story | Nevada | Crawford | Girard |
| Tama | Toledo | Decatur | Oberlin |
| Taylor | Bedford | Dicldnson | Abilene |
| Union | Crestin | Doniphan | Troy |
| Van Buren | Keosauqua | Douglas | Lawrence |
| Wapello | Ottumwa | Edwards | Kinsley |
| Warren | Indianola | Elk | Howard |
| Washington | Washington | Ellis | Hays |
| Wayne | Corydon | Ellsworth | Ellsworth |
| Webster | Ft Dodge | Finney | Garden City |
| Winnebago | Forest City | Ford | Dodge City |
| Winneshiek | Decorah | Franklin | Ottawa |
| Woodbury | Sioux City | Geary | Junction City |
| Worth | Northwood | Gove | Gove City |
| Wright | Clarion | Graham | Hill City |
| | | Grant | Ulysses |

## KANSAS

| County | County Seat | County | County Seat |
|---|---|---|---|
| | | Gray | Cimarron |
| Allen | Iola | Greenley | Tribune |
| Anderson | Garnett | Greenwood | Eureka |
| Atchison | Atchison | Hamilton | Syracuse |
| Barber | MedicineLodge | Harper | Anthony |
| Barton | Great Bend | Harvey | Newton |
| Bourbon | Ft Scott | Haskell | Sublette |
| Brown | Ifiawatha | Hodgeman | Jetrnore |

| County | County Seat | County | County Seat |
|---|---|---|---|
| Jackson | Holton | Reno | Hutchinson |
| Jefferson | Oskaloosa | Republic | Belleville |
| Jewell | Mankato | Rice | Lyons |
| Johnson | Olathe | Riley | Manhattan |
| Kearney | Lakin | Rooks | Stockton |
| Kingman | Kingman | Rush | La Crosse |
| Kiowa | Greensburg | Russell | Russell |
| Labette | Oswego | Saline | Salina |
| Lane | Dighton | Scott | Scott City |
| Leavenworth | Leavenworth | Sedgwick | Wichita |
| Lincoln | Lincoln | Seward | Liberal |
| Linn | Mound City | Shawnee | Topeka |
| Logan | Oakley | Sheridan | Hoxie |
| Lyon | Emporia | Sherman | Goodland |
| Marion | Marion | Smith | Smith Center |
| Marshall | Marysville | Stafford | StJohn |
| McPherson | McPherson | Stanton | Johnson City |
| Meade | Meade | Stevens | Hugoton |
| Miami | Paola | Sumner | Wellington |
| Mitchell | Beloit | Thomas | Colby |
| Montgomery | Independence | Trego | Wakeeney |
| Morris | Council Grove | Wabaunsee | Alma |
| Morton | Elkhart | Wallace | SharonSprings |
| Nemaha | Seneca | Washington | Washington |
| Neosho | Erie | Wichita | Leoti |
| Ness | Ness City | Wilson | Fredonia |
| Norton | Norton | Woodson | Yates Center |
| Osage | Lyndon | Wyandotte | Kansas City |
| Osborne | Osborne | | |
| Ottawa | Minneapolis | | |

# KENTUCKY

| County | County Seat |
|---|---|
| Pawnee | Lamed |
| Adair | Columbia |
| Phillips | Phillipsburg |
| Allen | Scottsville |
| Pottawatomie | Westmoreland |
| Anderson | Lawrenceburg |
| Pratt | Pratt |
| Ballard | Wickliffe |
| Rawlins | Atwood |
| Barren | Glasgow |

| County | County Seat | County | County Seat |
|---|---|---|---|
| Bath | Owingsville | Grant | Williamstown |
| Bell | Pineville | Graves | Mayfield |
| Boone | Burlington | Grayson | Leitchfield |
| Bourbon | Paris | Green | Greensburg |
| Boyd | Catlettsburg | Greenup | Greenup |
| Boyle | Danville | Hancock | Hawesville |
| Bracken | Brooksville | Hardin | Elizabethtown |
| Breathitt | Jackson | Harlan | Harlan |
| Breckinridge | Hardinsburg | Harrison | Cynthiana |
| Bullitt | Shepherdsville | Hart | Munfordville |
| Butler | Morgantown | Henderson | Henderson |
| Caldwell | Princeton | Henry | New Castle |
| Calloway | Murray | Hickman | Clinton |
| Campbell | Newport | Hopkins | Madisonville |
| Carlisle | Bardwell | Jackson | McKee |
| Carroll | Carrollton | Jefferson | Louisville |
| Carter | Grayson | Jessamine | Nicholasville |
| Casey | Liberty | Johnson | Paintsville |
| Christian | Hopkinsville | Kenton | Covington |
| Clark | Winchester | Knott | Hindman |
| Clay | Manchester | Knox | Barbourville |
| Clinton | Albany | Larue | Hodgenville |
| Crittenden | Marion | Laurel | London |
| Cumberland | Burkesville | Lawrence | Louisa |
| Daviess | Owensboro | Lee | Beattyville |
| Edmonson | Brownsville | Leslie | Hyden |
| Elliott | Sandy Hook | Letcher | Whitesburg |
| Estill | Irvine | Lewis | Vanceburg |
| Fayette | Lexington | Lincoln | Stanford |
| Fleming | Flemingsburg | Livingston | Smithland |
| Floyd | Prestonburg | Logan | Russellville |
| Franklin | Frankfort | Lyon | Eddyville |
| Fulton | Hickman | Madison | Richmond |
| Gallatin | Warsaw | Madison | Richmond |
| Garrard | Lancastre | Magoffin | Salyersville |

| County | County Seat | County | County Seat |
|---|---|---|---|
| Marion | Lebanon | Todd | Elkton |
| Marshall | Benton | Trigg | Cadiz |
| Martin | Inez | Trimble | Bedford |
| Mason | Maysville | Union | Morganfield |
| McCracken | Paducah | Warren | Bowling Green |
| McCreary | Whitley City | Washington | Springfield |
| McLean | Calhoun | Wayne | Monticello |
| Meade | Brandenburg | Webster | Dixon |
| Menifee | Frenchburg | Whitley | Williamsburg |
| Mercer | Harrodsburg | Wolfe | Campton |
| Metcalfe | Edmonton | Woodford | Versailles |
| Monroe | Tompkinsville | | |
| Montgomery | MountSterling | | |

## LOUISIANA

| County | County Seat |
|---|---|
| Morgan | West Liberty |
| Mublenberg | Greenville |
| Nelson | Bardstown |
| Nicholas | Carlisle |
| Ohio | Hartford |
| Oldham | La Grange |
| Owen | Owenton |
| Owsley | Booneville |
| Pendleton | Falmouth |
| Perry | Hazard |
| Pike | Pikeville |
| Powell | Stanton |
| Plaski | Somerset |
| Robertson | Mount Olivet |
| Rockcastle | Mount Vernon |
| Rowan | Morehead |
| Russell | Jamestown |
| Scott | Georgetown |
| Shelby | Shelbyville |
| Simpson | Franklin |
| Spencer | Taylorsville |
| Taylor | Campbellsville |

| County | County Seat |
|---|---|
| Acadia | Crowley |
| Allen | Oberlin |
| Ascension | Donaldsonville |
| Assumption | Napoleonville |
| Avoyelles | Marksville |
| Beauregard | De Ridder |
| Bienville | Arcadia |
| Bossier | Benton |
| Caddo | Shreveport |
| Calcasieu | Lake Charles |
| Caldwell | Columbia |
| Cameron | Cameron |
| Catahoula | Harrisonburg |
| Claiborne | Homer |
| Concordia | Vidalia |
| De Soto | Mansfield |
| East Baton Rouge | Baton Rouge |
| East Carroll | Lake Providence |
| East Feliciana | Clinton |
| Evangeline | Ville Platte |
| Franklin | Winnsboro |
| Grant | Colfax |

| County | County Seat |
|---|---|
| Iberia | New Iberia |
| Iberville | Plaquemine |
| Jackson | Jonesboro |
| Jefferson | Gretna |
| Jefferson Davis | Jennings |
| Lafayette | Lafayette |
| Lafourche | Thibodaux |
| La Salle | Jena |
| Lincoln | Ruston |
| Livingston | Livingston |
| Madison | Tallulah |
| Morehouse | Bastrop |
| Natchitoches | Natchitoches |
| Orleans | New Orleans |
| Ouachita | Monroe |
| Plaquemines | Pointela Hache |
| PointeCoupee | New Roads |
| Rapides | Alexandria |
| Red River | Coushatta |
| Richland | Rayville |
| Sabine | Many |
| St Bernard | Chalmette |
| St Charles | Hahnville |
| St Helena | Greensburg |
| St James | Convent |
| St John the Baptist | La Place |
| St Landry | Opelousas |
| St Martin | St Martinville |
| St Mary | Franklin |
| St Tammany | Covington |
| Tangipahoa | Amite City |
| Tensas | St Joseph |
| Terrebonne | Houma |
| Union | Farmerville |
| Vermilion | Abbeville |
| Vernon | Leesville |
| Washington | Franklinton |
| Webster | Minden |
| West Baton Rouge | Port Allen |
| West Carroll | Oak Grove |
| West Feliciana | St Francisville |
| Winn | Winnfield |

## MAINE

| | |
|---|---|
| Androscoggin | Auburn |
| Aroostook | Houlton |
| Cumberland | Portland |
| Franklin | Farmington |
| Hancock | Ellsworth |
| Kennebec | Augusta |
| Knox | Rockland |
| Lincoln | Wiscasset |
| Oxford | South Paris |
| Penobscot | Bangor |
| Piscataquis | Dover-Foxcroft |
| Sagadahoc | Bath |
| Somerset | Skowhegan |
| Waldo | Belfast |
| Washington | Machias |
| York | Alfred |

## MARYLAND

| | |
|---|---|
| Allegany | Cumberland |
| Anne Arundel | Annapolis |
| Baltimore | Towson |
| Calvert | Prince Frederick |
| Caroline | Denton |
| Carroll | Westminster |
| Cecil | Elkton |
| Charles | La Plata |

| County | County Seat | County | County Seat |
|---|---|---|---|
| Dorchester | Cambridge | Alger | Munising |
| Frederick | Frederick | Allegan | Allegan |
| Garrett | Oakland | Alpena | Alpena |
| Harford | Bel Air | Antrim | Bellaire |
| Howard | Ellicott City | Arenac | Standish |
| Kent | Chestertown | Barap | L'Anse |
| Montgomery | Rockville | Barry | Hastings |
| Prince | | Bay | Bay City |
| George's | Upper Marlboro | Benzie | Beulah |
| QueenAnne's | Centreville | Berrien | St Joseph |
| Somerset | Princess Anne | Branch | Coldwater |
| St Mary's | Leonardtown | Calhoun | Marshall |
| Talbot | Easton | Cass | Cassopolis |
| Washington | Hagerstown | Charlevoix | Charlevoix |
| Wicomico | Salisbury | Cheboygan | Cheboygan |
| Worcester | Snow Hill | Chippewa | Sault Ste Marie |
| | | Clare | Harrison |

## MASSACHUSETTS

| | | | |
|---|---|---|---|
| Barnstable | Barnstable | Clinton | St Johns |
| Berkshire | Pittsfield | Crawford | Grayling |
| Bristol | Taunton | Delta | Escanaba |
| Dukes | Edgartown | Dickinson | Iron Mountain |
| Essex | Salem | Eaton | Charlotte |
| Franklin | Greenfield | Emmet | Petoskey |
| Hampden | Springfield | Genesee | Flint |
| Hampshire | Northampton | Gladwin | Gladwin |
| Middlesex | Cambridge | Gogebic | Bessemer |
| Nantucket | Nantucket | Grand Traverse | Traverse City |
| Norfolk | Dedham | Gratiot | Ithaca |
| Plymouth | Plymouth | Hillsdale | Hillsdale |
| Suffolk | Boston | Houghton | Houghton |
| Worcester | Worcester | Huron | Bad Axe |
| | | Ingham | Mason |
| | | Ionia | Ionia |

## MICHIGAN

| | | | |
|---|---|---|---|
| Alcona | Harrisville | Iosco | Tawas City |
| | | Iron | CrystalFalls |

| County | County Seat | County | County Seat |
|---|---|---|---|
| Isabella | Mount Pleasant | Roscommon | Roscommon |
| Jackson | Jackson | Saginaw | Saginaw |
| Kalamazoo | Kalamazoo | SanilacIsle | Sandusky |
| Kalkaska | Kalkaska | Schoolcraft | Manistique |
| Kent | Grand Rapids | Shiawassee | Corunna |
| Keweenaw | Eagle River | St Clair | Port Huron |
| Lake | Baldwin | St Joseph | Centreville |
| Lapeer | Lapeer | Tuscola | Caro |
| Leelanau | Leland | Van Buren | Paw Paw |
| Lenawee | Adrian | Washtenaw | Ann Arbor |
| Livingston | Howell | Wayne | Detroit |
| Luce | Newberry | Wexford | Cadillac |
| Mackinac | St Ignace | | |
| Macomb | MountClemens | | |

## MINNESOTA

| County | County Seat |
|---|---|
| Manistee | Manistee | Aitkin | Aitkin |

| County | County Seat | County | County Seat |
|---|---|---|---|
| Manistee | Manistee | Aitkin | Aitkin |
| Marquette | Marquette | Anoka | Anoka |
| Mason | Ludington | Becker | Detroit Lakes |
| Mecosta | Big Rapids | Beltrami | Bemidji |
| Menominee | Menominee | Benton | Foley |
| Midland | Midland | Big Stone | Ortonville |
| Missaukee | Lake City | Blue Earth | Mankato |
| Monroe | Monroe | Brown | New Ulm |
| Montcalm | Stanton | Carlton | Carlton |
| Montmorency | Atlanta | Carver | Chaska |
| Muskegon | Muskegon | Cass | Walker |
| Newaygo | White Cloud | Chippewa | Montevideo |
| Oakland | Pontiac | Chisago | Center City |
| Oceana | Hart | Clay | Moorhead |
| Ogemaw | West Branch | Clearwater | Bagley |
| Ontonagon | Ontonagon | Cook | Grand Marais |
| Osceola | Reed City | Cottonwood | Windom |
| Oscoda | Mio | Crow Wing | Brainerd |
| Otsego | Gaylord | Dakota | Hastings |
| Ottawa | Grand Haven | Dodge | Mantorville |
| PresqueIsle | Rogers City | Douglas | Alexandria |

| County | County Seat | County | County Seat |
|---|---|---|---|
| Faribault | Blue Earth | Otter Tail | Fergus Falls |
| Fillmore | Preston | Pennington | Thief River Falls |
| Freeborn | Albert Lea | Pine | Pine City |
| Goodhue | Red Wing | Pipestone | Pipestone |
| Grant | Elbow Lake | Polk | Crookston |
| Hennepin | Minneapolis | Pope | Glenwood |
| Houston | Caledonia | Redwood | Redwood Falls |
| Hubbard | Park Rapids | Ramsey | St Paul |
| Isanti | Cambridge | Red Lake | Red Lake Falls |
| Itasca | Grand Rapids | Renville | Olivia |
| Jackson | Jackson | Rice | Faribault |
| Kanabec | Mora | Rock | Luverne |
| Kandiyohi | Willmar | Roseau | Roseau |
| Kittson | Hallock | Scott | Shakopee |
| Koochiching | International Falls | Sherburne | Elk River |
| | | Sibley | Gaylord |
| Lac Qui Parle | Madison | Stearns | St Cloud |
| Lake | Two Harbors | Steele | Owatonna |
| Lake of the Woods | Baudette | Stevens | Morris |
| Lyon | Marshall | St Louis | Duluth |
| Le Sueur | Le Center | Swift | Benson |
| Lincoln | Ivanhoe | Todd | Long Prairie |
| Mahnomen | Mahnomen | Traverse | Wheaton |
| Marshall | Warren | Wabasha | Wabasha |
| Martin | Fairmont | Wadena | Wadena |
| McLeod | Glencoe | Waseca | Waseca |
| Meeker | Litchfield | Washington | Stillwater |
| Mille Lacs | Milaca | Watonwan | St James |
| Morrison | Little Falls | Wilkin | Breckenridge |
| Mower | Austin | Winona | Winona |
| Murray | Slayton | Wright | Buffalo |
| Nicollet | St Peter | Yellow - | |
| Nobles | Worthington | Medicine | Granite Falls |
| Norman | Ada | | |
| Olmsted | Rochester | **MISSISSIPPI** | |

| County | County Seat | County | County Seat |
|---|---|---|---|
| Adams | Natchez | Lafayette | Oxford |
| Alcorn | Corinth | Lamar | Purvis |
| Amite | Liberty | Lauderdale | Meridian |
| Attala | Kosciusko | Lawrence | Monticello |
| Benton | Ashland | Leake | Carthage |
| Bolivar | Cleveland | Lee | Tupelo |
| Calhoun | Pittsboro | Leflore | Greenwood |
| Carroll | Carrollton | Lincoln | Brookhaven |
| Chickasaw | Houston | Lowndes | Columbus |
| Choctaw | Ackerman | Madison | Canton |
| Claiborne | Port Gibson | Marion | Columbia |
| Clarke | Quitman | Marshall | Holly Springs |
| Clay | West Point | Monroe | Aberdeen |
| Coahoma | Clarksdale | Montgomery | Winona |
| Copiah | Hazlehurst | Neshoba | Philadelpia |
| Covington | Collins | Newton | Decatur |
| DeSoto | Hernando | Noxubee | Macon |
| Forrest | Hattiesburg | Okibbeha | Starkville |
| Franklin | Meadville | Panola | Batesville |
| George | Lucedale | Pearl River | Poplarville |
| Greene | Leakesville | Perry | New Augusta |
| Grenada | Grenada | Pike | Magnolia |
| Hancock | BayStLouis | Pontotoc | Pontotoc |
| Harrison | Gulfport/Biloid | Prentiss | Boonesville |
| Hinds | Jackson/Raymond | Quitman | Marks |
| Holmes | Leidngton | Rankin | Brandon |
| Humphreys | Belzoni | Scott | Forest |
| Issaquena | Mayersville | Sharkey | Rolling Fork |
| Itawamba | Fulton | Simpson | Mendenhall |
| Jackson | Pascagoula | Smith | Raleigh |
| Jasper | Bay Springs | Stone | Wiggins |
| Jefferson | Fayette | Sunflower | Indianola |
| Jefferson Davis | Prentiss | Tallahatchie | Charleston |
| Jones | Laurel | Tate | Senatobia |
| Kemper | DeKalb | Tippah | Ripley |

**Adoption Searches Made Easier**

| County | County Seat | County | County Seat |
|---|---|---|---|
| Tishomingo | Luka | Christian | Ozark |
| Tunica | Tunica | Clark | Kahoka |
| Union | New Albany | Clay | Liberty |
| Walthall | Tylertown | Clinton | Plattsburg |
| Warren | Vicksburg | Cole | Jefferson City |
| Washington | Greenville | Cooper | Boonville |
| Wayne | Waynesboro | Crawford | Steelville |
| Webster | Walthall | Dade | Greenfield |
| Wilkinson | Woodville | Dallas | Buffalo |
| Winston | Louisville | Daviess | Gallatin |
| Yalobusha | Water Valley | DeKalb | Maysville |
| Yazoo | Yazoo City | Dent | Salem |
| | | Douglas | Ava |

## MISSOURI

| County | County Seat | County | County Seat |
|---|---|---|---|
| | | Dunklin | Kennett |
| Adair | Kirksville | Franklin | Union |
| Andrew | Savannah | Gasconade | Hermann |
| Atchison | Rock Port | Gentry | Albany |
| Audrain | Mexico | Greene | Springfield |
| Barry | Cassville | Grundy | Trenton |
| Barton | Lamar | Harrison | Bethany |
| Bates | Butler | Henry | Clinton |
| Benton | Warsaw | Hickory | Hermitage |
| Bollinger | Marble Hill | Holt | Oregon |
| Boone | Columbia | Howard | Fayette |
| Buchanan | St Joseph | Howell | West Plains |
| Butler | Poplar Bluff | Iron | Ironton |
| Caldwell | Kingston | Jackson | Independence |
| Callaway | Fulton | Jasper | Carthage |
| Camden | Camdenton | Jefferson | Hillsboro |
| Cape - Girardeau | Jackson | Johnson | Warrensburg |
| Carroll | Carrollton | Knox | Edina |
| Carter | Van Buren | Laclede | Lebanon |
| Cass | Harrisonville | Lafayette | Lexington |
| Cedar | Stockton | Lawrence | Mount Vernon |
| Chariton | Keytesville | Lewis | Monticello |

| County | County Seat | County | County Seat |
|---|---|---|---|
| Lincoln | Troy | Saline | Marshall |
| Linn | Linneus | Schuyler | Lancaster |
| Livingston | Chillicothe | Scotland | Memphis |
| Macon | Macon | Scott | Benton |
| Madison | Fredericktown | Shannon | Eminence |
| Maries | Vienna | Shelby | Shelbyville |
| Marion | Palmyra | St Charles | St Charles |
| McDonald | Pineville | St Clair | Osceola |
| Mercer | Princeton | St Francis | Farmington |
| Miller | Tuscumbia | St Genevieve | Farmington |
| Mississippi | Charleston | St Louis | Clayton |
| Moniteau | California | Stoddard | Bloomfield |
| Monroe | Paris | Stone | Galena |
| Montgomery | Montgomery City | Sullivan | Milan |
| Morgan | Versailles | Taney | Forsyth |
| New Madrid | New Madrid | Texas | Houston |
| Newton | Neosho | Vernon | Nevada |
| Nodaway | Maryville | Warren | Warrenton |
| Oregon | Alton | Washington | Potosi |
| Osage | Linn | Wayne | Greenville |
| Ozark | Gainesville | Webster | Marshfield |
| Pemiscot | Caruthersville | Worth | Grant City |
| Perry | Perryville | Wright | Hartville |
| Pettis | Sedalia | | |
| Phelps | Rolla | | |

## MONTANA

| County | County Seat |
|---|---|
| Pike | Bowling Green |
| Platte | Platte City |
| Polk | Bolivar |
| Pulaski | Waynesville |
| Putnam | Unionville |
| Ralls | New London |
| Randolph | Huntsville |
| Ray | Richmond |
| Reynolds | Centerville |
| Ripley | Doniphan |

| County | County Seat |
|---|---|
| Beaverhead | Dillon |
| Big Hom | Hardin |
| Blaine | Chinook |
| Broadwater | Townsend |
| Carbon | Red Lodge |
| Carter | Ekalaka |
| Cascade | Great Falls |
| Cbouteau | Ft Benton |
| Custer | Miles City |
| Daniels | Scobey |

| County | County Seat | County | County Seat |
|---|---|---|---|
| Dawson | Glendive | Sheridan | Plentywood |
| Deer Lodge | Anaconda | Silver Bow | Butte |
| Fallon | Baker | | |
| Fergus | Lewistown | | |

# MONTANA

| County | County Seat |
|---|---|
| Flathead | Kalispell |
| Gallatin | Bozeman |
| Garfield | Jordan |
| Glacier | Cut Bank |
| Golden Valley | Ryegate |
| Granite | Philipsburg |
| Hill | Havre |
| Jefferson | Boulder |
| Judith Basin | Stanford |
| Lake | Polson |
| Lewis and Clark | Helena |
| Liberty | Chester |
| Lincoln | Libby |
| Madison | Virginia City |
| McCone | Circle |
| Meagher | White Sulphur Springs |
| Mineral | Superior |
| Missoula | Missoula |
| Musselshell | Roundup |
| Park | Livingston |
| Petroleum | Winnett |
| Phillips | Malta |
| Pondera | Conrad |
| Powder River | Broadus |
| Powell | Deer Lodge |
| Prairie | Terry |
| Ravalli | Hamilton |
| Richland | Sidney |
| Roosevelt | Wolf Point |
| Rosebud | Forsyth |
| Sanders | Thompson Falls |

Montana (second column):

| County | County Seat |
|---|---|
| Stillwater | Columbus |
| Sweet Grass | Big Timber |
| Teton | Choteau |
| Toole | Shelby |
| Treasure | Hysham |
| Valley | Glasgow |
| Wheatland | Harlowton |
| Wibaux | Wibaux |
| Yellowstone | Billings |

# NEBRASKA

| County | County Seat |
|---|---|
| Adams | Hastings |
| Antelope | Neligh |
| Arthur | Arthur |
| Banner | Harrisburg |
| Blaine | Brewster |
| Boone | Albion |
| Box Butte | Alliance |
| Boyd | Butte |
| Brown | Ainsworth |
| Buffalo | Kearney |
| Burt | Tekamah |
| Butler | David City |
| Cass | Plattsmouth |
| Cedar | Hartington |
| Chase | Imperial |
| Cherry | Valentine |
| Cheyenne | Sidney |
| Clay | Clay Center |
| Colfax | Schuyler |
| Cuming | West Point |

| County | County Seat | County | County Seat |
|---|---|---|---|
| Custer | Broken Bow | Lincoln | North Platte |
| Dakota | Dakota City | Logan | Stapleton |
| Dawes | Chadron | Loup | Taylor |
| Dawson | Lexington | Madison | Madison |
| Deuel | Chappell | McPherson | Tryon |
| Dixon | Ponca | Merrick | Central City |
| Dodge | Fremont | Morrill | Bridgeport |
| Douglas | Omaha | Nance | Fullerton |
| Dundy | Benkelman | Nemaha | Auburn |
| Fillmore | Geneva | Nuckolls | Nelson |
| Franklin | Franklin | Otoe | Nebraska City |
| Frontier | Stockville | Pawnee | Pawnee City |
| Furnas | Beaver City | Perkins | Grant |
| Gage | Beatrice | Phelps | Holdrege |
| Garden | Oshkosh | Pierce | Pierce |
| Garfield | Burwell | Platte | Columbus |
| Gosper | Elwood | Polk | Osceola |
| Grant | Hyannis | Red Willow | McCook |
| Greeley | Greeley | Richardson | Falls City |
| Hall | Grand Island | Rock | Bassett |
| Hamilton | Aurora | Saline | Wilber |
| Harlan | Alma | Sarpy | Papillion |
| Hayes | Hayes Center | Saunders | Wahoo |
| Hitchcock | Trenton | Scotts Bluff | Gering |
| Holt | O'Neill | Seward | Seward |
| Hooker | Mullen | Sheridan | Rushville |
| Howard | St Paul | Sherman | Loup City |
| Jefferson | Fairbury | Sioux | Harrison |
| Johnson | Tecumseh | Stanton | Stanton |
| Kearney | Minden | Thayer | Hebron |
| Keith | Ogallala | Thomas | Thedford |
| Keya Paha | Springview | Thurston | Pender |
| Kimball | Kimball | Valley | Ord |
| Knox | Center | Washington | Blair |
| Lancaster | Lincoln | Wayne | Wayne |

| County | County Seat | County | County Seat |
|---|---|---|---|
| Webster | Red Cloud | | |
| Wheeler | Bartlett | | |
| York | York | | |

## NEVADA

## NEW JERSEY

| County | County Seat | County | County Seat |
|---|---|---|---|
| Carson City | Carson City | Atlantic | Mays Landing |
| Churchill | Fallon | Bergen | Hackensack |
| Clark | Las Vegas | Burlington | Mount Holly |
| Douglas | Minden | Camden | Camden |
| Elko | Elko | Cape May | Cape May |
| Esmemlda | Goldfield | Cumberland | Bridgeton |
| Eureka | Eureka | Essex | Newark |
| Humboldt | Winnemucca | Gloucester | Woodbury |
| Lander | Battle Mountain | Hudson | Jersey City |
| Lincoln | Pioche | Hunterdon | Flemington |
| Lyon | Yerington | Mercer | Trenton |
| Mineral | Hawthorne | Middlesex | New Brunswick |
| Nye | Tonopah | Monmouth | Freehold |
| Pershing | Lovelock | Morris | Morristown |
| Storey | Virginia City | Ocean | Toms River |
| Washoe | Reno | Passaic | Paterson |
| White Pine | Ely | Salem | Salem |
| | | Somerset | Somerville |
| | | Sussex | Newton |
| | | Union | Elizabeth |
| | | Warren | Belvidere |

## NEW HAMPSHIRE

## NEW MEXICO

| County | County Seat | County | County Seat |
|---|---|---|---|
| Belknap | Laconia | Bernalillo | Albuquerque |
| Carroll | Ossipee | Catron | Reserve |
| Cheshire | Keene | Chaves | Roswell |
| Coos | Lancaster | Cibola | Grants |
| Grafton | North Haverhill | Colfax | Raton |
| Hillsborough | Manchester | Curry | Clovis |
| Merrimack | Concord | DeBaca | Pt Sumner |
| Rockingham | Exeter | Dona Ana | Las Cruces |
| Strafford | Dover | Eddy | Carlsbad |
| Sullivan | Newport | | |

| County | County Seat | County | County Seat |
|--------|-------------|--------|-------------|
| Grant | Silver City | Clinton | Plattsburgh |
| Guadalupe | Santa Rosa | Columbia | Hudson |
| Harding | Mosquero | Cortland | Cortland |
| Hidalgo | Lordsburg | Delaware | Delhi |
| Lea | Lovington | Dutchess | Poughkeepsie |
| Lincoln | Carrizozo | Erie | Buffalo |
| Los Alamos | Los Alamos | Essex | Elizabethtown |
| Luna | Deming | Franklin | Malone |
| McKinley | Gallup | Fulton | Johnstown |
| Mora | Mora | Genesee | Batavia |
| Otero | Alamogordo | Greene | Catskill |
| Quay | Tucumcari | Hamilton | Lake Pleasant |
| Rio Arriba | Tierra Amarilla | Herkimer | Herkimer |
| Roosevelt | Portales | Jefferson | Watertown |
| Sandoval | Bernalillo | Kings | Brooklyn |
| San Juan | Aztec | Lewis | Lowville |
| San Miguel | Las Vegas | Livingston | Geneseo |
| Santa Fe | Santa Fe | Madison | Wampsville |
| Sierra | Truth or Consequences | Monroe | Rochester |
| Socorro | Socorro | Montgomery | Fonda |
| Taos | Taos | Nassau | Mineola |
| Torrance | Estancia | New York | New York |
| Union | Clayton | Niagara | Lockport |
| Valencia | Los Lunas | Oneida | Utica |
| | | Onondaga | Syracuse |
| | | Ontario | Canandaigua |

## NEW YORK

| County | County Seat | County | County Seat |
|--------|-------------|--------|-------------|
| Albany | Albany | Orange | Goshen |
| Allegany | Belmont | Orleans | Albion |
| Bronx | Bronx | Oswego | Oswego |
| Broome | Binghamton | Otsego | Cooperstown |
| Cattaraugus | Little Valley | Putnam | Carmel |
| Cayuga | Auburn | Queens | Jamaica |
| Chautauqua | Mayville | Rensselaer | Troy |
| Chemung | Elmira | Richmond | Staten Island |
| Chenango | Norwich | Rockland | New City |
| | | Saratoga | Ballston Spa |

**Adoption Searches Made Easier**

| County | County Seat | County | County Seat |
|---|---|---|---|
| Schenectady | Schenectady | Carteret | Beaufort |
| Schoharie | Schoharie | Caswell | Yanceyville |
| Schuyler | Watkins Glen | Catawba | Newton |
| Seneca | Waterloo | Chatham | Pittsboro |
| St Lawrence | Canton | Cherokee | Murphy |
| Steuben | Bath | Chowan | Edenton |
| Suffolk | Riverhead | Clay | Hayesville |
| Sullivan | Monticello | Cleveland | Shelby |
| Tioga | Owego | Columbus | Whiteville |
| Tompkins | Ithaca | Craven | New Bem |
| Ulster | Kingston | Cumberland | Fayetteville |
| Warren | Lake George | Currituck | Currituck |
| Washington | Hudson Falls-Salem | Dare | Manteo |
| | | Davidson | Leidngton |
| Wayne | Lyons | Davie | Mocksville |
| Westchester | White Plains | Duplin | Kenansville |
| Wyoming | Warsaw | Durham | Durham |
| Yates | Penn Yan | Edgecombe | Tarboro |
| | | Forsyth | Winston Salem |

## NORTH CAROLINA

| County | County Seat | County | County Seat |
|---|---|---|---|
| | | Franklin | Louisburg |
| Alamance | Graham | Gaston | Gastonia |
| Alexander | Taylorsville | Gates | Gatesville |
| Alleghany | Sparta | Graham | Robbinsville |
| Anson | Wadesboro | Granville | Oxford |
| Ashe | Jefferson | Greene | Snow Hill |
| Avery | Newland | Guilford | Greensboro |
| Beaufort | Washington | Halifax | Halifax |
| Bertie | Windsor | Harnett | Lillington |
| Bladen | Elizabethtown | Haywood | Waynesville |
| Brunswick | Bolivia | Henderson | Hendersonville |
| Buncombe | Asheville | Hertford | Winton |
| Burke | Morganton | Hoke | Raeford |
| Cabarrus | Concord | Hyde | Swanquarter |
| Caldwell | Lenoir | Iredell | Statesville |
| Camden | Camden | Jackson | Sylva |

| County | County Seat | County | County Seat |
|---|---|---|---|
| Johnston | Smithfield | Surry | Dobson |
| Jones | Trenton | Swain | Bryson City |
| Lee | Sanford | Transylvania | Brevard |
| Lenoir | Kinston | Tyrrell | Columbia |
| Lincoln | Lincolnton | Union | Monroe |
| Macon | Franklin | Vance | Henderson |
| Madison | Marshall | Wake | Raleigh |
| Martin | Williamston | Warren | Warrenton |
| McDowell | Marion | Washington | Plymouth |
| Mecklenburg | Charlotte | Watauga | Boone |
| Mitchell | Bakersville | Wayne | Goldsboro |
| Montgomery | Troy | Wilkes | Wilkesboro |
| Moore | Carthage | Wilson | Wilson |
| Nash | Nashville | Yadkin | Yadkinville |
| New Hanover | Wilmington | Yancey | Burnsville |
| Northampton | Jackson | | |
| Onslow | Jacksonville | **N O R T H  D A K O T A** | |
| Orange | Hillsborough | Adams | Hettinger |
| Pamlico | Bayboro | Barnes | Valley City |
| Pasquotank | Elizabeth City | Benson | Minnewaukan |
| Pender | Burgaw | Billings | Medora |
| Perquimans | Hertford | Bottineau | Bottineau |
| Person | Roxboro | Bowman | Bowman |
| Pitt | Greenville | Burke | Bowbells |
| Polk | Columbus | Burleigh | Bismark |
| Randolph | Asheboro | Cass | Fargo |
| Richmond | Rockingham | Cavalier | Langdon |
| Robeson | Lumberton | Dickey | Ellendale |
| Rockingham | Wentworth | Divide | Crosby |
| Rowan | Salisbury | Dunn | Manning |
| Rutherford | Rutherfordton | Eddy | New Rockford |
| Sampson | Clinton | Emmons | Linton |
| Scotland | Laurinburg | Foster | Carrington |
| Stanly | Albemarle | Golden-Valley | Beach |
| Stokes | Danbury | Grand Forks | Grand Forks |

| County | County Seat | County | County Seat |
|---|---|---|---|
| Grant | Carson | | |
| Griggs | Cooperstown | **O H I O** | |
| Hettinger | Mott | Adams | West Union |
| Kidder | Steele | Allen | Lima |
| LaMoure | LaMoure | Ashland | Ashland |
| Logan | Napoleon | Ashtabula | Jefferson |
| McHenry | Towner | Athens | Athens |
| McIntosh | Ashley | Auglaize | Wapakoneta |
| McKenzie | Watford City | Belmont | St Clairsville |
| McLean | Washburn | Brown | Georgetown |
| Mercer | Stanton | Butler | Hamilton |
| Morton | Mandan | Carroll | Carrollton |
| Mountrail | Stanley | Champaign | Urbana |
| Nelson | Lakota | Clark | Springfield |
| Oliver | Center | Clermont | Batavia |
| Pembina | Cavalier | Clinton | Wilmington |
| Pierce | Rugby | Columbiana | Lisbon |
| Ramsey | Devils Lake | Coshocton | Coshocton |
| Ransom | Lisbon | Crawford | Bucyrus |
| Renville | Mohall | Cuyahoga | Cleveland |
| Richland | Wahpeton | Darke | Greenville |
| Rolette | Rolla | Defiance | Defiance |
| Sargent | Forman | Delaware | Delaware |
| Sheridan | McClusky | Erie | Sandusky |
| Sioux | Ft. Yates | Fairfield | Lancaster |
| Slope | Amidon | Fayette | Washington Court House |
| Stark | Dickinson | Franklin | Columbus |
| Steele | Finley | Fulton | Wauseon |
| Stutsman | Jamestown | Gallia | Gallipolis |
| Towner | Cando | Geauga | Chardon |
| Trail | Hillsboro | Greene | Xenia |
| Walsh | Grafton | Guernsey | Cambridge |
| Ward | Minot | Hamilton | Cincinnati |
| Wells | Fessenden | Hancock | Findlay |
| Williams | Williston | Hardin | Kenton |

| County | County Seat | County | County Seat |
|---|---|---|---|
| Harrison | Cadiz | Putnam | Ottawa |
| Henry | Napoleon | Richland | Mansfield |
| Highland | Hillsboro | Ross | Chillicothe |
| Hocking | Logan | Sandusky | Fremont |
| Holmes | Millersburg | Scioto | Portsmouth |
| Huron | Norwalk | Seneca | Tiffin |
| Jackson | Jackson | Shelby | Shelbey |
| Jefferson | Steubenville | Stark | Canton |
| Knox | Mount Vernon | Summit | Akron |
| Lake | Painesville | Trumbull | Warren |
| Lawrence | Ironton | Tuscarawas | New Philadelphia |
| Licking | Newark | Union | Marysville |
| Logan | Bellefontaine | Vinton | McArthur |
| Lorain | Elyria | Warren | Lebanon |
| Lucas | Toledo | Washington | Marietta |
| Madison | London | Wayne | Wooster |
| Mahoning | Youngstown | Williams | Bryan |
| Marion | Marion | Wood | Bowling Green |
| Medina | Medina | Van Wert | VanWert |
| Meigs | Pomeroy | Wyandot | Upper Sandusky |
| Mercer | Celina | | |
| Miami | Troy | **OKLAHOMA** | |
| Monroe | Woodsfield | Adair | Stilwell |
| Montgomery | Dayton | Alfalfa | Cherokee |
| Morgan | McConnelsville | Atoka | Atoka |
| Morrow | Mount Gilead | Beaver | Beaver |
| Muskingum | Zaneesville | Beckham | Sayre |
| Noble | Caldwell | Blaine | Watonga |
| Ottawa | Port Clinton | Bryan | Durant |
| Paulding | Paulding | Caddo | Anadarko |
| Perry | New Lexington | Canadian | El Reno |
| Pickaway | Circleville | Carter | Ardmore |
| Pike | Waverly | Cherokee | Tahlequah |
| Portage | Ravenna | Choctaw | Hugo |
| Preble | Eaton | Cimarron | Boise City |

**Adoption Searches Made Easier**

| County | County Seat | County | County Seat |
|---|---|---|---|
| Cleveland | Norman | Murray | Sulphur |
| Coal | Coalgate | Muskogee | Muskogee |
| Comanche | Lawton | Noble | Perry |
| Cotton | Walters | Nowata | Nowata |
| Craig | Vinita | Okfuskee | Okemah |
| Creek | Sapulpa | Oklahoma | OklahomaCity |
| Custer | Arapaho | Okmulgee | Okmulgee |
| Delaware | Jay | Osage | Pawhuska |
| Dewey | Taloga | Ottawa | Miami |
| Ellis | Arnett | Pawnee | Pawnee |
| Garfield | Enid | Payne | Stillwater |
| Garvin | PaulsValley | Pittsburg | McAlester |
| Grady | Chickasha | Pontotoc | Ada |
| Grant | Medford | Pottawatomie | Shawnee |
| Greer | Mangum | Pushmataha | Antlers |
| Harmon | Hollis | Roger Mills | Cheyenne |
| Harper | Buffalo | Rogers | Claremore |
| Haskell | Stigler | Seminole | Wewoka |
| Hughes | Holdenville | Sequoyah | Sallisaw |
| Jackson | Altus | Stephens | Duncan |
| Jefferson | Wauiika | Texas | Guymon |
| Johnston | Tishomingo | Tillman | Frederick |
| Kay | Newkirk | Tulsa | Tulsa |
| Kingfisher | Kingfisher | Wagoner | Wagoner |
| Mowa | Hobart | Washington | Bartlesville |
| Latimer | Wilburton | Washita | Cordell |
| Le Flore | Poteau | Woods | Alva |
| Lincoln | Chandler | Woodward | Woodward |
| Logan | Guthrie | | |
| Love | Marietta | | |
| Major | Fairview | | |

## OREGON

| County | County Seat |
|---|---|
| Baker | Baker City |
| Benton | Corvallis |
| Clackamas | Oregon City |
| Clatsop | Astoria |
| Columbia | St Helens |

(continued from Marshall column)

| County | County Seat |
|---|---|
| Marshall | Madill |
| Mayes | Pryor |
| McClain | Purcell |
| McCurtain | Idabel |
| McIntosh | Eufaula |

| County | County Seat | County | County Seat |
|---|---|---|---|
| Coos | Coquille | Armstrong | Kittanning |
| Crook | Prineville | Beaver | Beaver |
| Curry | Gold Beach | Bedford | Bedford |
| Deschutes | Bend | Berks | Reading |
| Douglas | Roseburg | Blair | Hollidaysburg |
| Gilliam | Condon | Bradford | Towanda |
| Grant | Canyon City | Bucks | Doylestown |
| Harney | Burns | Butler | Butler |
| Hood River | Hood River | Cambria | Ebensburg |
| Jackson | Medford | Cameron | Emporium |
| Jefferson | Madras | Carbon | Jim Thorpe |
| Josephine | Grants Pass | Centre | Bellefonte |
| Klamath | Klamath Falls | Chester | West Chester |
| Lake | Lakeview | Clarion | Clarion |
| Lane | Eugene | Clearfield | Clearfield |
| Lincoln | Newport | Clinton | Lock Haven |
| Linn | Albany | Columbia | Bloomsburg |
| Malheur | Vale | Crawford | Meadville |
| Marion | Salem | Cumberland | Carlisle |
| Morrow | Heppnery | Dauphin | Harrisburg |
| Multnomah | Portland | Delaware | Media |
| Polk | Dallas | Elk | Ridgway |
| Sherman | Moro | Erie | Erie |
| Tillamook | Tillamook | Fayette | Uniontown |
| Umatilla | Pendleton | Forest | Tionesta |
| Union | La Grande | Franklin | Chambersburg |
| Wallowa | Enterprise | Fulton | McConnellsburg |
| Wasco | City of The Dalles | Greene | Waynesburg |
| Washington | Hillsboro | Huntingdon | Huntingdon |
| Wheeler | Fossil | Indiana | Indiana |
| Yamhill | McMinnville | Jefferson | Brookville |
| | | Juniata | Mifflintown |
| **PENNSYLVANIA** | | Lackawanna | Scranton |
| Adams | Gettysburg | Lancaster | Lancaster |
| Allegheny | Pittsburgh | Lawrence | New Castle |

| County | County Seat | County | County Seat |
|---|---|---|---|
| Lebanon | Lebanon | Providence | Providence |
| Lehigh | Allentown | Washington | West Kingston |
| Luzerne | Wilkes Barre | | |
| Lycoming | Williamsport | | |

## SOUTH CAROLINA

| County | County Seat |
|---|---|
| McKean | Smethport | Abbeville | Abbeville |

| County | County Seat | County | County Seat |
|---|---|---|---|
| McKean | Smethport | Abbeville | Abbeville |
| Mercer | Mercer | Aiken | Aiken |
| Mifflin | Lewistown | Allendale | Allendale |
| Monroe | Stroudsburg | Anderson | Anderson |
| Montgomery | Norristown | Bamberg | Bamberg |
| Montour | Danville | Barnwell | Barnwell |
| Northampton | Easton | Beaufort | Beaufort |
| Northumberland | Sunbury | Berkeley | Moncks Corner |
| Perry | New Bloomfield | Calhoun | St Matthews |
| Philadelphia | Philadelphia | Charleston | Charleston |
| Pike | Milford | Cherokee | Gaffney |
| Potter | Coudersport | Chester | Chester |
| Schuylkill | Pottsville | Chesterfield | Chesterfield |
| Snyder | Middleburg | Clarendon | Manning |
| Somerset | Somerset | Colleton | Walterboro |
| Sullivan | Laporte | Darlington | Darlington |
| Susquehanna | Montrose | Dillon | Dillon |
| Tioga | Wellsboro | Dorchester | St George |
| Union | Lewisburg | Edgefield | Edgefield |
| Venango | Franklin | Fairfield | Winnsboro |
| Warren | Warren | Florence | Florence |
| Washington | Washington | Georgetown | Georgetown |
| Wayne | Honesdale | Greenville | Greenville |
| Westmoreland | Greensburg | Greenwood | Greenwood |
| Wyoming | Tunkhannock | Hampton | Hampton |
| York | York | Horry | Conway |
| | | Jasper | Ridgeland |

## RHODE ISLAND

| County | County Seat |
|---|---|
| | | Kershaw | Camden |
| Bristol | Providence | Lancaster | Lancaster |
| Kent | Warwick | Laurens | Laurens |
| Newport | Newport | Lee | Bishopville |

| County | County Seat | County | County Seat |
|---|---|---|---|
| Lexington | Lexington | Deuel | Clear Lake |
| Marion | Marion | Dewey | Timber Lake |
| Marlboro | Bennettsville | Douglas | Armour |
| McCormick | McCormick | Edmunds | Ipswich |
| Newberry | Newberry | Fall River | Hot Springs |
| Oconee | Walhalla | Faulk | Faulkton |
| Orangeburg | Orangeburg | Grant | Milbank |
| Pickens | Pickens | Gregory | Burke |
| Richland | Columbia | Haakon | Philip |
| Saluda | Saluda | Hamlin | Hayti |
| Spartanburg | Spartanburg | Hand | Miller |
| Sumter | Sumter | Hanson | Alexandria |
| Union | Union | Harding | Buffalo |
| Williamsburg | Kingstree | Hughes | Pierre |
| York | York | Hutchinson | Olivet |
|  |  | Hyde | Highmore |

## SOUTH DAKOTA

| County | County Seat | County | County Seat |
|---|---|---|---|
| Aurora | Plankinton | Jackson | Kadoke |
| Beadle | Huron | Jerauld | Wessington Springs |
| Bennett | Martin | Jones | Murdo |
| Bon Homme | Tyndall | Kingsbury | De Smet |
| Brookings | Brookings | Lake | Madison |
| Brown | Aberdeen | Lawrence | Deadwood |
| Brule | Chamberlain | Lincoln | Canton |
| Buffalo | Gann Valley | Lyman | Kennebec |
| Butte | Belle Fourche | Marshall | Britton |
| Campbell | Mound City | McCook | Salem |
| Charles Mix | Lake Andes | McPherson | Leola |
| Clark | Clark | Meade | Sturgis |
| Clay | Vermillion | Mellette | White River |
| Codington | Watertown | Miner | Howard |
| Corson | McIntosh | Minnehaha | Sioux Falls |
| Custer | Custer | Moody | Flandreau |
| Davison | Mitchell | Pennington | Rapid City |
| Day | Webster | Perkins | Bison |
|  |  | Potter | Gettysburg |

| County | County Seat | County | County Seat |
|---|---|---|---|
| Roberts | Sisseton | DeKalb | Smithville |
| Sanborn | Woonsocket | Dickson | Charlotte |
| Shannon | Hot Springs | Dyer | Dyersburg |
| Spink | Redfield | Fayette | Somerville |
| Stanley | Fort Pierre | Fentress | Jamestown |
| Sully | Onida | Franklin | Winchester |
| Todd | Winner | Gibson | Trenton |
| Tripp | Winner | Giles | Pulaski |
| Turner | Parker | Grainger | Rutledge |
| Union | Elk Point | Greene | Greenville |
| Walworth | Selby | Grundy | Altamont |
| Yankton | Yankton | Hamblen | Morristown |
| Ziebach | Dupree | Hamilton | Chattanooga |
| | | Hancock | Sneedville |

## TENNESSEE

| County | County Seat | County | County Seat |
|---|---|---|---|
| | | Hardeman | Bolivar |
| Anderson | Clinton | Hardin | Savannah |
| Bedford | Shelbyville | Hawkins | Rogersville |
| Benton | Camden | Haywood | Brownsville |
| Bledsoe | Pikeville | Henderson | Lexington |
| Blount | Maryville | Henry | Paris |
| Bradley | Cleveland | Hickman | Centerville |
| Campbell | Jacksboro | Houston | Erin |
| Cannon | Woodbury | Humphreys | Waverly |
| Carroll | Huntingdon | Jackson | Gainesboro |
| Carter | Elizabethton | Jefferson | Dandridge |
| Cheatham | Ashland City | Johnson | Mountain City |
| Chester | Henderson | Knox | Knoxville |
| Claiborne | Tazewell | Lake | Tiptonville |
| Clay | Celina | Lauderdale | Ripley |
| Cocke | Newport | Lawrence | Lawrenceburg |
| Coffee | Manchester | Lewis | Hohenwald |
| Crockett | Alamo | Lincoln | Fayetteville |
| Cumberland | Crossville | Loudon | Loudon |
| Davidson | Nashville | Macon | Lafayette |
| Decatur | Decaturville | Madison | Jackson |

| County | County Seat | County | County Seat |
|---|---|---|---|
| Marion | Jasper | Wayne | Waynesboro |
| Marshall | Lewisburg | Weakley | Dresden |
| Maury | Columbia | White | Sparta |
| McMinn | Athens | Williamson | Franklin |
| McNairy | Selmer | Wilson | Lebanon |
| Meigs | Decatur | | |
| Monroe | Madisonville | **TEXAS** | |
| Montgomery | Clarksville | Anderson | Palestine |
| Moore | Lynchburg | Andrews | Andrews |
| Morgan | Wartburg | Angelina | Lufkin |
| Obion | Union City | Aransas | Rockport |
| Overton | Livingston | Archer | Archer City |
| Perry | Linden | Armstrong | Claude |
| Pickett | Byrdstown | Atascosa | Jourdanton |
| Polk | Benton | Austin | Bellville |
| Putnam | Cookeville | Bailey | Muleshoe |
| Rhea | Dayton | Bandera | Bandera |
| Roane | Kingston | Bastrop | Bastrop |
| Robertson | Springfield | Baylor | Seymour |
| Rutherford | Murfreesboro | Bee | Beeville |
| Scott | Huntsville | Bell | Belton |
| Sequatchie | Dunlap | Bexar | San Antonio |
| Sevier | Sevierville | Blanco | Johnson City |
| Shelby | Memphis | Borden | Gail |
| Smith | Carthage | Bosque | Meridian |
| Stewart | Dover | Bowie | New Boston |
| Sullivan | Blountville | Brazoria | Angleton |
| Sumner | Gallatin | Brazos | Bryan |
| Tipton | Covington | Brewster | Alpine |
| Trousdale | Hartsville | Briscoe | Silverton |
| Unicoi | Erwin | Brooks | Falfurrias |
| Union | Maynardville | Brown | Brownwood |
| Van Buren | Spencer | Burleson | Caldwell |
| Warren | McMinnville | Burnet | Burnet |
| Washington | Jonesborough | Caldwell | Lockhart |

| County | County Seat | County | County Seat |
|---|---|---|---|
| Calhoun | Port Lavaca | Dimmit | Carrizo-Springs |
| Callahan | Baird | Donley | Clarendon |
| Cameron | Brownsville | Duval | San Diego |
| Camp | Pittsburg | Eastland | Eastland |
| Carson | Panhandle | Ector | Odessa |
| Cass | Linden | Edwards | Rocksprings |
| Castro | Dimmitt | El Paso | El Paso |
| Chambers | Anahuac | Ellis | Waxahachie |
| Cherokee | Rusk | Erath | Stephenville |
| Childress | Childress | Falls | Marlin |
| Clay | Henrietta | Fannin | Bonham |
| Cochran | Morton | Fayette | La Grange |
| Coke | Robert Lee | Fisher | Roby |
| Coleman | Coleman | Floyd | Floydada |
| Collin | McMnney | Foard | Crowell |
| Collingsworth | Wellington | Fort Bend | Richmond |
| Colorado | Columbus | Franklin | Mount Vernon |
| Comal | New Braunfels | Freestone | Fairfield |
| Comanche | Comanche | Frio | Pearsall |
| Concho | Paint Rock | Gaines | Seminole |
| Cooke | Gainesville | Galveston | Galveston |
| Coryell | Gatesville | Garza | Post |
| Cottle | Paducah | Gillespie | Fredericksburg |
| Crane | Crane | Glasscock | Garden City |
| Crockett | Ozona | Goliad | Goliad |
| Crosby | Crosbyton | Gonzales | Gonzales |
| Culberson | Van Horn | Gray | Pampa |
| Dallam | Dalhart | Grayson | Sherman |
| Dallas | Dallas | Gregg | Longview |
| Dawson | Lamesa | Grimes | Anderson |
| Deaf Smith | Hereford | Guadalupe | Seguin |
| Delta | Cooper | Hale | Plainview |
| Denton | Denton | Hall | Memphis |
| DeWitt | Cuero | Hamilton | Hamilton |
| Dickens | Dickens | Hansford | Spearman |

| County | County Seat | County | County Seat |
|--------|-------------|--------|-------------|
| Hardeman | Quanah | Kimble | Junction |
| Hardin | Kountze | King | Guthrie |
| Harris | Houston | Kinney | Brackettville |
| Harrison | Marshall | Kleberg | Kingsville |
| Hartley | Channing | Knox | Benjamin |
| Haskell | Haskell | Lamar | Paris |
| Hays | San Marcos | Lamb | Littlefield |
| Hemphill | Canadian | Lampasas | Lampasas |
| Henderson | Athens | La Salle | Cotulla |
| Hidalgo | Edinburg | Lavaca | Hallettsville |
| Hill | Hillsboro | Lee | Giddings |
| Hockley | Levelland | Leon | Centerville |
| Hood | Granbury | Liberty | Liberty |
| Hopkins | Sulphur Springs | Limestone | Groesbeck |
| Houston | Crockett | Lipscomb | Lipscomb |
| Howard | Big Spring | Live Oak | George West |
| Hudspeth | Sierra Blanca | Llano | Llano |
| Hunt | Greenville | Loving | Mentone |
| Hutchinson | Stinnett | Lubbock | Lubbock |
| Irion | Mertzon | Lynn | Tahoka |
| Jack | Jacksboro | Madison | Madisonville |
| Jackson | Edna | Marion | Jefferson |
| Jasper | Jasper | Martin | Stanton |
| Jeff Davis | Ft Davis | Mason | Mason |
| Jefferson | Beaumont | Matagorda | Bay City |
| Jim Hogg | Hebronville | Maverick | Eagle Pass |
| Jim Wells | Alice | McCulloch | Brady |
| Johnson | Cleburne | McLennan | Waco |
| Jones | Anson | McMullen | Tilden |
| Karnes | Karnes City | Medina | Hondo |
| Kaufman | Kaufman | Menard | Menard |
| Kendall | Boerne | Midland | Midland |
| Kenedy | Sayita | Milam | Cameron |
| Kent | Jayton | Mills | Goldthwaite |
| Kerr | Kerrville | Mitchell | Colorado City |

| County | County Seat | County | County Seat |
|---|---|---|---|
| Montague | Montague | San Jacinto | Coldspring |
| Montgomery | Conroe | San Patyicio | Sinton |
| Moore | Dumas | San Saba | San Saba |
| Morris | Daingerfield | Schleicher | Eldorado |
| Motley | Matador | Scurry | Snyder |
| Nacogdoches | Nacogdoches | Shackelford | Albany |
| Navarro | Corsicana | Shelby | Center |
| Newton | Newton | Sherman | Stratford |
| Nolan | Sweetwater | Smith | Tyler |
| Nueces | Corpus Christi | Somervell | Glen Rose |
| Ochiltree | Perryton | Starr | Rio Grande City |
| Oldham | Vega | Stephens | Breckenridge |
| Orange | Orange | Sterling | Sterling City |
| Palo Pinto | Palo Pinto | Stonewall | Aspermont |
| Panola | Carthage | Sutton | Sonora |
| Parker | Weatherford | Swisher | Tulia |
| Parmer | Farwell | Tarrant | Ft Worth |
| Pecos | Ft Stockton | Taylor | Abilene |
| Polk | Livingston | Terrell | Sanderson |
| Potter | Amarillo | Terry | Brownfield |
| Presidio | Marfa | Throckmorton | Throckmorton |
| Rains | Emory | Titus | Mount Pleasant |
| Randall | Canyon | Tom Green | San Angelo |
| Reagan | Big Lake | Travis | Austin |
| Real | Leakey | Trinity | Groveton |
| Red River | Clarksville | Tyler | Woodville |
| Reeves | Pecos | Upsbur | Gilmer |
| Refugio | Refugio | Upton | Rankin |
| Roberts | Miami | Uvalde | Uvalde |
| Robertson | Franklin | Val Verde | Del Rio |
| Rockwall | Rockwall | Van Zandt | Canton |
| Runnels | Ballinger | Victoria | Victoria |
| Rusk | Henderson | Walker | Huntsville |
| Sabine | Hemphill | Waller | Hempstead |
| San Augustine | San Augustine | Ward | Monahans |

| County | County Seat | County | County Seat |
|--------|-------------|--------|-------------|
| Washington | Brenham | Salt Lake | Salt Lake City |
| Webb | Laredo | San Juan | Monticello |
| Wharton | Wharton | Sanpete | Manti |
| Wheeler | Wheeler | Sevier | Richfield |
| Wichita | Wichita Falls | Summit | Coalville |
| Wilbarger | Vernon | Tooele | Tooele |
| Willacy | Raymondville | Uintah | Vernal |
| Williamson | Georgetown | Utah | Provo |
| Wilson | Floresville | Wasatch | Heber City |
| Winkler | Kermit | Washington | St George |
| Wise | Decatur | Wayne | Loa |
| Wood | Quitman | Weber | Ogden |
| Yoakum | Plains | | |
| Young | Graham | | |

## V E R M O N T

| | |
|---|---|
| Zapata | Zapata |
| Zavala | Crystal City |

| County | County Seat |
|--------|-------------|
| Addison | Middlebury |
| Bennington | Bennington |
| Caledonia | St Johnsbury |
| Chittenden | Burlington |

## U T A H

| County | County Seat |
|--------|-------------|
| Beaver | Beaver |
| Box Elder | Brigham City |
| Cache | Logan |
| Carbon | Price |
| Daggett | Manila |
| Davis | Farmington |
| Duchesne | Duchesne |
| Emery | Castle Dale |
| Garfield | Panguitch |
| Grand | Moab |
| Iron | Parowan |
| Juab | Nephi |
| Kane | Kanab |
| Millard | Fillmore |
| Morgan | Morgan |
| Piute | Junction |
| Rich | Randolph |

| County | County Seat |
|--------|-------------|
| Essex | Guildhall |
| Franklin | St Albans |
| Grand Isle | North Hero |
| Lamoille | Hyde Park |
| Orange | Chelsea |
| Orleans | Newport |
| Rutland | Rutland |
| Washington | Montpelier |
| Windham | Newfane |
| Windsor | Woodstock |

## V I R G I N I A

| County | County Seat |
|--------|-------------|
| Accomack | Accomack |
| Albemarle | Charlottesville |
| Alleghany | Covington |
| Amelia | Amelia |

**Adoption Searches Made Easier**

| County | County Seat | County | County Seat |
| --- | --- | --- | --- |
| Amherst | Amherst | Greensville | Emporia |
| Appomattox | Appomattox | Halifax | Halifax |
| Arlington | Arlington | Hanover | Hanover |
| Augusta | Staunton | Henrico | Henrico |
| Bath | Warm Springs | Henry | Martinsville |
| Bedford | Bedford | Highland | Monterey |
| Bland | Bland | Isle of Wight | Isle of Wight |
| Botetourt | Fincastle | James City | Williamsburg |
| Brunswick | Lawrenceville | King & Queen | King & Queen |
| Buchanan | Grundy | King George | King George |
| Buckingham | Buckingham | King William | King William |
| Campbell | Rustburg | Lancaster | Lancaster |
| Caroline | Bowling Green | Lee | Jonesville |
| Carroll | Hillsville | Loudoun | Leesburg |
| Charles City | Charles City | Louisa | Louisa |
| Charlotte | Charlotte | Lunenburg | Lunenburg |
| Chesterfield | Chesterfield | Madison | Madison |
| Clarke | Berryville | Mathews | Mathews |
| Craig | New Castle | Mecklenburg | Boydton |
| Culpeper | Culpeper | Middlesex | Saluda |
| Cumberland | Cumberland | Montgomery | Christiansburg |
| Dickenson | Clintwood | Nelson | Lovingston |
| Dinwiddie | Dinwiddie | New Kent | New Kent |
| Essex | Tappahannock | Northhampton | Eastville |
| Fairfax | Fairfax | Northumberland | Heathsville |
| Fauquier | Warrenton | Nottoway | Nottoway |
| Floyd | Floyd | Orange | Orange |
| Fluvanna | Palmyra | Page | Luray |
| Franklin | Rocky Mount | Patzick | Stuart |
| Frederick | Winchester | Pittsylvania | Chatham |
| Giles | Pearisburg | Powhatan | Powhatan |
| Gloucester | Gloucester | Prince Edward | Parmville |
| Goochland | Goochland | Prince George | Prince George |
| Grayson | Independence | Prince William | Manassm |
| Greene | Stanardsville | Pulaski | Pulaski |

| County | County Seat | County | County Seat |
|---|---|---|---|
| Rappahannock | Washington | Grant | Ephrata |
| Richmond | Warsaw | Grays Harbor | Montesano |
| Roanoke | Salem | Island | Coupeville |
| Rockbridge | Leidngton | Jefferson | Port Townsend |
| Rockingham | Harrisonburg | King | Seattle |
| Russell | Lebanon | Kitsap | Port Orchard |
| Scott | Gate City | Kittitas | Ellensburg |
| Shenandoah | Woodstock | Klickitat | Goldendale |
| Smyth | Marion | Lewis | Chehalis |
| Southhampton | Courtland | Lincoln | Davenport |
| Spotsylvania | Spotsylvania | Mason | Shelton |
| Stafford | Stafford | Okanogan | Okanogan |
| Surry | Surry | Pacific | South Bend |
| Sussex | Sussex | Pend Oreille | Newport |
| Tazewell | Tazewell | Pierce | Tacoma |
| Warren | Front Royal | San Juan | Friday Harbor |
| Washington | Abingdon | Skagit | Mount Vernon |
| Westmoreland | Montross | Skamania | Stevenson |
| Wise | Wise | Snohomish | Everett |
| Wythe | Wytheville | Spokane | Spokane |
| York | Yorktown | Stevens | Colville |
| | | Thurston | Olympia |

# WASHINGTON

| | | Wahkiakum | Cathlamet |
|---|---|---|---|
| Adams | Ritzville | Walla Walla | Walla Walla |
| Asotin | Asotin | Whatcom | Bellingham |
| Benton | Prosser | Whitman | Colfax |
| Chelan | Wenatchee | Yakima | Yakima |
| Clallam | Port Angeles | | |

# WEST VIRGINIA

| Clark | Vancouver | | |
|---|---|---|---|
| Columbia | Dayton | Barbour | Philppi |
| Cowlitz | Kelso | Berkeley | Martinsburg |
| Douglas | Waterville | Boone | Madison |
| Ferry | Republic | Braxton | Sutton |
| Franklin | Pasco | Brooke | Wellsburg |
| Garfield | Pomeroy | Cabell | Huntington |

| County | County Seat | County | County Seat |
|---|---|---|---|
| Calhoun | Grantsville | Randolph | Elkins |
| Clay | Clay | Ritchie | Harrisville |
| Doddridge | West Union | Roane | Spencer |
| Fayette | Fayetteville | Summers | Hinton |
| Gilmer | Glenville | Taylor | Grafton |
| Grant | Petersburg | Tucker | Parsons |
| Greenbrier | Lewisburg | Tyler | Middlebourne |
| Hampshire | Romney | Upshur | Buckhannon |
| Hancock | New Cumberland | Wayne | Wayne |
| Hardy | Moorefield | Webster | Webster Springs |
| Harrison | Clarksburg | Wetzel | New Martinsville |
| Jackson | Ripley | Wirt | Elizabeth |
| Jefferson | Charles Town | Wood | Parkersburg |
| Kanawha | Charleston | Wyoming | Pineville |
| Lewis | Weston | | |
| Lincoln | Hamlin | | |

# WISCONSIN

| County | County Seat |
|---|---|
| Logan | Logan |
| Marion | Fairmont |
| Marshall | Moundsville |
| Mason | Point Pleasant |
| McDowell | Welch |
| Mercer | Princeton |
| Mineral | Keyser |
| Mingo | Williamson |
| Monongalia | Morgantown |
| Monroe | Union |
| Morgan | Berkeley Springs |
| Nicholas | Summersville |
| Ohio | Wheeling |
| Pendleton | Franklin |
| Pleasants | St Marys |
| Pocahontas | Marlinton |
| Preston | Kingwood |
| Putnam | Winfield |
| Raleigh | Beckley |

| County | County Seat |
|---|---|
| Adams | Friendship |
| Ashland | Ashland |
| Barron | Barron |
| Bayfield | Washburn |
| Brown | Green Bay |
| Buffalo | Alma |
| Burnett | Siren |
| Calumet | Chilton |
| Chippewa | Chippewa Falls |
| Clark | Neillsville |
| Columbia | Portage |
| Crawford | Prairie Du Chien |
| Dane | Madison |
| Dodge | Juneau |
| Door | Sturgeon Bay |
| Douglas | Superior |
| Dunn | Menomonie |
| Eau Claire | Eau Claire |
| Florence | Florence |

| County | County Seat | County | County Seat |
|---|---|---|---|
| Fond Du Lac | Fond Du Lac | Rusk | Ladysmith |
| Forest | Crandon | Sauk | Baraboo |
| Grant | Lancaster | Sawyer | Hayward |
| Green | Monroe | Shawano | Shawano |
| Green Lake | Green Lake | Sheboygan | Sheboygan |
| Iowa | Dodgeville | St Croix | Hudson |
| Iron | Hurley | Taylor | Medford |
| Jackson | Black River Falls | Trempealeau | Whitehall |
| Jefferson | Jefferson | Vernon | Viroqua |
| Juneau | Mauston | Vilas | Eagle River |
| Kenosha | Kenosha | Walworth | Elkhorn |
| Kewaunee | Kewaunee | Washburn | Shell Lake |
| La Crosse | La Crosse | Washington | West Bend |
| Lafayette | Darlington | Waukesha | Waukesha |
| Langlade | Antigo | Waupaca | Waupaca |
| Lincoln | Merrill | Waushara | Wautoma |
| Manitowoc | Manitowoc | Winnebago | Oshkosh |
| Marathon | Wausau | Wood | Wisconsin-Rapids |
| Marinette | Marinette | | |
| Marquette | Montello | | |

## WYOMING

| County | County Seat | County | County Seat |
|---|---|---|---|
| Menominee | Keshena | Albany | Laramie |
| Milwaukee | Milwaukee | Big Horn | Basin |
| Monroe | Sparta | Campbell | Gillette |
| Oconto | Oconto | Carbon | Rawlins |
| Oneida | Rhinelander | Converse | Douglas |
| Outagamie | Appleton | Crook | Sundance |
| Ozaukee | Port Washington | Fremont | Lander |
| Pepin | Durand | Goshen | Torrington |
| Pierce | Ellsworth | Hot Springs | Thermopolis |
| Polk | Balsam Lake | Johnson | Buffalo |
| Portage | Stevens Point | Laramie | Cheyenne |
| Price | Phillips | Lincoln | Kemmerer |
| Racine | Racine | Natrona | Casper |
| Richland | Richland Center | Niobrara | Lusk |
| Rock | Janesville | Park | Cody |

| County | County Seat |
|--------|-------------|
| Platte | Wheatland |
| Sheridan | Sheridan |
| Sublette | Pinedale |
| Sweetwater | Green River |
| Teton | Jackson |
| Uinta | Evanston |
| Washakie | Worland |
| Weston | New Castle |

# State Governors

## ALABAMA
Governor's Office
State House
Montgomery, Alabama 36130
(205) 242-7100

## ALASKA
Governor's Office
P.O. Box 110001
Juneau, Alaska 99811-0001
(907) 465-3500

## ARIZONA
Governor's Office
State House
Phoenix, Arizona 85007
(602) 542-4331

## ARKANSAS
Governor's Office
State Capitol
Little Rock, Arkansas 72201
(501) 682-2345

## CALIFORNIA
Governor's Office
State Capitol, First Floor
Sacramento, California 95814
(916) 445-2841

## COLORADO
Governor's Office
State Capitol
Denver, Colorado 80203-1792
(303) 866-2471

## CONNECTICUT
Governor's Office
210 State Capitol Avenue
Hartford, Connecticut 06106
(203) 566-4840

## DELAWARE
Governor's Office
Legislative Hall
Dover, Delaware 19901
(302) 739-4101

## FLORIDA
Governor's Office
State Capitol, PLO5
Tallahassee, Florida 32399
(904) 488-2272

## GEORGIA
Governor's Office
State Capitol
Atlanta, Georgia 30334
(404) 656-1776

## HAWAII
Governor's Office
State Capitol
Honolulu, Hawaii 96813
(808) 586-0034

## IDAHO
Governor's Office
State Capitol
Boise, Idaho 83720
(208) 334-2100

## ILLINOIS
Governor's Office
State Capitol
Springfield, Illinois 62706
(217) 782-6830

## INDIANA
Governor's Office
206 State House
Indianapolis, Indiana 46204
(317) 232-4567

## IOWA
Governor's Office
State Capitol
Des Moines, Iowa 50319
(515) 281-5211

## KANSAS
Governor's Office
Capitol Building, 2nd Floor
Topeka, Kansas 66612-1590
(913) 296-3232

## KENTUCKY
Governor's Office
700 Capitol Avenue
Frankfort, Kentucky 40601
(502) 564-2611

## LOUISIANA
Governor's Office
P.O. Box 94004
Baton Rouge, Louisiana 70804
(504) 342-7015

## MAINE
Governor's Office
State House
Augusta, Maine 04333
(207) 289-3531

## MARYLAND
Governor's Office
State House
Annapolis, Maryland 21401
(301) 974-3901

## MASSACHUSETTS
Governor's Office
State House
Boston, Massachusetts 02133
(617) 727-9173

## MICHIGAN
Governor's Office
P.O. Box 30013
Lansing, Michigan 48909
(517) 373-3400

## MINNESOTA
Governor's Office
130 State Capitol
St. Paul, Minnesota 55155
(612) 296-3391

## MISSISSIPPI
Governor's Office
P.O. Box 139
Jackson, Mississippi 39205
(601) 359-3100

## MISSOURI

Governor's Office
P.O. Box 720
Jefferson City, Missouri 65102
(314) 751-3222

## MONTANA

Governor's Office
State Capitol
Helena, Montana 59620
(406) 444-3111

## NEBRASKA

Governor's Office
State Capitol
Lincoln, Nebraska 68509
(402) 471-2244

## NEVADA

Governor's Office
State Capitol
Carson City, Nevada 89710
(702) 687-5670

## NEW HAMPSHIRE

Governor's Office
State House
Concord, NH 03301
(603) 271-2121

## NEW JERSEY

Governor's Office
State House, CN 001
Trenton, New Jersey 08625
(609) 292-6000

## NEW MEXICO

Governor's Office
State Capitol
Santa Fe, New Mexico 87503
(505) 827-3000

## NEW YORK

Governor's Office
State Capitol
Albany, New York 12224
(518) 474-8390

## NORTH CAROLINA

Governor's Office
State Capitol
Raleigh, North Carolina 27603
(919) 733-4240

## NORTH DAKOTA

Governor's Office
State Capitol, 600 E. Boulevard
Bismarck, North Dakota 58505
(701) 224-2200

## OHIO

Governor's Office
77 South High Street, 30th Fl.
Columbus, Ohio 43266-0601
(614) 466-3555

## OKLAHOMA

Governor's Office
State Capitol, Room 212
Oklahoma City, OK 73105
(405) 521-2342

## OREGON

Governor's Office
Office of the Governor
Salem, Oregon 97310
(503) 378-3111

## PENNSYLVANIA

Governor's Office
225 Main Capitol Building
Harrisburg, Pennsylvania 17120
(717) 787-2500

## RHODE ISLAND

Governor's Office
State House
Providence, RI 02903
(401) 277-2080

## SOUTH CAROLINA

Governor's Office
P.O. Box 11369
Columbia, SC 29211
(803) 734-9818

## SOUTH DAKOTA

Governor's Office
500 East Capitol
Pierre, South Dakota 57501
(605) 773-3212

## TENNESSEE

Governor's Office
State Capitol
Nashville, Tennessee 37243
(615) 741-2001

## TEXAS

Governor's Office
P.O. Box 12428, Capitol Station
Austin, Texas 78711
(512) 463-2000

## UTAH

Governor's Office
210 State Capitol
Salt Lake City, Utah 84114
(801) 538-1000

## VERMONT

Governor's Office
109 State Street
Montpelier, Vermont 05609
(802) 828-3333

## VIRGINIA

Governor's Office
State Capitol
Richmond, Virginia 23219
(804) 786-2211

## WASHINGTON

Governor's Office
Legislative Building
Olympia, Washington 98504
(206) 753-6780

## WEST VIRGINIA

Governor's Office
State Capitol
Charleston, WV 25305
(304) 348-2000

## WISCONSIN

Governor's Office
P.O. Box 7863
Madison, Wisconsin 53707
(608) 266-1212

## WYOMING

Governor's Office
State Capitol
Cheyenne, Wyoming 82002
(307) 777-7434

# State Police

## ALABAMA
Alabama Dept. of Public Safety
State of Alabama
Post Office Box 1511
Montgomery, Alabama 36192

## ALASKA
Department of Public Safety
State of Alaska
Post Office Box N
Juneau, Alaska 99811

## ARIZONA
Department of Public Safety
State of Arizona
2102 West Encanto Boulevard
Phoenix, Arizona 85005

## ARKANSAS
Department of Public Safety
State of Arkansas
Three Natural Resources Drive
Little Rock, Arkansas 72215

## CALIFORNIA
State Department of Justice
State of California
Post Office Box 944255
Sacramento, Califomia 94244

## COLORADO
Bureau of Investigation
State of Colorado
690 Kipling Street
Lakewood, Colorado 80215

## CONNECTICUT
State Police Department
State of Connecticut
294 Colony Street
Meriden, Connecticut 06450

## DELAWARE
Delaware State Police Dept.
State of Delaware
Post Office Box 430
Dover, Delaware 19903

## DISTRICT OF COLUMBIA
Department of Public Safety
District of Columbia
Post Office Box 1606
Washington, D.C. 20013

## FLORIDA
Dept. of Law Enforcement
State of Florida
Post Office Box 1489
Tallahassee, Florida 32302

## GEORGIA
Department of State Police
State of Georgia
Post Office Box 370748
Decatur, Georgia 30037

## HAWAII
Department of Public Safety
State of Hawaii
465 South King Street
Honolulu, Hawaii 96813

## IDAHO
Department of State Police
State of Idaho
6083 Clinton Street
Boise, Idaho 83704

## ILLINOIS
Department of State Police
State of Illinois
260 North Chicago Street
Joliet, Illinois 60431

## INDIANA
Indiana State Police
State of Indiana
100 North Senate Avenue
Indianapolis, Indiana 46204

## IOWA
Department of Public Safety
State of Iowa
Wallace State Office Building
Des Moines, Iowa 50319

## KANSAS
Kansas Bureau of Public Safety
State of Kansas
1620 Southwest Tyler
Topeka, Kansas 66612

## KENTUCKY
Kentucky State Police
State of Kentucky
1250 Louisville Road
Frankfort, Kentucky 40601

## LOUISIANA
Department of Public Safety
State of Louisiana
Post Office Box 66614
Baton Rouge, Louisiana 70896

## MAINE
Maine State Police
State of Maine
36 Hospital Street
Augusta, Maine 04330

## MARYLAND
Maryland State Police
State of Maryland
1201 Reisterstown Road
Pikesville, Maryland 21208

## MASSACHUSETTS
Department of Public Safety
State of Massachusetts
One Ashburton Place
Boston, Massachusetts 02108

## MICHIGAN
Department of State Police
State of Michigan
714 South Harrison Road
East Lansing, Michigan 48823

## MINNESOTA
Department of Public Safety
State of Minnesota
1246 University Avenue
Saint Paul, Minnesota 55104

## MISSISSIPPI
Department of Public Safety
State of Mississippi
Post Office Box 958
Jackson, Mississippi 39205

## MISSOURI
Department of Public Safety
State of Missouri
1510 East Elm Street
Jefferson City, Missouri 65102

## MONTANA
Department of State Police
State of Montana
303 North Roberts
Helena, Montana 59620

## NEBRASKA
Nebraska State Police
State of Nebraska
Post Office Box 94907
Lincoln, Nebraska 68509

## NEVADA
Department of Public Safety
State of Nevada
555 Wright Way
Carson City, Nevada 89711

## NEW HAMPSHIRE
New Hampshire State Police
State of New Hampshire
10 Hazen Drive
Concord, NH. 03305

## NEW JERSEY
New Jersey State Police
State of New Jersey
Post Office Box 7068
West Trenton, NJ. 08628

## NEW MEXICO
Department of Public Safety
State of New Mexico
Post Office Box 1628
Santa Fe, New Mexico 87504

## NEW YORK
New York State Police
State of New York
Executive Park Tower
Albany, New York 12203

## NORTH CAROLINA
Department of Public Safety
State of North Carolina
407 Blount Street
Raleigh, North Carolina 27602

## NORTH DAKOTA
Bureau of Investigation
State of North Dakota
Post Office Box 1054
Bismarck, North Dakota 58502

## OHIO
Department of Investigations
State of Ohio
Post Office Box 365
London, Ohio 43140

## OKLAHOMA
Department of Public Safety
State of Oklahoma
Post Office Box 11497
Oklahoma City, OK 73136

## OREGON
Oregon State Police
State of Oregon
3772 Portland Road
Salem, Oregon 97310

## PENNSYLVANIA
Pennsylvania State Police
Commonwealth of Penn.
1800 Elmerton Avenue
Harrisburg, Pennsylvania 17110

## RHODE ISLAND
Department of Public Safety
State of Rhode Island
72 Pine Street
Providence, RI 02903

## SOUTH CAROLINA
Dept. of Law Enforcement
State of South Carolina
Post Office Box 21398
Columbia, SC. 29221

## SOUTH DAKOTA
Criminal Investigations
State of South Dakota
500 East Capitol Avenue
Pierre, South Dakota 57501

## TENNESSEE
Department of Public Safety
State of Tennessee
1150 Foster Avenue
Nashville, Tennessee 37224

## TEXAS
Texas State Police
State of Texas
Post Office Box 4143
Austin, Texas 78765

## UTAH
Department of Public Safety
State of Utah
4501 South 2700 West Avenue
Salt Lake City, Utah 84119

## VERMONT
Vermont State Police
State of Vermont
103 South Main Street
Waterbury, Vermont 05676

## VIRGINIA
State Police of Virginia
State of Virginia
Post Office Box 27272
Richmond, Virginia 23261

## WASHINGTON
Washington State Police
State of Washington
Post Office Box 2527
Olympia, Washington 98504

**Adoption Searches Made Easier**

## WEST VIRGINIA

West Virginia State Police
State of West Virginia
725 Jefferson Road
South Charleston, WV 25309

## WISCONSIN

Law Enforcement Bureau
State of Wisconsin
Post Office Box 2718
Madison, Wisconsin 53701

## WYOMING

Criminal Investigation Bureau
State of Wyoming
316 West 22nd Street
Cheyenne, Wyoming 85002

# _Notes_